D1354491

Foundations of Social Theory

Foundations of Social Theory

JAMES S. COLEMAN

The Belknap Press of Harvard University Press

Cambridge, Massachusetts, and London, England

First Harvard University Press paperback edition, 1994

Library of Congress Cataloging-in-Publication Data
Coleman, James Samuel, 1926–
Foundations of social theory / James S. Coleman.
p.   cm.
Bibliography: p.
Includes index.
ISBN 0–674–31225–2 (alk. paper) (cloth)
ISBN 0–674–31226–0 (pbk.)
1. Sociology—Methodology.   I. Title.
HM24.C63   1990
301'.01—dc20
89–33792
CIP

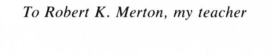

To Robert K. Merton, my teacher

Contents

Part III / Corporate Action

Part IV / Modern Society

Part V / The Mathematics of Social Action

Preface

"Social theory," as taught in the universities, is largely a history of social thought. An unfriendly critic would say that current practice in social theory consists of chanting old mantras and invoking nineteenth-century theorists. Meanwhile, however, societies have been undergoing an organizational revolution. Just as the forests and fields of the physical environment are being replaced by streets and skyscrapers, the primordial institutions around which societies have developed are being replaced by purposively constructed social organization. Given those changes, we may wonder: Are we going where we want to go? Can we modify the direction? How do we choose a direction? But before we can ask these questions, we need to know where we are going, and for that, we need a robust social theory. Such a theory requires a strong foundation, and that is what this book is intended to provide.

Several institutions were important to this book, because of the insulation they provided from more immediate concerns. The first of these, in 1970–71, was Churchill College, Cambridge, where I took the first steps toward writing this book. Another was Wissenschaftskolleg zu Berlin, in 1981–82, and a third was the Russell Sage Foundation in the fall of 1982. At the Van Leer Institute in Jerusalem during the summer of 1986, most of the chapters of the book first came into being, and in the Regenstein Library at the University of Chicago the manuscript took its final form.

I am indebted to many people for aid and valuable comments. Erling Schild read and discussed with me most of the chapters at a critical stage, as did Gudmund Hernes at another critical point. Others whose comments on individual chapters have been particularly helpful are Michael Braun, Norman Braun, Jon Elster, Michael Inbar, Edward Laumann, Richard Posner, Pamela Rodriguez, Arthur Stinchcombe, Tony Tam, Edna Ullmann-Margalit, and Jeroen Weesie. I have profited from discussions on matters related to the book with Lingxin Hao, Michael Hechter, Yong-Hak Kim, Siegwart Lindenberg, Stefan Nowak, Kim Scheppele, and Piotr Swistak. Gary Becker and the Faculty Seminar in Rational Choice that he and I have led at the University of Chicago for the past six years have also been important for the book, as have my colleagues in the Department of Sociology at Chicago.

My secretary, Debra Milton, heroically managed the organizational details that go into preparing a long and complex manuscript and typed most of the chapters through numerous revisions. Cassandra Britton provided supplementary word-processing support. George Rumsey was responsible for all the artwork.

My debt to Robert K. Merton is only partially acknowledged in the dedication, for he has encouraged me to continue in what has sometimes seemed an endless task. I also want to thank Michael Aronson of Harvard University Press, for keeping after me until the manuscript was completed. Finally, I am deeply indebted to my wife, Zdzisława, who has patiently read, encouraged, argued over, redirected, and altogether helped shape this book throughout its construction.

Because this book concerns a theory of action, the text is replete with sentences in which "the actor" is the subject or object of action, or appears as a possessor of something. Thus there are many occasions in which a third person singular pronoun is necessary. I would prefer to use gender-neutral language in these cases, but I have found no way of doing so consistently without using neologisms that distract attention from the content of the sentence and often become awkward. Lacking a satisfactory solution, I have, following tradition, used masculine pronouns to refer to actors for whom no gender identity is intended. My goal throughout has been to focus the reader's attention on content without linguistic distraction, a goal that cannot be fully achieved when conventions are not settled.

Passages from *The Merchant Bankers,* by Joseph Wechsberg, copyright © 1966 by Joseph Wechsberg, are reprinted by permission of Little, Brown and Company; material from *Corporate Take-over,* by Andrew Hacker, copyright © 1964 by The Fund for the Republic, Inc., is reprinted by permission of Harper & Row, Publishers, Inc.; paragraphs from *Crisis at Columbia,* by the Cox Commission, copyright © 1968 by Random House, Inc., are reprinted by permission of the publisher; quotations from *The History of English Law,* volume 1, by F. Pollock and F. W. Maitland, originally published in 1898 and republished in 1968, are reprinted by permission of Cambridge University Press; and passages from *Alienation and Charisma: A Study of Contemporary American Communes,* by Benjamin Zablocki, copyright © 1980 by The Free Press, a division of Macmillan, Inc., are reprinted with permission of The Free Press. Table 22.2, from my article, "Social Capital in the Creation of Human Capital," *American Journal of Sociology* 94 (supp. 1988): S95–S120, Table 1, S112, is reprinted with permission of the University of Chicago Press.

Foundations of Social Theory

Metatheory:
Explanation in Social Science

A central problem in social science is that of accounting for the functioning of some kind of social system. Yet in most social research, observations are not made on the system as a whole, but on some part of it. In fact, a natural unit of observation is the individual person; and in the development of quantitative methods of research, the dependence on individual-level data—most often interviews, but sometimes administrative records of behavior, direct observation, or other forms of data—has increased greatly. This has led to a widening gap between theory and research: Social theory continues to be about the functioning of social systems of behavior, but empirical research is often concerned with explaining individual behavior.

This focus on individual behavior as the thing to be explained is not completely misplaced in social science. Much of contemporary social research focuses on explaining individual behavior. Voting behavior, consumer choice, occupational choice, attitudes, and values are all taken as phenomena to be explained. Factors used in explanation include both characteristics of the individuals being studied and characteristics of their social environments, ranging from family to friends to larger social contexts. One method of explanation in sociology is statistical association, used in much quantitative research aimed at explaining individual behavior and ordinarily based on samples of individuals who differ both in the behavior to be explained and in characteristics which are potential sources of explanation of that behavior.

A second method of explanation, used in both qualitative and quantitative research, depends on examining processes internal to the individual. Sometimes knowledge of these processes is arrived at through introspection or sympathetic understanding on the part of the observer; sometimes it is arrived at through quantitative monitoring of changes within the individual, as is done in some branches of psychology. In principle, these observations may be carried out with only a single individual.

These two modes of explanation differ in more than method. The former uses as explanatory factors principally factors external to the individual or factors characterizing the individual as a whole. The latter uses principally factors internal to the individual and focuses on processes through which these internal changes lead to behavior.

I will have more to say about explanation of individual behavior later in this book, for it bears a more complex relation to social theory than is immediately apparent. At this point, however, I want merely to note that the focus on explaining individual behavior, found in much social research, often leads away from the central problems of social theory, which concern the functioning of social systems.

Explanation of the Behavior of Social Systems

The principal task of the social sciences lies in the explanation of social phenomena, not the behavior of single individuals. In isolated cases the social phenomena may derive directly, through summation, from the behavior of individuals, but more often this is not so. Consequently, the focus must be on the social system whose behavior is to be explained. This may be as small as a dyad or as large as a society or even a world system, but the essential requirement is that the explanatory focus be on the system as a unit, not on the individuals or other components which make it up.

As with the explanation of individual behavior, there are two modes of explanation of the behavior of social systems. One depends on either a sample of cases of system behavior or observation of the behavior of the system as a whole over a period of time. The analytical methods are based on statistical association between the behavior of interest and other characteristics of the social system as the context for that behavior. An example of research involving a sample of cases is factor analysis, sometimes carried out at the level of nations to account for political change or economic development. An example of research involving observation of a system over a period of time is the "natural history" approach in sociology or business cycle analysis applied to aggregate economic data (see, for example, Burns and Mitchell, 1946).

A second mode of explanation of the behavior of social systems entails examining processes internal to the system, involving its component parts, or units at a level below that of the system. The prototypical case is that in which the component parts are individuals who are members of the social system. In other cases the component parts may be institutions within the system or subgroups that are part of the system. In all cases the analysis can be seen as moving to a lower level than that of the system, explaining the behavior of the system by recourse to the behavior of its parts. This mode of explanation is not uniquely quantitative or uniquely qualitative, but may be either.

This second mode of explanation has certain points to recommend it, as well as certain special problems. Because this is the mode of explanation I will use throughout this book, it is useful to list some of the points that favor its use before turning to its major problem. In order to have a label to designate this mode, I call it the internal analysis of system behavior.

Points Favoring the Internal Analysis of System Behavior

1. A major problem of data adequacy exists in confirmation of theories based on system-level data when the systems are large in size and few in number. There are too many alternative hypotheses which cannot be rejected by the data. In part for this reason, research data in the social sciences are often gathered at the level of units below the level of the system whose behavior is of interest. Perhaps the most common point of observation is the individual, whether by interview, direct observation, or another method. Much sociological research is based on sample surveys of individuals, and nearly all demographic research is based on individual-level data. Data used in the study of economic systems are ordinarily gathered from individual firms and individual households, though the data are often aggregated before being used in research.

Because data are so often gathered at the level of individuals or other units below the level of the system whose behavior is to be explained, it is natural to begin the explanation of system behavior by starting at the level at which observations are made, then "composing," or "synthesizing," the systemic behavior from the actions of these units.

2. Just as observations are often most naturally made at levels below that of the system as a whole, interventions must be implemented at these lower levels. Thus a successful explanation of system behavior in terms of the actions or orientations of lower-level units is ordinarily more useful for intervention than is an equally successful explanation which remains at the level of the system itself. Even where an intervention is at the level of the system, such as a policy change made by a nation's government, its implementation must ordinarily occur at lower levels, and that implementation is what determines the consequences for the system. Thus an explanation of system behavior which goes down as far as the actions and orientations of those who will implement the policy is likely to be more useful than one which does not.[1]

3. An explanation based on internal analysis of system behavior in terms of actions and orientations of lower-level units is likely to be more stable and general than an explanation which remains at the system level. Since the system's behavior is in fact a resultant of the actions of its component parts, knowledge of how the actions of these parts combine to produce systemic behavior can be expected to give greater predictability than will explanation based on statistical relations of surface characteristics of the system. This need not be so, of course, if the surface characteristics are quite proximate to the behavior to be explained. In meteorology, for example, predictions based on immediately prior weather conditions in the vicinity may be better than predictions based on interactions among many component parts (various air masses and land and water

1. Schultze (1977) gives a number of examples in which a statutory change at the level of the federal government, not based on a theory or understanding of the orientations of those responsible for implementation of the statute, had consequences quite different from those intended.

surfaces). Similarly, macroeconomic predictions based on leading indicators having known statistical association with subsequent system performance may give better predictions than will economic models based on interactions among parts of the system. These illustrations, however, depend both on the incompleteness of the explanation (or "theory") based on internal processes and on the proximity of the system-level indicators. As the latter become less proximate, their predictive value falls off rapidly.

4. As point 3 suggests, an internal analysis based on actions and orientations of units at a lower level can be regarded as more fundamental, constituting more nearly a theory of system behavior, than an explanation which remains at the system level. It can be said to provide an understanding of the system behavior which a purely system-level explanation does not. Still, this raises the question of what constitutes a sufficiently fundamental explanation. Is it any explanation that goes down to a level of units below that of the system itself? Is it one that goes down to the level of the individual person? Is it one that does not stop at the level of the person but continues below that level?

I will not attempt to answer this question in general, except to say that point 2 provides a satisfactory criterion in practice. That is, an explanation is sufficiently fundamental for the purpose at hand if it provides a basis for knowledgeable intervention which can change system behavior. Later I will suggest that a natural stopping point for the social sciences (although not psychology) is the level of the individual—and that, although an explanation which explains the behavior of a social system by the actions and orientations of some entities between the system level and the individual level may be adequate for the purpose at hand, a more fundamental explanation based on the actions and orientations of individuals is more generally satisfactory. For example, an analysis of the functioning of an economic system based on the actions and orientations of firms and households may be quite satisfactory, but for other purposes those actions and orientations of the firms and households must be explained in terms of the actions and orientations of individual persons who play some part in controlling them.

5. The internal analysis of system behavior is grounded in a humanistically congenial image of man. This cannot be said for much of social theory. For many social theorists social norms are starting points of theory. The image of man demanded by a theory that begins at the level of social systems is *homo sociologicus*, a socialized element of a social system. The questions of moral and political philosophy which address the fundamental strain between man and society cannot be raised. The freedom of individuals to act as they will, and the constraints that social interdependence places on that freedom, nowhere enter the theory. Problems of freedom and equality cannot be studied. Individuals as individuals enter only via their conformity to or deviance from the normative system. With this image of man as a socialized element of a social system, it becomes impossible, within the framework of social theory, to evaluate the actions of a social system or a social organization. Germany under Hitler or

Russia under Stalin is indistinguishable as a nation-state from Switzerland in any evaluative sense, and Charles Manson's and Jim Jones's communes, which were directed toward death, are morally indistinguishable from an Israeli kibbutz, which is directed toward life. This is especially curious, since many sociologists hold values that sharply distinguish among social organizations on the basis of humanitarianism yet are content with social theory that blinds them to these very values—a stance which probably derives more from intellectual superficiality than from any lack of moral righteousness.

There is, of course, a reaction against social theory which begins at the level of a social system and against the image of man it presents, both within social science and outside it. The wide popularity of works by social scientists and others that explicitly open the question of human freedom (*Escape from Freedom* [Fromm, 1941], *The Lonely Crowd* [Riesman, Glazer, and Denney, 1953], and *The Organization Man* [Whyte, 1956]) and the question of human rights and the alienation of those rights (the works of Marx, Engels, and Marcuse) indicates the importance of these questions to persons in society.

The theory presented in this book is, as suggested above, not unique among social theories in taking individuals as its starting point. The problems it addresses are, however, just as close to those raised by the seventeenth- and eighteenth-century political philosophers Hobbes, Locke, and Rousseau as they are to questions dealt with by much of current social theory. More than any other single question, this theory addresses the question of the peaceful coexistence of man and society, as two intersecting systems of action.

A Note on Methodological Individualism

Those readers familiar with debates and discussions on methodological holism and methodological individualism will recognize that the position taken above on explanation is a variant of methodological individualism. But it is a special variant. No assumption is made that the explanation of systemic behavior consists of nothing more than individual actions and orientations, taken in aggregate. The interaction among individuals is seen to result in emergent phenomena at the system level, that is, phenomena that were neither intended nor predicted by the individuals. Furthermore, there is no implication that for a given purpose an explanation must be taken all the way to the individual level to be satisfactory. The criterion is instead pragmatic: The explanation is satisfactory if it is useful for the particular kinds of intervention for which it is intended. This criterion will ordinarily require an explanation that goes below the level of the system as a whole, but not necessarily one grounded in individual actions and orientations. This variant of methodological individualism is perhaps closest to that used by Karl Popper in *The Open Society and Its Enemies* (1963), although Popper is primarily concerned with explanation of societal-level phenomena, rather than behavior of social systems of any size.

The Major Problem

The major problem for explanations of system behavior based on actions and orientations at a level below that of the system is that of moving from the lower level to the system level. This has been called the micro-to-macro problem, and it is pervasive throughout the social sciences. In economics, for example, there is microeconomic theory and there is macroeconomic theory; and one of the central deficiencies in economic theory is the weakness of the linkage between them, a weakness papered over with the idea of "aggregation" and with a ubiquitous concept in macroeconomic theory, that of the "representative agent."

In this section I will show some of the problems involved in making a proper micro-to-macro transition, point to some instances where the transition has been correctly made, and indicate steps toward making the transition correctly in some areas where this has not been successfully done.

MAX WEBER AND THE SPIRIT OF CAPITALISM   To show something about what is involved in making a proper micro-to-macro transition, I will turn first to an instance in which it was not made properly. This example is a classic in sociology, Max Weber's *The Protestant Ethic and the Spirit of Capitalism* (1958 [1904]).

At one degree of detail, Weber is simply expressing a macrosocial proposition: The religious ethic which characterized those societies that became Protestant in the Reformation (and particularly those that were Calvinistic) contained values that facilitated the growth of capitalist economic organization. Diagrammatically, the proposition can be put as shown in Figure 1.1. This proposition, if there were nothing more, would exemplify the first mode of explanation described earlier, which remains at the level of the system. For any degree of confirmation the proposition would require one of two kinds of evidential basis. One would be a systematic comparison of the economic systems of Protestant and non-Protestant societies to determine if the former were more likely to be capitalist. A second basis would be an examination over time of the economic organization of societies which became Protestant, to determine whether capitalism developed shortly after the advent of Protestantism. Weber presents evidence of both these sorts, comparing countries according to their religious composition and the degree and timing of their capitalist development. This evidence, however, is far from conclusive, and Weber does not base most of his effort on it.

The deficiencies of this approach are among the points described earlier as favoring internal analysis. The empirical deficiencies (point 1 given earlier) are probably the most glaring: The societies that can be compared are few in number, and those in which capitalism developed most rapidly differed not only in

|Religious values
of a society | Economic organization
of a society |

Figure 1.1   Macrosocial proposition: Calvinism encourages capitalism.

religion but in many other ways as well. Statistical comparisons would be subject to many different interpretations, *even if* the association between Protestantism and capitalism were high.

But Weber does not remain with this proposition alone. He examines the content of Calvinist doctrine, in particular, the kind of moral prescriptions it imposes on its adherents. Then he examines the "spirit" of modern capitalism and, using a number of other periods and other economic institutions for comparison and contrast, singles out the idea of diligence in performing one's duty in a calling (p. 54) and opposition to traditionalism (pp. 58–63) as the central elements which distinguish it. Finding the same antitraditionalist orientation and the same precept of diligence toward one's calling in Calvinist doctrine, he uses this as evidence that the growth of this religious doctrine provided the value system which allowed capitalism to develop. This second kind of evidence allows further specification of the relation shown in Figure 1.1. The content of the Protestant ethic can be described as values deriving from the religious beliefs of a society, and the content of what Weber calls the spirit of capitalism can be described as values governing the economic activities of the society. These values are two components of the value system of a society, governing activities in two different institutional areas.

When Weber's thesis is seen in this way, some of its vulnerabilities to criticism become apparent. A major criticism, expressed by Tawney (1947) as well as others before and since, is that the shared content of the religious and economic values is not evidence of the effect of the former upon the latter, but may be an indicator of other changes which altered both religious and economic value systems. Alternatively, the shared content could arise from an effect of new values in economic activities in reshaping those religious values that were most susceptible to such an effect, that is, the values of Calvinists.

Part of Weber's discussion in support of his argument goes far beyond comparisons between nations to include comparisons between regions within nations, religious subgroups within regions, and even individuals in families (see especially his footnotes in chapter 1). For example, he quotes extensively from the writings of Benjamin Franklin to express the essence of the spirit of capitalism and points to the religioethical precepts taught to Franklin by his Calvinist father. Weber also compares the taxable wealth of Protestants and Catholics in a region in Germany.

The use of this material raises further questions about just what kind of proposition Weber was attempting to demonstrate and, in particular, what unit or units were involved in the proposition. Did he really mean to specify the proposition at the individual level? It appears, from his use of this individual-level evidence and from some of his statements, that this is exactly what he intended.[2] If so,

---

2. For example, Weber states that "this peculiar idea . . . of one's duty in a calling is what is most characteristic of the social ethic and capitalist culture, and is in a sense the fundamental basis of it. It is an obligation which the individual is supposed to feel and does feel towards the content of this professional activity" (p. 54). In later chapters Weber shows that this sense of "duty in a calling" was central to Protestant, and particularly Calvinist, doctrine.

then the proposition of Figure 1.1 must be revised. The single proposition breaks into three: one with an independent variable characterizing the society and a dependent variable characterizing the individual; a second with both independent and dependent variables characterizing the individual; and a third with the independent variable characterizing the individual and the dependent variable characterizing the society. Thus the proposition system begins and ends at macro levels, but in between it dips to the level of the individual. The three propositions may be put, somewhat crudely, as follows:

1. Protestant religious doctrine generates certain values in its adherents.
2. Individuals with certain values (referred to in proposition 1) adopt certain kinds of orientations to economic behavior. (The central orientations to economic behavior are characterized by Weber as antitraditionalism and duty to one's calling.)
3. Certain orientations to economic behavior (referred to in proposition 2) on the part of individuals help bring about capitalist economic organization in a society.

Figure 1.2 shows a way of diagramming such multilevel systems of propositions. The upper horizontal arrow represents the macro-level proposition. The three connected arrows—of which the first begins at the same point as the macro-level proposition and goes down to a lower level and the third goes back up to the final point of the macro-level proposition—represent the three linked propositions.

In this set of propositions, the third is of most interest, because it moves back up from the individual level to the societal level. The independent variable characterizes an individual, and the dependent variable characterizes a social unit, in this case the society. Obviously, a proposition of this sort, unless it is

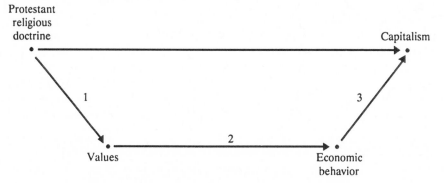

Figure 1.2   Macro- and micro-level propositions: effects of religious doctrine on economic organization.

one of those historical propositions which attribute major social changes to particular individual leaders, is not suggesting that a single individual's attributes are effective in bringing about social change. Rather, some sort of combined or joint or aggregate effect of the economic behavior of many individuals in bringing about capitalistic development is being proposed. It is here, however, that Weber's analysis is almost totally silent.[3] What kind of combination or aggregation brought about the development, even supposing the propositions of Figure 1.2 to be correct?

Whose economic behavior is at issue here—that of prospective workers in capitalist enterprise, that of prospective entrepreneurs, or that of both? And if that of both, is it proposed that the religious values were precisely appropriate for the economic behavior of the workers *and* for that of the entrepreneurs? For some values, particularly the antitraditionalism central to the "spirit of capitalism," it is clear that Weber is arguing that this is so. But the absence of a serious consideration of this question shows a major element to be missing from his theory.[4] What is necessary to account for the growth or occurrence of any social organization, whether capitalist economic organization or something else, is how the structure of positions constituting the organization comes into being, how persons who come to occupy each of the positions in the organization are motivated to do so, and how this interdependent system of incentives is sustainable. These are the central problems of the analysis of social organization. Marx's analysis of the emergence of capitalism from feudalism, polemically marred though it was, came closer to doing this than did Weber's analysis in *The Protestant Ethic*.

A considerable body of theoretical work, which might be called cultural psychology, attempts to explain social change by use of culture or values alone, without reference to social organization. Possibly the work of Abram Kardiner (1945) expresses this orientation most fully, but it can also be found in the work of other cultural anthropologists, such as Margaret Mead and Ruth Benedict. Just as in proposition 3 of Figure 1.2, essential elements of an explanation are

3. This is not to say that Weber said nothing about these matters elsewhere. The example being used here is a particular work, not Weber's total works. Yet the very fact that Weber's thesis has been questioned almost from the beginning indicates that his further work did not lay to rest the doubts raised by this work.

4. It could well be argued, and Weber's text would in many places support the argument, that Weber was concerned in this work only with showing the effects of the content of Protestant religious values on the content of values characteristic of capitalist enterprise. But this interpretation leads to other problems. Showing that two sets of values held by individuals have shared content does not provide evidence that either set affected the other; and the absence of any excursion from the realm of values to mundane activities means no mechanism is provided through which such effects might take place. On the other hand, if the "spirit of capitalism" is to be regarded as not merely a property of individuals but a property of the society, that is, a shared norm, then Weber has failed to show the processes through which the individuals' beliefs give rise to the social norm (as well as to demonstrate the relevance of such a norm to the actual practice of capitalism).

missing—precisely those elements that constitute the analysis of social organization.

THEORIES OF REVOLUTION   A contemporary instance of the attempt to make the micro-to-macro transition through simple aggregation of individual attitudes or orientations can be found in certain theories of revolution. These are theories which can generally be termed frustration theories.

The problem addressed by frustration theorists of revolution is the puzzling one of why revolutions often seem to occur during periods of social change in which conditions are generally improving. The frustration theorists resolve this problem by arguing that the improving conditions in the society create frustration on the part of individual members of the society, leading to revolution. Like Weber's propositions in *The Protestant Ethic,* there are three linked relations: The first is from the system level to the individual level; the second is wholly at the individual level; and the third is from the individual level to the system level. Figure 1.3 shows these propositions diagrammatically.

The first relation takes several forms, depending on where the theorist sees the frustration arising: from short-term setbacks, relative deprivation, rising expectations induced by rapid change, or some other cause (see Chapter 18). The second relation is merely a frustration-aggression proposition from psychology. The third relation is implicit, a simple aggregation of individual aggression to produce a social product, that is, a revolution. Yet a revolution involves organization and the interplay of actions on the part of a number of actors.

In both the analysis by Weber and that by the frustration theorists of revolution, the micro-to-macro transition is made simply by aggregation of individual orientations, attitudes, or beliefs. If, however, the theoretical problem is one involving the functioning of a social *system,* as it is in explaining the rise of a capitalist economy or the occurrence of a revolution, then it should be obvious that the appropriate transition cannot involve the simple aggregation of individual behavior.

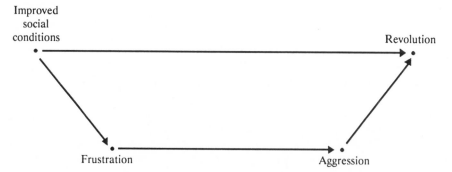

Figure 1.3   Macro- and micro-level propositions: effects of improved social conditions on potential for revolution.

Components of the Theory

There are three kinds of components to any theory in which system behavior derives from actions of actors who are elements of the system. These correspond to what are shown as relations of types 1, 2, and 3 in Figure 1.2. Relations of types 1 and 3 involve movement from macro to micro and micro to macro, respectively, and relations of type 2 are based on the principle of action describing actions of the actors. This principle of action constitutes a necessary fixed kernel, which gives rise to different systemic behavior—that is, different social phenomena—when located in different social contexts and when different persons' actions combine in different ways.

There is, in fact, a good rationale for arguing that social theory, as distinct from psychological theory, consists of theory about the working out of various rules within which sets of persons act.[5] This view, as well as the character of macro-to-micro and micro-to-macro transitions, can be understood by imagining a social-simulation game of the sort that is sometimes used in education.[6] Such a game is composed of the following:

A set of roles that players take on, each role defining the interests or goals of the player

Rules about the kinds of actions that are allowable for players in each role, as well as about the order of play

Rules specifying the consequences that each player's action has for other players in the game

If the playing out of the game is viewed as simulating the behavior of some aspect of a social system (as it will if the game is well constructed), then there are two naturally separable components: the players and the structure of the game. The players contain within themselves some principle of action (which could hardly be described as other than purposive), and the game comprises the structure which sets in motion these actions and combines them to produce behavior of the system.

It is this structure which corresponds to the two transitions I have described: macro to micro and micro to macro. The first of these transitions is mirrored in the game by all those elements that establish the conditions for a player's action: the player's interests, given by the goal established by the rules; the constraints on action, which are imposed by other rules; the initial conditions, which provide the context within which action is taken; and, after the game is in play, the new context imposed by others' actions. The second transition is mirrored by

5. See Brennan and Buchanan (1985, pp. 1–18) for a discussion of the role played by rules in a social order.

6. It was the development and use of such social-simulation games which led me away from my previous theoretical orientation, of a Durkheimian sort, to one based on purposive action. It seemed clear that both in development of the rules of the game and in observation of the consequences of those rules in play of the game, an enterprise leading in the direction of the development of social theory was taking place.

the consequences of the player's action: how it combines with, interferes with, or in any other way interacts with the actions of others (which in the play of the game as in reality may be simultaneous with or precede or follow the given player's action), thus creating a new context within which the next action takes place.

But if this description of the play of the game is intended to mirror transitions from the macro to the micro level and back again, where is the macro level? Although it is clear that the play of the game can represent the micro level, there is no tangible macro level. The answer is that the macro level, the system behavior, is an abstraction, nevertheless an important one. If, for example, the game is *Diplomacy*®, a commercial game in which the players represent the European powers in 1914, the "system behavior" is the alliances and conflicts that develop, the emergence of war, and the changes in the map of Europe as a consequence of the players' actions.

It is useful to interject that in *Diplomacy*® the players represent not individual persons but nations, exemplifying the case in which the actors at the micro level are not individuals but corporate actors. In this game the macro level is the level of Europe as a whole, and the micro level is that of the individual nation. One objection to such diplomatic games, in which a nation is represented by a single goal-oriented player, is that they do not mirror reality sufficiently well, that, in reality, actions of nations may express some internal conflict. For example, the point is commonly made that rulers sometimes provoke external conflict to generate internal cohesion.[7] For this reason, in more complex diplomatic games nations are sometimes represented by more than one player, with each player responsible for certain internal activities of the nation, activities which may affect the nation's actions toward the outside. In such a configuration the nation itself is treated as a system of action, which is in effect an actor in the larger system of action.

The system behavior, the macro level in the terminology of this book, sometimes is appropriately conceived as being merely the behavior of a system of actors whose actions are interdependent. In some cases the system behavior can be regarded as the action of a supraindividual actor, for example, the action of a nation resulting from the interdependent actions of actors internal to the nation. Similar to this is the case in which the macro level is a formal organization and the micro level is made up of departments in the organization or persons occupying positions in it.

Somewhere between the case in which the system behavior is purely an abstraction resulting in certain macro-level outcomes (such as changes in the map of Europe) and the case in which the macro level is a formal organization that can be conceived of as an actor is the case in which no unitary actor emerges at the macro level but there are well-defined properties or concepts characterizing

---

7. See Lederer (1940) for a discussion of Mussolini's venture against Ethiopia prior to World War II as such an action.

that level. The determination of price in an economic market is an example which illustrates this case well. The micro-level actors are the individual traders, and the price of each good gives the exchange rate (relative to some medium of exchange, or numeraire) for that good when there is equilibrium, that is, when no additional trades will take place beyond those already arranged. The relative prices of two goods as a concept characterizing the market as a whole (rather than merely the exchange rate at which a transaction involving those goods takes place between two particular traders) is an abstraction made possible by the fact that market competition compresses the various exchange rates for the same pair of goods among different trading partners toward a single rate, as each trader attempts to get the best exchange possible for the good or goods that trader holds.

The Individual-Level Theory of Action

The examples introduced earlier do not use the same theory of action. The frustration theorists of revolution use a model of expressive action, with aggressive behavior being the expression of frustration, unmodified by any goal or purpose. The psychological model underlying the study of suicide carried out by Emile Durkheim (1951 [1897]) was similar to that of the frustration theorists. Durkheim's analysis regarded suicide as an expressive act resulting from a psychological state brought about by one's relation to one's social environment. Max Weber's analysis of Protestantism and capitalism, in contrast, implicitly assumed that persons act purposively toward a goal, with the goal (and thus the actions) shaped by values or preferences. For Weber economically productive actions were modified by Calvinism through its effect on values that were relevant to economic actions. The economic actions followed directly as "reasonable" or "understandable" or "rational" actions for persons holding the values embodied in Calvinism.[8]

The individual-level theory of action I will use in this book is the same purposive theory of action used in Weber's study of Protestantism and capitalism. It is the theory of action used implicitly by most social theorists and by most people in the commonsense psychology that underlies their interpretation of their own and others' actions. It is ordinarily the dominant model of action we apply when we say we understand the action of another person: We say that we understand the "reasons" why the person acted in a certain way, implying that we understand the intended goal and how the actions were seen by the actor to contribute to that goal.

For some purposes in the theory of this book, nothing more than this commonsense notion of purposive action is necessary. For much of the theory, however,

8. This statement does not take into account the micro-to-macro problem discussed in the preceding section. The actions of an individual depend not only on preferences or values but also on opportunities and incentives provided by the environment. The growth of capitalism involved changes in these opportunities and incentives.

a more precise notion is required. For this I will use the conception of rationality employed in economics, the conception that forms the basis of the rational actor in economic theory. This conception is based on the notion of different actions (or, in some cases, different goods) having a particular utility for the actor and is accompanied by a principle of action which can be expressed by saying that the actor chooses the action which will maximize utility.

There are a number of points of clarification to be made about the use of this somewhat narrowly conceived version of purposive action as the individual-level component of a social theory. Some of these are in the form of caveats. First, this is clearly a particular specification of the broader idea of purposive action; other specifications are also compatible with that broader idea. For example, Tversky's (1972) theory of elimination by aspects (which appears to correspond better than standard rational choice theory to the way certain choices are made) implies that purposive choice is made in stages, with selection at each stage made according to a particular dimension or aspect on which the objects of choice differ. The standard theory of rational choice has no way for such dimensions to emerge, and no place for hierarchically structured choice.

In other work Kahneman, Tversky, and others (see, for example, Kahneman, Slovic, and Tversky, 1982) have shown conclusively that persons, when intending to act rationally, have systematic biases that lead their actions to be less than rational, according to some objective standard. That is, individuals act systematically to yield outcomes they regard as less good than outcomes that would have been obtained from other actions. One such systematic bias is the overestimation of probabilities of unlikely events.[9] Another is allowing one's perception of a situation in which a choice must be made (and thus the choice made) to be influenced by elements in the description that are irrelevant to the outcome.[10]

Another deviation from rationality lies in the inconsistency between resolving not to carry out some action and then later carrying out that action (in which case it might be said that one has "succumbed to temptation"). Elster (1979) describes such cases, cases in which persons may precommit themselves in order not to succumb. In these cases, as in the cases that can be explained

9. For example, people tend to overplay long shots in betting on races or choose to play a lottery having a larger prize but a lower expected value than another lottery.

10. For example, Tversky and Kahneman (1981) used an experimental situation in which it is stated that the United States is preparing for the outbreak of a rare disease that is expected to kill about 600 persons. Version 1 of the hypothetical situation is stated as follows: If program A is adopted, 200 people will be saved. If program B is adopted, there is a probability of 1/3 that 600 people will be saved and a probability of 2/3 that no one will be saved. Which program would you favor? Version 2 of the hypothetical situation is stated as follows: If program C is adopted, 400 people will die. If program D is adopted, there is a probability of 1/3 that nobody will die and a probability of 2/3 that 600 will die. Which program would you favor? In their experimental work Tversky and Kahneman show that many fewer persons choose program B than choose program A, but many fewer choose C than choose D; yet the situations in versions 1 and 2 are the same.

through a hierarchical structuring of choice, it appears that choice may be better conceived as resulting from an organization of components of the self than from a simple maximization of utility.

Apart from different specifications of how individuals act purposively and deviations from the objectively best action when intending to act rationally, there are other actions which appear to be better described as expressive or impulsive (that is, without a goal in mind), actions which lead to outcomes the actor does not prefer, even actions that can be described as self-defeating. The frustration-aggression hypothesis discussed earlier and Durkheim's theory of the impact of social context on psychic states leading to suicide are attempts to capture this. Although I will argue in Chapter 18 that the frustration-aggression model of action is incorrect as a component of theories of revolution, this does not mean that frustration never leads to aggression. Without commitment to a position for or against the thesis that such actions can be reconceptualized in a way that is compatible with purpose or rationality, one must accept that certain actions are most straightforwardly described in a way that does not involve purpose.

Still another objection to purposive action as a basis for social theory is an objection to the use of teleology in any theory of action. The concept of purpose is explicitly teleological. It explains current states in terms of (desired or intended) future states, rather than in terms of antecedent states. It gives rise to explanations based on final causes rather than on proximate causes. It is antithetical to the usual causal explanations in science. In other disciplines teleological explanations, when they have proved useful at all, have served as way stations, or intermediate points on the way to a theory which eliminates teleology.[11]

Given these and other deviations from, exceptions to, and objections to either the very concept of purposive action or the narrow conception of rationality given by the principle of maximization of utility, what is my rationale in using it as a basic component of social theory? The question can be divided in two: Why use a theory of purposive action at all, rather than a theory that is agnostic concerning individual action? Why use the narrow and especially simple specification of purposive action developed by economists, that is, maximization of utility?

11. An example used by Nagel concerns the question of why the angle of reflection of light from a surface equals the angle of incidence. A teleological explanation is that the reflection occurs in such a way as to minimize the total distance traveled from source to receptor. This obviously is only a superficial explanation, if it can be called an explanation at all. It leaves unanswered the question of why the distance should be minimized (unless the answer is given as a generalization of Le Châtelier's principle of least effort, a teleological principle used in chemistry) and serves, in effect, merely to describe a regularity in the behavior of light. See Nagel (1970) for a more extended discussion of teleological principles in science, their logical character, and their role in scientific theory.

WHY USE A THEORY OF PURPOSIVE ACTION?   The objection to the use of teleological principles in scientific theory is in general well taken. There are two reasons, however, why it has much less force in this case.

First, the methodological individualism which characterizes the theory to be presented here vitiates much of the antiteleology case. The action to be explained is at a higher level of social organization than the level at which purpose is specified. If it were not, if the theory were holistic, that is, remaining at the level of the system, then introduction of teleology at that level would explain a component of the system in terms of the function it performs for the system. This assumes what should be problematic for social theory—the integration and organization of the system. Such explanations, or "theories," are labeled functionalism in social science, and functionalist explanations are subject to all the objections made against teleological explanations.[12]

Psychological theories intended to explain the actions of individuals are subject to the same objections if they are purposive, for in that enterprise purpose is introduced to characterize the action to be explained, not an action at some lower level.[13] Theories in psychology which use the concept of reward are of this sort, since reward is defined in terms of its function, thus yielding an explanation that is at least partly circular in character. When the actions treated as purposive are actions of individuals, however, and the action to be explained is the behavior of a social system, behavior which derives only very indirectly from the actions of the individuals, then the explanation of system behavior is not in terms of final causes but in terms of efficient causes.

A second reason why a purposive theory of action at the level of individuals and based on a teleological principle is not harmful to social science, but desirable, lies in the peculiar relation of social science to its object of study. Social scientists are human beings, and the object of their study is actions of human beings. This means that any other kind of theory of human behavior poses a paradox for the theorists themselves. The paradox can best be seen by supposing a fully developed theory of human behavior which is not based on purposive action but on a causal framework into which individual goals or purposes never enter.

For example, consider approaches to social theory which base social change on technological change or on forces of nature. If such a theory is taken seri-

12. For discussion of functional analysis in social science, see Stinchcombe (1968) and Nagel (1970).

13. Some work in psychology suggests that it is not a difference in levels of action that is crucial but any difference between the action to be explained and the action for which purpose is invoked. Berne (1964), for example, showed that apparently irrational adult behavior can be explained in terms of actions learned at a young age, when they constituted rational responses to the child's social environment. In that explanation teleology is involved in accounting for the early behavior (for example, the child's goal of escaping punishment or gaining a reward), but it is the learning of such actions, and the assumption that they are not easily unlearned, which constitutes the explanation for actions that are not rational in a subsequent and different social context.

ously, this implies a fatalistic view of the future, in which humans are the pawns of natural forces. Still other theories do not have an individualistic base but have their foundation at a macrosocial level, taking as given the very social organization that is problematic in a theory based on purposive action of individuals. In theories of this sort the proposed causes of action are not persons' goals or purposes or intents, but some forces outside them or unconscious impulses within them. As a consequence, these theories can do nothing other than describe an inexorable fate; they are useful only to describe the waves of change that wash over us. At the mercy of these uncontrolled external or internal forces, persons are unable to purposefully shape their destiny.

The paradox arises because such theories imply that the theory itself, a result of purposive action, can have no effect on future action. Any attempt to use the theory purposefully will consequently be, according to the theory, destined to fail. A further paradox lies in the image of man implied by a nonpurposive theory. Since the conception is one into which purpose, goal, and will do not enter, it is incompatible with the very orientation of the theorist, who sets as a goal the development of such a theory. All of this arises because the subjects of the theory are persons, and that includes the theorists and the users of the theory.

There is another closely related value to basing social theory on purposive actions of individuals. In a certain range of scholarly endeavor, including ethics, moral philosophy, political philosophy, economics, and law, theory is based on an image of man as a purposive and responsible actor.[14] Among these fields there exists a degree of fruitful interchange which has been denied to most sociologists, simply because sociologists have not chosen to ground their theoretical work in that same way. Moral philosophers from Kant to Rawls have grounded their work in a conception of purposive responsible individuals, as have political philosophers such as Bentham, Rousseau, Mill, and Locke. Some theorists, such as Bentham and Hayek, have been able to span all these fields because of the common conceptual base. Social theory which uses that base stands to profit from the intellectual discourse this common ground makes possible.

It is also important to answer the objection that individuals do not always act rationally. I will not dispute the point, for it is clear that persons sometimes act self-destructively and at other times act with questionable rationality. I will say this, however: Since social scientists take as their purpose the understanding of

14. Throughout these disciplines there is a terminological problem which should be made explicit here. Often, especially in philosophy, one who acts is termed an "agent," and indeed is the agent of action. However, the term "agent" is also used in another way in economics and in law. The law of agency concerns principals, agents, and third parties, and the economic analysis of agency concerns the relation between principal and agent. In these branches of law and of economics, an agent is explicitly a person other than a principal, in whose interest the agent acts. Because I treat problems of principal-agent relations in this book, I will restrict use of the term "agent" to this meaning. I will use the term "actor" to refer to the individual (or corporate actor) who takes action. Thus I will be using actor to mean what philosophers refer to as agent.

social organization that is derivative from actions of individuals and since understanding an individual's action ordinarily means seeing the reasons behind the action, then the theoretical aim of social science must be to conceive of that action in a way that makes it rational from the point of view of the actor. Or put another way, much of what is ordinarily described as nonrational or irrational is merely so because the observers have not discovered the point of view of the actor, from which the action *is* rational.

The position I will take in this book, then, is that success of a social theory based on rationality lies in successively diminishing that domain of social activity that cannot be accounted for by the theory. Another way of viewing a theory based on rational actors is to specify that the theory is constructed for a set of abstract rational actors. It then becomes an empirical question whether a theory so constructed can mirror the functioning of actual social systems which involve real persons.

WHY USE MAXIMIZATION OF UTILITY? Even if purposive action is accepted as the appropriate principle of individual action for social theory, this does not imply the narrow specification of purpose as maximization of utility. First, I need to say that neither in the qualitative form of the theory (as developed in Parts I through IV of this book) nor in the use of this qualitative theory in research is the idea of maximization of utility explicitly introduced. The assumption of utility maximization is necessary only for the quantitative development of the theory (carried out in Part V), both for mathematical modeling and for the quantitative research which makes use of those models. Nevertheless, it is useful to spell out here the two reasons why such a narrow specification is valuable for social theory.

First, by making precise what is meant by "purposive action," such a specification provides greater power. Any teleological principle which specifies that some quantity is to be maximized or minimized is more powerful than a less specific principle. This is apparent for the teleological principle (see footnote 11) that light will be reflected from a surface in such a way that its total length of path is minimized. This principle allows precise prediction of the angle of reflection of light from any surface: It will equal the angle of incidence since that is the angle which minimizes the total length of path. This predictive power of a minimization or maximization principle is somewhat vitiated when measurement of the quantity to be minimized or maximized is less unequivocal than it is in this physical example, as is the case for utility.[15] Nevertheless, the increased power is not entirely vitiated since utilities are not free to change arbitrarily or capri-

15. There are parallels in natural science. Le Châtelier's principle of least effort, which states that a system will react to any change in such a way as to minimize the effect of the change, was long subject to objections based on equivocation about what was minimized. The principle was nevertheless used in chemistry, because of its heuristic value in suggesting how physical systems react to external actions upon them. (See Glasstone, 1946, for a discussion of Le Châtelier's principle.)

ciously, and the principle thus lends greater predictive power to those theories in which it plays a part.

A second reason favoring the use of this narrow specification of purposive behavior lies in its simplicity. For a social theory made up of three components—a macro-to-micro component, an individual-action component, and a micro-to-macro component—it is especially important that the individual-action component remain simple. This does not imply, of course, that the specification of purposive behavior is the best one of those at the same degree of simplicity. It is true, however, that a trade-off between complexity in the other two components and complexity in this component must be made if the overall theory is to remain manageable. I have chosen to trade off as much psychological complexity as possible in order to allow introduction of greater amounts of complexity in the other two components of the theory, the "social organizational" components. Even so, as Chapter 2 will show, this principle of action, when employed in the context that will be used here, gives rise to several different types of action, and these different types of action constitute building blocks for different kinds of social organization.

The Macro-to-Micro and Micro-to-Macro Transitions

The two other components of the type of social theory under consideration, through which the transition from macro to micro and the transition back to the macro level occur, can be conceived of as the rules of the game, rules which transmit consequences of an individual's action to other individuals and rules which derive macro-level outcomes from combinations of individuals' actions. How a theory might encompass this can be seen by examining somewhat more deeply the three-part paradigm for explaining macro-level phenomena, which consists of type 1, type 2, and type 3 relations: the macro-to-micro transition, purposive action of individuals, and the micro-to-macro transition.

For many macro-level relations this paradigm provides precisely the appropriate imagery. The relation between improving economic conditions and revolutions, used as an example earlier, illustrates this appropriateness. But in other cases what is to be explained at a macro level is not a relation between one macro-level variable (such as change in economic conditions) and another (such as revolutionary activity). Instead, a macro-level phenomenon is to be explained. The following example will illustrate.

In England in 1720 it appeared that a kind of speculation madness had infected a part of the population. Speculation in the stock of the South Sea Company, which had been formed to engage in trade with islands in the Pacific and the Spanish colonies of Chile, Mexico, and Peru (Mackay, 1932 [1852]), was widespread, and a host of minor stock companies had arisen as well. Slowly, trust in the company's directors and in the ability of the company to succeed was withdrawn, and the bubble of speculation collapsed, despite extensive moves by the Bank of England and the British government to prevent that. In this case what is to be explained is not a macro-level empirical generalization with independent and dependent variables, but the rise and fall of widespread stock speculation in England around 1720. This is a macro-level phenomenon, and the theoretical task is to account for it by going down to the level of individual actions and coming back up to the macrosocial level, as suggested in the diagrams of Figures 1.2 and 1.3. In this case the explanation might consist of a system involving micro-level actions, their combinations, the feedback from those combinations that affects further micro-level actions, followed by further combinations, and so on, producing the bubble of speculation and then the bursting of the bubble.

This example illustrates a more general situation, in which the theory describes the functioning of a system of action from which the three types of relations are not easily separable. Although such explanatory systems involve both individual-level actions and system-level behavior, they are not appropriately conceived of as the linking together of relations of these three types. Relations of the sort described by Figure 1.1 or Figure 1.2 are ordinarily best thought of as macro-level empirical generalizations which might be predicted as deductions from a theory. The theory which can generate such relations as specific propositions may be thought of as a theory of individual action together with a theory of how these actions combine, under specific rules, to produce systemic behavior.

Interdependence of Actions

There are various ways in which actions combine to produce macro-level outcomes, and it is useful to discuss some of these briefly. This cataloging of forms of interdependence of actions is not intended to be exhaustive.

A simple case is that in which one actor's independent action imposes externalities (positive or negative) on others and thus changes the structures of incentives confronting them. An example is the classic "tragedy of the commons" (see Hardin, 1968), in which the grazing of each farmer's sheep reduces the availability of pasture for the sheep of other farmers. But there are many very different kinds of examples. Such phenomena as the South Sea bubble or the panics that may be caused by theater fires also illustrate the case.

A second case is that of bilateral exchange, as in union-management bargaining. The resulting "system" is composed of only two actors, but there are systemic outcomes: the exchange agreements or contract arrived at by the two parties.

A third case is the extension of bilateral exchange to a competitive structure in a market. The outcomes of the market, that is, prices and transactions, depend on the particular institutional rules within which the market operates; for these rules govern the form of interactions between actors (for example, closed bids or open bids, presence or absence of recontracting, price-setters and price-takers, barter, exchange with a numeraire, and so on). (See Plott and Smith, 1978, and Smith, 1982, for results with experimental markets.)

A fourth case is that of collective decisions or social choice, in which the systemic outcome is the result of votes or other expressions of preference by individuals, combined by means of an explicit decision rule and resulting in selection of a single alternative.

A fifth case is the structure of interdependent actions that constitutes a formal organization producing a product. The organizational structure consists of a set of rules and incentives, which give rise to asymmetric interdependencies that could not come about through two-party exchange.

A sixth case is the establishment (through some poorly understood process) of a collective right to exercise social control over certain actors' actions, via norms enforced by sanctions. Once established, these norms come to constitute auxiliary "rules of the game," enforced more or less fully by the actors in the system.

These several forms of interdependence of actions show the wide variety of ways in which the micro-to-macro transition occurs. The macro-to-micro transition is in some of these cases implicitly contained in the interdependence of actions. In other cases, however, it is not. For example, in a market there is extensive variation in the flow of information by which offers are communicated throughout the system. The transmission of information from the macro level to individual actors can greatly affect the actions they take and thus affect system behavior. More generally, in any large system information is transmitted via media which are themselves actors in the system, with their own interests. This shapes the quantity and character of the information available to other actors, and different communication structures will alter this information in different ways.

The variation in information transmitted from the macro level to individual actors is just one example of possible variations in the macro-to-micro transition. In general, the environment, or social context, in which a person acts affects the relative benefit of different actions; and it is the macro-to-micro transition which shapes this social context.

Conceptions of the Relations between Micro and Macro Levels

Before going on, in Chapter 2, to explicit development of the theory itself, I will indicate here just how the proper conception of the relation between individual and systemic levels can be important to social research.

A first observation is that good social history makes the transitions between micro and macro levels successfully. Good social history attempting to establish a causal connection between, for example, the advent of Calvinistic religious doctrine and the rise of a capitalist economy in the West would show not only how the doctrine gets transmitted to individuals and then has an effect on their behavior, but also how that behavior comes to be combined, that is, how the social organization which constitutes capitalist enterprise takes place. After reading such history the reader would not be left in doubt about the character of the argument—about whether a change in workers' behavior, an increase in entrepreneurial behavior, more diligent behavior on the part of managers, all of these, or something else, was claimed to be the result of Calvinism and to lead to the growth of capitalism.

But it is one thing to be able to trace the development of social organization in a particular instance, as a historian might do, and quite another to develop generalizations about such processes. It is still another to construct models of the macro-to-micro and micro-to-macro processes. Quite clearly, some form of interdependence must be modeled in cases like those I have described, for the phenomena to be explained involve interdependence of individuals' actions, not merely aggregated individual behavior.

One arena which has some similarities to economic markets and in which some work has been done is the so-called marriage market. There is a demographic phenomenon known as the marriage squeeze. When there is a sharp increase in the birth rate, as there was, for example, after World War II, a problem exists for the cohorts of females born about the time of the increase or shortly thereafter—there will not be enough men for them to marry. Men marry women who are, on average, two years younger than themselves. This means that the normal mates for females born in 1946 would be males born in or around 1944. But the 1946 cohort was large, and the 1944 cohort was small. Thus there was a marriage squeeze for women beginning in the mid-1960s, with a larger number never marrying and a larger number marrying younger men or much older men who were divorced or widowed. Something like the reverse occurs if there is a sudden drop in the birth rate—a subsequent marriage squeeze for men.

The problem lies in the fact that when there is a marriage squeeze produced by a sudden birth-rate change, it is not at all clear what will give, that is, how the scarce men will be distributed among the surplus women. (Nor is it clear what other kinds of effects will occur; how the availability of large numbers of marriageable women will affect the divorce rate, for example, or how it will affect standards of sexual morality.)[16] The absence of a model for assortative mating by age when there are fluctuations in cohort size means that demographers have been stymied in their goal of developing what is called a two-sex population model for moving a population forward through generations.

It is clear that marriage can be seen as taking place in a kind of market, but one that is quite special, with each actor having only one commodity—himself or herself—to barter and with exchange rates governed by the constraint of monogamy, which prevents variations in quantity to achieve equal value in exchange. Models for the micro-to-macro transition in marriage markets have been developed, and there are theorems about the stability of particular matching algorithms. (See Gale and Shapley, 1962; Becker, 1973, 1974; Schoen, 1983; and Roth 1984a, 1985a.) Thus a beginning has been made—but only a beginning—

---

16. In *Too Many Women?* (1983) Guttentag and Secord argue that such periods lead to looser standards of sexual behavior for women.

toward solving the marriage-squeeze problem of demographers, facilitating a two-sex population model.[17]

In this chapter I have examined what I see as the structure theory should have in the social sciences. The chapter constitutes a background to, and a rationale for, the theory to be presented in this book. In Chapter 2 I begin to lay out the theory in qualitative verbal form and will continue that enterprise throughout the remaining chapters of Parts I to IV.

17. An illustration which shows the feasibility of models relating micro and macro levels in matching markets is the procedure by which graduates of medical schools are matched with hospitals for residency training. Hospitals submit lists of first choices, second choices, and so on, for their residency positions, and applicants submit rank-ordered choices of hospitals. A computer algorithm, in use since 1957, matches hospitals and applicants. The algorithm constitutes a matching process, and a stability theorem for this process has been proved, showing that, assuming no changes have occurred in preference orders, no resident and hospital would prefer each other to the hospital and resident, respectively, with which they have been matched (see Roth, 1984b).

PART I

Elementary Actions and Relations

Actors and Resources, Interest and Control

In the preceding chapter I presented a general orientation to social theory. This involved explaining behavior of a social system by means of three components: the effects of properties of the system on the constraints or orientations of actors; the actions of actors who are within the system; and the combination or interaction of those actions, bringing about the systemic behavior.

This general metatheoretical structure can be described as a conceptual framework for social theory. A framework of this sort can serve a useful purpose in evaluating and guiding research, as the examples in Chapter 1 indicated. It would be possible to stop here, before explicit theory construction, and devote the remainder of this book to examining the implications of this conceptual framework for research on various social phenomena. To do so, however, would be to stop short of theory itself. This would provide a less useful basis for the development of knowledge about social systems than will the explicit development of social theory within this conceptual framework.

I will proceed to develop a more explicit theory in two steps. Parts I through IV of this book set forth a verbal and qualitative specification of the theory, and Part V contains a formal specification. This partitioning of the task has two values. First, the usefulness of the theory for research can be partitioned into a portion which does not depend on formal modeling and a portion which does. It appears desirable to separate these two so that the results which do not depend on formal modeling are not obscured by those which do. Second, I have been able to carry the qualitative development of the theory further than I have the formal model, so the formal development of the theory covers only a subset of the phenomena treated in the qualitative development.

An indication of the way the conceptual framework laid out in the preceding chapter will be carried toward a more explicit theory is provided by considering the functioning of an economic market through a system of tentative contracts, as described by Walras (1954). Here the idea of system behavior is something of a reification, because each actor's actions have direct effects only on those with whom that actor has discussed contracts, and each actor's changes of contracts might depend only on comparison of exchange rates with those in the immediate vicinity, unless an institution exists to ensure full communication of information about all tentative contracts. Yet, in this case of a market, the reification becomes more and more a reality as the spread of information leads various contracts to converge toward a single set of exchange rates for each pair of goods. The market price is an emergent property of the system that arises from the pairwise interactions.

As this example indicates, it may be more useful in the emergence of at least some system behavior to conceptualize the feedback processes that produce that behavior not as explicit micro-to-macro and macro-to-micro relations but as interdependencies among the actions of different actors. In the various developments of the theory throughout this book, I will sometimes conceptualize these processes in one of these two ways and sometimes in the other, depending on which appears more useful.

In this chapter I will develop the conceptual base for interdependence among actions of individual actors. With this conceptual structure the only *action* takes place at the level of individual actors, and the "system level" exists solely as emergent properties characterizing the system of action as a whole. It is only in this sense that there is behavior of the system. Nevertheless, system-level properties will result, so propositions may be generated at the level of the system.

The Elements

There are two kinds of elements in the minimal system and two ways in which they are related. The elements are actors and things over which they have control and in which they have some interest. I will call these things resources or events, depending on their character. The relations between actors and resources are, as just implied, control and interest.

It is useful to consider briefly the concept of interest, for it has an extensive history in social thought. Hirschman (1986) locates its conceptual origins: "The term was originally pressed into service as a euphemism serving, already in the late Middle Ages, to make respectable an activity, the taking of interest on loans, that had long been considered contrary to divine law and known as the sin of usury" (p. 35). As Hirschman points out, the concept of interest, or self-interest, had an extraordinary growth in the sixteenth, seventeenth, and eighteenth centuries. It encouraged, beginning with Machiavelli's counsel to the prince, the emergence of the practice of statecraft unfettered by moral constraint; it aided the insights of the emerging discipline of economics in the work of Adam Smith and others; and it played a role in the conceptual revolution in ideas about the relation of self to society that was part of the French Revolution.

In the eighteenth century some saw interest as *the* central concept for the social world. The French philosopher Helvetius expressed this view: "As the physical world is ruled by the laws of movement so is the moral universe ruled by the laws of interest" (quoted by Hirschman, 1986, p. 45). The concept has had a checkered history since that time, both in its social-scientific role and in the regard in which it is held in society at large. Interest will play a central role in the theory presented in this book. The role it plays is close to that envisioned by

Helvetius in the eighteenth century. In Chapters 19 and 34, however, I will examine the possibility of dissolving this concept through analysis of the internal structure of the actor.[1]

If actors control all those resources that interest them, then their actions are straightforward: They merely exercise their control in a way that satisfies their interests (for example, if the resources are food, control is exercised by consuming the food). What makes a social system, in contrast to a set of individuals independently exercising their control over activities to satisfy their interests, is a simple structural fact: Actors are not fully in control of the activities that can satisfy their interests, but find some of those activities partially or wholly under the control of other actors. Thus pursuit of one's interests in such a structure necessarily requires that one engage in transactions of some type with other actors. Those transactions include not only what is normally thought of as exchange, but also a variety of other actions which fit under a broader conception of exchange. These include bribes, threats, promises, and resource investments. It is through these transactions, or social interactions, that persons are able to use the resources they control that have little interest for them to realize their interests that lie in resources controlled by other actors.

A minimal basis for a social system of action is two actors, each having control over resources of interest to the other.[2] It is each one's interest in resources under the other's control that leads the two, as purposive actors, to engage in actions that involve each other. A diagram of that minimal basis, shown in Figure 2.1, gives a sense of why it can be regarded as a system of action, rather than merely a pair of independent actors. It is this structure, together with the fact that the actors are purposive, each having the goal of maximizing the realization of his interests, that gives the interdependence, or systemic character, to their actions.

Forms of Interdependence

Friedman (1977) characterizes three kinds of interdependence among actors. The first he terms structural interdependence, in which each actor assumes the others' actions are independent of his own. In this form of interdependence each

1. In the formal theory developed in Part V, interest is defined in terms of a specific utility function, known in economics as the Cobb-Douglas utility function. This specification is introduced there to facilitate quantitative research utilizing the theory. In using the term "interest," I acknowledge its long and controversial history in social science, in particular, the continuing debate since Marx over the concept of objective interests as perceived by an outside observer. In other theories, such as theories of political pluralism, the notion of subjective interest, from the point of view of the actor, has played an important part. I will not pursue the controversy here, but interests are discussed in some detail elsewhere in this book, especially in Chapter 19.

2. This statement will have to be modified slightly for a special case to be treated later, involving an actor's unilateral transfer of control over his actions to another actor, but to do so here would constitute an unnecessary complication.

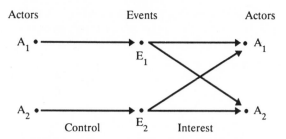

Figure 2.1   A minimal system of actors in control of and affected by events.

actor, in deciding on a course of action, can take the environment as fixed rather than reactive. A buyer's action in a market where prices can be regarded as fixed (that is, if that buyer is sufficiently small relative to others in the market that his actions do not affect prices) exemplifies structural interdependence. When a system involves only structural interdependence, rationality is well defined. Since the social environment is noncontingent, either rationality under certainty (when the outcome follows the action with certainty) or rationality under risk (when the outcome follows only with a certain probability less than 1.0) provides the appropriate model for rational action.[3]

The second form of interdependence Friedman terms behavioral interdependence. In behavioral interdependence the actions of each actor are conditional on those of others at an earlier point in time. This implies that an actor must base his action on more complex considerations than apply in structural interdependence. He must recognize that his action may have consequences for him not only directly but indirectly through another whose action may be affected by his own. Furthermore, because of this effect on the other's action, his own subsequent action may be affected, which can lead to an effect on him that constitutes a second-order indirect effect of the current action. This sequence of indirect effects can continue into the indefinite future. In such a setting, the question of what is rational for the actor depends on his information, both about the number and character of future choices and about the kinds of strategies that will be pursued by others. In this form of interdependence the definition of what strategy is rational for an actor is not independent of the strategies used by others with whom he is interdependent.

3. The form of interdependence that exists in a single-play game is formally structural interdependence, though action is based on consideration of what one player believes the other will do, which in turn is based on what the second player believes the first will do. For example, one player may carry out a strategic analysis as follows: If, in a two-person zero-sum game which involves only a single play, I can find the action which maximizes my gain under that action of the other which is the other's best reply to my action, then this is the action I should take, assuming that the other will act rationally. (This is the minimax strategy, which is the solution to a zero-sum game, proved by von Neumann and Morgenstern, 1947.) Even though there is no sequence of actions, the rational player will base his action on consideration of such "best replies," because he knows that the other player, acting rationally, will do the same.

An example of behavioral interdependence is bargaining between two or more actors, a process in which one's strategy depends on knowing not only the other's interests but also the other's strategy (which ordinarily will include assumptions about one's own strategy). Another example is the development of expectations and obligations between two persons over time, a process which depends on what each assumes about (or learns about) not only the other's interests but also the other's strategies.

A third form of interdependence identified by Friedman is evolutionary interdependence. In evolutionary interdependence there is behavioral interdependence over a sufficiently long period of time that, through selective survival, the mix of strategies in a population changes toward some "equilibrium of strategies"—which need not be a unique equilibrium point. Ideas of evolutionary biology, in particular the concept of evolutionarily stable strategies as developed by Maynard Smith (1974), have been introduced to aid in the analysis of evolutionary interdependence.

Most of the work in this book (as well as, I conjecture, the most important parts of social theory) is limited to the first and simplest form of interdependence, structural interdependence. Chapters 9 and 33, in which actors make unilateral transfers of control in an environment where actions of others are contingent on their own (for example, in a panic), are concerned with behavioral interdependence. Chapters 30 and 31, which treat the evolution of stable reallocations of rights, are concerned with evolutionary interdependence.

A Note about Self-Interests of Purposive Actors

For some social scientists (depending in part on the norms and assumptions of their discipline) my insistence on beginning a theory of action using as elements persons who are assumed to be not only rational but also unconstrained by norms and purely self-interested may appear to be a serious error. Certainly norms do exist, persons do obey them (though not uniformly), and persons do often act in the interests of others or of a collectivity, "unselfishly" as we would say.

Because of all this, it is useful to clarify the sense in which I begin with norm-free, self-interested persons as elements of the theory. My intent is not to suggest that everywhere and always persons act without regard to norms and with purely selfish interests. It is, rather, to indicate that at some point in the theory I take as problematic genesis and maintenance of norms, adherence of persons to norms, development of a moral code, identification of one's own interest with the fortunes of others, and identification with collectivities. To begin with normative systems would preclude the construction of theory about how normative systems develop and are maintained. Chapter 11 of this book would be pointless. To assume adherence to norms would impose a determinism that would reduce the theory to a description of automata, not persons engaged in voluntary action. To assume that persons come equipped with a moral code would exclude all processes of socialization from theoretical examination. And to assume altruism or unselfishness would prevent the construction of theory about how persons come to act on behalf of others or on behalf of a collectivity when it goes against their private interests.

To begin with persons not endowed with altruism or unselfishness and lacking a shared normative system does not mean that in every part of the theory the persons who are actors are assumed to be without these added components of the self. To the contrary, most parts of the theory will assume that actors possess some of these components, although the assumptions are largely implicit. In general, the more universally held a norm or the more widespread a moral precept, the more likely I will be to overlook it, to take it always and everywhere as given, thus necessarily diminishing the scope of the theory. Some norms are not so widely shared and are therefore more readily recognized.

Actions and Transactions

In the parsimonious conception of a system of action that I want to establish, the types of action available to the actor are severely limited. All are carried out with a single purpose—to increase the actor's realization of interests. There are, of course, different types of action, which depend on the situational constraints. It is useful to describe these types here.

The first type of action is the simple one of exercising control over those resources one is interested in and has control over, in order to satisfy one's interest. This action, however, is socially trivial (unless it has effects on others) and can be ignored, since it involves no other actors.

The second type of action is the major action that accounts for much of social behavior—an actor's gaining control of those things that are of greatest interest to him. This is ordinarily accomplished by using those resources he has, by exchanging control over resources that are of little interest to him in return for control over those that are of greater interest. This process follows the overall purpose of increasing one's realization of interests under the assumption that those interests can be better realized if one controls something than if one does not. Ordinarily, it may be assumed that control of a resource by an actor makes it possible to realize whatever interests that actor has in it.

A third type of action that can be and is widely carried out in social systems is unilateral transfer of control over resources one is interested in. Such transfer is carried out when the assumption on which the second type of action is predicated (that one can best satisfy one's interests by gaining control of resources one is interested in) no longer holds. That is, an actor transfers control over resources unilaterally when he believes that another's exercise of control over those resources will better satisfy his interests than will his own exercise of control. The conditions under which unilateral transfer is carried out are discussed at length in other chapters, and I will not go into them here, except to emphasize that the transfer is made, just as are all other actions, purposively—in the expectation that the actor will better satisfy his interests by so doing.

Types of Resources

The resources each actor has which are of interest to others include a wide variety of things. The most obvious of these are what economists call private goods. Neoclassical economic theory describes the functioning of systems in which each actor has control of certain private divisible goods that are of interest to other actors in the system. But private divisible goods are only one of several kinds of things over which actors have control and in which they are interested.

Actors may have control over events that have consequences for a number of other actors (that is, events in which other actors are interested). In the case in which control over such an event is partitioned among two or more actors, as when a collective decision is made by taking a vote, each actor has only partial control over the event.

Actors may have control over their own actions, and if the actors have certain attributes, such as skills or beauty, in which others are interested, they may give up rights to control certain of their own actions. Note that in this case I have used the phrase "give up rights to control" rather than "give up control." The reason is that direct control over one's own actions cannot be given up; it is inalienable. What can, however, be given up is a *right* to control the action. Physical inalienability from one's self is not the only kind of inalienability. Legal rules may also dictate inalienability of rights of control over physically alienable things. For example, for many collective decisions votes are made inalienable by rules of the system, but in some systems votes are alienable through the use of proxies.[4]

Actors may also have control over resources which are not of direct interest to others but are effective in determining, or partially determining, the outcomes of events in which others are interested. There are further variations in the resources that actors control. For example, some resources, as part of a transaction with another actor, can be delivered only in the future or over a period of time in the future, whereas others can be delivered in the present. Another variation is that some resources exhibit the property of conservation; there is a fixed quantity of the resource. If one individual controls (or consumes) one portion of the resource, the total available for others to control (or consume) is diminished by just this portion. The property of conservation is usually possessed by those things we think of as goods, but the general class of resources that individuals control include many without this property. For example, infor-

---

4. Although the vote is alienable in voting systems that allow proxy voting, often the right to transfer the vote is not alienable. That is, the proxy must be voted by the individual to whom it has been first transferred.

mation, as a resource over which actors have control, ordinarily does not exhibit conservation. Information which is passed on to another continues to be held by the original possessor as well. Still another property of certain resources is that their consumption or use has no consequences for actors other than the actor who consumes or uses them. Resources that are not like this but instead have inseparable consequences for more than the one actor are said to have external effects, or externalities.

That there is this wide variety of resources over which actors may have control and in which actors are interested (or which affect events or resources in which actors are interested) creates a terminological difficulty. I will ordinarily refer to the general class as resources, using the term to include what I have referred to above as goods, resources, and events.

As is evident in the above, there are several properties that distinguish types of resources, properties that have important consequences for the kinds of systems of action that emerge. These properties are divisibility, alienability, conservation, time of delivery, and absence of externalities. Economists, who ordinarily conceive of economic systems as involving goods, have employed a distinction between private goods and public goods. In terms of these properties a private good has no externalities and exhibits conservation. A public good does not exhibit conservation and is at the extreme of possessing externalities in that it has consequences for all (or, to use economists' terminology, is a good that cannot be supplied to one without being supplied to all).[5] The prototypical private good also is divisible, alienable, and currently deliverable; that is, it has each of the properties described.

Structures of Action

Differing kinds of structures of action are found in society, depending on the kinds of resources involved in actions, the kinds of actions taken, and the contexts within which those actions are taken. Most of the chapters of Parts I through III of this book are directed at examination of the properties of one of these structures of action. Here I will characterize these different structures as a way of locating each of the chapters of Parts I through III in the map of the structures of social action (Figure 2.2).

The matters treated in these chapters are all contained within the domain of purposive action. This is represented by the area in the map that is enclosed by the largest circle, labeled A. Many, though not all, of the actions treated can be described as transfers of control of resources or of rights to control resources. This is the area in Figure 2.2 that is enclosed by the second largest circle, labeled B. Some, but not all, of these transfers are made in exchange, whereas

5. See Samuelson (1954) for the classic definition of a public good in terms of the two properties of nonconservation and nonexcludability. The word "all" as used here may refer only to all within a given domain defined by geography, citizenship, organization membership, and the like.

others are made unilaterally. Those made unilaterally are enclosed by a circle labeled C, and those made in exchange lie outside that circle but within circle B. One particular transfer is a transfer of rights to control one's own actions, represented by the area enclosed by circle D. This area is wholly within B, partly within C (that is, unilateral transfers), and partly outside it (that is, transfers made in exchange). In all of these, transfers of control or of rights to control are

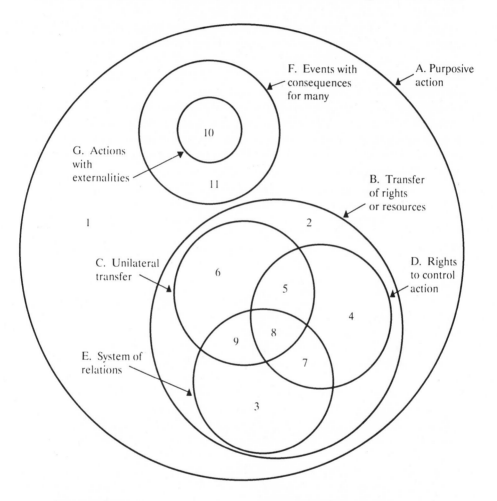

1. Private actions
2. Exchange relations
3. Market
4. Disjoint authority relations
5. Conjoint authority relations
6. Relations of trust
7. Disjoint authority systems
8. Conjoint authority systems
9. Systems of trust, collective behavior
10. Norm-generating structures
11. Collective-decision structures

Figure 2.2 **Map of the structures of social action.**

sometimes made as isolated transactions, sometimes as part of a system of relations (for example, in a market or proximate in space or time, as in collective behavior). The area enclosed by circle E represents those transfers made as part of a system of relations.

The region of Figure 2.2 labeled 1 is purposive action that is scarcely social. It does not involve transfer of rights or resources either unilaterally or in exchange, nor does it have consequences for others. Because it is so minimally social, it is only treated implicitly in Chapter 3 of this book, which treats rights to act quite generally, but is not examined separately. The problems for social science in this region are those treated by cognitive psychologists in studies of deviations from rationality. Chapter 19 has a brief discussion of this work.

Region 2 of the figure is transfer of rights or resources that is exchange but is not within a market or other system of exchange. This is what most of so-called exchange theory in sociology deals with. It is discussed in this chapter and is treated formally in the first half of Chapter 25. It is, however, the least interesting part of social action theory, because little can be said about it which has deductive power.

Region 3 is exchange relations within a system of exchange but not involving a transfer of rights to control one's actions. This is the defining criterion for a market not involving authority relations and encompasses not only economic markets, but also systems of exchange of resources that are less tangible and that are not exchanged for money. The exchange of intangibles that takes place in social groups is included in this region. Such systems are discussed in Chapter 6 and, formally, in the second half of Chapter 25 and in Chapters 26 and 27.

Region 4 is exchange in which one actor gives up rights to control his actions, the kind of exchange that creates an authority relation. Another kind of authority relation, of which the best example is a charismatic authority relation, is represented by region 5, in which one actor unilaterally gives up to another the right to contɾol his actions. The relations represented by regions 4 and 5 are examined in Chapter 4, which treats authority relations generally. Chapter 5, on relations of trust, also examines the kind of unilateral transfers of authority that are represented by region 5.

Region 6 is relations that involve a unilateral transfer of resources, tangible or intangible. Such a transfer ordinarily involves trust and, insofar as it does, is treated in Chapter 5. These trust relations are treated formally in Chapter 28.

Region 7 and region 8 involve systems of action in which authority over one's action is one of the resources involved in the exchange. The distinction between these regions (and between regions 4 and 5) is that in region 7 actors give up authority over certain actions in return for some extrinsic compensation, whereas in region 8 authority over one's actions is given up unilaterally. Region 8 is exemplified by charismatic authority systems, and region 7 is exemplified by Weber's rational authority and traditional authority. Both are treated in Chapter 7, which discusses authority systems. Region 8, however, includes phenomena that are also covered in Chapter 8, on systems of trust, and in Chapter 9, on collective behavior. The material in these two chapters is also treated formally in Chapters 28 and 33.

Region 9 is systems of relations that arise through unilateral transfer of resources. These are also discussed in Chapters 8 and 9, along with the phenomena in region 8.

Region 10, which represents actions with externalities, is the class of actions for which norms tend to arise. Chapter 10 examines these kinds of actions, and Chapter 11 examines the social conditions ûnder which this tendency for norms to arise becomes a reality. Chapter 30 extends this work formally.

Finally, region 11 covers events with consequences for many actors, which is the class of phenomena that gives rise to collective decisions and to the formation of corporate actors to carry out combined action. This important class of phenomena is treated in many places in this book. Chapter 13 examines the conditions under which rights will be vested in a corporate actor to carry out a unitary action for the collectivity as a whole. Chapters 14 and 15 examine the problems of collective decision making when rights to decide on such actions are not held dictatorially by one actor. Chapters 16, 17, and 18 examine special problems that arise for corporate actors. Some of these problems are discussed formally in Chapter 31 and some in Chapter 34.

Social Exchange

One property of the theoretical system developed here is parsimony. Actors are connected to resources (and thus indirectly to one another) through only two relations: their control over resources and their interest in resources. Actors have a single principle of action, that of acting so as to maximize their realization of interests. Such action can be simply consummatory, to realize the actor's interest; if it is not, the maximization principle leads most often to a single kind of action—exchange of control (or rights to control) over resources or events. Under some circumstances, however, it may lead to unilateral transfer of control (or right to control) to another. (Later in the book, in Chapter 19, I discuss another possible form of action, changing one's interests, but this is unnecessary for much of the theoretical development.)

The simplest system of action using the concepts described is a pairwise exchange of resources that have all the properties of private goods. Although such exchanges may occur in competition with others, as they do in a barter market, they need not. Social exchange is pervasive throughout social life. Indeed, some social theorists, such as Homans (1958) and Blau (1964), have constructed social theories based principally on exchange processes of this sort. In social exchanges of resources other than economic goods, the resources exchanged may not have all the properties of private goods, but this will not matter for certain qualitative deductions. In this section I will discuss the behavior of such systems and point to some of the qualitative deductions that can be made.

Exchange in social life can become complicated, for in many areas of social life institutions to facilitate exchanges of control (especially those exchanges that require more than two parties) are not as well developed as are institutions for the exchange of economic resources.[6] Nevertheless, in this first and simplest system of action that I will outline, I make the assumption that such exchanges can be made.

The restriction to an exchange process is not as constraining as it initially appears, once the exchanges are no longer limited to economic goods. In an exchange of economic goods, each actor, in offering an exchange, can only improve the lot of the other actor, which is why we usually think of such exchanges as both voluntary and mutually beneficial. But when events of other types are included, exchange can also be used to characterize phenomena that are ordinarily conceived of as coercion; threats are included along with promises. When a parent threatens a child with a spanking if the child disobeys, the parent is giving up temporarily the right to strike the child (which the parent continuously holds by virtue of the parent's physical and legal control of the child) in return for the child's satisfying the parent's interest.

In addition, many phenomena that are ordinarily viewed not as exchange but as deployment of resources are predictable by a rather simple form of the theory. For example, Dahl (1961) notes in his study of New Haven, and other political scientists have noted elsewhere, that many potentially powerful actors in a community do not exercise their power in community decision making. The end result is often that decisions are made without the influence of the most powerful actors in the community, a somewhat puzzling phenomenon. But because political resources are often capable of being used on any of a number of events and are partially consumed in use (for example, popular support for a corporation having a plant in a town will be reduced if the corporation uses its power in opposition to a popular policy), selective deployment may be the way for an actor to maximize realization of interests.

The idea of a system within which exchanges arise spontaneously can be illustrated by Figure 2.1. In the system represented there, actor A_2 is interested in resource E_1 but has no control over it. The action principle for each actor in the system is one which leads him to gain control over the resources that interest him by giving up resources he has. The resource held by A_2 is control over E_2. Actor A_1 is interested in E_2, so A_2 should be able to gain some control over E_1 by giving up some control over E_2.

Social Equilibrium

Through exchanges such as those described above, there is a reduction in the discrepancy between interest and control, to the point where an equilibrium

6. There are, of course, institutions of various sorts which aid this. Ostrogorski (1964 [1902]) describes the functioning of the political machine in American politics in the 1890s to bring about a three-way exchange among legislators (who got constituents' votes), business firms (who got legislators' votes) and constituents (who got money and services the machine could purchase with money).

occurs—a point at which there are no exchanges that can increase the expected realization of interests for both actors. At this point each actor will have maximized his expected realization of interests to the degree allowed by the resources with which he began.

Under certain conditions, such as in a system with a small number of actors, there may not be a *single* equilibrium point. For example, in the case of two actors, each with control over a set of things of some interest to himself and of some interest to the other, there will be a whole set of equilibrium points, each of which would be better for both actors than the initial point (and better than any point outside this set) but none of which would be better for both actors than any other point in the set. There are a number of different exchange rates that would make both parties better off than before the exchange, and in the absence of a market it is indeterminate which of these will occur.[7] The equilibrium point that is achieved in such a small system of exchange can be described as a property of the system, that is, a macro-level property, just as price is in market exchange. For example, Blau's (1963) study of the exchange of deference for advice in a government agency suggests that the amount of deference paid for a particular quantity and quality of advice constituted a property of the social system of the agency.[8]

The end result of the exchange process is a redistribution of control over events, a redistribution that will give outcomes which are in a certain sense optimal. After an exchange each actor is in control of those events that most interest him, subject to the power of his initial resources, and since he will exercise that control toward achieving the outcome he prefers, there is no way that greater satisfaction can be achieved, given the initial distribution of control and of interests. In this sense the outcome is optimal.

To make such a statement as the last one appears to engage in a fallacy that has dogged welfare economics since the utilitarians, the fallacy of assuming some common metric which allows interpersonal comparison of utility. That is, making a statement about aggregate satisfaction, as is done above, implies a comparison which balances different persons' satisfactions so that satisfaction can be aggregated over those persons. As has been shown over and over again in the economic literature, such a comparison, carried out by an analyst, is meaningless. What is not meaningless, however, is the comparison that is carried out by social processes themselves. It is this kind of comparison that is intrinsic to social systems and to the model described above. The comparison which gives a common metric to the satisfactions of different persons is that which derives from the resources with which they begin. Thus, considering a

7. In the mathematical model presented in Chapter 25, a determinate equilibrium point is found as part of the deductions. This is a simplification based on the assumption that there is a perfect market for the exchange process, an assumption which comes increasingly close to being met as the number of actors with interests in each event increases.

8. Because there was not a perfect market, the "price" of advice may have varied within the agency, making the system-level property a distribution of rates around a central tendency rather than a precise rate of exchange.

patriarchal family as a system, what is meant by maximum aggregate satisfaction is an aggregate that weights the satisfactions of the male head of the household more heavily than those of his wife, because of his greater control over resources. In a matriarchal household the wife's satisfactions are weighted more heavily than the husband's in arriving at the maximum aggregate satisfaction, because of her greater power. Such maximizations cannot be normatively justified, except *within the set of values implied by the initial distribution of control among the actors in the system.*

A first implication of the theory to be developed in this book, then, is that systems of exchange mirrored by the theory do achieve a maximum overall satisfaction, but one that is specific to the initial control. I will call this control the constitutional control regardless of whether there is a formal constitution among the actors. This control expresses the constitution of the social system, whether implicit or explicit, through its expression of the rights and resources held by each of the actors.[9] Such an aggregation of the various actors' interests might be a very different one from that which an outside observer would wish to see. For example, the aggregate satisfaction that is being maximized in a patriarchal household might not accord with that judged desirable by an outside observer. But it is the only aggregation that will be maximized in that system, because the aggregation is given by the distribution of constitutional control among the different actors in the system.

In fact, a confusion between the values that the observer would wish to place on each person's interests (for example, equality), on the one hand, and the internal functioning of the system (which because of constitutional control sets values on different persons' interests), on the other hand, has led to confusion about interpersonal comparisons of utility in welfare economics. There is no meaning to interpersonal comparisons carried out by an observer (except that they satisfy the observer), but there is a meaning to those carried out internally in a system of action. Those comparisons occur in the actual transactions that take place.

The idea of a social equilibrium introduced in this section has led to another term, a social optimum. Because this term will be important in the theory to be developed and because the concept of a social optimum differs in the various regions of the map of the structures of action, it is important to examine briefly what is meant by a social optimum in these different regions.

The Social Optimum

Adam Smith expressed the principle that an individual, intending only his own gain, is "led by an invisible hand to promote an end which was no part of his intention" (1937 [1776], p. 423). Although Smith did not imply that this leads to a

---

9. Constitutions of actual social systems do, of course, contain more than an expression of the distribution of control among existing actors in the system. See Chapter 13.

social optimum, he did go on to say, "By pursuing his own interest he frequently promotes that of the society more effectively than when he really intends to promote it" (p. 423). Neoclassical economists went further and showed that when certain highly restrictive conditions were met (costless exchange of goods that have no consumption externalities), pursuit of one's interest in exchange leads to an improvement for all those involved in the exchange with no loss to others. When no more voluntary exchanges are possible, a social optimum has been achieved. In this way, the grounding of economic theory on a principle of individual maximization of utility subject to resource constraints has made possible normative statements based on the theory. Some work in moral and political philosophy (Rawls, 1971; Nozick, 1974; Gauthier, 1986) has taken the same foundation from which to derive normative theory.

Sociological theorists have not followed this path. The absence of an explicit normative principle at the level of the individual, such as the principle of maximization of utility, has thus denied sociological theory the possibility of making normative statements. A property of the theoretical structure on which this book is based is that it contains the potential for making such statements. Yet to do so requires recognition that the conception of when a system is "better off" and the notion of a social optimum differ depending on which region of the map of the structures of action (Figure 2.2) the system is in. It is useful to describe the concepts of social optima that are relevant to different regions.

1. *Regions 2 and 4: voluntary exchanges outside a competitive market.* When voluntary exchanges of resources without externalities take place, both parties improve their lot and no one is hurt. When these exchanges occur outside a competitive structure, the exchange rate is indeterminate within a certain range. In such a setting an optimum exists when no other feasible exchanges are of interest to the two actors that would be parties to them. Such an optimal point is a Pareto optimum; and because the exchange rates are indeterminate (because of lack of competition), many Pareto optima are possible.

2. *Regions 3 and 7: voluntary exchanges of resources without externalities and within a competitive market.* When voluntary exchanges take place within the context of a competitive market, the number of mutually acceptable exchange rates shrinks to a single rate, so each resource can be said to have a particular value in the system. The multiple social optima possible outside a competitive market are reduced to a single point, which economists call the competitive equilibrium. As the preceding section indicated, this social optimum depends, as do all social optima, on the initial resource distribution. Thus each resource distribution is associated with a particular equilibrium point.

3. *Region 10: actions with externalities in a closed system.* Here the external effects (positive or negative) imposed by actions on others who have no control over those actions mean that voluntary choice no longer naturally achieves a social optimum. There is an intrinsic conflict of interest, created by the external effects. The social optimum depends on which interest is stronger, in the sense

discussed in the preceding section. If the interests opposing those of an actor are stronger than the actor's, a social optimum is achieved when there is an effective norm or law, with rights to control the action held by those other than the actor. Achievement of the social optimum in this region when the action is unobserved and thus cannot be policed by external sanctions requires internalization of the rights of others, or socialization. This internalization is commonly achieved within institutions such as the family and religious organizations.

4. *Region 11: events with consequences for many in a closed system.* This region of the map of the structures of action is another one in which there is conflict of interests. A social optimum is achieved when the outcome of the event is that favored by the stronger set of interests. This may be achieved when rights to control the action are distributed among all those with interests in the action (though, as Chapter 15 indicates, the achievement of a social optimum through collective decision making is not easily assured through allocations of rights). In this region there are often potential gains from action that is coordinated among two or more actors. The social optimum is achieved when the gains resulting from an additional unit of output are just compensated by the additional cost of bringing about that additional output. The structures within which this social optimum is achieved are ordinarily formal organizations having positions (occupied by actors) among which components of the action are distributed. The sanctions applied to actors occupying the positions either result from external policing of the action or are internal sanctions depending on the product of the action (see Chapters 7 and 16).

The importance of the concept of a social optimum to a social theory lies in the capability it brings for evaluating different social arrangements. No such evaluation is possible without a way of assessing when a system is "better off" or "worse off." The way in which this can be done is, of course, not evident in the brief descriptions given above, but will be addressed in subsequent chapters.

The Absence of a Social Equilibrium

In certain cases actions designed to bring about an individual equilibrium do not lead toward a social equilibrium. A social equilibrium results from exchanges of control of resources among actors; but when actors transfer control of resources to others unilaterally, in attempting to achieve individual equilibrium (utility maximization), the result may not lead toward a social equilibrium but away from it. (In Figure 2.2 this is represented by circle C, enclosing regions 5, 6, 8, and 9.) Unilateral transfer of control by one actor may lead, for example, to unilateral transfers of control to the same actor by others. There is nothing about unilateral transfers of control, even when they are voluntary and rational, which necessarily leads toward a social equilibrium. There may, for example, be increased concentration of power or dispersion of power.

Unilateral transfers of control over resources or events lead to structures of action that are ordinarily characterized as collective behavior. Collective behavior includes such phenomena as mob behavior, systems of trust, public opinion, social movements, emergent charismatic authority, audience behavior, fads, and fashion. It is a major source of social change.

Simple and Complex Relations

There is one additional distinction to be made before examining in detail the structures of action shown in Figure 2.2. This is the distinction between simple and complex relations among actors.

Social relations between two persons are, of course, the building blocks of social organization. But matters are not so straightforward as this might seem to imply. Certain social relations are self-sustaining in the sense that incentives to both parties to continue the relation are intrinsic to the relation. The incentives are generated by the relation itself, and continuation of the relation depends on its generating sufficient incentives for both parties. Many of what we think of as social relations are like this: primordial social ties, relations of friendship, "informal" social relations of all sorts, and authority relations such as those of master and servant or father and son. These relations can be seen as building blocks for much of social organization. Social organization that grows, as in a community or a sprawling social network, is an amalgam of such relations. These may be called simple relations to distinguish them from a second class of relations.

The second class of social relations are those that are not self-sustaining but depend on a third party for their continuation. Incentives to one or both of the two parties to continue the relation are not intrinsic to the relation but must be supplied from the outside. This is the kind of relation on which formal organizations are built. Social organization consisting of such relations does not just "grow," because one (or both) of each pair of parties has no incentive to establish such a relation. This kind of organization must be built, because it is based on more complex structures of incentives, involving three or more parties for each two-actor relation. The organization is a structure of relations made up of obligations and expectations, but there is not the requirement, as there is in a social organization composed of simple relations, that each person's obligations and expectations bring about a positive account balance in each of the person's relations. Each person need have only one positive account balance covering the total set of actors involved in this complex structure of incentives. This form of social relation I will call a complex relation.

The social environment can be viewed as consisting of two parts. One is the "natural" social environment, growing autonomously as simple social relations develop and expand the structure. A second portion is what may be described as the built, or constructed, social environment, organizations composed of complex social relations. The constructed social environment does not grow naturally through the interests of actors who are parties to relations. Each relation must be constructed by an outsider, and each relation is viable only through its connections to other relations that are part of the same organization. (The related concept of viability for corporate actors is discussed in Chapter 16.) The structure is like a house of cards, with extensive interdependence among the different relations of which it is composed. Unlike structures that grow from simple relations, structures that are built of complex relations have a well-defined boundary, distinguishing what is inside, what is part of the complex structure of interdependent incentives, from what is outside that structure.

The most common example of a constructed social environment is the modern corporate actor, composed of positions occupied by persons. Such corporate actors are examined at length in this book; they include corporations, government bureaus, trade unions, and other forms. Much of the social environment surrounding persons in modern society is a constructed social environment, just as most of the physical environment around persons in modern society is a constructed physical environment, made up of buildings and streets. The economic goods on which modern life depends are products of the constructed social environment, which is based on complex relations. Yet it appears quite possible that the constructed social environment, as we know it, is only the beginning of even more complex forms of social organization, forms that have not yet been invented.

« 3 »

Rights to Act

In the preceding chapters I described the quantities being exchanged as resources or events, but sometimes also as rights and resources. It is important, before proceeding to other forms of social exchange and social action, to examine the concept of rights more carefully. This concept will play a central part in many of the systems of action examined in the succeeding chapters.

It is sometimes assumed that economic exchanges involve physical things: goods, commodities, property. Social exchange outside of economic systems, such as that which occurs within systems of political governance or that which occurs in informal social organization is seen, in contrast, as exchange of intangibles. Yet that seems hardly to be a definitive difference, as the following example shows.

After World War II a veteran returned to the rural area of West Virginia where he grew up. Shortly afterward, he and the other heirs to his father's small piece of land sold it at auction, and he bought it. He built a house on it and a country store and settled there. At first, he took great satisfaction in stepping out his front door onto the land he grew up on and now owned. But just what does he own? An inspection of the deed shows that he does not own the mineral rights; those are owned by another. The county wants to widen the road, and he learns they have the right of eminent domain, that is, the right to take his land and compensate him at market price. The other heirs demand a right of way to the family cemetery. He offers the right of access, but they reject this. Subsequently a court decides that they have the right to construct a road up to the cemetery and the right to use it without hindrance. After all this, as he steps out his front door onto the land on which he grew up, he feels less pleasure because he's not sure what he owns.

This example merely scratches the surface of the possible partitioning of the bundle of rights which are ordinarily termed property rights or rights of ownership. This bundle ordinarily includes rights of use (in various ways), rights of consumption (if the good is consumable), and rights of disposal (see Honoré, 1961). It is because these rights are commonly bound together that systems of exchange of private goods operate as they do: The usage or consumption rights provide the incentive to obtain a good, and the disposal rights make possible exchange of the good.

For goods which are not finely divisible or for which there are several types of uses (such as land) or for indivisible events in which a number of persons have an interest (such as location of a road), the allocation of rights is more problematic than it is for divisible private goods. Rights over goods which have several types of uses may be allocated (bought and sold or allocated in another way) so that the usual bundle of rights that constitutes ownership is dispersed into the hands of more than one actor. Good examples may be found in cases like that described above, which concern rights over land. In rural areas a right of way across a piece of land is often held by someone other than the owner. Mineral rights for a piece of land are often held by someone other than the person generally regarded as the owner. A landowner will sometimes sell the lumbering rights to a piece of land or will rent the right to farm the land. In the city air rights over a piece of property are sometimes sold. In some U.S. cities a practice inherited from England is that of separating ownership of a house from ownership of the land on which it is built; the owner of the land collects "ground rent" but has sold the right to occupy the land for a long period of time (such as ninety-nine years). In feudal and postfeudal periods there was an explicit division of ownership rights over land among several levels: An overlord had rights to certain taxes; the lord had rights to certain other taxes; and the freeholder of the land had rights to till it and reap its harvest, subject to the various taxes (which were sometimes more extensive than the two types mentioned here). Each of these rights could be independently bought and sold. (See Denman, 1958, for further discussion of property rights in the Middle Ages.)

Many of these divisions of rights over simple physical goods are sources of conflict and dispute. The conflicts appear to arise for several reasons. In some cases, such as air rights or rights of way, the physical location of a piece of property gives the person who owns the right (for example, the owner of the property) monopoly control over what is of interest to another. In some cases the title to certain rights is in dispute, when "ownership" of the property has passed through several hands. In still other cases one use, whose rights are held by one actor, will have negative externalities for other uses, whose rights are held by other actors.

Other partitionings of rights over goods are more systematized and generate less dispute. For example, in the stock market there is a wide range of rights. A share of common stock is a right to a share of the profits of the organization, a right to a fraction of the assets if it dissolves, and a right to vote for directors of the company. A share of preferred stock lacks the last of these rights. A stock option, which may itself be bought and sold, is a right to buy shares of stock at a particular price.

The various examples of cases where different rights to the same good are held by different actors suggest that a theory of social exchange should conceive of what is being exchanged as a right to carry out certain actions rather than as a physical good. Sometimes this right will contain most of the rights ordinarily associated with ownership, but not always. In some cases even the concept of ownership is inappropriate with respect to what is being bought or sold. For example, a worker who exchanges the rights to control his labor for a wage is exchanging a certain specific set of rights of control to which the concept of ownership hardly applies. The exchange may or may not include the right to exchange those rights with a third party (contracts of professional athletes often include such a right, allowing the team owner to "sell" the player to another team).

The conception of ownership becomes especially important when a good or event in which more than one person has an interest is indivisible. One class of such indivisible events or goods consists of those which generate externalities when they are used. Coase's (1960) paper on the problem of social cost gives a number of examples of ways in which certain activities by one party impose externalities on another. A pub which maintained its own brewery created unpleasant odors that affected the owners of the neighboring property. The machines of a candy manufacturer in a certain building created extensive disturbance for a physician in a neighboring flat. In these cases some *use* of property by one person created negative externalities for others, and it is the right to carry out this use which is at issue. As Coase points out, such rights may be bought or sold apart from general ownership of the property or good in question.

In other cases of events or indivisible goods, the right to control the outcome of the event or use of the good may be divided up in any of a variety of ways. In a country where an automobile is too expensive to be bought by one person or one family, it may be jointly owned, with usage rights divided by time (days of the week or some other arrangement). The right of disposal may be a right to dispose of the usage right (that is, to sell the right to use the car on Saturdays) or a right to dispose of the good; in the latter case the disposal right is ordinarily held jointly, and a collective decision is necessary to sell or otherwise dispose of the good. The same principle of division of ownership rights to property by time has recently come into use for vacation property. A person "owns" the right to use a given property for two weeks per year, a right which may be bought or sold just as is true for full-time ownership.

The right to control outcomes of events may be divided by time as well. When a divorce results in joint custody of a child, this is ordinarily realized by the child's being under one parent's control for part of the time and the other's control for part of the time. In the military certain actions may be taken only by collective decision in peacetime but may be decided on by a single field commander in wartime; also, decisions that are ordinarily made at a higher level may be made at a lower level in a field of battle. A pilot has control of a plane during its flight, but when the plane is within a certain distance of an airport, rights of control pass to air traffic controllers; similarly, a captain of a ship has control of the ship during its voyage, and when the ship enters a harbor, rights of control pass to the harbor pilot.

In some cases control of an indivisible good or event is divided by giving each of a number of actors a chance at complete control. This occurs where rights to direct actions of a collectivity are vested in a leadership position (a "dictator's role"), and then there is competition for access to that position.[1] The case takes its purest form when the leader or dictator is chosen by casting lots. The same principle applies when chances on a prize are sold or otherwise allocated.

The most frequent division of rights of control over an indivisible event in which more than one actor has an interest is a distribution of partial control—in the form of a vote on a collective decision—to each of a number of actors (for example, each actor who has an interest in the outcome). The collective decision is made through application of a decision rule, such as majority rule, unanimity rule, or some more complex rule (for example, that which applies to the enacting of legislation in the U.S. federal government). This allocation of partial rights of control over an indivisible event presents numerous problems, because the implications of how these rights of partial control combine to produce a decision are not straightforward.

As indicated in all of the above, the allocation of rights is central to the functioning of a social system.

A major source of change in the functioning of social systems is innovation in the allocation of rights. For example, Berle and Means (1933, p. 8) state that the modern corporation, with its separation of ownership and control, has split the atom of private property. That split was a major innovation which involved separation of the rights to use a set of capital resources from the rights to benefit from them and dispose of them. It is also true that a restriction of rights can change greatly the functioning of a social system, as the enclosure laws in England, by restricting the rights to common use of land, changed greatly the functioning of the economic system.

For a certain class of economic goods, the idea that what is exchanged is a right to carry out actions in a certain way appears cumbersome and not especially useful. These are the classic private, divisible, alienable goods with no externalities. For such goods purchase of the good ordinarily implies purchase of the right to use it as desired, since its use imposes no externalities on others. Although this is true, there are many goods which initially appear to fall into this category but which do not carry unrestricted rights. The purchase of a gun does not allow its use for hunting, or the purchase of an automobile does not allow its

1. Zablocki (1980) describes a commune in which something like this authority structure existed: "Astar was anarchistic in the sense of wanting to avoid authoritarian rules and relationships as much as possible. The business organization of the commune, however, was complex enough to make this difficult. Those who had seniority tended to gravitate toward positions of authority simply because they knew more of what was necessary to make the farm work. In an attempt to find a creative response to this dilemma, the Astar commune developed a paradoxical form of dictatorship in the service of anarchism. According to this policy, each person in the commune, male or female, was required to take dictatorial control and responsibility for the entire operation of the commune for a one-week period. It was felt that, once the commune had gone through two or three rounds with everyone taking a turn at dictator, the members would be sufficiently imbued with a sense of the needs of the entire operation to be able to return to the desirable condition of an anarchistic commune, based on each person's taking responsibility for his or her own share" (p. 233).

being driven. Those uses require purchase of the relevant licenses. Even the purchase of food does not include purchase of the right to eat the food anywhere, without restriction—for example, in a retail store. That right is controlled by the store owner.

Thus, although it is cumbersome in the case of certain goods to think of what is being acquired or given up as a right to act, it is conceptually correct and often useful to do so.

What Are Rights?

Perhaps the most highly regarded classification of rights, and one of the most perceptive examinations of rights in general, is that of the legal theorist Wesley Hohfeld (1923). Hohfeld distinguished between "claim-rights" and "liberty-rights." Rights to act, under examination here, are in Hohfeld's terms liberty-rights. The right to control another's action, in contrast, is a claim-right in Hohfeld's terms. Thus, when an actor's right to act is transferred by that actor (or by others, as a later section will show is possible) to another actor or actors, the first actor loses the liberty-right and the other or others come to have a claim-right toward him.

Hohfeld's examination, however, does not pursue the question of the nature of a right in the direction most useful to this discussion, necessitating a step-by-step examination. Unfortunately for this examination, the most extensive analyses of rights have been carried out by moral philosophers, whose concern is with the normative question of how rights ought to be distributed, or what the *right* distribution of rights is. (Some notable contributions to this discussion have been those of Nozick, 1974; Steiner, 1977; and Lomasky, 1987.) As will be indicated shortly, an implication of the theoretical position to be developed here is that this question can have no answer.

In order to conceive of rights as being exchanged, it is first necessary to examine the question of just how to conceive of what a right is. First, a formally or constitutionally defined legal right can be quite simply described. If a person has a legal right to take an action or to use or dispose of a good or a resource or to control the outcome of an event, this implies that the person may do so without interference from legal authorities. If a right is protected by law, then interference by another actor with an actor's exercise of that right will be constrained by authorities.

None of this causes any trouble. The problems that arise lie in the broad area of rights that are *not* covered by law. What constitutes a right in such cases? One element of the answer is that the concept of a right intrinsically involves more than one person. If person A feels that he has the right to smoke at a given place and time but person B does not, it cannot be said that A has the right, despite the fact that he believes he does. It can only be said that the right to smoke at that time and place is in dispute. It is, in fact, those cases in which rights are in dispute that help most in illuminating just what is meant by a right. When all agree that a right exists (such as the right to a glass of water when one orders a meal in a restaurant) or that a right does not exist (as in the case of breaking into a line of people waiting to be seated in a restaurant), then the essential character of the right remains obscure.

It can be said provisionally that an actor has a *right* to carry out an action or to have an action carried out when all who are affected by exercise of that right accept the action without dispute. But this has very strong implications for a theory of action. In the preceding chapter I treated the structures of (rights of) control as objective structures, existing apart from particular actors. Yet this provisional definition of rights implies that that is not so; that rights imply inter-subjective consensus. This conception of rights implies that there is not a single "objective" structure of rights of control, but a structure of rights of control subjectively held by each actor in the system, and that we may speak of a right of control over an event being held by an actor only when that right exists in the subjective structures held by each of the actors affected by exercise of that right.

There are, in effect, as many private worlds as there are actors. The private world of an actor consists of the full distribution of rights as perceived by that actor, together with the actor's interests. There are two sources of conflict in such a system of private worlds. One source is a difference in perceptions of where rights lie: One actor perceives a right to be in his hands, and a second actor perceives the right to be not in the first actor's hands, but in his own. A second source is a conflict of interests that can exist even when the locus of rights is perceived the same by all. When the perceived distributions of rights are alike for all actors in a system, there is a single distribution of rights, and conflicts are confined to the second type, conflicts of interest.

In this conception there is not a single system of action, but as many systems of action as there are actors. Each actor has a set of interests in events, as well as a subjective conception of the rights of control for all events in which he has some interest (direct or derived through the dependency on the events of other events in which he has a direct interest). The interests of different actors taken together produce an overall structure of interest.

The structures of rights of control as held subjectively by each actor do not, however, consist merely of that actor's rights, which taken together with others' rights produce an overall structure of rights. Each actor's subjective conception of rights covers all events in which he has some interests, as well as some in which he does not. This is a portion of the overall structure of rights that overlaps extensively with that of others; and the different conceptions may be inconsistent. A smoker and a nonsmoker together in the same room may have different conceptions of who holds rights over smoking in that situation. There are four possibilities in this simple case. They are shown in Table 3.1, which also lists the actions that would take place in each case.

There is a general tendency for the conceptions of different persons about who holds the rights to come into agreement over time. The actions that take place in cells 2 and 3 of the table tend to bring conceptions into consistency. The dispute that arises in cell 2 leads each actor to recognize that his conception of rights is

Table 3.1 Configuration of smoker's and nonsmoker's conceptions of who holds the rights over smoking.

		Nonsmoker's conception of who holds the right	
		Smokers	Non-smokers
Smoker's conception of who holds the right	Smokers	1	2
	Nonsmokers	3	4

Cell	Who holds smoking rights?		Action
	Smoker's conception	Nonsmoker's conception	
1	Smokers	Smokers	Smoker lights up; nothing more happens.
2	Smokers	Nonsmokers	Smoker lights up; nonsmoker objects.
3	Nonsmokers	Smokers	(a) Smoker does not smoke; or (b) smoker asks permission for the right to smoke, and nonsmoker replies he already has the right to do so, without asking.
4	Nonsmokers	Nonsmokers	(a) Smoker does not smoke; or (b) smoker asks permision for the right to smoke, which nonsmoker may or may not grant.

not universally held. If the dispute involves more than two persons, one side will recognize that it is in the minority and may yield to the majority. In cell 3 the actions of the actors produce a less strong movement toward consistency, because there is no confrontation. There will, however, be a recognition that one's own conception of rights is not universally held, and some movement toward the local majority can be expected.[2]

2. Different persons, different families, and different cultures have widely varying likelihoods of carrying out actions associated with cells 2 and 3. If both actors have some uncertainty about who holds the rights and both are timid, they will for safety act so as to be in cell 3. If both

In the case of smoking, exogenous changes (such as increased concerns with health, coupled with evidence about the negative effects of smoking on the health of smokers and that of others nearby) have moved the conceptions of smoking rights in many settings out of cell 1, an equilibrium state, and into cell 2 or 3. If nonsmokers are, as might be expected, more health conscious and quicker to accept evidence of negative health effects of smoking than are smokers, the movement will in most instances be from cell 1 to cell 2. As long as the exogenous effects continue to move people from a conception that smokers have the right to control smoking to the conception that nonsmokers have it, majorities against smokers' rights to smoke will develop in both cells 2 and 3, and this will move the system toward the new equilibrium, in which all agree that nonsmokers control those rights. Once the new equilibrium is established, it is meaningful to say that nonsmokers hold the rights regarding smoking—just as it is meaningful to say that smokers hold the rights regarding smoking when there is an equilibrium in cell 1. It is not meaningful to speak of a right "being held" when the configuration represented by cells 2 and 3 is widely found.

The dependence of a right on both power and recognition by others is shown by the claiming of a right. An actor may claim a right to carry out a certain action, but unless others recognize that claim, he has no right. Under what conditions will others recognize such a claim? If they have no interest in the consequences of the action, they may recognize the claim. If they do have an interest in those consequences, they still may recognize the claim if the actor has sufficient power to enforce it. Even if he does not, they may recognize the claim as part of a more general claim that a number of actors have the right to carry out actions of that class, if the interest and power of those actors are sufficient to enforce the claim. The way in which location of a right is socially established is intimately connected with the way in which a norm emerges (treated in Chapter 11) and with the outcome of collective decisions with natural decision rules (treated in Chapter 14).

In a formal organization the way power and interests shape the allocation of rights is less amorphous than the imagery of consensus in the preceding paragraphs suggests. An example is provided by a memorandum distributed by a library administrator to faculty members who had studies in the University of Chicago library in the fall of 1988:

Memorandum

In re: Smoking in Faculty Studies

I have been asked to request that faculty who smoke in their studies please keep the study door closed. It seems a reasonable request and so I am

---

are aggressive, they will act so as to be in cell 2. It is easy to see that if both are timid, the matter may remain unresolved longer than it will if both are aggressive. If one is aggressive and the other timid, the aggressive actor may claim (and thus locally acquire) a right that the timid actor will not dispute.

distributing this note and asking that smokers cooperate with their neighbors.

I also wish to remind everyone that smoking is not permitted in the cor-
ridors.

Thank you.

As this memorandum indicates, formal authority over actions of faculty members in their library studies that affect others is held by library administrators.
The right of control over actions is implicitly given up by a faculty member in
acquiring a study. For certain actions the library officials do not themselves
directly determine the direction but either leave the right in the hands of the
actors or take it from them by implicitly weighting the interests of the actors
(smokers in this case) and those affected by the action. This appears to be the
process by which the rights allocation specified in the first paragraph of the
memorandum was arrived at. The second paragraph refers to a fully consolidated right, one that was earlier transferred out of the hands of the actors and
is no longer in question.

In view of the theory of rights as based on power-weighted consensus, one
may ask, what can be said about how rights ought to be distributed. That is, what
distribution of rights is *right*? The implication of this theory is that the question is
unanswerable in general; it can be answered only in the context of a particular
system of action, and there the answer is that the existing distribution of rights is
right. To go beyond this implies a vantage point outside the system under consideration, and the theory is explicit that there is no such vantage point. What is
right is defined within the system itself, by the actors' interests and relative
power in that system. The theory implies that moral philosophers searching for
the right distribution of rights are searching for the pot of gold at the end of the
rainbow.

How the Free-Rider Problem
Is Reduced for Rights

The creation of a conjoint norm, as discussed in Chapter 10, involves a transfer
of rights of control of an action from an actor in a system to others. Each gives
up the right of control over actions that impose externalities on others, in return
for partial rights of control over the others' actions. In Chapter 13 the creation of
a constitution in a collectivity is treated; the essential action involved is an
implicit social contract, a transfer of individually held rights of control to the
collectivity. There would appear to be one potential defect in this, however.
How does a given actor have any assurance that if he gives up a right, others will
follow suit? In a state of anarchy, in which each actor claims the right to attempt
to avenge wrongs experienced, how can one actor give up that claim without
suffering loss? It is in the interest of each actor to let others give up their rights
without giving up his own. Thus, although each has an incentive to induce others

to give up their rights to the collectivity, each also has an incentive to withhold his own.

It is this difficulty that led Hobbes (1960 [1651]) to pose the problem of bringing about order through a social contract. But Hobbes saw the problem as more serious than it actually is. Here the consensual character of a right becomes extraordinarily useful, for the determination of who holds a right is not under individual control. If an actor attempts to give up the right to avenge wrongs, he does not lose that right altogether until others follow suit. He loses temporarily by refraining from avenging wrongs; but if, when a wrong is done him, he decides to reclaim that right, he can do so without being sanctioned—since in the eyes of others who have not relinquished their right he still retains that right. Thus he suffers the loss of not exercising the right, but not the loss of being sanctioned if he does attempt to exercise it.

A right is inherently a social entity and, as discussed earlier, exists only when there is a high degree of consensus about where the right lies. For clarity it is important to distinguish between the control of a right and the right of control of an action. The right of control of an action of actor A may be individually held by actor A or may be collectively held or may be held by some actor other than actor A or may be in dispute. But control of the right itself is always held collectively. If all actors affected by an action agree on who should have the right to determine whether the action is taken, a right exists. If they do not, then the right is under dispute. All actors who have power to back up their positions in such a dispute have some control over the right, and all who have an interest in the outcome will exercise that control.

The result of this consensual character of a right is that each individual is not in an exposed position in giving up the right to control his own action. The individual actor already is not in full control of that right, for he holds it only at the pleasure of all those affected by the action and with some capacity to dispute it, just as he has partial control of the rights of others. Thus the giving up of rights over individual control of actions is not a set of individual actions, each subject to a free-rider problem, but is an implicit collective decision about rights to act—a collective decision to transfer a set of rights from individuals to the collectivity.

How Does New Information Bring About a Change in the Allocation of Rights?

The allocation of rights in a social system is a fundamental aspect of the constitution of that system. It is difficult to imagine, in the abstract, how mere information may change the allocation of rights. Therefore, an example may be useful in giving a sense of how this may occur.

The example concerns a right mentioned earlier, the right to smoke in public. There has been an extensive transfer of this right in most subsystems in the United States, beginning in the late 1970s and accelerating in the 1980s. Rights once held by smokers have been transferred to persons in the vicinity of smokers. The range of places in which smokers hold the right to smoke has, throughout this period, steadily shrunk. Of the possible reasons for this change, the one that appears most probable is the increase, over a period of time beginning in the 1960s and continuing through this period, in information about the harmful effects of smoking on health. Two kinds of information have differential relevance to the transfer of rights from smokers to nonsmokers. One kind, the information that first became available, was information about the effects of smoking on the smoker. The second kind of information became available only some time later, in the 1980s; it concerned the effects of smoking on others in the vicinity, so-called passive smoking. It is information of this second kind that has direct relevance to the change in rights.[3] If information about the effects of passive smoking brings about a widespread change in belief, from a belief that smoking has no effects on nonsmokers in the vicinity to a belief that it has a negative effect, this creates a conflict of rights where none existed before. The conflict is between the right to smoke in public and the right not to be involuntarily harmed by another's action.

Both of these rights are forms of the right to liberty, but the example suggests that the right to liberty is asymmetric with regard to the subject of action and the object of action. That is, the example suggests that, other things being equal, the liberty of the subject of action to act in a given way to his benefit is dominated by the liberty of the object of action not to be harmed by that action. The example, however, may be defective: Other things are not equal if the health costs (weighted by the power in the system of those affected by the action) are greater than the pleasure benefits (weighted by the power of the actor).

How is it possible to evaluate whether the costs or benefits are greater? One way is to perform the trick of turning interpersonal comparison of utility into intrapersonal comparison by devising a mental experiment in which the same person is the subject of an action and the object of others' comparable action (see Hare, 1981). The two liberties balance when the costs (amplified by the number of actors experiencing the costs) equal the benefits. For a smoker the pleasure of smoking must outweigh the subjective health costs of inhaling another's smoke, since it outweighs the even greater subjective health costs of smoking itself. For the nonsmoker things are less certain: The subjective health costs of smoking itself do outweigh the pleasure of smoking; it seems likely, but is not certain, that the subjective health costs of others' smoke do so as well. Thus the mental experiment suggests that for nonsmokers the subjective harm is greater than the benefit and for smokers the benefit is greater than the harm. The interpersonal-to-intrapersonal trick did not resolve the conflict of interest. The

3. The objective correctness of the information is not relevant here; what is relevant is the subjective correctness, that is, the general acceptance of the information as correct, which brings about a general change in belief about the effects of the action. The role of information in changing rights through changing beliefs suggests a major source of the power inherent in the control of information.

conflict remains an interpersonal one, and the outcome depends on the (weighted) interests favoring the action and those opposing it. The effect of information in the case of smoking has been to change smokers' internal balance of costs and benefits, leading some smokers not to smoke, and to strengthen the interests of nonsmokers against smoking. This has, in many settings, changed the outcome of this conflict of interests so that rights are no longer held by the actor.

This example of the way in which information changes the allocation of rights shows one path by which such a change occurs. Information changes beliefs; the new beliefs show a conflict of rights; the conflict of rights comes to be resolved by a change in one or the other right. There may be other paths, but the path illustrated by this example, shown in Figure 3.1, seems to be a general one.

Another example, in a very different area, shows the same path. The example concerns racial integration of schools in the United States. The allocation of rights prior to the mid-1960s was one in which local school officials held the right to assign children to schools and parents held the right not to have their children assigned to a distant school on the basis of an arbitrary ground (such as race), as well as the right for their children to have equal educational opportunity. The latter rights were affirmed in the 1954 decision of the Supreme Court in the case *Brown v. Board of Education,* which was brought by a black parent whose child was assigned to an all-black school, despite the closer proximity of another school attended by white children. A government research report issued in 1966, *Equality of Educational Opportunity,* contained information that affected beliefs about the process of achievement in school. The report presented evidence that children of lower socioeconomic status achieved more highly in schools that had a high proportion of children of higher socioeconomic status. This initiated a change in belief that brought into conflict the right to equal educational opportunity and the right of parents not to have their children assigned to a distant school on the basis of an arbitrary ground such as race or socioeconomic status. The evidence indicated that educational opportunity depends on a child's schoolmates and therefore, for some children, on attending school outside their neighborhood. The outcome of the conflict is not clear. Busing decisions which assigned children to schools so as to bring about racial balance across school

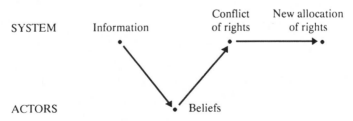

Figure 3.1   Macro-to-micro and micro-to-macro processes in the effect of information on rights.

districts were grounded on findings that school boards had taken actions that violated the right to equal opportunity and thus did not address the conflict directly. Despite this, it is clear that the information provided by the research report added weight to the arguments that busing policies should be instituted.

The general effect of information in changing rights allocations by changing beliefs so as to create a new consensus on rights suggests how research on public opinion can be important in the study of rights in society. The source of the importance, of course, lies in the consensual character of rights.

How Does a Right Change Hands?

Saying that an actor holds a right to carry out a certain action implies that a set of relevant other actors (leaving undefined at this point the precise meaning of "relevant," a question to be examined later) agree that the actor holds this right. The actor cannot be said to hold the right under either of two conditions: (1) when the relevant actors disagree over whether he holds the right, or (2) when the relevant actors agree that someone else holds that right.

Even if it can be said that the actor does hold the right, however, it is not the case that holding the right implies that he holds something free from encumbrances by the relevant others. An actor does not hold a right to act in the same way that he can hold a physical object. This is most transparently evident in the case of formally chartered corporate actors, whose very right to existence comes into being when they are chartered. When the British Parliament chartered the South Sea Company in 1712, it created a set of rights and placed them in the hands of a de facto corporate actor, which until then had no rights. These rights had great value (as later sales of South Sea Company stock show), but the rights were held at the pleasure of Parliament.

If the agreement that constitutes the right dissolves, then the right no longer exists, without the actor's having done anything. If a young man in a village has the right to court a girl from a certain family, he may lose that right without any action on his part, because the family (which by assumption constitutes the relevant other actors in this case) no longer accords him that right. The right has passed out of his hands without his transferring it, because he holds the right *only at the pleasure of the relevant others*. If the British Parliament revokes the charter of a company, all rights held by that company (including the ultimate right, the right to existence) pass out of its hands.

How then can one speak of an actor transferring authority over his actions to another? How can one speak of an actor's giving up to another the right to control his actions within a certain domain? If an actor holds a right only at the pleasure of a set of relevant others, how can that actor transfer that right at his own volition? How can a right become a resource that is exchanged like any material commodity?

It is evident that when an actor contracts to work for another, giving the other the right to control certain actions, the actor does treat the right to control his actions as a resource, exchanging it for something of greater interest to him. Only by recognizing that an actor does not always and everywhere have this right (one ordinarily does not have the right to sell oneself into slavery, for example) is the consensual character of this right made obvious. Even more elementary than prohibitions on the transfer of rights that an actor clearly *does* hold are cases in which an actor cannot give up to another the right to control an action because he does not hold the right. If there is no right to smoke in a given room, then I cannot say to another person in the room, "I give to you the right to tell me when I can smoke." An actor holds a right only if it has been accorded to him by the relevant others or if it has been transferred to him by another who properly held it (and also held the right to transfer it).

An actor may, under a wide range of circumstances, give up the right to control his own actions, but only when (1) he already *holds that right* (at the pleasure of the relevant others, of course) and (2) he *holds the right to dispose of the right,* as is often but not always the case (as prohibitions against slavery show).

Thus a right may change hands in either of two ways. The simplest way is for an actor to give up a right to another, as he would transfer a material resource. But this can occur only if the actor holds the right and also holds the right to transfer it. As is evidenced by the fact that, when the actor does transfer the right, he ordinarily receives something of value for it in return, these two rights are resources that have value in the system of action of which they are a part. The less simple way in which a right may change hands occurs when the relevant others at whose pleasure an actor holds the right stop according him that right. They may do so by consensually moving the right to another actor, thereby taking a resource of value from one actor and giving it to another; or they may do so by losing the consensus which is the necessary (and sufficient) condition for the existence of the right. In this latter case the right goes out of existence, and a resource of value is lost. The reverse process, of course, brings a new right into existence.

Who Are the Relevant Others?

In this formulation I have left unspecified the relevant others at whose pleasure a right is held. In the example of a village boy courting a girl, I indicated that the relevant others were the girl's family; in the case of the chartering of the South Sea Company, the relevant others were essentially a single actor, the British Parliament. More generally, however, the set of relevant others is not so clearly specified.

The general definition of the relevant others is a simple one—they are those with the power, collectively, to enforce the right. In practice, this is a less than fully satisfactory definition because it does not give criteria for determining where this power lies in a specific case. Nevertheless, it does locate the source of rights in power. The power itself may be constrained by the prior existence of other rights. For example, if in a social system there is a general consensus supporting liberty in the sense that John Stuart Mill (1926 [1859]) defined it, one actor may have the power to force another to give up his right to practice the religion of his choice, but that power is constrained by the prior right to liberty, enforced by a general consensus which the first actor does not have the power to overturn.[4]

How Are Rights Partitioned, and How Might They Be?

In some cases rights of ownership are bundled together; in other cases they are partitioned into different hands. In some nomadic tribes of the Sahara, rights to a camel are partitioned extensively: rights to ride, rights to milk, rights to the meat if the animal is killed, and rights to the skin. Among Eskimos hunting polar bears, rights to a portion of the carcass were held by each member of the hunting party, with special rights being held by the hunter whose spear was the first one into the bear.[5]

Rights over different kinds of goods tend to take different forms and tend to be partitioned differently. I will discuss what I see as the most fundamental differences and then examine for each class the form that rights characteristically take and the way these rights may be partitioned.

The most fundamental distinction, in its implication for the form that rights take, is between uses or actions that can be carried out independently without externalities for others and those that cannot. Rights to the former uses or actions may be partitioned without difficulty and may come to be held by different actors. What are thought of as divisible goods without externalities due to usage generally fall into this class. When a divisible good has one principal use (such as being consumed), then its divisibility and lack of externalities mean that different actors can hold different amounts of it and exercise their usage (or consumption) of it without interference with others' rights. When the divisible good has multiple uses, these are alternative uses and mutually exclusive. For example, money may be thought of as a finely divisible good or right with an enormously wide range of multiple uses—but mutually exclusive uses. If money is spent by someone on a concert ticket, that money is used up for that actor and cannot be spent for renting a squash court.

4. Moral philosophers will recognize here a point that is relevant to what are ordinarily called external interests. The question of whether external interests are to "count" can be seen to be easily resolvable through application of the ideas discussed in this section. An external interest counts if the actor with the interest has the power to make it count. This is, of course, an unacceptable solution for most moral philosophers, for in most of their work resolution of an issue in terms of the power of the participants is no resolution at all.

5. The existence of special rights for the hunter whose spear first enters the bear exemplifies an allocation of rights designed to create a socially beneficial incentive: It is to the interest of all members of the village that hunters be motivated to overcome their fear of the danger involved in first attacking a bear. Such a right will be allocated by common consent because of the common benefit it provides.

For indivisible actions consequences cannot be restricted to a single actor. Two or more actors are inextricably linked together, having either conflicting or concordant interests in the same event or action or good. If rights to act are ordinarily held by one actor, the action is said to have externalities, and other actors have an interest in gaining control of the right (for example, those who experience air pollution have an interest in gaining control of the right to pollute). If rights to act are ordinarily held collectively, then some partitioning of this collective right is necessary (for example, into votes).

It is useful to concentrate on these sharply different forms of rights: money as the prototype of a right over divisible actions, with a wide range of mutually exclusive uses, and a vote as the prototype of a partial right over an indivisible event or action. With the first form of rights the partitioning occurs through partitioning into smaller quantities. A smaller quantity of money still gives full rights to act, but to acquire or use or consume a smaller quantity of things.[6] In the case of the indivisible action, the partitioning of the right to act is a partitioning into partial rights over a single action. But are there different ways in which these rights can be partitioned? It is useful to consider this question because an answer may suggest new forms that rights might take in social systems. I will extend here the directions I examined in an earlier work (Coleman, 1986a, chapter 7).

Money, Vouchers, and Services

In many societies there are certain positive rights that are made available to all citizens or residents, although these rights are privately consumed. The most common of these is the right to free schooling for a certain number of years or up to a certain age. Another, available in fewer societies, is the right to free health care. Other rights are available for individuals or families with incomes below a certain level: housing (full or partial support), food (full or partial support), and others.[7]

Such rights are characteristically provided in one of three forms:

1. As government-provided services (or, equivalently, government-supported monopolies, privately operated under a franchise)
2. As subsidies to private suppliers of services, reducing the price to consumers
3. As rights in a form that can generally be called vouchers, by which the consumer chooses among privately supplied services and pays for the ser-

6. It is the case, however, that because some purchasable goods are indivisible, a larger amount of money has a wider range of uses, not merely the capability of buying greater quantities of the same divisible goods.

7. Reich (1964) examined the growth of these rights as the "new property," that is, as a substitute for property rights in the welfare state, and raised questions about their viability as they come to replace classical property rights.

vice with a government-provided voucher or coupon which is redeemed by
the supplier of the service

A fourth broader right is sometimes provided to income-deficient individuals or
families:

4. A cash income supplement

There are numerous examples of each of these forms of the provision of rights.
Government-provided services include schooling in most countries, public housing in many, government-provided health-care services in some, and free food
(bread lines) in still fewer. Subsidies to private suppliers are frequently provided
for housing and for food. Vouchers are provided for food (food stamps), housing
(housing allowances), and health care (physician and hospital are chosen from an
approved set and an eligibility card is used as a health services voucher). In a
few places (for example, the Netherlands), a school voucher or its equivalent is
provided. Finally, in some cases cash welfare payments are made to individuals
or families with little or no income. (The well-known income maintenance experiment in the United States in the 1960s and 1970s was an attempt to assess the
feasibility of making a single cash payment to all low-income families. See Rivlin
and Timpane, 1975; Rossi and Lyall, 1976.)

What is most interesting about these forms of government provision is that
going from form 4 to 3 to 1 (ignoring 2, which is equivalent to 3 except that
provision of the subsidy to producers prevents restriction to a particular class of
consumers) each provision contains a decreasing fraction of the power inherent
in money. Form 4 contains the full power of money, form 3 contains the full
power of money within a restricted realm of choice (education, food, or housing), and form 1 contains a more restricted right, the right to consume a service
that is collectively provided. In providing form 3 rather than 4, governments
retain the right to determine by collective action the nature of the service to be
consumed but give to consumers the right to choose within this domain. In
providing form 1, governments hold collectively all rights contained in money
except the right to consume the service.

It is clear, then, that for the kind of right under discussion here, a privately
consumable, divisible right that is collectively provided, there is a wide range of
variation in partitioning the right between its collectively held component and its
individually held component. At one extreme everything about the service is
collectively determined, with consumption of the service the only right to act
remaining to the individual. At the other extreme everything is individually
determined.

The specific characteristics that differentiate vouchers from both votes and
money can be clarified by imagining a voucher system in which the redistributive
aspect is removed. Suppose that a collectivity, a nation with a currency system,
makes a collective decision of the following sort. It determines a number of
activity areas, including those that are not individually consumed, such as public

administration and national defense. It then determines the fractions of individual income payments that are to be made in currencies that are usable only in various areas of consumption—health, food, housing, recreation, and others—and perhaps a fraction to be made in a currency usable in any area. It does not allow consuming individuals to exchange one currency for another at the government bank but does allow producing institutions, which receive one type of currency but must pay employees a currency mix, to do so, at fixed rates. In such a system, the vouchers, or area-specific currencies, are exactly like money except that their range of power is limited to a specific area. The income earner has lost one degree of power, the power to allocate his income among areas according to personal tastes. Within each area the vouchers have the full power of money.

One might ask why even this degree of power should be removed. Assuming that all children living in a country have a right to a free education, why does the society not decide (in a democratic society the self-governing character of the society makes it reasonable to say that the society decides) to allocate for every child a sum equal to the current cost of educational services, to be paid to the child's parents or guardians in cash? The theory of rational action would conclude that all families would reach a higher point of satisfaction if given the additional freedom represented by cash in place of an area-specific voucher. But the theory of rational choice would also predict (assuming a reasonable utility function) that many families would achieve that higher point of satisfaction through spending most of the cash on things other than education (that is, allocating the extra income in approximately the same ways as their current income is allocated).

Then why, collectively, should members of a society decide to restrict themselves in ways that bring about lower satisfaction? The answer probably lies in part in the public good character of education. The family will not experience many of the costs and benefits that the child, as an adult, will bring, and thus these costs and benefits will not influence the family's current decisions concerning expenditures.

It may also be true, however, that even without the public good character of education, members of a society will collectively (that is, through representatives in a legislature) restrict themselves by distributing vouchers rather than cash. Education is an expenditure for which the benefits come at some distance in the future. It may be easier to precommit collectively to that expenditure than to do so individually. This manipulation of oneself through precommitment is inexplicable by standard rational choice theory (see Elster, 1979). Persons will precommit themselves to future expenditures that seem to them beneficial because they know that later they would, in the absence of a precommitment, make other expenditures instead, ones that they currently judge less beneficial. The standard approaches to rational choice theory cannot account for this reversal of preferences, although efforts have been made to introduce modifications that would do so (Lowenstein, 1985; Ainslie, 1986).

A nonredistributional voucher system as described above, in which all income is paid in area-specific currencies, may appear exotic, but portions of it already exist. Social security deductions from paychecks and subsequent payments constitute an area-specific currency, defined not by type of consumption but by time of consumption; and in some countries initial acceptance by the population of social security was largely on grounds of precommitment (which in this case can alternatively be described as forced savings).

The partitioning of the power or rights inherent in money is widely used within governments and organizations generally. Budgets, approved at the level of the collectivity or organization as a whole and then fulfilled at the level of the department or division, constitute a partitioning of the power of money so that different portions of that power are in the hands of actors (or agents) at different levels of the collectivity or organization. When a legislature approves a global budget for a department of a government, that is comparable to general income for an individual; when a legislature approves a budget by separate line items, that is comparable to area-specific currency for an individual. Thus the principles underlying budget construction for the corporate actor and the principles underlying area-specific income for individuals are alike: A portion of the rights inherent in money is held collectively (perhaps different portions held at different levels of a collectivity or organization), and a portion is held individually, at the point where consumption takes place.

It is obvious from this discussion that even for the prototype of a private divisible good, that is, money, it is possible to partition rights so that they are held in part collectively and in part individually. At one extreme all rights are held by the individual; at the other all rights but that of consuming a collectively determined service are held collectively. The latter extreme is experienced by those who serve in the military or in a religious order and by those who live in company towns. The psychic benefits and costs of living in these kinds of situations are described in literature on these settings.[8]

Just as one can ask how rights to divisible goods may be partitioned, one can ask how rights to indivisible goods may be partitioned. This question, however, cannot be adequately treated without some prior discussion of corporate actors and is therefore reserved until Chapter 17.

Those resources involved in economic, social, and political exchange have one attribute in common: They all consist of rights to act, or in some cases bundles of rights to act in several ways. The essential quality of a right lies in its social base. Rights come into existence, vanish, and are taken from one actor and given to another by social recognition. Yet rights are dependent on power for their enforcement, either the power of the holder of the right to protect his claim or the power of actors other than the holder to enforce their allocation of rights.

---

8. The existence of psychic benefits arising from a restriction on choice is a phenomenon that ˙ɜ inexplicable using current rational choice theory.

Resources, as bundles of rights, may be used, partitioned, and exchanged. The central difference in the use and transfer of resources lies in whether they are divisible and without externalities, that is, whether they can be divided so that the action which inheres in the right (use or consumption of the good or outcome of the event) has consequences only for the actor. For such resources there is a wide array of possible partitionings of the bundle of rights. Some of these are illustrated by the variety of ways in which the rights inherent in money are partitioned, as indicated by the examples given above. Those resources that have the character of indivisible events create special difficulties in partitioning, as well as in transfer and use.

« 4 »

Authority Relations

In a study of communes Zablocki (1980) describes the daily functioning of one:

> At Mandala, as in all Eastern spiritual communes, the major ideological problem was the residual autonomy of individual members: each individual ego was to become conscious of its illusory nature and thus was to be subsumed into the collective ego. At a meeting every morning, everyone accounted for how all of his or her time was to be spent. Each person was responsible for fulfilling the contract specified by this morning report and, furthermore, was subject to criticism and pressure from the group if what he or she was intending to do with the day did not seem to meet communal needs.
>
> The Mandalans attempted to govern themselves by consensus, all individuals being bound by decisions made by the group. In addition, individuals were bound by several communal rules built into the charter of the community that could not be changed: absolute prohibition of coffee, alcohol, and drugs; vegetarian limitations on diet; and severe limitations on the access of the commune to visitors.
>
> In its attempt to discover the right path toward spiritual enlightenment, Mandala had placed itself loosely under the care of an absentee guru who served not as an authority but as a source of advice and guidance. Real day-to-day authority over the life of the commune rested in the hands of a young, energetic charismatic leader who was one of the commune's founders. Directly under him in authority was his wife and several other commune founders.
>
> Under them were those members who had made a long-term commitment to the life. The lowest tier in the hierarchy was for new members or those still tentative in their commitment. (p. 210)

An even more extreme example of transfer of the right to control to a single leader is evident in "the Family," Charles Manson's commune, some of whose members later engaged in brutal murders at his command. One member of that commune later described his feelings.[1]

1. Despite the extent of authority that Manson held over commune members, Watson's statement indicates that it was not coercive. Watson saw himself as better off inside the commune than in the outside world.

Sometimes I felt as though [Manson] were always with me, thinking my thoughts for me—or *his* through me . . . It was as though Charlie kept pulling me back, slowly but persistently, even though we'd had no contact since I walked out the back door of that Topanga Canyon cabin. I tried to fight it, but it was no use, he wouldn't let go of me. I'd seen the world I was living in and he'd warned me, and I found it just what he'd said it would be. (Watson, 1978, p. 81)

As these passages indicate, social action does not consist merely of transactions among independent individuals within a competitive, or market, context. Individuals often act under another's authority, although generally not in as extreme a form as in these communes. Social structure involves organizations and groups of people which engage in action as entities: nations, families, associations, clubs, and unions. These entities, viewed from the outside, may be regarded as actors no less than individuals are. Nevertheless, viewed from the inside, they may be characterized as authority structures.

The most fundamental question regarding authority structures is the question of how they can exist at all—or how, within the conceptual system developed in the preceding chapters, they can be conceived to exist. How, if the theoretical foundation is of a set of independent individuals, each controlling certain events or resources of interest to others, can there develop a social structure in which certain individuals' actions are not under their control but under the authority of another actor (an individual or a corporate actor)? This question is easily answered if it is recognized that among those resources over which individuals have control are their own actions. Individuals may, under threat or promise or because they otherwise see it as in their best interests to do so, give up the right to control certain of their actions. It is the right to control another's actions that is the usual definition of authority; this is what I will mean by authority in this book. One actor has authority over another in some domain of action when the first holds the right to direct the actions of the second in that domain.

This chapter examines the implications of this answer. A first way of doing so is by returning to the properties of events or resources discussed in Chapter 2. In simple systems of social exchange all events or resources over which actors gain or give up control are alienable. Yet although the classic private goods of economics are ordinarily alienable—that is, they can be physically transferred when an exchange is effected—many goods or events or resources over which actors have control are not. Of these the most important are an actor's own actions. An actor may well have, in his actions, various skills or capabilities or potential services that are of interest to others. Yet an actor cannot physically transfer actions to another actor in the way that he can physically transfer a pound of sugar or a pair of shoes. He can only transfer to others such intangibles as a promise to act in a certain way or the right to control his actions within certain specified limits. Given this conception of rights to control an inalienable resource—one's own actions—an authority relation may be defined: An authority relation of one actor over another exists when the first has rights of control over certain actions of the other.

Conceiving for the present of rights as being represented by pieces of paper, actor 2 has authority over actor 1 when 2 holds a piece of paper with a statement something like the following: "The actor holding this paper has the right to direct certain actions of actor 1. This right is subject to the following limitations (on classes of actions, time, place, or other dimensions)."[2] At the outset that right may be held by actor 1, who has de facto control of his own actions; in such a case an authority relation arises only when actor 1 transfers that right to actor 2. In some cases, however, the right is held by actor 2 at the outset (as a parent holds rights of control over a child's actions at birth or as the state holds rights of control over certain actions, defined as illegal, of its citizens), and the authority relation exists until revoked by actor 1. (The question of *whether* actor 1 can unilaterally revoke the authority relation, can unilaterally withdraw the right to control, is another question, which goes back to the consensual character of rights, as discussed in Chapter 3. I will turn to that question later in this chapter.)

It may appear odd to begin a discussion of authority, a relation in which a superordinate directs or governs the actions of a subordinate, by describing actions of the actor who becomes the subordinate. Yet this is essential to a conception of authority that is consistent with the theory of this book: Authority must be vested in a superordinate before the superordinate can exercise authority. Authority exists only when the superordinate holds this right.

The Right to Control One's Own Actions

What is the condition under which an individual holds the right to control his own actions? A naive answer to this question might be that the individual always holds this right, unless he has already transferred it to another. But this is not correct, as numerous examples make clear. A child born to a slave in slaveholding Rome or the slaveholding South of the United States was a slave, without the rights of free persons. Any child born in our society lacks certain civil rights; rights of control over certain actions are held by the child's parents. A citizen of a state who has full civil rights nevertheless has those rights circumscribed by law and does not hold an unlimited right to act as he wishes.

More generally, a person may not hold the right to control his actions for either of two reasons: The right may be held by another, even without having been transferred by the person to the other; or the right may not exist. This follows from the definition of a right, as given in Chapter 3. A right exists only when there is general consensus among the relevant actors about which actor holds the right. When that consensus is absent, then the right does not exist. And when that consensus places the right to control actor A's actions in the hands of

2. This is a simplification, of course, since rights are consensual in character, as discussed in Chapter 3. I will examine this simplification later in this chapter.

actor B (as, for example, consensus ordinarily places many rights to control children's actions in the hands of their parents), then actor B holds the right. To the question of which actors are relevant in determining whether there is a consensus, the answer is that power and interest determine relevance: An actor is relevant to the determination of where the right is lodged only if he has an interest in the action or event in question and has the power to support his claim to relevance; and the importance of an actor's voice in determining the locus of the right is determined by the amount of his interest, amplified by his power.

When, in a particular social system, persons are legally regarded as "free," this implies that after childhood (which I will return to shortly) there is a broad class of the person's actions in which no other actor (including the state) has a legitimate interest. This would not be true if the person were regarded by law as "unfree," that is, as the property of another actor. As the other's property, the person's actions would be of legitimate interest to the other; the law would give the other the right to control the person's actions.

Short of legally defined slavery the constitutions (implicit or explicit) of many social systems have legitimized other forms of involuntary subjection to authority. The most common of these is a form involving women. In some societies daughters are held to be subject to the authority of the father, who may sell the daughter to a prospective husband (for what is called a bride price). The wife then becomes the property of the husband, who has a legitimate right to control a broad range of her actions.[3]

Disregarding slavery, chattelism, and legally defined childhood, the constitutions of many social systems give no actor legitimate interests in a person's actions unless those actions have a clear effect on the other actor. There is an efficiency rationale for this, in that rights of control of actions are placed in the hands of those with strongest interests in the actions, and thus the strongest interest in exercising that control in a way that satisfies those interests. As long as those interests are not in opposition to a widely spread, although weak, interest in the actions on the part of numerous others, there is no strong rationale for placing the right elsewhere than in the person's own hands.

There is a second virtue, from the perspective of a functioning social system, in rights to control actions being held by the actor. This allocation of rights is self-policing, because it places rights of control in the hands of that actor with de facto control. That is not true for any other allocation: Slaveholders must police the actions of slaves; parents must supervise the actions of children; the state must police those actions of citizens over which it holds rights of control (for example, prison inmates). In other words, authority that is not voluntarily vested by an actor in another must be backed by coercive power if it is to be enforced. Consistent with this is the fact that the authority of parents over a

3. It is true, of course, that in some such social systems the interests of women are socially recognized, in that a husband's exercise of authority is limited by the society and he may be subject to social sanctions for overstepping the limits. Nevertheless, the authority, even if circumscribed, is present.

child diminishes over time, as their coercive power over the child—that is, the power to make the child who does not obey worse off—diminishes.[4]

When the principle that rights to control actions are held by the actor unless those actions have a clear effect on other actors is raised to the level of a political philosophy, it is that of liberalism. John Stuart Mill (1926 [1859]) expressed this philosophy:

> As soon as any part of a person's conduct affects prejudicially the interests of others, society has jurisdiction over it, and the question whether the general welfare will or will not be promoted by interfering with it becomes open to discussion. But there is no room for entertaining any such question when a person's conduct affects the interests of no persons besides himself, or need not affect them unless they like (all the persons concerned being of full age and the ordinary amount of understanding). In all such cases, there should be perfect freedom, legal and social, to do the action and stand the consequences. (pp. 141–142)

Mill's statement can be regarded as the statement of a political philosophy contending for position in the constitution (implicit or explicit) of a social system. Although Mill's statement is expressed as what "should be," or ought to be, it is merely one political philosophy among others contending for incorporation into a constitution.

There is a close association between the political philosophy of liberalism and a philosophical position that arose in the seventeenth century and holds that all persons are endowed with a set of natural rights. That is, all persons begin with, at minimum, a particular subset of resources, a subset that is labeled "rights" or "natural rights" or "inalienable rights." Such a philosophical position may be seen as motivated by the same aim that leads to inclusion of a bill of rights in constitutions of states—the aim of providing some ultimate grounding for distribution of rights among individuals. Such a grounding, however, must always be based on some external criterion or value outside the constitution of the system. It is the constitution, implicit or explicit, that embodies the social consensus upon which any allocation of rights is based.

Vesting of Authority

As indicated above, an individual may or may not hold the right of control over a particular class of his own actions. Only if the individual holds that right and, in

4. Also consistent with this is the fact that those parents whose coercive power is based on more than relative physical strength, such as on ownership of land or possession of other wealth, are able to maintain authority over their children far beyond the age when the child's strength matches that of the father. When the family has nothing to give or withhold from the child, the family's authority depends almost entirely on physical strength. This also suggests why familial authority is maintained over daughters for a longer time than over sons, especially in those families in which authority must rest principally on physical coercion.

addition, holds the right to transfer that right to another, can he voluntarily vest authority in another. Holding these two rights can be seen as equivalent to holding the piece of paper described earlier containing the words "The actor holding this paper has the right to direct certain actions of actor 1 . . ." The examination of authority throughout this chapter assumes that actors begin with this resource, which may be of some value to others and may therefore be used in exchange. It is also a resource which the actor may prefer to have held by another and thus may voluntarily transfer to another (as a young woman in taking vows to become a nun transfers authority over a large class of her actions to the church).

The assumption that actors hold rights of control over their actions and rights of transfer is never true for all actions of persons in a social system. It is only for those actions (which will differ from system to system) to which actors hold these rights that the vesting of authority is of interest. Before turning to those actions, I will examine briefly authority relations that are involuntary, where rights of control are held not by the actor, but by others.

Involuntary Authority and Divestment

The state retains rights of control over certain actions of even adult persons. In such authority relations the decision to vest authority does not arise, but divestment, or revoking, of authority does arise, as it does for the authority held by parents over children. In both cases the consensus on where rights lie is embodied in the legal system, which circumscribes persons' civil rights and enforces parental authority over children. Because the right to control the action and the right to transfer that right are not held by the actor, the right to divest authority also does not lie with the actor. In such a case, when the right to control the actor's action is constitutionally held not by the actor but by another, divestment cannot be carried out without invoking the coercive power of the state, which enforces the constitutionally defined consensus.

Nevertheless, persons do attempt to divest themselves of that authority: Children run away from home, citizens leave (or attempt to leave) a country, and groups of citizens sometimes engage in revolts. These actions can succeed only when the state, holding coercive power, allows them to (in most states the right of free emigration is held by citizens) or when the state does not have the power to enforce its own or parents' authority. (The case of revoking authority by overthrowing the existing authority structure is of special importance in social systems and is examined in Chapter 18.) Actors may also act to disobey authority, that is, to act contrary to authoritative directives, without withdrawing rights from the authoritative other. Such an action may be a test of the power of enforcement on which authority depends.

As Simmel (1950) points out in his discussion of authority, coercion is never absolute.

> Even in the most oppressive and cruel cases of subordination, there is still a considerable measure of personal freedom. We merely do not become aware of it, because its manifestation would entail sacrifices which we usually never think of taking upon ourselves. (p. 183)

Choice always exists even for persons subject to the most despotic authority.[5] Thus the question of why a given person submits to authority always arises. The answer may in some cases be easily given: because the authoritative other holds sufficiently extensive resources and is sufficiently willing to use them that the alternative would lead to serious negative consequences. As that answer indicates, even coercion may be regarded as a transaction. As Simmel notes, if a despot accompanies an order by a threat of punishment or an offer of reward, this indicates that the despot is willing to be bound by the results. The subordinate thus has a *claim* on the despot, contingent on the subordinate's actions. In authority relations that must be backed by coercion, the exchange is a somewhat special one in that the superordinate agrees to withhold an action that would make the subordinate worse off in return for the subordinate's obeying the superordinate.

It is, of course, true that many authority relations that require coercion for enforcement are ones in which the initial vesting of authority is done voluntarily. The necessity for coercion in such a case is like the enforcement invoked in a long-term contract, entered into voluntarily but binding on the parties. Such authority relations are entered into when, despite the absence of threat, the actor who becomes the subordinate transfers control because he believes he will be better off by doing so. The fief in feudal times exemplifies this relation. Enfeoffment was a contract in which one actor, who became the vassal, put himself under the authority of another, who became his lord. In doing so, the vassal promised absolute loyalty in return for protection. In many cases this relation was established when one man was seen as most powerful in the vicinity; therefore others would enfeoff themselves to him, establishing him in authority over them as vassals. This gave the lord certain rights of control over the vassals' actions, such as the right to collect taxes and to conscript them for military service. But the enfeoffing was done voluntarily, for the prospective vassal saw himself as better off with this protection than without it.

There is another phenomenon that is nearly the opposite of an authority relation entered into voluntarily but observed only when it is enforced. This is the case of involuntary authority (for example, family or state) or pure exercise of power, which, when exercised effectively in directions partially in accord with a subordinate's interests, comes to be accepted by the subordinate as legitimate.

---

5. Even Max Weber, who does not emphasize the choice involved in the authority relation, says in his definition of authority that "imperative coordination (control) was defined above as the probability that specific commands (or all commands) from a given source will be obeyed by a given group of persons . . . A criterion . . . is a certain minimum of voluntary submission" (1947 [1922], p. 324).

That there is such a phenomenon is widely recognized. The specific conditions under which it occurs are not well known.

Voluntary Vesting of Authority

Not all authority results from a voluntary vesting, as the preceding discussion indicates. However, in most social systems there is a broad class of actions over which rights of control are held by the actor, who also holds the right to transfer those rights. For this broad class of actions, it becomes possible to ignore the consensual character of rights (unless that consensus is called into question) and to treat the rights as though they were a tangible resource held by and usable by the individual. Thus it becomes possible to conceive of the vesting of authority, as was done in the beginning of this chapter, as the transfer of a piece of paper embodying a right.

The answer to the question of why persons vest rights of control over their actions in others differs sharply for two broad classes of authority relations. In the first class one actor vests authority in another because the first actor believes that he will be better off by following the other's leadership. He vests rights of control unilaterally, without extrinsic compensation. In the second class the actor transfers rights of control without holding this belief, but in return for some extrinsic compensation. In the first class the actor's transfer of rights of control over certain actions can be seen as unilateral transfer of the piece of paper described earlier; in the second class the transfer occurs only as part of an exchange.

Conjoint and Disjoint Authority Relations

Authority in the communes described at the beginning of this chapter is seen by the members of the commune to be in accord with their fundamental interests, even though that authority may be exercised to discipline a member or may go against a member's wishes in specific instances. When such vesting of authority occurs, it is ordinarily because the actor making the transfer sees the interests of the person (or corporate actor) to whom the transfer is made to be sufficiently like his own that the exercise of authority will bring benefits. Thus a rational actor makes a transfer in the expectation that he will be better off as a result of the exercise of this authority.

Besides communes, there are many other authority systems in which an actor makes a transfer without an extrinsic payment and with the expectation that the very exercise of authority by the other will bring benefits. Such an authority system is exemplified by an association such as a trade union. Each union member gives up control over certain actions (the right to sign a contract with the employer, for example) along with rights of taxation (union dues) in the expectation that actions on the part of the union will bring benefits (wage negotiations may bring greater income, for example).

It is useful to note that I do not make the distinction here that Max Weber (and others) made between associative groups, which he saw as based on rational common interests, and communal groups, which he saw as based on nonrational attachments. In the conceptual structure being presented here, both what are ordinarily described as communes and what are ordinarily described as associations are authority systems in which actors transfer authority without receiving an extrinsic payment. This is a subjectively rational transfer of authority when it is based on the belief that the exercise of the authority will be in the actors' interests.

The matter is altogether different for another class of authority structures, best illustrated by a formal organization composed of employees working for pay. In such an organization transfer of the right to control is made in exchange for payment of a wage or salary. There is no assumption that authority will be exercised in the interest of the actors (the employees) who have transferred the right—although in the actual workings of such organizations demands are sometimes made that the exercise of authority be made partly in the interest of those subordinates. For example, the closing of a plant and resulting loss of jobs may be protested, and demands for management attention to employee interests with respect to working conditions are often made. It is also sometimes believed by the superordinate in such relations that its long-term interests are in part in common with those of its subordinates.[6]

Weber's conception of bureaucracy as one ideal type of authority system portrays it as a system in which each official or employee exchanges the right to control his actions (in a limited realm of events) for a monetary wage and in which all actions of the organization are taken in the interest of the central authority at the top. Although a bureaucracy contains other attributes, and thus is only one form of authority system in which there is an extrinsic payment to the subordinates, it is a particularly good example of an authority system involving extrinsic payment. The legal system (which for present purposes can be regarded as a set of principles expressing the processes of a largely internally consistent social system) contains another example, in the law of agency. The law of agency defines three parties: principal, agent, and third party. In return for compensation the agent gives the principal the right to control his actions in a well-defined set of events, putting his services at the disposal of the principal.[7]

6. For example, Carl Kaufmann, of the public relations department of E. I. Du Pont de Nemours, describes the renovation of a plant which had made cellophane to produce other products: "Du Pont could have squeezed a bit more profit out of one or two of these newer products by producing them at other locations . . . They were considering the corporation's relationship to long-service employees, and to the community. (Of course, one can respond to this by saying that this policy, followed long-range, is the way to maximize profits, an argument with which I would agree.)" (1969, p. 237).

7. There are two forms of the law of agency: the independent contractor form, and the master-servant form. Only in the latter is a transfer of rights to control action made, and thus an authority relation established. (See Mecham, 1952 [1933]; see also Chapter 7 for a further discussion of agency.)

The law explicitly recognizes that the interests of the agent are different from those of the principal, and much of the law of agency is concerned with adjudication between principal and agent when actions of the latter may have been taken in his own interests rather than in those of the principal.

The two kinds of situations in which actors transfer rights of control over their own actions lead to different types of authority structures, as is illustrated by contrasting communes and trade unions with bureaucratic organizations and agency relations. The first of the two types, in which the transfer is made with an assumption that exercise of authority will benefit the subordinate, I will call a conjoint authority relation. The second, in which there is no such assumption, I will call a disjoint authority relation. Because actors are conceived to be rational, conjoint authority relations are ordinarily established by a unilateral transfer of rights of control, whereas disjoint authority relations are established only when compensation is paid. The terms "conjoint" and "disjoint" refer to the correspondence between the interests of the subordinate and the directives of the superordinate. In a conjoint authority relation the superordinate's directives implement the subordinate's interests. In a disjoint authority relation they do not; the subordinate's interests must be satisfied by extrinsic means.

Before turning to an examination of the properties of conjoint and disjoint authority relations, I want to make a distinction between an authority relation and an authority structure. An authority structure may be composed of a single authority relation or a number of authority relations. An authority relation is brought about by a transfer from one actor to another of the right to control certain actions. Thus, to be precise, it is only individual authority relations that may be described as conjoint or disjoint. Given these complexities, it is nevertheless helpful for the purpose of exposition to apply the terms "conjoint" and "disjoint" not only to authority relations but also to authority structures, as I will do in Chapter 7. Many authority structures consist primarily of one of the two types of authority relations, and as a consequence I will write of authority structures as though they do consist of only one.[8]

The genotypic distinction between conjoint and disjoint authority relations is introduced not only because it corresponds to phenotypically different forms of authority, but because the difference leads to different kinds of behavior and, in particular, to different kinds of problems for these two types of authority relations.

8. In a disjoint authority structure, such as a business firm, subordinates at a given level often have similar interests. It is this similarity of interests among those subject to the same authority that gives rise to joint actions, such as unionization. This similarity also leads to efforts on the part of superordinates to introduce conflicts of interest. One example is a story, possibly apocryphal, that circulated among union organizers in the 1930s, about an employer who paid alternate workers on the assembly line at different wage rates to introduce divergent interests. (See also Dreyfuss, 1952, on hierarchical grading in department stores.)

The Puzzle of Conjoint Authority Relations

When an actor vests the right to control his actions in another in exchange for extrinsic compensation, the potential gain to the actor is self-evident. This is not so when an actor vests rights of control without compensation. If the superordinate directs the subordinate to take actions he would not take voluntarily, then the subordinate would appear to be worse off than if he could act under his own authority. If the superordinate does not direct him to take such actions, then there seems to be no reason to vest authority in the first place.

There are, however, certain cases of conjoint authority relations in which the reason for vesting authority is clear. For example, if I am lost and I believe that another person knows the way, then it is rational for me to vest authority in that person. This appears to be a special case, yet it merits further examination. If I vest authority in another, I believe that the other has some qualities that I do not, qualities that make it possible for him to lead me to take actions that have an outcome more satisfactory to me. This circumstance may arise because social conditions are particularly disordered or confusing, because I am particularly disordered or confused (for example, if I am undergoing great changes), or because the person in whom I vest authority appears to have special qualities— or because of some combination of these.

Social disorganization, personal disorganization, and special qualities of a person are conditions which are seen by social theorists as leading to a phenomenon often regarded as outside the bounds of rational action, the peculiar phenomenon of charismatic appeal. Max Weber emphasizes the personal qualities of the "charismatic person" and overlooks both the characteristics of the person vesting authority and the characteristics of the situation. Following Weber, it has been common to regard charisma as wholly a quality of the person in whom rights of control are vested.[9] But other theorists have identified social disorganization as a source of the charismatic transfer (Zablocki, 1980; Bradley, 1987). Zablocki (1980) infers from his study of communes that "alienation from a coherent structure of values makes a collective action difficult. Charisma is a collective response to the need for action in the presence of alienation. In the presence of shared articulated values, collectivities are able to mobilize resources to achieve action" (p. 273). The charismatic leader is the instrument through which the members of a commune are able to mobilize one another so that collective action can take place, making each member better off. (Yet even

9. Weber, who developed the concept of charismatic authority, is not clear about whether the charismatic endowment is something the person *has* or something the person is *seen to have*. This confusion is evident in Weber's ambivalence about Joseph Smith, the leader of the Mormons, who, Weber says, "cannot be classified in this way [as a charismatic leader] with absolute certainty since there is a possibility that he was a very sophisticated type of deliberate swindler" (1947 [1922], p. 359). Because it is the actions of the followers that make a charismatic leader, however, what is essential is that the person be *seen* to have the endowment.

if this statement is accepted as true, it expresses a misplaced concreteness. The members do not act as a body, but as individuals. What remains unanswered is why one person will vest authority when he experiences costs by doing so, even though he experiences benefits from others' doing so. I will come back to this question, which at this point must be regarded as unresolved.)

Another condition which can, in principle, lead to extensive vesting of authority in another is personal disorganization or extensive personal change. There are a number of incidental observations that suggest the importance of personal disorganization and change as precursors to the vesting of authority in another. Religious penitents (who vest control over their actions in God) are characteristically seen as persons who are "lost," who cannot find for themselves a satisfactory mode of existence. The members of the Jonestown community, who vested such extensive authority in their leader that they drank a deadly poison at his command, have been described as persons who had little to live for before they joined the community. Persons who are engulfed by romantic love and "give" themselves to another seem characteristically to be at a point of extensive personal change, in particular, the point of leaving childhood and entering adulthood, leaving their families of origin and entering a wider world.[10]

These sociopsychological phenomena may also encourage strategic action on the part of those in whom authority is to be vested. That this does occur is suggested by the "stripping" process which often occurs when a person first enters a social order from which authoritative direction will flow, such as a religious order, the military, or a fraternity. Stripping of previous associations and resources encourages the new member to vest total authority in the institution.

Apart from the various research questions which follow from the above points, there remains one puzzle of apparent irrationality. In the case of social disorganization, where the fundamental problem is the inability to carry out collective action (not the inability of the individual to carry out individual action that will prove satisfying), a rational individual, acting individually, will not vest authority in another if others' vesting of authority will lead to collective action without his doing so. Nor will he vest authority if others' vesting of authority will not lead to action even if he does. An individual's vesting of authority is rational only if he is the decisive person, whose vesting of authority makes the difference in whether collective action occurs or not. Yet if all individuals in a system are

10. The existence of such points of extensive personal change suggests potential research hypotheses, for example: (1) if the age of psychological loss of parental authority lowers, the age at which romantic love first occurs will be lowered; (2) children in families with strong social relations and strong parental authority extending into young adulthood will not fall in love as soon or as fully (because physiological changes will have passed by the time parental authority is relinquished); (3) men will fall in love again when they begin to lose their sexual powers, as will women, unless they are absorbed in their children; (4) the less extensive the social ties in a society, the more its members will vest authority in some other, a charismatic person or a love object.

rational in this way, each will wait for the others, and no collective action will take place.

The question of how this puzzle is solved in any particular case is an open one, but there are at least the following four possibilities:

1. The individual's personal disorganization is sufficiently great that, apart from any benefit to be experienced from collective action, he will experience benefit from having his own action directed by another.[11] This implies that when there is a vesting of authority in another those first to so vest will be persons whose personal disorganization is great, who are undergoing change, or who have "nothing to lose."

2. Despite the absence of social organization that can bring about collective action, there is sufficient density of social relationships and closure of social networks that individuals can, making their vesting of authority mutually contingent, vest authority together, sanctioning those who do not.[12] (The specific ways in which this might occur are subject to detailed empirical investigation.)

3. Vesting of conjoint authority may be "rationally contagious." That is, if a number of persons have vested authority in a particular other actor, and if vesting authority in *someone* is little or no more costly than retaining authority to oneself, and if all else is equal, then it is rational to vest authority in that same person (to increase the likelihood of effective collective action) rather than another.

4. In a social system the right to control one person's action cannot be withheld by that person if all others have vested authority in an actor and regard the right to control that person's action as also being held by that authoritative actor. (If a subset is socially insulated from the larger system, members of the subset can withhold authority for all activities save those that bring them into contact with the larger society.) Thus the consensual character of a right makes it impossible for a person to unilaterally withhold the right to control his action from another if all others regard that right as held by the other. This point is, of course, relevant only when the vesting of authority in another is nearly universal and cannot account for small charismatic movements within a social system.

The Fundamental Defect of the Subordinate's Actions in a Conjoint Authority Relation

In a conjoint authority relation the subordinate sees his interests as coincident with those of the superordinate. If a number of persons have subordinated

11. Zablocki (1980) gives a case which appears to illustrate this: "If Will told me to do something, even if I may not agree with it, I have to trust that God speaks to me through Will . . . If Will's vetoing whatever this thing is that I want to run out and do, there's a reason that God does not want me to do it . . . God can change your authority if your authority is wrong . . . God will change Will. I don't try to change Will . . . I submit to him [Will] as the authority, as unto God, knowing that God is ultimately in control" (p. 281).

12. See Chapter 12.

themselves to the same superordinate (which may be a corporate actor such as a commune or a person acting as a leader), then each sees his interests as coincident with those of all. This means that the interests of each are as fully satisfied by the actions of another as by his own actions. It means also that the interests of each are as fully satisfied by the actions of those in authority as by his own actions. Thus, if the subordinate's actions in the direction of satisfying his own interests require effort or are in some other way costly, he may be better off not acting for himself, but leaving action to the leader. The authority's actions or those of others under the same authority are just as effective in satisfying the subordinate's as are his own, and they achieve this result without cost to him. A subordinate may, of course, have transferred away the right to direct his own action, and therefore be subject to the authority that he has given up. Yet in many conjoint authority structures, such as communes or associations of persons with similar interests, the general transfer of authority does not carry with it the prescription of what to do in each circumstance. It will be to the interest of each in any specific circumstance to let the leader do all the work.[13] If authority has been transferred to a collectivity such as a commune, it will be to the interest of each to let the others do all the work. It will be, on the other hand, to the interest of each to encourage others to further the collective goals and to support norms which encourage all to work in the public interest. Thus such kinds of authority structures should exhibit the greatest divergence between public norms concerning corporate goals and private behavior aimed toward those goals.

Casual observation suggests that one can find such divergence in many conjoint authority structures. In large conjoint collectivities such as nation-states, there is ordinarily a widely held norm that it is desirable to become informed about politics and to vote, yet most persons remained uninformed and many do not vote. In trade unions, composed of members with common interests with respect to their employers, there are similar norms concerning participation in union affairs, yet there is generally little participation by average members. More generally, it is in conjoint authority structures that what has come to be known as the free-rider problem is found extensively. As shown in Chapter 11, this free-rider problem might be overcome when norms supporting the common interest develop. The norms, however, can lead to *excessive* action in the direction of the common interest, as shown in Chapter 11.

There is another possible defect of the subordinate's actions in conjoint authority relations, one that has been little explored. This is the possibility that common interests, leading to mutual support for actions that further those interests, will lead each individual to transfer greater rights of control to a central authority than is in his interest. There may thus come to be in conjoint authority

---

13. This is the character of some religions, in which the transfer of authority to God is accompanied by an assumption that "God will take care of all" and thus one can merely "leave oneself in the hands of God."

structures a systematic bias from this source, in the direction of more rights being vested in a central authority than each individual, acting independently, would find it in his interest to vest. (This is explored more fully in Chapter 13, where the rational basis for deciding what rights to vest in a collectivity is examined.)

A serious limitation of conjoint authority relations is that they depend on a coincidence of goals between the actor who makes the transfer of authority and the actor who becomes the superordinate. Although this transfer may be valuable to the actor who thereby becomes a subordinate, it has severe limitations. The creation of an authority structure consisting of many such relations depends on the coincidence of many actors' interests, as well as consensus about who can best further those interests. By definition, all the components necessary for the structure must be intrinsic to the particular interests in question. No use of extrinsic payments is made to build the complex structure of interdependent actions that in a disjoint authority structure furthers achievement of corporate goals. Thus conjoint authority structures tend to be rather simple, consisting of few levels and having little internal differentiation.

The Fundamental Defect of the Subordinate's Actions in a Disjoint Authority Relation

In an authority relation the subordinate has transferred to the superordinate the right to control his actions. But because actions are an inalienable resource, the subordinate cannot transfer the actual performance of the action. It is the dependence of outcomes on both the directive given by the superordinate and the performance of the subordinate that makes an authority relation different from a transient exchange of goods and gives it some continuity in time.

The fundamental defect of the disjoint authority relation is that the outcomes of actions are dependent in part on actors (subordinates) who have no intrinsic interest in those outcomes. The broad usefulness of disjoint authority relations in social systems depends on this fact, but the defect also lies there. Thus, unless authority can be exercised over every detail of the actions or unless there is some easily observable indicator of the degree to which the subordinates' actions pursue the interest of the superordinate, the subordinates may fail to perform in the direction of the superordinate's interests. In some cases outcomes of events, that is, the products of the subordinates' actions, provide an easily observable indicator which can be used to monitor the action, but in many cases this is not so. Then policing is necessary, at some cost to the superordinate and with less than total compliance.

Many kinds of behavior in bureaucracies derive from this fundamental defect: stealing from an employer, loafing on the job, featherbedding (in which two persons do the work of one), padding of expense accounts, use of organizational resources for personal ends, and waste. There are other kinds of actions which are not as obviously derivative from this source but which nevertheless stem from it. The behavior of the so-called bureaucratic personality, which focuses on rules rather than organizational goals, is an example (Merton, 1968, p. 249). Rigidity and attention to rules are pursued by a bureaucrat as a policy that is safe, because, whatever the outcome, he is protected by having followed the rules; an action against the rules but having a better expected outcome for the organization would expose the bureaucrat to loss of position or other discipline if it was not successful.

Here, as in the more obvious cases, the defect results from the fact that the performance of the subordinate remains in his own hands, and his own interests have not been eliminated by transferring the right to control his actions to the superordinate. When these interests would lead to performance inimical to the interests of the superordinate and when policing by the superordinate is ineffective, then the actions taken will not be those that pursue the superordinate's interests. Incentive systems in formal organizations and work in economics on agency are directed to attempting to overcome this fundamental problem of disjointness, which is that performance remains in the hands of an actor whose interests are unrelated to the superordinate's interests. (Work in this direction is discussed more fully in Chapters 7 and 16.)

The defects of a subordinate's behavior in conjoint and disjoint authority relations show some similarity. In both cases the subordinate's interests lead, in the absence of special correctives, to reduced levels of performance. But other aspects of the behavior differ markedly. In conjoint authority structures the subordinates' interests lead to public support of norms encouraging high performance, even though private behavior may not accord with these norms; in disjoint authority structures subordinates' interests lead to no such norms, except in the presence of special incentive structures, such as group piece rates. In fact, if there is a class of subordinates having similar interests and among whose performances the superordinate makes comparisons, those interests, disjoint with the interests of the superordinate, often lead to support of norms that discourage high performance.[14] Thus conjoint and disjoint authority relations generate distinctive forms of behavior by subordinates, which constitute defects to the relations.

Defects in the Behavior of Superordinates

The defects described above for conjoint and disjoint authority relations concern failures of performance on only one side of the relation—the side of the subordinate. There are defects on the side of the superordinate as well. Some are inherent in any authority relation, and others are specific to conjoint or disjoint authority relations.

The source of the defects in the superordinate's behavior is the fact that authority relations are contracts (implicit or explicit) extending over time, thus

---

14. See, for example, the extensive work in industrial sociology on limitation of output, including the classic work by Roethlisberger and Dickson (1939).

giving to the superordinate a set of continuing rights. A result is that these rights of control, once transferred, can sometimes be used to bring about further aggrandizement of control. When private goods are exchanged in a one-time transaction, the goods given up in the exchange are physically transferred and are not connected to other resources still held. But in authority relations the right to control certain actions continues over time and is not so easily separable from other rights. It may sometimes be used to gain other rights against the subordinate's will. The subordinate is to some extent "under the power" of the superordinate as a result of the original transaction.

An example of this process is evident in what is called sexual harassment on the job. The most common form that sexual harassment takes is that of a male superior using his position of authority (in which the domain of rights vested by the subordinate is explicitly limited to work-related actions) to make demands outside the range of that authority, in the area of sexual behavior, on a female subordinate, explicitly or implicitly threatening her with loss of her job. It is the close relationship between the actions over which rights have been transferred and those over which rights have not been transferred that facilitates such demands. It is the continuity over time of the authority relation that makes the threat possible. This example only illustrates a very general process, evident in both conjoint and disjoint authority relations. The rights to control actions gained by the superordinate give the superordinate the opportunity to extend that control.

The defects specific to conjoint and disjoint authority relations are not in principle different from nonperformance in other kinds of transactions. The superordinate in a conjoint authority relation may act in ways inimical to the subordinate's interest rather than in ways beneficial to that interest, and the superordinate in a disjoint authority relation may fail to make the extrinsic payments promised as part of the transaction. These failures of performance are possible in any transaction that requires future payments; because an authority relation always does so, such failures are always possible.

Transfer of One Right or Two: Simple and Complex Authority Relations

A second fundamental distinction concerning types of authority relations lies in the difference between those in which one right is transferred and those in which two rights are transferred. Earlier in this chapter I indicated that an actor could vest in another actor rights of control over a certain class of actions only when the first actor held two rights: the right to control his own actions in that class, and the right to transfer that right.[15] If the right to control certain of one's actions

15. The case in which the first right but not the second is held is exemplified in some socialist countries, where a citizen may employ his own labor but does not have the right to exchange that labor for pay with a prospective employer other than the state, unless that employer has less than a certain number of employees (such as twenty).

is transferred to another, this makes possible the *exercise* of authority by the resulting superordinate over the subordinate. If, however, the subordinate transfers the second right, the right to transfer the first right, this gives the superordinate the possibility of an additional action, that of *delegating* the first right to another actor, a lieutenant.

The possibility of transferring the right to control a subordinate's actions creates two types of authority relations. In the first, authority is exercised by the same actor in whom it is vested. In the second, authority is exercised by an actor (the lieutenant) other than actor in whom it is vested (the superordinate). I will call the first of these two types, that requiring only two actors, a simple authority relation, and the second, requiring three actors, a complex authority relation. Simple and complex authority relations are subsets, respectively, of simple and complex social relations, discussed in Chapter 2.

Examination of the differences between these two types of authority relations is deferred until the examination of authority systems in Chapter 7, because the principal differences lie in the kinds of structures these two types of authority relations generate.

Limitations on Authority

Although no restrictions or limitations on authority have yet been discussed, they exist in every authority relation and may take a number of different forms.

A first restriction, shared by nearly all authority relations that are voluntarily entered into, is that the subordinate retains the right to revoke the authority over his actions held by the superordinate. Those relations for which this is not true are rather special, as a few examples will illustrate.

In social systems of the past it was more often true that subordinates could not terminate an authority relation. Throughout the Middle Ages and for some time after, most persons did not have the right to revoke a vesting of authority, whether that of the family or of larger social units, but could do so only by going outside the law, becoming an outlaw. In nearly any society today a citizen or subject may revoke the authority of a subunit within it by changing residence and may revoke the authority of the nation-state itself by leaving its territory.[16] Until quite recently women in most societies not only were subject to the broad authority of their fathers or husbands but lacked the right to revoke the authority by terminating the relation. That structure continues to be found in large parts of the less developed world. Children have always been in such an authority relation with respect to their parents, without the right of revoking it, although the age at which this authority relation is terminated continues to decline.[17] It is true

16. A few nation-states, most notably those organized on Marxist-Leninist principles, forcibly prevent exit, and some others require citizens to go through formalities when leaving.

17. An unusual case illustrating this phenomenon is that of a lawsuit brought in Chicago on behalf of a 12-year-old boy who wanted to remain in the United States despite his parents' intention to take him with them back to the Soviet Union. The judge ruled in favor of the boy's

in the case of children that parents' authority is not unlimited; however, the limitations give rights to usurp parental authority not to the child but to the larger society.[18]

Aside from exceptions of the sort just described, a subordinate in any authority relation retains the right to revoke the authority. When that right is wholly absent, the general principles discussed in this chapter concerning the divesting of authority do not hold.

The limitations on authority relations may take any of several forms:

1. *Limitations on the domain or scope of activities over which authority is to be exercised.* For example, in an employer-employee relation, the kinds of activities for which the employer has the right to direct the employee's actions are ordinarily limited to those directly related to the purpose of employment. Some collective bargaining agreements limit the tasks that skilled workers may be asked to do to those directly in their trade. As a result of the women's movement, some secretaries refuse to bring coffee to their bosses.

2. *Limitations on the time at which authority may be exercised.* Again, in most employment relations the right of the employer to exercise authority over an employee is limited to specific times, or working hours. The authority of a school system over a child attending school is limited to the period of the day during which school is in session. In contrast, a family's authority over a child or the authority of the state over a citizen is not time limited in this way.

3. *Limitations according to the physical location of the subordinate.* The hegemony of nation-states is defined both by the persons who are citizens and by geographical territory covered. That is, a state's authority is exercised over all persons within its territory, although certain authority is also exercised over citizens outside that territory. A physical or geographic scope of authority may in some cases override a time limitation. For example, an employee may be subject to certain authority of his employer while on the employer's property, even outside of working hours, or a student may be subject to the authority of the school system on school property, even outside of school hours.

4. *Limitations on the prescriptiveness of authority.* In general, the vesting of authority gives to the superordinate either the right to prescribe that the subordinate obey certain commands or the lesser right to proscribe certain actions on the part of the subordinate. The authority of a purposive organization is ordinar-

---

right to revoke his parents' authority and remain in the United States. It appears quite likely, however, that the judge's decision had less to do with the general principle of parent-child relations than with the fact that the boy was choosing the United States and his parents the Soviet Union. If the choices had been reversed, it is hard to imagine the American judge ruling in favor of the boy's right to go against his parents' choice.

18. The threshold at which the right to usurp parental authority arises differs in different societies. In Western societies that threshold has recently been moving downward. In Sweden, for example, a law was recently passed removing from parents the right to physically punish their children. Chapter 22 examines this broad change in the structure of rights held within families.

ily prescriptive, and that of a state over its citizens is largely proscriptive. Hayek (1973, p. 124) contrasts the prescriptiveness of some parts of public law, which command citizens to carry out certain actions such as paying taxes and sending their children to school, with the proscriptive character of private law, which is designed merely to maintain order among citizens.[19]

Although limitations on authority can arise from any of the sources described above (as well as possibly others; I do not claim that these are exhaustive), the principal dimensions on which different authority systems differ are the first and the fourth, the domain of activity over which authority is exercised and the prescriptiveness of authority.[20] Authority within organizations designed to accomplish a purpose is ordinarily very narrow with respect to the domain of activity covered but highly prescriptive within that domain. At the other extreme, the authority of a nation-state over its citizens covers a very broad domain of activity but is largely proscriptive. Disjoint authority relations are ordinarily narrow and prescriptive, whereas conjoint authority relations may cover either a narrow domain of activity (as in the case of those collectivities called associations) or a much broader domain of activity (such as the proscriptive authority found in a society and embodied in laws or norms which express the common interests of members).

Hayek (1973, pp. 35–39) distinguishes sharply between two sources of order that correspond to these two different forms of limitation on authority. The first he calls organization, or "made order," and the second he calls "spontaneous order." The first, as he points out, is ordinarily constructed for a purpose, whereas the second arises out of the continuing activities of different actors in contiguity with one another. Although the accomplishment of a purpose requires prescriptive commands, the maintenance of a spontaneous order generally requires nothing more than that the relevant actors abstain from certain actions. Hayek's distinction between spontaneous order and made order corresponds closely to the distinction made in Chapter 2 between organization based on simple social relations, constituting the natural social environment, and organization based on complex social relations, constituting the built social environment.

19. Hayek (p. 176) quotes J. C. Carter (1907, p. 234): "Legislative commands thus made, requiring special things to be done, are part of the machinery of government, but a part very different from that relating to the rules which govern ordinary conduct of men in relation to each other. It is properly described as *public law*, by way of distinction from private law."

20. The forms of limitation of authority listed in the text are limitations on what is exercised, not on how it is exercised or on who is exercising it. Limitations on how authority is exercised consist principally of limitations on the sanctions that can be used to ensure compliance, with the extreme being the use of force or violence. Limitations on who will exercise authority take a variety of forms and are designed primarily to prevent the accretion of excessive power in any one actor's hands. Among these are the balance of power among branches in many governments and limitations on the period during which a single person can occupy a position of authority. As another example, in republican Rome two consuls governed simultaneously, each subject to the other's veto. I will not discuss these limitations in this chapter.

Although these two forms of limitation on authority give rise to two phenotyp-ically characteristic kinds of authority systems, the logical independence of prescriptiveness as one dimension and the domain of activities over which au-thority is exercised mean that there are in fact four extremes rather than two, as expressed in Table 4.1. Authority systems of types 2 and 3 have limitations of one kind, not of the other. Type 3 is the purposive organization as described by Hayek, and type 2 is Hayek's spontaneous order, exemplified by a society or liberal state (although such a society also has limitations on the domain of activities its authority covers and is thus between type 1 and type 2). Authority systems of types 1 and 4 differ in the *amount* of limitation on authority, type 4 having very little limitation on authority and type 1 having authority limited on both dimensions. Type 4 is exemplified by a purposive commune of the sort described by Zablocki at the beginning of this chapter, although a society with an activist state, operating under Rousseau's principle of general will, moves to-ward this extreme. Type 1 is exemplified by the authority system governing a customer who has entered a store which has certain rules of conduct.

Thus the existence of these two major means by which authority is limited does not imply that authority systems all have similar degrees of limitation and differ only in type of limitation. There is immense variation in the limitations on authority. The statement by Charles Watson about the Manson commune quoted earlier in this chapter indicates that some authority systems are both broad and prescriptive. They can pervade every aspect of a person's activities and prescribe every action. A novitiate, on entering a religious commune, often goes through a ritual which symbolizes a total shedding of any interest in things outside and a total giving of control over oneself to the will of God (as that will is manifested through the community).

At the other extreme, authority over one's dress may be lodged in a multilevel implicit authority structure that is both narrow and nonprescriptive, involving

Table 4.1   Four types of authority systems formed by two types of limitations on authority.

| | | Domain of activities | |
		Narrow	Broad
Prescriptiveness	Proscriptive	1	2
	Prescriptive	3	4

fashion houses, magazines, and other persons around one.[21] The source of authority over physicians' behavior in prescribing drugs is similarly lodged in a narrow, nonprescriptive, multilevel structure involving drug companies, teaching hospitals, and other physicians in the community.[22] The structure of authority for a New Yorker's political beliefs may involve partial transfer to the *New York Times,* the *New Yorker,* and the *New York Review of Books.*

The last three examples consist of simple authority structures, even where multileveled, because authority over an actor's behavior is exercised, even if without intention, by another actor in whom the first has placed that authority. It is clear from all these examples that persons transfer widely varying amounts of authority over their actions to other actors, leading to authority structures which differ greatly in their inclusiveness and prescriptiveness.

Slavery

Why does the law prohibit certain kinds of transactions in which individuals might wish to engage? Generally, when a transaction is entered into voluntarily, both parties to it are better off, and if there are no negative externalities of the transaction for others, then the transaction is a Pareto-optimal action, and any law constraining such transactions reduces satisfaction of the two parties to the exchange without benefiting anyone. Yet the law does not recognize certain transactions as valid and cannot be used to enforce certain contracts. I will not address the general question of how this class of transactions is defined, but rather the narrower question of why certain transactions involving the selling of oneself into slavery are almost universally not recognized as valid by law and why they were recognized as valid in earlier societies. What is there about this kind of transaction which causes it to be regarded as different from the selling of one's labor for a wage, that is, selling rights to control a certain delimited set of one's actions?[23]

It is useful, in attempting to see what is special about this transaction, to examine how slavery is defined by students of the subject. Patterson (1977) gives as a definition of slavery "that condition in which there is an institutionalized alienation from the rights of labor and kinship" (p. 431). This definition appears too weak considering the kinds of actions toward slaves by masters that have been permitted by law in slaveholding societies. Masters ordinarily have had free sexual access to slaves; they could punish them physically, even brutally;

21. See Katz and Lazarsfeld (1955) for an examination of that authority structure for women in the United States in the 1940s.

22. See Coleman, Katz, and Menzel (1966) for an examination of that authority structure for physicians in four Midwestern communities in the 1950s.

23. Certain Marxists regard the latter as "wage slavery," not distinguishable in principle from slavery. Yet even they regard selling one's labor to the state for a wage as not a case of wage slavery, because the other partner to the transaction is not a private party but the state, that is, the people as a whole. (See MacPherson, 1964, for a forceful statement of this position.)

and in some slaveholding societies, they could even put a slave to death. Thus a slave loses more rights than the two which Patterson cites.

Finley (1983) appears to get closer to the heart of the matter when he says, referring to Greek and Roman slavery:

> The slaveholder's rights over his slave-property were total in more senses than one. The slave, by being a slave, suffered not only "total loss of control over his labour," but total loss of control over his person and his personality: the uniqueness of slavery, I repeat, lay in the fact that the labourer himself was a commodity, not merely his labour or labour-power. His loss of control, furthermore, extended to the infinity of time, to his children and his children's children. (pp. 74–75)

Finley implies that in slavery, rights of control to the very self have been alienated, and for all time. How is this different from other transactions?

A perspective on the matter may be gained by considering the analogous action on the part of a corporate actor. Ordinarily a corporate actor will buy factors of production and sell products in markets, doing so in order to maximize its gain, however defined. But under certain conditions corporate actors are themselves sold: a corporation may sell itself or be sold to another corporation. When a corporation does so, it loses independent identity and capacity as an actor. It becomes the property of another actor, and *all its actions* from that time forward are, according to the distribution of rights, to be taken in the interests of the owning corporation.[24]

How, then, can a corporation's selling itself be regarded as a rational action? By the definition of rational action, an actor carries out that action which maximizes his utility or interest, subject to constraints on him. But after a corporation sells itself to another, there is no longer an independent actor. After the transaction there remains an agent of action, but the object self, in whose interests the agent acts, no longer exists as an entity with legitimate, legally protected interests. Thus it might be conjectured that a corporation's selling itself can never be regarded as a rational or reasonable act, from the point of view of that corporation as actor. From an external perspective, the perspective of the shareholders in the corporation, the action can, of course, be seen as a rational action. *They* may benefit as individuals, even though the corporation itself loses independent existence as an actor forever.

Yet the matter may not be so simple. If the corporation which sells itself maintains a distinct identity and is not merely broken up in pieces, then the interests of the owner may require that the interests of the dependent entity be attended to. If the alternative for the corporation which sells itself is that it

---

24. If the corporation continues to exist as an independent entity, then, by virtue of the general principle that agents may divert resources to their own interests (Michels's [1949] principle that when organizations come into existence, they come to have interests of their own), it may not act fully in the parent corporation's interests. A similar point holds for a slave.

would cease to exist altogether, then selling itself and losing all independent rights is preferable.

The case of slavery is, I think, similar. It might seem that a transaction involving the selling of a person into slavery cannot be regarded as rational from the point of view of the person who becomes the slave, because by the transaction that person loses the independent self in whose interests he must act as an actor. The very recompense a slave might receive as part of the transaction becomes the property of his owner, for a slave and all he owns is the property of the owner. If the recompense goes to someone other than the slave (captors, slave traders, or parents), the transaction can be seen as rational for them as actors, although not for the slave.

Yet, as in the case of a corporation, this initial conjecture does not consider the alternative. In ancient Greece and Rome the alternative to taking slaves was to put the vanquished persons to death. Slavery was then regarded, and given that context would be so regarded today, as the preferable alternative. Slaves had hope, and a master, acting purely self-interestedly, sometimes found it necessary to attend to the interest of his slave. Certainly it is true that accounts of Greek and Roman slaves do not describe it as "a fate worse than death" but an existence often quite tolerable, and sometimes even pleasant.

The question posed at the beginning of this section was this: Why does law in most societies currently prohibit the selling of oneself into slavery, and why was this not always the case? The theoretical structure of this book answers the first half of the question by suggesting that the answer lies in the fact that such a transaction violates the fundamental premise of voluntary transactions: that both parties are made better off. But the second half of the question also requires an answer. The theoretical structure of this book implies that if the only alternative is death, as it was in ancient wars, slavery is very likely the preferable alternative. In such a case "selling oneself into slavery" is not the appropriate description for the transaction, but rather "buying one's life," by accepting slavery as the alternative to death.

Authority without Intentional Exercise

At the opposite extreme from the case of slavery is authority without intentional exercise: One transfers the right to control one's actions, and thus lets oneself be directed by another, without the other's intentionally exercising that authority. This is evident in the case of the lieutenant of a leader in a commune studied by Zablocki (1980):

> A small group of born-again Christians, following the lead of a charismatic pastor, attempting to keep one foot inside the church while revitalizing it from without, moved into the slums of Atlanta and asked the Lord to tell them what to do next . . . At times these relationships became so intense that the personalities of some seemed to melt into those of others. This was

particularly striking in the case of the charismatic leader (male) and his chief lieutenant (female). The two were seldom observed together without the female follower's positioning herself in such a way that she could observe his every expression. She mirrored his expressions and gestures, seemingly oblivious to her mimicry. (pp. 214–215)

Although most of what are ordinarily seen as authority relations involve intentional exercise of authority, this is not essential to such a relation. If a person transfers control over his political actions to news commentators on television or the editorial staff of a newspaper, he may be guided or directed by them without their knowing of his existence. If a person transfers control over some of his activities as a scientist to the author of a book which captures his attention, he is being guided or directed by that author's authority. There is a large class of authority relations of this sort, which are ordinarily called structures of influence. There is no need, however, for that term here, because the transfer of control over actions that a person makes in such cases is no different from that which he makes in any conjoint authority relation. A person makes such a transfer without extrinsic compensation, because he believes he will be better off by accepting that authority. These cases are by definition simple authority relations, for the person accepts authority from the actor (person or corporate actor) in whom he has vested it. The network or hierarchy of authority (influence), however, may be very complicated, from the compounding of these simple authority relations. Authoritative control (which, of course, may cover a very narrow domain of activity if the person depends on several other actors to guide his action) is accepted without being exercised. In some such cases it may be too strong a statement to say that there is no exercise of authority or no intention to exercise it. There are, however, clearly cases at the extreme in which there is no such intention (a girl passes on the street, and a younger girl attempts to imitate the way she walks; a baseball player has a certain batting stance, and a boy adopts that stance).

Thus it is necessary to recognize that authority may be vested without being intentionally exercised and that the essential actor in the authority relation is neither the superordinate in whom authority is vested nor the actor who exercises the authority (whether the superordinate or a lieutenant), but the subordinate. It is the subordinate's transfer of control over his actions to another that allows an authority system to function, and it is the accompanying transfer of the right to transfer that control that allows a complex authority structure to develop.

The above discussion moves toward developing a rationally grounded theory of authority systems. It is important to note, however, that this chapter has been confined to examining authority *relations* between two actors, not systems or structures of authority. Authority of one actor over another exists when the first has the right to control certain actions of the second. Such a right, as a consensual quantity, is in some authority relations initially held by the superordinate. Many authority relations in modern society, however, come into being when the right to control an actor's actions, held by the actor, is voluntarily vested in another to create such a relation.

The right may be transferred unilaterally (which a rational actor will do only in the expectation that the authority exercised by the other will benefit him more than would his own exercise of the right), or it may be transferred in exchange for some extrinsic compensation. The first case I have labeled a conjoint authority relation, and the second, a disjoint authority relation. There are characteristic defects associated with conjoint and disjoint authority relations, which were described in this chapter.

A second distinction concerning the kind of transfers made is that between transfer of only the right to control one's actions and transfer of both that right and the right to transfer that right. The transfer of the two rights makes possible a complex authority relation, in which authority may be exercised by an actor other than the actor in whom it is vested. This complex authority relation constitutes the beginning of an authority system, or structure. It is possible to build authority structures from concatenations of linked simple authority relations, but most authority structures are based on complex authority relations. These structures, or systems, of authority have as their building blocks the relations discussed in this chapter; just as a building is qualitatively different from the bricks of which it is constructed, however, an authority structure is different from the relations of which it is constructed. Chapters 7 and 16 pursue the steps involved in creating the structure from the relations.

« 5 »

Relations of Trust

One way in which the transactions that make up social action differ from those of the classical model of a perfect market lies in the role of time. In the model of a perfect market, transactions are both costless and instantaneous. But in the real world transactions are consummated only over a period of time. In some cases this means that the delivery of goods or services by one party occurs only after the other party has made delivery. In others it means that delivery by both parties occurs in degrees over a period of time. In still others the return to both parties is some product of their actions, so both must invest resources but neither receives a return until some later time. In still other cases an actor makes a unilateral transfer of control over certain resources to another actor, based on a hope or expectation that the other's actions will satisfy his interests better than would his own actions; yet he can only be certain at some time after he has made the transfer. For example, the transfer of control over one's actions in a conjoint authority relation, as discussed in Chapter 4, must occur at some time before the expected benefits can be realized.

Time asymmetries in delivery introduce risk into a unilateral action or transaction for the party or parties who must invest resources before receiving a return. Sometimes the risk may be reduced by use of contracts that are enforceable by law, but, for a variety of reasons, contracts cannot always serve this purpose. Especially in noneconomic transactions, where value is not precisely calculated and there is no numeraire (but in some economic transactions as well), enforceable contracts cannot easily be used, and other social arrangements are necessary. The usual arrangement is simply an incorporation of risk into the decision of whether or not to engage in the action. This incorporation of risk into the decision can be treated under a general heading that can be described by the single word "trust." Situations involving trust constitute a subclass of those involving risk. They are situations in which the risk one takes depends on the performance of another actor.

Before defining more precisely the way I will use the word "trust," I will present some illustrations within this class of situations and raise some questions about each. The illustrations will serve to indicate some of the empirical questions that arise surrounding what we think of as trust.

A first example is taken from a book titled *The Merchant Bankers*, by Joseph

Wechsberg (1966). The scene is a Friday afternoon in the City of London, the financial center where merchant bankers ply their trade, in the office of the manager of the Norwegian department of the merchant banker Hambros.

> Suddenly the phone rang: the operator told the Norwegian manager it was an urgent, personal call from a big city in Norway. A prominent shipowner was on the line. He needed help, at once. To be exact, he needed two hundred thousand pounds within the next half hour.
>
> He told the manager that one of his ships had undergone repairs at a big Amsterdam shipyard. A few minutes ago he'd had a call from his captain. The Amsterdam yard would not release the ship unless a cash payment was made of £200,000. Otherwise the ship would be tied up for the weekend, and the owner would lose at least twenty thousand pounds—the cost of two days of charter and expenses for the crew of twenty-two. Not to mention the loss of profit.
>
> The Hambros man looked at the clock and said, "It's getting late but I'll see whether I can catch anyone at the bank in Amsterdam . . . Stay at the phone."
>
> Over a second phone he dictated to a secretary in the bank a telex message to the Amsterdam bank: "PLEASE PAY £200,000 TELEPHONICALLY TO (NAME) SHIPYARD ON UNDERSTANDING THAT (NAME OF SHIP) WILL BE RELEASED AT ONCE." This done, he put down the second receiver and told the Norwegian on the long-distance phone to have a little patience.
>
> Within three minutes the second phone rang. Somebody in the bank in Amsterdam confirmed that they had already telephoned to the shipyard that £200,000 was at their disposal. The Hambros man said, "Thanks," put down the receiver and told the Norwegian over the other phone that payment of £200,000 had been arranged in Amsterdam, and that the yard would release his ship any minute.
>
> "Call your captain and give him your sailing orders," said the Norwegian manager. He listened with a smile. "Glad we could help you . . . Oh, no bother at all."

This case clearly involves trust. The manager of the Norwegian department at Hambros placed trust in the Norwegian shipowner who telephoned him—trust to the extent of £200,000 of Hambros's money. There was no contract signed, no paper involved in the transaction, nothing more substantial than the shipowner's intention to repay the money and the Hambros man's belief in both the shipowner's honesty and his ability to repay. Similarly, the bank in Amsterdam trusted Hambros to the extent of £200,000, again merely on the basis of a verbal request over the telephone. It committed £200,000 of its money on the assumption that Hambros would, on Monday morning, repay the sum.

What is problematic about this case? This can be seen by looking at the incident through the eyes of a young German bank manager who, Wechsberg reports, was spending some time at Hambros to learn how they did business. Wechsberg reports his reaction to the telephone calls:

"I could give you half a dozen reasons why I would be immediately dismissed from my bank if I had done what you did," he said to the Hambros man. "How can you be sure that you really talked to that shipowner in Norway? It's easy to imitate a voice over the phone. How do you know he's good for two hundred thousand pounds? Furthermore, you sent the order out over the telex, and there can easily be a misunderstanding. And worst of all, you didn't even check with your superiors! Two hundred thousand pounds!"

So the first point that is problematic is why the Hambros man placed trust in the shipowner on the basis of such insubstantial security. There is another question as well: Why was Hambros necessary in the first place? Wechsberg again quotes the young German bank manager:

"Why didn't the Norwegian shipowner call the Amsterdam bank directly? Surely he must be known there."

The second point that is problematic, then, is why a telephone call from Hambros could produce £200,000 from the Amsterdam bank when the shipowner's call could not.

A second example involves farmers.

A farmer was baling hay, and he had broken a needle in his baler. The weather looked unpromising, with rain likely. He did not know what to do. He had just bought the farm, this was his first crop of hay, necessary to winter his cattle, and now it appeared that this field of hay would be ruined. A neighbor who was helping him proposed a solution. "I'll go down and ask ———, who has a baler and could bale the field for you."

The farmer wondered at this, assumed it would cost him something in hay or money, but anxious to save his hay, readily assented. The neighbor did as he had proposed, and a little while later the second farmer arrived with tractor and baler. He proceeded to bale the hay, and all the hay was in the barn when the rain finally came.

The first farmer, who had not even known the farmer who baled his hay, was still puzzled, and asked of his neighbor what was due the second farmer for baling the hay in this emergency. The neighbor replied, "Oh, all he wants is the gasoline it took to bale the hay."

For this case there seems to have been a placement of trust by the second farmer in the first—trust that in a situation of need or time of trouble, when he might call on the first farmer, that farmer would provide help, as he had in this case. Although the second farmer did not know the first, he did know the neighbor and the farm which the first had just purchased.

What is problematic about this case can again be seen by looking through the eyes of someone who is unfamiliar with the setting, this time the first farmer, who was puzzled about why the second farmer would do this extensive favor (requiring an afternoon's work) for someone he did not even know. This is the question here: Why would the second farmer be willing to give up an afternoon in a busy time of year to help someone he had never seen—even if he expected that he would be repaid at some time in the future? Why would he have such trust?

A third example involves a high-school girl.

M—— did not go out very much although she was pretty. She was not one of the popular girls in school, probably because she was an immigrant. There was one boy, however, whom she did not know well, but who seemed interested in her. One afternoon he asked if he could walk her home. Pleased because of the attention, she said yes. As they walked and talked, they came to a woods. He suggested they take a short-cut through the woods to her house, and she assented. Suddenly he said he wanted to make love to her. Startled, she said no and began to run. He chased her and caught her. As she fell, a rock cut her foot, which began to bleed slightly. She began to cry; the boy roughly pulled her clothes off, sexually assaulted her, and then ran off.

When she could bring herself to do so, she got up, found her clothes and put them on, then limped home. Her mother asked her, when she saw her, what was wrong, but the girl, shocked and embarrassed and ashamed made no reply and went to her room. Later she told the story for the first time to a man whom she had come to trust, who asked about the scar on her foot.

This is a special case of a classic circumstance involving trust. A girl or a woman, ordinarily less physically strong than a boy or a man in whom she has an interest, must decide whether to trust him, in effect, giving him the opportunity to gain control over her body through seductive or violent means. Sometimes, as in this episode, that trust is misplaced.

One might say that nothing is sociologically problematic about this case, because it illustrates a classic and well-known pattern of interaction. One might, however, ask several things: Why did the girl agree to let the boy walk her home and to walk through the woods with him, when she hardly knew him? Why did he choose her, rather than another girl?

The final example involves a series of responses to a question asked, over a period of fourteen years, of representative samples of the adult American population (*Public Opinion*, 1979). The question that was asked was this (with minor variations): "As far as people running [major companies], would you say you have a great deal of confidence in them, some confidence, or only a little confidence?" Figure 5.1 shows the proportion of persons who responded "a great deal of confidence" not only in people running major companies but in people running each of the following eight other institutions:

Labor
Medicine
Military
Press
Organized religion
Congress
Executive branch of the U.S. government
Television news

The graph shows that confidence in only one of these nine institutions (television news) increased over the period, one (the press) remained approximately stable despite ups and downs, and all the others declined. The declines were most dramatic for certain years (1966 to 1971) and for certain institutions (major companies, the military, and Congress). One of the institutional areas, medicine, declined less precipitously, over a longer period of time, than did the other six that declined. The question is this: Why was there a general decline, affecting all institutional areas except the mass communications media in a similar way?

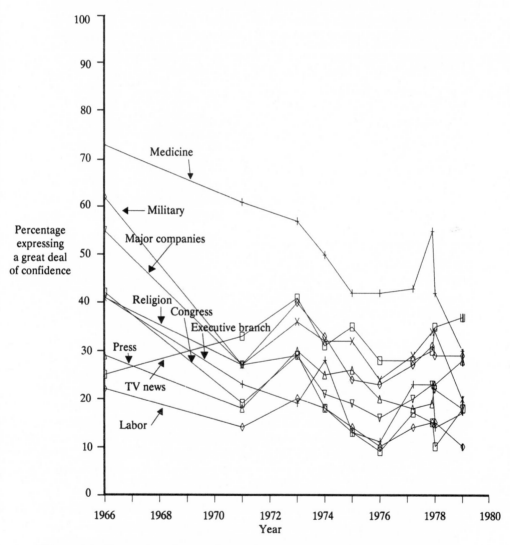

Figure 5.1 Percentage of respondents who had "a great deal of confidence" in people running nine institutions in the United States, 1966–1979.

What these four examples have in common is trust of some sort. In the last case, to be sure, all that is involved is a verbal expression of confidence in a given set of leaders; no explicit action is evident. In the other three cases, however, there are definite actions: Hambros extends a guarantee of the ship-owner's credit, and the Amsterdam bank accepts that guarantee; the second farmer trusts the first (or trusts the judgment of the neighbor about the first); and the high-school girl trusts the boy.

In this chapter I will present a conception of trust that will aid a better understanding of these examples, a conception that will help solve the puzzles apparent in them and will allow a better understanding of actions involving trust that are nothing like these examples.

In a trust relation there are, at minimum, two parties: trustor and trustee. I will assume both to be purposive, having the aim of satisfying their interests, whatever those might be. From this perspective one cannot account for the events of the third example merely by calling the girl naive and the boy malicious. One must assume that each actor is purposeful, and attempt to account for each actor's actions as reasonable ones in pursuit of purposes that an actor in such a situation might have. The potential trustor's decision is nearly always problematic—to decide whether or not to place trust in the potential trustee. In the examples under consideration these decisions can be stated as indicated in Table 5.1.

It is not only the potential trustor whose decisions must be considered. In many cases the trustee has a choice between keeping the trust and breaking the trust. (This is not always so; sometimes what is being trusted is not the trustee's willingness or intention to keep the trust but ability to do so.) The trustee may, in certain cases, find it is to his benefit to break the trust, when he stands to gain financially or otherwise from doing so. The trustee may, of course, stand to gain in the short run but lose in the long run by never again being trusted by that trustor. If the first farmer, whose hay was baled by the second farmer, later refused without good reason to help the second when he needed help, then the first could hardly expect help if his baler broke down again (or if a cow became sick or if any of the multitude of other farmers' problems arose). On the other hand, if the first farmer had just sold the farm and would be leaving the region, he would have little or nothing to lose by not repaying the obligation. Similarly, if the boy had a further interest in the high-school girl or if he assumed that she would tell others what happened, he would stand to lose by breaking her trust.

Also, the trustee may engage in actions explicitly designed to lead the potential trustor to place trust. I will not, however, have much to say about these actions, except that to be successful they must be based on an understanding (intuitive or explicit) of the potential trustor's basis for deciding whether or not to place trust.[1]

---

1. These actions are often extensive, complementing the potential trustor's search for information that can serve as a guide in deciding whether to place trust. Much advertising can be described as actions of this sort on the part of a potential trustee.

In some sequences of actions an actor may be both a trustor and a trustee. For example, the Norwegian shipowner's ability and intention to repay were trusted by the manager of the Norwegian department at Hambros, whose judgment was trusted by Hambros's directors, whose ability and intention to cover the credit extension were trusted by the Amsterdam bank. In such a case the trustor-trustee may be confronted with a decision both as trustor and as trustee: as trustor, whether to place trust, and as trustee, whether to keep or break the trust. Three-party transactions, with one party acting as both trustor and trustee, play a special role in social, economic, and political systems, and I will discuss them later. At this point it is necessary to ask how to conceive of the action that takes place. To answer this I will focus first on the placement of trust by the potential trustor.

The Placement of Trust

The first point to note is that the placement of trust allows an action on the part of the trustee that would not have been possible otherwise: for the shipowner,

Table 5.1 Examples of potential trustors and the nature of their decision.

Example	Potential trustor	Problematic decision in placing trust
1	Hambros officer	Whether or not to trust the shipowner
	Hambros directors	Whether or not to trust the judgment of their officer
	Amsterdam bank	Whether or not to trust Hambros
2	Second farmer	Whether or not to trust the first farmer to reciprocate later
3	High-school girl	Whether or not to trust the boy to respect her right to control use of her body
4	Surveyed American adults	Whether or not to maintain confidence in elected officials (for example, whether to reelect them), union leaders (whether, as a union member, to follow their directions), military leaders (whether to support their requests for appropriations), business leaders (whether to defer to their economic judgment), religious leaders (whether to follow their directives), physicians (whether to accept bad medical outcomes as unavoidable), the press (whether to trust its reportage), television news (whether to trust its reportage)

getting his ship operating; for the first farmer, getting his hay baled and in the barn; for the boy, engaging in sexual intercourse with the girl; for the leaders in American institutions, pursuing policies without interference from citizens. Placement of trust involves putting resources in the hands of parties who will use them to their own benefit, to the trustor's benefit, or both.

The second point is that if the trustee is trustworthy, the person who places trust is better off than if trust were not placed, whereas if the trustee is not trustworthy, the trustor is worse off than if trust were not placed. Hambros stands to make a profit, in terms of interest on future transactions with the shipowner (but also stands to lose £200,000). The second farmer stands to gain the help of the first farmer when he needs it in the future (but also stands to lose a day of valuable time). The lonely high-school girl stands to gain the attentions of a boyfriend (but also takes the chance of suffering a sexual assault). The American adults can turn their attention to other matters if their trust in elites is well placed. If it is not, the political, military, and social affairs in which they are interested may turn out less well than if they had paid attention to them.

The third point is that, in at least the second and third examples, the action of placing trust involves the trustor's voluntarily placing resources at the disposal of another party (the trustee), without any real commitment from that other party. The second farmer gave control over his time and equipment to the first farmer without any commitment from the latter; the high-school girl gave the boy control over the route by which they walked home, also without any commitment from him. Trust may be involved in explicit exchanges, such as the extension of credit in return for interest, but, as in these two cases, placement of trust may also be done unilaterally. For example, if I am walking along a street intending to enter a large hall where an event attracting many people is to take place and I do not know the direction to the entrance, I may "follow the crowd," placing my trust in their knowledge of where the entrance is. In such a case I have made a unilateral transfer of control over my direction to the crowd, with no awareness on the part of the members of the crowd that I have done so.

A fourth point is that each of these examples involves a time lag. Each has to do with future actions on the part of the trustee. There are many devices designed to overcome this time problem and thus reduce the necessity for placing trust. One is escrow, by which a third party holds a first party's payment until a second party delivers the goods. Another is bills of exchange, by which a potential trustee (ordinarily a buyer in a commercial transaction) offers the potential trustor (ordinarily a supplier in a commercial transaction) a note of another merchant, sometimes one more trusted than the buyer. More common than either of these is the contract, which takes many forms but always involves a promise to pay or deliver, ordinarily is legally enforceable, and often provides for some collateral in the event of default. Yet in many situations involving the placement of trust, particularly political and social situations, the parties involved cannot use such devices, often because there is no agreed value attached to the things the trustor gives up. For example, the farmer who bales the other farmer's hay cannot ask him to sign a contract promising to pay some unspecified service in the future.

All these points are rather elementary but important. The first and second indicate that the decision of the trustor fits the paradigm that decision theorists call decision under risk. The third point indicates that, unlike those social exchanges which require the voluntary action of two parties, placement of trust may be a voluntary action of one party alone, the trustor. The fourth point indicates something of the range of devices designed to reduce the necessity for placing trust.

A further analysis of these examples and of other cases involving decisions to place trust shows that the elements confronting the potential trustor are nothing more or less than the considerations a rational actor applies in deciding whether to place a bet. The actor knows how much may be lost (the size of the bet), how much may be gained (the amount that might be won), and the chance of winning. These and only these are the relevant elements. If he has no aversion to or preference for risk, it is a simple matter for him to decide whether to place the bet. It can be expressed in this way: If the *chance of winning,* relative to the *chance of losing,* is greater than the *amount that would be lost* (if he loses), relative to the *amount that would be won* (if he wins), then by placing the bet he has an expected gain; and if he is rational, he should place it.

This simple expression is based on the postulate of maximization of utility under risk. The potential trustor must decide between not placing trust, in which case there is no change in his utility, and placing trust, in which case the expected utility relative to his current status is the potential gain times the chance of gain minus the potential loss times the chance of loss. A rational actor will place trust if the first product is greater than the second or, stated otherwise, if the ratio of the chance of gain to the chance of loss is greater than the ratio of the amount of the potential loss to the amount of the potential gain. Below are shown the three essential elements and the way they combine to lead an actor to place a bet or a potential trustor to place trust.

p = chance of receiving gain (the probability that the trustee is trustworthy)

L = potential loss (if trustee is untrustworthy)

G = potential gain (if trustee is trustworthy)

Decision: yes if $\dfrac{p}{1-p}$ is greater than $\dfrac{L}{G}$

indifferent if $\dfrac{p}{1-p}$ equals $\dfrac{L}{G}$

no if $\dfrac{p}{1-p}$ is less than $\dfrac{L}{G}$

It is useful to compare the concept of the placement of trust as I have described it here with another conception that has been widely used in social psychology, that of Deutsch (1962). Deutsch defines trusting behavior as actions that increase one's vulnerability to another whose behavior is not under one's control in a specific type of situation, a situation in which the loss one suffers if the other (the trustee) abuses that vulnerability is greater than the gain one receives if the other does not abuse that vulnerability. (See also Zand, 1972.) If "actions that increase one's vulnerability to another" are identified as voluntarily placing resources at the disposal of another or transferring control over resources to another, then the actions involved in Deutsch's concept are the same as those discussed here. Deutsch's definition, however, restricts trusting behavior, or placement of trust, to those situations in which the potential loss (L) is greater than the potential gain (G); the definition I have given makes no such restriction.

It is true that in many cases that would be identified as involving the placement of trust L is greater than G. In the first three of the four examples given above, this criterion is met, but less clearly so in the fourth. There could be some rationale for limiting the idea of placement of trust to those situations in which L is greater than G (or, equivalently, the potential trustor's estimate of p is greater than .5). But one of the classic circumstances in which trust is involved—the placement of trust in a confidence man—does not fit Deutsch's definition. A confidence man ordinarily offers a trustor the prospect of extraordinary gains, much larger than the potential loss. One can then say, based on the inequalities given above, that even when p is less than .5 the trustor may place trust in the confidence man—that is, may transfer control over resources to the confidence man—if G is sufficiently larger than L. It is clear that such a case involves placement of trust and that it lies outside Deutsch's definition.

Another example that concerns the placement of trust in a circumstance that does not accord with Deutsch's definition is taken from a detective novel by Raymond Chandler (1955). The person speaking is a movie actor's agent.

> "One of these days," he said, "I'm going to make the mistake which a man in my business dreads above all other mistakes. I'm going to find myself doing business with a man I can trust and I'm going to be just too goddamn smart to trust him." (p. 118)

What makes this statement striking is its reversal of what would be said in many cases. The mistake a banker dreads, the mistake a lover dreads, the mistake a friend dreads is to place trust in someone who is not to be trusted. But the mistake this fictional actor's agent dreads is to *fail* to place trust when he should do so.

The difference, as explained by the paradigm which I have introduced in this chapter, lies in the values of L/G and p at which the actor's agent characteristically finds himself and the values of L/G and p at which bankers, lovers, and friends characteristically find themselves. The latter three types of trustors experience high values of potential loss relative to potential gain and, therefore, high critical values of p. Misplaced trust results in a great loss; the potential gain sacrificed in failing to place trust in a trustworthy borrower, lover, or friend is much smaller. Figure 5.2 shows the relation between the ratio of loss to gain for these cases involving placement of trust and the critical value of *p*. The movie actor's agent, if I am correct, is in a situation in which the potential loss is low

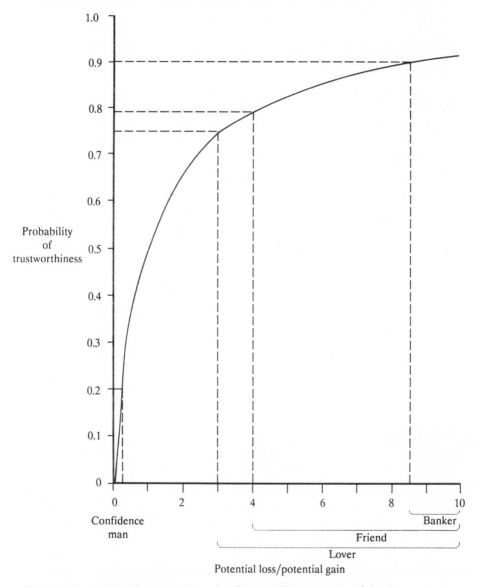

Figure 5.2 Relation between the ratio of potential loss to potential gain when placing trust, and the critical value of the probability of trustworthiness.

relative to the potential gain, and the critical value of p is much lower. In such a case the cost of an error of the first kind, placing trust when one should not have, is quite low. An error of the second kind, failing to place trust when one should have, has a high cost in terms of gains forgone. According to the movie actor's agent, in his business it is not merely that one can afford to take chances—one cannot afford *not* to take chances.

The Trustor's Information about p, L, and G

In various circumstances the three quantities p, L, and G are known to different extents. Often the amount to be lost is well known: in the Hambros example, £200,000; in the farming example, an afternoon's time and effort (though there was also the possibility of damage to the second farmer's equipment, a possibility he minimized by operating it himself). In some cases it is not well known: In the example concerning public confidence in various elites, the adults surveyed do not know what they may have lost by placing confidence in one presidential candidate rather than another or one set of congressional representatives rather than another. In the case of the high-school girl as well, the loss is not clear: She may not have anticipated the possibility of sexual assault. Even if she did, she did not know what the experience would be like physically and had no way of knowing what the psychological aftereffects would be.

The potential benefits or gains from placing trust are also sometimes well known: When a bank makes a loan at a fixed rate of interest, it knows just how much it will earn if the loan is repaid. In many other cases, however, the amount to be gained is less well known than the amount to be lost—as in the first and second examples presented earlier. In the first example the manager of the Norwegian department at Hambros knows precisely the potential loss to his bank; the potential gain is future business from the shipowner, which is less precisely calculable. In the case of the second farmer, the service that he might ask from the first farmer in the future is quite vague compared to the definiteness of what he gives up. In the case of the high-school girl, however, the potential gain to her is probably better known than the potential loss. That gain consists of attention from the boy and being able to go out on dates in the future, rather than staying at home as she has in the past.

Often the least well known of the three quantities involved in making a decision about whether to place trust is the probability that the trustee will keep the trust. When a voter votes for one candidate rather than another, he knows what both candidates are promising to deliver, for that is the substance of their campaigns. But he knows much less well just how likely it is that each would in fact deliver. Among merchant bankers the probability of repayment is the major unknown, as it is for banks generally. Wechsberg (1966) quotes the department manager at Hambros, who is explaining his quick decision to lend £200,000 to the shipowner:

> We translate this request into what it means to us here. A simple mathematical equation with one unknown quantity: Will it work out? The banker's

usual gamble. I make my decision and tell him either that we will do it or we won't. (p. 24)

This explains the central importance of information to an investment bank. The Hambros department manager says,

Actually, the risk isn't as terrible as it seems to you. I know the company, I know the ship, I even know the cargo. It's my job to know all these things. Admittedly, one has to be careful. Other banks have burned their fingers in this business. One has to keep a lot of useful information in one's head. (p. 24)

A merchant banker lives on his information and I try to get all the available information in my territory. (p. 32)

Information will have the effect of changing one's estimate of the probability of gain, that is, of moving one's estimate of the probability of gain as far as possible above or below the critical point at which the decision could go either way—the point at which the trustor would be indifferent between making a positive decision and a negative one. The farther from this point the trustor's estimate of the probability of gain is, the greater will be his certainty that his decision is the correct one. And the closer his subjective estimate of that probability is to the actual probability, the more likely his decision is to be correct.

It is principally for this reason that parents of high-school girls want to meet and know as much as possible about the boys their daughters go out with. And it is because a boy has less to lose from going out with the "wrong" girl that parents of high-school boys are less concerned with meeting and having full information about the young women their sons go out with. There is, of course, trust involved on the boy's side as well, for the "wrong" girl—one who would make a bad wife—might use sexual involvement and pregnancy to draw a young man into marriage. Nevertheless, the usual asymmetry of physical strength imposes a greater necessity for trust on the girl's part.

Not only is the probability that the trustee will keep the trust often the least well known of the three quantities, but the importance of knowing it depends greatly on the other two quantities: the possible gain and the possible loss. If the sum of the possible gain and the possible loss is small (as it is in the case of a boy's decision about whether to go out with a particular girl, relative to a comparable decision for a girl), then it is less important that the decision be a correct one, and a rational actor will carry out a less extensive search for information and will in other ways be less careful in making the decision.[2] An investment bank, for example, will assign only decisions involving relatively small amounts of money to an inexperienced officer. Only after the officer has "proved him-

2. It would seem that unduly conservative decisions will result from the use of experience in this way, for seldom is the outcome of the risk known for the cases in which trust is not placed. The exception is when another trustor does place trust in the trustee in question and the first potential trustor, who declined to place trust, is able to observe the outcome. But in many cases trust is not placed by any trustor, and the possible errors of omission are not observed, although the errors of placing trust when it should not have been placed are known.

self" at this level of risk will he be allowed to make decisions involving larger investments.

Thus it is not only the ratio of possible loss to possible gain, measured against the probability of the trustee's keeping the trust, that affects the action; the amount of the possible gain and the possible loss also should affect the extent of the search for additional information. The search should continue so long as the cost of an additional increment of information is less than the benefit it is expected to bring. That benefit increases with the sizes of the possible gain and the possible loss.

Why Are Persons Slow to Trust a Friend and Quick to Trust a Confidence Man?

The general paradigm presented in this chapter states that individuals will rationally place trust if the ratio of the probability that the trustee will keep the trust to the probability that he will not is greater than the ratio of the potential loss to the potential gain, or if $p/(1 - p)$ is greater than L/G. But this raises a question: When a person meets someone new who might become a friend, why is it generally said that it takes some time to develop trust? Why should the initial estimate of the probability of trustworthiness be an *underestimate* of the true probability rather than an overestimate? Why does it take time to learn to trust rather than taking time to learn to distrust?

There are examples, of course, which suggest that the estimate of p is not always an underestimate, but is sometimes an overestimate. That some confidence men can be quite successful despite the fact that they are totally unknown to the people who trust them suggests that at least some persons, some of the time, start with an overestimate of trustworthiness rather than an underestimate. The girl who was sexually assaulted by the boy with whom she walked home through the woods is another example of a person who began with too much trust rather than too little. Nevertheless, the generalization holds reasonably well: The process of getting to know another person well is ordinarily seen to include a process of developing trust in that other person. This appears to be especially true for close and intimate relationships, in which trust develops only over an extended period of time, on one side or on both.

A possible solution to this puzzle may lie in the values of the potential loss and the potential gain. Assuming that a person has a standard estimate of the probability of trustworthiness, p^*, for the average person he meets, based on past experience, then when in a situation calling for placement of trust in someone new, he will place trust if $p^*/(1 - p^*)$ is greater than L/G. When it is said that a person must come to develop trust in another, however, the context is ordinarily that of a relatively close relationship, in which the potential loss from taking another into one's confidence or exposing one's weaknesses is especially great. The potential gain from a close relationship may also be great, but since there are many other potential friends who might provide a nearly equivalent gain, the relevant comparison is not between the absolute potential loss and the absolute potential gain, but between the absolute potential loss (such as a violation of one's confidence or abuse of one's body) and the *difference* in gain expected from this friend and that from another. For a close relationship this ratio can be quite high compared to that for the usual circumstance in which one has an occasion to decide whether to place trust in another person. This means that the value of $p/(1 - p)$ necessary to surpass this ratio—which I will for close relationships call $(L/G)^*$—may be quite high, considerably higher than one's standard estimate, $p^*/(1 - p^*)$. The process of developing trust, then, may be nothing more than a move (through experiences with the other person, using occasions where L/G is not so high, or where the magnitude of L and G are both sufficiently small that, even though L/G may be high, the magnitude of possible loss is small) from one's standard value of $p/(1 - p)$ to a value that is greater than $(L/G)^*$. Thus, if this conjecture is correct, the relations for which it is said that there is a necessity for developing trust are those in which the potential loss relative to the potential gain is especially high.

But if this is so, how does it explain the fact that people will place trust in a confidence man they have never seen before? The answer in any specific case, of course, depends on how the confidence man manipulates a person's perception of the chance of loss and of the magnitudes of potential loss and potential gain. The usual proposition presented by a confidence man, however, is one in which the potential gain is quite large compared to the potential loss. The confidence man confronts the person with a proposition in which L/G is quite low. My conjecture here is that the proposition is one in which L/G is considerably lower than an average person's standard estimate, $p^*/(1 - p^*)$. Even if the person modifies his estimate downward somewhat from the standard value, it (according to this conjecture) will still be above L/G. The person will therefore place trust when he should not because the value L/G means that his estimate of trustworthiness must move *downward* from his standard estimate. The person must develop distrust in this case if p is to move to an accurate estimate; in contrast, for the case of trusting a friend, $(L/G)^*$ is so high a ratio that the person must develop trust, with p moving upward from its standard value.

If these conjectures are correct, various empirical implications can be drawn. One is that persons who lack alternative potential friends in whom to place trust (and therefore anticipate a large gain from a given friendship) should be far more trusting and require far less time to develop trust in a potential friend than persons who have many alternative potential friends. Another is that, in general, persons are likely to overestimate trustworthiness in situations in which the potential gain is especially high relative to the potential loss and to underestimate trustworthiness in situations in which the potential gain is especially low relative to the potential loss. If empirically true, this implication suggests extensive opportunities for swindlers, as long as the potential gain they hold out is great compared to the potential loss. A third empirical implication (merely a special case of the preceding one) is that long shots will be overplayed in race-track betting, and favorites will be underplayed.

Placement of Trust in Market and Nonmarket Settings

Why is it that in some arenas of action trust is placed in a diverse range of trustees, having different levels of trustworthiness, but in other arenas placement of trust is concentrated in one or a few trustees? As an example of the latter, the history of the emergence of money which does not inherently contain its value, as does commodity money, but depends for its value on a third-party guarantee, shows that the notes of certain goldsmiths or banks came to be accepted as currency in preference to personal notes and, in effect, drove out other notes by becoming the general currency. The result was that out of the proliferation of currencies issued by individual banks in a country, there came to be a single currency (see Ashton, 1945). The single currency seems to arise in this way: Commercial transactions are consummated by the buyer's giving the seller not commodity money, which inherently contains its value, but a note constituting a promise to pay. Suppose A buys from B and gives B his note in the transaction. Then, when B buys something from C, B can give C his own note, or he can transfer A's note to C. C will accept A's note in preference to B's note if C sees A as more trustworthy than B. Thus A's notes will circulate (which is to A's benefit as well, since that means they will not be presented for payment). Within such a setting, then, A's notes will become the single currency, if A participates in enough transactions that his notes are in sufficient supply.[3]

I believe the answer to the question at the beginning of this section lies in the fact that in some arenas of action the placement of trust occurs in a market structure, in which differing potential trustees offer promises in terms of the same commodity (for example, gold) or commodities which have a specifiable exchange rate (for example, silver and gold), whereas in other arenas promises involve goods that are not completely fungible in a market or are only incompletely so (for example, a promise to return a favor).

In a market with costless transactions, if two actors offer the same goods with promises of future delivery under the same terms but one actor is more trustworthy than the other, it is clear that rational actors will trade with the more trustworthy of the two. The result will be one of the following:

3. This tendency is illustrated in international trade (in which, however, the move to a single currency is inhibited by national sovereignty, which requires by law acceptance of national currencies in transactions within national boundaries). The U.S. dollar currently fulfills the dual requirements of being seen as trustworthy and being plentiful enough to be widely used as the unit of account and the medium of exchange in international transactions. Before the 1950s the English pound played this role. The tendency for good currency (that is, trustworthy trustees) to drive out bad is directly opposed to Gresham's law. Gresham's law derives from the interests of the party who passes currency, and the tendency described here derives from the interests of the trustor. Gresham's law can operate only when the two currencies in question are both legal tender, that is, when the trustor is required to accept either.

The more trustworthy actor will specialize in such promises, and the promises may even become fungible, passed on in further transactions.

The less trustworthy actor will be able to dispose of his promises only at a discount, reflecting the difference in trustworthiness.

The less trustworthy actor will be able to engage in transactions only after the goods of the more trustworthy one are exhausted.

The matter may be clarified by referring to the comparison that a potential trustor must make when confronted with two alternative transactions for which the potential loss and the potential gain are the same. He will engage in the transaction for which the probability of trustworthiness is greater, even though both probabilities are greater than the potential loss relative to the loss plus the potential gain. But when the potential trustor is in a situation in which the sources of potential gain and loss have no market value because there is no market, then the two transactions are offering different things. They differ in more than p_1 and p_2, the estimates of the trustworthiness of the two actors. What is to be gained and lost in the first transaction and what is to be gained and lost in the second are not fungible. G_1, offered by the first actor, and G_2, offered by the second, have no exchange rate fixed by a market. If they did, the less trustworthy actor would be forced out of the market; since they do not, he remains in it, trusted by some (for whom his offerings are of particular interest) and not by others.[4]

The Need to Place Trust

Actors sometimes have a strong need to place trust. An example is the case of the girl who trusts the boy to walk with her through the woods. She is lonely in school and needs companionship. That companionship is potentially available, but only if she places trust. For the comparison that is made in deciding whether to place trust, in this case G is quite large. This means that L/G is much smaller than it would be for another girl, so the girl in question will place trust even if p, the probability that the trust is justified, is relatively small. Women like this are often recognized by men interested in sexual conquests as being quite vulnerable, precisely because their need to trust is so great.

The most extreme case of a need to place trust is that of a person in a desperate situation from which he cannot extricate himself without help. If he is offered help by another, it is rational for him to accept it, even if he believes the chance is near zero that the other will in fact help him. This is true simply because he has nothing to lose: L is zero in this case because the help cannot make him worse

---

4. If the trustor is indifferent between actor 1 offering G_1 and actor 2 offering G_2, then if G_1 and G_2 are fungible and if actor 1 is seen as less trustworthy by the potential trustor, his indifference implies that G_1 is of greater value than G_2; that is, actor 1 must offer more than actor 2 for the same goods. Unless actor 1 can compensate by being more productive with those goods, he is driven out of the market.

off than he will be without it. In such a case a person who places trust is sometimes said to be "grasping at straws." Another way of putting this is that if there is nothing else to grasp at and unless one grasps something one is lost, then it is rational to grasp at straws. In general, many situations fall short of this extreme case yet have a ratio of potential loss to potential gain that is so low that a rational individual will place trust even when the chance of its being justified is very low. In such circumstances individuals may appear irrational in their placement of trust; they are properly characterized not as irrational but as having a strong need to trust.

Actions of the Trustee

I have said nothing about the behavior of the prospective trustee. Sometimes the trustee's actions are not in question—if, for example, the outcome in which the trustor is interested depends only on the trustee's ability, not on his intention or effort. For the large number of cases in which the outcome does depend on the trustee's voluntary actions, however, he has the choice of keeping or breaking the trust. Suppose he has something to gain by breaking the trust. What, other than an internalized moral constraint, might keep him from breaking it? In the case of the high-school girl, the boy who broke the trust might have experienced some direct harm if the girl had told her mother, who had reported to the school and civil authorities (or if the girl's father had taken matters into his own hands). In a case where a borrower has put up collateral for a loan and then defaults, the lender has the legal right to take possession of the collateral.

In most cases, however, particularly ones involving social or political trust, there is no such direct liability. What is often most important is that the trustee may have something to gain from being trusted in the future—either by the same trustor or by another to whom his actions may be communicated. For example, the trust that an electorate puts in an elected official may be withdrawn and the official impeached or otherwise driven out of office (as was Richard Nixon from the U.S. presidency and, in effect, Lyndon Johnson as well) or defeated in the next election. Two important implications follow from this central consideration on the part of the trustee. First, the trustee can expect to lose more in the future if the relationship with the trustor is a continuing one than if it is a single transaction. Thus the longer the relationship with the trustor and the greater the benefit the trustee desires from that relationship, the more trustworthy the trustee will be. Second, the more extensive the communication between the trustor and the other actors from whom the trustee can expect to receive placements of trust in the future, the more trustworthy the trustee will be.

Both of these implications help explain phenomena that otherwise seem puzzling. For example, a young man in military service was hitchhiking home to spend his leave with his family. Another hitchhiker, also a serviceman but from another base, got a ride in the same car. When the first serviceman got out because his route diverged, the second asked if he could borrow a dollar. The first made the loan; the second took his name and address and said he would certainly repay the dollar. When the first serviceman arrived home and mentioned the incident to his father, the father said, "Forget the loan, and be happy it was so small. It is likely you will never see it again." The mother chided the father, telling him he had no faith in human nature. The father replied that it was precisely his knowledge of human nature that led to his prediction. The second serviceman, having nothing to gain in the future by remembering the loan, would never be reminded of it, however honorable his intentions, and it would fade into oblivion.

The implication that a close community among potential trustors leads to greater trustworthiness also makes understandable certain other somewhat surprising phenomena. For example, about the very close community of merchant bankers in the City of London, Wechsberg (1966) writes:

> The visitor in the City is impressed by the absolute confidence placed in the spoken word. A press photograph of the floor of the stock exchange was titled "Where a word is as good as a contract." A lot of business is done with very little paperwork. Every day countless verbal promises, involving millions of pounds, are made over the telephone. "However tired you get of hearing that an Englishman's word is his bond, London's custom of verbal contracts is one of the planks of its reputation," writes Paul Ferris. The merchant banker's business is based on this anatomy of trust. (pp. 40-41)

Wechsberg also quotes a man from Hambros as saying

> [In New York] no one would talk to me without first consulting his lawyer . . . We don't talk to a lawyer before making a verbal promise . . . The City isn't big and you know who belongs here. (p. 41)

An even closer community is that of diamond dealers, another place where trustworthiness is extraordinarily high. Wechsberg describes the behavior in the diamond district of London (a description which holds for New York's diamond district as well):

> Men walk around Hatton Garden with a hundred thousand pounds worth of diamonds that were handed over to them in trust. In a dingy office a man shows another man a number of stones that cost him a fortune, and then goes away while the buyer inspects them carefully. No contracts are made. Nothing is written down. All deals are settled verbally. (p. 83)

In both of these close communities, verbal agreements suffice both because the reputation for trustworthiness is of central importance in these businesses and because that reputation is quickly communicated among all those on whom the trustee depends for future business, that is, for future placement of trust. The concern with integrity, trustworthiness, and reputation is almost an obsession among merchant bankers in the City of London, as their own statements, quoted by Wechsberg (1966) show:

> If a man has been an old customer and friend we'll do anything for him. Even when money is tight, we won't take advantage of him. We are very jealous of our name. (p. 80)
>
> [Merchant banking is] a sense of commercial honor, an absolute fairness in all dealings, willingness to suffer pecuniary loss, if need be, rather than tarnish by one unworthy act the good name of the firm . . . Confidence, absolute confidence, at first between father and son, later between brothers and still later between the partners. (p. 13)
>
> If you ask for one requirement only, it must be integrity. Without complete integrity there cannot be complete confidence. This confidence, our good will, is our most important asset. (p. 352)

These are, of course, the kind of apparent platitudes that are common in many milieus. But the frequency of their occurrence among merchant bankers suggests that for them living up to such words is not a matter of abstract morals but pure self-interest: A merchant banker will no longer be trusted, no longer be allowed to participate in the flow of credit, if his integrity in keeping agreements is not trusted, and his business will rapidly decline if his judgment concerning investments is not trusted.

It also seems likely that the otherwise difficult to explain phenomenon of keeping merchant banking in the family by employment of relatives and intermarriage with other merchant banking families derives from the importance assigned to maintaining closeness and continuity (and thereby insurance for trustworthiness) in the community. If this is true, there should be even more inbreeding among diamond merchants, for whom the closeness of their community is even more important.

In other markets, even those that are regarded as closest to being perfectly competitive, there is extensive evidence that trust and trustworthiness are important to market functioning. For example, Baker (1983) finds that cohesive groups of traders in the Chicago Options Exchange function as systems of mutual trust, even to the extent of driving out newcomers from other groups.

In legislatures there is an interesting phenomenon that also seems to show the importance of a close community. Logrolling occurs when legislation that is of special interest to one member but whose cost will be borne by all constituencies is voted for by the legislature as a whole—as a result of agreements made by the sponsoring legislator that he will vote for others' legislation. More generally, voting agreements are made to gain passage of bills which individually would be of benefit to only a minority of legislators' constituencies.

Some political theorists have found the existence of stable legislation of this sort inexplicable, for political theory based on rational choice behavior predicts that such stability should not exist. Different coalitions should form, based on defections from the original coalition, to replace the legislation in question with a different bill. For example, Schwartz (1981) expresses the result as follows:

> Assuming a majority rule and separability of preferences, an outcome (a position package) for which generalized exchange is essential—one obtainable only through generalized exchange—must be *unstable* in this sense: some actors have the joint power to overturn it in favor of an outcome they like more. (p. 488)

Yet political scientists find a high degree of stability in legislation. Why? Some authors (for example, Shepsle and Weingast, 1981) have seen this as resulting from institutional constraints in voting systems that induce stability. Although this undoubtedly occurs, it is also true that legislatures are close communities with a high degree of continuity. Legislators will suffer costs in terms of unwillingness by their fellows to make agreements with them in the future if they default on agreements (either vote trading or coalitions) in which they have been trusted. Consequently, a correct understanding of rational behavior under such circumstances will recognize that it is often not rational to defect and thus lose the benefits of future agreements (see Coleman, 1982a).

The kinds of actions and reactions by potential trustees and trustors described in the preceding examples can be considered as a game. A trustor must make a decision about whether to place trust in a potential trustee; there is the chance of loss if he places trust and the trustee is untrustworthy, and the chance of forgone benefits if he fails to place trust and the potential trustee would have proved trustworthy. The trustee, in turn, wants to keep the trust if it is to his long-term benefit to do so, but to break it if it is not. The trustor must use information, and perhaps search for more information and revise his views over time, as in an adaptive control system. Beyond all this, however, it is to the trustor's interest to create social structures in which it is to the potential trustee's interest to be trustworthy, rather than untrustworthy.[5]

A principal structure of this kind is a close community such as that found in London's financial center or in the diamond districts. The employment of close relatives within a firm, as occurs among merchant bankers, serves a similar function. Legal contracts and the enforcement potential of the law form another such structure. Each of these has its costs, as does every social structure, although the costs are of different kinds for different structures. The use of the legal system has as one of its costs the additional effort that must be employed to produce the same amount of effective action (or the same quantity of decisions, which is another way of saying the same thing).

Employment of close relatives has as one of its costs the lower average quality of performance among persons selected or promoted from the very small pool of

5. The creation of such social structures is, of course, a micro-to-macro transition. The question of how they are created is treated in Chapter 8.

close relatives than among persons selected from a very large pool on the basis of ability. For example, in the computer and semiconductor industry, no one would think of employing only relatives in sensitive positions, despite the importance of trade secrets and, therefore, trustworthiness of employees. In that industry a company's success depends on the brilliance and creativity of its employees, and a small company that restricted its personnel to close relatives of the owner would quickly be outdistanced by other companies. Firms in that industry use various security measures to reduce the necessity of placing trust in employees. One of these is the practice of telling a person who is being fired on his last day of work, after he has left the office, so that he cannot take with him any material that contains company secrets. Even so, firms in that industry suffer extensive losses due to employees moving to competitors and taking with them company secrets.

A close community with strong norms, such as the financial community in London, brings with it still different costs. One of these is lack of innovativeness. For example, in some industries in which trade secrets are important, there is a general norm against hiring an employee who has left a sensitive position in a competing firm until a certain period of time, such as two or three years, has passed. This practice reduces innovativeness because many good ideas remain unexploited within the firm in which they originated. If the person who has an idea or another person who knows of it is prevented by such community norms (or by trade-secrecy laws) from moving to another firm and exploiting the idea or creating a new firm to exploit it, then the idea remains unexploited.[6]

Studies of innovativeness in industry have shown that the movement of technical employees among firms is an important source of innovativeness (Baram, 1968). And trade-secrecy laws, which prevent employees from using trade secrets of a former employer in their new employment, further impede innovation (Stephenson, 1980).

It might seem that norms of the sort just described are beneficial to a firm within which new ideas originate but necessarily harmful to the system as a whole (the industry). This may, however, be incorrect. The norm may be beneficial to the industry as whole in this way: If new ideas have the property of nonexcludability, as they do in the absence of effective secrecy or patents, then the principal incentive for the generation of those ideas (to capture a part of the social value they create) would be absent. Thus, as with public goods generally, no one would be motivated to produce them. In such a case a firm would find the

---

6. In industries with high fixed capital costs, the impossibility of a person's leaving a firm to begin a small firm of his own is probably a major reason for the lack of innovativeness. An example is the automobile industry, which is composed of a few large firms with a high degree of vertical integration (except in Japan). If there were less vertical integration, there would be a greater possibility of employees' leaving a firm and beginning a new enterprise with the intellectual capital gained while employed there. (It is probably safe to say that most ideas which would prove commercially successful remain unexploited in the automotive firm in which they originate.) The result is an industry less innovative than it would be if this possibility were greater.

maintenance of a research department not in its interest, and no one would spend the time and money necessary to generate new ideas.

An illustrative case is the career of Howard Head, who was employed in the aircraft industry by Martin Marietta but left that firm, taking with him his knowledge of metal fabrication, which he used to invent metal skis. Head later had the idea of creating an oversized tennis racket using lightweight materials, a type of racket which proved to be an enormous commercial success. To implement his idea, he invested money in having a private tennis court built and paying fees for tennis lessons and invested time in learning to play tennis. He would never have done so if he had not had the prospect of developing a new type of tennis racket and of capturing some of the commercial value created by his idea, which he was able to do with a patent.

Another value of such norms is the facilitation of transactions. In the community of diamond merchants, the norms effectively facilitate diamond transactions. In an industry where trade secrets are important, the norms restricting transmission of information outside of a company facilitate the free flow of ideas within the company by increasing the trustworthiness of the recipients of information.

There are, then, clearly both benefits and costs to norms that can make it in the interest of each party in a transaction to be trustworthy. The optimal strength and character of such norms (or of laws, which can be legally enforced) is consequently not a simple question. In any particular case the social institutions designed to increase trustworthiness may do so either too effectively or not effectively enough, from the point of view of efficient social functioning.

One may ask why complete trustworthiness (never disclosing information belonging to the firm or using it outside of the firm) and a resulting complete trust do not necessarily give a social optimum, as they do in the simple system of an exchange involving two parties. One reason is the absence of optimal organization in a firm. An illustration of this is a case in which a joint enterprise, such as an automobile manufacturer, fails to pursue an idea which, if exploited, would bring benefits to others through product or process innovations. In this case the interests of the enterprise and of those outside it are not opposed, but the enterprise is not appropriately organized to maximize its own interests.

Other cases, however, illustrate a different source of suboptimality. Although trustworthiness provides a social optimum for a joint enterprise consisting of two persons, the actions of the joint enterprise may impose costs on others not party to the transaction. An example is the criminal organization known as the Mafia. Various enforcement procedures, including threats of death, are used to ensure the trustworthiness of members of this organization. The result is a high degree of trustworthiness without the aid of legal enforcement. Yet this does not imply that the larger social system is better off than it would be if the Mafia were unable to function effectively. In fact, the opposite would seem to be true.

More generally, the conflicts of interest in any social system make optimization (for example, through the elimination of mistrust) by one pair of actors involved in an exchange not beneficial to all, that is, not a Pareto-optimal move. This is most directly apparent in exchanges of votes within legislatures. Legislator A, who intensely wants to defeat bill X, promises to vote against bill Y, which legislator B intensely wants to defeat, in return for B's vote against X. If this exchange succeeds in defeating both bills, the gain of A and B is at the expense of those favoring the bills, who would otherwise have been the majority. There has developed an extensive literature showing that exchanges of votes can yield outcomes that by reasonable criteria are worse than the outcomes that would result in the absence of such exchanges (see, for example, Riker and Brams, 1973; Schwartz, 1975; Mueller, 1979).

Another institutional area where an increase in trustworthiness does not increase the general welfare is an oligopolistic industry. When oligopolistic agreements are made to maintain or raise prices above the competitive level, trustworthiness with respect to such an agreement is at the cost of lower prices to consumers of that industry's products.

The general question of what is the optimum level of norms, laws, and sanctions to maintain trustworthiness on the part of trustees is a complex one. The optimum, from the perspective of the social system as a whole, depends on the whole set of costs and benefits that result from trust and trustworthiness on the part of a particular pair of actors—not just costs and benefits for the particular actors but costs and benefits for others affected by the keeping or breaking of trust.[7]

The overall pattern of strategic actions in a system of exchange where mistrust can enter should now be clear. The potential trustor decides at any point whether or not to engage in a further search for information and, once the information search is finished, whether or not to place trust in the other party by engaging in a transaction. The potential trustee must first decide whether or not to provide information to the potential trustor that would help bring about a placement of trust and, if trust is placed in him, whether or not to be trustworthy. The trustor may then revise his estimate of the trustee's trustworthiness, using information from the trustee's actions. Furthermore, the trustor may, on the basis of his expected gains from greater trustworthiness, attempt to establish social institutions which increase the trustee's trustworthiness.

The situation may be one in which a given actor is only a potential trustor, without the opportunity to show untrustworthiness, or only a potential trustee, without the need to place trust. On the other hand, the situation may be one in which a given actor is in both the capacity of trustor and the capacity of trustee. In such a case the institutions that develop (for example, social norms with sanctions against those who are untrustworthy) may be ones which increase the overall welfare of each actor at the expense of the immediate gain that each would experience by being untrustworthy. The various industrial communities

---

7. See Chapters 10, 11, and 30 for examination of the emergence of norms with sanctions and discussion of the optimum level of norms.

which have been able to impose norms with sanctions exemplify this case. The case is also illustrated by an exchange of promises by two persons that they will not divulge a shared secret, when either of them might profit, at the expense of the continuity of the relation itself, by doing so. In both these types of situations the level of trustworthiness is generally far from perfect, showing that immediate interests are sometimes stronger than sanctions.

Multiple Trustors and Public-Goods Problems

If a trustee's behavior is affected by the application of sanctions, then a trustor's decision about whether to place trust in that trustee another time should be based not simply on his estimate of the probability of the trustee's keeping the trust, but also in part on the use of negative sanctions. This is illustrated by the following example.

An investment banker in New York, acting as an intermediary in finding investors for a company formed to produce a film, committed a breach of ethics by failing to inform the potential investors that there existed a dispute over film rights to the book on which the film was to be based. After investments were made it turned out that the company could not obtain the film rights. The fact that the investment banker knew of the problem and failed to disclose it became known to the investors, each of whom suffered the loss of a portion of the money invested. Later the same investment banker approaches one of the same investors with a very attractive proposition. The investor calculates that the overall probability of success, even after taking into account the investment banker's previous failure to disclose information, is still sufficiently high that there is an expected gain. Should he or should he not make the investment?

By not making the investment the investor forgoes an expected gain, but may discipline the investment banker so that he does not in the future violate the trust of investors. If a refusal to invest will impose a serious cost on the investment banker, then the investor can estimate the disciplining effect of such a refusal and thus his future expected gain from the increased trustworthiness of that banker. Deciding whether to make the investment is more complicated in such a situation than merely calculating the expected return on the transaction; the investor can optimize his long-term expected return only by taking the disciplinary effect into account.

When there are other investors available at little cost to the investment banker, however, the disciplinary effect of a refusal to invest by any one of them will be very small. It is then to the interest of each, *whatever the others do*, to make the investment if it seems profitable. If all the others invest, then one investor's refusal, having little disciplinary effect, will result merely in that one's forgoing the expected gains from the investment. If all the others refuse to invest, then one investor's refusal, which will represent only a small part of the funds the banker needs, will have little additional disciplinary effect and again will result merely in that investor's forgoing the expected gains from the investment. As a consequence, each investor is motivated to maximize his gains on the investment directly confronting him. The investment banker experiences no disciplinary effect, except that the decrease in the probability of his trustworthiness as adjudged by each investor means that his next offer must be slightly more attractive than it would otherwise be, in order to compensate for this reduced probability. This example illustrates the general point that sanctions constraining actions that impose externalities on others benefit not only the sanctioner but others as well. Such a sanction is a public good.

In a system in which there is a close community, of the sort that Wechsberg describes in the London financial district, a set of norms which overcomes the problem of supplying this public good can come into being. The first norm must be something like this: "Do not engage in transactions with a party who has violated the code of ethics." And that norm must be backed up by sanctions, which in such an informal community may necessitate another norm, something like the first: "Do not engage in transactions with a party who engages in transactions with a party who has violated the code of ethics."

Many such normative systems exist outside the economic system, and their functioning is similar. If girls in a high-school community are trusted not to engage in sexual relations and if the community is close, the norms are strong, and the sanctions effective, then a girl who does engage in sexual relations will be ostracized by the girls with whom she would otherwise interact, and a boy who dates such a girl will find that other girls refuse to date him. Yet few such normative systems among high-school students are perfectly effective, since, as in all normative systems, it is to the interest of each to violate the norm as long as sanctions can be avoided (although it is also to the interest of each that others observe the norm). Such a normative system is difficult to maintain unless the community is very close and very homogeneous in interests.

PART II

Structures of Action

Systems of Social Exchange

Social exchange often occurs not in isolated two-person transactions but within the context of systems of exchange, in which there is competition for scarce resources. These social markets sometimes resemble economic markets, although they often show major differences. An idea of both the similarities and differences can be gained by examining the role of money in economic systems—for as much as any other single difference, it is the absence of money that sets off noneconomic exchanges from economic ones.

What Is Money?

In barter exchange there must be what Edgeworth (1881) called a double coincidence of wants. That is, not only does A have something that B wants, but it is also true that B has something that A wants, and both want what the other has more than they want what they themselves have, which they are willing to give up in exchange. This, however, is a formidable requirement. Money is one means by which the necessity for the double coincidence of wants is overcome.

Money has been defined in numerous ways: as a store of value, a medium of exchange, and a unit of account. It is, of course, all of these. There are, however, different forms of money which perform these functions. For the purposes of this book, a distinction among three forms is useful: commodity money, which contains its value; fiduciary money, which is a promise to pay; and fiat money, which is less than such a promise. The currency which is used by one person in a transaction with a second is often regarded as fiduciary money, a promise by a third party, the government, which is accepted by the second in lieu of a promise by the first. This, however, is not correct. Currency issued by a government is no longer a promise to pay in a commodity which contains intrinsic value (such as silver or gold) but merely fiat money, a declaration by fiat that the currency is legal tender for all debts within the domain of the government. Fiat money exposes the full nakedness of money. Fiat money is accepted not because it is a promise to pay, for it is not, but for two reasons:

1. Its acceptance is legally required (although the value of the money in terms of the quantity of goods and services it will buy is not legally fixed).

2. It is accepted at a particular value because of the quantity of other goods
and services it will buy, that is, because others will accept it in return for
goods and services (although its value for certain uses, such as paying
taxes, is fixed by government fiat).

That is, B accepts a particular amount of currency for the goods or services he
provides to A because of the amount of goods or services that the money will
buy from C. The explicit promise of the government to "pay the bearer on
demand" in commodity money has been replaced by an implicit promise not to
issue fiat money at a more rapid rate than the rate of growth of goods and
services in the economy. It is the violation of this implicit promise which reduces
the value of fiat money.

In private transactions money enables two parties to break apart the two
halves of the double coincidence of a barter transaction. For example, B can
engage in one half of a transaction with A, by providing services to A (in return
for money), and then engage in the second half with C, who provides B with
services "in return" for those B provided to A (concretely in return for money B
earlier received from A). B need not discover a D, who both needs what he can
provide and has what he needs. Obviously, what is necessary for such half-
transactions to occur is some set of persons each of whom will accept money for
approximately the same set of goods or services. What is also necessary is some
stability in the rate at which money is valued, so when B goes to C, he finds that
the money he received from A will buy the goods he anticipated. This requires
some balance between the amount of goods and services traded per unit time in a
society and the amount of money traded per unit time (a product of the stock of
money in circulation and its average velocity, that is, the value of transactions
per unit time per unit of money stock). If the amount of money traded per unit
time increases more rapidly than the amount of goods and services, there will be
a continuing decline in the value of money (due to an increase in either the
quantity of money or its velocity), that is, inflation.[1]

The role of money in transactions in which the government engages is a special
one, since the government issues the fiat money with which it pays its own
debts. It is the role of money in transactions between private parties that is of
interest here. By allowing the breaking apart of the two halves of a transaction,
money substitutes for promises of one party involved in the exchange. Fiat
money is the most recent stage in an evolution which began with promises or
debts and went on to negotiability of debts (that is, exchange of a third party's
promises) and then to a competition among issuers of promises (that is, notes).
Gradually the less trusted issuers were driven out by the most trusted, which in
most settings was (or became) the society's central bank. As this happened, the
need for a promise vanished altogether, since the trusted third party was the
combined government and economy. This development paved the way for fiat

1. See Friedman (1956) for a discussion of the relation of velocity, quantity, and value of
money.

money, by which the promise to pay became a (less explicit) promise to maintain a balance between growth in goods and services and growth in money supply. The next stage in the evolution is one toward which credit cards are a significant step. Sometimes termed the cashless society, it merely consists of what has always been the theoretical alternative to money, a central clearinghouse of debts, made practicable by electronic transfer of information concerning transactions. When a half-transaction takes place, a customer buys a good or service and gives a card number as compensation. Where is the seller placing trust? No longer, of course, in the customer himself; it is not his promise that the seller trusts. It is the promise by the central clearinghouse that it will pay (that is, give credit for any residual balance left after the seller has made his purchases for the day). Thus for the cashless society the identity of the trustee and the nature of the trust that is placed are the same as for fiat money.

The stages of movement away from barter exchange are shown diagrammatically in Figure 6.1. Figure 6.1(a) represents direct exchange of goods and services; all other parts of the figure represent half-transactions, with goods and services flowing in only one direction. Figure 6.1(b) represents exchange in which a promise from one party allows nonsimultaneity between two halves of a transaction. Figure 6.1(c) represents negotiability of that party's promise, allowing not only nonsimultaneity but expansion of the half-transactions beyond the initial pair. Figure 6.1(d) represents the extension of this to the case in which a single central bank's promises (P_a in the diagram) constitute the medium of exchange used as the other half in all transactions. Figure 6.1(e) represents a cashless system, in which a central clearinghouse balances accounts and balances are paid to or received from the clearinghouse.

I have engaged in this examination of the role of money in economic systems to aid understanding of impediments to exchange in economic systems and of the way money, in its various forms, helps overcome at least one of those impediments: the fact that at any given time and place only one party of a pair who might engage in a transaction has an interest in what the other party has. The various changes in character that money has undergone, and is still undergoing, give an idea of different ways in which this impediment has been overcome in economic systems, possibly providing some hints for how similar impediments might be overcome in social and political exchange systems.

A last question will be useful for this examination of money: Why does barter exchange, for example, barter between nations as it occurs today, arise even in the presence of advanced forms of money? The first point to note is that in many of these barter exchanges one or both of the countries that engages in the exchange has a currency that is not freely exchanged and therefore lacks currencies that are freely exchanged (that is, hard currencies). This means that if it wishes to buy goods from a country with a hard currency, it cannot do so: Its promises, as embodied in its currency, are not valued by hard-currency countries at their nominal rate. If such a country's currency were to be traded in the open market, its value would sink below its nominal value. One solution for a

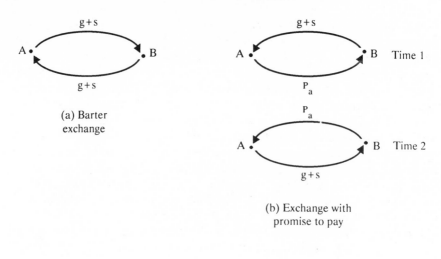

(a) Barter exchange

(b) Exchange with promise to pay

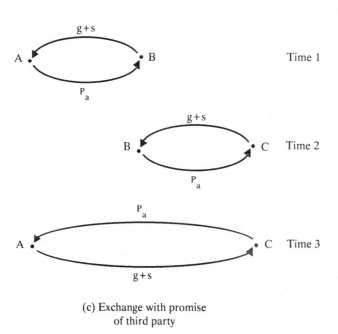

(c) Exchange with promise of third party

Figure 6.1 Structures through which exchange takes place.

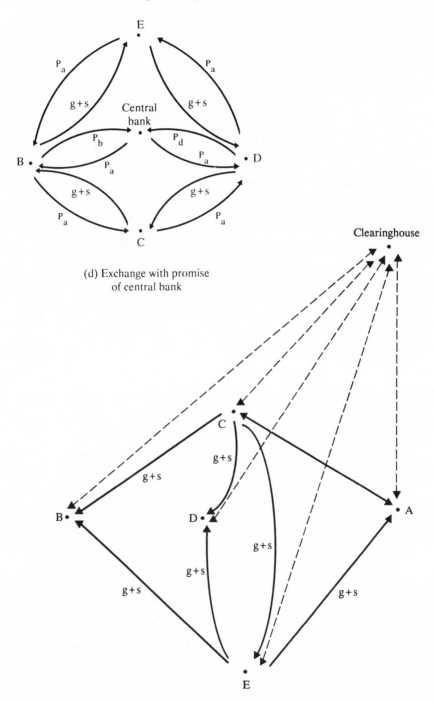

(d) Exchange with promise
of central bank

(e) Cashless system with central clearinghouse of accounts

country with this problem is to pay for goods in which it is interested not with its promises (that is, its currency) but with its goods.

A second source of barter arrangements lies in the fact that for those goods that are overproduced there are national surpluses at world market prices, and a preferable alternative to selling these goods below the market price or keeping the surplus may be to sell them not for money, but for other goods. Or, to put it differently, when there is an oversupply, one country may offer another, as an incentive for purchasing its goods rather than those of a competitor, the willingness to accept goods rather than money in exchange.

Barter exchange may also be seen as a kind of transaction system which exists in the absence of a common medium of exchange. Although national currency systems are in the advanced stages described above, of fiat money and beyond, this is not true at the international level. There is no single third party whose promises drive out all others, precisely because of the fiat moneys that are created by national governments. Dominant currencies, such as the pound sterling before World War II or the U.S. dollar since then, play this role in many transactions (that is, someone in country A uses U.S. dollars to pay someone in country B, and neither A nor B is the United States); and within the hard-currency area the currencies are exchanged as commodities, at rates which more or less reflect international confidence in a country's promises (that is, its production relative to its issuance of promises, or currency). Thus in international trade, just as in certain primitive economies with only limited forms of money (see Einzig, 1966, for an extensive examination), the limitations of a system of economic exchange without a well-developed monetary system are evident.

Media of Exchange in Social and Political Systems

It should be clear from the discussion in the preceding section that once money evolves beyond commodity money and becomes negotiable promises (third-party promises) or legal tender by fiat or is replaced altogether by a clearing-house of debts, it is fundamentally different from what it pays for. It pays for real goods and services, that is, things of intrinsic value. One may ask, then, whether there are any things in social and political systems that play a part in transactions and, like money, have no intrinsic value in themselves. One can quickly see that there are, for promises play an extensive role in social and political systems quite apart from their role in economic exchange.

A second question has to do with the first step toward fiduciary money: Are third-party promises traded? Does B, who has received a promise from A, trade it to C? The answer appears to be that this seldom happens in noneconomic systems; promises appear not to be negotiated or, if they are, only very minimally. Why not? That is a question I will return to later. At this point I will only say that in a few circumstances promises do appear to be traded minimally. In close communities, for example, where nonmonetary exchanges are very dense, some chains of obligation are found. It is commonplace in such communities to

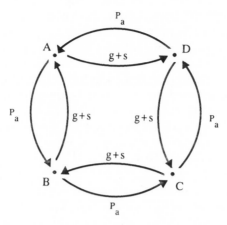

Figure 6.2 Circular exchange of a promise for goods and services in a close-knit community.

hear something like this: "John owes me a favor. Tell him I said to ask him to give you a hand"; or "Mary said you'd let me have this if I told you she sent me." But these chains are generally short, even in close communities. In some legislative bargaining and in some negotiations for cabinet positions among parties in coalition governments, there are deals among three or more parties, deals which involve the carrying of promises back and forth. But both of these types of exchanges occur in a very close and contained setting, so they represent only minimal moves in the direction of negotiable promises.

More generally, in some social settings where A and B are negotiating some transaction, A will make the statement "I've got C's promise that he will do X if . . ." In such a case A is using C's promise as a resource in negotiating with B. C's promise is not fully negotiable (it is seldom true that A could trade off that promise to B, who could then use it in a negotiation with D), because it is a promise specifically to A, not to just anyone. Such exchange of third-party promises is, in some societies, rather well developed. For example, in Germany the word *Ringtausch* describes this practice, which in some locales is widespread.[2] *Ringtausch* involving four actors is illustrated in Figure 6.2. The flow of the promise (P$_a$) is in one direction around the ring, and the flow of goods and services (g + s) in the other.

It is relevant to note that before the advent of fiduciary money economic debts were regarded as private debts and not negotiable. For example, Einzig's (1966) examination of primitive economies does not turn up any where such debts were used as a medium of exchange. Thus the near absence of negotiability of prom-

2. The classical example of a form of *Ringtausch*, of course, is Malinowski's (1922) identification of the Kula ring among Pacific islanders.

ises in social and political systems does not in itself imply that they are fundamentally incapable of being negotiable.

In addition, in some rural communities something analogous to a dual economy appears to exist. For transactions that involve goods imported from outside the community, legal tender is used to balance the half-transactions. For all others, involving locally produced goods (or more often services), some form of a promise of future payment of goods and services (one's own or a third party's) is used in payment. Such a dual economy appears to arise in communities where the value of time is very low relative to that of money, that is, where unemployment or underemployment is extensive.

Other than negotiable promises, the most prevalent device which can make half-transactions possible in social and political systems appears to be nontransferable promises, analogous to Figure 6.1(b). In social and political systems there is generally extensive use of obligations of this sort, for which some kind of account is kept formally or informally. This device provides one degree of freedom less than does money: It allows extension of transactions over time but not across persons. Sooner or later, the indebted party must pay off the debt to the party with whom he incurred it. He cannot use his credit with another party to pay off his debt to the first party—as is done, for example, in a moneyless economy through electronic transfers of debts and credits to a central clearinghouse. One clear reason why promises are not negotiable appears to be that which plagues any system without a general unit of account: There is no widely recognized unit in which accounts can be balanced. This may be intrinsic to the kinds of goods and services exchanged outside economic systems. It may be that their value depends on the particular relation and is intrinsically connected to the identities of the two parties involved.[3]

Another device which facilitates exchange in social and political systems when two-party barter is not possible is the intermediary, or middleman. Ostrogorski (1964 [1902]) describes the way the political machine in American cities at the turn of the century operated as an intermediary.

> For voters the machine provided money and jobs in return for votes for legislators.
> For legislators the machine delivered votes from the voters in return for passage of legislation favorable to business.
> For business the machine obtained favorable legislation in return for money which it used for buying votes.

This is another setting in which the double coincidence of wants is missing, but here this lack cannot be remedied by merely deferring payment through incurring obligations—because the barrier that must be overcome here is not the nonsimultaneity but the noncomplementarity of interests for any two of the three

---

3. In some cases, such as the buying and selling of votes or sexual favors, the transaction is outside the economic system because of legal barriers, a reason irrelevant to this principle.

parties. Thus the machine provides the service of bringing together the three
parties that, taken together, do have complementary interests, and thereby
brings about the transactions. The diagram of Figure 6.3 shows the transactions
involved.

Various social and political entrepreneurs do something similar to this. People
in certain positions in the U.S. Congress, such as the Speaker of the House or
the Majority Leader of the Senate, accomplish multiparty transactions on a
regular basis, although the parties differ from transaction to transaction. These
may be the best examples, but there are examples of entrepreneurship throughout political systems, which serve to bring about deals that require more than
two parties.

Note that little trading of promises is necessary in a system such as that shown
in Figure 6.3. For two of the three transactions, both halves could take place at
the same time. What is necessary, however, in the absence of extensive use of
negotiability of promises, is some "priming" of the system. The machine must
accumulate resources of some sort to use in the transactions, since the three sets
of transactions do not take place at the same time.

The structure of this transaction system is similar to that in Figure 6.1(e) for an
economic system in which there is a central clearinghouse to balance accounts.
It differs, however, in that the central clearinghouse deals only with residual
balances; most transactions are carried out directly. An analogous structure for

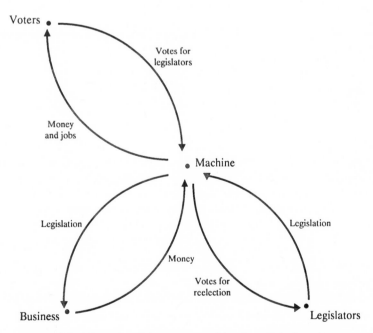

Figure 6.3 The role of the party machine in political exchange.

voters, legislature, and business is shown in Figure 6.4. In such a structure the machine's role is reduced to that of clearing residual credit balances by requiring one or two of the parties to provide additional quantities of votes, legislation, or money, sufficient to bring about future payments by the other parties. It is clear, however, that the machine does much more than this, by organizing the transactions. Because of free-rider problems as well as other problems, none of the parties to this set of transactions could easily carry out its part on its own, even if there were some form of political money or credit account.

To return to the general problem of making possible half-transactions, as money does in economic systems, probably the most important device in social and political systems other than money is the productive formal organization. I will not examine it in detail here but will simply describe the structure: In a formal organization a person in one position performs a task or service for the person or persons in another position; for example, a photocopying machine operator makes copies of documents for all persons in an office whose job requires that they have copies of those documents. Those persons, however, perform no compensating task or service for the operator; the organization does so, by paying a salary or wage. It is true that in many cases the organization imposes a direct charge for the service, not on the *person* but on the position or the department that receives it. There may be, for example, a debit from one line in a budget and a credit to another. Because, however, this balancing of debits and credits does not ordinarily affect any person's compensation but serves only for organizational accounting, it does not provide motivation to individual persons for engaging in half-transactions. That is provided by the organization in the form of a wage or salary, along with a specification of the duties of each position. Of course, the use of money is involved in this structure, but money alone, without the organization, would not bring about this complex of half-transactions. The structure is something between that of Figure 6.3 and that of Figure 6.4. As in the latter, the half-transactions are carried out directly between

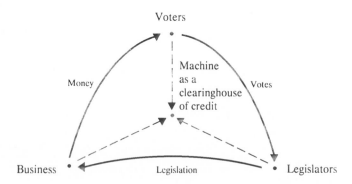

Figure 6.4   The party machine as a credit institution in the political system.

actors; but, like the machine in Figure 6.3, the corporate actor is necessary to organize the set of transactions and ensure fulfillment of them.

The productive organization is thus not a substitute for money but a supplement to it. Money allows single half-transactions to take place; but productive activity often requires an organized complex of half-transactions, for which money alone is not sufficient.[4]

Social Status as a Substitute for Money

One other general device which serves to balance transactions in social and political systems, in part by making possible half-transactions and in part by balancing otherwise unequal transactions, is the granting of status or the showing of deference by one party to another. Blau (1963), in the study referred to earlier, shows how this operates in a government agency. Certain of the agents had more knowledge or skill than did others. Blau observed a systematic pattern of transactions taking place. Some agents would regularly turn to others for advice. These transactions were quite asymmetric, and "debts" were not paid off over time through reciprocal advice giving. They were paid off through the showing of deference toward the advice-givers by the advice-seekers. The result was a status hierarchy in which different agents were recognized as having differing status, or levels of prestige.

Here is another example: A banker in a small town can make a loan to a potential borrower or refuse to do so. Even though the banker makes such a decision principally on the basis of potential profit, he takes into account the needs and intentions of the prospective borrower. If the borrower has no alternative sources of funds, the banker is in full control of the event, and the borrower has little to offer if the demand for loans is greater than the supply. The power is quite asymmetric, and the potential borrower is in the position of a supplicant, being dependent on the decision of the banker. He can, however, give to the banker, along with his note to the bank for repayment of the loan, a kind of generalized credit granting the banker power over various events that the borrower might in the future have control of. That is, he gives the banker, in effect, a credit slip of status, which means that in various contexts he will defer to the banker or give special privileges to the banker. If he is a shopkeeper, he will make certain that the banker and his family get the best service; he will be pleasant and deferential to the banker on the street and in church; he will be es-

---

4. An unresolved issue is just when a formal organization with the sanctions it can impose, rather than an informal organization with informal sanctions, is necessary for a particular productive activity. Williamson (1975) gives some of the pertinent factors. It is evident from comparing Japanese industry with that in Europe and America that technical constraints are not wholly determining, for a much greater fraction of manufacturing in certain Japanese industries (such as the automobile industry) is carried on in a market, rather than within a vertically integrated firm.

pecially pleased if his daughter dates the banker's son. In a multitude of ways he will provide the banker with psychic income in return for the benefit received from the banker or to elicit benefits; the awarding of status thus derives from the unequal resources brought by the two parties to the transaction.

This example is a special case because it involves an event in which the person who awards status has a direct personal interest. However, status is often awarded on the basis of events that do not directly affect the person who awards status. In a high school the boy with the highest status is often the star football player. In society generally movie stars and other entertainers have high status. In a group of hunters the man who kills the most game has high status. Among boys, those who are especially successful in getting dates and in inducing girls to do their bidding have high status. Among girls, those who are especially successful in getting dates and in inducing boys to do their bidding have high status.

This more general phenomenon of status is not the result of specific interactions such as that between the banker and the borrower, in which one member redresses the asymmetry by awarding status. The awarder of status may never even have met the recipient. In cases such as those mentioned above, the general structure is as follows: One person has special control (due to ability or any of numerous other causes) over events in which another has special interest. I do not question here the source of either the control on the part of one person or the interest on the part of the other. But when this configuration does arise, the person with interest in the activity gives a credit slip of status to the person with control over it. This is a kind of account against which the status-holder can draw, deposited against the possibility of a situation in which the status-holder can aid the status-awarder in gaining control over the desired events. This can come about in either of two ways: when the status-holder can directly aid the other who has paid him deference (as when a boy who is successful in obtaining dates can aid another less successful) or when the status-holder can aid a collective activity in which the other has an interest (as in the case of an athletic star helping a high school team to win a game).

All these examples point to a very general process in society. Differential status is universal in social systems; in fact, the awarding of status to balance unequal transactions or to make possible half-transactions appears to be the most widespread functional substitute for money in social and political systems. The foregoing examples indicate various benefits that status can bring, but status, or recognition from others, has long been regarded by psychologists as a primary source of satisfaction to the self. That is, an interest in status can be regarded as being held by every person.

Status, however, is not like money, but has properties peculiar to itself. For an individual, status in the eyes of one person may mean little, but status in the eyes of another means much. Thus, even though a beggar may show great deference, bowing and saying "Thank you, sir," the deference he grants has low value to most persons. Status is complex, for although it constitutes a general medium that can be and is widely used in exchange, it does not have a single denomination that is independent of the particular awarder-recipient pair. There is a general tendency within a given closed social system for the value of a particular person's deference to be similar for all recipients. But among the interpenetrating open social systems of which modern society is composed, there are often wide discrepancies. Suppose that a renowned historian and a renowned physicist are dining in the same restaurant, each basking in the attention of several admirers at his table. If these two with high status switched tables, the other persons at each table would show little deference, and any that was granted to the physicist by the historian's admirers would mean little to him—and vice versa. Each would be, so to speak, "a fish out of water." Even within a university, which has some properties of a coherent social system, a phenomenon similar to this may be observed, except that departments in the university replace the tables of the restaurant.

Within a closed social system status has a characteristic that makes it somewhat like money: The value of a particular act of deference from a person is proportional to his own status. It is as if he has a particular quantity of status and pays out a certain fraction of it through the act of showing deference to another. People with high status will be very hesitant about performing such acts, for ordinarily an act of deference toward another not only increases the other's status but takes away from one's own: It demeans one, in common parlance.

This examination of money and alternative ways of facilitating exchanges makes it possible to consider the kinds of transactions that occur outside of economic systems. That is, money in economic systems and the other devices discussed here outside economic systems serve to facilitate transactions, but they are not the "stuff" of transactions. With the possible exception of status, which may be something of interest in itself, these devices merely make it possible for things that are of interest to move from one person to another whose interest in them is greater.

Exchanges within Systems

Pairwise exchanges in social life do not take place in a vacuum. They occur in a setting in which there is competition for the resources held by each actor. In a high school a date between a girl and a boy depends not only on their interest in one another, but also on their interest in others and others' interest in each of them. Also, the exchange rate that exists for a particular high-school student between grades and school performance depends not only on the student's interest in grades and the teacher's interest in the student's performance, but also on the performance of other students (the competition among students for grades) and the alternative uses for the student's time (the competition among activities for the student's time).

A particular set of activities within an overall social system can ordinarily be examined by circumscribing a set of actors and a set of resources or events as a relatively closed subsystem. Within a subsystem exchanges are interdependent because of competition for the resources. Actors and resources outside the subsystem may be treated as its environment. For example, exchanges in a school between students' performance and their grades may be treated as a subsystem for analysis. Although there is competition for students' time from actors and resources outside this subsystem, those actors and resources can be treated as the environment for the purpose of the analysis. (A broader analysis might incorporate the external demands on different students' time, thereby providing a partial explanation of why, in the subsystem involving grades and performance, some students appear to have a greater interest in keeping control of their time than do others.)

Three elements are necessary to define a subsystem (or a system, for simplicity) for this analysis:

1. Actors
2. Resources or events
3. The constitution, that is, the initial distribution of control of resources among the actors

That is, actors, resources, and a constitution define a system.[5] The interests of actors lead them to carry out exchanges that redistribute the resources contained in the system. Students begin with control over their own time, and a teacher begins with control over grades. The students devote some of their time toward performance in school, and the teacher distributes grades. Students' allocation of time to schoolwork depends on their interest in learning and in grades. The teacher's allocation of grades to students depends on the teacher's relative interest in different students' performance. (If the teacher is fair, this means that the same performance from different students will receive the same grade. The fact that some teachers are not fair, that some students are teachers' favorites, means that a teacher's interest in performance may be student-specific.) The overall level of grades allocated by a teacher is often referred to as the teacher's "ease of grading." Insofar as the teacher is in a monopolistic position with respect to the students, the teacher has control of the ease of grading within a certain range, just as does a monopolist in an economic market. If the teacher is in competition with other teachers or with nonscholastic activities for student time, that monopoly is broken, of course.

In a high-school dating system the actors are the boys and girls attending the school. The resource with which each begins is control of his or her own attention. The interests of various boys in the attention of certain girls and vice versa result in the dating patterns, that is, the redistribution of attention.

It becomes possible in such a system to speak of the power of each actor, for power is a measure of the value *within a system* of the resources with which each

5. As mentioned earlier, in certain cases events or resources in which actors are interested are dependent on other events or resources. In such a case the structure of dependency is also one of the components defining the system.

actor begins (with that value itself deriving from the interests of other actors in those resources), and thus of the weight that the system applies to that actor's interests in the aggregate satisfaction that is realized.[6] More explicitly, there are complementary definitions of the power of actors and the value of events in such a system. These correspond to intuitive conceptions of what power and value should mean in a social system:

The power of an actor resides in his control of valuable events.
The value of an event lies in the interests powerful actors have in that event.

Although this pair of definitions is circular, the concepts of value and power thus defined are not empty of content. As Chapter 25 will show, knowledge of the distribution of interest in events and the distribution of control over events allows calculation of each actor's power and each event's value. As implied by this discussion, the power of an actor is one of the principal derived macro-level concepts for any system of action. Power by the definition given above is a property of *the actor in the system*. It is not a property of the relation between two actors (so it is not correct in this context to speak of one actor's power over another, although it is possible to speak of the relative power of two actors). Such a system of action, with initial individual-level concepts of interest and control and a derived system-level concept of power, suggests a kind of social theory in which social norms are not initial descriptors of a system, although they may constitute phenomena generated by it (see Chapter 10, for example). This suggestion will prove to be well-founded as the nature and implications of the theory become more apparent.

The quantity that plays the same role for resources as power plays for actors in the theory is the value of a resource in the system. As stated above, the value of a resource in a given system resides in the interests that powerful actors have in it. The value of a resource differs from the interest that a given actor has in it, for the value is a property of the resource *in the system as a whole*. The difference between a person's interest in a resource and the value of that resource is merely the difference between the utility a good holds for a person and the market value, or price, of the good. (As Chapter 25 will show, a perfect economic market of exchange of private goods is a specific realization of the system of action described here.) Thus the value of a resource lies in what an actor who controls it can gain from exchanging it, and the interest a resource holds for an actor lies in the potential it has for affecting his satisfaction.

The discussion so far has indicated that in a simple system of action containing only an exchange process, one can link together four concepts: interest and control, both of which specify the relation between an actor and a resource; and power and value, which characterize actors and resources in relation to the system of action as a whole.

What this means in practice is that if one knows the distribution of interests

6. See Chapter 25 for derivation of these properties in a formal model.

and control in a system, one can, through the definitional relations, determine the power of actors and the value of resources. People do this all the time in their everyday assessments of social functioning: The power that various actors have in a system is inferred from what they control and how interested others are in those things; and how valuable something is is determined by how interested those who have some resources are in gaining control of it. Other derivations may also be made for such a system, however. Knowing each actor's initial interests as well as his power and the values of resources makes it possible to determine just how much control each actor will have over each event at equilibrium, that is, when no further exchanges of control are possible. Alternatively, knowing both the initial distribution of control and the equilibrium distribution of control allows one to determine interests, power, and value.

Having an idea of how much control each actor would have over each resource or event at equilibrium provides in some cases (when resources or events are like divisible private goods and can be divided up among those who compete for them) a direct prediction of what the system will be like at equilibrium. But when resources or events are indivisible (such as issues that will have one outcome or the other), then the equilibrium distribution of control tells only what influence each actor will have on the outcome. This set of derivations can be diagrammed as shown in Figure 6.5, which gives a kind of causal structure of the theory: Actors have initial control over resources and initial interests. This distribution leads to exchanges, which in a market structure allow specifying the value of each resource. Then each actor's power is the value of all those resources that he controls, and the amount of each resource that an actor holds at equilibrium is determined by his interest in that resource, his power (that is, the value of the resources he controls), and the value of that resource itself.

Some of the possible empirical uses of the theory follow this causal sequence. That is, one begins with knowledge of initial interests and control and, from that, predicts outcomes of events. One simple qualitative example is Waller's (1938) principle of least interest, which states that in courtship the person with less

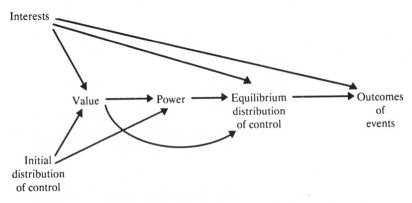

Figure 6.5 Relations among concepts in the theory of social action.

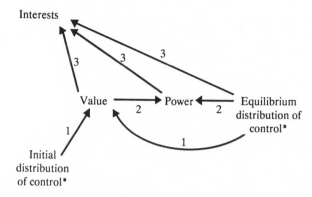

Figure 6.6 Calculations of value, power, and interests from knowledge of initial and equilibrium distributions of control.

interest in the other has greater control over the relation and can get his or her way concerning events about which their interests are opposed. Stated more generally, in a two-person relationship where each has control over his own actions (that is, the resources of the system), the person with less interest in the other has less interest in the resources controlled by the other. This gives him greater power and therefore greater ability to dictate the outcome of new events affecting both parties to the relationship.

For another setting Miller (1970) carried out a different kind of inference, again beginning with interests of different actors and their control of resources. Using an assessment of the interests in particular issues of groups having control over sufficient resources to make them regarded as having some power in the system, Miller predicted the outcomes of decisions on those issues.

Another example of the qualitative use of knowledge of interest and control to predict outcomes of events is the group interest theory of politics put forth by Bentley (1953 [1908]). Bentley made such an inference the central one of his theory of government, although he was not explicit about structures of control. According to Bentley's theory, social and economic activities generate interests, and these interests in conjunction with constitutional control (for example, voting rights) determine policy outcomes.[7]

Although these three examples involve inferences that go in the direction of causal flow, empirical use of the theory may involve starting not with observations of interests and control but with observations of other elements. For example, if one knows initial and equilibrium distributions of control, it is possible to work backwards and find the value of resources, the power of actors, and the interests of each actor in each resource. Figure 6.6 illustrates the steps in such an

7. A strong assumption of Bentley's, that interests lead to actions in pursuit of those interests, follows from the rationality assumption only in the case of private goods. Policies, however, are public goods for those parties interested in them. This deficiency in Bentley's theory led to a major challenge of it by Olson (1965). The public-goods problems pointed to by Olson are examined at various places throughout this book.

analysis; asterisks designate what is observed, and numbers on the arrows indicate the first, second, and third steps in the analysis. The final step in this analysis is inferring the interests that actors would have had in order to lead them from the observed initial distribution of control over resources to the observed equilibrium distribution.

The configuration of data in which initial control and equilibrium control of resources are known is probably the most frequently occurring configuration from which inferences can be made. In the remaining sections of this chapter, I will illustrate uses of the theory in which this configuration of data constitutes the starting point. The examples given will show the results of quantitative analyses (described in Chapter 26) and were chosen for purposes of exposition. As Waller's principle of least interest indicates, qualitative applications of the theory are possible as well.

Exchanges in the Classroom

Earlier in this chapter I described how one might conceive of students exchanging time and effort for grades, with the school as the system of action. This of course abstracts a single market from the total relations in which these actors are involved (with each other and with others), but such an abstraction is tenable for the purpose of analysis. For example, within a classroom itself, exchanges other than the exchange of effort for grades are also occurring at the same time. Students themselves are engaged in exchanges of attention, and the configuration of those exchanges affects the student-teacher exchange. Those exchanges may account for why it is that some students show little interest in grades and others show a great deal, but the effort-for-grades exchange can, as a starting point, be studied alone.

Such an analysis begins by conceiving of each student as being initially in control of his or her own time and effort and the teacher as being in control of grades. At equilibrium, control of students' time and effort and of grades is observed as the time and effort that students have given up to the teacher and the grades that students have received from the teacher.

A quantitative example is provided by observations regarding time spent on homework and school attendance (resources that each student has given up) and grades received (resources that the teacher has given up) made in two schools with twenty tenth-grade students, as shown in Table 6.1.

If it is assumed that each student begins with the same amount of time and that the two components of time, school time and out-of-school time, are distinct resources because of the legal requirement of school attendance, then data in the first two rows of Table 6.1 may be used to determine the fraction of school time and the fraction of out-of-school time each student has given up. In this analysis, grades are seen as the one resource students receive in this exchange, although in reality there are other resources (such as parents' approval or teacher's attention) that in a richer analysis would be included as well.

Table 6.1 Resources given up by twenty tenth-grade students (time doing homework and attendance at school) and by a teacher (grades) in student-teacher exchanges at two schools.

	School 1			School 2		
Student	Homework	Absences	Grades	Homework	Absences	Grades
1	8	2	7	5	0	6
2	5	4	7	1	20	2
3	8	4	7	8	10	4
4	5	25	4	5	4	4
5	5	4	4	13	0	8
6	8	0	6	8	4	6
7	8	0	5	1	0	3
8	13	0	5	1	10	5
9	8	2	6	3	25	4
10	5	4	7	8	0	5
11	3	4	5	0	4	5
12	8	4	4	8	0	6
13	1	0	7	5	0	5
14	8	2	5	1	10	4
15	8	0	8	5	4	4
16	5	2	7	8	2	7
17	13	0	5	8	4	6
18	5	4	6	1	4	7
19	5	4	5	1	10	5
20	5	4	6	13	0	7

Source: Data are from *High School and Beyond,* 1980 study of high-school sophomores and seniors. (Analysis is carried out in Chapter 26.) For grades, 8 = A, 7 = A/B, 6 = B, 5 = B/C, 4 = C, 3 = C/D, and 2 = D. Homework is hours per week, and absences are number of days in the fall of 1979.

If these were simple pairwise exchanges, in which there was no competition for grades, the exchange rate between student effort (reflected in time spent on homework and attendance) and grades would be a negotiated rate unique to each student. However, in a system of exchange in which there is competition for grades, grades may be seen as a common resource—those given to one student reduce those available to others. In other words, a teacher cannot give all A's but is limited in the total number of high grades given out. In such a system student effort (or possibly student performance) is also a common resource, of interest to a teacher whether it is put forth by one student or another.

In a system like this a common rate of exchange develops between student effort and grades. This common rate of exchange is precisely what is meant by relative price in an economic system or relative value in the theory described in this chapter. The common rate of exchange may be one that is, in effect, negotiated by the teacher and the body of students or one that arises from market competition. If it is the latter, then the structural asymmetry, with one teacher on one side of the market and twenty students on the other side, suggests that the exchange rate will be a monopoly rate favoring the teacher, rather than a competitive market rate. That, however, is a question that need not be resolved at this stage of the analysis.

STAGE 1: ESTIMATION OF VALUES   However the single exchange rate, or relative value, is arrived at in each school, the assumption of a competitive market, and therefore a common rate of exchange for all students, means that the data in Table 6.1 may be analyzed to find that set of exchange rates, or values, which are best fit by the data. In this system there are two independent exchange rates, which can be described in any of several ways (for example, as the exchange rate between student effort and grades, and the relative value of homework and attendance, or, alternatively, as the exchange rate between homework and grades and the exchange rate between attendance and grades). I will express them as relative values which sum to 1.0.

The methods derived in Chapter 25 and applied in Chapter 26 are used to calculate the best-fitting values in school 1 and school 2, shown in Table 6.2. (There are three relative values listed, but only two independent values, that is, exchange rates, because the values listed have been normalized to sum to 1.0. An alternative normalization could be used, such as setting the value of grades equal to 1.0.)

Several points should be noted about these results. First, they depend on assumptions made, in the absence of data, about the total amount of out-of-school time and the total amount of school time each student has, as well as about the total amount of grades each teacher can give out. If I had made different assumptions or if data on these aspects of the system had been available, the calculations would have yielded different results.

Second, comparison of school 1 and school 2 reveals differences in functioning. In school 1 the exchange rates are slightly more favorable for the teacher: The teacher gets a better combination of homework done and attendance for a given grade than is true in school 2. And in school 2 the value of time spent on homework, in getting good grades from the teacher, compared to the value of good attendance, is greater than in school 1.

Third, the calculated values in Table 6.2 are characteristics of the system, not

Table 6.2   Values of homework, attendance, and grades in two high schools.

	School 1	School 2
Homework	.37	.42
Attendance	.27	.24
Grades	.35	.33

of individuals. In terms of a diagram like Figure 1.2, these values characterize the systemic, or macro, level, and the processes implied by the derivations are processes of the social system (that is, exchanges between actors), not processes within the individual. In contrast, the coefficients obtained from a linear regression analysis using (as in this case) individual-level data are parameters of an individual-level process, which are in effect averaged over all individuals in the sample. In a regression analysis using individual-level data, the set of individuals on whom observations are made is conceived of as a representative sample of a population of independent individuals. In the analysis being carried out here, the set of individuals on whom observations are made is conceived of as representative participants (or, in the example being used, all participants) in a competitive exchange market. Thus, although relations between individuals are not observed, the process for which the parameters are estimated is a social process, not an individual one.

A fourth point is that, although the estimated values are based on the assumption that there is a common rate of exchange, some students get higher grades than others for a given amount of homework and attendance. This can be regarded as caused by imperfect measurement of what is being exchanged or as an imperfection in the market, leading to differences among the rates for different students' exchanges. In either case the result has implications for the power in the system: The varying exchange rates for different students means that some students gain power through the exchange process, and others lose power.

STAGE 2: ESTIMATION OF ACTORS' POWER IN THE SYSTEM   All students begin with the same resources in this example (the same amount of out-of-school time and the same amount of school time). Since the power of actors is equal to the value of the resources they control, all students start with equal power in this system. But because some get higher grades than others for the same amount of homework and attendance, power after exchange will differ for different students. In this example the total amount of out-of-school time for each student was assumed to be 25 hours per week, the total amount of in-school time was assumed to be 30 days, and the total amount of grades at the disposal of the teacher was assumed to be equivalent to giving everyone a B. Based on these assumptions, the relative power of each student (where the total power of all students and the teacher in each school is taken as equal to 1.0) is given in Table 6.3. This power is the sum of the value of the out-of-school time not devoted to homework, the value of the school time when the student was absent, and the value of the grade received. In each school the teacher's power is the value of grades, or, equivalently, the sum of the value of time students spent on homework, the value of attendance, and the value of grades that could have been given out but were not.

A comparison of Table 6.3 with Table 6.1 brings out some points about the most and least powerful students. The two least powerful in school 1 are students 8 and 17, both of whom spent a lot of time on homework, were never

Table 6.3   Power of each student and the teacher in the two high schools.

Student	School 1	School 2	Student	School 1	School 2
1	.034	.034	11	.033	.037
2	.037	.034	12	.026	.031
3	.035	.030	13	.038	.031
4	.038	.030	14	.028	.036
5	.028	.032	15	.036	.030
6	.030	.033	16	.036	.035
7	.027	.029	17	.024	.033
8	.024	.038	18	.034	.041
9	.031	.040	19	.031	.038
10	.037	.028	20	.034	.030
Teacher	.354	.322			

absent, and yet received only B/C grades. In school 2 the least powerful, student 10, shows a similar profile. The most powerful show varying profiles: In school 1 student 13 got high grades and did little homework but was never absent, and the equally powerful student 4 had a lot of absences and got low grades. In school 2 the most powerful, student 18, got high grades with little homework and some absences; the next most powerful, student 9, shows a profile like that of student 4 in school 1.

In this example the differential power among students represents differences in the exchange rates for different students. (More generally, of course, different actors enter a system with different resources, so each actor's exchange rate is measured by power at equilibrium relative to initial power.) The excess or deficient power for particular students remains to be explained as due to individual characteristics or relations with the teacher.

STAGE 3: ESTIMATION OF THE INTERESTS OF DIFFERENT ACTORS   For estimation of the value of resources and the power of actors, no assumptions were made about the way the common exchange rate in the system was arrived at, for example, by negotiation, by monopolistic competition, by perfect competition (that is, teachers compete for student effort, just as students compete for grades), or by a different process. Furthermore, no assumption was made about the form of actors' utility functions. But assuming that there is a perfectly competitive market and that the utility functions take a particular form (the Cobb-Douglas utility function, which specifies that an actor will always spend the same fraction of his resources on a good, independent of the amount of his resources and the price of the good) and that actions are not affected by normative constraints allows estimation of actors' interests on the basis of their power, the value of resources, and the amount of each resource each actor holds at equilibrium. These assumptions are spelled out in Chapters 25 and 26; the estimates of interests are made as described in Chapter 26.

It is possible to give a heuristic sense of the way an actor's interests are related to the values of resources and the power of the actor in the system. Figure 6.6 shows that the interest of an actor in a resource may be found from the value of the resource, the power of the actor, and the amount of the resource held by the actor at equilibrium. Assuming a Cobb-Douglas utility function and a perfectly competitive market, the product of the actor's interest in the resource and his power is equal to the product of the quantity of the resource he holds at equilibrium and its value. That is, maximization of utility subject to budget constraints means that an actor will acquire a resource until the value of the resource equals that fraction of his total resources (his power) equal to his interest in the resource. From this, interests may be estimated. With respect to the analysis being carried out here, interests of students and teachers in the two schools in each of the resources are given in Table 6.4. (Interests are normalized to sum to 1.0, since all that can be estimated are *relative* interests in the different resources.)

Interests, in contrast to values and power, are properties of individual actors, that is, micro-level characteristics. Conceptually they are independent of the system under consideration; therefore, they may be related to, and explained by,

Table 6.4 Estimated interests of students and teachers in the two high schools in leisure time, school time, and grades.

	School 1			School 2		
Student	Leisure time	School time	Grades	Leisure time	School time	Grades
1	.37	.03	.61	.50	.00	.50
2	.40	.05	.55	.60	.24	.16
3	.36	.05	.59	.49	.14	.38
4	.39	.30	.31	.57	.05	.37
5	.52	.06	.42	.31	.00	.69
6	.42	.00	.58	.44	.05	.51
7	.46	.00	.54	.71	.00	.29
8	.38	.00	.62	.53	.11	.36
9	.40	.03	.57	.47	.25	.28
10	.40	.05	.55	.51	.00	.49
11	.49	.06	.45	.58	.04	.38
12	.48	.07	.45	.46	.00	.54
13	.46	.00	.54	.55	.00	.45
14	.45	.03	.52	.57	.11	.31
15	.35	.00	.65	.57	.05	.37
16	.41	.03	.57	.42	.02	.56
17	.38	.00	.62	.44	.05	.51
18	.43	.05	.52	.49	.04	.47
19	.47	.06	.47	.53	.11	.36
20	.43	.05	.52	.34	.00	.66
Teacher	.28	.69	.03	.26	.60	.14

characteristics of the individual. Table 6.4 shows that the distribution of students' interest in grades is somewhat broader in school 2 than in school 1: Ten students in school 2 show interest below .4, compared to one in school 1; and two students in school 2 show higher interest in grades than shown by any student in school 1.

EXTENSIONS OF THE ANALYSIS   Although I will not pursue the example, it is useful to indicate how the analysis might be expanded beyond the simple situation examined here. It would be possible to predict the effect on students' allocation of out-of-school time of a change in teachers' interest in grades (equivalent to a teacher's grading "harder" or "easier"). It would also be possible to predict the effect on other students' grades, homework, and attendance (assuming their interests remain the same) if particular students (say the three with the highest grades) left the school. If the system were expanded to include other uses of out-of-school time besides doing homework (working, playing sports, watching television), then the relative interest in particular activities could be estimated, and the effect of making certain activities more or less available could be predicted. Those activities involve transactions in which time is spent and other things of interest are received in return. Appropriate data would allow those transactions to be incorporated into the system under analysis. If that were done, the analysis would become much richer, in showing how the system of activities in which students are embedded affects their allocation of resources to achievement in school. It would explain effort devoted to schoolwork in terms of characteristics of the system and of the match between the activities of the system and the individual's interests, rather than merely in terms of characteristics of individuals. Some of the activities competing for a student's time are social activities with other students. Thus one extension of the analysis would allow study of the way a high school's social system and scholastic system interrelate and affect each other.

Exchanges in Labor Markets

An area to which a theory of social exchange in a competitive market can naturally be applied is labor markets. Discourse about labor markets generally refers to the resources that a worker brings to the job market and the various kinds of attractions that a job holds for workers. The imagery underlying this discourse is one in which both workers and jobs bring resources to the market and a match occurs between a worker and a job that bring resources of equal value to the market. It is true that actual labor markets involve more complicated processes, as a result of factors such as collective bargaining, the two-stage sequence involving occupational choice followed by job choice within occupation, segmented markets, local markets, and various other institutional modifications of a perfectly competitive market. It is also true that because a labor market involves matches between a person, who constitutes a bundle of

Table 6.5 Personal and job resources of five workers.

Worker	Personal resources		Job resources	
	Education	Age	Prestige	Income
1	16	32	76	$60,000
2	16	30	52	11,275
3	20	32	51	27,500
4	13	29	45	21,175
5	18	29	62	27,500

Source: Data are for the first five respondents on the 1986 *General Social Survey* file (Davis and Smith, 1986).

resources, and a job, which constitutes another bundle, there are special constraints on the competitive market. Despite these institutional and structural modifications, an analysis of labor markets may be carried out by use of the assumption of a perfectly competitive market. This analysis, however, as will become evident, takes a different form than does that ordinarily carried out by sociologists or economists studying labor markets.

This way of studying labor markets involves taking a representative sample of workers in jobs in a given economy and treating this as a single labor market in equilibrium. The system is treated as if there were market clearing, even though some jobs go unfilled and some workers remain unemployed. (A modification would involve treating unemployment as a separate occupational category, with each unemployed person receiving a certain set of resources deriving from unemployment, such as money income from unemployment benefits or welfare payments, medical care, food stamps, occupational prestige associated with unemployment, and so on). From such a sample information is available on certain resources that each worker brings to the job (such as education, experience, and skills) and certain resources that each worker obtains from the job. For example, Table 6.5 lists several personal and job resources of five workers, taken from the *General Social Survey* (Davis and Smith, 1986).

The theory may be applied with the assumption that the value brought to the market by the worker (consisting of that worker's personal resources) equals the value received in the market by the worker (consisting of the resources of that worker's job). This assumption allows estimation of the relative value of each resource in the market. It is assumed here, unlike in the school example, that the resources on each side are wholly given up in the transaction.[8]

Table 6.6 shows the value of each personal and job resource for the average

8. An alternative, perhaps more realistic, assumption is that one commodity is given up on each side (time by the worker and a job by the employer), and that the value of the worker's time is a function of the various personal resources he brings to the job and the value of the job is a function of the job's resources. This alternative, discussed in Chapter 26, can be described by the same formal model.

Table 6.6 Value in the labor market of education and experience resources and value received in earnings and prestige for the five workers in Table 6.5.

	Value of personal resources				Value of job resources		
	Education	Experience	Constant	Total	Earnings	Prestige	Total
Average person or job	.232	.051	.434	.717	.663	.054	.717
Worker 1	.276	.037	.434	.747	.736	.101	.837
2	.276	.032	.434	.742	.624	.069	.693
3	.346	.037	.434	.817	.683	.068	.751
4	.225	.035	.434	.694	.666	.064	.730
5	.311	.035	.434	.780	.683	.082	.768

Note: The value of earnings is calculated as v_e [ln (earnings)/ln (average earnings)]. The value of each of the other resources is calculated as v_j [(quantity of resource j)/(quantity of resource j for average job or worker)].

worker and average job in the labor market analysis, based on *General Social Survey* data for 923 workers (like the data for five workers in Table 6.5). Listed in Table 6.6 is the value of each personal resource and each job resource for the five workers, as well as the total value of personal resources and job resources for each worker.

Table 6.6 gives a sense of the kind of results achieved by this theoretical approach to the study of labor markets. I will not carry the example further here. The analysis is carried out as described in Chapter 26.

« 7 »

From Authority Relations
to Authority Systems

Chapter 4 examined the vesting of authority by an actor in another. By giving another rights of control over a certain class of actions, the actor makes himself a subordinate of the other, either in return for extrinsic compensation from the other or because he expects the authority relation to provide intrinsic benefits. The creation of this asymmetric relation constitutes a step from the micro to the macro level, a creation of an acting unit consisting of two individuals in place of two separate and independent units.[1] Small though this move may be, it is worthwhile to ask how the resulting structure functions as a behavior system distinct from the actions of the individual actors, that is, what its special properties are. In examining this question, I will consider systems involving disjoint authority relations rather than conjoint ones and will limit the examination to the case in which authority is exercised by the superordinate in whom it is vested. It will be useful to look at the law of agency, at the principal-agent problem in economics, and at work on incentive systems in sociology.

The first important point is that the resulting structure, after authority has been vested, has one essential property: The subordinate's actions seem to violate the principle of rational action in that they are directed toward maximizing realization of the superordinate's interests rather than his own. The reason, of course, is that the superordinate, holding rights to control the subordinate's actions, attempts to exercise those rights so as to maximize realization of his own interests. Yet this reason should not obscure the unnatural character of the relation: An actor, the subordinate, acts so as to maximize the realization of interests of another actor, not himself. It is not surprising that such a relation has special deficiencies and generates special problems.

Law is particularly useful for uncovering deficiencies and problems in various forms of social organization. Civil law deals with cases that ordinarily involve problems concerning rights in action and liabilities for action. Thus examining how such cases are resolved brings to light two things: where problems arise in

---

1. As indicated in Chapter 4, dual authority relations are sometimes created through symmetric commitments by two actors, each of whom gives the other authority over certain of his actions. But this is best conceptualized as two asymmetric relations which in certain instances are balanced.

social organization, and what principles govern, within a given social system, the way that rights in action and liabilities for action are allocated.

The Law of Agency

A general class of activities in society is related to the disjoint authority relation as I have described it: One actor who wants to accomplish a certain goal but lacks some of the skills or capacities necessary to do so finds another actor with those skills or capacities and obtains the latter's services in return for remuneration of some sort. The first actor may employ the second over a period of time, or he may merely contract for a particular service; there is a wide variety of patterns in which this type of relation is manifested. The general property which all these patterns have in common is that one actor (the second party in the above discussion) carries out actions (often directed toward a third party) which are intended to fulfill the interests of the first party.

This class of social transactions is fundamental, for it provides a means by which interests can be pursued far beyond the capacities of the original interested party. It is not the only such means, but it is frequently used when an actor with interests to pursue has a sufficient quantity of resources, but not those of the appropriate kind to realize the interests (for example, has money but not the appropriate skills). He may then wish to use those resources to provide a kind of extension of self.

This class of transactions is treated in a broad branch of law known as the law of agency. The set of common law precedents that have been established in the law of agency allows the development of a coherent conceptual scheme. Even though the law contains conflicting precedents in many areas, it nevertheless evolves toward an internally consistent set of principles concerning social relationships. Although those principles are nowhere set down in concise form as a social theory, the theory (perhaps with some ambiguities) is implicit in them as they have been generated through the resolution of particular cases.

Why use English and American common law as a source for identifying elements of social structure from which a theory might be constructed? Why not use French law, or the Code Napoléon on which it is based? Why not Muslim law, or law as it has developed in Eastern Europe and the Soviet Union? The answer is in part that English and American common law, which develops incrementally through precedent, has a stronger claim to reflect the actual structure of social relations in a society than does a formal code, on which European legal systems are based (see Pollock and Maitland, 1968 [1898], vol. 1, pp. 558–573; Hogue, 1985 [1966], pp. 185ff). A second part of the answer is that it may not matter very much which legal system is used. The law can be used to identify central elements in a social structure through the problems that are brought to the courts. The law of a given country should not, of course, be accepted as providing the optimum solution for all these problems. Law in different countries will resolve the same problems in different ways, but the problems that arise, and the elements of social structure to which they point, will differ much less from one legal system to another.

An example will illustrate the latter point. Before the legal principle of limited liability developed in English common law, co-owners of an enterprise were responsible for all the obligations of the enterprise; their personal assets were not insulated from claims by creditors. Under that earlier legal system cases were of course decided differently than they have been since the advent of limited liability. But examination of cases under both systems shows that the central problem is that of liability, whether to conceive of the joint activity as a separate entity which could have liability "on its own," so to speak, thus limiting the liability of the co-owners, or as a joint venture of persons who are directly involved (and thus directly liable). Neither the earlier decisions which denied limited liability nor the later ones which affirmed it were optimal except from the point of view of particular goals. The later legal decisions led to a different social structure than the earlier ones would have produced if continued, for neither the publicly held corporation nor the multimember association, which together make up much of the structure of modern society, would have been possible. Thus differing decisions in law lead to different kinds of social structures, which facilitate different kinds of activities; regardless of how such decisions are made, however, the problems that arise in law point to central elements of the social structure.

The law of agency in English and American law has arisen out of cases in which one person (the principal) employed another (the agent) to carry out some action for him. Often the action involved contracts or negotiations with another person (the third party) who was buying from or selling to the principal. Thus the law of agency grew up to govern the rights and responsibilities of three persons: the principal, the agent, and the third party.

The minimal authority system consists, of course, of only two actors: superordinate and subordinate (or principal and agent, in the terminology employed by the law, which I will use for the rest of this chapter). The necessity for introducing a third party into the system lies in the fact that often the domain of events and resources over which authority is transferred includes events or resources that concern a third party. (This was particularly true during the early history of the law of agency, where the agent's function was often to contract with a third party on behalf of the principal.)

As it developed, the law of agency grew to cover a much wider variety of cases than those in which it was first used. It came to cover the employer-employee relation, although that relation has more recently come to be governed in considerable part by statutory law.[2] It also covers the relation between a principal and those who perform professional or other services for a fee, commission, or

2. Statutory law, consisting of legislative statutes, is much less useful than common law for the development of social theory. The latter, proceeding through the process of case resolutions, continually evolves incrementally toward internal consistency. Statutes undergo such an evolution in large jumps.

retainer, on a one-time or continuing basis. The law of agency is applied in cases in which any or all of the principal, agent, and third party are not natural persons, but corporate actors. Both principal and agent may be, for example, business firms. The law of agency is coming to be part of a broader segment of the law, covering organizations and associations generally. For example, in a book used in some law schools, *Enterprise Organization* (Conard and Siegel, 1972), dealing with the law covering all sorts of organizations and associations, one of the major sections treats the law of agency.

Servants and Independent Contractors

English and American common law recognizes two forms of agency, which have been termed, in the usage of the courts, the servant and independent contractor forms. These two forms have been distinguished in order to clarify the differing rights and responsibilities of the principal and agent under different conditions. This is obviously necessary because the agency relation is manifested in a very broad array of relationships, ranging from those in which the principal directs every last detail of the agent's actions to those in which the agent is wholly independent of any supervision by the principal. In order to answer the question of who is legally responsible for actions of an agent, the law has split this continuum of supervision into two categories: If the principal "supervises the physical conduct" of or has the "right of control" over the agent, the agent is termed a servant; if the principal does not, the agent is termed an independent contractor (Mecham, 1952 [1933]). The term "servant" remains from the earlier law on master and servant and, although anachronistic, suggests the essential attribute of the role: The servant is subject to control of his physical conduct by the principal. Conard and Siegel (1972) discuss this criterion.

> A number of problems arose with the independent contractor concept. First, there was a problem of identifying the true criterion by which independent workmen should be distinguished from dependent ones, or (in the argot of the courts) how "independent contractors" should be distinguished from "servants." The earlier cases suggested a number of tests, involving the expertise required for the job, the adherence of the workman to a separate craft, the repeated or occasional nature of the service, the control exercised. In the course of time, all these visible, factual elements became subordinated to a construct called "right of control." This "right," which must be distinguished from actual exercise of control, is a legal conclusion which cannot be directly proved or disproved, but must be inferred by the judge. (pp. 127–128)

The reason for making the distinction between independent contractor and servant in the law is not (as is often the case in academic social science) merely to provide conceptual nicety; it is because the cases are resolved differently. If an agent is a servant, subject to the direct control or supervision of the principal, the principal is liable for the agent's actions. If the agent is an independent contractor, the principal is not liable. There are further refinements, but the essential functional difference is the simple one of liability. For purposes of this discussion, whether the principal has the right of control of the agent's actions distinguishes those cases of agency in which there is an authority relation from those cases in which there is not. This chapter is concerned only with the servant form of agency.

The Relations of Principal, Agent, and Third Party

The law deals with one of the central concepts of agency, the right of control, through use of the terms "independent contractor" and "servant," but other concepts must be arrived at through examining the precedents established and the principles expressed in those precedents. The cases which establish principles can be grouped into five classes: those involving the relation between principal and agent; those involving the relation between principal and third party; those involving the relation between third party and agent; those involving the relations among principal, one agent, and a second agent; and those involving the relations among principal, agent, and subagent. Since the latter two go beyond the minimal authority system consisting of a single relation between superordinate and subordinate, they are not relevant to the present examination. The usefulness of the law of agency with respect to this examination lies in what it has to say about the first three of these classes of relations, ones involving principal, agent, and third party.[3]

The first principle that is evident from the examination of precedents concerns the agent's actions in that domain of events covered by the agency relation. Those actions are not to be affected by the agent's interests but are to serve only the interests of the principal. This is exemplified in precedents of the following sort:

1. An agent may not make use of confidential information which he has received in the course of his agency. "The owner of a trades directory employed two commercial travellers to canvass traders for the purpose of obtaining advertisements for insertion in it. At the end of their period of employment they proposed to use the information and materials, which they had acquired during the agency, in assisting a rival publication. The owner sought an injunction to prevent them from so acting" (Ivamy, 1971, p. 17). The court granted the injunction.[4]

3. In arriving at these points, I have used primarily three sources: *Restatement of the law second agency 2nd* (American Law Institute, 1958), the section on agency in *Enterprise Organization* (Conard and Siegel, 1972), and *Casebook on Agency* (Ivamy, 1971).

4. The legal questions surrounding use of information obtained in the course of employment by an employee for personal gain are becoming more important than ever before, because of the increase in the fraction of labor devoted to generating information. See Chapter 17 for a discussion of possible reallocation of rights to information between principal and agent.

2. An agent must not put himself in a position in which his interest and his duty will be in conflict. "A client instructed a stockbroker to buy 600 shares in a company known as Champion Gold Reefs of West Africa, Ltd. The stockbroker did not buy the shares on the open market, but sold [the client] 600 shares which he himself owned" (Ivamy, 1971, p. 10). The court held that the sale of the shares would be set aside because the broker had allowed his interest to conflict with his duty.

3. If an agent receives express instructions from his principal, he is guilty of a breach of duty if he disobeys them. "HMS Daffodil rendered salvage services to the Hermione which had struck a mine. Commander Noakes, of the Daffodil, instructed Stillwell and Sons who were the ship's agents, to prosecute a salvage claim on behalf of himself and his crew, and to settle it for not less than £10,000. Stillwell and Sons settled the claim with the Hermione's owners for £100 only" (Ivamy, 1971, p. 1). The court held that the agents were guilty of a breach of duty.

4. If an agent has received a bribe, he can be dismissed instantly. "A managing director of a company was paid a sum of money by a third party as an inducement to place an order for ice for use in the company's ships" (Ivamy, 1971, p. 12). The court held that the company was justified in dismissing him without notice.

5. An agent can receive payment from both parties to a transaction only if he has their full knowledge and consent to such representation. "If Messrs. Fullwood or any public-house broker want to get two commissions, they must fulfill the two conditions of the law by making a full disclosure to each party of the exact nature of their interest before they make the alleged agreement" (Ivamy, 1971, p. 23).

A second principle that is evident in legal precedents is that the principal, not the agent, is liable for all actions taken by the agent that are within the domain of his agency.

1. "If A is known to be an agent of P, then a statement [by the agent] which causes a contract to be made causes the principal to be liable" (American Law Institute, 1958, p. 640).

2. A principal is liable to a third party with respect to any acts falling within the usual authority of the agent. A secret limitation of the agent's authority is of no effect. "Humble owned the Victoria Hotel. He sold it to Fenwick, who employed him as manager, and allowed his name to remain over the door. Fenwick forbade Humble to buy cigars on credit. But he bought some on credit from Watteau, who discovered the existence of Fenwick, and claimed their price from him" (Ivamy, 1971, p. 69). The court held that Fenwick, the principal, was liable; Watteau's claim succeeded.

3. If an agent indicates that he is contracting as such, he cannot be made liable on the contract. "Houghton and Co. sold 2000 cases of oranges to Gadd, the 'sold note' stating: 'We have this day sold to you on account of James Morand

and Co. . . . ' and being signed 'Houghton and Co.' The goods were not delivered, so Gadd sued Houghton and Co. for damages for non-delivery" (Ivamy, 1971, p. 126). The court held that the suit failed because Houghton and Co. was acting as agent and had stated so.

4. If an undisclosed principal knowingly allows an innocent agent to make a false representation which induces a third party to enter into a contract, the third party can hold the principal liable for damages. "Love knowingly allowed his son, who was unaware that some sheep had rot, falsely to represent to Ludgater that they were in sound condition. Ludgater bought them and later found out the true facts. He sued Love for damages for fraudulent misrepresentation" (Ivamy, 1971, p. 118). The court held that Love was liable.

These two principles—that the agent must not allow his interests to affect actions covered by the agency relation, and that the principal, not the agent, is liable for actions taken by the agent in the course of agency—are based on an underlying structure of concepts. If principal, agent, and third party are conceived of as each having resources and interests, then there are two relations in which actors' interests are involved: that between principal and third party, and that between principal and agent. The agent's interests, according to this structure of concepts, can in no way enter into any interaction between the agent and the third party. There cannot be an exchange involving satisfaction of interests between agent and third party. In this structural system the agent's interests are absorbed by his relation with the principal. Thus the principal-agent combination becomes a *single* corporate actor in relation to the outside world, an actor with augmented resources but a single set of interests.

The problems involving the agency relation that are brought before the courts appear to arise because of difficulties with this construction: The agent lets his own interests affect his actions in the domain covered by the relation; the agent's action is not clearly identified as being in the principal's interests; a third party incorrectly attempts to make the agent liable; the principal-agent construct is incompletely formed; the agent disregards the principal's directives; the principal gives ambiguous directives. A number of these problems arise from misperceptions of the principal-agent combination on the part of the outside world. Some misperceptions are intentionally fostered by principal or agent; some are unintentional. All are made possible by the fact that this is a peculiar entity involving one actor's actions and another's interests.

The most fundamental problem, however, is internal to the agency relation: Because actions are inalienable and the agent can do no more than transfer *rights* to control his actions, a given action itself is the joint result of the principal's exercise of those rights and the agent's implementation of the action. Some of the difficulties this occasions can be addressed by the courts, but others cannot be. Within the terms of any contract, there is a wide range of actions that an agent may carry out, and even a directly supervised agent may devote more or less effort toward the outcome desired by the principal. As long as the principal's and agent's interests are disjoint, the agent's actions, even under direction of the principal, will be different from those the principal would carry out if he had the agent's resources (such as skills or knowledge) and were in the agent's place. This creates a fundamental problem for the principal.

On the other side of the relation, the principal has leeway as well. The very rights of control which have been transferred may facilitate the principal's extension of control beyond the domain covered in the relation; and the principal often has an interest in such extension. This creates a fundamental problem for the agent.

Once a transaction has been made, in which the principal satisfies interests of the agent (for example, through a monetary payment) in return for the agent's using his actions to pursue the principal's interests, a social system has been created. The system contains two self-interested, utility-maximizing actors, and knowledge of the functioning of self-governing systems leads to the recognition that outcomes of events in such a system will in general be different from outcomes in the case of a single actor. Obviously, however, the extent of the difference in outcomes will depend on the way in which the two-actor system is organized.

The Principal's Problem

The principal is ordinarily interested in the achievement of certain outcomes through the agent's actions. Because extrinsic compensation to the agent is part of the transaction and because the principal gains rights to control the agent's actions, there are two methods by which the principal's interests in the agent's actions may be satisfied. The rights of control may be exercised to direct the agent's actions, or the extrinsic compensation may be made contingent on the outcome of the agent's actions, as an incentive to shape those actions. (If rights of control are completely forgone through sole use of the latter means, there is no authority relation at all, and the agent is an independent contractor. Short of that, however, contingent compensation may be substituted for a portion of the rights of control.) The first of these can be called attending to actions, and the second attending to outcomes.[5]

Both methods have defects. Policing the agent's actions entails supervision costs and is not entirely effective. Attending to outcomes ordinarily means rewarding the agent for an outcome that is only partly due to the agent's actions (and partly due to chance, for example, or to actions of fellow employees or of third parties) and is thus an imperfect incentive.

It is possible to formulate the principal's problem as a special case of the general paradigm of rational action, that is, as the problem of maximizing utility (or interests, the term I use here) subject to certain constraints. A body of work

---

5. For complex organizations, discussed in Chapter 16, the terms "forward policing" and "backward policing" are used to describe these two strategies of a principal.

has recently been developed in economics that poses the problem in this way. (See Groves, 1973; Jensen and Meckling, 1976; Lazear and Rosen, 1981; Rosen, 1988.) The problem is specified as follows, in its simplest form: A product is produced as a function of the agent's work effort and of random disturbances. The principal's net income is the value of the product minus the policing costs and the compensation he must pay to the agent. The agent's utility increases with the compensation he receives but decreases with his work effort. The agent's work effort, in turn, is an increasing function of the level of policing. (In a more general formulation the level of policing may also affect directly the agent's utility.) The principal's utility increases with his net income. His task, then, is to set the levels of policing and compensation in such a way as to maximize his utility, given that the agent will put forth work effort so as to maximize his own utility.

Posed in this way, the structure is one of mutual contingency of actions, and the principal's problem is to maximize his realization of interests, given the mutual contingency.[6] This formulation has the virtue of extending the framework of rational action by a small step, from the micro level of individual action in a noncontingent setting to the level of mutually contingent actions of two actors. The formulation contains, in principle, all three components of explanation of system behavior (where the system is the pair of actors and the events relevant to the transaction). Rational action at the micro level is the principal's maximization of utility and the agent's maximization of utility. The micro-to-macro transition comes about through the quantity of product produced by these actions and the distribution of income between the principal and agent. The macro-to-micro transition is the feedback process through which the quantity of product and the distribution of income (and other conditions in any practical application) enter into the utility functions of the principal and the agent and affect their actions. This, of course, is the smallest possible behavior system, but the essential elements are present.

The limitations of such a formulation lie in the practical difficulties of making use of it given the current state of the art for capturing the many variations that exist in authority relations, in the way control is exercised, and in the kinds of incentive systems that may be used by the principal in compensating the agent. There is, however, a body of literature within industrial sociology on employee compensation and methods of incentive pay to employees (see Miller and Form, 1980). The extent of this literature suggests that there is no perfect solution, in which the employee's actions are made wholly consistent with the principal's

---

6. The problem could be said to be that of a non–zero-sum game between principal and agent. I choose not to describe it in that way because that problem as traditionally posed in game theory has certain imposed constraints, such as a single play with simultaneity of action, with both players knowing the other's payoff but not the other's action. The fact that the principal-agent problem in economics did not arise out of work in game theory, but independently, indicates the effects of these constraints. The formulation of the problem is, however, more compatible with work in differential games and work in repeated games.

interests. I will not go into this literature in detail here but will discuss only a few points that illuminate the kinds of divergences that can arise.

In the usual employment relation, where the worker contracts to put his time and effort under the control of the employer, there are two basic methods of compensation, with a large number of variations. The employee may be paid on the basis of time spent (which is the major way used by employers for policing actions) or on the basis of work accomplished.[7] The first is termed straight-time payment, and the second is variously termed piece work, incentive pay, commissions, bonuses, or other terms. Straight-time payment gives the worker no interests (except through other events that the principal might control, such as firing, promotion, or pay increase) in the outcomes of interest to the principal (that is, in production) and thus can lead to low expenditure of effort, resulting low quantity, and poor work quality.[8] It is generally recognized by employers that, in producing any complex product, inspection of product quality is a poor substitute for workers' attention to quality as they work. Piece work or incentive pay makes an employee's interests more consonant with those of the employer, but unless the criteria for payment are precisely in accord with the criteria that affect the principal's interest (for example, including measures of quality as well as of quantity), the employee's actions will not maximize the employer's interests.

At the top executive levels of corporations, and middle-management levels as well, incentive payments are widely used as supplements to a straight salary. These take various forms, such as bonuses, stock options, and payment in stock, and are clearly designed to make the interests of management, as agents, more fully aligned with the interests of owners (that is, the principals). Although such incentives are generally regarded as somewhat successful, subtle differences of interests remain. For example, the specific conditions of stock options may lead top executives to attempt, through corporate actions, to manipulate stock prices in a way having maximum benefits for them, at the cost of benefits to existing stockholders. Bonuses can have similar consequences. Further complexities are introduced by takeover attempts, in that stockholders may stand to gain by the takeover and executives to lose. And this situation is further complicated by the deficiencies of the majority decision rule, which pits the interests of stockholders who sell early (at the offered price) against the interests of those who do not.

Before turning to the agent's problem in the next section, I will mention

7. It is interesting that in nineteenth-century cotton mills in Germany workers were paid in terms of labor input, whereas in England workers were paid in terms of product output (see Biernacki, 1988).

8. In some machine-controlled operations, such as assembly line work, the pace of work is controlled by the machine rather than the employee. Such operations make it difficult to offer incentive pay; however, incentive pay has been used in such circumstances as a supplement to straight-time payment, often paid on a group basis to the set of employees working on a particular machine-controlled operation and associated with quality rather than quantity. For example, automobile manufacturers have used supplementary pay as an incentive to assembly line employees, based on a quality index for the finished automobiles.

another possible component of the principal's interests. Under some circumstances the principal has an interest in extending his control beyond the scope of the authority vested in him by the agent. The rights transferred by the agent may facilitate this. The prototypical case is that of an employer requiring an employee to run personal errands, or an employer expanding the domain of duties required of the employee beyond the domain initially agreed on.[9] This use by the superordinate of the rights of control acquired in the authority exchange to gain control over events outside that domain will be considered in the next section.

The Agent's Problem

The agent's problem, at the highest level of generality, is the same as that of the principal: to maximize his realization of interests. But the constraints under which the agent acts are different from those affecting the principal, as are the ways the agent's interests are realized. The agent's interests depend on the amount of compensation and the costs that he experiences from the actions he takes for the principal (called his work effort above). In addition, however, just as the principal may have an interest in extending control over the agent beyond the authority vested by the agent, the agent has an interest in limiting the principal's control to the domain in which rights have been vested or reducing it to less than that domain. Setting aside for the present this interest in limiting the principal's control, one can examine the agent's problem in terms of the formulation of the principal's problem given earlier. First, the agent can increase or reduce the effort put forth to further the principal's interests. The effect of this on the agent's interests depends on the policing and on the effect of his efforts on the product, in conjunction with the degree to which the principal has made the agent's compensation contingent on the quality or quantity of the product.

All of this leads to something often observed of individuals' work for others: loafing on the job, putting in less than a full day's work, and generally working at a low level of effort. There are, however, other actions that are evident in practice but are obscured by the formulation of the problem as given above. One of these is transmitting false information back to the principal, for the agent often has partial control over the information the principal receives about the agent's actions or about the product. The agent can pretend to work if the principal incompletely polices his actions; he can cover up mistakes in the product or provide false information about the product if the principal makes compensation contingent on the product.

9. The conditions of the initial exchange agreement are, of course, important here. There is, however, one clear demarcation: If an employee is employed by a corporate actor having a structure composed of positions, the rights of control have been transferred to the corporate actor and can be delegated only to a position or office, not to a person. If the occupant of the supervisory position to which those rights have been delegated demands personal services from a subordinate, services that are not relevant to the position, this is outside the domain of the events covered by the authority relation.

Besides adjusting his effort to maximize his interests, the agent ordinarily has another way of increasing his realization of interests. The fundamental point is that, in order to gain his ends, a principal must in many cases give to an agent rights to use certain resources. In other words, the principal retains the rights to benefit from use of the resources, the benefit rights, and the agent acquires the rights to use them, the usage rights. The agent's actions *together with* those resources bring about those ends which the principal desires. This gives the agent an opportunity to use those resources for his own ends—possibly harmful to the principal's interests and possibly not, but in either case benefiting his own. Examples are numerous: an employee's use of a company car for personal purposes, use of tools or office materials for personal ends, use of an expense account to maximize personal satisfactions rather than corporate ends, and use of information gained as an employee to benefit oneself. (See Chapter 17 for a more extended discussion of the drift of value from principal to agent, that is, from the holder of benefit rights to the holder of usage rights.)

The agent's use of the principal's resources in futherance of personal ends (or other ends outside the domain of events covered in the authority relation in which the agent has an interest) is directly analogous to the principal's use of rights of control over certain of the agent's actions to expand control beyond that domain. In both cases a party to the relation is attempting to increase his gains without cost. In both cases the continuing nature of the exchange through time makes the attempt possible. But because the resources exchanged are of different forms (actions versus materials, or labor versus capital), the principal's attempt and the agent's attempt take different forms.

Modifications of One Another's Interests by Principal and Agent

In the preceding examination of the authority relation from the points of view of both superordinate and subordinate (principal and agent), one avenue for achieving goals that was neglected is the changing of interests. If, as superordinate, I can change the interests of my subordinate so that satisfaction of my interests is satisfying to him as well, then he becomes a true extension of myself. The conflict of interests is removed, and I have no need to worry about policing or providing appropriate incentives.

The same potential opportunity exists for an agent. If the principal comes to take my interests as his own, then, as agent, I can pursue my own interests and simultaneously satisfy the principal's interests. Indeed, the same satisfactory state would be achieved for both, whether it was the agent or the principal whose interests changed.

Some flaw is obviously hidden in these simple solutions, for otherwise every authority relation would arrive at such a mutually satisfactory state. There are constraints on interests that prevent such solutions from being easily achieved. In general, throughout this book, except in Chapter 19, I assume that interests are unchangeable; in a theory based on purposive action interests must be taken as given before a rational course of action in pursuit of those interests can be charted.

Sympathy and Identification: Affine Agents

I will continue to use the term "principal" for the superordinate who wants or needs to mobilize resources beyond his own and to use the term "agent" for the actor who comes to be a subordinate and to act in the principal's interest. In the mode of organizing action discussed in this section, however, there is no principal-agent exchange, as there is in the other structures discussed in this chapter. I will call the agent in this mode an affine agent and the mode itself affine agency.

It is useful to clear up a possible point of confusion before proceeding. There is ambiguity in describing an actor's interests as being the same as those of another, for two different things may be meant. The phrase may mean that both actors are satisfied by receiving the same things; by this meaning, two farmers have the same interests. Or it may mean that the second actor is satisfied when the first actor's interests are satisfied. The latter case is what is meant here. The extreme instance would be an actor who acts only to promote the interests of another, his principal, and is oblivious to any other interests. That is, his interests have *become* his principal's interests, and he acts as agent for the principal fully as if he were the principal.

In an example concerning a commune that was first given in Chapter 4, this sort of relation is exhibited:

> At times these relationships became so intense that the personalities of some seemed to melt into those of others. This was particularly striking in the case of the charismatic leader (male) and his chief lieutenant (female). The two were seldom observed together without the female follower's positioning herself in such a way that she could observe his every expression. She mirrored his expressions and gestures, seemingly oblivious to her mimicry. (Zablocki, 1980, p. 15)

Social structures in which this kind of identity of interests exists are unusual. Nevertheless, something approximating it is found in certain situations. A head of state often has as his closest advisor someone he feels he can trust absolutely. He seeks out such a person because he must transfer a great deal of control to someone, primarily control over who has access to him. But the optimal condition for transferring control to another is one in which the other's interests are one's own, meaning that he will act just as one would in the same situation.[10] Thus the closest advisor of a head of state is often someone with few evident

---

10. A close advisor to President Nixon (though not one of the very closest) once described the person closest to Nixon as one who acted as a "second skin" to the president. Yet, after Watergate, the absence of full identity of interests became evident, as Nixon was finally abandoned by even his closest advisors and associates.

qualifications—his one unnoticed qualification is nearly total identification with the head of state.

Phenomena of this sort but short of this extreme are widespread in social organization. The phenomena can be described very simply in terms of the concepts of this book: One actor has adopted, or taken up, the other's interests. Thus the first actor acts as the agent of the other (and himself) without the necessity of policing by the other (the principal) and with payment only sufficient to cover his needs. His interests, being those of the principal, do not lead to actions inimical to the principal's interests. He is as attentive as is the principal himself to waste, inefficiency, bureaucratic rigidity, and all the other problems against which principals must guard.

What makes this mode of organizing action an important one is not that many organizations are largely based on it. Few principals manage to find other actors who will incorporate their interests without regard to self.[11] There are, however, a few important examples of this mode. One, which apparently has been created by evolutionary forces rather than rational action, is the organization of action that arises when a woman has a baby. Through some processes as yet imperfectly understood, the mother comes to identify herself with the child. This means that in the earliest period of life, at a point when a baby is not yet able to be an effective agent on behalf of its own interests, there is automatically a powerful agent acting for those interests. Apparently a structure of action of the sort under discussion here has evolved naturally. It is interesting to note that nature has "chosen" this mode of organizing action as the most effective for such a situation. It is a mode which needs no policing (since the mother will harm her own interests by harming the baby's) and engages a major portion of the mother's energies in the baby's behalf.[12]

Except in certain special social structures such as the one just described, the organization of action through identification, which I call affine agency, seems to operate in conjunction with, and as a supplement to, the mode of agency discussed in earlier sections of this chapter. I will give a number of illustrations of affine agency, which show its operation to different degrees.

1. *Identification with a close relative.* Among the processes in which immediate family members participate (including exchange of control, change of

11. The phenomenon under consideration here is different from charismatic authority. Charismatic authority involves a unilateral transfer of control by the followers to the leader, and they blindly follow his lead. Identification involves an incorporation of the other's interests, but without transfer of rights of control over one's actions. One may feel that one is better able than the other to act so as to satisfy those interests. A mother who is highly identified with her baby does not desire to transfer control to the baby.

12. It is not clear how much of this orientation of the mother is physiologically induced, as implied in this paragraph, and how much is due to the structure of interaction between a baby and the person who is most fully engaged in its care. See Ainsworth et al. (1965) for a review of research in this area.

interests, and unilateral transfer of control), the process of identification is an important one. It is evidently important for organizing the continued and intensive sort of action that is involved in family life, since it plays such a strong part in that life, arising at different points and in different members.[13] Identification of parent with child is strong from the time of birth, and identification of child with parent seems to be an important mode of implanting interests in the child.

2. *Identification with the nation.* Perhaps the most important mode by which a nation organizes action for its defense is that of identification. In wartime many young men volunteer for military service, despite low wages and a high risk of death. Once in the military, some volunteer for the most dangerous missions, for which there is little chance of escaping alive. (These cases may be close to Durkheimian altruistic suicide, with the Japanese kamikaze pilots in World War II a nearly pure example.) Identification with the nation is clearly (unlike identification in the family) purposively engendered by leaders of the nation. This does not answer the question of why those citizens who identify do so (how does it help them increase realization of their interests?) or the question of what conditions make the identification strong or weak. In the next section I will have something to say about the first of these questions (which will also help answer the second), for it is a fundamental one that arises concerning this mode of organizing action. Although this mode certainly benefits the principal, how does it benefit the agent?

3. *Identification with employer.* In most business firms there is loyalty to (that is, identification with) the company on the part of the employees. Sometimes this reaches extreme levels, approaching the identification some persons have with the nation or even the identification with family members or the family itself. This identification is the reason for the frequent use of the term ''family'' to refer to all who work for a firm. As with patriotism, it is to the interest of the principal to engender such identification. It overcomes many of the problems discussed in the preceding sections and in Chapter 16. In fact, some analysts argue that without some degree of identification on the part of employees, business firms have a difficult time operating effectively; the ordinary agency relation without some identification may be insufficient to maintain an effective organization. In any case, in the absence of close surveillance on the part of the principal or superordinate agents, it is clear that loyalty or identification on the part of employees is a valuable resource for the employer. It is true, of course, that employees sometimes have a negative identification with the firm, that is, they see their interests as opposite to those of the firm. As with the nation, those most benefited by the organizational structure come to be most identified with it, and

---

13. For example, a mother's identification with her baby probably declines over time. A child in turn begins to identify with the mother and father as socialization proceeds, a process whose effects increase for some period of time. One relationship involving extensive identification that is especially interesting but still imperfectly understood is that of twins.

those least benefited by it (low socioeconomic groups in the nation, lowest-level workers in a firm) often remain least identified with it.

4. *Identification with a master.* Although the employment relation is sometimes described in law with master-servant terminology, the relation between a domestic servant and his master is demonstrably different from that between most employees and their employers. The identification of the servant with the master is a classic and long-recognized phenomenon, written about in novels and plays and taken as a matter of course. Yet, like the other cases of identification, and more so than some, its rationality is not immediately apparent.

5. *Identification with a powerful captor.* Perhaps the most striking, because the most incongruous, example of identification is that of identification with a powerful captor. Bettelheim (1953) wrote of this occurring in one extreme situation, a Nazi concentration camp in which inmates came to identify with the SS guards. The behavior of some American prisoners of war in camps in North Korea exemplifies the same phenomenon. Although such behavior has been explained in terms satisfactory to at least some psychologists, it seems far from exemplifying the behavior of purposive actors. On the surface these cases seem most difficult to account for in rational terms.

6. *Identification with a community.* Some communes and intentional communities engender in their members extensive identification with the community. Zablocki's descriptions of communes (quoted above and in Chapter 4) reveal some of the mechanisms by which this change of interests is brought about, mechanisms that show some similarity to those used by captors to engender identification in their captives. The end result is a psychic life for community members very different from that outside the community, including, for example, periods of overwhelming collective euphoria and joy. The occurrence of such emotional benefit may be sufficient to account for this identification in rational terms; however, since the phenomenon here is similar to that in the other examples, which lack the collective euphoria, there must be an element in their explanation which is relevant here as well.

7. *Identification of a corporate actor with others.* All of the preceding examples have been illustrations of persons identifying with other actors, either other persons or corporate actors. But there is also a mechanism by which a corporate actor may come to take on the interests of another actor (ordinarily another corporate actor). If one corporation buys into another (assuming, for the present discussion that this occurs without any attempt at control), then a portion of the first organization's interest become identified with those of the second. Thus, in order for the first to pursue *its* interests, it must also pursue those of the second. The first corporation will, if it acts rationally and its interest in the second corporation is more than minimal, modify its actions so that they will benefit the second corporation. The greater its interests in the second, the more its actions will be modified—purely to benefit itself. Its behavior with respect to events affecting the second corporation will be like the behavior of persons with respect to events affecting other actors with whom they are identified.

Why Do Persons Identify with a Principal?

It is obvious that, as a mode of organizing action, affine agency is beneficial to the interests of the principal. A principal receives more services from an affine agent than he would obtain in an exchange with an ordinary agent. What is not immediately clear is how this mode benefits the affine agent, who identifies with the principal and thus does more to further the principal's interests than he would in the absence of this identification.

From another perspective the question almost answers itself. Given that the process of changing one's interests involves internal costs, and thus ordinarily proceeds more slowly than the process of exchanging control over events or resources, then *if* these costs are overcome, an agent who changes his interests by identifying with a principal is subjectively better off than one who does not. Having changed his interests, the agent is satisfying his own interests when he acts to satisfy those of the principal. And when the principal's interests are satisfied, the pleasure of the principal gives the agent a further satisfaction. If in addition the agent receives exchange benefits from the principal, in the form of material rewards such as wages or gratitude, then he has still further benefits (this time satisfying some of his interests that are not identical with those of the principal). Thus he is subjectively far better off than he would be if he had not modified his interests and had experienced only this last source of satisfaction.

This effect can be seen especially clearly in the case of a commune whose members periodically experience an overwhelming euphoria. If each member is identified with the community, then the actions of each to benefit the community are both self-rewarding and rewarded by the other members of the community. Thus there is a system with positive feedback, in which each action brings forth more pleasure, both internal and socially induced.

But such an explanation may explain too much, because the next question is why such identification is not universal and total. The answer presumably lies in the costs of acting in another's interests. As observation makes clear, although the theory does not have a way of reflecting this, interests are not arbitrary, to be shaped at the will of the individual, but are held in place by constraints, some of which are physiological.

The example presented earlier of identification on the part of a corporate actor gives some insight into this answer. If a corporation, having bought into another, acted solely in the interests of the second, it would not be able to maintain itself as a separate enterprise. Its costs would exceed its returns, and it could subsist, if at all, only through the benefits it received as a partial owner of the other corporation. It must either include its own narrow interests in its organization of action or cease to exist as an enterprise, with its owners becoming merely partial owners of the second enterprise. Persons, however, cannot make this choice, unless they choose to cease existence. If they do this (as is apparently the case in altruistic suicide), then they are in the same position as the corporation which chooses to cease to exist.

This discussion of why persons come to identify with others merely opens the question. The matter is carried somewhat further in Chapter 19, where I discuss changes in the self.

Simple and Complex Authority Structures

In Chapter 4 a distinction was made between a vesting of authority in which an additional right, the right to transfer the authority to another actor, was transferred, and a vesting of authority in which that additional right was not transferred. This is the distinction between simple authority relations and complex authority relations, as I called them in Chapter 4. The difference can be described in terms of two aspects of the authority relation: the vesting of authority and its exercise.

A simple authority relation is one in which authority is and must be exercised by the actor in whom it has been vested. The right to control actions is held by the superordinate, but not the right to transfer that right to another. A complex authority relation is one in which there is both a transfer (from the prospective subordinate to the prospective superordinate) of the right to control and a transfer of the right to transfer that right of control to another (a lieutenant).

This conception is independent of any philosophical position taken about the origin or ultimate location of rights. For the philosophical notion of natural rights, in which sovereignty is seen as held by natural persons, the starting point is the subordinate-to-be's decision to transfer the right of control to a superordinate-to-be. According to an opposing political philosophy, widely held in the Middle Ages and in many social systems before that, all sovereignty is held at the top, by the king (who received this grant of authority from divine sources). In this case the processes are the same, but at the starting point rights are already in the hands of authorities. Ullmann (1966) describes these two conceptions as the ascending and descending theories of government. There are variations on these ideas, one of which is Rousseau's general will, which has its descendants in state socialism, an application of the ascending theory which in practice often resembles the descending theory. Gierke's (1934 [1913]; 1968 [1900]) theory of sovereignty being held by intermediate natural associations, or *Genossenschaften*, is another philosophical position, which is consistent with common law in central Europe in the Middle Ages.

The definition of simple and complex authority systems under these political philosophies does not differ from that given above, as long as it is recognized that the original vesting of authority in the superordinate may occur in different ways. The different political philosophies, of course, constitute intellectual justifications for differing initial allocations of rights. The allocations of rights, however, arise not through political philosophies but through social consensus, backed up by power, as described in Chapter 3.

A simple authority system may consist of a number of levels, but the nature of this hierarchy differs from that found in a complex authority system. The institution of the fief in the Middle Ages exemplifies this. In enfeoffment the vassal pledged loyalty (and either military or agricultural services) to his lord, and the lord pledged protection to the vassal. Authoritative commands (for example, concerning military service) were given to the vassal by his lord. But the lord could enfeoff himself as a vassal to a more powerful lord, pledging loyalty (including some part of those resources he received from his own vassals) in return for the other's more encompassing protection. In such a system the higher lord did *not* hold authority over the intermediate lord's vassals. Those vassals had no relation to the higher lord, but only to the lord to whom they had pledged loyalty and from whom they received directives. The authority of the higher lord over the intermediate lord might affect the content of those directives, but they were issued to a vassal on the authority of the lord to whom that vassal had pledged fealty. This structural form did not vanish completely with the end of the Middle Ages. At the level of the household this structure of authority persisted for a long period in France, being embodied in law under the Code Napoléon. All members of a household were subject to the authority of the head, who alone was regarded as a subject-citizen of the state.

The implications of this kind of structure are numerous. For example, in feudal society the lord had complete power over his vassals, and they had no right to appeal beyond their lord's court to a higher lord's court or the king's court.[14] As Simmel (1950) describes it, the resulting social structure within which the individual found himself was one of concentric circles of authority, with the innermost being the head of the household and the outermost being the king. Only the circle closest to an individual had any direct impact on him; unless he was head of a household, for example, he was subject to the head, not the lord directly. The head was subject to his lord, that lord to his lord, and so on up to the king.

One might expect such an authority system to arise when resources are dispersed, there is little communication and poor transportation, there is anarchy at a societal level, and protection is valuable. Such conditions were characteristic of the early Middle Ages, when commerce was blocked by Muslim control of the Mediterranean, when markets were restricted to local areas, and when land was the principal productive resource.

There is another attribute of this period that is compatible with a simple authority system and may have helped maintain such a system: There was no conception of a corporate actor as distinct from a natural person. All resources were seen as being held by persons. If authority was exercised indirectly, it was through a servant transmitting the commands of his master. Thus, since all productive resources were seen as permanently held and all authority relations were viewed as being between natural persons, the notion of acting with an-

14. Such a right of appeal was first introduced in England by William the Conqueror after 1066. By so doing, he took to himself that authority which had been held by the lords, an action which led to a great increase in the king's power and a decline in that of the lords. This change ultimately led to a reaction by the lords and the issuance of the Magna Carta.

other's authority (which is a necessary element in complex authority structures) was an unconventional one, unless the person so acting was seen as a virtual extension of the self of the authoritative person. This latter conception was widespread in ancient authority systems which required several levels of command.

Although the feudal social structure provides a good example of the way that a multilevel macrosocial system can be constructed from simple authority relations, most examples of simple authority systems are flat or nearly so. The most common general case is that of a charismatic authority structure. Because, just as in the fief, the transfer of control is made directly to the person, the authority relation exists directly between the charismatic person and each follower.[15] There are cases, of course, in which the transfer is made to the charismatic person and then authority is exercised through agents (lieutenants), such as when charisma is seen to reside in a head of state (for example, Adolf Hitler). The charismatic relation, however, exerts a force toward a simple authority structure, because the charisma is seen to be embodied in the person himself. Lieutenants are often viewed by followers as interfering between themselves and the charismatic leader, for their transfer of authority to that leader does not include a right to transfer that authority to another. The followers cry for the "master's voice."

A broad class of authority relations can be classified as charismatic, although only a few exhibit the extreme of total dedication of self to the charismatic other. A disciple, as epitomized by the disciples of Jesus, makes such a total commitment. Fans of a movie star, in contrast, transfer to the star only authority over certain aspects of their dress and behavior.

Because of the nature of the authority transfer, the charismatic leader maintains a direct relation with the followers. It may well be that in all transfers of authority to a natural person, there is some charismatic quality (that is, the follower believes the person has some special endowment). If so, this exerts a force to keep the authority relation a simple one, because that endowment is generally seen as not transferable.

A final example of a simple authority structure that is not often recognized as such, but that has much in common with charismatic authority, is love. A person who has fallen in love with another has, in effect, committed himself to the other, has transferred control over many of his actions to the other. This kind of relation to another is much the same as that exhibited by the follower of a charismatic leader, and like the follower, the person in love often sees his object as possessing special qualities not possessed by any other. There are major differences, of course. For example, the charismatic leader has many followers, whereas love objects tend to be different for different persons; also, the person

---

15. There is some confusion in the work of Max Weber about the source of the charismatic endowment, as indicated in his discussion of Joseph Smith, founder of Mormonism (see footnote 9 in Chapter 4).

in love tries to draw the other to him, or to incorporate the other, but the follower, if anything, seeks to be incorporated by the charismatic leader.[16]

When the object of love also falls in love with the one who first loves, there is a unique authority structure of two persons, inwardly directed but with each individual under the control of the other. A disconnected and symmetric authority system of this sort seems to have special properties unlike that of any other and often produces bizarre and exotic behavior. Unfortunately, although this phenomenon has been richly described by novelists, it has been left largely unexamined by social scientists.

The Fundamental Problem of the Simple Authority Structure

In a simple authority relation the resource transferred from the subordinate to the superordinate is one that can be used (the authority can be exercised) but not transferred. This imposes an even greater constraint than that which exists for commodities in a barter market in economic exchange. The fundamental problem of a simple authority structure is the problem of how to cope with this constraint, which is, in effect, like that imposed on primitive forms of animal life by their very form. Invertebrates, for example, are limited in their functioning by the absence of a vertebra.

The effects of this constraint are exhibited in research on the span of control, which shows that in organizations where this constraint does not exist (that is, bureaucratic organizations) the number of subordinates under the direct supervision of a supervisor or manager is quite small (see Simon, 1957, and Blau and Schoenherr, 1971). Thus a simple authority structure, with one superordinate and $n - 1$ subordinates, is misshapen as a productive organization except when n is very small.

Multilevel authority systems compounded of several layers of simple authority structures, such as the institution of vassalage in the Middle Ages, constitute one means of overcoming the size-and-shape constraint, although not a highly successful means. The complex authority system, in which vested authority has a degree of fungibility, removes this constraint.

Properties of a Complex Authority Structure

A complex authority structure is, as defined earlier, one in which authority over a subordinate is exercised by an actor other than the actor in whom authority was vested. There are necessarily at least three actors in such a structure. As stated earlier, in a complex authority structure there is a form of action not present in a simple authority structure. This is the transfer (by the actor in authority) of

16. Although I cannot go into the various psychological intricacies of love and the transfer of authority to a charismatic leader, a property of some such transfers which seems less characteristic of love is that the charismatic leader is seen as a channel or a path toward an external goal (such as divinity); the love object is an object in itself.

authority over another (that is, rights of control over another) to a third party, who, for present purposes, may be termed a lieutenant or an agent.

There are, then, at least three levels in a complex authority structure: the superordinate, the lieutenant (or agent), and the subordinate. But the relation among these levels differs fundamentally from that in a multilevel simple authority structure of the feudal sort. In a feudal structure there is a direct exchange between each pair of adjacent levels: a transfer of authority to the level above, that is, the level at which that authority is exercised.[17] The actor at the next higher level is irrelevant to that relation. But in a three-level complex authority structure, there is a single relation involving three actors: The subordinate vests authority in the superordinate, who transfers it to the lieutenant, who in turn exercises it toward the subordinate.[18] The relation is not complete without any one of these three actors.

As is evident, the three-level complex authority structure exhibits the minimal degree of complexity. Yet it contains all the elements from which highly complex authority structures are built. A simple authority structure involves only two actions: vesting of authority by S (subordinate) in A (authority), and exercise of authority by A over S. A complex authority structure involves two additional actions: transfer from S to A of the right to transfer A's authority to a third party, L (lieutenant), and then the actual transfer of that authority from A to L. The authority over S is then exercised by L.

The rights that are transferred to create a complex authority structure can be given concrete form, as might be done in a game. First, for the transfer of rights that creates a simple authority structure, what might be transferred by an actor (S) to another (A) is a slip of paper saying something like this: "You (actor A) have the right (right 1) to exercise control over my (actor S's) actions within the following limitations . . ." What is important about this slip of paper is that it specifies a particular actor, actor A, as the superordinate. If actor A passes this slip of paper to actor L, he gives nothing of value to actor L. The paper does *not* state that "the holder of this paper has the right . . ." Such a right cannot be transferred; it is not fungible, to use economists' terms.

In order for a complex authority system to develop, an additional right must be transferred, the right to transfer the first right. This may be concretized by a slip of paper stating something like the following: "You (actor A) also have the right (right 2) to designate other actors to exercise all or a portion of the control

17. In the feudal structure there was an exchange in which benefits of protection were given in return for the transfer of control, but this need not be the case. Multilevel simple conjoint authority structures are also possible.

18. The defects in functioning exhibited by complex authority structures will be discussed later. But two examples of a shift from a simple to a complex authority structure illustrate those defects. Some analysts argue that the discontent among peasants in the provinces of France prior to the French Revolution arose when nobles left their lands for Paris and left the running of their estates in the hands of foremen. And it is similarly argued that the economic decline of the plantation as a social structure in the American South began when the second generation of plantation owners left for the city and exercised their authority as absentee landlords through foremen.

specified in right 1 and to transfer right 2 to another actor.'' If S gives this second slip of paper to A along with the first, it means that A may not only *exercise* right 1, but may write out another slip of paper: ''Actor L has the right to exercise control over S's actions within the following limitations (the same as expressed for right 1 or narrower) and to transfer that right to another, subject to the following limitations.'' This gives L the same (or narrower) rights to exercise control over S's actions as S had given to A, as well as the right to further delegate that authority.

There are, in fact, two forms that right 2 can take, only one of which leads to a complex authority structure. In the one form right 2 is stated as given above. This form of right 2 gives A the right to delegate authority, but A retains overall authority. This form of right 2 is what creates a complex authority system. The superordinate, actor A, transfers this right to actor L with specified conditions attached, such as obligations on the part of L to produce certain results or to exercise the authority thus delegated in the interests of A. This is ordinarily done as part of a disjoint authority relation in which L receives payment from A.[19]

The second form of right 2 is less interesting from a social-structural viewpoint because it does not lead to a complex social structure. It introduces full fungibility of right 1 by stating something like this: ''The term 'actor A' in right 1 is to be interpreted as the actor who holds that slip of paper (and this one).'' Or, more simply, right 1 can simply be changed by replacing the specific ''actor A'' with ''the bearer of this paper.'' With this more extended right, actor A may in effect sell the contract of actor S to another actor, thus completely removing himself from the relation. Such a right exists in professional athletics, in some areas of entertainment, and in systems of slavery. It does not exist, however, in most authority structures. In the usual employment relation, in fact, the subordinate is not bound to a particular length of employment but may terminate the relation at any point in time.[20] Thus, because it is not binding, a contract with a subordinate has little value for which a third party will pay.

The Problem of the Complex Authority Structure and the Emergence of Positions

A's delegation to L of authority vested in him by S poses a problem for A: How to delegate the authority without its being commandeered by L and lost to A?

19. Such delegation of authority sometimes occurs in conjoint authority structures as well. In such structures the lieutenant is expected to exercise the delegated authority to benefit the common interest.

20. This asymmetry of the employment relation could be usefully investigated, but I will not do so here. The superordinate is often bound, either by law or by collective agreements that are enforceable by law, not to terminate the relation except for certain specified reasons or to follow a specified sequence in termination of employees, such as terminating first the last one hired. This asymmetry is quite possibly a response to the structural asymmetry that has arisen with the emergence of large corporate actors as major employers in modern society, as described in Chapter 20.

There are, in fact, two problems: how to express the delegation of authority to L so that L may use the authority without having ownership rights to it, and how to ensure that L, having the right to use the authority vested in A, uses it for purposes consonant with A's interest rather than his own.

The second of these problems is, in a slightly different guise, a particular instance of the principal's problem in a principal-agent relation, as discussed earlier in this chapter. The first, however, is a conceptual problem. It has been solved by modern corporate actors using a simple social invention—the conception of a structure composed of persons is replaced by the conception of a structure composed of positions, with persons being merely occupants of the positions. Rights and resources delegated by the authority thus are not the property of a person to whom they are delegated; they are the property of the position to which they are delegated.

A hint of this development can be found even in structures composed of persons, in the etymology of the word "lieutenant." The word was originally French and is composed of two parts: *lieu*, or place, and *tenant*, or holder. Thus a lieutenant is a placeholder, acting in lieu of, or in place of, the actor in authority.

It is necessary, from the point of view of the superordinate, for the transfer of authority from superordinate to lieutenant to be a transfer to a position rather than a person. For if it were otherwise, the lieutenant could take that authority and use it for his own purposes.[21] If the authority is delegated to, and resides in, the position or office, the officeholder does not have the right to use it on his own for his own purposes (except insofar as he disguises them by, or associates them with, the goals of the actor in authority).[22]

With the creation of a complex authority structure, through the superordinate's transfer of the authority vested in him, that authority no longer contains a personal identification. It may remain identified with the actor (or actors) over whom authority is to be exercised, and it is identified with the office or position from which authority is to be exercised, but it has lost any identification with the

21. Simmel (1950) reports the case of a ruling prince who asked one of his advisors about a lieutenant: "'Is the man indispensable to us?' 'Entirely so, your highness.' 'Then we shall let him go, I cannot use indispensable servants'" (p. 199). The story illustrates how indispensability gives power to a subordinate, which reduces the authority of the superordinate.

22. The use of the authority of a position for personal purposes remains a serious problem in complex authority structures, partly because it is often easy for the officeholder to associate his own purposes with those of the higher authority (for example, the organization) and, in fact, sometimes difficult to dissociate his own purposes from them. Characteristically officers on a military base rely on enlisted men for a variety of personal services, although flagrant cases of this are punished. In most political systems higher officials are able to use their authority to gain a variety of personal benefits, ranging from chauffeur services for personal activities to secretaries who arrange personal as well as official affairs. Priests and ministers, as "servants of divine authority," sometimes receive extensive personal services from church members, because of their authoritative position. Yet they are only occupying a position in a religious authority system, a system in which the authority is vested by the followers not in the priests but in God.

person by whom authority is to be exercised.[23] This change is similar to the change that occurred in economic transactions when personal notes came to be accepted as transferable, that is, as a form of money (see Ashton, 1945).

Among all sociologists, Max Weber was most sensitive to the emergence of this new form of corporate actor in modern society. His bureaucratic organization, although it is an ideal type consisting of several dimensions, contains those elements that distinguish corporate actors whose structures are composed of positions-in-relation from those whose structures consist of persons-in-relation. His definition includes

The notion of a hierarchy of offices

Clearly defined spheres of jurisdiction for each office

Filling of offices via appointments on the basis of merit or educational qualifications

Payment in the form of a monetary salary

Limitation of the authority over the occupant of an office to official duties

Nonownership of the office or position by the occupant

Furthermore, Weber (1947 [1922]) saw the development of this form of corporate actor in modern society:

The development of the modern form of the organization of corporate groups in all fields is nothing less than identical with the development and continual spread of bureaucratic administration. This is true of church and state, of monies, political parties, economic enterprises, organizations to promote all kinds of causes, private associations, clubs, and many others. Its development is, to take the most striking case, the most crucial phenomenon of the modern Western State. (p. 337)

Although Weber was pointing to empirically the same phenomena that I am examining here, the fact that for him bureaucracy was an ideal type with a number of dimensions led him to apply the term widely, for example, to the New Kingdom of ancient Egypt and to the Chinese empire (although he saw both as having strong patrimonial elements; see Weber, 1968 [1922], pp. 1044–1051). These cases do show some elements of the bureaucratic ideal type, but the concept of office, as distinct from person, was only partially developed. The pharaoh's agents were his slaves for life, and in the Egyptian kingdom there appears not to have been that separability between person and position which

---

23. The authority does not lose the identification with the actor in whom it was vested, if the vesting of authority by the subordinate is expressly personal, as in a charismatic authority structure. In that case lieutenants often use the words "I require this in the name of . . ." Perhaps the best example is that of divine authority, which must be exercised by lieutenants, or "servants of God," who exercise authority over followers "in the name of God." These are cases in which the second right, the right to transfer the authority, has not been vested by the subordinate.

allows persons to leave positions without collapse of the structure. In the Chinese empire, however, there was a greater separation of office and person; some parts of the structure seem to have consisted of positions, and other parts consisted of persons.

Weber's analysis differed from the analysis here in another important way. He was concerned with modes of authority and therefore viewed the structure, and the processes which create and maintain it, from the perspective of the actor holding authority. My perspective, on the other hand, is that of actors who transfer rights or resources to others and thereby either give others authority over their actions or else vest rights of control in a particular position. I begin, conceptually, with a system in which no authority exists, but only individuals holding rights; Weber begins, conceptually, with a social system in which authority is present, and he goes on to develop concepts that describe parsimoniously the functioning of such a system.

As these comments suggest, most complex authority structures are structures composed of positions rather than persons. It is the positions that possess delegated authority and other resources. The person occupying a position may use its resources to accomplish the goals that are also a property of the position. The correspondence between complex authority structures and positions as the elements of such structures is not perfect, because authority has been conceptualized as detachable from particular persons only after difficult birth pangs involving a series of partial separations. Until the invention of the modern bureaucracy, multilevel authority systems necessary to govern a kingdom or the church were either of the feudal type (that is, compounded of layers of simple authority structures) or, if complex, involved the giving of prebends and benefices held for life or some similar arrangement.[24]

The difference between an authority structure composed of persons and one composed of positions might be seen in the following way. Suppose there are two games mirroring the two cases, and in each a superordinate delegates authority.

Game 1: The structure is composed of persons. The superordinate will pass to various persons (lieutenants) slips of paper stating something like this: "You (name) have the right (right 1) to use resources as specified below and to exercise authority specified below over (names). (Specifications follow.)" If a lieutenant is to have the second right specified earlier, he would receive a second slip of paper: "You (name) have the right (right 2) to transfer the rights and resources specified for right 1 to another, at your volition." There can of course be a large number of variations on the specifications, indicating the class of actors to whom

---

24. The transition from feudal society to corporate society involved the creation of an organizational structure composed of offices occupied by persons, in place of a structure composed of persons having (permanent) responsibilities and resources. This can be regarded as one of the most important social inventions in history. See Coleman (1970b) for further discussion.

the rights might be transferred or the disposal of rights in case of the death of the holder—for the contract might be written so that the rights reverted to the superordinate on the death of the actor to whom they had been transferred.

Game 2: The structure is composed of positions. The only right given to persons by the superordinate is one that specifies something like the following: "You (name) have the right to occupy position X, and this right may be revoked under conditions as specified. (Specifications follow.)" The substantive rights are, however, attached to positions. The new occupant of a position will find at that position a statement something like the following: "The occupant of position X has the right to use the resources specified below and to exercise the authority specified below over the occupants of positions Y and Z. (Specifications follow.)"

From the point of view of the actor establishing a complex authority structure, the defect of the deployment of resources to persons lies in the fact that the resources, including the right to exercise authority over subordinates, pass out of the hands of the superordinate and into the hands of the actor to whom they have been transferred. This was, in fact, a major defect of the authority structures of the late Middle Ages; there was the concept of offices with particular authority and obligations, but the offices were given as benefices to particular persons, and their occupancy could not thereafter be revoked.

The importance of the fact that the structure of a complex authority system is composed of positions to which authority is delegated, rather than persons, lies in the structural stability this brings. Otherwise there would occur decomposition into a multilayered simple authority structure, with each level having full and independent authority over the level immediately below it.

The implications of an authority structure composed of positions are numerous. One is that there comes to be a structure of relations that is independent of persons; the persons merely supply a necessary resource for the functioning of the system.[25] This was a major social change, one that is explored in some detail later in this book. At this point it is sufficient to note that complex authority structures composed of positions rather than persons have become increasingly numerous in the past century and constitute the principal form of stable authority structure in modern society.

Ordinarily, in a disjoint authority structure, in which the subordinate receives his benefits extrinsically, the transfer of authority is accompanied by the right to transfer this authority to an agent. For example, in the employment relation, which is the most common example of a disjoint authority structure, the employee who makes a transfer of control over his time and effort does not expect that the authority will necessarily be exercised by the person with whom he makes the exchange. In fact, in modern organizations he makes the exchange

---

25. A major implication is that if this resource can be supplied by a nonhuman agent (a machine of some sort), a person is unnecessary at that position in the structure.

with an intangible corporate actor, the organization itself, which must exercise its authority through persons (managers, officials, or other agents).

When the right to transfer the authority to an agent does not accompany a transfer of authority, the authority is transferred directly to the person. This ordinarily occurs in conjoint authority structures, where the subordinate believes authority will be exercised in a way that will benefit him. There are, of course, many conjoint authority structures in which the right to transfer authority is granted. Nation-states whose citizens elect or otherwise come to have a leader are conjoint authority structures—but under the leader is a complex structure of government to which and through which authority is transferred. Also, in a trade union, another conjoint authority structure, a set of officers is appointed by the leader in whom the union's authority is vested.

Although there are many such cases, conjoint authority structures are less easily transformed from simple ones to complex ones than are disjoint authority structures, for in some conjoint authority structures authority is transferred directly to a person, who can transfer it to a lieutenant only with difficulty. Even in a nation-state the choice of a leader will often be accompanied by the transfer of authority from the populace to the charismatic leader personally, and the populace will want to be ruled directly, to hear commands from the leader himself.

The Internal Morality of an Authority System

As I have indicated elsewhere, the vesting of rights of control by a set of persons in an actor who thereby acquires authority over certain of their actions provides that actor with a set of resources. How those resources are used is one element affecting whether a subordinate will continue to vest authority, rather than divesting. It is sometimes the case, however, as examples in this and later chapters illustrate, that even after divestment those who have held authority continue to retain power, which is overcome, if at all, only by the use of force.

In some social systems the divesting of authority can lead directly to the divesting of power through the institutions of the authority system itself, but in others it cannot. The capacity of a political system to bring about the defeat of incumbents seeking reelection to office indicates what I mean. In many authority systems, whether formally democratic or not, at the societal level or below, incumbent officeholders cannot be removed from office through the political institutions of the system. If there is a set of institutions through which such removal can in principle be effected, the subordinates in the system may lack sufficient social capital (as defined in Chapter 12) to use those institutions to overcome the incumbents' power.[26] In some systems no such institutions exist.

A first test of the internal morality of an authority system is whether widespread withdrawal of legitimacy (that is, rights of control) by subordinates in the

---

26. This will be discussed further in Chapter 12.

system can be followed, within the institutional framework of the system, by removal of incumbent officeholders from power. If this criterion can be met, the system exhibits internal morality; if it cannot, the system cannot be regarded as having internal morality.

What do I mean by internal morality, and how is it distinguished from the overall morality of an authority system? Internal morality has nothing to do with a social system's or an individual's meeting some externally imposed moral standard. The criterion for internal morality is based on a structural property of the system. Internal morality is absent when individuals are unable to recover actual control over their actions by withdrawing rights of control through use of institutions within the system of authority.[27] If the withdrawal of rights of control is done by a large fraction of the subordinates, then the inability of this fraction to remove incumbents using institutions of the system indicates a system that is internally immoral.[28]

Such a test would appear to show that the authority system of the Shah's reign in Iran had internal morality, for the Shah was ousted without bloodshed or violence. Yet the extreme violations of civil rights during the Shah's regime, including torture and disfigurement of political prisoners, would suggest a lack of internal morality. Those indicators are correct, for the Shah was not deposed through the institutions of the system. The absence of bloodshed was due to the Shah's giving up power by leaving the country. Thus the criterion is not the absence of violence, but the use of institutions of the system.

Other authority systems illustrate the difference between internal morality and external morality. For example, some trade unions in which members are unable to unseat their officials do not meet the criterion for internal morality, however virtuous the external actions of the unions may be seen to be from a particular viewpoint. Nation-states in which incumbent heads of state are able to remain in office despite withdrawal of legitimacy by the population fail the test as well.

Another way in which subordinates in an authority system may regain control of their actions after withdrawing rights of control is through removing power from the incumbent, rather than removing the incumbent from power.[29] This provides a second test of the internal morality of an authority system. If the institutions of the system can be used to limit the power of those in authority, this test is passed. The transition from an absolute monarchy to a limited monarchy is an example. The authority system in England failed this test at one point, when the divesting of King Charles I's power was accomplished only with the aid of the revolution of 1640; but later the English system passed the test, when the monarchy ceded power to Parliament.

---

27. The internal morality of an authority system bears the same relation to its external morality as the internal consistency of a theory bears to its external validity.

28. This implies an authority system in which all subordinates have approximately equal rights. For differentiated systems, in which different persons have differing rights, a more complex test is required.

29. I am indebted to Erling Schild for pointing this out.

A third test for internal morality concerns a single individual's withdrawal of rights: Is he able to follow his withdrawal of rights by exiting from the authority system at low cost? If so, then the system passes this test of internal morality. Those nation-states which forcibly prevent exit of their citizens fail this test.

The tests of the internal morality of a complex authority system concern the revocability of rights and the possibility of returning to conditions that existed before the authority was vested. The first two tests have to do with the collective revocability of rights through removing the incumbent from office or removing power from the incumbent. The third test has to do with individual revocability through withdrawal from the system at low cost.

« 8 »

Systems of Trust and Their Dynamic Properties

It is useful to gain a sense of macro-level phenomena involving trust, for in these are found combined the three components of a system of action: the purposive actions of individual actors, deciding to place or withdraw trust or to break or keep trust; the micro-to-macro transition through which these actions combine to bring about behavior of the system; and the macro-to-micro transition through which some state of the system modifies the decisions of individual actors to place trust and to be trustworthy. Some examples will give a sense of these macro-level phenomena.

1. In the 1660s a Jew named Sabbatai Sevi from Smyrna began to proclaim himself as the Messiah (Scholem, 1973). Soon a large number of Jews in Europe began to believe in him and became his followers. This extensive expansion of trust in Sabbatai Sevi as the Messiah was brought to a halt and collapsed when he was converted to Islam after having been held by the Turks.

2. Over a period of years beginning in the 1960s, the population of Poland withdrew trust from its leadership, periodically refusing to accept price increases, wages, and working conditions and participating in revolts of some sort in 1970 and 1976. Finally, strikes began in Gdansk in August 1980 and spread throughout the country, leading to the formation of the trade union Solidarity. Following the withdrawal of trust by the Polish population in their government, there was an extraordinary expansion of trust in the Solidarity movement and its leader, Lech Walesa, from August 1980 up to the Solidarity's congress in Gdansk in September 1981. In a country with a population of 35 million, Solidarity claimed a membership of 13 million workers and farmers. Unity in Poland was unlike anything in the previous two decades, and unlike anything since.

3. In 1717 a Scotsman named John Law, who had just succeeded in introducing paper money in France, got the French regent to charter the Mississippi Company for exploitation of the Louisiana Territory (Mackay, 1932 [1852]). There was an extraordinary spurt of stock speculation; hundreds of stockjobbers set up stalls in the gardens of the Hôtel de Soissons in Paris, and Paris society invested fortunes in Law's Mississippi Scheme. The trust placed in him was so great that, according to one report, at its zenith he became the most influential person in France.

175

4. In 1095 and 1096 a man known as Peter the Hermit went throughout Europe, having first convinced Pope Urban II that he had a true mission, preaching for a recapture of the holy city of Jerusalem from the Turkish infidels (Mackay, 1932 [1852]). Peter the Hermit gathered several hundred thousand men, women, and children, who followed him through Hungary to Constantinople and toward Jerusalem. Nearly all of them perished along the way; but this was the beginning of the crusades.

5. In the 1960s a declaration became popular among American youth: "Don't trust anyone over 30." This was associated with their extensive withdrawal of trust from the dominant adult culture.

6. In and around Nuremberg, West Germany, some of the artisans who make musical instruments have decided, after painful experience, not to hire and train young apprentices but to let their craft die with them. They have come not to trust the young, *as a class,* to be able to accept the necessary authority during the long period required to learn the exacting skills of instrument making. As a consequence, they have elected not to hire young persons to teach them this craft.[1]

7. In the 1970s in the United States and Europe, there was an extensive expansion of some religious groups and cults, which gained many new members among the young. Hare Krishna was one such group, the sect of the Reverend Moon another, and Zen Buddhism another; once-secular young Jews grew pious and entered yeshivas in Israel; and there were some localized cults, such as that of the Reverend Jim Jones, who established Jonestown.

8. An example of a periodic expansion and contraction of trust in a small social system occurred in a graduate department of sociology in the early 1950s. There was a peculiar phenomenon involving faculty members' evaluations of graduate students: For a time a given graduate student's reputation would rise rapidly among the faculty, in a fashion that appeared mysterious to the rest of the graduate students. Then, equally mysteriously and even more rapidly, one day that reputation would be deflated; all faculty members would seem to lose confidence in the student's abilities simultaneously.

All of these illustrations are macro-level phenomena involving trust. Typical "explanations" for such phenomena remain at the macro-level, are more or less ad hoc, and are based on some single macro-level variable. But even if such an explanation is correct as an explanation of the events in question, it may still have the defects of leaving a large void between purported cause and its effect and of providing at most a weak basis for generalization beyond the given case. For example, an explanation sometimes offered for the phenomenon described in the fifth example, the popularity in the United States in the 1960s of the declaration "Don't trust anyone over 30," is the baby boom, which produced large cohorts of young people in their teens and twenties in the mid- and late

1. I am grateful to Professor Henrik Kreutz, University of Erlangen-Nuremberg, for this example.

1960s, due to a dramatic increase in the birth rate beginning in 1946. But even if this is a cause, in the sense that without the increased cohort size, the withdrawal of trust would not have occurred, it is only one of a number of causes, in the sense of necessary conditions. Most important, it leaves unexamined the system of action through which the perceived macrosocial change had its effect. There is no macro-to-micro transition and (in this case, less problematically) no micro-to-macro transition.

In this chapter I will initiate an examination of systems of action involving trust, beginning with the trust relation as described in Chapter 5. That chapter discussed trust relations that contain only two actors: one in the role of trustor or potential trustor, and the other in the role of trustee. There are, however, three kinds of systems of trust more complex than this. First, two actors may be in two relations: The first trusts the second and is a trustee for the trust of the second. This is mutual trust. Second, the same actor may serve as trustee for one actor and as trustor for another. This actor is, in effect, an intermediary in trust. Third, there are situations in which an actor will not accept another actor's promise but will accept the promise of a third actor. This promise may be used in a transaction between the first and second parties. This is third-party trust. In this chapter I will discuss systems of these three kinds, beginning with systems of mutual trust, which are least relevant to the macro-level examples given earlier but do have important systemic properties.

Mutual Trust

Consider a girl, Kay, and a boy, Jay, in a system of mutual trust. That is, Kay trusts Jay, and Jay trusts Kay. According to the analysis in Chapter 5, rational grounds for Jay's keeping or breaking Kay's trust depends on the immediate benefits from breaking the trust (for example, by being unfaithful to Kay in order to strengthen a relationship with another) balanced against the forgone benefits due to Kay's not trusting him in the future. But since Kay is also the trustee for Jay's trust, there is an additional potential cost to his breaking trust with her: She may not only withhold trust in the future but also retaliate by breaking trust with him (or may simply find it no longer to her benefit to keep the trust). This would not only cost Jay the future benefits arising from Kay's trust, but it would also impose losses from Kay's breaking trust. The fact that Kay is trusted by Jay gives her a resource to prevent Jay from breaking trust.

The condition of mutual trust affects Jay's cost-benefit considerations not only as a trustee, but also as a trustor. As trustor, Jay must compare the probability of Kay's keeping trust with the ratio of potential loss to potential gain. The fact that she also trusts him affects both sides of this comparison: It both increases the probability that she will keep the trust (for the reason described for Jay above) and increases his potential gains from placing trust, since his placement of trust will increase the likelihood of her trusting him.

The situation confronting an individual is summarized in Table 8.1 as incen-

Table 8.1   Incentives for trustee and trustor in asymmetric and symmetric
relations of trust.

Choice of action	Incentives in asymmetric relation	Additional incentives in mutual relation
Keeping or breaking trust	Benefits lost because other will not place trust in the future.	Other, as trustee, will break trust if I do.
Placing or not placing trust	Expectation of gain (pG) from other's trustworthy actions is greater than expectation of loss ($[1 - p]L$).	p is increased by one's sanctioning power in breaking trust if other does; G is increased by future benefits from other as trustee.

tives for keeping trust and incentives for placing trust, in an asymmetric trust relation (where the individual is only trustor or trustee) and in a relation of mutual trust (where the individual is both trustor and trustee). A system of mutual trust is one with positive feedback, indicating that the dynamics lead to increasing levels of placement of trust and trustworthiness.

The additional incentives that exist for placing and keeping trust in a relation of mutual trust lead to two predictions: First, trustors involved in an asymmetric trust relation will have an incentive to transform that relation into one of mutual trust (if Kay wants to trust Jay, she has an interest in trying to get him to trust her). Second, if a relation involves mutual trust, both parties should be more likely to be trustworthy than is the trustee in an asymmetric trust relation (if Kay and Jay both trust, then neither is as likely to defect as is the trustee in a relation in which one trusts). One way the trustor, Kay, may induce the trustee, Jay, to place trust in her is to attempt to bring about situations in which Jay becomes the trustor (by inducing him to do a favor for her, for example) when such opportunities do not naturally arise. This, if it succeeds, will create an obligation on Kay's part, an obligation which she can use to constrain Jay's potential untrustworthiness. It is also, as Jay might recognize, an obligation that Kay will have an incentive to honor.

Another avenue for Kay as trustor is paradoxically almost the opposite: to increase greatly the benefits she provides for Jay. A person deeply in love with another (that is, with expectations of large gains from the relation) will sometimes "do anything" for the person who is the love object. It would be rational for Kay to so act if by so doing she can make Jay "need her as she needs him," that is, create a set of expectations on his part for continued performance (not in this case by creating obligations owed to the other, but by unilaterally benefiting the other).[2] Success in creating such expectations lies in prevention of a with-

2. For a discussion of this strategy and some of its dangers, see Norwood (1985).

drawal from the relation on the part of the other. The danger lies in establishing terms of exchange for future transactions with the other that are extremely unfavorable to oneself. A related danger is that one may be maintaining relations with those who would not continue a symmetric relation.

The fawning behavior toward superordinates that is sometimes observed in subordinates may have such a motivational foundation. The fawning subordinate, needing favorable actions from the superordinate in the future (and knowing that he cannot withdraw from the authority relation except at high cost, and knowing that the superordinate knows this), unilaterally gives benefits to the superordinate in the hope that the latter will come to depend on such benefits and will act favorably toward him in order to keep them coming.

The trustee also has certain strategies available. If the trustee in an asymmetric relation *does* intend to keep the trust and does see benefits in extending the density of transactions in the relation, then he has avenues open to him. If Jay is confronted with an alternative of placing trust in Kay, who has already placed trust in him through other actions, and May, who has not, he is more likely, all else being equal, to place trust in Kay than in May. His belief that Kay will be trustworthy is increased, as indicated in Table 8.1, by the fact that he holds a potential sanction over her, the threat of not being trustworthy himself.

Another means by which the trustee can convert the asymmetric relation into a symmetric one involves the repayment of obligations. When repaying an obligation (such as a personal favor), a trustee needs to do only slightly more than the trustor's expectation, which is what it cost the trustor to do the favor. But if he can bring about an event worth much more than that to the trustor, he may simultaneously repay his obligation and create an obligation on the trustor's part. An obligation will certainly be created if the return favor is not only worth more to the trustor but costs the trustee more than the original favor was worth to him. If this is the case, the trustee will have incurred a loss on the first transaction, but the obligation he has generated on the part of the other (the original trustor, now the trustee) can be expected to bring him gain when his return favor is repaid. As long as there is an extensive potential for gains from trade between these two actors (which depends on what they can do for one another and what it costs them to do these things), the investment made by simultaneously repaying an obligation and creating a new obligation stands to be a profitable one; and, in addition, it creates the potential for more extensive placement of trust by the other in the future.

The pattern of "overpaying" when fulfilling an obligation appears particularly characteristic of rural areas. This would seem to follow from rationality: In those areas persons are especially likely to need to ask others for aid, and such overpayment creates obligations which constitute insurance that the others will be responsive to one's request. Anthropologists have often noted this pattern in primitive societies. The best-known case is that of the potlatches of Indians in the Pacific Northwest.

The dynamics of asymmetric and symmetric relations of trust between two actors are complex, almost defying verbal analysis, as the preceding discussion indicates. These dynamics are examined more extensively through mathematical treatment in Chapter 28, where the effects of asymmetries in initial conditions (such as what each has to gain or lose by the maintenance of the relation) on the resulting character of the relation are examined.

The analysis of social relationships as systems of continued, and in some cases reciprocal, placement of trust and repayment of trust suggests a number of empirical and theoretical avenues by which our knowledge of the statics and dynamics of those relationships can be augmented. It appears that placement and repayment of trust are important to both the creation and the breaking of social relationships. It also appears that combined empirical and theoretical work on the dynamics of trust in social relationships should be productive.

Intermediaries in Trust

In two of the examples presented at the beginning of Chapter 5, those concerning the shipowner and the farmers, the single transaction involved a chain of trust. For the shipowner example the chain can be described as consisting of either two links or three. The two-linked chain is as follows: The Norwegian shipowner is trusted by the merchant banker Hambros, who in turn is trusted by the Amsterdam bank. The three-linked chain is this: The shipowner is trusted by the Hambros manager, who is trusted by the Hambros directors, who are trusted by the Amsterdam bank. For the farming example there are two links: The first farmer is trusted by the neighbor, who is trusted by the second farmer.

In both cases an activity was facilitated that would otherwise not have been carried out. The final trustor (the Amsterdam bank or the second farmer) would not have directly trusted the final trustee (the shipowner or the first farmer) in the absence of the intermediary (Hambros or the neighbor). The final trustor was quite willing, on the other hand, to trust the intermediary. What Hambros did as intermediary in the shipowner example was to provide a kind of guarantee which facilitated a flow of resources from final trustor, the Amsterdam bank, to final trustee, the shipowner. The neighbor as intermediary did not provide a guarantee, but he at least provided sufficient security that the second farmer was willing to do the favor for the first.

It is useful to distinguish three different kinds of intermediaries in trust, all of which can be exemplified in merchant banking and can also be found in wholly noneconomic activities in political and social systems. Intermediaries in trust can be described as advisors, guarantors, or entrepreneurs. The neighbor's role as intermediary in the farming example may have been as advisor to the trustor, the farmer who placed confidence in the neighbor's judgment.[3] This advisory function is often found in politics. In Washington, D.C., for example, there are a

3. Some merchant bankers, such as S. M. Warburg, another one described by Wechsberg (1966), specialize in this role.

number of individuals who act as a certain kind of lobbyist. They introduce interested parties (the potential trustees) to public officials (potential trustors). The potential trustors (congressional representatives or executive agency officials) invest time and attention in listening to the interested parties, trusting the lobbyist's judgment that they stand to benefit from doing so, and sometimes also come to place trust in the interested parties, based in part on their trust of the lobbyist's judgment.

The intermediary as guarantor is exemplified in the shipowner example, for Hambros incurred an obligation to the Amsterdam bank for the £200,000 it advanced. There is an important difference between the guarantor and the advisor as intermediary. The advisor's only stock in trade is the credibility of his advice, and if his advice proves incorrect, his loss is in the trustworthiness of his judgment in the eyes of those he has advised. The guarantor, in contrast, experiences a loss of resources if the final trustee violates trust, but his own trustworthiness in the eyes of the trustor is not diminished.

The entrepreneurial function is one in which the intermediary induces the trust of several trustors and combines these resources, ordinarily placing them in the hands of one or more other actors who are expected to realize gains for the original investors. Some investment bankers in New York have come to act primarily in this capacity—Lehman Brothers is an example discussed by Wechsberg (1966, p. 318). The entrepreneurial function is also often found in political systems. In legislatures such as the U.S. Congress, in which there is little party discipline, certain legislators come to be skilled as entrepreneurial intermediaries in trust. Sam Rayburn, as Speaker of the House, and Lyndon Johnson, as Majority Leader of the Senate, were persons whose integrity in adhering to promises was well known and whose positions made them natural centers of communication. As political entrepreneurs, they could call on a large number of representatives or senators to vote for either a legislative proposal initiated by the executive branch or a specialized bill in which only a small minority was interested. Successful passage of such a bill would create obligations on the part of either the executive branch or those representatives or senators who were interested in the bill's passage. If such a political intermediary is skillful, the credit that will have been extended to the trustors who have given him control over their votes on a given issue will be less than the obligation that will have been gained from the trustee to whom he delivered the votes.

The kind and amount of trust placed in each of these three kinds of intermediaries differs. For the advisory as intermediary, the trustor trusts the advisor's *judgment,* leading him to place trust in the ability and integrity of the trustee, as can be seen in Figure 8.1. The arrows in the figure are labeled J for trust in the intermediary's judgment or P for trust in performance capability (that is, the capability and integrity of the final trustee). It is the trustor's trust in an advisor's judgment that leads to placement of trust in the performance capability of the ultimate trustee. For the guarantor or entrepreneur as intermediary, the

trustor places trust in the performance capability and integrity of the intermediary, as the intermediary does in that of the trustee. In both of the latter
cases, the intermediary must trust highly his own judgment if he is to be able to
act as intermediary. He must in fact have good judgment if he is not to lose
resources as an intermediary.

As Figure 8.1 shows, the advisory intermediary is not a full intermediary, as
are the other two. The trustor must still place trust in the trustee, but in the other
two cases the trustor trusts only the intermediary. If the intermediary is an
advisor and the trustee proves untrustworthy, then the trustor loses resources,
and the intermediary loses reputation. If the intermediary is a guarantor or
entrepreneur and the trustee is untrustworthy, then the trustor loses nothing.

Finally, for the entrepreneurial intermediary several trustors, sometimes having different kinds of resources, must place trust; and part of the performance
capability of the entrepreneur may involve the proper deployment of resources
among the trustees who jointly produce the benefits of the activity. One may

(a) **ADVISOR**

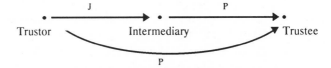

(b) **GUARANTOR**

(c) **ENTREPRENEUR**

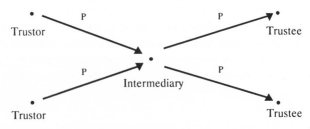

Figure 8.1   Three types of intermediaries in trust.

recognize in this last function the role of the economic entrepreneur who constructs an organization to produce a product, with each employee as a trustee as shown in Figure 8.1.

As with placement of trust generally, placement of trust in intermediaries is based on G, L, and p, the anticipated gains and losses and the trustor's estimate that the other will prove trustworthy. These considerations take their simplest form in the case of a guarantor as intermediary. For the ultimate trustor (the Amsterdam bank in the Hambros example) the estimate of potential gain or loss is the same whether trust is placed in the ultimate trustee (the Norwegian shipowner) or in the intermediary. The difference lies in the estimate of trustworthiness. The Amsterdam bank's estimate of the final trustee's trustworthiness is not sufficiently high to place trust; its estimate of Hambros's trustworthiness is sufficiently high to do so, and Hambros's estimate of the shipowner's trustworthiness is also sufficiently high to allow placement of trust.[4]

The Hambros example also illustrates the basis on which a guarantor can be successful in the capacity of intermediary. If the guarantor did not have a higher estimate of the performance trustworthiness of the ultimate trustee than did the ultimate trustor, he would be unlikely to serve as a guarantor, for he confronts the same potential loss as does the ultimate trustor and, in many cases, the same potential gain. If he *incorrectly* has that higher estimate, he will serve as guarantor but will often lose from placing trust in an actor who proves untrustworthy. Thus in order to be successful as a guarantor, an actor's principal asset (besides resources that can serve as the guarantee) is information about the potential trustee's trustworthiness. Unless his information about this is superior to that of others with whom potential trustees might engage in transactions, he has no possibility of gain through activity as intermediary.

For the ultimate trustor the considerations applied when using an advisory intermediary are similar to those for a guarantor. The advisor (whom I assume to be in a position similar to that of the trustor) has either placed trust or not, based on assessment of potential gains or losses from the trustee's actions, similar to those the trustor confronts. If the trustor believes the intermediary's judgment is better than his own, and better than that of others who have made the opposite decision about trusting the trustee, he will place trust in the intermediary's judgment and follow his action (placing trust or not doing so, withdrawing it or not doing so). The intermediary himself may or may not be active in an advisory capacity, for it may be his own action toward the trustee which leads him to be used as an exemplar by the actor who places trust in his judgment.

One important difference separates the entrepreneurial intermediary and the other two forms. Although this difference is critically important for the dynamics of trust in political systems, I will illustrate it by considering a purely social case, a hostess in diplomatic circles who is planning a party. The persons she invites

---

4. In this case as in others involving guarantors as intermediaries, the intermediary may also have more to gain by placing trust.

are the potential trustors, and each must ask introspectively, "What do I stand to lose by attending, what do I stand to gain, and what is the chance that I will gain rather than lose?" (In terms of the symbols used in Chapter 5, What is L, what is G, and what is p?) A critical element in the assessment of G and p on the part of each person invited is knowledge of who else will be there. In short, the resources provided by certain prospective guests increase the likelihood that other guests will place trust by attending, and only if most do attend will there be a gain for all rather than a loss.

Who are the final trustees in this case? The same persons are trustors, as individuals, and trustees, as a collectivity. The hostess, like a business entrepreneur, trusts the people who will constitute a "good combination" to come, and each of the people who do come trusts the hostess to have invited and been able to attract the "right people." The successful hostesses come to be trusted, and their parties are well attended, precisely because those who attend find them to be well attended and thus enjoyable. The unsuccessful hostesses are those in whom some persons place trust by attending their parties, but whose parties are found to be poorly attended and thus unenjoyable, leading to a loss of trust on the part of those who initially placed trust. Successful hostesses use various strategies to ensure the attendance of certain important people and to communicate to others the fact that these people will attend and even to generate a demand among relatively important people to be invited to their parties.

As another example, if a person convinced that political developments are detrimental to world peace attempts to organize a demonstration, it may or may not gain enough support to be held and, if held, may or may not give a participant a net psychic benefit. The participants have placed trust in the entrepreneur's ability to organize a demonstration that will be, in their view, successful. As the many cases of poor turnouts at demonstrations indicate, those who do turn out may have placed trust in an entrepreneur who cannot deliver, an entrepreneur who in this sense is untrustworthy.

Perhaps the most pervasive form of the intermediary in trust is the advisor. This form of intermediary exists in all areas of social life. For example, professors write letters of recommendation to prospective employers about students, and persons seeking a job or a loan list other persons who will recommend them. The acceptance of a recommendation by a prospective employer or creditor is a placement of trust in the judgment of the intermediary, which allows a placement of trust in the ability of the prospective trustee to perform as expected. If the latter defaults, then the trustor's trust in the intermediary's judgment is reduced.

The presence of some form of recommendation in many areas of social life indicates the broad scope of this form of intermediate activity in the placement of trust. Yet the nature of the intermediary differs in different societies. In premodern societies, including farming communities, where persons occupy relatively fixed positions in the social structure and most relations are between persons, the trustor is a person, the trustee is a person, and the intermediary is a person. In modern societies, however, the intermediary, whose judgment serves as the basis for trust, is often a corporate actor, such as a business organization or a government agency. This function of intermediary is made possible principally through one of two relations of a person to a corporate actor: as an employee and as a debtor.

If a person is an employee of an organization, this implies that the organization has placed trust in his performance as an employee; and the higher his position within that organization, ordinarily the greater the trust that has been placed in him. Or if a person owes money to an organization, this implies that the organization has placed trust in his ability and intention to repay his debts. A potential other trustor, whether a person or a corporate actor, can use this information; and the more trust this potential trustor has placed in the organization's judgment, the more likely the information will lead him to trust the employee or the debtor.

The importance of the relation of employee or debtor in establishing intermediaries in trust is apparent from the very widespread use—in job applications, in applications for credit, in applications for a telephone or a lease on an apartment, and in other areas—of both employment references and credit standings (credit cards held, loans outstanding and from what institutions, and so forth). The result is a skewed distribution of trust placement in persons, by other persons and by corporate actors. Certain persons, such as those employed in managerial positions in large respected organizations, find that trust of all sorts is readily placed in them. Their path in life is cleared of the kinds of obstacles that can be removed through the placement of trust by others. In contrast, there is a large set of other persons for whom this is not true: young persons, persons who are out of work, women who do not work outside the home, self-employed persons such as writers and artists, and retired persons. All these persons have more difficulty in carrying out even the everyday activities of life which require some trust on the part of others.

In societies of the past there was a different skewness, which is found even today in some societies and in some premodern areas of all societies. This was a skewness based on the family. Trust was more nearly placed by persons in families than in individuals, and because families exercised responsibility for their members' actions, trust of a family encompassed all its members. Different families had different "trust ratings," which were reflected in their social positions and transmitted to all their members. Thus even a child or a ne'er-do-well from the right family could obtain credit from the local store, and great deference would be paid to even the small children from especially important families. This skewness has almost entirely been replaced in modern society by a skewness due to large corporate actors' being the intermediaries between trustor and trustee.[5]

5. When I opened a bank account in a small town in rural West Virginia, the bank asked for names of persons in the community as references. When I opened an account in Chicago, the bank asked only for my employing organization and organizations with whom I had credit.

Third-Party Trust

Another form of trust relation is similar to that involving a guarantor as inter-mediary in a transaction, but the third party plays simultaneously a more passive role and a more central one. Economic transactions best illustrate the process.

For example, imagine a community in which economic transactions of various sorts take place. A wants something which B is willing to sell or trade to him, but A has, at the moment, nothing B wants. A can promise B to pay him something in the future, but accepting this promise of course requires B to place trust in A. Suppose, however, there is a third party, C, with whom both A and B have had numerous transactions and who is very highly trusted. Suppose further that A holds an obligation (that is, a promise to pay) of C's. Then if B trust C's promise as much as or more than he trusts A's, A can pass C's obligation on to B, and B will readily accept it.

As discussed in Chapter 6, this is a principal way in which paper money emerged and banks evolved from goldsmiths and merchants (see Ashton, 1945, for an account of this emergence in England, and Mackay, 1932 [1852], p. 10, for the events in France). If a merchant's obligations were generally acceptable throughout a community, a member of the community who wanted to borrow money for some purpose could promise to pay the merchant a given amount at some point in the future; the merchant would give him in return notes (that is, promises to pay), and the borrower could exchange these (where he could not use his own notes) for the resources necessary for his purposes. If the recipients of these notes continued to trust the merchant, and the merchant's obligations continued to be widely acceptable in the community, the notes could further circulate as a medium of exchange—based on trust of the merchant who issued them. Thus in each transaction the necessity for one party to place trust in the promise of the other party is replaced by trust in a third party, who is not involved in the transaction at all. Today, commercial paper, bonds, and govern-ment securities are money of this sort (although, of course, they are often traded against some other forms of money rather than actual goods). What is commonly thought of as money today, that is, paper currency, is exactly this sort of note or promise, issued not by merchants or banks but by national governments. Accep-tance of that money is based on placement of trust in the national government.[6]

It may be useful to be more explicit about the difference in form between third-party trust and a trust relation with a guarantor as intermediary. In a transaction involving third-party trust, party A wants something from party B and holds an obligation of a third party, C, which A can use directly in the transaction with B.

6. One key difference, however, is that a national government has a monopoly regarding the legal use of force, and all governments require acceptance of official currency at face value to settle economic obligations. This does not prevent inflation, of course, if the government issues too much money relative to the goods and services of which the society's economic transactions are composed.

The fungibility of C's obligation is brought about by the fact that B is more willing to place trust in C's note than in A's.

The guarantor as an intermediary in trust, exemplified by Hambros in the shipowner example, is a step toward such fungibility, but the direct participation of the intermediary is still required. The final trustee (the shipowner in the example) does not hold a fungible obligation of the third party (Hambros) that can be used in any transaction, but must go to that party and ask it to obligate itself to the final trustor, in a specific transaction between the final trustee and the final trustor. In contrast, if the shipowner had held a given quantity of credit from or drawing rights on Hambros, he could have used that directly at Amsterdam, without calling Hambros. Hambros's notes, in such a case, would be functioning like government-issued money, with Hambros as a silent third party. This is precisely the role played by credit card companies in modern economies.

The transition from guarantor as intermediary, the role played by Hambros in the shipowner example, to third-party trust, in which the third party is wholly passive, is rare in noneconomic social systems. Third-party trust in economic systems seems to be viable only in conjunction with a generally accepted unit of account, so that some value can be placed on the obligations of the third party to make them fungible in exchange. The same interests in making use of third-party obligations exist outside economic systems; the question that arises is what kind of social invention is necessary to facilitate this use.

Something close to such an invention is the formal organization based on complex relations involving stable obligations and expectations. (A complex relation, as defined in Chapter 2, is one in which the incentives to the two parties are not generated intrinsically by the relation.) In a formal organization each employee takes directions from a particular superior, trusting that he will be paid, at some regular interval, not by the superior but by the organization, with which he initially contracted to work. (The fact that he is paid in government-issued notes or in bank credit, rather than in notes issued by the organization, is irrelevant for the purposes of this illustration.) Thus the continuity of work depends on a placement of trust by a subordinate, not in the capabilities of the person occupying the supervisory position but in the capabilities of the organization as a whole. If he begins to lose confidence in the organization's viability, he will look around for another job and, if he finds one, will withdraw his placement of trust in this organization.

The formal organization is, however, somewhat different from a bank in the way that it functions as a third party. Its promises to pay are not issued in return for currency or even goods, but in return for services from employees. Its viability does not depend, as does that of a bank, merely on its success in judging the probability of trustworthiness of a prospective trustee. Its viability rests on its success in a more complex set of activities: first, judging the trustworthiness (in the performance of desired services) of prospective employees, to whom it entrusts its resources; and, second, organizing the services of its employees so as to provide a product (or service) and to sell it for a sufficient amount of money to cover its obligations. Some of the most interesting changes in organizations have been the result of innovations in the kinds of resources that are entrusted to different parts of the organization, in some cases replaced the hierarchical structure of authority (see Chapter 16).

Large Systems Involving Trust

In examining systems of trust, I have to this point treated only the components of these systems, either relations involving two actors or those involving three. The macro-level phenomena described at the beginning of the chapter, however, involve large numbers of individuals. Analysis of these phenomena requires going beyond the two- or three-actor systems discussed in the preceding sections, but it can be done through the use of these components as building blocks. I will discuss two kinds of larger systems constructed of these building blocks. The first type is the community that is composed of interconnected relations of mutual trust. The second is a system constructed of relations of advisory trust.

Communities of Mutual Trust

A common circumstance gives rise to a system of mutual trust that is in some respects a generalization of the mutual trust relations discussed above and in some respects a special case. This occurs where a number of actors (a group I will call a community here for convenience) are all engaged in an activity that produces an outcome in which all have a similar interest. In addition, each has an interest in not sacrificing other interests to engage in the activity of common interest. This social structure is a generalization of the two-actor system of mutual trust, but involves a greater number of actors; it is a special case in that the activity in which each actor is engaging (and for which trust on the part of others is necessary) is the same. If there is a leader, this is the kind of social structure I called a conjoint authority structure in Chapter 4. In such a system, unless each actor can directly and fully observe the actions of each other actor, each must trust to some degree that the other will do his part. Consequently, each is trustor of the others and trustee of the others.

In many such communities the actors are also engaging in a more general system of exchange, involving goods or events for which there is differentiated control and differentiated interest. What is observed in such communities is that trustworthiness is reinforced by social norms having sanctions attached. Sometimes the sanctions involve actions of one sort or another, but in communities which are bound together by a relatively rich set of social transactions, probably the most common sanction is the restriction of exchanges with the offending actor.

As stated above, the formal character of this social structure is an extension of the two-party system of mutual trust in that each actor is both trustor and trustee. As trustor, each makes his contribution to the activity of common interest, trusting that others will as well; as trustee, each decides whether to keep the trust of the others or to break it by withholding his contribution. There is, however, a special property of some such systems (one that is also shared by some two-party systems of mutual trust): The action in which an actor places trust and the action by which he maintains trustworthiness are one and the same. For example, if the members of a high-school class are collecting newspapers to finance a class party, a given class member acts in a trustworthy way by giving up time in order to work at this activity. But this same resource, the time given up to work, is also the resource through which the class member places trust in the others, by giving it up.

This extension of mutual trust relations throughout a community creates system behavior having special and sometimes bizarre properties. Such systems are unique and will be treated separately, in the discussion of free riding and zeal in Chapter 11.

Large Systems Involving Advisory Intermediaries

The intermediate process I have described as an advisory function seems operative on a widespread basis: A trusts the judgment of B; B trusts the performance capability of T, the final trustee; and this leads to A's trusting T's performance capability. There is an additional element of positive feedback to the process, however. What makes this possible is that the process does not stop there: C trusts the judgment of A and thus comes also to trust the performance capability of T. And then B, who trusts the judgment of C, observes C's trust in T and increases his own. The process is shown in Figure 8.2. If the process is undisturbed, it leads to all members of the system having total trust in T. And in some cases this extreme is reached, generally in a community with a highly charismatic leader. There are often attempts to keep the process of reinforcement from being disturbed. In religious, political, or communal movements, attempts are made to cut the members off from all "distracting," "faith-destroying," or "worldly" influences by segregating them physically in an isolated location, such as a cloister.

Information and the Fluctuation of Trust

The structure of communication that confronts potential trustors may have an important effect on the expansion and contraction of trust. The components of this structure can be understood by considering the example concerning the mysterious pattern of rise and fall of graduate students' reputations in one sociology department in the 1950s. In the department communication between faculty and students was minimal, but there was extensive communication among faculty about students, since they had to evaluate the students for fellowship and job recommendations, for student aid, and other purposes. Thus in the

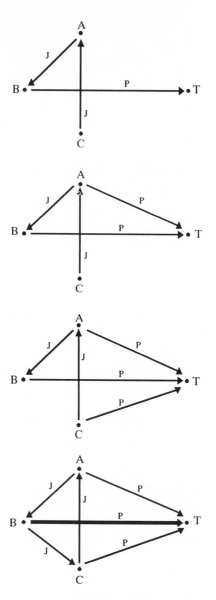

Figure 8.2 Growth of system of trust through trust in intermediaries' judgment.

absence of direct contact with the students, the faculty members placed a high
degree of trust in one another's judgment. Professor A would base his evaluation
of a student's capability on Professor B's judgment; then Professor C would use
A's judgment in making his evaluation; and B, finding that C's apparently independent evaluation was as positive as his own, would place even more trust in

the student's abilities. The process would often operate in reverse when a student's actual performance came to the attention of a faculty member who found it not up to the level of the trust that had been placed. This bit of negative information would reverberate throughout the system to bring about nearly simultaneous loss of trust in that student.

This example illustrates the three essentially different sources of information that affect the placement of trust in a single trustee:

1. The trustee's performance itself (for example, that of the graduate student being evaluated or a charismatic leader)
2. Others who have a position similar to the trustor's and similar interests in the placement of trust (for example, other faculty members, other members of a commune, or other members of a political movement)
3. Others who have a position different from the trustor's and lack the similar interests (for example, other graduate students or the persons seen as "worldly" or "heretical" by those within a movement)

Information from these three sources will characteristically differ. Information from source 2 will often lead to the same decision about placement of trust as that made by the person or persons whose judgment was trusted. Information from source 3 will often provide more independent evidence for the decision. Information from source 1, passing through no intermediary at all, will be most likely to lead to a correct assessment.

It appears that the extent of expansions and contractions of trust—that is, the extremity of fluctuation—depends very much on the mix of these three sources of information. First, social systems with a high degree of internal communication, providing a lot of information from source 2 (that is, others with similar interests in the particular placement of trust) are those in which trust in the judgment of others will lead to rapid expansion of trust. Second, in communication structures of this sort, punctuated infrequently by information from source 1 (that is, the trustee's performance) is apparently where the most rapid contraction of trust occurs. For example, in the South Sea Bubble in England and the Mississippi Scheme in France, contraction followed after bits of news about the company's failures entered the amplification system of the communication structure.

Certain short-term changes in structures of communication appear to be responsible for some expansions and contractions of trust. Among these is the change in structure of intergenerational communication that occurred in the 1960s and 1970s. Because of the postwar baby boom, the ratio of children to adults increased, and therefore the average young person, especially the average young person not on the leading edge of this boom but in the interior, experienced an increased proportion of communications from those of the same age. In addition, the widening influence of television, movies, and popular music meant that communication from adults was less often from parents, neighbors, and kin and more often from commercial interests aimed at the youth audience. This change in the mix of information sources appears in part to be responsible both for the withdrawal of trust from adults ("Don't trust anyone over 30") and for the extensive placement of trust in spontaneously emergent leaders of youth in matters of politics (such as Abby Hoffman in the United States or Rudi Dutschke in Europe), music (the Beatles), and dress (Mary Quant and Twiggy).

The changes in the structure of communication between generations during this period can be seen simply by using statistics on the age structure of the population. Although the phenomenon occurred in a number of countries after World War II, statistics for the U.S. population will suffice to illustrate. For the average 18-year-old in 1950 through 1984, how many persons were there in the population around his own age (say 15–24) compared to the number around the age of his parents (say 35–44)? If the tendency of persons to communicate differentially with others close to them in age is neglected completely, this ratio represents the age distribution of his communication partners. The curve showing the ratio of the sizes of these age groups from 1950 to 1984 is labeled A in Figure 8.3. If differential communication is factored in by assuming that the 18-year-old is twice as likely to communicate with someone near his own age than with someone the age of his parents, given equal availability in the population, this gives a curve (labeled B in Figure 8.3) showing an even more marked rise in the 1960s. These graphs show a rise in age-homogeneous communication for the average 18-year-old during the decade of the 1960s. This change in the communication structure, together with intermediary trust of the advisory type, provides a setting in which it is understandable that the declaration "Don't trust anyone over 30" would arise among youth.

The implications of population composition for the placement of trust, and thus for the content of judgments and evaluations, provide a valuable avenue for research. Actors place trust, in both the judgment and performance of others, based on rational considerations of what is best, given the alternatives they confront. But the distribution by age, gender, race, and other characteristics of those with whom they associate and the underlying distribution of those characteristics in the population determine what alternatives they confront. For example, as the ethnic composition of a population changes, unless association is tightly enclosed within ethnic groups, the ethnic distribution of persons in whose judgment trust might be placed changes for each member of the population. Research can measure both the distribution of association and the overall population distribution that partly determines association. Such structural information can help explain the placement of trust and predict changes in that placement. The examples given at the beginning of this chapter indicate that the consequences of differential placement of trust can be significant and suggest the importance of research which investigates it.

There also seem to be long-term changes in trust placement due to the increased extent of communication at a distance. Fads, mass delusions, and extraordinary levels of trust placed in persons and in corporate bodies seem to have been much greater before the middle or late nineteenth century than since (as some of the examples of Chapter 9 suggest). Accounts of the spread of

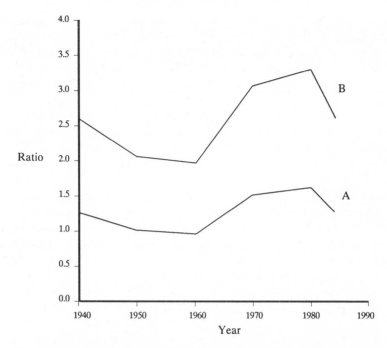

Figure 8.3   Changes in age structure of U.S. population 1940–1988 and implications for structure of communication between generations. Curve A
plots the ratio of the size of the U.S. population aged 15–24 to the
size of the population aged 35–44. Curve B plots the ratio of the frequency of communication of those aged 15–24 with one another to
the frequency of their communication with those aged 35–44 (assuming twice as much communication with each person in same age
group as with each person in other age group).

information and misinformation during speculatory booms such as the South Sea
Bubble suggest that person-to-person communication, unchecked by independent sources, allowed the development of extreme mass delusions about the size
of the potential gain. There have been such delusions in the twentieth century,
but most appear to have been confined to small close communities such as
Jonestown or the stockbrokers dealing on the floor of a stock exchange. It seems
likely that the incidence of mass delusion in unconfined populations has been
reduced by technological developments such as the telegraph, telephone, radio,
and television, which allow rapid communication without intermediaries.

Although the advent of the mass media may have reduced the occurrence of
massive expansions of trust based on widespread delusion, there appears to be a
recent change in those media leading toward the contraction of trust. A sense of
this change can be gained by returning to the example in Chapter 5 concerning
the contraction of adult Americans' trust in institutions. Figure 5.1 shows a rapid
decline in public confidence in various institutions in the United States during

the period 1966–1976 (a decline not found for the media of communication, as represented by television news and the press). A person's information about these institutions, with the exception of religion, comes in part from source 2 listed above, that is, other potential trustors (in this case other members of the public), and in part from source 3, that is, other actors with differing interests (in this case the media), and periodically from source 1, that is, the performance of the trustees (in this case the people running the various institutions). If that performance showed a declining rate of success during this period, this could account for the widespread withdrawal of trust by the public.

But does this fully account for the general withdrawal of trust? For example, the lack of success of the U.S. government in its conduct of the Vietnam War cannot be fully responsible for the decade-long decline in public confidence in the government, which continued until 1976. The growth of confidence in television news and the stability of confidence in the press suggest that the decline of confidence in other institutions may be due to the increasing power of the media—particularly television—as an information source of type 3 and also as the interpreter of information from source 1.

Increasingly, it appears, the mass media constitute the intermediary in whose judgment persons place trust. Along with this acceptance of the media as intermediaries whose judgment is to be trusted has come an aggressive independence on the part of the media where they are not state-controlled. This has sometimes been termed investigative journalism. The mass media can expand their audiences (and perhaps increase the amount of trust placed in them) when they expose defects in the trusted elites; therefore they have an interest in giving selective attention to those defects, leading to withdrawal of public trust in the elites.

In certain areas of social life, of which public schooling is an example, social research appears to have had a similar effect. Since 1966, when the first national research report showed the ineffectiveness of public schools in the United States in bringing about equality of educational opportunity and gave indications of their more general ineffectiveness, there has been a steady loss of public confidence in the schools (exhibited both in yearly Gallup polls and in the increasing failures of school bond referenda since 1966). This is in part due to dissatisfaction with policies directly experienced and in part a carryover from loss of trust in other institutions, but is also likely in part due to the generally poor performance documented in research reports. In this case social researchers constitute the advisory intermediaries whose judgment is trusted. For the social researcher, of course, the same incentive operates as for the journalist (although the researcher is more constrained by evidence): Exposure of defects in the functioning of the system expands the research's audience. (See Chapter 23 for further discussion.)

CONSEQUENCES OF THE EXPANSION AND CONTRACTION OF TRUST   As indicated earlier, placement of trust gives resources to the trustee, facilitating the power to act; and if the trustee is trustworthy, placement of trust also brings gains to the trustors. Overexpansion of trust, that is, the widespread placement of trust in a trustee who is not trustworthy, does the first of these but brings losses rather than gains to the trustors—as exemplified by John Law's Mississippi Scheme in the early eighteenth century in France, by Peter the Hermit and his crusade, by Hitler in Nazi Germany, or by Jim Jones and his followers in Jonestown.

To give an idea of the consequences of withdrawal of trust, I will first list a few examples of how the actions of elites have been constrained by withdrawal of trust—without attempting to answer the question of whether that withdrawal was in fact based on a correct assessment.

1. Before 1965 political analysts in the United States said that the most consistent regularity of presidential elections was the benefit that incumbency brought for reelection. Since that time incumbency appears to be a presidential candidate's greatest handicap. Between 1968 and 1984, all but one incumbent president of the United States was either forced out of office or defeated for reelection: In 1968 Lyndon B. Johnson was forced to withdraw as a candidate for reelection because of opposition to his Vietnam policies. In 1972 Richard Nixon was reelected but was shortly thereafter forced to resign because of Watergate. In 1976 Gerald Ford was defeated by a political unknown, Jimmy Carter. In 1980 Jimmy Carter was defeated for reelection by Ronald Reagan. The one exception was the reelection of Ronald Reagan in 1984.

2. Loss of confidence in public schools in the United States in the 1960s and 1970s has led to more frequent defeats by voters of school bond issues and school tax increases, constraining schools' ability to function and leading to increased use of private schools.

3. Nuclear power generation, which was steadily increasing in the United States and Europe, nearly ground to a halt in many countries even before the nuclear power plant accidents of the 1980s, because of loss of confidence of some persons in risk assessments carried out by scientists for political elites.

4. The reduction of trust by American and West European citizens in political elites' judgment about armaments has in the 1980s greatly constrained the elites' actions with respect to the Soviet Union.

5. In the case of the instrument makers of Nuremberg, their withdrawal of trust in the younger generation has led to a reduction in opportunities to do work of just the sort that some of the young see as most desirable.

All of these examples illustrate a general point: Simultaneous withdrawal of trust by many persons at once—a contraction of trust—sharply reduces the potential for action of those who had been trusted. In some of these cases the trustee is in effect an entrepreneur, making joint use of the trust placed by many persons. The example of the diplomatic hostess introduced earlier illustrates a further consequence: The capacity of such a hostess to throw a successful party that will bring gains to the participants depends on resources they themselves provide through their trust. More generally, it is true that in many circumstances the very resources the trustee needs to perform successfully are those received from the trustors: the freedom a political leader has to act without being called to account; the business entrepreneur's ability to produce profits using financial resources from investors; the ability of a bank to function using the money its depositors provide; and so on.

One can immediately see that this kind of dependency can lead to instability. Either placement of trust provides the power that leads to success and thus generates further placement of trust (which helps lead to further success); or withdrawal of trust by the trustor reduces the resources necessary for success. A case in point is the trust of U.S. citizens in their government's conduct of the Vietnam War. Initially low levels of trust placement led to less freedom of action for the government in pursuit of victory in the war than would have been the case if there had been a high degree of trust. The ineffective conduct of the war in turn even further reduced the levels of trust placed in the government, which led to even less power to achieve success, and so on.

There is also an effect of withdrawal of trust on the trustor, for it eliminates the potential gains he expected to receive through placement of trust. The consequence seems to be, whatever the arena of life in which trust is withdrawn, that there is placement of trust *elsewhere*. Here are a few cases referring to earlier examples:

1. In Poland the extraordinarily rapid growth in Solidarity membership and in trust in Lech Walesa followed a long period of withdrawal of trust from the Communist Party and the government.

2. The withdrawal of Americans' trust in certain institutions, shown in Figure 5.1, was accompanied by placement of trust not in a single other person or elite, but in a diverse array of other institutions, including religious sects and communes.

3. There seems to be extensive evidence that the rise of a charismatic leader (such as Sabbatai Sevi, Peter the Hermit, or Adolf Hitler) is likely to occur in a period when trust or legitimacy has been extensively withdrawn from existing social institutions. A potential leader with some attributes having widespread appeal is eagerly sought by a population that no longer experiences the gains arising from institutions vested with the power to act (see Bradley, 1987, for examples of this in communes).

Altogether there seem to be three kinds of consequences of expansion and contraction of trust. First, the expansion of trust leads to increased potential for social action on the part of those who are trusted, elites or otherwise, and the contraction of trust has the opposite effect. Second, the very dependence of a trustee's power to succeed on the amount of trust that has been placed means that expansion of trust tends to bring further expansion and contraction leads to further contraction; therefore the process is unstable. Third, extensive contraction of trust in one set of elites produces a pressure favoring placement of trust elsewhere.

« 9 »

Collective Behavior

The eclecticism—or, one might say, the intellectual disarray—of the microfoundation of sociological theory is evident from a comparison of the received wisdom about bureaucratic authority and the received wisdom about collective behavior (that is, phenomena such as riots, mobs, panics, crowd behavior, fads, and fashions). The ideal type of bureaucracy is envisioned as having a single purposive actor at the top of the hierarchical structure, with the remainder of the structure occupied by entities that differ little from the parts of a machine. *Their* purposes or interests never play a role in the classical theory of organizational functioning. The conception of the official or the employee in the bureaucracy is like the conception of the agent in the legal theory of agency: The interests of the agent are not to affect the agent's action when acting in the position of agent. Max Weber's plaintive cry about bureaucratic man, quoted in Chapter 16, is not really about modern man but about Weber's conception of modern man—a robot in the employ of the bureaucracy. Yet these "robots" are the same persons concerning whom observers of collective behavior have a wholly different conception. They are described as "excitable," "emotional," or "suggestive"; their behavior exhibits "contagion"; they are subject to "hypnotic effects of the crowd." That is, they are irrational, disorderly, unpredictable, and spontaneous, close to the opposite pole from the bureaucratic man Weber envisioned as the typical man of the future.

Such an intellectual disarray is one that sociologists have learned to live with. Social theory has too often taken the easy path of creating, conceptually, exactly that kind of creature at the micro level that by simple aggregation will produce the observed systemic behavior—whether that systemic behavior is the orderly and mundane functioning of a bureaucracy or the spontaneous and emotional outbursts of a crowd. The correct path for social theory is a more difficult one: to maintain a single conception of what individuals are like and to generate the varying systemic functioning not from different kinds of creatures, but from different structures of relations within which these creatures find themselves.

In this chapter I consider a type of systemic functioning that is especially difficult to reconcile with the microfoundation on which the theory of this book rests. Weber's theory of bureaucracy at least conceived of rationality at *one* point in the system. Most of the theorists of collective behavior could not be

197

further from such a conception; their individual is a kernel of emotion, with no hint of rationality. The reason for the latter conception, of course, is as indicated above: Since the systemic behavior being studied seems to exhibit certain properties, the simplest social theory to account for that behavior is one that generates the system as merely an aggregate of persons having the same properties. This chapter begins to account for a system marked by these properties by use of the same conception of the individual actor as is postulated for more orderly and stable organizational forms. As it will turn out, the kind of action that is involved in going from rational individual actors to the wild and turbulent systemic functioning called collective behavior is a simple (and rational) transfer of control over one's actions to another actor. As in some authority relations, this transfer is—in the phenomena known as collective behavior—made unilaterally, not as part of an exchange.

This, however, is looking too far ahead. It is useful to begin in a more straightforward fashion, by stating just what is to be comprehended under the term "collective behavior." In doing so, I begin at the system level, with the system behavior that is to be explained. Later I will descend to the micro level of individual actors.

General Properties of Collective Behavior

The systemic phenomena loosely grouped under the heading of collective behavior have several elements in common:

> They involve a number of people carrying out the same or similar actions at the same time.
> The behavior exhibited is transient or continually changing, not in an equilibrium state.
> There is some kind of dependency among the actions; individuals are not acting independently.

This class of phenomena is broad. It includes runs on banks, panic in a crowded theater when a fire alarm is sounded, behavioral fads of the sort that sometimes sweep through a population of children (such as the hula hoop or skateboard craze), acquisitive manias such as the stock speculation that occurred in France with John Law's Mississippi Scheme (see Chapter 8), hostile unorganized demonstrations, riots, crowd behavior, the spread of fashions in clothing, and religious frenzies or mass conversions. Beyond the three elements listed above, these diverse phenomena have little in common. Some appear quite spontaneous; others involve premeditation and calculation. Some are one-time events; others recur in somewhat different forms. They involve various emotions: fear, hate, attraction, enthusiasm, or avarice. Yet listing these phenomena together accords with common sense. They all appear to be based on processes that are similar.

What makes these phenomena so fascinating and so puzzling is that they are so transient, evanescent, and apparently unpredictable. They go beyond the bounds of stable obligations and expectations which make up much of social organization, and they do so with reinforcement that is internal to the system itself, sometimes leading to "explosive" results. Periods of change, when institutionalized structures have broken down or are in the process of doing so, are especially likely to give rise to such transient and effervescent social phenomena. Thus an understanding of these phenomena is particularly useful for the study of social change. For example, revolts and revolutions (discussed in Chapter 18) usually are marked by many instances of collective behavior.

A strong basis of knowledge about such phenomena is important but has not been developed. In times of social stability it is difficult to imagine wild and uncontrolled social behavior, and there is a comfortable feeling that such things "will never happen." Yet they do occur, however sporadically or infrequently. When they do, attention is fully occupied with the case at hand; when that manifestation is over, the relief that order is restored often leads to a turning away from such upsetting events—until the next time. Social scientists are not immune from these tendencies, with the result that less attention is given by them to periods of disequilibrium than is warranted by the importance of such events, both for social theory and for social practice. Thus the general area of collective behavior holds potentially great rewards for theory development and empirical research.

Some suggestion of the processes involved in collective behavior was provided by the examination of systems of trust in Chapter 8. This chapter will build on that one but will focus more explicitly on the dynamics of collective behavior and will examine the differences among the various kinds. The individual action on which systems of trust and relations of trust (see Chapter 5) are based is unilateral transfer of control over actions, and it is that transfer which will constitute the micro-level kernel of the explanations of collective behavior provided in this chapter. I will explain why persons purposively make this transfer when they do, as well as how this individual behavior combines to produce the sometimes spectacular macro-level phenomena which constitute the various forms of collective behavior.

In terms of actors and events the micro level can be seen as one in which each actor begins with control over one event, that actor's own actions. For collective behavior to result there must be a change from this situation, with each individual in control of his own actions, to one in which he has transferred control over his actions to others. The way in which this can occur is illustrated by the following incident:

One day in church, in the middle of the sermon, we heard a fire engine drive into the church parking lot, next to the sanctuary. There was an uncertain feeling—were we in danger? The obvious impulse to get out of the place was countered by the obviously inappropriate character of any such behavior in the sacred setting of the church. I found myself looking to left and to right to see whether other people looked frightened, to see whether anyone was doing anything about the situation. I looked at the minister to catch any gestures which might indicate his feelings. What I saw was a lot of other people also looking about, presumably in the same way I was! (Turner and Killian, 1957, p. 59)

In this situation, each person was attempting to find others to whom he could transfer control over his actions. Why does this happen? Understanding why will help in predicting the conditions under which it will happen.

What Does the Individual Do in Collective Behavior?

It is useful to ask what persons do that give rise to collective behavior. How can their actions be described generally? For this purpose I will turn to Brown's (1965) comprehensive overview and synthesis of work on collective behavior.[1] Brown focuses on crowd behavior, including panics of escape or acquisition and hostile or expressive outbursts. He also includes in his consideration panics which do not occur in face-to-face crowds, such as stock market panics, but for all cases his prerequisite is that the persons must influence one another.

As Brown points out, one of the major problems confronting theorists of collective behavior is that the actions of the members of a crowd are not in any way the average of the actions that members would take individually; there is some emergent behavior. He quotes Le Bon:

Contrary to an opinion which one is astonished to find coming from the pen of so acute a social philosopher as Herbert Spencer, in the aggregate which constitutes a crowd there is in no sort a summing up of or an average struck between its elements. What really takes place is a combination followed by the creation of new characteristics just as in chemistry certain elements when brought into contact—bases and acids, for example—combine to form a new body possessing properties quite different from those of the bodies that have served to form it. (Le Bon, 1960 [1895], p. 27)

The difficulty is that, although Le Bon recognizes the emergent properties of the crowd, he analogizes rather than analyzes the emergent behavior. As Brown (1965) says, "Science must explain . . . the emergence in crowds of primitive emotional behavior and must account for the way in which that behavior sweeps through the crowd to produce a homogeneity of thought and action" (p. 734).

Le Bon and others have made some suggestions as to how to explain the emergence and the contagion, suggestions which are close to a notion of transfer

---

1. The most comprehensive sociological theory of collective behavior is that of Smelser (1963). Smelser's theory has a base that borrows from economic theory: Stages in the development of a phenomenon of collective behavior are seen as contributing "value added," leading to a final product, the collective behavior.

of control. Brown summarizes the explanations offered by various authors for the homogeneity of behavior, that is, the contagion:

Le Bon: "suggestions and hypnotic effects"
McDougall: exciting of an instinct in one individual by another's expression of the same emotion
Allport: "social facilitation"
Miller and Dollard, and Blumer: "circular reactions"
Park and Burgess: "rapport"

Brown adds some explanation himself, but before turning to that, I will note that each of these explanations refers to some effect, either using a descriptive term, such as social facilitation, circular reaction, or rapport, or invoking some causal process located near the boundary between psychology and physiology. In no case is the crowd behavior explained in terms of meaningful, purposive action on the part of the members of the crowd. On the contrary, the collective behavior is generally seen as explicitly "irrational." Yet looking at the notions of contagion, circular reaction, suggestion, and social facilitation not in terms of the effects but in terms of the actor's orientation makes it clear that in the situations these terms describe members of the crowd have transferred large portions of control over their actions to one another.

For example, around 1950 a black family moved into all-white Cicero, Illinois, causing a riot which spread from initial rock throwing by teenagers at the family's apartment (Abrams, 1951). The phenomenon could certainly be described as "social contagion" or a "circular reaction" or "spreading throughout the crowd," as it was by various commentators. But it could equally well be described as having taken place in a group in which many members had transferred large portions of control of their actions to the various other members and were simply waiting for some action on the part of those others that would determine what they themselves would do. The advantage of looking at such behavior from this other side is that, since transfer of control is a positive action taken by a purposive actor rather than a reactive response to a stimulus or an effect of an outside cause, it paves the way for asking why and under what conditions a rational actor will make such a transfer.[2] This in turn can lead both to prediction of when collective behavior of various sorts will arise and to knowledge about how it can be controlled or prevented.

Also, looking at the action from the side of the actor makes it apparent that the difference between a group that has a potential for extreme collective behavior such as a panic or a riot and one that does not is simply the difference between a

2. In addition, because control over an actor's action exhibits the property of conservation and social contagion or influence does not, some potential benefits for theory construction arise with such a conceptualization. The question of where control over each actor's action is located is ever present, and the answer to that question is critical for determining the behavior of the system. See Elkana (1974) for a discussion of the discovery of the principle of conservation of energy for physical systems.

group in which the members have transferred large amounts of control over their actions to one another and one in which the members have not done so. In addition, *for some actions* members of a crowd will have transferred large portions of control over the action to others, but for other actions they will not have done so. For example, in a crowded theater members of the audience may have transferred control over their movements to exit in case of a fire alarm to other members of the audience and may have transferred smaller, but still substantial, portions of control over their reactions to the stage performance, laughing, crying, clapping, or shouting when other members of the audience do so. But they will have transferred to other members of the audience less control over their actions toward their seat partners, which for some may be holding hands, for others whispering about where to go after the theater, for still others gazing into each other's eyes, and so on.

It is important to note that widespread transfer of control to others in a group does not necessarily result in panic or mob behavior; it can as well be compatible with an orderly dispersal, depending on the initial actions of those who take action on their own without transferring control. Thus, if there is a fire in a crowded theater, there may be orderly movement to the exit, not because persons have not transferred control to one another, but because the initial actions were calm, and thus orderly movement was picked up by those who had transferred control to whoever took an initial action. It is precisely this unpredictability and volatility that is characteristic of collective behavior: Similar situations, triggered by different initial actions, will lead to collective behavior of quite different sorts. A bank panic may be initiated on the basis of the slightest evidence of bank insolvency; or it may be halted by an astute bank manager who facilitates withdrawals by ostentatiously putting more tellers on duty and making statements that the bank will remain open until every depositor who wants his money has received it.

Unilateral Transfer and Disequilibrium

At one level of understanding it is easy to see why the phenomena described here as collective behavior do not lead to stable equilibria. But individual maximization of utility leads to a stable equilibrium in many social situations, so why not in these? The question is addressed in greater detail in Chapter 33, and the formal properties that distinguish these phenomena are given there. It is useful to give some indication here of what is different about them.

In an exchange of private goods, rational actors maximize utility by giving up some goods they hold in order to get other goods in which they have greater interest. Goods are in scarce supply, and each actor carries out exchanges with others until he can no longer make mutually profitable ones. This is the point of economic efficiency, an equilibrium at which no actor can do better, given his resource constraints. The individual maximizes his utility by balancing his interests in one good against his interests in another; this individual balancing leads to a system balance.

In the phenomena under consideration in this chapter, however, each actor is not giving up something to get something, in competition with others. Each actor is attempting to maximize utility by making a unilateral transfer of control over his own actions. Maximization of utility does not occur through using resources to acquire other resources (or control over events) that are demanded by other actors. The individual attempts to maximize utility, but the action that does so is not a balancing among goods that are in scarce supply. Because that action is instead a unilateral transfer of control, individual maximization no longer necessarily leads to system equilibrium.

Escape Panics

The escape panic was modeled in a classic experiment by Mintz (1951). Mintz, who wanted to show that panic behavior was due to the structure of rewards inherent in the situation rather than to some mysterious "mob psychology," created the following situation:

> A narrow-necked bottle had aluminum cones inside it, each with a string attached, leading out of the bottle. Each person in the group held the string to one cone, and each was rewarded if his cone when removed was dry but was fined increasing amounts according to the amount of water on his cone. Water entered the bottle from below, and the level slowly rose toward the cones, which could be removed through the neck of the bottle but only one at a time. Thus the cones removed toward the end were likely to get wet.

Mintz found that with this situation, which presented to each participant what he called an unstable reward structure, there was always jamming of the cones, resulting in the wetting of many. Jamming occurred less often, but still with some frequency, when the group had a chance to plan for orderly escape beforehand.

Brown (1965) accounts for these results by using a prisoner's dilemma game with two players. In this application the person whose decision is problematic may be considered as one player (A_1), and the others all together as the second (A_2). Each has two options: to rush to exit, or to take turns. The game matrix is shown in Table 9.1. In the cells are given the payoffs to A_1: high, medium, low, and very low. In other words, for A_1 the expected rewards go in decreasing order for the combinations of actions shown in Table 9.2. This is the reward structure for the game.

Inspection of the game matrix and reward structure shows that if the others take turns, A_1 is better off rushing, and if the others rush, he is also better off rushing. Consequently, it would appear that no matter what the others do, he is better off rushing. The paradoxical aspect of the game, of course, is that each

Table 9.1　Reward structure for A_1 in an escape panic, contingent on his and others' (A_2's) actions.

		A_2	
		Take turns	Rush
A_1	Take turns	2　Medium	4　Very low
	Rush	1　High	3　Low

person is confronted with the same reward structure, so that each person will find it to his benefit to rush. Therefore, rather than all receiving the medium reward, which all could expect to receive if they took turns, all will rush, an entrapment will occur, and the expected reward for each will be low (for example, in a fire-initiated panic many will be killed, as in the Iroquois Theater fire in Chicago in 1903 in which 602 died in a panic).

Game-theoretic analyses (including Brown's analysis) argue that in such a situation the only rational action is to rush. There are important differences, however, between the situation described here and the classical prisoner's dilemma. In the latter case the two prisoners are separated and not allowed to communicate. Each makes a single binding decision—to confess (comparable to rushing here) or to hold out—and each does so unilaterally. Because they cannot communicate, there is not an unstable reward structure, as there is for Mintz's experiment. The reward structure is quite stable: The only rational thing to do is to confess. That is not the case in Mintz's experiment, for each person can see what the others are doing.

Not only is the communication structure different; there is a sequence of action and reaction throughout the period during which the cones are being

Table 9.2　Actions of A_1 and others (A_2), and expected rewards to A_1.

Actions	Expected reward to A_1
1. He rushes; others take turns.	High: definitely escapes
2. He takes turns; others take turns.	Medium: probably escapes
3. He rushes; others rush.	Low: probably gets wet
4. He takes turns; others rush.	Very low: definitely gets wet

pulled from the bottle. Each could monitor carefully what the others were doing and react to the others' actions. But this is the same as saying that each has the possibility of transferring partial control over his actions to the others, precisely the action discussed in Chapters 5 and 8. But is it rational to do so, and if so, under what conditions is it rational? Why, in the presence of communication and advance planning, do the subjects in Mintz's experiment sometimes not pull up their cones rapidly, resulting in a jam?

The conditions under which it is rational to transfer control rather than to rush to exit are shown in Chapter 33. It is possible to state the general result here, however, and to give an intuitive sense of the rationality of transferring control. Suppose player A_1 knows that each of the other players will act independently, regardless of what he or anyone else does. Then it is to his benefit to move as rapidly as he can, pulling his cone through the neck of the bottle as quickly as possible—*because he knows that his actions will not affect what anyone else does*. In contrast, if he knows that others' actions are contingent on his own, then he knows that pulling his cone rapidly to escape may trigger similar actions from others and lead to a jam. Only if he is especially close to the exit will he avoid the jam and escape. If others' actions are wholly contingent on his, it is to his advantage to dictate a fixed order of exit (again, unless he is especially close to the exit). Thus in this case it will be to his advantage to make an orderly exit— *because he knows that others have fully transferred control to him and to do otherwise would create a jam, to his disadvantage.*

If, however, he assumes that each of the others will not act independently and have not transferred control to him alone, but have transferred partial control to each of the members of the group, including himself, then the situation is different. He may feel he is better off if he rushes independently of what others do, or if he makes an orderly exit independently of what others do, or if he begins with an orderly exit but makes his subsequent action contingent on those of others. This depends on just how much control others have transferred to him, on the chance that they will rush anyway (through the control they have transferred to one another), and on the difference in payoff that different outcomes have for him.

Ordinarily, of course, he would not make an orderly exit independently of what others do, because if others run while he walks, that implies that they have not transferred control completely to him. Yet their transfer of full control to him is the only condition under which it is rational to make an orderly exit ignoring what they do. The two alternatives that are not dominated are these:

1. To run unilaterally, independently of what others do
2. To begin by walking, and then make one's subsequent action contingent on that of others, that is, to transfer control to others

This makes the game a different one, with the pairs of actions and outcomes (taking a two-person panic for simplicity of exposition) shown in Table 9.3.

Table 9.3   Actions of A_1 and others (A_2), outcomes, and expected rewards to A_1 and others.

Action		Outcome	Expected reward to—	
A_1	A_2		A_1	A_2
Transfer[a]	Transfer	Orderly exit, escape from danger	High	High
Run[b]	Transfer	Jam, but A_1 has advantage	Low	Lowest
Transfer	Run	Jam, but A_2 has advantage	Lowest	Low
Run	Run	Jam, neither has advantage	Lower	Lower

a. Transfer = begin by walking, and run contingent on others' running.
b. Run = begin by running, and run independently of others' action.

Table 9.4   Reward structure for a two-person escape game in which each player can transfer control to the other or run.

A_2

	Transfer	Run
Transfer	a	c
Run	b	d

A_1

The game matrix is shown in Table 9.4, with cells labeled *a, b, c, d*. The order of payoffs from highest to lowest for A_1 and A_2 is

A_1: *a   b   d   c (lowest)*
A_2: *a   c   d   b (lowest)*

This game does not have the structure of the prisoner's dilemma for either player. Neither action dominates for either player. If A_2 will transfer, then A_1 is better off transferring; and if A_2 will run, then A_1 is better off running.

If A_1 estimates that, with probability p, A_2 will transfer control, then should A_1 run? If A_1 transfers, the expected value of the outcome for him is $pa + (1 - p)c$. If he runs, the expected value is $pb + (1 - p)d$. Examination of these quantities shows that A_1 should transfer if $p/(1 - p)$ is greater than $(d - c)/(a - b)$. This can be analyzed in the same way as used in the analysis of trust, if p is taken as comparable to the probability that the trustee will be trustworthy. For $d - c$ is the amount that A_1, the trustor, has to lose by placing trust if the trustee, A_2, is not trustworthy (in this context, if he runs rather than walks at the beginning), and $a - b$ is the amount that A_1 has to gain by placing trust if the trustee is trustworthy.

For example, suppose the outcomes have the payoffs shown in Table 9.5; then

$$\frac{d - c}{a - b} = \frac{1}{8}$$

This means that A_1 should transfer control if he believes there is more than one chance out of eight—that is, $p/(1 - p)$ should be greater than $\frac{1}{8}$—that the other will begin by walking and will run only if A_1 runs himself. But although this is A_1's optimal strategy, it is also (because of symmetry in this case) A_2's. This puts A_1 and A_2 at a peculiar impasse, in which the rational action of each depends on his belief about what action the other will take.

The interdependence in this situation is described as behavioral interdependence (Friedman, 1977). There is mutual contingency of action, in which an actor's action has consequences for him not only directly but also through the effect it has on the action taken by the other (or others). A central feature of situations where there is behavioral interdependence is that a rational strategy cannot be defined in the absence of knowledge (or assumptions) about the strategies of the actor or actors one confronts. Classical game-theoretic solutions for two-person games are based on the assumption that the other will make the best reply to what the other assumes will be one's own best reply to each of the possible actions of the other. If these best replies converge to a single pair of strategies, those are the equilibrium strategies.

For the situation shown in Table 9.5, a similar line of reasoning for A_1 is as follows: "A_2, reasoning as I do, sees that it is to my interest to begin by walking if I believe he will do so. He believes that I believe he will do so, because he sees

Table 9.5 Payoffs for both players for the two-person escape game of Table 9.4.

		A_2	
		Transfer	Run
A_1	Transfer	0, 0	-11, -8
	Run	-8, -11	-10, -10

me as a rational person like himself, and he knows my reward structure. There-fore he believes that I will begin by walking. This will lead him to begin by walking. Therefore it is to my interest to begin by walking.'' Such reasoning is similar to, but differs from, that of classical game theory, which would find two equilibria in such a game, one in which both players walk and the other in which both run. Both this reasoning and that of game theory, however, are based on assumptions that may be tenable in certain circumstances but not in others. It is not always correct to assume that the other reasons as one does oneself; if one holds evidence to the contrary, it is rational to use that evidence.

Another line of reasoning for A_1 in this situation is to assume that A_2, being in the same situation, has high probability of transferring control (that is, of begin-ning by walking). As in the trust analyses, A_1 in effect compares his estimate of that probability with the critical probability—(determined by the ratio $(d - c)/(a - b)$; if the former is greater, A_1 will place trust (that is, will begin by walk-ing). But A_1 will also use any other evidence he may have to modify his estimate of the probability of A_2's beginning by walking. This reasoning does not give a determinate "solution," but it does allow qualitative predictions. For example, the greater A_2's potential loss from walking (that is, placing trust) given that A_1 runs (that is, is not trustworthy), the more likely it is that A_2 will run (for both direct and second-order reasons) and that A_1 will run. Similar logic holds true for the effect of an increase in the potential gain from walking (placing trust). This reasoning also predicts certain actions that a game-theoretic solution would not, for example, that A_1 and A_2 will be greatly attentive to possible evidence about what the other will do. Such reasoning accounts for the benefit of fire drills as partly due to their changing each person's expectation about what others will do (that is, changing each one's estimate of the others' probability of walking), which in turn makes each more likely to begin by walking rather than running.

There are, however, unsatisfactory aspects to these results. Perhaps the most unsatisfactory concerns their extension to larger groups. If p is A_1's estimate of the probability that A_2 will make his action contingent on A_1's, then p must of necessity decline as the number of persons increases. For the situation shown in Table 9.5, where the critical value of $p/(1 - p)$ is ⅛, this implies that in a homogeneous group of nine persons the maximum value of p that each could estimate for each of the others is ⅛. This is exactly the critical value. Thus any group of more than nine members would be predicted to always panic under this reward structure. And for any setting this analysis would predict a drastic and unavoidable rise in the probability of panic as group size increases. In general, for a group of size n, the critical value of p would have to be less than $1/(n - 1)$ if the members are to make their actions contingent on those of others. Although it is probably true that the likelihood of panic increases in a situation of con-strained escape as the number of persons increases, the connection hardly ap-pears to be as direct and inevitable as the analysis indicates.

The question, then, is whether a deeper analysis might yield a way out of this difficulty. A possible clue is that in a crowd it appears likely that each member sees himself as not affected individually by the other members but by "the crowd," as something more than a set of separate individuals. Either of two ways of looking at this possibility seems reasonable. The first is that each member sees the crowd as a single entity. A given individual's action (for example, beginning to run) is not seen as irrelevant if $(d - c)/(a - b)$ is greater than $1/(n - 1)$, as the above analysis would predict. It is instead seen as an indicator, or signal, of what the crowd will do. Thus each member may make his action contingent on what the crowd as a single entity is doing, using individuals' actions as evidence which affects his estimate of the probability that the crowd will exit in an orderly fashion. To act in this way appears reasonable, for the individual is affected not by each individual, but by the crowd as a single acting entity, which either is progressing in an orderly fashion to the exits or is turbulent and disordered.

The second way of looking at this possibility is to assume that individuals continue to assess how individuals will act, rather than how the crowd as an entity will act, but that they see other individuals' actions as not only possibly contingent on their own actions but contingent on the others' actions as well. Thus, in a group of size n, A_1 may assess that A_n's action may be partly contingent on his own, but also partly contingent on that of A_2, A_3, or others. This means that if his running would set off that of A_2 and A_3, others whose actions were highly contingent on that of A_2 or A_3 would begin to run, and in a sequential fashion, the whole crowd might begin to run.

This analysis obviously requires the technical aid of a formal model, which will be presented in Chapter 33. It probably provides a more adequate description of the situation than does the holistic treatment, especially for cases in which the crowd is geographically dispersed and persons find it rational to make their actions more contingent on the actions of those close to them than on the actions of those further away.

Another important point is based on the fact that fire drills appear to be quite effective. Under circumstances of an orderly exit, there appear to be normative constraints which inhibit an actor from the deviant action such as running. Thus under certain circumstances in panic-generating situations the processes discussed in Chapters 10 and 11 appear to be operative. Because it is to the interest of each that others do not run, each has an interest in sanctions being imposed on a person who begins to run. Whether those sanctions are imposed or, instead, each begins to run depends on factors discussed in Chapter 11.

The additional complexity introduced by greater numbers of persons and by the possibility of sanctions being imposed to inhibit running indicates the necessity for detailed empirical investigations and further theoretical work.

It is necessary to ask why the results from this analysis of a panic situation differ from the game-theoretic solution to the prisoner's dilemma. The structure of rewards for the outcomes is the same, yet in the two-person case the results differ.[3] The central reason lies in contingency, for contingency of each actor's action on the other's implies that there is both communication of what the other does and some sequence of action, neither of which occur in the prisoner's dilemma situation. If A_2 transfers control to A_1, this means that A_2's action must take place after that of A_1 and that A_2 must know what A_1 did. And the reverse is true if A_1 transfers control to A_2. Clearly, both the conditions (communication and a sequence of actions) are characteristic of an escape panic. Action takes place over a period of time, resulting in each individual's being able to modify actions based on what he sees others do.

However, in an *iterated* prisoner's dilemma, there is a sequence of play and communication of the actions of each player after each play in the sequence, thus making contingency of action feasible. There have been both empirical results and theoretical analyses of the iterated prisoner's dilemma. The theoretical analyses conclude that if it is not known in advance on which round play will end, it becomes rational to take an action other than continued defection.[4]

Of the empirical results, one set is especially relevant. This is the work carried out by Axelrod (1984), who, for an iterated prisoner's dilemma of indeterminate length, set up two tournaments involving matches between pairs of computer programs written by various social scientists, computer scientists, and game theorists. Each match between two programs consisted of a sequence of pairs of actions; each action could be either cooperate (C) or defect (D). Thus the first three rounds of a sequence might go like this:

A_1: C   D   C
A_2: D   C   D

After each round information about the outcome was available to each program. Thus for a given round each of the programs' strategies could incorporate all the information about what had happened on all the rounds that had gone before. The payoffs were determined for each round, and the overall score was the sum of the payoffs at the end of the sequence of play.

The sequences of play for the matches generally appeared similar to the sequence of actions found in escape panics. For example, some matches showed cooperation (corresponding to orderly exit) throughout. Others began with defection and got locked into it for the whole sequence. Others began with cooperation but then subsequently got locked into defection (corresponding to panic

3. The structure of rewards which defines the prisoner's dilemma is that (D, C) (D = defect, C = cooperate) has the greatest payoff, (C, C) the next greatest, (D, D) the next, and (C, D) the least, where the rewards are specified for the player whose action is listed first. In an iterated prisoner's dilemma, there is a further constraint that the payoff for (C, C) is greater than half of the sum of the payoff for (D, C) and the payoff for (C, D). This constraint is necessary to prevent alternating patterns of (D, C) and (C, D), that is, so that the pattern of alternating (D, C) with (C, D) is less attractive than (C, C).

4. See Kreps et al. (1982). The first result in this direction was that of Luce and Raiffa (1957), who argued, by backward induction, that only if play were infinite would a strategy other than always defecting be rational.

which develops after an orderly beginning). There were no cases in which an initial sequence of mutual defection was followed by mutual cooperation.[5] The programs which were first to defect (characterized by Axelrod as "nasty" strategies) generally had the lowest total payoffs, and those which were not first to defect ("nice" strategies) generally showed higher payoffs. The strategy with the highest payoff of all was one of "tit for tat," which is equivalent to transferring control to the other (taking the action which the other took on the preceding round).

What is especially interesting is that the tit-for-tat strategy did not attain the highest score through victories over its opponents in individual matches. In every individual match this strategy either did marginally worse than its opponent or had the same score; in none of its matches did it come out ahead. Yet its total score from all matches with other strategies was higher than that of any other strategy.

How could this happen? The simplest way of accounting for how this cccurred is to say that the tit-for-tat strategy (or transferring-of-control strategy) gained the highest overall score *by inducing cooperative behavior from those with whom it played.* But such an explanation seems inapplicable because the matches were played by computer programs whose strategies were determined in advance of play. How could a preprogrammed strategy induce cooperative behavior from other preprogrammed strategies? The answer is that it did so through the contingency of its actions on prior actions of its opponent and the communication of that contingency, making it rational for the opponent, if it also was a contingent strategy, to take the cooperative action rather than defecting. Two tit-for-tat strategies playing each other—that is, two strategies each of which will transfer control to the other's prior action—would induce cooperative actions in one another, with no defection throughout the whole sequence of play.

Asymmetry in Escape Panics: Stable and Unstable Equilibria

A further examination of the asymmetry apparent in the iterated prisoner's dilemma as well as in escape panics is useful.[6] The system behavior in a panic-generating situation often goes from orderly exit to panic, but seldom goes in the reverse direction. This asymmetry was assumed in Tables 9.4 and 9.5 as shown by the absence there of the strategy of beginning by running and then making one's subsequent action contingent on that of the other. Although the asymmetry is certainly understandable, this is not quite the same as being explainable by an internally consistent theory. The question, then, is why the asymmetry

5. There was one pattern, like the sequence shown above, in which alternating cooperation and defection "echoed" back and forth. This is an artifact of the discrete form of play.

6. Asymmetry in an iterated prisoner's dilemma depends, of course, on the particular strategy. A tit-for-tat strategy is wholly symmetric; many of the strategies used in iterated prisoner's dilemma games are not symmetric.

exists. To specify that individuals have "transferred control" to others in an escape panic has no asymmetry about it, yet asymmetry is characteristic of such situations: It is easy for a panic to arise; it is hard to quiet one that is in existence.

The reason for this can be seen by again referring to an iterated prisoner's dilemma. Consider two situations in which there is a sequence of actions, with each player having transferred control to the other, simply repeating the action used by the other on the last round. In one situation both are cooperating, and in the other both are defecting. In the third round A_1 suddenly changes his action to the opposite. Table 9.6 shows the sequences of actions with the payoffs to each player in parentheses and the deviant action indicated by an asterisk.

As this table shows, the deviation from a cooperating equilibrium (orderly exit) brings an immediate benefit to the deviant, changing his payoff from medium to high. Deviation from a defecting equilibrium, however, brings an immediate loss to the deviant, changing his payoff from low to very low. There is no incentive for the nondeviant to follow suit, for that would reduce his payoff. There is thus an incentive to defect from the cooperating equilibrium and an incentive to stay with the defecting equilibrium. An equilibrium of the first kind can be described as unstable, or non-self-policing. An equilibrium of the second kind can be described as stable, or self-policing. A panic in a crowded theater when a fire alarm is sounded is a stable, or self-policing, outcome, because a deviant experiences an immediate cost from deviating. An orderly exit is an unstable, or non-self-policing, outcome, because the deviant experiences an immediate benefit from deviating.

It is also useful to examine the role of time in the context of a situation that can generate an escape panic. Consider a person in a crowded theater when a fire alarm is sounded. If he keeps control over his actions, he will either rush to an exit or walk at an orderly pace, whichever he has decided on previously (or independently decides on at the moment). If he transfers such control, however, he will watch to see what others do. If they begin to run, then it is imperative for him to do so as well, in order that he not be last out—unless his running will increase the congestion and thereby reduce, rather than increase, the chance

Table 9.6   Actions and payoffs for an iterated prisoner's dilemma with deviation by A_1 in the third round. Payoffs to each player are in parentheses; the deviant action is indicated by an asterisk.

Deviation from mutual cooperation (betrayal)
A_1:   C (medium)   C (medium)   D* (high)
A_2:   C (medium)   C (medium)   C (very low)

Deviation from mutual defection (turning the other cheek)
A_1:   D (low)   D (low)   C* (very low)
A_2:   D (low)   D (low)   D (high)

---

that he will get out in time. His expected loss is zero if he gets to the exit before a certain point in time; it increases as the time moves beyond that, as shown in Figure 9.1. If he is to minimize his costs, he must minimize the expected time it will take to get out. If running has no effect on congestion (and thus on the time it will take him to exit), then running will get him out at time t_r, which will minimize his expected costs. But if others' actions are conditional on his own, then running will increase his expected time beyond t_r. If the effect is sufficiently great, the expected time will be t_r', greater than t_w, the time at which he would get out if he walked. In that case, when the contingency of others' running on his running makes the expected costs of running greater than those of walking, he is better off if he walks. But if a few others begin to run, this may reduce the effect of his running on others. That reduced contingency may change the situation so that t_w becomes greater than t_r', making it no longer to his benefit to walk.

There is another effect of time. If the person sees that the number of people running is increasing, then he is better off if he runs immediately, rather than waiting. This can be seen in Figure 9.2, which shows the expected benefits as a function of the fraction of others running when he begins to run (including any effects his running might have on those expected benefits). The benefits are shown as negative, because in an escape panic he is minimizing his losses. The figure also shows the marginal benefits. Because the benefits decline as the proportion of the crowd running increases, the marginal benefits are negative. At every point his losses increase as the proportion running increases, which makes it to his interest to run before that proportion gets even higher. If the decline in benefits has the general shape shown, the marginal losses are especially high when the fraction running is small. Thus if the fraction is small but increasing, the urgency is especially great.

Figure 9.2 is based on the assumption that he should run despite the contingency of others' action on his own. That may not be so. But whatever he does,

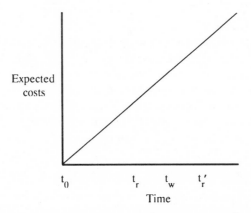

Figure 9.1 Expected costs as a function of time taken to exit in an escape panic.

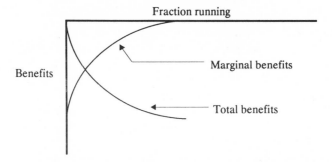

Figure 9.2 Marginal and total benefits of an individual's beginning to run as a function of the fraction of others already running.

he should decide quickly. There is a cost to delaying a decision. This has two effects. First, it increases the incentive to transfer control of one's action to others, an effect which both increases the potential for an orderly exit and increases the instability of the outcome. Second, if the number of others running is increasing, then he is better off making an error of running too soon than making the reverse error. The cost of the error of running when he should still be walking is less than the cost of the error of walking when he should be running.[7] This means that persons will tend to err in the direction of running early, which can lead those who had made a correct assessment to find it in their interest to also run.

Thus, despite the mutual contingency of actions, which may make it rational for all to walk, an orderly exit is an unstable outcome which can quickly give way to a panic, through errors of judgment on the part of a few, which then makes it rational for all to run.

Heterogeneity in Power

In situations which can lead to escape panics, there are variations in the homogeneity of the crowd. In a story by Damon Runyon of a fire in a burlesque theater, the strip-tease performer prevents a panic, attracting attention and quieting the rush to the exit, by stripping all the way. In real life there are similar cases. In the panic at the Iroquois Theater in Chicago in 1903, comedian Eddie Foy, who was performing that evening, made extensive attempts from the stage to quiet the crowd and bring about an orderly exit. Although he failed, why did he even try, while members of the audience rushed to exit? The answer may have been that he had access to a separate, nonjammed exit which meant that he could defer leaving without serious danger, while exhorting others to leave in an

---

7. This aspect of time, I suggest, the high cost of taking time to make a decision, is what creates the emotion labeled "panic" among persons in such a situation.

orderly fashion. But even if this were not so, it might be rational for him not to run and to attempt to quiet others through a demonstration effect, but rational for others to run. This follows if the transfer of control is sufficiently asymmetric. That is, if all members of the audience had transferred a high degree of control over their actions to him (because of his greater visibility on stage), then he, by his actions, could bring about an orderly exit and have a better chance of escaping himself. None of the others were in such a position.[8]

The implications of this are straightforward, both for prediction from theory and for practice. For prediction, this implies that the greater the heterogeneity in the distribution of attention (or power) in a crowd, the more likely it is that control will be transferred in a way that makes it to someone's interest not to run—and the more likely that this example will be followed, leading to an orderly exit. The more equal the distribution of attention (or transfer of control), that is, the more homogeneous the crowd, the more likely it is that there will be a panic outcome. (The theory predicts just the opposite for hostile expressive crowds, as will be discussed in a later section.) For practice, the implication is that in a setting in which an escape panic might occur, the chance of such a panic can be reduced by providing a natural focal point for attention, to which persons will naturally look for direction, that is, to which they will transfer control.

Bank and Stock Market Panics

A run on a bank or a panic to sell stocks that are falling in price has a structure similar to that of a physical escape panic, but the reward structure is somewhat different, leading to differences in systemic behavior. For a bank panic the two actions are to withdraw deposits or leave them, withdrawing being comparable to running in a physical escape panic.

How dependent is the ultimate fate of a bank or a stock on a run? If a stock's price accurately reflects the firm's value, the fall in price due to widespread selling will be only temporary. If the bank is sufficiently sound that it can borrow enough cash to meet a liquidity crisis brought about by depositors' demands, it will survive, and depositors will get their money, whether they withdraw or wait. If, however, the firm is overvalued or the bank cannot meet the liquidity crisis, there will be consequences at both the macro and micro levels, that is, at both the level of the firm or bank and the level of the individual investor or creditor.

At the macro level widespread selling of a stock may lead to the failure of a firm which is temporarily in distress but could survive if the falling stock price had not destroyed its ability to borrow. Or the firm might have failed even in the absence of the panic. A run on a bank might lead to the failure of a bank whose loans are fundamentally sound, but which could not meet the liquidity crisis. Or the bank might be fundamentally unsound, with failure only a matter of time. At

---

8. It is principally for this reason, I suspect, that the general rule has evolved that the captain should be the last to leave the ship in cases of shipwreck.

the macro level, then, a panic will make a difference for failure or success in an intermediate circumstance (category 2) when the firm or bank is strong enough to succeed in the absence of a monetary crisis, but too weak to succeed when there is one.

At the micro level the individual investor or depositor is just as well off not participating in the run if the firm or bank is in the first category. If it is in the second or third category, however, where the run will bring about a failure or there will be a failure anyway, then the individual is better off the sooner he sells his stock or withdraws his money.

The individual, however, is not in a position to know which of these three categories is confronting him. The reward structure of a bank run as he perceives it can be characterized as shown in Table 9.7, where the actions are numbered to correspond to the cells of Table 9.1. Clearly this structure of rewards is like that of the prisoner's dilemma or the physical escape panic. At this first level of analysis, the individual's only rational action is to withdraw his money.

But at a deeper level of analysis it was apparent in the physical escape panic (as in the iterated prisoner's dilemma) that it may not be rational to rush to the exit. Because of the possible contingency of others' action on his own, a contingency which is rational if his action is contingent on theirs, it becomes rational for the individual to make his action contingent on others'.

Is a bank panic like that? I believe the answer is no. There is no reason for the individual to transfer control to others' actions as there is in the physical escape panic. For if the bank is unsound, or if it is sound but has a liquidity crisis, he will be better off if he withdraws his funds, whatever the others do and whether or not they transfer control to him and follow his action. Unless he advertises his decision to withdraw before doing so, he will not be less likely to receive his money because of "congestion" resulting from their following him. He can make his withdrawal before his action has any effect on others. Unlike the physical escape panic and the iterated prisoner's dilemma, the bank run does not have a sequence of actions in which an individual's action at an early stage can affect the contingencies he confronts at a later stage. The individual's situation

Table 9.7   Reward structure in a bank panic.

Action	Expected reward to A_1
1. He withdraws; others do not.	High: no loss
2. He does not withdraw; others do not.	Medium: no loss if bank is in category 2
3. He withdraws; others withdraw.	Low: loss if he is late and bank is in category 2; loss if bank is in category 3
4. He does not withdraw; others do.	Very low: loss if bank is in category 2 or 3

in a bank panic is that of the player in a single-play prisoner's dilemma, not an iterated prisoner's dilemma.

Why, then, if there is no need to transfer control to others in this case, does the bank run share characteristics with physical escape panics in which it is rational to transfer control and in which there is evidence that such transfer is widespread? The answer can be found by looking more closely at what happens in a bank panic. Depositors hear a rumor that their bank is about to fold and, if they believe the rumor, flock *independently* to the bank to make withdrawals. They use others' actions as evidence of the bank's soundness, not as evidence of how "the crowd" will behave. They are not acting in response to the others' actions, except as those provide additional information about the bank's soundness. If they believe the bank is unsound, it is rational for them to rush to withdraw, whether others do or not. Although they may rush faster because they believe others will, in order to get a better place in line, it is not rational to transfer control on the basis that others' contingent actions would have consequences for oneself. That is, even if others do not withdraw, it is rational for a person who believes the rumor of the bank's unsoundness to withdraw.

The critical difference between the two types of panic is that in the bank panic there is a single action, and in the physical escape panic there is a continuous sequence of actions. In the latter case there can be a reciprocal transfer of control in which each individual lets his action be controlled by others' prior actions. In the former case each may let his action be guided by information from others, and some may let their actions be guided by the actions of others. But since an individual experiences no indirect consequences of his action (due to the contingency of others' subsequent actions on his own action), an individual need not be concerned about indirect consequences. His dependence on the others is solely for information which aids him in making the decision to withdraw or not to withdraw.

A simple way of conceptualizing this is to use the idea of placing trust in another's judgment, as presented in Chapters 5 and 8. When there is a single action, such as a bank withdrawal, only the direct consequence of the action is relevant. One may place trust in another's judgment concerning what action to take. The other's action affects one's estimate of the probability of unsoundness, but one's own action does not affect what one gets through the other's action. For the bank run it is impossible to say whether it is rational to place trust in the judgment of the particular source from which the rumor of unsoundness was heard. It is clear, however, that even if one's belief is at a low level (that is, one believes that the chance that the rumor is false is substantial), the small cost of withdrawal compared to the potential loss due to nonwithdrawal is likely to make placement of trust in the source from which the rumor was heard a rational action (as discussed in Chapter 5).

This raises a question as to what differences there are in behavior when there is a single action as in a bank panic and when there is a continuous flow of action, or sequence of actions, on the part of each individual. First, in the case where there is a sequence of actions (for example, when there is a fire in a crowded theater), there should be much more variability or unpredictability in the outcomes of objectively similar situations. In one fire there will be orderly exit; in another, a panic. The outcome will depend highly on the initial actions of those who took some action on their own—whether they rushed or called for order. Second, this very dependence on early actions means that it can be valuable to have a trained force who will take decisive control. In a situation with only a single action (for example, a run on a bank), the existence of trained and strategically located leaders should do less good—not only because their impact will have fewer long-range indirect effects, but also because the rationality of one's action does not, in this case, depend on what others are doing. In much the same way, training of a group, such as in fire drills, which leads each person to anticipate that the group will behave in an orderly way, should be effective in reducing the likelihood of a panic outcome in physical escape situations. Training of a bank's depositors, however, should not be effective in preventing a bank panic.

These and other differences that can be predicted for situations that differ as a theater fire differs from a bank failure provide a potential starting point for research into specific kinds of situations that are panic-generating as well as for developing techniques of controlling particular kinds of panics.

Acquisitive Crazes

The tulip craze in seventeenth-century Holland (which Brown, 1965, discusses), the Florida land boom, and other speculative ventures differ somewhat from the escape panics discussed above. Although the late phases of these crazes resemble a stock market panic or a run on a bank, in the early phases the reward structure confronting an individual appears to be different in that it offers the individual the possibility of great gains, not great losses.

The actions possible for the avaricious investor are to act—to buy the stock, buy the tulip bulbs, buy the land—or not. The urgency to act lies in the possibility that purchases by others will drive up the price or will exhaust the supply. If the gain the potential investor expects is more than the opportunity costs of the use of the money, then it is rational for him to buy. What makes it rational for him to believe the seller? If he has transferred control over his beliefs about investments to others, and if these others confirm the claims of the seller (ordinarily by their own investments), then, if it was rational to make that transfer of control, it is rational to believe the seller.[9] Note that the investments of others confirm the claims of the seller in two ways: first, by providing evidence that the investment is sound, and second, by confirming that the opportunity may soon be lost.

---

9. The transfer of control can be said to be rational if past experience has shown the investor's interests to be better satisfied when control was transferred than when it was not.

The analysis of placement of trust carried out in Chapter 5 is useful for examining the situation confronting the potential buyer. This is a situation in which the potential gain *(G)* is very great compared to the potential loss *(L)*. The criterion for placing trust is that the perceived chance that the gain will be realized, relative to the chance that it will not, must be greater than the ratio of loss to gain; that is, $p/(1 - p)$ must be greater than L/G. In this case (as in that of the person confronting a con man in Chapter 5), L/G is small. Thus it is rational to place trust, even if the chance of success is not especially great.

This does not explain, of course, why acquisitive crazes expand so greatly, beyond the point at which it is rational (from the perspective of an outside observer) for individuals to continue to buy. An explanation of that depends on some special aspects of transfer of control in such a situation. Why does this overexpansion occur? One element of crazes of this sort that brings about overexpansion and reduces stability is the dependence of p on others' actions. The subjective probability of gain, as held by each actor, depends not only on objective circumstances but also on others' actions. Thus, as long as others continue to buy, that subjective probability is high. If buying stops, this provides information that leads many to lower their subjective probability.

The question of how this overexpansion and subsequent withdrawal come about must be left for theory development and research. It is clear that, in forming a judgment about the wisdom of an investment, each person uses others as advisory intermediaries, to use the terminology of Chapter 8. When many are taking the same action, there is a cognitively homogeneous social environment (after the acquisitive craze has developed) which constitutes a system of positive feedback, in which each person is using others' actions as evidence about the probability of gain. This, of course, can produce the explosive phenomenon. What is left unexplained, however, is how intendedly rational action leads to a system of action in which there is far too much investment to correspond to the true opportunities for gain. Also, no indication is given as to when and how such a bubble will burst, and turn into an escape panic similar to a bank run.

Contagious Beliefs

Another kind of collective behavior which appears to have some elements in common with acquisitive crazes is known as contagious belief. It is exemplified by belief in flying saucers, ghosts, and other strange but widely accepted phenomena. The behavior obviously involves a transfer of control over belief. No actions are ordinarily taken in these cases; there is merely a belief that spreads much like an epidemic. What happens in these cases? What leads to the apparent transfer of control over belief by many persons in the population?

Of the experimental research in social psychology that is relevant to these phenomena, the most directly so is Sherif's (1936) experiment with the autokinetic effect. When an individual is placed in a dark room, with no visual cues to spatial location, and a fixed pinpoint of light is shown at the other end of the room, the point of light appears to wander. The apparent movement is a consequence of the absence of a visual frame of reference and is termed the auto-kinetic effect.

Sherif carried out such an experiment with two individuals, one a confederate of the experimenter who reported out loud a particular direction of movement. The autokinetic effect was present for the other subject, but the direction of movement he perceived was very similar to that reported by the confederate. Clearly the naive subject in Sherif's experiment can be described as transferring control of his perception to the confederate, in a situation in which there are no physical cues. When he has no basis for determining the validity of a perception, he transfers control to another's perception. This could be described as rational action, even though nothing much is gained from it. Since the action occurs at the perceptual level (that is, the individual is unaware of his dependence on the other), I will simply take it as a given psychological fact.

This work gives a possible clue concerning the conditions under which contagious beliefs such as belief in flying saucers might arise. It suggests that they might arise in a circumstance in which there is instability in the structure of authority and in the usually stable structure of transfer of belief or trust in judgment. Anthropological research on the conditions under which cults arise (such as the cargo cults of New Guinea) is consistent with this, showing that cults often arise at a time when the society is undergoing rapid social change and a breakdown in the traditional structure of authority.[10]

As with acquisitive crazes, further research into contagious beliefs is necessary before an explanation of such behavior systems can be integrated into a general theory of action.

Hostile and Expressive Crowds

A system of behavior quite different from panics and crazes is that of a crowd which engages in hostile, destructive, or expressive acts which no member would have engaged in alone. It is for this kind of behavior that the term "mob" is used. The violent outburst that soldiers sometimes engage in when occupying a village—looting, raping, destroying—exemplifies this phenomenon. A lynch mob, such as were formed in the South to take vengeance on an accused black, is another example. Others are looting mobs which occur after a flood, tornado, or other natural disaster and crowds which engage in riots, such as the race riots that erupted in North American cities in the 1940s, the violent demonstrations that broke out on college campuses in the 1960s, the ghetto riots in the 1960s, or the race riots in South Africa in the 1980s.

10. See Berndt (1965, pp. 99–100) and Lawrence (1967). In the foreword to Lawrence's book, J. K. McCarthy (head of the Department of Native Affairs in Port Moresby, New Guinea, at the time) writes that (in 1963) "there is hardly a month that passes without somewhere in the vastness of New Guinea, another prophet arising among its two million souls to preach the cult of cargo" (p. vi).

In all of these collective phenomena, one element is present: A group engages in an action together that no member would have engaged in alone. In discussions of this kind of behavior, this point comes up again and again. It is described as behavior that violates the norms, or behavior that ignores established authority.

One example from the late 1960s is the student revolt at Columbia University on April 23, 1968 (to be discussed again in Chapter 18). The Cox Commission (1968) report describes what occurred:

The SDS demonstration was scheduled for the Sundial at noon. Apparently, the gymnasium was not to be an issue on that particular day.

Yet when the demonstration began about noon the presence of black students was noteworthy. SAS and SDS had not previously cooperated. All told, the unusually large crowd numbered about 500 including many curious bystanders as well as the number who intended to challenge the Administration by marching into Low Library. To the north on Low Plaza were stationed about a hundred students opposed to the Sundial demonstrators. Another group of about 50 pickets organized by the Students for a Free Campus stood blocking the path of the proposed march.

The rally began with speeches by Ted Gold and Nick Freudenberg on University discipline and IDA. Cicero Wilson, SAS President, then attacked the construction of the gymnasium. Apparently, his participation and the presence of numerous black students resulted from last-minute consultation. SAS had recently become concerned with the gymnasium.

Mark Rudd then began to speak but the cry was raised, "To Low, on to Low." The crowd surged up the steps toward Low Library. No one can say how many were committed demonstrators and how many were merely spectators.

As the marchers approached the library, they paused and swerved to the east, thereby avoiding any serious collision with the counter-demonstrators gathered at the top of the steps. A few demonstrators sought to force entrance through the southeast security door, but the Administration had had it locked in anticipation of trouble. Most of the crowd milled around, unsure what to do next. The demonstration seemed to have lost all sense of purpose. Mark Rudd climbed atop an overturned trash can near the door and began a rambling discussion of possible courses of action. Several witnesses recall thinking that SDS had failed once again in its efforts to mobilize the student body.

But again chance intervened. A voice from the crowd cried for a march to the site of the proposed gymnasium and most of the group, with black students among the leaders, moved eastward toward the excavation at Morningside Drive and 114th Street. A lesser number, among whom were Gold and Rudd, went back to the Sundial for more speeches.

It was 12:30 P.M. when the main body of demonstrators numbering about

300, arrived at the excavation. Some students began to pull down a section of the fence. Three policemen appeared and tried to block access to the gym site, but they were quickly overwhelmed by the students. More policemen came up; there was a scuffle, and one student was arrested. There was argument over the arrest. A policeman was knocked down and kicked before the students were driven backwards.

On the way back to the campus they encountered the Sundial group which was marching to the gym site. The two groups merged and made their way to the Sundial.

Up to this point, the course of the demonstration had been entirely haphazard. The planned indoor demonstration had not been held. Except for Mr. Rudd's successful effort to avoid further trouble with police at the gym site, the crowd had responded to the calls of unknown members rather than its leaders. After moments of indecision and frustration at the Sundial in front of Low Library, and again at the gym site, there was still a crowd of about 500, many of them looking for some kind of showdown with the Administration.

Back at the Sundial, Mark Rudd spoke once more. He noted that one of the protesters was held as a hostage (apparently referring to the student arrested at the gym site), and suggested that the crowd take a hostage of its own. The meaning of the statement, as reported, seems hardly clear, but the crowd understood it to mean a sit-in and began an orderly march into nearby Hamilton Hall, a classroom building, which also houses the administrative offices of Columbia College. The 450 people who entered the building included opponents of the protest as well as its sponsors and supporters. It was now 1:35 P.M. (pp. 100–103)

This began the occupation of Hamilton Hall, which initiated an outburst involving the occupation of five university buildings for seven days and ended with violence when police were brought in to clear the buildings; 103 persons were treated for injuries at two hospitals, and 692 were arrested.

Involved in these events were a large number of persons who, for different reasons, were opposed to the actions of the university administration. The SDS nucleus was principally opposed to actions in support of the Vietnam War, including the use of campus offices for armed forces recruiting. The black SAS nucleus was principally opposed to plans for construction of a new university gymnasium. And many students held private grudges. Thus the structure of the situation was one in which many students had an interest in some action against the university.

If a student had transferred no control over his actions to others, then he could express this interest in whatever way he desired: acts of vandalism, individual disruption of classes, or other actions against the university. Students had, however, transferred rights of control over their actions, as part of their enrollment in the university, to the authority of the university and to civil authority.

Thus most actions expressing their interest were barred to them, so long as that transfer of control was maintained. If, individually, they had withdrawn rights of control from university and civil authorities and had pursued their antiuniversity interests, they would have been punished.

When students were surrounded by others with antiuniversity interests, there arose the possibility of something which would allow realization of their interests: a withdrawal of rights of control from the authorities to which they had been transferred and a simultaneous transfer of that control either to the crowd as a corporate actor or to its members, with greatest control being transferred to those who appeared to lead an antiuniversity action. The period during which such a shift takes place is one that has been noted by many observers of such crowds, whether in student revolts, race riots, or lynching mobs—a period of milling around, during which nothing happens. This milling period was strikingly evident at Columbia University on April 23.

Brown (1965) suggests that the milling period is one in which members of the crowd "feel one another out" to determine the degree of common sentiment. In the Columbia University case the milling period did appear to include this, but also seemed to include a number of trial actions by potential leaders. None of these got a response from the members of the crowd, but then one did.

In terms of the conceptual framework of this book, the formation of the crowd and the milling process facilitated the withdrawal by crowd members of rights of control over their actions from the authorities. They retransferred rights of control, it appears, partly to the crowd itself and partly to those leaders who initiated action in a direction that satisfied their antiuniversity interests. This withdrawal of rights of control, occurring in a setting in which a number of others are doing so at the same time, illustrates the consensual character of a right, as discussed in Chapter 3. If the rights to control certain actions of a student are, by consensus (or the crystallization of consensus in law), held by university authorities or civil authorities, then a student cannot individually withdraw those rights without being wholly "in the wrong" by doing so. Only if there is another collectivity (the crowd of demonstrators in this case) who develop a different consensus about where rights of control are held (for example, by the collectivity itself or by a particular leader) can the individual members effectively transfer those rights. When there is such a body, there are conflicting definitions of where rights lie, or of what is "right."

Chapter 18 examines the revoking of authority in a longer-term sense, as occurs in a revolution. That discussion makes it clear that authority cannot ordinarily be revoked by individual action; what is required is collective action, which is of course subject to free-rider problems. In a mob or hostile crowd setting, there is revocation of authority, and, as in revolutions, the consequences for the individual are highly dependent on what others do. There is a widespread structure of mutual (positive) externalities: "If I am the only one to act, I will be punished by the authorities, and perhaps even by others. If I am one of many, I will not be negatively sanctioned, either by authorities or by others." The milling around that is observed can thus be seen as a process of creating collective action from individual actions, a period during which individuals assess the contingencies of others' actions: "If I take the first step, who will follow me?" Since these contingencies will differ for different types of actions, in part the milling is a search for arenas or types of action that will allow a number of persons to transfer control of their actions to a leader or to the collectivity.

For a hostile or expressive crowd, it appears that the *number* of participants plays a different and more important role than for the forms of collective behavior discussed previously. Brown (1965) cites the common observation for such phenomena of an impression of "universality" among participants. As the number of persons with common sentiments increases, each person feels less and less controlled by the pre-existing norms which governed his behavior and feels increasingly that the new behavior is normal. Approval of his acts by a large number of persons appears to give him courage to act, apparently by releasing him from the control exercised by pre-existing authority or norms. And each additional person who coordinately engages in the action with him reduces the potential cost, since punishment by the authorities becomes less likely.

As was done for other forms of collective behavior, it is possible to construct a table representing the reward structure confronting a member of a crowd if he engages in the hostile or expressive action or he does not. In this case, because the others' actions shield him from punitive authority and are more likely to do so as the number of others engaging in the action increases, the table should show how his rewards vary as that number varies.[11] It is also important when constructing such a table to recognize that for some reason (antagonism to the university, rage at white authority in the ghetto, rage at the accused black in a lynch mob, easy availability of goods in an unattended, flood-damaged store in a looting riot) the individual member has a strong interest in acting against the norms or laws. In Table 9.8 this is reflected by a zero reward for not acting and a positive reward for acting in the absence of restraining norms or authority. A negative number in a cell indicates that if he acts he will be punished through a sanction (such as suspension from the university); if he is not punished, there is a positive number.

As Table 9.8 illustrates, if no others are acting, the individual crowd member receives no reward if he does not act, remaining frustrated.[12] If he does act in that situation, he is very likely to be punished and thus receive a net reward of -4. As the number of others acting increases, the likelihood of his being pun-

11. It may be that, as suggested in the preceding paragraph, two types of persons are important: those who actually engage in the action, and those in authority who silently indicate approval of the action (or at least indicate that no sanctions will be applied). Studies of lynch mobs indicate that the latter group, consisting of leading members of the community who tacitly consent to the lynching, is critical for the action to proceed.

12. The zeros in the first row of the table reflect the assumption that there are no negative sanctions imposed by those who are acting on those who are not.

Table 9.8 Reward structure for member of a hostile crowd.

		Number of others acting						
		0	1	2	3	4	5	6
Crowd member	Not act	0	0	0	0	0	0	0
	Act	-4	-3	-2	-1	0	1	2

ished decreases, until, with a certain number of others acting (four in this table), the net result if he acts is psychically no worse than if he does not act. For any number greater than that, he will have an incentive to act, because the chance of punishment, as he sees it, is sufficiently small that the satisfaction from the action outweighs the expected loss from possible punishment.

Thus, as in the case of a physical escape panic (although the reward structure there is quite different), the crowd member is best off neither if he acts nor if he fails to act, but if he makes his action contingent on that of others. In other words, it is to his interest to transfer control to others to a specific extent; in this example, if three or fewer members of the crowd act, he does not act, but if five or more act, he does.

Hostile or expressive crowds differ, however, from physical escape panics in that it is to the individual's interest to make his action contingent on that of others, regardless of whether their actions are contingent on his. This can be seen in stylized form as a two-player game matrix in which A_1 is the individual and A_2 is the others. The reward structure in Table 9.9 is quite different from that of a prisoner's dilemma. As the Table shows, for A_1 the strategy of making his action contingent on others' actions dominates both the strategy of not acting and that of acting.

Two additional important points are illustrated by Tables 9.8 and 9.9. First, if the members of the crowd are heterogeneous with respect to their reward structures (that is, one person crosses the threshold of net benefits even if no other persons are acting, a second crosses it contingent on one other person acting, a third contingent on two others acting, and so on), the crowd will be more likely to act than if the members have homogeneous reward structures, even if the heterogeneous crowd has a higher average threshold. Thus a few "wild men" in a heterogeneous crowd can set it off even if most persons in the crowd require a fairly large number of others acting in order to provide a shield from punitive

Table 9.9   Reward structure for member (A₁) of a hostile crowd as a two-player game matrix.

| | | A₂ (others) | | |
		Not act	Act	Act contingent on A₁
A₁	Not act	0	0	0
	Act	-10	10	10
	Act contingent on A₂	0	10	10

authority.[13] This prediction that a hostile expressive crowd is more likely to erupt into action if it is heterogeneous than if it is homogeneous appears to be the opposite of the prediction about heterogeneity in the case of escape panics. The basis for this difference will be examined in the next section.

Second, as Table 9.8 indicates, it is not only to the individual crowd member's interest to transfer control to others in the manner just described; it is also to his interest to do what he can to increase the number of others acting. In the table his potential net rewards increase as the number of others engaging in the action increases. Consequently, *quite apart from* his own action, he has an incentive to encourage others to act. It is this aspect of the reward structure that leads to the commonly expressed encouragement in such situations: "Go ahead and do it. I'm right behind you." It is also likely that the milling around that often precedes such actions is a period in which this encouragement of each by others takes place.

Figure 9.3 is a diagram of the benefits of an individual's action in an expressive crowd as a function of the number of persons already acting. Although the diagram is analogous to Figure 9.2 for escape panics, it shows a very different pattern of benefits as a function of the number engaging in the action.[14] Here the

13. Granovetter (1978) has examined collective behavior of this sort using the notion of differing individual thresholds discussed here (but without the general underlying framework of transferring control that is present in this chapter). He has examined the epidemiological consequences of variations in threshold distributions, showing that major consequences can result from very minor differences in distribution.

14. For escape panics I used the fraction of the crowd rather than the number of persons. The use of the number engaging in the action for hostile crowds is based on the fact that it appears that this number is a more important determinant of benefits than is the fraction of the crowd. In the case of escape panics, it is less clear.

benefits rise with the number engaging in the action, but they begin below zero. The number n^* is the break-even point, above which the member of the crowd finds it beneficial to act. The marginal benefits are always positive, though declining (assuming the benefit curve is convex to the origin, as shown).

The behavior of a hostile crowd is like that in a physical escape panic and unlike that in a bank panic in that there is a sequence of actions. This implies that the individual crowd member's early actions may have some effects on others' subsequent actions, which can affect his benefits in later stages. Thus, besides being rational for him to make his action contingent on theirs, independent of what they do, it is also rational for him to attempt to induce others to act. Table 9.9 or Figure 9.3 shows that he is better off when both he and others act than he is when both he and others do not.

Thus the reward structure for this form of collective behavior differs sharply from that for the others already examined. There is something new here: an interposition of others, a collectivity with a new consensus, between a person and the authority to which he had previously transferred rights of control over his actions. This interposition in effect shields him from that authority, allowing him (or even directing him) to withdraw the rights of control and to transfer them to another actor whose actions express his current interests. In some cases this interpositional role is played by a party different from the one to whom control is finally given when the mob action gets started. For example, in violent mob actions directed against blacks in the southern United States, there appeared to be two roles played by two different sets of whites: Lower-class, disreputable men carried out the violence; respected, established men in the community did not take part but gave their silent approval, indicating that there would be no punishment. In this case the respected white men were those in whom the

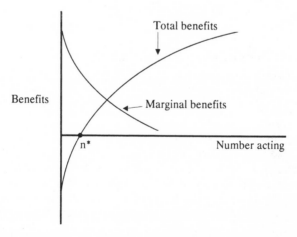

Figure 9.3 Marginal and total benefits of an individual's action in an expressive crowd as a function of the number of others already acting.

disreputable ones had previously placed rights of control over their actions (which is implicit in the adjective "respected"), and this control was used to counteract the control that had been lodged in higher authorities (at the state or federal level). Thus the disreputable white men were freed from the control of civil authorities and could transfer control to those among themselves who expressed most fully their violently racist sentiments.

There appear to be, then, in the case of hostile crowds or mobs, two different processes that take place: a release, due to the crowd's providing a new consensus, from the authority or the normative control that had existed by virtue of the stable or institutionalized transfer of control over their actions that persons had made; and an action by one or more persons that leads members of the crowd to transfer that control to those persons. Sometimes these two activities are carried out by the same persons (the crowd or the mob); sometimes they are carried out by two different sets of persons.

The withdrawal of the rights of control from the authorities may not result from anyone's action but may be a result of wholly external events. In that case the events do not establish a new consensus and thus a new (that is, competing) allocation of rights. Instead, they destroy the existing allocation of rights to the authorities, leaving an absence of control over rights to act in which individuals are free to act in satisfying their interests. The events make it difficult or impossible for those in authority to apply sanctions that would enforce the rights and thus to retain control. For example, after a natural disaster such as a tornado, flood, or fire, there is often widespread looting. In these cases, it is the disaster itself which has removed the civil authority that has previously prevented looting; it is not an action by any person or corporate actor. (That this removal of authority is what facilitates looting is confirmed by the severity of punishment threatened for looters after a disaster, which is out of proportion to the severity of the crime: "Looters will be shot on sight!" is a familiar statement. Such action is an attempt to reinstate authority, that is, not to let the rights of control dissolve.)

The kinds of collective behavior that fit this general pattern also include those that are expressive and antinormative, but not destructive or hostile. Panty raids in college dormitories are an example. The processes are the same: Control is withdrawn from existing authority with the aid of support from others; then this control, temporarily withdrawn from authority, is transferred to certain leaders.

Further insight into the processes involved in hostile, destructive, and expressive behavior by crowds can be gained by considering ritual orgies or other ritualized collective violations of norms that have been practiced in a number of societies. In these the same release from the control of everyday norms takes place, but in a different way. Members of the group do not withdraw the control over their actions they have placed in authorities' hands; instead, the authorities maintain control but transform the content of the norms within a rigidly defined frame of time and place. Thus, although the overt behavior may be similar to that in spontaneous mobs, it takes place without a withdrawal of control from existing authority and is in fact directed and guided by existing authority.[15] A comparison of the same sort can be made concerning drug use in communal settings. Although use of hallucinatory drugs declines among those entering communes, the use that does occur in some communes is highly institutionalized and carried out under the explicit control of the communal authority.

Why Does Heterogeneity Have Opposite Effects for Expressive Crowds and Escape Panics?

The prediction that a heterogeneous crowd will be more likely to erupt in expressive action than will a homogeneous one is based on the particular definition of heterogeneity as composed of differences among individuals in the strength of normative constraints on them emanating from existing authority. The prediction concerning escape panics is based on a different kind of heterogeneity, heterogeneity in the distribution of attention or transferred control, which is predicted to reduce the likelihood of panic. Thus the two predictions are not in direct opposition.

The theory being developed here would also predict, however, that in an expressive crowd heterogeneity of the second sort, that is, in distribution of attention, is more likely to lead to action than is an egalitarian or homogeneous distribution of attention or transferred control. A hostile crowd with leaders is more likely to erupt into action than is a leaderless crowd, but in a panic-generating situation a crowd with a leader is less likely to erupt into panic than is a leaderless crowd.

Again the predictions are not in direct opposition; this time it is not because the independent variables differ, but because the dependent action differs. A panic that arises in a panic-generating situation represents complete disorder, with each person seeking his own escape. When a hostile crowd under a leader erupts into action, the action may be violent and extreme, but it is ordinarily coherent and directed toward a common goal. When a leaderless hostile crowd erupts into action, as in a riot or in looting, it is *this* action which is most comparable to the individualistic action of the escape panic.

In an escape panic leadership encourages action in accord with normal authority (orderly exit); in a hostile crowd leadership encourages action opposed to normal authority (demonstration or organized violence). In both cases the theory of this book predicts that the transfer of control will be more extensive and

---

15. It would appear, deductively, that such ritual orgies could take place only among populations in which the norms are maintained by external controls and not internalized. For if they are internalized, it would seem that the authorities to whom control has been transferred would be unable to transform the content of prescribed (or permitted) action in such a way that it violated existing norms. The conjecture is speculative but suggests a possible avenue for research. It appears to go against empirical evidence, for ritual orgies and similar phenomena are found in tribal societies, where internalization of the content of norms would seem to be most pronounced.

effective when it focuses on a single leader or on a few persons. But in the case of an escape panic this effectiveness leads away from collective behavior, and in the case of a hostile crowd it leads toward collective behavior. In both cases leadership aids in the realization of interests, by coordinating the action. In the escape panic it does so by inhibiting actions that depart from normal activity. In the hostile crowd it does so by facilitating actions that depart from normal activity. This may be seen by the direction in which normative sanctions are applied (if any are) by members of the crowd toward one another: In the escape panic these will be negative sanctions against the action which contributed to the eruption of panic; in the hostile crowd they will be positive sanctions that encourage the action which contributes to the eruption of violence.

This examination of hostile and expressive crowds leaves many questions unanswered, as was true for the earlier examination of panics and crazes. One of the most important concerns the conditions that may facilitate or bring about the withdrawal of control from institutional authority. Such unanswered questions indicate that work in this area is in its infancy.

Fads and Fashions

A form of collective behavior different from both panics and hostile crowds is the broad category of fads and fashions. Fads (as I will call them) show a particular pattern over time: They develop, starting slowly and then gathering momentum, until they reach a peak; then they decline until they are gone. There is a growth curve and a decay curve, but I will not be concerned here with the precise forms of these curves. It is useful simply to note that this type of collective behavior is differently distributed over time than is either the behavior of a crowd in an escape panic or the behavior of a hostile crowd.

Some fads rise and fall as distinct and unique phenomena, for example, the hula hoop craze in the United States in the late 1950s. Others, such as popular music and fashion in women's clothing, are part of an ongoing cycle in which one song or fashion arises and replaces another and, in turn, is replaced by the next. Some linguistic fads, in which a new term is coined, becomes very widely used, and vanishes, are like the hula hoop fad; however, some terms remain in usage after having entered the language via this route. For example, Mackay (1932 [1852], p. 623) describes the origin of the term "flare up" as a description of the burning of Bristol in riots. Usage of this term then grew explosively in England, becoming common in everyday speech. Unlike many linguistic fads, it did not die out, but remains in everyday usage today.

Concentrating on linguistic fads and dress fashions makes apparent an element that is very likely present in all fads. This is that one's linguistic usage or style of dress is carried out with the response of others in mind. This may result in simply making the style or usage acceptable or understandable to others: dressing in a way that others will approve of, or speaking in a way that others will accept and understand. In such a case the behavior is often said to be controlled by norms. In other cases the style or usage may be designed to startle, to cause others to notice the action (and thus the actor) or to produce a particular effect. It is sometimes said that a person who acts this way is flouting the conventions.

These two patterns of behavior appear to perform different services for the actor. The first allows the actor's action to take place without disturbing ongoing action, without attracting attention away from other actions in the system. The words are spoken for maximum understanding and clarity; the clothes selected are intended to be inconspicuous, unremarkable, and acceptable. The second pattern does quite the opposite, attracting attention to the action or actor and leading the others who are witnessing it to respond to that action itself.

In a study of how opinions in fashion and other areas come to be formed, Katz and Lazarsfeld (1955) identified two forms of behavior that are compatible with this conception. They coined the term "opinion leaders" for those persons who attempt to be the first to wear a new fashion or to know the latest political news, or who always know the top ten or top forty popular songs. These opinion leaders (who differ for different areas of expertise) are complemented by other persons who are their followers. Such opinion leaders make extensive use of those mass media which are informative in their area of expertise, and their followers do not. Katz and Lazarsfeld formulated from this pattern a notion of a two-step flow of communication, from the media through the opinion leaders to the followers.

This behavior is on the borders of what is properly called collective behavior, for it is highly institutionalized: The opinion leaders maintain their leadership over a reasonable period of time, and the followers maintain a stable relation to their opinion leaders in each area of expertise or fashion. But despite its near institutionalization, the behavior seems to be similar to that which goes on, sometimes with less stable roles for leaders and followers, in the phenomena I have labeled fads. Even though the leaders and followers remain the same, new fads and fashions continue to emerge and pass through the system. The process in the institutionalized areas of clothing fashions and popular songs is that the leaders maintain the attention of their followers (in competition with others who would supplant them) by being first to exhibit the new behavior (first to wear a type of dress, adopt a new hair style or makeup, or know a new song). Thus, as a fashion comes to be widespread, they must, to maintain their position, abandon it for a new fashion.

In terms of the conceptual framework of this chapter, some persons, the followers, have transferred extensive control to particular others, their opinion leaders. In different areas of action and opinion, they have transferred different amounts of control and have transferred it to different leaders. But not everyone has transferred control extensively to others within the system. The opinion leaders have transferred partial control to others outside the system under consideration, that is, to various mass media which focus on topics relevant to their area of expertise. In a negative way, however, they also transfer partial control to others within the local system. There are certain followers (or persons

Table 9.10   Reward structure for leader (A₁) and followers (A₂) in a three-player
fashion game.

		A_3 (mass media)			
		Fashion 1		Fashion 2	
		A_2 (followers)			
		Fashion 1	Fashion 2	Fashion 1	Fashion 2
A_1 (leader)	Fashion 1	2, 2	3, 0	0, 2	1, 0
	Fashion 2	1, 0	0, 2	3, 0	2, 2

who follow a different style) whom they endeavor *not* to be like. For example, a woman may be heard saying, "I wouldn't be caught dead wearing things like ——— wears." When the fact that one person acts in a given way makes another less likely to do so, then it is quite correct to say that the second has transferred some control (negatively) over his action to the first.

If the system described is viewed in the form of a game matrix, the reward structure is different from that for the escape panic. First, there are (at the simplest level) two different reward structures: one for those whose interests are structured so as to make them followers, and one for those whose interests are structured so as to make them leaders. For a leader, however, it is a three-player game, in which the two other players are followers (considered all together) and mass media. In Table 9.10 the outcomes according to the interests of leaders are given as 0, 1, 2, or 3, ranging from a very low-valued outcome to a high-valued one. For the followers the outcomes are given as 0 and 2, for low- and high-valued outcomes. Because the mass media are irrelevant for the followers, the values of outcomes for the followers are independent of the media's actions. Each of the three players is assumed to take one of two actions, called fashion 1 and fashion 2.

As the game matrix indicates, the followers have an interest in doing whatever the leader does; their rewards are high whenever their fashion is the same as the leader.[16] It is, then, to the follower's interest to transfer control to the leader.

16. The interest underlying this is the benefit experienced from being not different from others (the leader and other followers). This interest may derive from a desire to be inconspicuous or a desire to direct one's attention elsewhere by dressing or speaking acceptably without incurring the cost of making decisions, or from something else.

The leader has two interests: first, in adopting the same fashion as the media do; and, second, in having a fashion different from that of the followers. (In reality, it is probably more nearly true that leaders have an interest in seeing the followers adopt their fashion, but also an interest in being different once a certain fraction of followers have adopted it. Only the second of these interests is reflected in Table 9.10.)

With interests like those described, the rational strategy for a leader is to transfer control partly to the media (positively) and partly to followers (negatively). A sequence of action can be seen as follows: The media adopts fashion 2 while the followers are still exhibiting fashion 1; this moves the outcome from one in which the rewards are medium for the leader and high for the followers to one in which they are low for the leader and high for the followers. The leader then finds it in his interest to adopt fashion 2, both to follow the media and to separate himself from the followers. According to Table 9.10, he receives a high reward. Then his followers, acting on the basis of their reward as shown in the table, adopt fashion 2 as well. This gives them high rewards, but reduces the leader's rewards to medium. (When the media again change to a new style, his reward is changed from medium to very low, and he must change to the new style also, to regain a high reward. This initiates a change in followers, and so on.)

As long as the external sources change their actions, for whatever reasons, the process as described will generate a sequence of change within the social system. The structure of a single leader-follower relation is obviously a simplification of reality; there can be various types of structure. The dichotomy between leader and follower is also a simplification of reality. There are varying degrees of leadership and followership, that is, varying degrees to which control is transferred. And even if only the extremes are considered, there are logically four types of persons, as indicated in Table 9.11. In the cells of the table are terms

Table 9.11   Roles generated in a social system by various combinations of transfer of control.

| | | Others' transfer of control to oneself | |
		Yes	No
One's transfer of control to others	Yes	Amplifier	Follower
	No	Leader	Independent

which characterize the role of the person in the system. Besides leaders and followers, there are those to whom others have transferred control but who themselves have transferred control to others; these persons merely act as amplifiers for existing opinions or fads in the system. And there are those who have maintained control over their own action, just as the leaders have, but to whom nobody listens—that is, to whom no one has transferred control. These are independents.

The question of why rational persons would either transfer control or not do so can be answered by recognizing that there are potential costs to not transferring control, as well as potential benefits for doing so. The potential costs lie in part in the amount of time and effort required to remain knowledgeable in certain areas. Acquiring expertise and leadership may require hours of poring over magazines, listening to records, memorizing baseball statistics, reading the *New York Times* and *Washington Post,* practicing the hula hoop, or cultivating an esoteric vocabulary, for example. Transferring control to others can save great amounts of time and effort that would otherwise be spent in areas where one's interests are not great, but not zero: A woman can just note what a particular other woman wears; a girl can simply ask a friend what song is at the top of the charts; a man can simply ask someone at work what the standing of the local baseball team is.[17] In some areas major costs of not transferring control to others may include disapproval from others because one's behavior is different. For example, wearing a dress seen as "old-fashioned" may generate disdain; at the other extreme, daring departures from current fashion, such as miniskirts were when they were first worn, may bring disapproval. Ostentatious use of an unfamiliar word may be regarded as "putting on airs" and thus disapproved of. Even when disapproval is not forthcoming, a person may feel a degree of uncertainty about others' response to an action or opinion which is different, whether it is regarded as outdated or unconventional or new. For some persons this uncertainty is a serious cost. It may be sufficient, for example, to keep a person from uttering a previously unexpressed opinion in a conversation.[18]

On the other hand, the benefits of not transferring control can also be great. A new or unconventional action may attract followers and may, if practiced over a period of time, draw a set of followers who pay special attention to one's actions and show deference. Such deferential attention from others is a direct gratification for most persons. In contrast, if one transfers control to another in a given area, one may find it necessary to pay deference or even "play dumb" in order to extract desired information from the other ("Oh is that so? I didn't know that most Eastern Jews in Israel support the Likud Party. Tell me more.").

It is understandable, then, that, because of differing interests, for some persons the costs of maintaining control will outweigh the benefits, and they will

17. In Chapter 33 I show that, all other things being equal, one can realize a higher level of satisfaction by concentration of one's interests.

18. See Chapter 10 for a discussion of how norms may develop among a set of rational actors.

transfer control over their actions to others; for others the benefits will outweigh the costs. And depending on whose leadership has proved beneficial to them in the past, various persons will transfer control to different others. Thus there should be both a distribution of the amounts of control transferred over the action and a distribution of the points to which it is transferred.[19]

A question I have put aside until now is this: Under what conditions do fads arise? It is one thing to describe fads, and related behavior, in terms of control over actions or beliefs being transferred to others. It is quite another to account for a fad. What is the structural condition that should lead to explosive fads? The answer is clearly that the system must include many persons of the amplifier type (see Table 9.10): persons who transfer control to others and thus will pick up a fad, and to whom at the same time others have transferred control. Once an amplifier has picked up a fad, it is spread to others. When there are large numbers of such persons, any new activity, however it may enter a system, is greatly amplified by the structure of transferred control.

In the English public schools of the nineteenth century, a number of new games developed that later spread beyond their confines, as well as some that did not: Harrow fives and Eton fives spread to Oxford and Cambridge and are the precursors of handball; racquets spread minimally but spawned squash; rugby began at Rugby school; Eton's field game and wall game have remained confined to that school; and there were more. Boarding schools constitute one of the few contexts in which a new game can receive sufficient amplification, without disturbance from the outside, to develop and to acquire devotees.[20] Deciding to play a game requires some rather extensive transfer of control because consensus on the rules is necessary; as long as that transfer does not extend beyond the boundaries of a nearly closed group, the game can be played many times and its popularity amplified.

This illustration suggests that widespread transfer of control alone is not enough to allow a new action to gain the initial momentum within a social system sufficient to lead to its becoming a fad. The transfer must occur within a group having a high degree of closure, in order that the activity not be displaced by some new competitor entering from the outside. Note, however, that for the activity to spread more widely, the subsystem within which it develops cannot

19. I have said nothing, and will say nothing here beyond this footnote, about the transfer of control to actors other than persons, in particular, various media such as newspapers, television, and magazines. This obviously affects, however, the dynamics of opinion, belief, fashion behavior, and other activities for which there is widespread transfer of control. (In Chapter 33 I discuss these matters.) Because of the potential importance of these media in initiating opinions, fashions, and fads and in controlling these phenomena, it is important to carry out empirical research on the transfer of control to these actors, as well as mathematical examination of the effects of the kind of structural intervention they represent in the epidemiology of fads.

20. A physical manifestation of this amplification is the existence at Eton of fifty curious-looking courts for Eton fives, each a replica of an asymmetric section of Eton's fifteenth-century chapel, where the game was first played. Eton fives is also played outside Eton, but only in a few places.

be totally insulated from the outside. It must be relatively closed to the outside, but outsiders must have transferred some control to it. It is probably no accident, for example, that Eton fives, Harrow fives, and rugby developed within three of the most prestigious of the English public schools. It is likely that boys in other schools transferred more control over games and other activities to boys in these schools than to their counterparts elsewhere.

Thus the conjecture here is that a fad or a social innovation can best develop in a system whose structure has a great amount of transferred control and has pockets, or subsystems, with two properties: a high degree of closure to outside control, and a large amount of control transferred to them from outside.

There may be parallelism between the inward-directed subsystem, serving as the initiating nucleus of a new activity or fad, and the individual person as a system. If the person transfers almost no control over his actions to others but receives all his direction from some wholly separate source (such as his inner self, his dreams, revelations from God), he may serve as the starting point of a movement. Sabbatai Sevi, the initiator of the Sabbatian movement among many Jews of the seventeenth century, who believed him to be the Messiah, was one such person. In fact, Scholem (1973) shows convincingly from contemporary evidence, including first-hand accounts, that Sevi was a manic-depressive. During the manic periods he manifested a supreme confidence in himself, which gave force to the beliefs picked up by others. A passage from Scholem indicates how this developed:

> Coenen reports that according to Sabbatai's fellow citizens of Smyrna, certain manic states began to manifest themselves in the period before his marriage. "He would quote Isaiah 14:14, 'I will ascend above the heights of the clouds; I will be like the most high' . . . , and once it happened that he recited this verse with such ecstasy that he imagined himself to be floating in the air. Once, when he asked his friends whether they had seen him levitate and they truthfully answered, 'No,' he retorted: 'You were not worthy to behold this glorious sight because you were not purified like me.'" . . . According to Coenen it occurred to Sabbatai a number of times before his first messianic self-revelation. Shortly afterward he revealed to the members of his circle who shared his studies and ascetic exercises that great things might be expected from him. One hint was added to another until, at last, he revealed himself as the messiah son of David. (p. 127)

Scholem continues:

> After the beginning of the mass movement in 1666, the believers no longer spoke of an "illness." This term disappears. In their view both phases of the disease were divine dispensations for which they employed theological terms, traditional ones as well as new coinages, corresponding exactly to the modern terms "depression" and "mania." The new vocabulary . . . speaks

of periods of "illumination" and of the "hiding of the face" respectively. (p. 130)

The case of Sabbatai Sevi suggests that the kind of psychic state described as mania can constitute the extreme of the nontransfer of control which makes a person a possible initiator of a fad or a movement. The internal functioning of a person who has a manic-depressive personality might mirror in a sense the internal structure of a group having much transfer of control within it but little to the outside.

It is clear that persons find it more rewarding to transfer control to others under certain social conditions than under others. In his discussion of the Sabbatian movement, Scholem (1973) suggests why Jews would be particularly vulnerable to messianic movements, that is, would be very quick to transfer control over their religious lives from the rabbinate to a self-proclaimed Messiah:

> In the peculiar conditions of Jewish existence, messianism was the expression not so much of internal Jewish struggles—class or otherwise—as of the abnormal situation of a pariah nation. The sense of insecurity and permanent danger to life and property . . . (p. 462)

Even if this suggestion is correct, however, it does not show why such a movement emerged in the seventeenth century.

Research on the emergence and development of fads, messianic movements, and other phenomena that involve extensive transfer of control is necessary if the theory of collective behavior is to develop. At this point I can only indicate that the question of what social conditions lead to the extensive transfer of control should be a focus of that research activity.

Influence Processes in Purchasing Decisions, Voting, and Public Opinion

An area that lies at the border of phenomena called collective behavior is that of individual decision making in unstructured settings which contain other actors making similar decisions. Consumers' purchasing decisions are probably the most common examples. Another is deciding how to vote in an election.[21] Still another is the development of opinions on current events. The general area of behavior exemplified by such decisions is only a step removed from fads and fashions. Although the behavior does not necessarily exhibit the cyclical[22] char-

---

21. I will not discuss here the decision concerning whether to vote or not to vote. That constitutes a special problem, for one person's vote is very unlikely to affect the election's outcome. Thus, if it costs him anything to vote, it appears irrational to do so. This problem is addressed in Chapters 11 and 30.

22. See Kroeber (1973) for an examination of the cyclical pattern of fluctuations in women's dress lengths.

acter or wild fluctuations found with fads and fashions, the individual decision making is similar in the two types of situations. In fact, points can be assigned on a continuum between volatile fads and ongoing stable systems of individual decision making. For example, there certainly are fads in children's toys and cyclical patterns of fashion in women's clothes, but not so much so in children's clothes and in women's food purchases, although these are all purchasing decisions in a social context. What probably determines the point on the continuum at which a given type of purchasing decision lies is the exhaustibility of the market for the particular product (for example, a particular type of toy has a limited market, since it will not be repurchased for the same children but must either wait for the maturing of a new cohort or give way to another toy) and the degree to which the use of the product provides rewards for differentiation (as seems to be true for women's fashions with respect to fashion leaders, as discussed in the preceding section). Such a reward structure (coupled with the complementary reward structure for followers) provides a generating system for cyclical change. If that structure were not present, the generating system would be missing an essential component.

In this section I turn to systems of decision making in which a sizable fraction of a population makes choices from among the same alternatives within a limited span of time. These decisions may be frequently repeated, as are those concerning the purchase of consumer nondurables such as food products; or they may be repeated only infrequently, as are those concerning the purchase of consumer durables such as washing machines or automobiles and those concerning what presidential candidate to vote for.

In these systems of decision making, there can sometimes be precisely the same benefits from transferring control to others that were discussed earlier. For example, an individual must make a decision about buying something and does not know the consequences of acting in one way rather than another. He may engage in an extensive search for information, especially if the decision will have important consequences for him, for example, if it involves purchase of a consumer durable such as a car. If the decision will not have important consequences, if it concerns, for example, whether to buy one brand of yogurt for 55 cents or another for 60 cents, or, more generally, the purchase of any consumer nondurable where he can change brands next time, then he may not engage in an information search because it is costly, and the most cost-effective means of acquiring information is to purchase the item (or even both alternatives) and learn from experience.

For purchases for which the cost of a bad decision is high, a rational actor will engage in a search for information before deciding. But along with his information search, he will place trust in the judgment of others. If there are others whose judgment he trusts (as described in Chapter 8), he will give them partial control over his decision. In a situation in which many have placed trust in the judgment of others, the behavior of the system will differ from that of a system in which few have placed trust in others. It will show more volatility than will a system of independent opinions (because all will tend to move in the same direction at the same time), and if there is closure in the system (that is, A trusts B's judgment, B trusts C's judgment, and C trusts A's), extreme misjudgments can be made with high confidence, as discussed in Chapter 8. Since the specific character of such systems requires the use of mathematics, they will be examined in some detail in Chapter 33.

For a system of action in which there are many actors making comparable decisions, partly depending on one another for information and judgment and partly depending on other actors such as (in the case of consumer goods) the producers who advertise or salespeople, it is possible to conceive of a distribution of ultimate control over the outcomes or, to put it differently, power in determining outcomes. That is, since A_1's decision is partly controlled by A_2 and A_3, and theirs in turn is partly controlled by others, and so on, it is easy to conceive of a closed system of action in which each actor, including actors such as producers of consumer goods, has a certain amount of power to determine outcomes. If the degree to which each actor's action is controlled by each other actor could be measured, it is intuitively apparent that the ultimate power of each actor in the system could be determined. This would be an attractive and useful possibility because it would allow the design of an optimal strategy for an actor to use to affect the distribution of outcomes.

Specific Predictions about Collective Behavior

The various forms of collective behavior examined in this chapter obviously have differing properties. Based on the analysis at the micro level of the structure of these systems, it is possible to make predictions about the systemic behavior, that is, the macro level. The analysis of escape panics and hostile crowds in particular yielded several predictions that were referred to earlier in the chapter; it is useful to restate them here with several additions.

1. In a physical escape panic the greater the focus of attention on one or a few persons (that is, the greater the heterogeneity with respect to focus of attention), the less likely a panic will occur.
2. In a bank panic (single stage of action) there should be no such effect.
3. In a hostile crowd the greater the focus of attention on one or a few persons, then the more likely it is that the crowd will take some hostile or expressive action, and the more organized that action will be.
4. In a hostile crowd the greater the heterogeneity among individuals with respect to their normative constraints (holding constant the average degree of normative constraint and the commonality of interests), the more likely it is that the crowd will break out into hostile or expressive collective action.
5. Training persons to exit in an orderly fashion and to direct attention to a designated leader will be valuable for preventing escape panics (sequence of actions) but not bank panics (single stage of action).

6. In an escape panic the more prominent an individual's position in the crowd (the greater the attention directed to him), the more likely he will be to exhibit orderly exit behavior.
7. The larger a crowd is in absolute numbers, the more likely it is to break out into hostile or expressive collective action.
8. The larger a crowd is in absolute numbers, the greater is the likelihood that a panic will occur in a physical escape situation.
9. Such a relation will not hold for bank panics.
10. Physical escape panics (sequence of actions) should show greater variability in outcome when circumstances are similar than is true for bank panics (single action).
11. Contagious beliefs should arise at times of extensive social change, when rights of control have been withdrawn from institutions that have power.

« 10 »

The Demand for Effective Norms

Much sociological theory takes social norms as given and proceeds to examine individual behavior or the behavior of social systems when norms exist. Yet to do this without raising at some point the question of why and how norms come into existence is to forsake the more important sociological problem in order to address the less important. Whatever the reason for neglect of this question (and it differs for different theorists), I will show in this chapter and the next that two simple conditions, taken together, are sufficient for the emergence of norms. The first of these, to be examined in this chapter, is a condition under which a demand for effective norms will arise. The second, to be examined in the next chapter, is a condition under which that demand will be satisfied. Both conditions may be described as social-structural.

As much as any other concept in the social sciences, a norm is a property of a social system, not of an actor within it. It is a concept that has come to play an extensive role in theories developed by some sociologists. The reasons are fundamental. The concept of a norm, existing at a macrosocial level and governing the behavior of individuals at a microsocial level, provides a convenient device for explaining individual behavior, taking the social system as given. This device has been especially useful for those sociologists characterized by Sorokin (1928) as members of the sociologistic school of social theorists, of which Emile Durkheim was the most prominent member. Durkheim began with social organization and in a part of his work asked, "How is an individual's behavior affected by the social system within which he finds himself?" Answering this requires not the three components of social theory that I outlined in the first chapter of this book but only one—the transition from macro to micro. For many social theorists, Durkheim among them, the concept of a norm provides a means for making this transition.

For another school of social theory, of which Talcott Parsons is the most prominent member, the concept of a norm provides a basis for a principle of action whose role in the theory is comparable to that of maximizing utility in rational choice theory. The principle, something like "Persons behave in accordance with social norms," leaves examination of the content of norms as the theoretical task at the macro level. Whereas rational choice theory takes individual interests as given and attempts to account for the functioning of social systems, normative theory takes social norms as given and attempts to account for individual behavior.

Apart from its role in social theory, the use of the concept of a norm is important in describing how societies function. This is especially so for the description of traditional stable societies. A description of the functioning of the caste system in India that did not use the concept of dharma, which means something like "duty" or "appropriate behavior" or "behavior in accordance with accepted norms," would hardly be possible.[1] Stable or slowly changing norms constitute an important component of a stable society's self-governing mechanisms.

Both the evident importance of norms in the functioning of societies and the importance of a norm as a concept throughout the history of social theory underlie the importance of this concept in contemporary social theory. It has not one but two entries in the *Encyclopedia of the Social Sciences* (both written by sociologists), and one of them begins with this sentence: "No concept is invoked more often by social scientists in explanations of human behavior than 'norm.'" For example, Dahrendorf (by no means one of those sociologists most wedded to the concept), in an essay on the origin of social inequality, states, "The origin of inequality is thus to be found in the existence in all human societies of norms of behavior to which sanctions are attached . . . the derivation suggested here has the advantage of leading back to presuppositions (the existence of norms and the necessity of sanctions) which at least in the context of social theory may be taken as axiomatic" (1968, p. 104).

Norms may be taken as axiomatic by many sociologists, but for others they constitute an unacceptable deus ex machina—a concept brought in at the macrosocial level to explain social behavior, yet itself left unexplained.

Some rational choice theorists, armed with maximization of utility as a principle of action, regard the concept of a norm as altogether unnecessary. To take this stance, however, is to ignore important processes in the functioning of social systems and thus to limit the theory. It is one thing to refuse to take norms as starting points for social theory; it is quite another to ignore their existence altogether. In this book I refuse to take norms as given; in this chapter I ask how norms can emerge and be maintained among a set of rational individuals.

Social norms enter the theory developed here in the following way: They specify what actions are regarded by a set of persons as proper or correct, or improper or incorrect. They are purposively generated, in that those persons who initiate or help maintain a norm see themselves as benefiting from its being observed or harmed by its being violated. Norms are ordinarily enforced by sanctions, which are either rewards for carrying out those actions regarded as correct or punishments for carrying out those actions regarded as incorrect.

1. See O'Flaherty and Derrett (1978).

Those subscribing to a norm, or, as I will say, those holding a norm, claim a right to apply sanctions and recognize the right of others holding the norm to do so. Persons whose actions are subject to norms (who themselves may or may not hold the norm) take into account the norms, and the accompanying potential rewards or punishments, not as absolute determinants of their actions, but as elements which affect their decisions about what actions it will be in their interests to carry out.

In the preceding paragraph I do not give an explicit definition of a norm but only indicate its function. The explicit definition is, however, important because it derives from the conception of rights discussed in Chapter 3 and because it may not include everything that is ordinarily meant by the concept of a norm. I will say that a norm concerning a specific action exists when the socially defined right to control the action is held not by the actor but by others. As discussed in Chapter 3, this implies that there is a consensus in the social system or subsystem that the right to control the action is held by others. By the definition of authority, this means that others have authority over the action, authority that is not voluntarily vested in them, either unilaterally or as part of an exchange, but is created by the social consensus that placed the right in their hands. The right that is relevant to the definition of a norm is not a legally defined right or a right based on a formal rule imposed by an actor having authority. It is, rather, an informal or socially defined right. It may exist in the absence of a legally defined right or in opposition to a legally defined right, as is the case when a norm is in conflict with a law.

With this definition, the question concerning the conditions under which an effective norm will arise becomes a question concerning the conditions under which there will come to be a consensus that the right to control an action is held by persons other than the actor, and the conditions under which that consensus can be enforced.

It is important to note that this definition is a very specific and perhaps narrow one. No norm exists as long as the individual actor holds the right to his own action, and no norm exists if no right has come into existence. A norm exists only when others assume the right to affect the direction an actor's action will take. But *when* does this happen? This chapter is aimed at answering this question. There are, however, additional questions to be answered if norms are to be fully understood.

A norm may be embedded in a social system in a more fundamental way: The norm may be internal to the individual carrying out the action, with sanctions applied by that individual to his own actions. In such a case a norm is said to be internalized. An individual feels internally generated rewards for performing actions that are proper according to an internalized norm or feels internally generated punishments for performing actions that are improper according to an internalized norm. How and when does this happen?

There is interdependence among norms such that many norms are part of a structure of norms. The most elaborate of such structures are those described by dharma in India and analogous systems in other societies with long cultural traditions. How do these structures come into being?

These questions pose substantial tasks for the theorist. First is the task of establishing the conditions under which a norm with a particular content will arise. This includes determining why a norm does not always arise when the existence of an effective norm would be in the interests of all or most persons. Related to this are the tasks of specifying who will come to hold the norm and whose actions will be the target of the norm. Another task is determining the strength and prevalence of sanctions, recognizing that applying a sanction may entail costs for the sanctioner. Related to this is determining what kinds of sanctions will be applied, since there are a variety of sanctions that may be applied (and it is empirically evident that various kinds of sanctions are applied, ranging from those that damage or enhance reputations to those that impose physical damage or provide material benefits). In addition, there are theoretical tasks concerning the internalization of a norm. Why do persons attempt to induce internalization in others in the first place? Under what conditions will those who hold a norm attempt to induce internalization, and under what conditions will they use only external sanctions? Why will a person be receptive to attempts by others to internalize norms? Finally, there is the task of describing and accounting for interconnections among norms. What kinds of relationships exist among norms, how do those relationships arise, and how is the role that norms play in a social system affected by these relationships?

It is useful to begin by locating the concept of a norm, as well as the theoretical activity of this chapter, in the context of the three components which I have proposed as necessary to social theory: the macro-to-micro transition, purposive action at the micro level, and the micro-to-macro transition. Norms are macro-level constructs, based on purposive actions at the micro level but coming into existence under certain conditions through a micro-to-macro transition. Once in existence, they lead, under certain conditions, to actions of individuals (that is, sanctions or threat of sanctions) which affect the utilities and thus the actions of the individuals to whom the sanctions have been or might be applied. Thus norms constitute a social construction which is a part of a feedback process, involving either negative feedback, which if effective discourages and dampens certain actions, or positive feedback, which if effective further encourages certain actions.

The emergence of norms is in some respects a prototypical micro-to-macro transition, because the process must arise from individual actions yet a norm itself is a system-level property which affects the further actions of individuals, both the sanctions applied by individuals who hold the norm and the actions in conformity with the norm. A diagram analogous to Figure 1.2 but illustrating the emergence of a norm begins at the micro level and ends there as well, with individual sanctions and conformity to the norm, as shown in Figure 10.1.

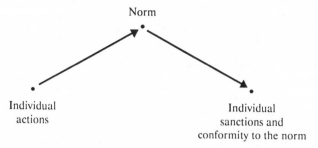

Figure 10.1   Relations of micro and macro levels in the emergence of a norm.

Examples of Norms and Sanctions

Some sense of what is meant by norms and sanctions can be gained by considering several examples.

1. A three-year-old child, walking with its mother on a sidewalk in Berlin, unwraps a small piece of candy and drops the cellophane on the sidewalk. An older woman who is passing by scolds the child for dropping the cellophane and admonishes the mother for not disciplining the child. A three-year-old child, walking with its mother on a sidewalk in New York City, unwraps a piece of cellophane and drops the paper on the sidewalk. An older woman is passing by but says nothing, not even noticing the action of the child. Several questions are raised by this example: Why does the woman in Berlin assume the right to scold the child and admonish the mother? Why does a woman in a similar circumstance in New York City not do the same? Does the woman in New York not feel she has the right to scold the child, or does her failure to act arise from other sources?

2. In an organization which provides free coffee and tea to its employees, one employee who drinks tea goes down with his cup to the hot water dispenser. All the tea bags are gone, but he expresses no dismay, remarking to another person standing there, "This often happens, but I have taken some tea bags back to my office just for such occasions." The other person responds in a disapproving way, "It's people like you, stashing tea bags away, who create the problem." This example also raises questions: How did the second person come to acquire a right to express disapproval? And why did the first person leave himself open for such a comment, by his remarks? Furthermore, why does he accept the disapproval of the second person, apparently acknowledging the right of the second person to impose this sanction?

3. A high-school girl on a date at a beach house finds herself in a crowd in which the others, including her date, are smoking marijuana. The others encourage her to do so as well, showing disapproval and disdain of her reluctance. That reluctance, in turn, is produced by her knowledge that her parents would disapprove. This example raises questions about conflict: Can there be two conflicting

norms governing the same action? If so, then what determines which one, if either, will govern? And if conflicting norms do occur, in what class of situations do they arise?

4. Among the Sarakatsan nomads in northwestern Greece, norms are very strong. Campbell reports (restated in Merry, 1984, p. 283): "In one very poor family, the father failed to defend his son against the insult of being pelted with dung by another little boy, displaying to onlookers his inability to protect the honor of his family in more important ways. The same man looks dirty and uncouth despite gossip about his unkempt appearance, and his wife is criticized for laughing and joking, as it implies that she may be guilty of sexual immodesty. Although their daughter is apparently virtuous and chaste, she is tainted by her mother's immodesty, and no honorable man seeks her hand." This example raises a question about the effectiveness of norms. There are apparently normative sanctions imposed by others against various actions of this family, but the sanctions appear less effective than one might expect.

5. In Gush Emunim settlements of the West Bank in Israel, strong norms require the men of the community to form a minyan of ten or more and pray in the synagogue each day. Some men do, and some don't. Those who don't claim to be busy with their work. They stay indoors at the time when others are going to pray. This example raises the issue of the conflict between the demands of daily life and the demands of norms. How are norms maintained in the face of such conflicts? The demands of daily life are ever present and are associated with interests that have material consequences. Norms often demand, such as in cases like this, actions which are unrelated to consequences that the individual, or even the whole group, will experience. How are the norms maintained?

6. Elias (1982) traces the evolution of norms concerning table manners in French provinces, using writings about etiquette. Elias shows how these norms, which began by proscribing only the most offensive actions (such as coughing up a piece of meat at the table) evolved into the most elaborate prescriptions of what to do at the table. Furthermore, the norms differed in different social groups, and there was a hierarchy of elaboration, corresponding to social status and having its peak at the king's court. This example raises questions about how and why norms become increasingly elaborate over time, as well as why manners are more elaborate in groups of higher social status.

Distinctions among Norms

The diversity among the examples above suggests that it is useful to make some classifications of norms. Although this cannot be fully done at this point in this exposition, a start may be made.

First, norms are directed at certain actions, which I will call focal actions. In the example about the three-year-old and the cellophane candy wrapper in Berlin, the focal action is dropping the wrapper on the sidewalk (more generally, any action that has the effect of littering the sidewalk).

Some norms discourage or proscribe a focal action, and I will call these proscriptive norms. Other norms, such as the norm to smoke marijuana among the young people at the beach house or the norm among members of Gush Emunim settlements to form a minyan and pray every day at the synagogue, encourage or prescribe a focal action. I will call these prescriptive norms. Proscriptive norms provide negative feedback in the system, damping out the focal action; prescriptive norms provide positive feedback, expanding the focal action. When there are only two possible actions, of course, one is prescribed and the other is proscribed by the same norm. For example, the norm of walking to the right when encountering another pedestrian walking in the opposite direction is simultaneously prescriptive and proscriptive. The distinction is meaningful only when the number of alternative courses of action is greater than two.

For any norm there is a certain class of actors whose actions or potential actions are the focal actions. The statement "Children should be seen and not heard" specifies a norm for which children constitute this class. I will call members of such a class targets of the norm, or target actors. There is also a class of actors who would benefit from the norm, potentially hold the norm, and are potential sanctioners of the target actors. These are actors who, if the norm has come into being, assume the right to partially control the focal action and are seen by others who would benefit from the norm to have this right. For the norm specified by the statement above, parents, or adults more generally, are those who hold the norm. It is possible that children also hold the norm, but the operation of the norm and its supporting sanctions does not depend on this. I will call those who would benefit from the norm and thus assume the right to control the target action (who are also ordinarily the potential sanctioners) beneficiaries of the norm. The current beneficiaries of the norm may be those who initiated it, or they may have merely continued the enforcement of a norm initiated by persons who preceded them.

For some norms, such as the one concerning children mentioned above, the targets of the norm and the beneficiaries are not the same persons. The norm benefits one set of actors and is directed toward actions of another set. I will label such norms disjoint norms because the set of beneficiaries and the set of targets are disjoint, resulting in a physical separation of opposing interest. The beneficiaries have an interest in the norm being observed, and the targets have an interest in the focal action being unmodified by the norm.

For many norms, however, including all those described in the earlier examples (except for the norm about not smoking marijuana held by the parents of the high-school girl), the set of beneficiaries of the norm coincides with the set of targets. In such cases, the interests favoring observance of the norm and those opposing its observance are contained within the same actors. Each actor is simultaneously beneficiary and target of the norm. I will call norms of this sort conjoint norms.

The distinction between disjoint and conjoint norms reflects only the extremes of the variations that may occur. Figure 10.2 shows those extremes, along with

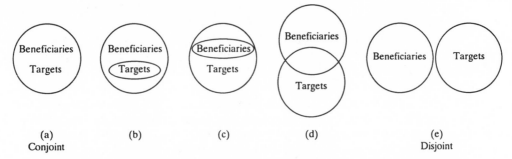

Figure 10.2   Inclusion relations of beneficiaries and targets of a norm for different
types of norms.

intermediate cases. In cases b, c, and d, some persons are both beneficiaries and
targets. In case b there are also some beneficiaries who are not targets. An
example is the norm against sexual relations before marriage, which is held not
only by unmarried persons, the targets, but also by married persons. In case c
there are targets who are not beneficiaries. For example, norms about proper
behavior held by members of a community are directed not only at community
members as targets, but also at strangers. In case d some beneficiaries are not
targets, and some targets are not beneficiaries.

A clarification of what is meant by the term "sanction" is also useful. If
holding a norm is assumption of the right to partially control a focal action and
recognition of other norm holders' similar right, then a sanction is the exercise of
that right. A sanction may be negative, directed at inhibiting a focal action which
is proscribed by a norm, or positive, directed at inducing a focal action which is
prescribed by a norm. I will use the terms "sanction" and "effective sanction"
interchangeably, indicating by either an action on the part of a beneficiary which
has some effect in moving the focal action in the direction intended by the
sanctioner.

One final distinction concerns selection of a focal action, an action to be
discouraged or encouraged by a norm, from a set of mutually exclusive actions.
In some cases the selection of the focal action is largely arbitrary, but in others it
is not. The former is exemplified by the convention of driving on the right side of
the road (or, in England and Australia, on the left). It is arbitrary whether the action defined as correct is driving on the right or driving on the left. Once the
convention has been established, however, all are better off if each follows the
convention. The interests in a particular direction of action depend on whether it
is the action being carried out by others. If a convention has established the
direction of a norm, I will call the norm a conventional norm.[2]

2. Ullmann-Margalit (1977, p. 97) calls these coordination norms and distinguishes between
those that arise through convention and those adopted by decree. I will not make use of this
distinction.

For many norms the focal action has not been arbitrarily selected. The targets' interests lie in the direction of action opposing observance of the norm, and the beneficiaries' interests lie in the direction of action favoring observance of the norm. These interests in particular directions of action would remain, whether or not the norm existed and independent of others' directions of action. In this case the direction of the norm depends on more than convention. I will call these essential norms. This last distinction can be illustrated, as Ullmann-Margalit (1977) has done and as I will do shortly, using simple payoff matrices from the theory of games.[3]

The First Condition: Externalities of Actions and the Demand for a Norm

In Chapter 2 I indicated that one distinction which is important for the functioning of social systems is that between events that have consequences only for those who control them and events that have external consequences (that is, externalities) for actors who have no control over them. The latter events are intrinsically of interest to actors other than those who control them. When such events are actions, there are two kinds of externalities of actions: When an action benefits others, the action has positive externalities; when an action is harmful to others, the action has negative externalities. If an action benefits some and hurts others, then its externalities are positive for the first set of actors and negative for the second.

An action that has externalities generates interests in the action among those actors who experience the externalities. Yet there is no general way in which the consequences of the action for those affected actors can enter the utility function of the actor taking the action. Actors harmed by an action that benefits the actor in control of it experience negative externalities, as exemplified by nonsmokers sitting near a smoker. Those benefited by an action that benefits the actor controlling it experience positive externalities, as exemplified by passersby who benefit from a householder's removing snow from the sidewalk in front of his house. The problem for those other actors in the first situation is how to limit the action which is harming them (and how much to limit it). The problem in the second situation is how to encourage and increase the action (and to what level it should be encouraged).

A special case of the latter problem is that of paying the cost of a public good when each actor's action has beneficial consequences for others, by helping to bring about the public good, but the benefits to himself are less than the costs he will incur. Only if enough actors can be induced jointly to carry out the action to

3. Ullmann-Margalit distinguishes three kinds of norms, which she calls prisoner's dilemma norms, coordination norms, and norms of partiality. These correspond approximately to what I have termed essential norms, conventional norms, and disjoint norms, respectively. Essential norms, however, to use my terminology, may be disjoint or conjoint, whereas Ullmann-Margalit's three classes are mutually exclusive.

make the benefits exceed the costs for each will the public good be provided. A parallel problem exists for a public bad; for example, in overgrazing of a commons, each herd-owner's increase in grazing will increase his own benefits, but at a cost to others. Only if all the herd-owners with access to the commons can be induced to limit grazing by their animals will the grazing be reduced to the level at which the land will produce maximum nutrition.

When an action generates externalities for others, they may be able to make their interests felt through wholly individualistic means. For example, one of them may engage in an exchange with the actor whose action imposes the externalities, offering or threatening something to bring about the outcome he desires. But this may not be possible if the externalities are spread among several actors, no one of whom can profitably make such an exchange.

When exchange is possible, this gives a solution which is a special case of that described by Coase in "The Problem of Social Cost" (1960). The general solution is a market in rights of control, in which the actors who do not have control of the action may purchase rights of control from those who do, the former being limited only by their interest in the action and their resources. It is easy to see that if there are no transaction costs in such a market, the outcome will be a social optimum (which is defined only relative to the initial endowments of resources of the various parties in the market), at which no further exchanges are mutually beneficial. Those hurt by the level of action existing at the outcome would be even more hurt by parting with the resources that the actor controlling the action would take to limit it further.

In the case of a public good, each of the actors who is benefited by the actions of others would exchange rights of control of his own action for rights of partial control of the action of each of the others. For example, each resident in a town might agree to the building of a public park and to contribute an equal fraction of the cost. This constitutes a multilateral exchange in which each gives up the right not to contribute in return for the giving up of the same right by each of the others. (I put aside for the present the question of how such a multilateral exchange might be organized.)

Similar markets have been developed in regulation of environmental pollution. The amount of total pollution allowed is not set by market forces, but marketing of rights to pollute occurs among those who operate pollution-generating plants (see Noll, 1983). Yet there are many activities in society in which markets in rights of control cannot easily come into being, for one reason or another. In a social situation in which one person is smoking and another finds it irritating, the second can hardly say to the first, "How much will you take to stop smoking?" A high-school girl at a party where all others present would like her to smoke marijuana but who knows her parents would not can hardly ask for bids from the two opposed sets of others for control of her action. There is a wide range of situations in which an action has extensive externalities but a market in rights of control of the action is either impracticable or illegal.

The condition under which interests in a norm, and thus demands for a norm, arise is that an action has similar externalities for a set of others, yet markets in rights of control of the action cannot easily be established, and no single actor can profitably engage in an exchange to gain rights of control. Such interests do not themselves constitute a norm, nor do they ensure that one will come into being. They create a basis for a norm, a *demand* for a norm on the part of those experiencing certain externalities.

The externalities created by the action may, as indicated earlier, be positive or negative. In high schools, for example, positive externalities are created by athletes who contribute to the success of a team, which in turn contributes to the school's general standing in the community (which in turn contributes to the other students' feelings of well-being or pride). Often a norm does arise, one which encourages potentially good athletes to devote their energies to interscholastic sports. In contrast, students who get especially high grades create negative externalities for other students, insofar as the teachers grade on the curve. High-performing students increase for other students the effort necessary to receive good grades, thus making matters more difficult for others. Often a norm arises in this case also; students impose a norm that restricts the amount of effort put into schoolwork.[4]

How a norm actually comes into being once a demand is created by externalities is a matter which I will examine in Chapter 11. But the genesis of a norm is based in externalities of an action which cannot be overcome by simple transactions that would put control of the action in the hands of those experiencing the externalities.

Several points follow from this central premise. One implication is that the potential beneficiaries of the norm will be all those who are affected in the same direction by the action. If a norm does arise, it will be those persons who will claim a right to have partial control over the action and who will exercise their claim by attempting to impose normative sanctions on the actor performing the action to induce the direction that benefits them, often at that actor's expense. A further implication is that a potential conflict of norms arises when an action has positive externalities for one set of persons and negative externalities for another. In the example of the high-school girl whose friends' approval is contingent on her smoking marijuana and whose parents' approval is contingent on her not doing so (or on their ignorance of her doing so), there are such opposing externalities. If she does not smoke, she dampens the party, destroys the consensus, and perhaps reminds some of those present of their similar normative conflicts. If she does smoke and her parents learn of it, they are made unhappy as their pride and trust in her are undercut.

The structure of interests created by externalities in which norms have their genesis may be presented more systematically by using simple situations whose

4. Of course, when academic activities are organized interscholastically, this can generate a prescriptive norm concerning studying. Striking cases of this may be found in a description of statewide competition in academic subjects among rural schools in Kentucky (Stuart, 1950, p. 90).

Table 10.1   Payoff matrix for two-person joint project.

		A₂	
		Contribute	Not contribute
A₁	Contribute	3, 3	-3, 6
	Not contribute	6, -3	0, 0

outcomes can be described by payoff matrices such as are used in theory of games. For example, suppose that two persons are told separately, "You may take either of two actions: contribute $9 to a common project, or contribute nothing. For each $3 that is contributed, an additional $1 will be earned by the project (that is, there will be a return of $4 for each $3 contributed). The final total will be divided equally between the two of you, regardless of who made a contribution." Each can assess the net gains or losses for himself and for the other, for each combination of actions. These are expressed in Table 10.1, where the values of the outcome (in dollars) for each of the persons (A₁ and A₂) are given in each cell.[5]

If neither contributes, there is no gain or loss for either. If A₁ contributes and A₂ does not, A₁'s contribution of $9 plus the $3 earned will be divided equally, giving $6 to each. For A₂ this will be a net gain, as indicated in the upper-right-hand cell of the table. But for A₁ the original $9 contribution must be subtracted, giving him a net loss of $3. The gain and loss are reversed for the case in which A₂ contributes and A₁ does not.

This situation creates a pair of actions, each having externalities for the other actor. As Table 10.1 indicates, A₁'s action (of contributing or not contributing) makes a difference of $6 (between 3 and −3 or between 6 and 0) to A₂, and A₂'s action makes a difference of $6 to A₁. Furthermore, in both cases the externalities go in the direction opposite to the actor's own interests. Each actor is better off by not contributing (whichever action the other takes), but not contributing makes the other actor worse off. Finally, the external effects of the other's action are greater for each than are the direct effects of his own action.

5. This payoff structure is that of a prisoner's dilemma. See Luce and Raiffa (1957) or Rapoport and Chammah (1965) for a discussion of this game.

A_1's action makes a difference of only \$3 to him, but A_2's action makes a difference of \$6—and similarly for A_2.

The result of this situation is that each has an incentive not to contribute (since he will lose \$3 by so doing), and if both do not, each gets nothing. Yet if both did contribute, each would gain \$3. The optimal action for each actor gives a social outcome which is not an optimum. Both would be better off if both took the action which is *not* individually optimal, that is, if both contributed to the project.

Much has been written about this structure of outcomes, but most of it is not of interest here. (For references to some of this literature, see Axelrod, 1984.) What is of interest is Ullmann-Margalit's (1977) discussion of this structure as calling for or generating one type of norm, which she calls prisoner's dilemma (or PD) norms. Her argument is that such a structure of outcomes creates an incentive for all parties involved to set up a norm that will constrain the behavior of each in the direction of carrying out the action that is better for the others (in the example above, contributing to the joint project). In the terminology introduced earlier, such a structure of interdependence of actions creates externalities for each and thus an interest on the part of each in the creation of a norm.

In situations of this sort, however, where two persons' actions affect each other in the way shown in Table 10.1, a norm is not necessary at all. Either person can propose an exchange in which each gives the other rights of control to his action and gets rights of control of the other's action.[6] Each has resources (his own action) that are of more value to the other than the resources held by the other (the other's action). Thus by exchanging rights of control each gets something that is worth more to him than what he gives up. Each will exercise the control over the other's action in the direction which benefits himself, and in so doing will bring about a social optimum. In the example above A_1 will contribute A_2's \$9, A_2 will contribute A_1's \$9, and both will gain \$3 as the outcome.

Where there is a pair of interdependent actions for which the self-interested action of each imposes negative (or positive) externalities on the other that are greater than the benefits (or costs) that the other's own self-interested action brings, a mutually profitable exchange is always possible in principle. Logistics may, of course, preclude such exchange. In the game-theoretic analysis of the prisoner's dilemma, the possibility of exchange is excluded, because by assumption the players cannot communicate. But no such constraint is necessary here. Norms can arise only where there is communication; thus bilateral exchange is possible in all those two-actor cases where the possibility for a norm exists.

---

6. As far as I know, Erling Schild and Gudmund Hernes were the first (independently, in 1971) to point out that the simplest social solution to the prisoner's dilemma is exchange of control between the two players, an action which is rational for each. Bernholz (1984) has shown that Sen's paradox of a Paretian liberal (discussed in some detail in Chapter 13), where the payoff structure is that of a prisoner's dilemma, is solved in the same way. If the exchange is not instantaneous, of course, but requires a promise on the part of one or both, it becomes necessary to introduce some form of retribution.

There is an apparent exception in those cases where communication exists before and after the action, but not during the action itself. However, any agreements reached before the action or any retributions taken after the action need make no reference to a norm, but can be treated wholly within the framework of bilateral exchange—although possibly of course requiring introduction of notions of trust and mutual trust, as discussed in Chapter 5.[7]

The one true exception, in which the social optimum is not attained by an individualistic solution or by a bilateral exchange, is where the actions are pairwise, but the two actors are not in contact either before or after the action (or will meet only in the distant future), and thus have no opportunity either to make an agreement or to carry out the terms of a prior agreement.[8] In that case a norm, in which sanctions are imposed by others who are in contact with the actors after the action, can bring about a social optimum; bilateral exchange cannot.

It is best to clarify what the word "exchange" implies in the current context, for the example may otherwise be misleading. The imagery evoked by exchange in the context of this example is that one actor approaches another with an offer, "You let me make your decision, and I will let you make mine" or "Let us contribute together" or something similar. This is certainly what happens in some cases. In an examination of the emergence of norms, however, it is appropriate to conceive of a succession of comparable projects, extending over time, in which a new decision arises each time. This expands the possibilities to incorporate exchanges, implicit or explicit, that cover two or more projects (for example, "If you fail to contribute this time, I will not contribute next time"). This conception is especially relevant for those cases in which it is not logistically possible to exchange control or rights to control on a given occasion. It is also relevant for those cases in which there is no project involving simultaneous contribution but separate actions of each actor which exhibit the same pattern of internal and external effects. For example, a person must decide whether to take an action, such as watching his neighbor's house while the neighbor is away, that has a net cost for him but benefits his neighbor. His neighbor, in a similar situation, must make the same decision.

---

7. Whether or not such bilateral exchanges are considered to be norms is purely a matter of convention. I choose not to consider them to be norms because they do not exhibit the fundamental problem that must be overcome when no mutually profitable two-person exchange is possible but some n-person exchange is possible, where n is greater than 2. This fundamental problem, called the second-order free-rider problem, is discussed in Chapter 11.

8. This is a fundamental point on which Axelrod (1984, p. 49), who discusses the growth of cooperation between two players in iterated prisoner's dilemmas, exhibits confusion. At some points he seems to be asserting that pairwise interactions in large populations, where the same two parties will meet only very infrequently, will generate the same cooperation as found in his pairwise "tournaments." In general, however, Axelrod's work in that book demonstrates the point made here: that bilateral exchanges, explicit or implicit, are sufficient, without introduction of a norm, to arrive at a social optimum in pairwise interactions with externalities. See Coleman (1986b) for examination of social-structural conditions under which contact among individuals does not allow such agreements, implicit or explicit, to be effective.

Another type of implicit exchange, which may be more common empirically, is not precisely equivalent to those described above. If two actors have a social relationship, which as described in Chapter 12 consists of a set of obligations and expectations (assumed for the present to be symmetric), various actions by each may affect the outcome of an exchange. If A_1 wants to prevent an action of A_2, which imposes a cost on him of \$6 but benefits A_2 by only \$3, A_1 has only to introduce into the negotiations some other event which he controls that has a cost for him of less than \$6 and a benefit for A_2 of more than \$3. A promise or a threat with respect to this event may serve A_1 as well as, or better than, the action which is analogous to the action of A_2 he wants to control. To state it differently, one actor need not use as a sanction for another actor the same kind of action as the action he is sanctioning. For example, if one actor is late for a meeting, the other need not show up late for the next meeting; he can express disapproval, or he can threaten to break off the meetings altogether (if the meetings are of sufficient interest to the first actor to make this a credible threat). The other events may include some for which the costs to the sanctioning actor are very small yet the other actor's interest may be sufficiently great that the sanction is effective.

It is important to recognize these additional possibilities that actors may have for sanctioning one another because they lend importance to the existence of other events linking the actors. Attention to these additional possible sanctions is also important because of the potential asymmetries in sanctioning that may result from inequalities in actors' control of events of interest to others.[9]

Systems of More Than Two Actors

It is when pairwise exchanges cannot bring about a social optimum that interests in a norm arise. This may be illustrated by expanding the joint project described earlier to a common project involving three actors. Again, each has the alternative of contributing \$9 or nothing. For every \$3 contributed, the product will be \$4. The total product will be divided equally among the three. Table 10.2 shows the outcomes for each combination of actions. Since the situation is symmetric for the three actors, these outcomes can be summarized more compactly, as shown in Table 10.3.

The situation here is fundamentally different from that shown in Table 10.1. It is not possible for two of the three actors to exchange control over their actions and gain by so doing. If there are no contributions, giving no net gain or loss to each, and then A_1 exchanges control with A_2, each contributing for the other,

9. Another source of asymmetry is hidden by the symmetry of this example. Even for activities for which all actors' similar actions impose externalities on the others, the externalities may be unequal, providing sanctioning opportunities for some actors that do not exist for others. This is related to interpersonal comparison of utilities, and, as will be evident later, a correct untangling of that issue will be important for the analysis of norms as well as other aspects of the social system.

Table 10.2   Payoff matrix for three-person common project.

	A_3			
	Contribute		Not contribute	
	A_2		A_2	
	Contribute	Not contribute	Contribute	Not contribute
Contribute	3, 3, 3	-1, 8, -1	-1, -1, 8	-5, 4, 4
A_1 **Not contribute**	8, -1, -1	4, 4, -5	4, -5, 4	0, 0, 0

they end up losing $1 while A_3 gains $8. If A_3 is contributing, A_1 and A_2 each gain $4 without an exchange. If they exchange control, with each contributing for the other, the gain for each is $3, making each of them $1 worse off than they would be without the exchange.

Only if *both* A_2 and A_3 can be induced to change their actions from not contributing to contributing, contingent on A_1's contribution, does it become profitable for A_1 to join in such an arrangement. In such a case the outcome for each changes from no gain to a gain of $3. Thus a compact among the three is necessary to bring about a gain to each. One form of compact is a norm, by which the right to contribute or not is no longer held by each actor, but for each is held by the other two. It is in this way that it can be said that each comes to have interests in a norm.

The structure of interdependence in this case is one in which, if a norm arises at all, it will be a conjoint norm, with the same actors being targets and beneficiaries. It will be an essential norm, not a conventional one, because there

Table 10.3   Summary of outcomes for three-person common project.

Number of contributions	Gains or losses to—	
	Contributors	Noncontributors
0	—	0
1	−5	4
2	−1	8
3	3	—

is one direction of action that benefits each (contributing) and one that does not. It would be possible to construct a similar artificial example and matrix of outcomes for which interdependence would generate interest in a conventional norm. But that is straightforward and self-evident, and I will not present it here.[10] For a disjoint norm the matter is somewhat different, and I will put aside examination of such norms until a later point. It is, however, useful to examine a question that arises concerning some conventional norms, where the externalities imposed by one actor's action on the others are not immediately apparent.

Do Norms Arise Only When There Are Externalities of Actions?

There are some norms which seem not to be generated by an action's imposition of externalities on others. For example, in high schools certain subgroups of girls or boys will have strong norms about how their members dress.[11] In the 1950s ducktail haircuts constituted observance of a norm by certain groups of boys. Certain groups of girls wore bobby socks (or even a particular color of bobby socks); certain groups of boys wore white bucks, and others black leather jackets. In Jerusalem some women keep their heads and arms covered, and some men wear black yarmulkes, reflecting membership in an orthodox Jewish community characterized by a particular set of religious observances. In Cairo some women dress wholly in black with heavy black veils covering their faces, reflecting membership in a Muslim community characterized by a particular set of religious observances. In rural Pennsylvania some women wear bonnets and plain-colored clothes without buttons, reflecting membership in an Amish community characterized by a particular set of religious observances.

10. A table of payoffs that can generate a conventional norm, exemplified by the norm of walking to the right or to the left when passing on a sidewalk, is as follows:

		A_3			
		Left		Right	
		A_2		A_2	
		Left	Right	Left	Right
A_1	Left	0, 0, 0	-4, -6, -4	-4, -4, -6	-6, -4, -4
	Right	-6, -4, -4	-4, -4, -6	-4, -6, -4	0, 0, 0

11. See *The Adolescent Society* (Coleman, 1961) for various examples among high-school students.

All these norms about dress are conventional norms, despite the doctrinal rationale for the direction that some of them take. But how is it that a member's action in conformity with the particular norm creates a positive externality for other members of the group? For persons who have come to constitute a group and want to differentiate themselves from others, common dress constitutes a very efficient means of doing so. Each member's obeying the norm strengthens the expression of group solidarity and the differentiation from others. Observance of rules about dress is similar to observance of dietary norms, rules of etiquette, and other differentiating characteristics (see Goode, 1960; 1978).[12] Observance by fellow members aids and supports each member, and failure to observe constitutes a threat to the solidarity of the group. This is an instance in which a derivation from theory can aid research. Measurement of the strength of dress codes and their degree of observance in a particular subgroup can show the strength of interest of the members in subgroup membership.

Dress codes illustrate a form of conventional norm for which externalities do not exist prior to and independent of the norm. They contrast with conventions such as driving on the right, for which negative externalities exist in the absence of the norm and the norm provides benefits by reducing them. Dress codes exist where the strength of members' interest in group membership is sufficiently great that an opportunity for positive externalities exists. The dress code makes possible those positive externalities by prescribing dress that will declare one's group identity to other members and to nonmembers.

Status Groups, Norms of Etiquette, and Standards of Speech

Norms of etiquette, such as those studied by Elias (1982) and mentioned earlier in this chapter, are somewhat different from norms about dress maintained by a group such as a religious group. As Elias showed, elementary norms of etiquette are essential norms, constraining the target actor's behavior so that it is attentive to the interests of those interacting with that actor. At the same time, however, norms of etiquette create a status group composed of those who conform to them. Because their actions attend to the interests of others in the vicinity, they can make a claim to be "better" than those who do not observe the norms. Action in conformity with a norm of etiquette creates a positive externality for members of the status group, who hold the norm, by differentiating them from those who do not hold it—just as in the case of religiously prescribed dress codes. Since membership in the status group is defined by conformity to the norm, however, anyone who acts in conformity with the norm can enter the group. The norm will not give a positive externality for members of the group unless conformity to the norm is sufficiently difficult that outsiders cannot easily enter the group.

---

12. Dietary restrictions may be more than conventional. Some have arisen for reasons of health or reasons of scarcity. For an examination of the use of rules of etiquette in differentiating one group from another, see Elias, 1982.

Thus the norm, which at the outset only constrains actions having negative externalities, has the potential to induce actions that bring positive externalities by creating a status group of those who hold the norm. That potential is realized, however, only if the norm is elaborated in such a way to make entry into the status group difficult. If a set of actors is capable of establishing a norm of etiquette to meet the demand for reducing negative externalities in interaction, then this set of actors, comprising a status group, is also capable of elaborating the norm to maintain the distinctiveness of that group. (The question of whether the set of actors will be able to establish a norm of etiquette is, of course, an open one, which cannot be answered merely by specifying that persons have common interests in eliminating negative externalities or encouraging positive ones. I will examine that question in Chapter 11.)

It is not only norms of etiquette that can be generated and used by status groups as described above. Standards of speech, elaborate norms of dress, or norms of fashion are used in the same way. A social system may contain a hierarchy of status groups, in which members of a group that is neither at the top nor at the bottom attempt both to conform to the norms of the next higher group and to maintain the norms of their group in order to keep out those below.

What I have outlined in this section indicates that sets of persons develop norms not only to serve as protective devices against actions that impose negative externalities, but also to perform positive services. This is more conjectural than much of the theory in this book and clearly requires empirical study, in order to test the theory and elaborate its details.

A Note on the Concept of Function in Social Theory

In the preceding examination of the use of norms by sets of actors, I have avoided using the term "function," although it would be natural to have written, for example, that "sets of persons develop norms not only to serve a protective function against actions that impose negative externalities, but also to perform positive functions for them." I have avoided using the term because of the confusion surrounding its use in social theory. In particular, radical versions of functional analysis have purported to explain the existence of a phenomenon by its function. In this context that would mean explaining the emergence of a norm by the functions it serves for the set of actors who hold it.

It should be clear, however, that the functions a norm serves for those who hold it, or, in the terms I have used, their interests in the norm, are not sufficient as an explanation of its emergence or continued existence. The fact that a set of actors is interested in gaining the right to control the actions of individual actors is not sufficient as an explanation for their coming to gain that right. In the explanation of the emergence of norms given in this book, that is only the first of two necessary conditions. The condition under which those interests will be realized, to be examined in the next chapter, is the second half of the explanation.

The common tendency of many theorists carrying out "functional analyses" to explain a phenomenon solely by its function is the principal failing of functional analysis as a theoretical paradigm. For a theorist to go beyond this, to examine how a phenomenon has come into existence, requires going from the macrosocial level down to the level of actors, thus abandoning the paradigm of functional analysis for a paradigm that, like the one used in this book, contains actors and a theory of action.[13]

What Constitutes Social Efficiency?

Most of the analysis of the preceding sections has been concerned with conjoint norms, for which the set of persons experiencing externalities from the focal action is the same as the set of persons who carry out the focal action and thereby impose externalities on others. In such a circumstance and with a group which is homogeneous, exemplified in Table 10.2, the concept of social efficiency, or a social optimum, is straightforward, because interests for and against the action are contained within the same actors. If the benefits that each obtains from his own action are less than the costs imposed by all others' similar action, then the emergence of a norm is socially efficient. All will be better off if there is a norm.[14] The achievement of social efficiency in this case lies in a redistribution of rights of control over each action to the group as a whole.[15] But with a group that is not homogeneous, it becomes more problematic to define social efficiency. The balancing of positive and negative interests in each actor's action is no longer straightforward. The difficulty is most easily seen by turning to disjoint norms, where the externalities are imposed by a set of actors disjoint from those experiencing the externalities, who are the potential holders of the norm.

How can one say whether a norm is socially efficient? In the case of a conjoint norm within a homogeneous group, the establishment of the norm either brings a gain to each member and is socially efficient or brings a loss to each and is inefficient. But establishment of a disjoint norm makes the beneficiaries better off (through the rights they gain) and the targets worse off (through the rights they lose). At this point Coase's 1960 paper on the problem of social cost becomes directly relevant. Coase was not concerned with norms but with the question of how cases involving externalities imposed by one actor on another should be decided in law. Who should pay the social costs? That problem is

13. See Nagel (1970) and Stinchcombe (1968) for examinations of the logic of functional analysis.

14. By a socially efficient state or a social optimum, I mean the analogue to economists' notion of economic efficiency. I do not mean the much weaker concept of a Pareto optimum. For a disjoint norm, both the existence of the norm and its absence are Pareto-optimal points, since no move from either state to the other can be made without hurting either the beneficiaries of the norm or its targets. Only one of the two states, however, is socially efficient. See Chapter 2 and Chapter 29 for fuller discussions of social efficiency.

15. This statement is given greater precision in Chapter 30.

closer to the problem of disjoint norms than is at first apparent—for law and social norms are close relatives in the family of social control mechanisms, and the structure of the situation examined by Coase (one actor or set of actors imposing externalities on a different set) is, according to the theory presented in this chapter, exactly that in which a demand for a disjoint norm arises.

Coase (1960) argued that legal allocation of rights to the actor or actors carrying out the activity that produced the externalities or to the actor or actors experiencing them was irrelevant to the question of whether the activity would continue (the Coase theorem). If the activity was economically efficient, it would continue (with rights to impose the externalities purchased by the actor producing them, if necessary); if the activity was not economically efficient, it would not continue (with rights to produce the externalities purchased from the actor producing them, if necessary). There are conditions attached to the Coase theorem, such as absence of transaction costs, the existence of a market value for the costs imposed by the activity, and negligible effects of the legal allocation of rights on the distribution of resources within which economic efficiency must be defined. The theorem is directly relevant to the case of disjoint norms, however, for Coase's point is that there is an economic value to the activity that produces the externalities and an economic cost created by the externalities, and if (but only if) the former exceeds the latter, the activity will continue, independent of who pays the costs. The possibility of transactions outside the context of the externalities themselves (that is, the possibility of purchase of rights by one party or the other) is what brings this about.

The implication of this theorem for disjoint norms is that if the externalities imposed by the activity are sufficiently great that the persons experiencing them are motivated to induce the actor to cease, and if those persons have the resources to make that motivation effective, then they will do so, whether or not a norm is in existence (that is, whether or not the informal rights to control the action are held by them). This implies that a norm (or a law) is superfluous and would make the existence of norms or laws inexplicable.

How is the logic of Coase's argument consistent with the existence of norms and laws? The answer lies in the assumption on which the Coase theorem is based—that there are no transaction costs in inducing the actor to cease carrying out the action when he has the rights.[16] There are, however, transaction costs in real social systems, and a norm can reduce the transactions necessary to achieve socially efficient outcomes. When rights are held by those experiencing the

---

16. There are other problems with the Coase theorem. If rights allocation does not matter, then the right to steal or to kill without fear of sanction should lead to outcomes no different from the outcomes arising in the absence of such rights: The potential victim need only buy off the predator at a mutually satisfactory price. In such a social system physical strength and access to weapons become the principal resources of value. More generally, the Coase theorem neglects the fact that rights allocations can affect the incentive to impose externalities on others (for example, in the form of threats); it treats externalities as necessary by-products of activities :arried out for other purposes.

externalities and those rights are recognized by the target actor, then the action is inhibited without any transaction occurring. Sanctions are unnecessary and will be applied in only two circumstances: when a target actor misinterprets the situation and incorrectly believes his power is sufficient to allow him successfully to ignore the norm; and when the target actor does have sufficient power, but the norm holders misinterpret the situation, believing they can successfully sanction the action.

The Importance of Other Resources for Disjoint Norms

Enforcement of what is socially optimal through the reallocation of rights and the threat of sanctions implies the possibility that the actors who experience the externalities can use their control over events *other than* the actions creating the externalities—events in which the target actor has an interest. It is their control of such events that allows the events to be used as sanctions or potential sanctions, and it is the importance (or "value") of those events that determines whether the sanctions will be effective.

When the social optimum is that an action not take place, the action will be constrained and the social optimum achieved only if those experiencing the externalities have the requisite social relationships to both bring a potentially effective norm into existence and make it effective. I will discuss this problem in the next chapter and will show some of the ways in which the potentially effective demand for a norm may be realized. The absence of social relationships among those experiencing the externalities will prevent the social optimum from being attained, if that optimum is observance of the relevant norm.

There is, however, a more important qualification, which concerns the existing distribution of rights and resources, that is, of control of events by actors. Just as in the case of economic efficiency, the social optimum is defined relative to an existing distribution of rights and resources (see Chapter 30). If that distribution is highly unequal, this implies that the interests of some actors count for much more than do the interests of others. Those actors having more power will be able to impose disjoint norms to govern the actions of those having less power, and they will be able to counter effectively norms imposed to govern their actions and to resist sanctions applied to enforce those norms.

This situation is illustrated by two kinds of examples from traditional societies. One concerns norms governing the actions of women. In many such societies there are stringent and effective norms governing the behavior of unmarried women, the behavior of married women, and the behavior of widows, but not similar norms governing the behavior of men. The target actors are women, but the actors benefiting from the constraints and ensuring that sanctions will be applied to violators are generally men of all ages and women older than the target actors, that is, actors other than the targets. Do these norms, together with their observance, give a social optimum? Social anthropologists with a functionalist orientation argue that they do (see Gluckman, 1955; 1963). That answer is correct, but only for the distribution of power that exists in such societies, a distribution in which men and older women have a great deal of power. If that highly unequal distribution of power were not taken as given, it could not be said that the norms result in a social optimum. (See Chapter 30 for further discussion.)

The second example that illustrates this point is the fact that even when a norm exists for which they are among the target actors, wealthy and powerful members of traditional societies are often not subject to effective sanctions. Their actions are less impeded by the norm because, given the distribution of power, the sanctioner or sanctioners cannot apply the sanctions without losing more than is gained by bringing about observance of the norm. This result is not due to an inability to share the cost of the sanction; it occurs because the total costs of applying the sanction to a powerful person are greater than the benefits achieved by the sanction, merely because of the differential power.

Do Similar Results Hold for Conjoint Norms?

In the case of disjoint norms, control over events other than the focal action is important. What about conjoint norms? In examining those norms, using the example of the common project, I directed attention principally to the focal action itself, with the social optimum defined only in terms of those actions which produced a public good or public bad. The implications of the preceding section, however, are that *all* the events controlled by target actors or by beneficiaries of the norm that are of interest to actors in the system become relevant in defining the social optimum. Analyzing conjoint norms as if the only resource an actor has at his disposal is the action of contributing or failing to contribute to a common project ignores those other events.

The resources relevant to defining the effective demand for a norm consist of actions that have nothing to do with the norm. They are primarily disapproving statements and withdrawal of respect, actions which are of differential interest to a target actor depending on who the sanctioner is and who the target actor is.

Consider an example introduced earlier, the one about tea bags. Assume that observance of an antihoarding norm makes each person better off.[17] The norm is a conjoint norm. Suppose that there is one person in the organization who has sufficient power (the boss) that his disapproval of a sanction would outweigh the benefits of the sanction; there is no distribution of sanctioning costs that will make the benefits for each outweigh the costs to each. If that is the case, this actor, the boss, could hoard tea bags without being sanctioned, but all other tea drinkers in the organization would be sanctioned by one another. Only if the

---

17. This may not be the case. Hoarding merely transfers the common stock to individual stocks. But absence of the norm may reduce availability in another way, since individuals may use stock from their hoards elsewhere.

boss had internalized a norm against such an action would he not hoard. This scenario bears a striking resemblance to those traditional societies in which the wealthy and powerful are able to ignore certain norms without being sanctioned.

The question, then, is this: Is a social optimum achieved if the norm is violated by this one actor, through an unsanctioned action which reduces availability of tea bags for all others? The answer is yes, just as it was for the case of a disjoint norm discussed earlier. The social optimum is the state in which the powerful actor does not ever experience reduced availability of tea bags, but even has them during temporary shortages, and each of the others experiences slightly reduced availability. But, just as in the example from traditional societies, this social optimum is based on the existing distribution of rights and resources (that is, control over events) held by members of the organization. The statement that a social optimum is achieved when the availability of tea bags to the average actor is maximized is incorrect if it contains the implicit assumption that the availability of tea bags to each actor should be weighted equally in arriving at the availability to the average actor. Only if the powerful actor is given a weight proportional to his power in the system is there a correct definition of availability. In the mathematical model described in Part V, the differential weights are derived from the power of different actors: the equilibrium (that is, the socially efficient state, or the social optimum) is based on the initial distribution of resources.

Certain implications that are not obvious follow from the differential power of actors to exercise sanctions and to violate a norm. Perhaps the most straightforward is the implication that those who because of greater power would be likeliest to impose a sanction on others (because an equally effective sanction would cost them less) would also be those most likely to violate the norm (because others would have less power to sanction them). The same implication follows from differential interest in the focal action. For example, a person for whom the availability of tea bags is especially important should be more likely to violate a norm against hoarding and should also be more likely to sanction others for violating such a norm. There is, however, the fact that violating a norm can put one at a disadvantage with respect to sanctioning others, so norm violation and sanctioning tend to preclude one another. Thus it is probably more correct to state these implications as follows: Norm violation and sanctioning should both be positively associated with power in the system, although possibly not with each other; and norm violation and sanctioning should both be positively associated with interest in the focal action, although possibly not with each other.

The various issues surrounding the emergence and observance of norms and sanctioning as discussed in this chapter are difficult to describe precisely with words. This is especially true for issues involving relative power and the use of resources that go beyond the focal action. The results given here, together with others that require formal derivation, are shown more precisely in Chapter 30, where these questions are reexamined with the aid of a formal model.

Systems of Norms

Throughout this chapter I have examined norms one by one, as though they existed independently. Some norms are relatively independent, but this is not generally true. Norms, like laws, are related to one another; in some cases these relations are hierarchical and in some cases due to overlapping jurisdictions. The exploration of such relations constitutes a major task in itself, one that is beyond the scope of a treatment of the foundations of social systems.

A question that necessarily arises in such an investigation is whether an analysis of systemic relations of norms must make the descent from macro to micro level and the ascent from micro to macro level. That is, must actors be brought in as intervening elements, or can a system of norms be analyzed as relations among norms per se? The question is comparable to one concerning the relations among laws that make up a system of common law: Does the study of common law have to go outside the body of laws itself and examine the actions of individual actors? One answer to this question is obtained by observing the way construction of legal theory is actually carried out. It is carried out by examination of cases, cases involving actors taking actions, other actors experiencing the consequences of those actions, and judges giving justifications for the resolution of disputes about liability for those consequences. In carrying out such examination, legal theorists infer a general principle (that is, the common law) from the resolution of specific cases. Each of these cases involves a descent to the micro level, even though the law itself, the principle as it has evolved, is a system-level property.

In the examination of jurisdictional questions and questions involving conflicts between different laws, legal theorists proceed in the same way, carrying out examinations at the micro level of specific cases of actors and events, control and interests, in order to make generalizations about the relations between laws.

These purely methodological issues do not enter into the substance of theory concerning systems of laws or systems of norms. The conclusion I draw from the character of legal scholarship is that research on systemic relations among norms is also best carried out not through analyses (whether formal or not) of the abstract content of norms, but by moving back and forth between micro and macro levels at each interface between two norms, examining the way the conflict (or other contact) between norms comes about and how actors resolve normative conflict.

11

The Realization
of Effective Norms

In the preceding chapter I examined the conditions which lead to the demand for a norm, that is, to interest in the creation of a norm and in the imposition of sanctions to bring about its observance. I said nothing about the conditions which allow this demand to be realized by bringing into being a norm and sanctions. The question which must still be answered is this: What is required to get from interests in a norm to the actual existence of a norm backed by sanctions?

It is useful to clarify what I mean by the qualification "backed by sanctions." In the preceding chapter I defined the existence of a norm as the state in which a socially defined right to control an actor's action is held not by the actor but by others. If a norm exists, it may be generally observed by target actors even though they find it against their immediate interests to do so. Sanctions may seldom be necessary. But unless the beneficiaries of a norm have the capability of applying effective sanctions when necessary, it is meaningless to say that they hold the right to control the action. (To say that there is an effective sanction does not imply that the sanction is always effective or effective for all target actors, but that it is effective for at least some target actors some of the time.) Thus, when I use the terms "effective norm" and "effective sanctions," I mean that the potential for enforcement exists for at least some of the focal actions.

The fundamental problem exhibited in the common project involving three actors used as an example in the preceding chapter is one of social organization. In the two-actor project (Table 10.1), each person has the resources to prevent the other from imposing negative externalities on him (or, equivalently in this case, to induce the other to act in a way that brings about positive externalities).[1] This is not so in the three-actor project (Table 10.2). No single actor can exchange control with a single other to their mutual benefit. The externalities of the actions of each for any one of the others are less than each actor's own effect on his gains. If a social optimum is to be achieved in such a case, something beyond pairwise exchange is necessary.

For a project like that of Table 10.2, one solution is a sequence of pairwise

---

1. As indicated earlier, when there are only two alternative actions, as in this case, there is no distinction between prescriptive and proscriptive norms.

exchanges among the three actors (A_1, A_2, and A_3), in which actors A_1 and A_2 first exchanged rights of control, and then A_2, having the right to control A_1's action, exchanged *this* for the right to control A_3's action. After these exchanges the rights of control are distributed as follows (where E_i refers to the contribution of A_i):

A_3 controls E_1

A_2 controls E_3

A_1 controls E_2

If these exchanges took place, then each actor would exercise the control he possessed in a way that benefited him (as well as one of the other two): A_3 would commit A_1; A_2 would commit A_3; and A_1 would commit A_2. But the first exchange, between A_1 and A_2, would take place only if both actors knew that a second exchange was possible—for without that further exchange each would be giving up something worth more to him than what he received. Furthermore, after the exchange between A_1 and A_2 had been made, A_3 would find it *not* to his benefit to exchange control with either. Thus the transactions would end after the exchange between A_1 and A_2, and both would end up losing while A_3 gained.

This solution depends not only on A_3's willingness to carry out the second exchange, but also on a condition often not found: the knowledge on the part of A_1 and A_2 that further transactions will be available to make an initially unprofitable exchange a profitable one. As is evident from the study of primitive systems of economic exchange, the development of such a sequence of exchanges (by which objects come to have a value in exchange apart from their utility for the actor, leading the actor to acquire them for further exchange) is not simple (see Einzig, 1966).

An Action-Rights Bank

The similarity of the fundamental problem of the three-actor project to one confronted in economic markets where there is no medium of exchange or central bank raises the question of whether there are other possible solutions analogous to what has come about in economic markets. One possibility is suggested by the fact that the rights of control of each actor's actions have for him a particular value, as well as having a particular value for others in the system. For example, in the project of Table 10.2 the contribution of A_1 has for him a value of (minus) $5, and it has for the other two actors, taken together, a value of $8. Suppose all actors agree that each actor will deposit in a central "bank" the right to control his action in this event. Then this action-rights bank issues two types of shares in the right to determine A_1's action, which it sells at $1 per share: shares for the right to use the right in a positive direction, that is, to make a contribution; and shares for the right to use the right in a negative direction, that is, not to make a contribution. Each actor in the system may offer to buy any number of shares in each right. Whichever set of shares, positive or negative, is more heavily subscribed is sold to the offerers, who pay the central bank (the actors on the other side get their money refunded) and receive the positive or negative right.

In the specific case being considered, the right to control A_1's action in a positive direction is worth $4 to A_2 and $4 to A_3. Assume that A_2 and A_3 make an agreement that each will offer to buy $3 worth of shares. That $6 is more than it is worth to A_1 to offer for negative shares; they are worth only $5 to him. Thus if he has bought $5 worth of negative shares, his $5 is refunded to him, the positive right is given to A_2 or A_3 (it doesn't matter which since it must only be used to bring about a positive action), and the $6 is given to A_1. Next A_1 is required to contribute $9, as a result of the positive right's being exercised by A_2 or A_3. Then each actor gets $4 back as a return from that contribution. The result is that A_2 and A_3 gain $1 each, having paid in $3 and recovered $4, and A_1 gains $1 ($6 − $9 + $4). Similar transactions involving rights to control A_2's and A_3's contributing would result in A_1, A_2, and A_3 each gaining $3 overall.

Such a system would create a social optimum through a device comparable to a central bank and a market with a medium of exchange. The procedures of the action-rights bank have, in effect, overcome the public-good problem confronted by A_1, A_2, and A_3. The mental construction of such a device gives some insight into the character of the problem to which norms are addressed.

Although such an action-rights bank may seem strange, a majority voting system in which actors vote for passage or defeat of a project has striking similarities to it. In both cases each actor has partial rights of control over the action at issue. The depositing of rights of control over an action in the action-rights bank is analogous to the constitutional decision that certain rights will be held collectively rather than individually. These rights of control are then partitioned into votes, or shares of partial control. In casting a vote, a voter is exercising a right in the direction of a positive outcome or a negative outcome, as in the case of the action-rights bank.

There are, of course, also differences. In collectivities where actions are decided on by majority vote, shares in the right to control the action are distributed on a basis whereby each qualified member or citizen receives one share, not through the sale of shares. A member or citizen cannot alter his fraction of control over the event, as an actor can in the case of the action-rights bank, except by casting or not casting his vote, an action which has trivial costs for him. This has two implications: His control over the event is independent of his resources, that is, his wealth; and his control over the event is independent of his interests in it. (In certain cases the costs in time are not trivial. This makes voting dependent both on interests [positively] and on earnings [negatively]. For an examination of such a case in India, see Goel, 1975.) This suggests possible directions of modification of voting systems in ways that would make each voter's control of the event dependent on his interests but still independent of his wealth. (Tideman and Tullock, 1976, and Groves and Ledyard, 1977, have proposed a "demand-revealing" method for arriving at a social choice that has the first of these properties. See Margolis, 1982, for criticism of their device.) All of this, however, goes beyond the subject of norm emergence being addressed here.

There is an alternative sometimes used by individuals who anticipate benefits from a common activity but have difficulty in overcoming the free-rider problem. They may vest rights of control over their actions in a leader, creating a conjoint authority system. This requires, of course, a high level of trust in the leader to act in terms of the followers' interests, trust which sometimes is placed when a potential leader is viewed as having charismatic qualities.

Social Relationships in Support of Sanctions

In the absence of an externally imposed solution to the public-good problem, some kind of combined action is necessary if a social optimum is to be attained. The combined action can be the mutual transfer of rights that constitutes establishment of a norm; but for the norm to be effective there must also be an effective sanction to enforce it, if any of the actors should give indications that he will not contribute. This in turn depends on the existence of a social relationship between two actors affected by the actions of a third. Fig 11.1 shows two cases: In part a actor A_1's action has an effect on A_2 and A_3 (as shown by the arrows), who have no social relationship with one another. Their social relations are with other actors, A_4 and A_5. In part b there are the same effects of A_1's actions, but actors A_2 and A_3 have a social relationship (the content of which I will discuss shortly).

In the case depicted in Figure 11.1(a), any sanction by A_2 or A_3 to direct A_1's action so that it is not inimical to their interests must be applied by either independently. As is shown for the three-actor common project in Table 10.2, neither can do so: A threat to A_1 by A_2 not to contribute if A_1 fails to contribute hurts A_1 by only \$4, and A_1's not contributing gains him \$5. In contrast, as shown in Figure 11.1(b), a social relationship between A_2 and A_3 may make it

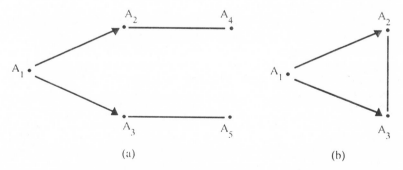

Figure 11.1　Structures of relations among actors that have differing potentials for the emergence of a norm.

possible to impose a sanction on A_1 through some form of joint action that neither A_2 nor A_3 could impose alone. Similarly, if there exists some social relationship between A_1 and A_2, it may be possible to impose a sanction on A_3, and similarly with a relationship between A_1 and A_3.

But two related questions arise: First, what kind of sanction might be applied which could not be applied by either of the actors separately? Second, what is meant by the unanalyzed term "social relationship"?

There are two aspects of a social relationship that can lead to an effective sanction. One is simply communication that allows the possibility of joint action. If A_2 and A_3 pool their contributions, they together offer a sanction that is effective toward A_1: Their combined contribution makes a difference of \$8 to A_1, and his own failure to contribute benefits him by only \$5. Thus a joint threat by A_2 and A_3 to not contribute is sufficient to bring about a contribution from A_1.

Second, the social relationship between A_2 and A_3 may contain some other possibilities, some interests and control which give one or both actors leverage over the other. These are the obligations and expectations examined in Chapter 8 as components of a certain kind of system of trust. Because social relationships consist of obligations and expectations, held either asymmetrically or symmetrically, and because each actor continues to control some events in which the other is interested, there exists inherently in each social relationship leverage which can be used for the purpose of developing sanctions. If, in the case depicted in Figure 11.1(b), A_2 has obligations toward A_3, then A_2 may pay off a portion of those obligations by sanctioning A_1. But he can do this only if he can threaten A_1 with some event that could make a difference of \$5 or more to A_1. A_2's own contribution makes a difference of only \$4, which is not enough. A_2 must have some obligation toward A_1 that he can threaten not to honor, if his sanction is to be effective. Even a threat which costs him more than he benefits from A_1's contribution may be viable, because of the compensation he receives from A_3. Or if A_2 has control of some event in which A_3 is interested (which may be nothing more than A_2's approval), A_2 and A_3 can carry out an implicit exchange, in which A_3 incurs the cost of sanctioning A_1 in return for control of the event currently controlled by A_2.

This use of social relationships to facilitate the employment of sanctions constitutes a solution to a general problem, to which I now turn.

The Second-Order Public-Good Problem for Norms

The sanctioning problem has been called the second-order public-good problem or the second-order free-rider problem. The problem can be conceptualized by considering one of Aesop's fables, known as "The Mice in Council." The council meeting was called to discuss a problem faced by the mouse society, that of how to control the cat who was slowly decimating the population. In the terms used in this book, the cat's action was imposing severe externalities on the mice and constituted, in effect, a public bad, creating constant danger for each mouse. This is the first-order public-good (or in this case public-bad) problem.

The second-order public-good problem is indicated in the statement of the wise old mouse who finally rose in the council, after a proposed solution (that a bell be put around the cat's neck to warn of its approach) had been roundly applauded. He suggested that the council consider how the bell was to be fastened about the cat's neck and who would undertake the task. The second-order public-good problem lies in the fact that, just as the cat's action imposes externalities on all, an effective sanctioning of the cat's actions also has externalities (positive in this case) for all those experiencing the benefits of the sanction; yet the benefits to the mouse who would undertake to bell the cat would not be sufficient to overcome the costs.

For the case of the three-actor project shown in Table 10.2, the first-order public-good problem lies in the fact that each will benefit only from the contribution of others; and the second-order public-good problem is that if A_1 does not contribute, then the sanctioning of A_1 is a public good for A_2 and A_3, but neither receives sufficient benefits from his own sanctioning action to compensate the costs of sanctioning A_1. The problem may not appear to be a serious one for the three-actor common project. The second-order public-good problem for sanctioning one actor's failure to contribute to a three-actor common project is reduced to a two-actor joint project. This may be solved whenever there is the possibility of exchange between the two actors who experience externalities from the third. One can compensate the other for the net costs of applying the sanction (in this case, for instance, the costs to A_2 of sanctioning A_1, less the benefits that A_2 will derive directly from the effects of the sanction). More generally, the second-order public-good problem of sanctioning always involves one actor less than the first-order public-good problem.

The sanctioning problem for the case in Table 10.2 is shown in Table 11.1, where it is assumed that A_1 proposes not to contribute and that A_2 and A_3 have contributed. Since A_1 gains \$5 by not contributing (the difference between \$3

Table 11.1   Payoff matrix for two potential sanctioners in three-person common project.

		A_3	
		Sanction	Not sanction
A_2	Sanction	.5, .5	-2, 3
	Not sanction	3, -2	-1, -1

and \$8), it will cost A_2 or A_3 (or both together) whatever is equivalent to \$5 for A_1. Making up the \$5 for A_1 is not possible for either A_2 or A_3 to do within the framework of the common project, since either alone can only make a difference of \$4 to A_1 by contributing or not contributing. It is further assumed for Table 11.1 therefore that A_2 and A_3 each have a relation to A_1 that makes it possible to hurt A_1's interests by \$5 and that the cost of such a sanction is equivalent to \$5 to either A_2 or A_3.[2]

These assumptions make it possible to specify for A_2 and A_3 a set of payoffs for the second-order public-good problem posed by the question of how to sanction A_1. If neither A_2 nor A_3 sanctions, they lose \$1 each (from Table 10.2). If only A_2 sanctions, it costs him \$5 to induce A_1 to contribute (again, the difference between \$8 and \$3). In that case A_3 gains \$4 (the difference between − \$1 and \$3) and ends up with \$3. Similarly, if only A_3 sanctions, it costs him \$5, and A_2 gains \$4. If both sanction, it costs each \$2.50 and each gains \$4, leaving each with a net of \$1.50 after subtracting the cost of the sanction and thus with \$0.50 for the total project.

There are four points of importance to note about this sanctioning problem. First, the structure of payoffs illustrates the fact that the necessity to employ a sanction is costly to the sanctioners. Even though the right to control A_1's action is held by A_2 and A_3, enforcement of that right is costly. The fact that enforcement is possible, at a cost to A_2 and A_3 less than the benefit they can gain from the effects of the sanction in bringing A_1 into line, makes the threat of sanction credible, and the norm viable.

Second, the sanctioning problem involves, as stated earlier, one actor fewer than the original public-good problem. When the original problem involves three actors, the sanctioning problem involves two and can ordinarily be resolved by exchange. With large numbers of actors, of course, the benefit of this size reduction is small.

Third, the sanctioning problem involves a smaller cost to the actors involved than does the original problem. This can be seen in two ways. The difference between the social optimum of a payoff of \$0.50 each and the outcome of − \$1 that results from each taking his individually optimal action is only \$1.50; this difference is \$3 for the original problem. Also, from A_3's perspective, if he sanctions, the difference that A_2's sanction makes for him is only \$2.50, compared to \$4 in the original problem. Thus the sanctioning problem is less costly than the original problem.

Fourth, if the second-order sanction is a positive one, rewarding the sanctioner, then even though it is less costly than the first-order sanction, it must be

2. That the cost of the sanction to A_2 or A_3 and its benefit to A_1 are equal implies interpersonal comparison of utility, which I have fixed here by fiat by specifying homogeneity among the actors. More generally, however, if A_2 is more powerful than A_1, he may have available the means to sanction (that is, control over another event), something worth little to him and much to A_1, making it possible to sanction A_1 with little cost. These differences are discussed in subsequent sections.

provided whenever the right action (sanctioning the initial offender) is taken; a negative sanction must be applied only when the wrong action is taken. If there develops a norm that one must sanction the violator of the initial norm, then the negative second-order sanction for not applying the first-order sanction must be applied only when that sanctioning norm is violated. This cost reduction to norm beneficiaries may give them an interest in establishing a sanctioning norm.

It is now possible to state the second condition for emergence of an effective norm, the condition under which the demand for an effective norm will be satisfied. Stated simply, this condition is that under which the second-order free-rider problem will be overcome by rational holders of a norm. To put it differently, the condition is that under which beneficiaries of a norm, acting rationally, either will be able to share appropriately the costs of sanctioning the target actors or will be able to generate second-order sanctions among the set of beneficiaries that are sufficient to induce effective sanctions of the target actors by one or more of the beneficiaries. This condition depends on the existence of social relationships among the beneficiaries.

Free Riding and Zeal[3]

The theory developed in this and preceding chapters can be used to solve an empirical puzzle. It is first necessary to restate the free-rider problem: When a number of self-interested persons are interested in the same outcome, which can only be brought about by effort that is more costly than the benefits it would provide to any of them, then, in the absence of explicit organization, there will be a failure to bring about that outcome, even though an appropriate allocation of effort would bring it about at a cost to each which is less than the benefits each would experience.

The puzzle lies in the fact that there are many empirical situations in which just the opposite of free-rider activity seems to occur, even though the circumstances are those in which free riders would be predicted to abound. That is, there is an outcome in which a number of persons are interested, which requires effort whose costs are not fully compensated by the benefits the outcome will bring to any of the persons. Yet in some such situations what is found is the opposite of free riding, that is, an excess of zeal. In the fever of patriotic zeal during wartime, men will volunteer for military service; in the military they will volunteer for front-line duty; and at the front line they will volunteer for dangerous missions. Even among those who are opposed to violence, there are some who will volunteer for front-line duty in providing medical aid to the wounded. In all of these cases the costs that are borne are extreme, including a greatly increased probability of being killed.

Similarly extreme costs are borne by persons in small groups who engage in militant or even terroristic acts on behalf of what they regard as a public good.

3. An earlier version of this section appeared in *Sociological Theory* (Coleman, 1988a).

Examples include the IRA hunger strikers in Northern Ireland, some of whom fasted until death; Mohandas Gandhi and his followers in India, who endured extreme hardship for a cause; the Red Guards in Italy, who engaged in terrorism designed to bring down the system; activists in the PLO in the Middle East; and leaders and activists in the Solidarity movement in Poland. In all these cases a number of persons experienced extreme costs to bring about a result from which they personally could hardly expect to benefit sufficiently to justify those costs.

Another area where free-rider behavior might be expected but zealous activity is often found instead is in team sports. Since the benefits of winning are experienced by all team members, one would expect, by free-rider logic, to find little or no activity by team members. Yet both in practice and in games, team members often work harder than do participants in individual sports (such as track and field events). Even if one accepts the caveat that is often introduced in predictions about free-rider activity—that it does not occur in small groups— this does not explain the higher levels of effort in team sports. It would predict equal levels of effort. What seems instead to occur in team sports is some free-rider activity, that is, some greater amount of loafing than occurs in individual sports, but also zealous activity at a greater level than occurs in individual sports. The overall average level of effort is probably higher in team sports than in individual sports.

Rationality of Free Riding and of Zeal

How can the two phenomena, free riding and zeal, coexist? How can similar situations produce free riding and zeal?

The rationality of free riding is straightforward: If a number of persons' interests are satisfied by the same outcome, and if the benefits that each experiences from his own actions that contribute to the outcome are less than the costs of those actions, he will not contribute if he is rational. If others contribute, he will experience the benefits of the outcome without incurring costs. If others do not contribute, his costs will outweigh his benefits. Yet in much the same situation another rationality leads to zealous activity. If a number of persons' interests are satisfied by the same outcome, then each has an incentive to reward the others for working toward that outcome. Each may in fact find it in his interest to establish a norm toward working for that outcome, with negative sanctions for shirking and positive sanctions for working toward the common goal. If the norm and sanctions do become established, then each person has two sources of satisfaction when he works for the outcome: the objective achievement of his interests through the contribution of his actions toward the outcome, and the rewards provided by the others for helping to achieve that outcome. Thus one's efforts directly help to satisfy one's interests (even if not enough to outweigh the costs of those efforts), and they also bring benefits from others for helping to satisfy *their* interests. The combination of these two benefits can be greater than the costs of the effort one expends.

The rationality of free riding and the rationality of zeal arise under the same structure of interests. This is not the structure of interests that characterizes most situations, where the interests of different persons are complementary and are realized through some kind of social exchange. Nor is it a structure in which interests are opposed, so one person's interests are realized at the expense of another's. Rather, it is a structure of common interests; that is, the interests of all (or at least all in the vicinity) are realized by the same outcome (winning a war or a game, or achieving a political or community goal). It is in these sorts of situations that both free riding and zeal can be found.

How can these two rationalities be made consistent in a way that will allow prediction as to when one or the other will prevail? To answer this requires looking at the similarities and the differences between the rationality of free riding and the rationality of zeal. The rationality of zeal has the same incentive that leads to free riding, but with a second incentive superimposed on the first. The second incentive, however, becomes effective only through an intervening action: encouragement of others, or positive sanctions, which may overcome the deficiency of the first incentive. It is this intervening action that makes the difference between the deficient incentive leading to free riding and the excess incentive leading to zeal. Thus the condition under which free riding occurs and the condition under which zeal is exhibited are delineated by the absence or presence of this intervening activity.

What are the conditions under which the intervening activity is present? When this intervening activity, which I have described as encouragement of others, is examined more closely, it can be seen to be one of a general class of activities that are described as sanctions in enforcement of a norm. (There can be, as I will indicate later, encouragement of others' activity in the absence of a norm, but this can be effective only under special circumstances, which I will specify.) That is, the activity is a certain kind of sanction which *encourages* the action rather than *discouraging* it, and the norm is of a certain kind, one which *prescribes* a certain action rather than proscribing it. But to say that a norm arises under those two conditions is to beg half the question. The existence of externalities is a necessary condition for the existence of an effective norm, but not a sufficient one—if it were, free riding would not exist when actors have common interests.

The Closure of Networks and the Emergence of Zeal

An earlier section showed the importance of social structure in supporting the employment of sanctions. It has also been suggested that it is social structure that can transform free ridership into zeal. How this occurs can be understood by examining differences among social networks, as shown in Figure 11.2. In part a of the figure actors A_1, A_2, and A_3 are not part of the same network. Whatever social relations they have are not with each other. In parts b and c

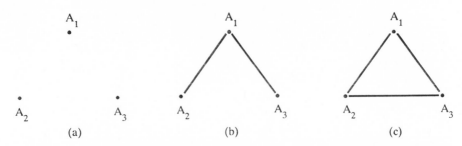

Figure 11.2 Structures of relations among actors that have differing potentials for the growth of zeal.

actor A_1 is connected to actors A_2 and A_3. In part b actors A_2 and A_3 are not connected, but in part c they are.

Suppose some circumstance arises which fits the incentive structure for both free riding and zeal. That is, there is an activity in which the action of each actor benefits all three, although the benefits to each actor of his own action are insufficient to overcome the costs of that action. The common project introduced in Table 10.2 and discussed in both Chapter 10 and this chapter illustrates such an activity.

In a social structure such as is shown in Figure 11.2(a), each actor has no possibility of influencing the contribution of either of the others. They have no relations, and thus they cannot provide the encouragement or impose the sanctions that will induce the others to contribute. It would be irrational for any of the three to contribute.

In a social structure such as is shown in Figure 11.2(b), matters are more problematic. If A_1 proposes not to contribute, but to free ride on the contributions of A_2 and A_3, then A_2 would like to induce him to contribute; and in part b, unlike part a, A_2 (and A_3 as well) is in a social-structural position that facilitates this. As shown earlier in connection with Figure 11.1, however, in some circumstances, A_2 cannot do so if he must compensate A_1 in some common medium of exchange in order to encourage him to contribute. There are, of course, public goods for which inducement by A_2 would be sufficient to lead A_1 to contribute while still providing a net benefit to A_2. (For example, suppose in the three-actor common project A_1's contribution of $9 brought a benefit of $6 to each. Then A_2 could induce A_1 to contribute by offering him any amount more than $3 and would benefit if he offered A_1 any amount less than $6.) It may also be true that A_2 can compensate A_1 with something worth little to him but worth a lot to A_1. A_2 could offer this to A_1 with a net surplus for both parties. For example, if A_2 is highly respected by A_1, then A_2's gratitude to A_1 for contributing may fulfill this condition.

In the social structure shown in Figure 11.2(c), there is an additional possibility. If a sanctioning of A_1 would cost A_2 (or A_3) more than he would benefit from it, then with this structure the second-order sanctioning problem could be overcome, as described in the discussion concerning Figure 11.1.

Is There an Excess of Zeal?

The above discussion simply restates the earlier result that closure of social networks can overcome free-rider activity through the creation of norms and sanctioning systems. The discussion does not indicate, however, how the contributions (of money or effort or time) can be *greater* than would occur if the three actors were each engaged in producing a private good. In the common project the norm brought the contributions back to what they would have been if the return had been purely private goods; that is, if each had received $12 for his $9 investment but none from the others' investments. In principle, the existence of a norm with sanctions does what formal organization does in the presence of externalities: It internalizes the externalities.

Social networks, and the norms they facilitate, do more than this, however. Under certain circumstances they generate the excessively zealous activity which indicates not a deficiency of incentives to contribute, but an excess. What leads members of an interconnected group to engage in the opposite of free riding?

Earlier I indicated that if A_2 held something that was worth little to him and much to A_1, he could induce A_1's contribution without loss, even in the social structure of Figure 11.2(b). And in the social structure of Figure 11.2(c), there is the additional possibility of gains from A_3's holding something of greater value to A_2 than to himself, which he could use in place of money for the second-order sanctioning of A_2. The relationships of which social structures are composed contain such possibilities in abundance. An expression of encouragement or gratitude for another's action may cost the actor very little but provide a great reward for the other. The shouts of encouragement to an athlete from his teammates may cost them little but provide him with rewards that lead him to work even harder. Or a girl's smiling at the athlete may cost her little but impel him to new heights of determined effort.

When there are such differentials, the social structure does more than merely internalize externalities. The social system has within it a potential, analogous to the potential in an electrical system. That is, when one actor carries out an action, thus experiencing costs, and others receive the benefits, the return that the actor experiences is not merely those benefits transmitted back to him through the social structure but those benefits amplified by this potential that exists in the structure.[4] Thus when an actor's activity levels off at the point where marginal cost equals marginal return, that point is at a higher level because of the amplified returns he has received, which were in turn produced by the potential that exists in the structure. The potential lies in the difference between the cost to the sanctioner, in each of the relations that transmits rewards back to an actor, and the benefits the sanctioner gains through the increased activity of the actor who is being (positively) sanctioned.

---

4. This amplification, although it has hardly been studied by social scientists, appears to offer promise for understanding several social-psychological phenomena, such as the intensity of pleasure in new relationships as compared to old ones.

The Impact of Social Structure

The networks shown in Figure 11.2 exhibit two components of a social structure that are important for the existence of norms which can transform a deficiency of incentive into an excess of incentive. The first of these two components is the existence of social relations between an actor and those for whom he generates externalities. Even if those others are disconnected members of an audience witnessing his actions, their connection to him may mean that they can provide rewards, at a cost to themselves that is below their benefit from his actions, that spur him on to greater efforts. It is for this reason that a performing athlete, musician, or actor may experience far greater motivation than will a book author, who cannot see the reactions of his audience.

The second component of a social structure that is important for the existence of norms is exhibited by the difference between parts b and c of Figure 11.2. This is the closure of the network, the existence of relations between those who experience externalities from another's action. From the example of the common project in conjunction with Figure 11.1, it is clear how these relations can make a difference between a system in which there is a deficient incentive to act and thus a suboptimal level of activity, and a system in which there is an excess incentive to act and thus a manifestation of zeal. More generally, closure of the network gives increased potential for amplifying returns to the actor. Thus a system in which others have connections to the actor may exhibit a strong potential that induces higher levels of activity, but a system that in addition has high closure has an extra potential, due to the benefits that each of those who experience externalities of the actor's action receive from one another. There is an amplification that occurs even before the rewards get back to the actor himself.

Heroic versus Incremental Sanctioning

Examination of the ways in which norms are characteristically enforced makes it clear that a common mode of sanctioning can be characterized as incremental sanctioning. This is exemplified in unions by "putting in Coventry" scabs and others who seriously violate union norms; that is, other members refuse to speak to the transgressor (Lipset, Trow, and Coleman, 1956). It is also exemplified by the development of a "reputation," which is followed by avoidance or snubbing. In incremental sanctioning the cost incurred by each sanctioner is small, and the effect of each sanctioning is small as well, but the effects are additive, giving a large total effect.

Aesop's fable "The Mice in Council," however, is a reminder that it is not always possible to sanction incrementally. To bell the cat was not an activity that could be engaged in by additive increments. It required what I will call a heroic sanction, that is, a sanction whose total effect occurs through a single actor's action. In the examples of norms and sanctions given earlier in this chapter, the sanctions were imposed by single individuals.

In this section I will use the three-actor common project to examine the different structures of action when sanctions are heroic and when they are incremental, carried out by all the actors in the collectivity other than the one being sanctioned.

Table 11.1 is based on the assumption that a sanction is all or nothing: The sanctioner (assuming only one) must pay the full costs of inducing A_1 to contribute, that is, something worth $5 to A_1 (which in this homogeneous case is assumed to cost A_2 or A_3 the equivalent of $5). If the sanctioner is A_2, he benefits by $4 from A_1's contribution, but his cost of $5 creates a net loss of $1. This is a heroic sanction, because A_2 brings about the total effect by his action alone. Unless it is possible to divide the costs with A_3 by both simultaneously sanctioning (see upper-left cell of Table 11.1), he loses $1 by sanctioning. This $1 loss may be made up by A_3 as a reward to A_2, from the $4 A_3 has gained from A_2's sanctioning. Thus, when only a heroic sanction is possible, a sequence of two steps is necessary if the heroic sanctioner is to end up with a net benefit from his sanctioning. First A_2 must sanction A_1, and then A_3 must give a reward to A_2 to compensate for the loss incurred.

If, however, sanctions can be additive in their effects, as empirical evidence suggests they are in many cases, A_2 can bring about a contribution of half of the $9 from A_1 through a sanctioning action costing A_2 $2.50 and bringing a benefit of $2 to A_2 and to A_3. The net cost to A_2 is only $0.50. This payoff structure is shown in Table 11.2. There is a prisoner's dilemma structure here, but one with extensive possibilities for mutually beneficial arrangements, due to the disparity between the sanctioner's net loss (only $0.50) and the other's gain ($2) from the sanctioning.

This example, however, does not show the differences between heroic and incremental sanctions in a structure of action as clearly as does a case with a

Table 11.2 Payoff matrix for two potential incremental sanctioners in three-person common project.

		A_3	
		Sanction	Not sanction
A_2	Sanction	.5, .5	-1.5, 1
	Not sanction	1, -1.5	-1, -1

Table 11.3 Net gains for each actor from six-person common project.

Number of contributions	Net gain (in dollars) for—	
	Noncontributors	Contributors
6	—	3
5	10	1
4	8	−1
3	6	−3
2	4	−5
1	2	−7
0	0	—

larger number of actors. Consider the same common project but with six partici-pants, rather than three. Each contributes nothing or $9, and $1 is earned for every $3 contributed; the total product is divided equally among the six. The net gain for each contributor and noncontributor for each configuration of contribu-tions is shown in Table 11.3. The net loss incurred by contributing is no longer $5, but $7. (For example, if five are contributing, the noncontributor's gain is $10. If he contributes, there are six contributing, and he ends up with $3, making him $7 worse off.) The net gain experienced by the others from one actor's sanctioning of a noncontributor is no longer $4, but only $2. (For example, if the sixth actor does contribute, the others' net gain goes from $1 to $3.)

If sanctioning cannot be incremental, the heroic sanctioner in this six-actor project must incur a cost of $7 to achieve a benefit of only $2. He has a net loss of $5, whereas the heroic sanctioner in the three-actor project has a net loss of $1. Furthermore, this net loss of $5 cannot be made up by another who benefited without that other's experiencing a net loss, because each actor's benefit from the heroic action is only $2. Even two others could not provide sufficient re-wards to the heroic sanctioner to make his action anything other than foolhardy; if they rewarded him with their gains, he would still have a net loss of $1. It would take three others, that is, all but one of the four who gained by the heroic sanction, to make up for the heroic sanctioner's net loss.

If the sanctions can be incremental, the degree of exposure of the sanctioner is much less. A_2 as sanctioner, for example, incurs a cost of $7/5, or $1.40, and gains from his sanctioning alone $0.40 from the incremental contribution made by A_1, the actor sanctioned (although A_2 gains $2 altogether if others sanction as well). Thus each actor experiences a net loss of $1 by sanctioning. It is again possible for this to be made up by a sequence of rewards from others, of $0.40 each, which would require participation by at least three of the other four. Alternatively, additional incremental sanctions from the others can make up A_2's loss, each incremental sanction reducing the loss by $0.40. If all sanction incre-mentally, A_2 gains $0.60. Thus if incremental sanctions are to pay the sanctioner, some prior collective decision that all (or at least many) will sanction is required (as in the consensus Merry, 1984, p. 279, describes as the second phase of gossip).

For example, suppose all members of a club are expected to clean up after meetings, but one member consistently fails to help. If one person expresses disapproval, this might induce a small effort on the offender's part, but would also have a negative effect on the relationship between these two, an effect that might be more important to the potential sanctioner than the benefit from the offender's efforts. But if all concurred in expressing disapproval, inducing the offender to make his full contribution, the benefits to each would outweigh the costs of each one's worsened relation with the offender.[5]

Returning to the six-actor common project, suppose there is not a binding collective decision, and all but one have sanctioned. Then the sanctions can go one stage deeper. Suppose that A_1 is the noncontributor and A_2 is the nonparticipant in incremental sanctioning. Each of the others has provided an incremental sanction, and A_1 has made four-fifths of his total contribution. A_2, who is $1 better off by not sanctioning, can be induced to sanction either by a heroic second-order sanction of $1, which works out to a net cost of $0.60 to the second-order sanctioner, or by incremental sanctions of $0.25, which work out to a net cost of $0.15 for each of the sanctioners.

The overall difference between the heroic sanction and the incremental sanctions lies in the magnitude of the costs incurred by the sanctioners at every stage. At the first stage in the six-actor project, A_2, the heroic sanctioner, must incur a net cost of $5, a loss five times that incurred by each incremental sanctioner. At the second stage, for A_3 to reward the heroic sanctioner alone imposes a net cost of $3 on A_3. If sanctioning is incremental, the free-rider problem remains, but at a greatly reduced magnitude. The net cost to each sanctioner is $1, rather than $5. If the second-stage sanction (the reward to the incremental sanctioner) is heroic, the second-stage heroic sanctioner incurs a net cost of only $0.60, rather than $3. If the second-stage sanction is incremental, the net cost to each of the four sanctioners is only $0.15.

What this means in practice is that in many circumstances in which heroic sanctions are beyond the resources of any sanctioner, the resources for incremental sanctioning are readily available. These resources may, as indicated earlier in this chapter, be other events which are controlled by each of the potential sanctioners. The values specified above indicate only the costs that sanctioning will impose on the sanctioner, if the cost to the sanctioner is the same as its cost to the person being sanctioned (as in the case of a parent who tells a child that a punishment "hurts me as much as it hurts you"). When the sanctions have the small cost that incremental sanctions come to have in a group of any size, a positive sanction may consist of nothing more than a "credit slip"

---

5. Empirically the costs might also be reduced, since disapproval from all might lead the offender to accept the collective verdict and not to respond unpleasantly to the members expressing disapproval. In the example of Table 11.3, however, the net gain from incremental sanctioning by all does not depend on such reduced costs.

in the form of gratitude for what the other has done, or a negative sanction may consist of nothing more than a withdrawal of credit in the form of displeasure ("Just wait till you ask me to do something for you!").

Other possibilities exist with incremental sanctioning. If there is some heterogeneity among the potential sanctioners, then, as Chapter 30 shows, the free-rider problem may be overcome at some stage and in any case will constitute less of an obstacle.[6] The complex possibilities that exist can only be alluded to here. In Chapter 30 they are examined in some detail, with the aid of a formal model which facilitates inclusion of the full set of resources available to each actor, not merely those in the common project itself.

I must point out that here the term "heroic" refers to a single sanctioning by one sanctioner sufficient to bring about a noncontributor's contribution. If the set of five contributors (or a large enough subset) can act as a single actor, a single sanction from that set can be sufficient to bring about the contribution and yet bring a net benefit to each. Many communes hold meetings once a week or at some regular interval, at which the whole membership gathers to give self-criticism or hear criticism by others. This phenomenon suggests that, in such settings, this method of sanctioning is easier to organize than either heroic sanctioning or sanctioning by independent increments.

How Are Sanctions Applied in Society?

The preceding analysis indicated the logical character of the sanctioning problem. The theory construction can be aided by examining some ways that sanctioning is commonly done. This review is not exhaustive, but is only a means of discovering some ways that the second-order public-good problem of sanctioning is solved.

It is useful to begin with some of the examples introduced at the beginning of Chapter 10. In the example involving the dropping of a candy wrapper on a Berlin sidewalk, the sanction was imposed by one woman, without apparent social support. In the example involving the hoarding of tea bags, the sanction was again applied by a single person, another tea drinker in the same organization. Did neither of these sanctioners need any additional support? Was the sanction so near to being costless that it could easily be applied, despite the fact that the direct benefits the sanctioner might experience were uncertain and weak at best, and despite the unpleasantness that might ensue when the disapproval was voiced?

The question cannot of course be answered for these cases in the absence of evidence, but two observations may be made. First, in both cases the sanctioner may paradoxically have depended on some implicit support from the person

6. On the other hand, if the target actor is more powerful than the sanctioner, a sanction that hurts the target actor a little will hurt the sanctioner a lot, thus exacerbating the sanctioning problem.

being sanctioned, that is, the sanctioner may have felt that the person accepted the normative definition of what action is right and recognized that the action carried out was wrong. Second, the sanctioner in either case may have been able to bring up the event in subsequent discussion with others who shared the same opinion or feeling about the event and would provide encouraging comments in support of the disciplining that the sanctioner carried out. If so, this introduces a third actor, comparable to A_3 in Figure 11.2(c), with whom the sanctioner has a relation and in whose approval the sanctioner has some interest. Thus, when it appears that sanctioning is carried out heroically, by a single person without social support, there may in fact be support from other actors on whom the target actor's actions would impose externalities. It is also true that such support for the sanctioning is less costly than the sanctioning itself, and thus has no potential for bringing about unpleasantness, which the original sanctioning might produce for the sanctioner.

This is a general result: Where sanctions are applied in support of a proscriptive norm and are consequently negative sanctions, the second-order public-good problem of providing positive sanctions for the sanctioner is more easily overcome, because positive sanctions incur lower costs than do negative ones.

Another observation concerning these two examples is that whether the sanctioner depended on implicit support from the target actor or on subsequent approval from a third actor, there was an assumption concerning what is right. That is, both mechanisms on which the sanctioner may have depended for support are based on a norm defining what is the right action or (as in these cases) what is the wrong action. The norm, prescribing what is right or proscribing what is wrong, gives a sanctioner some presumption that his action will elicit approval from those who hold the norm. He has a presumptive right to impose the sanction. Thus the existence of a norm provides for a potential sanctioner some expectation of receiving approval from the holders of the norm. However, this expectation is highly contingent on the social relations between the potential sanctioner and other holders of the norm, because establishment of the norm and vesting of the right to sanction can be achieved only by some form of collective decision, implicit or explicit. One difference between the older woman in Berlin and the older woman in New York City may have been that the former spent evenings with others like herself, with whom she could discuss the shortcomings of the younger generation's child-rearing practices and arrive at consensus about what is right, and the latter spent evenings in an apartment alone.

Another example from Chapter 10 involves a different kind of sanctioning than that found in the two examples discussed above. In the case of the poor family among the Sarakatsan nomads in Greece, gossip appears to have played an important part in generating sanctions. Merry (1984), in a review of studies of the role of gossip in social control, suggests that there are three distinct phases.

> The first is the circulation of information about an event or action. The second is the formation of some consensus about the moral meaning of that event; how it is to be interpreted, and which rules are to be applied . . . The

third phase is the implementation of the consensus, the transformation of shared opinions into some form of action. This action can range from individual acts of snubbing to collective decisions to expel. (p.279)

Gossip appears to be an important element in the enforcement of norms in many contexts. Why should this be so? It appears that gossip is a means of generating sanctions that could not be applied by individuals in the absence of or before the gossip. If there are three phases of gossip, as Merry suggests, the first two phases appear to be motivated by the potential aid that a consensus provides for the application of a sanction. The consensus either establishes a norm (that is, a definition of what is right or what is wrong, and the assumption of rights to partially control the action) or establishes the application of an existing norm to the action in question.

Each person who has an interest in the maintenance of the norm and the application of sanctions to those who violate it comes thereby to have an interest in the spread of information that can lead to a consensus on legitimate sanctions. This means such a person will be interested in listening to gossip and interested in passing gossip. If the consensus leads to a collective decision to expel the offender, or to cut off communications with him, as occurs in some communes (see Zablocki, 1971), then the second-order public-good problem is overcome. If it does not, the consensus nevertheless provides the basis for support by members of the community of heroic sanctions applied by individuals. This overcomes the second-order problem by a second stage consisting of positive sanctions rewarding the heroic sanctioner. The consensus also increases the effectiveness of incremental sanctions which are sufficiently small that the cost they impose on each sanctioner is minimal—for these sanctions taken together may be very powerful. The combined effect of individual acts of snubbing can mean isolation of the individual, whereas one individual's snub would constitute an ineffective sanction.[7]

Gossip, then, constitutes a device which both aids in establishing a norm and overcomes the second-order public-good problem of sanctioning. It leads to sanctions that may have little cost for the beneficiary of the norm, the one who passes gossip or the one who receives it, and also brings him potential benefits. The benefits lie in the facilitation gossip provides, through the consensus it brings about, for sanctions that might not otherwise be possible. A typical comment that suggests this goes something like this: "Knowing that you feel the same way about what he did gives me the courage to speak to him about it." When such consensus is amplified by many others who feel the same way, the "courage" it provides to each can be great.

But gossip depends on two conditions: First, similar externalities must be experienced by a number of actors, who thereby come to be beneficiaries of

---

7. Although internal sanctions are not introduced until a later section, it is useful to note here that if the target actor has internalized others' evaluations of him, the very knowledge that gossip is circulating about him can be a strong sanction.

the same norm. If they are all to find benefits in the spread of gossip and the consensus it helps bring about, they must share interests in prescribing or proscribing the action. Second, gossip depends on there being relatively frequent contact among the persons who are affected similarly by an actor's action (and thus are motivated to pass gossip). The benefit that any individual beneficiary can expect to gain from spreading or receiving gossip is relatively small. The costs of doing so must be correspondingly small if persons are to be motivated to spread gossip. Ordinarily these costs are small only if the opportunity to pass gossip is a by-product of relations formed and maintained for other reasons.

This second condition does not involve merely the extent of social relations but the degree to which these relations close in upon themselves as well. Comparison of parts b and c of Figure 11.2 shows that it is the closure of the structure which distinguishes the two. More precisely, what I mean by closure is the frequency of communication between two actors for whom another actor's action has externalities in the same direction.

Empirical studies of gossip confirm the importance of closure. Merry (1984), in a review of work in this area, gives the following generalization:

> Gossip flow⌣ most readily in highly connected, morally homogeneous social networks, and it is here that its impact is greatest. For gossip to occur, the two participants must know a third party in common. The more mutual friends they have, the more people they can discuss. Every individual is at the center of a network of people he or she knows. The extent to which the members of this network know one another, independent of their relationship to ego, can be described as their "degree of connectedness." Gossip flourishes in close-knit, highly connected social networks but atrophies in loose-knit, unconnected ones.
>
> Moreover, only when the gossipers share moral views is the soil fertile for gossip. The person sharing a juicy tidbit expects the listener to join in condemning that behavior, not to approve it. If only minor differences in norms exist, gossip can forge consensus, but where fundamental ideas of proper behavior differ, gossip will be stunted. (p. 277)

It is evident that both sanctions that have a foundation in gossip and sanctions that do not are more likely to be applied in social structures which exhibit the property of closure than in those which do not. Empirical work shows this, and there are theoretical grounds for such a conclusion. Closure reduces the net costs of applying a sanction, because the consensus that occurs in structures having closure provides the legitimacy (that is, the right) for actors to apply sanctions. This ensures that there will be some compensation (in the form of approval) for the costs incurred in imposing a sanction.

It is clear, however, that gossip itself does not constitute a sanction. Even if gossip analytically has two elements, communication concerning an action and consensus concerning it (the first two phases specified by Merry), neither of these necessarily constitutes a sanction for the target actor. For some persons in some societies, merely being aware of others talking "behind one's back" constitutes a powerful sanction; gossip can spread, however, without the person who is being gossiped about knowing of it. As indicated earlier, the consensus lowers the costs for any holder of the norm to apply a sanction, but does not ensure that the sanction will be applied.

One social characteristic possessed by a potential target actor is reported by anthropologists and sociologists as reducing the likelihood that sanctions will be imposed: especially high status or power in the social system which contains the norm holders (see, for example, Frankenberg, 1951, p. 156; Bailey, 1971, p. 283). This provides confirmation of the view that the act of sanctioning imposes costs on the sanctioner, since such costs can be expected to be especially high if the target of the sanctioning is someone with whom a continued relation is of special interest to the potential sanctioner. A clear example of this situation is exhibited in the story by Hans Christian Andersen about the emperor who had no clothes. Almost all the inhabitants of the kingdom were so subject to the king's authority that they were afraid to point out the absence of clothes. Only a child was free of such feelings of dependence and thus able to state the truth.

This implies that even a conjoint norm, for which the targets and the holders are the same actors, may be differentially applied because of the varying costs of sanctioning different actors. The consequence is that those actors with greater power in a social system are less constrained by norms than are those with less power. There are, in fact, institutionalized excuses and indulgences available to high-status persons who fail to obey norms. A high-status person may merely be said to be eccentric, whereas the same behavior would bring severe sanctions upon a lower-status person.

At the other extreme there is little cost to applying sanctions to persons whose status is considerably below one's own. Black (1976, p. 57) suggests that legal systems have often meted out harsher punishments to lower-status persons than to higher-status persons for the same violations. Garnsey (1973, pp. 162–164) gives various examples of this in the Roman Empire. If sanctioning of a lower-status person or a member of a small minority can be done without cost, it can be done irresponsibly, as in the case of scapegoating.

A Note on Compliance with Norms

In general, I will have little to say about compliance with norms, because, in this theory, compliance or noncompliance is merely the result of the application of the principle of maximizing utility under different constraints. There are, however, some empirical results concerning compliance that are closely related to the structural and positional factors discussed above. The points of relevant evidence are these:

1. Powerful persons in a community are not only less likely to be sanctioned, but also less likely to obey the norms than are those of lesser power (Bailey, 1971, p. 20; Starr, 1978, p. 59).

2. Those lowest on the social ladder, although not less likely to be gossiped about or to be negatively sanctioned by others, are less complaint with norms and sanctions than are those above them (Pitt-Rivers, 1971).
3. No matter what degree of closure exists among the holders of a norm, those targets of a norm who have contacts with others outside who are not norm holders, are less likely to be compliant with sanctions (Bott, 1971; Pitt-Rivers, 1971; Merry, 1981).

The first of these empirical results follows from the logic that inhibits those of lesser power in applying sanctions to those of greater power: The latter, recognizing this inhibition, can deviate from norms with less fear of being sanctioned than is true for those below them. Although their position means they have a great deal to lose, it also means they will be less likely to be called to task for deviant actions.

The second empirical result is consistent with the fact that negative sanctions related to social respect can have no effect on those who are at the bottom of the social ladder because they have nothing to lose. This relative disregard of negative sanctions among those without social position should be limited to certain kinds of sanctions, such as disapproval. For other kinds, such as physical punishment, the effectiveness should not be lower among those without social position.

The third empirical result, the imperviousness to norms among those with contacts outside the group of norm holders, is almost transparent. Those with greater mobility can escape sanctioning either physically (as did one young man in Merry's study [1984, p. 292] of an urban neighborhood who simply moved a few blocks away) or psychologically by reducing interest in the community in which sanctions are imposed, increasing them in areas of their lives that lie outside this community.

The third empirical result concerning compliance with norms has implications for the conditions under which norms emerge. Norms emerge as a result of purposive actions on the part of actors who experience externalities from others, potential beneficiaries of the norm. This means that even if there is sufficient closure in the social network of potential beneficiaries, there will be little incentive to bring a norm into being if the potential target actors have sufficient mobility to escape the effect of sanctions. This structural condition exists in some disorganized lower-class urban neighborhoods (as well as among highly mobile high-status persons).

Why Accept a Norm as Legitimate?

I turn now to a question which introduces more explicitly than before the different interests that arise on the part of different actors when there is some heterogeneity in their control and their interests: Why do persons accept the legitimacy of others' claim to a right to control their action when this acceptance constitutes an immediate disadvantage? It may be that not all such acceptance can be accounted for by rational choice theory as currently constituted. For example, social psychologists such as Asch (1956) show that a person's very perceptions can be altered by others' reports of different perceptions of the same objects; and Sherif (1936) has shown that judgments may be easily altered by the frame of reference supplied by another. In at least some cases, however, acceptance can be explained by rational choice principles. Although a person may see acceptance of the right of each to partially control the actions of others as being to his *immediate* disadvantage, he may well see it as being to his long-term advantage. If the norm is a conjoint norm, the person may, on some occasions, be in the position of the person expressing this right, that is, in the position of a person affected by another's action of the same type. Acceptance of the legitimacy of others' rights to partially control his action is necessary to establish the norm that gives him a legitimate right to control others' similar actions. Rejection of that legitimacy constitutes a rejection of the norm, an action against the legitimacy of his right on those other occasions. For example, if residents of a dormitory attempt to establish a norm that one cannot use the public telephone for more than 10 minutes if others are waiting, then if one resident of the dormitory rejects the legitimacy of such control, he thereby rejects the norm and cannot claim the right to sanction others when they make long telephone calls. Thus with a conjoint norm a person may rationally accept others' claims to partially control his action, for he stands potentially in the position of sanctioner of others' actions. Acceptance of others' claims is necessary to establish the norm which aids him in controlling their actions which affect him.

It is clear, however, that even for conjoint norms such as that governing telephone calls in a dormitory, there are asymmetries. Some persons, who make many short calls, will often be in the position of sanctioner, and others, who make a few long calls, will often be in the position of target. Depending on a person's perception of how often he will be in these two positions, he may or may not find it to his long-term advantage to accept the norm regarding the length of calls.

Recognition of the fact that persons differ with respect to the relative frequency with which they will be in the position of sanctioner or target can give guidelines for prediction of who will accept a norm as legitimate and who will not. It is less likely to be in the interests of a person who often finds himself the target actor, being constrained by the norm, to accept it as legitimate. The norm is less likely to benefit him in the long run. For example, the claim in a community of a right by the members to constrain—through expressions of disapproval—the bathing suit styles worn at the community swimming pool will be more likely to be regarded as legitimate by the older and less attractive members of the community, who will seldom wear bathing suits that would be challenged, than by the young and beautiful ones, whose swimwear is more likely to be challenged.

It also follows from rationality that those who fail to observe a norm will be less likely to impose the norm on others—for if a person fails to observe the norm, imposing a sanction on others for not observing it increases the likelihood of being sanctioned oneself. If a girl wears a revealing bathing suit that violates the norm, she is less likely to disapprove of another girl's revealing suit than she would be if she herself wore a conventional suit. If a man is among a group of men, all of whom are wearing ties in a setting where wearing a tie is normatively prescribed, that man's reaction to a newcomer's wearing or not wearing a tie will depend on whether he himself is wearing one.

With a disjoint norm—for which those who are targets of the norm are not beneficiaries of it, such as children whose actions are sanctioned by adults or smokers whose actions are sanctioned by nonsmokers—giving up the right to control one's action must arise from considerations beyond the focal action itself. Giving up that right must be the result of a transaction that can take place because the beneficiaries of the norm (or some subset of them) are powerful; that is, they control some events of interest to the target actors, and they can exchange that control (including exchanges involving threats) to gain rights of control over the focal action.

With a norm that has been internalized, the situation is somewhat similar to that with a conjoint norm. If a person comes to *identify with* a socializing agent, that is, to see his interests as identical to those of the agent, then the claim by that agent of a right to control will be seen as legitimate, because it is a claim deriving from interests the person sees as his own.

Emergence of Norms about Voting

The act of voting poses a deep and serious problem to students of the rational calculus of behavior. If a voter is viewed as a rational actor who has an interest in the outcome of an election, but for whom the act of voting itself constitutes a small cost of time and effort, then the act of voting does not directly follow, even though his interest in the outcome may be very great. Straightforward considerations will lead the voter to recognize that if there are many others voting, his own vote is very unlikely to affect the outcome. The small cost in time and effort that voting will incur must outweigh the very minor chance that the act of voting will bring gain. As a consequence, a reflective voter must conclude, as he is going to the polling place, that whatever impels him there, it is not the impact of his vote on the outcome.

This sort of analysis has been carried out by many students of the rational calculus of voting. Downs (1957) discusses the problem; Riker and Ordeshook (1973) examine it at length, as do Ferejohn and Fiorina (1974), Margolis (1982), and many others. The empirical fact to be explained is, of course, that although the above considerations seem reasonable, many persons do vote, even in elections involving great numbers of voters. Indeed, even a weaker prediction from rational considerations, to the effect that whatever the level of voting, it should certainly decline as the number of voters increases, does not seem to hold. This problem is so puzzling that it has been described as the paradox of voting (and has received attention second only to that given Arrow's or Condorcet's paradox). The paradox in this case is not logical, but empirical: Why do so many persons vote when it is clearly irrational to do so?

The problem can be expressed more precisely in simple mathematical form. Suppose a person experiences a certain cost, c, from the act of voting. And suppose he would experience a benefit, b, from the election's having the outcome he prefers. Suppose further that he expects that outcome to occur with probability p if he does not vote and with probability $p + \Delta p$ if he does vote. Then he can calculate the expected return if he does participate and the expected return if he does not. His expected return if he participates is $b(p + \Delta p) - c$. His expected return if he does not participate is bp. If he is rational, in the usual meaning of the term, he will participate if and only if the first of these two expected returns is greater than the second, that is, if $b(p + \Delta p) - c$ is greater than bp. This reduces to $b\Delta p$ is greater than c, or Δp is greater than c/b. That is, he should participate only if the increment in the probability of his desired outcome, due to his vote, is greater than the ratio of the costs of voting to the benefits of the desired outcome.

It is obvious that whenever the number of voters is large, Δp is quite small, so an individual's voting can be explained as rational only if the costs of voting to him (c) are nearly zero or the benefits (b) are enormous.[8] Few political scientists would suggest that either condition is met for most voters, and thus the puzzle of apparently nonrational voting remains.

Various authors have tried to "rationalize" voting in a variety of ways. One is to assume that the act of voting may not only incur some costs, but also bring some benefits. For example, if voting is highly approved by a person's friends and not voting is disapproved of, the outcome of the election does not have to be of interest to the person in order for him to vote, nor does he have to believe that his vote will affect the outcome. In that case, if the psychic benefits he experiences from approval are b^* and the costs he experiences from disapproval are c^*, his expected return from voting is $b(p + \Delta p) - c + b^*$ and from not voting is $bp - c^*$. This changes the inequality that must be satisfied if the person is to vote: $b\Delta p + b^* + c^*$ must be greater than c. This inequality may be fulfilled even if he believes his vote will have no effect on the outcome, that is, even if Δp is zero. All that is necessary is that the sum of the psychic benefits from approval for voting and the psychic costs from disapproval for not voting be greater than the direct costs of participation.[9]

8. Another definition of rationality, the minimax regret principle, might also lead a person to vote, as pointed out by Ferejohn and Fiorina (1974). However, this principle can be regarded as rational only in games with a strategic other. The situation under discussion, on the other hand, is a game against nature, a nonstrategic other.

9. The decision to vote can be due to another process discussed in a later section of this chapter and in Chapters 7 and 19, that of coming to identify with a nation or with a political party. This can result in the act of voting itself being rewarding, despite its minimal effect—and even in the absence of approving friends. This analysis of voting behavior would lead to somewhat different predictions than those discussed in this section. For development of a variant of this point, see Margolis (1982).

This explanation of voting has certain virtues. One is that it gives rise to differential predictions about whether persons will vote in different circumstances and can thus be empirically supported or disconfirmed. For example, one prediction would be that persons removed from the company of their friends or persons in the company of those who do not express approval for voting and disapproval for not voting will be much less likely to vote than others.

This explanation has certain unsatisfactory aspects as well. A principal one is that it provides no answer to the question of why others express approval for participation and disapproval for nonparticipation. Those others are presumably subject to the same rational considerations, which should lead them not to vote themselves, as well as not to apply sanctions to others for not voting. Thus the above explanation merely pushes the problem back one step: Why should there be expressions of approval of voting and disapproval of not voting on the part of others?

What is necessary is an explanation of voting that is consistent with the one given above, but takes the further step of explaining why others, despite their similar circumstances, express approval and disapproval. Such an explanation is given in Chapter 30, based on a mathematical model, which provides certain results beyond those possible with a verbal exposition. It is possible, however, to express the general ideas without resort to mathematics.

Assume there is a system of actors, each of whom has an interest (which corresponds to b in the above discussion) in the outcome of an election and a negative interest in the act of voting itself (which corresponds to c in the above discussion). The latter may of course be very small relative to the former. Each actor has some small fraction of control over the outcome of the election, through his vote. In such a circumstance each actor's action is of interest to each other actor; that is, the actions have externalities. There will be, in accord with the principle discussed in Chapter 10, a demand for a norm to vote. And, according to the principle presented in this chapter, satisfaction of that demand depends on the existence of social relationships among potential beneficiaries of the norm if the second-order free-rider problem is to be overcome. When those conditions are met, there will be a general transfer of rights of control over the action of voting or not voting, by each to all.

The end result of this transfer of rights of control will be a system in which each actor has given up a large portion of rights of control over his own action (that is, voting or not voting) and has gained in return a small portion of rights of control over the action of each of the other actors. This constitutes, as discussed in an earlier section, the emergence of a conjoint norm. Each actor will exercise the rights gained in the direction of others' voting, but he may exercise the remaining control he holds over his own action against his own voting (because of the cost to him). His exercise of rights of control over others' voting can be enforced through the exhibiting of approval or disapproval. If each actor has given up most of the control over his own action to others, then the potential approval for voting and disapproval for not voting may be sufficient to overcome the costs each will incur by voting.

One might argue that this conjoint norm would be restricted to a subgroup within the system whose members all support the same candidate, since votes for an opposition candidate impose negative externalities. Since persons generally associate with those whose political sentiments are like their own, the application of such a norm (that is, sanctions of approval for voting or disapproval for not voting) will be toward inducing voting among those who will vote in the same direction as oneself. In fact, the observation by students of voting that persons under so-called cross-pressure are less likely to vote may result from differential application of the norm. (See Berelson, Lazarsfeld, and McPhee, 1954, for a discussion of cross-pressures.) The reduced likelihood of voting among persons who are in surroundings different from those to which their background or interests predispose them may result from reduced application of normative sanctions that would lead to voting.

A further implication may be drawn. Since these normative systems are composed of supporters of each candidate, their strength depends on the degree of closure of each. Unless the social networks that link persons together are somewhat distinct, so there is a correlation between the political preferences of friends, these normative systems cannot function. Thus one prediction based on this theory is that the lower that correlation, so that social networks are largely random with respect to political preference, the lower the proportion of the population voting. By a small additional step, a low correlation between social relations and political preference should lower the rate of voting most for those candidates in a minority position in the system under consideration (for example, a city or town).

The central element of this explanation, which was missing in the earlier one, is the giving up of partial rights of control over one's own action and the receiving of partial rights of control over the actions of others, that is, the emergence of a norm. The end result is that control over the voting of each, which was initially held by each alone, becomes widely distributed over the whole set of actors, who exercise that control in the direction of approval for voting and disapproval for not voting—despite the fact that each has some reluctance to vote himself.

Internalization of Norms

To examine the process by which norms are internalized is to enter waters that are treacherous for a theory grounded in rational choice. Asking the question of how individuals come to have the interests they exhibit is ordinarily not possible in constructing such a theory. Despite the fact that anyone knows, if only through introspection, that interests change, theory based on purposive action must start with purpose, and the theoretical apparatus is applied to realization of that purpose, whatever it may be. A theory based on rational action thus has the same deficiency at the level of the individual (considered as a system) as a theory which begins with societal purposes or social norms has at the level of the social system. This individual-level deficiency is, as I have indicated in Chapter 1, far less debilitating to social theory than is the deficiency created by a starting with a social purpose or a set of social norms.

It is nevertheless a deficiency, because individual interests do change and individuals do internalize norms. It would be possible to ignore the latter fact and construct a theory that assumed all sanctions were externally imposed. But such a theory would be weaker, because it could not be used to predict the conditions under which and the degree to which norms would be internalized, and less correct, because predictions based on it would fail to take internalization of norms into account. Thus, acknowledging the dangers in going beyond the usual limits of theories based on rational action, I will in this section examine some questions concerning internalization of norms.

I will not use "internalization of a norm" to mean merely accepting a norm as legitimate, accepting the right of others' to partially control one's actions—nor is this the common way in which the term is used. If internalization of a norm were to mean nothing more than that, it would not inhibit the individual's deviant action that is unobserved by others. In this discussion internalization of a norm will mean that an individual comes to have an internal sanctioning system which provides punishment when he carries out an action proscribed by the norm or fails to carry out an action prescribed by the norm.

The question that then arises is that of how the internal sanctioning system comes to be established. This question can be divided into two: First, assuming that internalization of a norm can take place, what are the conditions under which other actors will attempt to bring about an actor's internalization? Second, what are the conditions that will lead an actor to respond to those attempts by internalizing the norm? Only the second of these questions involves going beyond the usual confines of a theory based on rational action, for answering it requires examining why and how individuals change the motivational structure within themselves (motivation is the role that utility plays in a theory of rational action). This second question will be deferred until Chapter 19. The first question, concerning the socializing agents, will be addressed next.

Under What Conditions Will Actors Attempt to Bring About Internalization?

The question to be considered here, then, is why a beneficiary of a norm, or more generally an actor interested in exercising control over another's action, will attempt to establish an internal sanctioning system within a target actor rather than merely using external sanctions as the occasion warrants. The answer is immediately apparent if one takes the perspective of a parent of a small child or that of a police officer coping with crime in a neighborhood. The existence of an internal sanctioning system within the small child or within each person in the neighborhood would make unnecessary the continual external policing of actions. Thus if internalization can be brought about at a sufficiently low cost, it is a more efficient means of social control than is external policing of actions. The question then becomes, just what are the conditions under which creation of an internal sanctioning system is likely to be more efficient than maintaining external policing of actions?

A first point to recognize is that since norms are devices for controlling actions in the interests of persons other than the actor, internal and external sanctions constitute two forms of policing: internal policing and external policing. The process of creating an internal policing system is part of a broader process which is ordinarily called socialization. It is the installation in the individual of something which may be called a conscience or a superego; I will call it an internal sanctioning system. Persons for whom socialization has been ineffective, in the sense that they have failed to internalize many social norms, are called sociopaths. Those persons and small children are perhaps the most prominent categories of individuals whose internalization of norms is minimal, whose actions are subject to little, if any, internal policing.

Under what conditions is it rational to attempt to bring about an internal sanctioning system? A step toward an answer is to recognize that it is rational to do so when such attempts can be effective at reasonable cost. Thus part of the answer depends on knowledge of the conditions under which attempts at establishing internalization will be effective. Part of the question, however, may be addressed by assuming some receptivity in the individual. In examining this part of the question, I will move back and forth between empirical observation and theoretical argument, using the former to suggest the nature of processes that do not derive directly from a principle of rational action.

First, I must make some general points. Deciding whether internalization of a norm in another actor is rational must involve balancing the cost of bringing about the internalization to a given degree of effectiveness against the discounted future cost of policing to bring about the same degree of compliance, where the degree of compliance is selected by balancing the costs of noncompliance against the costs of sanctioning by the most efficient means (internal or external).

It is also important, of course, to know whether a real distinction exists between different socialization strategies, in that some constitute more nearly external sanctioning and others constitute more nearly internal sanctioning. The literature on socialization practices certainly appears to indicate that the distinction can be made (see, for example, Miller and Swanson, 1958, and Kohn, 1977), and the differences are not esoteric or observable only to initiates. It is relatively easy to distinguish external sanctions from attempts to instill an internal sanctioning system. A parent who slaps a child's hand or withdraws a pleasure to punish an action or who gives the child something, such as candy, to reward an action is employing an external sanction. A parent who shows that an action of a child has hurt or disappointed the parent or who exhibits happiness and expresses love for the child when the child has carried out an action is employing a sanction that both assumes the existence of an internal sanctioning system and attempts to strengthen that system.

Turning back to the question of the conditions under which internalization will be attempted, I begin with an empirical observation. It appears that socializing agents do not simply attempt to inculcate specific norms. A major component of socialization is an attempt to get the individual to *identify* with the socializing agent. This occurs not only in the socialization of children by parents, but in other cases as well. Nation-states use public education as well as various nationalistic events and patriotic propaganda to encourage the individual to identify with the nation, to take its interest as his own. Some business firms (most prominently in Japan but elsewhere as well) attempt to get their employees to identify strongly with the company. Professional schools and graduate schools socialize a candidate into a profession or discipline, leading him to identify himself with the profession or the discipline (to "become a sociologist," for example). Religious orders, the army, and other institutions use various techniques to socialize entering individuals, to give each a new identity. In all these cases it appears that the socialization activities are attempts to create a new self so that the individual's actions will be dictated by the imagined will or purpose of the actor he has identified with: parents, nation-state, company, · religious order, profession, or academic discipline. It is then that will which generates the internal sanctions for future actions.

The empirical evidence suggests, then, that a major strategy taken by actors in attempting to internalize norms in another actor is to do so by modifying the self whose interests the actor will attempt to maximize by his actions. This is an indirect strategy, for it does not attempt to inculcate directly the belief that certain actions are right and others wrong. The strategy is to change the self and let the new self decide what is right and what is wrong (for example, by imagining what one's mother would say about a particular action).

Another perspective on this strategy can be gained by examining the problem that exists for corporate actors in motivating agents to act in their interests. This was described in Chapter 7 as the problem a principal has in getting an agent to act in the principal's interest. A major question the principal must ask is whether to engage in external policing, that is, supervision, or to attempt to bring about internal policing by the agent himself. The means by which the latter is attempted are numerous. Those which use directly economic incentives include stock options, stock ownership, piecework, performance bonuses, commissions, and other means. The first two of these are designed to make the agent's interest largely coincide with that of the principal (in that the agent's interest is satisfied through the outcome or product that also satisfies the principal's interest). The other three tie the agent's interest to what he does for the principal. In addition to economic incentives firms use other means which, like stock ownership, lead agents to identify directly with the firm. Collective activities such as sports clubs, company outings, and various company-sponsored entertainments exemplify these. Creating an expectation of long-term employment with the company is another means.

These actions on the part of corporate actors to induce identification in their agents, or to induce their agents to act in a way that will be best for the corporate actor, appear to apply a strategy similar to that used by actors engaged in socialization of individuals. The strategy is to attempt to align the agent's interests so fully with those of the principal that the agent's self-interest comes to coincide with the principal's interest. Some of the means used appear to carry out this alignment in a more fundamental way than do others. The strategy of the socializing agent and the strategy of the principal appear to be similar in that neither is an attempt to create internal sanctions for a particular action, that is, to inculcate a norm with respect to one action, a norm with respect to a second action, and so on, on a case-by-case basis. Each strategy goes a level deeper, by modifying the interests of the individual being socialized or of the agent of the principal. The socialization strategy, as well as certain of the economic and noneconomic means used by corporate actors, appears to go yet another level deeper, by creating a new self which takes another's imagined will as the basis for action. The similarity of these two strategies, one bringing about changes within an individual actor and the other bringing about changes within a corporate actor (also in part by bringing about changes within individual agents), suggests that a global strategy may in some circumstances be more efficient than a case-by-case strategy. Assuming that this is so, it is possible to ask about the conditions that would affect the efficiency of internalization.

First, internalization becomes increasingly efficient the greater the number of different types of actions that the socializing actor, such as a parent, wants to control using norms. The basic process of creating identification with the socializing agent constitutes in effect a capital cost, and there is an additional marginal cost for each different action that is to be subject to a normative constraint. The capital cost seems to be the larger by far of these two types of costs, so the total cost to the sanctioning agent of subjecting a large number of actions to normative constraints is not much greater than the total cost of doing so for a small number of actions. Thus, for example, once a mother has brought about a condition in which her daughter has internalized the mother's wishes, the mother can extend the number of prescriptions and proscriptions contained in her wishes without incurring great cost.

This implies that authority systems that, like religious orders, aim to penetrate all aspects of the member's or subordinate's life will be more likely to attempt to bring about identification through creation of a new self than will authority systems that attempt to exercise less broad social control. A similar but less obvious prediction is that parents whose desired scope of authority over their children is broad will make more use of internalization than will parents whose desired scope of authority is narrower. More particularly, parents who have an egalitarian ideology about raising children, leading to a laissez-faire parental authority system (few prescriptions and proscriptions), will find it less efficient to bring about identification and instill internalization of norms in a child than will parents whose desired scope of authority is broader and more rigid. Thus children of egalitarian parents should show less internalization of norms, or be more nearly sociopathic, than children of authoritarian parents. This prediction counters the commonsense assumption that "enlightened" parents are both more egalitarian and more likely to use internal sanctions than external ones; that assumption leads to the prediction that the correlation between parental egalitarianism and use of internal sanctions is positive.

A second point is that parents (or other actors) who are in a position to establish an internal sanctioning system do not reap all the benefits from it. Parents must pay the costs of internalization, but others will experience some of the future benefits. It is true that parents experience some benefits during the period the child is at home. Since these are only a fraction of the benefits, however, there is an expected underinvestment in internalization from the perspective of the total set of benefits to others that internalization will bring about (reduced policing and fewer negative externalities). This underinvestment should be especially great for internalization of norms which have least to do with a child's actions in the home and are primarily concerned with actions toward others later in life.

This underinvestment in internalization is comparable to and derives largely from the same interests as business firms' underinvestment in human capital (see Becker, 1976, for a discussion of underinvestment in human capital). A firm recovers only a portion of the investment in human capital, depending on the length of tenure of the employee.[10] In the literature on human capital, a distinction is made between specific and general human capital. A firm is able to capture all the benefits of investments in specific human capital (firm-specific knowledge or skills) but not able to capture the benefits of general human capital, which can be used in other firms to which an employee might move. This distinction is similar to the distinction between norms covering a child's actions in the home and norms covering actions outside the home or later in life. The implication of this distinction is that there will be less underinvestment in internalization of a norm prescribing honesty, which is part of the child's actions in the home, than in internalization of a norm prescribing fairness to peers, a trait manifested largely outside the home, on the playground, and in school. There should be even greater underinvestment in internalization of norms proscribing sharp practices, which are exhibited primarily in business later in life.

A further prediction is that underinvestment in internalization of norms should be greater in cultures or settings in which children leave home at a younger age. In such settings a parent, engaging in the socialization of children, will experience a smaller fraction of its total benefits and thus will find the investment in internalization to have a lower payoff. One specific prediction is that in modern societies, where the typical household is two-generational, there should be greater underinvestment than in traditional societies, where there tend to be

10. There is at least this difference: The investment in human capital makes the employee more valuable in the labor market, increasing the chance that he will leave the firm and further decreasing the firm's return on its investment. There is no analogous situation for the socialization of children.

three-generational households or extended families. A second specific prediction is that an increase in divorce rates should decrease the investment in internalization, and children of divorced parents should show a lower degree of internalization. Either divorced parent expects to spend less time with a child and will thus find it less costly to use external sanctions in cases where, if there were a more extended payoff period, the creation of internal sanctions would be more efficient.

A third point is that parents can increase the return on their investment in internalization of norms by identifying with the child and continuing to inform themselves about the child's actions later in life. Such identification, together with information about the child's actions that accord with a parent's wishes and gain approval from others, can bring satisfaction to the parent and thus make an investment in internalization profitable. This would lead to the prediction that the use of internal rather than external sanctions by a parent will be greater if the parent expects that the future associates of the child will hold the same values as the parent does (for instance, as occurs in a stable society).

A specific prediction that follows from this general point is that persons in America and Europe who grew up in the 1960s and experienced a great gap in values between themselves and their parents can be expected to find identification with their own children as they grow up a less profitable investment, and thus a weaker spur toward increasing the investment in creating internal sanctions in their children.

A fourth point concerns different families in the same society. Some families have a strong interest in their status in the community and see family members' actions, throughout life, as affecting that status. Other families have little status in the community, and thus little to lose by the deviant behavior of family members throughout life. Parents in the latter type of family can be expected to seriously underinvest in creating internal sanctions, and parents in the former type can be expected to invest much more heavily in creating such sanctions. Studies of socialization practices of different social groups are quite consistent with this prediction, showing that the lower the social status, the less internal sanctions are used (see Kohn, 1977). Further predictions could be tested as well. Any aspect of social structure which reduces the degree to which the child's later actions will benefit or harm the family's interests (such as residence in a more anonymous urban setting as compared to a small-town setting, or geographic mobility and discontinuity in family life) should weaken the relation between the family's interest in its status and the degree to which socialization practices incorporate internal sanctions. Thus, as these conditions proliferate, families of the same social status will use internal sanctions less often and external sanctions more often; persons in future generations will be decreasingly socialized.

A fifth point makes use of a result from the literature on the economics of agency. The efficiency of supervision (that is, external policing), relative to some incentive system that provides internal policing, is reduced as the actions subject to observation become more costly to observe. Thus a worker in a cottage industry is more likely to be paid by the piece and less likely to have supervision than is a factory worker making the same product, and an outside sales representative is likely to receive a higher fraction of compensation as commissions and have less supervision than is an inside salesperson or sales clerk. This principle leads to the prediction that the trait of honesty, which is often difficult to observe, will be more likely to be internalized than will the trait of cleanliness or orderliness, both of which are more easily observed and thus more readily subject to external sanctions.

These five points concerning conditions which will lead parents to instill internal sanctions rather than using external policing lead to predictions that are not at all trivial. Certain of the predictions, if they are borne out by research, have strong implications for social control in the future, for they point to decreasing levels of internalization of norms among future generations, assuming that the family continues as the principal agency of socialization. This implies that either use of external policing systems will increase or there will be lower levels of social control.[11]

11. These predictions, and the points which generate them, make evident the naiveté of certain assumptions, such as "Increasing levels of education will increase the viability of democracy" or "Increasing enlightenment through education will result in parents raising better-socialized children."

12

Social Capital

In preceding chapters I have examined certain kinds of relations among actors in society. Actors are seen as beginning with resources over which they have some (possibly total) control and in which they have interests. Social interdependence and systemic functioning arise from the fact that actors have interests in events that are fully or partially under the control of other actors. The result of the various kinds of exchanges and unilateral transfers of control that actors engage in to achieve their interests is, as shown in preceding chapters, the formation of social relationships having some persistence over time. Authority relations, relations of trust, and consensual allocations of rights which establish norms are the principal ones that have been examined here.

These social relationships which come into existence when individuals attempt to make best use of their individual resources need not only be seen as components of social structures, however. They may also be seen as resources for the individuals. Loury (1977; 1987) introduced the term "social capital" to describe these resources. In Loury's usage social capital is the set of resources that inhere in family relations and in community social organization and that are useful for the cognitive or social development of a child or young person. These resources differ for different persons and can constitute an important advantage for children and adolescents in the development of their human capital. (See also Bourdieu, 1980, and Flap and De Graaf, 1986, who have used this term in a similar fashion.) The relations of authority and of trust and the norms examined in earlier chapters are forms of social capital. This chapter will examine more directly various kinds of social capital and the ways in which it is generated.

There is a broadly perpetrated fiction in modern society, which is compatible with the development of the political philosophy of natural rights, with classical and neoclassical economic theory, and with many of the intellectual developments (and the social changes which generated them) that have occurred since the seventeenth century. This fiction is that society consists of a set of independent individuals, each of whom acts to achieve goals that are independently arrived at, and that the functioning of the social system consists of the combination of these actions of independent individuals. This fiction is expressed in the economic theory of perfect competition in a market, most graphically in Adam Smith's imagery of an "invisible hand."

This fiction derives in part from the fact that the only tangible actors in society are individuals and in part from the extraordinary impact that Adam Smith and other classical economic theorists, as well as political philosophers of the seventeenth and eighteenth centuries, have had on the way we think about social and economic life. It also derives in part from the fact that social changes have moved modern society toward a structure in which individuals act more independently than they did in the past, in which individuals' goals are more independently arrived at than they were in the past, and in which individuals' interests are more self-directed than they were in the past.

Hobbes and his followers, political philosophers of the seventeenth and eighteenth centuries, extolled the virtues of self-interest as an antidote to the passions generated by religious and ethnic identity, as Hirschman (1977) describes.[1] Self-interest was not only seen as a beneficial force that moderated fierce group loyalties; it was justified by a philosophy that natural rights inhered in each person. That philosophical position continues to the present.[2] The philosophical and economic arguments of the seventeenth and eighteenth centuries were followed by extensive social changes in the direction of individualism, and these changes have not abated.

Despite these changes the fiction is just that—for individuals do not act independently, goals are not independently arrived at, and interests are not wholly selfish.

Recognition of this individualist bias in neoclassical economics has led to a number of economists to attempt some modification. As mentioned above, Loury introduced the concept of social capital into economics to identify the social resources useful for the development of human capital. Also, Ben-Porath (1980) has developed ideas concerning the functioning in exchange systems of what he calls the F-connection. The F-connection is composed of families, friends, and firms; and Ben-Porath, drawing on sources in anthropology and sociology as well as economics, shows the way these forms of social organization affect economic exchange. Williamson has, in a number of publications (for example, 1975; 1981), examined the conditions under which economic activity is organized in different institutional forms, that is, within firms or in markets. There is a whole body of work in economics, referred to as the new institutional economics, which attempts to show, within neoclassical theory, both the conditions under which particular economic institutions arise and the effects of these institutions (that is, of social organization) on the functioning of the system.

1. Holmes (1989) extends Hirschman's examination, showing the role these philosophical positions played in transforming the common view of the fundamental nature of man.

2. It is true, of course, that the opposition of the philosophical ideals of self-sufficiency, self-interest, and individualism on the one hand, and social responsibility, benevolence, charity toward others, and humanitarianism on the other goes back to the Greeks. The Epicureans set forth the first set of virtues. The second set were held by the Stoics during the Hellenistic period and were taken over by the Romans during their empire-building period (see Sabine, 1937, pp. 132-153).

There have also been recent attempts by sociologists to examine the way social organization affects the functioning of economic institutions. Baker (1983) has shown how relations among floor traders in the highly rationalized market of the Chicago Mercantile Exchange develop, are maintained, and affect trading activity. More generally, Granovetter (1985) has engaged in a broad attack on the "undersocialized concept of man" that characterizes economists' analyses of economic activity. Granovetter criticizes much of the new institutional economics as crudely functionalist because it often explains the existence of an economic institution merely by the functions it performs for the economic system. He argues that there is a failure even in the new institutional economics to recognize the importance of concrete personal relations and networks of relations—what he calls the embeddedness of economic transactions in social relations—in generating trust, in establishing expectations, and in creating and enforcing norms.

Granovetter's notion of embeddedness may be seen as an attempt to introduce into the analysis of economic systems social and organizational relations, not merely as a structure that springs into place to fulfill an economic function, but as a structure with history and continuity that give it an independent impact on the functioning of the system.

Lin, in a number of papers (Lin and Vaughn, 1981; Lin, 1982; 1988), has built on Granovetter's work showing how persons use social resources in accomplishing their goals, particularly in occupational attainment. Lin has shown that persons act instrumentally, using their social ties (especially more extended, or "weak," ties) to gain occupational mobility beyond that predicted by their structural position. Flap and De Graaf (1986) have extended this work in their comparative examination of the United States, West Germany, and the Netherlands.

I want to incorporate this general set of ideas into the framework presented in earlier chapters. I will conceive of these social-structural resources as a capital asset for the individual, that is, as social capital. Social capital is defined by its function. It is not a single entity, but a variety of different entities having two characteristics in common: They all consist of some aspect of a social structure, and they facilitate certain actions of individuals who are within the structure. Like other forms of capital, social capital is productive, making possible the achievement of certain ends that would not be attainable in its absence. Like physical capital and human capital, social capital is not completely fungible, but is fungible with respect to specific activities. A given form of social capital that is valuable in facilitating certain actions may be useless or even harmful for others. Unlike other forms of capital, social capital inheres in the structure of relations between persons and among persons. It is lodged neither in individuals nor in physical implements of production.

Defining social capital more precisely will be facilitated by first considering several examples which illustrate some of its different forms.

1. The *International Herald Tribune* for June 21–22, 1986, had a front-page article about radical student activists in South Korea. The article describes the

development of such activism: "Radical thought is passed on in clandestine 'study circles,' groups of students who may come from the same high school or hometown or church. These study circles . . . serve as the basic organizational unit for demonstrations and other protests. To avoid detection, members of different groups never meet, but communicate through an appointed representative." This description of the basis of organization of this activism illustrates social capital of two kinds. The "same high school or hometown or church" provides social relations on which the study circles are later built. The study circles themselves constitute a form of social capital—a cellular form of organization which appears especially valuable for facilitating opposition to a political system that is intolerant of dissent. Any organization which makes possible such oppositional activities is an especially potent form of social capital for the individuals who are members of the organization.

2. Traditionally, the relation between physician and patient has been one in which the patient places trust in the physician, and the physician employs medical skills in the interest of the patient. Recently in the United States that trust has broken down, as evidenced by the great increase in the number of malpractice suits brought by patients against physicians who have treated them. This has led to an increase in the cost of medical care for certain treatments, due to the cost of malpractice insurance, to abandonment of private practice by some physicians, and in at least one town to the refusal of obstetricians to accept female attorneys or wives of male attorneys as patients. This decline in trust and the increased willingness to file suit against a physician after a medical treatment has had a bad outcome result from a lack of those social relations on which trust depends and lead to increased cost and reduced availability of medical care.

3. A mother of six children, who moved with her husband and children from suburban Detroit to Jerusalem, describes as one reason for doing so the greater freedom her young children have in Jerusalem. She feels it is safe to let her eight-year-old take the six-year-old across town to school on the city bus and to let her children play without supervision in a city park, neither of which did she feel able to allow where she lived before. The reason for this difference can be described as a difference in the social capital available in Jerusalem and in suburban Detroit. In Jerusalem the normative structure ensures that unattended children will be looked after by adults in the vicinity, but no such normative structure exists in most metropolitan areas of the United States. One can say that families in Jerusalem have available to them social capital that does not exist in metropolitan areas of the United States.

4. In the central market in Cairo, the boundaries between merchants are difficult for an outsider to discover. The owner of a shop which specializes in leather, when queried about where one can find a certain kind of jewelry, will turn out to sell that as well—or what appears to be nearly the same thing, to have a close associate who sells it, to whom he will immediately take the customer. Or a shopkeeper will instantly become a money changer simply by turning to his colleague a few shops down. For some activities, such as bringing a customer to a friend's store, there are commissions; others, such as money

changing, merely create obligations. Family relations are important in the market, as is the stability of proprietorship. The whole market is so infused with relations of the sort just described that it can be seen as an organization, no less so than a department store. Alternatively, the market can be seen as consisting of a set of individual merchants, each having an extensive body of social capital on which to draw, based on the relationships within the market.

As these examples indicate, social organization constitutes social capital, facilitating the achievement of goals that could not be achieved in its absence or could be achieved only at a higher cost. There are, however, certain properties of social capital that are important for understanding how it comes into being and how it is destroyed or lost. A comparison of social capital with human capital followed by an examination of different forms of social capital will be helpful for seeing these.

Human Capital and Social Capital

Probably the most important and most original development in the economics of education in the past thirty years has been the idea that the concept of physical capital, as embodied in tools, machines, and other productive equipment, can be extended to include human capital as well (see Schultz, 1961; Becker, 1964). Just as physical capital is created by making changes in materials so as to form tools that facilitate production, human capital is created by changing persons so as to give them skills and capabilities that make them able to act in new ways.

Social capital, in turn, is created when the relations among persons change in ways that facilitate action. Physical capital is wholly tangible, being embodied in observable material form; human capital is less tangible, being embodied in the skills and knowledge acquired by an individual; social capital is even less tangible, for it is embodied in the *relations* among persons. Physical capital and human capital facilitate productive activity, and social capital does so as well. For example, a group whose members manifest trustworthiness and place extensive trust in one another will be able to accomplish much more than a comparable group lacking that trustworthiness and trust.

The distinction between human capital and social capital can be exhibited by a diagram such as Figure 12.1, which represents the relations of three persons (A, B, and C); the human capital resides in the nodes, and the social capital resides in the lines connecting the nodes. Social capital and human capital are often complementary. For example, if B is a child and A is an adult who is a parent of B, then for A to further the cognitive development of B, there must be capital in both the node and the link. There must be human capital held by A and social capital in the relation between A and B.

Forms of Social Capital

Using the concept of social capital will uncover no processes that are different in fundamental ways from those discussed in other chapters. This concept groups

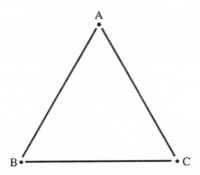

Figure 12.1   Three-person structure: human capital in nodes and social capital in relations.

some of those processes together and blurs distinctions between types of social relations, distinctions that are important for other purposes. The value of the concept lies primarily in the fact that it identifies certain aspects of social structure by their function, just as the concept "chair" identifies certain physical objects by their function, disregarding differences in form, appearance, and construction. The function identified by the concept "social capital" is the value of those aspects of social structure to actors, as resources that can be used by the actors to realize their interests.

By identifying this function of certain aspects of social structure, the concept of social capital aids in both accounting for different outcomes at the level of individual actors and making the micro-to-macro transition without elaborating the social-structural details through which this occurs. For example, characterizing the clandestine study circles of South Korean radical students as constituting social capital that these students can use in their revolutionary activities is an assertion that the groups constitute a resource which aids in moving the students from individual protest to organized revolt. If a resource that accomplishes this task is held to be necessary in a theory of revolt (as it is in Chapter 18), then the study circles can be grouped with other organizational structures, of different origins, which have fulfilled the same function for individuals with revolutionary goals in other contexts, such as the *comités d'action lycéen* of the French student revolt of 1968 or the workers' cells in czarist Russia described and advocated by Lenin (1973 [1902]).

It is true, of course, that for other purposes one wants to investigate the details of such organizational resources, to understand the elements that are critical to their usefulness as resources for a given purpose, and to examine how they came into being in a particular case. But the concept of social capital can allow showing how such resources can be combined with other resources to produce different system-level behavior or, in other cases, different outcomes for individuals. Whether social capital will come to be as useful a quantitative concept in social science as are the concepts of financial capital, physical capital, and human capital remains to be seen; its current value lies primarily in its usefulness for qualitative analyses of social systems and for those quantitative analyses that employ qualitative indicators.

In other chapters (principally in Part III) the concept of social capital will be left unanalyzed (as it was in the brief descriptions given above as examples). In this chapter, however, I will examine just what it is about social relations that can constitute useful capital resources for individuals.

Obligations and Expectations

As described in Chapter 5, if A does something for B and trusts B to reciprocate in the future, this establishes an expectation in A and an obligation on the part of B to keep the trust. This obligation can be conceived of as a "credit slip" held by A to be redeemed by some performance by B. If A holds a large number of these credit slips from a number of persons with whom he has relations, then the analogy to financial capital is direct: The credit slips constitute a large body of credit on which A can draw if necessary—unless, of course, the placement of trust has been unwise, and the slips represent bad debts that will not be repaid. In some social structures (such as, for example, the neighborhoods discussed by Willmott and Young, 1967) it is said that people are "always doing things for each other." There are a large number of these credit slips outstanding, often on both sides of a relation (for these credit slips often appear to be not fungible across different areas of activity, so credit slips from B held by A and those from A held by B are not fully used to cancel each other out). The market in Cairo described earlier in this chapter constitutes an extreme case of such a social structure. In other social structures where individuals are more self-sufficient, depending on each other less, there are fewer of these credit slips outstanding at any time.

Two elements are critical to this form of social capital: the level of trustworthiness of the social environment, which means that obligations will be repaid, and the actual extent of obligations held. Social structures differ in both of these dimensions, and actors within a particular structure differ in the second.

A case which illustrates the value of trustworthiness is the rotating credit association found in Southeast Asia and elsewhere. These associations are groups of friends and neighbors who typically meet monthly; each person contributes the same amount of money to a central fund, which is then given to one of the members (through bidding or by lot). After n months each of the n persons has made n contributions and received one payout. As Geertz (1962) points out, these associations serve as efficient institutions for amassing savings for small capital expenditures, an important aid to economic development. Without a high degree of trustworthiness among the members of the group, such a credit association could not exist—for a person who received a payout early in the sequence of meetings could abscond, leaving the others with a loss. One could not imagine such a rotating credit association operating successfully in urban areas marked by a high degree of social disorganization—or, in other words, by a lack of social capital.

Another situation in which extreme trustworthiness facilitates actions that would not otherwise be possible is that of heads of state. Various accounts of the experiences of heads of state suggest that for persons in this position it is extremely valuable to have an extension of one's self, an agent one can trust absolutely to act as one would in a given situation. Many heads of state have such a person, who may not occupy a formal position of power but may be a member of a personal staff. The fact that these persons are often old friends, or cronies, rather than persons who have distinguished themselves in some political activity, is derivative from this: The most important attribute of such a person is that trust can be placed in him, and this requirement often dictates choosing a long-term personal friend. Such persons often come to have enormous power due to their proximity to a head of state and the trust placed in them; and there are many recorded accounts of the use of that power. What is of interest here is the social capital this relation provides for the head of state, assuming that the trust is well placed. The trusted other is virtually an extension of self, allowing the head of state to expand his capacity for action.

Still another case that illustrates the importance of trustworthiness as a form of social capital is a system of mutual trust. The extreme example of such a system is a couple, each of whom places extensive trust in the other, whether they are deeply in love or not. For both members of such a couple, the relation has extraordinary psychological value. Each can confide in the other, can expose inner doubts, can be completely forthright with the other, can raise sensitive issues—all without fear of the other's misuse of the trust.

Differences in social structures with respect to the extent of outstanding obligations arise for a variety of reasons. These include, besides the general level of trustworthiness that leads obligations to be repaid, the actual needs that persons have for help, the existence of other sources of aid (such as government welfare services), the degree of affluence (which reduces the amount of aid needed from others), cultural differences in the tendency to lend aid and ask for aid (see Banfield, 1967), the degree of closure of social networks, the logistics of social contacts (see Festinger, Schachter, and Back, 1963), and other factors. Individuals in social structures with high levels of obligations outstanding at any time, whatever the source of those obligations, have greater social capital on which they can draw. The density of outstanding obligations means, in effect, that the overall usefulness of the tangible resources possessed by actors in that social structure is amplified by their availability to other actors when needed.

In a farming community such as that of the example in Chapter 5, where one farmer got his hay baled by another and where farm tools are extensively borrowed and lent, the social capital allows each farmer to get his work done with less physical capital in the form of tools and equipment. Such a social structure is analogous to an industrial community in which bills of exchange (that is, debts) are passed around, serving as money and effectively reducing the financial capital necessary to carry out a given level of manufacturing activity. (See Ashton, 1945, for a description of this in Lancashire in the 1790s, before a centralized monetary system was well established in England.)

Individual actors in a social system also differ with respect to the extent of credit slips on which they can draw at any time. For example, in hierarchically structured extended family settings, a patriarch often holds an extraordinarily large set of such credit slips, which he can call in at any time to get done what he wants done. Another clear example occurs in villages in traditional settings that are highly stratified, where certain wealthy families, because of their wealth, have built up extensive credits on which they can call at any time. (It is the existence of such asymmetries that can make some families immune to sanctions that can be used to regulate the actions of others in the community, as occurred in the example about the Sarakatsan nomads of Greece in Chapter 10.)

Similarly, in a political setting such as a legislature, a legislator in a position that brings extra resources (such as the Speaker of the House of Representatives or the Majority Leader of the Senate in the U.S. Congress) can, by effective use of those resources, build up a set of credits from other legislators so that it becomes possible for him to get legislation passed that would otherwise be defeated. This concentration of obligations constitutes social capital that is useful not only for the powerful legislator, but also in increasing the level of action of the legislature. Thus those members of legislatures who have extensive credit slips should be more powerful than those who do not because they can use the credits to produce bloc voting on many issues. It is well recognized, for example, that in the U.S. Senate, some senators are members of what is called the Senate Club, and others are not. This in effect means that some senators are embedded in a system of credits and debts, and others (outside the Club) are not. It is also well recognized that those in the Club are more powerful than those outside it.

Another example showing asymmetry in the sets of obligations and expectations is the one presented earlier about the crisis in medical care in the United States due to liability suits. Traditionally physicians have been in control of events having literally life-and-death importance to patients, who in turn often felt unable to adequately compensate them for the extreme benefits they brought about. Part of a physician's payment was in the form of gratitude, deference, and high occupational prestige. These constituted a felt obligation to the physician, a form of social capital which inhibited patients dissatisfied with the outcome of their medical treatments from taking action against the physician.

But several factors have changed. One is that physicians' monopoly on medical knowledge has been lessened by an expansion of education. A second is a reduction in the likelihood that there is a personal relation between physician and patient, since a patient is less likely to use a family doctor or even a general practitioner and more likely to see specialists for particular medical problems. A third is the high income of many physicians, which reduces the perceived asymmetry between service and compensation. A fourth is the increased use of liability insurance, which transfers the financial cost of a lawsuit from physician to insurer. The combination of these and other factors has reduced the social capital that protected the physician from becoming a target when patients experienced undesirable medical outcomes.

WHY DO RATIONAL ACTORS CREATE OBLIGATIONS? Although some of the variation in the extent of outstanding obligations arises from social changes of the sort described above, some appears to arise from the intentional creation of obligation by a person who does something for another. For example, Turnbull (1972), who studied the Ik, a poverty-ridden tribe in Africa, describes an occasion when a man arrived home to find his neighbors, unasked, on the roof of his house fixing it. Despite his not wanting this aid, he was unable to induce them to stop. In this case and others there appears to be, not the creation of obligations through necessity, but a purposive creation of obligations. The giving of gifts has been interpreted in this light (see Mauss, 1954), as have the potlatches of the Kwakiutl tribe in the Pacific Northwest. In rural areas persons who do favors for others often seem to prefer that these favors not be repaid immediately, and those for whom a favor is done sometimes seem anxious to relieve themselves of the obligation.

Although the motives for freeing oneself from obligations may be readily understood (especially if the existence of obligations consumes one's attention), the motives for creating obligations toward oneself are less transparent. If there is a nonzero chance that the obligation will not be repaid, it would appear that rational persons would extend such credit only if they expect to receive something greater in return—just as a bank makes a loan only at sufficient interest to realize a profit after allowing for risk. The question then becomes whether there is anything about social obligations to make a rational person interested in establishing and maintaining such obligations on the part of others toward himself.

A possible answer is this: When I do a favor for you, this ordinarily occurs at a time when you have a need and involves no great cost to me. If I am rational and purely self-interested, I see that the importance to you of this favor is sufficiently great that you will be ready to repay me with a favor in my time of need that will benefit me more than this favor costs me—unless, of course, you are also in need at that time. This does not apply when the favor is merely the lending of money, since a unit of money holds about the same interest to a person over time.[3] When the favor involves services, expenditure of time, or some other nonfungible resource, however, or when it is of intrinsically more value to the recipient than to the donor (such as help with a task that can be done by two persons but not by one), this kind of mutually profitable exchange is quite

---

3. It is interesting that, for persons whose interest in money fluctuates wildly over time, this sort of exchange is possible. In a rural county in West Virginia, the county clerk would lend money to the three town drunks when their need for money was great and then collect from them, with exhorbitant interest, when they received their welfare checks, when money was of less interest to them.

possible. The profitability for the donor depends on the recipient's not repaying the favor until the donor is in need.

Thus creating obligations by doing favors can constitute a kind of insurance policy for which the premiums are paid in inexpensive currency and the benefit arrives as valuable currency. There may easily be a positive expected profit.

There is one more point: A rational, self-interested person may attempt to prevent others from doing favors for him or may attempt to relieve himself of an obligation at a time he chooses (that is, when repaying the favor costs him little), rather than when the donor is in need, because the call for his services may come at an inconvenient time (when repaying the obligation would be costly). Thus in principle there can be a struggle between a person wanting to do a favor for another and the other not wanting to have the favor done for him or a struggle between a person attempting to repay a favor and his creditor attempting to prevent repayment.

Information Potential

An important form of social capital is the potential for information that inheres in social relations. Information is important in providing a basis for action. But acquisition of information is costly. The minimum it requires is attention, which is always in short supply. One means by which information can be acquired is to use social relations that are maintained for other purposes. Katz and Lazarsfeld (1955) show how this operates for women in several areas of life; for example, a woman who has an interest in being in style but not at the leading edge of fashion can use certain friends, who do stay on the leading edge, as sources of information. As another example, a person who is not deeply interested in current events but who is interested in being informed about important developments can save the time required to read a newspaper if he can get the information he wants from a friend who pays attention to such matters. A social scientist who is interested in being up to date on research in related fields can make use of his everyday interactions with colleagues to do so, if he can depend on them to be up to date in their fields.

All these are examples of social relations that constitute a form of social capital in providing information that facilitates action. The relations in this case are valuable for the information they provide, not for the credit slips they provide in the form of obligations that one holds for others' performance.

Norms and Effective Sanctions

Chapter 10 discussed the problems of establishing and maintaining a norm and the sanctions which give it effectiveness. When an effective norm does exist, it constitutes a powerful, but sometimes fragile, form of social capital. Effective norms that inhibit crime in a city make it possible for women to walk freely outside at night and for old people to leave their homes without fear. Norms in a community that support and provide effective rewards for high achievement in school greatly facilitate the school's task. A prescriptive norm that constitutes an especially important form of social capital within a collectivity is the norm that one should forgo self-interests to act in the interests of the collectivity. A norm of this sort, reinforced by social support, status, honor, and other rewards, is the social capital which builds young nations (and which dissipates as they grow older), strengthens families by leading members to act selflessly in the family's interest, facilitates the development of nascent social movements from a small group of dedicated, inward-looking, and mutually rewarding persons, and in general leads persons to work for the public good. In some of these cases the norms are internalized; in others they are largely supported through external rewards for selfless actions and disapproval for selfish actions. But whether supported by internal or external sanctions, norms of this sort are important in overcoming the public-good problem that exists in conjoint collectivities.

As all these examples suggest, effective norms can constitute a powerful form of social capital. This social capital, however, like the forms described earlier, not only facilitates certain actions but also constrains others. Strong and effective norms about young persons' behavior in a community can keep them from having a good time. Norms which make it possible for women to walk alone at night also constrain the activities of criminals (and possibly of some noncriminals as well). Even prescriptive norms that reward certain actions, such as a norm which says that a boy who is a good athlete should go out for football, are in effect directing energy away from other activities. Effective norms in an area can reduce innovativeness in that area, can constrain not only deviant actions that harm others but also deviant actions that can benefit everyone. (See Merton, 1968, pp. 195–203, for a discussion of how this can come about.)

Authority Relations

If actor A has transferred rights of control of certain actions to another actor, B, then B has available social capital in the form of those rights of control. If a number of actors have transferred similar rights of control to B, then B has available an extensive body of social capital, which can be concentrated on certain activities. Of course, this puts extensive power in B's hands. What is not quite so straightforward is that the very concentration of these rights in a single actor increases the total social capital by overcoming (in principle, if not always entirely in fact) the free-rider problem experienced by individuals with similar interests but without a common authority. It appears, in fact, to be precisely the desire to bring into being the social capital needed to solve common problems that leads persons under certain circumstances to vest authority in a charismatic leader (as discussed in Chapter 4 and in Zablocki, 1980, and Scholem, 1973).

Appropriable Social Organization

Voluntary organizations are brought into being to further some purpose of those who initiate them. In a housing project built during World War II in a city in the eastern United States, there were many physical problems caused by poor construction, such as faulty plumbing, crumbling sidewalks, and other defects (Merton, n.d.). Residents organized to confront the builders and to address these problems in other ways. Later, when the problems were solved, the residents' organization remained active and constituted available social capital which improved the quality of life in the project. Residents had available to them resources that were seen as unavailable where they had lived before. (For example, despite the fact that there were *fewer* teenagers in the community, residents were *more* likely to express satisfaction concerning the availability of babysitters.)

Members of the New York Typographical Union who were monotype operators formed a social club called the Monotype Club (Lipset, Trow, and Coleman, 1956). Later, as employers looked for monotype operators and as monotype operators looked for jobs, both found this organization to be an effective employment referral service and utilized it for this purpose. Still later, when the Progressive Party came into power in the New York Typographical Union, the Monotype Club served as an organizational resource for the ousted Independent Party. The Monotype Club subsequently served as an important source of social capital for the Independents, sustaining their party as an organized opposition while they were out of office.

In an example used earlier in this chapter, the study circles of South Korean student radicals were described as being groups of students who came from the same high school or hometown or church. In this case also, organization that was initiated for one purpose is appropriable for other purposes, constituting important social capital for the individuals who have available to them the organizational resources.

These examples illustrate the general point that organization brought into existence for one set of purposes can also aid others, thus constituting social capital that is available for use.[4] It may be that this form of social capital can be dissolved, with nothing left over, into elements that are discussed under other headings in this section, that is, obligations and expectations, information potential, norms, and authority relations. If so, listing this form of social capital is redundant. But the phenomenon of social organization being appropriated as existing social capital for new purposes is such a pervasive one that separate mention appears warranted.

Intentional Organization

A major use of the concept of social capital depends on its being a by-product of activities engaged in for other purposes. A later section will show why this is so, why there is often little or no direct investment in social capital. There are,

_____

4. A classic instance of this is described by Sills (1957). The March of Dimes was originally dedicated to the elimination of polio. When Salk's vaccine virtually eradicated polio, the March of Dimes organization did not go out of existence but directed its efforts toward other diseases.

however, forms of social capital which are the direct result of investment by actors who have the aim of receiving a return on their investment.

The most prominent example is a business organization created by the owners of financial capital for the purpose of earning income for them. These organizations ordinarily take the form of authority structures composed of positions connected by obligations and expectations and occupied by persons (as described in Chapter 4). In creating such an organization, an entrepreneur or capitalist transforms financial capital into physical capital in the form of buildings and tools, social capital in the form of the organization of positions, and human capital in the form of persons occupying positions. Like the other forms of capital, social capital requires investment in the designing of the structure of obligations and expectations, responsibility and authority, and norms (or rules) and sanctions which will bring about an effectively functioning organization.

Another form of intentional organization is a voluntary association which produces a public good. For example, a group of parents whose children attend a school forms a PTA chapter where one did not exist before. This organization constitutes social capital not only for the organizers but for the school, the students, and other parents. Even if the organization serves only the original purpose for which it is organized and is not appropriated for other purposes, as is the case for organizations described in an earlier section, it serves this purpose, by its very nature, for a wider range of actors than those who initiated it. Such an organization is, concretely, of the same sort as those described earlier. The PTA is the same kind of organization as the Monotype Club, the residents' association formed to deal with faulty plumbing, and the church groups of South Korean youth. All are voluntary associations. As it functions, however, the organization creates two kinds of by-products as social capital. One is the by-product described in the preceding section, the appropriability of the organization for other purposes. A second is the by-product described here: Because the organization produces a public good, its creation by one subset of persons makes its benefits available to others as well, whether or not they participate. For example, the disciplinary standards promulgated by an active PTA change a school in ways that benefit nonparticipants as well as participants.

Relative Quantities of Social Capital

It is possible to state more precisely the resources that social capital provides for those who have it. That will be done in Chapter 30, but I will introduce here some of the results of that chapter. In Figure 12.1 the nodes A, B, and C represent persons and the lines connecting them represent relations; human capital is found in the nodes and social capital in the lines. But the "relation between A and B" is to be taken to mean, as indicated in earlier chapters, that A controls some events of interest to B and B controls some events of interest to A. If the events controlled by each actor are seen as credit slips held by that actor, expressing obligations of the other, then this diagram corresponds directly

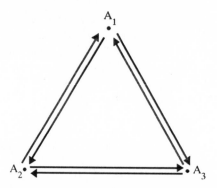

Figure 12.2   A three-actor system with full closure.

to the first form of social capital discussed earlier, obligations and expectations. Other interpretations of events correspond to other forms of social capital, although the correspondence is not perfect.

If an arrow from A_1 and A_2 denotes A_2's interest in events controlled by A_1 or A_2's dependence on A_1, a system of three actors with full closure is represented by Figure 12.2.

If there is no relation between A_2 and A_3, relations among the three can be represented as shown in Figure 12.3.

If A_3 depends on A_2, but A_2 has no dependence on A_3, the diagram of Figure 12.3 is modified as shown in Figure 12.4.

For Figure 12.2, if each actor controls events of equal interest to each of the others, then the power of each, as calculated in Chapter 25, will be equal, by symmetry. In Figure 12.3, A_2 and A_3 are in reciprocal relations with A_1 but have no relations with one another. If these relations are thought of as credit slips (that is, expectations and obligations), then the situation diagrammed in Figure 12.3 can be described by saying that the debits and credits of each pair of actors

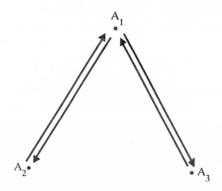

Figure 12.3   A three-actor system without closure.

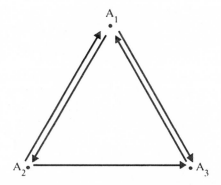

Figure 12.4   A three-actor system with near closure.

are balanced, but A_1 has twice the volume of debits and credits that A_2 and A_3 have. Figure 12.3 represents, then, a situation in which A_1 has more social capital available to him than does either of the other actors. The equilibrium state of the linear system of action is used in Chapter 25 to show that the power of A_1 in the system reflects this. Calculations in that chapter show that if the events that A_1 and A_2 control are of equal interest to each other and similarly for A_1 and A_3, the power of A_2 or A_3 in this system is only .707 times that of A_1.

For Figure 12.4, which is like Figure 12.2 except that A_2 has no obligations to A_3, the calculations of Chapter 25 show that A_2's power is equal to A_1's—A_2 has the same social capital available to him as A_1 does. The absence of any obligations from A_2 and A_3 means that A_3's power is reduced to .618 of that held by A_1 or A_2.[5] Thus the power of an actor in the equilibrium linear system of action is a direct measure of the social capital available to the actor within that system. Examples of the way closure of the system affects the power of actors within it is shown both later in this chapter and in other chapters (see Figure 11.1).

The Public-Good Aspect of Social Capital

Social capital has certain properties that distinguish it from the private, divisible, alienable goods treated by neoclassical economic theory. One of these, discussed by Loury (1987), is its practical inalienability. Although it is a resource that has value in use, it cannot be easily exchanged. As an attribute of the social structure in which a person is embedded, social capital is not the private property of any of the persons who benefit from it.

Another difference, deriving from the public-good aspect of social capital, can be seen by comparing it with physical capital. Physical capital is ordinarily a private good, and property rights make it possible for the person who invests in

5. Cook et al. (1983) have used similar measures to show the power of actors in different structures of constrained communication.

physical capital to capture the benefits it produces. Thus the incentive to invest in physical capital is not depressed; there is, as an economist might say, not a suboptimal investment in physical capital, because those who invest in it are able to capture the benefits of their investments. For human capital also—at least human capital of the sort that is produced in schools—the person who invests the time and resources in building up this capital reaps the benefits that persons anticipate receiving from schooling: a higher-paying job, more satisfying or higher-status work, or even the pleasure of improved understanding of the surrounding world.

But in most of its forms social capital is not like this. For example, the kinds of social structures which make possible social norms and the sanctions to enforce them do not benefit primarily the persons whose efforts are necessary to bring the norms and sanctions into existence, but all those who are part of the particular structure. For example, where there exists a dense set of associations among some parents of children attending a given school, these involve a small number of persons, ordinarily mothers who do not hold full-time jobs outside the home. Yet these mothers themselves experience only a subset of the benefits of this social capital generated for the school. If one of them decides to abandon these activities, for example, to take a full-time job, this may be an entirely reasonable action from a personal point of view, and even from the point of view of her household and children. The benefits of the new activity for her may far outweigh the losses which arise from the decline in associations with other parents whose children attend the school. But her withdrawal from these activities constitutes a loss to all those other parents whose associations and contacts are dependent on them.

As another example, a family's decision to move away from a community because of a job opportunity elsewhere may be entirely correct from the point of view of that family. But because social capital consists of relations among persons, others may experience extensive losses due to the severance of relations with members of that family, a severance over which they had no control. Such losses may entail the weakening of norms and sanctions that aid law enforcement and of those norms that aid parents and schools in socializing children. The total cost each family experiences as a consequence of the decisions it and other families make may outweigh the benefits that come from those few decisions it has control over. Yet the beneficial consequences to the family of those decisions it does have control over may far outweigh the minor losses it experiences from them alone.

Underinvestment of this sort does not only occur in voluntary associations such as a PTA or a Monotype Club. When an individual asks a favor from another, thus incurring an obligation, he does so because it brings him a needed benefit. He does not consider that the other experiences a benefit as well, from having the chance to add to a drawing fund of social capital available at a future time of need. If the first individual can satisfy his need through self-sufficiency or through aid from some external source (for example, a government agency), without incurring an obligation, he may do so—and thus fail to add to the social capital outstanding in the community. Similarly, in choosing to keep trust or not (or choosing whether to devote resources to an attempt to keep trust), an actor does so on the basis of costs and benefits he himself will experience. That his trustworthiness will facilitate others' actions or his lack of trustworthiness will inhibit others' actions does not enter into his decision making.

A similar but more qualified statement can be made about information as a form of social capital. An individual who serves as a source of information for another because he is well informed ordinarily acquires that information for his own benefit, not for any other who might make use of him. This is not always true, however. As Katz and Lazarsfeld (1955) show, opinion leaders in an area acquire information in part to maintain their position as such. This is to be expected if the others who use them as information sources pay deference or gratitude for the information they get, even if the opinion leaders initially acquired information solely for their own use.

[margin note: gossip queens at the school gates!!]

Norms also suffer only in part from underinvestment in public goods. Norms are intentionally established, as means of reducing externalities, and their benefits are ordinarily captured by those who are responsible for establishing them. But as Chapter 11 showed, the capability of establishing and maintaining effective norms depends on properties of the social structure (such as closure) over which one actor does not have control, yet which may be affected by one actor's action. These properties affect the structure's capacity to sustain effective norms; yet individuals seldom take this fact into account when taking actions that can destroy these structural properties.

Some forms of social capital have the property that their benefits can be captured by those who invest in them; rational actors consequently will not underinvest in these forms of social capital. Organizations that produce a private good constitute the outstanding example, as indicated earlier. The result is that there will be in society an imbalance between the relative investment in organizations that produce private goods for a market and in organizations (often voluntary associations) from which the benefits are not captured—an imbalance in the sense that if the positive externalities created by such social capital could be internalized, it would come to exist in greater quantity.

The public-good aspect of most social capital means that it is in a fundamentally different position with respect to purposive action than are most other forms of capital. Social capital is an important resource for individuals and can greatly affect their ability to act and their perceived quality of life. They have the capability of bringing such capital into being. Yet because many of the benefits of actions that bring social capital into being are experienced by persons other than the person so acting, it is not to that person's interest to bring it into being. The result is that most forms of social capital are created or destroyed as a by-product of other activities. Much social capital arises or disappears without anyone's willing it into or out of being; such capital is therefore even less recognized and taken into account in social research than its intangible character might warrant.

The Creation, Maintenance, and Destruction of Social Capital

In this section I will suggest some factors, themselves the consequences of individuals' decisions, which help create or destroy social capital. Because there is some redundancy with earlier chapters, the treatment will be brief.

Closure

In Chapter 11 I indicated the importance of closure of social networks for the emergence of norms. Closure is also important if trust is to reach the level that is warranted by the trustworthiness of the potential trustees. This is evident especially in the case of systems of trust that involve intermediaries in trust, as discussed in Chapter 8 and shown in Figure 8.2. A's placement of trust in T's performance is based in part on A's trust in B's judgment. B's placement of trust depends in part on his trust in C's judgment, and C's in turn depends in part on his trust in A's. These closed systems can, of course, lead to inflationary and deflationary spirals in the placement of trust; despite this instability that can result from extreme closure, some degree of closure is a valuable asset to individuals who must decide whether or not to place trust.

In some systems of trust intermediaries can constitute a substitute for closure. If A must decide whether to place trust in T but has no relation with T, then B's relation to T, together with A's trust in B's judgment, can allow A to make a more accurate assessment of T's trustworthiness, and thus to reach a better decision.

The effect of closure can be seen especially well by considering a system involving parents and childen. In a community where there is an extensive set of expectations and obligations connecting the adults, each adult can use his drawing account with other adults to help supervise and control his children. If A and B are adults in a community and a and b are, respectively, their children, then closure in the community can be pictured as in Figure 12.5(a), where arrows from one actor to another again represent the dependence of the second on the first through events the first controls. Lack of closure is shown in Figure 12.5(b), where the parents, A and B, have their friends outside this community. In a community like that represented in Figure 12.5(a), A and B can both use their mutual obligations to aid them in raising their children and can develop norms about their children's behavior. Actions of either child, a or b, impose externalities, direct or indirect, on both A and B in both communities; but only in the community represented by Figure 12.5(a) is there the closure which allows A and B to establish norms and reinforce each other's sanctioning of the children.

For Figure 12.5, if all obligations are assumed to be balanced and all interests

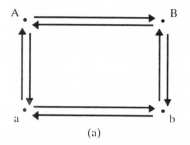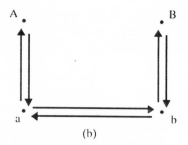

Figure 12.5 Representation of two communities: (a) with and (b) without intergenerational closure.

to be equal, then it is possible, as for Figures 12.2, 12.3, and 12.4, to calculate the relative disadvantage faced by parents in the community without closure. In the community depicted in Figure 12.5(a), each child and each parent have equal power, by symmetry. In the community depicted in Figure 12.5(b), the parents, though continuing to hold just as much direct control of events which interest their respective children, have only .618 of the power their children have, purely because of the relations between those children and the absence of relations between the parents. In other words, the parents in the community without closure have only .618 as much power relative to their children as do the parents in the community with closure—the deficiency is due to the lack of relations between the parents.

The variation in closure exhibited in Figure 12.5 can be generalized to any social structure in which actors can be classified as two different types and have relations both with actors of the other type and with actors of the same type. For example, instead of parents and children, the types may be unmarried men and unmarried women. The men and women will date one another, and, in addition, the men may have extensive networks of relations, and the women may have extensive networks of relations, as shown in Figure 12.5(a). Or it may be that the women, for example, have extensive networks of relations with internal closure, but the men do not, as shown in Figure 12.5(b). In that case the women will have more social capital than the men do. They can give the men reputations (good or bad), establish rules or norms that may strengthen a woman's power relative to a man's on dates, and use their social capital in other ways.

This example, as well as the case of parents and children, suggests that where one type of actor is weaker in a relationship (as children are with respect to parents or women with respect to men or students with respect to faculty), the actors of that type will be likely to develop social networks that have closure, in order to strengthen their position relative to the more powerful type of actor. There are, of course, other factors that facilitate closure in such networks, such as the social proximity that schools provide for children.

One setting in which closure in a network is especially important is in certain communities of corporate actors. In a case where firms in one industry (represented by A and B in Figure 12.5) are suppliers for firms in a second industry (represented by a and b in Figure 12.5), there are supplier-customer relations (analogous to parent-child relations), possibly relations among firms within the first industry, and possibly relations among firms within the second industry. Relations among supplier firms constitute a potentially valuable form of social capital, sometimes leading to collusion and resulting in price fixing. Relations among customer firms also constitute valuable social capital, sometimes resulting in boycotts or embargoes.

Figure 12.5 illustrates variations in closure in a social structure with role differentiation; Figures 12.2, 12.3, and 12.4 show variation in closure where there is no role differentiation. When there is closure in the latter structures, as in Figure 12.2, norms and reputations can develop that keep the actors in the system from imposing externalities on one another. When closure is not present, as in Figure 12.3, those norms and reputations cannot develop.

Stability

A second factor which affects the creation and destruction of social capital is the stability of social structure. Every form of social capital, with the exception of that deriving from formal organizations with structures based on positions, depends on stability. Disruptions of social organization or of social relations can be highly destructive to social capital. The social invention of organizations having positions rather than persons as elements of the structure has provided one form of social capital that can maintain stability in the face of instability of individuals. Where individuals are relegated to being simply occupants of positions, only the performance of the occupants, not the structure itself, is disturbed by mobility of individuals. But for every other form of social capital, individual mobility constitutes a potential action that will be destructive of the structure itself—and thus of the social capital dependent on it.

Ideology

A third factor affecting the creation and destruction of social capital is ideology. An ideology can create social capital by imposing on an individual who holds it the demand that he act in the interests of something or someone other than himself. This is clear in the effects religious ideology has in leading persons to attend to the interests of others. One indirect and somewhat surprising effect has been noted from comparisons of religious and secular schools. Religiously affiliated private schools in the United States, despite their more rigid disciplinary standards, have dropout rates much lower than those of secular private schools or public schools (Coleman and Hoffer, 1987). The apparent cause is a quantity of social capital available to the religiously affiliated school that does not exist for most other schools, private or public. This depends in part on the social-structural connections between school and parents, through the religious community. In part, however, it depends on the precept derived from religious doctrine that every individual is important in the eyes of God. A consequence of this precept is that youth are much less likely to become administratively "lost" through inattention. The signs of alienation and withdrawal are more quickly responded to, because of the religious ideology held by the school's principal, members of the staff, and adult members of the religious community associated with the school.

There are also ways in which ideology can negatively affect the creation of social capital. An ideology of self-sufficiency, such as that espoused by the Epicureans in classical Greece, or an ideology emphasizing each individual's separate relation to God, which is a basis of much Protestant doctrine, can inhibit the creation of social capital. Durkheim (1951 [1897]) examined the factors leading to individualism (roughly what he described as *égoïsme*) and its effects on the tendency to commit suicide.

Other Factors

Although there are various additional factors which affect the creation and destruction of social capital, only one broad class of these is especially important. This is the class of factors which make persons less dependent on one another. Affluence is one important member of this class; official sources of support in times of need (government aid of various sorts) is another. The presence of these alternatives allows whatever social capital is generated to depreciate and not to be renewed. For despite the public-good aspect of social capital, the more extensively persons call on one another for aid, the greater will be the quantity of social capital generated. When, because of affluence, government aid, or some other factor, persons need each other less, less social capital is generated.

Finally, it is useful to mention that social capital is one of those forms of capital which depreciate over time. Like human capital and physical capital, social capital depreciates if it is not renewed. Social relationships die out if not maintained; expectations and obligations wither over time; and norms depend on regular communication.

PART III

Corporate Action

13

Constitutions and the Construction
of Corporate Actors

Norms and Constitutions

Chapters 10 and 11, on the emergence of norms, began a transition in this book. Norms constitute a supraindividual entity, a recognized set of rights of some individuals to constrain or otherwise shape the actions of individuals who are targets of the norms. In many cases beneficiaries and targets of norms are the same individuals, reflecting the fact that it is in the interest of individual rational persons to collectively constrain certain actions (and encourage others) that any individual might engage in. Chapter 10 argued that it is the negative externalities imposed on others by some actions and the positive externalities created for them by other actions that create the demand for norms (but do not ensure their existence).

The supraindividual character of norms lies not merely in the fact that sanctions are sometimes imposed collectively, as is the case when members of a group shun an individual, generate a reputation for an individual, or heap adulation on an individual. It lies also in the fact that rights to control a certain class of actions of an actor are regarded, by actors in the system, as held not by the actor but by others. To state it differently, the norm and the use of sanctions to enforce it are held to be legitimate by each of the beneficiaries. This legitimacy is evident not only because actors do claim the right to sanction target actors, but also because target actors accept the definition of an action as wrong and accept a sanction that could be resisted. In extreme cases, such as can be found in primitive societies, the power of a norm is made evident by the fact that a violator may even feel unable to continue living.[1]

Where a conjoint norm exists, a right has been given up by the individuals as individuals and assumed by them as a collectivity. This is the right to control one's own actions, a right examined in Chapter 4. That chapter showed how rational individuals may give up certain rights of control of their own actions, either for extrinsic compensation or in the expectation that the very exercise of authority will benefit them. In the creation of a conjoint norm, individuals who

---

1. See, for example, Park (1974, pp. 42–43), who describes a case from Jane Richardson's fieldwork with the Kiowa, a North American prairie tribe, in which a man died of shame after sanctions imposed by women of the tribe.

are simultaneously the targets of the potential norm and its beneficiaries in effect establish an authority relation: As individuals, they become the subordinates, having given up the right to control a certain class of action. And as a collectivity, they become the superordinate, having acquired that right as a collectivity or a corporate actor.

In some self-contained villages, communes, and tribal societies, there is no authority beyond this. The authority of the village or the commune or the tribe lies in the rights it holds, through norms accepted by all, to constrain certain actions and encourage other actions. The collectivity or the corporate actor consists of nothing more than this set of norms and sanctions. In such settings norms do everything that formal laws do in more legalistic societies, and community sanctions do everything that legal sanctions and governmental actions do in a society with institutionalized government.

Not all actions can be governed by the application of sanctions by members of a collectivity, however. Even in such closed communities there is often a more formal governing body, as is apparent in Zablocki's (1980) descriptions of communes (see Chapter 4). This governing body is concerned with ensuring that certain tasks necessary for the common welfare get done (a problem corresponding to that for which prescriptive norms are sometimes established) and with constraining actions that produce negative externalities (a problem for which proscriptive norms are sometimes established).[2]

It might well be said that in settings such as these, an implicit constitution has been brought into being by the members of the community through their establishment of norms (that is, their transfer to the collectivity of rights to control certain of their actions) and their establishment of procedures to implement these rights, together with sanctions to enforce the norms and rules.

But Chapter 11 showed that certain social-structural conditions are necessary for the establishment and maintenance of effective norms. In many settings, especially in large dispersed groups but also in many smaller ones, those conditions are not met. What is carried out informally in settings of the sort described above must be carried out more explicitly and formally in other settings if individuals want to achieve benefits analogous to those they obtain from conjoint norms in small social systems with a high degree of closure.

It is for this reason that explicit attention to constitutions is necessary, in both social practice and social theory. Formal constitutions in more formally organized social systems can be seen as the analogue of the informal sets of norms and rules that emerge in small social systems with a high degree of closure. That a formally written document titled "Constitution" for a group, organization, or larger social system corresponds only loosely to what social scientists refer to as

---

2. The literature on communes suggests that in many communes, once a set of rules concerning the performance tasks for the common good is determined through a formal procedure, informal community sanctions form the principal governing device to ensure that these actions are done, as well as for constraining negative externalities. (See Kanter, 1973; Zablocki, 1980.)

the constitution of such a system reflects the fact that formal constitutions have their sociological origins in informal norms and rules. The effective constitution of a group, organization, or social system is far broader than the written document and includes the unwritten norms and rules, as well as the written ones. Thus the examination of constitutional questions in this chapter will be grounded in the sociological ancestry of constitutions (in norms) and the results of the examination of norms in Chapters 10 and 11. It is when the social structure will not support a norm that is sufficiently effective to satisfy the interests of the potential beneficiaries of the norm that the question arises of constructing an explicit corporate entity having greater powers than does a norm or set of norms.

Conjoint and Disjoint Constitutions

Norms are conjoint when the beneficiaries and the targets are the same persons, and disjoint when these are different persons. As indicated in Chapter 10, there are intermediate cases, but here I will limit attention to these two extremes.

Corresponding to conjoint norms are constitutions in which the beneficiaries of corporately held rights are also the potential targets of corporately generated constraints or demands. It is this structure that is ordinarily implicit in theories of constitutions as social contracts: Those engaging in the social contract are forming a compact to govern *themselves*. When constructing a constitution in this sort of structure, the same persons see themselves in two capacities with respect to the corporate body they create: as beneficiaries and as targets. A single actor can be seen as representative of the whole, for the interests of beneficiary, leading to a strong corporate body, and the interests of target, opposed to a strong corporate body, are found in each person. Constitutions based on this kind of structure I will call conjoint constitutions. Membership groups and organizations that are brought into being by their members exemplify corporate bodies with conjoint constitutions. The U.S., Polish, and French constitutions were perhaps the first constitutions of nation-states that had as an ideological base a social contract among equal citizens. Reality, of course, fell short of this ideal, because of the differing social positions of different citizens.

At the other extreme are constitutions constructed by one set of actors to create a corporate body that will impose constraints and demands on a different set of actors. The beneficiaries and targets are different persons. In this case, there can be no representative member, because each is either beneficiary or target, having only one set of interests. Constitutions based on this kind of structure I will call disjoint constitutions. Examples are found throughout history. In feudal society the rules were made principally by the nobles to govern the peasants. The ideology surrounding the formation of Marxist socialist states emphasizes that socialism is dictatorship of the proletariat; that is, state and constitution are established by and for the workers as beneficiaries, with other social classes as targets of the demands and constraints imposed by the state. The realization of this concept also fell short of the ideology, but the ideology is that of a disjoint constitution, which specifies that the society is governed by a particular class, in contrast to the ideology underlying the U.S. Constitution.

There are also examples of disjoint constitutions within nation-states. Perhaps the most common is the constitution of a school, which is established by the community of teachers, administrators, and parents, and whose constraints and demands are imposed on the children attending the school. (In a later section I will examine a major constitutional change occurring in American high schools.)

The establishment of a corporate body by means of a conjoint constitution does not provide a setting for interpersonal or intergroup conflict, because any conflict of interests lies within the individual. In contrast, the establishment of a corporate body by means of a disjoint constitution must occur through coercion, either that implicit in an existing authority structure (as in feudal society or in schools) or that resulting from the outcome of a civil war (as in class-based revolutions).

Conjoint Constitutions and Social-Contract Theory

The correspondence of the situation in which there is a demand for conjoint norms to the situations treated by moral and political philosophers is perhaps best seen in social-contract theory, such as that of John Locke. Locke (1965 [1690]) argues that rational individuals, each possessing natural rights, will engage in a joint social contract to give up to a central authority those rights which if held and exercised centrally will make them better off. They sacrifice the unrestricted right to control their own actions in return for the benefit they expect from the establishment of the same restriction on the rights of others.

Nozick (1974) has followed Locke's framework in generating a theory of the minimal state. In Nozick's formulation neighbors begin with mutual-protection associations, to which they relinquish certain minimal rights, the right to use force and the right to be taxed for common defense involving the use of force. Because of increased benefits from further combinations, these associations become larger until something like a minimal state comes into existence. Nozick says, "Out of anarchy, pressed by spontaneous groupings, mutual-protection associations, division of labor, market pressures, economies of scale and rational self-interest there arises something very much resembling a minimal state (1974, pp. 16–17).

It is useful to examine this emergence using the three-actor common project treated in Chapter 10. I will modify the example slightly so that it will better correspond to Nozick's discussion of mutual protection. Three individuals, A_1, A_2, and A_3, propose to form a mutual-protection association, to which they will each contribute $9. Without the association they are subject to a predation which takes $12 from each. If the association is formed and all contribute, they are each $3 better off, since they contribute $9 each and do not experience the predation of $12 each. If only one contributes, the predations are reduced by $4 for each, and if two contribute, the predations are reduced by $8 for each. The outcomes

Table 13.1 Payoffs to three actors for contributing and not contributing to a mutual-protection scheme.

		A_3			
		Contribute		Not contribute	
		A_2		A_2	
		Contribute	Not contribute	Contribute	Not contribute
A_1	Contribute	-9, -9, -9	-13, -4, -13	-13, -13, -4	-17, -8, -8
	Not contribute	-4, -13, -13	-8, -8, -17	-8, -17, -8	-12, -12, -12

for each are as shown in Table 13.1. (This table has the same structure as Table 10.2, as can be seen by adding 12 to each number in this table.)

As Table 13.1 shows, all three are $3 worse off if they fail to form the association to which all contribute than if they do form it. The contribution of each actor constitutes a positive externality worth $4 to each of the others; the contribution of each actor makes that actor $5 worse off, because it is worth $4 to him but costs him $9. If they can form the mutual-protection association merely through informal sanctions sufficient to ensure contribution by all, then they are all better off than without it.[3] If they cannot, then they are motivated to form a corporate actor (Nozick's minimal state) which does not depend on the social-structural conditions necessary for the emergence of norms. That is, if sanctions alone are insufficient to induce contributions from all, they have an incentive to form a corporate actor to which they give up rights sufficient to realize that common goal.

An agreement among all three actors to give up control of their actions to a central authority would be beneficial to all if the central authority is costless and if all three can be assured that the central authority will require each to contribute $9. Thus each sees potential gain from a voluntary vesting of rights in a

---

3. Perhaps the best example of such an association found in practice is the voluntary fire department that exists in some small towns. Having control only of informal sanctions, such associations have sometimes experienced difficulties in obtaining sufficient contributions to purchase equipment or volunteers to man the equipment. One sanction that has sometimes (although rarely) been employed is to fail to respond to a fire alarm from the residence of a noncontributor.

central authority. But as the payoff structure shows, each stands the chance of being worse off than he would be if he acted alone. In a situation with this structure, an authority relation is created. In effect, the three individuals agree to create a new actor with the right to act for all. I will call this new actor a corporate actor, for it is a corporate entity which holds rights vested in it by its members.

The structure I have described is, I believe, equivalent to that which the social-contract theorists such as Locke describe as leading to formation of a state. It is also the structure used by individuals who see some opportunity for mutual protection (or mutual gain) to create a social contract that leads to a voluntary association. Trade unions, joint-stock business firms, trade associations, professional associations, and other corporate actors are in principle created in this way.

Given that some authority systems are created in this way, the newly created corporate actor can be seen as the superordinate, and the members who have voluntarily given up to the corporate actor certain rights to control or constrain their actions can be seen as the subordinates. This kind of authority system is a special case, however; since the members retain the right to control the actions of the corporate actor (for example, through collective decisions in which each has voting rights), they have created an actor with authority over them but whose actions they jointly have authority over. It is both superordinate over them and subordinate to them. If nothing more were to be said, this could be regarded as an ingenious social invention to achieve the benefits of common action at no cost.

Of course, there is more to be said. How is the new corporate actor to come to take the action that benefits the members? The simplest case is illustrated by the mutual-protection example, in which it is clear which action is to the common interest of the three members of the association. There is a constitutional task, then, for the new corporate actor, that of determining the decision rule to be used for arriving at corporate actions. The corporate actor must have a means of deciding on its actions since each member of the collectivity, as well as each subset of members within it, has interests that partially conflict with those of other members and other subsets. For example, the ranking of the outcomes given in Table 13.1 for each individual is as shown in Figure 13.1.

Individuals have interests that are partially in conflict and partially in agreement. Thus, if the decision rule for the corporate actor is majority rule, A_1 and A_2 might engage in a coalition to choose DDC, their second choice but the last choice of A_3. Coalitions are also possible between A_1 and A_3 and between A_2 and A_3. If the decision rule is unanimity, then some rule must be introduced to cover the situation when unanimity is not reached. If that rule is (as seems possible) that DDD will be the outcome, then, unless unanimity can be reached on another choice (such as, CCC), the collectivity is no better off than if its members acted individually, for the outcome would be DDD in that case.

This problem, where each individual is in a similar situation, can be resolved by a meta-rule that would be to the interest of all, to the effect that persons in similar situations are to be treated similarly, or that laws are not to distinguish among persons. This problem remains unsolved, however, when individuals are not in the same situation. If, for example, A_1, A_2, and A_3 have different amounts of wealth, a meta-rule might specify that they are each to pay a tax, but that payment can no longer automatically be \$9 for each. The decision about how much each should pay remains to be made.

This is the kind of complication that arises in even the simplest situation. In a more complex situation, in which a larger number of individuals (still in a conjoint structure, where each is target and beneficiary of the potential norm) propose to create a corporate actor to cope with a number of different kinds of externality-generating actions, the complications are more numerous. Examining these complexities and seeing how they might be addressed can be done by returning to the situation which constitutes the basis for norms. There are potential targets and potential beneficiaries of a norm, and in the case of a conjoint norm these are the same actors. The target actors have interests, and the beneficiaries have interests. The interests of the target actors are the interests of the individuals, as subordinates to the corporate actor they have created. The interests of the beneficiaries are the interests of the corporate actor, the superordinate to which they have given authority over their actions.

Examining the interests of actors as targets and beneficiaries and weighing these interests against each other can be done by adopting a device used by Rawls (1971), that of rational, self-interested actors standing behind a veil of ignorance about their futures. I will use that device in asking what kinds of

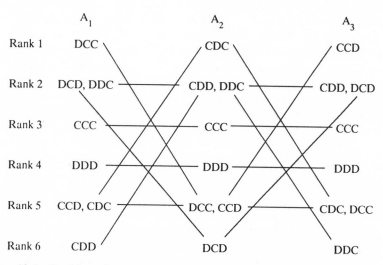

Figure 13.1   Ranking of outcomes by A_1, A_2, and A_3 for mutual-protection scheme shown in Table 13.1.

principles will guide the consideration of rational individuals in the construction of a corporate actor, that is, in the creation of a constitution. I will first describe Rawls's use of the device, to distinguish it from my own.

Rawls used the device as a way of asking what kind of society an individual would choose if he had no knowledge of what position (or set of positions over a lifetime) he might occupy. Rawls argued that the first question such an individual would ask himself is this one: What amount of liberty would be optimal? The answer Rawls gives is very much like that given by John Stuart Mill—the maximum liberty compatible with equal liberty for all. The second question, according to Rawls, would be this: What amount and kind of inequalities are optimal? Rawls's answer is that only those inequalities are just which operate to the benefit of the least advantaged.[4] Rawls argues that each rational individual, motivated wholly by selfish concerns, will answer in this way because he himself might come to be in the position of the least advantaged. Thus, each person, by imagining himself in a variety of possible social positions, arrives at a rule which will be socially just, because it "balances" the discomforts he would feel in various social positions. As numerous authors have pointed out, Rawls's balancing is equivalent to a minimax game-theoretic strategy—the strategy that minimizes the maximum possible loss. Implications of this strategy have been the source of damaging objections to this formulation. Nevertheless it is an impressive intellectual device for producing a rule which generates equity among persons, a rule arising from each person's considerations about what rule is best for him in an uncertain future. The device translates the problem of interpersonal comparison of utility into that of intrapersonal comparison. Something like this formulation is basic to the fairness of the rules of a game, for in a similar way those rules must be established before each player knows what role he is to play. Rawls in fact titled the paper in which the original (somewhat different) version of this principle was stated "Justice as Fairness" (1958).

The veil of ignorance envisioned by Rawls is one of a class of devices used to transform interpersonal comparison of utility into intrapersonal comparison. An early device of this sort was introduced by Thomas Hobbes, who gave in his *Leviathan* what he called a "Rule, by which the Laws of Nature may be easily examined." This rule was, according to Hobbes, an "easie sum": "Do not that to another, which thou wouldst not have done to thyself." Hobbes describes this as follows: "When weighing the actions of other men with one's own, . . . to put them into the other part of the balance, and his own into their place, that his own passions, and self-love, may adde nothing to the weight" (1960 [1651], XV, p. 35).

---

4. In his earlier article "Justice as Fairness" (1958), Rawls arrived at a less precise principle: Only those inequalities are just which operate to the benefit of all. This earlier principle is close to the criterion of Pareto optimality and to the Kaldor principle of compensation (discussed later in this chapter) and is also much closer than Rawls's subsequent principle to the criterion that rules of a game must meet.

Immanuel Kant's categorical imperative ("Act only on that maxim through which you can at the same time will that it should become a universal law") is another device for transforming interpersonal comparison of utility into intrapersonal comparison. The categorical imperative is a relatively minor modification of Hobbes's rule (although Kant argued that it is very different), and both are very similar to the Golden Rule. Hobbes's imagery of a balance, which allows one to discover the "Laws of Nature," is similar to the idea of balancing the interests of the beneficiaries of a norm or corporate action and the targets of that action. Hobbes, however, was envisioning an interaction between two persons, and, as Baumrin (1988) points out, his rule, or "easie sum," is predicated upon both persons' interests having equal weight. The idea of balancing interests as target and as beneficiary allows any number of actors on each of the two sides and makes no assumption that different actors' interests have equal weights.

In asking how it is that rational actors do create constitutions (not, as did Hobbes, Kant, or Rawls, asking what they *should* do), I will assume that they carry out the balancing of their interests behind a veil of ignorance like that of Rawls. Yet the derivation of the constitution-generating situation from the norm-generating situation shows that the questions Rawls poses for rational actors are not at all appropriate for devising a constitution for a corporate actor—whether a state or an organization. The appropriate questions derive from two sets of interests: the interests actors will have as subordinates to the corporate actor thus formed (analogous to the interests of target actors in the case of norms), and the interests of the corporate actor itself (analogous to the interests of beneficiaries of a norm). The veil of ignorance in this case is a special one: After posing to himself the questions generated by his interests as target and as beneficiary, each individual knows, for a given class of events, the number of targets of corporate action and the number of beneficiaries, and each knows the cost of corporate action to the targets and the benefit of the action to the beneficiaries. What each does not know is his own position as target or beneficiary, either for a particular event or over all events of that class that he will experience. The individual does not know whether he will always be a target, will always be a beneficiary, or will sometimes be target and sometimes beneficiary with the frequency expected for the population.

The problem each individual confronts is simple and straightforward: What rights are to be held corporately, and what rights are to be held individually? For each class of actions, is the right to control actions of that class to be held corporately or individually? This problem might be seen as one variant of the problem that arises for the subordinate-to-be when an authority relation is created, as discussed in Chapter 4. Should he vest authority over a particular class of actions or retain the right of controlling them himself? To see the problem in this way is to take the perspective of a philosophy of natural rights, in which rights originate with individuals and are held corporately only after each individual transfers them to a newly created corporate actor.

The problem, however, is not best seen from this philosophical position, for in the absence of some kind of consensus, no rights exist, as argued in Chapter 3. The appropriate position for viewing the problem is that rights originate with consensus and are nonexistent in the absence of consensus. Rights do not inhere in individuals but originate only through consensus; yet consensus itself requires recourse to individuals. The problem remains one that rational individuals, in creating a constitution, must confront at the outset. The answer depends on the balance, as seen by an individual, of his interests as a target of corporate action for that class of events and his interests as a beneficiary of such action.

For a single class of common projects like that of Chapter 10 or a single class of predatory actions like that which leads the mutual-protection association of Table 13.1 to be formed, the problem can be solved simply. But for any organization or any state, there are possible various common projects, as well as various predations from without and various types of individual actions which impose externalities on others (including negative externalities such as those imposed by stealing or positive externalities such as those resulting from heroic actions). As the example of the common project in Chapter 10 and the example of the mutual-protection association in this chapter illustrate, joint activities can also be regarded as being composed of individual actions that impose externalities on others.

Some externality-producing actions result in strong externalities, and some do not. For each class of actions the individual must assess, from behind a veil of ignorance, the relative strengths of his interests as a potential target of corporate action, and as a potential beneficiary of corporate action.

The question can be put in the same terms as the general question of Chapter 4: For which actions is it in my interest to vest rights of control in a corporate actor? This question asks for a balancing of the individual's interests as target of corporate action and his interests as beneficiary of corporate action. As long as all individuals are alike in their expectations of being target or beneficiary of corporate actions—and they are if the veil of ignorance is taken as a given—they will arrive at the same decisions concerning which actions should have rights of control held by individuals and which actions should have rights of control vested in the corporate actor.

What criterion will a rational actor use to determine those actions over which rights of control are to be transferred to the corporate actor? He will use the criterion of rationality: Rights with respect to an action will be transferred to the corporate actor if the benefits (or costs) experienced in carrying out the action aggregated over all the occasions when one expects to be in that position are less than the costs (or benefits) experienced from externalities of the action aggregated over all the occasions when one expects to be in that position. If rights over the action are transferred to the corporate actor, the first of these two positions is that of the target actor, and the second is that of the beneficiary of corporate action.

Note that this criterion has the same structure, but not the same content, as that of Rawls. The individual, behind the veil of ignorance, weighs the costs of rights being held corporately (in those circumstances in which he would be the target of corporate action) against the benefits of those rights being held corporately (in those circumstances in which he would be the beneficiary of corporate action). Here, as in Rawls's formulation, interpersonal comparison of utility is transformed into intrapersonal comparison. Rawls *assumes* that rights are held corporately, however, and asks a subsidiary question ("What inequalities are just?") predicated on this allocation of rights; I ask the question which logically precedes the allocation of rights. One might see my answer as being no different from the first principle that Rawls sees as emerging from behind the veil of ignorance, the principle of maximum liberty. But if Rawls had taken that principle seriously, his second principle concerning the optimal level of inequalities would have to have been based on a determination of what rights the individuals proposed to give themselves corporately, that is, what liberties they proposed to restrict. The answer to that question would then have prescribed limits to the rights available to the collectivity to reduce inequalities in the society. For example, as several authors have pointed out, Rawls's second principle implies eliminating the inequalities imposed by the family, which implies that the state has the right to take children from parents at or near birth.[5] This implies loss of parents' rights to the state, or, in Rawls's terms, restriction of a liberty. It is questionable at best whether this is a restriction to which individuals behind a veil of ignorance would agree.

It is important to be clear about this limitation on rights of control transferred through the social contract to the corporate actor, for some theorists are not. Rousseau is oblivious to this issue (making him, according to Talmon, 1952, the father of modern totalitarian democracy), as is Rawls. Apart from the criterion of rationality, an additional reason to be clear about the limitation of rights will become apparent later in this chapter when I examine the capacity of corporate actors, once in existence, to acquire coercively through their agents more rights from those who brought them into being.

Sen's Paradox

A sense of the importance of the distinction between rights held individually and rights held corporately can be gained by examining a paradox described by Sen (1970). Sen attempts to show that a political philosophy of liberalism is incompatible with the criterion of Pareto optimality. What makes this incompatibility, if it does exist, serious and paradoxical is that Pareto optimality is a criterion that evaluates policies according to their consequences for each individual separately, whereas liberalism is a political philosophy that judges policies according to the liberty they permit for each individual. Thus by neither criterion is one

5. Implementation of Rawls's second principle would require the state to exercise virtually unlimited authority in stamping out inequalities that originated in the family and elsewhere. See Coleman (1974a) for a discussion of this essentially totalitarian implication of Rawls's theory.

individual's welfare of liberty balanced against that of another (as is the case with utilitarianism, for example). It would be a serious charge against liberalism if it were in fact found to be incompatible with Pareto optimality.

To illustrate his paradox, Sen presents the case of two persons who disagree about reading D. H. Lawrence's *Lady Chatterley's Lover*. Sen calls the two Prude and Lascivious. Lascivious prefers that they both read the book. Prude wants neither to read it. Second best in Lascivious's view is that Prude read the book, if both cannot. Prude also prefers to read the book rather than to have Lascivious read it, if one of them must. The preferences can be tabulated as shown in Table 13.2.

Prude's preferences are outcome D, B, C, and A, in that order, and Lascivious's are A, B, C, and D. A constitution based on a political philosophy of liberalism would give each the right to determine what he reads. That is, Prude would have the right to select either the upper or the lower row of the matrix. Lascivious would have the right to select either the left or the right column of the matrix. Under this distribution of rights, Prude will decide not to read *Lady Chatterley's Lover,* and Lascivious will decide to read it, giving outcome C. But as Sen points out, both prefer outcome B over C. Outcome C is not Pareto-optimal, because both participants like it less than outcome B (Prude reads *Lady Chatterley's Lover* and Lascivious does not).

The disturbing aspect of this apparent incompatibility lies in the general motivation behind the idea of Pareto-optimal moves, and its similarity to the motivation behind liberalism. The idea is that if a move from one policy to another makes one person better off, he will prefer to see that move made, and if it hurts no one else to make such a move, then there should be no objections to it. It will be socially desirable, resulting in a state that is better than the original state. At least one person is better off, and no one is worse off. The same imagery of individuals exercising choices to express their preferences underlies the political philosophy of liberalism. Yet the two conceptualizations are in apparent conflict. Why?

Table 13.2   Choices and outcomes for Prude and Lascivious according to Sen's paradox.

		Lascivious reads	
		Yes	No
Prude reads	Yes	A	B
	No	C	D

As Bernholz (1987) has shown, Sen's paradox is easily resolved if the usual definition of liberalism is used rather than the narrow one Sen uses. By the usual definition individuals are free to exchange rights and resources. Both Lascivious and Prude have an interest in an exchange giving Prude rights of control over what Lascivious reads in return for Lascivious having rights of control over what Prude reads. Then Prude would dictate that Lascivious not read *Lady Chatterley's Lover*, and Lascivious would dictate that Prude read it, and the Pareto-optimal outcome, B, would be realized.

Despite this easy resolution, a fundamental difference between Pareto optimality and individual rights is shown by Sen's paradox. The key to the inconsistency between liberalism and Pareto optimality lies in the distribution of rights implied by each. For it to be always possible to make a Pareto-optimal move, this means that, except under special conditions (conditions that might entail very complex exchanges), all policy moves must be centrally controlled, despite the apparent individualism on which the idea of Pareto optimality is based. If the change which is an improvement for a given person and not harmful to others is not under the control of that person, then, in the absence of a benevolent despot there is no one who is motivated to make the move and has sufficient power to do so. In the case of Prude and Lascivious, both can be made better off by a change from outcome C to outcome B, but neither has the right to make such a move. It would require a collective decision by the two to make that Pareto-optimal move, but with the distribution of rights specified by Sen, rights are held individually rather than collectively, corresponding to liberalism.

A digression concerning terminology is necessary here. When I refer to a benevolent despot, I mean not only a single ruler vested with all governmental power, but also the *people* vested with all governmental power. In an absolute democracy (where all rights are held collectively), the people may be as coercive and arbitrary as an individual despot. The essential distinction for understanding Sen's paradox is that between control of action by a single corporate actor and control by individuals. The distinction between a single governmental actor directed by a collective decision in which individual preferences play a part and a single governmental actor directed by the will of a single ruler is secondary.

What Sen has done is to establish a system in which Lascivious has rights of control over the choice that is of most importance to Prude (whether or not Lascivious reads the book) and Prude has control over the choice that is of most importance to Lascivious (whether or not Prude reads the book). In this situation the external effects of the other's action on one's satisfaction are greater than the direct effects of one's own action, and this is true for both parties. This is precisely the condition under which Pareto optimality and liberalism (as Sen defines it) are in conflict. Pareto optimality implies that adjustments are to be made with attention to each individual's *benefits*, or preferences among outcomes, and liberalism implies that individuals *control* their own actions. The individualism of Pareto optimality is individualism of benefit, but the individualism of liberalism is individualism of rights of control.

A benevolent despot having total control can make the move to the outcome having Pareto optimality while maintaining individualism of benefit—making sure that increasing one person's satisfaction will not lessen another's. Individualistic control can accomplish that only when persons control those events that have outcomes of most interest to them or are able to gain control of those events through exchange. The character of this difference can be better understood by considering three political philosophers—Jeremy Bentham, Jean Jacques Rousseau, and John Stuart Mill—and the economist-sociologist Vilfredo Pareto.

Bentham visualized a single social optimum, "the greatest good for the greatest number." This optimum is arrived at through an implicit interpersonal comparison, made by a benevolent despot. But the despot is not bound by Pareto's principle, the principle of individualism of benefit, because the interpersonal comparison allows him to say whether one person's gain is greater than another's loss, and thus to impose a loss on some to obtain a greater gain by others. For Bentham the benevolent despot is a legislature; in his *Constitutional Code* he says, "Why render the legislature omnicompetent? . . . Because it will better enable it to give effects to the will of the supreme constitutive, and advancement to the interests and security of the members of the state . . . Any limitation is in contradiction to the general happiness principle" (1983 [1841], p. 119).

For Rousseau individual control characterizes the state of nature; in creating a social contract, however, each individual gives up this right of control to the general will. Like Bentham, Rousseau visualizes a single social optimum, which is created by a benevolent despot, the general will. As is true for Bentham's, Rousseau's social optimum may sacrifice the good of some. In contrast to Bentham, Rousseau does not see the benevolent despot using individual utilities as criteria in establishing the social optimum. In making the social contract individuals have given up not only individual rights to control, but also individual utilities. There is not only a general will which takes action for the collectivity; the social optimum is defined in terms of utility for the collectivity as a supraindividual entity.

Mill is at the other extreme from Rousseau. Like Rousseau, Mill begins, in his *On Liberty* (1926 [1859]), with individuals having the rights to control their own actions. But for Mill individuals retain most such rights; the consequences for other individuals provide the criterion for determining what rights should be transferred to the collectivity. Except when the consequences for others are great, relative to the consequences to oneself (and here Mill implicitly uses the same interpersonal comparison Bentham does but at the earlier constitutional stage), the rights to control the action remain in the individual's own hands.

Pareto's criterion of optimality is like that of Bentham in that its realization may require a benevolent despot; it differs from that of Bentham in that its realization is achieved by separate, individual-by-individual examination of benefits, or preferences about outcomes. Thus for Pareto there is not a single social optimum, as there is for Bentham, but a set of social optima which cannot be compared unless the despot is willing to decrease one person's benefits in order to increase another's, which he is not willing to do under Pareto's criterion. It is in this sense that Pareto optimality is based on individualism of benefit.

These four theorists can be compared on three dimensions:

1. Control of action is held individually or collectively.
2. Benefits of outcomes characterize individuals or the collectivity.
3. If the benefits characterize individuals, they are evaluated separately or comparatively.

In Table 13.3 the four theorists are located in six cells created by these three dimensions in accord with the discussion above.

A comparison of Bentham and Rousseau indicates their similarities and differences on the dimensions of this table. Rousseau makes it quite clear in *The Social Contract* (1950 [1756]) that, although the general will originates in individual preferences in the constitutional stage, all rights of control in the postconstitution stage are vested in a single governmental actor, whose task is to absorb the general will and act in its name. Bentham is less clear about this matter, because the collective decision, through a legislative assembly, remains as the energizing force for governmental action in the postconstitution stage. This difference is what places Bentham under "Benefits characterize individuals" in Table 13.3 and Rousseau under "Benefits characterize the collectivity." That Bentham is located in the collective control row, along with Rousseau, reflects his criterion of the greatest good for the greatest number, as well as his explicit statements such as that quoted earlier.

If actions had no externalities, Mill and Pareto would be in the same cell in Table 13.3. If the action of each affects only himself, then control of their actions

Table 13.3   Classification of political philosophers by individualism of control and of benefits.

	Benefits characterize individuals		Benefits characterize the collectivity
	Benefits evaluated individually	Benefits evaluated comparatively	
Control held individually	1	2 Mill	3
Control held collectively	4 Pareto	5 Bentham	6 Rousseau

by self-interested individuals will produce the same actions as control by a benevolent despot. It is when actions do have externalities that are sufficiently great that Mill and Pareto differ. Because of such externalities, Pareto must be in cell 4, preserving individualism in evaluation of benefits at the expense of individualism in rights of control. Mill, however, is in cell 2, preserving individual rights of control while allowing comparison of the size of internal effects and externalities.

Both of these positions pose difficulties, however. For Pareto the question becomes this: How can individuals express their relative evaluations of different outcomes if they cannot carry out an action expressing this preference? For the example used by Sen and described earlier, how can it become known that Prude prefers outcome B (see Table 13.2) to outcome C if, under Sen's allocation of rights, Prude can only choose between the pair of outcomes A and B and the pair of outcomes C and D. The principle of revealed preferences means that preferences can only be known by their revelation, that is, by the exercise of choice. And to move from outcome C to outcome B in this case, as Pareto optimality implies, requires removing the right to exercise choice and assuming a benevolent despot, with neither Prude or Lascivious able to express a preference.

This difficulty suggests that indiscriminate application of the criterion of Pareto optimality to outcomes, or social states, is equivalent to ignoring rights to control particular components of such states. The absence of an explicit recognition of rights of control from the concept of Pareto optimality forces the conception of a despot with full rights to control any moves, but one that is benevolent and liberal, making a move only if no one is harmed and someone is benefited.

Mill's position also poses difficulties. Mill's notion (expressed in the quotation in Chapter 4) is that rights are to be held individually in the postconstitution stage, except where a comparison of the direct effects and external effects of the individual's action indicates that the latter are sufficiently great that control should be held collectively. But this implies, at the constitutional stage, just the opposite of Mill's liberalism: Although rights are held individually at this stage, some sort of collective decision, comparing direct effects of an action with externalities, is necessary to determine which rights are to continue to be held individually in the postconstitution stage and which have sufficient externalities that control should be vested centrally.

Some further insight into these problems can be gained by locating other political philosophers within Table 13.3. For example, from Rawls's *A Theory of Justice* (1971), it is clear that the implementation of his two principles (maximum liberty commensurate with equal liberty for all, and elimination of all inequalities except those which make the least advantaged better off) would require all rights to be centrally held in the postconstitution stage. For if they were not, there would be no way of eliminating undesirable (by Rawls's criterion) inequalities that arise in the course of everyday activities, such as inequalities due to family background. Thus, Rawls fits in the bottom row of Table 13.3. It is not clear in which column he fits, however. Considering the utility of only the least advantaged is akin to considering benefits that characterize the collectivity, because the utility of the least advantaged individual constitutes a single criterion for the collectivity as a whole and does not consider the utility of each individual. Consequently, Rawls's position has something in common with that of Rousseau, who is located in cell 6 of Table 13.3. On the other hand, since a comparison of levels of utility is (implicitly) necessary to determine which individual is least advantaged, Rawls has some elements in common with Bentham, who is in cell 5. But Rawls's assumption that individuals at the constitutional stage choose behind a veil of ignorance implies that rights are held individually and benefits are evaluated individually, a position that seems to fit in cell 1. For Rawls what gives rise to an agreed-upon principle, rather than pure anarchy, in the postconstitution stage is that since each is behind a veil of ignorance, all will arrive independently at the same principles of justice. The fact that Rawls appears to belong in cell 1 at the constitutional stage but in cell 5 or 6 at the postconstitution stage suggests why his theory seems to mean all things to all people.

This examination of Sen's paradox and the positions of various political philosophers on the dimensions of action it contains indicates the importance of the allocation of rights in the construction of a constitution. It also indicates the central position of externalities—either external diseconomies or external economies—in a theory of constitutions, for it is only in the presence of externalities that the most critical issues arise, those which distinguish different philosophical positions. Only the existence of externalities distinguishes a philosophy in which there is individualism of control, such as Mill's liberalism, from one in which there is individualism in the evaluation of consequences, such as with Pareto's criterion of optimality.

Corporate Action to Prevent Public Bads and Promote Public Goods

Each individual behind the veil of ignorance about his future position balances interests as beneficiary against interests as target, and that balance will differ for different classes of actions. This results in a constitution in which certain rights are held by individuals as individuals and certain rights are held by those same individuals collectively, that is, by the corporate body. If the corporate body is a state, the rights held individually constitute civil liberties; those held collectively constitute the powers of the state. In the Constitution of the United States, the Bill of Rights, along with later amendments, specifies the core of rights held by individuals. Other parts of the Constitution specify rights held by the United States.

A distinction between broad classes of action has important consequences for the balancing of targets' and beneficiaries' interests. The two broad classes are actions that generate negative externalities and those that generate positive externalities. The difference can perhaps best be seen by examining positions held by certain political philosophers.

John Stuart Mill considers only negative externalities. Mill poses this question: "What, then, is the rightful limit to the sovereignty of that individual over himself? Where does the authority of society begin?" (1926 [1859], p. 88). If this question is asked not only *about* individual sovereignty but *by* the individual at the constitution-constructing stage, how does a rational individual answer it? For Mill the individual gives up sovereignty only when his actions seriously harm the interests of others. As Mill says, "there is no room for entertaining any such question [of interfering with a person's conduct] when a person's conduct affects the interests of no persons besides himself, or need not affect them unless they like" (1926 [1859], p. 89).

But there is a second way of answering this fundamental question, a way related to positive externalities. This can be seen by examining the work of Nozick (1974), who is sometimes regarded as no less a libertarian than Mill. Nozick begins with natural rights as the starting point, as does Mill, but his question takes a different perspective: What rights and resources will rational actors voluntarily give over to a collectivity? Nozick's answer is that they will not remain in a state of anarchy but will give over some minimal rights and resources to what he refers to as a dominant protective association, because of the gains to each resulting from positive externalities for one another of the protective actions of each. Nozick does not recognize negative externalities of actions other than that of the predatory action against which the dominant protective association is intended to act.[6] But the rights and resources necessary to ensure contribution to the dominant protective association may be much greater than those necessary merely to prevent negative externalities.

The question posed by Nozick is an instance of a broader question: For an individual interested in achieving certain ends, what allocation of rights to a collective body will create the mix of collective action and individual action that will best realize those ends? This question, like that posed by Mill, assumes that the individual has interests as a beneficiary of corporate action (that is, as beneficiary of the common projects) and as a target (as contributor to the common projects). But in the answer to this question, the interests of the beneficiary of corporate action ordinarily are stronger, relative to those of the target, than for Mill's question. Nozick's question essentially conceives of the corporate body as an instrument (or agent) of the members of the collectivity. It recognizes the action of the corporate body as an alternative to individual action and asks what allocation of rights between these two agents will most effectively achieve the individual's ends.

The problem, of course, is that Mill's question and Nozick's question concern

6. The similarity of Nozick's dominant protective association to the protection rackets operated by gangs in some nearly anarchic areas of cities raises the question of just what institutions would exist in Nozick's ideal system to prevent the coercion that such dominant protective associations can impose—a coercion directly opposed to Nozick's notion of individual rights. Nozick's lack of attention to such danger is indicative of a general blindness to the importance of social institutions on the part of moral philosophers, whose attention is almost exclusively directed to abstract principles.

the same set of rights, although they raise different questions about them. It may well be that the allocation of rights which is optimal for constraining negative externalities is far from optimal for bringing about positive externalities.

The criterion used by Mill to determine when society should have the right to intervene with regard to actions that impose negative externalities on others, that is, to constrain the individual's sovereignty, is simple and straightforward: "As soon as any part of a person's conduct affects prejudicially the interests of others, society has jurisdiction over it" (1926 [1859], p. 89) because "the evil consequences of his acts do not then fall on himself but on others—and society, the protector of all its members, must retaliate on him, must inflict pain on him for the express purpose of punishment, and must take care that it be sufficiently severe" (p. 94).

Nozick's question, however, conceives of the corporate body as an instrument of the members to realize some of their goals and is thus concerned solely with positive externalities which individuals' actions can have for one another. The most frequent goal of this sort for which governments have been formed is mutual defense. The positive externality lies in the fact that defense is a public good for a set of geographically proximate individuals. One person in defending himself also defends others in the vicinity.

In other forms of social organization, purposively entered into, something comparable to common defense can be the equivalent public good. Those working at a craft may organize into benevolent associations that provide insurance against adversity (see the discussion of printers' benevolent associations in Lipset, Trow, and Coleman, 1956), and workers in a trade or industry may organize into a union to engage in collective bargaining with their employer. In other cases the goal of organization is financial gain, as it is for a set of investors who start up a business. In all these cases the constitution or charter of the corporate body reflects the common interest in pooling resources and the goal of providing the corporate body with a set of rights sufficient to enable it to achieve the common goals.

There are, then, two fundamental parts to the constitutional question a rational actor will pose, and for each he must see himself as both beneficiary and target of corporate action. The principal problem is that these two parts of the question cannot be answered independently. The sovereignty which the rational individual may give up to constrain negative externalities—or, as Hayek (1976, p. 8) puts it, to establish and enforce "rules of just individual conduct"—may not be sufficient to achieve the collective benefits that the same rational individual wants to gain through the joint transfer of rights to the corporate actor. Furthermore, the rights may necessarily include those that, once given up to the corporate body, could be used against him, in fact used to take away coercively other rights he has reserved to himself.

The very character of a public good is such that the rational individual will not contribute voluntarily to its supply. Consequently, freedom from coercion with respect to a certain class of actions may well be one of the rights he will give up in the constitutional stage in order to achieve positive externalities. For example, the rational individual may consent to a military draft instituted in order to achieve the common defense in wartime. The right to be taxed, with coercive enforcement, will almost necessarily be one of the rights the rational individual will give up in the constitution-constructing stage, in order to gain the benefits provided by combining individual resources for achieving common goals. This right is given up not only in civil societies but in voluntary organizations such as trade unions where there are required dues and strike assessments.

The giving up of rights such as these opens a Pandora's box, for the corporate body that has unrestricted rights of taxation can commandeer all resources necessary to achieve some goal it has. As Hayek (1976) puts it,

> Though the maintenance of a spontaneous order to society is the prime condition of the general welfare for its members, . . . we must briefly consider another element of the general welfare. There are many kinds of services which men desire but which, because if they are provided they cannot be confined to those prepared to pay for them, can be supplied only if the means are raised by compulsion. Once an apparatus is given the monopoly of coercion, it is obvious that it will also be entrusted with supplying the means for the provision of such "collective goods" . . . The whole history of the development of popular institutions is a history of continuous struggle to prevent particular groups from abusing the governmental apparatus for the benefit of the collective interest of these groups. This struggle has certainly not ended with the present tendency to define as the general interest anything that a majority formed by a coalition of organized interests decides upon. (pp. 6–7)

Thus, examining the full constitutional question which the rational individual puts to himself leads from a limited corporate body, empowered only to maintain the rules that constrain individuals from harming one another, to a corporate body having rights and coercive power to extract from individuals the resources necessary for whatever goals the corporate body may entertain. This kind of body is not merely Nozick's dominant protective association, a minimal state to which only rights to common defense have been given. It is a full-bodied corporate actor, with coercive power over its members. The question then becomes just how the goals of the corporate body can be constrained to satisfy the interests of the rational individual as both beneficiary and target of corporate action.

Positive Social Theory

The devices that moral and political philosophers find useful in establishing the set of rights held corporately and that held individually (easie sum, categorical imperative, veil of ignorance) have a fundamental flaw from the perspective of positive social theory. This flaw derives from the role of these devices in transforming interpersonal comparison of utility into intrapersonal comparison. Each person weighs the benefits (or costs) he will experience as the actor from an action against the costs (or benefits) he will experience as one of those affected by externalities of action. But if this weighing is to be used to transform all interpersonal conflicts of interests into conflicts within each individual, then it must be assumed either that each person is totally ignorant about his future activities or that all persons will in fact have the same mix of future activities. Both assumptions are patently false in existing societies. Furthermore, if positive social theory were held to these assumptions, it could not explain interpersonal or intergroup conflict occurring when corporate bodies are established.

If these assumptions are set aside, there remains the weighing by each actor of interests as beneficiary of corporate action and interests as target, but the mix will differ among persons in different positions depending on the expected mix of interests as beneficiary and target in that position.[7] The differing mixes of interests among persons create differing preferences regarding the vesting of rights in the corporate actor; and these differences in preference create interpersonal conflicts of interests. There is a weighing of interests across the social system as a whole, but power counts in this weighing: Each actor's interest favoring beneficiary or target is weighted by that actor's power. The resolution of this conflict of interests, as shown in Chapter 31, tends toward the allocation of rights that has the greatest weighted interests in its favor. The resolution will occur without overt conflict if the weaker side correctly perceives its relative strength. It will occur after overt conflict if the weaker side sufficiently overestimates its relative strength.

Thus moving from the normative considerations of political philosophy to a positive social theory entails tearing away the veil of ignorance, as different individuals anticipate different mixes of interests as beneficiary and target. This raises an important question.

What If Not Every Individual Is Equally Beneficiary and Target of the Corporate Action?

The scenario visualized earlier, where constitutional choice takes place behind a veil of ignorance, is much more like that which occurred for Polish nobles in the sixteenth century in deciding how extensive a set of rights to vest in their king than that which involved the wife of a serf of one of those nobles—or that which occurred for middle-class Poles in 1948 when they saw a state being created over them through the intervention of a neighboring country, the Soviet Union. The serf's wife would have seen the vesting of authority in the king as being merely the cap on the top of a hierarchical authority structure which already existed, in

---

7. The distinction between person and activity, or person and position, is also important here. Insofar as a person may see himself in a different position in the future, his mix of expected interests as beneficiary and target may vary.

which she was below her husband, who in turn was below the noble. The middle-class Pole of 1948 would have seen the creation of the state as coercive action taken either by one class in the society, the workers, to establish (with the aid of the Soviet Union) a central authority under the control of this class and implementing its interests or by a neighboring country, the Soviet Union, to establish a central authority under its control and implementing its interests. Either of these scenarios differs greatly from the creation of a conjoint constitution as envisioned by political philosophers who begin with a set of independent individuals, each having full control of rights over his actions. Yet states can be said to begin in this way.

Most states, it can reasonably be argued, are established by a set of individuals along the lines of the Hobbesian scenario, but imposed coercively over another set of individuals with too few resources to prevent such an establishment. The set of individuals who establish the state (only after the partial conflicts of interest and problems of social choice described in the preceding sections) may be, for example, nobles with large estates and even villages subject to their authority, as in sixteenth-century Poland; or white, propertied, male heads of households, as in the formation of the United States in the eighteenth century; or landed aristocracy, as in England at the time of the Magna Carta or in some South American countries today; or the proletariat, as in Russia after the 1917 revolution. But in any case the state is established as an agent of only a subset of those whom it will subsequently govern. Despite the engaging imagery of Hobbes's war of each against the other, it is not the only starting point from which states with authority over citizens' actions emerge. They often emerge through the exercise of coercive power by one subgroup or class over another. That is, a state often emerges through a revolution, coup d'état, or conquest—some activity involving the use of force.

Despite the fact that force was required to establish a state, the state may come to gain legitimacy even among those who opposed its establishment. If, for example, all are better off under the authority of the state than before, even though some have gained more than others, then legitimacy (that is, the vesting of authority in the state) is likely to be forthcoming. For example, consider the payoff matrix of Table 13.4. If prior to the establishment of an authority system, the actions chosen by the three actors were D, D, and D, there are four possible combinations of actions for a corporate actor to take that would be at least good for all and better for some: CCC, CCD, CDC, and CDD. An authority system may be established only by coercion following a struggle, because the outcomes are ranked quite differently by each. Actor 1 ranks CCC highest, actor 2 ranks CDC highest, and actor 3 ranks CCD highest. Whatever the outcome of the struggle, if any of the three wins and gains control of the authority system, the outcome will be better for each than was the starting state. Authoritative control by actor 1, 2, or 3 (as in an aristocracy) will make each better off than before, through the productivity achieved with outcome CCC, CDC, or CCD, compared with the starting state, DDD. Even though actors differ in the degree to which

Table 13.4 Payoffs to three actors under collective authority with asymmetric outcomes.

		Actor 3			
		Contribute		Not contribute	
		Actor 2		Actor 2	
		Contribute	Not contribute	Contribute	Not contribute
Actor 1	Contribute	24, 6, 6	12, 15, 3	12, 3, 14	0, 12, 12
	Not contribute	24, -6, -6	12, 3, -9	12, -9, 3	0, 0, 0

they are likely to be beneficiaries and targets of corporate action, all will be net beneficiaries, and all can be expected to vest rights of control over this action in the corporate actor.

When force is involved in establishing an authority structure, however, the outcome need not be one which makes each better off. Table 13.5 shows a case in which no other outcome makes all actors better off than the anarchic outcome DDD, even though each other state is more productive (as measured by the sum of the payoffs). A struggle for creation of state authority could be expected to occur in such a circumstance. If actor 1, 2, or 3 gains control, the outcome will be DCC, CDC, or CCD, respectively. If actors 1 and 2 gain control jointly, DDC will be the outcome; if actors 1 and 3, DCD; and if actors 2 and 3, CDD. None of these is the most productive outcome, and for each, one actor is worse off than under anarchy. Such a configuration cannot be expected to gain legitimacy in the eyes of the actor who is made worse off. Under a normative theory of the formation of conjoint constitutions as social contracts entered into behind a veil of ignorance, no constitution could be created in such a case. Any theory of constitution construction under such circumstances must be one in which coercion plays a part—not merely in the postconstitution stage, after rights have been vested in the corporate actor, but in the constitutional stage.

Empirical examination of the period of formation of states in many cases reveals a distinction between those individuals for whom the role of beneficiary of the corporate action is felt most strongly and those for whom the role of target of the corporate action is felt most strongly. The former comprise the relatively small set of persons who bring the state into being, persons generally regarded as

Table 13.5 Payoffs to three actors under collective authority where at least one is always worse off than with outcome DDD.

		Actor 3			
		Contribute		Not contribute	
		Actor 2		Actor 2	
		Contribute	Not contribute	Contribute	Not contribute
Actor 1	Contribute	-2, 3, 3	-4, 6, 1	-4, 1, 6	-6, 4, 4
	Not contribute	4, -1, -1	2, 2, -3	2, -3, 2	0, 0, 0

the "founding fathers." For the United States this set was a portion of the political and economic elite from the thirteen colonies and the leaders of the war of independence, from among whom were selected the drafters and signers of the Constitution. For the Soviet Union it was the leaders of the Bolsheviks, who had planned the revolution and had played important roles in its execution. For England it was the landed aristocracy. For Israel it was kibbutz members, members of the Zionist movement and the socialist labor movement, and leaders in the war of independence.

For all these persons the dominant considerations are those of the beneficiary of the corporate action. For them Louis XIV's statement "L'état, c'est moi" is the prototypical stance. Their identification with the new state is stronger than their attention to the interests of themselves and others as targets of state action. Because these persons control the writing of the formal constitution and the establishment of governmental institutions, the constitution will ordinarily be biased toward beneficiaries' interests rather than targets' interests. Thus, although one can conceive of a social contract among rational individuals as resulting in an optimal constitution, the existence of heterogeneity among individuals with respect to power and with respect to the mix of beneficiary and target interests will almost certainly lead to an excess of rights being transferred to the corporate actor. It may be, for example, that the omission of a statement of fundamental rights of individuals from the Constitution of the United States (an omission soon rectified by the addition of the Bill of Rights as the first ten amendments) was due to this asymmetry.

The early history of many states organized as democracies shows a period during which elections reflect a high degree of trust in the founding fathers; there are almost no appeals by candidates to individual interests, and extensive appeal to common interests—that is, the interests of the nation-state as a corporate actor. This period is often terminated by a critical election in which a candidate is for the first time elected on the basis of partisan appeals to a particular social group, defined by region, social class, immigrant status, or some other criterion. In the United States that occurred with the election of Andrew Jackson in 1828. In Israel the election of Menachem Begin in 1977 was characterized by partisan appeals made for the first time to Jews of Eastern origin. In Britain, where the governing elite were not founding fathers of a new state but carriers of the traditions of the landed gentry, the change was marked by the Labour Party's rise to replace the Liberals as one of the two major political parties.

Change in a Disjoint Constitution: American High Schools

The constitutional process described so far in this chapter is relevant to conjoint constitutions, established by the set of actors who will be subject to the corporate actor's authority or by a subset of those actors. There are, however, also disjoint constitutions; those who establish the constitution, implicit or explicit, are disjoint with those who come to be subject to the corporate authority. That is, the principal beneficiaries of corporately held rights and the principal targets are disjoint. It is the principal beneficiaries who establish the constitutional scope of authority, and it is the principal targets who are subject to the authority. The example below will suggest that in the case of a disjoint constitution a change in the relative power of targets and beneficiaries can have a strong effect in changing the number of rights held corporately. The example concerns the implicit constitutions that exist in high schools in the United States. (A change similar to the one I will describe has also occurred in some other Western societies, but I will not extend the discussion to those cases.) Among the changes in those constitutions in the period 1960–1980, I will focus on what is probably the most important one: the extent of the staff's authority over the students.

The implicit constitution of a high school is not created by a process of construction as described in earlier sections of this chapter. There is no transfer of rights by children to the school; the children's parents or legal guardians have transferred their rights to control the children's actions to the school. Schools have traditionally operated under a principle of *in loco parentis*, exercising authority in place of parents. The delegation of authority creates an implicit constitution; the school becomes a corporate body having certain rights over students' actions that can be exercised by its head or by agents of the head. The set of rights held by a school is only partly fixed by law; a considerable part of it is established by a constitution internal to the community. This constitution is established, in effect, by parents of the students, acting through the school board and other bodies that, in interaction with the head, define the set of rights held by the school. Individual parents implicitly assent to the constitution when they enroll their children in school.

As new cohorts of children enter school, they have an authority relation to their parents different from that of their predecessors. There are also changes in the amount of authority delegated by parents to the school. For example, corporal punishment—hitting a student on the hand with a ruler or on the backside with a belt—was within the authority held by the school fifty or more years ago. But then there was a constitutional change, removing that right from the corporate authority of the school in school after school, as increasing numbers of parents no longer wished to delegate that authority to the school. Finally, the authority to administer corporal punishment was withdrawn from schools by law.

Since World War II, and especially since the early 1960s, three social changes have greatly modified the effective constitutions of schools. The result is that corporately held rights have diminished, to the point where many schools find themselves in a reversion to a Hobbesian state of anarchic war of every one against every other.

The first of these changes resulted in a reduced extent of authority exercised by parents over their children and a lowering of the age at which authority over many of their children's activities is given up by parents. Authority over children's consumption, leisure pursuits, dress, and sexual activities was, until sometime in the 1960s, exercised by most American parents throughout high school. Since then, increasing numbers of parents have relinquished authority over these domains in the early or middle years of high school. The implicit constitution of the family has changed, due principally to the increased power of children, whose resources relative to parents have been augmented by the decline in social structure based on the extended family and the neighborhood, and the rise in commercially generated leisure activities. When parents no longer hold authority over children, they cannot delegate that authority to the school.

A second change has brought about a decreased basis for consensus among persons living in the area from which a school's students are drawn. The basis on which local consensus depended was a functional community focused around a place. That neighborhood-based community is now in decline, principally because of the growth in transportation, which allows separation of work and residence, and secondarily because of the extensive movement of women into the labor force, which removes much of the foundation of community-based associations. With this decrease in local consensus, variation in parental authority, which would otherwise be between communities, is *within* them. A large number of high schools have within their districts some parents who have relinquished extensive authority over their teenaged children and do not delegate that authority to the school.

A third change is the increased use of litigation, which can be initiated by a single actor, as a means of resolving disputes (again in part a consequence of the decline in consensus-generating structures).

A result of the three changes taken together is that for many schools there are one or more parents who are willing to contest in court a school's exercise of authority over their child. In the 1960s there was a succession of court cases brought by parents contesting a school's disciplining of their child in matters of dress. Boys' long hair was an important issue; legal precedents were finally established that allowed schools much less authority over student dress than before. On a variety of issues involving school authority, court cases continue to be brought by parents. The authority of the school continues to shrink as parental authority over children shrinks. It is clear that the viability of schools as institutions deriving their constitutional authority from that of the parents in the geographic area surrounding the school is vanishing.

These three changes in social structure outside the school have, in effect, destroyed the conditions on which the implicit constitutions of American high schools have been based. The constitutions have been, in effect, social contracts among parents residing in limited geographic areas. Two directions toward new constitutions for high schools appear feasible, one more radical than the other. The less radical alternative is to retain a disjoint constitution with parents as the contracting parties (thus maintaining the principle of *in loco parentis* as the basis of the school's authority over children) but to eliminate "resident in the local geographic area" as the defining property for the parents among whom the social contract is made. The social contract instead would be made by parents who chose a particular school for their children. Children would attend schools not according to area of residence, but according to parental choice, as private schools under a voucher system or magnet schools in the public sector are chosen.[8]

This direction, however, is viable only if two conditions hold: The population density of the area must be great enough that choice among schools is feasible without long-distance travel; and the parents of the high-school students must retain sufficient authority to delegate it to the school. If the first condition does not hold, there is no possibility for choice (although high schools may of course be smaller than at present). If the second does not hold, parents are the wrong parties to the social contract, since they do not hold the authority. In that case the appropriate type of constitution is a conjoint constitution, with the high-school students themselves as parties to the social contract. Because there would undoubtedly still be a general adult-imposed requirement of school attendance up to age 16, the constitutions would not be wholly endogenous (as they are in youth gangs, for example) but would conform to certain legally imposed constraints. Contracts could be devised by school principals or staff, conforming to legal requirements, and youth (not parents) would choose among contracts offered by different schools.

This constitutional change in high schools shows how a change in the relative power of different actors (parents and children in the example) has strong implications for a disjoint constitution. The example is an especially interesting one

---

8. In some magnet schools the social contract is explicit; the parent (and in some schools the child as well) signs a contract containing the rules to which the signer agrees.

since a school is an extreme case of a corporate actor constructed by means of a disjoint constitution. The change is also of special interest because it may lead eventually to a conjoint constitutional base for the school.

An Optimal Constitution

If norms are viewed as the precursors of constitutions, the question of optimality can be raised about a constitution just as it can for a norm. For a single class of externality-generating actions, there are two relevant states of rights allocation. In one, rights are held by the actor; in the other, rights are held by those experiencing the externalities. The second state is one in which (using the definition of norm given in Chapter 10) a norm can be said to be governing that class of actions. This state, in which a norm exists, is optimal if the cost (or benefit) of the externalities to those experiencing them is greater than the benefit (or cost) of the action to the actor. This is the condition under which one might speak (given two outcomes, one favoring the actor's interest and one favoring others' interests) of the outcome which favors the actor's interest as being inefficient, or nonoptimal.

This implies, as indicated in earlier chapters, that the interests (or utilities) of different persons can be compared, and that, in turn, implies that there is some set of resources held by each actor, and transactions involving these resources, that give relative power to each. It is the relative power that provides weights for actors' interests in this comparison. (All of this is spelled out more precisely in Chapters 30 and 31).

It is possible to go beyond the social efficiency of outcomes to consider the social efficiency of an allocation of rights. Socially efficient outcomes may require the purchasing of rights from those actors to whom they are originally allocated, by others for whom they have greater value. A socially efficient allocation of rights—between the individual and the collectivity—is that which requires fewer purchases of rights in order to achieve socially efficient outcomes.

The idea of a socially efficient or optimal constitution is merely a generalization of the above conceptualization from one to many classes of actions. For each class the same question may be asked, leading to an allocation of rights over that class of actions—placing them in the hands of the individual who takes the action or in the hands of the collectivity. In the case of an explicit constitution of a formally organized corporate actor (from an association to a state), what were norms in the informal social system become rules or laws in the formal corporate body.

Three Levels of Optimality

There are three levels of optimality for the allocation of rights for a given class of events. Two of these correspond to conjoint constitutions, in which beneficiaries and targets of corporate action are the same actors, and one corresponds to disjoint constitutions, in which beneficiaries and targets are different actors. The three levels of optimality are individual optimality, utilitarian optimality, and imposed optimality.

1. *Individual optimality.* If an allocation of rights is individually optimal, every actor is either better off with that allocation or at least as well off as he would be with another allocation. If a right that is corporately held is individually optimal, each actor's interests as beneficiary of corporate action are as great as or greater than his interests as target. For example, it is reasonable to suppose that corporate control of the right to kill a person (to carry out that action or to constrain and sanction it) will make each person in the collectivity better off than if there were individual control of that right. If a right that is held by individuals is individually optimal, each actor's interests as target of corporate action are as great as or greater than his interests as beneficiary.[9] For example, it is reasonable to suppose that if each has the right to meet with others in private gatherings, each will be better off than if only the corporate body has the right to call such meetings, and to prevent others from doing so and sanction those who participate in them.

For this level of optimality no interpersonal comparison of utility is necessary: All of the conflict of interests between targets and beneficiaries occurs within individual actors. This corresponds to what is called in Chapter 30 a pure conjoint norm.

2. *Utilitarian optimality.* If the criterion of individual optimality is not met, some actors are better off if a right is allocated to the corporate body, and some are better off if the right is allocated to individuals, although interests favoring both allocations (that is, interests as beneficiary and as target) can be found in the same actors. This optimality is defined as that allocation of rights which has the greater interests in its favor. To determine which allocation this is, interests are weighted according to the power of actors in their regular transactions, that is, the value of the resources they bring to these transactions.

For this level of optimality interpersonal comparison is necessary: Only part of the conflict of interests between targets and beneficiaries lies within individual actors; part lies between actors. The definition in Chapter 30 of a conjoint norm (not pure) corresponds to this rights allocation.

3. *Imposed optimality.* If some actors are beneficiaries of corporate action and others are targets, then interests of different actors are opposed, and all conflict lies between actors. In this circumstance an optimal allocation of rights is that which favors the stronger set of interests, that is, the interests held by actors having resources of greatest value.

For this level of optimality the allocation of rights favors one set of actors at

9. If the corporately (individually) held right is not also to be individually optimal, the two statements should include "and at least one actor's interest as target (beneficiary) is greater than his interest as beneficiary (target)."

the expense of the other set. One might ask why, if the rights were allocated to the corporate actor, those who would be targets of corporate action would agree to such a constitutional allocation. There are three possible answers: First, what is described here is the rights allocation for a single class of actions; the actors who are targets for this class may be beneficiaries for others and thus may find it in their overall interest to agree to the constitution.

Second, it may be that, although the targets would be better off with rights held individually than with rights held corporately, they would be better off with rights held corporately than with no rights allocation at all. Their lack of valued resources, which is why their interests can be overridden in the constitution, might lead to vulnerability in the absence of a rights allocation, perhaps making them worse off.

Third, it may be that the targets do not agree to the constitutional allocation. Their lack of power may prevent effective opposition to the constitution, which comes into being in spite of their opposition. In the case of a constitution that meets only the criterion of imposed optimality, conflict of interest only arises between actors, and the winners of the conflict can impose the constitution on the losers.

Economic Efficiency

The criteria for optimality of constitutions as I have described them are based on the same conceptual structure as the criterion of economic efficiency. Because this is so, it is important that these criteria not be interpreted narrowly in efficiency terms, a possibility that can take different forms. The criteria do not involve economic efficiency in the sense of the efficient allocation of rights having a monetary value.

This caution is important because of the theoretical position in law which states that judges' decisions ought (and tend) to allocate rights in common law to the party to whom they are of greater economic value (see Posner, 1986). Although this is sometimes consistent with the criteria of optimality given earlier, it is not always because some resources of value (that is, those that help determine outcomes) are not marketed, not ordinarily exchanged for money, and not ordinarily appraised in monetary terms.

Also, optimality as I have described it is not to be confused with efficiency from the perspective of a single actor or from the perspective of a single set of interests. It involves a weighing of opposed interests rather than efficiency in the sense of the most efficient means to a given end. That sense of efficiency is exemplified by a conjecture of Posner (1987) that the reason for the absolute prohibition of the use of torture by the state in the U.S. Constitution lies in torture's not being an efficient means for extracting information. Not only is the correctness of the embedded proposition thrown in doubt (by the widespread use of torture to extract military information from captured enemy soldiers, and the belief of some military authorities that the only way to provide effective resistance against this means of extracting information is to provide officers with self-administrable poison capsules to ingest if they are being tortured); this use of efficiency as a constitutional criterion takes only the perspective of a state with a goal of extracting information. It seems more likely that the constitutional prohibition of torture arose from the balance of actors' interests as beneficiary and as target of this corporate action, with interests as potential target weighing more heavily than those as potential beneficiary.[10]

How Is an Optimal Constitution Achieved?

The criteria for an optimal constitution have been stated above as though the weighing of interests were done automatically or some outside benevolent despot were carrying out the weighing. Neither of these is true: The weighing is done by the actors whose interests are involved and who will be governed by the corporate actor they create.

If the allocation of rights for a class of actions meets the criterion for the highest level of optimality, individual optimality, then in principle that section of the constitution could be written by any single actor drawn at random from those who form the collectivity. If this were true for all classes of actions, each actor would embody all the interests in the collectivity, and the entire constitution for the collectivity could be written by any one actor, who would produce a constitution with optimal allocations of rights.

From the highest to the second and then the third level of optimality, the relative power of various actors becomes increasingly relevant. If power were definable independently of the allocation of rights, it could be said that the allocation of rights would be optimal if actors' participation in constructing the constitution was in proportion to their individual power in the system (and assuming that each actor's participation in constructing the constitution expressed equally well that actor's interests). This cannot, however, be said, for postconstitution power depends on control of resources, and rights allocated in a constitution are among the resources that are important in determining power. What can be said is that a constitution will have an optimal allocation of rights if power in the postconstitution system of action is distributed in proportion to each actor's participation in construction of the constitution. But because power in the postconstitution system is in part determined by the constitutional allocation of rights, a number of different constitutional allocations could be optimal, depending on who wins the constitutional struggle. These allocations would create somewhat different systems; however, a constitution is optimal if in the system that results, rights for each class of actions are allocated in accordance with the interests of those who, postconstitutionally, have power-weighted interests that are stronger than the opposing power-weighted interests.

10. This supposition gains some support from the fact that there are some states in which torture is used on noncitizens but not on citizens, but none (that I am aware of) in which the reverse is the case. Noncitizens are parties neither to the construction of the constitution nor to its continual modification by current citizens of the state, and their interests thus do not play a part in the weighing of interests as beneficiary and as target.

An optimal constitution may contain extensive restriction of rights, because different actors have differing inalienable resources. In socialist systems, for example, an obvious problem exists if private property is abolished but rights of emigration remain in the hand of individuals. Since the personal resources of skills and experience vary and since actors can find other societies in which they retain rights to capture the benefits of production resulting from employment of those skills, then, unless the state restricts emigration, the most resourceful members will emigrate. (Because these personal resources are productive, that is, create value in the system, there will be places where persons can capture a portion of their value. That is, some form of property rights will emerge through competition by different states or localities for the most productive persons.) Thus, if a subordinate class eliminates property rights following a revolution, they must also effectively eliminate emigration rights. This may, however, eliminate the incentive for individuals in the next generation to acquire the personal resources that make them productive, so such a system may be foredoomed to a lower level of productivity.

As this example illustrates, an imposed optimality can create a largely, but not wholly, arbitrary allocation of rights. The winners in a conflict can create a system in which they and their successors are largely the beneficiaries of the corporate actor's actions, and the vanquished are largely the targets of those actions. The winners cannot, however, ignore the inalienable personal resources of the vanquished, which give them the potential for overturning or modifying the constitution. Slave uprisings and mutinies, among other types of revolt, exemplify this.

Interests of Members in Controlling Agents of a Corporate Body

The one interest most fully shared by the member as beneficiary of corporate actions and the member as target of those actions is an interest in controlling the agent. Even such a simple system as the earlier example of a corporate actor having three members, A_1, A_2, and A_3, can show the structural possibilities for agents to benefit at the expense of members. Assume that, having created the corporate actor with rights to control their contributions, the members appoint a nonmember as agent to execute corporate actions. For the outcomes as ranked in Figure 13.1, how is the executive to be motivated to choose CCC, giving the payoffs of the upper-left cell of Table 13.1, rather than another combination of actions? For example, A_1 has an incentive to induce the executive to choose DCC, for that reduces A_1's net loss to $4, at the same time increasing the net loss of each of the other two to $13. A_1 thus has a potential surplus of $5 if the DCC outcome is chosen rather than the CCC outcome, and some part of that could be used to induce the executive to choose DCC. A_2 or A_3 has the same motivation to bribe the executive to choose CDC or CCD, respectively. This gives the executive the potential to gain by favoring one of these three special interests and sharing in its gain. A lesser gain can be realized by the executive from a coalition of two members. Any two have together a surplus of $2 with which to induce the executive to choose the outcome of common interest to them. Establishing a coalition of two requires some organization, however.

This example has its counterpart in actual practice in relations between occupants of government positions, elected or appointed, and actors being governed. Since the occupants *do* have interests, as do all individuals, and since individual members of the collectivity, or intermediate corporate actors within it, can experience a gain from governmental actions which favor them at the expense of others, the potential exists for collusion between the occupants of government positions and a portion of the governed. The collusion can lead to suboptimal collective actions. In the example the only option that remains available to the member or members against whose interest the executive acts is to withdraw from the collectivity—an action that under the circumstances is rational, since one loses less as an independent actor ($12) than if one continues one's membership in the collectivity ($17 or $13). Only if this option can be exercised (that is, each member retains the right of withdrawal without additional cost) does the executive have an incentive to ignore special interests and attend to common interests.

Use of the option of withdrawal as a means of giving an agent an incentive to act in the common interest is an instance of a more general strategy: structuring the agent's incentives to lead him to act in the common interest. If the interests of the executive can be properly structured, his interests can be conjoint with the common interests of the members. That is, if in the case of the example of Table 13.1 the executive's interests can be fixed so that outcome CCC ranks highest for him, his interests will be conjoint with the common interests of the members of that collectivity. It is this outcome which provides the greatest gains from collectivization, and, coincidentally, it is this outcome in which each member gains. As a consequence, in this case, there is no question about which choice best furthers the common interest. The only problem for the collectivity is that of establishing incentives for the executive which will rank outcome CCC first for him (and rank CCD, CDC, or DCC second, and CDD, DCD, or DDC third, and DDD fourth).

This is the problem discussed in Chapter 7, the principal's problem of establishing the optimal incentive for an agent. In this simple example the ranking of outcome CCC as first and DDD as fourth for the executive can be brought about by simply setting up a rule that each member of the collectivity retains the right to withdraw without cost. Since the only outcome that is beneficial for each member is CCC, choosing that is the only action of the executive which would lead to no withdrawals (and DDD is the only action that would cause all to withdraw). This rule would, however, induce the executive to rank CDD, DCD, or DDC second, and CCD, CDC, or DCC third (favoring the majority at the expense of the minority), rather than the reverse. If the rule allowing withdrawal is combined with a tax which compensates the executive with a percentage of the profits of each individual who realizes a net gain from the collective action, the optimal ranking can be achieved (but at a cost to the members).

In this example there is one outcome, CCC, which provides both the greatest net gain from collective action and the distribution of gains that is most equal. That these two properties are found in the same outcome is specific to this example, which corresponds to the case in a society in which the policy that leads to the greatest economic growth is also the policy in which the gains are most equally distributed. The example of Table 13.1 shows that such a coincidence of policies is possible. But when the criteria of maximum productivity and distributional equity are not both satisfied by the same outcome, the problem of establishing an optimal incentive structure for the executive becomes more complex than it is in this simple case. Because there is not a single principal, the conflicts between the criteria are not internally resolved within an individual as principal, but must be resolved among individuals constituting the collective body.

Here the interests of target and of beneficiary diverge. As beneficiary of the corporate action, the individual has an interest in maximizing the corporate product—in the example being considered, maximizing the gains from mutual protection. As target of the corporate action, the individual has an interest in minimizing his potential contribution as a member. These interests correspond to two principles for arriving at a corporate action. One was proposed by Kaldor (1939) and specifies that a proposed policy change should be made if those who will gain from the change are able to compensate those who will lose and still be better off than before. This criterion ranks the outcomes of the example in the order of total benefit to the collectivity, that is, in the order CCC, CCD, CDD, DDD (with the permutations of CCD and CDD ranked with those two outcomes in second and third place respectively). Inspection will show that a move from any lower-ranked outcome to any higher-ranked one results in a gain, if not to all three members, to one or two, and the one or two can compensate the other(s) for losses due to the move and still be ahead.

The Kaldor principle is ambiguous about whether compensation should in fact be carried out. If the principle is interpreted as saying that compensation should be carried out, then it can be described as one which uses both the criterion of maximum productivity and that of distributional equity but applies the criterion of productivity first.

Rawls's (1974) difference principle is the second principle for resolving the conflict of efficiency and equity in arriving at a corporate action. This principle specifies that (subject to the provision of equal liberty for all) the just policy is the one which most benefits the least advantaged. If Rawls's principle is viewed as ranking actions in terms of their proximity to a wholly just policy, it ranks the outcomes of the example in the order CCC, DDD, CCD, CDD.[11] This ranking differs sharply from that arrived at by applying the Kaldor principle; in particu-

---

11. The payoffs for these four outcomes are -9, -9, -9 for CCC; -12, -12, -12 for DDD; -13, -13, -4 for CCD; and -17, -8, -8 for CDD. The first payoff listed for each outcome is to the "least advantaged," and this order ranks the outcomes according to this payoff. Note that Rawls's principle assumes interpersonal comparison of utility to decide who is least advantaged.

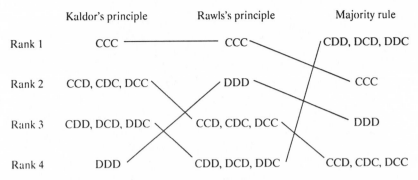

Figure 13.2   Ranking of outcomes by Kaldor's compensation principle, Rawls's principle, and majority rule.

lar, outcome DDD moves from last to second place because of its equity. Rawls's principle can be described as one which uses both the criterion of maximum productivity and that of distributional equity but, in contrast to Kaldor's principle, applies the criterion of equity first.

A third principle for resolving the conflict between efficiency and equity in choosing a corporate action can be described as the principle of democratic choice through majority rule. (This can be regarded as the principle by which the executive is elected or through which a rank order is chosen by direct vote.) This principle ranks the outcomes in the order CDD, CCC, DDD, CCD. This ranking differs from the other two even more than they differ from one another (see Figure 13.2). It can be described as a principle which gives higher priority to equity than to efficiency, but limits the set of individuals for whom equity is evaluated to a majority of the members. The result for the example is to rank as first that action which is ranked last by Rawls's principle.

These three principles constitute three possible bases for guiding corporate action. As the differences between these principles indicate, the conflicting interests of the individuals who come together to create a corporate actor lead to widely differing principles to guide its actions.

The members' problem of controlling the agent (that is, the officials) of the corporate actor is a general one to which I turn next.

Maintaining Effective Control of Agents of a Corporate Actor: Internal and External Social Capital

Once a corporate actor is established by individuals with interests in common (for example, persons with the same occupation establish a trade union, or members of a social class establish a state after a class-based revolution) and officials are put in place as its agents, the members are often unable to control the agents. How and why this comes about can be seen by examining a body of sociological research that begins with that of Robert Michels.

Michels studied the German Social Democratic Party, with a single question in mind: How was it that this political party, which had an explicitly democratic constitution, was in fact controlled by a small oligarchy composed of the highest officials? Despite the democratic provisions of the party's constitution, the incumbent leaders were able to pursue the policies they themselves preferred (expansion at the expense of principles and cooperation with bourgeois parties to maintain party stability, for example, by forming a coalition government), were able to stay in office, and were able to effectively take from the members the rights of self-government they held constitutionally.

Michels's (1949 [1915]) answer to the question was a pessimistic one, which he formulated as his "iron law of oligarchy": "It is organization which gives birth to the dominion of the elected over the electors, of the mandataries over the mandators, of the delegates over the delegators. Who says organization says oligarchy" (p. 401). He showed that the very creation of organizational authority does two things: First, it creates a set of interests that are distinct from those of the members as a whole and that include but are not limited to leaders' interests in maintaining their positions. Michels expressed the principle this way: "By a universally applicable social law, every organ of the collectivity, brought into existence through the need for the division of labor, creates for itself, as soon as it becomes consolidated, interests peculiar to itself. The existence of these special interests involves a necessary conflict with the interests of the collectivity" (p. 406).

Second, creation of organizational authority gives to those leaders most of the resources inherent in the organization: a monopoly of the means of communicating with the membership, a monopoly over sources of personal status and of visibility before the membership, control over the actions of intermediate officials (who will be dependent on the leaders for furtherance of their careers), and control of the treasury of the organization.

Michels showed two things about the German Social Democratic Party. First, the creation of the party had given social capital to the leaders, in the form of the organizational resources necessary for corporate action. Second, despite constitutional allocation of rights to the members to act collectively in keeping their leaders accountable, neither the social structure of the party nor its internal political organization provided sufficient social capital to the members to allow them to pursue their interests when those interests ran counter to the interests of the small elite who controlled the organization.

In the late 1940s Seymour Martin Lipset, dismayed by Michels's pessimistic conclusions and by the corroborating evidence of oligarchic control in the Soviet Union and in other socialist countries in Eastern Europe, searched for evidence that the iron law of oligarchy was not universal. The result was a study (Lipset, Trow, and Coleman, 1956) of the International Typographical Union (ITU), where Michels's law did not hold. Contrary to the usual pattern of oligarchic control in trade unions, the ITU had the continuing presence of an opposition party, frequent turnovers in office, and new leaders rising from the ranks. It was nearly unique among North American trade unions in its internal democracy. The pattern of an ongoing opposition party was initiated by secret societies within the union, which existed *despite* a union rule established in 1896 making such societies illegal (p. 38). The formal structure of the ITU thus contained elements inhibiting institutions conducive to democratic control and protection of members' rights. Yet democratic control flourished in the ITU, and members' rights were preserved. In contrast, in many other unions constitutional provisions specifically designed to ensure preservation of members' rights to control union policies have been unsuccessful in preventing oligarchic control.

Research on the ITU showed that the principal continuing source of protection for members' control of their union lay in the social capital provided by the social organizations established within their occupation. Many printers were associated with one another in various organizations, including secret societies that existed in the early days of the union and various clubs which provided valuable services for members. For example, the Monotype Club was the unofficial employment agency for monotype operators in the New York City area (Lipset, Trow, and Coleman, 1956, p. 227). These organizations provided the social capital that enabled an opposition party to survive and remain strong while its adherents were out of office. Thus, within the larger local unions, members had the social capital necessary to control local officials through democratic political processes. This political activity within the large locals made those officials dependent on membership support, rather than on patronage from the international officials. This independence allowed the locals to serve at the international level as the clubs did at the local level, as social capital for political opposition. For example, the San Francisco local was for many years a strong base for the Independent Party, and the New York local was a strong base for the Progressive Party.

The case of the ITU showed that Michels's iron law of oligarchy did not always hold and provided a set of conditions (perhaps not the only set) under which it did not. If it is accepted that officials in control of the governing apparatus will come to have interests differing from, and in some cases conflicting with, those of the individuals being governed, the problem becomes one of overcoming the second component necessary for Michels's law to hold: the officials' monopoly of control of the available social capital, which allows them to maintain their power and subvert the members' rights to control the collectivity. In the ITU this monopoly was broken by organization among the members, which at the highest level took the form of an opposition party able to compete effectively with incumbents for the allegiance of the membership. But this highest level of organization had its foundation at lower levels (social clubs and union locals). Organization at these intermediate levels in turn had its foundation at the lowest level, in social capital generated by the interactions of members, social capital that lay outside the control of union officials.

Thus an exception to Michels's law is provided, paradoxically, by a form of organization itself. Organization may bring oligarchy, but the antidote for oligarchy is organization within organization (such as opposition parties that can maintain themselves when out of power). The possibility of so organizing is not always present, for such organization requires social capital that is independent of the official structure. In the ITU this was provided by the strong and active locals and clubs, which fulfilled important functions for the members and maintained their independent strength. For many other trade unions the members' occupation does not generate the requisite social capital.

At every level of organization, there is the danger of oligarchy, that is, the danger that leaders may subvert the interests of members and may take away some of their rights. This danger can in principle be countered by organization at the next lower level and down to the lowest level, which allows an effective opposition to these leaders to be mounted; then tne intermediate levels of organization depend on the members below, not on the officials above.

An organized opposition party which presents the membership with an alternative that can overcome the oligarchic monopoly of agents of the corporate body is a public good, which no member or set of members will have the incentive to bring into existence. But other organizations, which exist by virtue of providing private goods for members (the best example in the ITU is the Monotype Club), can constitute the social capital for overcoming the free-rider problem. If they do so at the lowest level, this brings about at least partial independence of the officials at that level from those at the next higher level. These independent officials provide a base for overcoming the free-rider problem at the next higher level, and so on. All this appears to depend, however, on overcoming the free-rider problem at the lowest level, the grass-roots level, for this creates the dependence of the successively higher levels on the members below, rather than solely on the higher-level officials.

It is true that once a structure of opposition is in existence, it gains legitimacy, and officials who attempt to destroy it may suffer at the hands of members, through the ballot box.[12] But the legitimacy that comes about in this way arises as a consequence of the organization and is not by itself effective. Once in existence, such a structure of opposition gains many supports that help keep it in place; the more serious problem is how it can come into existence in the first place.

This question then arises: Is the problem posed by Michels overcome in ways other than that shown by the research on the ITU? Can the oligarchic tendency of governmental organization be overcome in the absence of grass-roots social organization which provides the social capital necessary for effective opposition to whatever set of officials is in power?

There is evidence which suggests that the social capital to counter that held by officials can arise from another source—from outside the corporate actor and its membership. Two examples will illustrate this. One, at the national level, is the

12. An example of this occurred in the ITU in 1919, when a strike initiated by the New York local was put down by the International officials. This action led to the ouster of the president of the ITU in the next election.

effect of international public opinion and its manifestation in trade boycotts and other actions on the attention of the government in South Africa to rights of blacks. A second, at the organizational level within a nation, is the codetermination law of 1976 in Germany, whereby the state intervened in the organizational structure of business firms to specify constitutional rights of workers and institutional structures to protect those rights. In these two cases outside actors had some effect in increasing individual rights or protecting those rights against incursions by the governing body. The effect is like that of the independent internal social organization discussed above. The position of the actors outside the corporate actor in question provides an independent organizational base for partial control of the actions of incumbent officials.

The potential of externally generated social capital as an instrument for controlling officials of a corporate body will probably increase in the future. New communications media have made boundaries of organizations, even nation-states, far more permeable than in the past.

Constitutional Strategies for Members' Control of Agents

The preceding section described two sources of social capital for individuals to use in controlling officials of a corporate actor of which they are members: Social capital can be provided by organization internal to the membership but independent of control by officials; or social capital can be created by external organization but made available for members' benefit. There are, however, other means by which members can control officials, some of which are incorporated in constitutions. The first of these is the constitutional limitation on corporate power by reserving certain rights to individuals, as described in earlier sections. Such constitutional statements of individual rights are of value only when complemented by the presence of persons or groups having the resources to make use of the rights (that is, having social capital, as discussed in the preceding section). The constitution of the Soviet Union, for example, specifies a greater range of individual rights than does the U.S. Constitution. Yet the government of the Soviet Union has been able to negate many of these rights.

I will describe several other constitutional strategies below.

SETTING AGENTS' INTERESTS IN OPPOSITION   One means for controlling agents that has been proposed in political theory and used in practice is employing the very power resulting from governmental organization to control governmental power. The means is an articulated form of government composed of different branches which act to check and balance one another. This idea was developed in English and French political philosophy in the seventeenth and eighteenth centuries, stated as a principle by Montesquieu (1977 [1748]) and most extensively realized in the U.S. Constitution.[13] Contained in such a struc-

---

13. More primitive forms of this idea can be found in ancient political systems. Adcock (1964), for example, describes a form of government in early Rome in which there were two magistrates ruling simultaneously, each able to exercise a veto over the other's actions.

ture is the possibility that the branch designed to constrain negative externalities imposed by individuals on one another—ordinarily the judicial branch—may treat the acting branch of the government (executive or legislative or both) as an individual capable of imposing negative externalities on individuals who are members of the collectivity, and thus subject to legal constraints like those imposed on those individuals. For this potential to be realized, of course, a minimum requirement is that the government not have immunity from prosecution, a condition which is often far from being true.

The articulated, or branched, form of government is a political invention that applies Michels's insight that the creation of organizational units with specialized functions creates interests specific to the units. Each branch of government comes to have interests that are to some degree in conflict with those of other branches. A major question is whether this conflict of interests between different branches of the authority system serves to protect the rights of individuals. The answer is not clear. Parliamentary systems, which govern most European countries, are a less articulated form of government, with fewer checks and balances, than is the trifurcated system of the United States. Yet the societies they govern have as strong an independent economic base as that of the United States and probably no less protection of individual rights.

POWER-LIMITING DECISION RULES   Another constitutional device to control agents is the use of decision rules that limit the corporate actor's power to act. The most extreme such limitation is a constitutional provision that the corporate body (or its agents) can act only under unanimous approval of the members. Buchanan and Tullock (1962) and Buchanan (1975) discuss this principle in some detail, and Wicksell (1958 [1896]) argued for it on questions of taxation in Sweden at the turn of the century, foreseeing a future when a majority composed of the dispossessed would use a majority rule as a confiscating device.

The use of a decision rule which limits the power of a corporate body to act has been a common practice. A decision rule by which one individual can commit the corporate body to action is at one extreme; a rule that calls for unanimity is at the other. Rules that call for majorities less than unanimity but greater than a simple majority provide some constraint, but less than a rule of unanimity.

A major defect of the use of power-limiting decision rules is that they reduce the capacity of the corporate actor to act in the members' interests. Thus one constitutional strategy is to allow the limitations on the power to act to vary over time. Since interests in goals to be individually achieved and those to be collectively achieved fluctuate over time, the constitution may provide for contingent and temporary grants of power to the corporate actor, including some mechanism for rescinding the grant when conditions warrant. In most constitutions there is some such provision, such as provisions for the declaration of martial law or the War Powers Act in the United States. One danger, of course, is that, unless the rescinding mechanism is robust, the very power that comes into the agents' hands will allow them to prevent a return to the status quo ante and will thus bring about a progressive loss of individual rights.

CONSTITUTIONAL DEFERENCE TO HIGHER AUTHORITY   One shield of protection against the state that has proved important is constitutional recognition of a set of "higher laws," as discussed by Buchanan (1975, p. 13), for example. In political philosophy this recognition may be found in the theory of natural law, developed primarily by Aquinas and other Catholic scholars to characterize divine authority or the authority of the church in relation to secular authority. In practice religious allegiance has been widely used to counter the force of the state, as discussed in Coleman (1956); recent examples are the Solidarity uprising against the state of Poland in 1980, fueled by the Catholic Church, and the overthrow of the Shah in Iran in 1979 by religiously inspired Muslims. In both of these cases there was not only a set of beliefs which acted as a counterforce against the authority of the state, but also religious organization within the society to sustain those beliefs and an outside referent (the Church in Rome, the Ayatollah Khomeini in Paris). The second of these two examples illustrates the importance of constitutional recognition of higher authority in a reverse way: In a state based on religious law, such as the post-1979 state of Iran, the state represents religious authority and need not defer to higher authority. It thus becomes difficult to invoke higher authority to counter state authority.

JURISDICTIONAL REACH AND MULTIPLE ACTORS   Externalities of different actions are not coextensive; some have a greater reach than others. This creates serious questions for construction of a corporate actor. In particular, voluntary associations within a state (such as trade unions, professional associations, and trade associations) have natural boundaries defined by the coextensivity of a number of positive and negative externalities for those within the association (sharing an occupation or industry). Thus there is a natural basis for an individual behind a veil of ignorance to say "The association should extend so far, and no farther; and I should transfer to it these rights of control, and no others."

A similar natural basis for a state may be a shared language or ethnic background or both.[14] Yet the existence of a nation-state, with a monopoly of force over a well-defined population, is not something that obviously and necessarily results from the choices of rational actors responding to externalities imposed on

14. In a more fundamental sense the problem of membership does exist for states. The claim by Welsh nationalists to sovereignty and comparable claims by Lithuanians, Basques, or Armenians, for example, raise the question of where these boundaries should be if the state is to be regarded as created by sovereign individuals. This question was raised by Woodrow Wilson at the end of World War I, and resulted in the creation of new states in Central Europe. It was not raised effectively at Yalta at the end of World War II, and this resulted in the subordination of Eastern Europe to the Soviet Union.

them by one another, including the positive externalities of common defense. It is conceivable that alternative social constructions might be preferred. One such alternative would be governments that have a monopoly of force in a given geographic area but no defined population, that is, no citizenry; each individual would be able to choose at any time the jurisdiction he wishes to be under. Another alternative, which has been characteristic of nomadic populations throughout history, is clan-based governments that have a monopoly of force over the related members of a group but no defined geographic territory.

Given that a state is in existence, what is the optimal reach of its jurisdiction over particular subsets of actions? That is, what degree of federalism or decentralization of government is optimal for the individual being governed? A part of the answer to this question concerns principally the reach of the externalities. The reach of a jurisdiction will be defined by the reach of the externalities, and the number of actions covered by it will be determined by the coincidence of the reach of externalities for different actions, as well as spillovers between different actions. Other factors, such as efficiencies or inefficiencies of scale, also must be considered. The most important issue, however, which is not addressed by examining the reach of the externalities, is the effect of either consolidation or decentralization on the power of the corporate actor to act on behalf of its members and on the agents' power to subvert the members' interests. It seems likely that no general principle concerning this can be stated; that is, the possible use of multiple corporate actors to reduce the power of the agents of any one of them probably needs to be investigated on a case-by-case basis.

It is clear that in certain social systems in which there is a high degree of social and economic interdependence, the number of jurisdictions is very great and overlapping. For example, one study identified approximately 1,400 governments in the New York City area, such as the New York Port Authority or the Scarsdale School District, each with a different jurisdiction (Wood, 1961). There has been some work by economists on the question of optimal jurisdiction (see Breton, 1974; Breton and Scott, 1978). The questions concerning the optimal size of school districts and schools are special cases of this question. In practice the sizes of school districts and schools have been principally based on attempts at optimization not over all of the various capacities in which individuals find themselves (students, parents, teachers, or taxpayers), but only over the last of these capacities, modified by the convenience of administrative authorities.[15]

A final issue concerning the optimal jurisdictional reach of corporate actors to

15. Evidence shows, for example, that in the United States the optimal size of a high school is below 500 students for "good outcomes" for the average student and around 1000 for economic efficiency. (See Coleman and Hoffer, 1987, for indirect evidence on the former and direct evidence on the latter.) Yet central governmental authorities impose consolidation to bring about school sizes larger than either of these optima, resulting in schools that are optimal neither for the student nor for the taxpayer. The power of authorities to do this is an instance of the aggrandizement of power that arises when corporate actors are created, as discussed elsewhere in this chapter.

which rights of control are transferred concerns externalities that cross national borders. Acid rain falling in one country because of manufacturing activity in another and depletion of the worldwide population of whales due to whaling activity of one or two countries are examples. International bodies with greater or lesser coercive power have been established to have jurisdiction over some of these areas—raising again the question of whether rational individuals behind a veil of ignorance would give a monopoly of force to a single body, the state. The answer may very well be no; the current existence of the nation-state as a mode of organizing social activity may be a residue of the historical origins of coercive social organization in kinship groupings such as clans and tribes. As kinship comes to be a less prominent basis of social organization, the way may be opened for social constructions quite different from the modern nation-state.

Who Are the Elementary Actors?

In the above treatment I have assumed natural persons as the elementary actors; a constitution has been seen as a means of partitioning rights between a corporate actor and natural persons. But this may not be the case. In the construction of the constitution for a given corporate actor, it may be that certain other corporate actors are the elementary actors. For example, when the U.S. Constitution was constructed, there were thirteen well-defined colonies which had been the principal corporate actors in the system up to that time. The U.S. Constitution recognized two sets of elementary actors explicitly by establishing two representative assemblies: the House of Representatives, in which each citizen was to be equally represented, and the Senate, in which each state was to be equally represented by two senators, regardless of the number of citizens within it. In addition, residual rights not explicitly specified in the Constitution reverted to the states. In fact, the debates of the Constitutional Convention of 1787 concerned not the balance between the rights of persons and those of the federal government, but the balance between the rights of states and those of the federal government. For most purposes, one can say that in the constitutional deliberations leading to the formation of the United States, the constituent states were more nearly the relevant individuals than were natural persons.

Similarly, at the formation of the modern state of Lebanon in 1945 there was explicit constitutional recognition of the main religious groups as actors, with representation specified for Christians and Muslims separately, although the government is not explicitly federal. There are other cases in which corporate entities within a body are regarded as the elementary actors of which the larger corporate entity is composed. Within the United Nations nation-states are the elementary actors. According to the charters of corporations, either kind of actor, individual or corporate, owning shares of common stock is an elementary actor in the governance of the corporation, with a share of control proportional to the shares of stock held. In trade associations the members are themselves corporations.

In all these cases what I have called elementary actors may be regarded as
elementary for a single reason: The corporate body of which they are members
does not have the right to determine their internal functioning. All such rights are
held by each member.

Functional Parts as Intermediate Actors

There is, however, another class of corporate actors in which the existence of
corporate entities within the larger corporate actor is explicitly recognized but
the rights to determine the internal functioning of those entities are held by the
larger actor. An example of this occurred in West Germany after new laws were
passed in the early 1970s in the various states concerning the governance of
universities. The law in West Berlin, for example (which was subsequently
struck down in 1982), required that the governing body of a university have one-
third representation from professors, one-third from students, and one-third
from nonprofessorial faculty. The procedures by which each of these three
groups selected their representatives was determined by the law, not by the
group or by the university. Within the National Academy of Sciences in the
United States, collective decisions on admitting new members are carried out by
a three-stage voting procedure. The first selection is made within disciplines
(organized into "sections"), then groups of disciplines (organized into
"classes") select among these candidates, and finally there is an election by the
entire membership, with quotas by class. As another example, in the early
history of the International Typographical Union, most major decisions were
made by an executive council consisting of the president and vice-presidents
elected by each craft represented in the union. Here again the procedure for
elections within the subdivisions was specified at the level of the union as a
whole, not within the subunit.

For none of these examples can it be said that the corporate entities within the
larger corporate body are elementary actors, as is true for the earlier examples of
the United Nations and trade associations. Rather they are subordinate corporate actors with rights of partial control over the actions of the larger corporate
actor, which in turn has rights of control over their internal functioning. Such
subunits ordinarily appear to constitute what could be described as functional
components of the larger actor: the professors, other faculty, and student body
are three important functional components of a university, just as employees and
stockholders (labor and capital) are the two major functional components of a
business corporation. The conception of rights of control over corporate actions
in such entities is not one in which those rights are held by individual actors,
such as the professors in a university or the employees in a corporation. Rather,
they are held corporately by the subunits themselves, the subordinate corporate
actors: the body of professors or the firm's employees as a whole. This is easily
seen by the weight that an individual's vote has. For example, if a university
with the governing structure described earlier had forty students per professor,

one might be tempted to say that a student had, by constitutional intent, a fortieth of the power that a professor had. But a quick mental experiment shows that this is an erroneous conception: If the student body declined to half its size, the student representation in university government would remain the same, giving each student a twentieth of the power of a professor. The correct way of viewing such a structure appears to be to view the rights to control the larger corporate actor (the university) as lodged in the intermediate or subordinate corporate actor (the student body). In turn, the rights to control the intermediate corporate actor are lodged in the individual members—and it is the larger corporate actor, not the intermediate one, which determines how those rights are allocated.

Although the foregoing appears to describe correctly the allocation of rights, it does not make clear when such functional substructuring of a corporate actor is necessary or useful. In general, the substructuring appears to be important when corporate action is the result of some functional interdependence among the intermediate parts, each of which plays a particular role in the corporate action, but substitution of individuals within each part is possible. This is true for the German university or industrial corporations. In cases like the National Academy of Sciences, however, the substructuring appears to occur for a different reason: not because of functional interdependence among different roles, but in order to prevent the existing social structure (which leads each individual to vote according to one interest only—academic discipline, in this example) from producing domination by one subgroup. In Lebanon the importance of religion in the social structure appears to be responsible for the provision for representation by religion in the constitution.

There is another pattern in addition to those described above. This is exemplified by community decision making, as described in studies by Dahl (1961), Banfield and Wilson (1963), and Laumann and Pappi (1976). Community decisions over where to locate a hospital or an airport or similar decisions over which explicit control is held by the mayor or city council may be informally controlled by the few actors in the community whose interest will be directly affected. Ordinarily these are not natural persons or intermediate corporate actors subordinate to the community government. They are, rather, corporate actors independent of that government: banks, local business firms, branches of national business firms, or agencies of the national government. The rights of control of such actors are not formally recognized through a procedure such as voting or sign-off. Instead these rights may be regarded as part of the informal constitution of the community, as is the case when a mayor knows that he must "get an okay" from a certain actor in the community before proceeding with a project.

It may be most useful not to include as part of the informal constitution the processes of influence and social exchange through which the collective decision gets made in such cases, but rather to leave those as separate processes for explicit analysis. It is sufficient here to observe that these independent corporate actors within a community may be regarded as not having formal rights of control over actions of the community, but having resources that may be of interest to those who do have formal control, and thus the possibility of gaining control over the outcome.

The response to the question of who is the elementary actor with rights of partial control over corporate action can be summarized as follows: In many cases the elementary actor is a natural person. In others (such as the United Nations) the elementary actor is itself a corporate actor. In some cases (such as a corporation with both natural persons and corporations as stockholders) the elementary actor may be either a natural person or a corporate actor. There are, however, more complex cases such as those described above, in which intermediate actors may be functionally interdependent with respect to the corporate action or the social structure on which the corporate actor is superimposed. The lack of complete sovereignty of many intermediate corporate actors is shown by the fact that ordinarily their constitutions, which specify how they themselves are controlled by their members, are established at the level of the superordinate corporate actor.

« 14 »

The Problem
of Social Choice

Chapter 11 showed how the existence of actions with externalities is the basis for the rationality of transferring rights to an action-rights bank. And Chapter 13 showed conditions under which rational individuals will find it in their interest to transfer rights to control certain of their actions to a corporate actor. All such transfers are made under the assumption that those rights will then be exercised in a way that makes the individuals better off than if they had held the rights individually.

Thus, as those earlier chapters showed, even if rights are initially held by individuals (or are seen to be so held from a philosophical perspective of natural rights), those individuals will not continue to hold all their rights individually. Each will make a contingent transfer of some of the rights to a corporate actor, which springs into being upon the acquisition of those rights. But in many cases it is not rational for individuals to make such a transfer unless they retain some control over the actions the corporate actor takes, since those actions constitute or give rise to events that have consequences for them. The problem is just how control over those corporate actions can be partitioned among a number of individuals.

This problem arises in a wide variety of settings. Collective decisions within democratic nation-states and voluntary organizations are the most prominent cases, but the problem also exists for communes, which must make decisions about communal affairs, and for corporations, which must make decisions about economic affairs. The absence of uniform success in solving this problem can be seen in a number of phenomena: the fall of the government in some nation-states, sometimes through revolution; the breakup of a commune split by factions; the hostile take-over of a firm.

Partitioning of Rights to Indivisible Goods

It is possible to partition the rights inherent in divisible goods in the range of ways described in Chapter 3. But what about the rights inherent in an indivisible action or event? How can those rights be partitioned?

Suppose there is a constitution with the following properties:

The set of rights to be held collectively rather than individually has been constitutionally fixed.

The distribution of rights of control over the collectively held rights has been constitutionally fixed (for example, equal control for all those persons qualifying as members or citizens).

The specific form of the rights of control is not constitutionally fixed.

The constitution gives each person equal control over collective actions but leaves open the question of whether these rights of control are to be exercised through a more or less continuous plebiscite, through a legislature whose representatives are elected in periodic elections, through a single executive who is elected periodically, or in some other way. A sense of the structure of rights inherent in collective actions may give some insight into each of these forms of exercising rights as well as other possible forms.

To establish a foothold for addressing this problem, I draw attention to several matters:

1. For almost any collectivity there is not a single collective action to be taken, but a stream of actions over time. This fact establishes partial divisibility of collective actions over time, since the actions in this stream are separate actions.[1]

2. Different collective actions are of varying interest to different members of the corporate body. At the extreme an action may be of no interest to all but a subset of members. This fact introduces the possibility that rights to control certain collective actions may be transferred (with or without a compensating exchange of rights) to subgroups in the collectivity.

3. A common means used to partition control of corporate actions among members is a vote, but a vote can transmit the members' interests to the level of corporate action only imperfectly. It is deficient in various respects (to be examined later in this chapter), but one is rather subtle: A vote recognizes only individuals as having rights and therefore partitions control over corporate actions in such a way that social capital (see Chapter 12), which exists differentially for different members, is ignored. Thus, by default, much more power is given to those who have social capital available to them than to those who lack social capital. Another way of describing this defect is to note that a corporate action is a public good and that the individual is the wrong acting unit, in the sense that individual maximization leads to collective suboptimization (that is, individual maximization leads each individual not to cast a vote). Still another

---

1. Various systems of governance have taken advantage of this divisibility over time of collective actions. One example is that of the Astar commune studied by Zablocki (1980, p. 233), in which each member had dictatorial control over decisions of the commune for a week in regular rotation.

way to describe this defect of a vote is that social scientists have been led astray by the utilitarian vision of Jeremy Bentham, who saw maximization of social welfare as simply the aggregate of individual utilities. This imagery leads to simple aggregation of votes, with the attendant problems noted above.

4. It is sometimes assumed that for a collective decision involving two alternatives, the only device by which the right of an individual to partially control the corporate action can be realized is a vote, which is a binary action. But this is not so. It is possible, for example, for the constitution of the corporate body to dictate a multi-stage procedure, with the individual having constitutional rights at each of the stages. The U.S. Constitution, for example, requires a multi-stage decision procedure for enacting laws. A citizen, with the right to vote in congressional and presidential elections, has partial control over each of the bodies involved in the decision making: the House of Representatives, the Senate, and the president. This is merely one possible structure through which a multi-stage decision procedure can extract multiple, and thus more richly informative, inputs from individuals.

5. In collectivities which continue over a period of time, decision making is not carried out as an isolated event. It is accompanied by extensive electioneering, organization, and often party formation. Clearly these activities occur because they are regarded by those who engage in them as useful in implementing their interests, that is, in getting the outcome in which they are interested. But these activities are not provided for in constitutions; in some cases they are even discouraged by rules forbidding parties or factions. That the theoretical premises which are the basis for the allocation of rights (that is, allocation of votes) do not provide for such activities, which occur widely nonetheless, suggests that these premises, and thus the allocation of rights, are defective. What this means for practice is not wholly clear, but minimally it means that the individualistic right to cast a vote in an undifferentiated single-stage collective decision ignores those rights in which social context or social organization plays a role.

These points concerning the character of indivisible corporate actions suggest ways of partitioning rights to control those actions, ways that are not generally in use in formal decision rules. For example, the fact that there is generally a stream of corporate actions rather than an isolated action means that individuals might be given rights which extend over a class of those actions and allowed to allocate them as they see fit within that class. This possibility provides an additional degree of freedom for individuals' allocation of resources over a set of collective actions. If the number of persons were very small and the number of actions were very large, this would constitute a means by which the constraint of indivisibility of actions would effectively vanish: One person would use his resources to gain control of those collective actions that most interested him, another would gain control of those which most interested him, and so on.

One collectivity in which the number of persons is small and the number of actions is large is the family, and this is the way many family decisions are made:

Given the initial constitutional distribution of rights that determine relative power (a distribution which may of course be inegalitarian), the husband and father comes to have control of those collective activities which most interest him, the wife and mother comes to have control of those collective activities which most interest her, and the children come to have control over those collective activities which most interest them (for example, what the family does on Saturday)—all relative to their initial power.

In a collectivity for which there is a large number of corporate actions and a small number of members, the free-rider problem inherent in a vote is overcome. In a larger collectivity the free-rider problem is inherent so long as the maximizing entity is the individual and he maximizes his individual interests, because the large number of individuals means that an individual's own action has very little effect on his expected benefits, but the actions of all the others taken together affect his expected benefits greatly.

Constitutional Issues in Partitioning Rights to Control Corporate Actions

Some of the problems of partitioning rights of control over corporate actions are addressed at the constitutional stage. Rules, including partitioning of the right to control corporate action, under which the corporate actor takes action are established at this stage. Some problems remain for the individual even after those rules are established; these are problems concerning how to exercise one's rights rationally.

The problems which exist for the corporate actor at the constitutional stage can be stated as follows (they are not wholly independent, as is evident from the list).

1. Given that rights to partially control the corporate action are distributed among various individuals, what form should these rights take? A vote in a collective decision, subject to a particular decision rule, is the usual form of such a right, but there are other alternatives, as indicated in the preceding section. Also, it will become evident that votes as rights have some undesirable properties.

2. Whatever form these rights take, there will be differences among the various individuals who hold them about which action the corporate body should take in any given case. What rules or procedures will resolve these differences in a way that meets the following criteria?

   a. The rules which lead to corporate actions should meet some criteria of consistency or rationality. A set of such criteria is the axioms given by Arrow (1951), who proved that there is no rule for aggregating votes that satisfies all of his axioms. I will call Arrow's set of axioms the criterion of consistency. A large body of work has subsequently been carried out in search of a means of aggregating votes that will be least unsatisfactory by this criterion.[2]

    b. The rules should lead to corporate actions which reflect well the interests of the members. I will call this the criterion of veridicality. (Such a criterion is included in Arrow's axioms as the condition that there be a positive association of individual and social values. That is, however, substantively distinct from the criterion of collective rationality. Arrow's axioms together establish criteria of citizen sovereignty and consistency, or collective rationality, as Arrow points out [1951, p. 31].)

    c. The rules should lead to corporate actions that will be implemented with sufficiently strong force that they will be effective. I will call this the criterion of action-potential.

    d. The rules should lead to actions that will not destroy the corporate actor by causing secession or revolt on the part of some members. I will call this the criterion of nondivisiveness.

3. The free-rider problem that exists for any indivisible event tends to lead each individual in a large collectivity not to exercise his right to partially control the actions of the collectivity. One of the consequences of the free-rider problem is that it is irrational for an individual to vote in any but the smallest collective decisions if the act of voting imposes a cost on him. The fact that many individuals do vote at some cost of time and effort and in the face of their vote's having a negligible effect on the outcome is sometimes referred to as the paradox of voting (see Riker and Ordeshook, 1973). The way in which this apparently irrational behavior can be explained through the rational emergence of a norm to vote was examined in Chapter 11 (and will be further analyzed in Chapter 30). That explanation, however, merely describes how a norm may arise among rational individuals to bring about voting. It does not point to a way for a corporate actor to overcome the paradox of voting, and even less does it overcome the general free-rider problem for decision making by corporate actors.

These problems can be seen as part of the problem of making the micro-to-macro transition for the corporate actor. Rights to determine the direction of action are to be held at the level of individuals, but action is to be taken at the level of the corporate actor. The micro-to-macro problem here is a problem of institutional design: how to combine these rights of partial control to give as a result a direction for corporate action that meets the criteria of consistency, veridicality, action-potential, and nondivisiveness.

2. Much of this work appears in the journals *Public Choice, Journal of Economic Theory, Social Choice and Welfare,* and *American Political Science Review.* The term "consistency" has also been used in a narrower sense in the literature on social choice (see Young, 1975; Fishburn, 1977), where a choice is said to be consistent if the set of alternatives chosen by a combined group consists of those chosen separately by both of two subgroups of which the larger group is composed. Here I use the term to mean transitivity of social choice to provide a preference order for the collectivity.

This problem is sometimes described as a problem of aggregation, where the rights being aggregated are votes. To describe the problem in this way is incorrect in two ways. First, just as for any other micro-to-macro transition, the combining of individual-level rights or resources to give a macro-level outcome is not simply a matter of aggregation but involves interactions of some sort. The fact that the problem of institutional design *has* been seen as merely a problem of aggregation is one source of defects in institutions for arriving at collective decisions.

Second, this description of the problem is incorrect in its assumption that the rights held by individuals must be in the form of votes as currently defined. This assumption forecloses a search for a form of right which would allow the solution to the micro-to-macro problem to better meet the four criteria given above. Votes constitute a defective and archaic means for making the micro-to-macro transition, better in only some respects than a lottery in which the winner dictates the corporate action (and in fact worse than a lottery in some respects).

Because it is a problem of institutional design, this micro-to-macro problem is of a somewhat different character than most of the others discussed in this book, which are less a matter of optimal design than a matter of appropriate conceptualization of an existing micro-to-macro transition. The intellectual task remains in part, however, that of appropriate conceptualization of autonomous processes, for some collective decisions are made in the absence of explicit institutional design. The examination of these will help in the development of institutional design. In addition, even in the presence of institutions constitutionally defined so as to produce social choices, other institutions arise through the purposive actions of individuals in the system. Political parties, for example, are not called for or specified in most constitutions (and some constitutions specifically outlaw them), yet they arise spontaneously in many political systems. An understanding of why such institutions emerge can give some insight into the overall process through which the micro-to-macro transition is made, as well as into the deficiencies of existing institutional structures for making the transition.

This chapter will examine the first two of the three problems of the corporate actor listed above. (There is some treatment of the third problem in Chapter 31.) After examining some naturally emerging institutions in settings that lack formal decision rules, I will examine first the problem of establishing an institutional structure which produces "good" outcomes. The relative goodness of an outcome is evaluated as the extent to which it meets the four criteria of consistency, veridicality, action-potential, and nondivisiveness. I will turn then to the first problem listed above, that of what form the rights of partial control held by individuals should take.

Intellectual Puzzles concerning Social Choice

Ever since the American and French revolutions created contexts within which formal collective decisions by the populace or their representatives replaced some of the decisions made by single heads of state, the questions surrounding collective decisions have created intellectual puzzles with direct relevance for social action. Two of the earliest theorists of collective decisions, the Marquis de Condorcet and Jean Charles de Borda, were stimulated by the French Revolution and the intellectual foment preceding it. Much of the subsequent work on collective decisions has been directed to the task to which their efforts were directed, that of devising a decision rule which accurately reflects, under all conditions, the will of the people.

Earlier democratic decision procedures, such as those used in classical Greece and the British Parliament, apparently did not stimulate such intellectual activity. There have, however, been other settings which, like the American and French revolutions, provided a stimulus for addressing these puzzles. One was in the colleges of the English universities of Oxford and Cambridge, where the necessity for electing masters led Lewis Carroll and others to address the question of how to find decision rules with desirable properties.[3] Black (1970) has reviewed the early history of these intellectual developments.

It was the French Revolution, more than any other event, which stimulated intellectuals to give attention to the question of how the will of the people, or Rousseau's common will, might best be discovered through election procedures. There are two components to this problem. One is definitional: Just what is meant by the "common will"? The other, postdefinitional, problem is how, once a definition is given, the common will can be realized through a procedure or set of rules which elicits some behavior on the part of individuals and aggregates that behavior in some fashion.

The notion of finding that direction for collective action which expresses the common will, or the will of the people, reflects in at least one aspect earlier forms of social choice, perhaps best exemplified by the institution of trial by ordeal. The conceptual basis for trial by ordeal is the notion of a supernatural force which would protect the accused from the forces of nature *if* he was innocent. In the early conceptions of popular sovereignty, and certainly in Rousseau's writings which constituted part of the origins of those conceptions, the notion of a supraindividual will, which had only to be discovered, was evident.

Despite the fact that theoretical work in social choice has abandoned such a notion, it is important to recognize that its being popularly held could itself have some value for creating a "good" decision procedure. It could give legitimacy to the choice arrived at, even though the procedure used might in fact be defective. The argument may be put as follows: As long as rights were seen to be of divine origin, and to descend from God to the monarch, the legitimacy of the monarch's actions—as well as that of actions taken under the monarch's delegation—was assured. Rights could always be traced to God, from whom they emanated, and

---

3. These elections have proved a continuing source of interest in how collective decisions are made. C. P. Snow constructed a novel, *The Masters* (1951), around a fictional election of a new master in a college in Cambridge. In Chapter 17 an incident from that novel is referred to in raising a question about the legitimacy of certain transactions in collective decisions.

any action taken by the holder of those rights had legitimacy. As the doctrine of natural rights and popular sovereignty began to make itself felt in the seventeenth and eighteenth centuries, this path through which corporate actions could be assured of legitimacy was gone. But the shifting of sovereignty to the people did not eliminate the need for some ultimate source of legitimation of corporate actions. This need was satisfied by the conception of the common will, or the will of the people, as something that existed prior to and independent of the procedures used to make social choices. Any such procedure was merely the device by which the common will was discovered.

But other, no less genuine, problems remain. The most important is Condorcet's paradox, which is that consistent individual preferences can produce, with a majority decision rule, inconsistent social choices. Arrow (1951) proved that no decision rule by which consistent (as defined by his axioms) individual preferences or votes are aggregated will always result in consistent social choices.[4]

It is useful, before turning to an examination of this paradox and some of its implications, to examine more carefully the differences between partial rights of control over indivisible events and ownership rights over goods that are private, divisible, and alienable. This can be done by comparing the micro-to-macro transition in the two cases. For ownership rights over private goods, the market is one major means by which such a transition occurs. The system begins with individual holdings and preferences and ends with a new distribution of holdings determined by prices which are emergent from the transactions at the micro level. (The market is not the only means through which such redistribution occurs; redistribution through the intervention of a central authority, by means of rationing or price control, is another alternative.)

The comparison of social choice with an economic market is instructive. The starting point in the case of the market is the individual having control (or rights of control) of some fraction of each of a number of private and divisible goods. The institutional setting is one in which agreements are enforced (or self-enforcing if there is simultaneous delivery), and the rights of private property are honored. Related institutions, such as banks, media of exchange, systems of credit, escrow, and so forth, may emerge, but these emergent institutions should be distinguished from the basic rules necessary to begin the process. In such a setting individuals do not control all that interests them, but since the goods are divisible, have no externalities, and are alienable, the individuals can use their resources to satisfy their wants, within the budget constraints imposed by the resources with which they begin. In doing so, they generate the systemic outcome, which is the distribution of goods resulting from exchanges. This outcome

---

4. Condorcet's proposed procedure for arriving at a collective decision in the face of this paradox retained the conception of a "correct" choice, with individual votes seen as merely individuals' judgments and possibly in error. Condorcet proposed to break the cyclical chain at the weakest link, which involved counting the fewest votes as errors (Young and Levenglich, 1978; Young, 1987). See Chapter 15 for further discussion.

emerges incrementally, as individuals make exchanges that bring them increasingly closer to the new equilibrium distribution.

For social choices concerning indivisible events, the matter is different. The resources with which individuals begin ordinarily have the form of rights of some kind to affect the outcomes of decisions of the corporate actor. Voting rights are probably the most common form of these rights. But individuals are not in a situation in which they can satisfy their wants with respect to these decisions in the incremental way they can in economic markets. They cannot buy control over a decision that is of interest to them, as they can buy a private, divisible good—not only because buying votes is illegal. Two properties of the outcome of a social choice result from the indivisibility of the event. The first is that the outcome of the event is all-or-none, so the principle of declining marginal utility does not hold. The second is that the consequences of the event have the properties of a public good. One's control of the outcome, partial or total, provides one with no more benefits than does control by someone else who favors the same outcome.

The question concerning the individual's action becomes that of how, if at all, these two differences in resources will affect his motivation and thus his action. The absence of declining marginal utility means that his incentive to gain an additional unit of control does not decline incrementally as he gains more control. If, for example, there is a majority decision rule, his incentive to control an additional vote probably increases as he comes closer to controlling half the votes, and then becomes zero after that point.[5]

Just how fundamental the absence of declining marginal utility is to votes as resources is shown by a mental experiment. Suppose the decision rule were as follows: If n_1 out of n votes are cast for a positive outcome and $n - n_1$ votes are cast for a negative outcome, then a probability mechanism determines whether the outcome will be positive, with probability n_1/n, or negative, with probability $(n - n_1)/n$. With such a decision rule how is a rational individual's incentive to control more votes affected by the number he already controls? The answer is not at all. The effect of each vote on the expected outcome (and thus on the individual's expected utility) is the same, independent of the number he already controls.

For a decision rule based on votes to incorporate declining marginal utility, the probability of an outcome in agreement with the individual's preference would have to increase incrementally, but at a declining rate, as the number of votes he controls increases. Such a decision rule is possible but is not currently found in practice. If such a decision rule were used, it would mean that there was some incentive to acquire control of additional votes besides one's own (although no more incentive, overall, than with current decision rules) *and* that this incentive declined with the number of votes controlled so that some kind of equilibrium

5. I say "probably" here because his incentive depends on his assessment of others' actions. See Coleman (1968b) for an extended examination of the marginal utility of a vote.

would be possible. As I will show in Chapter 31, however, such a condition is not necessary for an equilibrium to exist.

The second troublesome property of an event which is to be decided by collective decision is that the consequences of the event for an individual may be the same whether or not he controls the outcome. The consequences are not restricted to those who hold and exercise control over the outcome. If others who favor the same outcome as I do control the event, then I gain the benefits of that outcome, just as though I had held and exercised control myself. If others who favor a different outcome control the event, I experience the consequences of that outcome. One's control of a vote is of no more benefit to one than is control by someone who will cast the vote in the same way. The difference in incentive produced by this second property can be very great, depending on the number of persons who have partial control over the collective decision. If the number is large, then the outcome (and thus the consequence for the individual) is almost independent of the individual's own vote.

Another mental experiment will give a better sense of just how a collective decision concerning an event with consequences for all differs from individual control of private, divisible goods. Suppose a collective decision must be made concerning an event with n possible outcomes and under the control of n individuals. Outcome i represents individual i receiving a consumable good. Each individual has an interest only in whether or not he receives the good; that is, individual i has an interest only in outcome i as against all other outcomes. The decision rule can be any reasonable rule, so majority rule can be assumed. The event is indivisible, as before, thus leading to the absence of declining marginal utility and giving no basis for reaching an equilibrium by exchanges. In contrast, the second property of the event, which distinguished it from a private, divisible good, no longer does so. Only if the individual controls the event will he experience the outcome he is interested in. Thus there is no longer a free-rider problem.

If contracts were revocable in a tatonnement process and if each individual had other resources which he could use for acquiring votes, then sufficient votes would be acquired by one of the individuals to gain control of the event. This would be the individual who had both sufficient resources to allow purchase of others' votes and high interest in the good that was being distributed by the collective decision. The process would be formally equivalent to an auction in which the winning bid was divided equally among all other bidders, with the right to bid constitutionally determined. (The formal treatment in Part V will show that the individual gaining control of the event will be the one for which, in terms of the concepts introduced in Chapter 2, the product of power and interest is greatest.)

Given the differences just described between ownership rights in private goods and rights of partial control over an indivisible event, how does social choice come about in the absence of formal decision procedures?

Emergent Processes and Institutions for Social Choice

It is useful to see how social choice occurs in various settings in which formal institutions for decision making are absent or minimal. One of these is the small group.

Natural Decision-Making Processes in Small Groups

One case of small-group decision making occurs in communes. Communes are closed systems of action, with few connections to the outside. Members are often undifferentiated in terms of formal power; there may be some qualification for membership in the commune, reaching a certain age or being accepted as a new member from the outside through a collective decision of the current members. Many communes have no formal decision rule. Any decision is arrived at by consensus, after extended discussion and argument, but without any formal procedure through which preferences are assessed and then aggregated. There is an extended process of decision making, starting from initial disagreement and resulting finally in agreement.

Such a decision-making process is not confined to communes, but characterizes many informal small groups and committees. The process is familiar to anyone who has sat on committees or been a member of a small group which must come to a decision; I will state only the central points without elaboration or example. First, there is not a formal decision rule. Second, there is a general desire among members to reach consensus, that is, to arrive at a final decision that all agree on. Third, there is often a desire on the part of all or most members to avoid a vote. Fourth, the process involves not only declaring one's position but also extended discussion. Members usually have different "weight," and sometimes when a person who has great weight argues in favor of an alternative early in the discussion, certain others who might have spoken out against it do not do so.

What does the theory of this book have to say about a collective decision of this sort? To answer this requires returning to the conceptual structure described in Chapter 2. There (and more formally in Chapter 25) the concept of an actor's power in a system of action is defined as the actor's control over those things that actors in the system have interests in. A simple and direct application of the theory can predict the outcome of a collective decision in a small-group setting: If there are two alternatives, with no modifications possible, and if some of the members have interests favoring the one outcome and others have interests favoring the other outcome, the outcome chosen will be the one for which the sum of the weighted interests of members is greater. The weight of an actor is his power, as defined earlier.

How does such an outcome come about, according to the theory? The question is especially pointed when the theory leads to the prediction that a minority will prevail, for to go from a minority favoring an outcome to unanimity in favor of that outcome is an extreme change. The most straightforward prediction would be that the position initially held by the majority will in the end prevail. The prediction that a minority position will prevail can arise because, loosely speaking, those in the minority have greater weight, that is, greater power or greater interest in the outcome, or both. More precisely, according to the formal theory as described in Part V, it is because the minority has greater weighted interests in the outcome than does the majority. The processes by which a minority position ends with unanimous support are, according to the theory, processes in which actors engage in exchanges, calling in credit or making promises. In any of those activities the interest of an actor plays a part, in determining how much of his resources to commit to influencing the decision; and the power of an actor plays a part, for his power is determined by the extent of his resources, including the value of his promises and the amount of credit he can call on. His power is equivalent to his budget constraint in a system of exchange of divisible goods.

The theory yields a second and possibly different prediction, also requiring a return to the conceptual structure of Chapter 2, where it was pointed out that outcomes of events may have implications for other events in which actors are interested. These implications, which constitute dependencies between events, allow the content of the event in question to have an effect in the following way: Since the event is not seen by the members of the collectivity as independent of all others in which they are interested, additional interests may come to be activated if the implications of each outcome for other events of interest to the members are made evident in the discussion. According to the theory, the role of extended discussion is to make explicit the dependence of other events on the decision being made.

If there is extended discussion, interests in other events are brought into play. The outcome may be different than it would be in the absence of the discussion. Although the weights of the various members remain the same, a greater portion of the interests of some or all of them comes into play, and therefore the weighted interests may be different. The decision may be regarded as having been made more nearly on the basis of the content of the event in question than on the basis of a pure exercise of power, but power remains important. The only difference is that the implications of the decision for various other events enter into the decision-making process.

Thus the theory of this book predicts two possible outcomes for a collective decision by a small group, depending on whether or not there is extensive discussion about the implications of the decision for other interests. Unanimity is important for Kaldor's compensation principle (see Chapters 13 and 29). Unless those who lose from a corporate action can be compensated by those who benefit from it, so there are no overall losers, the action may not be the correct one to take from the point of view of the corporate actor as constituted (that is, with the particular joint distribution of power and interests found among its membership). The compensation here is the calling of obligations by members who, by virtue of the credit they hold, have power in the system. In other words, it can be said that the corporate action has externalities for each of the members of the collectivity. Unless the (weighted) positive externalities of the action are greater than the (weighted) negative externalities, the outcome of the collective decision results in a net loss. Unanimity after exchange ensures that there will not be a net loss.

One point should be noted about the actions that members of small groups take in the extended discussion that makes evident the implication of a decision for other events of interest to members. A new kind of action, not discussed before, takes place. Actors either introduce new events into the system or introduce linkages of dependence between the outcome of the particular social choice and other events confronting the collectivity or its individual members. Thus, by drawing attention to previously ignored events or previously ignored dependence of other events on this one, they change the system of action in which the social choice occurs. As will become evident later in this chapter in the discussion of community conflicts, this kind of activity is extensive in some kinds of conflicts surrounding social choice.

The two predictions made above have certain unsatisfactory aspects. One is that neither suggests what would happen when there are three or more alternative outcomes. Yet it is this circumstance that has been the focus of scholarly examination, from Condorcet's paradox in the 1790s to Arrow's theorem in the 1950s to the search for incentive-compatible voting schemes in the present. I will return to this aspect later.

A second unsatisfactory aspect of these predictions is that neither seems to take into account what appears, from empirical observations, to be an important element in the decision making of conjoint collectivities. This is the distinction that members make between self-interests (or selfish interests) and group interests. Members appear hesitant to bring up self-interests and sometimes express disapproval when another member does so. The distinction between what is good for the individual and what is good for the group is a common one, not only in small groups but in large collectivities and even (though less often) in disjoint corporate actors such as business corporations.

It appears that a normative process is often operating in the deliberations that precede collective decisions. The norm operates, if I am correct, to constrain members from expressing interests that are not shared by others in the collectivity. Can the theory account for the emergence of such a norm? The answer is clearly yes. Collective decision making is a setting in which each actor's action, insofar as it affects the outcome, imposes externalities on each other individual actor and has consequences as well for the corporate actor. In such circumstances a norm which is to the benefit of all is a conjoint norm that says that no one should take a position that cannot be justified in terms of benefits to the collectivity or to all its members. Such a norm will be in opposition to divisive actions because they can hurt members in two ways: First, they hurt the interests of some members of the collectivity as individuals; and second, they hurt the interests of all in maintaining a strong and effective collectivity.

Since such a norm is in the interest of all members of the collectivity, it can be expected to emerge and to have some strength. This leads to a prediction that in general differs from the two stated earlier: The outcome of a collective decision will be more in the direction of interests that members have in common or goals toward which the collectivity is directed than an outcome given by either of the two predictions made earlier.

But is it possible to say whether one outcome is in some sense "better" than the others? This is the kind of question that moral philosophers examine, and it is useful to take their perspective. Doing so will lead to questions closely related to those examined in Chapter 3.

Ethical Theory: How to Determine the Right Action

Moral philosophers have as their central concern the determination of what is right. For some moral philosophers this is principally a personal question; they ask how an individual, a natural person, may know what is the moral thing to do. Kant's categorical imperative is the best-known answer to this question. For other moral philosophers, such as Rawls (1971) or Nozick (1974), the question is a social one; they ask what policy or law is moral, or right, or just. This question is asked not for a person but for a corporate actor, ordinarily a society with a governing agent and a set of laws. It is a question to be asked for (or by) those who have some influence on the policies of the corporate actor.

Does this central concern of moral philosophers have anything in common with the notion of right as I have discussed it or, more generally, with positive social theory? The answer, I believe, is that it does, despite the contrast between normative theory and positive theory. In fact, the framework of ideas introduced here provides a way of evaluating some of the arguments of moral philosophers on behalf of some way of determining what is the right action or the right policy.

Moral philosophers often take as their starting point some fundamental principle defining what is right or how to know what is right.[6] Perhaps the most durable of such principles is the set of variations on Kant's categorical imperative, which itself is a variant of the Golden Rule: "Do unto others as you would have others do unto you." Such a principle does not specify what is right but gives a procedure by which one may distinguish between a right action and a wrong action. A principle of this sort goes one step deeper than a principle which identifies particular actions as right or wrong (such as the specification that killing another person is always wrong or that helping another is always right). Because it leads to a decision on what is right or wrong based on consideration of actions in particular social contexts, a principle of this sort is potentially compatible with a positive theory of social action.

---

6. See Herzog (1985) for an argument that an appropriate system of moral philosophy cannot begin with such a principle.

Efficiency and Ethics

Many foundational principles in ethical theory are somewhat similar to the Golden Rule. Such a principle involves a person (or more than one person) imagining himself as object of the action, in the position occupied by one or more other persons and evaluating the action from that perspective. This was perhaps most explicitly stated by Hobbes as his "easie sum" (described in Chapter 13). This principle may be found not only in many normative theories, where it determines what an actor *should* do, but also in many positive social psychological theories. Cooley's (1902) looking-glass self, Adam Smith's (1976 [1753]) concept of sympathy, and similar concepts of other social psychologists all express the idea that many of actions of individuals are shaped by a prior evaluation of the proposed action from the perspectives of others. Rawls's (1971) social contract scenario of persons behind a veil of ignorance about their future positions utilizes this principle, although it is transformed into something closer to self-interested rationality.[7] (Rawls's veil of ignorance makes it unnecessary to put oneself in another's place. Because of the veil of ignorance, putting oneself in the range of places one might occupy in the future is approximately equivalent to imagining oneself in positions occupied by others.)

If each person were perfectly accurate in placing himself in the positions of others and evaluating an action or a policy from those perspectives, then all would agree on the effect of a given action or policy on a person in a given position. Suppose, for simplicity of exposition, that there are only two relevant positions with respect to a certain policy: the position of being a man and the position of being a woman. If the policy is to be evaluated directly and each person has an equal voice in the evaluation, the outcome will depend on whether men or women are in the numerical majority. If, however, each man and woman places himself or herself in the position of others in the system, then each, whether man or woman, will balance the benefits (or costs) to men against the costs (or benefits) to women. This means that each will take into account not only the numbers of men and numbers of women affected by the policy, but also the strength of the effect. Each will weigh the interests of those benefited against the interests of those harmed by the policy, and each will arrive at the same overall evaluation. The issue will be resolved by consensus, since all will see the policy in the same way—having internalized the interests of all others in the system. Self-interests will count for no more than the interests of any other. Each will speak in the name of the whole.

This is the goal of collective decision making in many small groups and close communities. It is reflected in the consensus decision rule found in many communal groups and in members' distaste for calling a vote in such groups.

In such a decision-making process, it is not the case that the interests of each as internalized by another are regarded by that other as counting equally. It is

---

7. Nozick's (1974) moral philosophy, however, does not include this process of imagining oneself in the position of others.

the importance of each to the system as a whole (that is, what I have called power in the system) that constitutes the weight attached to another person's interests as internalized.

The above description is an idealization of the decision-making process that occurs in small, tightly knit groups. It is an idealization in the sense that there is seldom or never the complete elimination of self-interests envisioned above. It is also an idealization in that seldom is each member of a collectivity perfectly accurate in assessing the interests of the others and in assessing the importance of each of the others to the functioning of the collectivity. But it is not only an idealization of the process that goes on; it is a description of the normative ideal that each member of the group holds about how actions and policies should be evaluated.

Suppose this ideal is realized in a specific case. Then, I contend, the decision-making process will give a socially efficient outcome, in a way that is precisely analogous to the market for externalities envisioned by Coase (1960) as a means by which a socially efficient outcome is achieved. In Coase's analysis interests favoring and opposing a given outcome are weighted according to the resources (money) that those favoring and opposing the outcome are willing to devote to securing that outcome. The importance of an actor, constituting the weight applied to his interests, is his wealth. This weighting of his interests occurs automatically through the amount of money he is willing to give up to gain the outcome he prefers (ignoring, of course, free-rider problems).[8] For the efficiency arrived at through the internal balancing process that leads to consensus in decision making, the importance of an actor is his importance to system functioning as perceived by each of the persons doing the internal balancing. This is what I have described as power in Chapter 2 and will define formally in Chapter 25.

What, then, is the ethical or morally correct outcome? It is, I suggest, the outcome arrived at through such a process of internal weighing of interests on the part of each of the actors. No longer is each acting in terms of self-interest; each is acting in terms of the interests of the collectivity, conceived of as a corporate actor. Assuming that each actor perceives the interests and importance of each other actor correctly, each will favor the same outcome, the socially efficient and morally correct outcome, which is optimal for the collectivity as a corporate actor. This is the outcome given by the third prediction in the preceding section. According to that prediction, a conjoint norm arises in which each actor gives up to the others as a collective the right to determine his action (that is, his support of a particular social-choice outcome). Yet norms often fail to emerge even where there is demand for them unless there is high closure, and

8. In Chapter 30 and 31, this is expressed in the formal model by a property of the Cobb-Douglas utility function: The value of the resources that an actor will devote to an event is equal to a fraction of his total wealth (or power), where the fraction constitutes his interest in the event.

for the same social-structural reasons such an ideal is likely to be approximated only in small groups.

An implication of this reasoning is that the morally correct or ethical outcome is endogenously determined, by the members of the system itself. For example, if the members of the Jonestown community in Guyana knew what they were doing and went through the internal weighing process described above when they followed Jim Jones's directive to drink the poisoned Kool-Aid, the outcome was a morally correct one.

A further implication, however, is that there can be other systems from which an action can be observed, providing external observation points for judging an action's morality. In those systems the process operates just as it does within the system where the action takes place. Thus, for example, each of the persons within American society as a whole might weigh the action at Jonestown in the fashion described earlier, and there might be a consensus that the action is not efficient, not socially optimal, not correct. This would make the action a morally wrong action *from the perspective of the external system.* It is important to emphasize that every such observation point is that of a particular social system. *There is no absolute observation point, outside any social system, from which moral judgment may be made.*

Executive Decision Making

Certain characteristic processes found in executive decision making may add insight concerning social choice. One phenomenon which is characteristic of many executive decision-making processes is that of high consensus on a course of action. What often occurs appears to be something like this: A dictator (whom I will call an executive) is faced with making choices for the corporate actor whose actions he directs. The alternatives to choose among must somehow arise, and they may be put forth by persons around the executive (whom I will call courtiers). If it is assumed that courtiers are motivated solely by personal advancement (analogous to a political party's motivation to get candidates elected) and that advancement is conditional on providing or supporting the alternative that will ultimately be chosen by the executive, then each courtier will attempt to present or justify that alternative which he believes will be chosen by the executive. Thus, if there is perfect information, all will converge on the single point, the executive's most preferred position. This leads to what is ordinarily characterized as sycophancy, or being yes-men. A phenomenon frequently observed in hierarchical organizations, an executive surrounded by yes-men, is the natural result. A courtier who supports an alternative that differs considerably from the preferred position of the executive, when the other courtiers support the executive's preferred alternative, will be left in isolation. The executive notes that the other courtiers agree that the position he originally favored is the correct one. He regards his opinion as confirmed and the courtiers who confirm it as wise, insightful, and perceptive. He is, of course, right about their wisdom, perception, and insight; what he fails to notice is that their objective is to support the alternative that he prefers, rather than to present an alternative that will prove best in the long run.

It is possible to see something comparable to the sycophancy of courtiers in forms of social choice other than executive decision making. In decision making in small groups each member may be seen as a combination of executive (holding rewards for the others) and courtier (interested in rewards from the others). In other words, the group member has a preferred outcome, which he believes will be objectively best, but in addition he has an interest in rewards from the other group members (analogous to the courtiers' interest in advancement).

In this case the symmetry of the structure suggests that, if all positions are initially equidistant and all members are equally powerful in the benefits they hold for each other, all group members should move toward a central point, which will be the final decision outcome. In fact, there is unlikely to be such pure symmetry in the balance between positional interests and interests in rewards or in group members' possession of rewards (that is, power) or in the distance of positions from one another. If one group member has greater interest in his preferred position than do others, their greater relative interest in rewards will tend to lead toward his position. If one member holds rewards of greater interest to others, their interest in these rewards will tend to lead toward his position.[9] All this, however, is merely another way of describing the functioning of weighted interests, as discussed earlier.

Decision making in small groups is not the only form of social choice in which a structure comparable to that of an executive surrounded by courtiers is present. Political parties in a two-party system may be seen as courtiers to the median voter, following the general framework introduced by Downs (1957). Downs, drawing on earlier work by Hotelling, showed that in a two-party system if there were a single dimension of importance, if the parties took as given the positions of citizens on that dimension, and if the parties had no objective other than to gain office, both parties would present platforms or candidates at the position occupied by the median voter. The paradox in this, of course, is that the two parties, acting rationally, would be presenting alternatives to voters which minimize their opportunity for choice. And although one might hope that the final outcome of a collective decision in which two parties were positioning themselves rationally and voters were choosing rationally would be an outcome

9. Janis (1972) gives various cases of group decision making where the outcomes appear (to him) not to be optimal. He terms the processes which lead to these outcomes "groupthink." It is likely that arriving at consensus on an outcome which is not optimal is a result of the power being quite unequally distributed in the system thus leading the outcome to depend greatly on the initial position of the actor with greatest power. One of Janis's examples is the Bay of Pigs invasion: One actor was President Kennedy and another was his brother Robert. If the president's initial position or his brother's (whose power was also high) favored invasion, the result would be led strongly in that direction. As this example illustrates, the case of an executive and courtiers shades over into this more general case if some of the courtiers have independent power.

in which the total distance between policy and voters' positions was minimal, this does not occur except in special cases. In this sense rational behavior in such a structure leads to a perverse outcome.[10] Thus, to the degree that Downs's work accurately describes the behavior of political parties in a two-party system, they can be seen as courtiers who are sycophants to the median voter.[11]

Structured Dissent

In the case of the executive and courtiers, it is useful to ask about responses to sycophancy. The rational executive, who is unconcerned about which of his courtiers get advancement but wants to choose an alternative that will have good consequences for the corporate body, has an interest in overcoming sycophancy. One institution that can be used to do that is what I will call structured dissent.[12] This varies somewhat in different cases, but one variant of it is as follows: A general discussion is held among executive and courtiers, or among courtiers alone, to elicit possible alternatives. In this discussion alternatives are not put forth to be defended, so there is no competition among courtiers to support the preferred alternative. After all alternatives are on the table, each feasible alternative is assigned arbitrarily to a courtier, whose task is to prepare a position paper which examines the consequences of that alternative, both favorable and unfavorable. (In another version of the process, the courtier has the task of propounding and arguing for the assigned alternative.)

This institution of structured dissent is one which detaches the courtier's interest in advancement from the actions of finding and supporting the alternative that will be accepted by the executive, and attaches it to a different task: showing the consequences of an arbitrarily assigned alternative. The courtier is put in a position in which sycophancy no longer aids his interest in advancement, which is furthered instead by acumen in characterizing the consequences of the assigned alternative.

10. On the other hand, although the parties will not in general have chosen that alternative which is at the mean of voters' tastes, they will have chosen the median position, anticipating what voters' choices will be. The condition under which this would not be true is that both parties have misperceived the position of the median voter; then *both* would present a candidate who is to one side of the median.

11. There has been a considerable amount of work since that of Downs in modifying his theory to fit better the actual behavior of parties. For example, I show elsewhere that if a party is no longer viewed as a monolithic actor taking an action to maximize its chance of gaining office, but as an ideologically skewed subset of the population of voters, each of whom wants to maximize the expected satisfaction he gets from the outcome, and if there is some uncertainty about just where the median voter lies, then the outcome will be the election of candidates that are not at the median voter's position but somewhere between that point and the median voter of the party they represent (Coleman, 1971).

12. This institution has emerged in the U.S. presidency during the administrations of several presidents and elsewhere in the U.S. government. In NASA a variant is called "nonadvocacy policy review."

Community Decision Making and Conflict

An examination of the processes which characterize community decision making that occurs outside of institutionalized channels can provide further insight into the micro-to-macro transition which results in a social choice. A conflict within a community typically arises over a particular event, concerning which a social choice must be made. In *Community Conflict* (Coleman, 1957) I examine a number of such conflicts. The event in many of the cases was a decision on whether or not to fluoridate the community's water system. In others it was a school-related event. In some cases formal authority for making the social choice rested with citizens, through referendum. In others it rested with a representative assembly, the city council or a school board. In still others it was held by an executive, such as the mayor or the school superintendent.

Thus the decision-making process in such situations begins not with a set of actors and events, as assumed in applications of the theory in earlier chapters, but rather with an event. The actors and events that may be involved in the outcome of the event are not fixed in advance. The event around which the action is focused in this kind of situation, the event concerning which a social choice is to be made, I will call the conflict event. What other events and actors are brought into the process may depend on the strategic actions of actors who have an initial interest in the outcome of the conflict event.

For example, around 1950 a small group of citizens in Pasadena, California, was opposed to the superintendent of schools and wanted either to remove him from office or to change the "progressive" educational practices he had instituted in the system (Hurlburd, 1950). These two events—his continuation or removal as superintendent, and the continuation or change of his educational practices—may be thought of as events concerning which a social choice was to be made. The superintendent had authority over the latter event, and the school board had authority over the former. The small group of citizens included no school board members and had only a very small portion of control over election of the school board, since the group had fewer than ten members. One of their actions was to call a meeting of "concerned parents" (they were not themselves parents of children in school) to discuss the problems that children were having with learning to read. In that meeting, to which a number of parents came, the members of the instigating group did not attempt to find others who shared their interest in opposing the superintendent and his progressive practices; instead they focused attention on another event in which the parents were interested: their children's failure to learn to read. They presented what they viewed as two causal linkages: the dependence of the progressive practices on the superintendent, a dependence that was not difficult to establish; and the dependence of the children's failure to learn to read on those progressive practices, a less conclusive dependence, but one which these particular parents were predisposed to accept. Thus, through the meeting, they introduced a new set of actors (concerned parents) and a new event (children's performance in reading) into the system of action. They did so by establishing two new cognitive links: a perceived dependence of the new event, the event these new actors were interested in, on the two conflict events they themselves were interested in.

In this example, which typifies one class of actions taken in community conflicts, a set of actors not in control of a pair of conflict events brought into the system of action a new event and new actors, giving those actors an indirect interest in the conflict events. This is not the only way new actors and events are brought into community decision making, but it appears to be one of two general ways.

The second way in which interested parties characteristically expand the set of actors and events begins with the same asymmetry of structure: One actor or set of actors holds control over an event, and another actor or set of actors has no control over the event but is interested in the opposite course of action from the one being taken by the actor in control. From this point the action taken by the interested parties differs. They find other actors who have some obligation to them or over whom they have some power, and who in turn have some power over the actor or actors controlling the conflict event. In an example which is not a typical community conflict but is nevertheless a noninstitutionalized social choice, one actor was the Polish government, which had control over the conflict event: issuance of a passport to a Polish citizen. The actor interested in the passport's issuance was the Polish citizen's husband, an American. He brought in another actor, a counselor to the U.S. president, who had some control over some things of interest to the Polish government. Thus the new actor was brought in, not by linking events in which he was interested to the conflict event, but by the interested party's using generalized control over the new actor (due to unspecified credit or obligations) to induce him to use his control over events of interest to the Polish government. In this situation the set of events over which the interested party had control was very diffuse, taking the form of either past actions which gave him a kind of credit balance with the new actor or future events over which he would have control and that might be of interest to the new actor. The set of events over which the new actor had some control and in which the Polish government was interested was similarly diffuse. In some sense, then, these can be considered institutionalized relationships, one between two corporate actors (the U.S. and Polish governments) and one between two persons. The system of action as a whole however, is not institutionalized. The husband, not in control of the event he was interested in, had no institutionalized relation to the Polish government; there was no circumscribed set of events and actors with a set of possible exchanges such that a recognized and accepted power ranking existed among the actors. And the outcome of the conflict event obviously depended on just what other actors and events were brought into the system of action.

It is possible, in accounting for behavior such as is exhibited in the above two examples, to maintain a purposive framework based on a principle of maximization. The maximization that each actor achieves, however, will be maximization within a particular set of limitations, those established by his own repertoire of strategies and other intellectual attributes. The two examples presented above can illustrate what is meant by this. In the first example the small group of persons interested in getting rid of the superintendent may have followed this plan of action: First, they thought of ways that partial control over the conflict events might come to be held by actors sharing their interest, coming up with both the strategy of establishing a dependency of other actors' existing interests on the conflict events and the strategy of finding actors over whom they had some control, who in turn might be able to gain control over the conflict events. Then they selected the first of these two general classes of actions, the one which appeared to give the maximum potential return on their investment of time, effort, and other resources. Having carried out this maximization, they proceeded to act within the first class of actions (establishing a dependency of other actors' existing interests on the conflict events) by choosing those actors and events which appeared to maximize the return on investment of resources.

Although the above plan of action would appear to be a reasonable strategy, perhaps it is not as good as another. Perhaps a single-stage maximization would have led to a different course of action that would have given a greater return. Or perhaps a better strategy would have been one entirely different from the two described above, a totally different general class of actions. Thus the Pasadena group had what might be described as limited rationality, which is characteristic of actors in general. Actors may aim to be rational, but they are more or less sophisticated in realizing that aim. As the complexity of the task they are faced with increases, their actions may deviate increasingly from the objectively most efficient action. A part of this human frailty arises from the necessity of dredging up through recall the possible actors and events that may be linked to the conflict event and the possible ways of linking them. Since persons differ in their ability to recall and in the accuracy of their estimates of these matters, they will differ in the efficiency with which they realize their aims, even apart from differences in the general strategies they consider.

An example similar to the Pasadena conflict over the school superintendent can, by comparison, illustrate this: The conflict occurred in Scarsdale, New York, at about the same time and over a similar issue (Shaplen, 1950). There was a small group of citizens ("The Committee of Ten"), which was opposed to inclusion in the school library of a book by Howard Fast, an American author who was a professed communist. The committee wanted this book and others removed, but the school librarian had control over that and refused their request. Then they attempted to gain control over the conflict event by demanding that the school superintendent fire the librarian. He refused. Next, they attempted to change other persons' attitudes toward the conflict event (inclusion of the book in the school library) by reading passages from the book at meetings.

This strategy, however, gained them few converts, because they made the mistake of assuming that many other persons in the community shared their interest in eliminating writings of communists from the school library. If they had proceeded as the Pasadena group did, by finding an event in which many other persons in the community were already deeply interested and then attempting to link *that* event to the conflict event (or to the superintendent, who controlled the controller of the conflict event), they might have been more successful. The strategy they did use was not successful.

In conflicts over community decisions it is generally the case that introduction of new issues is a major part of the strategy of the nuclei of actors most interested in achieving a particular outcome. In terms of the conceptual framework of this book, introducing new issues means establishing the dependence of certain events on other events. Ordinarily, as in the Pasadena conflict, the new events thus introduced are events in which some persons are interested but which have previously not been causally connected to the event for which a social choice is to be made. The principal new issue in the Pasadena example was children's lack of reading proficiency, introduced by establishing in parents' minds its dependency on progressive education. What issues are introduced strategically will obviously depend on where formal authority over the outcome of the conflict event resides. If it resides in a set of citizens as voters, then the issues introduced (the new events brought into the system) will ordinarily be more numerous than if it resides in a body such as a city council or in a single executive; this is because of the wider range of events in which voters are interested. Sometimes, as in the Pasadena example, formal authority resides in a kind of hierarchy: The superintendent had authority over the curriculum, the school board had authority over the superintendent's tenure in office, and the citizens had authority over the composition of the school board.

The strategies that have been described in this section are shown in parts b, c, and d of Figure 14.1. E_1 is the conflict event concerning which a social choice is to be made; A_1 is the actor (or actors) with formal authority over this event; and A_2 and A_3 are actors interested in the outcome of the event. The strategy shown in part b is that of introducing new issues into a community decision for which formal authority is held by the citizens as voters. A_2 introduces the dependency link between E_1 and E_2 as a new issue. The aim of A_2 in doing so is to create a derived interest on the part of actor A_1 in E_1, that is, to induce A_1 to favor the same outcome of E_1 that A_2 favors. The strategy shown in part c is that used by the small group in Pasadena and is a variant of the strategy shown in part b. Here A_1 is the superintendent, and A_3 represents citizen-voters. The introduction by A_2 of the link between the curriculum (E_1) and reading proficiency (E_2) is designed to bring A_3's interest into the social choice, since A_3 has control (indirectly, through the school board) of A_1's tenure in office. The strategy shown in part d is that used in the Polish passport example, and is fundamentally different. A_2 brings in A_3, with whom A_2 has some social credit (E_2). A_3 is an actor who has control over something of interest to the authoritative actor, A_1.

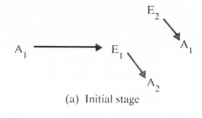

(a) Initial stage

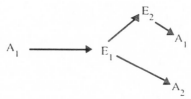

(b) Introducing dependency of E_2 on E_1

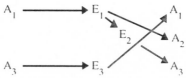

(c) Introducing dependency of E_2 on E_1 by a variant strategy

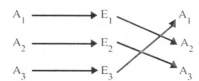

(d) Introducing actors over whom one has some control

Figure 14.1 Strategies for gaining control over a conflict event (E_1).

Characteristics of Noninstitutionalized Social Choice

Several general characteristics of the micro-to-macro transition can be extracted from this chapter's examination of processes in social choice which go beyond or lie outside formal institutional structures.

1. There is ordinarily a calling in of credit (that is, a use of power) held either directly or indirectly from actors who have rights of control or partial rights of control over the social choice. This process is evident in small-group decision

making, in community decision making, and in cases like the Polish passport example.

2. The relevance of actors' potential power is apparent, even when the power is not used, in the support given to particular alternatives, as well as in the introduction of alternatives. This is evident in the sycophancy shown by courtiers to executives and by weak members of small groups to powerful members. The sycophancy of political parties to the median voter is a similar phenomenon, but the parties are attentive only to the power embodied in the vote, not to extraconstitutional power. This process, like that just above, is not based on any of the four criteria for the goodness of an outcome given earlier in this chapter. It derives from self-interests of members rather than the interests of the corporate body.

3. There is normative pressure toward consensus, against supporting outcomes that cannot be justified in terms of the collective good, and against taking a vote on the decision. This is evident in small-group decision making. The source appears to be two of the criteria for the goodness of an outcome: that it have a high action-potential and that it be nondivisive. These pressures, however, appear to be much less strong in larger collectivities and less cohesive collectivities (such as a residential community, as compared to a commune). The decline in pressure toward consensus where individuals are less identified with the group appears to result because each individual acts more fully as agent for his own self as object and less as agent for the corporate actor as object (see Chapter 19 for a discussion of complexities in the self).

4. There is often some institution for eliciting information about implications of the alternative outcomes that is insulated from personal interests of the actors providing that information. The most common such institution is open discussion of the implications of outcomes. When power is highly skewed, however, those with less power have an incentive to engage in sycophancy in unstructured discussion. Use of an institution to counter that incentive may be in the interest of a powerful executive (although not in the interest of powerful members of a group when none have sufficient power to dictate a decision) and may be evident in an executive's introduction of some form of structured dissent. The aim on the part of the executive appears to derive from the second of the criteria for goodness of an outcome, that is, the criterion of veridicality.

5. In the period preceding a decision, there is a focusing of attention on the dependency of other events on the outcome of the social choice. This can also be described as making explicit the indirect implications of outcomes. It is evident in the extended discussion of small-group decision making, in the introduction of new issues into the community decision-making process, and in executive decision making where an institution of structured dissent is operating. This process appears to help the outcome meet the criterion of veridicality.

Focusing attention on the dependency of other events on the event whose outcome is to be decided by social choice appears to be related to the agenda, an area of work that has begun to show great importance in the formal theory of social choice. One source of the importance of an agenda lies in the interdependence of different events about which a given collectivity must make decisions.[13] Because of this interdependence, control of the agenda can constitute the most important element in determining outcomes.

13. When there is a vote exchange, there is a second source of interdependence of events on the agenda: If actors i and j have exchanged promises to vote on two events, and if the event on which i has promised his vote is first on the agenda, he must deliver first on his promise.

« 15 »

From Individual Choice
to Social Choice

Chapter 14 examined collective decisions carried out in the absence of formal institutions for translating individual preferences into a social choice. This chapter will examine some aspects of formal rules by which corporate actors arrive at choices based on their members' expressions of preference. These formal rules are mechanisms for moving from the micro level of individual action (such as voting) to the macro level of social choice. The simplest of such mechanisms are rules about the form in which votes are cast, the way they are counted, and the criterion for deciding which candidate has won.

The problems examined in this chapter are among those dealt with in the extensive body of literature on social choice. I will focus on how collectivities achieve (or fail to achieve) something close to consistency in social choice (the first of four criteria for the goodness of an outcome, given in Chapter 14), when there is disagreement among those members of the collectivity, each of whom has a right to affect the outcome. The problem of achieving consistency can be expressed as an intellectual puzzle, the Condorcet paradox, which has occupied theorists of social choice. An example of the paradox can be stated as follows: If there are more than two candidates running in an election, then, under some distributions of preferences among voters, if the election is carried out as a sequence of pairwise contests and each loser is eliminated, the outcome will depend on the order of the contests. This can be seen in its simplest form for an election with three voters, Tom, John, and Steve, and three candidates, Barbara, Carol, and Denise, with a majority rule. Suppose the preferences of Tom, John, and Steve are these:

	Tom	John	Steve
Rank 1	Barbara	Carol	Denise
Rank 2	Carol	Denise	Barbara
Rank 3	Denise	Barbara	Carol

Then in one sequence of pairwise contests to determine the winner, Barbara beats Carol with Tom's and Steve's votes, and Denise beats Barbara with John's and Steve's votes. But this seems wrong because Carol would beat Denise with Tom's and John's votes. If the sequence had begun with a different pairwise

397

contest, the outcome would have been different. Arrow (1951) proved that it is not possible to have a decision rule by which, if voters express their preference orders (or cast votes in accordance with their preference orders), the Condorcet paradox never arises. Gibbard (1973) and Satterthwaite (1975) extended this result to show that no decision rule is strategy-proof.

The Problem of Independence from Irrelevant Alternatives

But Arrow's axioms, which define what is to be regarded as a consistent (or rational) social choice, include one that has been controversial: independence from irrelevant alternatives. This axiom states that the social choice between two alternatives should not be affected by changes in preferences regarding other alternatives in the set, as long as individuals' preferences regarding the two alternatives do not change.

This axiom makes inadmissible certain decision rules that seem reasonable. For example, it excludes aggregation procedures that allow members of the collectivity to express the relative intensities of their preferences. These procedures are excluded because intensity of preference is always relative to the alternatives under consideration, and if the position of one alternative in a preference order is changed, the intensities of preferences for others will change, differentially for different members.[1] If the axiom of independence from irrelevant alternatives is violated, collective actions may fail to attain the sort of consistency ordinarily required of individual actions described as rational. This means that the way is blocked to conceiving of a corporate actor as a rational actor obeying the same principles of action as does a rational individual, unless either of two conditions is met: The corporate actor follows the will of a single individual (a dictator), or the composition of the corporate actor is restricted so that the interests of all of the members have a certain coherence.[2]

The most frequent way of illustrating independence from irrelevant alternatives is by considering addition or elimination of an alternative. This is not formally equivalent to a change in position of an alternative already in the set,

---

1. One might naively think that, since cardinal utilities express intensity, it would be possible to have a decision rule by which members' utilities are added up for each alternative, and the alternative with the highest score wins. Such a procedure would appear to take intensities into consideration without violating the independence axiom. But the procedure neglects the fact that for decisions among a given set of alternatives, it is not the absolute utility of an alternative that matters for intensity of preference, but its utility as the outcome relative to that of other alternatives in the set. The intensity of a member's preference for one alternative over another may become insignificant if a third alternative becomes sharply different from those two or may increase if the utility of the third no longer differs greatly from that of the other two. Arrow (1951, pp. 32–33) illustrates this with an example using von Neumann–Morgenstern utilities.

2. This coherence, when expressed in terms of preferences, can be described as a single-peaked preference order. The constraint, first introduced by Black (1958), has been examined by many authors. Kramer (1972) shows that when more than one dimension of choice exists, this constraint is strengthened to allow only the trivial case of complete unanimity.

because the set of alternatives changes. Nevertheless, the same anomalies arise; and the illustrations in this chapter involve adding or deleting an irrelevant alternative.

Do the actions of individuals obey the axiom of independence from irrelevant alternatives? If the apparent irrationality or incoherence that is found at the corporate level is also found at the individual level, the fault may lie not with the social-choice procedures but with the axiom itself.

Independence from Irrelevant Alternatives in Individual Decisions

A paper by Tversky (1972) is a useful starting point for examining independence from irrelevant alternatives in individual choice. Tversky presents an impressive array of evidence to show that persons' choices under certainty violate the principle of independence from irrelevant alternatives. He says:

> ... data show that the principle of independence from irrelevant alternatives is violated in a manner that cannot be readily accounted for by grouping choice alternatives. More specifically, it appears that the addition of an alternative to an offered set "hurts" alternatives that are similar to the added alternative more than those that are dissimilar to it. (p. 283)

Even a simple mental experiment can show that theories of probabilistic choice which follow from axioms of rationality violate common sense. Tversky presents an example (originally from Debreu, 1960) in a criticism of Luce's probabilistic theory of choice behavior: "Suppose you are offered a choice among the following three records: a suite by Debussy . . . and two different recordings of the same Beethoven symphony . . . Assume that the two Beethoven recordings are of equal quality and that you are undecided between adding a Debussy or a Beethoven to your record collection" (p. 282). It follows from Luce's theory and the chooser's indifference between the two Beethoven recordings and between either of those and the Debussy recording that the probability of his selecting the Debussy recording from among the three should be about ⅓. But, as Tversky goes on to say, this conclusion "is unacceptable on intuitive grounds because the basic conflict between Debussy and Beethoven is not likely to be affected by the addition of another Beethoven recording" (p. 283).

Tversky then introduces a theory of choice, which he terms elimination by aspects, to account for the observed behavior. The general idea of the theory he expresses as follows:

> Suppose that each alternative consists of a set of aspects or characteristics, and that at every stage of the process, an aspect is selected (from those included in the available alternatives) with probability that is proportional to its weight. The selection of an aspect eliminates all the alternatives that do not include the selected aspect, and the process continues until a single

alternative remains. If a selected aspect is included in all the available alternatives, no alternative is eliminated and a new aspect is selected. Consequently, aspects that are common to all the alternatives under consideration do not affect choice probabilities. (pp. 284–285)

As Tversky shows, something like this rule seems to be used in individual choice. Yet choices made in accordance with this rule violate the axiom of independence from irrelevant alternatives.

Thus obedience to the axiom does not distinguish individual choice and social choice. If individuals choose by sequentially using as criteria aspects of the alternatives, as Tversky argues, and if no one aspect wholly dictates the choice (that is, no aspect is dictatorial), then individuals' choices also violate the axiom. This suggests that even if it *were* possible to find a social-choice procedure which did not violate the axiom of independence from irrelevant alternatives, persons would not regard it as reasonable—just as they would not regard as reasonable the prediction from Luce's theory for the example of choosing between Debussy and Beethoven recordings.

Yet individuals appear to have devised better algorithms for resolving multiple-alternative choices than have collectivities. In the example involving Debussy and Beethoven recordings, the addition of a second similar Beethoven recording does not change the likelihood of the Debussy being chosen or the likelihood of *some* Beethoven being chosen, although any one Beethoven is less likely to be chosen. The following example shows that the existence of multiple alternatives can have more extensive consequences for social choice.

Social Choice among Three Candidates: An Example

In Chicago in 1983 there were three candidates in the Democratic mayoral primary: Jane Byrne, Ritchie Daley, and Harold Washington. Byrne and Daley were whites, and Washington was a black; voting was largely along racial lines. Daley was the last of the three to enter the race; in opinion polls that pitted Byrne and Washington against one another, Byrne came out ahead, reflecting the fact that black voters, although a large minority, were a minority.[3] But in the primary itself, in which the winner was determined by plurality among the three candidates, Washington won. Figure 15.1 is a diagram expressing the macro-level relations and the macro-to-micro and micro-to-macro transitions.

The macro-to-micro transition in this case is simple: The alternatives available in the contest (that is, at the macro level) determine which alternatives in the overall preference order are relevant to the individuals' action (that is, voting). The micro-to-macro transition in this case is different from ones examined in earlier chapters. It does not involve interactions among actors (as in a market) or the creation of a norm or other micro-to-macro processes that occur in social

3. These poll results also reflected Byrne's incumbency. In 1987, when Washington was the incumbent, he defeated Byrne in a two-candidate Democratic primary.

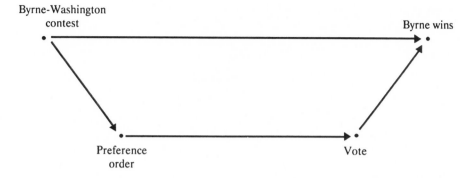

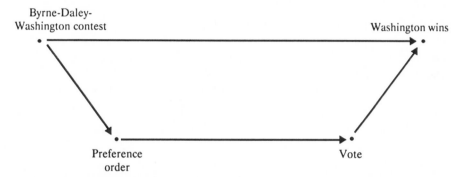

Figure 15.1 Micro-to-macro diagrams for two- and three-way contests in Chicago mayoral primary.

systems to give rise to an emergent macro-level phenomenon. It is, rather, a simple aggregation of votes for each of the candidates to give an outcome for the contest, with the voting procedure and the procedure for deciding the winner (plurality in this case) established by institutional rules.

From the macro-level relations alone, the two outcomes appear paradoxical: The entrance of a third candidate into the contest (who came in third in the primary) reversed the order among the other two candidates, changing the outcome of the election. What may appear paradoxical at the macro level (but will not seem so to any student of elections) can be resolved by descending to the micro level. The observed outcomes would result if the preference order of a large number of voters (but less than a third) had Daley first, Byrne second, and Washington third, and only a small number put Daley first, Washington second, and Byrne third. As long as Daley was not in the contest, most of the larger group of voters would give Byrne their votes. When Daley entered, their votes went to Daley. As long as fewer voters had Daley first, Washington second, and Byrne third as their preference order, Daley's entering the race took away more votes from Byrne than from Washington. (As a student of elections would put it, Daley split the white vote, which gave the election to Washington.)

One can immediately see from this example that a plurality rule does not have the property of independence from irrelevant alternatives. Yet the consequence of this violation for a social choice differs from that of the analogous violation at the individual level. In both cases the addition of a new alternative had the consequence described by Tversky (1972): ". . . the addition of an alternative to an offered set 'hurts' alternatives that are similar to the added alternative more than those that are dissimilar to it" (p. 283). But the result for individual choice seems reasonable: Although the presence of a new alternative reduces the likelihood of the individual's choosing the similar alternative, it does not *increase* the probability of his choosing the dissimilar alternative (the Debussy recording). At most that probability remains constant. The reduction in the probability of choosing the similar alternative benefits the alternative it is similar to, not the dissimilar alternative. But in the example of a social choice, it was the dissimilar alternative, Washington, that benefited.

Political Parties and Tournament Elimination

If the Chicago election had been a general election, rather than a primary, the pair of outcomes observed would have been less likely, because the contest might have been narrowed to the candidates of the two major parties, and there would not have been a three-way race (although three-way races do sometimes occur in general elections in the United States). In general, the two major political parties introduce a stage into the process which reduces the final contest to a two-candidate race. The parties transform what is constitutionally defined as a single-stage decision into a two-stage decision. For individual choice Tversky argues that individuals transform a single-stage choice into a multi-stage choice through an elimination process. Thus it may be that political parties constitute a move toward a structure for social choice that is similar to the structure individuals have developed internally for individual choice.

But the parallel between what parties do and what Tversky's theory of elimination by aspects specifies that individuals do breaks down. Tversky's theory specifies that individuals first select an important aspect or dimension (composer in the Debussy-Beethoven example) and then make a choice regarding that aspect (Debussy or Beethoven), moving successively to less important aspects. The party system does the opposite. The division between the parties ordinarily represents the dominant dimension which divides the voters, and the choice between nominees of the parties is the *last* stage in the process. A second difference, of course, is that the parties only break the selection process into two stages, whereas individuals, according to Tversky's theory, go through as many stages as are necessary to narrow the choice down. This second difference, however, seems less than fundamental, for there are often factions within a party, differing on a dimension less major than party difference, and in some cases sects within factions, differing on a still more minor dimension.

Tournaments as Institutions for Social Choice

The central difference between the structuring of social choice that occurs via political parties and the structuring of individual choice according to Tversky's theory concerns the direction of elimination: In the case of elections as a social choice, elimination occurs along successively more important dimensions within each faction and then within each party; according to Tversky's theory, for individuals, elimination occurs along successively less important dimensions, beginning with the most important. This produces two different structures. The structure for social choice, insofar as it is elaborated into multiple stages, is like tournament elimination, and Tversky's theory gives a structure for individual choice that is the reverse of a tournament elimination.

Suppose, for example, that there are eight alternatives (A, B, C, D, E, F, G, and H) and that adjacent alternatives are most alike. A tournament elimination structure that embodies the process of choice by factions within parties and sects within factions can be diagrammed as shown in Figure 15.2. The process of social choice via political parties moves from left to right: First are four contests between candidates of sects within factions, then two contests between factional

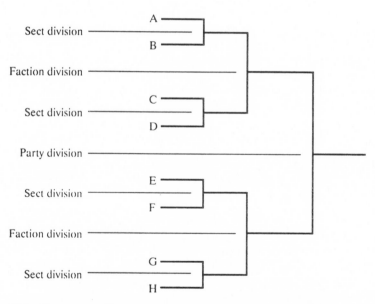

Figure 15.2   Tournamentlike structure of an election in a two-party system with factions within each party and sects within each faction.

candidates within parties, and then the final contest between party nominees. Elimination by aspects moves from right to left: The individual first selects the upper or lower half, then one branch of that half, and finally one of the two remaining alternatives.

There are several points to make about the two procedures. First, tournament elimination is at each stage selection between concrete alternatives, whereas elimination by aspects is selection based on an abstract dimension between classes of alternatives (until only two remain). Second, because of this, tournament elimination is less efficient. Seven contests between pairs of alternatives are necessary to decide the winner of the tournament elimination diagrammed in Figure 15.2, but only three selections are necessary to choose among eight alternatives with elimination by aspects. Third, however, elimination by aspects can lead an individual to regret his choice. For example, suppose, for a choice among three recordings, that two dimensions or aspects are together more important than composer, but either one alone is less important. One Beethoven recording is on a compact disc (which the individual prefers) and is digitally recorded (which he also prefers). If composer is the dominant aspect, and he prefers Debussy, elimination by aspects will mean that he chooses the Debussy. But he might prefer the Beethoven digital compact disc to the Debussy analog record.

My conjecture is that it is not only social choice which proceeds according to tournament elimination or something like it; individual choice does as well when the number of alternatives is not large.[4] If an individual chooses according to aspects, an alternative that the individual prefers might be eliminated even though its total set of aspects taken together outweighs the single dominant aspect responsible for eliminating it. In addition, interactions between different qualities or aspects could make an alternative's attractiveness even less determined by the attractiveness of its aspects considered independently. The central difficulty lies in the fact that it is not until the last stage of elimination by aspects that—according to Tversky's theory—the individual finally compares concrete alternatives. Thus an alternative which would have been the overall winner because of its combination of qualities could, if the individual chooses as that theory says, be eliminated at an early stage.

In contrast, if the individual chooses by a process similar to tournament elimination, he will eliminate first those alternatives that are clearly dominated by another (as in the first round of a tournament). Then he will again compare alternatives which are most alike, eliminating the less preferred; he will continue in this way, always comparing concrete alternatives, until he ends up with a single alternative. It is probably true that as the number of alternatives increases, efficiency becomes more important and may outweigh the cost of errors that the procedure of elimination by aspects can entail. Thus it may be that

4. The conjecture that individuals use different procedures when choosing among different numbers of alternatives is supported by experimental evidence in work by Payne (1976).

individuals use tournament elimination, eliminating concrete alternatives by comparing them with particular other concrete alternatives, unless the number of alternatives is so great as to make the cost of that procedure (in time and effort) outweigh its benefit (of accuracy).

Note, however, that if individuals use *either* of these two choice procedures, they are not using the simple procedure of choosing their most preferred alternative in an overall preference order. As Newell and Simon (1972) argue, and as they show in research on problem solving, individuals confronted with complex tasks use algorithms or heuristics that involve compromises between information-processing limitations and attainment of the most satisfactory outcome. These compromises can lead to outcomes that fail to conform to any simple set of axioms for rational choice. One might say that procedures for social choice similarly constitute a compromise between limitations on the information-aggregation capabilities of the corporate actor and attainment of the most satisfactory outcome. Seen in this way, the search for better procedures for social choice is an attempt to improve on the information-aggregation capabilities of the corporate actor.

Is the two-stage elimination resulting from the party structure a better procedure than the analogous single-stage elimination? Party-structure elimination is like one stage of tournament elimination, and it is clear that introduction of a tournament elimination structure (including factional eliminations within the party, as shown in Figure 15.2) would do away with the anomaly shown in Figure 15.1. The social choice would, like the individual choice, be consistent or reasonable; the addition of a new alternative might hurt alternatives close to it, but it would not help those distant from it, as occurred in the Chicago primary.

Multi-Stage versus Single-Stage Processes for Social Choice

The virtue of both elimination by aspects and tournament elimination lies in the benefits that a multi-stage process brings. A multi-stage conceptualization of individual choice allows theory to reflect the way a new alternative hurts those close to it. Both individuals' behavior and the predictions of the theory result in what is regarded as reasonable or rational actions, despite the fact that the axiom of independence from irrelevant alternatives may be violated by the behavior.

For social choice the introduction of a structure that transforms a single-stage procedure to a multi-stage procedure brings the same benefits. As the example of the primary election in Chicago shows, however, this structural elaboration is not well developed beyond the first stage, the party itself. There is a second defect as well: Party structures have great inertia, with the result that they will continue far beyond the point at which they represent the major dimensions of political cleavage in the system. Furthermore, the major dimensions of political cleavage may fluctuate from election to election, so no structural division with continuity in time, such as parties have, could track them. One can ask whether there might be other means by which the benefits of multi-stage election processes, in which only one alternative were eliminated in each contest, might be realized. In particular, might a procedure be possible in which preferences are elicited in a single stage but aggregation is done in a way that corresponds to a multi-stage tournament elimination?

This direction of effort is also suggested by work on formal theory in social choice, as well as by the results of the examination in Chapter 14 of emergent processes in collective decisions. The results of formal theory that are directly relevant concern the great importance of the agenda in determining outcomes (see Plott and Levine, 1978; Shepsle and Weingast, 1984). In effect, what these results show is that control of the agenda can, under a wide range of distributions of preferences, determine the outcome. The agenda can be seen as analogous to the pairings of a tournament, and the officials who control the pairings can be seen as analogous to the procedure (via the chairman or the rules) that establishes the agenda in social choice. As is well recognized among tournament officials, pairings of competitors can be quite important in determining the outcome of a tournament. For example, A, B, and C are the top-seeded players in a tournament, and if the records of past performances show that A wins over B more than half the time and loses to C more than half the time and that B beats C more than half the time, the officials must favor one of these three in setting up the pairings. If A and B are in one bracket and C is in the other, C will be more likely to win (A beats B, then C beats A); if A and C are in one bracket and B is in the other, B is favored (C beats A, then B beats C); if B and C are bracketed together, A is favored (B beats C, then A beats B).[5]

This background allows a question to be raised concerning whether there is a procedure for eliciting and combining choices which will correspond to the multi-stage tournament elimination created by an agenda in committees or (imperfectly) by political parties in elections. The central element of such a procedure is that the preferences will serve not only to choose between alternatives but also to establish the agenda.

Social Choice via Implicit Multiple Stages: Criteria for Elimination

The aggregation of preferences (votes or rank orderings or some other expression of preferences) is ordinarily carried out as a single-stage process. In some cases, such as runoff elections when no candidate among several has received a majority of votes, there is an explicit two-stage election process, in which all candidates but two are eliminated in the first stage. Practical considerations

---

5. There is a literature in economics on tournaments (see Lazear and Rosen, 1981; Rosen, 1988), in which the assumption is made; Rosen states that ". . . the rules themselves evolve to maximize the social value of the game" (1988, p. 77). Except for a brief treatment by Rosen (1986, p. 710), however, this literature has not examined optimal pairings (pairings designed to be fair to all players), which would make it useful for the agenda problem. An examination of the principles used by officials in athletic tournaments to pair contestants might be helpful in this context.

ordinarily make it infeasible to have more than two stages of voting; in principle, however, it would be possible.

If it is possible in principle to have multi-stage elections based on some initial pairings, with one alternative of each pair eliminated in each contest, then it is also possible in principle to do so with only a single stage of voting but multiple stages in the aggregation of preferences. In an explicit multi-stage election process, each voter can be seen as consulting his preference order and providing information to the election officials based on that preference order. An implicit multi-stage election process would differ from that only in eliciting from the voters at one time all the information that in the explicit process is elicited in stages. This information would be fully contained in each voter's rank ordering of the alternatives. This is not to say that a voter would have no interests in these alternatives beyond that expressed by the rank ordering, for he may have different intensities of preference. But an implicit multi-stage election process may be devised using only information from ordinal preferences.

Clearly, if a sequence of pairings is established, election officials could arrive at the outcome through a multi-stage elimination process, based on a single-stage expression of preferences by voters in the form of rankings. At each of the implicit stages, the officials, rather than the voters, would consult those rank orders, counting a vote for the alternative which is ranked higher. What is critical, of course, is the establishment of the agenda, or the sequence of the pairings. As is made clear by the various examples used earlier in this chapter, as well as the research and theory on agendas, the agenda is an important component of social decision making and, with certain distributions of preferences, can determine the outcome. Therefore, the proper sequence of implicit contests for a social choice when there are multiple alternatives is not one imposed from without, but one generated by the preferences themselves. In short, what seems appropriate for such social choices is to let the preferences of voters determine the agenda.

One principle which appears to be used by individuals in making choices is that of similarity; that is, they first eliminate one of the two most similar alternatives. I will call this decision procedure elimination by similarity. It can be described as follows:

1. Given m alternatives, the first contest is between the two alternatives that are closest, as determined by the distribution of preferences. Distance between alternatives is the sum, over all members, of the number of other alternatives separating them.
2. After the winner of that contest is determined, thus eliminating one alternative, the closest pair among the remaining $m - 1$ alternatives is selected for the second contest.

This process continues until one alternative remains.

For example, for an election with three candidates (A, B, and C) and a hundred voters, Table 15.1 lists the six possible rank orders, with their hypothetical

Table 15.1   Possible rank orders of three candidates (A, B, and C) and their frequencies for a hypothetical election involving 100 voters.

Rank order	Frequency	Type
ABC	20	1
BCA	19	2
CAB	24	3
ACB	15	4
CBA	10	5
BAC	12	6

frequencies. In this case, if the contest between A and B occurs first, C wins; if the contest between A and C occurs first, B wins; if the contest between B and C occurs first, A wins. Thus there is the cyclical majority of the Condorcet paradox. There is no Condorcet winner.[6] But looking at the frequency with which pairs of alternatives are adjacent in the rankings shows that A and B are adjacent in 66 cases, A and C are adjacent in 70, and B and C are adjacent in 64. Thus A and C are most similar, and the contest between A and C is first. C wins this contest, and then B defeats C in the second and final contest.

It is useful to examine this case more fully. By elimination by similarity B is the winner; yet B is in first place for the fewest voters and in last place for the most voters. If the voting rule were a majority rule with a runoff election after a first-round elimination, B would receive only 31 votes in the first round and be eliminated. The victory would go to C in the runoff election. With a plurality rule, as used in the Chicago primary, A would be the winner, with 35 first-place votes versus 34 for C and 31 for B. Another possible decision rule is a Borda count, in which a first-place rank counts 2, a second-place rank counts 1, and a third-place rank counts 0. With this rule A would win with a count of 106; C would have a count of 102, and B a count of 92.

Elimination by similarity has another undesirable property. One of Arrow's axioms is the positive-association axiom: An alternative should not fall in the social preference order if nothing changes except that it moves up in an individual's preference order. Suppose three voters whose ranking of the candidates was ACB (type 4 in Table 15.1) move B up by changing their ranking to ABC (type 1). Then A and C are no longer most similar; A and B are most similar. Thus the first-stage contest is between them, and A wins. Then C defeats A in the second stage. Thus elimination by similarity violates both the axiom of

6. A Condorcet winner is an alternative that is preferred by a majority to each of the other alternatives in pairwise contests. Whenever there is a cyclical majority, there is no Condorcet winner. That a decision rule should always select the Condorcet winner when one exists is therefore a criterion for a desirable decision rule—yet is quite weak, for many decision rules satisfy it.

independence from irrelevant alternatives (as does individual-choice behavior) and the axiom of positive association.

There is another problem with this decision procedure. Elimination by similarity was introduced in part to overcome a particular defect exhibited by some decision rules: The addition of a new alternative can hurt the alternatives to which it is most similar, not merely by benefiting itself but by benefiting the more dissimilar alternatives. Note, however, what happens under the distribution of frequencies given in Table 15.1 when first A and B are the alternatives and then a new alternative, C, is added. Before the addition, A wins with 59 votes. But A and C are most similar, so in the two-stage elimination by similarity B is the final winner. The defect which elimination by similarity was designed to overcome is still present. The introduction of C not only hurts its neighbor, A, but helps the more distant alternative, B.

Thus this multi-stage procedure in which the voters' own choices are allowed to establish the agenda is not a good decision procedure by a variety of criteria. Yet it should not be dismissed without examining why it behaves as it does—for it not only seems to parallel the process individuals use but also embodies the principle evident in the institution of political parties.

The three alternatives form a cyclical pattern, as evidenced by the Condorcet paradox: B defeats C who defeats A who defeats B. With the distribution of frequencies given in Table 15.1, A and C are closest, but after three voters whose ranking of the candidates is ACB move B from third to second place, A and B are closest (see Figure 15.3). The situation is analogous to one in which, with the initial distribution and A and C in one party, A is eliminated in the primary, and then C loses to B in the general election. With the changed distribution, preferences of the voters have shifted, and A and B are now in the same party, and the primary contest between A and B is won by A, who goes on to lose to C in the general election.

This does not seem strange in the context of political parties, for nothing is inappropriate about elimination of one of the two candidates who are most similar. Even the fact that B's elimination is brought about by B's replacing C as

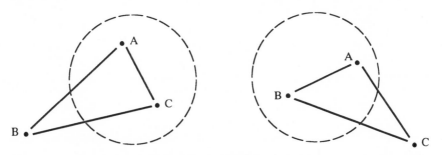

Figure 15.3   Shift in distances between candidates leading to a change of outcome in two-stage collective decision.

the second preference of those whose first preference is A is not unusual: What brings A into the party, requiring an elimination, is the shift of some A supporters away from C and toward B. But this expands the party, causes a primary, and thus disadvantages B. (In the party context in most political systems, although not here, that would result in a different electorate for the primary, with the party shifted in A's direction. This would give even greater cause for B's disadvantage.) When considering such a structure, it does not seem inappropriate that the nonperversity axiom is violated; it certainly would be in the two-stage election with parties as described in the above scenario.

It should be noted that the strange result that B wins given the rankings and frequencies shown in Table 15.1 comes about because the first stage is like the California primary: The voters who most prefer B are eligible to vote in the first-stage contest between A and C. It is their bias toward C that gives C the victory in this primary. If the first-stage contest were limited to those voters for whom one of its contestants is most preferred, then B's second-stage victory would vanish. A would win the primary and the final election.

It is clear that as a decision rule elimination by similarity has undesirable properties. Another procedure analogous to the operation of some two-stage elections with parties is restriction of the distance count for pairs of alternatives to those who rank one of the two alternatives first. The first contest is between the two alternatives most similar among all members who rank one of the two first, and the voting is restricted to those who rank one of these two alternatives first. This would be similar to a system with party primaries in which only party members vote. In the example the contest between A and C is most similar among those who place one of the two first (39 adjacent out of 69 comparisons), and among those members A wins the "primary" by 35 to 34. A goes on to defeat B among the total members (59 to 41). If the distribution is changed as described earlier, by three members changing their ranking from ACB to ABC, then the first contest is between A and B. A wins that, 35 to 31, and is defeated by C at the second stage. For this example the modified elimination-by-similarity procedure is better than the unmodified version. If, however, no attempt is made to mimic the two-stage procedure of party primaries, there are numerous other ways of establishing an agenda.

In considering what such ways might be, it is useful to point out that Condorcet himself proposed a procedure for arriving at an outcome when his paradox seemed to be operating. His procedure involved eliminating the weakest link in the cycle (see Young and Levenglich, 1978; Young, 1987). In the hypothetical election considered above, C beats A by 53 to 47; B beats C by 51 to 49; and A beats B by 59 to 41. Condorcet's procedure eliminates not one of the alternatives, but a pairwise contest, in this case, the contest between B and C. Then A beats B and C beats A; the winner is C. Thus Condorcet's proposal establishes an agenda, just as elimination by similarity does. With Condorcet's proposal, however, the agenda is not arrived at through elimination of alternatives but through elimination of pairwise comparisons. For a selection among three alternatives, elimination of the weakest link in the cycle, the most balanced contest, leaves two contests which cannot exhibit the cycle. With a greater number of alternatives, consistency may require elimination of a greater number of contests.

A procedure similar to that of Condorcet may be used to establish an agenda by eliminating alternatives. I will call this procedure Borda elimination. Assume, as before, that the election is based on obtaining all voters' rank orders of the proposed alternatives. The alternative which has least support over all implicit pairwise contests is eliminated. (Among m alternatives, each alternative enters $m - 1$ pairwise contests, and its total support is determined by the sum of the votes received in these implicit pairwise contests.) After one alternative is eliminated, the same process is carried out with the remaining $m - 1$ alternatives, and repeated until only one alternative remains. That is the winner.[7] Applying this procedure to the hypothetical case of Table 15.1 eliminates B first and gives C as the overall winner. This procedure may be seen as a way of establishing an agenda, that is, a sequence of elimination. Whether this agenda would be the one chosen by rational members of a collectivity for eliminating alternatives is unknown; but it is a reasonable candidate.

I call this procedure Borda elimination because it can be seen as an inversion of a Borda count: The alternative with the lowest score in the Borda count is the same as the alternative with the fewest supporters in the implicit pairwise contests. An alternative's Borda count is the number of supporters it has in implicit pairwise contests. When the Borda count is repeatedly used (recalculating it each time) to eliminate the weakest remaining alternative successively until only one alternative remains, this is Borda elimination.

Borda elimination is a modification of a procedure proposed by Nanson (1883), which is called Nanson's method in the literature. In Nurmi's terminology Borda elimination is Modification 1 of Nanson's method; its properties have been investigated by Fishburn (1977), Nurmi (1987), and Niou (1987). The procedure has some desirable properties, but some undesirable ones as well. A major virtue is that it always gives the Condorcet winner if one exists; but, like all social-choice functions, it has defects that become apparent when no Condorcet winner exists.

A summary of the outcomes of a social choice among three alternatives under different decision rules is given in Table 15.2.

7. A simple extension of Borda elimination can be used for elections in which candidates from a single list are to fill multiple posts. After the first post is filled, via the procedure as described, that candidate is eliminated from the rank orders, and the procedure is repeated to fill the second post. This process continues until all posts are filled. The Hare system is also based on a rank-order voting procedure but employs a different counting procedure. With the Hare system each voter casts a vote for his first-ranked candidate. If no candidate receives a majority, the candidate receiving the fewest votes is dropped, and the votes of his supporters are given to their second-ranked candidates. For elections with multiple candidates the Hare system establishes a quota for election; if a voter's first-ranked candidate has already reached that quota when the voter's vote is tabulated, his vote is cast for his second-ranked candidate.

Table 15.2   Outcomes of a three-alternative social choice under different decision rules.

	Under distribution of frequencies given in Table 15.1	If three voters change their ranking of the alternatives from ACB to ABC
Single-stage decision rules		
Plurality	A	A
Borda count	A	A
Multi-stage decision rules		
Elimination by similarity	B	C
Modified elimination by similarity	A	C
Majority in runoff election	C	C
Elimination of balanced contest		
(Condorcet's procedure)	C	A
Borda elimination	C	C

It is useful to compare tournament elimination with Borda elimination. The principle by which the agenda (that is, the pairings of contestants) is constructed in tournaments is not one of similarity (which has no immediately evident meaning in the case of a tournament), but one of strength. The two strongest contestants are placed in the brackets farthest from one another, and the progressively weaker contestants are placed in increasingly closer brackets. If the number of contestants is not a power of 2, then the stronger contestants get byes. Typical pairings for a tournament with ten players are given in Figure 15.4, where the players are ranked from 1 to 10. With these pairings the four weakest contestants go through a first stage, and the other contestants receive a bye. The second-stage pairings are arranged so that contests between those who are both strongest and similar in strength are deferred as long as possible.

Tournament elimination has some correspondence to Borda elimination. With Borda elimination alternative 10 would be eliminated first, and subsequent eliminations would be dependent on how the rankings changed after each elimination. Generally, however, the lower-ranking alternatives would be eliminated earlier than the higher-ranking ones.

Overall, Borda elimination appears to hold some promise as a procedure for arriving at collective decisions. It is an implicit multi-stage selection procedure that shares the virtues of two explicit multi-stage procedures: party systems and tournaments. It would not be feasible in large collectivities in the absence of modern information processing techniques. According to the criteria introduced at the beginning of Chapter 14, it does well in terms of consistency and reasonably well in terms of veridicality, but its performance in terms of action-potential and nondivisiveness has not been examined.

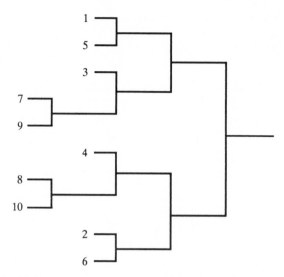

Figure 15.4 Pairings by strength in a hypothetical tournament including ten contestants.

The search for a decision procedure which meets the criterion of consistency has gone through several steps leading in the direction of a good procedure:

1. Tversky's analysis of individual decision making makes it apparent that individuals' decision procedures which are seen as being reasonable do not fulfill the condition of independence from irrelevant alternatives. Thus it appears wise not to search for procedures for social choice which meet this condition, but to search for procedures that give results that can be regarded as reasonable. For example, it is reasonable that a new alternative hurts alternatives that are close to it, but not by giving the victory to an alternative that is more distant.

2. Tversky's theory of elimination by aspects suggests that individuals faced with multiple alternatives proceed in a sequence of stages involving elimination. Mental experiments, however, lead to the conjecture that when the number of alternatives is not too large, individuals eliminate alternatives in a sequence of pairwise contests (a tournamentlike elimination), rather than eliminating classes of alternatives based on dominant aspects, or dimensions.

3. Some procedures for social choice (as in the 1983 Chicago primary) exhibit the phenomenon of a new alternative hurting another close to it but not in a way that seems reasonable, for the new alternative may do so by changing the outcome from victory of the closer alternative to victory of a more distant one.

4. Examination of endogenous institutions for social choice shows that polit-

ical parties and factions serve to transform a single-stage process of choosing among multiple alternatives into a multi-stage process of pairwise choices, a procedure similar to tournament elimination, where the pairwise contests are between alternatives which are closest in preference among those who most prefer them.

5. Work in the formal theory of social choice shows the importance of agendas in determining outcomes. The pairings which occur in the multi-stage selection procedure created by parties and factions within parties implicitly constitute a fixing of the agenda, that is, the sequence of the pairwise contests.

6. Since the multi-stage procedure created by parties and the factions within them are based on nothing more than individuals' preference orderings, it is in principle possible to have a procedure for social choice consisting of a single stage of registering of preferences by voters followed by multi-stage procedures for the aggregation of those preferences. The aggregation would involve some form of elimination in pairwise contests. It would have the virtue, which party structures lack, of corresponding to current comparisons among alternatives by voters rather than to dimensions of party divisions which are not currently important but are maintained by organizational inertia.

7. The use of such a procedure would give to the electorate the power which inheres in the agenda, because in the procedure by which the sequence of pairwise contests is established, the voters' preferences determine not only the outcome of the pairwise contests, but also the sequence of contests.

8. Although the above points are stated in terms of individuals' preference orders, the separation of the process by which information about those preferences is obtained (how the voters express preferences or interests) from the process by which this information is combined to give an outcome (via a multi-stage procedure) means that the points are applicable if more information can be obtained from voters (such as information about intensity of preferences).

9. The procedure of elimination by similarity (analogous to elimination by party primary) has properties that lead to outcomes that are low in veridicality, that is, do not correspond well to members' preferences.

10. Borda elimination (or Modification 1 of Nanson's method), an implicit multi-stage procedure, shows some of the properties of tournament elimination and elimination by party primary. It appears to give outcomes that are high in veridicality and consistency.

The Nature of Rights in Social Choice

In all of the discussion in this chapter, I have assumed that rights held by members of a collectivity making a social choice must be embodied in the form of preference orders or, something even less informative, a vote for the most preferred alternative. Yet the examination of natural decision processes in Chapter 14 indicates that in the absence of formal decision rules, both interest in the outcome (that is, intensity of preferences) and power in the social system play a part in the outcome. This raises two questions: First, *should* interest and power (or interest but not power) play a part in the outcome of collective decisions? Second, if the answer to that question is yes, how can a procedure for collective decision making appropriately take into account differential interests in the outcome and differential power?

Voting transmits to the collectivity a very small amount of information about individuals' interests, and in some contexts where a corporate action must be decided on it is clear that more information could be transmitted. One of those contexts is where there is, as is true for an ongoing corporate actor, a stream of actions to be taken corporately. In such a case decision-making rights might be distributed quite differently, as I will indicate shortly.

If the context is that where a single corporate action is to be chosen from three or more alternatives, there are various means of transmitting more information about interests from the individual level to the corporate level. Collective decision-making procedures which elicit preference orders from members (rather than votes) and use a Borda count, the Borda elimination procedure, or a Hare system (see footnote 7) for aggregating preferences constitute one such means. Another is a system of approval voting, which consists of indicating which alternatives one approves of (see Brams and Fishburn, 1978; 1983).

Intensity and Approval Voting

A comparison of approval voting with election procedures that are based on members' preference orders can be used to illustrate the different kinds of information that members may provide in an election. For a choice among four alternatives, there are six implicit pairwise contests. By ranking the alternatives a member expresses a preference in each of the six pairwise contests. Suppose a member ranks the four alternatives A, B, C, and D from most to least preferred as C, B, A, D. The information provided for the six implicit pairwise contests is as follows:

C preferred to D   B preferred to D   A preferred to D
C preferred to A   B preferred to A
C preferred to B

Approval voting provides some of this same information, as well as additional information concerning the intensity of preferences, which is not shown in a ranking of the alternatives. Three members whose preference order is C, B, A, D may, in approval voting, give the following patterns of approval:[8]

---

8. It is also possible to approve none or approve all. Neither of these votes, however, provides any information that is useful for selecting among the four alternatives.

Member 1: approves C only
Member 2: approves B and C
Member 3: approves A, B, and C

These ballots provide information about different subsets of the implicit pairwise contests, as follows:

Member 1: C preferred to A
           C preferred to B
           C preferred to D
Member 2: C preferred to A   B preferred to A
           C preferred to D   B preferred to D
Member 3: C preferred to D   B preferred to D   A preferred to D

Member 1's approval of C and member 3's approval of A, B, and C both provide information about preferences in three of the six pairwise contests, and member 2's approval of B and C provides information about preferences in four of the six contests. But each ballot provides additional information as well. Member 1's ballot indicates a preference for voting in the contest between C and A, the contest between C and B, and the contest between C and D, rather than in the contest between B and D or the contest between B and A or the contest between A and D. This implies that member 1's preference for C over his next best alternative is stronger than any other preference. Member 2's approval of B and C is a choice to vote in the contests involving C and A, C and D, B and A, and B and D, rather than the ones involving C and B, and A and D. This tells nothing about member 2's preferences between B and C or between A and D, but implies that the preference for the less preferred of C and B over the more preferred of A and D is stronger than any other preference. Similarly, member 3's approval of A, B, and C implies that the preference for the least preferred among them over D is stronger than any preferences among those three alternatives.

If, as stated earlier, all three members have the preference order C, B, A, D (although that information is not provided by approval voting), and assuming that the alternatives have utilities for the members, the information provided by approval voting can be expressed as utility differences: For member 1 the utility difference between C and B is greatest; for member 2 the utility difference between B and A is greatest; and for member 3 the utility difference between A and D is greatest. The scales of the relative utilities of the four alternatives for the three members might look like Figure 15.5.

Thus approval voting, which does not give full information about a voter's preference order, does give some information about the relative strength, or intensity, of preferences.

Pairwise Rights

Approval voting can be interpreted as providing information about relative utility differences, but might more complete information about utility differences, or the intensity of preferences, be provided through voting? Figure 15.5 suggests the possibility that this might be done, and the examination in Chapter 14 of natural decision processes suggests that it should be done, to satisfy the criteria of action-potential and nondivisiveness.

If there are n alternatives for a collective choice, there are $n(n - 1)/2$, or m, implicit contests between pairs of alternatives. Suppose each member of the collectivity is given m votes, one for each implicit contest. He has the right, however, not to cast a vote in each implicit contest but to cast any of the m votes in any of the m implicit contests. If he desires, he can cast all votes in a single contest or can distribute them among contests. The justification for this is that since any contest among n alternatives can be seen as a set of $n(n - 1)/2$ implicit pairwise contests, there is no reason why a member of a collectivity should not have a right associated with each implicit contest. And to allow him a further right to decide which of those contests are most important to him (and thus to which to allocate his votes) increases the information about his interests that he expresses through casting votes.

Suppose each member is conceived of as having the right to vote in each of the pairwise contests and, further, the right to allocate votes across contests depending on the contests' relative importance to him. If it is specified that a member's provision of information about preferences need not take the form of a vote, it is possible to divide the process into two parts: The member provides information about preferences to the officials; the officials use that information to cast votes in the implicit contests, following the member's implicit instructions.

One way this can be done is to ask each member to rate the alternatives, giving the most preferred alternative a rating of 10 and the least preferred a rating of 0. In the kind of information it provides, this method is a combination of rank ordering and approval voting. Based on Figure 15.5, members 1, 2, and 3 might

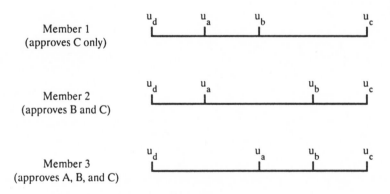

Figure 15.5   Relative utilities consistent with ballots of three members in approval voting.

give ratings as follows:

Member 1: 10 for C, 5 for B, 2.5 for A, 0 for D
Member 2: 10 for C, 7.5 for B, 2.5 for A, 0 for D
Member 3: 10 for C, 7.5 for B, 5 for A, 0 for D

If these ratings are treated as votes in the six implicit contests, the unadjusted net votes are simply the differences in the ratings. These votes may be adjusted, since the ratings give different numbers of implicit votes depending on the variation among a voter's ratings. All the ratings shown above give implicit vote totals of 32.5. The minimum is 30, when the two intermediate alternatives are both rated 0 or 10. The maximum is 40, when one intermediate alternative is rated 10 and the other is rated 0. To give each member the same number of votes in the six implicit contests, each rating can be multiplied by a factor to make the sum of votes equal (for example, 6). This would give member 1 the following votes: 1.85 for C, .93 for B, and .46 for A (from multiplying the ratings by 6/32.5). For a member who rated C as 10, B as 10, A as 0, and D as 0, the votes would be 1.5 for C, 1.5 for B, 0 for A, and 0 for D (from multiplying the ratings by 6/40).

Unfortunately, even if voters knew their ratings would be adjusted to give a fixed number of total votes in pairwise contests, this procedure would still not be incentive-compatible, that is, without any incentive to misstate preferences for strategic purposes. If a voter believes that his vote for any alternative is equally likely to make a difference for that alternative's winning, he will maximize utility by concentrating his votes in the contests that are most important to him.

This incentive to concentrate votes, thereby not revealing true utility differences, arises because the expected marginal utility of a vote does not decline as the number of votes the member casts increases. An artificial decline in marginal utility can be designed, however, to offset exactly the incentive to concentrate votes on the most important contests. This is done by discounting votes according to their concentration. The more concentrated his votes are, the fewer total votes the voter receives. In Figure 15.5 members 1, 2, and 3 have the same degree of concentration, with the largest difference between utilities equal to .5 and the other two equal to .25 each. The discount that would give these voters no incentive to concentrate their votes would be the same for each of them: The counted votes would be the adjusted votes multiplied by .943. If member 1 rated the alternatives 10, 5, 2.5, and 0, as indicated earlier, the counted votes would not be the adjusted votes 1.85, .93, .46, and 0, but 1.74, .88, .43, and 0. This discounting is designed to give a member with the utilities shown for member 1 in Figure 15.5 no incentive to rate the alternatives other than 10 for C, 5 for B, 2.5 for A, and 0 for D.[9] A defect of this procedure, however, is that the discount

9. The general equation for finding the discount to be applied to an adjusted vote in a four-alternative election is

$$d_4 = \left[\frac{100(20/9)}{100 + r_2^2 + r_3^2 + (10 - r_2)^2 + (10 - r_3)^2 + (r_2 - r_3)^2} \right]^{1/2}$$

applied to eliminate the incentive to concentrate votes by giving extreme ratings penalizes those voters whose utilities are in fact extreme. They end up with a smaller number of votes than those voters for whom the alternatives are equally spaced.

Fungible Rights over a Set of Corporate Actions

Another set of rights, similar to the pairwise rights described above, is as follows: If each of a number of corporate actions, say *n,* is to be determined by collective decision, the usual procedure is for members of the collectivity to vote for each in turn. An alternative procedure is to provide *n* votes to each member, to be cast in any way he likes. At one extreme all votes may be cast in one contest, or at the other extreme one vote may be cast in each. Suppose there are *n* bills to be voted on in a legislature. Like the voting procedure with pairwise rights, this procedure would lead a rational voter to concentrate all votes in the contest for which the difference between the utilities of alternatives is greatest. A discount can be applied in this case as well. If there are *n* votes to be distributed among *n* bills and cast for or against, the discount is $(n/\Sigma_j c_j^2)^{1/2}$, where c_j is the number of votes cast on bill *j.* Again there is a defect: The discount to make the voting incentive-compatible gives fewer votes to those voters whose interest is concentrated in one or two bills. Even with this penalty, however, the rational voter maximizes utility by concentrating his votes to reflect his concentrated interests.

An Income of Votes to Be Spent as Desired

Corporate actions to be decided by collective decisions do not ordinarily come in discrete batches as assumed in the preceding suggested procedure. An extension of that procedure to cover the case in which there is an unpredictable sequence of corporate actions extending into the future is what I have described elsewhere as a bank account of fungible votes (Coleman, 1986a, p. 186). It would operate as follows: Each member of the collectivity would be given a number of votes in an

---

where the voter ranks his most-preferred and least-preferred alternatives as 10 and 0, respectively, and then ranks the two intermediate alternatives r_2 and r_3 where $0 \leq r_3 \leq r_2 \leq 10$. For a three-alternative contest the discount is

$$d_3 = \left[\frac{100(3/2)}{100 + r_2^2 + (10 - r_2)^2} \right]^{1/2}$$

These discounts are found by writing the expected utility of a member's ratings as a function of the utilities of the alternatives and the ratings, translated into discounted adjusted votes (assuming that each pairwise contest is equally likely to be decisive for the outcome and that the member's vote in each pairwise contest is equally likely to be decisive for that contest). The equation is solved for that discount which will make the relative differences in ratings proportional to the utility differences among alternatives.

account in a vote bank. As corporate actions came up for collective decision, each member could draw on his account by casting as many votes as desired, up to the total number in his account. To maintain a fixed quantity of votes in the system, the votes cast would be recycled by returning to the accounts of each of the n members $1/n$ of the total votes cast for each collective decision. The justification for this procedure is that it retains the general constitutional provision that each member has equal rights of control over the corporate action and provides members with an additional right: the right to express the amount of their interest in a given corporate action by allocating votes according to that interest.

« 16 »

The Corporate Actor
as a System of Action

A natural person encompasses two selves, object self and acting self, or principal and agent, in one physical corpus. A minimal corporate actor is created when principal and agent are two different persons. With this same minimal structure, the principal may be a corporate actor, or the agent may be a corporate actor, or both may be corporate actors (as when a corporation owns another corporation). The most extensively developed corporate actor is one with multiple principals, constituting the object self, and multiple agents, constituting the acting self. This is the way a publicly owned corporation is conceived of in modern society. The principals are the multiple owners, the shareholders of the corporation; the agents are all those employed by the corporation, from its chief executive officer to its production workers. (In Chapter 21 questions will be raised about this conception of the publicly held corporation, but for present purposes it will aid analysis.) In a trade union the two halves are the members, who constitute the dispersed principals, and the officials and staff, the agents through whom the union takes action. In a nation-state the citizens constitute the principals (the "sovereigns" in whom rights are seen to originate), and the governing officials and employees of the state constitute the agents.

If such a full-fledged corporate actor is to be regarded as acting purposively, it must deal with two fundamental problems: the problem of collecting the resources and interests of the multiple principals to create a coherent set, and the problem of deploying the resources via the configuration of agents in a way that realizes the interests. These two problems exist for many forms of corporate actor. They are sufficiently distinct that there are often separate constitutions for the two halves of the organization. In the United States, for example, a business corporation is formed under a charter issued by one of the fifty states; this charter constitutes the constitution for the principals (the object self of the corporation) but says nothing about the rights and responsibilities of the agents (the acting self). The constitution for the agents is internal to the corporation and concerns the structure of relations among them.[1]

---

1. The internal constitution dealing with rights and responsibilities of agents is extensively constrained by both statutory and common law. In some countries (such as Germany, discussed later in this chapter), the internal constitution for agents is largely determined by statutory law.

In this chapter I will examine the functioning of the acting self of a complex corporate actor. For this purpose the problem of collecting resources and interests of the dispersed principals will be regarded as having been solved. There is a single principal with the problem of taking action, where the action is complex, involving interdependent actions among many agents.

Although this chapter applies to many kinds of formal organization, it focuses on the modern corporation, because it appears to be in active evolution and exhibits a range of variations and innovations that can show fundamental aspects of organizational functioning.

Weberian Bureaucracy in Theory and Practice

The evolution of the classic hierarchical formal organization raises serious questions about the dominant conceptual model of bureaucratic authority on which formal systems of authority have been based. This conceptual model, first crystallized by Max Weber as an ideal type, has long provided both a practical model for the construction of formal organizations and a theoretical model for social scientists studying the development of formal organizations. The conception is of an authority structure composed of positions; the activities for each position are directed by the position above it in the hierarchical structure. The fundamental flaw in this theory and practice of organization (for the theory describes the practice, and the practice is limited by the conceptions expressed in the theory) lies in the fact that persons have interests as well as resources. They can be led to give up control over certain of their resources (that is, to alienate their labor) under certain circumstances, but those circumstances are not always present. Also, they never give up such control completely, nor is it possible to establish an exchange of resources which will ensure that they do so. Their interests will always be present and can never be alienated from them. Their interests will ordinarily be opposed to full employment of their resources by the corporate actor, because that full employment would prevent those resources from being used elsewhere. Consequently, in every organization composed solely of this kind of exchange, there is a limitation to output, a manifestation of the fact that the agents' interests are not fully directed toward the goals to which their resources (their labor) are being applied by the authority structure.

Max Weber saw, as clearly as did Karl Marx, the alienating character of the form of organization that he described and provided the conceptual base for:

> It is as if . . . we were deliberately to become men who need "order" and nothing but order, who become nervous and cowardly if for one moment the order wavers, and helpless if they are torn away from their total incorporation in it. That the world should know no men but these: it is in such an evolution that we are already caught up, and the great question is therefore not how we can promote and hasten it, but what we can oppose to this machinery in order to keep a portion of mankind free from this parcelling-out of the soul, from this supreme mastery of the bureaucratic way of life. (quoted by Mayer, 1944, p. 97)

But Weber had no conception of "rational" organization which is not composed in this way. For him the fundamental exchange is one by which the resources of men, alienated from their control, are employed toward corporate ends determined by a purposive actor at the top of the authority system. The fundamental flaw in his theory is that only this central authority is treated as a purposive actor. The fact that the persons who are employed to fill the positions in the organization are purposive actors as well is overlooked. That oversight has never been wholly rectified.

Michels (1949 [1915]) documented certain consequences of this oversight and summarized them as his iron law of oligarchy: that entities which are established to carry out the will of a corporate actor come to have interests of their own. Michels neglected to note, however, that some of the same processes that lead to oligarchical control by the leaders over the members of a collectivity also lead the employees of a corporate actor to implement their interests. He saw the principle he enunciated as a deviation from perfect organization that occurs at the top of the structure, rather than seeing it as a fundamental property of social organization that operates throughout an organization, and implies a basic fault in the bureaucratic model on which organizational practice is based.

Other theorists of organization, in particular Barnard (1938) and Simon (1947), have pointed out that the inducements offered by a corporate actor for a person's services must be high enough that the person is motivated to contribute to the corporate actor, and the contributions of the person must be sufficient to cover the cost of the inducement offered by the corporate actor. The fundamental conceptions are expressed as follows by Simon, Smithburg, and Thompson (1951, pp. 381–382):

1. An organization is a system of interrelated social behaviors of a number of persons whom we call the participants in the organization.
2. Each participant and each group of participants receives from the organization inducements in return for which he makes to the organization contributions.
3. Each participant will continue his participation in an organization only so long as the inducements offered him are as great or greater (measured in terms of his values and in terms of the alternatives open to him) than the contributions he is asked to make.
4. The contributions provided by the various groups of participants are the source from which the organization manufactures the inducements offered to participants.
5. Hence, an organization is "solvent"—and will continue in existence—only so long as the contributions are sufficient to provide inducements in large enough measure to draw forth these contributions.

Here the conception that the individual gives up control over his resources in return for certain inducements has remained the same. The conception of a different sort of exchange is still missing.

Other authors (Merton, 1940; March and Simon, 1958, Chapters 3 and 4) have examined motivational problems that arise and persist in organizations because the conception of the person in the theory of rational organization is that of an actor without interests—and because there is no well-developed theory of rational organization in which the interests of persons play a part. Empirical research has shown how those interests play a part in persons' behavior when they are acting as agents for a corporate actor (see especially Blau, 1963, 1964; Crozier, 1964). This research, together with everyday observation, indicates the importance of halting the process, in theory of organizations and in organizational practice, of continually repairing a structure based on a fundamental conceptual error. The appropriate conception, as I have described it above, is beginning to be realized; what is necessary is to recognize that it represents a dismantling and reconstruction of the theory of rational organization as well as of actual organizations that are constructed with that theory as the guiding principle.

Why has the Weberian flaw persisted so long and generated such a productive—although flawed—economic machine? Part of the answer is that the practice of organizations has never totally followed Weber's theory and has come in recent years to deviate widely from it. The deviations have occurred principally in upper levels of organization and are of two kinds. The first is composed of the class of activities termed incentive payments, ranging from production incentives at the plant level to bonus systems and stock options at the upper managerial level. Yet even if a person is receiving some kind of incentive payment, he remains in a position in a hierarchical authority structure; thus this deviation does not fully conform to the conception stated above, nor does it succeed in engaging all of the agent's interests. It cannot do so, so long as he remains in control of only a portion of his resources. For if the agent is to employ his resources most effectively, he must be in control of them.

This leads to the second kind of deviation from the Weberian model: the explicit vesting of control over corporate resources in a person's hands. Despite the absence of such a principle as part of the rational theory of organization, corporate actors are forced, by their very nature, to do this for nearly all intermediate positions in the authority structure—that is, for all levels of management. The corporate actor, by placing a manager in charge of a department, vests in him control over some of its resources. Although it has removed from him control over some of his own actions, it has at the same time placed in his hands rights of control over a larger set of actions—those of his subordinates—and has necessarily left him with a large measure of control over his own actions because he must direct those below him. Thus he has gained rather than lost control. The larger realm of control he enjoys must necessarily engage his interest, since it is a resource available to him. If the corporate actor can design the returns to the manager from his actions so that they are contingent on his fruitful use of the corporate resources he controls, it will ensure that his interests will guide the employment of those resources in directions compatible with corporate goals.

Recently, as will be discussed elsewhere in this chapter, there has come to be a widespread change in organizational practice away from the Weberian model toward the conception stated above, in a variety of situations. It is, however, true that the old model, of the corporate actor as a machine with human agents as parts, is still widely manifested at lower levels of organizations and in some bureaucracies (notably public agencies and firms in industries with old technologies). Some insight into why this is the case can be gained by considering another reason why the Weberian flaw has persisted for so long.

I indicated earlier that persons can be led to give up control over their own labor under certain circumstances. When industrial development began and since then, almost up to the present time, those circumstances were present. Quite simply, persons held few material resources, and the material inducements they were offered to give up control over their labor constituted a great improvement in their material welfare. This is no longer generally true. Material welfare has reached such a high level in many societies that without working at all persons are supported by the state—at a higher level than they once attained through hard labor. Thus the conditions under which persons will give up control over their labor and submit to the will of another are disappearing in developed societies.

This change has created difficulties for managers of organizations, who find it more difficult to motivate employees. This change also imposes a constraint on a society organized according to the political philosophy of liberalism, a constraint that removes from such a society the element to which MacPherson (1964) points as Marx's central objection: the alienation of man's labor from him. The change imposes on those who organize corporate actors a more difficult task of organizing interests and may well make certain activities unprofitable. The resulting society, however, promises to be one in which labor is done largely under the individual's own direction.

A concomitant change that has occurred is the increase in the personal resources that enable persons to productively employ capital resources at their own command. Education and the growth of technical and intellectual skills have made productive a form of organization that vests its resources in largely autonomous agents. The creation of such an organization is difficult in some cases, because the exercise of authority over another's activities is not easily given up, even when that exercise is not successful. But, slowly or rapidly, the Weberian form of rational organization is being replaced by a form which acts largely as an investor, facilitator, and guide to the successful employment of the resources it invests.

The Formal Organization as a Specification of Transactions

A formal organization, in the form of a hierarchical authority structure, is often seen as an alternative to a market as a way of organizing economic activities. Williamson (1975) in particular has examined the conditions under which market organization of such activities is optimal and those under which hierarchical organization, as is found in corporations, is optimal. I will focus on a contrast I see as fundamental to all the benefits and costs inherent in formal organization, relative to a market organization consisting of independent agents.

A perfectly competitive market is a system of action in which each actor is a potential partner for a transaction with each other actor. The social structure is one in which relations among actors are limited only by the interests of each actor and the resources controlled by each actor. A formal organization is, in contrast, a system of action in which relations among actors are highly constrained by the social structure. The organization consists of positions occupied by persons. Each position stands in a particular relation to other positions. Certain relations are prescribed by rules, and many are proscribed. The occupant of one position has certain obligations toward occupants of specific other positions, and certain rights concerning what he can expect from occupants of specific other positions. Relations as an agent (that is, "on company business") with most of the other positions in the organization are discouraged or forbidden, and a relatively small number of relations are permitted without being required. Requests and other communications must "go through channels."

The contrast between the model of formal organization and that of a market organization could not be a sharper one. Also, as the next section will show, the relations which are prescribed for each position in a formal organization have a peculiar character, providing another contrast with market organization.

Modes of Maintaining Viability in Formal Organizations

Consider the following situation. An entrepreneur who possesses capital establishes a manufacturing firm. He is to be chief executive officer and to manage the plant. He determines that the organization also requires a bookkeeper, a secretary, three supervisors, one secretary-clerk to be shared by the supervisors, and six machine operators under each supervisor. Altogether there will be twenty-five positions within the organization. The entrepreneur advertises for and hires persons to fill all of the positions other than his own. Each person in a position has a set of obligations that are associated with that position. Some of these are obligations to persons in specific other positions, such as obligations of the secretary-clerk to the three supervisors. Some are obligations to the firm as a corporate actor, such as the obligation to put in a full day's work at the tasks specified for that position. Each person in a position also has a set of expectations that are associated with that position. Some of these concern persons in specific other positions, such as the expectation of one machine operator that the parts coming to him from another operator will meet quality specifications and be provided in proper quantity. Some expectations concern the firm itself, such as the expectation that the wage and working conditions specified at the time of employment will be met. In other words, each position has a certain set of goals or tasks, provides a certain set of resources with which to accomplish them, and requires the occupant to observe certain rules. The structure of the organization makes the products of one position's activity the resources for those in other positions.

What has occurred to bring about a scenario like this one? Of course, a disjoint complex authority structure has been established by the entrepreneur, in which each employee has exchanged the right of control over certain actions in return for wages and other benefits and has also given to the employer the right to transfer the right of control (see Chapter 4). But beyond this, a structure of positions has been created that exists independently of the occupants of those positions. Even the position of general manager can be filled by another; the owner might hire someone else to occupy that position or might sell the firm to another owner. What exists is a structure composed of positions in relation, not persons in relation. The positions are not permanently associated with particular persons; persons are only temporary occupants of the positions.

The invention of this form of social structure was a critical development, for it had the effect of freeing persons. This social structure exists independently of the persons occupying positions within it, like a city whose buildings exist independently of the particular persons who occupy them. The ecological structure of the dwellings is fixed, and individuals may move in and out. The difference between a social structure of positions in relation and a social structure of relations among persons is equivalent to the difference between a city with fixed dwellings successively occupied by different residents and a nomadic clan, whose tents have no fixed location or patterns of relations independent of their owners but are merely possessions that move with them.

In an organization that consists of positions in a structure of relations, the persons who occupy the positions are incidental to the structure. They take on the obligations and expectations, the goals and resources, associated with their positions in the way they put on work clothes for their jobs.[2] But the obligations and expectations, the goals and resources, exist apart from the individual occupants of positions. As described in Chapter 4, the necessity for these to remain associated with the position, the resources remaining the property of the corporate actor, is created by the impermanence of the employment relation. Otherwise, the resources used to establish the corporate actor are quickly dissipated, as the first employees leave and take them along.

There is one way in which a structure of positions in relation differs fundamentally from a structure composed of persons in relation: the condition that must be met for viability of the structure. Consider a market in which goods are ex-

---

2. A widely used management-training game, called the in-basket game, illustrates this point. The trainee is told that it is Monday and he is replacing the plant manager, whose last day was the preceding Friday. The trainee is given a set of letters and memoranda, which are the contents of his predecessor's in-basket. The task is to decide how (and whether) to act on each of the items, most of which are directed to the position of manager, but some of which are directed to the previous occupant personally, and some of which involve both person and position.

changed. Both parties to any transaction must benefit if the transaction is to take place. The relation must be mutually beneficial, or, as I will say, the relation must show *reciprocal viability*. The exchanges are self-contained pairwise relations, and any imbalances in a relation must be corrected in that relation itself, through the use of deference as a residual credit balance where necessary.

In modern authority structures composed of positions in relation, reciprocal viability of each relation is not necessary. For example, the secretary-clerk has certain obligations to each supervisor, but a supervisor's obligations to the secretary-clerk need not balance those, nor is the imbalance adjusted by a residual credit balance of deference. Instead the imbalance is compensated for by the corporate actor, for each position in relation has certain obligations and expectations to the corporate actor itself. In effect, the modern corporate actor has come to constitute a third party in relations between its positions, eliminating the necessity of reciprocal viability between them. What is necessary instead is what I will call *independent viability*.

In a market structure both parties in each relation must realize a gain from their interaction. In a modern corporate structure a third party has been introduced to balance debits and credits. In a structure of n persons in relation, such as a barter system, there are $n(n - 1)/2$ potential relations, for each of which the criterion of reciprocal viability must be met if a transaction is to take place. In a structure in which there are n occupants of positions and a "corporate entity" serving as a third party in each relation between positions, there need be only n viable relations. For each of the n persons employed by a firm, the relation between employee and firm must be profitable to the firm and to the employee.

In describing the role of money in an economic market, Edgeworth (1881) pointed out that in a pure barter system a double coincidence of wants is necessary. It is not enough that one party wants something offered by another; the first party has to offer in return not merely something of equal value, but something wanted by the party who possesses what he wants. Thus reciprocal viability is necessary for each transaction that occurs. This is changed, however, when money (or, alternatively, a clearinghouse of credits and debits) is introduced into the system. The criterion of viability for transactions takes a less restrictive form than the double coincidence of wants necessary for a barter system. Independent viability, of each individual's account with the bank, replaces reciprocal viability in each transaction—just as independent viability replaces reciprocal viability in a formal organization.

The difference between elimination of the restriction of reciprocal viability in an economic market and its elimination in social organization will be discussed shortly. First, however, it is important to see just what the criterion of independent viability implies.

The difference between reciprocal viability and independent viability becomes more pronounced the larger the social structure. A complete network of relations among 4 persons comprises 6 relations; reciprocal viability requires mutual benefit for all of these, or 12 positive accounts. In a formal organization having 4 positions, independent viability requires only 4 mutually beneficial relations (one between the organization and each of the 4 persons occupying the positions), or 8 positive accounts. In a barter system in which all the relations among 25 persons are active, there must be 300 mutually beneficial relations ($25 \times 24/2$), with 2 positive account balances for each relation, or 600 positive account balances. In a formal organization this is reduced to 25 relations, with 2 positive balances for each, or 50 positive accounts.

The criterion of independent viability is exactly what Barnard (1938) specified as necessary for the viability of a firm: a balance of inducements and contributions. The inducements to each employee must be of greater value to him than what he must give up to continue as an employee, and the employee's contributions must be of greater value to the firm than what the firm must give to him as inducements.

The criterion may, however, be weaker than one saying that n relations must have independent viability. Since the same actor, the corporate actor, is on one side of each relation, it can make up its losses from some of the n relations by gains from others. It need have only a single balance sheet showing a profit, rather than one for each employee. Only 26 positive balances are necessary, one for each of the employees and one for the global account of the corporate actor. I will call this weaker criterion *global viability*. What it implies is that each of the employees receives inducements of greater value to him than the time and effort he gives up—as in the case of independent viability—and the corporate actor receives contributions which taken together are of greater value to it than what it must give up in wages and benefits, thus maintaining its viability.

The Danger in Global Viability

Global viability provides much greater flexibility for a corporate actor, for if the corporate actor consists of n positions filled by n individuals, only n relations must meet the criterion of independent viability, and since the corporate actor is a participant in each, it can balance off losses in one relation against gains in another to bring about global viability. Yet there is a danger for the corporate actor, for if especially profitable relations (that is, especially valuable contributors) fail to provide excess value, the whole system becomes nonviable. If the excess value produced by some employees is due to their characteristics as individuals and if there is a market for the services provided by those individuals who provide excess value, then they are likely to receive more beneficial offers from other employers and leave, which will make the corporate actor nonviable.

If the only compensation received by individuals is money and all of their contributions can be measured in monetary terms, then payment of each individual according to his marginal contribution will avert this danger for the corporate actor by reintroducing independent viability. This is the solution arrived at in economic theory (see Hicks, 1957 [1932]). In such a case the corporate actor is assumed to be capable of adjusting the compensation to each individual employee so that it is equal to that employee's marginal contribution to the corporate actor. The payment to each individual of a wage equal to his marginal contribution gives him a market wage, ensuring that he will not receive a better offer elsewhere, unless another employer can get more value from his services.

But the assumptions underlying this solution are seldom met in practice. The difficulty for the corporate actor lies in three areas: First, not all compensation in disjoint authority structures is in the form of money wages (for some corporate actors none is). Second, because of the interdependence of activities and because many employees' activities consist primarily of overseeing a production process, it is often difficult to separate out the marginal contribution of each actor. And third, because of collective bargaining agreements (and other social constraints), the firm is powerless to pay each employee an amount equal to his marginal contribution.

Alternatives to Global Viability

A number of devices have evolved within organizations to maintain viability in another way. Three of these can be termed divisional viability, forward policing, and backward policing. I will examine each of these briefly.

DIVISIONAL VIABILITY   A management practice for large business firms, developed first by General Motors and Du Pont in the 1930s, is the creation of divisions, each of which has to justify its products for "make or buy" decisions of the firm (see Chandler, 1962). The principal innovation here was the partial introduction of the market into the firm, by using the market outside the firm as a benchmark of the competitive viability of divisions within the firm. An extension of this practice has been the introduction of internal transfer prices; each division within the firm "sells" its services or products to other divisions of the firm. Such a practice, if a way can be found to establish a market price for each product or service, allows the firm to measure the contribution of each division to the firm and compare it to the costs of that division. This makes it possible to replace global viability with divisional viability, that is, global viability for each division separately. (In some cases transfer pricing constitutes only an accounting device used to measure each division's performance; in other cases divisions' budgets are determined in part by their shadow profits or losses. Obviously only the latter constitutes a movement from global viability to divisional viability.)

Within a division the practice of transfer pricing can allow the determination of departmental contributions, and thus departmental viability. In principle, transfer pricing can be carried all the way to the level of the individual. For some jobs in some firms, this occurs through the payment of a portion of wages as bonuses, with the size of the bonus dependent on an evaluation of the individual's contribution. This can be seen as approximating the solution described earlier of making compensation equal to the employee's marginal contribution.[3]

One serious weakness of divisional viability is the difficulty of establishing appropriate transfer prices for goods and services for which there is no external market price to serve as a benchmark (see Eccles and White, 1986, for a discussion of this problem). A second weakness appears to be a lack of incentive, except to central management, for establishing and maintaining an internal set of accounts. The incentive to central management to establish such a system is the need for measuring the performance of various units of the firm. But this incentive is not shared by those units unless they are sanctioned based on the level of their performance, through receiving a share of the profit or loss they bring the firm as a whole.

FORWARD POLICING   The classic means of attempting to ensure viability has been through the exercise of authority over the actions of employees, from the highest authority in the firm downward. In such a system viability is determined through a feedback loop that goes from the final product back to the starting point of the process, the highest authority. On the basis of this feedback, modifications are introduced to increase viability, with authority continuing to be exercised downward. If, for example, defects are found in the product by customers, there is feedback to the firm as a unit, which is then transmitted down to the locus where the defect arose. This means may be called forward policing because it is policing of actions. In a production system actions at time t produce outputs at time $t + 1$ throughout the sequence of actions constituting the production process. Thus the policing of actions constitutes policing of a forward process.

BACKWARD POLICING   Around 1980, when the general manager of the Pontiac Division of General Motors wanted to learn why quality control at Honda was so successful, he studied that company's production process. He learned that Honda employed a form of backward policing, which operated according to a simple principle: Each unit involved in the process of production and shipping of the automobiles had the right to reject inputs to it and was held strictly accountable for its outputs by the unit next in line, which had the right to reject them as its inputs. If parts coming into a production line did not meet specifications, the unit which operated that line, or any member of that unit, could reject those parts, even if this meant shutting down the line. The unit supplying the parts would be held accountable for the downtime. Each unit had an inspector, not at the end of its stage of the process, but at the beginning.

3. Frank (1985, pp. 80–98), however, argues persuasively that incentive pay schemes are greatly influenced by the fact that workers evaluate their wages relative to others in the same location. This would prevent incentive payments from approximating the wage that corresponds to marginal productivity.

Another property of the system, which appeared to be a consequence of this reallocation of rights, was that there was a much lower ratio of supervisors (forward policing) to operators. A third property of the system, again an apparent consequence of the reallocation of rights, was that operators themselves who were held accountable for the quality of the product, acted as their own inspectors, for both the inputs to their stage in the process and the outputs.

What Honda used in quality control was policing of the product at each stage of the process, rather than of the actions which produced the product. The policing thus operated backward—from the final product backward to the first stages of the production process. A long feedback loop from the final customer at the end of the process characterizes forward policing; with backward policing that loop is broken into a large number of very short feedback loops by giving each unit the same rights of rejection as are held by the final customer. Nothing more—or less—is involved in the shift from forward to backward policing than a reallocation of rights and accountability in the organization.

Further Consequences of Global Viability

If the transactions between each employee and corporate actor have independent viability, as occurs when wages and benefits equal marginal productivity, then each of these internal transactions is self-policing. If the employee's contributions decline, the wage declines; if the contributions increase, the wage increases. If the wage is below an employee's marginal contribution and there are competing corporate actors which do pay the marginal wage, the employee can move to such a competitor.

If an organization is to maintain global viability, two devices are necessary: There must be detailed constitutional specification of the obligations of the occupant of each position, and there must be extensive policing of actions to ensure that the correct ones are taken. If only the first of these devices were employed, the second would become necessary to ensure that the specified actions would in fact be performed. And if only the second device were employed, constitutional prescriptions of correct actions would necessarily become part of the policing.

Thus, if a means can be found to move from global viability back to independent viability, the corporate actor is relieved of two tasks: first, the detailed constitutional specification of what actions are required in each position; and second, the policing of actions to ensure that this set of obligations is in fact fulfilled. At Honda backward policing came close to bringing about a move from global to independent viability for a production process that consisted of a sequence of stages. This was largely due to a reallocation of rights, which in turn modified the interest of workers. The reallocation of rights gave production workers rights of control over the inputs to their productive activity. These rights, held by workers at one stage, gave those at the preceding stage interests in maintaining high quality in the outputs of their activity.

Backward policing appears to be a satisfactory means of moving from global viability to independent viability in some forms of productive activity, such as that found in the automobile industry. It is not apparent how widely applicable backward policing is, but what does appear widely applicable is the reallocation of rights that brings about backward policing. In the employment transaction the employee-to-be gives up rights of control over his actions in a particular realm covered by the employment contract. The reallocation of rights which gives rise to backward policing redistributes a portion of those rights, giving them not to an intermediate level of management, as occurs in the delegation of authority, but back to their original owner, the employee. In return, the corporation assumes the right to make compensation contingent on productivity. Another portion of the rights, the right to reject the product of the employee's activity, is given to the employee who must use this product, that is, the worker at the next stage in the production process. Policing of quality is inherent in those rights given to workers at the next stage in the production process.

There is, however, another kind of evolution in organizational form, which goes all the way back to the reciprocal viability of two-party exchange.

The Reintroduction of Reciprocal Viability

Much social organization of the past was based on two-party transactions between a principal and an agent—particularly in the use of land. The owner of large amounts of land, which he could not himself use productively, would carry out a transaction with a set of peasants, tenants, or sharecroppers. They would have use of the land in return for a certain portion of its product. If sovereignty was held by a king, he made land grants to nobles in return for a royalty or tax. The fact that the nobles made further transactions concerning use of the land was not relevant to this transaction, because the king delegated these rights to the nobles. The rights held by the ultimate tenants varied under different systems of land tenure. In England during the feudal period, some held land as a feudom (or "in fee") and had rights of alienation of the land (subject to the lord's consent). These were freemen, although they gave services and taxes to the lord in return for protection. But other lands were held directly by the lord and tilled by villeins, who could not leave the land, and were therefore not free. In pre-feudal England such direct bondage was absent, or at least less widespread, and lords held a smaller set of rights (see Denman, 1958, pp. 46ff).

In modern society this simple form of two-party exchange is still used where other forms of organization have failed to function well. In a hotel, for example, the restaurant manager, the barbershop manager, and the manager of the valet service may not be employees of the hotel but independent operators. The hotel has contracted with them to use its physical facilities in return for a share of the restaurant's or barbershop's or valet service's income or for a fixed fee. Another example is found in modern supermarkets and drugstores. Some of the items sold in these places are being sold by rack-jobbers, so named because items, ordinarily convenience items, are displayed in racks in the store. The supermarket or drugstore provides the space for the display, the rack-jobber arranges it, keeps the rack filled, takes inventory, and collects from the store for those items sold. For some smaller groceries food-processing firms perform a similar function for the principal food items.

Perhaps the most common form of organization of this sort is the franchise, where a corporation, operating in a market, franchises an agent to sell its goods or to engage in a joint enterprise as an independent contractor. The traditional franchise was in the form of a dealership or a distributorship covering a particular territory, with the interaction between the two parties involving the normal elements of a two-party exchange, supplemented by a contractual agreement giving the franchisee exclusive rights to operate in a given geographical area. The new form of franchise, however, best exemplified by fast-food chains such as McDonald's, involves a transaction in which the franchiser performs a number of activities within the franchisee's organization: training of personnel, establishing product specifications, and designing and supervising construction of the premises. Nevertheless, the franchiser-franchisee relationship is not analogous to backward policing, which introduces independent viability; it is one for which the criterion is reciprocal viability. There is an extensive set of transactions between franchiser and franchisee, and these must be profitable for both parties engaging in them. There is no third party to balance the transactions, as there is in a production process with either forward or backward policing.

Each of the cases described above represents a return to reciprocal viability in the relationship between principal and agent. If the restaurant in a hotel cannot make a profit, it goes out of business and is replaced by another organization. Or if the restaurant fails to provide appropriate services for the hotel's guests, or projects an image the hotel regards as inappropriate, or provides too little income, then the hotel terminates the relation. If a given supermarket does not constitute a profitable location for a rack-jobber's wares, the relation is terminated. Thus these relations are subject to the classic criterion of reciprocal viability. The benefits of weakening the requirement of reciprocal viability to that of independent viability are missing, but the drawbacks of global viability are also avoided.

Global Viability in a Corporation and in a State

It has sometimes been noted that the centrally held authority in a modern corporation and the centrally held authority in a modern socialist state are familiar. A corporation which maintains central authority and forward policing of employees' actions (and the long feedback loops this entails) is operating according to the criterion of global viability. Such a firm must determine what allocation of wages and benefits will maintain its global viability while providing sufficient inducements to keep its employees. In addition, it must engage in the constitutional specification of duties and continuous policing of actions to ensure that these duties are carried out. Extensive central planning is necessary to coordinate activities, to allocate resources, and to determine production quotas.

A nation-state maintaining central control over prices and wages and exercising central authority over production and distribution is also operating according to global viability. Actors within the state, whether corporate actors producing a product or persons employed in some task for the state, need not maintain independent viability. In a firm which functions according to global viability, unproductive workers may continue to be employed as long as there are others sufficiently viable to maintain the firm's global viability; similarly, unproductive enterprises can continue unimpeded in a state which operates according to global viability. Independent viability of each enterprise, which arises automatically in a market system, is missing in the socialist state as a criterion for assessing enterprises. Thus the system is without a self-policing structure. An extensive policing mechanism becomes necessary.

Structurally, then, a capitalist corporation which operates according to global viability and a socialist state are similar. A principal difference is that the state has monopoly control over population and land and can therefore survive even though it would not be viable without this monopoly power. A corporation is disciplined by the market, even if it does not extend that discipline internally, and cannot survive if it fails to maintain its global viability.

CENTRALIZED WELFARE AND GLOBAL VIABILITY   Certain phenomena in the modern state lead to the gradual replacement of independent viability by global viability. Perhaps the best example is the state's replacing the family as the major social welfare institution of society. This phenomenon is discussed in more detail in Chapter 22; here I will simply note that it also means that the criterion of independent economic viability of the family is being replaced by the criterion of global viability, and the interest of the family as a corporate actor, in maintaining independent viability through support and care for its unproductive members, is being eliminated. The end result is the same as in the large corporation or the socialist state: an extensive constitutional specification of what perquisites are allowable (families on welfare are allowed to have a television set and telephone but a new video recorder or home computer would be challenged, for example) as well as extensive policing. The remedy lies, as it does for the large corporation or the socialist state, in reintroducing into the system the criterion of independent viability, applied not to each individual but to small subunits in the society which have the possibility of continuous viability (for example, extended families may have continuous viability, whereas individual persons and nuclear families do not, because of age, infirmity, or incapacity).

Explicit and Implicit Constitutions

A corporate actor with a structure composed of positions rather than persons must specify two sets of rights and obligations in relation to its agents, that is, its employees. One set can be conceived of as a constitution specifying rights and obligations of the occupant of each position, both in relation to occupants of other positions and in relation to the corporation itself. These I will call positional rights and obligations. The second set concerns the relations between the corporation as a corporate actor and the employee as a natural person. This second set may be conceived of as contractual rights and obligations between two contracting parties. These are governed by civil law, including both common law and statutory law (in the United States examples of the latter are the National Labor Relations Act, the Occupational Safety and Health Act, and the Freedom of Information Act).

As the conception of the corporation changes, however, there is a blurring of the distinction between these two kinds of constitutions. It is not possible to fully separate the two sets of rights and obligations because the conception of the corporation which allows that separation no longer holds for the corporation as it has evolved. This evolution can be seen by referring to the legal concept of agency discussed in Chapter 7. The principle that can be abstracted from common law concerning the agency relation is that the agent's skills and services are employed *in the principal's interest.*

The evolution of the corporation has made this classic concept of agency no longer applicable to the employment relation, or only after considerable revision. According to the concept, the actions of the agent could be insulated from his personal interests by appropriate compensation, possibly even incentive compensation according to performance. The functioning of the corporation as a formal organization could be described, like that of a machine, in terms of the functions of each of the parts for others (the obligations and expectations associated with positions). But the evolution of the corporation has so fully intertwined and combined interests of the corporation and interests of the persons who work in it that such a separation becomes increasingly difficult. The modern corporation can increasingly be seen not as a machine with parts but as a system of action comparable to an unconstrained market, a system whose organizational structure lies not in defining expectations and obligations and exercising authority, but in structuring reward systems and providing resources.

Such a system must still address a set of constitutional questions that are comparable to those facing states as authority systems. Corporations continue to constitute authority systems, even though the authority is increasingly diffuse and decreasingly hierarchical. Thus issues have arisen concerning the way in which those persons in the system who are subject to corporate authority—including all those who are employees—come to have their interests taken into account in the exercise of that authority. These issues are comparable to those for the construction of constitutions in conjoint authority systems, as discussed in Chapter 13. I will not repeat here that discussion concerning institutional structures through which interests of subordinates come to be taken into account, although the issues are relevant for corporations. I will instead examine three constitutional innovations with origins in Japan, Germany, and the United States, respectively.

Quality Circles and QWL Programs

In a number of American firms a program patterned after Japanese quality circles has been initiated. Sometimes termed a quality of work life, or QWL, program, it involves an extensive restructuring of the organization of a manufacturing plant, in which supervisors' activities are largely replaced by the collective decisions of work teams of from seven to fifteen persons engaged in interdependent activities (for example, a section of an assembly line or a group of stamping machines). Each team meets regularly, ordinarily once a week during work time. After first electing a chairman and deciding how it will conduct its business, the team proceeds to do so. Its business ranges from modifying the work structure to resolving interpersonal problems among members of the team.[4]

A peculiar pattern characterizes QWL programs which are initiated when plants first open. There is a period, lasting several months, during which a small group composed of people from management (ordinarily including the future plant manager), people from the production line (including union leaders in unionized plants), and a QWL advisor meets on a full-time basis, working out the organization of the new plant. A major product of this group, which may subsequently be framed and hung on the wall, is a jointly agreed upon statement expressing the operating philosophy of the plant. What is surprising is that the operating philosophies of different plants are quite similar and appear to an outside observer to consist mostly of platitudes. It seems reasonable to question the function of this intensive preparation period since the output is no different from that which could have been directly borrowed from another plant.

The answer, I believe, is that this period is one of arriving at a constitution, a set of rights and obligations supported both by the core of the production-line workers and the core of management. (Ordinarily the rest of the managerial and production work force is hired and trained by this group or a group derived from it. A major question posed to prospective employees concerns their agreement with the plant's operating philosophy and form of organization.) The nature of the constitution, that is, the structure of rights and obligations, is largely the result of suggestions from the QWL advisor, who serves as a channel of information from other QWL programs. But the intense collective effort involved in arriving at the constitution is a process by which members of the core group of employees come to commit themselves to the constitution. Such commitment is necessary to ensure commitment from the other employees, who will subsequently be indoctrinated by the core group as they are hired. That commitment, in turn, is necessary in order to ensure that the allocation of rights provided by the constitution will be enforced by all who work in the plant. The period of meetings by the core group and the elaborate procedures for induction of new employees help bring about legitimacy of the authority system under which all will work.

---

4. A somewhat different work-restructuring movement arose in Europe in the 1970s in Philips, Volvo, and other firms. It grew out of demands for industrial democracy, not, as in Japan, out of concern about improving quality.

Why were such procedures not used (and possibly not useful) in the past? The answer lies in the changed character of the authority system. In the classic hierarchical form of authority which formerly characterized most industrial production, legitimacy of authority was intrinsic to the labor contract. The employee gave rights of control over his actions to the employer and received a wage as compensation. Authority was either exercised directly or delegated by the employer to an intermediate agent who exercised it. When collective bargaining arose, the employment transaction took a different form, and the terms of the transaction changed. Some rights were reallocated to the collective body of workers, a new corporate actor created through formation of a union. But the principal change was that a smaller set of rights of control were transferred to employer by employee.

In plants operating according to a QWL program authority is diffused, with a large portion of it being held and exercised collectively by the teams. This implies that not only must employees accept the collective authority of their peers, but they must exercise authority collectively. The allocation of rights in such an organization includes an allocation to each team as a corporate actor; and the members of the team must accept that allocation and exercise those rights.

Thus an allocation of rights that in the traditional labor market was accomplished through a single employment contract is becoming much more complex. The acceptance of this new allocation of rights presupposes an understanding of the more complex structure; and because the functioning of the system is dependent on the acceptance and exercising of the allocated rights by all workers, a period of indoctrination is valuable to increase commitment to the constitution.

Codetermination in German Corporations

In Germany in 1976 a comprehensive codetermination law *(Mitbestimmung)* was enacted, giving new rights to workers. This law (which had been preceded by similar laws for specific industries enacted after World War II by the British during the occupation and by an even earlier tradition in Germany of workers' councils) made extensive changes at two levels. At the level of the board of directors, it fixed the size—at twenty members for large firms—and specified that half should be representatives of stockholders and half representatives of employees. The law also specified the details of the procedure by which employees' representatives are elected. It specified the role that the board of directors plays in the corporation, including the kind of information to be made available to board members, the minimum frequency of meetings, and the kind of management decisions that must have board approval.

At the level of the workplace, the law required creation of workers' councils and specified both procedures for the election of representatives and the councils' powers, such as those concerning workers' grievances. The powers of these councils include some which previously belonged to management and were exercised through supervision. The councils and the newly constituted boards of directors greatly increased workers' power in organizations.

Germany's codetermination law (which has counterparts in Scandinavia) is a manifestation of a general movement in Western societies (particularly in Western Europe) toward industrial democracy. The law and the movement behind it reflect a modified conception of the corporation, which parallels somewhat the direction of the autonomous evolutionary developments in corporations described earlier.

Ownership Rights to Innovations

In capitalist corporations the standard employment agreement for persons engaged in activities which might result in patents includes the assignment of patent rights to the corporation. The agreement also places restrictions on the employee's right to work or consult for competing firms for a period of time after termination of employment. The employment agreement for comparable employees of state-owned enterprises is similar, containing a provision that patent rights will be assigned to the government. In effect, such an agreement vests ownership rights to innovations developed by an employee in the corporation or the government.

In contrast, by the terms of faculty appointments at most universities in the United States, rights to innovations ordinarily reside with the person, the faculty member. The source of this difference is probably the earlier origin of the university—prior to the conception of the modern corporation and prior to the conception of the employment relation that is intrinsic to that conception (see Coleman, 1973). Ownership rights to ideas and innovations that originate in universities are vested in the person or persons who develop them, not in the university, although a contract with a government, corporation, or other source of research funds may specify otherwise. This has led to proliferation of what may be termed professorial spin-offs: One or more faculty members who have developed new ideas as part of their research form a corporation to bring the ideas to commercial realization. This has occurred not only in the physical sciences (it is especially evident in electronics), but also in the biological sciences (firms in genetic engineering have been formed by groups of faculty members, sometimes in a joint venture with existing corporations) and even in the social sciences (notably firms producing data bases in law and in economics, and statistical software).

In some corporations the principle that ownership rights to ideas and innovations lie with the corporation has begun to erode. One corporation in which this change came early is 3M. Within 3M there is an implicit acceptance of the principle that ownership rights to ideas and innovations are shared by the corporation and the originating person or group. Schon (1970) describes the structure:

> They got Scotch tape out and it seemed to work and they sold a lot of it. Then along came . . . research with magnetic tape. They said, "We know how to make tape. We'll make magnetic tape." . . . They had an invention

along with this: the invention was that the man who developed the idea would go off and take a piece of the business and become in effect a semi-autonomous firm based around the product which he had developed. The company then kept P & L—profit and loss—control over that division, but in no other way attempted to manage that man.

And pretty soon what you had was a constellation of forty semi-autonomous firms surrounding a bank and a development facility. And if you asked what business [3M] was in you could not say as long as you remained on the substantive product level. They are a company that makes money out of exploiting and commercializing entities that come from development. And the entities that come from development are organically related to one another and bear what Wittgenstein would call family resemblances to one another which reflects that organic process. But there's no Aristotelian basis for saying what the firm is, that is to say there is no set of characteristics which all and only products of the firm possess. (pp. 9–10)

It is the personal computer industry in which the problems of ownership rights to ideas and the resulting variations in structure are greatest. In this industry ideas are easily transportable, for several reasons. First, the production processes necessary to implement an idea require little capital and few persons, so a person or group may resign from a firm and without great difficulty start a new firm. Second, there are many small firms in the industry, so an extensive flow of persons (carrying with them ideas) among firms can occur. In this industry spinoffs of the sort that Schon described in the case of 3M have been one result of the high transportability of ideas. Another has been that firms often give partial ownership of the firm to an employee who creates an especially valuable intellectual product.

Another possibility is to give organizational autonomy, that is, to allocate corporate resources with interference from above, to a group engaged in product innovation. A successful example of this occurred when IBM established a protected unit in Boca Raton, Florida, for the development of a personal computer; the group had nearly autonomous control over design decisions for the new product. This resulted in a computer that departed dramatically from IBM's product philosophy in having so-called open architecture, a departure that was largely responsible for its success.

Another evolutionary change is evident in high-technology and biological industries, especially in genetic engineering firms. A kind of joint activity is created: University faculty members, working on their own time, make use of a company's laboratories and other facilities under a contractual arrangement by which ownership of resulting ideas is regarded as being shared by the person and the corporation. The increased incidence of high-technology industrial parks and industrial research parks in the vicinity of large universities is in part evidence of professorial spin-offs and in part evidence of the symbiotic relation between faculty members and corporations under a variety of property-rights arrangements.

Such new organizational structures seem especially evident in certain industries, such as those I have mentioned, but almost nonexistent in others, such as the automobile industry and other heavy industries. This absence may have less to do with the nature of the product than with the traditions of the corporations in these industries, which were born in a period before the concept of shared ownership rights between corporation and employee became widespread.

Like the reallocation of rights to bring about backward policing in place of forward policing, this reallocation of ownership rights to innovations appears to have extensive consequences for the corporation as a system of action. Empirical observations suggest that a major effect of the change has been to increase the rate of innovation. University laboratories, where ownership rights to ideas ordinarily reside with the originating person, appear in the United States to be a much richer spawning ground for new processes and products than corporate or government laboratories. Industries in which there is extensive theft of ideas from firms by those who originated the ideas (by resigning and forming a new firm or a new unit with special rights in a competing firm) show very high rates of innovation. The microcomputer hardware and software industries are perhaps the best examples. The rate of innovation in the computer industry since the invention of minicomputers and microcomputers (both of which had their origins when innovators broke away from larger firms) has been increasing explosively.

Another effect of the sharing of ownership rights to innovations between the corporation and the originating person or group appears less salutary to organizational functioning. This is the potential divisiveness that such an allocation of rights can give rise to. If ideas become effectively the property of their originator, they are less likely to be openly shared and to be worked on jointly. Disputes about ownership of ideas may even arise within a unit of an organization. The potential for divisiveness can, however, be reduced or eliminated by vesting ownership rights not in an individual, but in a group which works in a given area.

In effect, the shift of ownership rights to the innovating actor or group can be seen as a partial rejoining of the "split atom of private property," which Berle and Means (1933, p. 8) described as the major consequence of the modern joint-stock corporation. This shift reunites ownership and control, the two halves of private property that were split apart, but does so in a different way than has been envisaged by theorists of the corporation such as Berle and Means. The reunion has come about through vesting of partial ownership rights (the rights to benefit from the action) in the corporation's agents, rather than from returning control to those who hold ownership rights or to a broader community (as envisaged by Berle and Means).

Societal Origins of Changes in Corporate Constitutions

It is useful to examine the three innovations in corporate constitutions in relation to the societies in which they originated. There is an important similarity and an important difference between the Japanese quality circles (or their American derivatives, the QWL programs) and German codetermination. Both the quality circles and codetermination constitute changes in the implicit constitution of the corporation, and both give additional rights to production workers. But they do so in different ways. Codetermination does not challenge the conception of the corporation as having two classes of employees: a class of managers and a class of workers. It establishes, in fact, an organizational structure which emphasizes that division and the distinct interests on each side. It does not alter the structure of authority through which work is carried out, but formally introduces the interests of the workers into that authority structure by giving them a voice in controlling its activities. It is more compatible with forward policing than with backward policing. The Japanese quality circles deemphasize the division between management and labor, are based on a conception of common interests throughout the corporation, and utilize consensual decision making for production decisions. Quality circles are more compatible with backward policing than with forward policing and with authority exercised collectively through group norms than with authority exercised hierarchically.

These two ways of redistributing rights within the corporation appear to reflect the differing ways in which the corporation as an organizational form emerged from feudalism in Japan and Europe. The Japanese corporation is more closely derived from the feudal estate; there was no intervening influence of Enlightenment philosophy (with its emphasis on individualism) or the revolutions that destroyed the vestiges of feudalism in eighteenth- and nineteenth-century Europe. In Japan, paternalism and the responsibility of the feudal lord for all in his demesne have been carried over in the modern corporation. For example, in Japan the corporation is responsible for a number of the welfare activities that are the responsibility of the state in Europe.

America lacks a history of feudalism but had an immigrant population who were descendants of European feudalism and Enlightenment. In America the corporation has a conceptual basis similar to that in Europe, but with more muted class divisions. The American corporation seems potentially hospitable to either of these reallocations of rights, although it is probably not accidental that neither had its origins in America.

The third constitutional change, involving ownership rights to innovations, differs from the first two in its vesting of rights in the individual rather than in a collectivity (subgroups within a conjoint collectivity in the case of Japanese quality circles and interest-based classes in the case of German codetermination). This vesting of rights in individuals rather than in groups or classes appears as closely related to American history and social structure as do the other two variations to Japanese and German history and social structure, respectively.

Structures That Link Interest and Control

The three constitutional innovations examined in previous sections may be regarded as modifications to the classical Weberian conception of bureaucratic organization as rational authority. If the corporation is viewed from a different perspective, however, as a system of action in which there is a distribution of control among actors and a distribution of actors' interests among events or resources, there are other examples of what goes on within such organizations that aid understanding of their functioning.

A concrete example in which ownership rights to an innovation, or rights of control over development of the innovation, were not vested in the innovator contrasts with some of the cases described earlier. An automobile manufacturer has an advanced product engineering division, which is to initiate and develop innovations to be incorporated as part of new product designs by the divisions responsible for manufacturing and marketing the automobiles. Around 1970 this division developed a cambering principle that was applicable to a range of vehicles, including scooters, motorcycles, and small three-wheeled vehicles. Because the head of the division was enamored with the idea, the division implemented the principle in a number of test vehicles, spending a great deal of attention, interest, and time on it. The division head attempted in vain to "sell" the idea of developing and marketing such vehicles, both to the corporation and to the automobile divisions. The decision not to proceed may have been a correct one for the corporation and the divisions. But the failure to either proceed or vest in the innovators the right to develop the idea outside the corporation resulted in the product engineering division's being partially diverted from other developments that would have been of interest to the automobile divisions. More generally, the existence of this structure, in which new design ideas were to originate within a unit that was not organizationally within a division that could carry any innovation through development, manufacturing, and marketing meant that design innovations seldom moved beyond the boundaries of that unit.

This example shows that a failure to have some continuity of control from innovative idea to final product not only can inhibit the development and commerial exploitation of innovations, but also can divert the interest and attention of units responsible for innovations (the research and development divisions of corporations) away from ideas that might be useful and toward "hobbies" that merely occupy their attention.

There is another phenomenon observed in corporations which lack continuity of control from innovative idea to final product. It is called the NIH syndrome, where NIH stands for "Not Invented Here." The behavior that is referred to by this epithet is a lack of motivation, interest, and effort concerning ideas that originated outside a group, either elsewhere in the firm or in another firm. The group's investigation into an idea that originated elsewhere seems often to result in only a catalogue of reasons why the idea will not be useful.

The NIH syndrome is the opposite of what generally occurs when an innovator is given control of the development of his innovation. With that control he has a strong interest in seeing the idea successfully carried through to implementation. If an idea is clearly another's, an actor appears to have an interest in seeing the idea fail. This interest appears to arise because the success or failure of others' ideas provides a benchmark for evaluating one's own performance: By demonstrating the defects in another's idea, one justifies not having had the idea oneself; by allowing the idea's potential to be realized, one would be relatively worse off, because that would raise the standard for evaluation of one's own work.

Interfaces between Components and between Agents

A general problem of the organization of action in corporate bodies concerns decision making at the interface between subunits. A particular case of this general problem exists when there is some project or purposive activity that involves more than one subunit, whether those subunits are individuals, departments, or divisions. The problematic interface is that between any two agents employed to act in the interests of the corporate actor.

In a manufacturing firm different divisions may be established to design and manufacture different components. Thus there can be many interfaces requiring technical design decisions. For example, in an automobile manufacturing corporation the steering assembly may be designed and manufactured by one division, and the front suspension designed and manufactured by another. The interface between steering assembly and front suspension requires design decisions that might be made one way by the engineer designing the steering assembly and another way by the engineer designing the front suspension. The first might wish to see the front suspension optimized, given the steering assembly design as a constraint, and the second might wish to see the reverse. How should the design decisions be made?

The question as I have posed it is very specific, intended to give concreteness to the problem. It can be put into more general form, relevant to any purposive activity of a corporate actor which is partitioned among its agents: What principles should govern the partitioning of a task among agents (departments or individuals), and what principles should govern the control of the process by agents among whom the task has been partitioned?

The preceding section implied that for an innovation, the person or group responsible for an innovative idea should play some part in the implementation of that idea. A principle similar to this holds for a project leading to some product. One agent has greatest interest in the project—that agent who will be held accountable for the product's success or failure. That agent should have final authority over all stages of the project. Components of the product should be structured in the same way. Thus an interface between steering assembly and front suspension creates an interface between the two engineers designing the components. One of these engineers should be within the unit which will be finally accountable for the automobile as a whole, and thus finally accountable for the design of the components. It is this engineer who has greatest interest in the success of the project as a whole and thus has an interest in designing the components so that optimization is attained for the vehicle as a whole, rather than designing them so as to achieve either of the constrained optimizations.

This is the engineer who should have rights of control over technical decisions at the interface.

But in what way should these decisions be made? The principle to be applied here might be called backward design and is similar to that involved in backward policing. The principle is the simple one of rational action: The actions are taken in a forward direction to reach the goal. But the criteria which shape those actions are dictated in a backward fashion, from the goal to the starting point. Just as backward policing involves short feedback loops from end result to action, backward design involves short feedback loops from final product to design decision. Backward design can be expected to achieve a result closer to total product optimization, since the process begins with product functioning and works backward.

There are, of course, other principles which affect the structuring of the system of action. If all agents have an interest in the corporate goal, then the allocation of authority over decisions at interfaces is less important. Although different agents may perceive the problem differently, their interests will not be different, but alike. As a result, decisions at interfaces will depend less on how rights of control are allocated. Yet the differential perceptions, induced by each agent's position in the process, still dictate the same basic structure, with authority exercised in a backward direction by that agent finally accountable for success of the project.

The problems at interfaces between agents of a corporate actor arise from the structure of a formal organization based on roles or positions. Such a structure erects barriers to transactions between many pairs of actors. As a consequence, there is a much greater necessity to shape those transactions that are allowable so that agents can come to have control over those events that are of greatest interest to them (that is, those outcomes for which they will be held accountable).

Agents' Internalizing of the Corporation's Interests

The problem of allocating control over design or production decisions in such a way that the decisions are optimal for the corporate actor as a whole rather than for a component of it is simplified greatly if the corporate actor is a largely conjoint authority system (in which all have many of the same interests) and the corporate actor's product is simply a realization of those interests. That, of course, is not the character of a corporate actor which creates a product and sells it in the market, for the only interest that agents of such a corporate actor have in common is maintaining its viability, on which the employment of each depends. In addition, each agent has diverse interests (in personal advancement, in departmental or divisional success, and in other benefits to subunits of the corporate actor) that may conflict with other agents' interests—and are certainly not interests held in common with them.

In such circumstances it is to the corporate actor's interest to attempt to bring about identification of each agent with the corporation, so that the agent will take the corporation's interests as his own. At the extreme the agent would become what I called in Chapter 7 an affine agent, an extension of the corporate actor, with interests indistinguishable from those of the corporate actor. Are there actions on the part of the corporate actor or on the part of the agent that might lead in this direction?

There appear to be a number of actions, some initiated by corporate actor and some initiated by the agent, that tend to bring about this identification, for example:

Singing of company songs by agents
Wearing of a uniform by the agent to identify himself as part of the company
Holding and attending company social events—outings, picnics, and so forth
Establishing company policies for job security and even lifetime employment
    to lead the agent to see the company's future as his own.

These actions and others indicate that corporate actors do attempt to induce in agents identification with corporate interests and that agents appear, under some circumstances, to find satisfaction in taking the corporate interests as their own.

General Principles for Optimizing the Corporate Actor's Internal Structure

The first point to be recognized is that, despite the value of agents' identification with corporate interests, those interests cannot be realized without giving different interests to different positions. Vigorous pursuit of positional interests by occupants of positions within a corporation can lead to internal conflicts of interest and to suboptimization of outcomes for the corporation as a whole. But less vigorous pursuit of positional interests would give outcomes even further from the corporate optimum. Mandeville's *Fable of the Bees* (1772 [1714]) is relevant here: It is the attention of each agent to his own interests that generates the energy necessary to realize corporate interests.[5]

The corporate actor, if it is structured appropriately, will have established for each position a set of interests such that pursuit of those interests will lead to satisfaction of corporate interests. This has been stated by Charnes and Stedry (1966) as follows:

Perhaps an ultimate goal is an organization whose control system is so designed that attainment of goals set for employees at all levels contributes to organizational goals. This is not to say that all employees in an organization need be committed to organizational goals—e.g., it is not necessary for the lathe operator to be committed to increasing the company's market share. Rather it is necessary to design for that lathe operator a set of goals

5. In Mandeville's fable the bees, by each pursuing its own goals, brought about a productive hive; when all were required to work for a common interest, the hive was overcome by sloth.

and rewards of such a kind that his pursuit of what he considers his own best interests, whatever the form of rational or irrational decision rules he follows, will contribute as much as possible to the attainment of organizational goals. (p. 163)

This is far from being a Weberian conception of rational organization, in which the interests associated with particular positions do not enter into the structural design. (Weber's organizational design is based on the assumption that officials' actions are either based on orders from above or naturally directed to the organization's goal.) The ideal described by Charnes and Stedry does not, however, address the question of how rights to control actions (including rights to make decisions at interfaces) are to be allocated for optimal corporate performance. In fact, the more fully the interests of the position are fitted to that position, as Charnes and Stedry recommend, the more serious the problem of potentially conflicting interests.

The examples introduced throughout this chapter lead to several intermediate-level principles. First, the fact that backward policing of a sequence of production activities appears to give organizational performance superior to that resulting from forward policing suggests the benefits of short feedback loops. A deeper analysis of the experience between short and long feedback loops indicates two important consequences for the organization: Short feedback loops give more rapid responses to disturbances and minimize the number of positions through which the feedback passes, thus minimizing distortion and minimizing transaction costs.

Second, the success of many corporate spin-offs (as well as the failure of the cambering principle to be implemented or the division head to abandon it) suggests that allowing control of an activity to remain with those who have a strong interest in its success, rather than passing that control from division to division in a design or production sequence, will result in better performance. The prevalence of the NIH syndrome reinforces this conclusion.

Third, the example concerning design decisions at an interface suggests that the agent with the strongest interest in the success of a corporate activity is the one who, if given authority over design and production decisions affecting that activity, will be most likely to optimize the outcome as a whole.

These three principles together suggest a higher-level principle, which may be introduced by reference to the theory of federalism mentioned in Chapter 13. A major question addressed by that theory concerns finding the governmental unit that would optimally be the authoritative entity for a particular activity (for example, sewage disposal, water service, port activities, or policing). The answer in its simplest form is that the governmental unit that leads to efficiency is one that covers exactly the actors directly affected by the activity in question. For a water system serving a city and some of its suburbs, this unit would not be the central city government or the wider county government, but a special-purpose governmental unit whose reach encompasses exactly those areas covered by the water system. Underlying this answer is the principle of internalizing the external effects of the given activity, thus making it possible to arrive at efficient outcomes without the necessity for transactions involving actors outside the decision-making unit. Under certain simplifying assumptions (including the assumption that there are no costs to adding special-purpose governmental units), it can be shown (Breton, 1974) that this solution leads to efficient outcomes.

If similar reasoning is applied to the structure of corporate actors, it leads to the following guidelines for structuring of authority over actions:

1. Taking the technical interdependence of activities as given, discover for each position what other agents are directly affected by the actions of the occupant of that position.
2. Give those agents rights of control over what interests that occupant, such as wages and promotions.

With such structuring of the corporate actor (backward policing is an example of its application to a linear production sequence), the hierarchical authority structure would be largely replaced by a complex exchange system among occupants of positions. In such an exchange system authority would be allocated in a way almost opposite to the way it is in hierarchical structures: The actors with rights of control over the incentives for an occupant of a position would be the actors directly affected by the actions of the occupant of that position. The role of upper management would largely be to design the structure of technical dependence among positions, to allocate rights and resources of the corporate actor among positions (thus structuring the incentives for persons occupying various positions), and to adjudicate conflicts of interest arising from corporate activities.

This principle of optimal rights allocation leads to a structure for which none of the modes of viability discussed earlier is appropriate. The reallocation of rights results in a structure in which the relation between corporate actor and employee (principal and agent) is largely replaced by supplier-customer relations between various positions in the organization. Each occupant of a position must achieve what might be called positional viability, that is, viability with respect to transactions with other positions in the corporate body. Overall viability of the corporate actor occurs when each position has high positional viability.

The Changing Conception of the Corporation

Max Weber's conception of bureaucracy, the legal concepts of principal and agent, the economic work in principal-agent theory, and some organization theory in sociology have one element in common. The corporation is seen as an extension of a single purpose; an owner or set of owners (or principals) brings together factors of production or officeholders (or agents) to implement this purpose. Employees fill the positions, become the agents, and constitute one of the factors of production. The authority system is seen as disjoint; the employees have no interest in the purpose of the owners, but they agree to act in the owners' interests in exchange for compensation. Employees, in this conception, acquire certain rights as employees, primarily ones occasioned by the specific kind of commodity, labor, which they bring to the marketplace.

For a productive corporation operating within a socialist state, the conception is somewhat different. The principal or owner is the state, and the employees are agents of the state. As "part owner" of the state, an employee is also one of the principals of the corporation. Thus, as theorists of state socialism say, the individual is not alienated from his labor because he, as worker, is employed by himself, as member of the society and thus part owner of the state corporation (see MacPherson, 1964).[6] The central fact, however, in either the socialist or capitalist economic system is that employees' (agents') interests and owners' (principals') interests are disjoint, even if the same person is both employee and one of many owners.

A society as an authority system is conceived differently: as a largely conjoint authority structure, in which citizens share some common interests as members of the society but also have interests that are not held in common. The theory of governance of such an authority structure was spelled out in some detail in Chapter 13. It is based on the conception that citizens are sovereign and, through a social contract, have given over to themselves corporately a portion of their sovereign rights, to be used in their common interests. This theory of governance includes specification not only of an institutional structure by which the society can take action corporately, but also of a set of institutions by which the interests of the individual citizen-sovereigns can direct the corporate actions of the society. Because of processes which give rise to oligarchical control by leaders of a collectivity (Michels's iron law of oligarchy), a portion of this theory of governance addresses the social and institutional conditions under which those in positions of authority, as agents of the citizen-sovereigns, can be controlled by them.

What, then, is an appropriate conceptual basis for the corporation, which I have termed a disjoint complex authority structure? As a related question, what is the appropriate conceptual basis for formal organizations other than corporations, such as government agencies or bureaus? The changes in modes of gover-

---

6. Such a statement ignores the fact that other citizens are also part owners of the state corporation. Thus if he is 1 out of 250 million citizens, only 1 part out of 250 million parts of his labor is not alienated. His interests as worker far outweigh his interests as part owner, since the latter are diluted by the size of the population. This statement also ignores the fact, recognized by Michels (1949 [1915]) that those who control the organizational apparatus come to have interests different from those of ordinary members of the collectivity (society in the case of state socialism, or the German Social Democratic Party in the case studied by Michels). But because the principal is the state itself, employees cannot easily use the state to control the power of the principal or to increase their own power through statutory legislation (such as the National Labor Relations Act or the Freedom of Information Act in the United States or the codetermination law in Germany).

nance described above move in a direction away from authority exercised by a superordinate, and toward a discipline imposed by the structure of incentives. Employees' acquisition of interest in the corporation itself, through a kind of identification, and the decline of shareholders' interest in the corporation except as a source of return on capital move the conception of the corporation away from one in which there is an owner as principal and employees as agents.

The appropriate conceptual basis for the corporation, the government bureau, and other formal organizations is, I believe, as a system of action that differs in only one respect from a self-constituting and self-governing social system. That is, the corporate actor should not be viewed as a hierarchical authority structure, as traditional bureaucratic theory would have it; instead it should be seen as a system of action composed of positions (not persons). In such a system the structure of relations among positions is not autonomously organized, as in a self-constituted social system, but is fixed by central management to bring about the achievement of certain goals, which constitute the purpose of the corporate actor. Actors within the structure pursue purposes of their own. If the structure is well designed, these pursuits will also achieve the purpose of the corporate actor.

I will not carry this conception further here but will take it up again in Chapter 21, where the corporation as a whole, including its owners, is examined in relation to the larger society in which it exists.

« 17 »

Rights and Corporate Actors

Chapter 3 examined the essential character of rights in social systems as well as ways of partitioning rights to divisible goods with no externalities. There are, however, special problems when rights concern corporate actions. Chapters 13 through 16 have addressed some of these issues. This chapter will examine three additional issues involving rights and corporate action. The first of these concerns the disparity between individual maximization of utility and corporate action: What effect does the way in which rights within a corporate actor are partitioned have on the seriousness of the public-goods problem created by this disparity? The second issue concerns exchanges of rights by individuals, when those rights involve corporate actors in one way or another: What are the conditions under which an individual's exchange of such rights is legitimate and the conditions under which this exchange is illegitimate? The third issue concerns the splitting of property rights: Berle and Means (1933) described how the modern corporation has split the atom of private property into two components, which can be described as the right to benefit from the property and the right to use it as a resource, or benefit rights and usage rights. How does this splitting of property rights into two components affect the distribution of power?

Allocation of Corporate Rights and the Public-Goods Problem

The disparity between individual maximization and corporate action creates a public-goods problem. This is perhaps the most serious problem facing a large collectivity, because it results in collective decisions being made by members who have no incentive to inform themselves, or even to act in accord with their interests—since any member's action in exercising his voting right has so minuscule a chance of affecting the outcome. The fundamental defect is that the maximizing unit is the wrong one: Individual maximization leads to suboptimization of corporate action.

Various directions might be taken toward rectifying this defect; one concerns the allocation of rights. The effect of such allocation on the free-rider problem can be illustrated by returning to an example introduced in Chapter 16. The example showed the difference between forward policing and backward policing in a manufacturing firm. With forward policing the right to reject inputs to a given unit's stage in the production process (for example, an assembly line) is not held by that unit but by a higher position, to which that unit is subordinate and to which an inspector reports. The right to halt the production process if mistakes are found is held, within the unit, by a foreman, who is responsible to the supervisor of the unit. With backward policing the right to reject out-of-specification inputs is held by the unit itself, and within the unit is held by each of the operators in the production line. The right to halt the production process if mistakes are observed is also held by each of the operators individually (each has a veto right). Each of these holders of the right is responsible to the unit as a collectivity. The unit, in turn, is responsible to the unit at the next stage of production, which holds the right to reject the inputs with which it must work.

As described in Chapter 16, forward policing results in a long feedback loop from consequence for the organization to the individual. The individual's input is one of many that create the corporate product, and if the individual feels consequences only from the product as a whole, an incentive to free-ride is created. Backward policing involves short feedback loops from individual actions to consequences for the actor. If the individual actors are engaged in individual maximization, forward policing produces a gross mismatch between the acting unit and the unit experiencing consequences, and thus generates the public-good, or free-rider, problem. Backward policing partially overcomes this mismatch and thus the free-rider problem.

Exercise and Exchange of Rights

In some settings an actor may exercise a right but does not hold the right to freely exchange that right. That is, exchanging the first right is illegitimate. Table 17.1 presents some cases in which exchange of a right is not legitimate along with analogous cases in which the actor and the right to be exchanged remain the same, but the exchange is now legitimate. What is the difference?

It is intuitively evident which of these transactions are illegitimate or illegal and which are legitimate. There is no mystery to these cases. Yet it is important to go a step beyond intuition and ask this conceptual question: What is the principle (or set of principles) which distinguishes the legitimate from the illegitimate exchanges?

For the transactions made by a legislator, the differences between illegitimate and legitimate ones can be clarified by recognizing that the legislator is a person filling the position of agent and his constituency as a corporate actor is the principal. The legislator's vote is a resource which is the property of the constituency, to be used by the agent in the constituency's interests. The illegitimate transactions are those in which the legislator gives up his vote, the property of the constituency, in return for goods that he will use personally.

The first two cases of the legislator's legitimate transactions raise some additional questions. A promise to vote in a way favored by constituents in return for their votes for reelection is the basic transaction between principal and agent and

Table 17.1 Illegitimate and legitimate exchanges of rights.

Illegitimate	Legitimate
1. Legislator exchanges a promise to vote for or against legislation in return for any of the following: a. Money for personal use b. Information about lucrative investments c. Promise of profitable business for his law firm	1. Legislator exchanges a promise to vote for or against legislation in return for any of the following: a. Promise by constituency groups of voters to support him and provide aid in next election campaign b. Promise from party leader of appointment to committee position c. Promise by government agency head that a new facility will be located in his constituency
2. Police officer accepts a money bribe for not issuing a traffic ticket.	2. Police officer tears up a traffic ticket of physician on a call.
3. Judge accepts a money bribe for giving a light or suspended sentence to a convicted criminal.	3. Judge gives a light or suspended sentence to a criminal with an extended family to support.
4. Zoning board official agrees to try to get a variance passed in return for a contribution to a political party.	4. Zoning board official agrees to try to get a variance passed in return for builder's agreement to create a public park in his development.
5. Purchasing agent accepts gifts from a sales representative and places a larger than usual order.	5. Purchasing agent agrees to place a larger order when a sales representative offers a larger discount.
6. Secretary trades sexual favors for job advancement.	6. Secretary works extra hours in conjunction with a promise of job advancement.
7. Union leader agrees to the terms of a contract after the factory manager mentions nominating him for country club membership.	7. Union leader agrees to the terms of a contract after management agrees to build a sports facility for employees.

is legitimate. It must be distinguished, however, from a transaction that appears on its face to be similar: a promise to a corporation doing business in the legislator's constituency to vote in a way favoring its interests in return for money for campaign support. Such a transaction is not legitimate, in the eyes of constituents, to whom, as principal, the legislator's vote belongs. The exchange is one in which an agent is using a resource of the principal in his capacity as agent in a way which may not coincide with the principal's interests. The illegitimacy lies both in the fact that money is not a resource that can legitimately play a part in this principal-agent transaction and in the fact that the actor with whom the exchange is made is not the principal. The principal here is a corporate body, the voters in the legislator's constituency; but because there are conflicts of interest within any constituency, the principal's interests on any given issue must be either the majority position on the issue or what the legislator believes is in the constituency's best overall interests.[1]

There is further complexity, however, because the legislator also has a second principal, whose interests may conflict with those of the constituency as principal: the society as a whole, of which the constituency is a part. During periods when this corporate body (for example, a nation-state) is under threat, it becomes illegitimate, in the eyes of members of this larger corporate body and members of the constituency, for a representative to act in any interest other than the interest of the larger corporate body.

The second, third, and fourth cases in Table 17.1, involving a police officer, a judge, and a zoning board official, have the same principle at base. In each case the official has certain rights to act, that is, certain resources, in his capacity as agent of the community (the city or other jurisdiction). These are the property of the community and can legitimately be used only to further the community's interests. But the agent's use of his judgment is within the latitude of his role as agent, and what makes some transactions legitimate is the fact that they can be regarded as the result of the agent's use of judgment about what is in the community's interest. This claim to legitimacy is reinforced because in each case the agent's own interests were not furthered by the exchange. If it were discovered that the agent's interests were involved, such a transaction would lose its claim to legitimacy.

Thus in all these cases there is a single principle involved: A particular right to act always has an owner. If the holder of this right is not the owner, or principal, but an agent, then the right can only be transferred if its transfer furthers the owner's interests as well as can be expected. A test of this, applied in agency relations generally, is whether the transfer furthers the agent's interests.

Two additional examples will illustrate this principle in cases where the owner of the right to act is a corporate actor, either formally defined or informally constituted.

The first example is a fictional conflict described in a novel by C. P. Snow, *The Masters* (1951). The conflict surrounds the election of a new master of a college at Cambridge University by the thirteen fellows. One college fellow, Nightingale, appears at one point in the conflict to hold the deciding vote. He desires to become a fellow of the Royal Society. A college fellow on one side of the

---

1. This distinction, of course, corresponds to that between a delegate, who votes as instructed by his constituency, and a representative, who is expected to vote in accord with constituents' interests but to use his skill and judgment as their agent. A similar distinction has evolved in the courts for distinguishing between independent contractor and servant as forms of agency (see Chapter 7).

conflict, a chemist, is a fellow of the Royal Society. Nightingale attempts, by offering to change his vote in the college election, to use his power with respect to that election to induce the chemist to nominate him to the Royal Society. The chemist does not accept the offer, and the offer is not seen as legitimate by the other fellows of the college. Nor would it have been regarded as legitimate by the fellows of the Royal Society.

In this example the fellows of the Royal Society had reason to be against the transaction corporately, because a decision intended to be made in the interests of the Royal Society would instead be made in the interests of another set of persons: the college fellows to whom Nightingale intended to sell his vote. In other words, a resource of the Royal Society, a fellowship, would not be used to advance the interests of the Royal Society, but would be stolen and used to advance the interests of persons outside the Royal Society. Examining the point of view of the college fellows requires distinguishing between the two sides of the conflict. Those fellows who were on the same side as the member of the Royal Society, considered corporately, had interests that would be aided by the proposed transaction. One of their members held a resource (nomination to a fellowship in the Royal Society) that he might be willing to add to their corporate resources to gain Nightingale's vote in the election for master of the college. Those fellows on the other side of the conflict, considered corporately, had interests that would be harmed by the proposed transaction. Neither of these two parties, these two corporate actors within the college, had constitutional claims on Nightingale's vote, however, and therefore neither could regard the transaction as theft of a resource. But as fellows of the college, considered as a corporate actor, they could (and did) regard Nightingale's proposed transaction as attempted theft of a resource. Nightingale's vote was a resource constitutionally given to him as a fellow of the college, to be used to further the corporate interests of the college as he saw them. To use this resource for private gain in effect deprived the college, as a corporate body, of that resource. Those college fellows who were on the side that would be harmed by Nightingale's proposed transaction pressed the claim of illegitimacy most forcefully, but even members of the other side recognized it, and some were not happy with the prospect of gaining Nightingale's vote in this way.

In this example the corporate body in which the position of master inheres and which constitutionally distributes control of that position to its fellows through votes would be the victim of a theft. There were four relevant actors in this potential action: two potential thieves and two victims of theft. The thieves would have been persons: Nightingale and the college fellow who was also a fellow of the Royal Society. They would have stolen a resource from the college and one from the Royal Society, using them to pursue private interests rather than the interests of those respective corporate bodies.

A second example involves a different structure but once more concerns exchanges across corporate boundaries to serve private ends. The case occurred in France at the time when it was governed by Charles De Gaulle, who was pressing for revaluation of gold against the dollar (after France had bought up large amounts of gold). De Gaulle attempted to negotiate the following exchange involving the Common Market (EEC) and the International Monetary Fund (IMF): consideration of Britain for membership in the EEC, in which France would withhold its veto, in return for support by other EEC members for revaluation of gold against the dollar. The EEC members were all members of the IMF, but not all members of the IMF were members of the EEC. The members of the EEC other than France favored Britain's entry; consequently, although the corporate interests of the EEC were opposed to the use of an EEC resource (a vote by France for or against Britain's membership), no individual member's interests were opposed to this use. On the other side some of the members of the IMF were not members of the EEC, and they regarded the proposed exchange (which did not take place) as illegitimate because it involved the use of IMF resources (votes by members of the IMF who were also members of the EEC) to further interests other than those of the IMF by withdrawing resources from the IMF for the use of actors who were members of another corporate body.

The Drift of Power toward Actors Having Usage Rights

Usage Rights in the Hands of Corporate Actors

As noted earlier, Berle and Means (1933) suggested that the modern corporation in the United States has split the atom of private property. What they meant is that private property consists of (at least) two rights: the right to use the property for the pursuit of any lawful purpose, and the right to benefit from the use of the property. They showed how, in the modern publicly owned corporation, the managers hold the usage rights (that is, have the power to determine the specific uses of the corporation's wealth) and the owners retain the right to benefit from that use, through dividends and increasing value of their stock, as well as the right to ultimate disposal of their stock, which entails the benefits of capital gains. What I have termed usage rights (and what Berle and Means called active property) are rights to determine the use of corporate resources. In many corporate bodies these rights are constitutionally dispersed among many members or owners, with each having some voice (ordinarily through voting, but also through other means, such as the right to speak at a union meeting or a stockholder's meeting) regarding the direction of the organization.

Both Berle and Means and Michels (1949 [1915]) have shown that, despite such constitutional rights, the effective voice of the members or owners is very weak. In the case of political parties examined by Michels and in the case of public corporations examined by Berle and Means, the principal mechanism for alienation of usage rights was the fragmentation or dispersal of the members or owners, which made them unable to collect sufficient power to counteract or constrain the power held by the top executives of the party or the corporation.

The general phenomenon has come to be more widely recognized in recent years, and a number of proposals designed to increase the power or voice of the members or owners of a corporate body with respect to the corporate body itself have been made. For example, Goldberg (1971) has argued that outside members of boards of directors (that is, those not associated with the corporation's management) should be provided with staff resources and access to management files to enable them to discharge their responsibilities to owners. Ralph Nader has argued for federal, rather than state, chartering of corporations, to ensure greater constraints on corporate executives. Hirschman (1970) has also argued for an increase in the effectiveness of voice in those corporate bodies in which the most centralized direction exists (that is, business corporations). The various and numerous proposals are in effect suggesting the restriction of the usage rights of the top management of corporate bodies, by giving more voice to the dispersed membership from whom the corporate resources originally came—or in some cases to other persons, such as employees, customers, or, more vaguely, the public.[2]

Still another way in which persons give up usage rights or direct control over their resources is by giving up to government a larger realm of control over their actions. Through the giving up of rights to be collectively held, via the representative process, persons surrender autonomy in order to achieve ends that they see as a collective benefit. They lose direct control of increasing amounts of resources and must trust to the mechanisms of representative government and the occupants of government positions to exercise that control in ways they desire. But the analyses of Michels and of Berle and Means hold here as well: Giving over those resources to government deprives persons of control over their employ; that control is largely held by the corporate bodies of government, which are partly insulated from the persons to whom the resources ultimately belong.

In its most general form the process that takes place in corporate bodies can be seen as a generalization of the phenomenon discussed by Berle and Means, the splitting of the atom of private property. All corporate bodies "split the atom" of whatever resources are vested in them, taking the usage rights and leaving to members or owners the rights to benefits from that use. Individuals in society, by vesting their resources in corporate bodies, elect to give up the direct usage rights over these resources in return for the greater benefits they expect to realize from the combined use. Thus the usage rights and benefits of resources in society are in different hands: The usage rights are increasingly in the hands of corporate bodies, and the benefits remain in the hands of individual persons. The result is a population that is increasingly alienated from direct control over its resources and increasingly supported by a set of corporate bodies in whom it has vested that direct control.

2. Berle and Means, at the end of their analysis, ask this question: To whom should the rights which have drifted to top management be returned? Their answer, given without a convincing rationale, is the community as a whole. There have also been recent proposals urging public representation on boards of directors of corporations.

This process may also be seen in the occupational shift from free professionals and free craftworkers to employed professionals and employed skilled workers. In making such a shift, a person loses control over the conditions of his work in return for greater or more secure income as an employee. The resistance of some groups, such as physicians, to making the shift from free professionals to employees must be seen as due in part to a reluctance to give up direct control over one's work activities, a control that is widely regarded as an important source of satisfaction in work.

Expressions of discontent—ranging from Goldberg's unhappiness with management control of boards of directors and Nader's attempts to impose greater accountability on managers of bureaucracies to the antagonism of some persons toward "the establishment" and increasing demands for greater control of work conditions—may be specific manifestations of a general reaction against this drift of control from individual persons to corporate actors.[3] Psychological evidence has shown that persons experience distress when they feel a loss of control and derive satisfaction and learn better when they have control over events that affect them (see Seeman, 1963, 1971; Rotter, 1966, 1971).

The shift of direct control from persons to corporate bodies creates a structural condition in society in which a large number of the events that individuals are interested in are not under their direct control. This suggests that society is moving in the direction of a dependent population of persons who experience benefits from a set of intangible corporate actors, which control the major resources and events. This structure may be an inevitable consequence of the increased interdependence of persons and the necessity to delegate many rights to act to corporate bodies, within which events affecting many persons are decided.

There may, however, be other means by which a large portion of control could be returned to persons, without sacrificing the benefits that accrue from delegation of power. Hirschman (1970) contrasts voice and exit as two ways in which persons may affect the actions of corporations. Voice corresponds to usage rights; that is, it entails taking actions that affect the disposition of resources. Exit is indirect control by making the choice to leave. For example, the existence of an efficient capital market makes it possible for an investor in a corporation to withdraw his resources at very little cost, in effect giving him a measure of control over the use of his resources. If the capital market were less efficient, an investment in the corporation would constitute a greater loss of control over his resources. On the other hand, no such market exists for union members who have invested resources of time and energy in their occupation and have paid

---

3. Examples of demands for greater control of the work situation can be found in a variety of places. Some law firms have found it necessary to promise to young law school graduates one day a week to engage in legal practice for the poor in order to attract the persons they want to hire. Philips Electronics and other firms have engaged in work restructuring, in which manufacturing tasks are grouped into larger sets so that a worker has a broader task and greater discretion about how he will organize his activities.

union dues. A union member is subject to a set of constraints that restrict his choices: whether to work overtime, decisions about how to pursue his job or about the range of activities that he will carry out as part of the job, control of bargaining over his wage and the decision of what wage to accept, and so forth. A member cannot generally withdraw his membership and shift to another union, except at the cost of losing those investments he has made in his occupation.

In general, among different kinds of corporate bodies there exists a continuum, ranging from those for which costs of withdrawal are zero to those for which costs of withdrawal are effectively infinite (that is, withdrawal can occur only at the cost of one's life). At one extreme are business corporations; because of an efficient capital market, owners (stockholders) may sell their stock at little or no cost. Trade unions impose a greater cost of withdrawal, because of the absence of competing unions among which a worker may choose. Nation-states impose a still greater cost of withdrawal on their members, and the cost is extremely high for those countries from which exit is forcibly restricted.

Thus there is probably an even greater range among corporate bodies with respect to the cost of exit than with respect to the degree to which owners' or members' voice is effectively heard. It is clear that as the cost of withdrawal from a corporate body increases, the necessity for some voice within it increases, since exit and voice are alternative means of controlling the corporate body. Thus internal democracy among the shareholders of a business corporation is less important for shareholders' control of the corporation than is internal democracy of a trade union for members' control of the union, which in turn is less important than internal democracy in a nation-state for citizens' control of the nation-state.

The broad control of social actions by corporate bodies has created the following situation: An increasing fraction of the events that are important to persons in society is under the control of corporate bodies that are only very distantly controlled by those persons. Thus a person living in a large city, working for a large firm, belonging to a large union or professional association, and having some interest in political affairs receives many benefits in the form of money, services, and other resources, but at the cost of having little control over those events which interest him. The individual in modern society has surrendered control of many of the activities of daily life to those corporate bodies that service him. The basic activities of society can be seen to be controlled more and more by intangible corporate actors.

If the above conclusions are valid, then the degree to which a person feels a sense of control over those activities and events whose outcomes are of interest to him should be a function of two elements: the degree to which his interests are confined to activities close at hand, and his actual control over various activities. In particular, those persons who have a high degree of interest in events controlled by large corporate bodies should have a lower sense of control than those who have interests in events controlled by smaller, more localized corporate bodies (family, neighborhood, and so forth). Furthermore, if persons' general levels of satisfaction are assumed to derive from their feeling of having control over those events that are of interest to them, the persons with the lowest levels of satisfaction should be found among those whose interests are in the most distant events.

A further hypothesized process, in conjunction with the foregoing, leads to further predictions. There is some indication that persons constitute homeostatic systems with regard to internal control or efficacy. As this control decreases, they act in ways to regain control over something. If persons' subjective experience of internal control depends on their having control of things in which they have interest, this means they can act to increase their control over corporate bodies that control events that interest them, or they can shift their interest from events over which they have little control to events over which they have greater control.[4] One implication of such a homeostatic process for a given population is that when certain events show themselves to be less subject to the control of bodies over which members of the population have some control, members will lose interest in those events. Furthermore, the loss of interest should be greatest among those whose interest in the events was initially greatest (for similar profiles of control) and greatest among those whose control over corporate bodies that have some control over the events is least (for similar profiles of interest).

Evidence of the extent of this homeostatic process of shifting interests in everyday life can be sought by using successive public opinion surveys to examine the relation over time between the perceived degree of control of events by corporate bodies and interest in those events. Evidence of the homeostatic effect will be present if reduced perceived control over a set of events is followed by reduced interest in those events. For example, if persons perceive that their government has less control over events in foreign affairs, a subsequent reduction of their interest in those events would be evidence of the occurrence of the homeostatic process.

One can see concretely how this hypothesized process may work by considering as an example the International Typographical Union (ITU) studied in the 1950s by Lipset, Trow, and Coleman (1956). In that union many members did not give up to the union as much control over the decisions involving their working conditions, wages, and so forth, as did members of other unions. Members of the ITU attended meetings, were often active in shop, local, and international election campaigns, and read about and discussed union politics and policies. In short, some members of the union exercised close control over the union's activities.

The hypothesis offered above would say that for two union members, both of whom had equal amounts of interest in occupational matters, the one who exercised active control of the union as described above would have a greater subjec-

---

4. In some respects this shift of interest is analogous to a stockholder's withdrawal of capital from one corporation and reinvestment of it in another.

tive sense of internal control and greater satisfaction with work activities—and the gap would be widest for those pairs of members who had the greatest interest in occupational activities. The homeostatic hypothesis of shifting interests also implies that those persons who have given up the most control to a corporate actor will lose most interest in the activities controlled by that actor. Although this homeostatic process makes the relation between active control and a sense of internal control and work satisfaction difficult to test, it implies that an inactive union member who starts out with a high interest in working conditions will—whether the inactivity is voluntary or imposed by an oligarchic structure in the union—lose interest in those conditions.

Usage Rights in the Hands of Agents

Corporate actors are intangible bodies; consequently they must employ persons as agents. Whether these agents are corporate executives and employees, union officials and employees, government officials and employees, or other types of agents, the corporate body must place in their hands usage rights to the resources it holds. This constitutes a kind of deployment of resources that is complementary to the concentration of resources that gives power to the corporate actor.

The vesting of usage rights in persons who occupy positions in a corporate body gives power to those persons, who act as agents. They, in turn, may use this power to divert some of the benefits to themselves. If a personnel manager has some discretion in hiring, he may use that discretion to hire his friends or to create obligations to himself. If a government official has information about a policy involving land acquisition, he may use that information to benefit himself, directly or indirectly. If a union official has the power to negotiate a wage contract, he may use it to gain a membership in a country club. If a worker has the right to use a set of tools or a sales representative has the right to use an automobile, the tools or automobile may be employed to serve personal ends. If an employee has use of an expense account, he may well use it to his own benefit.

All of these diversions of benefits stem from the necessity of a corporate body to deploy its resources in the hands of persons who occupy positions within it. Although some personal uses of corporate resources are preventable, others are not, without immobilizing the organization. And aside from questionable actions which use corporate resources for private gain, there are ways in which a person's position in a corporate actor provides automatic benefits. He has credit references for loans and credit cards, and he has in effect a co-insurer for many activities, as evidenced by the frequency with which the question "Who is your employer?" is asked as a means of establishing trustworthiness or legitimacy. In addition, a worker gains certain rights to his job over a period of time, perhaps somewhat comparable to squatter's rights but codified in seniority rights and protection against summary dismissal.

The process is exactly the same as that which gives power to a corporate actor in the first place: the drift of power to those who actually engage in the use of resources and away from those who have ultimate rights of ownership of those resources. This drift accounts for the gain in power of managers relative to owners or members, as described by Berle and Means (1933) and by Michels (1949 [1915]), and the gain in power of those persons in lower-level positions to which resources of an organization have been delegated.

Since a process that brings power back into the hands of persons is seen as an extension of a process that puts power into the hands of corporate actors, it would at first appear that no loss of power is sustained by persons. This is not so for two reasons. First, the resources that go into the hands of corporate actors for usage purposes are not primarily employed for the private gain of persons in positions in the organization but for corporate gain. The capability of corporate actors for preventing loss of power arising from delegation of usage rights is much greater than the capability of persons for diverting that power to themselves.

The second reason why these two processes bring about loss of power is that the persons who give up power to corporate bodies through delegation of usage rights are not the same persons as those who gain power from occupying positions in corporate bodies that give them usage rights to corporate resources. There are some persons who occupy no positions in corporate actors and thus have no use of corporate resources. The best examples of persons in this category are women who do not work outside the home. From the perspective of this theoretical framework, nonemployed women have particularly experienced loss of power as corporate bodies have increased their power in modern society. Young people who are old enough not to be wholly dependent but not yet occupying a corporate position are another example. Farmers are another. Women, youth, farmers, and others without a position as employee are in general in positions of greatest powerlessness, as society becomes increasingly organized around formally constituted corporate actors.

Empirical consequences of these two processes should show up in several ways:

1. Among those persons whose interests are equally highly focused on events and activities outside the home, unemployed women and youth should express the lowest sense of internal control and of general satisfaction, relative to persons who are employed.

2. The difference in perceived internal control between unemployed women and youth and employed persons should be greatest in those social structures where large formally organized corporate actors have greatest power, that is, in industrialized and urban areas. The difference should be least in small towns and rural areas, especially those areas that are not industrialized.

3. Persons' sense of internal control should be greater (given equal distribution of interests), the greater the amount of corporate resources invested in

them or delegated to them in their jobs. If jobs are scaled according to the extent of these resources, a person's sense of internal control should be related to that dimension of the job more than to other dimensions, such as the income it produces. If (as is probably the case) occupational prestige is to some extent a surrogate for the investing of corporate resources in a person, a person's sense of internal control should be more highly related to occupational prestige than to income (with interests controlled).

Obviously a given person's control is a resultant of both processes discussed in this and the preceding section: the drift of control from persons to corporate actors and the drift of a portion of corporate power to persons who act as a corporate body's agents. The hypotheses and implications, however, have treated these two processes independently. Any empirical analysis should take into account the joint operation of the two processes and include in a person's direct control of resources both the residue of control of his own resources and the control of resources placed in his hands by a corporate body which employs him.

Withdrawal of Usage Rights through Voice and Exit

When persons invest resources in corporate bodies, giving those bodies usage rights over the resources, they ordinarily gain a voice in, or certain rights of control over, the actions of the corporate body. These include voting rights, rights of petition and recall, and rights of access to certain information held by the managers of the corporate body. Under many conditions the investment of resources is accompanied by a placement of trust in the corporate body's management and an acceptance of the legitimacy of the corporate actions' being unfettered. Trusting in a corporate body means giving the corporate body free rein to act, without using one's potential control of the corporate body to constrain its action. For example, a citizen who trusts his city government will not engage in political activities designed to influence the actions of that government, but will employ his energies elsewhere. One can conceive of trust placed in a corporate body as an investment of rights to control parallel to the giving up of usage rights to tangible resources. But that investment of rights to control can be withdrawn, by withdrawing trust from those in whom one has placed it. One withdraws one's trust by exercising voice—by becoming politically active and by using one's resources in whatever way one can to influence the actions of the corporate body.

Thus what is ordinarily termed trust or confidence in a social institution or corporate body can be seen as a general measure of the investment of rights to control actions of the corporate body. The withdrawing of this investment can lead the individual either to exit or to exercise voice, either to withdraw his resources from the corporate body or to attempt to exercise control over its actions. For example, stockholders' loss of confidence in managers of a firm can lead to either voting those managers out or selling of their stock. Members' loss of trust in union leaders can lead to either voting the officers out or leaving the union. The action taken will depend on the relative costs of the two possibilities. These costs will be largely a function of the existence of alternative corporate bodies to which to transfer the resources and of the potential for opposition within the corporate body.

Recognizing all this makes it possible to use a measure of trust or confidence as an indicator of the degree to which individuals vest their rights to control in corporate bodies. What is problematic, however, is the relation between withdrawal of trust, on the one hand, and behavioral measures of withdrawal of rights to control, on the other. Behavioral measures include various indicators of political activity, such as demonstrations, resistance to a draft, and political acts of a newsworthy sort, and attitudinal measures as used in public opinion surveys. (For example, as presented in Figure 5.1, opinion polls showed reductions in public confidence in various governmental, political, and religious elites between 1966 and 1979; the reductions averaged 20% and ranged up to 43%.) This relation can be studied through observations of actions and through responses to surveys, at the level of the population as a whole and for identifiable subgroups such as racial, regional, and age groups. It may well be that there is a time lag between expressions of lower confidence or trust and behavior reflecting withdrawal of rights to control. Thus it is necessary to allow for the possibility of such lags in studying the relationship.

Such research would only establish a degree of correspondence between actions that are here interpreted as reflecting a person's withdrawal of rights to control vested in a corporate body and attitudes that show a person's withdrawal of trust. But since such actions can be important in the functioning of society, understanding of their genesis would be valuable in itself. If expressions of withdrawal of trust in various corporate bodies of society show up in attitude surveys and are followed by political demonstrations, destructive actions directed against corporate bodies, or actions designed to affect their decisions, the attitude change becomes not only an important social indicator of the level of trust in the corporate body, but also a predictor of behavior toward that body.

In examining the separation of usage and benefit rights brought about by modern corporate actors, I have tried to sketch several processes that affect the distribution of power in society. One is the process by which persons turn over usage rights associated with various resources to corporate bodies, in return for benefits (or the expectation of benefits) greater than they themselves could achieve by use of those resources. A major source of the increased benefits is the additional power that inheres in concentrated resources. But this very concentration gives the corporate actor power with respect to the investors, allowing its interests to be pursued, sometimes to the neglect of their interests. There is an overall drift of power from the natural persons to the corporate actors in which usage rights have been invested.

But the corporate actor must also vest usage rights to its resources in its agents. This brings some power back to persons, but the power is distributed differently than it was before investment in the corporate body. Certain persons in society are left relatively powerless, and if the theory presented here is correct, these persons should feel more powerless than their counterparts in whom corporate bodies have made some investment.

Finally, an additional transaction occurs. When persons give up to corporate bodies usage rights to various resources, they ordinarily gain a right to exercise a voice, to partially control the actions of the corporate body, through voting, for example. The placement of trust in a corporate body can be seen as an investment of these rights to control in those who presently control that body. Withdrawal of trust can simply constitute withdrawal of those rights to control, which are then exercised by the individual through political participation, or in some cases can also involve withdrawal of the tangible resources originally invested in the corporate body.

« 18 »

Revoking Authority

Authority systems are structures of rights. Those rights have the social character that all rights have: They exist through a consensus of the relevant actors, that is, all those who are part of the system. In the case of an authority system, this consensus is what is meant by the legitimacy of authority.

In many authority systems, although not all, individuals hold the right to revoke the authority by exiting from the system. This option, however, often entails costs that make it unattractive—for example, exit from a trade union may entail exit from the occupation, or exit from a nation-state may entail giving up most of one's social and material resources. To remain within a system and revoke its authority involves changing the allocation of rights in the system, and because rights are socially defined, this cannot be done alone. In an established authority system the consensual base on which authority rests is reinforced by a set of formal institutions, which may include the police and the military. These institutions provide physical control that supports the rights of control (the legitimacy) and impedes revocation of authority.

Nevertheless, it is often possible for a subset of actors in a system to weaken its authority by attempting to withdraw rights of control. One way of doing so is through a kind of internal emigration, by which a small group cuts itself off and exists in an isolated location as a self-contained society within the larger one.[1] In the United States in the 1960s, a number of such societies were established as rural communes. Such a possibility depends, however, on toleration by the state and the larger society, for such enclaves are sometimes seen as threats to the larger sociopolitical system.

Short of such full withdrawal, actors may attempt to remain within a society but to withdraw partial rights of control that are important to governance of the system. This may weaken the existing authority, because of its dependence on the compliance or active support of society's members. For example, a portion of the authority of the president of the United States lies in the willingness of subordinates to carry out his wishes and of citizens to follow his leadership. If this willingness does not exist, as it did not during Prohibition in the 1920s or the

---

1. The term "internal emigration" has sometimes been used to describe individuals' withdrawal from social participation in the Soviet Union, which restricts physical emigration.

Vietnam War in the 1960s and 1970s, the authority is undermined, and the president has lost a portion of his capacity to direct the country.

Even in the case of slavery, the most extreme system of authority, the subordinates' compliance and even active effort are necessary for the system to continue. Oppressive systems sometimes fail merely because of the passive noncompliance of a subject people.

Yet certain kinds of withdrawal of authority cannot be carried out by simple noncompliance. This is true especially with regard to state authority, which has the force of police power behind it. Unless a citizen has extensive support, he will be unable to refuse to pay taxes, to refuse to send his children to school, or to refuse to obey any of a multitude of civil and criminal laws. He may, depending on the state, be prevented by force from emigrating to escape the state's exercise of power. He may be prevented from joining with others in forming a communal enclave. And he cannot replace the authority system with another more to his liking. Even if there is a means of replacing those who exercise authority (for example, through elections), there is no simple way to replace the authority system itself.[2]

The constraints on the individual are generally fewer in authority systems less encompassing than that of the state, such as the authority system in one's workplace or local community. Even with less encompassing authority systems, a subordinate has investments that must be sacrificed if he withdraws authority by leaving the system.

Authority systems can sometimes be changed, however, and authority that was vested in one governing body can be transferred to another. In some instances this occurs without force. For example, in the Philippines the regime of Ferdinand Marcos was ended in 1986 upon the election of Corazon Aquino, without the use of force. After that election the constitution was suspended, and the existing legislature was dissolved, changes as extensive as those that occur after some violent revolutions. Another example of a change of government without force occurred when the Shah of Iran was deposed in 1979 by a widespread withdrawal of legitimacy, which was vested instead in the religious leaders, or mullahs, and ultimately in the Ayatollah Khomeini.

Yet even widespread withdrawal of legitimacy is ordinarily insufficient to bring about a change in regime. If the Shah had maintained control of the armed forces, the withdrawal of legitimacy from his regime would not have been sufficient to bring about its fall. In a neighboring state, Afghanistan, the widespread withdrawal of legitimacy from a regime supported militarily by an external state, the Soviet Union, has been accompanied by the use of force, but that force has been insufficient to overthrow the regime because its military power is reinforced by outside support. Similarly, extensive withdrawal of legitimacy

---

2. It might be argued that this is possible in a political democracy, if citizens can elect leaders who will transform the system. But my point is not that this is never possible, but that under most regimes in most circumstances it is not possible.

from Polish authorities by a large majority of the population and vesting of it in the independent trade union Solidarity were not sufficient to overthrow the regime in the face of the use of force by the head of state and support from the neighboring Soviet Union.[3]

It is clear from examples like these that widespread withdrawal of rights of control (that is, legitimacy) from an authority structure is often not sufficient to bring about a change in that structure or even in the way authority is exercised. (I will ask later whether it is a necessary condition.) But the difference between rights to control and power to exercise control means that whether or not there is a widespread withdrawal of rights to control by subordinates, changing an authority system requires revoking the actual power to exercise control. If that power is not given up voluntarily, it must be taken by force. Such an exercise of power against state authority can occur in a variety of ways, which can be termed revolt or revolution. In less encompassing authority systems, revolts by subordinates are a major means by which authority is changed. The history of trade unions shows this (see Lipset, Trow, and Coleman, 1956, p. 66), and studies of conflicts within communities indicate that one of the principal forms these conflicts take is the asymmetric form of a revolt against authority (Coleman, 1957).

In this chapter I will examine this important means of revoking authority. I will review what some theorists have had to say about the conditions under which revolts or revolutions arise and then sketch the basis for a theory of revolutions based on a microfoundation of rational action.

Theories of Revolution

Because revolution at the level of the society as a whole is not frequent but is important as a mechanism of change in authority, it has been the subject of study by many social scientists and social philosophers. A question that has been addressed frequently is that of when revolutions occur. That is, social scientists have been less concerned with predicting the outcome of a revolution or even describing the course it takes than with understanding its emergence.

In investigating this question, social scientists have principally used one method. They have focused on societies in which revolutions or revolts did occur and have examined those societies in the period preceding the conflict (for example, Russia in the late nineteenth and early twentieth centuries or France in the middle and late eighteenth century). This has led them to answer the question in terms of *changes* in a society that may lead to revolution. Answers have not characteristically been framed in terms of stable structural conditions that lead some social systems, but not others, to undergo a change of authority by way of revolution or revolt.[4] For example, suppose one structural difference

3. At the height of its strength Solidarity claimed a membership of 10 million in a country of 30 million, and membership in the Communist Party dropped precipitously.

4. This method has not always been used in the study of revolutions to the exclusion of others. Eisenstadt (1978), in his examination of the transformation of societies by revolution

between societies is the existence or nonexistence of institutional means by which subordinates can change the authority system, such as regular elections to change the persons in authority or rights of petition and referenda to change aspects of the authority structure. It seems clear from other research that such institutional differences are important (see, for example, Lipset, Trow, and Coleman, 1956, pp. 33–66). The bloodless accession of Aquino to the presidency of the Philippines and of Allende to power in Chile, establishing a socialist regime, were facilitated by the existence of democratic institutions. The methods employed in most research on revolution do not lead to such answers, however, because the precise question researchers are examining is not "For which social systems will revolutions occur?" but rather "In those social systems in which a revolution does occur, what are the changes that lead to its occurrence?"

It is possible to review the kinds of answers that various investigators have given to the latter question. The specificity of the query makes it clear that the results do not constitute a comprehensive theory of the occurrence of revolutions, but only a component of such a theory. That the work I will examine constitutes a narrow component of a theory of revolutions is evident for another reason. I will focus on changes at the level of individual persons, either the members of the society as a whole or a subset of those members. Yet most social systems have many institutions at various levels—and thus many actors can engage in a power struggle with central authorities. Replacement of government officials by nonconstitutional means, and even changes in the form of government, can occur with little change in orientation on the part of individual citizens, although this is more likely to be true in traditional societies than in modern ones.

Even when there is unrest or other change at the level of individual citizens, the picture of revolutions that is provided by the theoretical principles I will discuss is the too simple one of a structure consisting only of the authorities and one or more components of the population. Many of those whose work I will refer to are fully aware of this and do not claim to base a theory of revolutions on such a simplified picture lacking intermediate structure. Yet the element that I focus on in their work, the change in orientation of subordinates in an authority system toward those in authority which leads to their taking action, is important in the transition from one authority system to another. For such a transition implies a withdrawal of rights to control from one set of authorities and is only complete when those rights have been vested in a new set of authorities.

Changes that involve only struggles of power among elites (for example, a

---

and otherwise, uses an explicitly comparative approach which examines the generally ignored structural differences. Skocpol (1979), in studying the history of the French, Russian, and Chinese revolutions, uses, in addition to this method, some comparisons with other contemporary societies where revolution did not occur. This is one reason why she arrives at some conclusions about the causes of those revolutions that differ from what had been given before. Some authors have made cross-national quantitative comparisons and examined some of the structural differences leading to revolution. Their results will be discussed in a later section.

coup d'état by army officers) do not constitute a change of authority system, because there is no divesting and revesting of authority by the population as a whole, but only a change of officials at the top. That such a change may have occurred by nonconstitutional means, even involving the use of force, makes no difference.

It is useful to first scrutinize a concept that plays a central role in theories of revolution—legitimacy. Many theoretical works on revolution see a critical point in a revolutionary struggle as the point at which the existing system of authority loses legitimacy in the eyes of the population or of important segments of the population. Goldstone (1989) describes how authorities may lose legitimacy by engaging in actions regarded by the population as outside the ground rules governing authoritative actions. Authorities may also lose legitimacy when they become ineffective and unable to act authoritatively to provide the benefits that are part of the (implicit or explicit) constitutional contract.

Legitimacy, as has been often stated, constitutes the difference between authority and power: Authority is, it is sometimes said, legitimately exercised power. Eisenstadt and Curelaru (1976), for example, describe legitimate actions as those that are in accord with generally recognized ground rules.

In terms of the theory of this book, authority is the right to control another actor's actions, and power is the capacity to do so, with or without the right. It is the consensual character of a right that creates a correspondence between the right to exercise control and the legitimacy of authoritative actions. The right to carry out an action exists if and only if there is a general consensus that the particular actor in question has the right to carry out that action. Those in authority have the right to use certain actions in bringing about compliance if and only if there is general consensus that they hold that right. If authorities engage in actions other than those for which this consensus exists, they lack the right to do so, are acting illegitimately, and may lose legitimacy. That is, the rights to govern which they do hold may be generally withdrawn, leading to collapse of the consensus which gives legitimacy. If they take actions for which they do hold the rights but carry them out ineffectively, the rights may be withdrawn. For some other reason the consensus on which the right to govern rests may collapse, and the authorities may lose the right (that is, lose legitimacy)—in this case not through their own actions, but because of other factors which change people's conception of where the right lies.

Thus legitimacy is simply the right to carry out certain authoritative actions and have them obeyed. It rests on a consensus among those actors in a society relevant to the continued exercise of authority—which may be the population as a whole or only certain parts of it.

Does a Revolution Occur When Conditions Are Worsening?

Simple common sense suggests that a revolution will be more likely when citizens' living conditions are worsening. Such a proposition was part of Marx's theory of the transformation of capitalism to socialism: that the increasing impoverishment of the working class under capitalism would lead workers to become conscious of their interests and to revolt. This prediction, of course, was wrong in its premise, since workers have not become increasingly impoverished under capitalism. But there is extensive evidence to indicate that even if Marx's premises had been met, his conclusions would not have followed. In fact, almost the reverse has been true: When general impoverishment has increased, the population appears to have sunk into an increased passivity.

Some cases are more complex, however. Before the French Revolution in 1789, the economy in France as a whole was prospering, but the peasants' economic condition was worsening. The revolution, however, was not started by the peasants, but by those who were benefiting from the general economic growth—members of the Third Estate. Alexis de Tocqueville commented on the facts that during the period preceding the French Revolution France was enjoying a general increase in prosperity and that unrest was greatest in those parts of the country which had experienced greatest economic improvement. In addition, political conditions had improved. Louis XVI had introduced various political reforms. Tocqueville generalized that "it is not always when things are going from bad to worse that revolution breaks out. On the contrary, it more often happens that, when a people which has put up with an oppressive rule over a long period without protest suddenly finds the government releasing its pressure, it takes up arms against it" (1955 [1860], pp. 176–177).[5]

In Iran economic prosperity (following the worldwide rise in oil prices after 1973) and greatly increased opportunities to pursue higher education overseas were followed by overthrow of the Shah. There was a total transformation of the authority system from a monarchy to a theocracy with a parliamentary form; this was followed by violence and threats of revolt. In the Soviet Union dissidence rose to unprecedented levels in the post-Stalinist period, which was characterized by less political oppression and less economic hardship than were present during Stalin's regime. In Poland the protorevolutionary developments that began in August 1980 followed a period of greatly improved economic conditions and increased political liberalization. The unrest among blacks in South Africa intensified in the mid-1980s, after a decade and a half in which the share of disposable income of blacks in that country had risen from 32.3% to 44.5%, and real wages of blacks had increased while those of whites had remained constant.[6]

Revolts against institutions within a country show the same pattern. The student revolts of the late 1960s in the United States occurred during a period in which constraints on college students were being extensively relaxed. The principle of *in loco parentis* had been abandoned in many universities, coed dorms

5. One might say that Tocqueville's proposition about the conditions under which revolutions break out is directly opposed to Marx's supposition that increasing immiserization under capitalism will lead workers to revolt.

6. These are results of a study by Professor Piet Niel of Unisa's Bureau of Market Research, reported in *The Jerusalem Post*, August 22, 1986, p. 6.

had been instituted, curricular requirements for admission and graduation were relaxed, and grade inflation was widespread.

Theorists of revolution have reached a general consensus on the broad outlines of empirical reality: Revolution is more likely to arise during times of economic improvement for at least some parts of a population or at times of political liberalization, or both. The details are not clear, but the general outlines are. (For a review see Oberschall, 1978.) Common sense or rationality appears to be in eclipse, for common sense would lead to the opposite prediction.

The general character of the empirical phenomenon can be seen in Figure 18.1, where the vertical axis represents the level of economic, social, or political conditions and the horizontal axis indicates time. The general result found by most theorists of revolution is that the revolution does not happen at time P, when there is a stable low level of economic prosperity or political freedom, but at time R, after a period of improvement in these conditions. What makes this result so puzzling is that it does appear to fly in the face of rationality. Why should people revolt when things are getting better rather than worse? The fact that they do so appears to be a victory for irrationality. Here, as in other cases, however, a valuable theoretical strategy is to refuse to accept the apparent irrationality and instead to ask what perspective might make it rational to act in the way that people are observed to act.

The Frustration Theorists

A number of authors have pursued this task by taking different vantage points. Even though they differ, the vantage points can be described rather generally as theories in which revolution arises as a result of increased frustration. The

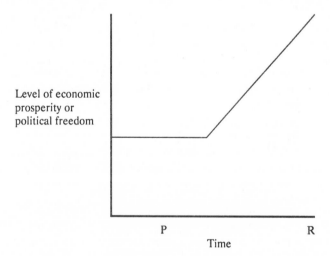

Figure 18.1   Conditions of stability or improvement as influencing likelihood of revolution.

theories differ in the way they address the obvious question of how frustration can be increasing when conditions are improving.

HOW CAN FRUSTRATION INCREASE WHEN CONDITIONS IMPROVE? The common element in the frustration theories of revolution is a positing of a subjective perspective of those subordinate to authority that differs from the perspective taken by external observers. From the point of view of this subjective perspective, things are getting worse, although the external observer's viewpoint would say they are getting better. Thus each of these frustration theories attributes to the subordinates in an authority system a perspective which makes the apparent anomaly vanish. I will briefly indicate what each of these perspectives is.

The theory of rising expectations. One theoretical perspective explains the apparent anomaly as follows: When there is a certain rate of improvement in objective conditions, economic or political, this creates rising expectations, so persons expect to be better off. But the expectations rise faster than the rate of improvement in the objective conditions. Thus there is an increasing gap between people's expectations and reality. The people view reality from the perspective of increasing frustration, which leads them to revolt. Brinton's (1965) generalizations from four revolutions (English, American, French, and Russian) include this general thesis. Brinton says that the strongest feelings "are roused in those who find an intolerable gap between what they have come to want . . . and what they actually get" (p. 250).

This theoretical perspective can be illustrated graphically as shown in Figure 18.2, where the solid line shows the level of economic prosperity or political freedom, as in Figure 18.1, and the dashed line represents the level of people's

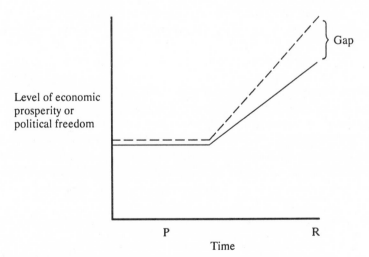

Figure 18.2   Predicted revolutionary potential: Gap created by rising expectations.

expectations. According to this theoretical position, the more rapid rise in expectations results in a widening gap between expectations and reality, which, when sufficiently wide, leads to revolt, at time R on the graph.

This thesis gains some support from the work of Emile Durkheim, an early social theorist whose interest was in other matters. Durkheim's explanation of suicide includes a type which he calls anomic suicide (1951 [1897], p. 241). The condition of anomie is one of normlessness; the usual norms that govern a person's expectations are removed, and expectations can become unbounded. This, according to Durkheim, produces a disorientation and despair which may lead to suicide. Suicide of course is different from revolt, but the psychic state Durkheim sees as produced by the unboundedness of expectations is similar to that posited by the theorists of rising expectations. There never has been a good empirical test of Durkheim's behavioral prediction of suicide under conditions of unbounded expectations, nor has there been a good test of the theory of rising expectations.

The theory of short-term setbacks. Davies (1962) has resolved the apparent anomaly of why revolutions occur when conditions are improving in a somewhat different way. He begins, as do the theorists of rising expectations, with a general improvement in economic or political conditions, although he focuses primarily on economic conditions. Expectations rise along with this improvement. The improvement is interrupted, perhaps by an economic recession. It is this setback which creates the gap between expectations and reality, since the expectations continue to increase at the same rate as before. As with the theory of rising expectations, this gap creates frustration, which leads to revolt.

This theoretical perspective, in the crude form in which I have presented it, can be illustrated as shown in Figure 18.3. The objective conditions are again represented by a solid line and the expectations by a dashed line. The change in objective conditions follows a different course from that posited by the theorists of rising expectations: There is not only general improvement in economic conditions over a period of time, but also a setback in that improvement.

Davies presents evidence of short-term setbacks prior to the French Revolution, as well as for other cases, and uses this evidence in support of his theory. Stone (1970) gives evidence supporting the theory of short-term setbacks for the English Revolution of 1640. There were economic setbacks in the export trade in cloth beginning in 1620 and poor harvests during the decade beginning in 1630. Zagorin (1982), studying the revolts and rebellions of the 1640s in Europe (in Portugal, Catalonia, Naples, Sicily, and France), examined data on harvests and economic conditions throughout Europe during this period, which yielded evidence of both general economic prosperity for some time prior to the revolts and economic setbacks in the period just preceding them.

Evidence supporting the theory of short-term setbacks may also be seen in the events of December 1970 in Poland. In a period of general economic development with improving economic conditions, food prices had been fixed for some time. Then, five days before Christmas, food prices were increased sharply by

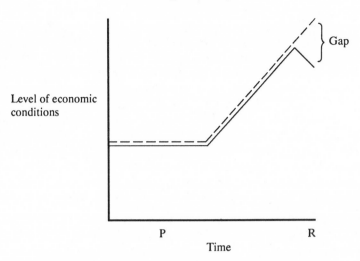

Figure 18.3 Predicted revolutionary potential: Gap created by economic reversal
after improvement.

the government, by as much as 50% for some items. Extensive riots in the port
cities of Gdańsk and Gdynia followed, leading to the ouster of Gomulka as first
secretary of the Communist Party. The theory of short-term setbacks does not,
however, account for the Solidarity uprising in Poland in 1980, an organized
uprising that was much closer to a revolution than were the riots of 1970.

It appears that short-term setbacks had occurred for urban blacks in the
United States in the late 1960s when riots broke out in a number of cities. Both
political and economic conditions for blacks in the United States had improved
more in the decade preceding the riots than in any previous period of American
history. But during the summers of 1966 and 1967, in which riots occurred, a
large number of urban blacks were unemployed. In April 1968, when Martin
Luther King, Jr., the most important leader of the black political movement, was
killed, riots broke out in a large number of cities.

Neither of these contemporary cases is compelling. It should be remembered
that there was no revolution in the United States in the late 1960s or in Poland in
1970. The outbreak of riots is not the same as the outbreak of a revolution.

The theory of relative deprivation. Another way of generating a subjective
perspective that gives rise to frustration in the presence of improvement is
presented by the theorists of relative deprivation, exemplified by Runciman
(1966) and Gurr (1970). Their point of departure is this: As long as there is no
change in objective conditions, all persons are in the same boat. But when there
is rapid improvement in conditions, those of some improve more rapidly than
those of others. Those for whom conditions are not improving very rapidly see
others, perhaps no more qualified, doing much better than they are. It is from
this perspective that they perceive a widening gap, which leads them to feel

frustration and thus to revolt. Given that in a period of economic improvement, there are often more persons left behind than getting ahead, these feelings of frustration can be widespread.

This theoretical position can also be presented graphically. Figure 18.4 shows an individual's conditions, ordinarily economic, as a solid line. The dashed line graphs the objective conditions of others with whom he compares himself, persons he sees advancing more rapidly than he is. Thus from this perspective his own conditions appear bad.

This theory gains some credibility from empirical findings regarding relative deprivation. In *The American Soldier* Stouffer et al. (1949) found that morale was higher among officers in the military police, where promotion was very slow, than among officers in the Air Force, where promotion was very rapid. The authors (as well as Merton and Rossi, 1950, who extended and elaborated the thesis) attributed this to the relative deprivation experienced by the large number of officers in the Air Force who were moving up less rapidly than the fastest. The many incidences of rapid promotion created a vantage point, a perspective, from which each of the less rapidly promoted men could view his own situation. There was no revolt in the Air Force, so the assumption that increased frustration leads to revolt was not tested. There was, however, strong evidence that the perceived gap created by the rapid promotion of some was responsible for the lower morale.

The conditions in France prior to the revolution of 1789 might appear on the surface to support the theory of relative deprivation. As prosperity in France increased during the period preceding the revolution, the economic conditions of peasants worsened. But this theory would predict that revolutionary activity

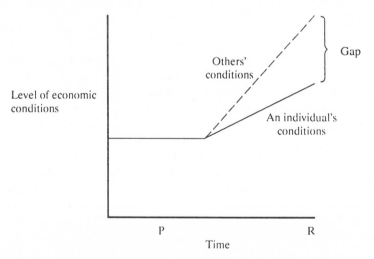

Figure 18.4 Predicted revolutionary potential: Gap created by relative deprivation.

would begin among the peasants. Instead it began among the Third Estate, whose economic conditions (but not political power) had improved. (The case in France actually appears to be more consistent with the next theory to be examined.)

The theory of status inconsistency. Another theoretical perspective on the genesis of frustration begins with the fact that in periods of rapid change status inconsistencies are created for a large number of persons. Many who have had little wealth or political power gain economic resources but find that their political position remains unchanged. Their improved economic circumstances lead them to expect a parallel increase in political power, an increase which does not come about.

Lenski (1954, p. 411) makes the general argument that when status inconsistencies are widespread, the population will support social change. Stone (1970), applying this to the English Revolution of 1640, shows that members of the gentry were experiencing increases in level of education, relative wealth, and social status, creating an inconsistency in their political power relative to that of the king. In his study of the English, American, French, and Russian revolutions, Brinton (1965) makes a similar argument, proposing that in all these societies there was a sense of being cramped or restrained among those who had become prosperous.

From this theoretical position the perspective from which one judges one's own situation as bad is created by a divergence of different aspects of one's condition. It is ordinarily the economic aspect that improves, while the political aspect remains unchanged. In Figure 18.5 the dashed line represents a person's

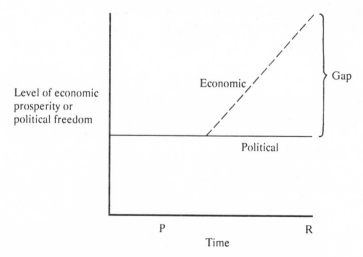

Figure 18.5 Predicted revolutionary potential: Gap created by status inconsistency.

improving economic condition, and the solid line represents his stable and low political position.

AN OVERVIEW OF THE FRUSTRATION THEORISTS   The theories described above have certain elements in common (and indeed are often grouped together). They agree that rapid improvement in conditions (political or economic for some, only economic for others) followed by a setback (for some, but not for others) generates a gap between expectations and reality. That gap in turn creates frustration. And the frustration in turn leads to aggression, which produces revolt. There are three links in the theoretical chain, corresponding exactly to the three kinds of relations involved in an explanation that goes from the macro to the micro level and back to the macro level, as shown in Figure 18.6.

The theories differ concerning only the first of these links, that is, in their hypotheses about the source of the expectations that differ from objective reality, generating the gap. These hypotheses are sufficiently distinct and precise that empirical evidence could be used to distinguish among them. It is tenable, of course, that all of them are true, that expectations divergent from reality may be created in any of the ways hypothesized by the frustration theorists. It seems more likely, however, that careful empirical examination would disconfirm some of these hypotheses. Whether an expectations gap is the first step toward revolution is another question.

It is worth noting certain additional points about these theories. The first of these is that they are wholly individualistic. It is true that the historians who make use of them do so as only one component of their explanations of particular revolutions. It is also true that some of the frustration theorists do introduce some nonindividualistic elements within their overall theories of revolution. For example, although I have characterized Gurr as one of the relative deprivation theorists, his more recent work (1986) is much more comprehensive and com-

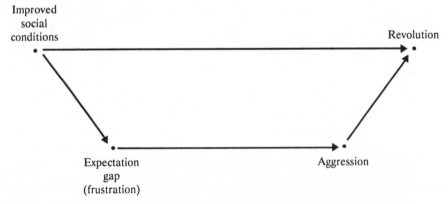

Figure 18.6   Micro-to-macro diagram for frustration theorists' explanation of revolutions.

bines a component of relative deprivation with elements from power theories of revolution (discussed in the next section). In addition, I have not fully presented the theoretical positions of the individual theorists, but have extracted from each the analytical components that facilitate comparison of different theoretical directions. Examination of work by the theorists themselves is necessary to gain an accurate picture of their overall theoretical positions.

Yet the kernel of these theories is the frustration-revolt hypothesis, which is individualistic. Frustration is a characteristic of individuals. A revolt or revolution is a social phenomenon. The micro-to-macro transition that is implicit in the frustration-revolt link is one of simple aggregation: The frustration simultaneously felt by a large segment of a population somehow aggregates or combines into the macro-social phenomenon known as revolt or revolution.

The general view of revolts that arises from this hypothesis is that they are spontaneous uprisings which are due to an aggregation of individual actions. But it is clear that revolutions are not like spontaneous riots, but are highly organized. Consequently, whatever the value of this theoretical approach, it does not explain revolts or revolutions. At most, it could account for the responsiveness of a population in general to an opportunity to revolt, an opportunity that is ordinarily created by an organized leadership.

Later in this chapter I will examine more closely the third link, the micro-to-macro transition. Focusing on the first link in the theoretical chain brings up a different objection to these theories. All of them begin with a macro-level empirical finding that presents an apparent anomaly—that revolutions occur when conditions are improving—and attempt to eliminate the anomaly while retaining the general proposition that a revolt occurs because people are more frustrated. The problem these theorists set for themselves is explaining how people can feel worse even though things are getting better. They do so in different ways, often ingeniously. What they do not question is whether in fact the improved conditions do make people feel worse.

The Power Theorists

If the idea that frustration is the precondition, at the level of individuals, of revolt or of support for revolutionaries is abandoned, it is no longer necessary to solve the puzzle of why improved conditions increase the level of frustration. But then it is necessary to have an alternative model of individual action which will account for the empirically observed phenomena of increased revolutionary activity and increased general support for this activity when conditions are improving, economically or politically. There is a group of theorists of revolution who have developed such an alternative model; I will call them the power theorists. They include Leites and Wolf (1970), Tullock (1974), Laqueur (1976), Oberschall (1978), and Tilly (1978). Others, including Goldstone (1986), share some of the power theorists' approach. My own work (Coleman, 1978a) has been in this direction.

If revolutionary activity and support for the revolutionary activity of others are regarded as rational actions, it becomes evident that such activity will be more likely to occur as those who have an interest in seeing the authority system replaced come to have a belief that they will succeed. And support for revolutionary activity among those who are committed to neither side but hope to be on the side of the winners will increase as their estimation of the revolutionaries' chances of success increases. It is irrational to revolt and dangerous to support those who do if the revolt will almost certainly be suppressed. There is an expected gain only when two conditions exist: when the expected gain if the authorities are overthrown is positive *and* the expectation of overthrowing the authorities is high. This can be put more precisely (in particular, it depends also on the expected costs of failure so long as there is a nonzero probability of failure), but the point should be clear: The likelihood of revolution should increase if either of these two factors increases.

Viewing revolutionary activity in this way allows one to interpret the widely observed empirical regularity described earlier in a different way. It raises the possibility that improved conditions might not increase frustration at all, and could even be decreasing it. The improved conditions might, however, increase the perceived chances of success of a revolution, for they add to the power and resources of those outside the regime.

Fanon (1972), in his call for revolutions of national liberation, argued that a principal effect of collective violence against European colonialists is to give the natives a belief in their ability to win. He implies that the principal deterrent to revolutionary activity is the absence of this belief and the holding of a belief in the omnipotence of Europeans.[7] The Tillys (Tilly, Tilly, and Tilly, 1975; Tilly, 1978), in their work on revolutions, have shown that revolutions are preceded by a variety of phenomena, including vacillation and weakness of the authorities, that give those interested in revolutionary activity a stronger belief that overt activity in opposition to the regime will be successful. Oberschall (1978) has drawn from the work of a number of investigators evidence that the period prior to overt revolutionary activity is one in which potential revolutionaries and political followers who see themselves as likely to be just as well off or better off under a different regime come to believe that a revolution can succeed.

The empirical regularity described earlier may therefore have a much simpler explanation than that offered by the frustration theorists. The effect of improved conditions may be to strengthen the belief of those opposed to the regime in their own power and potential for success, as well as to foster this belief among the

---

7. See also Jean-Paul Sartre's introduction in Fanon's book, which draws out the generalization more fully than does Fanon himself. Walzer (1977) argues that unfocused violence by rebels, or terrorism, if employed against civilians, is beyond the limits of the moral conduct of revolt. That may be, and Walzer's criticism of Sartre's fawning on the Algerian terrorists from the safety of the Boulevard St. Germain is well taken. Walzer does not, however, seem to recognize that the demonstration that those in authority are not all-powerful may be an important element in mobilization of support, especially among an oppressed people.

population as a whole, whose support in the end will go to the winning side. If this explanation of the empirical evidence is correct, the frustration theorists are completely wrong. Improved conditions make people feel better, not worse, but along with that better feeling comes an increased confidence in the likelihood of success of opposition to the regime. Unless the improved conditions greatly reduce dissatisfaction with the regime and thus undermine the belief that the regime is worse than one which might replace it (a belief which may not be easy to change, particularly if those in power represent a different class or ethnic group), the potential for revolution is increased.

A second point of the power theorists concerns the orientation of those in the general population who are not active in a revolt and who are uncommitted to either side. In societies with largely subsistence economies (such as Vietnam, El Salvador, or Nicaragua), that subgroup is likely to include most persons, unless the revolt is based on religious beliefs (such as the overthrow of the Shah in Iran in 1979), shared ethnicity, or national liberation. The power theorists assert that winning over the general population is unimportant; most persons' interest in the relative merits of different authority systems are far weaker than their interest in social order. That is, just as potential revolutionaries are mobilized into activity by a strengthening of their belief in their success, the support of those who have no interest in the outcome will be gained if they are seen as likely to succeed. Ultimately they will gain the right to exercise authority (that is, legitimacy) because of their power.

This means that revolutionaries' strategy should not be to win the support of the people, but to ensure that the people regard them as powerful. Leites and Wolf (1970) and Laqueur (1976) show that this was the strategy of terrorists and guerillas in Vietnam and elsewhere—not to win the support of the population but to immobilize it, to ensure through example that the population recognized that aid to the authorities would be swiftly and certainly punished. In such circumstances it seems unimportant whether the majority of the populace prefers the authorities or the revolutionaries; what is important is perceived power: what the people believe about the relative power of the two sides and about what will happen to them if they support one side or the other.

For the election in El Salvador in the spring of 1982, foreign journalists were unable to predict even the general direction of the outcome (which supported the rightist parties more than had been anticipated by the journalists). During the Vietnam War President Lyndon Johnson commissioned a survey of the population of South Vietnam, to discover the extent of support for the Viet Cong, for the South Vietnamese government, and for American intervention. The necessity for taking such a poll is evidence of the relatively passive stance of the population. The results indicated there was little support for the Viet Cong and somewhat more for the government; there was an absence of intense support for either side, an absence of patriotic fervor for defense against the North Vietnamese and of revolutionary fervor for overthrow of the regime. In both of these cases the absence of strong support for either the revolutionaries or the regime is consistent with the general thesis of the power theorists. The hearts and minds of the general populace seem not to have been fought over by the revolutionaries and the regime, nor did the people strongly support one side or the other.

The orientation of the general population is not, however, irrelevant to revolutionaries or authorities. The statement of Mao Zedong to the effect that rebels depend on the support of the people as much as fish depend on the water in which they swim expresses both the importance of the general population to the revolutionaries and its functional distinctiveness from the revolutionaries. The active protagonists in a revolutionary conflict need to be able to move freely without having their actions impeded. But they do not need the general population's active support. To gain the passive support that they need, imposing direct costs on the populace (which may use principally the incentive of fear) is more effective than setting up abstract goals which can provide only uncertain benefits in the future.

I have not yet discussed one problem addressed by the power theorists. I have described the potential revolutionaries as if they were wholly unified, in effect, a single individual who must decide whether it pays for him to act, a decision which depends on how likely it is that he will be able to overthrow the authorities. But the potential revolutionaries are not a single individual. The decision for each of them is one concerning his action only. He must ask how likely it is that the authorities will be overthrown if he joins in the revolutionary activity and if he does not. In effect, the revolution is a public good, and, like any public good, it gives rise to the free-rider problem. Its realization will depend on others' efforts as well as his own. Unless he is extremely important to the revolution's success, that success will depend much more on efforts of others than on his efforts; and the less important he is to the revolution's success, the less his contribution to that success will be a motivating factor for him.

It is possible to illustrate the motivational situation for the potential activist by using a device similar to the common project described in Chapters 10 and 11. Suppose that success of the revolution is worth 100 to the potential activist and that if others pursue revolutionary activity, he sees a 50% chance of the revolution's succeeding. His participation will, he estimates, increase that chance of success by 1 percent. But participation is dangerous (even if he neglects the cost of participation in terms of other activities forgone), because of the possibility of punishment by the authorities. Suppose he estimates the cost of that punishment as 20 (using the scale in which success of the revolution means 100 to him). Punishment is certain if others do not act, but has only a 50 percent chance of occurring if others do act. Then the net benefit for him of acting if others do not act is -20, and if others do act is $(50 + 1 - 20 \times .5) - 50$, or $41 - 50$, or -9. The net benefits for him, contingent on his acting and the others' acting, are shown in Table 18.1. The table shows that if others do not act, he has an expected loss of 20 if he acts, and if others do act, he still has an expected loss of 9. Thus whether others act or not, it is to his interest not to act.

Examining the decision facing each potential activist rather than treating all

Table 18.1 Net benefits to potential revolutionary contingent on his acting and on others' acting.

		Others	
		Act	Not act
Self	Act	41	-20
	Not act	50	0

the potential activists as though they were a single corporate actor raises a problem for a theory of revolution. This problem is ignored by most frustration theorists but is generally discussed by those theorists I have called power theorists (as reflected by the term "mobilization theorists" used by Oberschall, 1978, in his review of theories of conflict, to characterize them). Their treatment is weak, however, and the problem remains for revolutionary theory. It also arises in practice for opponents to authorities. Authorities have the social capital provided by the governing organization; there is no comparable source of social capital available to their opponents. Yet social capital is not the only means by which the problem of inducing participation is solved by those with an interest in overthrowing the regime. I will examine the various ways more systematically later in this chapter.

The Frustration Theorists versus the Power Theorists

There are, then, two major directions of theoretical work on revolutions, what I have termed frustration theories and power theories. The frustration theories differ in two ways from the theoretical orientation of this book. First, the micro-level component is that of expressive action rather than purposive action. Second, the micro-to-macro transition is implicitly made by simple aggregation and does not take into account problems concerning participation. These two differences are related: If the action of individuals is merely expressive, then there is no macro-level purpose. The overthrowing of authorities is merely an outcome of these actions taken together, and nothing more. It is possible, of course, to overlay purposive action on expressive action, by imputing strategic behavior to leaders and expressive behavior to the followers. That is what some frustration theorists have done.

The work of the power theorists is, in contrast, generally compatible with the theoretical orientation of this book. The compatibility lies in two areas: first, in a micro-level foundation that is purposive rather than expressive; and second, in a recognition that the micro-to-macro transition in the case of a revolt is problematic in both theory and practice.

In later sections I will build on these foundations and give the outlines of a theory of revolts and revolutions that follows directly the theoretical structure of this book. First, however, I wish to present one empirical puzzle and several empirical generalizations about revolutions.

A Puzzle: Is Frustration Increasing?

If the general thesis of the frustration theorists is not correct, how can the apparent empirical validity of the idea that frustration is increasing prior to a revolt be accounted for? It is clear from historical materials that the level of frustration is especially high before some revolutions. This can be seen especially well in the lists of grievances compiled at the local level preceding the French Revolution, as well as in numerous other cases.[8] It is on such empirical evidence that the ideas of the frustration theorists are based. The answer is, I believe, straightforward. If opponents of an authority system come to have a strong belief in their own power to overthrow the regime, one consequence will be a sense of frustration that the regime remains in power. But this frustration will be only an epiphenomenon, an incidental consequence of the opponents' increased belief in their own capabilities. The frustration is without consequence, despite its occurrence preceding the revolt. It does serve as a measure of the potential for action, but the consequences are not due to the frustration, but to the components that give rise to it: the existing dissatisfaction with the current authority system, and the newly acquired belief that there is some possibility of change.

A concrete example will make this point clearer. From 1967 through most of the 1970s, Palestinian Arabs of the West Bank were not supporters of the PLO. Following 1970 came a period of unprecedented prosperity for the West Bank, as a result of employment opportunities in Israel and the development (with the aid of Israeli authorities) of local industry. Then, in the late 1970s and 1980s, there were some acts of terrorism by West Bank youths, including actions against elected mayors of West Bank towns who served under overall Israeli authority. By 1986 a survey carried out under independent auspices showed widespread support for the PLO and opposition to the Israeli authorities. By 1988 that opposition had increased dramatically: Arab boys threw rocks at Israeli cars venturing into the West Bank, acts of arson were the cause of fires in Israeli forests, West Bank women sewed PLO flags, and acts of rebellion in West Bank towns increased in frequency. All of this follows the pattern noted by theorists of

8. See Markoff and Shapiro (1985) for analysis of the *cahiers de doleances*.

revolution and appears to show increased frustration despite a period of economic prosperity.

What happened in this case? The interest of West Bank Arabs in living under non-Israeli authority did not change during this period. Several other things did change, however:

1. The PLO gained increased legitimacy outside the West Bank.
2. The terrorist actions against Israeli-recognized mayors of West Bank towns and against Israeli occupation forces showed that the opponents to Israeli occupation had some power.
3. Certain actions that were taken by the authorities and by religious-nationalistic Jews (encroaching on land in the Muslim quarter of the Old City of Jerusalem, erecting a yeshiva in the center of an Arab residential area, destroying olive trees on land regarded by Arabs as theirs) were seen as illegitimate by West Bank Arabs.
4. New institutions (principally West Bank colleges), not controlled by the older generations through the family, came into being on the West Bank.

The first and second of these changes increased the legitimacy of the PLO within the West Bank, and the third decreased the legitimacy of the Israeli authorities and Israeli-recognized West Bank authorities. The second change increased the belief that opposition to Israeli authority was powerful enough to overturn it, and the fourth provided social organization that was controlled by the young, independent of family-based and Israeli-sponsored authority.

This case again shows that the observation that frustration with authorities grows during periods of economic prosperity is not incorrect. What is incorrect is the failure to recognize that frustration is not a cause of rebellion, that expressions of frustration are consequences of the same change that leads to rebellious actions. That change is ordinarily an increased belief that rebellious action will be successful, or at least will not be immediately punished.

One can see rebellious action as the product of two quantities: dissatisfaction with the existing social order, and belief that action in opposition to that social order will be successful. Why did West Bank Arab boys begin to throw rocks at Israeli cars, when they had not done so before? Because they came to believe they could "get away with it." Their parents and other adults in the village would not punish them for doing so, as they had earlier. Why would the adults no longer punish them? Because parents would no longer be punished by village authorities for their childrens' actions. Why would the parents not be punished? Because a new elite in the community, unrecognized by Israeli authorities, was challenging with some success the Israeli-recognized elite, based on patriarchal social structure and supporting the existing (Israeli-imposed) social order. Why did the population of the West Bank become receptive to an elite that challenged the existing social order? Because of actions taken by Israelis that undermined the legitimacy of their authority and of Israeli-approved West Bank authority. Why was the new elite able to take advantage of this opportunity? Because of organizational resources provided by new institutions (the West Bank colleges, newspapers, and new economic enterprises) and financial resources provided from outside.

In the French Revolution why did the peasants burn manor houses and crowds storm the Bastille in Paris? Because these people had longstanding dissatisfactions and grievances. But why did they not riot earlier? Because at the time they did there was a challenge, not immediately suppressed, to the existing social order (the existing allocation of rights) by the nobles and especially by the Third Estate. They began to believe they could "get away with it." The system of sanctions imposed by the existing social order had begun to show weakness. Why did the Third Estate challenge the existing allocation of rights? Because their social and economic resources had increased greatly, and the challenge to the king by the nobles led them to believe they could "get away with it."

These and other examples indicate that the puzzle facing the power theorists, that frustration is increasing prior to a revolt, can be satisfactorily resolved without assuming that increased frustration is responsible for rebellious action. If dissatisfactions are already present but have been suppressed by a set of sanctions imposed by the existing social order, then anything that weakens those sanctions will increase both the expressions of frustration and the likelihood of revolutionary activity, or rebellious action. Because the sanctions are upheld by a complex structure of authority, there are various types of changes that can weaken them.

Comparative Macrosocial Research: Inequality, Economic Development, and Repressiveness

An additional set of empirical generalizations relevant to revolutions is found in a body of research other than that I have discussed so far. This is comparative research on political violence, which takes countries as its units of analysis. Such analyses have used data on differing numbers of countries (ranging from 25 to 126) and have examined the statistical dependence of the amount of political violence (measured by deaths attributed to political violence) on inequality of income, level of economic development, and (in two analyses) repressiveness of the political regime. Analyses have been carried out by Sigelman and Simpson (1977), Weede (1981; 1987), and Muller (1985). The research discussed in earlier sections of this chapter examines changes in a society in the period preceding a revolution; this research examines stable structural differences in societies with differing amounts of political violence. It addresses different questions about the causes of revolution, ones that are nevertheless relevant to a theory of revolutions.

One branch of the frustration theorists of revolution discussed earlier argues that frustration arises from relative deprivation. It is this theoretical position to which inequality of income is most relevant. If such inequality is associated with political violence, this would provide some confirmation of that theoretical position. Among the five analyses only one, that of Muller (1985), shows a relation of any magnitude between inequality of income and political violence, in a regression equation in which level of economic development and amount of repression were statistically controlled. In a reanalysis Weede (1986) demonstrates the fragility of this result (its dependence on a particular lag structure) and in a subsequent analysis (1987) with three different data sets finds small and inconsistent relations. Thus analyses involving inequality of income give results inhospitable to the relative deprivation form of frustration theory.

The second property of societies examined in this comparative research on political violence is the level of economic development, and the results are not relevant to either the power theories or the frustration theories. Some of these analyses find a lower level of political violence where the level of economic development is higher, but others find the reverse. All that can be said is that these analyses show no consistent relation of level of economic development to political violence.

The third property, repressiveness of the regime, shows a curvilinear relation to political violence, a result first found by Muller (1985). Countries with high and low levels of repression have lower levels of political violence than do countries with intermediate levels of repression. Weede (1987) regards this result as evidence in favor of the power theories (it is irrational to rebel if repression is extremely great but may be rational to do so if it is less great), but my interpretation of the power theorists' position is that they would predict a monotonic decrease in rebellion as repression increased. In contrast, the frustration theorists would predict a monotonic *increase* in rebellion as repression increased. Thus the observed curvilinear relation is not, I believe, predicted by either theoretical approach.

It is, however, not reasonable to treat repression as exogenous. The amount of repression clearly depends on the potential amount of violence. This is not the only factor determining the level of repression, but it is certainly an important one. Thus it is incorrect to treat the repressiveness of a regime as independent of the political violence directed against the regime. When that is done, as it is in the analyses of Muller (1985) and Weede (1987), the apparent effects of repression on political violence will not be true effects. In the absence of better-specified models of what happens at the macro level (according to one or the other of the theories), the statistical relation between political violence and repression does not provide evidence for or against either theoretical approach.

Ideology in Revolutions

One other empirical generalization that must be noted is the importance of ideas, or ideology, in many revolutions. The two best examples in revolutions and revolts of the past four centuries are Protestant religious doctrine and Marxist political doctrine.

In the revolutions of the mid–sixteenth century throughout Europe, the role of

Protestantism in the overthrow of secular authority was natural, because the religious authority it challenged was extensively interwoven with that secular authority. The Protestant Reformation and its aftermath were central to three of the four (the Fronde was the fourth) great revolutions of the late sixteenth and seventeenth centuries: the English Revolution of 1640, the war of independence of the Netherlands from Spain, and the French civil war. Stone (1970) describes as one of the three most important preconditions of the English Revolution "the spread through large sectors of the propertied classes of a diffuse Puritanism, the most important political consequence of which was to create a burning sense of the need for change in the church and eventually in the state" (p. 96). Hume (1985 [1778]), writing in the middle of the eighteenth century about England in the seventeenth century, saw in the Puritans a combination of "enthusiasm" and an attachment to civil liberty that led to contempt for authority.

The linkage of Protestantism to twentieth-century revolts and rebellions is less obvious but nevertheless present. For example, in Africa the role of religion, particularly Protestantism, in the post–World War II anticolonial revolts appears to have been indirect, but significant. For example, there was a strong correspondence between Protestant missionary activity and anticolonial activity in Nigeria (James Smoot Coleman, 1958). The Protestant religious doctrine had no overt connection to secular revolt there; the missionaries did not preach anticolonial doctrine to the natives as their predecessors had preached against the state church in England and Europe in the seventeenth century. The connection appears to be more subtle than that. Earlier, in China, the connection between Protestant missionary activity and rebellion is unmistakable. The Taiping Rebellion of 1850 was initiated by missionary-educated Christians. The principal leader of the 1911 revolution, Sun Yat-sen, was a convert to Christianity. The student revolts in South Korea during the 1980s have some links to Protestant churches.

Although Protestantism is, among the world's religions, the most widely associated with revolution, there are many examples where other religions have been directly involved in revolts and uprisings. Fundamentalist and irredentist Islam not only was central to the bloodless revolution of 1979 in Iran, but also constitutes a potential revolutionary force in many Asian and African countries. In Ireland and in some Latin American countries, Catholicism is directly connected with revolt.

By far the most important ideology for twentieth-century revolutions, however, is not religious but secular—Marxism. Its role in Asian, African, and South American revolts and revolutions is apparent.

Why should this be so? What kind of role does religious ideology or Marxist ideology play in helping to bring about revolution? The answer appears to be in part that these ideologies provide a utopian vision, as an alternative to the existing allocation of rights in a society. In both Protestant religious ideology and Marxism, there is a vision of utopia; furthermore, the two visions have much in common: Both posit a world of equality, communal sharing, absence of internal social strife, and transformed human nature. The visions of utopia are definitions of what is right that come from authorities that can challenge existing authority: from God, as the supreme being; or from scientific socialism, as an objective source of truth.

Even in some internal revolts the role of utopian ideology is important, as it was in student revolts in Europe and America in the 1960s. For example, a report of the student revolt at Columbia University states,

> One of the causes of the April disturbances was the organized effort of a tiny group of students, within the SDS, whose object was to destroy the university as a corrupt pillar of an evil society . . . [T]here were many more, attracted to SDS, for sundry and idealistic reasons, who talked—and in April 1968 lived—revolution, half seriously and half in a dream world. (Cox Commission, 1968, p. 58)

As this quotation indicates, the utopian vision provided by some religions or (as in this case) Marxism appears important both for the nucleus of extreme activists and for a larger group which surrounds them and which is mobilized during the period leading up to the revolt.

It should be clear, of course, that religion does not always play the same role, even when it is important to the conflict. For example, the role of Catholicism in Ireland in the conflict leading to independence and later in Northern Ireland has clearly not been to provide an alternative utopian vision of what is right. It appears to have been to provide an organizational base reflecting the ethnic and economic divisions in the society.

If it is true that the utopian vision of Protestant and Marxist ideologies is the principal source of their importance for revolts and revolutions, a question still remains: Just what kind of role does that vision play and for which actors in the conflict? Where does it fit in a purposively grounded theory of revolution? That question will be addressed after the basic outlines of the theory are presented.

A Theoretical Framework of Revolution

The Social Structure of Revolts and Rebellions

Revolts and revolutions are not ordinarily mass uprisings. Typically a revolution involves only a very small part of the population as activists, either on the side of the revolutionaries or on the side of the authorities. The images evoked by some theories of revolution, particularly what I have described as the frustration theories, do not correspond to this reality, being images of a whole population engaging in a massive spontaneous revolt.

There are revolts in which large fractions of the population are involved, but these uprisings are preceded by other critical events. The initial actions are taken by a small set of activists who have already withdrawn rights of control over their actions from the authorities. The success of those actions, sometimes reinforced by weakness on the part of the authorities or by parallel withdrawal of legitimacy by elites on whom the authorities depend for support and for sanctions, may then lead to larger, more massive uprisings, among segments of the population with longstanding grievances. (The processes involved occur on a less-compressed time scale, but appear to be like those that occur in a hostile crowd or in looting, where the change preceding any mass action is withdrawal of rights of control from the authorities; see Chapter 9.) These massive uprisings then may feed back to strengthen the challenge to authority by the activists. But any such massive uprisings are only part of a social process initiated by actions of a few activists. And in many revolutions, such as those in Southeast Asia in the 1960s, 1970s, and 1980s and those in Latin America in the 1980s, the fraction of the population ever actively involved is small.

In revolts against the authority of institutions within a state (such as the student revolts of the 1960s), the fraction of those potentially involved who ever actually become involved is also ordinarily small. In the Columbia University crisis of 1968, which was one of the largest campus revolts, less than 10% of the student body was involved as active participants in the conflict; the SDS, which constituted the principal activist body, was composed of only about 50–100 students, out of a total student body numbering 13,000. Within the SDS it was "a tiny group of students" (Cox Commission, 1968, p. 58) whose aim was wholly revolutionary: to destroy the university as part of the authority structure of society. The Cox Commission report estimated (p. 165) that at the height of the conflict, on April 29, there were 700–1,000 students inside the buildings and 2,000 outside. Most of those outside were not active participants.

Similarly, in community conflicts which constitute revolts against local government or school authorities, the fraction of the population that is actively involved is small—despite the fact that such conflicts are ordinarily resolved by a vote by the citizens, creating strong incentives for the authorities and their opponents to mobilize the population. Here, as in the case of other revolts, the logic of free riding makes it not in the interest of an individual to act, unless the costs are very low or there are some benefits from participation generated by those in the immediate vicinity (as described in the discussion in Chapter 11 of the conditions under which the logic of free riding is transformed into the logic of zealotry).

As these cases indicate, revolts do not involve a simple two-party structure, with the authorities as one party and the population, considered as a homogeneous mass, as the other. The opponents of the authorities are ordinarily a very small subgroup of the population at the beginning of a revolt, and most of the populace is not active on either side. But even those who are initially uninvolved differ in various ways relevant to the conflict. They cannot be characterized according to a single dimension alone (such as their relation to the means of production, which is how Marxist theory characterizes them). Any population is differentiated in many ways: region, ethnicity, age, class, economic status, and so forth. What is relevant from the point of view of a theory of revolution is the relation of members of the population to authoritative actions. If government policy distinguishes (or could distinguish) among ethnic groups, economic classes, sexes, or regions, then these distinctions will be relevant to a revolt—for the distinctions that government policy makes create different interests in government actions.

For example, prior to the French Revolution the interests of the nobles, the Third Estate, and the peasants were all different: The nobles wanted the king to share authority with them; the Third Estate had an interest in gaining representation in governance commensurate with its increased economic power; the peasants wanted economic benefits. These interests did not produce the same actions from the three groups, but the actions of each group in opposition to the king interacted with the actions of the others to bring about a revolution. At Columbia University in 1968 the SDS activists were opposed to the university's indirect involvement in the Vietnam conflict. The black community groups were opposed to construction of a university gymnasium on city park land. The members of SAS, who were black, as well as some white students, wanted to show solidarity with the black community groups. Other students had miscellaneous grievances against the university authorities. It was the interaction between the actions of these different groups that led to the revolt in the spring of 1968.

The social structure often changes over the course of a revolt; a number of the nonparticipants may come to actively support the opponents of the authorities, and in some cases others come to actively support the authorities. (In the student revolts of the late 1960s, there was ordinarily a group of students who actively supported the university authorities. At Columbia University these were known as "the jocks"; in the 1968 revolt of French university students at Nanterre, they were known as "Occident.") Yet even at the height of a revolt or revolution, inactive members of the population continue to constitute the largest segment. This inactive group, however, may have some impact on the outcome of the revolt. Although they are not engaged in overturning the authority structure, they will either continue to vest rights of control in the authorities or withdraw those rights. Whichever they do may in turn have an effect on others' actions.

Two kinds of questions must therefore be asked concerning the micro level of a revolt as a system of action. One is about an individual's decision to take some action in support of the revolt, and the other is about an individual's decision to continue to vest rights of control in the authorities. I will examine these in turn.

The Costs and Benefits of Acting for the Individual

It is important to clarify the position that the individual is in with respect to costs and benefits that may result from taking action. First, there is the impact of the existing authorities' policies on his interests as he defines them (and his perceptions of what will be the policies of the opponents). Second, there are the potential actions that may be taken by the authorities or the opponents to encourage participation on their side or discourage participation in support of the other side. Finally, and this may be most important for many persons, there are positive or negative sanctions that may be imposed by others in the immediate vicinity, in response to actions in support of the authorities or the opponents. If those in the immediate vicinity have not withdrawn legitimacy from the authorities, these sanctions will encourage support for the authorities and discourage support for the opponents. If they have withdrawn legitimacy without giving it to the opponents, the sanctions will discourage any actions. If they have transferred legitimacy to the opponents, the sanctions will encourage actions supporting the opponents and discourage those supporting the authorities. This aspect of the situation confronting the potential activist is described by Mao Zedong's statement that revolutionaries depend on the support of the people as fish depend on the water in which they swim.

For individuals who have some interest in seeing the power of the authorities overturned, the question of whether to take action toward that outcome depends on the estimated costs and benefits of such action. The potential costs may arise from any of several sources, but as a starting point it can be assumed that they are due to the authorities quelling the revolt and punishing the participants. The anticipated costs, then, are these potential costs modified by the perceived chance that they will in fact be experienced. The potential benefits also may come from various sources, but it can be assumed that they come only from seeing the authorities' power overturned. The anticipated benefits from acting are those potential benefits modified by the difference that the individual believes his action will make toward achieving this outcome.

These elements can be put in the form of a simple inequality, similar to that proposed for a potential trustor in Chapter 5. The terms of the inequality are as follows:

L is the possible losses (costs) from engaging in revolutionary activity.

G is the possible gains (benefits) from engaging in such activity.

p is the individual's estimate of the probability that the revolt will be successful *if* he participates ($p - q$ is the probability of its success without his participation).

q is the individual's estimate of the probability that *his action* will bring about the success of the revolt.

r is the individual's estimate of the probability that he will be punished for participation, if he participates and the revolt is unsuccessful.

If the total expected costs of participation are assumed to be those resulting from possible punishment by the authorities, then the individual's expected costs are $r(1 - p)L$. If punishment is certain, then the anticipated costs of taking action are $(1 - p)L$, and the anticipated benefits are qG. It is rational to engage in revolutionary activity if and only if qG is greater than $r(1 - p)L$.

But here, unlike the case of placing trust, q and $r(1 - p)$ do not sum to 1.0. The chance that the individual will be punished by the authorities if he participates,

$r(1 - p)$, is not simply the complement of the chance that his action will bring about overturn of the authorities, q. In fact q is in nearly all cases extremely small. Unless the individual believes the revolution is reasonably likely to succeed and sees his participation as central to that success, q will be quite small. Even if he thinks the revolution is very likely to succeed, unless his participation will make a reasonably large difference to that success, q will be small. On these grounds it would appear that a revolt would never be initiated by rational individuals, no matter how strongly they opposed the authorities.

Some other points are pertinent, however. The authorities may be unlikely to punish participation (because of humanitarian reasons, because the regime is ineffectual, because enough of the population has withdrawn legitimacy from the regime that participation is protected, or because those on whom the authorities depend for sanctioning actions against them have been terrorized into not cooperating with the authorities). If this is the case, then r is much less than 1, and the anticipated cost, $r(1 - p)L$, is low, even if the revolution appears likely to fail. Or punishment may be minimal (because of humanitarian reasons or because of widespread protest by a population that has withdrawn legitimacy from the regime). If this is the case, then the anticipated cost is low, even if punishment is nearly certain. Thus whatever might reduce the anticipated costs of participation can lower the threshold that the anticipated benefits must exceed to make participation reasonable.

More generally, if there are some benefits that do not depend on the value of the individual's participation for the revolution's success, then revolutionaries or authorities can develop strategies to induce participation. If there are some costs that do not depend on overall success or failure of the revolt, then revolutionaries or authorities can develop strategies to suppress participation.

THREE SETS OF BENEFITS ASSOCIATED WITH REVOLUTIONARY ACTIVITY It is useful to distinguish three major sets of benefits an individual may receive as a result of participating in revolutionary activity.

The first set of benefits, G_1, is composed of those already discussed, the benefits that the individual expects if there is a change in the regime. These benefits are almost independent of the individual's participation: They will be gained with probability p if he participates and with probability $p - q$ if he does not, where q is ordinarily very small. Thus, if one does not participate, one's expected benefits from this source are $(p - q)G_1$; if one does participate, one's expected benefits are pG_1. The incentive to participate is qG_1. This will ordinarily be very small because q is so small.

The second set of benefits, G_2, comprises those that are dependent both on individual participation and on the success of the revolt. The principal benefits in this set are those that result from the revolutionaries' gaining power, such as a position in the new regime. These are material benefits and are in scarce supply. They can only be offered to individuals whose participation is relatively important to the success of the revolt. These benefits are analogous to what Olson

(1965) calls selective incentives, which are available only to participants but not to all participants, because of the limited supply. These benefits, when they exist, are contingent both on participation and on success of the revolt. Thus the motivation they provide for a participant is pG_2, which is directly dependent on the perceived chance that the revolution will succeed.

The third set of benefits, G_3, is composed of those that result from participation alone and are *independent* of whether the revolt is successful. These benefits ordinarily derive from two sources, and it is important to distinguish between them.

One source is the individual's friends and immediate associates, who provide part of the social capital available to the individual. If friends are participating, the reciprocal rewards can constitute a substantial benefit from participation, one that is contingent on nothing but participation and the simultaneous participation of those close to one. But as the discussion of zealous action in Chapter 11 shows, such mutual reinforcement depends not only on action, but on a shared goal toward which each is acting. In the case of a revolution, of course, this goal is success of the revolution. Thus the existence of a common goal among persons in a structure with a high degree of closure appears to be a prerequisite for this source of benefits.

It may be here that utopian ideology plays a role. A vision of utopia held by all members of a group in close association can promote a setting within which heroism and zealotry blossom.[9] If this conjecture is correct, then the role of utopian ideology is an extremely important one. The ideology provides the content which allows the closed group to generate reciprocal rewards—a set of rewards that is not conditional on one's estimate of the success of the revolt or on the size of one's own contribution toward that success. If this source of benefits is an important one, then that implies that a revolutionary cadre should be exceedingly tightly knit, with a high degree of closure. Unity of purpose and unity of action among those in association, with no dissension about overall aims, can provide mutual rewards. Records of this are found in accounts of revolutionary and rebellious activity. For example, students who engaged in occupation of university buildings or other prolonged collective actions during the protests of the 1960s have reported afterward that the spirit and the collective euphoria they experienced made the period a high point in their lives.[10]

A second source of benefits which derive from participation alone is internal. As described in Chapter 11, internalized norms and the sanctions supporting them can exert a force of their own. If one has come to hold an ideology containing a utopian vision, then working toward the realization of that vision generates internal psychic rewards, independent of the surrounding social capital. Again, if this conjecture about the role of utopian ideology is correct, the

9. The heroism and zealotry are induced by the rewards provided by others for actions that bring positive externalities, as discussed in Chapter 11.

10. This is evident in writings such as those presented by Avorn (1968) describing the events at Columbia University in the spring of 1968.

importance of such ideology can be great because the benefits it generates depend only on participation, not on success of the revolt or on effectiveness of the individual's participation in bringing about that success.

THREE SETS OF COSTS ASSOCIATED WITH REVOLUTIONARY ACTIVITY There are also three sets of costs, or losses, an individual may experience from participation in a revolt.

A first set of possible costs, L_1, comprises those discussed earlier, costs due to punishment by the regime for participation if the revolt fails. These costs are ordinarily high for leaders of the revolt but may be low for peripheral participants, especially if the fraction of the population participating is large.

A second set of possible costs, L_2, is composed of those due to sanctions imposed by the authorities or by supporters of the authorities during the course of the conflict. These costs do not depend on the chance that the revolt will fail but on whether some supporters have withdrawn legitimacy from the authorities, on the regime's benevolence, incompetence, or weakness, and on the degree to which the individual's actions are insulated from the sanctions because large numbers of persons have withdrawn legitimacy from the regime or have become fellow participants. These costs also depend on the individual's position in the social structure, as long as others have not withdrawn legitimacy from the authorities. Those with the least to lose with regard to social position (such as young people) have the lowest costs of this sort. This second set of costs is uncertain: Sanctions may occur even if the revolt ultimately succeeds, because there is the possibility of punishment during the course of the revolt. Sanctions may not be imposed if the revolt fails, because of various reasons mentioned earlier (benevolence or incompetence of the regime, or support from nonparticipants who have withdrawn legitimacy from the regime). Thus the chance of incurring this set of costs can be taken as roughly equal to the chance that the revolt will fail, but greater or less than that chance because of particular characteristics of the authorities or other factors.

A third set of costs, L_3, consists of the various personal costs associated with participation and independent of the success of the revolt and sanctions from others. These include the giving up of activities, associations, and friendships that are inconsistent with or irrelevant to participating in the revolt.

THE PUZZLE OF MASS PARTICIPATION There is an important empirical puzzle that I must address directly. This is the problem of mass participation. Because the outcome of a revolt is almost independent of any individual's participation (unless the individual is a leader of the revolt or a high authority), the benefits of that outcome are almost independent of an individual's participation and provide him with no incentive to act. In fact, participation is often costly and sometimes even leads to death. Yet in some revolts there is mass participation. How can this be?

The earlier discussion of the benefits that arise from participation alone, together with the discussion in Chapter 11 of free riding and zeal, indicates how mass participation can occur in this structure, which would otherwise generate free-rider behavior. If the costs or benefits one experiences from others in the immediate vicinity is important and if those others have vested legitimacy in the revolutionaries, then participation in support of the revolt will elicit the rewards. Thus, if there is homogeneity of individuals' orientation to the revolt within groups showing extensive internal communication, zealous action that is collectively self-sustaining can arise. The same setting would, in the absence of that homogeneity, generate free riding, that is, nonparticipation.

The Divesting of Authority

In every system where revolt against authority occurs, there are many persons who have vested rights of control in the established authority. Some of these may come to be involved in the conflict in the ways described above, either on the side of those engaged in revolt or on the side of the authorities. But for many the anticipated costs of acting for either side are greater than the anticipated benefits. For these persons another question arises: whether to divest authority, to withdraw from those in authority the right to control their actions. As indicated earlier in this chapter, this withdrawal alone is seldom sufficient to modify greatly the power of those in office. Nevertheless it can have considerable consequence, depending on the circumstances. If one's approval or disapproval constitutes a sanction for others, then one's withdrawal of legitimacy from those in authority can be important in freeing others to do the same or to participate actively in the revolt. Thus divesting of authority can be contagious, through the processes described in Chapter 9.

Those who continue to regard the authority structure as legitimate must decide on some basis for or against continuing to vest authority in those who have been in authority and continue to hold power. In contrast to active participation, which may carry heavy costs of types L_1, L_2, and L_3, an individual's withdrawal of rights of control from authorities may involve only a few costs of type L_3 if not accompanied by overt support of the revolt.

The question of whether to divest authority leads back to the question of why authority is vested in the first place, in creating a corporate actor such as a state, a trade union, or a voluntary association. As discussed in Chapter 13, the reason lies in the elimination of negative externalities that exist in a Hobbesian war of each against all and in the realization of positive externalities from joint action (such as common defense). Authority, or the right to control certain actions, is vested in a corporate actor when the individual expects that such vesting will have these results.

What can lead to divesting of authority? Stated most generally, the answer is a loss of confidence that the investment continues to be a good one. This loss of confidence can occur with respect to the intentions of the authorities or their capability of continuing to govern effectively. There are numerous sources of such loss of confidence. The multiplicity of ways in which this loss of confidence can arise partly accounts for the individuality of various revolts and revolutions. In some cases loss of confidence is due to weakness of the state in external relations, economic or political. Skocpol (1979) points to the importance of such weakness in the period preceding the French, Russian, and Chinese revolutions. The loss of confidence in governing institutions in the United States between 1966 and 1979, as indicated by the poll results graphed in Figure 5.1, was clearly due, at least in part, to the failure of the government to prosecute the Vietnam War effectively.

In many cases the loss of confidence is due to weakness or vacillation manifested by the authorities in internal affairs. Histories of prerevolutionary periods are full of examples of such vacillation and weakness. The loss of confidence by many Americans during the early 1950s in their government's ability to cope with internal subversion was so great that it could have been a component, if other circumstances had been propitious, of an organized revolt. Instead it led to, among other things, the election as president of Dwight Eisenhower, a wartime general in whom many had confidence. The vacillation of the president of Columbia University in the fall of 1967 and early 1968 in coping with the disturbances by the SDS on the campus led to a loss of confidence in his administration on the part of many students and faculty members. At the same time it increased the confidence of the SDS in its own capabilities. This case also illustrates a common error on the part of authorities, which compounds the loss of confidence: using compromise from a position of weakness as a tactic for pacifying dissident groups, an action that is seen as a further sign of weakness.

When there is a growing challenge to existing authority, in the form of a revolutionary cadre or other structure, the very existence of an alternative may lead those who have not done so before to question their current vesting of authority. Thus the growth of an active opposition can itself help bring about a withdrawal of rights of control from existing authorities on the part of those who are not, and never will be, activists.

As a revolutionary movement develops, its viability as an alternative to the existing authority structure can lead persons not only to divest authority from the existing regime but to vest authority in the challengers. The extent to which this occurs depends primarily on the estimated probability of success of the revolt (labeled p earlier). This estimated probability, in turn, may depend for many persons on the trust they place in the judgment of intermediaries, as discussed in Chapter 8. Thus there can be a contagious or bandwagon effect if many persons have placed trust in the judgment of others regarding public affairs.

Both evidence of external weakness and evidence of internal weakness can lead to loss of confidence in authorities' capability of governing effectively. Ordinarily a given class or ethnic group or status group loses confidence that the authorities will attend to their interests. This can arise when a group gains economic power or other resources without gaining positions of authority or a voice in the corporate body. For example, in Lebanon in the early 1970s the size of the Muslim portion of the population had increased greatly relative to the Christian part, but the government structure had not changed to reflect this; positions were still allocated on the basis of a demographic balance that existed at the time of the state's founding. The ensuing revolts, beginning in 1972, reflected the Muslims' dissatisfaction with this condition. Before the English Revolution of 1640, there was extensive loss of confidence in the capability of King Charles I to govern effectively, but there was also extensive growth in the economic power of the gentry, which induced in them a lack of confidence in the king's attention to their interests. Prior to the French Revolution, the growth in wealth and power of the Third Estate, accompanied by the lack of any increase in its formal role in the authority structure, encouraged a loss of confidence in the king's attention to its interests. As a more recent and lower-level example, the city manager form of government, which had been instituted in many cities in the United States, was subsequently overthrown in a number of these cities after certain groups lost confidence in its attention to nonbusiness interests (Stene and Floro, 1953).

Divesting of authority is not, however, entirely dependent on confidence in a regime's ability to govern effectively. There are, in fact, two actions under consideration here. One is a divestment from an existing regime and the other is subsequent vesting in another regime. The former can occur without the latter, as happened when the public lost confidence in various authorities in the United States in the late 1960s and early 1970s (see Figure 5.1). But divestment can also occur because an alternative set of ideas and ideals arises to contend for legitimacy. This is a role that ideology plays, particularly religious ideology that is either nonhierarchical or utopian in character and Marxist ideology. Ideological challenges to the authority of a given regime can bring about both actions at once: divestment and reinvestment of legitimacy.

It is important to note the divesting of authority and revesting of authority may not take place among most of the populace until after a revolt has succeeded. In coups de'état, which occur quickly, the divesting and revesting of authority merely legitimate the transfer of power. The more general principle which this exemplifies is that the vesting of the right to control depends in part on the *existence* of control. If an actor holds effective power over others, the right to exercise that power is often forthcoming from them; if an actor is not able to exercise power, the right to do so is often withdrawn.

The estimate, by a potential activist, of the probability of punishment at the hands of the authorities for revolutionary activity is an important element in deciding to engage in such activity. This estimate, which changes over time as the fortunes of the revolt shift, is closely related to confidence in the capacity of the authorities to govern effectively. As the possibility of success of the revolt grows, both the likelihood that an activist will be punished by the authorities and the confidence of nonactivists in the authorities' capacity to govern effectively decline.

Thus legitimacy may be withdrawn from the authorities not only before any organized revolt or at the end of a revolt (as acknowledgment of a fait accompli), but over the period of the revolt itself, as the authorities lose strength. Insofar as this withdrawal has in turn an effect on the outcome of the revolt, bringing it about should become a component in the activitists' strategy.

Assumptions and Omissions at the Micro Level

The theoretical treatment in the preceding sections has concerned almost exclusively the micro level. I did not discuss explicitly the movement from micro to macro, which I will examine in the next section. After describing the structure of a typical social system prior to a revolt (omitting the particular aspects, such as class, status, race, or ethnic divisions, which may be present in a given authority system), I focused on two kinds of decisions that have to be made by the large body of the population. The first kind is the decision to participate in the revolt or not. The second kind of decision has analytically (and often in practice as well) two parts: whether to divest authority from the regime which holds both legitimacy and power, and then whether to vest legitimacy in those engaged in revolt.

By confining the micro-level examination to these components, I implicitly make an assumption and leave open certain questions. I implicitly assume the existence of a nucleus of committed activists opposing the regime. One can alternatively think of such a nucleus as persons who have already made the two decisions described above, but the important part of the assumption is that there is nonhomogeneity among persons in the system with respect to support of (or opposition to) the authorities, and there are some existing opponents whose opposition is taken as given in the theory. Such a nucleus of opposition is ordinarily present, even in authority systems of small communities (see Coleman, 1957); in large social systems there may be several such nuclei, as there were in Russia prior to the 1917 revolution.

I have left open the question as to how currently inactive individuals decide whether to participate actively in support of the authorities. This decision parallels in form the decision concerning whether to participate on the side of the revolt. Thus its components can be inferred from the discussion of the benefits and costs of that decision, and an extended examination of it would be redundant. I should point out that it is logically possible (and sometimes occurs empirically) for an individual to find it to his benefit to participate on both sides, assuming that it is logistically possible to do so. For example, a mercenary's participation depends wholly or primarily on material benefits that can be provided by the authorities or the revolutionaries or both.

I have also left open questions concerning the actions of the nuclei on opposite sides of the conflict: the authorities and the opponents of the authorities. The actions of the authorities and their active supporters and those of the committed opponents fall under the general category of strategy in conflict, which is outside the domain of a theory directed toward explaining the emergence of revolt in a structure of authority. Nevertheless, an important set of strategies can be derived directly from the theoretical points made in this chapter concerning participation decisions and divestment decisions by members of the population. These points of strategy are presented in the next section.

From Macro to Micro and Back Again

Any theory intended to explain the emergence of revolutions cannot remain at the micro level, as the preceding sections may appear to do. That appearance, however, is somewhat misleading. Transitions from the macro to the micro level and from the micro to the macro level are in part built into the foregoing analysis of individual decisions. This occurs in two ways: First, some of the factors that affect the decision on participation and the decision on divesting are conditions that exist at the level of the system in question. Second, certain of those factors are actions of other actors in the system: authorities, opponents, or other members of the population making the same decisions.

Figure 18.7 shows the various types of gains and losses involved in the decision to participate and the factors that affect these, as discussed earlier. It also shows the outcomes of the decision to divest and the decision to revest as rectangular boxes. Beside each of the factors is a number indicating the type of actor who controls that factor: 1 for authorities, 2 for their opponents, 3 for active loyalists, and 4 for the passive majority. When the factor is under the joint control of two actors (as, for example, the early successes in a revolt are under the joint control of authorities and opponents), both numbers are listed. When a factor is a macro-level property of the system that is not directly under any actor's control, an M appears beside it instead of a number.

In this theory the macro-to-micro and micro-to-macro transitions arise through the effects of various actors' actions on other actors' actions. This also leads directly to the question of strategy on the part of authorities and on the part of their opponents. Both of these actors have control of particular actions and, knowing their effects as shown in Figure 18.7, should use that control in such a way as to maximize their expected gains. Although some of these actions may not be applicable in a particular revolt, they constitute practical recommendations for authorities or their opponents that can be derived from this theory.

The recommendations for action derived from the theory discussed in this chapter are listed below in three categories. In the first category are recommendations that apply to both authorities and revolutionaries; in the second category are recommendations addressed specifically to authorities; and in the third category are recommendations addressed specifically to revolutionaries.

Both Sides
1. Attempt to achieve successes to provide a display of power as early as possible in the revolt.

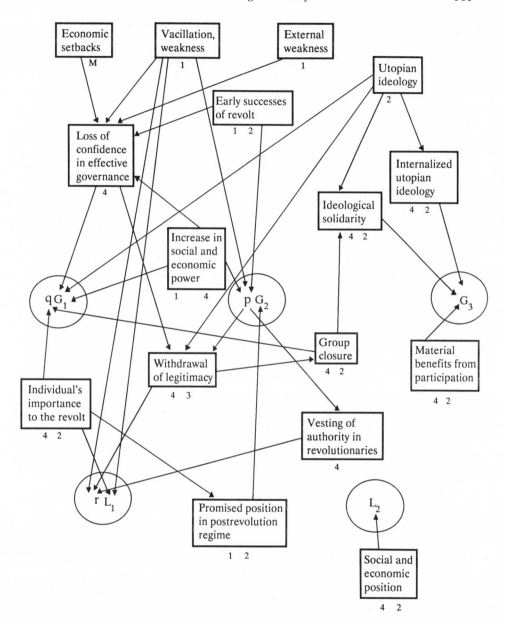

Figure 18.7   Postulated causal diagram for initiation of a revolt.

2. Threaten and implement certain and severe punishment for acting in support of the other side.
3. Provide material inducements (both current and promised for after the revolt) to potential participants who might be important to success.
4. Do not engage in indiscriminate terror.

Authorities
1. Maintain strength externally.
2. Do not let an internal challenge to authority go unmet. If unable to meet a challenge, divert attention through compensating use of power in another area.
3. Show no indecisiveness.
4. Undermine alternative ideologies.
5. Reduce opportunities for closure of social structure among members of the opposition.
6. Develop institutions for addressing grievances of the population on a one-by-one basis (that is, without providing a setting for communication and amplification of grievances).

Revolutionaries
1. Find and promulgate a utopian ideology that challenges the values expressed by the current authority structure, and provide an alternative vision for the future.
2. Use any means other than actions universally regarded as illegitimate to demonstrate authorities' weakness.
3. Cut potential recruits off from contact with nonsupporters of the revolt; develop a high degree of closure within groups of supporters.
4. Incorporate existing grievances of the population into proposals for change.
5. Obtain all possible external support.

« 19 »

The Self

Any theory of action requires a theory of the elementary actor. The elementary actor is the wellspring of action, no matter how complex are the structures through which action takes place. For the theory of this book, the elementary actors as described so far constitute extraordinarily simplified abstractions of human individuals. They are hedonic creatures, who experience satisfaction to differing degrees from the outcomes of various events and from the acquisition or consumption of various resources. The expectancy of such satisfaction leads an individual actor to act in a way intended to increase it.

More precisely, in this book an actor has been described as related to the outside world of resources and events by two properties: interest in some resources and in the outcomes of some events, and control over some resources and events. The actor's relation to other actors is even more tenuous: It lies only in his interest in resources or events over which other actors have control, and his control over resources or events in which other actors have interests. The principle of action used by this actor is the simple one of attempting to maximize utility or satisfaction. In many cases this involves sacrificing some resources over which the actor has control in order to get control of others. In other cases it occurs through deploying the resources he controls (such as the right to control his own actions), placing them into the hands of other actors who may be better able to act in ways that satisfy his interests.

The attempt to maximize utility may not be wholly successful. The theory assumes the elementary actor has a certain modicum of intelligence, but not perfect intelligence; limitations exist. Especially for complex strategic situations involving double contingency of action, limitations on rationality are assumed (and in some such situations where the strategy of others is not well known, even the definition of full rationality is open to question, as discussed in Chapter 33).

The actor presented in the preceding chapters has nothing beyond this, in particular no relations to other actors except through the media of resources and events. The concept of an actor having this minimal structure is applicable not only to natural persons but also to corporate actors.

Problems Inherent in a Unitary Actor

In a theory based on purposive action, the actor is a kind of homeostatic or goal-seeking entity. Even the simplest such device must have two parts: (1) a receptor of signals from the environment, and (2) an actuator which takes action toward the environment, using information from the receptor. Implied in this two-part structure is some kind of intelligence, even if it is nothing more than a comparison operation which links the signals from the receptor and the actions of the actuator. The receptor, linkage, and actuator constitute a kind of control system, and the perfect purposive actor could also be described as an optimal control system.

The two parts of the structure of the simplest possible actor correspond to what I have called in earlier chapters the object self (receptor) and the acting self (actuator); interests constitute the linkage between the two. For corporate actors the same distinction is evident in the terminology of principal (receptor) and agent (actuator).

For both the natural person and the corporate actor, the linkage between the two components of the self can be problematic. The actor may not be guided by an optimal control system, for a variety of reasons. And when the environment is complex, demanding greater complexity from the actor, the possibility that the control system will be nonoptimal is greater. For example, when the object self (principal, or receptor) is benefited or harmed by a number of different aspects of the environment, the actor may act differently, depending on which aspects of the environment capture his attention.

Thus the first problem inherent in the conception of a unitary actor is that of how to fit together the components necessary to carry out the separate functions which constitute purposive action. Ultimately the unitary actor must be regarded as a structure composed of parts if the malfunctioning of the actor is to be studied.

There are other ways in which actors are not unitary. For example, the interests to be satisfied may involve other persons, leading one to act in a way that makes another happy, even at a cost to oneself.[1] Or, just as a person may unilaterally transfer control of his actions to another person who then exercises authority over him, he may transfer control to an actor he has known only in imagination (such as Jesus) or in the past (a parent long dead). Thus both the object self and the acting self may be multiple. But given that there is a multiplicity of object selves and acting selves, there must be some way of selecting what self is to be activated.

Much of this chapter is directed toward these problems of the structure of the self. In addition, as a way of gaining greater insight into the question of how best to conceive of the self, I will address some questions of change. Actors change in various ways, and in a theory of purposive action these changes must be accounted for as being purposively made. The same problem exists and can be

1. It is easy to get caught up by language. What does "oneself" mean here?

seen more readily for corporate actors. The constitution of a corporate actor in effect defines the actor. A theory for the way corporate actors change their constitutions expresses the general principle that is needed, but such theory appears intrinsically difficult to construct. There are, of course, theories of individual change: socialization theory, learning theory, and various social-psychological theories of change. The problem lies in seeing change as purposively attained rather than as arising from some environmental or other external forces. A portion of this chapter is directed toward examining this problem.

One class of problems concerning the actor will not be addressed directly in this chapter, although some of them will be touched on in treating the problems described above. This is the class of problems having to do with apparent irrationalities or inconsistencies of individuals. An extensive body of work in cognitive psychology is concerned with individual behavior that violates predictions based on the theory of maximizing expected utility under risk or those based on the theory of maximizing utility under conditions of certainty. One kind of deviation found experimentally is the effect of framing, which leads an individual's choice of action to be highly dependent on the particular frame of reference in which it was cast (Tversky and Kahneman, 1981). Another empirical finding is that people will lay out small amounts to make bets that would give them large gains if they won, which is inconsistent with their laying out small amounts to purchase insurance that would protect them against large losses (which the same persons in fact do), assuming that they perceive the probabilities correctly and have a utility curve with declining marginal utility (Friedman and Savage, 1952; Kahneman and Tversky, 1979; Lowenstein, 1985). Another class of phenomena concerns time: Individuals will take actions at a given time to prevent themselves from "succumbing to temptation" later or will otherwise precommit themselves (Elster, 1979). When two alternatives are presented and they choose the one that is more distant in time, they change their choice to the nearer alternative as the time for it approaches (Ainslie and Herrnstein, 1981; Ainslie, 1986).[2] Individuals act as if the self is an organization with one component in control (albeit imperfect control) of other components (Thaler, 1980; Thaler and Shefrin, 1981). Individuals will exhibit addictive behavior, appearing to get greater increments of pleasure from a substance the more of it they consume (Becker and Murphy, 1988).

Some of these deviations from rationality appear to result because the organization of the self is more complex than is assumed for the unitary actor in rational-choice theory. Precommitment, for example, can be seen as resulting from an internal structure that allows one part of the self to be in control at one

2. My own conjecture is that a satisfactory resolution of the apparent irrationality implied by preference reversal requires recognizing that the individual has only a single channel of attention at a given time and will ordinarily act to satisfy that interest which is at the top of his attention list. It requires recognizing as well that interests have different temporal profiles. Interest in food, for example, has peaks and valleys, depending on the actor's physiological state, and will capture attention when it is at a peak but not when it is in a valley.

time and another at a later time. I will discuss such internal structures later in this chapter.

Other deviations from rationality appear to result from imperfections in the intelligence that links receptor and actuator. If this intelligence has adapted in an evolutionary fashion, and if its capabilities are limited, it may be possible to trick the actor into acting in ways that are not beneficial to him by creating a setting that differs from those that he will have naturally encountered (for example, the deviations from rationality discussed by Herrnstein (1982) appear to arise for this reason). This intelligence may very well depend on experience in learning how to act in one's interest in complex situations (as is evident to anyone who has dealt with children), and actors' experiences, and therefore their capacities to act in their own interests, do differ.

An extreme example of these limitations is provided by two prisoner's dilemma computer tournaments carried out by Axelrod (1984). A number of game theorists, computer scientists, evolutionary biologists, and social scientists submitted computer programs that incorporated their strategies for playing an iterated prisoner's dilemma with specifications established by Axelrod. Despite these persons' extensive experience with such games and with prisoner's dilemma games in particular, they submitted programs embodying a wide range of strategies and having a wide range of success. They did not converge on a single strategy, as might be expected if it was assumed that action was always and everywhere rational. Even a much weaker assumption—that game theorists, attempting to act rationally in a well-defined and restricted situation, would be able to do so—is inconsistent with these results.

One justification for disregarding deviations from rationality in this book (which may or may not be valid) is that they do not substantially affect the social theory developed here. To put it another way, my implicit assumption is that the theoretical predictions made here will be substantially the same whether the actors act precisely according to rationality as commonly conceived or deviate in the ways that have been observed. (This, of course, is not entirely correct. Chapter 20 describes systematic phenomena of some importance that arise in modern society as a consequence of natural persons' weakness of will.) Their importance in this chapter lies principally in what they can suggest about complexities in the internal structure of the individual as actor.

Some gains in understanding these apparent deviations from rationality will very likely arise from the explicit introduction of a component of the self that governs attention. The standard conception of rational action assumes that all alternatives are known without cost; yet in reality some selectivity of attention is always involved in action. Simon (1955) pointed to the need for both search activities and fixation activities if an individual is to behave effectively. In many cases attention is greatly affected by the environment and by responses, perhaps physiological in origin, to certain changes in the environment. There is a close parallel between the importance of the agenda for outcomes in social choice (see Chapters 14 and 15) and the importance of attention for outcomes in individual choice. There is a similar parallel between the relative neglect of agenda by actors involved in making social choices and the neglect of attention by actors engaged in making individual choices. Neglect of the agenda by committee members is a principal reason why a chairperson can have so much control over the outcome of committee activity. Young children's lack of ability to maintain attention is the reason why the easiest way to change a young child's actions is by distracting the child, causing a shift of attention.

Functional Components of the Self

Because the actor both acts and is an object of others' actions, it appears useful to conceive of the self as consisting of at least two parts: an object self, which experiences satisfaction or the lack of it; and an acting self, which is in the service of the object self, attempting to bring it satisfaction. A similar conceptual separation can be found in the work of some social psychologists. Mead (1934), for example, had two concepts of the self, which he called the me and the I. These correspond quite closely to the concepts of the object self and the acting self.[3] Adam Smith, in *The Theory of Moral Sentiments* (1976 [1753]), formulated a separation of the self into three components. Two correspond to the object self and the acting self, and a third is the "judge," who stands apart and evaluates the agent's action and the actions of others.

There has been an extensive concern with the concept of the self in the last several years in psychology. Some of this work is merely an extension of earlier work in social psychology under other labels: the study of attitudes and values, the study of motivation, and so on. There are, however, some questions being asked that were not asked in the preceding period. For example, Lecky's (1945) brilliant essay on self-consistency has been resuscitated. The question of how— and indeed whether—a person acts, as Lecky argued, in such a way as to maintain consistency of his self-conception (even, as Lecky would have it, if that self-conception is a negative one) has been revived. More generally, this new orientation is one in which the self is seen as a differentiated and active entity, with agency being one part of that differentiated structure (see, for example, Bandura, 1982; 1986). The self is seen as being an entity of parts, with some parts acting on, or making use of, other parts (see Swann and Read, 1981). This new orientation in psychology is much more compatible with optimal control theory and with organization theory of the sort presented in Chapters 4, 7, and 16 than was the approach of the preceding several decades.

For Mead, Smith, and other social psychologists and philosophers, the agent of the self (the I in Mead's terms) carries out purposive action. The agent does

---

3. Freud proposed three components of the self: the ego, the id, and the superego (or, as Bettelheim, 1982, translates from Freud's original German, the I, the it, and the over-I). This set of components does not seem to correspond closely to the object and acting self. All three seem to be components of what I have termed the object self, leaving no component for the acting self.

not experience anything but only acts; it is the self as object of action, whether one's own action or that of another, which has experiences. If one pinches one's own arm, the self as agent does the pinching, and the other self, the object of action, experiences the pain.[4]

This separation between two selves is a separation of function, for two very different functions of the individual as a social being are involved: the function of acting on the environment, and the function of being acted on by the environment (of sensing or experiencing the results of some action). Leaving aside other aspects of the self (such as the judge suggested by Adam Smith) and the other functional components of purposive action discussed earlier in this chapter, I will adopt this dichotomy between the acting self and the self as object of action.

For natural persons as actors I will assume that ordinarily there are no problems in transmitting consequences from the object self to the acting self. It is for this reason that individual persons can as a first approximation be regarded as primitive elements, as unitary actors—for a unitary actor is, analytically, a degenerate case of the corporate actor, one for which the complexities of internal structure can be disregarded.

It is useful to point out here a major interface between psychological theory and the theory of social action. That interface is a conception of the internal structure of the individual which connects the object self with the acting self. The fact that these separate concepts of the self have been distinguished by various social scientists indicates that their integration as a solidary unit cannot always be taken as given. In fact, some psychological pathologies can involve separation between the object self and the acting self. But, pathologies aside, the analytical separation of these two elements, as well as the development of a theory of the psychic organization that connects them, can be valuable for understanding how changes arise within the individual.

For the individual as an actor, the idea of there being an object self and an acting self is fully compatible with the conceptual framework of action discussed above. The acting self has control (partial or total) of certain events in a given system. The object self has interests in certain outcomes of events. The acting self acts in view of the interests of the object self, so as to further those interests.

The distinction between two components of the self implies that, besides actors who have both control over events and interests in events, social systems should contain two sets of parties, each of which has one, but not the other, property of a full actor. One set has interests in events but cannot themselves take action, either because they are outside the system of actors under consideration or for some other reason. These parties are objects of action; for them certain outcomes of events have positive or negative consequences. The second set of parties consists of agents of action, without interests.

---

4. The difference in these two components of the self is revealed in statements persons make about themselves. Some young persons express their main aim in life as "experiencing everything," in effect letting the world act on them in all the varieties of ways it can. Others express their main aim as "doing something important," that is, acting on the world in a powerful way.

These two partial actors may be found in the law, which recognizes entities which have only one of these two components, either an object self or an acting self. In the law of agency these two functional components are distinguished as principal and agent. Other special categories of persons are distinguished elsewhere in the law. Infants are examples of partial actors with object selves; the law says they have interests (that is, object selves) but are not capable of acting in their own behalf. Legally, the other half of an infant's self is the infant's guardian or trustee, who, in actions affecting the infant, is expected to act wholly as an agent for the infant's interests and not in his own interests. Early common law in England made numerous distinctions among classes of persons before the law, as Pollock and Maitland (1968 [1898], p. 407) describe. In fourteenth-century English common law the infant was the purest case of an actor who has only an object self before the law, who cannot take action. In addition, women, serfs, monks, and nuns were among the categories of persons described by Pollock and Maitland as only partial actors, with little more than an object self and unable (or nearly so) to take action before the law. For all these categories of persons an extrinsic party had to constitute the acting self: the guardian for the infant, the husband (or father if she is unmarried) for the woman, the master for the serf, the Church for the monks and nuns.

In corporate actors this separation of the self corresponds to physically different parties: the principals (members or owners) as the object self, and the agents (officers or employees) as the acting self. For a corporate actor the connections between these two aspects of the "self"—the object self and the acting self, or the principals and the agents—are highly problematic, and much of organization theory is concerned with them.

The separation of active property and passive property (or benefit rights and usage rights) which Berle and Means (1933) pointed to in the modern corporation is a split between the object self and the acting self. There is extensive disagreement among theorists of organization as to the correctness of the position of Berle and Means (those opposing their conclusions focus on the efficiency of stock markets and the possibility of hostile take-overs). For present purposes what is pertinent is simply that theorists do recognize the existence of these two components of the corporate self.

The Dual Role of Interests

This conceptual separation of two components of the self, whether the actor is a corporation or an individual, means that there must be some reconnection between the two. In the theory of this book the concept of interests provides this reconnection. This in turn implies that the concept of interests plays two roles in the theory. For the object self, interests indicate the levels of satisfaction contingent on the outcomes of certain events or control of certain resources. For the acting self, interests indicate the relative amounts of resources that will be committed to gaining control over the event; they serve as the driving forces for action.

The dual character of the definition of interests is made possible by the principle of action that defines rationality, that is, maximization of utility. The utility being maximized is a property of the object self. The agent which carries out the action to realize this maximization is the acting self. There are certain circumstances, however, in which the actions of the acting self do not directly follow from the interests of the object self. It is possible that there are some important psychopathological conditions under which this is true: It is often said of a person that he is "working against his own interests" or "acting as if to spite himself." Whether such a conceptual distinction is useful in psychology, or whether it might be more fruitful to locate, in such puzzling cases, a deeper interest that is being satisfied, remains to be determined. But on a superficial level at least there seem to be numerous cases of irrational behavior, in which the object self's interests and the acting self's driving forces are different.

This discrepancy can be seen even more easily for certain kinds of corporate actors, especially those with long chains of authoritative command and numerous owners or members. The discussion in Chapters 16 and 17 of the separation between ownership and control (the thesis of Berle and Means) or that in Chapter 13 of the discrepancy between the interests of members of an association and the actions of its officers (the thesis of Michels) can be put in exactly these terms. The interests of the object self are the owners' or members' interests, and the driving forces for the acting self (that is, the officers or agents of the corporate actor) are distorted reflections of those interests. The amount of distortion may vary, depending on the kind of linkage between the agents' interests (that is, the interests that drive the acting self of the corporate actor) and the owners' or members' interests (the interests of the object self), as discussed in Chapter 16.

The discrepancy between interests and actions discussed above can be attributed to imperfect (possible inherently so) construction of the actor, whether natural person or corporate body. There are, however, other sources of the discrepancy, wholly within the confines of rationality. For example, it is obvious that there can be a shift from rationality in a noncontingent environment to a higher level, at which the contingency of the other's action on one's own is taken into account. At the higher level of rationality, the actor confronted with a potential conflict of interests does not blindly follow his interests oblivious of the other's action, but first compares his resources and interests with those of his opponent and then acts strategically, guided by his interests, but perhaps pursuing an indirect course to their realization.[5] What seems probable, then, is that only at the lowest level of rationality are interests necessarily pursued directly. In many cases there may be a separation between interests of the object self and apparent interests expressed through the actions of the acting self. The former may be better satisfied by a strategic deployment of resources than by a blind or direct pursuit.

5. It has been persuasively argued (Hirshleifer, 1987; Frank 1988) that persons employ their emotions strategically. That this is true in some circumstances is indicated by terms such as "crocodile tears" which implicitly recognize the existence of a strategy.

More generally, the dual role of interests means that the connection between interests as the criteria for satisfaction of the object self and interests as the springs of action for the acting self is not necessarily automatic or direct. It may be defective, leading to action that is ineffective in realizing the interests, or complex, in order that the action be effective in realizing the interests. For natural persons as actors questions arise about the psychological processes through which the connection occurs. For corporate actors the nature of the connection is a central problem for the theory of corporate action, the principal-agent problem—that of inducing the agent to act in the principal's interest.

Objective and Subjective Interests

There has been an extensive debate among social scientists, principally between Marxists and non-Marxists, over the idea of objective interests. Objective interests of the working class, as distinguished from subjective interests, play a central role in Marx's theory of social change. Without this distinction there could be no "false consciousness"; Marx would have had no basis for explanation of the failure of working classes or peasants to revolt against capitalism, and no process of creation of a consciousness of true class interests.[6]

A broader interpretation of objective interests would not limit them to class interests but would regard them as deriving from various aspects of the position in which an actor finds himself in a social system—not only his position relative to the means of production. Thus this broader conception would include not merely class interests, but interests associated with age, sex, religion, race or ethnicity, size of family, and many other aspects of a person's situation. This is not an extension Marxists would make, but it is a generalization of Marx's "objective interests."

The difficulty with both the narrower Marxist conception of objective interests due to class position and the broader conception of positionally generated objective interests is that a theorist invites danger in imputing objective interests to a person which differ from that person's interests as he perceives them. For who, other than the actor, can say what an actor's interests are? If an outside observer attempts to do so, the resulting "objective" interests may be merely a manifestation of the observer's wishes or desires for the actor in question.

Yet advocates of objective interests have a reasonable argument against their being dismissed altogether. Balbus (1971) notes, in a paper on this issue, that "to suggest that subjective interest alone is a sufficient political criterion is to deny the . . . possibility that an individual may be . . . unaware of, or may misjudge the

6. Some rational-action theorists speak—pejoratively—of the thin theory of rationality, as distinct from a more full-bodied theory. The former sees rational action as nothing more than consistency of behavior, whereas the latter defines rational action as action which brings long-term benefits to the actor. This distinction restates the debate on subjective interests versus objective interests in different language and differentiates the strain of rational theory originating in classical economics and the strain that has its origins in Marxist theory.

effect that something has on him . . . [This] leads one to the perverse conclusion that there is no normative problem of political representation with regard to individuals whose life chances are seriously affected by a given policy but who do not perceive any effect'' (pp. 152–153).

These two positions, one holding that objective interests are meaningful and knowable by outside observers and the other holding that only subjective interests are meaningful, are important in political theory. The notion of subjective interests and the view that each person is the best judge of his own interest are central to neoclassical economic theory and its use of the concept of utility, as well as to the political philosophy of liberalism. Thus this debate is not merely an academic one. The assumed existence of objective interests serves as the justification for state intervention in private affairs, which is carried out not only on behalf of the weaker actor in a transaction between two actors, but also for the citizen's ''own good.'' The opposite assumption, that nothing beyond subjective interests exists, serves as the individual's protection against the state, which, according to this thesis, cannot know his interests better than he does. The former position serves as a partial philosophical justification for state-directed socialism and central planning; the latter serves as a partial philosophical justification for liberal democracy and a market system. These two theoretical positions provide two opposing ways of arriving at normative statements for society: According to the former, normative statements derive from the perspective of the outside observer; according to the latter, normative statements derive from the perspective of the actors in the system themselves.

Both of these conceptions are found in daily life. For many activities of life, such as how persons spend their money, there is an implicit assumption that persons know their own interests best. Yet even here there are legal constraints to ''protect people from themselves'': laws forbidding the sale or purchase of certain drugs, for example, or taxes to provide for old-age pensions (to impose forced savings).[7] Deviations from rationality found in psychological research on preference reversal or precommitment are relevant here: the interests that govern a person's action are not those that the person would later (or earlier) claim to be his ''true'' interests.

A possible approach to resolving the conflict between an objective-interests position and the subjective-interests position can be found in what might appear to be an unlikely place: the work of the political theorist Arthur Bentley (1953 [1908]). Writing at the turn of the century, Bentley developed a theory which laid the foundation for the work of interest group theorists in modern political science. Bentley conceived of society as consisting of a large number of activities, economic and otherwise; he conceived of those activities as generating interests and the interests as generating interest groups. In the work of those who fol-

---

7. Laws constraining individuals' choices when the outcome will not hurt another are often vigorously protested, as, for example, the law requiring the use of seat belts and laws against pornography.

lowed Bentley, this first link was lost, and with it the possibility of linking objective effects and subjective interests. Bentley saw the activities of society as placing persons in certain positions relative to government policy (more generally, one might say, relative to any action of the persons' environment), so policy would have a particular kind of effect on them.[8] This effect then generated the subjective interests that led groups to exert political pressure.

This perspective provides a way to reconcile the difference between subjective and objective interests without imputing omniscience to an outside observer or leaving the person to the vagaries of fallible subjective assessment. The way out lies in conceiving of objective interests as generated by a person's position in a social system but not directly observable. Only subjective interests are directly observable; objective interests may be inferred only in one of two ways: by observing over time the increase or decrease in an actor's satisfaction brought about by his pursuit of subjective interests, or by knowing the systematic distortions that may exist in the connection between object self and acting self. The latter leads back to the deviations from rationality described earlier in this chapter. These constitute some of the ways in which the connection between the object self and the acting self can be imperfect. Insofar as these imperfections are systematic, that is, predictable, other actors can exploit them, as children will exploit one child's inability to control anger by teasing that child to evoke the anger.

This approach leads directly to what can be seen as a common research problem for personal actors and corporate actors: What are the sources of discrepancy between interests of the object self and interests pursued by the acting self? For corporate actors this problem has been addressed in work in sociology on incentive pay and in economics on the principal-agent problem. For persons it has been addressed by cognitive psychologists studying deviations from rationality and by research on psychopathology.

Corporate Actors and Optimal Control

For corporate actors the fact that the internal functioning is out in the open, in transactions between agents, allows a view of processes that are hidden for natural persons as actors. If there is a single dominant goal or interest, certain points concerning optimal control may be made. In this case it should be possible to specify the conditions, in terms of the distribution of interest and control among persons at particular positions, that must exist within the corporate actor if its actions are to be optimal from the perspective of that ultimate interest. In effect, this means specification of the properties of an optimal feedback system, when an entity is subject to dispersed control from several points, each having a

8. Balbus (1971) dismisses Bentley's approach but mistakes what Bentley meant by activity, seeing it as the political behavior generated by the interest of a group in a policy. In fact, for Bentley activity is the social and economic activity which places a person in a particular position relative to a policy.

given set of interests. The properties of such a system obviously must involve either the structure of control among the dispersed centers or the interests that each of the dispersed centers uses for guiding its action, or both. There are different ways of achieving optimal control in the above sense, all of which can be found in existing corporate actors.

LIKE INTERESTS   If the relative benefits of any corporate action for each of the actors having some control over the corporate actor are identical to the relative benefits of that action for the corporate actor as a whole, then each of those actors will, in favoring the action that most benefits him, favor the action that most benefits the corporate actor. An infamous expression of this correspondence was made by Charles Wilson, Secretary of Defense under President Eisenhower. Wilson, a former president of General Motors, when asked about potential conflicts of interest is said to have replied, "What is good for General Motors is good for the country." [9] The disfavor with which this remark was greeted arose not from the fact that it implies a complete correspondence of interests, but from the fact that the interests of the country appear to be derivative from those of General Motors, rather than the reverse. In a social system where all interests were wholly alike, such a remark would occasion no unfavorable comment, because all persons' interests would be identical not only to those of the country but to those of other actors in question (in this case General Motors).

A homogeneous organization, such as a new nation, has roughly this character: Each member is in a similar position relative to the external environment; consequently all members will be motivated to act in similar ways toward the environment. In such a case the structure of control for the corporate actor is unimportant. Each agent pursues the same set of interests. [10]

DIFFERENTIATED INTERESTS   If interests of actors within a corporate actor are not alike, then the structure of control does matter. In general, only one structure of control will be optimal relative to an externally specified goal. An intuitive idea of what is necessary is contained in the notion that there should be a correspondence between interests and power; those whose interests are closest to the corporate actor's interests (as determined by the ultimate criterion of survival) should have the greatest power over corporate actions. [11]

---

9. In fact, it appears that he stated the reverse: "What's good for the country is good for General Motors." But the uproar over the remark was due to its being reported as stated in the text.

10. It is possible for the effective interests of all members of a corporate actor to be nearly alike for short periods, for example, when the existence of the corporate actor is under severe threat. The theory in this book is not developed to the point of embodying such temporal changes.

11. This condition may be realized in either of two ways: by allocating power so that it corresponds to interests, or by modifying interests to correspond to existing power. An example of the latter is the provision of incentives to managers or others on whose efforts success most depends, to tie their success as closely as possible to success of the corporate actor (again, assuming the existence of a single goal).

More generally, differentiated interests, in contrast to like interests, characterize most social organizations. In most social organizations there is an explicitly structured differentiation of interests, produced by the different relations of the actors to productive activities (that is, to events, in the terms of this theory). For many corporate actors, however, it would be wholly incorrect to attempt to specify an overall goal or dominant interest from an external point of view. One could not start with the corporate actor's interests and say that optimal control occurs when (speaking loosely) those whose interests are closest to the corporate actor's interests have the most power. It would be necessary to reverse the implied causality and to say something like this: The (subjective) interests of the corporate actor, as reflected in its behavior, are most fully derivative from the interests of those who have the most power.

IDENTIFICATION WITH THE CORPORATE ACTOR   A third means of optimal control is attainable when members are highly identified with the corporate actor. Under this condition of identical interests, any structure of control will give the same results: The actions of each agent are based on the same set of interests. The collectivities that come closest to this ideal are small communes organized around religion, as described by Zablocki (1980) and Bradley (1987) and discussed in Chapter 4. As described in Chapters 7 and 16, however, many large corporate bodies composed of actors with differentiated interests depend in part on identification to induce members and agents to pursue directions of action that are in the corporate interest. National governments develop such identification in many ways, under the general rubric of patriotism. The existence of such identification offers a strong safeguard against actions that could have negative consequences for the corporate actor.

Structures involving like interests, differentiated interests, and identification with the corporate actor are all found in corporate actors, and each constitutes a different means for achieving optimal control. In other words, each of these types of structures is a means for bringing the interests as pursued in action into accord with the interest of the principal. Whether there are also different means of achieving optimal control within the natural person as actor is a problem that remains to be studied.

Processes of Change inside the Actor

In the theory being developed here there is as yet no basis for change within the actor. In Chapter 11 there was discussion of processes of internalization of norms, but there I simply assumed that such a change was possible in individuals and asked questions about the conditions under which various socializing agents would have an interest in attempting to internalize norms in others (such as children). Thus that process assumes the existence of internal change within the individual without providing a theoretical accounting for it.

One might first ask where interests come from. There are various answers to this question in psychological theory (although not all of them are consistent with rationality of the actor). One source of interests is obviously the primary needs of the organism. A second source, however, has to do with the means toward acquiring the intrinsically satisfying and necessary things. If the actor is conceived of as beginning as a very simple entity, with only a few primary needs for things required for survival, the course of events and action creates over time a whole superstructure of interests that were originally pursued as paths toward the satisfaction of more central needs. These come to be autonomous interests insofar as they satisfy, over some period of time, the more central needs. The term "functional autonomy of motives" has been introduced to describe this process (Allport, 1937; see also Merton, 1968, p.15).

The concept of secondary reinforcement in learning theory can be applied to these autonomously developed interests. Secondary reinforcement occurs when a subject is rewarded not with a reward that satisfies a primary need, such as food, but with a reward that has been strongly associated with receipt of the primary reward. Experiments have shown that secondary reinforcement is relatively weak for animals (see Hilgard, 1956). But animals differ from humans in their relative lack of cognitive associations. Consequently, although secondary reinforcements are weak when responses are unmediated by cognitive connections, this does not imply that they are weak in the presence of cognitive structures.

Since psychological theory is so forthcoming with theories of psychological change, it is necessary to ask why economics—the social science for which a theory of purposive action has been most central—has never developed or borrowed from psychology a theory of internal change of individuals. For some economists this is seen as merely an incompleteness of the foundations of economic theory; for others the fixity of utilities or tastes has substantive meaning and importance.[12] One reason such a theory has not been developed is the difficulty of introducing a theory that is compatible with the central principle of action, maximization of utility. If an actor's goals, or what goods and events he regards as satisfying him or as having high utility for him, cannot be specified, then there is no basis for maximization. The theory of rational action of purposive action is a theory of instrumental rationality, *given* a set of goals or ends or utilities. If a theory of internal change of actors is to be justifiable or consistent with the basic principle of action, it must do what appears to be impossible: to account for *changes* in utilities (or goals) on the basis of the principle of *maximization* of utility.

I introduce this cautionary note at the outset to indicate that the requirements for a satisfactory theory of internal change in actors are not easily met. The only satisfactory theory will be one in which change derives from application of the principle of action itself.

---

12. The former position is exemplified by work of Weiszacker (1971) which makes current tastes depend on past consumption. See Stigler and Becker (1977) for the latter position and Vanberg (1986) for an extension of it.

It is useful, in assessing how actors might change themselves, to step back and view the system of action. The essential aspect of action systems is that they are systems of *action:* Actors take action, modifying outcomes of events in the world, in order to make those outcomes more compatible with an order that exists inside each of them. That internal order has been represented in the theory developed here by the idea of interests, or internal states which specify how object selves are satisfied and (if the actor is well organized internally) constitute the motivations for action.

The actions are taken to affect outcomes of events taking place in the world outside an actor: But might not the desired compatibility be equally well achieved by changing the *internal* structure? In other words, if the actor is engaged in the task of maximizing the satisfaction of his interests, the task can be accomplished in either of two ways: He may take action to restructure the outside world, by gaining control over certain events that are important to him; or he may restructure the internal self, by gaining interest in some events and losing interest in others.

In effect, what may be envisioned is a kind of war between two worlds: the external world of events, which have their own sequence and structure as determined by others outside the actor; and a world internal to the actor. Changes in the first of these worlds constitute a system of observable action, with actors struggling to gain control over those events or resources that interest them. Changes in the second world, the internal one, do not appear as observable actions because they take place within the actor. These are psychic changes, and they might well be thought of as the psychic counterpart of action systems, in which the actor achieves satisfaction not by taking action to change the world, but by changing himself to be satisfied with the world.

Identification: Expansion of the Object Self

Under what circumstances might an actor carry out psychic changes? It can be argued that an important process that occurs throughout life is an expansion of the object self, to include larger and larger sets of social objects. Whereas persons early in life are relatively undisturbed by events having dire consequences for others nearby, they come later to experience the consequences of such events almost as if they happened directly to themselves. In effect, it is possible to conceive of the (object) self in such a way that events affecting others in the vicinity *do* in fact happen to oneself, that is, to the expanded self. This is not to say that the object self continually expands and never withdraws attachments. Such withdrawals obviously do occur at times as life situations change, even while the overall expansion of the object self continues. And evidence indicates that there are times, particularly during old age, when an overall contraction of the object self takes place.

The general nature of this conception is that the object self, in whose interests the agent acts, is ever changing and throughout much of life expanding. This conception makes unnecessary any deviation from the conception of a rational purposive actor on which the theory of this book is based. Acts of apparent altruism, acts which derive from sentimental attachments and appear to be against the actor's self-interests narrowly defined, are explicable through such an addition to the theory, the use of the notion of an expanded object self.

This theoretical device would be of no value, however, if the theorist were merely using it as a way of saving the theory. The first question is this: What does identification do for the person who identifies with another so as to lead him to do it? The second is this: What are the constraints which limit the process? Without any constraint every action could be explained trivially, merely by positing a degree and direction of identification which would lead to that action.

A step toward answering the first question is the recognition that there might be an expansion of the object self in the expectation that this will bring benefits. Suppose one's action, taken to benefit oneself or for another reason, benefits another actor. Or suppose one's action to benefit another, whether taken voluntarily or not, brings benefits to oneself. Then one can capture the extra benefits of one's action, the benefits the action brings to the other, if one incorporates the interests of the other as one's own. When a business firm does this, economists describe it as internalizing (positive) externalities. When a person does it, psychologists describe it as internalizing another's interests, or identifying with another.

Empirically identification appears to occur in this way, through *acting* to benefit others. This is most evident in a parent's identification with a child. The parent's identification with the child grows as the parent cares for the child and sees the child develop. It appears that this process operates even when the action is not spontaneously taken. A servant often comes to identify with his master, to feel the master's pleasures and pains, although he does not originally enter into the relation because he identifies with the master. Only a minimal response from the child or from the master, in recognition of the care given or the service provided, seems sufficient to encourage this identification.

A second process which leads to identification is as follows: If outcomes of events are benevolent to another actor, then one might find it possible to increase one's satisfaction by identification with that other. There is widespread evidence of this: People join fan clubs for movie stars, not fan clubs for handicapped persons. People identify with a sucessful hero and quickly drop that identification when the hero stumbles. What limits such identification with successful others? Why do individuals not simply live in a dream world, in which they live the lives of handsome princes and beautiful princesses? Although there are obvious limiting factors, it is difficult to state a general principle. Reality intrudes inexorably, confronting individuals with consequences they cannot escape. There may be more to be gained by attempts to shape real events than by continuing to identify with successful persons. This, however, is not a very satisfactory answer, and the problem must be regarded as unsolved.

There is a parallel for corporate actors: Corporations invest in other corporations that have been successful or seem likely to be successful in the future. Persons do this as well, when they invest money or another valuable resource in an activity. It is clear in these cases that investments by corporate actors or persons are limited by the quantity of their discretionary resources. Furthermore, these resources have an opportunity cost, and a rational actor will direct the investment to the actor or activity likely to be most profitable.

A third process through which identification appears to occur is the shared experiencing of the same consequential events. The more intense the experience, the stronger the identification, even if the experience was a bad one. The shared experience of soldiers who have "gone through hell together" often creates a strong bond of identification, so each one feels close to each of the others and experiences a great loss if something happens to one of them.

This process may be an instance of classical conditioning. In conditioning, one event constitutes a primary reinforcement for a subject, eliciting a response from him. A second event or object can, after cognitive association with the primary reinforcement (for example, due to contiguity in space or time), come to generate the same response on the part of the subject. This second object may be another actor. If one has been in close association with another actor over a period of time, experiencing the same events, then the occurrence of something good or bad to the other may induce feelings in oneself that are like those one would experience if the thing had happened to oneself.

A fourth and apparently powerful process by which identification occurs is being dependent on another. This can be seen in children's identification with parents or in the identification of hostages with their terrorist captors, of concentration camp inmates with their guards and of brainwashed prisoners with their "reeducators." (For a description of the last two of these, see Bettelheim, 1953, and Lifton, 1961.) Dependency can create not only strong identification but also hate—prisoners hate their captors, and children sometimes come to hate their parents. Nevertheless, the dependency itself appears to create identification, independently of any benevolence of the actor on whom one is dependent.

Finally, it appears that identification can occur as a consequence of the process of vesting control in another. A person gives another control over some portion of his actions, and then some degree of identification often follows. In the extreme case, if an actor vests control of his actions in a charismatic leader, he ordinarily comes to identify with that leader. The vesting of control which occurs when one falls in love leads to the love object being an object of one's gratification, but one also comes, over time, to identify with the person, to feel pain when that person feels pain to feel joy when that person feels joy.

Thus there seem to be at least five circumstances under which one actor may develop an identification with another:

1. When one acts to benefit the other
2. When the other is successful
3. When one has been affected by the same events as the other
4. When one is highly dependent on the other
5. When one vests rights of control of one's actions in the other

This constitutes only a list of distinct circumstances under which identification appears to come about. There is no theoretical principle to bring them together, and the most that can be said is that for each of the five, with the exception of the third, an actor can gain satisfaction by coming to identify with the other, that is, by taking the interests of the other to some degree as his own.

However it comes about and whatever functions it performs for the actor, identification is a form of psychic organization which has strong implications for social organization. In the external action system described in earlier chapters, the modes through which persons are related to one another are limited to the following:

1. Persons control events or goods of interest to one another and are thus useful to one another as means to goal achievement.

2. Because certain resources controlled by individuals (such as labor) are not alienable, in exchanges involving these resources what is exchanged are rights to control action, or promises to act in a certain way in a particular case. In addition, in the case of an unequal exchange, a generalized credit may be given by one actor to the other. These rights, promises, and credits constitute expectations and obligations which persons have toward one another.

3. Persons transfer rights of control to others, either unilaterally or in exchange, giving others rights of control over their actions over an extended or indefinite period. This creates a subordinate-superordinate relation, that is, an authority relation.

4. Because persons have interests in aspects of other persons that are intrinsic to those persons, the others can become ends in themselves. That is, other persons constitute some of the social objects over which persons are interested in gaining control.

These four kinds of social relations can be described as complementarity, claims, authority, and cathexis, respectively. The additional relation in which persons internalize the interest of others can be called sympathy (as Adam Smith did, when he identified this form of relation in *The Theory of Moral Sentiments*) or empathy (as others have done). I will, however, simply call it identification, meaning that one takes as one's own, to a certain degree, the interests of those with whom one identifies.

Identification with others is a particularly important kind of internal change actors undergo, but not the only kind. Another source of change is conflicts within the self. One body of work, balance theory, addresses such conflicts.

Balance Theory and Divestment

A widely used theory of attitude change in social psychology is balance theory. The original ideas for balance theory are due to Heider (1958); they were subsequently developed in varying forms by a number of social psychologists. Expressed rather crudely, balance theory specifies that if an actor has attachments to two social objects and those two objects (other persons, values, and so forth) are in conflict, the individual will change his orientation toward one or both in such a way that the conflict is reduced or eliminated. This theory is one of a large class of tension-reduction or least-effort principles in social and natural science. It clearly describes an important process of internal change of individuals.

Heider examines two kinds of relations. One is liking or disliking; the other he calls unit formation, by which he means that two social objects are seen as belonging together. Thus an actor may (according to Heider) like or dislike another person, and he may like or dislike an object that is not a person. He may see two social objects (persons or other objects) as belonging together or as not belonging together. He may also perceive another actor as liking or disliking another social object, and he may see himself as belonging together with another social object.[13] Heider goes on to argue that if there is "imbalance" or "disharmony" in the actor's orientation to these social objects and his perception of their orientation to each other, "the situation will tend to change in the direction of balance" (p. 207). He does not go beyond this. He does not indicate what will change or what is the basis for change, thus providing no basis for a rational theory of change within the self. Despite this, I will sketch the structure of such a theory.

Heider (1958, p. 176) uses an example to illustrate the kind of phenomenon with which balance theory is designed to cope. In an experiment carried out by Esch (1950), a set of 101 subjects (high-school students, college students, and others) were presented with short descriptions of social situations and asked, "What would happen nine times out of ten when something like this occurs?" One situation was as follows: "Bob thinks Jim is very stupid and a first-class bore. One day Bob reads some poetry he likes so well that he takes the trouble to track down the author in order to shake his hand. He finds that Jim wrote the poems."

The results of the experiment were as follows:

46% responded that Bob would change his mind about Jim and come to have a positive evaluation of him.

29% responded that Bob would change his mind about the poetry and come to dislike it.

5% responded that Bob would not accept the combination, for example, would not believe that Jim wrote the poems. (In Heider's terms these respondents refused to accept the unit formation composed of Jim and the poems.)

---

13. Certain irregularities in Heider's system have never been straightened out by balance theorists; one of these is revealed by the fact that in a triad consisting of three persons there are six relations of like or dislike, and for each relation, two perceptions of the relation (by each of the other actors). This results in much greater complexity than is reflected by the simple plus or minus associated with each pair of such a triad in balance theory. I only warn the reader of this and will not pursue it, because my aim here is simply to see what aid balance theory can provide for a theory of change internal to the self.

2% differentiated two aspects of Jim, saying that Bob would continue not to respect one and come to respect the other (that is, Jim's ability as a poet). 18% did not resolve the "disharmony."

Balance theory simply specifies that under such circumstances, when there is disharmony, persons will change in such a way as to eliminate it. Heider uses the example to show that most persons did remove the disharmony. Almost half stated that Bob would change his orientation to the other person; almost a third stated that Bob would change his orientation to the other object, in this case the poetry; a small percentage separated what Bob did not like from what he did, breaking apart the unit formation composed of Jim and the poetry or that composed of two parts of Jim.

How does the theory of this book treat this sort of internal change? First, it can be said that Bob's internal world, his cognitive and affective internalization of the external world, has a particular organization which provides him directives for acting in a way that will give him satisfaction. Two of the elements in the external world toward which Bob can act to gain satisfaction are the poems he has just read (toward which a positive action will provide satisfaction) and Jim (toward whom a negative action will provide satisfaction). If the first of these two actions is called E_1 and the second E_2, Bob is in the circumstance diagrammed in Figure 19.1, where A_1 represents Bob. Then, however, the outside world changes, and thus his cognitive mapping of it changes. He sees himself as no longer able to take separate actions, E_1 and E_2. There is a new event, E_3, a single action toward *both* Jim and the poetry. The other two actions can be seen as dependent on this action. If it is positive, he gains satisfaction from E_1 (action toward the poems) but loses satisfaction from E_2 (action toward Jim). If it is negative, he gains satisfaction from E_2 but loses satisfaction from E_1. This new situation can be diagrammed as shown in Figure 19.2.

This new structure among events, with E_1 and E_2 dependent on a single action, E_3, lowers Bob's level of satisfaction. It can be increased by any of several changes. One is a change in his orientation toward Jim (that is, his interest in E_2). Another is a change in his orientation toward the poetry (his interest in E_1). These are changes in his affective organization. Changes in his cognitive organization are also possible. He may refuse to recognize Jim's authorship, thereby

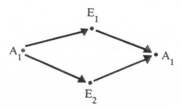

Figure 19.1   Positive action of Bob (A_1) toward poetry (E_1) and negative action toward Jim (E_2).

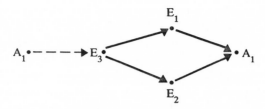

Figure 19.2   Single action (E₃) of Bob toward poetry and Jim.

maintaining a cognitive organization like that in Figure 19.1 so that he can act separately toward Jim and the poems. Finally, Bob may split the structure in a new way, into a part of Jim that he respects and a part that he does not.

The internal change that Bob undergoes as a consequence of a change in his external world agrees with the general principle of maximizing satisfaction, but does not come about in the way described elsewhere in this book, through actions which bring about changes in the external world. Those actions are either exchanges of control or unilateral transfers of control, but this internal change is one that accommodates to a change in the external world for which exchange or unilateral transfer is not feasible. The result is a change in interest on Bob's part, who will be likely to either change his negative interest in Jim to a positive interest or change his positive interest in the poetry to a negative interest.

This, however, is not a very satisfactory conclusion. It predicts that Bob will change his orientation toward one of the two social objects, but it does not predict which he will do or provide any basis for such a prediction. To go beyond this requires three steps taken in sequence: The first step is to gain some sense of just what, substantively, is the basis for the direction and amount of change. The second is to formulate these ideas in a fashion that is both internally consistent and consistent with the larger theory. The third step is to state predictions of the theory concerning actions appropriate for empirical testing and then to carry out the empirical tests. I will carry out the first step and begin the second step.

The essential substantive idea that serves as the basis of this theory of internal change is that the social objects in question are not only linked to one another, but also linked to other social objects, such that an action cannot be taken toward each separately. And the actor in question, Bob, has an orientation to these other objects (I will subsume these orientations under the general concept of interests). Thus a change in orientation toward either of the social objects in question, the poems or Jim, has implications for the satisfaction Bob can obtain from a whole set of actions.

This idea, of course, is not new. In both balance theory and other parts of social psychology, the idea that individuals make those changes which maximize the balance or harmony of the structure as a whole has been stated many times. There are, however, some differences; for example, in the theory being proposed here it is the necessity for action and the consequences of the action for levels of satisfaction that impose the pressure toward attaining balance or harmony or consistency. In most other versions of these ideas, action plays no role.

This conceptual difference leads to a difference in how the structure is diagrammed. For the case involving Bob, Jim, and the poems, suppose there is another class of actions based on Bob's orientations toward other social objects in which he has positive or negative interests. For example, suppose Bob developed his negative orientation toward Jim from comments by a friend. Coming to like Jim would then reduce his satisfaction from positive actions toward that friend. Suppose also that his pleasure from the poems was a pleasure shared with his girlfriend, who also enjoyed them. Coming to dislike the poems would then reduce his satisfaction from being with his girlfriend.

If Bob took positive actions toward his friend (E_6), resolved the disharmony concerning Jim and the poems by changing his mind about Jim and acting positively toward Jim and the poems (E_1) (by shaking his hand and congratulating him), and continued to read the poems with his girlfriend (E_7), the structure of action could be diagrammed as in Figure 19.3. This diagram, which shows a changed orientation of Bob toward Jim, contains a continuing disharmony, or source of dissatisfaction. Bob's positive action toward his friend (E_6) is implicitly a negative action toward Jim and is inconsistent with his positive action toward Jim and the poems (E_1).

If Bob had taken a negative action toward Jim and the poems, the dissatisfaction from E_6, his positive action toward his friend, would have been removed. Another source of dissatisfaction would have cropped up, however, in his actions toward his girlfriend. If Bob continued to read Jim's poems with her (E_7),

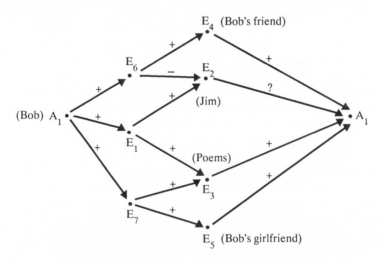

Figure 19.3 Additional elements of cognitive structure affected by Bob's action toward Jim and poetry.

the satisfaction from this action would be lower than before, because of its inconsistency with his action toward Jim and the poems.

If this were the whole set of actions and social objects connected directly or indirectly to Jim and the poems, it would predict two things:

1. Bob would take the action which reduced his satisfaction least, considering not just action E_1, but also E_6 and E_7.
2. There would remain a continuing tension in the system which would lead to some future external or internal change (such as eliminating action E_6 toward the friend, by losing interest in him, or discontinuing the reading of the poems with his girlfriend).

The second prediction illustrates how, according to this theory, tension, or a source of dissatisfaction in the internal structure when that internal structure is interfaced with the outside world, leads to change.

It may be useful to carry this sketch of a theory of the system of action within the self somewhat further. As Ainslie (1986) has suggested, "[if] the parts of the self can be clearly articulated, they may be suitable material for a model more microscopic than microeconomics, 'picoeconomics' perhaps, in which the elements that combine to determine the individual person's values can be described" (p. 139). One way of conceiving of a picoeconomics within the self is to conceive of the self as a system of action like that described in Chapters 6 and 25. The general idea is as follows: In a system of action as described in this book, there are actors having control over resources and events, and interests in resources and events. If a corporate actor (that is, an organization) is regarded as a system of action, the actors within that system are the various employees or agents occupying positions in the organization. Their interests are shaped by the incentive structure within the organization. The *actions* of the corporate actor are outcomes of events, which are determined by what is sometimes described as the internal politics of the organization and dependent on resources held by various actors within the organization, as well as their interests in the events. (This is stated more precisely in Chapters 30, 31, and especially 34.) If it is possible to regard the actions of a corporate actor as outcomes of events in a system of action internal to the corporate actor and to regard the agents of the corporate actor as actors within that system of action, then it should also be possible to regard the actions of a person as outcomes of events in a system of action internal to the person. What is necessary is to identify the "actors" within the person and their interests and resources. That is the general strategy I will pursue here.

It is useful to begin with the extreme case, a person who has so strongly internalized the goals or interests of others that the "actors" inside that person are simply reflections of actors outside; the system of action here is a kind of internal world mirroring the external world. The phrase is reminiscent of Cooley's (1902) term, "the looking-glass self," which is ordinarily interpreted in a narrow sense, that is, as seeing oneself through the eyes of others. But Cooley seems to have intended the term to be more encompassing, that is, the self as constituting an internal reflection of the system of action that exists outside the person. In this view the self contains within it a reflection of all the actors in the system outside, along with their interests. The person's action toward that outside system is an outcome of the balance of interests among the actors internalized from that system.

How then does the subjective world of action that is played out within a person, leading to that person's taking action, differ from the objective world? How is the subjective world of one person different from that of another? What appears to be a reasonable conjecture is that each person has, in effect, a different *constitution:* Each of the actors from the outside world who participates in a person's internal system of action is endowed with certain rights by the person. These rights are extensive if an actor (within a person) represents someone who is or was important in the socialization of that person, that is, someone whose directives or values the person has internalized. The internal system of action of a person is an egocentric one, in the sense that each person's constitutional allocation of rights differs from that of another person.

The rights in this conception are rights of partial control over various actions of the person. The rights can be "exchanged" by the internal actors; if one of them loses on one action over which it has partial control, it will gain a credit that makes it more likely to be able to control the next action in which it has an interest.

Such a conception of the self, however, brings up a number of difficulties. For example, if the person is rational, why does he gives up this internal control to the imagined interests of others? What is rational about this conception of action? It is, rather, action controlled by little people whose will the person has internalized. Such a person's action is merely controlled by the perceived wills of others—perhaps embodied in norms, perhaps not. It is not controlled by passions or appetites, or principles, or, apparently, rational consideration. This conception of the person merely brings back normatively controlled or externally controlled action.

Two points can be made. The first is that this conception of an actor is, as indicated earlier, an extreme. Moving away from that extreme allows the internal actors within the person's system to be not only other persons, but also appetites and general principles of action that are not associated with any particular person. This allows the person to act in a much more differentiated way, sometimes appearing to be controlled by norms, sometimes by passions, and sometimes by principles. This nevertheless continues to relegate rationality to a minor position, even if one of the principles by which the person is governed is that of maximizing his own utility or long-range interests.

The second point, however, is that rationality, generated by a kind of evolutionary feedback process within the individual, might enter at an earlier point, during construction of the constitution. According to this conception, the individual's constitution, which gives (partial) control over different actions to different internal actors, would arise from experiences in the particular world that this person inhabits. For example, a child whose mother gives extensive social-psychological rewards for helping around the house would "learn," through this internal evolutionary process, to give the mother, as an internal actor with perceived directives or values, extensive control over that class of actions, for doing so brings gratification.

This is a sketch of how a theory internal to the self (developed formally in Chapter 34) might be constructed. The model is a kind of picoeconomics, to use Ainslie's term, incorporating within the self a system like that outside the actor, but with a constitution all its own.

Corporate Actors' Changes in Self

In earlier sections of this chapter, I have suggested some parallels between persons' changes in self and corporate actors' changes in self. In this section I will focus wholly on a kind of change in corporate actors which is most difficult to understand as purposive: change in the very purposes or interests that are pursued.

The operational meaning of persons' subjective interests is as indicators of direction of action and level of motivation to act. Since subjective interests of persons (interests of the acting self) are operationally defined in this way, there is no insuperable barrier to using this concept for corporate actors. That is, although it is neither reasonable nor possible to specify the psychic state of a corporate actor, it is possible to determine its actions. The actions of a corporate actor are the actions of its agents, sometimes as implementation of corporate decisions and sometimes on the basis of their own decisions, using resources of the corporate actor.

For a corporate actor there are two ways of assigning these subjective interests; for a person there is only one. A corporate actor's interests can be inferred without peering inside it, from actions its agents take toward the external world; in much the same way a person's subjective interests may be inferred from the actions he takes. But there is a second method of inferring interests (and thus predicting behavior) of a corporate actor. This is an internal analysis of the corporate actor, inferring from the interests of various positions within it and the structure of control given by its constitution, the actions and thus the interests (or the interests and thus the actions) that can be expected from it.

A simple illustration of how this may be done qualitatively is provided by the examination of a change in the Ford Motor Company's internal structure of control, given in Chapter 34. Briefly, before the mid-1920s, Ford had been very successful through concentrating on manufacturing engineering. By the mid-1920s, however, the marginal return in sales from Ford's expenditures in manufacturing engineering was much lower than the marginal return from the company's expenditures in product engineering, body design, and style. Yet Ford, unlike General Motors, had not responded to this change in environment. Ford finally underwent a reorganization in which the manufacturing engineers lost power in the organization and the product engineers, designers, and stylists gained power. This reorganization made Ford responsive to the changed environment and thus saved the organization.

This corporation changed itself. How to characterize such a change conceptually is not clear, for either a corporate actor or a person. A general statement may be made that an internal revolution has occurred, or a description may be given of just what happened in the specific case. It is clear also that in some cases the control is so strong and rigid that an organization may fail to survive because of inability to change itself. Nevertheless, both in the case of corporate actors and in the case of persons, the conception of a differentiated self capable of changing the constitution through which it governs itself, is the necessary conceptual device.[14]

In the above illustration the effective interests of Ford before its organizational change (considered to be its subjective interests) were derivable from the structure of control and the distribution of interests within the corporation. Because the manufacturing engineers had effective control, it was their interests that were most important in determining the corporation's effective interests. After the structure of control changed, the effective interests of the organization changed, reflecting the changed structure of control.

Can it also be said that the first set of interests were the objective interests of the organization? Or did the new structure of control after reorganization bring the subjective interests into closer correspondence with the objective interests? These questions are not fully answerable because there is no single principal. The multiple principals in the case of Ford Motor Company were the members of the Ford family, who owned the company's stock. The interests of that nucleus in survival of the company were barely sufficient to effect a change. In the Ford Motor Company, as in other corporate actors, there were several object selves with competing or conflicting interests. In this respect corporate actors are no different from persons. A person has investments in many social objects, as suggested earlier, and the consequences of his actions for those objects determine his interests.

There does, however, remain the fact that Ford Motor Company was losing money and was on the verge of collapse until the change in control. Thus in an evolutionary sense, the company was better off after the change in control than it was before—merely on grounds of survival. And if a hierarchy of interests exists among those principals with some control of the internal structure, and survival is at the top of this hierarchy, then this allows some statement about objective corporate interests.

---

14. In human affairs conceptual gaps in theory are also manifested in conceptual gaps in practice. Thus there is no practical work in devising corporate actors capable of restructuring themselves in response to environmental changes, just as there is no body of theory about optimal forms of organization for achieving this.

PART IV

Modern Society

Natural Persons and the New Corporate Actors

Individual Sovereignty

Throughout much of this book I have envisioned a social system in which all rights and resources are initially held by individual persons as actors: Only their interests dictate the course of events. In any ongoing social system into which persons are born, this assumption is untrue: A great deal of power resides in corporate actors. Thus it might appear that the theory of this book is naive or excessively individualistic in its conception of social systems.

Neither charge is correct, however. The theory recognizes that within a given social system a large fraction of rights and resources, and therefore sovereignty, may reside in corporate actors. This fact may be to persons' benefit or harm, depending on how the actions of the corporate actor are derived from, or insulated from, the interests of those persons. If the theory failed to take as its conceptual starting point rights and resources—and therefore sovereignty—in the hands of individual persons, it would not be possible to address the question of just how that sovereignty becomes alienated from them and held by corporate actors that may not be fully responsible to them.

The matter is, of course, more complicated than this, not only empirically but conceptually. As discussed in Chapters 3 and 13, a right comes into existence only when there develops a consensus about its locus. Yet individual persons do have primacy, because it is persons, not corporate actors, whose consensus determines the initial locus of rights. In much of the exposition in the preceding chapters, in particular the chapters concerned with authority (Chapters 4 and 7), I have assumed the existence of rights and have assumed that they are held by individual persons. These assumptions allow the kinds of analyses carried out in those chapters, but it is important to recognize the origin of rights in consensus.

Quite apart from the locus of rights is the purpose for which theory construction is carried out. As persons, social scientists engage in theory construction to benefit persons; their interest in corporate actors is only instrumental. Corporate actors merit existence only insofar as they further the ends of natural persons. Thus only by starting conceptually from a point where all sovereignty rests with individual persons is it possible to see just how well their ultimate interests are realized by any existing social system. The postulate that individual persons are sovereign provides a way in which sociologists may evaluate the functioning of social systems.

It is useful to point out that the preceding paragraph explicitly contains in its second and third sentences the major value premise that will be used at certain points in this part of this book. Even though this is a small and solitary value premise, it will be possible to derive from it strong evaluative judgments about particular types of social systems.

Changing Conceptions of Sovereignty

The extensive philosophical arguments that have arisen since the seventeenth century about the origin of rights have been important in providing the philosophical basis for law and for social organization consistent with that law. If rights were divinely granted to a king, as in early conceptions of monarchy, or to the church, as in medieval canon law, then all rights would have their earthly origin in the king or the church and would revert to that origin unless expressly conceded to other persons or groups. If the state was the original locus of rights, as in Roman public law, then all persons and groups would have to justify their claim to rights in terms of a concession from the state. If the community (the folk) was seen as the original bearer of rights, as in the Dark Ages in Central Europe, then individuals would have rights only as members of that community, and there would exist no individual rights per se.

Not only the legal status of rights was at stake in this philosophic debate, but also the form taken by social organization. Under Roman law corporate bodies constituted, in effect, only subordinate organs of the state and were neither subject to private law nor recognized as independent entities in public law.[1]

The most interesting and perhaps best-documented struggle in law over these different conceptions of the origins of rights occurred in Central Europe, from the twelfth through the nineteenth century. Gierke (1934 [1913]) traces the origins of the German association (*Genossenschaft*, translated as fellowship by Maitland; see Gierke, 1968 [1900]) in medieval common law before the twelfth century. Such associations, of which one type was the tradesmen's guild and another the farm community *(Markgemeinde)*, did not wholly vanish during the feudal period but became a part of a hierarchical structure, mediating between individuals at the bottom and the monarch at the top. The waning of the Middle Ages saw a decline in the strength of that mediating structure, along with a drift of power to the monarch. Consonant with this change in real conditions was a change in political philosophy and legal constructions of reality. Gierke shows how the *Genossenschaft* and its autonomous rights were submerged in the fifteenth and sixteenth centuries by a new conception of the state, arising with the reception of Roman law in Germany, in which corporate bodies were wholly derivative from the state and had rights obtained by concession from the state.

1. See, for example, Lewis (1935, p. 48) and Mogi (1935, p. 5).

The introduction of Roman law also brought the idea of the corporate body, the *universitas,* as a juristic person, albeit a fictional one. The idea of corporate bodies that received rights from the state and were seen as nonautonomous under it but were subject to private law as fictional persons was followed in the seventeenth century by Hobbes's doctrine of natural rights and Rousseau's social contract, in which rights derived wholly from individuals, and corporate bodies had no independent existence. (Hobbes, however, brought back the corporate bodies under a concession from the state and fully subordinate to it, *after* individuals had given over sovereignty to the state, that is, Leviathan.) Finally, in the seventeenth, eighteenth, and nineteenth centuries, the idea of the corporate body as a legal person was reconstituted, but as a free subject of rights, not dependent on a concession from the state or in any sense an organ of the state. It required certification from the state after the fact of its existence, but natural persons also required certification as citizens. (I will use the legal term "natural person," or where there is no ambiguity "person," to refer to physical beings and "corporate actor" to refer to those corporate bodies that can be regarded as taking coherent action directed toward a goal.) In practice, however, associations in Germany never gained the degree of freedom from the state envisioned in Gierke's theory. It was in England and America that they came to have the greatest freedom from the state.

The medieval conceptions of corporate bodies, whether derived from Roman law or in German law or English common law, recognized an overall corporate unity of which such bodies were themselves parts. There was a fixed hierarchy of collective bodies, a nested structure built up from communities or associations, as described by Gierke (1968 [1900]) and Simmel (1950). The essentially new element which subsequently emerged in English and German law was the existence of corporate bodies that were independent and free, not part of an articulated structure but, like real persons, the subject of whatever actions they miglt choose to engage in. This severance of the modern corporation from a fixed place in a structure represents the most recent development in social organization. The severance is analogous to an earlier one—the severance of the individual from a fixed place in a social structure—which led to the philosophical thesis of natural rights inhering in sovereign individuals.

Gierke developed a legal foundation for rights that lay somewhere between the unitary tradition of all rights inhering in a single entity, whether an organismic state or a despotic ruler, and Locke's theory of natural rights, in which only individuals have sovereign rights. Gierke found a correspondence between the German association and the nineteenth-century theory of the corporation as a juristic person with legal rights, and attempted to develop a social theory based on these legal rights. His thesis was that natural rights inhere in all "persons," both natural persons and those corporate actors which are legal persons, because human beings exist both as individual persons and as parts of collective bodies. They should thus have natural (or sovereign) rights in both capacities, as natural persons and as parts or members of corporate bodies.

The only difficulty with this thesis from the point of view of the theory of this book, and social theory generally, is that it precludes investigation of certain questions. Since natural persons are free to join or leave corporate actors, to vest rights and resources in them or to divest, then for the theorist to take corporate actors along with individuals as starting points would shut off from investigation the question of how individuals make those choices, how they relate themselves to society through corporate bodies, and how these bodies constitute vehicles through which individuals exercise their rights. Also shut off from investigation would be the questions of how corporate actors are born when rights are vested in them and how they can be killed by divestment—for corporate actors are born, they do change, and they die.

Emergence of Corporate Actors in Social Organization and Law

Because corporate bodies are not physical entities, as natural persons are, the importance of treating corporate bodies as actors may not be immediately apparent. It is therefore useful to review the emergence of corporate bodies as actors in the past centuries. For it would not always and everywhere have been appropriate to develop a theory of social organization with this structure.

Just as modern economic systems developed from informal trading and barter arrangements in early societies, modern legal systems developed from the local customs, rules, and procedures which characterized such societies. The parallel is not perfect, however, because economic activities take place within systems of law and are dependent on them. Thus without the codification of laws the quantitative and systematic character of the modern economic system could not exist. Nevertheless, the legal system and the economic system in modern society have undergone parallel development in the direction of codification, calculability, and precision.

I emphasize this development because it is related to the potential development of the social sciences. In primitive economies only a primitive and qualitative theory of the functioning of the economic system could potentially be developed.[2] Transactions were casual and not made according to careful calculation of value; many of the institutions intrinsic to modern economic systems (for example, banks) did not exist. Thus the highest possible state that the science of economics *could* have attained was limited by the level of complexity and calculability that the concrete reality of the economic system had reached. Economics as a scientific discipline today mirrors the complexity of actual economic systems. It may fail to do so adequately, but the concrete reality constitutes a

---

2. In another context Joan Robinson (1956) says, "There is no advantage (and much error) in making definitions of words more precise than the subject matter they refer to" (p. 236). One might extend this to the structures of activities themselves, which are very loose and casual in primitive economies.

guide to, and sets limits on, the development of the discipline.[3] And economic systems are not fixed and immutable but always in the process of change.

One implication of this is that social theory must constantly undergo change, even in the mature state. As social reality changes, through the invention of new forms of organization and the development of new processes, social theory must be elaborated or changed.

Biology as a scientific discipline would in principle be in the same situation, considering the long course of biological evolution. Theories about biological processes such as photosynthesis could not come into existence before the processes themselves had developed evolutionarily. In practice, of course, biological organization can be regarded as stable because evolutionary movement is so slow relative to the time scale covering the period of theory development. This is not the case, however, for social organization. Social inventions occur in the same time scale as theory development. Theory must change as those inventions make possible new structures and new processes.[4]

In the same way that rationalization of the economic system constituted a guide for the development of economics, rationalization of the legal system should constitute a guide for the development of political science and sociology. It does so for certain parts of political science; for example, the study of government and the study of constitutional law are inextricably intertwined. Yet sociologists, conceiving of their discipline as behavioral, have largely ignored law. This neglect may be warranted for certain branches of sociology (for example, demography). But in the study of social organization it can lead the sociologist to ignore those very structures and processes that form the core of social organization in a given society.

An illustration of this can be seen in the following passage from Pollock and Maitland (1968 [1898]) describing an aspect of thirteenth-century constitutional law in England:

> Of the diverse sorts and conditions of men our law of the thirteenth century has much to say; there are many classes of persons which must be regarded as legally constituted classes. Among laymen the time has indeed already come when men of one sort, free and lawful men *(liberi et legales homines)*

3. Of course, when a real system shows the loose coupling and highly stochastic character that I have described, it could in principle be mirrored by a theory which contained a relatively greater indeterminacy. Such a theory would be even more complex than one that mirrors a more determinate system.

4. Some authors make much of the fact that sociological knowledge itself is an element in bringing about that change. For example, Merton (1968, pp. 183–184) points out that this creates a paradox in the development of theory because the knowledge changes the reality that the theory was designed to mirror. But the paradox exists only if current social theory is regarded as fixed and immutable. Friedrichs (1972) argues that the feedback makes usual scientific endeavor impossible. But so long as social theory itself is seen as subject to change, there is no problem.

can be treated as men of the common, the ordinary, we may perhaps say the normal sort, while men of all other sorts enjoy privileges or are subject to disabilities which can be called exceptional. The lay Englishman, free but not noble, who is of full age and who has forfeited none of his rights by crime or sin, is the law's typical man, typical person. But besides such men there are within the secular order noble men and unfree men; then there are monks and nuns who are dead to the world; then there is the clergy constituting a separate "estate"; there are Jews and there are aliens; there are excommunicates, outlaws and convicted felons who have lost some or all of their civil rights; also we may make here mention of infants and of women, both married and unmarried, even though their condition be better discussed in connexion with family law, and a word should perhaps be said of lunatics, idiots, and lepers. Lastly, there are "juristic persons" to be considered, for the law is beginning to know the corporation. (vol. 1, p. 407)

This passage indicates the kinds of persons who were counted as different under the law and who bore different relations to society's organization. A theory of social organization applicable to France or Germany in the thirteenth century would have required even more distinctions among persons of different estates than would one applicable to England. Both in England and on the Continent at that time, however, different persons were related to social organization in different ways. The law of that period recognized and detailed these distinctions, and a theory of social organization appropriate to that period would have had to make use of the functional distinctions these classifications implied.

A social theory appropriate to modern Western society might seem simpler in some respects than one appropriate to the Middle Ages. The estates have vanished, as have, or nearly so, the distinctions among classes of persons treated differently under the law. This apparent simplification is misleading, however, as will become evident later in this chapter. A higher level of complexity in social organization has developed; impersonal corporate actors exist in full flower, and much of social organization consists of relations between such actors. These corporate actors are composed not of persons but of positions, a fact which makes it possible for the same natural person to occupy *several* positions simultaneously. This constitutes a basic restructuring of society, and role theory in sociology (a type of theory inapplicable to the organization of social life in the Middle Ages) is a reflection of the new reality.

The full history of the restructuring of social organization that took place from the thirteenth to the twentieth century has yet to be written. That the beginning elements of the change were present in the thirteenth century is indicated by one of the "sorts and conditions of men" referred to by Pollock and Maitland above, the "juristic persons" in the form of corporations.

The conception of the corporation as a legal person and the reorganization of society around impersonal corporate bodies made possible a radically different kind of social structure. As long as society was seen as a fixed organic whole, the social differentiation of activities that emerged in the Middle Ages (trade, crafts, agriculture, and religion) implied a rigid differentiation of natural persons in fixed positions (as in the caste system in India but with less continuity through generations). But as this differentiation of activities increased, a new form of social organization slowly came into being, and the law reflected this invention. This form involved the corporation as a functional element, a juristic person which could substitute functionally for a natural person. A corporation could act in a unitary way, could own resources, could have rights and responsibilities, could occupy the fixed functional position or estate which had been imposed on the natural person (and later could be partially freed from that fixed position).

Natural persons, in turn, came to be free from the fixed estates, gaining mobility as structural stability began to be provided to society by the new fixed functional units, the corporations or corporate bodies. Persons no longer had to be one dimensional; they could occupy several positions in the structure at once and could change positions freely. It was the positions—as components of the new elements of society, the corporate actors—which provided the structural continuity and stability.

In this context it is easy to see why modern sociology could easily neglect the law and consider itself wholly behavioral. In contrast, a sociological science in the Middle Ages, built on a hierarchical whole of which natural persons were the most elementary units, would have defined persons' activities within narrow limits—limits imposed by the requirements of the unitary society. There was little range for behavioral choice because persons had not yet been freed from fixed functional positions by the philosophical theory of natural rights or the invention of the juristic person, the abstract and intangible corporate actor. To suggest that this invention arose all at once, or that it has even now fully replaced the old basis of social organization, would be mistaken. Modern sociology is complex because modern society contains two forms of social organization: that in which relations are between natural persons, and that in which corporate actors are the fundamental elements and natural persons act only as their agents. (Some of the ways in which these two forms of organization coexist and interrelate will be examined in subsequent chapters.)

It is useful to gain a sense of the way in which the concept of the corporation developed in the law. The law, of course, was attempting to keep pace with changes that were occurring in actual social organization. Pollock and Maitland (1968 [1898]) opened their discussion of corporations in this way:

> Every system of law that has attained a certain degree of maturity seems compelled by the ever-increasing complexity of human affairs to create persons who are not men, or rather (for this may be a truer statement) to recognize that such persons have come and are coming into existence, and to regulate their rights and duties. (vol. 1, p. 486)

The earliest clear development of the idea of elements of society other than natural persons or the state arose in Roman law as the concept of *universitas,* but it was not until the thirteenth and fourteenth centuries that the organization of Continental and English society required its use. By then persons were acting corporately and independently of any monarch, in such a way that the action could be seen as other than an act of the aggregate. Functionally, the whole came to be, not greater than, but different from the sum of its parts.

In certain places to be regarded as a corporate entity in law required a charter from the state, although this was not universal. In certain legal systems, as in ancient Roman law, judgment against a corporate body could not be imposed against the individuals who made it up, but again this was not everywhere the case. The history of laws of incorporation of joint-stock corporations reveals wide variability with respect to this principle. But as the corporate person has become more and more of an independent entity in society, the separation of corporate and individual liability has become more universal and explicit.[5] After reviewing the variations among corporate entities in which the whole does behave differently from its parts, Pollock and Maitland (1968 [1898]) described the essential qualities of the legal corporation:

> The core of the matter seems to be that for more or less numerous purposes some organized group of men is treated as a unit which has rights and duties other than the rights and duties of all or any of its members. What is true of this whole need not be true of the sum of its parts, and what is true of the sum of the parts need not be true of the whole. The corporation, for example, can own land and its land will not be owned by the sum of the corporators; and, on the other hand, if all the corporators are co-owners of a thing, then that thing is not owned by the corporation. (vol. 1, p. 488)

In the early development of the concept of the corporation in the twelfth, thirteenth, and fourteenth centuries in Germany and England, the churches played an important part. A problem arose as follows: A landowner would build a church on his property and then give over the church to the priest as a loan. But in so doing, he gave up certain rights to the land the church was on and came to be regarded as merely the patron of the church. The priest as agent of the church could not be rightly regarded as the owner of these rights, but only as their temporal guardian. Thus it became necessary to conceive of another actor, neither the patron of the church nor the priest, to hold these rights. For a time, the saint for which the church was named was regarded as that actor. Thus the church and the land it stood on became independent of the original owner-patron and came to be the property of a saint, with the priest as temporal guardian. Since the saint was no longer alive, it was only a short step to conceiving of the church as a corporate actor holding rights of ownership. And in any social

5. There has been, in some recent legal rulings in the United States, a movement back toward an earlier stage, an attempt to find individual liability when there is corporate liability—in some cases top managers have been held liable, and in others corporation directors (see Chapter 21).

system such rights bring with them responsibilities, the possibility of overstepping them, and thus the necessity to regard their holder as both an object of action and a subject. This came about slowly in the case of churches, but eventually they could have judgments passed against them for infringement of others' rights.

Other corporate actors began to develop in thirteenth-century England—the boroughs, or communities chartered by the king. These communities became both the object of action (often in suits brought by the king) and the subject of action, through ownership of lands and toll rights. In contrast to the corporate unity of the church, which began to develop through the church's becoming the subject of action (as the owner of property), the movement of geographic communities toward corporate status began by their becoming the objects of action. Maitland (1908) gives an example of the way this occurred for the hundred, historically an important geographic unit in England which never fully acquired the status of corporate actor:

> Under the law of the conqueror, if a man be found slain and the slayer be not produced, the hundred is fined, unless it can prove that the slain man was an Englishman. In the general administration of the law, the hundred is an important unit. In particular it is important in the system of trial by jury introduced by Henry II. (p. 46)

Thus social reality gave a unity of purpose and of action to geographic communities. Yet it was several centuries before legal theory caught up with reality, defined the corporate actor by its rights and responsibilities, and clearly distinguished it as a juristic person, a legal entity separate from its members. Maitland also indicates how legal theory developed in England with respect to the boroughs:

> In later times, in the fifteenth century and onwards, we can arrive at a legal definition of a borough: the notion of a corporation has then been found, a juristic person, which has rights and duties which are quite distinct from the rights and duties of its members . . . The greater boroughs, however, of Edward's reign have already in substance attained to all or almost all of those distinctive characteristics which the later lawyers regarded as essential to corporate unity. These characteristics are five—the rights of perpetual succession, the power to sue and be sued as a whole and by the corporate name, the power to hold lands, the right to use a common seal and the power of making by-laws. (p. 54)

Legal theory had difficulty distinguishing the aggregate, or the community, from the corporate actor. In a community natural persons with a common interest might bind themselves together to protect that interest jointly through collective action. But in a corporation a new entity has been created, whose interests and resources are distinct from those who brought it into being. Even if it, as a distinct entity, is liable, the natural persons who are its founders may not be. The corporation takes unitary action with resources of its own and is not merely a manifestation of a collective will or common purpose which draws its members into action. This distinction developed only through legal arguments and court decisions from the thirteenth century to the present, which provided rules concerning the new social phenomenon that began to emerge in the thirteenth century.

The distinction between corporate actor and natural person can perhaps best be seen when there is a single person with whom the corporate actor might be identified, a person who acts in two capacities. The best example is a king; the concept of corporation sole (a corporate entity consisting of only one person) was developed in order to be able to distinguish his acts as king from his acts as an individual. The doctrine of the king's two bodies—the physical body and the body politic—became established during the fifteenth, sixteenth, and seventeenth centuries to separate the two sets of actions (after the landed or ecclesiastical corporation as a legal person was established).

Many court cases were argued over actions of the king and the question of whether a given action should be regarded as an action of the body politic. For example, King Edward IV sold, when he was 9 years old and thus legally a minor, some lands in the duchy of Lancaster (Kantorowitz, 1957). If this action were judged by the laws applying to natural persons, it would not be legal because the king was a minor. But if it were regarded as an action of the body politic of the king, it would be legal, for the body politic had no birth or death, no age of minority or infirmity. The concept of the Crown as the body politic of the king, a distinct and separate person with interest and resources, emerged. The distinction made it possible for Parliament to revolt in 1642 against Charles I as a physical person while continuing to uphold the Crown. This distinction, which did not exist in France, made it possible for a King to be beheaded while the monarchy continued.

The concept of corporation sole makes it clearer that a corporation does not need a set of persons standing behind it, that it is not merely a representative of persons. The essence of the concept of the corporate actor lies in the existence of a separate set of rights and responsibilities and a set of resources and interests, which can neither be allocated to a single physical person nor be allocated among a set of persons. It is these properties of a corporate actor that are crucial to the functioning of social organization, as legal systems have recognized, and to the concept of corporate actor in social theory.

The concept of corporation sole also illuminates a sharp contrast between a theory involving corporate actors and role theory. During the emergence of the concept of corporation sole, jurists were grappling with a real problem: The same physical person might take actions that could not be appropriately handled by law unless they were attributed to two different actors. The problem arose because the king as a physical person had the attributes of any physical person (birth, death, infirmities and so forth) but the king as a corporate person did not. The functional significance of the king's actions thus differed, depending on whether they were taken in one or the other of his two capacities, even though these were not easily identifiable.

The functional significance of an action taken by a manager of a firm toward his secretary similarly differs, depending on whether he is acting in his capacity as an agent of the firm (in which case he has certain rights, within the constitution of the firm, to make demands on his secretary) or in his capacity as a personal actor (in which case he has such rights only if the secretary gives them to him). In the first case there is a relation between two agents, and the firm's explicit and implicit rules of organization specify their rights and responsibilities. The agents' positions may be called roles, and role theory is able to describe the relations between them. But putting such a situation, in which persons are acting as agents of a corporate actor, under the label "role," along with the heterogeneous collection of descriptive terms also so labeled (such as coward, friend, and Christian), destroys the functional differentiation between personal actions and actions as agents of a corporate actor. Role theory thus ignores the carefully worked out legal distinctions which have been found to be necessary to apply law in the functioning of society. Sociologists cannot ignore these legal distinctions, if only because of the fact that treating certain entities as entities before the law makes them functioning entities in the organization of society. Beyond that, however, the necessity for the law to create fictional persons (that is, corporate actors) suggests that a proper theory of social organization will also find it necessary to utilize that abstract concept.

Role theorists have recognized the same phenomenon that legal theorists recognized, that is, that the same person can act in different capacities on different occasions, with functionally important attendant consequences. But then in their haste to encompass all of social organization, and because they were never forced to act on their theories as jurists were, role theorists threw away the power that such a recognition offered. It is also useful to mention that the watering down of the basic distinction forced role theorists to abandon the concept of interests that inheres in the precise juridical concept of actors, or parties, and thus abandon with it any possibility of conflicts of interests. Since roles have no interests, but are like different hats which a person puts on in appropriate circumstances, role conflict within an individual cannot be conceived of as a conflict of interests between two actors in society.

Without serious reification, then, it can be said that there are, functionally, two types of persons or actors in society, and the theory of this book is a theory of action in which both appear. If a still newer form of social organization were to emerge, as the present form has arisen over the past few centuries, the present theory would no longer be appropriate. The theory is, as all theories of social organization must be, dependent on the social structures that actually exist. The development of corporate actors has meant that natural persons are no longer the sole social units among whom relations can be said to exist. This development constituted a frame for a radical reorganization of society, which has finally come to be pervasive in developed countries. It could, however, eventually be replaced by another form of social organization—perhaps one in which natural persons were even more fully absolved from the necessity of constituting the stable functional elements. If such a change in societal organization were to occur, it would necessitate changes in law and in social theory.

For the present, however, a social theory of purposive action must take as its elementary actors both natural persons and corporate bodies, because both have the essential properties of actors: control over resources and events, interests in resources and events, and the capability of taking actions to realize those interests through that control.

Examples of Interactions of Natural Persons and Corporate Actors

Some examples of interactions will show how corporate actors play a part through their agents. Interactions that appear to be between persons are not always so.

When a waitress waits on a customer in a restaurant, takes his order and serves him food, she is acting not as an individual actor but as an agent of the restaurant, which is a corporate actor. The menu she offers to the customer is not a set of choices which she as a personal actor is offering the customer, but a set of choices offered by the restaurant of which she is an agent. When she is paid for the meal, she cannot keep the money (although she may keep any tip left for her personally) but must transmit it to the cashier, another agent of the corporate actor, that is, of the restaurant. Thus the two actors in interaction in this situation are the restaurant, a corporate actor, and the customer, a natural person.

As another example, consider a foreman who asks the plant manager to change the arrangement of machines on the shop floor. There are two corporate actors here: the production unit of which the foreman is in charge; and the plant as a whole, of which the plant manager is in charge. The foreman is making the request as an agent of his unit, and the plant manager responds as an agent of the plant. The foreman makes the request, or is expected to do so, on the basis of the benefits the change will bring not to him personally but to his production unit, the corporate actor in whose name he is making the request. The plant manager assesses the request in terms of its costs and benefits to the whole plant, of which he is an agent, and not its costs and benefits to him personally. Thus their resources as natural persons and the consequences to them as natural persons play no legitimate part in the interaction between these two. Only the resources of and the consequences to the corporate actors whose agents they are are involved. This is a case of interaction between two corporate actors, one of which is subordinate to the other.

Both of these examples are distinct from an interaction in which a man asks a woman to go out for an evening. This is an interaction between two personal actors, and the man uses resources that belong to him personally to gain results of interest to him personally.

In an interaction in which one or both persons are acting as agents for corporate actors, there is always the possibility of an accompanying interaction between personal actors. The customer in the restaurant may engage the waitress in conversation, shifting at some point to an interaction with her personally by asking her about herself, or perhaps asking to meet her after work. The plant manager may refuse the foreman's request, not because of any considerations about the plant's benefit, but because of personal hostility which he feels toward the foreman. In both these cases a single concrete interaction can, for analytical purposes, split in two. In the first case, there is an interaction between a corporate actor (the restaurant) and a natural person and an interaction between two natural persons. In the second case there is an interaction between two corporate actors, one subordinate to the other (the production unit and the plant), and an interaction between two natural persons.

Social theorists have written widely about the informal social organization that springs up within formal organizations (for example, Homans, 1950; Blau, 1963). Such works have distinguished what in the present theory are conceived of as relations between personal actors from the relations between corporate actors that occur in the formal organizational structure when persons are acting in the capacity of agents for corporate actors. Although some social theorists distinguish role relations from personal relations, I distinguish between two kinds of actors involved in the relationships: corporate actors and natural persons.

In a concrete situation which involves an agent of a corporate actor, decisions must sometimes be made which show sharply the distinction between the personal actor and the corporate actor. For example, consider a young boy whose first job is behind the counter in a drugstore, serving ice cream cones and sodas to customers. At certain times he is confronted with a moral dilemma: When a friend comes into the drugstore, should he or should he not give his friend a larger than normal scoop of ice cream? The source of this dilemma lies in the fact that the ice cream is not the boy's but the drugstore's. This moral problem has a certain defining character: whether the boy can use resources that are physically under his control, that is, the ice cream, for his personal purposes. Legitimately he cannot. By the implicit terms of his contract with the drugstore, he must act as the drugstore's agent with regard to any of its resources over which he has control and must use those resources for furthering the drugstore's interests rather than his own.

Analytically it is clear that any person in such a situation has two sets of resources: his own, that is, his as a personal actor; and those of the corporate actor for whom he is an agent. Any employee of a firm traveling on the firm's business at its expense has two kinds of money, which he could, if he desired, physically separate into two pockets. In one pocket would be his own money, which he could spend however he desires. In the other pocket would be the firm's money, which he may use only for expenses that are incurred in pursuit of the firm's business. Because the agent has physical control of expenditures, a common occurrence is the use of the corporate actor's resources by the agent in his own interests. Numerous devices have been employed in social organizations to prevent this appropriation from occurring.

Such an appropriation of a corporate actor's resources is not the only type of confounding between personal and corporate actor that occurs when an individual acts as an agent for a corporate actor. Another frequent pattern is the apparent establishment of a personal relation (that is, a relation between personal actors) in which one of the parties is in fact acting as the agent of a corporate actor. A classic example is the female spy, who, acting as an agent for some government, appears to establish a personal relation but does so solely for the purpose of obtaining information for her principal. This type of deception occurs in other situations as well. A newspaper reporter may use a variety of techniques to establish a personal relationship with someone from whom he wants to obtain information for his newspaper that would not be forthcoming if he appeared to be fully an agent of the newspaper.[6]

Another example, a set of activities following a single incident, gives further insight into the distinction between personal actors and corporate actors and that between relations among persons and relations among positions that are part of the structure of a corporate actor. The activities raise difficult questions about the nature of social organization and about theory designed to account for such organization. The following episodes occurred after the death of a man in a small town and centered around the man's widow and son. The man had lived in the town for five years and had a number of friends there, but the widow was not well acquainted in the town, and the son was not known there at all. These activities will appear unusual to some readers and commonplace to others. This difference in reaction is itself closely related to the questions they raise about social organization.

1. The day after the death, as the body was being prepared and the widow was dressing for receiving visitors to the funeral home, she decided she needed a set of earrings. She went into a store on the town square, two blocks from the funeral home, to buy them. The saleswoman who waited on her began to show her earrings, and they engaged in conversation. When the widow could not decide, the saleswoman offered to lend her those she was wearing. The widow accepted.

2. As visitors arrived at the funeral home, one of them, a man who lived down the road from the dead man's farm, described how he had "kept an eye out" for disturbances at the farm whenever the owner was away. Just the past week, he mentioned, he had noticed lights, although he believed the owner to be away. So

6. There are many deceptions similar to this that involve no corporate actor at all. That is, an individual may establish a relationship with another person apparently for its own sake, but in fact for his own ends outside that relationship. In the cases mentioned here, however, a corporate actor is the final recipient of what is obtained in the relationship.

he had driven up toward the house far enough to see that the car parked there was the owner's car and not that of an intruder.

3. The next morning at 6 A.M., the widow and son prepared to leave the farm and discovered that the car would not start. Their reaction was to call the dead man's daughter, who lived about thirty miles away and to whose home they were traveling on the way to the funeral (to be held in another town), and ask her to pick them up. The daughter suggested that an hour's time would be saved if they asked a neighbor who had been a friend of the dead man to bring them down. They called the neighbor, and he quickly got dressed and took them to the daughter's home.

4. The disabled automobile was left at the farm, but neither the widow nor the son returned there that day. The widow called the friend, who arranged to have the car fixed and then, for safety, brought to his house to be picked up later by the widow and son.

5. The widow and son returned to the town several weeks later to meet with a lawyer (hired earlier by the dead man) to settle the small estate. The widow and son discussed with the lawyer common acquaintances and friends, discovering that several people known well to the lawyer were friends of the widow or the dead man. The widow and son were both concerned about possible overcharging by the lawyer. The lawyer, when asked about the costs for probate court, replied that they would be small, less than $100. When asked what his fees would be, he replied that he charged according to a fixed schedule declining from 5% to 2% as the size of the estate increased. Both widow and son were surprised, having heard of considerably higher legal fees elsewhere.

6. The widow and son had lunch with a friend at a nearby restaurant and discussed the lawyer with the friend. The friend indicated that she knew several people who had used him and were convinced of his honesty and skill and that the dead man had heard about the lawyer from a friend of his at a nearby loan company, who recommended the lawyer as someone he knew personally, who was honest and could be trusted.

In the first of these episodes, it was possible that either of two actors—both represented by the same concrete person, the saleswoman—would be activated. One was the store, of which the saleswoman was an agent; the other was the natural person. It was the natural person who engaged in the interaction of lending earrings to the widow. Apparently the relation between persons was activated because the conversation principally concerned relationships between persons (the saleswoman's friendship with the dead man and his relation to the widow) rather than the relation between the store as corporate actor and the widow as customer.

In the second, third, and fourth episodes, it was not a question of a conflict between two competing actors represented by the same person, but rather of whether or not a personal actor would act. The relationship between persons was strong enough that in all three cases the personal actor did act.

In the fifth episode there was again the possibility that either of two actors would be activated in the lawyer: a natural person or the agent of a law firm.[7] In fact, both were activated to some degree. But the initial discussion of the lawyer, the widow, and the son reinforced the structure of relationships between persons and deemphasized the structure of relations involving the corporate actor. The lawyer, in establishing his fees, might well have charged higher ones than were characteristic of the town because he was dealing with persons from outside the town. That he did not do so is not conclusive evidence that the natural person entered into the transaction, but it does suggest that possibility.

Whether or not that was the case, the conversation of the widow and the son with the friend in the final episode concerned only the personal relations in which the lawyer as a person took part, and not the relations or the activities of the corporate actor, the law firm.

All of these actions of natural persons as actors were benevolent. That need not have been so, of course; malevolent as well as benevolent actions can be directed from personal actors toward personal actors. The point is that the actions of these persons were activated by personal relations rather than relations involving corporate actors for which they were agents.

What emerges from these episodes is a picture of a community in which the principal relations are between persons. Persons know nearly everyone they meet as persons, not as occupants of positions. Memory resides in persons, not in office files, and the memories concern other concrete persons. Many of the activities in the community are ones in which persons and relations between them would not play a part in most communities; but in each of these episodes persons did emerge as actors. The community appears to be held together far more by relations among persons than by relations among corporate actors or between corporate actors and persons.

Types of Interactions Involving Corporate Actors and Persons

The existence of corporate actors as structural elements in a social system creates the possibility of types of interaction which have special characteristics. Two types of actors, corporate actors and persons, make possible three distinct combinations of types in a given two-party interaction:

1. Person with person
2. Person with corporate actor
3. Corporate actor with corporate actor

These can be seen in Table 20.1.

7. Law firms, like universities, are social anachronisms in that the corporate actor is not fully distinct from the members who make it up. Thus the term "agent" is not entirely appropriate here.

Table 20.1 Types of relations between actors.

		Object of action	
		Person	Corporate actor
Subject of action	Person	1	2a
	Corporate actor	2b	3

Type 1 Interactions

The first type of interaction is the kind into which people are socialized through-out childhood, the kind for which the Golden Rule or Kant's categorical impera-tive was constructed, the kind on which most commonsense notions about social interaction, as well as most work in social psychology, are based.

Type 2 Interactions

The second type of interaction is exemplified by customer-store relations, by employee-company relations (in the absence of a union or other bargaining agent), by client–social welfare agency relations, and by citizen-government relations. In all of these one actor is a personal actor, and the other is a corporate actor.

Such interactions pose a number of problems for social organization. Unlike relations between persons, type 2 interactions usually evince an asymmetry in the size of the parties, which tends to create, all other things being constant, a power asymmetry. A second problem arises because individuals are socialized into type 1 relations, but as adults find themselves living in a form of social organization in which they must frequently confront corporate actors in interactions.

Some of the problems of type 2 interactions have been noted by sociologists. Katz and Eisenstadt (1960), for example, show the kinds of problems that arose when Middle Eastern Jews, who had lived in familistic and primitive settings, first confronted governmental bureaucracies in Israel. They found it difficult to distinguish between the person with whom they dealt (who was not only a person but also the bureaucracy's agent) and the bureaucracy itself. They ex-pected to interact with the same person each time they dealt with the bureaucracy. They attempted to establish personal relationships with each of the various agents with whom they dealt. They attempted to get things done by the use of influence, that is, by claims of personal relationships through which they were connected to agents of the bureaucracy.

Other kinds of problems also arise for relationships between a corporate actor and a person. There is evidence that individuals do not feel bound by the Golden Rule in their intereactions with corporate actors (for instance, there are persons who will cheat the telephone company but not other persons). Problems are occasioned by the fact that in some circumstances corporate actors cannot respond differentially to persons, but must make the same response to all. And there are certain problems created by fundamental differences between natural persons and corporate actors. An important one of these concerns short-term and long-term interests.

EXPLOITATION OF THE CONFLICT BETWEEN SHORT-TERM AND LONG-TERM INTERESTS IN TYPE 2 INTERACTIONS   Certain properties of actors lead to special problems in exchanges involving type 2 relations. One of these problems is the conflict between short-term and long-term interests referred to in Chapter 19. One manifestation of this conflict is seen in the related notions of willpower and weakness of will (see Elster, 1979; Ainslie, 1986). The notion of willpower, or the power to prevent short-term interests from overwhelming long-term interests, has no place in standard theory of rational choice. Yet it is a common element in the actions of natural persons.

The only basis on which persons can precommit themselves and exercise willpower is that of experience, either real or vicarious. They must have been confronted at an earlier time with similar action alternatives and have seen the short-term and long-term consequences.[8] If persons were perfectly experienced, they would precommit themselves only in the right circumstances, that is, if and only if their longer-term interests in one action are greater than their shorter-term interests. However, they do not. Persons act indulgently, for which they are sorry later; they succumb to temptation and later regret doing so, even when succumbing brought all the benefits expected; they engage in impulse buying and compulsive eating.

In type 1 interactions both parties to a transaction are subject to weakness of will. Some may be able to withstand their impulses better than others, and thus may attain better outcomes in the long term. Some may even be able to exploit weakness of will in others and achieve more at their expense. Children in particular are characterized by inability to resist temptation, because they have not yet

8. Connections between actions and consequences must be cognitively perceived if the actor is to take a consequence into account when deciding on an action. For example, some children become irritable when they need to eat, before they experience the sensation of hunger. It may be, in fact, that the sensation known as hunger (including visions and thoughts of food) only arises after that irritability has been satisfied a number of times through eating food and experiencing its reduction.

experienced longer-term consequences of actions. It is in part for this reason—that is, to protect their long-term interests from actions that indulge their short-term interests and to protect them from others' exploitation of their short-term interests—that children have legal guardians. Weakness of will is a part of the human condition, however, to which all persons are subject. Precommitment, keeping in mind long-term consequences, and other mental efforts may reduce its effects, but it is a human characteristic.[9]

In type 2 relations one actor is a corporate actor, constructed differently from human beings. The consequence is that a corporate actor is in a unique position to exploit weakness of will in natural persons, even to exploit the potential for such weakness by encouraging impulsive action.

This would be merely an interesting academic point if there were not so many signs that this weakness of natural persons is widely exploited by modern corporate actors. In consumer markets the signs are abundant. Most evident is advertising which encourages impulse buying (advertising of this sort does not occur in markets where the consumers are corporate actors) or, more generally, any advertising which makes use of attention-getting devices that exploit appetites of natural persons. The widespread encouragement of the use of credit cards by corporations is another striking example of this exploitation.

The contrast between use of credit cards and lay-away buying is instructive. Buying through lay-away plans is a means of saving. It is precommitting oneself to making periodic payments until a certain sum is reached, when the goods are received. It is a commitment to forgo the immediate benefits of the small amounts of money which constitute the payments in order to realize a longer-term interest. In credit-card buying the time perspective is the opposite: One receives the good immediately and pays later. Saving is not positive, as with lay-away plans or related activities such as Christmas Clubs, but negative.

The general decline of the positive-savings forms of consumption and their replacement by negative-savings forms indicates an increase in the capability of modern corporate actors to exploit weakness of will in natural persons. This increase is evident as well in the high rate of personal bankruptcy in the United States. (The capacity of corporate actors to exploit weakness of will in persons is especially pronounced in the United States, where the rate of personal savings is lowest of any developed country and where credit-card purchasing is higher than in any other country.)

Exploitation of natural persons' weakness of will is not only done by corporations in consumer markets. Such exploitation is also carried out by governments. In democratic political systems with periodic elections, in which the government depends on assent from natural persons to remain in power, political scientists have noted that election-year economic policies often provide short-term boosts to the economy, and thus short-term economic benefits to the

9. Rotating credit associations, widespread in the Far East and discussed in Chapter 12, constitute a special form of precommitment involving others. Alcoholics Anonymous is another example of the use of other persons in sustaining precommitment.

voters. Governments of some socialist countries have been accused of setting low prices for hard liquor in order to gratify appetites and dissipate any organization of political unrest.

It is possible that natural persons will come to be better able to resist this exploitation by modern corporate actors through development of psychological devices such as precommitment. It is also possible that educational institutions will reduce the amount of actual experience necessary to overcome weakness of will. Because lifetimes are limited, however, there is a limited and varying degree of experience in any age-heterogeneous population of natural persons. Thus the potential for exploitation of natural persons' weakness of will by corporate actors will remain high. It may even be that the potential for such exploitation will increase because of natural persons' limited lifetimes and corporate actors' unlimited lifetimes.

The asymmetry between persons and corporate actors with respect to willpower is only one source of problems that arise in type 2 relations. Other sources are the fact that corporate actors and natural persons are differently constructed and the fact that many type 2 relations show a great asymmetry in size and power.

THE GROWTH OF TYPE 2 INTERACTIONS   The problems of type 2 interactions are of special importance for modern society. During the twentieth century there has been a great increase in the ratio of type 2 relations to type 1 relations for the average individual in society. It is likely that this ratio will continue to grow. Thus the problem for the functioning of social systems created by the great increase in interactions between persons and corporate actors is of current and future importance. This structural change is due, of course, to the substantial increase in the ratio of corporate actors to persons. Although there has been an increase in the number (and thus the density) of persons in societies, the increase in number and variety of corporate actors has been much greater. For example, a tabulation of the number of profit-making corporations in the United States filing an income tax return between 1916 and 1969 shows an explosive growth, as indicated in Figure 20.1.

Since natural persons are both the owners and agents of such corporate actors, it might at first appear that this growth is of little importance. But one consequence of the proliferation of corporate actors is that the frequency of interactions in which each individual engages as a person with a corporate actor (actually with an agent) has increased greatly. Thus each person's social environment has become not so much peopled by other individuals like himself as by impersonal entities for which individuals act as agents. Later chapters will examine some of the consequences of this change for the functioning of modern society.

Type 3 Interactions

The type 3 interaction is one that does not involve natural persons at all but occurs solely between corporate actors: firms, organizations, associations, or

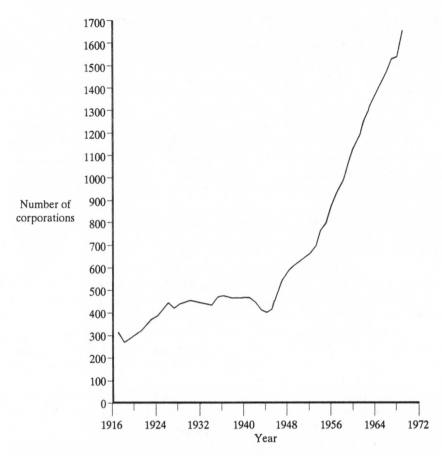

Figure 20.1   Number of profit-making corporations filing an income tax return in the United States, 1917–1969. (Data from Wu, 1974.)

other corporate entities. In type 3 interactions, individuals do not act as persons, but as agents of the corporate actors they represent. The earlier example of a foreman and a plant manager interacting as agents was such an interaction. Some of these transactions are wholly economic, involving exchange of goods and money. Others involve a variety of other resources; for example, the lobbying of a trade union against proposed legislation may involve use of the threat of nonsupport at the polls as a resource.

Obviously, with the proliferation of corporate actors, there has been a growth in the number of interactions of this third type. Thus, just as the average individual has come to be involved increasingly in type 2 interactions (either as a personal actor or as the agent of a corporate actor), he has come to be involved increasingly in type 3 interactions as an agent of a corporate actor interacting with another agent. Consequences of this trend will be discussed in succeeding chapters.

Displacement of Nature by Human Constructions

The emergence and growth of modern corporate actors can be viewed as part of a long-term historical development in which the primordial, natural environment is replaced by a purposively constructed one. The change occurs in both the physical environment and the social environment. The purposively constructed environment of the buildings and streets of a city (what has been called the built environment) has in the twentieth century displaced the natural environment of rural areas which in the nineteenth century constituted most persons' physical environment. Socially, primordial ties and the old corporate actors based on them (family, clan, ethnic group, and community) are increasingly displaced by the new, purposively constructed corporate actors and the relations generated by their existence.

This thesis, that there is progressive replacement of the natural environment by a purposively constructed one, is similar to Max Weber's thesis of a progressive rationalization of society. Both theses say that phenomena that in their uncontrolled state give rise to natural environments come to be subject to persons' control through a growth in human knowledge. In the thesis I am setting forth, replacement of the natural by the constructed constitutes a qualitative change, as the very form of social organization changes.

This general approach to historical development is not one that allows prediction of the future state of the constructed environment, either physical or social. That depends on inventions not yet made. The skyscraper depended on the invention of the elevator, and before that invention no one could foresee cities with central areas full of skyscrapers. The modern corporate actor, whose elements are positions rather than persons, was a social invention, and before that invention no one could foresee a social structure heavily populated with such actors. The modern corporate actor will not be the last social invention to be made. Thus the social structure as I have described it in this chapter is not the ultimate form of social organization. It will eventually be displaced. For the present, however, it is an intrinsic element of social theory: an important kind of actor in society, one which is itself a system of action.

« 21 »

Responsibility of Corporate Actors

Chapter 20 introduced the notion that the structure of modern societies is fundamentally different from that of earlier ones. Alongside natural persons is a newly evolved creature, the modern corporate actor, that acts and is acted on, pursues interests, and controls events. If this new society is considered from a naive point of view, a number of questions arise for the first time. One of these has to do with responsibility toward other actors in society. To whom are corporate actors responsible, and how is fulfillment of that responsibility ensured?

This question arises from three sources. The first is that the means by which responsibility toward others is induced in natural persons may not be available for these new creatures. If not, it becomes necessary to ask if there are existing or potential alternatives.

The second source of the question lies in the fact that many corporate actors are extraordinarily large and powerful. It is their money which sustains most of the expensive restaurants in modern society, most of the hotels, and all of the commercial airlines. They are the customers for much of the expensive art and sculpture, the luxury furniture, and the luxury high-rise construction. A transaction between a large corporate actor and a person is extremely asymmetric, because of the asymmetry in size and power. This asymmetry makes the attentiveness of the large modern corporate actor to the interests of others affected by its actions especially important.

The third source of the question is perhaps the most central: A corporate actor is by definition not a natural person. Thus, although it might be said that a person attending to his own interests is at least being responsible for himself, a similar statement cannot serve to justify a corporate actor's actions. It *must* serve the interests of some natural persons in society if it is to have a raison d'être. Who, then, are those persons whose interests it serves, and how does it affect the interests of other persons in doing so?

It is useful in addressing this question to focus on one set of corporate actors in capitalist society: the profit-making corporations. The rationale for this restriction is that this is the most complex case. For trade unions or other membership associations, the organizational goals are directly related to those of the members and stem from them. Whether those goals are in fact pursued effectively is another issue, and it is clear that they sometimes are not. Nevertheless, answering the above question is simpler for trade unions and other associations whose members are persons.

A sense of the fundamental character of this question of corporate responsibility can be gained by considering an extended hypothetical example. American Electric is a company invented by Hacker (1964) to illustrate the problem:

By 1972 American Electric had completed its last stages of automation: employees were no longer necessary. Raw materials left on the loading platform were automatically transferred from machine to machine, and the finished products were deposited at the other end of the factory ready for shipment. AE's purchasing, marketing, and general management functions could be handled by ten directors with the occasional help of outside consultants and contractors.

Beginning in 1962 AE's employee pension fund had started investing its capital in AE stock. Gradually it bought more and more of the company's shares on the open market, and by 1968 it was the sole owner of AE. As employees became eligible for retirement—some of them prematurely due to the introduction of automation—the fund naturally liquidated its capital to provide pensions. But instead of reselling its AE shares on the open market, the fund sold the stock to AE itself, which provided the money for pensions out of current income. By 1981 the last AE employee had died, and the pension fund was dissolved. At this time, too, AE became the sole owner of its shares. It had floated no new issues, preferring to engage in self-financing through earnings.

By 1982 the ten directors decided that AE would be well served by the passage of legislation restricting the imports of certain electrical equipment. They therefore secured the services of a public relations firm specializing in political campaigns. The objective was to educate the public and sway grass-roots sentiment so that Congress would respond by passing the required bill. The public relations firm was given a retainer of $1 million and told to spend up to $5 million more on advertising and related activities.

Within months the public began to hear about the dire consequences that would follow the importation of alien generators. National security, national prosperity, and the nation's way of life were threatened by a flood of foreign goods. The public relations firm placed several hundred advertisements in newspapers and magazines, and almost a thousand on television. At least fifty citizens' committees "spontaneously" arose to favor the legislation, and over two hundred existing groups passed resolutions in its support. Lectures were given to women's clubs, and films were shown in high school. By the end of the year—an election year—public sentiment had been aroused and hardly a Congressman was unaware of the popular ferment.

The bill was introduced in both chambers, and a good majority of senators and representatives, abiding by the wishes of their constituents, voted for it.

The President signed the bill, and it became law. AE's profits were substantially higher the following year.

A group of senators, however, were curious about what had been going on, and they decided to investigate AE's foray into the political arena. One of the directors was happy to testify, for he knew that no law had been violated. No bribes had been offered, certainly, and no contributions to legislators' campaigns had been made. Toward the end of the inquiry, after all of the techniques employed by the company and the public relations firm had been brought out, the following colloquy took place:

DIRECTOR: . . . And if we undertook these educational and political activities, it was our view that they were dictated by the company's best interests.

SENATOR: Now when you say that these campaigns were on behalf of the "company's" interests, I am not clear what you mean. Were you acting for your stockholders here?

DIRECTOR: I am afraid, Senator, that I cannot say that we were. You see, American Electric has no stockholders. The company owns all its stock itself. We bought up the last of it several years ago.

SENATOR: Well, if not stockholders, then were you acting as a spokesman for American Electric employees—say, whose jobs might be endangered if foreign competition got too severe?

DIRECTOR: No, sir, I cannot say that either. American Electric is a fully automated company, and we have no employees.

SENATOR: Are you saying that this company of yours is really no more than a gigantic machine? A machine that needs no operators and appears to own itself?

DIRECTOR: I suppose that is one way of putting it. I've never thought much about it.

SENATOR: Then so far as I can see, all of this political pressure that you applied was really in the interests of yourself and your nine fellow directors. You spent almost six million dollars of this company's money pursuing your personal political predilections.

DIRECTOR: I am afraid, Senator, that now I must disagree with you. The ten of us pay ourselves annual salaries of $100,000 year in and year out, and none of us receives any bonuses or raises if profits happen to be higher than usual in a given year. All earnings are ploughed back into the company. We feel very strongly about this. In fact, we look on ourselves as a kind of civil servant. Secondly, I could not say that the decision to get into politics was a personal wish on our part. At least eight of the ten of us, as private citizens that is, did not favor the legislation we were supporting. As individuals most of us thought it was wrong, was not in the national interest. But we were acting in the company's interest and in this case we knew that it was the right thing to do.

SENATOR: And by the "company" you don't mean stockholders or employees, because you don't have any. And you don't mean the ten directors because you just seem to be salaried managers which the machine hires to run its affairs. In fact, when this machine gets into politics—or indeed any kind of activity—it has interests of its own which can be quite different from the personal interests of its managers. I am afraid I find all this rather confusing.

DIRECTOR: It may be confusing to you, Senator, but I may say it has been quite straightforward to us at American Electric. We are just doing the job for which we were hired—to look out for the company's interests. (pp. 3–5)

Although there are no companies which have reached the limit exemplified by Hacker's American Electric Company, the general point of his example remains valid: There is no set of natural persons to whom the modern corporation is intrinsically and irrevocably responsible. The owners, including perhaps both persons and corporate actors, are the so-called residual claimants, but no one argues that they, and only they, are the actors to whom the corporation is, or ought to be, responsible. Thus the question of defining a responsible role in society for the modern corporation is an especially difficult one.

Responsible Actions of Natural Persons

As an initial approach to the problem, it is useful to reexamine the processes through which natural persons come to exhibit responsibility for themselves and others in their actions. Means by which persons' behavior is made responsible have evolved through the prehistory and history of human societies. Some of these involve external sanctions to bring about a minimum level of attention to the interests of others who may be affected by one's actions. Others are internal, such as identification with others brought about through socialization, as described in Chapters 11 and 19.

How is the action of a person controlled so that it is not totally irresponsible and oblivious to the interests of others? This question is an important one for natural persons, yet the conception of what constitutes responsible behavior is unstable. It varies for different members of a society. In broad outline, of course, responsible behavior can be defined as that which takes into account the interests and rights of others. Some actions which an actor expects to benefit his own interests slightly will bring about considerable harm to others.[1] Obviously everyone will be better off in the long run if such actions are not taken. How can this be achieved?

1. This statement implies interpersonal comparison of utility, which in general cannot be carried out (but see Chapter 29). In this context, however, interpersonal comparison of utility *is* carried out by each individual in deciding what yields greater harm to others than benefit to himself. From this perspective socialization which induces responsibility in a person may do so by increasing the weight of others' interests relative to his own. Persons characteristically differ in this: Young children give especially low weight to others' interests, whereas some adults are at the other extreme, "bending over backwards" to take others' interests into account.

The effort to establish controls over the behavior of natural persons is a major component of socialization. In addition, the importance of informal sanctions and criminal law as devices for social control of natural persons attests to the continuing importance of mechanisms of social control throughout adult life, beyond the period of childhood socialization.

The principal advantage of socialization over external sanctions is that once the internal change has been brought about, others' interests or rights will be taken into account even when no one else can observe the action. As a consequence, enforcement of responsible behavior, which may be costly, becomes unnecessary; rights and interests of others will be respected even in those situations in which enforcement is difficult or impossible. The external sanctions by which persons' actions are made responsible range from informal ones, such as expressions of slight disapproval or ostracism, to legal sanctions for breaking laws or regulations.

Another important consideration concerning the responsible actions of persons is the question of to whom an actor should be responsible. A person's environment contains many other persons, and responsible behavior toward one does not imply responsible behavior toward another. Members of tightly knit ethnic groups, families, or clans exhibit a high degree of responsibility toward others within the same group, but little toward outsiders. In primitive societies, where social worlds are sharply differentiated (for example, between tribes), this differential responsibility is even more pronounced.

Even when a person's sense of responsibility toward different others is not greatly different, there may be conflicts because an action that is responsible toward one party harms the interests of another. For example, children in growing up confront such conflicts between responsibility to family and responsibility to friends.

One way, then, of seeing how the actions of corporations might be guided in responsible directions is to gain some insight from the way in which society copes with natural persons. But first it is useful to note that social control of the actions of natural persons is far from universally successful. Some children are never socialized and grow up to be sociopaths, exploiting every situation for the tiniest bit of personal gain. Other adults are oversocialized, unable to function effectively because of too much attention to others' interests and too little attention to their own. The volume of behavior that can be termed irresponsible is another indication of the lack of universal success of institutions which induce responsible behavior.

All of this is useful for establishing an appropriate context for examining ways in which responsible behavior is induced in corporations and ways in which it can be induced. If corporate bodies are regarded as unitary actors, it is reasonable to use the social processes in which natural persons are involved as a context for asking questions about analogous processes for corporate actors.

It is not immediately obvious what institutions in society parallel (or might come to parallel if they currently do not) the socializing institutions and social norms that constitute constraints on individual actions and guide such actions in responsible directions. The legal system certainly constrains the actions of both natural persons and corporate actors, but there is no clear parallel to childhood socialization and to informal social norms.

Social Origins of Corporate Responsibility

A connection between natural persons and corporate actors might be made more apparent by a consideration of the origins of modern corporate actors that have no intrinsic connection to natural persons.

Chapter 20 emphasized the development of the modern corporate actor through changes in law and the organizational changes in society which accompanied the legal changes. But there was another source of modern corporate actors as natural extensions from an institution to which persons *are* intrinsically attached. The institution was a family—the Medicis. The Medici family branched out from Florence in the thirteenth century and became bankers for many parts of Europe. Doing this necessitated that the family take on many characteristics of the modern corporate actor. The Medicis' banking house had distant branches staffed by agents unrelated to the family. Nevertheless, action remained traceable to the family and ultimately to its head.

When corporate actors in society were of this sort, legal questions involving them were fundamentally simpler to resolve, because there was always a natural person at the end of the line of responsibility.[2] But as I indicated in Chapter 20, social practice, especially in England, changed from the thirteenth through the seventeenth centuries; first the chartering of towns gave them a corporate status independent of any of their citizens, and then the chartering of trading companies gave them a corporate status independent of the investors who brought them into being. Unlike the Medici banking house, these companies had no family base and thus were more readily distinguishable from natural persons. The question of responsibility for corporate action arose most forcefully after this separation occurred, for there was no longer a single natural person as principal to whom law and the community could attribute responsibility for actions. In fact, once the legal principle of limited liability became established, even multiple investors were protected from liability for the corporation's actions. The history of this development is perhaps best traced in England, principally by Maitland (1904; 1908; 1936).

When the concept of the corporation as an actor in its own right came to be

---

2. Because that natural person was subject to the mechanisms of social control that have been ever present for individuals—socialization, informal social norms, and laws—the social responsibility of the corporate actor was closely tied to the social responsibility of that individual. This is not to say that the clan or the tribe as a corporate entity was not sometimes held responsible for actions of its members. The retributive principle "an eye for an eye, a tooth for a tooth" has governed the relations between clans in many premodern and semi-anarchic societies. That is, any member of a clan is held responsible for the actions of one of the members which harmed a member of another clan.

accepted in common law, the question of corporate responsibility became more difficult and complex than it had been when corporate actors took on only simple forms. The corporation, by becoming detached from the family, has become freestanding, and the ideas of individual responsibility of natural persons and of corporate responsibility have become divorced. To illustrate what I mean, I will use two examples: corporate philanthropic activity in Minneapolis and the incident at Love Canal in upstate New York. The first illustrates the paths by which corporate responsibility has come about under the old, premodern corporate form, and the second the paths by which it comes about—or fails to come about—under the new, modern form.

Minneapolis has the highest level of corporate philanthropy of any large city in the United States. The Minneapolis Symphony Orchestra, the museums, and other cultural activities are better supported than comparable activities in other American cities. A sociologist at the University of Minnesota has studied the reasons for this and has tentatively concluded that the following process occurs (Galaskiewicz, 1985). In Minneapolis, as in most cities, the large corporations are controlled by professional managers—who, like most professional managers of corporations in the United States, come from middle-class and lower-middle-class backgrounds. The economic success of these managers is tied up with that of their detached, freestanding corporations. The large modern corporation, however, has none of the encumbrances, responsibilities, and informal community obligations that arose through the personal and family connections of the owner of the old, family-based corporation. But in Minneapolis there is one difference from most large American cities: The wealthy social elite of the city, who determine the bases of prestige and who control access to the inner circles of social status, maintain strong connections both to the civic and cultural activities of the city (as is true generally in American cities) and also (as is not the case in most large American cities) to the business community composed of these upwardly mobile managers. This strong connection allows the social elite to shape the norms and standards of behavior to which the managers who control corporations (as well as the newly wealthy owners of new enterprises) must adhere if they are to be socially accepted. Corporate philanthropy is encouraged by those norms. Thus a top manager's social success is in considerable part determined by the benevolence of the corporation he heads. In this way links between corporation and community, and the community responsibility this engenders, are maintained. These links were once maintained by the community ties of the families which both owned and controlled the corporations, but the separation of ownership and control of large corporations has severed them. A substitute has been found in Minneapolis, but one which probably will not be viable beyond another generation or two.

There are other cities with philanthropic traditions in the United States. In Rochester, New York, George Eastman, the founder of Eastman Kodak, helped to initiate norms favoring philanthropic activity that are to some degree maintained. In Wilmington, Delaware, there has been a strong tradition of community responsibility first on the part of E. I. Du Pont de Nemours and then on the part of other corporations in the vicinity. The list of business firms which have a philanthropic relationship with the city in which they began is a long one, but it becomes shorter each year, as conglomerates become more numerous and firms are taken over by or sold to larger corporations.

Love Canal is a different story. A canal was begun in upstate New York under the supervision of an engineer named William Love, but it was never completed. A number of years ago Hooker Chemical Company used the bed of the uncompleted canal as a site for disposing of chemical wastes. Houses were built on the landfill, and children of residents in the area have recently exhibited genetic defects, which may be a result of the presence of the toxic wastes. The persons at Hooker Chemical who made the decisions about waste disposal are long gone, and in fact the company itself has been taken over by a conglomerate, Occidental Petroleum. For the actions of Hooker Chemical at Love Canal, the interests of the community outside the firm did not serve to modify or constrain those actions, except as those interests were embodied in law. One might well argue that it could hardly be otherwise, that a chemical company which followed a more expensive but less potentially harmful mode of toxic waste disposal than that permitted by law would thereby suffer in the marketplace.[3]

These two examples illustrate two different points on a continuum of corporate responsibility toward parties outside the corporation. They indicate as well possible mechanisms by which corporations may come to act more or less responsibly toward a particular community or group. In addition, they suggest that such mechanisms are less widely available than they were when corporations were controlled by owners, and those owners had a position to maintain in a local community. They suggest further that, as corporations develop and become divorced from both their founders and local communities, the future will show decreasing availability of these mechanisms as means of generating corporate responsibility.

Internal Changes and Corporate Responsibility

The limited and declining availability of mechanisms through which corporations may exhibit social responsibility raises the question of just what other means there are of inducing responsible behavior by corporations. It will be helpful to keep in mind the parallel problem for natural persons and the means that have evolved to address that problem.

A rough parallel can be drawn between corporations and natural persons. Internal changes in a corporation are analogous to socialization of a natural person, and government laws and regulations to which the corporation must adhere under threat of punishment are analogous to the norms and laws which,

3. The market economy cannot, however, be held responsible for environmental pollution. Such pollution is far greater in East Germany, which lacks a market economy, than in West Germany, which has one; and in Kraków, Poland, where there is not a market economy, the pollution from nearby steel mills (and, until it was closed, an aluminum plant) is destroying the facades of centuries-old buildings.

accompanied by informal and formal sanctions, provide external control of the natural person. For the corporation there is, however, a much wider range of both internal changes and external constraints than for the natural person, because of the much wider range of structures and functions of organizations. External constraints in the form of regulatory statutes and court decisions that have upheld and enforced them have been widely used by governments, with a noteworthy flurry of activity in the 1960s and 1970s. The internal changes that naturally lead to more responsible behavior constitute a more elegant approach, but have been less fully studied.

What Is Social Responsibility?

It is useful to ask first what constitutes social responsibility, before considering potential internal changes in corporations. The answer lies in the kinds of relations the corporate actor has with its environment and the interests of the other party in those relations. As with natural persons, responsibility to one set of interests may conflict with responsibility to another. I have described elsewhere these kinds of relations and the interests they generate using illustrative federal regulatory agencies designed to protect some of these interests (Coleman, 1982b). The Food and Drug Administration (FDA) was designed to protect certain interests of the customer. The Occupational Safety and Health Administration (OSHA) was designed to protect certain interests of the employee. The Environmental Protection Agency (EPA) was designed to protect certain interests of the neighbors of the corporation (broadly, neighbors include all those persons, natural or corporate, who are affected or are likely to be affected by actions of the corporation). The Securities and Exchange Commission (SEC) was designed to protect the interests of owners or investors. These four sets of interests, in addition to those of the corporation itself as a conceptual entity, are the interests that may be affected by a corporation's actions.

Any corporation which acts effectively will act to satisfy some sets of interests, which may be a mix of the five types just listed. In effect, the question of corporate responsibility is one concerning how to change this mix—ordinarily by making changes away from satisfying the corporation's own interests toward satisfying one or more of the other four sets of interests, those of employees, customers, investors, or neighbors. But the multiplicity and diversity of the interests, within each set as well as between sets, suggest that the problem is not a simple one, even conceptually: There is no single group toward which the corporation may exercise social responsibility and simultaneously satisfy the interests of all those affected by its actions.

Who Is Internal to the Corporation?

A related conceptual difficulty in considering possible internal changes to the corporation is that of determining who is internal to the corporation. Responsibility of an actor to interests of those with whom it interacts must be seen in relation to the actor's own interests to which its actions are responsive. Determining what those interests are for a corporate actor is not simple.

The classic view of the corporation is as an owner of capital (or as a set of investors sharing ownership) which buys factor inputs such as raw materials, labor, and processing equipment, organizes their appropriate integration to yield a final product, and then sells the product to consumers. With this conception the inside of the corporation is the set of owner-organizers.

Two properties of the corporate structure have led to two conceptions which differ from the classic view. One property is the alienability of capital; the other is the nonalienability of labor. The alienability of capital has meant that it becomes merely another factor input. The functions of providing capital and organizing the factor inputs into a product have become divided. In the language used by Berle and Means (1933) the modern joint-stock corporation has split the atom of private property into two sets of rights: The rights to benefit from the use of the property are still held by the investors; the rights to control the use of that property are held by salaried managers. Investors do, of course, have rights to vote for directors, but they are seldom organized and often uninterested in exercising those rights, since they can, with little loss, move their capital from one corporation to another. Investors' interests lie almost solely in the economic benefits they derive from the corporation's activity, through dividends and increases in share prices. With this conception the inside of the corporation no longer contains the owners. They are seen as merely providers of a factor input, bought at a price which is approximately the interest rate for loans or the dividend rate for stocks.

There is, however, one property that differentiates shareholders from other providers of capital and from providers of other factor inputs. Shareholders are residual claimants; that is, their claims to the corporation's assets and earnings are met only after all other claims have been satisfied. This cuts two ways. Because the claims of other parties are fixed, shareholders have rights to whatever remains when those claims have been met. If the firm is especially profitable, their earnings are high. If, however, the firm fails, shareholders have last claim to the assets and stand the greatest chance of loss.

This generalization applies more directly to the reality of a small start-up firm than to that of an established corporation. For the latter the shareholders' dividend rate varies much less than does the firm's earnings. The variation in a shareholder's return on his investment is greater than, but not qualitatively different from, the variation in returns to other providers of capital, and even to providers of other factor inputs. Thus, although there is some basis for regarding shareholders as being the inside of a corporation, it is weaker than in the past and weaker for established corporations than for beginning ones.

The inside of a corporation might be thought to consist of the top management. If so, the board of directors should, if it is to be responsive to internal interests, be responsive to the interests of the top managers, who organize the factor inputs (including capital) into a final product. The difficulty with this implication is that the top management of a corporation consists not of persons but of the positions they temporarily occupy. Executives' interests as natural persons are not properly part of the interests of the corporation, since they are only its agents. Yet the de facto position of most boards of directors reflects this modified conception. Although there remains the legal fiction that directors are agents of the stockholders, they are most often the creatures of top management. Stockholders sometimes bring suits against directors for not attending to stockholders' interests; the fact that such suits can be filed implies that the old conception of the stockholders as being the inside of the corporation is not dead. Yet the fact that the suits are filed indicates that directors are often seen as the agents of management or of the corporation as an abstract acting unit (and see themselves that way). This of course leaves open the question of just how to conceive of the corporation's interests apart from those of any natural person (a question addressed in Chapter 19).

The control of boards of directors by top management of the corporation may currently be lessening in American firms, as evidenced by the increased number of hostile take-overs. Hostile take-overs are facilitated by new forms of borrowing (so-called junk bonds) in conjunction with something that has traditionally aided managers in controlling corporations: the majority decision rule, which gives control of the corporation to whatever faction can control more than 50% of the voting shares of stock.[4] Legal changes have made hostile take-overs more difficult, however, and counterstrategies designed to destroy the value of a firm after a hostile take-over have been carried out by some boards of directors.

The second property of the corporate structure mentioned earlier, the nonalienability of labor, means that although the role of capital has been reduced to that of little more than another factor input, the role of labor at all levels of the corporation has increased to something more than that of a factor input. The nonalienability of labor means that employees of a firm, being physically present to provide their input, are much less able to shift their services to another corporation than are investors to shift their capital. Thus employees acquire a stake in the organization, which they will lose if it fails. This stake is recognized in a number of ways; basing promotions or layoffs on seniority is perhaps the most evident. Other prominent evidence of the stake that employees acquire is the buy-out, by which employees can receive extensive severance pay plus pension benefits for retiring early. For example, Honeywell, Inc. offered to buy out employees in November 1982 when reducing its labor force in the United States. Those employees who accepted the corporation's offer received benefits

---

4. The majority rule can affect the likelihood of take-overs in this way: A take-over offer will be made to stockholders to buy their shares at a price above the market price; the offer stands until those attempting the take-over own 50% of the stock. Stockholders who sell at the offered price realize capital gains; those who fail to sell hold stock which after the take-over has less real value because of the debt incurred in purchasing the majority of the shares. Stockholders thus face two sources of incentive to accept the offer and sell their shares.

averaging $30,000 annually from that point on. Such payment, if accepted, can be seen as the value of the stake each employee has in the company.

With this modified conception the inside of the corporation is repopulated with natural persons, but they are no longer the owners. They are the employees who have acquired a stake in the organization through their service as employees. It is this conception that gives rise to a law such as the codetermination law in Germany. To conceive of the board of directors of a corporation as representatives of the various interests internal to the organization, as a legislative body which is the product of industrial democracy, implies that the corporation is seen as neither disembodied nor the creature of the owners, but as encompassing sets of interests of natural persons. In the case of codetermination in Germany these persons include both employees and the providers of capital. With the conception just described, it includes only employees.

According to the three different conceptions of what the corporation is, the board of directors serves different interests. Under the first, the classic, conception the board is the agent of the owners and must act in their interests. Under the second conception the board is the agent of the top management of the corporation and, as in Hacker's fictional example, properly acts in the corporation's own interests, which are distinct from those of any natural persons. Because top management is well equipped to act unitarily, the role of the board of directors is reduced to approving or advising the actions of the executives and only very rarely making decisions independently. Under the third conception members of the board are agents of the various constituencies internal to the corporation, and the board becomes a kind of legislative body taking actions that reflect the balance of power among these constituencies.

The conceptual questions of what constitutes social responsibility on the part of the corporation and what interests are internal to it precede any examination of possible internal changes. The changes themselves fall into three broad classes: One is composed of changes in the structure of governance of the corporation. The second is composed of changes in the incentive structure confronting its agents. The third is composed of changes in investments of the corporation.

Changes in the Governance Structure: Worker Representation

One type of change in the governance structure of corporations is worker representation on boards of directors. Worker representation is part of the movement to broaden the range of interests to which boards of directors, and the corporations they govern, are responsive. In Germany this has taken the form of the codetermination law of 1976. As described in Chapter 16, this law places workers' representatives on boards of directors, in number equal to those of stockholders' representatives. This law certainly provides the basis for a change in the content of corporate decisions.

For example, in the 1970s Opel, part of the multinational firm of General

Motors, made a decision to build a new automotive plant in Spain. The decision to locate the new factory in Spain rather than in Germany was made shortly before the codetermination law went into effect. Had it been made after the new law was effective, it is doubtful that the plant would have been located in Spain, or in any country other than Germany. A decision to build a new plant in a distant location where there was a cheaper or more tractable labor force would be less likely under the new law.

Codetermination in German corporations makes them more democratic, that is, more responsible and responsive to the interests of employees. A corporation may simultaneously become less responsive to stockholders' interests in increasing the firm's economic returns and to customers' interests in low prices. The firm could become noncompetitive and fail. However, if employees' representatives act rationally in their constituents' interests, the principal effect will be to increase the fraction of corporate earnings which go to workers, at the expense of the stockholders.[5]

Apart from the issue of economic viability, does internal democratization mean that the corporation becomes more responsible to other parties, the consumers of its products or its geographic neighbors? Speaking of the democratization of trade unions, John Dunlop addressed an analogous question: "It is sheer demagoguery to hold that we can have unions which are highly responsive to the rank and file and at the same time be responsible and businesslike" (quoted in Fiester, 1980, p. 236). What is true concerning the democratization of trade unions is no less true for the democratization of corporations. Responsiveness to the interests of employees and of owners does not in any way imply responsiveness to other interests, such as those of customers and of neighbors. In fact, it may make the corporation less likely to be responsive to interests of outside parties. It seems probable, for example, that corporations in Minneapolis would be less likely to support those cultural activities (such as a symphony orchestra) which are of little interest to the majority of their workers if they were governed via codetermination. If the process of cooptation of top managers based on their interests in acceptance by the local social elite does occur, as described by Galaskiewicz (1985), a reduction of those managers' power would reduce corporate philanthropy for cultural activities.[6]

It also seems unlikely that a broader distribution of corporate control would lead to more extensive socially responsible actions such as establishing and funding philanthropic foundations. The Ford Foundation was created by holdings concentrated in the Ford family. The holdings of the pension funds of Ford Motor Company's employees, which are also very large, have produced no

---

5. If, as is generally true, the board of directors has been controlled by upper management rather than by owners, the shift may be at the expense of reinvestment, which would be more likely to affect the economic viability of the corporation.

6. Something like this is also true for nations: The United States, the most responsive among large nations to general public opinion, is also lowest in public support for cultural activities such as music, theater, fine arts, and museums.

comparable foundation. General Motors Corporation, larger than Ford but with ownership always more widely diffused than that of Ford, has also never created a comparable foundation. Virtually all philanthropic foundations have been created in circumstances where wealth and power were concentrated in one person's or family's hands, not by corporate bodies subject to decisions made through processes of internal democracy. This result follows directly from rational choice theory if the proportion of income an actor spends on philanthropic interests increases with income.[7] Greater concentration of wealth or greater inequality of income would lead to greater levels of philanthropic giving.

Changes in the Governance Structure: Representation of External Interests

Worker representation on boards of directors is quite different from representation of constituencies that by all definitions are outside the corporation, that is, customers and neighbors. What kind of conception of the relation between corporation and society is compatible with representation of external interests on corporate boards? Entertaining the idea of representation of external interests on corporate boards requires consideration of two different kinds of representation.

OBEYING THE RULES OF THE GAME   One kind of representation of external interests would be designed to ensure that the corporation obeys the letter and spirit of the laws. Such representation would be intended to protect the interests of those actors in society for whom the corporation's action has some consequence: employees, investors, customers, and neighbors. The intent would not be to make the corporation benevolent or philanthropic, but to ensure that it does not violate laws and thus harm these other parties' interests. Such violations ordinarily occur when a corporation's actions cannot be scrutinized by outsiders, providing an opportunity for engaging in activity that illegally harms the interests of others. There are examples of such violations for each of the kinds of transactions in which corporate actors are engaged; what is not clear is whether outside representation on corporate boards could inhibit them.

The most frequent examples of violations are ones harmful to the interests which disclosure laws are designed to protect. Insider trading by persons occupying positions in upper echelons of management or by other persons close to them is the principal action, and the interests protected by the laws are those of other shareholders.[8] There are also examples where the principal interests af-

---

7. This would be inconsistent, however, with the utility function assumed in Part V (the Cobb-Douglas utility function), which implies that expenditure on a good is a constant proportion of income.

8. There is lively argument among economists as to whether insider trading should be made legal. One argument in favor of doing so is that no one in particular is hurt by insider trading. Another is that insider trading provides signals to others in the market of the high confidence of

fected are those of consumers. A common example is collusion among competitors to maintain or increase price levels, such as occurred for turbine generators and involved General Electric and Westinghouse. There are examples where the principal interests harmed are those of neighbors. It appears that in the United States some toxic waste disposal has been carried out by companies run by organized crime, which dispose of waste by bleeding the chemicals into oil sold for home heating. Finally, there are examples where the interests harmed are those of employees. Probably the most frequent of these occur when companies violate the regulations of the National Labor Relations Board in union representation elections. These violations, however, are ordinarily visible from the outside and not easily kept secret.

The basis for this first kind of outside representation on boards of directors is to make the corporation's actions more public so as to prevent infractions of the rules governing the various markets in which the corporation is involved. The function of such representation is like that of an outside auditor—to discover after the fact or to prevent before the fact actions which, by violating rules under which the market operates, give the corporation unfair advantage. The intent behind such representation is to ensure that the rules of the game are being obeyed and that corporate actors which obey the law are not penalized in the market for doing so. But is outside representation on the board of directors the appropriate tool to accomplish this?

What appears more appropriate is something analogous to the periodic external financial audits that publicly held corporations must undergo but addressed to a wider range of potential misdeeds than simply accounting irregularities. A law which required external functional audits addressing actions relevant to the various markets in which a corporation participates might be effective. The prototype already exists in the financial audits that are required by law. Something analogous might be required for corporations larger than a given size and covering the markets in which they engage where their actions are not visible from the outside. It is important to point out that such functional audits would not be patterned after the social audits which had some currency in the United States in the 1970s. The idea behind those was to show that the corporation was a "good citizen," philanthropic or benevolent or public-spirited. Unlike financial audits, those social audits were not designed to uncover irregularities, to open to outside scrutiny corporate actions which were improper or illegal.

This alternative of a functional audit would imply, rather than a general public director of the sort that Stone (1975) proposes, an external firm which would

---

upper-level management in a firm. The principal argument against legalizing insider trading is that the right to profit personally at the possible expense of the owner of the corporation, considered as a single actor, on the basis of superior knowlege about actions taken by oneself as agent is not compatible with the rights allocation of the principal-agent relation. A second is that allowing insider trading might introduce incentives for top management that would expand the conflict between executives' own interests and the corporation's interest.

undertake to examine the corporation's activities in all markets in which it participated, to ensure that those activities remained within the rules governing those markets. If functional auditing of this sort were required periodically by law, it could replace the investigatory and regulatory activities of government agencies, which (as any sociologist could predict) either take on an adversarial character that generates costly inefficiences or engender cooptation that reinstates the corporation's freedom to act.

ATTENTION OF THE CORPORATION TO INTERESTS OF THOSE OUTSIDE IT   The second kind of external representation on boards of directors is intended to make the corporation more socially responsible in general. The essence of the problem, I believe, is this: When a corporation is completely freestanding, controlled by managers whose social status lies outside the community and owned by a multitude of investors whose only interest is in high dividends and increased stock prices, then how can it be led to be a "good citizen"? That is, how can the corporation be induced to engage in public-spirited activities which are not required by law but which benefit a broader range of interests than those which are regarded as being internal to the corporation?

The family-based corporations that were common in the past but are rare today had internalized the interests of others through the family's connections to the community, no less so than natural persons come to internalize the interests of others through socialization. Is there any process which might bring about effects for modern corporations comparable to those of socialization of natural persons?

Socialization of children is the process of somehow getting them to bring the interests of other persons inside, so that the object self whose interests are the basis for action incorporates to some degree the interests of those others. This task would seem to be intrinsically simpler for corporate actors, because the positions which make up their structure are occupied by persons (that is, outsiders) who have their own interests and who have obligations to other persons outside. Thus the implanting of interests external to the corporate actor would appear to be intrinsically easier than the implanting of external interests in a natural person.

Actions that seem intended to "socialize" corporations in this way are sometimes taken. For example, in the United States socially responsible activities are sometimes seen to be augmented by appointing a woman or a black to a board of directors. Such an appointment very likely helps to draw the board's attention to issues in which women or blacks have an interest. For example, the appointment of Leon Sullivan, a black, to the board of directors of General Motors resulted in a set of racially impartial employment policies for General Motors in South Africa and established the Sullivan principle, which was applied for some time by other American firms with establishments in South Africa.

Although such an appointment probably does lead the corporation to internalize external interests to some extent, this raises a number of questions. First, if the corporation remains legally responsible to its shareholders, the pursuit of such external interests by the board subverts the interests of those whom they represent. A change in the law regarding corporations would appear to be a prerequisite for any actions which were clearly not in the shareholders' interests. Second, even if there were such a legal change, the pressures of the market would prevent extensive actions to benefit external interests, for corporations which pursued interests that increased their costs of doing business would find themselves disadvantaged in one or more of the markets in which they operate.

But how was it that in the past corporations that were closely linked to the local community could (as in Minneapolis) be more philanthropic or public-spirited without being disadvantaged in the market? The answer probably lies in part in market imperfections which allow deviations from efficiency and in part in the fact that since all or most corporations acted under this constraint, none were at a competitive disadvantage. This disadvantage only arises after change has released a number of corporations from this constraint.

WHAT EXTERNAL INTERESTS SHOULD THE CORPORATION INTERNALIZE? Even if the problems of feasibility described above were resolved, there still remains the question of just what external interests the corporation should internalize. "Interests of women" or "interests of minorities" are ad hoc answers without any theoretical justification. Answers given by theorists who study the modern corporation are usually vague; for example, Berle and Means (1933) at the end of their book indicate that the corporation should serve the interests of the community. I believe the question can be answered less vaguely. There are two parts to the answer. One has to do with restitution to interests that are indirectly harmed by the negative externalities directly imposed by unconstrained corporate action, and the other has to do with those negative externalities.

Restitution to interests indirectly harmed by the corporation. Chapter 22 deals with the conflict between modern corporate actors and the family. The modern corporate actor has extensively undermined the functioning of the family and has thus harmed the interests of those natural persons aided by the family but not the corporation. These persons include all those who are not employed by a corporation: housewives, the elderly, unemployable persons, and especially children. The interests harmed are those related to certain activities: socialization and child care, maintaining the household as a socially viable enterprise, and, generally, activities involving care for other persons.

These, then, are the external interests to which the modern corporation should be responsible in a positive sense. These interests have been harmed not so much by corporations' specific actions as by their very existence and their power. The harm has resulted from the alienation of first the husband and father from the household and subsequently the wife and mother. The consequence is that those products of joint production in the household—by-products of the adults' productive activity in the household—such as child care and care for other dependent persons have become uneconomic.

How can corporations provide restitution to those interests which are important for society but have been damaged by the rise of corporations? I will attempt to answer this question in Chapter 22, where I examine the impact of the corporation on the family.

Negative externalities directly imposed by corporate action. When persons interact as persons with others with whom they will continue to be in contact, as in a small community with high closure, they are subject to normative constraints, through sanctions generated by the processes discussed in Chapter 11. When this is not the case, as in an urban setting without closure, persons are released from norms and will often carry out actions they would never engage in in a setting with high closure. When persons are agents of corporate actors or of anonymous principals of such actors, they are no longer personal actors, but only agents. Thus they are largely freed from responsibility for the actions they take. These actions create any of a variety of negative externalities. Environmental pollution such as was caused by Hooker Chemical at Love Canal is one; pornography is another; violence on television is another; destruction of norms or codes of behavior is another.

Two questions arise, one normative and the other positive. The normative question is this: How free from normative constraints should corporate actors be? For example, should there be normative constraints on the content of television programs, and, if so, what should be the extent of the constraints? If the answer to the normative question affirms the desirability of some level of constraint, the positive question to be posed is this: How can the constraints be imposed? The answer to the normative question may in fact be contingent on the answer to this one. For example, informal constraints that lead a corporate actor to modify its own actions may be justifiable from a normative perspective that would regard legal constraints as not justifiable. As another example, in a 1973 decision on mass media censorship (*Miller v. California*), the U.S. Supreme Court ruled that local communities had the right to determine their own standards, within a certain range. This means that the Court implicitly accepted levels of censorship imposed by law at the local level that it would strike down if imposed by law at the federal level.

The only theoretically defensible response to the normative question is exemplified by the Supreme Court ruling, that is, an answer not in terms of the content of the norms but in terms of which actors should have the right to decide the content of the norms. In the case of children's exposure to mass media, the theoretical answer is straightforward: the actor with guardianship rights over a child has, as part of those rights, the right to decide to what media the child is exposed. In societies as currently constituted, for most children that actor is the parent or parents. Yet the principle is not easy to apply: If, for example, the content of television programming is unconstrained except at the level of the household, parents must engage in extensive monitoring in order to impose constraints, perhaps an unreasonable demand. Yet if the content is constrained at the source, to a level compatible with the strictest parental standards, this imposes constraints not desired by most parents. A technological solution might allow parents to choose the degree of constraint of content allowed into the household by choosing a television set that receives only certain levels or types of programming. In the absence of a technological solution, a constraint by some intermediate-level actor, such as the local community invoked by the Supreme Court ruling, is probably the closest to a solution based on guardians' rights.

The general problem of what constraints should be applied can only be resolved by reference to the problems discussed in Chapters 10 and 11 and the criterion proposed by Coase (1960), also discussed there. When an action has negative externalities, those actors whose interests are adversely affected by the action should be able to constrain it if their constitutional rights and resources are sufficient to allow this. As with the externalities considered by Coase, the fact that the externalities are experienced by many may impose high costs of organization. I have considered these problems in Chapter 11; the principal point to be added here derives from the asymmetry in size and power between corporate actors which impose externalities and individuals who experience them. Because this creates a bias in favor of corporate actors, a public-bad problem is created for the set of unorganized natural persons. Use of government institutions such as regulatory statutes and agencies (EPA, FDA, the Consumer Protection Agency, the Federal Communications Commission, and others in the United States, and their counterparts in other countries) is one general solution, which allocates rights to the society as a whole. Where the set of persons who experience the externalities of the corporation's action is identifiable, a superior solution would be to use powers of government to eliminate the costs of organization for that set of persons and to provide the organization with rights to tax all those who experience the externalities so that the offensive action, if uneconomic (in the broad sense that persons are willing to pay a tax sufficient to induce the corporation to refrain from it), would be eliminated.

According to the general principles developed in Chapters 30 and 31, a further step would be necessary to reduce transaction costs if, in most cases involving externalities, those experiencing the externalities were willing to tax themselves sufficiently to induce the corporation to limit the externalities. This step is a transfer of rights from the corporation generating the externalities to the actors experiencing them—thus reducing the transaction costs necessary to achieve socially efficient states. This is not the way governments have addressed these problems, but it is the means by which social efficiency would be achieved, whether that involves continuing the externalities or eliminating them.

Internal Corporate Changes Involving Agents' Incentives

Chapter 16 discussed forward policing of actions and backward policing of product. With backward policing agents are not supervised but are held accountable by the recipient for the quality and quantity of the products. Extension of backward policing across the interface of the corporation with the outside world can provide for the corporate actor something comparable to socialization for the natural person. An interaction of a customer or client with an agent of a large corporate actor (a corporation or government) is generally an impersonal interaction in which the agent remains nameless, hardly identifiable as a concrete person. If backward policing is put in effect at this boundary of the corporate actor, the customer or client becomes able to discipline the agent through nonacceptance of the service or through some other action whose consequence is felt directly by the agent. In this way the interest of the agent in using the corporate actor as a shield to deflect the consequences of his actions cannot be realized. The agent is thrust back into a situation similar to a person-to-person interaction in that he must personally experience some of the consequences of his actions.

Although backward policing is far from being the rule, a number of corporations have instituted some means of making the rewards and punishments of agents who serve customers more directly conditional on satisfaction of the customers' interests. Telephone operators often introduce themselves by name; some manufactured goods come with an inspector's slip marked not with a number but with a name; and a number of companies reward employees who win contests based on customers' votes or nominations. The general principle used is that of backward policing: to link more directly the employee's own self-interest with the satisfaction of the client's or customer's interests.

Backward policing of agents by customers addresses one particular kind of corporate responsibility, responsibility to the customer. For marketed goods and services this is already addressed by the structure of market competition which rewards corporations financially for satisfying customers. The value of introducing auxiliary reward structures at the level of agents becomes important under either of two conditions. One is when the corporation is large; large size makes the built-in incentives of the corporate hierarchy (satisfying one's superior) more important for most agents than the incentives of the market. The second condition occurs when the corporate actor is not in a market, as is true for a government agency. It is in such agencies that one would expect to find (and generally does find) low attention to clients' interests. Thus it is in such agencies that the introduction of backward policing of agents by clients could be most effective in increasing agents' attention to clients' interests.

Socially Responsible Investments

The third means, other than changes in governance and changes in incentive structures for agents, by which corporations could be made more socially responsible is through changes in their investments. I will discuss this only briefly; although it is a means for inducing social responsibility in corporations, it appears to be less widespread than the other two means I have discussed. The general principle is that by investing in an activity a corporation benefits the activity in two ways: first by providing resources which help support the activity, and second by acting so as to protect its investment by improving the functioning of the activity. (For example, a bank, to protect capital it has loaned, may provide some kind of managerial services intended to foster success in the enterprise to which it has made the loan.)

There are, of course, some corporations whose incorporators have socially responsible interests and implement those interests through their investment. For example, in the United States the Mutual Real Estate Investment Trust was organized by persons interested in racial integration to make loans for integrated housing. Such corporations, however, merely represent use of a corporate form to implement interests of investors; there is no manifestation of social responsibility that conflicts with investors' interests.

There are several defects of this means of inducing social responsibility. One is that the action taken in changing investments must be acceptable to those actors to whom the corporate actor is legally responsible. For example, for the divestment actions taken with respect to South African investments in the United States, these actors were stockholders (represented by boards of directors) in the case of corporations, boards of trustees in the case of universities, and city councils in the case of cities. A second defect of this means of inducing social responsibility is that it is dependent on public sentiment on particular issues, which may fluctuate wildly, and does not exercise a steady pressure toward an overall socially responsible portfolio. A third defect is that this means has principally been implemented through divestiture, not through positive investments. Thus the restitution to interests based in family activities (discussed in an earlier section) is unlikely to be brought about through this means.

Tax Laws and Social Norms

Another means for inducing social responsibility in corporate actors besides the internal changes discussed above is a change in the reward structure imposed by the environment. The principal way this may be done is through changes in the tax laws.

Is there anything analogous for the corporate actor to the informal social norms that encourage natural persons to act in ways that take into account others' interests? Those norms provide not only encouragement for actions that benefit others but discouragement of activities that harm others. Legal constraints on corporations do not function similarly, because they only provide punishment for proscribed actions. There is, however, a device which can function in a way analogous to informal social norms. This is tax policy. Relief from taxes can be allowed for activities which are not in the corporate actor's interest but are widely held to be in the public interest. In this way supporting, the activities may come to be in the corporation's interest. Something of this sort has been done in many developed societies. Contributions to charitable activities reduce a corporation's tax liability, so the corporation is in the position of the socialized person who has been induced to consider others' interests.

Tax laws in capitalist economies do allow for this; yet the contributions to socially beneficial activities appear less extensive than many would desire. This deficiency could be remedied by changes in tax deductions. There are a variety of tax havens for corporations; if these include too few of those which support activities regarded as socially beneficial, then the remedy lies in governmental decision making, not corporate decision making. Given the freestanding character of corporations, they will necessarily attend primarily to their internal interests; only by an appropriate reward structure can this wholly self-interested behavior be reshaped so that they attend to a broader range of social interests.[9]

For many corporations, examples such as those in Minneapolis notwithstanding, the fact that a dollar benefiting some activity defined as charitable costs the corporation much less than a dollar is an insufficient incentive for incurring the cost, reduced though it is. What is necessary to increase corporations' social responsibility is much more careful attention to the incentives and the results they produce. Tax law appears much more effective in inducing profitable corporations to acquire unprofitable ones, allowing tax write-offs to the profitable corporation, than it is in inducing contributions to socially beneficial activities.

The range of possibilities for tax relief to corporations would appear to be large indeed. Elsewhere (Coleman, 1982b) I raise the possibility that large corporations could be induced to become age-balanced, with a distribution of ages that mirrors the distribution in society as a whole. The inducement to the corporation would be tax credit or payment equal to the cost to the state of providing comparable services for children and the aged. The social benefits would be reduction of the age-segregation of modern society and provision of services on a smaller, less centralized, more humane scale.

Free-Rider Problems for Corporate Responsibility

Olson (1965) has shown that the logic of public-good supply implies that in industries composed of many small firms there will be less activity furthering the collective interest of the firms (for example, lobbying activity for legislation which benefits the industry) than in industries containing one or a few large firms. The activity of one benefits all, and for a small firm the consequences of its own activity will benefit it insufficiently to warrant the activity. For a firm which constitutes a large fraction of an industry, the activity will be worthwhile, even though it also benefits smaller firms in the industry.

A similar logic holds at two levels for the socially responsible activities of corporations. If a firm is only one of many in a city, its involvement in civic affairs will have little impact on the quality of life in the city. Its own workers will experience little impact, so its action will have little impact on its environment. In addition, the firm, and those who control its actions, will receive few social rewards, since the contribution to civic affairs is relatively so small. The

9. The use of tax policy to induce socially beneficial actions on the part of corporations is a philosophical position not reflected in the tax code changes introduced in 1987 in the United States, changes that reduced deductions for such actions. If the theory expressed in the text is correct, those tax changes are incorrect.

opposite is true when a firm is large relative to the city in which it is located. Its civic activities make a large difference. Philanthropic activity beyond legally required responsibilities brings the firm some benefits. This is probably why the cities mentioned earlier—Rochester, New York (where Eastman Kodak dominates) and Wilmington, Delaware (where Du Pont dominates)—have more philanthropic activity than do cities such as Baltimore, where industry is composed of a number of smaller firms. There is also a difference between the situation in Europe or the United States and that in Japan, where many firms have residential areas for their employees (see Clark, 1979). Providing amenities in those areas constitutes providing benefits directly for the firm's own employees, not for the city as a whole. Some part of the paternalism of Japanese corporations derives from the different incentives made possible by this ecological pattern.

The free-rider effect occurs for stockholders as well. A small stockholder has no incentive whatsoever to contribute, as an owner of a firm, to socially responsible activities. The small stockholder will receive no credit if the firm engages in such actions. A major stockholder identified as a firm's owner will receive credit for civic, socially responsible, or philanthropic activities of the firm. Thus in firms whose stock is widely dispersed, and in which no investors have major holdings, stockholders can be expected to pressure managers mainly to higher stock prices and higher dividends; in closely held firms owners' interests are more likely to include socially responsible activities.

Can free-rider problems be overcome, to lead corporations to act in ways that would be mutually beneficial but are unrewarding if engaged in alone? The answer is that they cannot, without some incentive that makes participation directly in the participant's interest. Olson (1965) calls these incentives that are contingent on participation selective incentives. The form they often take is punishment for nonparticipation, and participation is ordinarily in the form of taxation: government-imposed taxes, check-off payment of union dues, license fees for television stations to pay for publicly supported broadcasting, and taxes on gasoline to pay for roads.

Just as punishment for nonpayment of taxes is used as an incentive to induce individuals and businesses to support (through taxes) publicly provided activities, relief from taxation could be used as an incentive to induce corporations to support other socially beneficial activities. Thus, solution of the free-rider problems for socially responsible actions by corporations requires the kind of selective incentives that are provided by the strategy suggested earlier—the use of tax relief to encourage a wider range of socially responsible activities.

Corporate Responsibility in Sum

The modern corporation, owned by an anonymous set of investors and managed by professional executives, is a new kind of actor in society. It is recognized in law as a person, as the subject and object of action, but the traditional mecha-

nisms of social control for natural persons are not all available for encouraging it
to act responsibly. These mechanisms are the law itself, socialization (which
creates internal standards for behavior in the person), and informal social norms
(which provide external rewards and punishments). The detachment of corporations from individual persons and their construction instead around positions of
which natural persons are merely temporary occupants means that socialization
and norms applied to natural persons no longer constitute effective means for
ensuring responsible action on the part of corporations.

An increase in external regulation has been the principal trend in social control
of corporations, indicated by the explosive growth of regulatory agencies in the
1960s and 1970s in the United States. But it is reasonable to pose this question:
Are there alternative internal changes in the corporation that could lead it to act
more responsibly? In particular, are there changes in the composition and functioning of boards of directors which, if required by law, would bring about more
responsible behavior? My conclusion is that the answer differs for representation of those interests which, by some definition of the corporation, are internal
to it and those which are not. For the former, which includes interests of owners
or investors and of employees at all levels, a change in the composition and
functioning of the board of directors so as to include or better represent these
interests may well be effective. What remains uncertain, however, is whether
effective representation and pursuit of workers' interests will lead to actions that
make the corporation economically inefficient and thus hurt its competitive performance.[10]

For those interests that by any definition of the corporation are outside it, it
seems impossible to conceive of any composition and functioning of a board of
directors that would successfully blend attention to those interests with continued attention to internal interests. What appears a more promising approach
is a combination of two kinds of activities. The first is extension of the concept of
external auditing so as to incorporate the interests of those parties which legally
required audits currently inform poorly or not at all: consumers, labor (if it is
considered outside the corporation's interests), and neighbors (those directly
affected by the corporation's activity). The second is the more extensive use of
tax incentives for inducing corporations to support those interests and activities
external to it that are regarded by the public as socially beneficial but noneconomic. In addition to these mechanisms, others might benefit both the corporation and outside interests, for example, a greater measure of personal responsibility on the part of agents of the corporation in their interactions with outsiders.

---

10. Most examples of such actions are ones that result in maintenance of an inefficiently
large work force. However, this result may merely be due to a deficiency of imagination. An
enlightened firm directed in pursuit of investors' interests will, when it finds it has excess
capital, invest in new activities that are expected to be profitable. Similarly, an enlightened firm
directed in pursuit of both investors' and workers' interests should, when it finds it has an
excess of workers, see these as an asset and seek out new activities which would efficiently
employ the additional labor.

Because the law of agency has been slow to recognize joint responsibility of principal and agent for activities of the corporation pursued by its agent, it may have encouraged irresponsible actions on the part of agents which taken together add up to irresponsible behavior on the part of the corporation.

What Conception of the Corporation Is Best for Natural Persons?

In this chapter I have assumed that the conception of the corporation as an actor in society is both theoretically useful and normatively desirable. But the latter may not be correct from the point of view of natural persons. Certain economists have begun to conceive of the corporation as merely the intersection of a number of markets, with value created (or lost) at this intersection (Fama, 1980). Such a conception includes a set of residual claimants, who have rights to the residue after all market transactions (with customers, labor, suppliers, and capital sources) have been carried out and who stand to gain profits or incur losses depending on the outcomes of these transactions. This conception dissolves the corporation into its component parts. There is no inside and no outside; the issue of social responsibility does not arise because there is no actor who can be assigned the role of being socially responsible. There are only contending actors in each of the markets, and each of those actors is attending to his own interests and legitimately unconcerned with others' interests.

The legal conception, of course, has developed over the past several centuries; as discussed in Chapter 20, this conception arrogates to the corporation the role of a person with rights and interests, able to be plaintiff or defendant in court. Accompanying this conception was the necessity to separate the corporation's rights and interests from those of any natural person. This was accomplished largely through two devices: First, the law applied the servant form of agency to the corporation, so the principal (the corporation) and not the agent was held liable for actions of the agent, except in cases of criminal liability where the agent knowingly commits on the corporation's behalf an action which is illegal. Second, the principle of limited liability was created to provide protection for the set of natural persons engaged in a corporate venture.

A change in the conception of the corporation so that it would be seen as nothing more than the confluence of a number of market transactions would require a change in both of these legal principles. A set of natural persons would necessarily be held liable as persons for a corporation's actions. These would be either the set of agents who carried out the action or the board of directors. The latter would no longer be regarded as representatives of shareholders, and shareholders would be regarded as merely investors, not owners or residual claimants. Some sequence of claims to assets, in case of dissolution of the corporation, would be specified, as at present. The board of directors would become in effect a board of trustees, whose members were protected personally from liability claims by insurance (as is in fact increasingly true for directors). Liability insurance would also have to be provided for some agents, who would have greater personal liability for their actions than at present, if persons were to be motivated to fill the positions.

The law appears to be moving in this direction via court decisions which have increasingly imposed personal liability on directors and agents. But there is a question remaining: If directors are to become in effect trustees, in whose interests should they act?

One answer is that they should become trustees for interests of the society as a whole. For corporations that are internal to a particular nation-state, this in effect constitutes nationalization, although it would be less consequential than is nationalization of a corporation as currently conceived and legally constituted. For multinational corporations, the question of what interests the board of directors would become trustees for is less easily answered.

A second answer to the question of whose interests the trustees would serve is derived from a principle stated earlier: The trustees would serve the interests of those who experience negative externalities from the existence and power of corporations. I indicated earlier what some of those interests are: child care, youth socialization, and care of dependents and unemployable persons. However, a more detailed examination of corporations' negative externalities for persons in society would be necessary if such a criterion were to be used.

« 22 »

New Generations in the New Social Structure

Chapter 20 described an extraordinary change in the structure of society that has taken place over the last several centuries (and most dramatically during the last century and a half). This is a change in the basic elements that, in a theory of social action, must be regarded as the actors in society. As Chapter 20 indicated, this period has seen the growth of corporate actors of a new form, freestanding in society, without a fixed relation either to natural persons or to other corporate actors. In recent years these new corporate actors have come to be so pervasive that they threaten another structural element that has, since prehistory, constituted the basic building block of social structure—the family.

The conflict between these two components of social structure is in itself an interesting and important development in social history. But what gives the conflict crucial importance is that one of the components, the family, is the unit within which members of the next generation of society are nurtured and brought into adulthood. The new corporate actors are specialized and narrow-purpose entities, constitutive of a structure marked by a high division of labor, and have no place for childrearing. Thus a question arises: How will society reproduce itself when this new component of the social structure becomes even more dominant?

The Conflict between the Family and the Corporation

It is useful to begin by examining the way in which the conflict between the family and the new corporate structure of society manifests itself. The family has always been an entity within which multiple activities are carried out: economic production, joint consumption, procreation, socialization of children, and leisure pursuits. Generally it cannot be regarded as a purposive actor in the way the term is used in this book, for it cannot usually be described as having a purpose in terms of which it acts. It is, like society as a whole but on a smaller scale, a system of action composed of purposive actors in relation. Yet in some capacities the family may be usefully regarded as a purposive actor, for it is an entity in terms of whose perceived interests natural persons act; for example, sometimes persons say they are acting to "uphold the honor of the family." And in some cases a family does act as a unit, to attain ends that can be described as purposes or goals of the family.

It may be useful to clarify when and for what purposes a system of action should be called an actor. For example, in a swarm of insects hovering in the summer air, each insect is darting this way and that, apparently either randomly or in pursuit of its own ends. But the swarm as a whole will move this way or that, hover, expand or contract, and then fly off no less coherently than if it were a single organism. Biologists have long been fascinated by what can be described as non-physically-contiguous organisms, entities having physically separable components that together act as a coherent and purposive actor and could not survive alone. Thus, just as a swarm of insects may be considered an actor, the family may—sometimes—be considered an actor.

The multiple activities of the family have strong externalities for one another. Childrearing, for example, has always been carried out conjointly with other activities, in particular with economic production and consumption. In rural cultures children go to the fields with their mothers (as El Hakim, 1972, describes for a village in Chad) or their fathers (see Whiting and Whiting, 1975, for descriptions of variations in these activities in different cultures). Children have traditionally helped their mothers with household chores, thereby learning to work productively. In households where craft or trade activity occurs, children perform incidental tasks from early ages, moving toward more central roles as they become older (see Ariès, 1962, for descriptions). Older children in families are expected to care for younger children, and in doing so learn child-care skills.

Thus the household is characterized by joint production of several products, one of which has been childrearing. Childrearing may be thought of, in consequence, as a by-product of other activities in the traditional family.

The Industrial Revolution brought an important change in the traditional social structure, as a portion of the economically productive activity of the household was extracted from it. Cottage industry, by which productive activity remained within the household, was an early attempt to assimilate the technological change into the existing social structure (see Smelser, 1959). But the social structure gradually accommodated to the economic developments, making use of the new corporate form, the fictional person described in Chapter 20. That corporate form, giving rise to the modern corporation from about 1850 on, proved extraordinarily hospitable to technological change (and appears likely to continue as the principal social-structural vehicle through which such change is implemented). The new corporate actors removed a large portion of production from the household to some locus outside it: the factory or the office. This productive activity outside the household ordinarily took the form of the husband and father exchanging his labor for a wage and bringing back that wage to support his family.

An indicator of the scope and timing of this change is given by an indirect measure, the fraction of the male labor force working in agriculture. Farm work, although not identical to work within the household (since it excludes craft or trade activities which are carried out in a household setting or in close proximity to the household), is a rough approximation to it, if the household is regarded as encompassing the farm. Figure 22.1 shows that the fraction of the male labor force working in agriculture in the United States declined from about 87% in 1810 to about 3% in 1980. A similar decline has occurred throughout the developed world. Thus, in less than two centuries, the structure of the household has changed from one in which nearly all men's work was within the household to one in which almost none is. This radical change extracted from the household one of the various activities that were part of its joint production. In addition, certain aspects of childrearing, which were part of that joint production, suffered. The on-the-job training that children and youth, particularly boys, received in their own household or in nearby households to which they were apprenticed was increasingly less possible.[1]

During the same period of time, schooling was transformed from an elite activity engaging a small fraction of each cohort of children to a mass activity encompassing nearly the entire cohort. Figure 22.2 shows, superimposed on the line for the proportion of males working in agriculture, the proportion of boys aged 5–19 not attending school, from 1850 to 1970. The correspondence between two graphs suggests that the growth of mass public schooling is a response to the removal of job-training activity (for boys, at least) from the household when the husband and father went to work outside it in return for a wage. Although it would be a simplification to see mass schooling as wholly a response to the exodus of the man from the home, it was surely in part just that.[2] The result of that exodus is that households have lost two closely linked activities, which had both been carried out within them: the man's productive activity (and presence during the day), and the training of children for future productive activity.

The conflict between the family and the corporation was not clear-cut in its early days. The wage labor of men was often carried out in close physical proximity to the household, jobs were obtained through family connections, and many business enterprises emanated from the family and employed neighbors. But further changes occurred to increase the separation between the household and men's labor: increasing size of business enterprises, urbanization, and the rise of personal transportation. The increased size of factories and offices and the clustering of economic activities brought about urbanization. The density of population and economic activities in urban areas led to an effective social

1. The overall change depended, of course, on increases in farm productivity, so the labor of one farm household could feed increasing numbers of other households. Agricultural production has continued to be carried out largely as a household activity (except in fruit and vegetable farming, where, relatively recently, extensive use has been made of migrant labor, and farms can now be regarded as factories in the fields).

2. The fact that schooling for girls became common shortly after that for boys did, despite the fact that the productive activity of nearly all women and the prospective productive activity of their daughters remained in the household during this period, serves to indicate that the connection is not intrinsic.

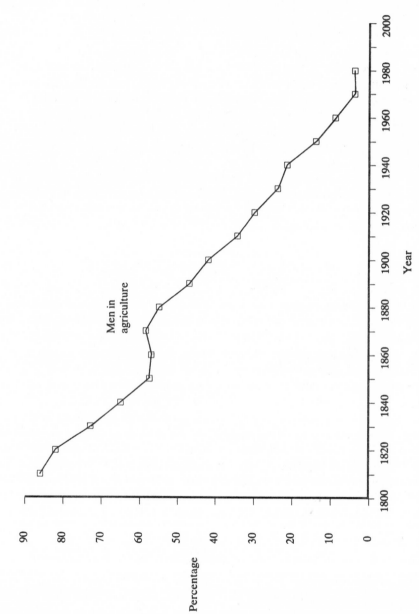

Figure 22.1 Percentage of male labor force working in agriculture, 1810–1980. (Data are from U.S. Bureau of the Census, 1975, Table 182–282; and U.S. Bureau of the Census, 1984.)

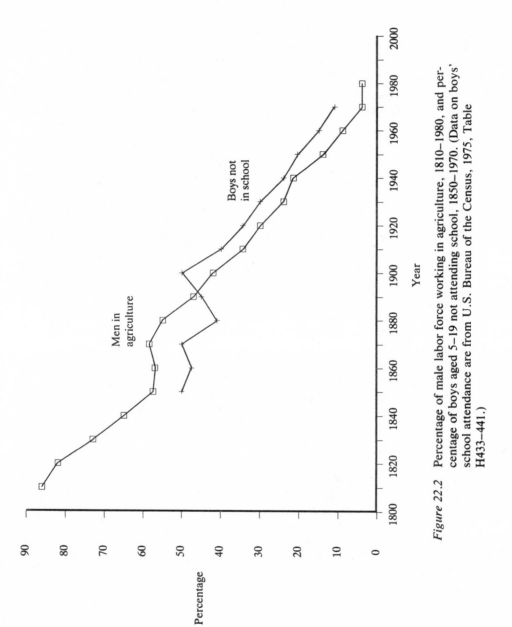

Figure 22.2 Percentage of male labor force working in agriculture, 1810–1980, and percentage of boys aged 5–19 not attending school, 1850–1970. (Data on boys' school attendance are from U.S. Bureau of the Census, 1975, Table H433–441.)

separation of the household and men's labor, even when the geographic distance from home to business was not great. When personal transportation in the form of private automobiles became widely distributed, from the 1930s on, the social separation between the household and men's labor was no longer dependent on the high density of urban central cities. Physical dispersion of residences into suburbs was compatible with the workplace being concentrated outside the household, in corporations that were not derivative from the household.

In modern industrial society there have come to be two parallel organizational structures: a primordial structure based on, and derivative from, the family; and a newer structure composed of purposive corporate actors wholly independent of the family. (I will call this the purposive structure, to contrast it with the primordial structure.) The primordial structure consists of family, extended family, neighborhood, and religious groups. The purposive structure consists of economic organizations (such as firms, trade unions, and professional associations), single-purpose voluntary associations, and governments.[3] One can still see in many less developed countries (for example, in Lebanon and other Arab countries of the Middle East) social systems in which economic and governmental organizations (even private armies) are extensions of the family and the clan. But that period of social development is long past in modern industrial society.

The creation of the purposive social structure, which is independent of the family and its derivatives, has facilitated a movement of various activities out of the household and the family-based primordial social structure into the purposive structure. Within the family mutual dependence between generations has consisted principally of two stages. First, children depend on their parents to provide nurturing and education—the latter either at the hands of the parents themselves or through support (financial and otherwise) for schooling. Second, parents, in their old age, have depended on their adult children. This mutual dependence has been curtailed, however, by the rise of pension funds and retirement insurance—which constitute an assumption of responsibility for care of the aged by the purposive structure, taking it away from the primordial structure. In different countries different parts of the purposive structure have assumed these responsibilities. In Japan, where the modern corporations are derived more directly from the paternalistic feudal household than they are in Europe (Japan not having had the intervention of revolutions to separate feudal from modern society), these responsibilities that were once the province of the family have been in greater part assumed by corporations; in Europe and the United States, these responsibilities have been principally taken on by the state. Variations in the onset and the rate of this shift from primordial structure to purposive structure are due to incidental differences, such as Bismarck's desire to tie per-

---

3. Schools are sometimes more nearly a part of the first of these structures, and sometimes more nearly a part of the second, for they are both agents of the family and the neighborhood and agents of the state and the larger society. (See Coleman and Hoffer, 1987, Chapter 1, for a further discussion of this.)

sons' allegiance to the new German state or the greater centralization of national government in England than in the United States.[4] But the shift has occurred in all industrial societies.

This shift of responsibility for the care of the dependent aged changes, of course, the incentives for the first stage of the relation of mutual dependency in the family. If children are no longer of value to support one in one's old age, their upbringing and education is no longer an investment in one's future. If children's success brings parents no concrete benefits, then parents' incentive to improve children's chances of success is reduced. This should have an impact in two ways: First, the incentive to have children should be reduced, leading to a lower birth rate, with couples who engage most in rational planning being least likely to have children. Second, the investment in childrearing should be reduced in that parents will be less concerned about, and willing to invest in, their children's education. The first of these implications has certainly been borne out throughout modern Western society; there the birth rate has sharply declined, and the bearing of children is increasingly concentrated in the lower classes. Evidence supporting the second implication is more ambiguous, but there is some support for the argument that parental investments in children have gone down as children have become less important for parents' future financial security.

This, however, is only part of the unbundling of activities that were once tied together in the family. The primordial structure is unraveling as its functions are taken away by the new corporate actors. For example, as more of the man's activity takes place in the purposive structure, in his place of employment, leisure activities are less likely to be linked to the extended family or neighborhood, and thus less likely to be cross-generational. Cocktail parties for the parents and rock concerts for the children replace shared leisure activities. Extensive commercially produced entertainment, targeting specific age groups, replaces the family- and neighborhood-based cross-generational structures that produced both childrearing and leisure satisfactions as by-products.

Another shift of activity from the household to the modern corporate structure has had an impact comparable to that of the man's leaving the household to go to an external workplace. This is the woman's leaving the household to go to an external workplace. In doing this, the woman shifts her daytime locus of activity from the primordial structure, the family, to the purposive structure, the world of corporate actors. Figure 22.3 shows, along with the movement of men out of agriculture, the movement of women into the labor force. This movement of women out of the home roughly parallels that of men but occurs about a hundred years later. This movement shows no signs of abating and is especially pronounced among mothers of children below school age.

---

4. Skocpol and Orloff (1986) give importance to the variation in governmental structure as affecting the assumption of welfare activities by the state. But more striking is the uniformity, over a longer sweep of history, of the assumption of these responsibilities by the social structure composed of modern purposive corporate actors. These responsibilities had been, throughout history and prehistory, responsibilities of the family and its extensions.

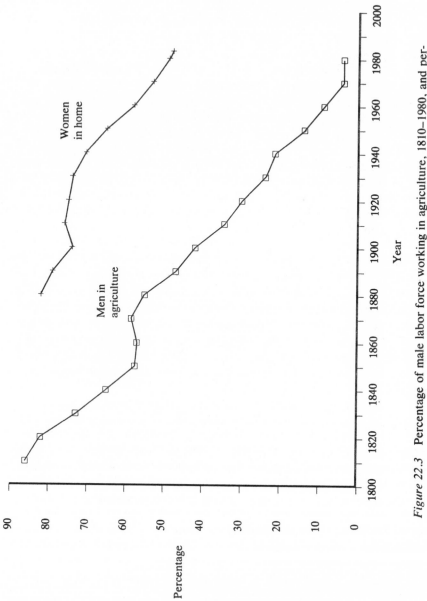

Figure 22.3 Percentage of male labor force working in agriculture, 1810–1980, and percentage of women not employed in paid labor force, 1880–1982. (Data on women are from U.S. Bureau of the Census, 1975, Table D49–62; and U.S. Bureau of the Census, 1984.)

The man's movement out of the household (and ultimately out of the neighborhood) to carry out productive activity in the purposive social structure had a profound effect on childrearing, constituting a major force leading to mass schooling of children. The woman's movement out of the household to carry out productive activity can be expected to have effects that are just as profound. The man's removal from the household left one adult there, but the woman's leaves none. The man's leaving the household removed the opportunity for boys' occupational training there or in the neighborhood, and the woman's leaving removes other elements. One way of describing the loss for children is to say that the removal of the woman from the household curtails many of those daily activities of which childrearing has been a by-product.

One major such household activity that is currently decreasing as more wives and mothers work outside the home is cooking meals. The explosive proliferation of fast-food restaurants (as well as other components of the low-cost segment of the food-service industry) indicates the rapidity with which the activity of eating meals is moving out of the primordial structure of the household and into the purposive structure of modern corporate actors. In some cases families still eat the restaurant meals together, but in others eating together has also ended.

Distribution of Income to Children in the New Social Structure

As modern corporate actors displace functions of the family, there is another consequence for future generations. This concerns the intergenerational distribution of income. Economists have examined consequences for inequality of bequests from parents to children (Becker and Tomes, 1979, 1986; Loury, 1981); these analyses have assumed the distribution of children in households. Here I will examine effects of the changes that have occurred in that distribution.

In a society consisting of households in a subsistence economy, each household produces most of what it consumes. Until about a hundred years ago, this was the economic structure for most households in even the most economically advanced societies. In such a structure problems for the distribution of economic goods are confined to the distribution of the resources (principally land) through which those goods are produced. Any inefficiencies in the functioning of society introduced by imperfect macrosocial institutions have relatively minor effects, because society consists of many small, weakly interacting social systems, each nearly self-contained.

As economies changed from subsistence household economies to exchange economies, the principal method of distribution of economic goods was merely an extension of what had already existed in the economic superstructure outside of households: an exchange of wages for labor, and a use of the labor (largely by the new corporate actors) to produce goods, which were then exchanged for the money that had been paid in wages. A single interdependent economic system replaced the multiple, largely independent, economic systems of households.

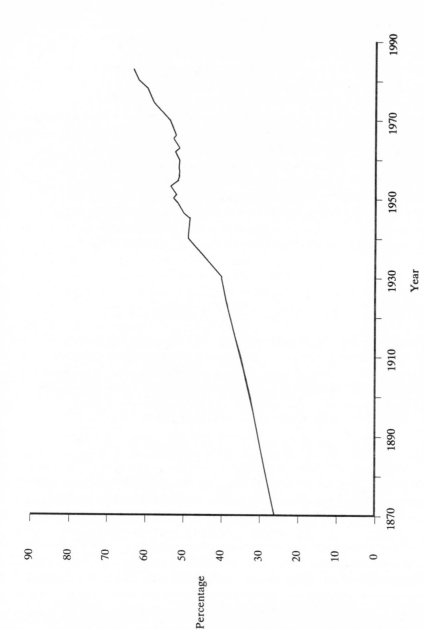

Figure 22.4   Percentage of households in the United States containing no children (persons under 18), 1870–1983. (Data for 1875 from Pryor, 1972, recalculated with all households as the base; data for 1930 from U.S. Bureau of the Census, 1930, interpolated because data are reported for persons under 21; data for 1940, 1946, 1947, and 1949 from U.S. Bureau of the Census, 1947, 1949; data for 1950–1970 from U.S. Bureau of the Census, 1975; data for 1971–1983 from U.S. Bureau of the Census, 1984.)

Only a portion of the household economy was replaced by the interdependent economy, however. Within the household there is a distribution system following a communal principle. In the household economy, all contributed to the joint products, and all consumed, without a balancing of individual accounts. (Communal distribution does not, of course, mean equal voice; it is compatible with highly centralized authority, as is evident in both patriarchal households and charismatic communes.) When the interdependent economy, with the exchange of labor for wages and wages for consumption goods, replaced the household economies that had preceded it, the communal distribution system of the household continued, but with certain necessary modifications. Income entered the household via one breadwinner (or in some cases several) and was distributed, along with other goods and services still produced within the household, to all members of the household.

For this communal distribution within the household to fully supplement income distribution through the labor market depends on households being sufficiently extended to cover all persons. That assumption is no longer valid. The household has been the unit within which wages—extracted by one member, the wage earner, or breadwinner, from a new corporate actor through labor—are redistributed communally for consumption. But the household has been fragmented along with the family. The first fragmentation came as the three-generational economic unit (which may have consisted of more than one household but was largely a single economic unit for consumption), containing a breadwinner in an income-earning stage of life, gave way to the nuclear family as the principal economic unit. The set of smaller units which replaced the extended economic unit did not all contain a wage earner: Those past the income-earning stage of life were without earnings, and those affine dependents, previously tucked away in corners of households, were cast adrift. The impact of this breaking up of the extended income-sharing unit was softened (and the breakup thereby hastened) through the intervention of pensions, both private (financed by a person's own earnings at an earlier age) and public (financed by the government via taxes on the earnings of all).

The next stage of the decline of the communal distribution function of the family arose as the nuclear family itself began to break apart, and as more children have come to be born and raised in households with no wage earner—either because of the dissolution of marriage or through the production of children in the absence of marriage. This stage, which began in the last ' third of the twentieth century, effectively destroys a large portion of the fami¹ ₂ communal income-sharing function.[5]

Figure 22.4 shows the percentage of households in the United States containing no children under 18, from 1870 to 1983. The fraction of the national income

---

5. The extremely high rate at which divorced income-earning fathers default on payment of alimony is a strong indication that income redistribution even to one's own children is ineffective once the household as an organic unit is broken.

distributed to households with children—and thus the fraction of that income available for the raising of children—has declined precipitously as the fraction of households with no children increases. This can be seen in Table 22.1, which shows what the per capita income for children would be, under certain assumptions, relative to that for the average adult, at three points in time, 1870, 1930, and 1983; for the table it is assumed that the income per household is equal, the number of adults in each childless household is two, the average number of children in households that have children is three, and income is shared equally within households but not between. Given these assumptions, a wage in a household with children must be divided into five parts, whereas the same wage in a childless household is divided in half. The assumptions are of course crude, but the table serves to show the impact of this one social-structural change on the capacity of the economic system to distribute resources to children.

Consequences of the New Social Structure for Social Capital

The loss to children from women's move out of the household and neighborhood to jobs in modern corporate actors can also be described as a removal from the household and the neighborhood of much of the remaining social capital on which children and youth depend—both for social and psychological support and for social constraint. Social capital that is important for childrearing is present in three aspects of social structure. One is the intensity of relations between adult and child, the second is the relation between two adults who have relations of some intensity with the child, and the third is continuity of structure over time. Figure 22.5(a) illustrates the first aspect; Figure 22.5(b)–(e) represents the second aspect, realized in four different ways; and Figure 22.5(f) represents the third.

Figure 22.5(a) may represent the relation between a parent and child. Two examples illustrate the importance of the intensity of that relation. The first concerns a father and son. John Stuart Mill was taught Latin and Greek by his father, James Mill, at an age before most children attend school, and later in childhood discussed critically with his father and with Jeremy Bentham drafts of the former's manuscripts. John probably had no extraordinary genetic endow-

Table 22.1 Proportion of households without children and relative per capita income of children.

	1870	1930	1983
Proportion of households without children	.27	.40	.64
Per capita income of children relative to that of adults	.71	.63	.51

Note: Based on assumptions of two adults in household, one of whom is a wage earner, three children per household containing children, equal income per wage earner, and equal sharing within households.

ments; and his father's learning was no more extensive than that of some other men of the time. The critical difference was the time and effort the father spent in intellectual pursuits with the child. The second example concerns a school district in the United States where textbooks were purchased by children's families. School authorities were puzzled when they discovered that a number of Asian immigrant families purchased *two* copies of each textbook their children needed. Investigation showed that the second copy was purchased so that the mother could study it in order to maximize the help she could give her child with school work. In this case the human capital of the parents, at least as traditionally measured as years of schooling, is low, but the social capital in the family available for the child's education is extremely high.

These examples illustrate parent-child relations of some intensity. That intensity is reduced in the new social structure. The removal of both father's and mother's productive activities from the household and the neighborhood not only removes the activities which produced childrearing as a by-product. It takes away from the child some of the psychic investment in the child by mother and father, psychic investment which is transferred to activities in the other structure, the structure created by modern corporate actors. If James Mill had

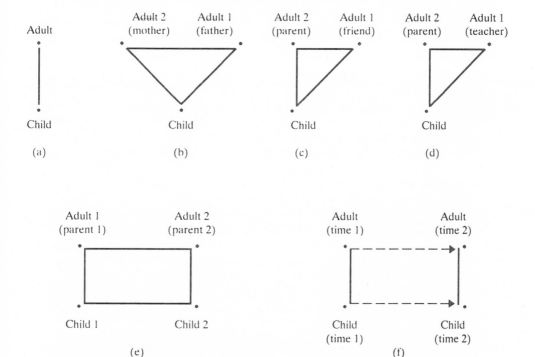

Figure 22.5 Social-structural forms through which social capital for childrearing is generated.

been working in an office rather than writing at home, his attention and time would not have focused so intensely on his son, and John Stuart Mill would probably not have been commenting on his father's manuscripts at age 12. If the Asian mothers were at work in a factory or office, they would not give the time and attention to their children's homework that they do.

The adult does not have to be a parent for the strong relation of adult and child to constitute social capital of benefit to the child. The social capital important for Bertrand Russell's growing up was not provided by a parent but by his grandmother (who, however, was a surrogate parent). In the case of some close-knit neighborhoods, the relation might involve an adult hobby enthusiast who persuades a neighbor boy or girl to take up the hobby. In the case of a youth organization, it may be an enthusiastic and sympathetic adult leader. It may be a teacher who takes a special personal interest in a child.

In terms of the diagram of Figure 22.5(a), the social capital lies in the capability of the relation between the two nodes, adult and child, to transmit from one to the other. Some relations can transmit emotional contact, or intimate feelings, whereas others can transmit a different range of content. Certain content is important for social-psychological reasons. These can be summed up crudely as protection against social isolation, although the ways in which intimate social relations are important to psychic health are of course complex. Emile Durkheim (1951 [1897]) was the sociologist who studied most fully the role of social isolation in mental illness, in his extraordinary *Suicide*.[6] Faris and Dunham (1939) pursued this examination further, in a study of mental illness in urban areas that were characterized by various kinds of living arrangements and thus different degrees of social isolation. In a later section I will show the importance of this form of social capital for another behavioral outcome among contemporary youth—not suicide, but a phenomenon which has some elements in common with it—dropping out of high school.

Social capital also lies in the capability of the relation between the two nodes to transmit a different range of content. The adult hobbyist who transmits excitement about his hobby, the swimming coach or violin teacher who transmits intensity of commitment to a goal, the parent who helps a teenager overcome some obstacle or who has carried out sufficiently effective socialization that the child has internalized the parent's goals—all of these adults illustrate the way in which social capital of the form generated by the relation diagrammed in Figure 22.5(a) can be important in a child's development.

The close relation with an adult can have a variety of effects on children and youth, some of which would not by any criterion be characterized as beneficial to the child. Sometimes a close relation between an adult and a child, if the adult

---

6. Durkheim's results are often misstated; there is confusion between what he called anomie, by which he meant absence of norms, and what he called egoism, by which he meant social isolation. In Durkheim's empirical results egoistic suicide was much more prevalent than anomic suicide, but the latter is most often seen as his principal focus.

is unconstrained by incest taboos or other normative constraints, can result in sexual exploitation of the child. Sometimes the emotional bond between child and parent can be so great that the parent has undue power over the child.[7] Yet even though the potential exists for such perverse effects, the existence of a strong relation between adult and child must be regarded, on the whole, as a source of social capital important for the development of the child.

Social capital of a second type is generated by relations diagrammed in Figure 22.5(b)–(e). Here the social capital derives from the existence of closure of a social network involving a child and two (or more) adults. Closure is present only when there is a relation between adults who themselves have a relation to the child. The adults are able to observe the child's actions in different circumstances, talk to each other about the child, compare notes, and establish norms. The closure of the network can provide the child with support and rewards from additional adults that reinforce those received from the first and can bring about norms and sanctions that could not be instituted by a single adult alone.

In Figure 22.5(b) closure depends on the strength of the relation between the child's parents. If that relation is strong, the parents can act consistently and as a unit toward the child. If it is weak or absent (as in the case of some single or divorced parents), the child's home environment contains many inconsistencies and conflicting signals. The parents will not be able to reinforce each other in disciplining the child. In the extreme case the child plays off one parent against the other.

In Figure 22.5(c) closure is attained by a relation between a parent and another adult. This relation can provide reinforcement for the parent in disciplining the child, if the other adult agrees, or a restraining influence, if the other adult's experience is different. It can allow the parent to transmit to the other adult information about actions that the parent approves or disapproves of, and can thus strengthen the approval or disapproval the child receives; and it can transmit similar information from the other adult back to the parent.

In Figure 22.5(d) closure is established by a relation between parent and teacher; this represents a special case of the network shown in Figure 22.5(c). It is important because in modern society school occupies a large portion of a child's time—and is the context for the major form of role-differentiation that characterizes modern childhood. A teacher sees and knows a child in the role of student and classmate to others of the same age. This is a different role from that observed by the parent. Thus teacher and parent have very different information about the child. Their sharing of this information with each other can lead them to take more consistent actions toward the child, can strengthen their respective actions when their observations point to a common conclusion, and again can lead to the creation of a norm enforced by both.

Figure 22.5(e) portrays a network with closure that is especially common. The

---

7. There are many examples of this. One class is composed of cases of child prodigies who go to pieces when the parent is no longer there.

network is composed of a child, a friend of the child, the friend's parent, and the child's parent. In this case the parents have similar tasks and goals in fostering the development of their children. If there were no relation between the parents, their common interests—some in support of their children's activities and some in support of one another in opposing their children's activities—could in no way be mutually reinforced. Their children have a relation, develop joint strategies, and support one another in their actions. When the children's interests or values or tastes are opposed to those of their parents, they have an advantage due to this mutual reinforcement if there is no comparable relation between their parents. When children's interests must be protected from other actors (such as the school), the absence of a relation between parents makes each parent less effective in opposing the other actor on the child's behalf.

The forms of closure illustrated by parts b–e of Figure 22.5 all exist in a community in which neighbors know each other, children go to the same school, and teachers are part of the community. Such a structure is part of the primordial social structure that has the family as its basic building block. In the purposive social structure based on modern corporate actors, closure taking these forms is often absent. There are other adults in society who have a reasonably strong relation to the child and to the parent, but they ordinarily turn out to be from the primordial structure: aunts, uncles, grandparents, or other members of the extended family; neighbors; parents of friends of the child; and sometimes fellow church members. The adults from the purposive structure with whom a parent has reasonably strong relations seldom have occasion to know the child well. The role-differentiation of parents' lives means that their work-related activities seldom intersect with their family-related activities.

Figure 22.5(f) represents social-structural closure with respect to time. Time-closure means that the adult in a given type of relation with a child at one time is the same adult that was in this relation with this child at an earlier time. To some degree all the relations in Figure 22.5 imply continuity over time, or time-closure, in that they have become established. Time-closure is important in itself, however, apart from the intensity it helps bring about. Time-closure has both prospective and retrospective effects. Prospectively, it encourages investments in the relation that will pay off only after some time as well as trustworthiness on the part of both the adult and the child (because each will have to confront the other in the future). Retrospectively, it gives the relation a past history in the memories of the two parties, which can provide the basis for placing trust, a potent form of social capital.

This depiction of closure in social structures is not merely empirical observation; it follows from the structural difference between a social system constructed of modern corporate actors and one consisting of multipurpose collectivities that produce many products and outcomes jointly. In principle, it would be possible for closure among parent, child, and other adults and time-closure to prosper in the purposive structure if the physical setting of parent-child activities intersected with the physical setting of work activities and if persons were long-term occupants of positions. In principle, closure would also be possible if there were extensive leisure activities which included parents, other adults, and children. But there is nothing inherent in the new social structure based on modern corporate actors that induces such closure; in fact, various aspects of the structure (such as physical separation of work and residence, short-term occupancy of positions, and the development of age-specific leisure activities and entertainment) discourage it.

Empirical Consequences of Lack of Social Capital for Youth

The preceding section indicated some possible forms of social capital that can aid children's social and intellectual development. Here I will describe consequences of variations in that social capital for achievement during high school and for staying in high school until graduation. There are various measures of the intensity of the parent-child relation; I will examine the following:

1. *The presence of both parents in the household.* When both parents are present, there will be, if all else is equal, a stronger parent-child relation than when only one parent is present.
2. *Number of siblings.* Attention and interest of parents in each child are roughly inversely proportional to number of children. Thus the social capital available to each child will be less, the greater the number of children in the family.
3. *Talking about personal matters.* If parents and child talk about personal matters, this indicates greater attention and interest of the parent in the child.
4. *Mother's working outside the home before child is in school.* If the mother works at an outside job before the child is in school, this reduces the strength of the mother's relation to the child by reducing the time she spends with the child during a formative period. This action may also reflect a greater focus of the mother's attention on a career and thus away from the child.
5. *Parents' interest in the child's attending college.* Other things being equal, parents who have an interest in their child's attending college are more interested in their child and concerned about the child's future than are parents who have no interest in their child's attending college.

These five indicators of social capital in the home have been measured in a nationally representative survey of 28,000 students in 1,015 high schools in the United States. In 1980, when they were sophomores, and again in 1982, the students responded to a questionnaire on which the above measures were based. A simple measure allowed examination of educational outcomes for these students: whether or not a student remained in school. Table 22.2 below shows the independent effects of each of the indicators of social capital on remaining in school, when each of the other indicators of social capital, as well as various

Table 22.2   Effects of various measures of social capital provided by the
parent-child relation on estimated percentage of students dropping out
(grades 10 to 12).

	Percentage dropping out	Difference in percentages
1. *Parents' presence*		
Two parents	13.1	6.0
Single parent	19.1	
2. *Additional children in family*		
One sibling	10.8	6.4
Four siblings	17.2	
3. *Ratio of parents to children*		
Two parents, one sibling	10.1	12.5
One parent, four siblings	22.6	
4. *Mother's expectation for child's education*		
Expectation of college	11.6	8.6
No expectation of college	20.2	
5. *All measures combined*		
Two parents, one sibling, mother expects college	8.1	22.5
One parent, four siblings, no expectation of college	30.6	

Note: All effects are significant at 5% level. (DEF of 2.0 is taken into account.) Analysis is carried out via a weighted logistic regression using nine variables. Results are calculated by subtracting from or adding to the overall percentage (14.4%) the effect due to deviation from the mean of the independent variable or variables in question. Table is taken from Coleman (1988b), based on analysis carried out by Hoffer (1986).

other characteristics of the student, is taken into account. The results are expressed as differences in the percentages of students dropping out of school between grades 10 and 12.

The same study also considered a measure of the social capital existing because of closure of social networks as shown in parts c, d, and e of Figure 22.5. This measure is less direct than those above, but nevertheless gives some indication of the social capital in the community available to the child. The measure is the number of times a child has changed schools because the family has moved. This measure is an indirect measure of all three forms of closure, because parents are less likely to have relations with teachers (Figure 22.5c) or with other parents of children in the school (Figure 22.5d), and the child is less likely to have relations with other adults in the community (Figure 22.5b) if the family has recently moved and the child has had to change schools. Table 22.3 shows the effect of residential stability, a form of social capital, or dropping out of school, analogous to the effects shown in Table 22.2.

Table 22.3 Effect of residential stability in providing social capital on estimated percentage of students dropping out.

Number of moves since fifth grade	Estimated percentage dropping out
No moves	12.6
Two moves	20.0

Note: Effect is significant at 5% level. (DEF of 2.0 is taken into account.) Analysis is carried out via the weighted logistic regression used for Table 22.2, with those nine variables as well as race, Hispanic ethnicity, socioeconomic status, and other variables statistically controlled. Results are calculated as for Table 22.2. Regression coefficients have been reported by Hoffer (1986).

The Direct Impact of the Two Social Structures on the Next Generation

The social structure of modern corporate actors has a portion of its effect on the next generation through the removal of the physical presence and interests of adults from the primordial structure within which children remain. Thus children and youth are isolated from the adults who constitute their principal socializing agents. Another portion of the effect, however, is manifested in the nature of the relations that children and youth have with natural persons and corporate actors outside the family.

In the primordial structure one prototypical corporate actor with which a child may have a relation is a religious body of which the parents are members. Another is the neighborhood community; its relation to children differs somewhat from that of a religious body, although may overlap with it. In the purposive structure one set of corporate actors with which a child has some relation is the set collectively responsible for television programming. Another set of corporate actors with which the child has some relation is that composed of producers of goods that the child consumes—toys, clothes, records, food, entertainment, and other items.

The difference in the impact of the two social structures on children lies partly in a fundamental structural difference: The elements of primordial corporate actors are persons, and the elements of purposive corporate actors are positions, of which persons are merely temporary occupants. This structural difference has major consequences for children.

Whole-Person versus Role-Segmented Structure

The purposive structure implies that each person occupies several positions in different corporate actors. The individual's relation with each of these corporate actors involves some kind of exchange of resources, of the sort described throughout this book. The corporate actor's interest is in the services or other resources the person provides, and the person's interest is in what he receives in exchange. The corporate actor may be a business firm, a governmental agency, or a voluntary association, and the individual may act in the role of employee, client or customer, or member; in any case each actor has an interest in something provided by the other, but not in the other per se.

If the social system were composed entirely of such corporate actors, the social structure could be viewed as containing two kinds of entities: individual persons holding positions in a particular set of corporate actors, and corporate actors composed of positions currently occupied by a particular set of persons. An approximation of this currently exists for a number of adult persons in modern society, who have no relations as whole persons with other persons, but only relations through occupancy of positions in corporate actors. Extreme examples are persons who die in accidents and whose bodies remain unclaimed at a morgue. The relations arising from occupancy of a position in an organization are not ones that would lead the other parties to those relations to claim the body.

A structure composed largely of this sort of relation has one consequence that is particularly important for children: There is no one to "claim the body," no person or corporate actor to take responsibility for the person as a whole. A child has a clear need for such a person or corporate actor. The need is recognized in law, which designates a legal guardian for each child regarded as a minor. In current and past social systems, the parents are ordinarily the legal guardians (or if there has been a divorce, one parent). In the absence of the natural parents, the state, adoptive parents, or relatives may become a child's legal guardian.

One question for the social structure of the future, then, is this simple one: Who will take responsibility for the whole child; who will be in a position to "claim the body"? If the family disintegrates, with natural parents performing only the function of procreation and then disappearing into their own networks of relations based on self-interest, there is no natural replacement. This does not imply that there is no possibility of creating purposive corporate actors in which attention is given to, and responsibility taken for, the child as a whole. These already exist in the form of boarding schools and summer camps, neither of which acquires its orientation to the whole person through derivation from the family.

There appear to be two general strategies that can be employed to ensure that in the society of the future the child will be attended to as a whole person. One is the nurturing or strengthening of the primordial relations of kinship, which have constituted the principal source of such attention and responsibility. The second is explicit creation of purposive organizations—that is, modern corporate actors—structured so that persons do give attention to and take responsibility for the whole child.

Interests of Primordial Corporate Actors in Children

The structural difference between primordial corporate actors and purposive corporate actors leads to systematic differences in their interests in children. It is useful to examine these and to assess how they might be expected to have an impact on corporate actors' actions toward children and youth.

The interests of a religious body or a local community in children are interests for which something about the child is an end in itself. These primordial corporate actors have an interest in the child becoming a moral being. The community has an interest in the child's growing up to be self-sufficient, sociable, and a contributor to the community. Both a community and a religious body have an interest in the child's obedience to norms that lead to actions benefiting others, and thus an interest in the child's internalizing such norms.

The interest of the community may be seen to derive from the selfish interest of each of its members in having fellow members whose actions will benefit him when possible and will otherwise do as little harm to him as possible. Because the community in this prototypical case is homogeneous except for age and sex differences, for many of the norms that develop, the beneficiaries and the targets are the same persons; that is, norms are conjoint (see Chapters 10 and 30). The interests of the community members who sanction children and attempt to bring about internalization of these norms are also the interests of the children, since for conjoint norms the interest in having the norm obeyed and in violating it are found in each person.

In many cases the norm is a disjoint one in that adults benefit from the child's adherence to it, and children are the targets. Because children will later become adults, such a norm may be in effect serially conjoint (each person being both target and beneficiary, but at different ages); however, there is no insurance, as there is with a pure conjoint norm, that such a norm is socially efficient (see Chapter 30). The costs to children due to the constraints of the norm may be greater than the benefits experienced by the adults—since adults, having already passed through the period of targethood, are not constrained by the possible future impact of the norm on them. Only insofar as children have some power to make adults uncomfortable, either through the family or outside it, can they oppose disjoint norms which impose hardships on them. Here, as elsewhere, the balance that is attained between different persons' interests depends on their relative power in the system of action.

Certain norms maintained by the community and imposed on children do not even have serial conjointness. These derive from power differences among different families or clans in the community. Such disjoint norms may be imposed only on children of less powerful groups. The example in Chapter 10 concerning nomads in northeastern Greece illustrates this.

There are also some conjoint norms induced by primordial corporate actors for which adults are targets and both children and adults are beneficiaries. The most prominent examples are norms against adults' exploitation of the physical, mental, or social control they can exercise over children: norms against incest, against sexual and physical abuse, and against blatant exploitation of the child's labor.

The interests of a religious body, distinct from interests of its members and from interests of the community with which it may largely coincide in membership, appear highly directed toward the development of the child as an end in itself. Since maintenance of a religious body requires belief and observance in each succeeding generation, a religious body has an interest in fostering in the next generation the beliefs or desires which will maintain the observance. This creates an intrinsic interest of the religious body in the kind of person the child is and will become.

Interests of Purposive Corporate Actors in Children

The interests of many purposive corporate actors with which children interact are quite different from those described above. The set of actors which produces television programs for children must be divided into two groups: those whose interests appear to have something to do with changes that a program produces in children, and those whose interests do not include changing children. Examples of programs produced by the former for American television are *Sesame Street, The Electric Company, Mr. Rogers' Neighborhood,* and some nature shows. Examples of programs produced by the latter group are much more numerous: cartoons, space adventure shows, various programs involving violent action, and so forth.

The interests of the corporate actors in the first group have some similarity to those of primordial corporate actors: Although they are interested in success, which is ordinarily defined as making money, they view that success as dependent not only on gaining the children's attention, but also on the perceived effects of the program on the children. The effects desired for most children's programs that are publicly funded have less moral content than is true of the aims of the primordial corporate actors discussed earlier, because there is little social consensus as to which values to inculcate. There is a much higher degree of social consensus concerning the development of skills or knowledge in children. Thus these programs usually have as goals adding to children's knowledge or developing their cognitive skills.

The interests of the second group of corporate actors which produce children's television programs lie solely in attracting the child's attention and, through that, in extracting money from the household (money spent on goods consumed by children). Any other effects, beneficial or harmful to children, are accidental. (This is illustrated by the investigations of, and disagreements about, the possibly negative effects on children of violence on television. Those corporate actors responsible for the programs which contain violence are not attempting to bring about either negative effects in children or positive ones. The interests of some of those actors are satisfied if the programs attract a large audience; the interests of others are satisfied only if products advertised on the programs are purchased.)

The interests of most other purposive corporate actors with which children come in contact—manufacturers and sellers of toys, cereals, candy, soft drinks, and clothing and purveyors of popular music and other commercial entertainment—appear also not to include any interest in effects on the child beyond that of inducing a preference for a particular product. Thus most of their effects, beneficial or harmful, are accidental and unintended. The intended effect can have a cumulative impact, inducing a young person to be very interested in clothes, certain foods (so-called junk foods), or popular music, and attracting interest away from other matters. This may have an overall shaping effect on the direction a child's or youth's life takes; however, the effect appears to be incidental to the corporate actors' aims.

There is a small set of corporate actors whose success does depend on causing changes in children's tastes or habits. These actors are related in some way to a set of actions for which the term "addiction" is used, actions that include smoking cigarettes, drinking alcohol, and taking drugs. The corporate actors who benefit from acquired dependencies on these things have a great interest in creating tastes for them. With cigarettes in particular, advertising has been very successful in creating the taste—which, once in place, generates consumption without further inducements. A set of corporate actors opposing these acquired tastes or habits also exists. These include governmental organizations, privately supported organizations, and even commercial organizations that receive their income from consumers (such as firms that manufacture substances that aid in stopping smoking).

The Balance of Interests with Which Children and Youth Are in Contact

For the two kinds of social structure, primordial and purposive, just what is the overall character of the interests of actors with which children come in contact? In neither case can it be said that interests are uniformly directed toward ends that further children's long-range interests. What can be said, however, is that in the purposive structure the interests of actors (primarily corporate actors) are more often unrelated and incidental to children's interests. There is much greater danger of unintended (although not accidental or unforeseeable) harm to the long-range interests of children and youth. Furthermore, when the interests of an actor in contact with a child are opposed to those of the child, they are less often moderated by indirect ties to the child (for example, through parents) in the purposive structure than they are in the primordial structure.

Thus it appears that interests of purposive corporate actors in contact with children and youth are more likely to be harmful to the interests of those persons than is true in the primordial structure. A part of the difference is related to the deviation from rationality described as weakness of will in Chapter 19. It can be assumed that a child has both short-term interests and long-term interests. This assumption seems fully warranted, because of deviations from rationality that have been shown experimentally to be exhibited in adult behavior (see the discussion in Chapter 19). The conflicts between these two types of interests are reflected in terms such as precommitment, weakness of will, and temptation. If there can be a conflict between short-term and long-term interests of an actor, then in an exchange setting another actor may be able to exploit this conflict to realize his own interest. By providing something which satisfies short-term interests (some of which are called appetites to suggest that they can be satisfied by immediate consumption), an actor may induce another to give up something of much greater long-term interest to himself.

The phenomenon is so common that it has been the subject of numerous stories, fairy tales, and folk tales. From these come such sayings as "He sold his soul to the devil" (in return for some temptation offered by the devil) or "He gave up his birthright for a mess of pottage." The phenomenon occurs daily and constitutes part of the events through which one learns by experience. It becomes a matter of social concern, as well as becoming of interest to social theory, when there are systematic distortions of this sort in the exchange process.

Perhaps the most serious of those systematic distortions has to do with children. One commonly observed characteristic of children is that they often pursue their short-term interests at the expense of their long-term interests. Since children lack long-term experience, this is quite understandable; their relatively short experience has not taught them that pursuit of a particular short-term interest may be harmful to one's interests in the longer term.

One of the ways certain actors whose relations with a child have time-closure (for example, parents) take a child's interests into account in their interactions with the child is to attend to the child's longer-term interests, often by opposing the child's pursuit of short-term interests. But if children are in extensive contact with (that is, engage in social exchanges with) actors whose relations with the children do not have time-closure, it is not in those actors' interests to attend to the children's long-term interests. When these actors do not take children's long-term interests into account, they are free to exploit children's short-term interests to their advantage.

The most prominent example of corporate actors which exploit children's short-term interests and ignore their long-term interests are those involved in the production of certain television shows, not only shows with an appeal based principally on thrills and violence, but also ones which have as their sole purpose attracting children's attention. Some such programs may not be harmful to children's long-term interests, but if they are not, this is incidental. Another thing many children are interested in is sweets of various sorts. This short-term interest is easily exploited by corporate actors who make and sell candies, soft drinks, cakes, ice cream, sugar-coated breakfast cereals, and so on. Moderate consumption of these foods may not be inimical to the child's long-term interests, but heavy consumption may be. A child's experience and physiological signals are often insufficient to limit the quantity consumed, and unless there is some guardian of the child's interest, consumption may be sufficient to be harmful.

Children's actions carried out principally to satisfy short-term interests, such as those satisfied by watching television, are much less conditioned by long-term interests than are actions of adults. Thus protection against harm to long-term interests, a protection that is imperfect even among adults, is largely absent among children. That protection has characteristically come from adult guardians, who are most often parents but may be other adults. If, however, a child is in relatively unconstrained interaction with certain corporate actors, as is true for many children with respect to watching television and for some children and youth with respect to other consumption activities, protection of long-term interests is missing.

The latter circumstance is especially applicable to many high-school students in modern Western society. Youth in their teens have become an important segment of the consumer market in certain areas such as music, clothes, and fast foods. The fraction of youth who work while attending high school and still living at home has increased in recent years in the United States, especially among middle-class youth, and is beginning to rise in Europe. The consequence of this is that high-school students have increasing amounts of discretionary income for which they need not account to their parents.

Conflicts of Interest over Childrearing

In every society there are conflicts of interest among different actors concerning the raising of children. These conflicts are inherent in the differentiated structure of a social system, but they are different in social systems in which the principal corporate actor is the family and its derivatives than they are in systems in which the principal corporate actor is the modern purposive corporate actor. It is useful to begin by considering the interests of actors who are affected by children. Although there are many such actors, it is possible as a first approximation to consider only two: the family, and all others outside the family who are members of the same social order.

The potential conflicts of interest between the family and society with respect to children's upbringing can be seen as occurring along three dimensions:

1. *The values, orientations, customs, language, norms, and culture of the family versus those of the broader social order.* An extreme example occurs where a family has one culture, religion, or language, and the broader society has another. Included in this dimension of potential conflict are all differences with respect to social norms. For example, a family engaged in crime or other deviant activity may have an interest in raising its children to impose similar harm on others outside the family.

2. *The family's interest in using its resources to educate its children versus the society's interest in using the resources of all families to educate all children.* This conflict only occurs between those families with more than average resources and the society as a whole (or, it might be said, between those with more resources and those with fewer). It is the conflict between publicly supported education and education supported separately by each family according to its

resources. In all developed societies this conflict has been resolved in the direction of the broader society's interest, in that education up through the late teens or beyond is publicly supported. Yet the issue remains alive.

3. *The interest of parents or potential parents in spending their resources on themselves versus the interest of the broader social order in spending their resources on the next generation.* This conflict of interest arises only when the intergenerational family is no longer the basic building block of the society, and persons in one generation are not dependent—financially or psychologically—on the success or failure of their own progeny, but on the overall success or failure of the generation that succeeds them in the society as a whole. This conflict of interest exists principally in the most advanced societies in Europe and America. One manifestation of it is the lack of interest of increasing numbers of adults in having children; another is the lack of interest of those who do become parents in depriving themselves of consumption goods and retirement savings to educate their children beyond the level of publicly supported education.

I will call conflicts along these three dimensions cultural conflict, educational conflict, and generational conflict, respectively. Each of these potential conflicts of interest raises certain policy issues, and for none of them does the resolution follow straightforwardly from a set of moral or ethical principles. There is, however, a fundamental difference between the first two types of conflict and the third. For the first two the unity of the family and the interest of the family in its children are taken as given. Thus these two conflicts of interest will clearly occur between two well-defined actors: the family as a unit having an interest in the children who are its members, and the broader society as a collectivity having an interest in all the children who are its members. For the third conflict there is on one side not the family, but the individual adult or the husband and wife. Here the family is no longer assumed as one actor, and thus the interest of the family in the children can no longer be taken as given. In fact, for generational conflict such an interest is assumed no longer to exist, having been replaced by each individual's interest in his own future or a couple's interest in their joint future— in both cases restricted to that generation. This means, of course, that one strategy open to the broader society is to attempt to rekindle that interest, to reconstitute the family as an entity with interests that span generations.

CULTURAL CONFLICTS AND ISSUES OF LIBERTY AND EQUALITY   The conflict over the values, orientations, religion, language, and culture that will be transmitted to children in educational institutions is a conflict over who is the appropriate guardian of a child. It is illustrated by the following example: On a wooded cliff in Kentucky, overlooking the Ohio River, a beautiful cedar house stood empty. The house was owned by an artist, who had moved with his family to another state because he and his wife wanted to educate their children at home, but the state of Kentucky did not allow children to be tutored at home by their parents instead of attending school. Does the state have the right to take children, against their parents' will, away from what may be a remarkable household and put them into one of its schools, of uncertain quality?

More generally, issues involving liberty and issues involving equality of educational opportunity are at stake. The special difficu.ty in resolving these types of issues lies in the intergenerational nature of the problem. The matter is more complex than the conflict between liberty and equality that forms the backbone of much of moral philosophy. Bringing a new person into the world creates a being whose goals and interests are unformed. Thus issues of moral philosophy or social policy cannot be limited to those in which the parties are assumed to have fixed and well-defined goals and interests. It is necessary to begin at an earlier point.

But granted this, how then to proceed?

FAMILY INTERESTS, OTHERS' INTERESTS, AND PROBLEMS OF EXTER-NALITIES   It is useful to see just how these issues of liberty and equality arise in two extreme settings: an isolated village and modern society. The principal corporate actors in the village are primordial, having the family as their ultimate foundation. The principal corporate actors in modern society are purposive, and independent of the family.

An isolated village. In an isolated village inhabitants' lives are circumscribed by the setting, and the next generation can be expected to live there from cradle to grave. Until the last century settings approximating this constituted the largest part of nearly all societies. Now such settings are difficult to find except in the least developed portions of the least developed societies. In such a setting the family is the principal welfare institution of the community. It is responsible for raising its children, for caring for its elderly and sick. It is a communal unit roughly adhering to the principle "from each according to his abilities, to each according to his needs." The village outside the family serves as a back-up welfare system, based largely on community norms which encourage charity.

In a setting of this sort, interests of others in a child can be described as, first, those of the family and, second, those of friends and neighbors throughout the village. The family's interests derive from all those activities in which the child can engage, as child or as adult, that affect members of the family. These include actions while growing up for which the family will be held responsible and, in addition, care and support for parents when they are old. Also, if family members have an interest in the family as an entity that exists for generations, apart from its individual members, then each family member has an interest in each child's upholding the family name and carrying on the family's cultural traditions.

These interests lead each parental generation to make heavy investments in children. If survival of children is (or in memory has been) problematic, or if there is little limitation on economic expansion, these interests may lead to production of large numbers of children. Under other conditions the same interests will lead to investments in the quality of each child. In all cases, of course, the investments in children must compete with consumption needs. For this reason, and because the payoffs from investments in children come in the future, some families (particularly low-income and low status families) can be expected to make low investments in children, with respect to both number and quality.

Interests of other villagers in a child derive from some of the same activities as do those of the family. The actions of the child, both currently and as an adult, will have consequences for the other villagers; many of those are essentially the same as the consequences for the family, but less severe. It is family members who will experience most strongly the consequences of the child's actions, and they therefore, appropriately, have primary control over the child's socialization and education.

There are four potential conflicts of interest between the family and other villagers. First, a cultural conflict may occur in times of change, when other villagers may have an interest in investing in different directions of development in the child. Second, the family's interests may lead to its limiting the scope of certain rules of conduct, such as telling the truth, not cheating, and the like, to the family itself.[8] Others have an interest in those rules of conduct being extended to cover actions affecting anyone in the village. Third, children from families who make low investments in them may be, from other villagers' viewpoint, too little socialized or too little educated. And fourth, villagers have an interest in maintaining their own positions of status and power, which may be in opposition to the interest of a family in a child's improving the family's position in the community. These are four ways in which the child's actions based on family socialization may impose negative externalities on other villagers. The pertinent questions are, first, what the appropriate degree of control of these externalities is, second, whether the villagers can control these externalities, and, third, what means they use to do so.

The answer to the second and third questions is that secondary control over a child's socialization and education resides with the villagers, by means of the daily interactions that the child has in the village. If the villagers hold the family responsible for the child's actions, this can reshape the family's interests to be more in accord with those of the villagers. Thus the villagers have two ways to control the externalities imposed by the child: direct sanctions on the child, and sanctions on the family.

Answering the question of what degree of control is appropriate is more difficult. Because the family is the principal welfare institution, having primary responsibility for the child's actions, primary authority over the child should remain within the family. It is worthwhile to note that the standard answer to such a question for an economic system is that the appropriate degree of control

---

8. A good illustration of this phenomenon is provided by gypsies. Accounts show that gypsy children are well socialized to be highly truthful and honorable within the band, but not in dealing with *gaje*, that is, nongypsies. See Yoors (1967).

is that which leads to maximum economic efficiency (defined only with regard to the given distribution of wealth), and that this arises naturally through the market if there are no transaction costs. There is never a change in the relative wealth of different actors in such a system. The analogous answer for the informally organized social system of the village is that the appropriate degree of control is that which leads to greatest satisfaction, with the satisfaction of each inhabitant weighted according to his power or resources in the system. (Distribution of power in this system corresponds to distribution of wealth in the economic system.) Furthermore, this optimum will naturally arise if there is full and free interaction, where sanctions can be imposed by persons on others to the degree that their power permits.[9]

This social optimum as an answer to what the appropriate degree of control is has its deficiencies. It leads to a wholly static community, to the absence of any social change that involves changes in the distribution of power. The result, in a closed and isolated system such as a village, will be a perpetuation of whatever distribution of power and status was established at the outset, with a lack of opportunity for those of new generations to change their family position. In practice, of course, such an extreme case is never found. Yet the oppressiveness and absence of freedom in closed communities that approximate this extreme can be seen both in some fiction (such as that of William Faulkner) and in ethnographic accounts of primitive tribes, traditional villages, and communes. It should be said, however, that the tight collective control may not be experienced as oppressive by those brought up in such a community, and subjective happiness may be at a high level (see Zablocki, 1971).

Modern society. Modern society differs extensively from the village social structure described above. The family is no longer the primary welfare unit. Responsibility for caring for the aged has been taken over by the society as a whole. Responsibility for medical care has been taken over by the state and employers. The next generation's productivity or dependency is experienced little more by the family than by the society as a whole. The family, greatly shrunken in size and function, has become incapable of carrying out many welfare activities: Dependency cannot be ameliorated by averaging income among household members, for increasingly households either have adequate individual incomes and no dependents, or are dependent as a whole. The state, greatly expanded in size and function, has taken on most welfare functions. The welfare state has replaced the welfare family.

Profound dilemmas for the raising of children have been created by factors, largely technological but political as well, which have destroyed the family's role

---

9. There is a small literature on the paradox of enforcement, which is based on the recognition that a sanction is a public good and that it will therefore be undersupplied, unless there are ways that the sanctioner can recover from others their share of the costs of sanctioning. See Laver (1976). In a stable, highly interactive community, however, there appear to be means for such cost recovery (see Coleman, 1985). The problem, nevertheless, is not well studied. See Chapter 11 for a discussion of this problem, also called the second-order public-good problem.

as society's fundamental building block and primary welfare institution. The family is no longer capable of, nor do its members have a strong interest in, taking primary and long-term responsibility for its members. The state has assumed responsibility for many dependent persons. This means that the responsibility for, and authority over, children has shifted from parents to agents of the state. Yet children's psychological and social development depends on their receiving personal care and attention from adults, not as agents but as persons (as exemplified by parents and other family members). There is, then, for children a continuing loss of parents' care and attention without a corresponding increase from another source. Agents of the state, whether day-care attendants, nursery-school teachers, school teachers, school counselors, or truant officers, cannot exhibit individualized care and attention because of the numbers of children under their supervision.

The first dilemma is this: Should social policy attempt to recreate the conditions which reinforce parents' natural interest in and responsibility for their own children or attempt to create conditions which will induce agents of the state to take a long-term personal interest in and responsibility for children who fall into their hands? The first alternative requires a reversal of certain individualizing and rationalizing tendencies in society. The second requires policies which no state has yet been able to devise and implement; no state has successfully substituted care and attention by agents of the state for that of parents. The prospects seem poor for either alternative. Yet if neither is pursued, increasing numbers of children will suffer from neglect and inattention.

The second dilemma arises as follows: The state has come to serve as a backup welfare institution for children when certain conditions of care and financial support do not exist within the family. The costs to families of providing appropriate care and financial support for children have increased. (For example, in the more populous and multifunctional household of the past, many child-care activities were jointly produced with other activities, at little additional cost. In the modern household child care is more often mutually exclusive with other productive activities, many of which are carried out outside the household.) The combined result of these two changes has been to increase the disincentive for having children for all but the wealthiest families and those at the lowest economic levels, that is, at levels where care and financial support of children fall below the level of state support. For the latter families there exists instead a positive incentive to have children since state support directed at children also provides support for the adult members of the family. The result of the change in incentives has been to reverse the longstanding positive correlation between income and number of children, making it increasingly negative. The change in incentives for low-income families can also be described as a separation of responsibility for children from authority over decisions concerning them. Authority remains in the family's hands, but responsibility for the consequences of childrearing decisions is taken by the state.

The second dilemma, then, is whether to reintroduce familial responsibility for children of low-income families or to remove familial authority since the responsibility has already been removed.[10] A related dilemma is whether to rebalance the incentive structure by creating policies that will give low-income families incentives comparable to those of higher-income families (as in the first alternative suggested above) or by creating policies that will give higher-income families incentives comparable to those for low-income families.[11] (The latter creates a separation of authority and responsibility at all income levels like that currently existing for low-income families.)

10. Murray (1984) has proposed the first of these alternatives, arguing that policies that have progressively removed responsibility have increased the incidence and severity of dependency by causing increasing numbers of persons to qualify for welfare support from the state.

11. Policies of this sort have been advocated by Garfinkel (1982).

The Relation of Sociology to Social Action in the New Social Structure

The social structure of the past might be described as a structure with persons as elements and primordial ties as the basic relations among the elements. In the new social structure the primordial relations have been driven to the periphery as the new corporate actors have come to take over many of their functions. The old social structure can be described as a natural social environment, and the new one in contrast a constructed social environment. In the nineteenth and twentieth centuries, a constructed physical environment composed of buildings and streets has displaced the natural environment of forests, rivers, and plains as the central physical environment in many persons' lives; a constructed social environment composed of modern corporate actors has displaced the natural social environment.

Sociology as a discipline came into being and grew during the period in which the constructed social environment began to grow and displace the natural social environment. This is not coincidental but grounded in a special property of the discipline. The discipline itself, as an object of investigation, falls within the scope of the subject matter of the discipline. That is, sociology is a reflexive discipline, whose subject matter encompasses itself. One implication of this reflexivity is that as long as the social environment is natural, the discipline cannot justify its own existence, except as an epiphenomenon, irrelevant to social functioning. It is when the change to a constructed social environment begins that sociology begins to be relevant, as an aid to that construction.

A second implication of sociology's reflexivity is that an unusual constraint is imposed on any social theory that seeks to be comprehensive. It must meet not only the two usual criteria for theory (that is, internal consistency and corre-spondence to reality) but also a third: The content of the theory must be such as to account for the action of engaging in the construction of social theory. If, in a theory of social change, there is no role for sociological knowledge in affecting social change, the theory cannot account for the act of theorizing itself. Theory construction in sociology must, according to such a theory, be purposeless, since it has no consequences. If the theorist claims a purpose for such a theory in helping to shape the future, the theory is self-contradictory. If, on the other hand, a theoretical approach does pass this test, if it does contain within it a means by which sociological knowledge affects social reality, it is reflexively consistent. By this criterion most classical social theory is purposeless, and some is self-contradictory. Little is reflexively consistent. One can begin to see this by looking at the work of three major theorists: Marx, Weber, and Durkheim.

The Social Role of Social Theory

The work of Karl Marx shows a curious paradox in his conception of how social science could shape society. As an activist political radical, he devoted a portion of his life to an attempt to bring about the next stage, as he saw it, in the historical development of society. Yet in his theory of such development, perhaps the most complete of any social theorist's, only material factors played a part. In oversimplified terms Marx held that technology determined the mode of economic production; the mode of production determined the structure of classes and their relation to the means of production and thus to one another; and this in turn generated, over time, their orientation to (for example, their alienation from) the system of production and led to their taking action which would transform it. The role of ideas and social knowledge in Marx's theory of history was as a dependent or derivative phenomenon, a superstructure generated by the conditions of material existence. In this respect Marx was the originator of the sociology of knowledge; he presented a specific theory about the way in which conditions of social existence bring about knowledge, beliefs, and values concerning social functioning—but no theory about the way knowledge, beliefs, and values might affect social conditions.

Perhaps the best place to look for the role of sociological knowledge in Marx's theory is in his predictions concerning the transformation of a social class from a class in itself to a class for itself, that is, the development of class consciousness. Certainly Marx's own activist efforts were directed to the attempt to arouse the working classes of nineteenth-century Europe to self-consciousness. Yet his theoretical statements about this transformation give the causal role to the social-structural conditions in which people find themselves. The general pattern by which a class gains class consciousness and the derivative position of ideas are perhaps most evident in Marx's discussion of the role of theory in the development of class consciousness:

> Just as Economists are the scientific representatives of the bourgeois class, so the Socialists and the Communists are the theoreticians of the proletarian class. So long as the proletariat is not sufficiently developed to constitute itself as a class, . . . these theoreticians are merely utopians who, to meet the wants of the oppressed classes, improvise systems and go in search of a regenerating science. But in the measure that history moves forward, and with it the struggle of the proletariat assumes clearer outlines, they no longer need to seek science in their minds; they have only to take note of what is happening before their eyes and become its mouthpiece. (1963 [1847], p. 125)

Note that in this statement the theoreticians' role is circumscribed by the state of the proletariat's consciousness, which itself is determined by the economic structure and the position within it of the proletariat. The theoreticians constitute merely a "mouthpiece" for describing the drama as it unfolds.

At one point Marx recognizes the role of knowledge and ideas in social change:

> . . . locomotives, railways, electric telegraphs . . . are products of human industry . . . the power of knowledge objectified. The development of fixed capital indicates to what degree, hence, the conditions of the process of social life itself have come under the general control of intellect and been transformed in accordance with it. (1973 [1858], p. 706)

Here, however, Marx is discussing the role of technological knowledge in changing industry; he seems not to have addressed the question of the role of sociological knowledge in changing social policy. Insofar as there is any nonmaterial force in Marx's theory of social change, this is where it is.

Yet this wholly undeveloped thesis gives no real point of departure for a theory of the social role of sociology. There is not, in Marx's work, any conception of the role of the ideas and leadership provided by disaffected members of higher classes (such as himself, Engels, and others) in moving the working classes toward class consciousness and socialism. Marx envisioned a rational, or constructed, society but did not theorize about the place of sociological knowledge in informing rational action, nor did he develop ideas about how the classless society would function.

Max Weber was another major social theorist whose theory lacks explicit ideas about the social role of social science. Weber was motivated in his sociological investigations, no less than Marx, by an interest in influencing social change. And his theoretical writings about social change provide a far more hospitable environment for a theory of the social role of sociology than does the work of Marx. Weber seems to have had two divergent theses about social change, and each provides, in different ways, a potential foothold for such ideas.

One of Weber's theses is manifested in his studies of the world's religions and is best seen in his study of Protestantism and the rise of capitalism (1958 [1904]). He thought that ideas, beliefs, and values, as embodied in a religion (Protestantism), could provide the basis to counter communal bonds and generate the individualistic spirit that would allow capitalism and industrial development to take place. But Weber did not extend his conception of the role of these ideal forces (as opposed to Marx's material forces) to a consideration of how sociological analysis might become an element of social change. He carried out sociological analysis, and he was motivated in his selection of problems by the values he held about society; but, like his contemporaries, he did not allow a role for sociological analysis in social change.

The other of Weber's theses about social change is his belief in the progressive rationalization of society. His study of authority systems shows a progression from traditional authority to rational authority (with charismatic authority as an unstable filler, so to speak, between stable authority systems), and he expresses in several places the conception of an increasing rationalization of markets (for example, in his discussion of the expanding role of money) and of authority systems. At one point Weber seems to despair about the future as he pictures the continuation of this rationalization:

> It is as if . . . we were deliberately to become men who need "order" and nothing but order, who become nervous and cowardly if for one moment the order wavers, and helpless if they are torn away from their total incorporation in it. That the world should know no men but these: it is in such an evolution that we are already caught up, and the great question is therefore not how we can promote and hasten it, but what we can oppose to this machinery in order to keep a portion of mankind free from this parcelling-out of the soul, from this supreme mastery of the bureaucratic way of life. (quoted in Mayer, 1944, p. 97)

The conception of social change held by Weber has in principle a place for sociological analysis as a force in social change. A component of rational action (whether action of a person, a bureaucratic corporation, or a bureaucratic government) is, as indicated earlier, the reception of information that may redirect action. And in fact social policy research has been so used by organizations (as I will describe shortly). But Weber did not include in his theory of rational authority any feedback mechanism to provide information that might affect action. Perhaps this was because his conception of rational or bureaucratic authority is a wholly static one: a fixed structure of positions, occupied by persons and functioning like a machine, with no mechanism for change. For whatever reason, however, Weber's theory of rational authority allows no role for information of the sort that is generated by social research as a guide to policy.

The work of another major social theorist, Emile Durkheim, provides even less room for such a theoretical direction. Whereas Marx saw economic conditions as the prime movers of change and Weber (in part of his work) saw values, Durkheim saw social and demographic conditions (as well as technological developments leading to an increasing division of labor). Like the other two theorists discussed above, and perhaps to an even greater extent, Durkheim was a student of society, but he did not raise the question of how his and others' sociological analyses might enter into the course of social change—or how sociological analyses might constitute an intrinsic component of social action in the future. He did conjecture about future social developments and even advocated certain ones (most prominently in the preface to the second edition of the *Division of Labor,* 1947 [1893], where he proposed the formation of occupational groups to replace the mechanical solidarity of the primitive community), but his conception of social change has no role for sociological analysis.

There have been some social theorists whose work is reflexively consistent, although deficient in other ways. One of these was Auguste Comte, who posed an explicit theory of the social role of sociology. Comte was motivated, as were nearly all early social theorists, by a desire to influence the course of society—as indicated in his famous statement, *"Savoir pour prévoir, pour pouvoir."* In contrast to most other early social theory, however, his philosophy of history contains a place for sociological knowledge. He conceived of that knowledge and the prediction it would allow as leading to a scientific humanism. But his conception of how this would occur was primitive and naive; he conceived of a utopia which was little different from that which Plato had proposed two millennia earlier. Comte believed that positive knowledge (as distinct from normative or ideologically inspired beliefs) about social functioning would provide the basis for rational social planning, with social scientists as the guiding elite. In the final phase of his work, he envisioned a religion of humanism in which social scientists would be the high priests. Thus, in Comte's overall conception of the society of the future, positive knowledge about societal functioning plays a central role, but only simple assumptions are made about how that knowledge has its effect.

Comte's work in its later stages may have constituted a kind of social science fiction, but that of other classical theorists allowed no role for social science in shaping society. It is perhaps understandable that most early social theorists had no place in their theories for a social role of sociological knowledge. In the nineteenth and early twentieth centuries, the degree to which conditions of human existence were shaped by knowledge was slight, compared to the present. Humans and animals were still the primary sources of mechanical energy for production; medical outcomes were seen as being "in the hands of God" rather than affected by medical science; and the physical surroundings of most persons still consisted of a larger component of the natural environment than of the constructed environment.

Today all this has changed. The conditions of human existence depend largely and increasingly on purposive actions taken by persons. Actions based on knowledge and decisions have come to replace, in an ever expanding range of areas, natural events beyond human control. The constructed social environment, consisting of purposive corporate actors and their agents, constitutes a large part of the social environment of most persons in modern societies. In such a setting the question of the social role of sociological knowledge cannot be ignored. Any social theory, then, must be subjected to the test for reflexive consistency. To pass this test, a theory must provide a location for sociological knowledge, and the activity which generates it, in the functioning of society.

Besides bringing about reflexive consistency, this component of social theory is useful for the further development of such theory and of social research. The directions in which social theory and research develop need not be guided only by the menu of unsolved problems as defined by current fashions in the field, or by contemporary social problems. Their development can also be guided by a vision of the current and potential role of sociological knowledge in the functioning of society. Thus, even if the current importance to society of sociological theorizing and research is, according to a theory, less great than that of some other set of activities, a self-conscious examination of their current and potential role can be of special value in guiding their future direction.

In the rest of this chapter, I will apply social theory to the reflexive task of examining the role of sociological knowledge in the functioning of society.[1] To simplify this task I will focus not on theory but on social research, and not on all social research but only on that research described as applied. To see why applied research, rather than pure research, is relevant requires an examination of two worlds: the world of social action and the world of sociology as a discipline.

The World of Action and the World of the Discipline

It is useful to make an analytic distinction between the structure of general knowledge and ideas that constitutes the discipline of sociology and the world of social action to which the discipline's knowledge and ideas apply. The value of this distinction is the aid it provides in distinguishing between two different purposes for which social research is carried out, two arenas to which sociological work is intended to contribute.

Some research in sociology is intended to contribute toward building the structure of knowledge and ideas that constitutes the discipline. The term "pure research" is sometimes used to designate work intended to contribute to this structure. I will instead use the term "discipline research" to refer to such research.

Other sociological research has the aim of illuminating some social phenomenon that can be affected by informed action. This research may also contribute to the structure of knowledge and ideas of the discipline, but any such contribution will be a by-product of its central aim, which is to provide information to affect action. The term "applied research" is often used to designate this second kind of research. Despite the diffuse meanings this term carries, I will use it to contrast with discipline research.[2]

Discipline research and applied research have differing relations to sociology and to social action. For both kinds of research, activities in the world of social action are the objects of attention. For applied research, however, the problem

1. I have begun this task elsewhere (Coleman, 1972b; 1978b; 1980), and others have engaged in the same sort of endeavor (see especially MacRae, 1976; 1985). The work is closely related to the sociology of knowledge and the sociology of science, on which there is an extensive literature. There is also literature on what has been called the sociology of sociology, consisting primarily of essays in which sociologists reflect on activities of sociologists or argue for or against certain directions of sociological theory or research. See, for example, Lynd (1939) and Mills (1959). This literature contributes to the reflexive task, although much of it is written as polemics in struggles for ascendance within the discipline.

2. The term "action research" would be more appropriate, but it has already been employed to designate research attached to an action program and designed to help implement the program. Elsewhere I have called this research policy research, a term I do not use here because it suggests limitation to government policy.

to be studied comes from the world of action, and the results of the study are fed back into the world of action. This contrasts with discipline research, for which the problem originates within the discipline and from which results are intended to go back to the discipline. For discipline research the world of action is the object of its attention, nothing more.

Applied research, then, spans the two worlds in a way discipline research does not. For applied research the problem originates in the world of action, the methods and design come from the world of the discipline, and the results go back to the world of action. Because applied research has this multiple connection with the real world, social theory is relevant in two ways: first for designing such research, and second for understanding the role it plays in society. Understanding this role allows seeing whether, for structural reasons, there are systematic biases in the kinds of research problems that are spontaneously initiated, and how these problems initiated in society will change as the social structure changes. It also allows understanding something about the effects on social functioning of feedback of information from applied research and the way those effects can differ depending on the point at which information is fed back into the system (for example, conflicts sometimes arise over whether the results of a research project are in the public domain, and therefore available to all, or are the private property of the actor which commissioned or sponsored the research).

In the following sections I will attempt to carry out a reflexive examination of the social role of applied social research. I will first examine the way the central directions of applied research have mirrored certain changes in society.

The Structure of Society and the Nature of Applied Social Research

The relation between the structure of society and the nature of applied social research can be seen by examining the rise and fall of schools of sociological thought. This examination will concentrate on applied social research in the United States, because it is there that applied social research flourished first and most fully and has taken the greatest number of forms.

Schools of sociology have grown, flourished, and declined in parallel with the life cycles of particular persons dominant in them, for example, Robert Park of the Chicago school or Paul Lazarsfeld of the Columbia school. But the schools' growth and decline are also related to broader changes in society. A focus on these changes gives insight into both social structure and the emerging role of social research in that structure.

The Chicago School and Its Decline

The Chicago school of sociology flourished during the first quarter of this century and into the second, maintaining its strength up until World War II. There were, at the beginning of this period, other sociologists in the United States whose credentials were as good as those of Albion Small at Chicago: Ross at Wisconsin, Giddings at Columbia, Cooley at Michigan, and Sumner at Yale. But the Chicago school, under Small, was dominant. This was in part due to the organizational independence of sociology within the university, but in part certainly due to its focus.

The sociology of the Chicago school was characterized by several elements: a focus on the city, on immigrants and their cultural adaptation, on marginal persons, and on deviant subcultures.[3] The Chicago school was associated with private philanthropy, which in turn was church-related, and with urban reform movements. Its members had a diversity of styles, but they shared interests in the city. Charles Henderson, an important member of the department at the time and chaplain of the university, was also a leader in municipal reform movements. At the other extreme was W. I. Thomas, a flamboyant agnostic who was deeply interested in the sociological problems of the city. Robert Park's major interest was the various forms that life took within the city. Many of the doctoral dissertations Park sponsored became books describing urban subcultures: *The Ghetto* (Wirth, 1928), *The Gold Coast and the Slum* (Zorbaugh, 1929), *The Taxi-Dance Hall* (Cressey, 1932), *The Gang* (Thrasher, 1936), *Black Metropolis* (Drake and Cayton, 1946), and others. A theory of urban ecology was developed by the Chicago school, based on the idea of concentric rings around the city center, containing different activities and with persons of higher status residing in the outer ones. The concept of the marginal man was also developed in the Chicago school and supported by many empirical studies of marginal persons and deviant subcultures: studies of prostitutes and pimps, of jazz musicians, and of persons who "passed," living black and working white.

In short, the Chicago school documented the turmoil, adjustment, marginality, and growth in American urban life. It reflected a particular period in American society, a period each society undergoes as it is transformed from a predominantly rural society into a predominantly urban one. The period had special features in the United States, stemming from the country's character as a new society. One such feature was the flood of immigrants, which swelled the cities more rapidly and produced more disorder than would have been the case if the only transition taking place had been from a rural to an urban society.[4] Chicago's population doubled between 1880 and 1890, and again between 1890 and 1910.

The decline of the Chicago school was not solely due to the demise of the powerful personalities who shaped it. It was due to a decline in the kinds of problems on which the school had focused. Immigration declined; urban life became somewhat more ordered; the number of marginal persons, principally

3. Empirical social research on the problems of the modern city had been carried out considerably earlier in England by Mayhew (1861) and Booth (1891).
4. Max Weber, on a visit to Chicago in 1904, reported that it was like looking at the human body with the skin removed (Weber, 1926, p. 299).

itinerant men, decreased because immigration declined and life became more settled. (In the early part of this century, for example, there were a number of occupations that were held by men who lived for a time in one locale and then moved on to another. Barbers were one such group, printers were another, miners were another, and there were many others.) The sex ratio of young adults equalized, men married and settled down—the number of unmarried adults declined sharply. Thus the problems on which the Chicago school focused gradually declined in importance. Cities had become more habitable; prosperity had increased; human misery had been reduced.

A Shift in the Structure of Interaction

Other social changes were meanwhile creating a new set of problems. These changes turned a nation composed of a set of local communities, largely internally focused, into a nation in which the focus was no longer local but national. Manufacturing changed in many product areas from local firms producing for local markets to national firms producing for national markets. Washing machines, made by a few national firms, replaced washtubs and washboards, made and sold locally. Packaged breakfast cereals, heralded by entrepreneurs with persuasive public relations skills, replaced locally grown cracked wheat and oats. National auto manufacturers emerged in the 1920s and 1930s from a plethora of local firms all over the country.

Perhaps most important, however, was the emergence of national communications media. National magazines became an important medium, gaining strength especially in the 1930s. Radio grew and movies flourished. These media were first of all the diffusion mechanisms for the new nationally marketed goods. Through their advertising they created national markets which facilitated manufacturing centralized for production at a national level. And they themselves had national audiences, focusing the attention of the population as a whole on the same objects.

One of the consequences of these changes was that a new set of sociological problems emerged. These problems were related to the new national markets and national audiences—and among them were problems of market research and audience research. Producers no longer had direct and informal contact with their customers, because they were separated from them geographically. The structural distance between producer and consumer had begun to transcend the ability of producers to assess their market informally, assimilate information about it, and plan on the basis of that. Advertising became important but was like scatter shot in the dark, and advertisers needed some knowledge of their audience. Mass communications media, especially radio, were in a similar situation. Broadcasters had no way of knowing even the size of the radio audience. And neither national radio broadcasters nor national magazine publishers knew the composition, attentiveness, or interests of their audiences.

The Columbia School: A New Relation of Social Research to Social Action

As these problems arose, a new school of applied social research arose, the Columbia school, built around Paul Lazarsfeld.[5] Beginning with radio research, moving into mass communications research in general, and on into market research, the Columbia school not only addressed these new problems but came to dominate American empirical sociology—which was almost synonymous with American sociology.

This domination arose, I believe, because methods and a general approach appropriate for these problems—random samples that were sometimes nationally representative, questions that were appropriate to the population as a whole, and general analytical relations intended to characterize the population as a whole—came to replace the local, geographically bound methods and problems that had dominated American sociology in the era of the Chicago school. These problems came to be of interest to sociologists, replacing earlier locality-specific interests, because the structure of society had changed. The society was no longer one in which relations and interactions were confined to localities. There had come to be a large body of interactions at the national level, between persons on the one hand and large corporate actors such as manufacturers, radio networks, and magazines on the other.

It was not simply force of personality, then, which brought about the dominance of the Columbia school, nor was it accidental that a school of sociology located in New York became dominant. New York City was the center of the emerging communications and advertising industries and the locus of newly national marketing decisions. The changed structure of social interaction in American society from locally bound to national focused the attention of sociologists on the substance of communications research and on the survey methods which accompanied its birth. The focus of attention subsequently shifted away from communications research, and survey methods were adapted to a wide variety of local as well as national problems, involving purposive as well as random samples. But a shift had taken place, first in the structure of social interaction itself and then in the research perspectives of sociologists.

Several characteristics of the new problems occupying social research sharply distinguished them from the problems addressed in the early part of the century by the Chicago school. One was that the new problems were not general social problems; they were problems of particular actors in the social system. Those actors—the manufacturers with national markets, the national magazines, the radio networks—were themselves newly emergent. The problems involved concrete decisions: Should a radio program be continued? What was the potential market for a given product? What made people buy a certain good? How many

---

5. Lazarsfeld did not import this new type of research from Europe. In fact, the research he carried out before he left Vienna, a study of a small community hit by unemployment (Lazarsfeld, Jahoda, and Ziesel, 1933), would have fit well within the Chicago school.

people were listening to the radio, and how did they differ from those not listening? How many people read a given magazine advertisement? What kinds of appeals would sell war bonds?

A list of these problems makes them sound mundane and trivial, of a lesser order of importance than the social problems investigated by the Chicago school. They are very narrow problems in that they ignore many of the continuing and ongoing conditions of disorder, adjustment, deviance, poverty, inequality, and conflict in society, which continued even after the early turmoil of urban life had subsided or had become commonplace. These problems were of interest to only a limited subset of actors in American society: mass manufacturers, advertising agencies, radio networks, and national magazines. Yet they marked an important change: They were problems of particular actors in society, and the answers offered by sociologists were of direct interest to those actors, who were prepared to act on them.

The era of the importance of communications, public opinion, and market research continued into and through the 1950s, as did the dominance of the Columbia school. But like the dominance of the Chicago school, that of the Columbia school came to an end; 1960 was perhaps the beginning of the end. And again the end was not solely due to the decline of certain personal careers. It was also due to a change in the nature of applied social research, itself responsive to another change in the structure of society.[6]

A Shift in the Structure of Responsibility

In the 1920s, 1930s, and 1940s, the United States underwent a change in the structure of social interaction, from a structure that was almost entirely local and personal to one that had a large component of national and impersonal interactions. World War II provided a stimulus to this change, by inducing an even higher rate of migration from rural to urban areas and, more generally, by inducing persons to move away from the locality and even the region of their birth. All this helped bring about a change which became evident in the 1960s: a change in the structure of responsibility from private and local to public and national.

As long as the principal interactions in society were confined to locality and were primarily between persons, the claims that persons had for care and attention when they were in need were largely made on other persons with whom they were in frequent contact. Adult children took care of aging parents; families exercised responsibility for their mentally defective members within the household; extended families aided out-of-work brothers, uncles, and nephews and provided homes for unmarried family members on a continuing basis. County homes housed the indigent aged.

6. The audience and market research on which the Columbia school was based has not vanished. It has merely moved outside universities, and largely outside the discipline of sociology, into freestanding commercial research organizations.

That the change in the structure of interaction brought with it a change in the structure of responsibility follows quite naturally. If two parties are involved in regular and continuing interaction, they begin to acquire rights in their relationship and can exercise claims on one another. This proposition is generally true for interpersonal interactions; I am asserting here that it is also true for interactions between persons and large corporate actors. Those interactions may be mediated by mass communications, as is true of the interactions between persons and the nation considered as a body, or by multiple layers in a bureaucracy, as is true of the relations between employer and employee. But despite this mediated character, rights are acquired in such relations, and claims come to gain legitimacy, creating a structure of responsibility that did not exist in the absence of the continued (even though indirect) interaction.

This changed structure of interaction increasingly generated claims on the national government and eventually brought about an assumption of new responsibilities by that government. The U.S. government had previously taken responsibility in isolated cases, for example, by providing pensions for Civil War veterans. And some other governments, in particular that of Germany, had introduced extensive welfare provisions in the nineteenth century. But these are exceptions that illustrate the point: The early welfare provisions of the German government were strategic actions of Bismarck, designed to create a state by creating dependency of the population on the national government. And the Civil War was an event at the national level, involving the U.S. government itself. By issuing pensions to veterans, the government was simply taking responsibility for consequences of an event in which it was itself one of the interacting parties.

Responsibility of the national government for the general welfare of the population was different from veterans' pensions and arose as the structure of economic interaction changed from local to national. Some measures, such as Social Security and emergency work programs, were taken in the 1930s, early in the shift from local to national interaction. These were certainly stimulated by the extensive need during the Great Depression, but the national government responded to the problem as it had not done in earlier depressions.

A particular instance of this change in the United States that is of special importance concerns blacks. Before World War II most blacks lived in the rural South. The only claims they could exercise in their local structure of interactions, a structure characteristic of the country as a whole at that time and especially of rural areas, were claims on the local black community (for example, through a church) or on the farm owner for whom they worked or share-cropped. After the war, and after the move to the urban North had taken place for the majority of blacks, they entered the national structure of interaction. They bought goods marketed nationally, were a component of the mass media audience, and were—as part of this structure of communication—increasingly subjects of mass media attention as well.

As blacks became part of the national structure of interaction, a broader set of

national responsibilities arose, because of blacks' objectively depressed conditions, the past discrimination that had generated those conditions, and the continuing discrimination in local interactions that were helping to maintain those
conditions. In the absence of a national structure of interaction, and the national
structure of responsibility that grew out of it, that discrimination would have
continued as it had in the past. In the presence of the new structure of responsibility, the special claims of blacks provided an additional impetus to the assumption of responsibility by the national government in areas where claims were
once limited to localities (as in education) or to private relations (as in health
care or housing).

This shift in the focus of claims and responsibility not only led persons increasingly to make claims at the national level but also made the population receptive
to new legislation, executive branch action, and court decisions which accepted
the legitimacy of the claims and assumed the existence of new national responsibilities. Although this increase in claims and in receptivity on the part of the
population as a whole was a continuous process, the actions at the national level
responsive to the change came in spurts. One was the 1954 decision of the
Supreme Court on school desegregation. A second was the Great Society legislation introduced by Lyndon Johnson beginning in 1964: the Civil Rights Act of
1964, the Elementary and Secondary Education Act of 1965, the creation of the
Office of Economic Opportunity, the Headstart program, Medicare, and other
programs. A third spurt came in a somewhat different area in the 1970s, with
occupational safety and environmental regulation. The national government began to exercise wide authority concerning matters of safety and air and water
quality, which had previously been viewed as individual or local responsibilities.
Air quality in large cities, water quality in some rivers, and occupational hazards
in some industries had all been worse at earlier periods in the United States, but
in the absence of a structure of national responsibility, they were not seen as
general societal problems.

A Third Phase of Social Research

As the structure of responsibility changed, social policies—as distinct from
economic policies—came into existence on a broad scale at the national level.
These were policies concerning health, education, welfare, and employment,
and some regulatory policies. Along with these policies came a new kind of
social research: social policy research. This research has taken a number of
forms, some with names that were unknown in 1960. Evaluation research is one,
large-scale social experimentation is another, and there are national longitudinal
studies of particular populations, such as high-school seniors of a given cohort.

The applied social research of the Columbia school served as a precursor to
social policy research. One body of research that provides a good illustration of
this transition was *The American Soldier*, research carried out for and within the
U.S. Army during World War II and published after the war (Stouffer et al.,

1949). This work derives directly from the communications, marketing, and public opinion research initiated in the 1930s, although it was directed at policy problems within the U.S. Army and not decisions in a market.

The American Soldier repays a perusal of its content, because it is clear in retrospect that the researchers were working on the boundary of an important change in social research. Some of the research was obviously carried out without any intent to address a policy problem of the army. This was in the mold of an earlier sociological tradition in which research problems were defined by the investigator's curiosity alone. But another large fraction of the research was obviously directed toward obtaining answers useful for making army policy. For example, research designed to learn the probable reactions of servicemen to various patterns of discharge was influential in an extremely important policy decision at the end of the war—the point system for discharge of servicemen. This research was designed to inform policy, and the information it provided was used in the formulation of policy.

Despite the early developments represented by *The American Soldier*, the growth in social policy research did not begin until the major shift in claims and responsibility in the 1960s. It was the social policies of the 1950s, 1960s, and 1970s that stimulated social policy research. The reasons why the growth of national social policy generated social policy research are several, but it is sufficient to note one: As the national government assumed public responsibility in matters where responsibility had been local and private, it was ill-equipped to discharge this responsibility. This deficiency stemmed largely from the structural distance between the national government and the activities for which it was exercising responsibility—a distance that mirrored the geographical separation and indirectness of the national structure of interaction. The situation in which the national government found itself was analogous to that of mass manufacturers and national communications media in the 1930s.

Research was necessary to learn how a social welfare program should be modified, whether it should be continued, even whether it was working in the manner intended. Because social policy was enacted at a national level and its execution occurred at a local level, the old, direct, informal methods of getting such feedback were no longer effective.

There was a period in the early days of the new social policies when federal agencies (such as the National Institute of Mental Health and the Office of Education) commissioned applied research initiated by researchers themselves and administered through grants which had very flexible conditions concerning the timing and character of the research products. During this period initiation characteristic of discipline research was used. This is based on a model in which there is a general growth of knowledge within the discipline, providing, as a by-product, new approaches to social problems. According to this model the impact of specific research on policy is an indirect one, a side effect of the general growth of knowledge.

This model was inappropriate for applied research in the new era of national social policies, because much more direct feedback was needed to inform the policies. In the late 1960s a more direct linkage of research and policy began to emerge. Research was initiated through requests for proposals (or RFPs), and contracts, more specific in their timing and product requirements, began to replace grants. Large projects, requiring the various skills of a research organization, replaced small projects that tolerated the narrower skills and lower reliability of a single investigator. Research began to be commissioned not merely by funding agencies (such as NIMH and the National Institute of Child Health and Human Development) but also by operating (that is, policy-making) agencies such as the Department of Housing and Urban Development, the Department of Transportation, and the Department of Labor. Funding agencies with no direct responsibility for policy making began to initiate demonstration programs and other "mini-policies" (on the principle that successful programs would be continued by local authorities or the principle that they would be incorporated into legislation at the national level).

With these changes social policy research came into existence. This form of research is not identified with a particular school, comparable to the Chicago school or the Columbia school, but it has come to play an increasingly dominant role in social research. It, however, is no more the final or equilibrium state of applied social research than the other phases have been. It is merely the latest form of applied social research that has been generated by changes in the structure of society. What, then, will the future direction of applied social research be?

The Future Direction of Applied Social Research

The future direction of applied social research depends in part on whether social change continues to be the principal means by which such research is generated. If instead there is some guidance based on theoretical analysis of structurally induced biases in the spontaneous generation of research, or if the content of the research becomes theory-driven in other ways, the kind of research carried out can be expected to change. The conjectural answer given in this section is based on the assumption that applied research will continue to be generated principally by change in the social strucure. The next section will begin the analysis that could provide theoretical guidance for applied social research.

The first point to note is that in the 1970s and 1980s there has been a change in the structure of economic production comparable to that which occurred in the 1920s and 1930s, when local economic production began to be replaced by national production. The current economic change is from national to international production. The associated shift in the structure of mass communications, however, is more complex than was the growth of nationwide media in the 1920s and 1930s. On the one hand, language differences among countries complicate matters greatly. On the other hand, new technology (such as television, satellite transmission, language dubbing, and other developments) has made the expansion from nationwide to worldwide communications technically feasible. A result is that a soap opera, for example, about a hypothetical family in Texas, is seen not only in North America but also in South America, Europe, Asia, and Africa. The same television variety show is viewed simultaneously throughout Europe. A direct implication of these changes is that a new wave of market, audience, and public opinion research, international in character, will occur. This development has already begun, largely outside the purview of academic social science. The research is carried out by international management consultant firms, international market research organizations, and consortia of polling organizations.

What can be predicted with some confidence about this form of applied social research is that it will continue to expand and that it will remain outside academia. The institutionalization of applied social research in commercial research organizations occurred at a national level beginning in the 1940s and carries over directly to the international level. The extension from national to international research is accomplished simply by the expansion of these commercial firms from national to multinational organizations. The implications for the kinds of corporate actions taken on the basis of the research are extensive, however. Products, including mass media vehicles of entertainment, will increasingly be designed (as some now are) for a worldwide market. As occurred earlier for national markets, segmentation of audiences and markets will no longer be based on geographic location, but on taste and other distinguishing characteristics.

The theory and methods of applied social research require little change to remain applicable through this extension in scope. There is no need for new techniques comparable to the population sampling and survey design techniques that accompanied the initial development of market and audience research and opinion polling. Multinational telephone surveys, for example, differ little in method from national telephone surveys.

The shift of economic production and mass communications from national to international will certainly be followed by an assumption of responsibility across national borders. How this will occur is clearly not through national governments, and very likely not through an international analogue such as the United Nations. A systemic solution short of a government, involving multiple international bodies of narrow scope, may constitute the means by which this international responsibility, once assumed, is met.

Actions to fulfill this responsibility will require social policy research. This research, however, will be of greater order of complexity than the comparable research at a national level. To conjecture about the character of that future research is beyond the scope of this chapter. It is sufficient to predict an extensive future development in the use of social policy research at an international level as an intrinsic component of feedback processes in the international social system.

Applied Social Research and the Theory of Action

A sense of just where applied social research fits within a system of action and what gaps there are in the current spontaneously generated research can be gained by applying the theory of action. Applying the theory of action to applied social research raises a question at the outset. Why did sociology arise when it did, and why has applied social research developed as it has? To answer this requires another look at the structural change in society produced by the growth of modern corporate actors.

Table 23.1 (presented previously as Table 20.1) shows the types of social interactions in a system populated by natural persons and corporate actors. The table allows applied social research to be categorized into the types listed below.

Research on systems of action
Type 1: research primarily focused on relations among natural persons
Type 2: research primarily focused on relations between natural persons and corporate actors
Type 3: research primarily focused on relations among corporate actors

Research on parts of systems of action
Type 2a: research on actions of natural persons directed toward corporate actors or in response to their actions
Type 2b: research on actions (policies or products) of corporate actors directed toward natural persons

This typology can be used to characterize social research of the three periods described in earlier sections. In the early period, as represented by the Chicago school in the United States or the work of Booth in England, society was populated largely by natural persons (and their extensions, families and clans),

Table 23.1 Types of relations between actors.

		Object of action	
		Person	Corporate actor
Subject of action	Person	1	2a
	Corporate actor	2b	3

with some modern corporate actors that were small and confined to a locality. Thus the relations that were most characteristic of that time were type 1; social research was also type 1. The new modes of production had crowded people into cities and changed the character of interpersonal relations from those characteristic of the village and the farm to those characteristic of the city, in settings such as the taxi-dance hall, the gang, the slum, the apartment house, and so on. It was these new forms of interpersonal relations, all of type 1, that were documented by the Chicago school. The resources that supported this research were resources of natural persons or, in some cases, of religious bodies, corporate actors of a premodern form. Their interest, ordinarily described as philanthropic, was in the welfare of natural persons who found themselves involved in these new forms of type 1 relations and in some newly generated type 2 relations.

The change in the structure of interaction that came about in the 1920s and 1930s, as described earlier, focused attention of sociologists on relations of type 2, those between persons and corporate actors. The structural change did not replace relations of type 1 with those of types 2 and 3, but it did increase the proportions of type 2 and 3 relations. In addition, type 2 relations were altered from being direct and face to face (such as the relation between a local family-run store and a customer) to being indirect and at a distance (such as the relation of national media of communication with their audiences or nationwide chain stores with consumers). It was this change that focused attention of social researchers on type 2 relations and brought about the extensive work of the 1940s and 1950s in mass communications, audience research, and market research.

This research was typically type 2a, focused on actions of natural persons in response to actions of corporate actors. A corporate actor would carry out an action (a radio network began a new series, or an advertising agency instituted an advertising campaign in a national magazine), and research would be carried out to study actions of type 2a, that is, the reactions of persons to the actions of the corporate actors. But there was a fundamental change with regard to the support for the research: The resources to study these actions were provided by an interested party, the client. The social researcher no longer stood outside society, but became a functional part of it.

Thus a major shift in the character of sociological research took place not only from the problems addressed by the Chicago school to the problems addressed by the Columbia school, but from research which was unfunded or funded by socially concerned philanthropists (natural persons or religious bodies) who were outside the relations being studied to research which was funded by corporate actors who were themselves one party to the relations being studied. These corporate actors funded such research because they could make use of the information it provided. This change from unfunded research, or disinterested funding, to financing of research by interested parties has never since been reversed, although there has been a change in the identity of the interested parties.

Who was the audience for the products of the Chicago school? Were there any parties for whom its applied social research provided directives for action? The answer, I think, is no. The products of the Chicago school were read by sociologists and by interested laypersons, and they certainly exercised some influence on social action. But that influence was diffuse, indirect, and even accidental. There may have been interested parties who could have made use of Wirth's *The Ghetto* (1928) or Zorbaugh's *The Gold Coast and the Slum* (1929), but there was no assurance that they were even aware of the books or research reports. In short, in that period the relation of sociological research results to social action was analogous to bread being cast upon the waters. These research products may have had effects on social action but not more than some novels—certainly not as much, for example, as the effect of *Uncle Tom's Cabin* in stimulating antislavery actions some seventy-five years earlier.

Thus the shift to communications and audience research was paralleled by a shift in the relation social research had to social action. This was a shift from accidental effects and general irrelevance toward a more direct linkage, with social research being designed to provide to one of the actors involved in a relation information about that relation. It would be incorrect to say that this research was always used in the decision making for which it was intended, or that the information it provided was always useful. The importance of the change lay in the fact that the intention had changed: The research was designed to provide information relevant to specific decisions, and the results were intended to aid specific decision makers. It would also be wrong to say that most sociological research was of this sort, for a large proportion was discipline research, initiated and carried out in the independent fashion that is characteristic of that form. But this new social research and the technical methods of survey design and analysis that it introduced came to occupy the center of the stage. Its methods and techniques came to have extensive influence on sociological research in general.

When the change in the structure of responsibility occurred, as described earlier, and the national government took over responsibilities that had been local and private, a new variation was introduced in type 2 relations. The interaction involved action at a distance, this time between government and natural persons. The interaction typically takes the form of a government program (for example, a job training program, health clinics, or educational programs for disadvantaged children) which is implemented locally and to which individuals respond in some fashion. The typical research is again of type 2a, focused on the reactions of individuals to the program.

Type 2a research, that is, market research or social policy research, is carried out on behalf of one actor in a relation (most often a corporate actor) to obtain feedback about the effects of its action. The earlier research of the Chicago school was initiated by parties who were outside the system being studied but had an interest in modifying that system in some way (ordinarily through social reform). As a consequence of this difference, research results might be expected to affect social functioning through different processes in the two periods. The implicit rationale behind the earlier research was that of the exposé: If social conditions generally regarded as undesirable were exposed, this would lead to indignation and concern on the part of elites or the general public, which in turn might lead to social reform, aimed at correction of the undesirable conditions. The implicit rationale behind market research and social policy research is based on there being a complex system of action in which an actor establishes feedback mechanisms to inform his actions. Applied social research—whether market, audience, or policy research—constitutes that feedback mechanism. Yet this implicit rationale is defective, just as was the earlier rationale of the exposé.

To see the defects requires an explicit application of the theory of action, and that requires providing answers to a number of questions:

1. What is the (sub)system of action which the applied research is designed to inform?
   a. Who are the actors that control resources and have interests in this system?
   b. What are the actors' interests?
   c. What are the actors' interests in information that might be supplied by social policy research?
   d. What is the distribution of control of resources relevant to this system of action?
2. What is the correct action of the sociologist who carries out the applied social research?
   a. Whose agent is the sociologist?
   b. What are the relevant considerations of the sociologist in deciding whether to enter a particular agency relation?
   c. What is the correct action in design of the research?
   d. What is the correct action in transmitting results of the research back to the world of action?
3. What determines the use of the results of the applied social research?
   a. Who uses it?
   b. Under what conditions is it used?

Certain of these questions, in asking what is correct, are normative in character. They assume the existence of a normative criterion as the basis for an answer. What, then, is an appropriate normative criterion? This question is itself normative in character, illustrating the fact that normative questions lead into an infinite regress, which can in practice be halted only when a point is reached at which there is general consensus, or, failing that, by an explicit statement of the values taken as normatively axiomatic in the system.

What Is the Appropriate Normative Criterion?

Normative questions can be addressed within a positive discipline of sociology, as long as normative statements are justified in terms of an explicit allocation of rights or a framework of values taken to be normatively axiomatic. The justification of the framework itself lies outside the discipline; but the framework, once established, serves as the source of justification for normative statements.

The implication of this for applied social research is that the constitutional allocation of rights (implicit or explicit) in a system serves as the set of normative axioms or the source of justification for various normative questions about the research. It does so through the following premise about the role of applied social research: Applied social research should, like the law, be neutral with respect to particular actors. It should not favor the rights held by one set of actors in a system. If the results of applied social research constitute a force to change the constitutional allocation of rights, the direction of that force should not be inherent in the design of that research.

The test of whether changes in the constitutional allocation of rights based on information from applied social research are appropriate is this: If information from the research, provided comparably to all interested actors in the system, brings about a change in the rights allocation, the change is an appropriate one. If a change occurs as result of differential provision of information to sets of actors in the system, the change is not an appropriate one. (The way in which a change in rights allocation can come about as a result of new information is described in Chapter 17.)

This normative criterion underlies all the normative statements I will make in response to the above questions.

Answering the Questions

The above questions may be asked for the entire range of applied social research carried out in a given social system or subsystem or for only a single piece of research. I will begin by answering them for the research that was dominant in the three periods described earlier: the community and neighborhood research of the Chicago school, the audience and market research of the Columbia school, and social policy research.

THE CHICAGO SCHOOL: COMMUNITY AND NEIGHBORHOOD RESEARCH
The systems of action studied by the Chicago school were composed primarily of relations of type 1 (see Table 23.1). The studies were not studies of single relations, or of individual actions, but of systems of action involving a number of actors: the social life of a neighborhood (*The Ghetto* and *The Gold Coast and the Slum*), the functioning of geographically bounded communities (*Elmtown's Youth* and *Middletown*), particular worlds existing within the life of the city (*The Gang* and *The Taxi-Dance Hall*). The sociologist was either the agent of no one or the agent of a humanitarian organization (ordinarily derivative from primordial corporate actors such as particular churches).[7] This sociological research

---

7. See Bulmer (1984) for a discussion of the church-related support of the Chicago school. The Lynds' *Middletown* (1929), akin in spirit to the Chicago school, was closely overseen by Reinhold Niebuhr, an influential pastor in New York City.

could hardly be considered part of the system of action it studied; it lay almost entirely outside the system, as an observer from Mars might study earthlings' activities without affecting them.

The sociological studies of the period dominated by the Chicago school constituted only a weak form of feedback for social action, only affecting the actions of certain primordial corporate actors (such as churches) which had lost much of their power to effect change, or the actions of no one in particular. Thus the questions posed above are hardly relevant to that research. It might be argued, in fact, that that research was not applied research but discipline research. The critical point is that the principal for the research (which was ordinarily the sociologist) was outside the system of action being studied and could use the information resulting from the research only in very indirect ways to affect the system of action. It was not until the advent of the Columbia school that this changed, and applied social research became a part of the system of action.

THE COLUMBIA SCHOOL: AUDIENCE AND MARKET RESEARCH   The advent of audience and market research made applied social research an explicit part of a system of action. The questions listed above can be answered with little difficulty for this research. The relevant system of action consists minimally of actors on two sides of an asymmetric market. On one side are a small number of corporate actors (ordinarily corporations), and on the other are natural persons. In the case of market research there are producers (ordinarily manufacturers rather than merchants) on one side and consumers on the other. In the case of audience research there are producers of mass communications (such as broadcasters or magazine publishers) on one side and consumers of mass communications on the other.

Whose agent is the sociologist? The sociologist carrying out market research is ordinarily the agent of a corporate actor who is a producer in an asymmetric market. Applied social research provides feedback to the producer in a system of action where relations are not face to face, and the feedback provided from them is insufficient to inform his action.

It is not always the case, however, that the sociologist carrying out the applied social research is the producer's agent. Reitz (1973a; 1973b) has examined 52 cases of applied social research that were characteristic of the Columbia school. Of these, 47 can be classified as examining type 2 relations, relations between a corporate actor (ordinarily a producer) and natural persons (ordinarily in the role of customers). Of the 42 cases for which it is possible to determine the role of the social researcher, in 25 the researcher was the producer's agent, either as employee or as independent contractor. In 12 cases the researcher was an agent of a third party (ordinarily a foundation or a government), and in 5 the researcher was independent. When the researcher was an agent of a third party, that party was in nearly all cases acting on behalf of consumers' (that is, natural persons') interests.

A further question is whether the social position of the researcher as agent

Table 23.2   Social position of researcher and perspective from which
             recommendation is made.

	Researcher's social position	
	Producer's agent	Third-party agent or independent
Studies in which recommendations or implications are presented from point of view of producer's interests	11	2
Studies in which recommendations or implications are presented from point of view of consumer's interests	12	13
Totals	23	15

affects the kind of research carried out, the kinds of results reported, and the recommendations made. For 38 of the studies examined by Reitz, I was able to make a crude classification of the recommendations as being from the perspective of the producer or that of the consumer (the corporate actor or the natural person). Table 23.2 shows the relation between the social position of the researcher and the perspective from which recommendations were made for those studies.

Table 23.2 indicates that the researcher's position as agent of the producer is almost a necessary condition, but by no means a sufficient one, for the study's recommendations to be from the perspective of the producer. It is likely that the personal values of the social researchers were more likely to favor interests of the consumer, creating the bias shown in the table.[8] This may be a special case supporting the general proposition that in a society populated by impersonal corporate actors and natural persons, each type of actor seems to give preferential treatment to its own kind. The evidence does suggest that for applied research on type 2 relations the researchers are likely to be agents of the corporate actor, and that the social position of the researcher affects the perspective from which recommendations are made.

What are the interests and information interests of the actors? The interests of producers and consumers in asymmetric markets are straightforward. Actors on both sides have the goal of maximizing utility. For producers this goal is ordinarily expressed as profit maximization. Various actions are taken to reach this goal, such as steps to increase market penetration. In most cases the producer's

8. For example, a study was done for AT&T concerning the growth in use of operator assistance rather than telephone books to obtain telephone numbers (a practice of consumers that was increasingly costly to AT&T). The researcher recommended that there should be a wider distribution of telephone books, *not* that some cost be imposed on the consumer, such as a charge or a delay, for information calls.

interest is purely an interest in the money value of sales; in the case of communications media, the matter is more complex. Commmercial electronic media are interested in sales, but they sell audience attention—both quantity of audience and type (or quality) of audience—to advertisers, who are other corporate actors. Nonelectronic media, that is, magazines, obtain part of their income in this way and part from selling the publication to consumers.

The interests of consumers in these markets are also straightforward. They maximize utility by obtaining the greatest possible satisfaction for their expenditure of money or time. This implies that they have interests in minimizing the expenditure of money or time necessary to attain a given level of satisfaction.

The information interests of actors on the two sides of the market derive directly from their overall interests. Consumers are ordinarily interested in information about the product. Consumer research of the sort reported in certain magazines (such as *Consumer Reports* in the United States and *Which?* in Britain) exemplifies this kind of information. Producers have an interest in learning as much about their market as possible, in order to increase their sales. This includes interests which are not opposed to consumers' interests (such as learning how to make consumers aware of products) but also some which are opposed to consumers' interests. Producers are interested in learning the weaknesses of various types of consumers (see Chapter 20); exploitation of such weaknesses can provide opportunities for increasing sales. For example, one such weakness of persons is a tendency to discount future value relative to present value: A person may choose one dollar today over two dollars tomorrow. This means that a sales strategy that makes possible purchases on credit (for example, through credit cards) will lead to increased sales. Another consumer weakness is a tendency to engage in impulse buying. This means that a corporation may increase sales and profits by directing attention to aspects of a product that appeal to consumers' appetites and by diverting production costs from those qualities of a good that are not evident at time of purchase (such as durability, safety, or nutritional quality) to those that are (especially packaging), beyond the point at which such a diversion is desirable to a rational consumer (that is, one who is not an impulse buyer).

Consumers' weaknesses lead them to act in a way that can be summed up by use of a term found in discussions of rational choice and cognitive psychology. The term is money pump; it refers to any deviation by an actor from rational action that would lead to the possibility of that actor's being economically exploited by another actor who makes use of that deviation. If an actor acts in such a way that he is a money pump, he may be so exploited until his money is exhausted or until he ceases to act in that way. This fact should lead the actor in the direction of self-correction, for the existence of continued exploitation makes it increasingly in the interest of the exploited actor to correct the deviation from rationality. But the limited lifetimes of natural persons and the fact that ontogeny recapitulates phylogeny mean that a population at equilibrium contains persons with varying amounts of experience in being money pumps.

The increased frequency of type 2 relations in modern society has made possible the systematic exploitation of consumers' weaknesses. Corporate actors have been successful in taking actions implementing the information obtained from market and audience research (advertising, sales strategies that draw attention away from cost, product design intended to satisfy immediate rather than long-term interests) to exploit the irrationalities in natural persons' actions. The result is a set of consumers whose consumption of goods provided by large corporate actors goes beyond the level that would maximize utility and who consume goods that are initially pleasing but later unsatisfactory. Consumption related to leisure activities can be divided into two classes: consumption of goods and services provided by large corporate actors in competitive markets (television programs, movies, music, clothes, toys and games) and consumption of noncommercial entertainment (use of parks, community and neighborhood activities, hiking, walking, folk games). The implication is that there is excess consumption of the first class and deficient consumption of the second, relative to the mix that would maximize utility of rational consumers (that is, consumers not afflicted with the deviations from rationality that are found in natural persons).

This situation suggests that there may be developing, in societies containing many large corporate actors, a condition which may be described as parasitism. Corporate actors are the parasites, and natural persons are the hosts. Although the parasites not only feed off the hosts but also provide food for them, the rationale for describing the relation as parasitism, rather than as a more symmetrical symbiosis between two components of a system, is that the corporate actors effectively control the system. Since corporate actors control the system, the state of the other parties, the natural persons, is such as to maximize the corporate actors' utility, rather than to maximize their own utility. They become, in effect, slaves, maintained at a level of satisfaction that is less than the maximum possible given their resources.

Social Policy Research and Its Effects on Social Functioning

A perspective on the feedback process in which market research and social policy research are involved can be gained by examining the feedback process that exists in interpersonal interactions, that is, interactions of type 1, and how this is modified in the asymmetric interactions of type 2. Figure 23.1 is a simple picture of a feedback process in a symmetric two-person interaction, with actor

Figure 23.1 Feedback process in symmetric two-person interaction.

A_1 carrying out an action that has an effect on actor A_2, who then acts in such a way as to lead A_1 to adjust his next action affecting A_2 based on A_2's response.

Figure 23.2 suggests, in a very simplified way, how this feedback process differs in an asymmetric interaction of type 2, where a government takes the place of actor A_1 and a government policy is the action analogous to A_1's first action in Figure 23.1. The structural characteristics of the type 2 interaction differ in certain ways from those of the type 1 interaction. First, the government's action is mediated or implemented by agents, each with its own interests. Second, the asymmetry of the type 2 relation means that the action affects not a single other actor, but many others. The greater the asymmetry, the more distant are the effects and the more complex the structure of agency through which they occur. As a consequence, the forms of feedback usually found in two-person, face-to-face interactions are nonexistent in the type 2 interaction. New forms of feedback are necessary, both so that the first actor (the government) will be able to modify its policies to realize its interests and so that the affected actors (labeled the policy recipients in Figure 23.2) will be able to realize their interests.

A variety of devices have been implemented to provide this necessary feedback, some of them part of the formal political structure and some less formal. One is political representation through elected representatives. Another is representation of interests through organized interest groups and lobbying. One important means by which feedback occurs is the congressional or parliamentary committee hearing. Yet all these devices remain less satisfactory, both for the government and for the persons affected by the policy, than the direct feedback processes that occur in two-person, face-to-face interactions. This is why, I suggest, governments have brought into being the new means of feedback known as social policy research.

A serious question naturally arises: Just what place in the structure of interaction does social policy research occupy? One answer is that the research is in effect an agent of government. If this is the case, the questions posed by the research are ones which government has about the effects of its policy; they are

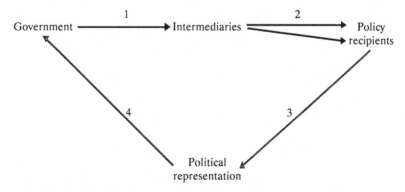

Figure 23.2   Feedback process in asymmetric type 2 interaction.

not questions asked by any other parties. The information obtained by the research is transmitted directly back to the government agency which carried out
the action, and only to that agency. This view of social policy research sees it as
a direct and immediate aid to the corporate actor who must take action in an
asymmetric social structure in which the usual feedback from action is missing
or severely curtailed. With this orientation, social policy research represents a
direct extension of market research from business to government.

This conception is illustrated by the structure diagrammed in Figure 23.3
(where the dashed arrows represent information). Intrinsic to this conception are
two elements. Arrow 8 in the figure indicates that research results are transmitted directly back to government, not to any other party. Arrow 5 indicates that
the design of the research is dictated by the government's information needs.
That is, the information (arrows 6 and 7) extracted by the social policy research
from the total set of effects of the policy is determined wholly by the government
body.

The structure in Figure 23.3 provides a feedback mechanism which is in addition to, and independent of, the feedback mechanism that operates through
political processes. This kind of structure is envisioned by social scientists who
believe policy making of the future will be "rationalized" by the introduction of
experimental policies accompanied by feedback of the sort that is provided by
policy research. For example, one social philosopher has described this vision of
the future in a paper titled "The Experimenting Society" (Haworth, 1960).
Another (Habermas, 1971) expresses the same vision but does not see it as
benign (as Haworth does); Habermas regards the bypassing of political processes of feedback as inherently dangerous to the functioning of a political
democracy.

There is another answer to the question of what place in the structure of
interaction social policy research will occupy. In this conception social policy

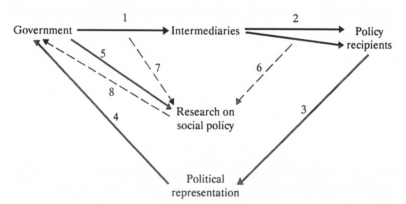

Figure 23.3   Feedback process in asymmetric type 2 interaction with social policy
            research.

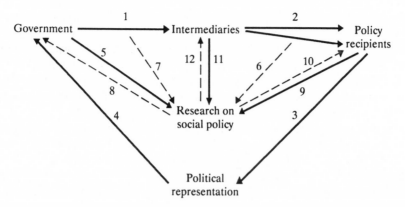

Figure 23.4   Feedback process in asymmetric type 2 interaction with pluralistic social policy research.

research is not under the monopolistic control of the government, but under pluralistic control. The questions posed in the research are questions that all interested parties, not only the government, have about the effect of the policy. And the information obtained by the research is transmitted openly, to all the parties which might have an interest in (that is, might be affected by) the policy. Figure 23.4 indicates these differences with arrows 9, 10, 11, and 12. Arrows 9 and 11 indicate that the research design is in part under control of the intermediaries and policy recipients, and arrows 10 and 12 indicate that results of the research are transmitted back to the other interested parties, as well as to the government. In this conception of social policy research (which I will call pluralistic policy research), the principal effect of the research occurs not through direct feedback (arrow 8) but indirectly, through informing interested parties outside government about those effects of the policy in which they have an interest (arrows 10 and 12). That information can lead them to modify the actions they take via political processes to influence policy in directions they favor.[9]

Rights in Decisions and Rights to Information

Which is the appropriate conception of social policy research? The answer to this question derives directly from the allocation of rights in the social system: If rights are allocated so that various interested parties have rights to influence the outcome of policy-making decisions, then these interested parties will equally have rights to influence the kind of information to be obtained and to the information once obtained. The danger of the conception which involves direct feedback to government, as shown in Figure 23.3, is that it changes the distribution

9. For research explicitly carried out using a pluralistic policy research design, see Coleman, Bartot, Lewin-Epstein, and Olson, 1979.

of rights by ignoring the rights held by actors outside government. This can increase the power of government relative to the power of all other interested parties in the social system, that is, natural persons and the corporate bodies independent of government in which persons have vested resources. This increase in power comes from both rights to additional production of information of primary use to government (relative to that which is of primary use to other interested parties) and rights to access to information.

There is another danger of seeing social policy research as direct feedback only to government. Access to information constitutes power within the governmental hierarchy as well as power of government relative to that of other parties. If information is transmitted solely back to government (that is, without redundant channels), the point at which it enters the governmental structure and its path through the structure will shape the way in which it is used, and even whether it is used. Evidence of misuse can be found for other types of information in government organizations. For example, security classification is often used to keep information out of the hands of an internal competitor (the army keeping information from the air force and navy, for example). Similarly, the use of files kept by internal security agencies by those with access to them to pursue personal interests is well known. Information generated by social policy research is no different. Interests of various actors inside government are helped or harmed by that information, and when it is in the hands of only some of those interested parties, the distribution of power within the organization is changed, and the information may be buried or used in inappropriate ways.

This does not imply that there are no conditions under which social policy research is appropriately carried out as shown in Figure 23.3. There is a kind of evaluation research called formative evaluation of a social program. This refers to a taking of the pulse of a program in progress to obtain information of use to a program manager in making administrative adjustments in the program when the goals are well specified.[10] The kinds of decisions for which formative evaluation is used are often termed administrative decisions, in contrast to policy decisions. That is, the existence of a well-defined policy with specific goals is assumed, and the decisions merely concern the implementation of that policy. Formative evaluation is intended to provide information that will facilitate modification of administrative decisions to better meet policy goals.

Social policy research of this sort (which may be termed administrative feedback) provides information for decisions that are legitimately made by administrators. The general public has no rights to participate in such decisions and consequently no information rights. Thus there is no justification for open publication of the research results. The research is appropriately carried out so that feedback is designed by, and directly reported to, the party who administers or implements a policy.

10. More precisely, formative evaluation is ordinarily initiated and controlled by those labeled intermediaries in Figure 23.3, and information is fed directly back to them.

The general principle, as indicated earlier, is clear. Rights to influence the kind of information obtained for policy-making activities and rights of access to that information once obtained should be distributed in the same way as are rights to influence policy decisions in that area. In some cases the distribution of rights to influence decisions is not precise, so this principle does not remove all ambiguity. It is clear, however, that current practice in social policy research does not adhere to this principle. There is a bias in the direction favoring government, which by initiating and funding policy research, has de facto control over the resulting information. Procedures for ensuring that policy research is pluralistically designed are not well developed, and neither are procedures for transmitting information to interested parties. The Freedom of Information Act in the United States and more or less analogous statutes in other developed countries have established the right of interested parties to gain access to information generated by social policy research. These laws, however, neither include procedures to aid that dissemination nor establish rights concerning what information is obtained. Government agencies are attentive to their own interests in information; they are not attentive to the interests of other parties.

Questions may be raised, however, about the theoretical principle that specifies that an allocation of rights to information should parallel the allocation of rights concerning decision making. Does application of that principle lead to outcomes more in the interests of those with rights to affect decision making? Answering this question requires first considering the question of who uses the results of social research and how they do so.

WHO USES SOCIAL POLICY RESEARCH AND WHEN?   An illustrative case is a particular piece of social policy research initiated by the federal government in 1965. The research led to the report *Equality of Educational Opportunity* (Coleman et al., 1966). That report was publicly available and was extensively used in court and school board proceedings by advocates of affirmative action for racial integration of the schools.[11] The report was widely held to have been instrumental in helping to bring about the busing decisions of the late 1960s and early 1970s in the United States. There are two pertinent empirical questions: Who used the report? What were the consequences of this use?

First, it was *not* used in the federal bureaucracy which undertook it or in the federal government generally. Grant (1973) describes the reactions of various parties in and out of government. The Department of Health, Education, and Welfare not only failed to use the research, but the principal sentiment in the department at the time of the report's release seemed to be a hope that it would pass unread into filing cabinets, or even a fear and uneasiness that it might not. This reaction might be attributed to the fact that the research was called for in an

11. The report showed that lower-status black children had higher achievement in predominantly middle-class schools than in predominantly lower-class schools. This fact was used as an argument in favor of affirmative integration of black children (predominantly lower class) with white children (more often middle class).

act of Congress rather than being initiated wholly within the agency. Similar reactions of research-funding agencies in circumstances where the research *was* initiated by the agency indicate that the reasons are deeper than that.[12]

Who, then, did use the report? In school desegregation cases it was used by plaintiffs in suits against local school districts; it was also used in school board controversies over desegregation plans by factions attempting to initiate comprehensive plans of racial integration. It was widely used in schools of education, and it became a part of the general discourse surrounding school desegregation. Its use was opposed by some, especially by some economists, who had particular disciplinary reasons for finding fault with the research.[13] Opposition to the report came to be regarded as opposition to school desegregation, however, and since that was not a popular position at the time, the opposition was muted.

Observations of the actions of the principal actors in the desegregation conflict lead to a generalization: The report was used by those without formal authority over educational policy or those with little such authority. It was not used by those in authority. This might have been an isolated case, but the same pattern of use by outsiders and nonuse by insiders can be found in other cases. There appears to be a sociological principle: The use of social policy research is principally by those without authority; if it is used by those with authority, this occurs when they are in a weak position.

Why is this so? The answer, I believe, lies in a single word—legitimation. Those who hold the authority of office ordinarily have, by virtue of that authority, power sufficient to formulate and implement public policy. The rights associated with holding office legitimate the power and eliminate the need for any other basis of legitimation. Those who do not have formal authority, but only rights as interested parties to influence the decision, need legitimation from other sources. One such source that has proved effective is social research, because of the information it provides.

A corollary of the proposition that social research is used by those who lack the legitimation based on authority is that social research is more likely to be used when there is an existing conflict over policy. If social research is used

12. For example, reaction of the Department of Education to a report on public and private schools from research the Department itself initiated was at least as fearful and uneasy, delaying open publication of the report for several months. See Coleman (1983) for a discussion of the case.

13. See Bowles and Levin (1968), Coleman (1968a; 1970a; 1972a), Cain and Watts (1970), and Hanushek and Kain (1972). The economists' disciplinary reasons lay in the fact that the study did not show a direct and unequivocal relation between inputs and outputs of schooling for a production function, which would show the percentage increase in achievement associated with (and due to) a given percentage increase in each input resource. But the production of achievement in schools depends on things other than the standard input resources. When the report made this manifest, it provoked a reaction from some economists. A subsequent review of educational research on this question by one of these critics (Hanushek, 1986) reports on numerous later studies that showed results like those reported in *Equality of Educational Opportunity.*

primarily for legitimation and if there is no conflict over policy, there are no parties who need social research to legitimate and strengthen their positions. Policy is formulated by those whose legitimation comes from their authority. They have no incentive to use social research unless their position of authority has been or may be threatened if a policy is unsuccessful.

A second corollary to the proposition is that there is one circumstance under which those in authority will make extensive use of social research (or more generally social science). This is when there is a major policy change for which the legitimation that comes with authority is insufficient. Then those in authority have an incentive to seek out additional sources of legitimation, not limited to social research or social theory, but including both.

But if social policy research is used primarily to legitimate already held positions, what can be said about its potential value? Does this imply that such research is merely an arbitrary weapon that can be used to provide legitimation for any policy? The answer is no; social policy research cannot be used to justify every policy. It justifies *some* already held position, but not any already held position. The results of social policy research, in providing justification for one direction of policy, undermine the justification for a different direction. The way they do so is instructive. Unlike legitimation that derives merely from positional authority, legitimation that results from research results has its grounding in more universally held values. For example, social policy research concerning school desegregation (a policy on which there is not high consensus) helps legitimate a policy of desegregation if it shows that desegregation leads to greater equality of opportunity. Equal opportunity is a goal on which there is much higher consensus than there is on desegregation, and if research establishes a causal connection from the latter to the former, the latter gains greater legitimacy as a goal.

There are, of course, other goals on which consensus is also high; achievement in school is one of these. If research showed desegregation to constitute a move toward equal educational opportunity, but only at the cost of a move away from achievement, then a policy of desegregation would not be given greater legitimacy by the research. Legitimacy is gained when research shows that a policy moves the system toward a goal on which there is high consensus, and legitimacy is lost when research shows that a policy moves the system away from a goal on which there is high consensus.

Applied Research on Systems, Relations, and Individuals

Table 23.1 has one property not previously mentioned: It characterizes actions of individual actors or relations between two actors, not systems of action. The table was first introduced in Chapter 20 to show the types of relations of which social systems are composed; it is also appropriate for characterizing research of the Columbia school or social policy research. The policies of corporate actors are actions of type 2b, and the responses of individuals (on which applied social research is generally focused) are actions of type 2a. The table, however, is not equally appropriate for characterizing research like that of the Chicago school. The research of the Chicago school did not focus on relations among individuals; it focused on social subsystems made up of those relations. None of the studies from the Chicago school referred to earlier concerned individual actor's actions or relations between pairs of actors. All were case studies of small subsystems of society. The shift to studying individuals' actions occurred when there was a shift to research designed to provide feedback to an actor, that is, market research and then social policy research.

Another way of describing this shift is to state that it was a shift from studying a system of action to studying one component of a system of action, that is, actions at the micro level. But this leads to a question about research adequacy: If the question to be answered is a macrosocial one, involving something about the system's functioning, can it be answered by studying actions of individuals? The answer to this depends of course on just how sophisticated the study of individuals' actions is. One fact should, however, constitute a warning: The study of actions of type 2a (for example, responses of natural persons to corporate actors' actions) is an analysis at the micro level. If the research question concerns the macro level, as it ordinarily does, then there is the problem of moving from micro to macro level.

The way this problem arises for social policy research can be illustrated by considering research on job training for disadvantaged youth. The assumption underlying legislation to provide this training is that a macrosocial relation holds: Legislation to provide job training for black youth, among whom unemployment is highest, will decrease unemployment. (See Figure 23.5a.) The research designed to evaluate a job-training program's effectiveness, however, ordinarily studies a micro-level question: Does enrollment in the job-training program increase an individual's probability of being employed?[14] Suppose the answer is yes. Then this effect may come about in any of three ways, shown in Figure 23.5(b):

1. The employment of a program-trained youth may displace another black youth who was not enrolled. This would leave the unemployment rate among black youth unchanged.
2. Employment may displace another person who is not a black youth. This would change the unemployment rate of black youth but would leave the overall unemployment rate unchanged.
3. Employment may occur without displacing anyone, through a new job

14. See, for example, a report from the National Research Council (1985), which reviews a number of studies of this sort in the United States in the late 1970s and early 1980s. The report finds that the answer is generally yes for the Job Corps program and indeterminate for other federally sponsored programs under the Youth Educational Development Program Act of 1977. Figure 23.5 indicates that a program may fail because of a lack of the first arrow in the sequence (that is, implementation of the legislation through establishment of actual programs) or the second (that is, actual enrollment of trainees).

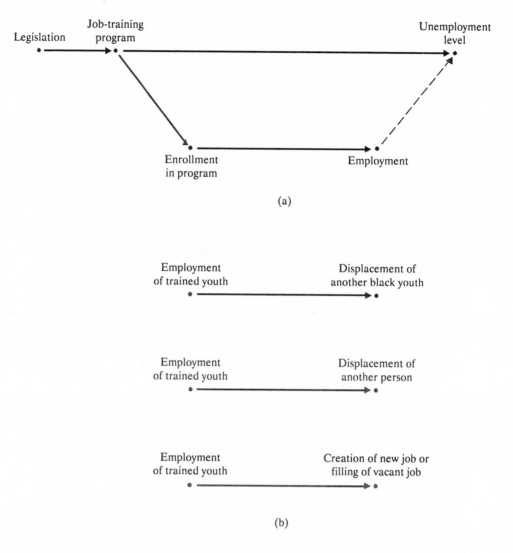

Figure 23.5 Possible alternative effects of job-training program.

created or a vacant job filled, making use of the newly created human capital.

Only if the third alternative is in fact what occurs will the macrosocial relation hold.

The question of which of the three alternatives occurs calls for additional research beyond finding out whether training an individual increases the probability of that individual's employment. The question is answerable, but answering it requires a completely different research design than that for answering the question of whether a job-training program is effective for the participants, or even for the target population as a whole.

Information that would help answer the question about the three alternatives might be described as follows:

Data on employment or unemployment of a representative sample of workers in the job market for which youth were being trained, before and after the training program

Data on occupancy or vacancy levels for a representative sample of jobs in the same markets, before and after the training program

These data appear in principle to be sufficient to determine the degree to which the job-training program affected the macrosocial outcome, that is, the degree to which the additional resources changed the equilibrium by filling vacant or new jobs rather than by displacing employed workers. These simple forms of data would not in fact be sufficient, however, given the complexities of the real world. Cyclical fluctuations in employment mask the effects of job-training programs, and it is ordinarily difficult to isolate labor markets to the extent assumed for the above data to be useful. Nevertheless, once the criterion that the training must increase the employment levels of trained youth without an offsetting effect on others' employment has been established, research can be designed that will address the macrosocial question.

An application of a linear system of action like that described in Chapters 6 and 26 would allow an investigation of the macro-level effect of a job-training program. Application before and after the program would result in two estimates of value of various resources held by individuals. One of the resources of individuals included in such an empirical analysis should be graduation from the job-training program or a measure of skills of the sort developed by the program. The several possible effects of the program would be identifiable as follows:

1. The program had no effect at the micro level; it was worthless for the persons who participated in it. Then graduation from the program would show no value as a resource, and the value of other resources (the quantity of which was unaffected by the program) would remain the same. If skills developed by the program but also arising from other sources (such as literacy skills or specific job skills) were measured, then the absence of any effect of the program would be identifiable by the absence of change in the total value of these skills for all individuals in the system, taken together. This would represent a decline in the value of each unit of skill, since the job-training program would have increased the total quantity of these skills in the system.

2. The program had a micro-level effect but no macro-level effect. Then graduation from the program would show some value as a resource. That value, denominated in dollars, would be an indication of the value of the program to

participants. But the absence of a macro-level effect would be evident in a compensating reduction in the value of some other personal resources, resulting in an unchanged total value of personal resources in the system. In individual terms this would mean that the trainees had gained resources of value in the labor market and had displaced others who had different resources, which were now worth less in the market.

3. The program had both a micro-level effect and a macro-level effect. Then graduation from the program would show value as a resource, and all or part of that value would show up as an increase in the overall value of personal resources in the system. The value of other personal resources would not be reduced. This increase in value might show up as an increase in the number of persons holding jobs or as higher wages for persons in jobs, or some combination of the two, bringing about higher total wages in the system. The total macro-level value of the program, that is, its value for the economy, could thus be measured by the increment in the total value of personal resources in the system.

For such programs an even more extensive accounting balance is necessary. The cost of such a program to the economy in jobs can be expressed in terms of number of job-years lost from the private sector, as estimated by the total tax cost divided by the income of the average employee within the distribution of persons and corporate actors on whom tax is levied. Jobs are created by the training program. Payments are made to trainees, and jobs are created (or vacancies saved from dying) because of added skills of the trainees. Thus there is a cost of the program in private-sector jobs and a benefit of the program in public-sector jobs, and possibly in private-sector jobs. Does the increase in jobs or in income among trainees exceed the decrease in jobs or the loss in income due to taxes? That question is answerable only through careful accounting that includes jobs lost due to private-sector taxation.

What Should Applied Social Research Be Like?

The example of research on job-training programs indicates a more general problem with applied social research of type 2a, that is, social policy research, audience research, and market research. The research question is at the macrosocial level: What is the effect of a particular corporate decision or government action (on the actions of the audience, the consumers, or the clients or on public opinion)? This can be expressed as shown in Figure 23.6.

In the case of social policy research, the interest of the government, as the agent of the society, is in the effects of a policy (an event at the macrosocial level) on the society (a consequence also at the macrosocial level). But social policy research is ordinarily focused on phenomena at the individual level. The implicit assumption is no different from that of Max Weber in his study of Protestantism and capitalism (described in Chapter 1): Individual actions aggregate in a simple fashion to bring about societal effects.

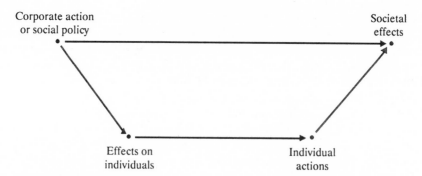

Figure 23.6   Macro-to-micro-to-macro relations in effects of social policies.

A similar disparity exists between the interest of the corporation and the usual methodology of market or audience research: The interest is at the macrosocial level, but the research takes as dependent phenomena individual actions and opinions. There is again an assumption of simple aggregation, which is not correct. Some of the research at the height of period of dominance of the Columbia school shows this well. *Personal Influence* by Katz and Lazarsfeld (1955) shows that in the 1940s societal reaction to what was presented in magazine articles and advertisements was not simply the aggregation of individual reactions. What occurred was what the authors called a two-step flow of communication, in which some persons used others as opinion leaders. It was the opinion leaders' reactions to the stimuli, percolating through the rest of the population, that generated the ultimate societal reaction. (See discussion in Chapter 9.) Coleman, Katz, and Menzel (1966), in research carried out in 1954 at Columbia, showed that the use of a new drug in medical practice by doctors (in four small Midwestern cities) was not a simple aggregation of individual responses to the drug company's advertisements and sales representatives. Instead doctors made extensive use of one another, not so much to get information as to share the risk of introducing the drug.

In the case of a governmental policy, the appropriate conception of the system is considerably more complex. Responses to (or effects of) the policy involve intermediaries that interpret and implement the policy. Unless the incentives confronting them are known, the differences between the policy as enunciated and the policy as implemented cannot be predicted. As Schultze (1977) shows, these incentives often lead to extensive differences. Then both participation in the program (in the case of a voluntary government program) and response to the program depend on the social structure existing among recipients (as in the cases of Katz and Lazarsfeld's two-step flow or the sharing of risk among doctors, but sometimes more complex than either of these).

These are various ways in which applied social research can overcome the error of simple aggregation. One is through use of modifications of survey techniques in ways that involve explicit introduction of social structure, as in the two studies referred to above. Another is to use the assumption that social exchange leads to general equilibrium, resulting in the methods described in Chapter 26. Those methods allow survey data to be used to estimate system-level properties, such as the value of particular resources and the power of particular actors.

Whatever the methods used, if applied social research is to give correct results, it is necessary not to remain at the individual level, but to carry out explicitly the aggregation that produces a societal response from the individual responses.

What Research Is Missing?

The above analysis of applied social research has left open the question of whether such research reflects the information interests of various actors in society equally well. The asymmetry of the modern social structure, consisting of large corporate actors with extensive resources and natural persons with much less extensive resources, suggests that the answer might very well be that it does not.

An example can serve to apply the question to a particular context, that of college admissions in the United States (Coleman, 1969). There are two sets of interested parties on two sides of a market: colleges on one side, and students on the other. For many colleges and many students, the information problem is not serious: The colleges draw applicants from a few local high schools and are easily able to evaluate the applicants' high-school transcripts. The applicants are choosing from among only two or three local institutions and have extensive knowledge about them from friends and relatives who are attending or have attended. But for some applicants and some colleges, the market is not local, but regional or national. For these colleges and these students, more information is needed than that furnished by high-school transcripts and interpersonal interaction.

The first colleges to confront a national market were those in the Ivy League and a few other elite institutions. These colleges, whose presidents were in frequent contact, joined together at the turn of the century to form the College Entrance Examination Board (CEEB), which has subsequently become the College Entrance Board (CEB). The express purpose of the organization was creating and administering a single examination to college applicants, to enable board members to better evaluate those applicants. Although not generally regarded as applied social research, the college board tests constitute an example of such research.[15]

As more colleges and universities came to operate in a broader market, more

15. The A-level examinations taken by many students throughout Great Britain at the end of upper secondary school have served much the same purpose, and the *Baccalaureat* in France and the *Abitur* in Germany have played a similar role. As university enrollments increased in these countries after World War II and applicants represented a broader range of social classes, universities confronted a problem like that which brought CEEB into existence in the United States. In England a response was the Common Universities Examination, similar in intent but different in form from the college board tests in the United States.

became members of CEEB and used the tests administered for it by its agent, the Educational Testing Service. A second testing program, the American College Testing Program, was created by another consortium of colleges. Nearly all U.S. colleges and universities with other than a local market (and many that have only local markets) currently use one or both of these two testing programs, which in effect carry out applied social research for the institutions. The research is financed by the applicants, who must pay to be tested.

As the market has expanded, has a similar need (that is, an interest in information) arisen for applicants? And if so, has analogous applied social research come into being to meet that need? The answer to the first question seems to be yes, both on presumptive grounds and on the basis of individual actions taken by applicants. Applicants' need for information would appear to be great. Choosing a college is an action most of them will take only once in their lives, and it has extensive consequences for the future. Empirical evidence also supports the existence of this need for information. Many applicants make trips to visit the colleges they have applied to, at considerable cost, to gain information about the colleges. Many spend a great deal of time and carry out extensive consultations with others in the same situation, when deciding which colleges to apply to and which one to attend, once admitted. The total number of person-years spent by applicants on these decisions is many times greater than the total number of person-years spent by admissions officers in selecting among applicants.

The second question, whether applied social research has come into being on applicants' side of the market, does not have a clear affirmative answer. Colleges distribute catalogs, informing prospective applicants about what the administrators want to show about the schools, and there exist some more objective guides to colleges, used by applicants and high-school guidance counselors. The CEB publishes information (subject to the colleges' granting of permission) on the distributions of Scholastic Aptitude Test (SAT) scores of entering students. There has been an attempt (see Pace, 1964) to create a college characteristics profile, based on surveys of samples of student bodies. Altogether, however, institutionalized gathering of information about colleges and universities (applied social research of type 2b) has been minuscule compared to that carried out on the other side of the market. Applicants cannot easily learn dropout rates, level of student morale, evaluations of faculty members, extent of drug use on campus, or postgraduation positions of students.

The answer to why this is so appears to be a simple one: the asymmetry of the market, along with the fact that information about the other side of a market is a public good for all those on one side of the market. The asymmetry means that the problem of how to organize to pay the cost of providing the public good is more easily overcome on the side of the market with fewer actors. In the example this problem was resolved on that side of the market when the CEEB was formed by the small set of elite institutions. On the other side of the market, the applicants are numerous and are in the market for only a short time; they have never satisfactorily overcome the problem of organization.

In some cases intermediaries may spring into existence to overcome the problem of organization for those on the more populous side of a market. One reason why they have not arisen more extensively in this case would appear to be that the power necessary to induce colleges and universities to allow access to their student bodies could be better wielded by an organization representing applicants than by an intermediary representing no one. In the case of product markets, that reason does not hold and cannot be used to explain why market research (type 2a) is so much more widespread than consumer research (type 2b). The reason may be that the public-good property of information is harder to overcome when there are large numbers of actors in the market. Information will readily disseminate among persons, making it to no one's interest to pay an appropriate share of the cost of obtaining it.

The example of the college admissions market illustrates how the asymmetry in modern society, which is composed of large corporate actors as well as persons, leads to an asymmetry in applied social research. In general, that asymmetry is one in which research of type 2a is not suboptimally provided, but that of type 2b is. How the public-good problem might be overcome is an important question, but answering it lies beyond the scope of this chapter.

Social theory must have reflexive consistency if its development is to be more than an idle pursuit. Examination of the role of sociological knowledge in the functioning of society is important both to guide sociologists' activities and to enable macrosocial theory to better characterize the functioning of modern society. If the examination shows that there is no effect of social research or social theory on society's functioning, then sociologists must seriously question their purpose. If the examination shows that there are effects, whether or not they bias functioning, then guidance is provided for optimal institutionalization of applied social research. As this chapter has indicated, the kinds of effects that one form of applied social research—social policy research—has as currently institutionalized may introduce biases into the functioning of society. A further task of social theory is to design an institutionalization of applied social research that eliminates such biases.

« 24 »

The New Social Structure
and the New Social Science

Purposive corporate actors, having an existence and internal structure independent of natural persons, could be found before 1850. Yet at that time most social organization still consisted of the natural social environment based on primordial ties: family, kin group, clan, neighborhood, community, and village. This was not social organization by design, but social organization by accretion. Corporate actors designed and constructed for specific purposes were peripheral to most of persons' social life.

In the almost century and a half since that time, constructed social organization, based on purposive corporate actors, has undergone extensive growth. During the first hundred years, until the 1940s, the new corporate actors established themselves as important components of the social structure, enormously enhancing the system's capacity to produce goods and services. In the last half-century purposive corporate actors have expanded their roles and functions in society, coming to occupy the center.

Purposive corporate actors, the constructed component of persons' social environment, have begun to displace families as welfare and childrearing institutions. Purposively constructed affinity groups based on common interests are no longer constrained by the necessity for physical proximity but are fostered by electronically assisted communication. Distant strangers share intimacies, and neighbors become strangers. Matchmaking is not kin-driven and parent-regulated but assisted by common membership in purposive organizations and by corporate actors (including computerized dating services) constructed for that purpose. Leisure activities are less likely to involve interactions with persons, more likely to involve interaction with corporately produced mass media and the constructed persona they supply. Even communal settings, the antithesis of bureaucratic purposive corporate actors, are increasingly intentional communities (constructed with a purpose by individuals) and decreasingly communities that grow from kin, clan, and primordial ties.

This change from a natural to a constructed social environment has been paralleled by a change from a natural to a constructed physical environment. The constructed physical environment has come to displace much of the natural surroundings that were once the setting for most persons' lives. Today's children play supervised games in constructed playgrounds while their parents work in factory or office buildings; their great-grandparents at the same age chased rabbits for fun in the fields and gardens while their fathers and mothers worked nearby. The stories and fairy tales of previous centuries that are still read to some children are rich in the fields, forests, and animals of the natural physical environment; the animated programs these children see on television reflect the constructed physical environment of the present and future, populated by strange new constructed creatures.

These two transformations—from natural to constructed physical environment and from natural to constructed social environment—generate a demand for new bodies of knowledge, disciplines that can provide a basis on which to construct the future. For the constructed physical environment the branch of physics known as mechanics, supplemented by organic and physical chemistry and to some extent by most of the physical and biological sciences, provides the foundation, and disciplines such as architecture and civil engineering provide the superstructure. The constructed social environment, the purposive social organization that now surrounds and penetrates most persons' lives, also generates a demand for new bodies of knowledge, disciplines that can provide a foundation and superstructure of knowledge to aid in constructing the future.

A new kind of social science has begun to emerge to meet that demand. This social science is not only a search for knowledge for the aesthetic pleasure of discovery or for the sake of knowing, but a search for knowledge for the reconstruction of society. As horizons become wider and possible directions of social progress multiply, knowledge about self and society, and their relation, gains a new importance and immediacy.

Demand for the new social science arises in part from the vacuum created as primordial social organization withers away. Primordial social organization has depended on a vast supply of social capital, on a normative structure which enforced obligations, guaranteed trustworthiness, induced efforts on behalf of others and on behalf of the primordial corporate bodies themselves, and suppressed free riding. That social capital has been eroded, leaving many lacunae. Perhaps the most important area in which erosion has occurred, the regeneration of society through nurturing of the next generation, was discussed in Chapter 22. The new social science is necessary, then, not as an accomplice of dark forces that would undermine traditional society, but as an aid in the reconstructive task of filling the voids created by the erosion of social capital and the mode of social organization it supported.

Conceived too narrowly, this new social science becomes science in the service of the powerful—which in modern society means large corporate actors, including but not limited to the state itself. Conceived more broadly, this new social science becomes science that extends its knowledge to the understanding of how power comes to be distributed and accumulated in society, and to the understanding of how natural persons can best satisfy their interests in a social system populated with large corporate actors. It is science that goes beyond questions concerning the optimal organization of a firm, the optimal policy to achieve a government's goals, the optimal marketing plan for introduction of a new product, the optimal bargaining strategy for a trade union, the optimal composition of a jury for defense or prosecution, or the optimal way to prevent (or make) a revolution.

One component of the new social science *is* directed to specific questions of this sort. This is the applied social research described in Chapter 23, research known as policy research, evaluation research, market research, and public opinion research. Even that component of the new social science, however, need not and should not be merely science in the service of the powerful, as Chapter 23 makes apparent. Conceived, designed, and reported properly, applied social research has its impact through its results, independently of its sponsors.

As Chapter 23 demonstrates, a second component is required to locate this new social science in the functioning of society and to discover what interests it benefits when it is institutionalized in one or another way. This theoretical component of the new social science is also important more generally. As the science of mechanics does for construction of the physical environment, the theoretical component of the new social science must provide a foundation for the purposive reconstruction of society.

It is to this foundational work that this book is directed. To provide an adequate foundation is a task that was begun long ago and will not soon be completed. What is of importance is the recognition by social theorists (and here I include not only sociologists but also theorists in economics, politics, psychology, philosophy, and law) that creating the new social theory is not a mere pastime or whim. It is, rather, the task of providing the foundation for constructing a viable social structure, as the primordial structure on which persons have depended vanishes.

In the remainder of this chapter, I will use some of the results of this book to raise questions about current social organization. Contemporary societies are not the product of long-term accretion and adjustment. They are more like modern cities of skyscrapers and tenements than like the honeycomb of dwellings on the island of Mykonos or the cumulated complexity of a coral reef. Because they are new, they contain much that makes them function less well than they might.

The Replacement of Primordial Social Capital

Throughout most of history persons have been born with some mix of three kinds of endowment: genetic endowments that, when developed, constitute their human capital; material endowments in the form of land, money, or other goods, which constitute their physical capital; and the social context surrounding and supporting them, which constitutes their social capital. As societies have developed, the mix of these three forms of capital possessed by persons in successive generations has changed. Of particular note are an increase in physical capital resulting from economic abundance and a decrease in social capital provided by the primordial social organization of family and community. The latter change (discussed in Chapter 22) reflects the growth of purposive corporate actors, which have replaced the household and community for an ever increasing range of functions and have thereby weakened those primordial corporate actors.

One property of the social capital provided by the primordial social structure is that it was generally widely enough distributed to cover times of dependency: when a person was young, sick, aged, or otherwise unable to be self-sufficient. It did not do so for everyone; there have always been persons cast adrift from others, lacking the social supports provided by family, friends, and neighbors. In addition, in times of social disruption due to war, plague, famine, mass migration, or natural disaster, many persons have been left isolated, bereft of the social capital provided by the social structure into which they were born.

These exceptions aside, the family and those social structures that grew directly out of the family provided for most persons most of the time an essential supplement to their economic productivity: These structures distributed resources internally largely on the basis of need. They supported persons during the periods of dependency at the beginning and end of life, as well as during the gaps in self-sufficiency that could occur at any time in between. They provided, especially for the dependent young, a special form of resource which for want of a better term I will call sustained attention. The family and its extensions constituted a communal unit that was both a second system of economic distribution beyond that based on productive activity and a system for distributing resources (such as sustained attention) of a sort that cannot readily be purchased in a market.

Human capital and physical capital have never been as equally distributed as social capital. Neither includes resources that can compensate for those provided by social capital, such as sustained attention. Nor do they have the insurance quality that social capital has. They are more easily squandered and thus less likely to cover times of need. As a result, neither is a full substitute for social capital.

What *does* constitute a substitute in the new social structure for the social capital that is eroding? A part of the answer lies in constructed social organization, narrow-purpose corporate bodies that cover some functions once served by family and local community: schools, medical insurers (either governmental or private), government agencies that provide old-age benefits or unemployment benefits. This answer is incomplete, however, because these organizations provide only a partial substitute for the family and community they have begun to supplant. This is most evident for childrearing, because the emotional and cognitive development of the child depends on particular properties of interaction with other persons that are not well supplied by schools, nurseries, or day-care centers.

The answer is not only incomplete but contains a serious flaw. This flaw can be seen by recognizing that primordial social organization generates the incentive structure that brings into being actions on behalf of another, norms, trustworthiness, and other components of social capital. The constructed social organization purposively created by governments and other modern corporate actors undermines that existing incentive structure (by encouraging free riding) and does not generate a comparable replacement. Even the incentive to provide for one's own needs is undermined if those needs can be provided for by some external agency. Incentives (for example, the incentive to care for particular others) are supplied through extrinsic means, ordinarily a wage payment for professional services (for example, those of a teacher, nurse, or day-care attendant). The knowledge of how to use these extrinsic rewards to bring about interest in, attention to, and care for others is weak.

The weakness lies at two points, one of which is in organization theory itself. As Chapters 7 and 16 pointed out, the theory of formal organizations has been impeded by a fixation on Max Weber's theory of bureaucracy, a theoretical orientation that recognizes purpose only at the apex of an organization and ignores the problem of connecting extrinsic interests of an employee to job performance. Also ignored are the free-rider problems created as externalities when government provides goods and services not contingent on an individual's own contribution. The fixation on bureaucratic theory is part of a broader problem: Theoretical questions concerning social organization have seldom been couched in terms of how to best organize action in order to accomplish a specific task without generating undesirable externalities.

The second point of weakness is an inadequate understanding of the task itself. What is it, for example, about parental care in early childhood that is especially important for emotional development and for cognitive development? I have used the term "sustained attention," but too little is known about the kind of attention necessary and about the importance of continuity of care-giver. Parental care cannot and need not simply be mimicked in constructed child-care institutions; some elements are extraneous to the child's development. Just what ones are not? Research has shown that children raised in institutions develop less well cognitively, emotionally, and even physically than do those raised by parents (Ainsworth et al., 1965; Bowlby, 1965; 1966), but what remains partially obscured is just what aspects of parental care or family life are necessary to optimal childrearing and how these change as the child ages. That knowledge would give understanding of the task to be accomplished in designing child-care organizations.

Additional questions arise once child care that is wholly removed from the family is envisioned. Are there structural aspects of primordial corporate bodies that are inimical to the child's development and therefore should not be replicated in constructed institutions? (For example, the authority structure of the nuclear family subjects the child to two fixed authorities, mother and father. Is this inferior to a more pluralistic authority structure? Is it inferior to a setting like a single-parent household, in which the parent may give up authority to gain the child's companionship?)

Is the very concept of optimal child care inappropriate in that there may be different environments suited to engendering different adult personalities? If so, then if knowledge of organizational design becomes sufficiently great, it would be possible to vary the personality structure of society by varying the mix of these different environments. But such a possibility raises another problem: how to make collective decisions on issues that were once decided by nature and out of human control. The necessity to design child-care institutions in the face of diminishing child care within the family forces recognition of an intrusive fact: The decline of primordial social organization and increased knowledge about constructing social organization bring into the public domain decisions that were once private and often made in ignorance. The chances of centralized social control, with its attendant dangers, increase radically.

Although childrearing is the most prominent form of social capital that is poorly provided by the current constructed social environment, it is only one such form. The forms of social capital that provide insurance for times of dependency throughout a person's life are all generated under the umbrella of family, clan, and community. As this umbrella decomposes, will there be a residual locus of responsibility for the person?

There are other forms of social capital beyond that necessary to provide care during dependency, such as that necessary for social order. As the norms and sanctions that proliferate in the primordial social structure have become ineffective in a massive social system based on purposive organization, the institutions designed to maintain social order have been poorly constructed. How to overcome anarchy without oppression remains elusive. In a system based on purposive constructed social organizations in which persons are transient occupants of positions, is it possible to create a structure of norms and sanctions that will undergird the formal system of social control? And can this come about in a way that avoids the monolithic control envisioned in *1984* or *Brave New World*?

All these questions regarding the replacement of the vanishing primordial social capital with constructed social organization are forced on social theory by social change. A failure to address these questions does not merely leave society where it was before. It places each of us and each of our children in the position of the "poor little rich kid," having an abundance of material resources but without the social resources necessary for satisfactory lives.

Independent Viability, Global Viability, and Distribution in the New Social Structure

In the shift which has occurred principally in the past century from subsistence economies of households to a single interdependent exchange economy, society has changed from one based on independent viability to one meeting only the criterion of global viability (see Chapter 16). The units, that is, households, which engaged in transactions within the larger society fulfilled the requirement of independent viability in that both the household (regarded as an actor) and the society (also regarded as an actor) realized a gain from the relation. If individuals within a household were net liabilities, the losses were made up by the household, which was the principal welfare institution. If households themselves were net liabilities, the losses were made up by the next larger social and economic unit: the extended family, the village, or (where the employment relation had a feudal or paternalistic quality) the employer.

Global viability has replaced independent viability as most economic exchanges of goods and services have moved outside the household in the double-exchange economy (the first exchange is labor for money; the second is money for goods and services). Persons have replaced households as the units engaged in economic transactions with the larger society, and the welfare activities of the family have come to be taken over by the state. One way of describing this change is to say that the state has become redistributive. A second is to say that the liabilities which make persons economically dependent are no longer absorbed by the corporate bodies most proximate to them (just as the economic exchanges of which persons are a part are no longer with actors most proximate to them) but by the state itself, which has become the major welfare institution. A third way of describing this change is to say that the society, as a corporate actor, has replaced the criterion of independent viability with that of global viability.

A question that may be asked is whether global viability can be maintained in the long run. A money wage can be regarded as a drawing right on the aggregate product of all the society's productive activities. But in a society not organized in families, a distribution of these drawing rights through productive work leaves a large fraction of persons without such rights. A second set of drawing rights is provided by redistribution through the political system. Thus the attainment of global viability is made especially precarious if the second set of drawing rights (welfare rights) reduces the value of the first set (rights to earned income on the basis of productive activity). If that occurs, disincentives to contribute are created.

Attempts to repair the increasingly extensive dependency in the social system have been almost exclusively through redistribution by the state. Taxation for redistribution can be seen as Okun (1975) has described it, as a second-round distribution that follows the first-round distribution made through the market, which allocates wages and other income. Seen in this way, taxation and redistribution imply a set of preferences on the part of those holding political decision-making rights for a greater degree of equality than is provided if the market is left to function freely. Okun's description of state-organized taxation and redistribution as a second-round distribution suggests a functional correspondence to the communal redistribution that has traditionally occurred through the family, the household, and the clan. Unlike that communal redistribution, however, the taxation-fed redistribution organized by the state divides households (and even neighborhoods) into two groups: the benefactors and the recipients, or the productive and the unproductive. The social structure necessary to suppress the disincentive to contribute is missing. An underclass is created that is not only permanent but gains new recruits without restraint. The redistribution creates incentives that tend to defeat those of the first round of distribution via wages for productive activity (for arguments about the importance of this effect in the United States, see Murray, 1984; 1988).

What has not been attempted is a consideration of alternative systems under which drawing rights on the aggregate product are provided in such a way that disincentives to contribute to the product are reduced. A first question is this: How has the family, as a communal unit, solved the problem of disincentives to contribute to its aggregate product? The family can be seen as the only social unit that has successfully carried out distribution principally on the basis of need rather than on the basis of contribution. How has it done so? It must first be noted that it has done so only imperfectly. There are wives who see their husbands as ne'er-do-wells and must struggle to provide sufficient financial support for their families. There are husbands who see their nonworking wives as sloths, interested only in consuming. Families often have difficulties in inducing children who are employed and living at home to contribute to the family budget. The extended families of the past often contained an uncle or cousin who was said to spend his life sponging off relatives.

Nevertheless, families appear to overcome the disincentives, or free-rider problems, better than other social units do. The means by which they do this appear to be largely social-psychological: the use of stigma to brand noncontributors and the conferring of status and power on those who contribute more than their share. These kinds of incentives appear to be effective only within very small social units. In fact, it may be that the size of the unit within which there can be communal redistribution based on need has been limited primarily by the scope of effectiveness of these social-psychological benefits and costs.

The social structure of a corporate economy of abundance (a structure in which persons need one another less and thus have fewer opportunities to accumulate social capital) is one in which the size of units within which social-psychological factors such as stigma, reputation, deference, and power are effective is small and becoming smaller. There may be some means of reconstituting groups within which these incentives will operate effectively, via the family or via a new institution, thus reviving communual redistribution as a robust complement to primary distribution via the double-exchange economy. Yet apart from scattered and generally short-lived experiments in urban communes by young people, there is little to suggest how such units might be constituted.

Nevertheless, one approach to the distribution problem in a double-exchange economy characterized by abundance is to accept that there is a necessity for a second round of distribution and to bring into being appropriate institutions that are proximate to the individual. The requisite institutions would have the resources necessary to shoulder the liabilities of dependent persons as well as the capacity to produce social-psychological incentives of the form that have proved effective in the family: stigma, status, deference, and power. This approach would entail creating around the individual new forms of social capital, microsocial institutions whose power would grow at the expense of the state, as they took over its redistributive activities.

Questions arise concerning this approach, however. How can such bodies be brought into being, and what would they be like? Most such proximate bodies are physically proximate; yet a decreasing fraction of persons' social relations are based on physical proximity. And what kind of reallocation of rights in society (away from the state or away from the individual) could provide sufficient resources to these proximate bodies so that they could absorb the welfare functions that were once the province of the family and are now the province of the state? What loss in equality might be created by the devolution of resources and responsibility to microsocial institutions? These are the kinds of questions the new social structure poses for a new social science.

Modes of Organizing Action

Throughout history some tasks in which persons have an interest have been beyond the capacity of a single person to carry out. In a wide range of such circumstances, the tasks have been carried out through the exercise of authority, with one or more persons acting under the direction of another, taking actions they would not have taken in the absence of authority.[1] Chapter 7 detailed different forms of authority systems; here I want to ask how action may be organized in the future and what role authority can be expected to play. There has been and continues to be a long-term decline in authority in social systems. Will this continue, and, if so, what will replace authority?

The most extreme form of authority, one with a long history, is slavery, in which the whole person is subject to another's authority. Less extreme types of servitude have also been prominent throughout history. Other forms of authority, such as those exercised within the family, household, or clan, have also encompassed the whole person. These forms, in which one person has authority over and responsibility for another, have become less pervasive over time, however.

It is also true that the kinds of persons created through socialization are becoming less socialized to authority. Socialization of children in modern societies has moved from an ideal of obedience to authority toward an ideal of self-regulation. This change is probably most pronounced in Germany following World War II, but can be found elsewhere as well. For example, using data from two studies done in Muncie, Indiana, in 1924 (*Middletown* by Lynd and Lynd,

---

1. There have always been tasks that are jointly carried out by associations whose members share a common purpose, perhaps beginning with hunting parties in primitive societies. These associations, when small, characteristically have only minimal authority relations.

1929) and 1978, Alwin (1988) reports the following comparison of parents' preferences regarding traits in their children:

	1924	1978	Difference
Strict obedience	45%	17%	−28%
Loyalty to church	58%	22%	−36%
Independence	25%	76%	+51%

These preferences are almost certainly reflected in parents' socialization practices; that is, socialization for an authority structure is being replaced by socialization for self-regulation.

The principal structural change in society with respect to the form of authority has been away from authority over the whole person and toward authority over activities. Bureaucratic authority is exercised over the activities of an occupant of a position, is limited by time, place, and task, and is nonexistent outside these bounds.

The legal concept of agency extends the modes of organizing action even further. Although the servant form of agency implies authoritative control by a principal, the independent contractor form eliminates authority altogether. There are also what I have called in Chapter 7 affine agents, who come to see their interests as coinciding with those of their principal and act wholly in those interests without any exercise of authority.

Chapter 16 describes corporate actors that have still other modes of internal organization. One, represented by codetermination in Germany, maintains the basic authority structure within the corporation but subjects it to democratic control through what is, in effect, a legislative assembly organized by estates (classes of workers and the shareholders). A second, represented by Japanese quality circles, changes the very structure of authority by reallocating to the work group as a collectivity the right to exercise authority over its members. A third, represented by shared ownership rights to innovations and originating in the United States, reallocates to a person or small group both rights to control certain organizational resources and rights to benefit from an innovative idea. Still another change in the structure of rights, examined in Chapter 16, is that from forward policing, which involves the exercise of authority over actions, to backward policing, which involves the right to reject the product of the activity.

Authority is not eliminated by these organizational changes, but it is greatly modified in form and in some cases sharply reduced. Codetermination represents a change from a monolithic to a pluralistic authority structure for the organization as a whole. The quality circles transfer the lower-level authority in an organization from individuals to small groups. The third and fourth organizational changes involve replacing authority by an incentive structure within which individuals act autonomously.

These organizational changes can be seen as design of a corporate actor through constitutional allocations of rights. Viewing them in this way allows posing a general question: With given resources (including human resources) and in a given environment, what is the allocation of rights (an allocation that creates an organization's structure) that will be most efficient in accomplishing a given task? An answer to this question, a sociologically naive one by current standards, was once assumed to be the allocation constitutive of a bureaucratic authority structure. From the present perspective that assumption can be seen as a stage in the evolution of modes of organizing action away from absolute authority and toward forms in which authority plays a lesser role.

In the design of purposive social organizations in a post-bureaucratic world, certain principles, discussed earlier in the book, are important. One is that the central defect of a disjoint authority system is that the agent will act in his own interests rather than those of the principal. Another is that the central defect of a conjoint authority system is that the agent, again acting self-interestedly, will free ride on others' actions taken toward the common goal. A third is the principle that the right to reject the product of an agent's action (or to otherwise provide feedback based on that product) is often an alternative to authority, that is, to the right to direct that action.

As these principles and other points in Chapter 16 make evident, conceiving of the corporate actor as a structure based on an explicit allocation of rights provides a powerful tool for the design and construction of corporate actors. For example, once the properties required for the tasks of childrearing become clearer, the design of corporate actors to provide these essentials can be aided by this conceptual tool. The tool itself, however, requires further development; and this is a task for the new social science.

Nation-States versus Multinational Corporations, or Voice versus Exit

Another set of questions that arises at the macrosocial level concerns the nature of the corporate actors of which the worldwide social system is composed.

The nation-state is a corporate actor of intermediate form, exhibiting some properties of premodern corporate actors based on primordial bonds and some properties of modern purposive corporate actors. Many nation-states evolved from an ethnically homogeneous people or nation, and some remain ethnically homogeneous. Many have a single religion or culture. A shared religion or culture has been responsible for many acts of oppression or hostility toward religious or ethnic minorities, as well as for wars of aggression in the name of religion or nation (see Hirschman, 1977; Holmes, 1989).

Even when nations are not ethnically or religiously homogeneous, they retain many characteristics of premodern corporate actors. The elements of which they are composed are persons, not positions. They take responsibility for the person as a whole and claim authority over the person as a whole. Yet many are organized through an explicit constitution, which is conceived of as a social contract among independent individuals who are joining together with a common purpose. This constitutional basis of a nation-state is conceptually in opposition to the primordial basis (ethnic, religious, or cultural), and the nation-state is often in uneasy tension between these two bases.

Multinational corporations are prototypically modern purposive corporate actors. They are composed of positions as elements, and persons are merely occupants of positions and agents of the corporation. Corporate purposes are embodied in products, and the corporations can reasonably be described as acting to maximize some objective function (such as profit or size).

Nation-states and multinational corporations are in fundamental conflict, as two modes of organizing the global social system. As the economic division of labor becomes international, the conflict between these two modes intensifies. Multinational corporations seek to move persons and goods with as little regard for national borders as possible. Nations guard their borders, restricting entry and exit of persons and goods. Nations have a monopoly over legitimate coercive power within their borders, which they exercise through police and military forces. Multinational corporations control economic power, although without a comparable partitioning into exclusive domains.

The contrast between multinationals' interests and nations' interests is illustrated by a quotation from a brochure of a multinational hotel chain that has several hundred hotels throughout Europe: "As we see it, Europe is a single vast nation made up of a number of regions—Germany, Italy, France, Austria, Great Britain, the Netherlands, Belgium, Luxembourg, and Switzerland." If this quotation does not seem to call into question national autonomy, suppose the chain expanded throughout Asia and put out a brochure which read: "As we see it, Eurasia constitutes a single vast nation made up of a number of regions— Germany, Turkey, Italy, the Soviet Union, France, Iran, . . ."

The conflict between nation-states and multinational corporations is not an overt one. Unlike struggles between nation-states or competition between corporations, it is not a conflict between particular corporate bodies for dominance; it is a conflict for dominance of a *form*. The first question, then, is whether the two forms are truly in conflict, rather than being complementary. Can nation-states continue to exist as sovereign entities when their economic systems merge into a single international economy? Or, can a single international economy come into existence as long as nation-states are dominant?

The principal points on which the two forms are in conflict have to do with movements of persons and goods. Corporations move goods and induce people to move for economic gain. For example, corporations in Northern Europe in the 1950s and 1960s relocated people from the Mediterranean rim (Greeks, Yugoslavs, Italians, Spaniards, Turks, and Algerians) to work in their factories, changing irrevocably the population distributions within nation-states. But nation-states maintain barriers to such movements, designed to preserve economic inequalities across nations and to maintain territorial sovereignty. As rich nations, which are part of the international economic system, become richer and

poor nations largely outside that system remain poor, and as the system becomes more international, the pressures to break down barriers to immigration
increase. If these barriers disappear completely, will national soveignty continue
to exist? If not, what will happen to persons' self-identification? Will they become detached from the now mythical nation? Will they become detached from
place altogether? Will they become attached to the corporation? But how could
that happen, since persons are merely temporary occupants of positions within
the corporation?

All these questions arise from the fundamentally different bases of organization on which nation-states have developed and multinational corporations have
been constructed. Answers to these questions will require greater knowledge of
the way the conflict between nations and multinationals is resolved in the minds
and actions of persons—for it will be the choices of persons, individually and
collectively, that will give dominance to one or the other form.

These questions may be examined from a somewhat different perspective, that
is, the way individual preferences affect corporate action. Insofar as persons
exercise control over the actions of nations, they do so through voicing their
preferences via some democratic institution of collective decision. Elections of
legislatures and chief executive officers and rights of petition and referendum exemplify these institutions. But insofar as persons exercise control over
the actions of multinational corporations, they do so through exiting. (See
Hirschman, 1970, for an examination of voice and exit as two ways of controlling
organizations.) As customers, they shift their custom to another supplier; as
employees, they leave and go to work for another firm. There are some modifications of these pure types: Collective bargaining and industrial democracy
introduce voice into the corporation, and emigration from a nation-state can
affect its government's policies.

Thus the conflict between nation-states and multinational corporations as
modes of organizing the world corresponds roughly to a conflict between voice
and exit, or a conflict between democracy and the market as ways of translating
individual-level preferences into macro-level outcomes. In these terms the conflict is one between two systems of rights allocation. The two systems differ not
in their approximation to equality of rights, but in the way rights are partitioned.
Democratic voice assumes that rights of control over corporate actions are
collectively held, with each member having some fraction of those rights. Individual exit assumes that rights of control over individual actions (that is, the
exercise of choice) are individually held, with the organization affected slightly
and independently by each action.

It is obvious, of course, that not all corporate actions can be organized according to democracy (or collective control) or according to the market (individual
control). Yet the latitude for substitution between voice and exit is very great,
and one mode or the other can come to dominate—manifested in the dominance
of nation-states or multinationals.

The New Social Science

As primordial corporate actors wither away and the social capital on which societal functioning has depended is eroded, the purposive social structure that replaces them presents both opportunities and problems. The three preceding sections have sketched the kinds of changes occurring, in order to provide some idea of these opportunities and problems. Those sections should also have given a sense of the necessity for the development of social theory and the pursuit of social research if society is to realize the opportunities and avoid the problems.

This is not the way institutional change has ordinarily been approached. The implicit assumption on which decision making in democratic societies has proceeded is that legislatures composed of responsible persons from various walks of life can design institutions that will satisfactorily cope with social change. Such an assumption may be valid when the social changes constitute minor adjustments within a stable structural form. But when the structural form itself is changing, as is currently the case, the assumption is no longer valid.

The assumption is invalidated for several reasons. The issues discussed here illustrate three of these. First, the change in structural form, from primordial to purposive, means that purposive organization replaces those functions that can be bought and sold in a market but not those which cannot. In other words, purposive organization reorganizes the production and distribution of private goods in such a way that the spillover benefits (or positive externalities, or by-products) for other activities are lost. The most prominent example is childrearing as a by-product of the production and consumption activities of the family.

The loss of these nonmarketable functions as a result of the replacement of primordial by purposive organization is what I have called a loss of social capital; and in this chapter I have described some of the consequences of that loss. It is improbable that legislatures (or government agencies) will effectively address this loss of social capital because legislators know no organizations other than formal organizations, which buy services on a market and resell them. Legislatures cannot buy sustained attention and have no organizational means to bring it about. Knowledge about such matters derived from social theory would use organizational forms not merely as a way of organizing and targeting services, but as a way of creating social capital to fill in the interstices left by the market.

A second reason for the invalidity of the assumption that legislatures can design a replacement for the social structure that has been lost is illustrated by the shift from household economies to a single interdependent economy. Legislatures, concerned only with global viability of a nation's economy, have no conceptual tools for making the transition from household economies to a single interdependent economy in a way that preserves the virtues of independent viability. Some progress toward developing such tools has been made in organization theory as applied to the internal economy of business firms; but to extend and reshape the tools for use on the economies of nation-states is a task that requires dedicated development of social and economic theory.

A third reason why legislatures cannot create a structure to replace the functions of that which is vanishing lies in the fact that some social changes tend to make national legislatures irrelevant. Multinational corporations, as prototypical purposive corporate actors, are representatives of an organizational form that is in conflict with that of nation-states. If the multinationals win, national legislatures will have lost control of the decision making that affects the organizational structure of society. In that circumstance the very question of how national legislatures can best further the reconstruction of society becomes irrelevant. Then the question goes up one level: What is the means, in a worldwide social system, by which the movement from primordial to purposive social organization can be carried out without sacrificing all the virtues of the former?

These questions, posed by changes in the very basis of social organization, constitute a demand for a new social science. The demand increases as the transformation of social organization continues, a demand for knowledge and ideas that will help realize the opportunities created by this transformation and avoid the problems it generates. The new social science must consist of both applied research and theory. The theory, if it is to be of value for this task, must cross the traditional bounds of the disciplines within which knowledge is ordered, for the transformation of society has changed the linkages among these institutional areas. In so doing, it becomes the new social science, appropriate to the new social structure.

PART V

The Mathematics
of Social Action

« 25 »

The Linear System of Action

Parts I–III of this book present conceptual foundations for social theory grounded in purposive action. To go beyond qualitative deductions from the theory requires a mathematical foundation, however. Such a foundation is particularly important because of the two-level character of the theory. The transitions between micro and macro levels in the conceptual system, whether achieved through simple aggregation (as in aggregation of votes), through the structure of interactions implied in a perfectly competitive market, or through an even more complex structure of interactions (such as occurs in the emergence of a norm), require mathematical structures which are isomorphic with the structures by which the transitions take place in reality.

This part is devoted to the development of mathematical structures to reflect the varied ways in which the transitions take place in social systems. These structures are all based on the simple conceptual foundations outlined in Chapter 2: actors and events as the two basic elements of a system of action, linked together by the control of actors over resources and events and the interest of actors in resources and outcomes of events (that is, the consequences of events for them).

The theoretical foundations for the actions of purposive individuals in such a setting have been developed in economics, and I will use these foundations as a starting point. The first section of this chapter will therefore be similar to an introductory text in microeconomic theory. Only after setting out these foundations will the mathematical structure come to have a distinctive form, one which can be modified to accommodate the various kinds of macro-to-micro and micro-to-macro transitions that occur in social systems.

I will begin with the simplest case: events that have the properties of a private good. For such events (I will refer to them as goods throughout this chapter) persons with limited resources must choose the amounts of each that they will hold (or consume). For example, each person chooses among leisure activities, perhaps between playing squash and listening to chamber music. Persons' choices ordinarily represent a mix of various amounts of time and money spent on different activities.

The essential behavioral regularity that nearly all persons obey nearly all the time can be expressed in the following way: The more a person has of a good, while remaining at the same level of satisfaction (because of having less of something else), the less of any other good he will be willing to give up to get still more of the good. I will take this as an assumption about behavior. The adoption of this regularity as a fundamental premise of microeconomic theory constituted a major development in economics, known as the marginal revolution. (See Schumpeter, 1954, pp. 1053–1073, and Black, Coats, and Goodwin, 1973, for the history of this development.) It was introduced independently in the 1870s by an English, a French, and an Austrian economist: W. Stanley Jevons, Leon Walras, and Carl Menger.

For a person who likes playing squash and listening to chamber music, a statement of the regularity would be this: Suppose the person lives in a city where squash is widely available and concerts less available, and the result is that he plays squash more than he attends concerts. Then he moves to a city where squash is less available but concerts are more available, and the result is that he attends more concerts than before and plays less squash, but is equally satisfied. He is asked in both circumstances how much squash he would be willing to give up in order to attend a concert. According to the behavioral regularity, he would give up more squash in the first city (city A), where he was playing a lot of squash and attending few concerts, than in the second (city B), where he was playing only a little and attending many. The amount of squash he would be willing to give up when he is at (A_s, A_c) to get one unit more of music and remain at the same level of satisfaction is more than he would give up when he is at (B_s, B_c). This is equivalent to the statement that the curve XX' (called an indifference curve in economics because the person is indifferent among all points on the curve) is convex to the origin as shown in Figure 25.1.

In classical economic theory this behavioral regularity was described as declining marginal utility. In neoclassical economics, however, the phrase "declining marginal rate of substitutability" or the term "convexity" has been used to indicate that this behavioral regularity can be expressed without assuming that the person in question has something called utility having a particular metric.[1] It nevertheless remains most convenient to describe this behavioral regularity as resulting from declining marginal utility of the good for the person.

In this book, when dealing with events that have the properties of a divisible good, I assume that this behavioral regularity holds. The kind of behavior that does not conform to this regularity is referred to by a special term, addictive

---

1. See Simpson (1975) for further discussion of the standard assumptions of economists about consumer preferences. Simpson expresses the declining marginal rate of substitutability in a straightforward way: " . . . the more one has of any one commodity, the utility index (i.e., satisfaction level) remaining constant, the lower will be the rate of substitution of any other commodity for it" (p. 3). Some economists such as Lancaster (1966) and Weiszacker (1971) have been willing to go beyond qualitative regularity and impose a specific functional form on the utility function. Others, such as Becker (1976), have made assumptions about the arguments of utility functions (for example, assumptions leading to an interdependence between the utilities of two persons who are friends).

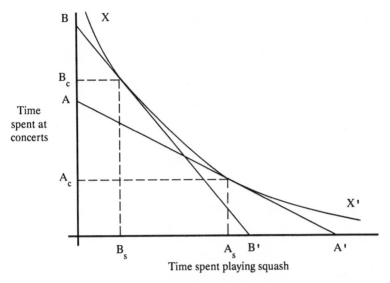

Figure 25.1 Combinations of time spent on two activities (playing squash and going to concerts) that give equal satisfaction in two cities (A and B).

behavior. This means essentially that the more a person has of a certain good, the greater his desire to have still more of it. Although addictive behavior can be characteristic of a person within a certain range of consumption of a good, it must give way to its opposite, declining marginal utility, at the extreme.[2]

In choosing the amounts of two or more goods to hold, a rational individual with resource constraints will act in the way described in the above example. The resource that is constrained in the example is leisure time, and the individual allots it between going to concerts and playing squash, depending on the satisfaction that each holds for him (as shown by the indifference curve XX') and the costs (in time and effort for this case) of each (as shown by the line AA' for city A and the line BB' for city B).[3] Such choices can be regarded as exchanges or trade-offs made by the individual with respect to a fixed environment. A social exchange, however, involves one or more other persons, like himself but perhaps having different tastes and beginning with different resources. The simplest

2. See Becker and Murphy (1988) for an examination of addictive behavior in the context of rational choice.

3. It need not be true, of course, that the costs of the two activities change in such a way as to leave the individual exactly as satisfied as before. It may well be that, for example, squash became less available while concerts became no more available. In that case the person would spend an increased fraction of his leisure time at concerts but would end up with lower satisfaction. Or both activities might become more available but to differing degrees, producing a resource constraint that is everywhere above AA' but with a different slope. Then he would end up with a higher level of satisfaction.

such situation is exchange between two persons outside the context of a market. When the exchange involves divisible goods that are not sold in a market, such as personal favors, this is the setting in which much social exchange takes place.

Two-Person Exchange System with Divisible Goods

Consider two boys, Tom and John, each interested in collecting baseball and football trading cards of the kind that children sometimes collect and trade. Suppose, for convenience, that there are 100 football cards and 100 baseball cards in the system. Tom has had access primarily to football cards and has 95 of them, along with 4 baseball cards, or 99 cards altogether. John has had greater access to baseball cards and has only 5 football cards and 96 baseball cards, or 101 cards altogether. Both Tom and John have preferences concerning baseball and football cards (like the individual's preferences concerning squash and concerts in the earlier example). Indifference curves representing the relative numbers of each kind of card that would give them equal levels of satisfaction are shown in Figure 25.2. Tom has a much greater interest in football cards (which constitute his primary holding), as shown by the asymmetry of the indifference curves in Figure 25.2(a). John, however, has equal interests in football and baseball cards, as shown by the symmetry of the indifference curves in Figure 25.2(b). The initial resources of Tom and John are shown as point X, at (95, 4) and at (5, 96); also shown are indifference curves passing through these points representing initial resources, as well as other curves showing higher levels of satisfaction.

A general way of representing this situation, which exhibits several aspects of

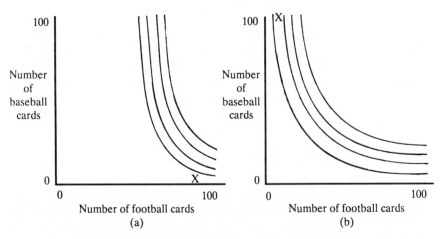

Figure 25.2 Indifference curves for football and baseball cards for (a) Tom and (b) John.

a two-actor exchange system, was developed by Edgeworth (1881), whose graphical representation has come to be called the Edgeworth box. The situations of Tom and John can be represented by an Edgeworth box, as shown in Figure 25.3. The graph for Tom's situation has the same orientation as in Figure 25.2(a), but that for John's is upended, with the zero point in the upper right-hand corner of the box. The upper and right-hand axes represent John's holdings; his holdings of football cards increase from right to left along the upper axis, and his holdings of baseball cards increase from top to bottom along the right-hand axis.

In Figure 25.3 the horizontal axes represent football cards, and the vertical axes baseball cards. The lower left-hand corner represents zero quantities of both for Tom, and the upper right-hand corner represents zero quantities of both for John. The total number of football cards in the sysem is 100, and before exchange Tom has 95 and John has 5. The total number of baseball cards is 100, and before exchange Tom has 4 and John has 96. The initial position of the two

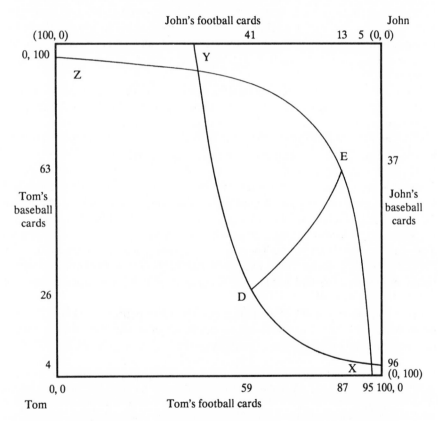

Figure 25.3 Edgeworth box and contract curve for exchange in a bilateral monopoly.

actors is characterized by point X in the diagram. The curve XY, an indifference curve for Tom, gives the locus of points that are equally satisfying to Tom as the beginning point X; and the curve XZ, an indifference curve for John, gives the locus of points that are equally satisfying to John as X. Thus the interior between the two curves contains all points at which the actors are better off than at the initial point X.

Some of these points are, however, dominated by others. That is, for some points one or more other points are just as good for one actor and better for the other. Thus one actor can be made better off without making the other worse off—or both can be made better off. There is one line, represented by DE in the diagram, that consists of the undominated points as defined above. That is, it is not possible to move from one point on the line DE to another point on the line without making one actor worse off. A move toward E makes John worse off, and a move toward D makes Tom worse off. This line thus consists of points that are Pareto-optimal and is called the contract curve.[4]

The principal demonstration for which the Edgeworth box is ordinarily used is to show that there is not a single price at which two such actors will exchange. Instead there is a range of exchange rates, represented by the curve DE. In the absence of further knowledge about the interaction, all that can be said about the final positions of the two actors is that they will be represented by a point somewhere on this line.

There are, however, some interesting conclusions that can be drawn from such systems. In Figure 25.3 the area enclosed by the indifference curves is skewed in the direction favoring Tom. The contract curve DE, as drawn, shows that the number of football cards he can expect to end up with ranges from 59 to 87 and the number of baseball cards he can expect to end up with ranges from 26 to 63. John can expect to fare worse. He will end up with the complement of Tom's position, that is, with somewhere between 13 and 41 football cards and somewhere between 37 and 74 baseball cards—despite the fact that he began with a slightly higher number of cards than Tom did. This, of course, is a consequence of John's having a greater interest in what Tom holds initially than Tom has in what John holds. There is a wide range of possible exchanges, as indicated by the contract curve DE, but for all of this range Tom ends up with a larger number of football cards, and for a part of it with a larger number of baseball cards as well.

In a two-person system of exchange outside a competitive market, as in this example, the outcomes are bounded by the levels of satisfaction of both parties on entering the exchange (the indifference curves of Figure 25.3), and they

---

4. The discussion that defines the contract curve implies that this curve is the locus of points enclosed by XY and XZ at which the indifference curves for the one actor and those for the other are tangent. Thus any move off a point of tangency is a move to an indifference curve at lower satisfaction for at least one of the actors, and any point that is not a point of tangency is below indifference curves for both actors that are tangent elsewhere (that is, somewhere on the line DE).

should fall somewhere on the contract curve where no further mutually profitable exchanges can be made. But that curve may represent a wide range of possible outcomes, as illustrated by *DE* in Figure 25.3. The particular position on that curve of the actual outcome is ordinarily said to be determined by the bargaining abilities of the two actors.

It is useful to view this two-person exchange system as a system of action, albeit a small one, and to ask about the macro-level properties and the transitions between micro and macro levels. The most clear-cut macro-level property emerging in this system is the exchange rate at which football and baseball cards will be traded. That rate, for the curves in Figure 25.3, could range from 59 baseball cards for 8 football cards at point *D* (the most favorable exchange rate for Tom) to 22 baseball cards for 45 football cards at point *E* (the most favorable exchange rate for John). A second emergent macro-level property is distributional: the final distributions of football and baseball cards for Tom and John.

The initial properties at the macro-level are of two sorts: institutional rules or norms, and distributional properties. The institutional rules or norms govern how exchanges take place. They may be minimal, such as a norm that private holdings are to be respected; or they may be more inclusive, for example, involving a specified rate of exchange. In large systems of exchange the institutional rules may be elaborate, involving specifications of how exchange rates are to be arrived at (for example, whether recontracting is allowable and, if so, how much time is allowed for it), how transactions are to be carried out (whether a central bank exists as a clearinghouse for bids and offers), whether there is a unit of account, whether some actor is established to balance off credits and debits or one good is used as a medium of exchange, and so forth.[5] In larger systems of exchange communication structures may also be macro-level properties, since the implicit assumption of full communication between actors often does not hold for such systems.

The initial distributional properties for the example are, of course, the initial distribution of trading cards and the initial distribution of preferences. These can equally well be described as properties of the two individuals, but that is true for distributions in general: The elements are properties of individuals, and the vector itself is a property of the system.

The macro-to-micro transition in this example is implicit because all initial macro-level properties are either institutional or distributional. Specifying the micro-to-macro transition, giving the exchange rate and equilibrium distribution, would require detailed knowledge of the transactions, for microeconomic theory is nonspecific about the outcomes, predicting only that they lie within a wide

5. See Cook (1982) for experiments in which different restrictions are placed on structures of communication in exchange systems. See Chapter 27 for models in which barriers to exchange are introduced. There is some literature in economics on these questions; see, for example, Hirshleifer (1978). There has also begun to be a literature in experimental economics, in which institutions of an experimental market are introduced and market outcomes examined; see Plott and Smith (1978) and Smith (1982).

range, that is, the whole length of the contract curve. More information about personalities or bargaining strategies, together with theory which would make use of such information, would be necessary to specify the micro-to-macro transition more precisely.

When there are additional actors, of course the situation changes. If there were two other boys with football cards, for example, they would be in competition with one another to exchange with John. The matter would be considerably more complex, and somewhat stronger statements could be made about the set of equilibrium outcomes. The matter becomes less complex again when there are larger numbers of competitors on both sides, and a full-fledged market for exchange comes into existence. This will become evident in a later section.

Restrictions on the Utility Function

The system of action described in the preceding section followed fully the assumptions of standard microeconomic theory. I will now part company with that theory by imposing further restrictions on the utility function. In the preceding section the only restriction specified was that of declining marginal utility. The utility can be specified algebraically as a function of the amount of each of m goods held:

$$U_i = U_i(c_{i1}, \ldots, c_{im})$$

where $U_i \equiv$ utility of individual i

$c_{ij} \equiv$ amount of good j held by individual i

The assumption that utility increases as the amount of the good held increases implies a restriction on the first derivative of U_i with respect to c_{ij}:

$$\frac{\partial U_i}{\partial c_{ij}} > 0, \quad j = 1, \ldots, m$$

The assumption of declining marginal utility implies a restriction on the second derivative of U_i with respect to c_{ij}:

$$\frac{\partial^2 U_i}{\partial c_{ij}^2} < 0, \quad j = 1, \ldots, m$$

The above restrictions are standard in microeconomic theory. In the theory presented here a specific utility function satisfying them will be assumed:

$$U_i = c_{i1}^{x_{1i}} c_{i2}^{x_{2i}} \cdots c_{im}^{x_{mi}} \tag{25.1}$$

where x_{ji} are parameters which express the contribution that good j makes toward the utility of individual i.

There are two constraints on x_{ji}:

$$x_{ji} \geq 0, \quad j = 1, \ldots, m \tag{25.2}$$

$$\sum_j x_{ji} = 1$$

The constraint $x_{ji} \geq 0$ implies that each good contributes positively, if at all, to individual i's utility. If good j makes no contribution to i's utility, then $x_{ji} = 0$. That $0 \leq x_{ji} \leq 1$ for all j implies declining marginal utility (except for the trivial case in which x_{ji} is equal to 1 for one good and 0 for all others).

This form of the utility function is known in economics as the Cobb-Douglas utility function. It is an analogue of the Cobb-Douglas production function, $P = K^\alpha L^\beta$, where K is capital, L is labor, and $\alpha + \beta = 1$. Economists have in general not assumed specific utility functions, although there are exceptions. Clements (1987) reviews several of these, dealing most fully with the Klein-Rubin (1948) specification, which is a slight generalization of the Cobb-Douglas function. In the Klein-Rubin function, c_{ij} in eq. 25.1 is replaced by $c_{ij} - b_j$, where b_j is the subsistence level of good j.

For the trading-card example the indifference curves were generated by values of x_{ji} as follows:

	Football cards	Baseball cards
Tom	.8	.2
John	.5	.5

The values for John (.5 and .5) reflect his equal interest in the two types of cards, giving rise to the symmetric indifference curves shown in Figures 25.2(b) and 25.3. The values for Tom (.8 and .2) reflect his greater interest in football cards, as indicated by the asymmetric indifference curves in Figures 25.2(a) and 25.3.

I impose the specifications given in eqs. 25.1 and 25.2 for two reasons:

1. To make possible the use of an algebraic model of a system of action which establishes a correspondence between the micro and macro levels
2. To facilitate the use of the model with quantitative empirical data (carried out in later chapters)

The specifications have a further value as well: The quantities c_{ij} correspond directly to control, as used in Parts I–IV of the book, and the quantities x_{ji} correspond directly to interest, as used there. In Chapter 2, I specified that the essential elements of the theory of this book are actors and events linked by interest and control. In this chapter the events are divisible private goods (football and baseball cards in the example), the actors are individual persons (Tom and John), and the two relations that link actors and events are given by c_{ij}, actors' control of each good, and x_{ji}, their interest in each good.

The fixing of a specific form for the utility function represents a compromise different from the one that has been made in economics. Economists have generally sacrificed the ability to characterize the general equilibrium for systems of many goods in order to prove results that assumed no restrictions on the utility function beyond the signs on the first and second derivatives. The theory of this book requires calculation of the general equilibrium for more than two goods (or events, in later chapters) and more than two types of actors. In order to do this I am sacrificing generality of results beyond the Cobb-Douglas utility function.

Calculation of Indifference Curves

Calculation of the indifference curves shown in Figure 25.2 can be carried out by use of eq. 25.1, specified for two goods, by first taking logarithms:

$$\ln U_i = x_{1i}(\ln c_{i1}) + x_{2i}(\ln c_{i2}) \tag{25.3}$$

The indifference curve consisting of all points that give Tom satisfaction equal to that at the starting point (for Tom 95 football cards and 4 baseball cards, or .95 and .04 of the total quantity of each, which is 100) is calculated by first substituting the starting values in the right-hand side of eq. 25.3 to find his satisfaction level (ln U_i) for this combination of goods. Then other values of c_{11} and c_{12} are found which provide the same satisfaction level, for values of c_{11} from 0 to 1.

$$.8(\ln .95) + .2(\ln .04) = -.685 \tag{25.3'}$$

$$.8(\ln c_{11}) + .2(\ln c_{12}) = -.685$$

Values of c_{11} and c_{12} which satisfy eq. 25.3' are shown in Figure 25.2(a) as the curve which contains the starting point X, (95, 4). Similar calculations for levels of satisfaction higher than $-.685$ give the other indifference curves in Figure 25.2(a), and carrying out the same calculations for John gives the indifference curves shown in Figure 25.2(b). For John the starting point gives a lower level of satisfaction, -1.518, because, unlike Tom, he does not have greater interest in the cards he already holds.

If Tom and John are confronted, not with each other, but with a market having a fixed exchange rate, as shown by the straight lines AA' and BB' in Figure 25.1, it is possible to determine the combination of cards each will end up with, as well as the level of satisfaction provided by this combination. For example, if $1:1$ is the fixed exchange rate, then $c_{12} = .99 - c_{11}$ is the market possibility line passing through Tom's initial endowment of cards.[6] The indifference curve which is tangent to this line (representing the highest satisfaction Tom can get by exchanging cards in this market) is found by taking the first derivative with respect to c_{11} of the general equation for Tom's indifference curve, $K = .8(\ln c_{11}) + .2(\ln c_{12})$. The result is this equation:[7]

$$0 = \frac{.8}{c_{11}} + \frac{.2}{c_{12}} \frac{dc_{12}}{dc_{11}}$$

Since the market exchange rate (the slope of the market possibility line), under the assumption of 1-for-1 exchange, is $dc_{12}/dc_{11} = -1$, the above equation becomes

$$0 = \frac{.8}{c_{11}} - \frac{.2}{c_{12}} \qquad \text{or} \qquad c_{11} = 4c_{12}$$

6. In general, the equation for the market possibility line is $c_{12} = a - bc_{11}$, where b is the exchange rate of good 2 for good 1.

7. The general equation is $dc_{12}/dc_{11} = x_{11}c_{12}/x_{21}c_{11}$

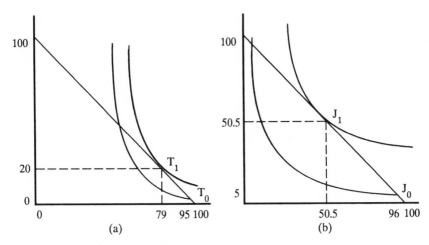

Figure 25.4 Positions of (a) Tom and (b) John, before and after exchange.

Substituting $.99 - c_{11}$ for c_{12} allows solving for c_{11} at the point of tangency, giving .79. Then c_{12} is found to be .20, and the satisfaction level has increased from $-.68$ to $-.51$. (Only the relative values of satisfaction are meaningful; the scale on c_{ij} determines the scale on satisfaction.)

Thus, if Tom is confronted with this market, he will trade in 15 of his football cards for baseball cards, ending up with 79 football cards and 20 baseball cards rather than the 95 and 4 with which he began. John, confronting the same market, will also exchange some of his baseball cards for football cards. A calculation similar to that carried out above would show that John will end up with equal numbers of the two types of cards, 50.5 and 50.5 (rounded off to 50 and 51). Note that in this market, in which the exchange rate is $1:1$, the ratio of the numbers of cards of each type that each boy ends up with is simply given by the ratio of his interests: $.8:.2$ for Tom and $.5:.5$ for John. The movements for Tom are shown in Figure 25.4(a) and those for John in Figure 25.4(b). The initial points are T_0 and J_0, and the positions after exchanges in the market are T_1 and J_1.

Bilateral Exchange: Calculating the Contract Curve

When Tom and John are not separately exchanging in a market in which exchange rates are fixed, the situation is that shown in Figure 25.3, which has been drawn to conform to the utility functions of Tom and John. The equation for the contract curve can be found by an extension of the means used in the preceding section. Since the contract curve is the locus of points of tangency of the two sets of indifference curves, and since John's holdings are the complements of Tom's ($c_{21} = 1 - c_{11}$ and $c_{22} = 1 - c_{12}$), the equation for the contract curve is found simply by setting the equations for the slopes of the two sets of indifference curves equal to each other:

Tom: $\dfrac{dc_{12}}{dc_{11}} = -\dfrac{.8c_{12}}{.2c_{11}} = -\dfrac{4c_{12}}{c_{11}}$

John: $\dfrac{dc_{22}}{dc_{21}} = -\dfrac{.5c_{22}}{.5c_{21}} = -\dfrac{1 - c_{12}}{1 - c_{11}}$

When the right-hand sides are set equal to each other, this equation for the contract curve results:

$$c_{11}c_{22} - 4c_{12}c_{21} = 0$$

The general equation is

$$x_{12}x_{21}c_{11}c_{22} - x_{11}x_{22}c_{12}c_{21} = 0$$

This equation allows drawing a contract curve such as that shown in Figure 25.3. The equation says nothing, however, about where the transactions between Tom and John will end, beyond specifying that they will end somewhere on the contract curve between the two indifference curves representing Tom's and John's initial endowments, as shown in the figure. It may be that some external factors, such as personalities, relative bargaining abilities, or a Schelling point will dictate how the exchanges go within the constraints.[8] Among the latter, two possibilities appear reasonable: 1 for 1, and 1 for 2. The second may be more likely because of Tom's not being very interested in baseball cards.[9]

It is useful to see just what the equilibrium would be if a particular exchange rate were to prevail, for example, 1 : 1. What number of each kind of card would each boy end up with? Note that the outcome will be in general different, and less satisfactory to one of the two, than if he were confronting a market with this exchange rate. This is because the transactions will end at the point at which the exchange rate is just tangent to the indifference curve of one of the two boys. Beyond that, he would have no more interest in a trade, although the other might well have.

There is no point on the contract curve of Figure 25.3 at which the common slopes of the indifference curves are -1, corresponding to an exchange rate of 1 : 1. What might occur, if such an exchange rate were in effect, is that cards would be traded until Tom was no longer interested in further exchange at that rate, which, as Figure 25.4 shows, would be after they had traded 16 cards, giving Tom a mix of 79 football cards and 20 baseball cards and John a mix of 21

8. A Schelling point is a point which presents itself as a prominent candidate. In this case a 1 : 1 ratio would be a Schelling point, as would a 1 : 2 ratio, but 1 : 1.07 would not.

9. Exchanges might begin at 1 for 1, and then, as the positions move toward the contract curve, Tom's reluctance will induce John to offer a better exchange rate, such as 2 for 1. Closer to the contract curve, however, John becomes less willing to offer a rate favorable to football cards because at that point he will no longer be overstocked with baseball cards.

and 80. At that point the transactions would end unless they could agree on a new exchange rate, such as $1:2$. If they could, they would continue to trade cards at that rate until they reached the contract curve, or one of them was no longer interested in exchanging at that rate. In the example they would reach the contract curve (or as close as they could approach with integral numbers of cards). The location on the contract curve where they would end up, beginning at $c_{11} = 79$ and $c_{12} = 20$ (after exchange of 16 cards at a $1:1$ rate), is $c_{11} = .704$ and $c_{12} = .372$, or, as the closest that exchange would bring them, 71 football cards and 36 baseball cards for Tom. That is, they would have exchanged 8 more football cards for 16 baseball cards. At this point trade would end. This is not, of course, the point at which they would have ended up if they had begun trading at a $1:2$ rate. The point they would reach on the contract curve in that case would be $c_{11} = .753$ and $c_{12} = .433$ (or 76 and 42, integers reachable by exchange). Thus Tom would end up with 76 football cards and 42 baseball cards, and John with 24 football cards and 58 baseball cards. Figure 25.5 shows both of these paths. The

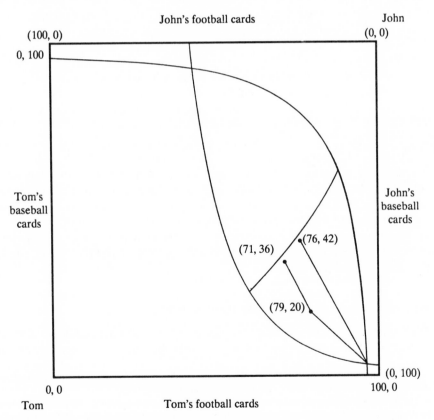

Figure 25.5 Two equilibrium points for exchange in a bilateral monopoly.

one path represents exchanges at $1:1$ to the point (79, 20) and then at $1:2$ to (71, 36). The other represents exchanges at $1:2$ to (76, 42).

There are, of course, many other possible paths that lead to some point on the contract curve, and there is nothing in the theory of exchange between two rational actors that allows prediction of which of these paths will be taken or which point will be the equilibrium point.

There is another issue related to the empirical use (rather than mere demonstration from the theory as I have done) of this theoretical apparatus. Even if the utility functions are assumed to take the form given in eq. 25.1, the values of the parameters x_{ji} are ordinarily not directly observed. Here I have assumed that football cards are worth four times as much as baseball cards to Tom ($x_{11} = .8$, $x_{21} = .2$), and the two kinds of cards are equally valuable to John ($x_{12} = .5$, $x_{22} = .5$). But without a series of experiments to see what exchanges these two actors would make or else believable statements from them about their relative interests in the two kinds of cards if they had equal numbers of each, these interests are not observable. Observation of a number of occasions of exchange between these two boys, or a number of occasions of exchange of each with other partners, or their transactions in a market with a fixed exchange rate, would make it possible to infer interests from the observed behavior.[10]

Thus, except for circumstances with unusual data, the analysis to this point is not directly useful empirically; its principal use is as a demonstration of how a minimal system of action with divisible goods will function. It is probably the case, however, that some use could be made of verbal expressions of interest, more than would ordinarily be trusted by a behaviorally oriented social scientist. For example, a question like this might be asked of Tom and John: If you had equal numbers of cards of each type, what rate of exchange would make you indifferent with respect to giving up one kind of card or the other? It is not unreasonable to expect that Tom would say something like 1 for 4 and John something like 1 for 1. The question could even be posed so that there was no necessity to imagine a change of position: What rate of exchange of football cards for baseball cards would leave you in a position equivalent to the one you are now in?[11] Some calculations, starting with the known quantities of each type of card held by each boy and using the responses to this question, could be done to estimate the values of x_{ji}.

Beyond a Two-Person System of Action

The contract curve, shown as DE in Figure 25.3, has another technical name. It is the core of the two-person exchange system. In general, the core consists of

10. In a market exchange only one observation would be necessary, under the assumption that eq. 25.1 describes the utility function, to estimate the interests.

11. In situations where a discrete choice is made under risky conditions, the posing of this kind of question has been assumed in order to measure utility under risk. See von Neumann and Morgenstern (1948); see Coleman (1964, Chapter 2) for applications within sociology.

all those allocations (that is, divisions of control among the different actors) which are unblocked. An allocation is blocked if there is another allocation such that each of a set of actors within the system who together have it in their power to bring about that other allocation finds it at least as good as the first; that is, in this case the first allocation is blocked by the second.

The core shrinks very rapidly as other competitors enter the exchange system. For example, if two more actors were added to the two-person system of the example, one similar to Tom and the other similar to John, the core would shrink at both ends to less than half the length of the curve *DE*. As more competitors are added, rapid shrinkage continues to occur, so with a relatively small number of actors (in a system with two goods) the core is a very small region.

What happens as the number of actors increases in a more general system, one with a number of goods? There is a particular point called the competitive equilibrium; Debreu and Scarf (1963) proved that, under quite general conditions, the core shrinks to this single point as the number of actors approaches infinity.

In most of the remainder of Part V, I will deal with only this single allocation, the competitive equilibrium. The justification for this restriction is that the core does shrink rapidly as the number of actors increases. Also, this point can be regarded as a kind of expected value around which, even in a system with a small number of actors, the equilibrium can be expected to be found. The virtue of restricting attention to the competitive equilibrium lies in the fact that calculation of the space occupied by the core is not possible except for the simplest systems, but calculation of the competitive equilibrium for a system in which actors have utility functions as given by eq. 25.1 is quite simple.

The Competitive Equilibrium and the Linear System of Action

The preceding sections lead to a consideration of a general system of action with divisible private goods or resources, which is the system that will be the basis for all subsequent models in succeeding chapters. In this section I will derive the competitive equilibrium for such a system with n types of actors and m goods.[12]

The starting point involves actors, goods, control, and interest:

$c_{ij} \equiv$ control of actor i over good j, where $i = 1, \ldots, n$ and $j = 1, \ldots, m$

c_{ij} is scaled arbitrarily so that control over each good sums to 1.0:

$$\sum_{i=1}^{n} c_{ij} = 1.0 \qquad (25.4)$$

$x_{ji} \equiv$ interest of actor i in good j, where $j = 1, \ldots, m$ and $i = 1, \ldots, n$

---

12. The derivation of the competitive equilibrium for the more general utility function is given in several expositions that use relatively simple mathematics. See Malinvaud (1972).

x_{ji} is scaled arbitrarily so that the interest of actor i sums to 1.0:

$$\sum_{j=1}^{m} x_{ji} = 1.0 \tag{25.5}$$

In matrix notation

$$\mathbf{C} = \|c_{ij}\| \quad \text{(an } n \times m \text{ matrix)}$$

$$\mathbf{X} = \|x_{ji}\| \quad \text{(an } m \times n \text{ matrix)}$$

Because a competitive equilibrium is to be calculated, it is useful to think of a very large number of actors of each of the types, so that the assumptions of a competitive market are realized. Then c_{ij} is the sum of the control of all actors of type i over good j.

In a competitive equilibrium each good has a single price, the rate at which it is exchanged in all transactions. Thus a new (macro-level) concept is introduced, which I will call the value of the good.

$v_j \equiv$ value of good j in the system, or the rate at which it is exchanged

$$\mathbf{v} = \|v_j\| \quad \text{(an } m \times 1 \text{ vector)}$$

The total value of actor i's resources is the sum of the values of each of the goods that he holds:

$$r_i = \sum c_{ij} v_j \tag{25.6}$$

Each actor is maximizing his utility subject to his resource constraint:

$$\max U(c_{i1}, \ldots, c_{im}) \text{ subject to } r_i = \sum_{j=1}^{m} c_{ij} v_j$$

The maximization can be carried out using Lagrange multipliers. The Lagrangian function is

$$L = \prod_{j=1}^{m} c_{ij}^{x_{ji}} + \lambda(r_i - \sum_{j=1}^{m} c_{ij} v_j) \tag{25.7}$$

The maximum is formed by setting the partial derivatives of L with respect to λ and each of the c_{ij} equal to zero, and then solving the system of $m + 1$ equations. The equations have the following form:

$$\frac{x_{ji}}{c_{ij}^*} U_i - \lambda v_j = 0, \quad j = 1, \ldots, m$$

$$r_i - \sum c_{ij}^* v_j = 0$$

where the asterisk on c_{ij} indicates that these are equilibrium values of c_{ij}. Dividing the jth equation by v_j and subtracting the equation for $j = m$ from the first

$m - 1$ equations gives, for the first $m - 1$ equations,

$$\frac{x_{ji}}{c_{ij}^* v_j} U_i - \frac{x_{mi}}{c_{im}^* v_m} U_i = 0 \tag{25.8}$$

Equation 25.8 implies that the ratio of the marginal utilities, $(x_{ji}/c_{ij})U_i$, equals the ratio of the values. The ratio of the values is the slope of the market possibility line (often called the budget line), and the ratio of the marginal utilities equals the marginal rate of substitution, so at the maximum the marginal rate of substitution equals the slope of the market possibility line.

The amount of resource j held at equilibrium by actor i when all actors are maximizing utility can be found by dividing eq. 25.8 by U_i and writing the result in this form:

$$\frac{x_{ji}}{c_{ij}^* v_j} = \frac{x_{mi}}{c_{im}^* v_m}$$

Since this equation holds for all $j = 1, \ldots, m - 1$, it can be written as

$$\frac{x_{ji}}{c_{ij}^* v_j} = \frac{x_{ki}}{c_{ik}^* v_k} \tag{25.9}$$

Multiplying through by the denominators and summing over j gives

$$c_{ik}^* v_k \sum_{j=1}^{m} x_{ji} = x_{ki} \sum_{j=1}^{m} c_{ij}^* v_j$$

But $\sum_{j=1}^{m} x_{ji} = 1.0$ by eq. 25.5, and $\sum_{j=1}^{m} c_{ij}^* v_j = r_i$ by eq. 25.6, so the above becomes

$$c_{ik}^* v_k = x_{ki} r_i \tag{25.10}$$

Equation 25.10 defines the quantity of c_{ik} held at competitive equilibrium, in terms of the power of actor i, the value of good k, and the interest of actor i in good k.

Equation 25.10 can be written in this form:

$$c_{ik}^* = \frac{x_{ki} r_i}{v_k} \tag{25.11}$$

Defining two diagonal matrices, $\mathbf{D}_r$, an $n \times n$ diagonal matrix with diagonal elements r_i, and $\mathbf{D}_v$, an $m \times m$ diagonal matrix with diagonal elements v_j, allows eq. 25.11 to be written in matrix form as

$$\mathbf{C}^* = \mathbf{D}_r \mathbf{X}' \mathbf{D}_v^{-1} \tag{25.11*}$$

Equation 25.11 gives the distribution of goods at the competitive equilibrium among the actors of each type. In the derivation the concept of the value of a good, v_k, was introduced, as was the concept of the power of an actor, as the sum of the value of all goods held by the actor (eq. 25.6). With eq. 25.11 the value can be expressed as a function of interests of actors and their wealth or power. Multiplying both sides of eq. 25.11 by v_k and summing over i gives (since $\sum_{i=1}^{n} c_{ik}^* = 1.0$)

$$v_k = \sum_{i=1}^{n} x_{ki} r_i \qquad (25.12)$$

The total amount of value in the system, whether expressed as the sum of powers of all actors or the sum of values of all goods, is arbitrary and is simply the unit in which accounting is done. For simplicity I will fix this total value as 1.0, thereby arbitrarily introducing a scale of value,

$$\sum_{i=1}^{n} r_i = \sum_{j=1}^{m} v_j = 1.0 \qquad (25.13)$$

If this model is used with data on initial distributions of control and of interest, the competitive equilibrium may be found after substituting the right-hand side of eq. 25.6 for r_i in eq. 25.12:

$$v_k = \sum_{i=1}^{n} x_{ki} \sum_{j=1}^{m} c_{ij} v_j \qquad (25.14)$$

or

$$\mathbf{v} = \mathbf{XCv} \qquad (25.14^*)$$

For a system with m goods there are $m - 1$ independent equations of the form of eq. 25.14. Since $\mathbf{X}$ and $\mathbf{C}$ are assumed to be known, these equations may be solved for the m quantities v_k, using eq. 25.14. Then eq. 25.6 can be used, with the known v_k, to find the power of actors, r_i. Finally, eq. 25.11 is used to find the distribution of control at equilibrium, c_{ik}^*, for all i and k.

Some sense of the way these equations are used to arrive at the competitive equilibrium may be gained by applying them to the trading-card example. Using interests and initial control gives one independent equation of the form of eq. 25.14:

$$v_1 = .8(.95v_1) + .8[.04(1 - v_1)] + .5(.05v_1) + .5[.96(1 - v_1)] = .704$$

$$r_1 = .95(.704) + .04(1 - .704) = .681$$

$$c_{11}^* = \frac{.8(.681)}{.704} = .773$$

$$c_{12}^* = \frac{.2(.681)}{1 - .704} = .461$$

Thus at the competitive equilibrium Tom would have 77 football cards and 46 baseball cards, having given up only 18 of his football cards to get 42 of John's baseball cards, an exchange rate of 7 baseball cards for 3 football cards. It could be said that in this system the football cards have a value of .7 (compared

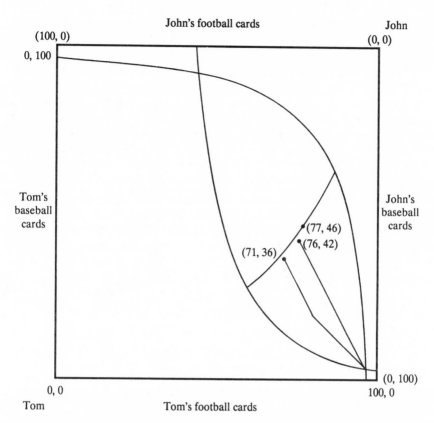

Figure 25.6   Three equilibrium points, including the competitive equilibrium, for exchange in a bilateral monopoly.

to .3 for the baseball cards) and Tom's power is .68 (compared to John's power of .32). The competitive equilibrium can be shown as an additional point on the contract curve of Figure 25.5. This point is shown in Figure 25.6.

The Macro-to-Micro-to-Macro Transitions in the Linear System of Action

Equations 25.6, 25.11, and 25.12 describe the linear system of action, and the trading-card example illustrates its application.[13] The linear system of action for the perfectly competitive market makes it especially clear how the macro-to-micro transition and the micro-to-macro transition are assumed to be made. The initial properties at the macro level are the distribution over actors of control of

---

13. Clements (1987, p. 10) shows how the analogous system using the Klein-Rubin utility function can be described as a linear expenditure system, a term by which it has been known in economics.

goods and the distribution over goods of interests of actors, as well as certain assumptions about how the exchanges will take place and about social and communication structures.

In much of the economic literature on the perfectly competitive market, the institutional and social-structural assumptions remain implicit. The general idea contained in these assumptions is that each actor can talk to all others and compare or make offers. But however the exchanges occur, it is assumed that no firm agreements are reached until an equilibrium price is achieved for all goods, when no further agreements can be made which are acceptable to both parties. Then all exchanges take place at this equilibrium price. Since there are no exchanges at other than the equilibrium price, the value of what each actor controls at equilibrium is the same as the value of what he controlled at the beginning.

The elegance, power, and importance of this intellectual achievement in characterizing the general equilibrium of a perfectly competitive market should not be underestimated. It constitutes an idealization of a set of processes for micro-to-macro transitions that are found not only in economic markets but in many social systems. Arrow and Hahn (1971) describe this contribution in a way that makes it virtually equivalent to the micro-to-macro transition in general:

> Whatever the source of the concept, the notion that a social system moved by independent actions in pursuit of different values is consistent with a final coherent state of balance, and one in which the outcome may be quite different from those intended by the agents, is surely the most important intellectual contribution that economic thought has made to the general understanding of social processes. (p. 1)

What is not ordinarily discussed in the economic literature is the quite complex structure of interactions that is assumed in this process of negotiations, tentative agreements, and final contracts.[14] This complex structure was noted by classical economists, who pointed to the improbability of the double coincidence of wants in a true barter economy (Jevons, 1875, p. 3). The double coincidence of wants exists when it is true not only that one actor has something of interest to another actor, who has goods of sufficient value to pay for it, but also that the goods which the second actor wants to use for payment are goods that are of interest to the first actor. In general, money as a medium of exchange or a centralized clearinghouse is necessary to overcome the need for double coincidence of wants (see Ostroy and Starr, 1974). The problem, of course, is particularly serious for social exchange, since there is in most social structures neither a central clearinghouse nor a medium of exchange for noneconomic exchanges.[15]

---

14. An exception is the work of Ostroy and Starr (1974) examining the implications of the system of a central bank or a medium of exchange in facilitating transactions which could not occur in a barter economy unless there were some clearinghouse for debts and credits.

15. In Chapter 16 I discussed the role of the organizational entrepreneur as a clearinghouse, allowing organization of activities that would otherwise be impossible.

In addition to the structural problems created by the need for a double coincidence of wants, problems of communication structure exist, as well as other frictions in transactions that economists put under the heading of transaction costs. In later chapters I will examine both the problems occasioned by the lack of a medium of exchange and those occasioned by variations in communication structure. The model of perfect competition will be modified to mirror some of these structural variations.

Further Derivations and Use of the Model

It is possible to start with certain subsets of the quantities defined in eqs. 25.4–25.6, 25.11, and 25.12 and calculate the remaining quantities. In particular, the three matrices C, X, and C^* are the matrix of initial control, the matrix of interests, and the matrix of equilibrium control, respectively. If the starting data give C or C^* and X, it is possible to calculate the distributions of power, r_i, among actors and of value, v_j, among goods. If the data consist of C and X, it is possible to calculate C^* as well as the power of actors and the value of goods; but if the data consist of C^* and X, then, since there are many values of C which could be starting points, the actual starting point is indeterminate.

It is also possible to start with C and C^* and calculate r, v, and X by using eqs. 25.6, 25.11, and 25.12. The first section below shows the calculations that begin with X and either C or C^*. The second section shows the calculations that begin with C and C^*. In the latter case the calculations are carried out assuming the data fits the model perfectly. In Chapter 26 use of the model with empirical data is examined, and methods are described for analysis to obtain estimates that are in a specific sense best-fitting.

Calculations Given C and X or C* and X

Equation 25.6 or 25.12 can be used to write the matrix equation

$$r = CXr \qquad (25.15)$$

or

$$v = XCv \qquad (25.16)$$

Equation 25.15 can be written as

$$0 = (I - CX)r \qquad (25.17)$$

where 0 is a vector of zeros and I is an identity matrix, both of appropriate size. If E_n is defined as an $n \times n$ matrix with elements $1/n$, and e_{n1} is defined as an $n \times 1$ column from this matrix, then $e_{n1} = E_n r$ since the elements of r sum to 1.0. Adding the left-hand and right-hand sides of this equation to the left-hand and right-hand sides of eq. 25.17, respectively, gives

$$\mathbf{e}_{n1} = (\mathbf{I} - \mathbf{CX})\mathbf{r} + \mathbf{E}_n\mathbf{r}$$

$$\mathbf{e}_{n1} = (\mathbf{I} - \mathbf{CX} + \mathbf{E}_n)\mathbf{r}$$

$$(\mathbf{I} - \mathbf{CX} + \mathbf{E}_n)^{-1}\mathbf{e}_{n1} = \mathbf{r} \qquad (25.18)$$

After eq. 25.18 is used to find the vector $\mathbf{r}$, eq. 25.12 can be used to find $\mathbf{v}$, and eq. 25.11 to find $\mathbf{C}^*$. These calculations were carried out in a previous section for the trading-card example.

The matrix $\mathbf{E}_n$ and the vector $\mathbf{e}_{n1}$ with elements $1/n$ are used in eq. 25.18, but an arbitrary matrix $\mathbf{A}$ and vector $\mathbf{a}_1$ with any identical elements may be used, since for an arbitrary matrix $\mathbf{A}$ and vector $\mathbf{a}_1$ with identical elements, $\mathbf{a}_1 = \mathbf{Ar}$, if the elements of $\mathbf{r}$ sum to 1.0. The matrix $\mathbf{E}_n$ with elements $1/n$ is used in eq. 25.18 (and $\mathbf{E}_m$ in eqs. 25.19 and 25.21) because of special properties that are useful in Chapter 27. For computational convenience in research of the sort described in Chapter 26, however, other constants may be preferable.

Equation 25.16 may be used in a manner similar to that demonstrated above to find $\mathbf{v}$. Here $\mathbf{E}_m$ is an $m \times m$ matrix with elements $1/m$, and $\mathbf{e}_{m1}$ is a column from that matrix.

$$\mathbf{0} = (\mathbf{I} - \mathbf{XC})\mathbf{v}$$

$$\mathbf{e}_{m1} = (\mathbf{I} - \mathbf{XC} + \mathbf{E}_m)\mathbf{v}$$

$$(\mathbf{I} - \mathbf{XC} + \mathbf{E}_m)^{-1}\mathbf{e}_{m1} = \mathbf{v} \qquad (25.19)$$

Then $\mathbf{v}$ may be used with eq. 25.6 to find $\mathbf{r}$ and with eq. 25.11 to find $\mathbf{C}^*$.

Calculations Given $\mathbf{C}$ *and* $\mathbf{C}^*$

Since eq. 25.6 holds for both c_{ij} and c_{ij}^*, it is possible to write

$$\mathbf{Cv} = \mathbf{C}^*\mathbf{v} \qquad (25.20)$$

This becomes

$$(\mathbf{C} - \mathbf{C}^*)\mathbf{v} = \mathbf{0}$$

Multiplying both sides of eq. 25.20 by $(\mathbf{C} - \mathbf{C}^*)'$, the transpose of $(\mathbf{C} - \mathbf{C}^*)$, gives

$$(\mathbf{C} - \mathbf{C}^*)'(\mathbf{C} - \mathbf{C}^*)\mathbf{v} = \mathbf{0}$$

Defining $\mathbf{E}_m$ and $\mathbf{e}_{m1}$ as above to be a matrix and vector of elements $1/m$, respectively, leads to $\mathbf{e}_{m1} = \mathbf{E}_m\mathbf{v}$.

$$(\mathbf{C} - \mathbf{C}^*)'(\mathbf{C} - \mathbf{C}^*)\mathbf{v} + \mathbf{E}_m\mathbf{v} = \mathbf{e}_{m1}$$

$$\mathbf{v} = [(\mathbf{C} - \mathbf{C}^*)'(\mathbf{C} - \mathbf{C}^*) + \mathbf{E}_m]^{-1}\mathbf{e}_{m1} \qquad (25.21)$$

After eq. 25.21 is used to find the vector **v**, eq. 25.6 can be used to find **r**, and eq. 25.11 to find **X**.

It should be noted that in order to calculate **v** and **r** it is not necessary that **C*** be used in this derivation. What is necessary for using eq. 25.21 is the distributions of resources at two different times, neither of which need be the equilibrium distribution. Only for the calculation of **X** is it necessary that one of the values used be **C***.

Calculations using **C** and **C*** may be more useful than those involving **X** and **C**, because often **C** and **C*** are both observed behavior, but **X** is a subjective state. For the trading-card example suppose Tom's and John's interests were not known, but it was observed that after exchange Tom ended up having 76 football cards and 42 baseball cards (which would have happened if the boys had exchanged at a 1:2 rate, as shown in Figure 25.5). Calculation using eq. 25.21 gives a value of .667 for football cards and .333 for baseball cards (a necessary reflection of the fact that cards were traded at a 1:2 rate). Tom's power would be .647 and John's would be .353, and the interests would be calculated as .78 in football cards and .22 in baseball cards for Tom and .45 and .55 for John. If the exchange rates had been first 1:1 and then 1:2, with Tom ending up with 71 football and 36 baseball cards (as shown in Figure 25.5), the values exhibited by this exchange would be even less favorable to the football cards: .57 for football cards and .43 for baseball. The power of Tom and of John would be .56 and .44, respectively, and the interests would be .72 and .28 for Tom, and .38 and .62 for John.

These different outcomes of course indicate differing value, power, and interest. In both of these cases, involving exchange rates of 1:1 and 1:2, assuming that the true interests were .8 and .2 for Tom and .5 and .5 for John, the strength of the ethical norm to trade at a rate more favorable to the weaker cards (or perhaps the strength of the Schelling point) was such as to reduce the effective power of Tom and the value of the football cards, as well as to impose apparent interests different from the true interests. One would ordinarily not, of course, know the true interests, but this hypothetical case shows how some external principle or norm governing exchange can have a strong impact by making the effective interests differ from the interests that would operate in the absence of the norm and by changing the effective power of actors and the value of goods.

Linear System of Action When Quantities of Goods Vary

The derivations in preceding sections treated the case in which the quantities of each good can be neglected. Although this is satisfactory for some action systems, it is not for others. Consequently, in this section I will show how the derivations are modified when the quantities of goods are not equal to 1.0. This is equivalent to abandoning the assumption that $\Sigma_i c_{ij} = 1.0$. Then the utility function given by eq. 25.1 no longer has the constraints that x_{ji} sum to 1.0 over events or goods and that c_{ij} sum to 1.0 over actors. The utility function is specified such that c_{ij} is in units of a good, and x_{ji} is the interest per unit of the good.

In the earlier derivation the constraints on the sum of x_{ji} and c_{ij} did not enter until eq. 25.10. Thus this derivation for the more general system will begin with the modification of eq. 25.10 and continue through the modification of eq. 25.21.

If r_i is defined as $\Sigma \, c_{ij}v_j$, as in eq. 25.6, and the sum of i's interests is defined as

$$x_i = \sum_j x_{ji}$$

eq. 25.9 becomes the following rather than eq. 25.10:

$$r_i = \frac{c^*_{ik}v_kx_i}{x_{ki}} \tag{25.10'}$$

Solving eq. 25.10' for c^*_{ik} gives

$$c^*_{ik} = \frac{x_{ki}r_i}{v_kx_i} \tag{25.11'}$$

Multiplying both sides of eq. 25.11' by v_k and summing over i gives

$$c_kv_k = \sum_{i=1}^n \frac{x_{ki}r_i}{x_i} \tag{25.12'}$$

or, dividing by c_k,

$$v_k = \sum_{i=1}^n \frac{x_{ki}r_i}{c_kx_i} \tag{25.12''}$$

where c_k is the total quantity of good k in the system. Note that in this case v_k and r_i are defined asymmetrically: v_k is the value of one unit of good k, and r_i is the total wealth of actor i.

Since the total wealth in the system is in arbitrary units, it may be fixed as 1.0, giving

$$\sum_{i=1}^n r_i = \sum_{j=1}^m c_jv_j = 1.0 \tag{25.13'}$$

An equation which eliminates r_i from eq. 25.12' may be obtained by substituting for r_i from eq. 25.6:

$$c_kv_k = \sum_{i=1}^n \frac{x_{ki}\sum_{j=1}^m c_{ij}v_j}{x_i} \tag{25.14'}$$

or

$$v_k = \sum_{i=1}^n \frac{x_{ki}\sum_{j=1}^m c_{ij}v_j}{c_kx_i} \tag{25.14''}$$

There are $m - 1$ independent equations of the form of eq. 25.14', and these and eq. 25.13' allow solving for the m quantities v_k. Then eq. 25.6 may be used to find the n quantities r_i and eq. 25.11' to find the quantities of k held by actor i at the competitive equilibrium.

It is then possible to give the modified forms of eqs. 25.15–25.21 by first defining $\mathbf{D}_c$ as a square $m \times m$ matrix with the quantities c_k in the main diagonal and zeros elsewhere (which makes the inverse $\mathbf{D}_c^{-1}$, a matrix with elements $1/c_k$ in the main diagonal and zeros elsewhere) and $\mathbf{D}_x$ as a square $n \times n$ matrix with elements x_i in the main diagonals and zeros elsewhere (making $\mathbf{D}_x^{-1}$ a matrix with elements $1/x_i$ in the main diagonals and zeros elsewhere). These definitions make it possible to write eq. 25.12″ in matrix form:

$$\mathbf{v} = \mathbf{D}_c^{-1}\mathbf{X}\mathbf{D}_x^{-1}\mathbf{r}$$

Then this equation may be used to substitute for $\mathbf{v}$ in $\mathbf{r} = \mathbf{C}\mathbf{v}$:

$$\mathbf{r} = \mathbf{C}\mathbf{D}_c^{-1}\mathbf{X}\mathbf{D}_x^{-1}\mathbf{r} \tag{25.15'}$$

Or substituting for $\mathbf{r}$ in eq. 25.12″ and left-multiplying by $\mathbf{D}_c$ gives

$$\mathbf{D}_c\mathbf{v} = \mathbf{X}\mathbf{D}_x^{-1}\mathbf{C}\mathbf{v} \tag{25.16'}$$

Equation 25.15' may be solved as before, defining $\mathbf{E}_n$ as an $n \times n$ matrix of elements $1/n$ and $\mathbf{e}_{n1}$ as an $n \times 1$ vector of elements $1/n$:

$$\mathbf{0} = (\mathbf{I} - \mathbf{C}\mathbf{D}_c^{-1}\mathbf{X}\mathbf{D}_x^{-1})\mathbf{r} \tag{25.17'}$$

$$\mathbf{e}_{n1} = (\mathbf{I} - \mathbf{C}\mathbf{D}_c^{-1}\mathbf{X}\mathbf{D}_x^{-1} + \mathbf{E}_n)\mathbf{r}$$

$$\mathbf{r} = (\mathbf{I} - \mathbf{C}\mathbf{D}_c^{-1}\mathbf{X}\mathbf{D}_x^{-1} + \mathbf{E}_n)^{-1}\mathbf{e}_{n1} \tag{25.18'}$$

After eq. 25.18' is used to find $\mathbf{r}$, eq. 25.12' may be used to solve for $\mathbf{v}$, and eq. 25.11' to find $\mathbf{C}^*$.

If eq. 25.16' is used to solve for $\mathbf{v}$, then, since from eq. 25.13' we have $\mathbf{e}_{m1} = \mathbf{E}_m\mathbf{D}_c\mathbf{v}$,

$$\mathbf{0} = (\mathbf{D}_c - \mathbf{X}\mathbf{D}_x^{-1}\mathbf{C})\mathbf{v}$$

$$\mathbf{e}_{m1} = (\mathbf{D}_c - \mathbf{X}\mathbf{D}_x^{-1}\mathbf{C} + \mathbf{E}_m\mathbf{D}_c)\mathbf{v}$$

$$(\mathbf{D}_c - \mathbf{X}\mathbf{D}_x^{-1}\mathbf{C} + \mathbf{E}_m\mathbf{D}_c)^{-1}\mathbf{e}_{m1} = \mathbf{v} \tag{25.19'}$$

Then $\mathbf{v}$ may be used with eq. 25.6 to find $\mathbf{r}$ and with eq. 25.11' to find $\mathbf{C}^*$.

Finding $\mathbf{r}$ and $\mathbf{v}$ may be done beginning with $\mathbf{C}$ and $\mathbf{C}^*$, rather than $\mathbf{C}$ and $\mathbf{X}$. First, from eq. 25.6

$$\mathbf{C}\mathbf{v} = \mathbf{C}^*\mathbf{v}$$

Subtracting $\mathbf{C}^*\mathbf{v}$ from both sides gives $(\mathbf{C} - \mathbf{C}^*)\mathbf{v} = \mathbf{0}$. Multiplying both sides of that by $(\mathbf{C}\mathbf{D}_c^{-1} - \mathbf{C}^*\mathbf{D}_c^{-1})'$, using $\mathbf{D}_c^{-1}$ to maintain dimensional consistency, gives

$$(\mathbf{C}\mathbf{D}_c^{-1} - \mathbf{C}^*\mathbf{D}_c^{-1})'(\mathbf{C} - \mathbf{C}^*)\mathbf{v} = \mathbf{0}$$

Then adding $E_m D_c v$ to the left-hand side and e_{m1} to the right-hand side (since $E_m D_c v = e_{m1}$) gives

$$[(CD_c^{-1} - CD_c^{-1})'(C - C^*) + E_m D_c]v = e_{m1}$$

$$v = [(CD_c^{-1} - C^* D_c^{-1})'(C - C^*) + E_m D_c]^{-1} e_{m1} \quad (25.21')$$

Equation 25.21' may be used to solve for v.

This completes the derivations if the quantities of goods vary. One use of this modification is to examine how values of goods in a system vary as quantities vary. The only differences between the dimensions of this modification and those of the basic model are in v_j, x_{ji}, and c_{ij}. The sum of power or wealth in the system remains 1.0, but v_j in the modified model is value per unit of the good, and x_{ji} is interest per unit of the good.

APPLICATION TO THE TRADING-CARD EXAMPLE An idea of the way this modification of the model may be used can be given by applying it to the trading-card example under two sets of conditions: first, the conditions specified earlier; and second, when there are 200 baseball cards rather than 100, distributed proportionally as before. Interest in each baseball card and each football card is the same for the two cases. In the original example Tom's interests were .8 and .2 for 100 of each type of card, which means .008 and .002 per card; John's interests per card are .005 and .005. The control and interest for the two cases are given in Table 25.1. Note that the constancy of interest per card means that the two actors have different total interests in case 2.

Calculations in an earlier section gave the value of cards, power of actors, and distribution of cards at competitive equilibrium for case 1. Applying eq. 25.18' to get the results for case 2 requires these matrices:

$$D_c = \begin{bmatrix} 100 & 0 \\ 0 & 200 \end{bmatrix} \quad CD_c^{-1} = \begin{bmatrix} .95 & .04 \\ .05 & .96 \end{bmatrix}$$

$$D_x = \begin{bmatrix} 1.2 & 0 \\ 0 & 1.5 \end{bmatrix} \quad XD_x^{-1} = \begin{bmatrix} .667 & .333 \\ .333 & .667 \end{bmatrix}$$

Note that after being normalized by inverses of the totals, the control matrix has remained the same; it is only the normalized interest matrix that has changed.

The results of applying eq. 25.18' and then calculating v and C^* are given in Table 25.2 for case 2, along with the results obtained earlier for case 1. The results show considerable change. The addition of 100 baseball cards, primarily held by John, increased his power from less than half of Tom's to slightly greater than Tom's. The total value of the baseball cards increased for two reasons: their greater number relative to the number of football cards, and the greater power of the person who is most interested in them. (If the additional cards had been principally in Tom's hands at the beginning of trading, these two factors would have worked in opposite directions.)

Table 25.1 Control and interests for two cases of the trading-card system.

	Case 1: 100 cards of each type				
	Control (C)		Interest (X')		
	Football	Baseball	Football	Baseball	Total
Tom	95	4	.8	.2	1.0
John	5	96	.5	.5	1.0
Total	100	100			

	Case 2: 100 football and 200 baseball cards				
	Control (C)		Interest (X')		
	Football	Baseball	Football	Baseball	Total
Tom	95	8	.8	.4	1.2
John	5	192	.5	1.0	1.5
Total	100	200			

Table 25.2 Value, equilibrium control, and power in the trading-card system

	Case 1: 100 cards of each type					
	Value of cards			Equilibrium control		
	Football	Baseball		Football	Baseball	Power
Total	.704	.296	Tom	77	46	.68
Per card	.0070	.0030	John	33	54	.32

	Case 2: 100 football and 200 baseball cards					
	Value of cards			Equilibrium control		
	Football	Baseball		Football	Baseball	Power
Total	.498	.502	Tom	66	66	.50(−)
Per card	.0050	.0025	John	34	134	.50(+)

The value per card is lower for both types of cards in case 2, since the total wealth in the system is 1.0 and there are 300 cards rather than 200. The value of each football card has gone down by a much larger fraction than has that of each baseball card—this effect is due, as indicated above, to the increase in power of the person who is most interested in the baseball cards. If the actors' power had not changed, or if their interests had been alike, the value of each type of card would have declined by the same fraction of the original value.

Economic and Psychological Properties of the Utility Function

As is evident earlier in this chapter, the single restriction imposed on the system of action considered here beyond those of standard microeconomic theory is the specification of the utility function, as given in eq. 25.1. It is useful to comment on the properties of this utility function and the interests x_{ji} which derive from it. These interests have two important implications for behavior, which can be described as income elasticity of $+1$ and price elasticity of -1. Stated more fully, these implications are as follows:

1. *The individual will devote the same fraction of his income to obtaining a good, independent of the amount of that income.* That fraction is given by x_{ji}. If his income increases by 10%, he will increase the quantity he holds of each good in the system by 10%. (A good with a price elasticity greater than 1 is a good on which he spends a greater fraction of his income as that income increases. A good with a price elasticity less than 1 is a good on which he spends a smaller fraction of his income as that income increases.)
2. *The individual will devote the same fraction of his income to a good, independent of the price.* That is, he will change the quantity of a good acquired inversely with price changes in such a way that the fraction of his income devoted to obtaining the good remains the same. If the price of a good increases by 10%, he will reduce the quantity of that good he holds so that he continues to spend the same fraction of his income on it.

These implications are shown in eq. 25.11: The amount of good k that individual i holds at equilibrium is proportional to his wealth, r_i, and inversely proportional to its price, v_k.

A psychological property of this form of the utility function is its correspondence to the Weber-Fechner law of psychophysics, which states that the change in an objective stimulus necessary to produce a change in subjective response is proportional to the existing level of the objective stimulus. For example, if the level of illumination is very low, a very small increase in illumination will produce a just noticeable difference; if the level of illumination is higher, a larger increment in illumination will be necessary to produce a just noticeable difference. If σ_j is the level of the objective stimulus and ρ_j is the level of the subjective response, the Weber-Fechner law states that

$$\delta\rho_j = K_j \frac{\delta\sigma_j}{\sigma_j}$$

where K_j is some constant. Dividing through by $\delta\sigma_j$ gives

$$\frac{\delta\rho_j}{\delta\sigma_j} = \frac{K_j}{\sigma_j}$$

Expressed in this way, the law states that subjective response resulting from a change in objective stimulus is inversely proportional to the existing level of the stimulus.[16]

16. The Weber-Fechner law is not really a law of psychophysics; it describes only approximately the relation between objective stimulus and subjective response. (For generalization of this "law" see Stevens, 1951; 1957.) It is a first approximation, however, and therefore useful for examining the psychological properties of the Cobb-Douglas utility function.

Considering an increment in satisfaction from good j as equivalent to the subjective response and the amount of good j held (c_{ij}) as the objective stimulus allows examination of the correspondence between the utility function and the Weber-Fechner law in terms of the relation between changes in control and changes in satisfaction.

In eq. 25.3 the logarithm of utility was taken as defining satisfaction for calculating indifference curves. If $\ln U_i$ is called the satisfaction of i, or s_i, then the change in satisfaction due to a change in control of j is given by the derivative of s_i with respect to c_{ij}. Assuming that the interest in good j is independent of the amount of good k held gives, from eq. 25.3,

$$\frac{ds_i}{dc_{ij}} = \frac{x_{ji}}{c_{ij}} \tag{25.22}$$

This equation has the same form as the Weber-Fechner law: The increment in satisfaction from a good due to an increment in the amount of the good held is inversely proportional to the amount already held.

These economic and psychological properties of the utility function specified by eq. 25.1 and used for the linear system of action show the empirical reasonableness of this function. There is no implication that all individuals respond this way to all goods. These properties suggest, however, that if a simple form of the utility function is to be chosen, with a single parameter for each good, the one given by eq. 25.1 is probably the most empirically adequate. The benefit of choosing a particular form lies, of course, in facilitating the micro-to-macro transition.

Open Systems

Interests in External Events

The question naturally arises whether it is possible to use the model described above to represent situations in which one or more actors have interests in events outside the system. Such a situation may be regarded as an open system. Substantively this means that there is a drain of resources away from the system, that one or more actors are taking out of the system some of the resources they have gained through control over events in the system. These withdrawn resources are not replenished from outside unless one or more actors also have some control over events of interest to those outsiders who control the external events in which those actors have interests.

Such a system can be treated in full detail by expanding it to include those external actors and events and then partitioning the expanded system into two parts, each an open system. For some purposes, however, it may not be feasible or even possible to specify the external events and actors, and it may be desirable only to characterize the original system, even though it is known that some interests of the actors lie outside the system (that is, they use some of the resources they gained within the system to control events outside), and some actors from outside have interests in events within the system (that is, they bring resources into the system). The effect of these imports and exports (for this is how they may best be conceived) on the relative power of actors in the system depends not only on the amount of interest each actor has in events outside the system, but also on the distribution of interests of the external actors in events within the system. Thus it may be desirable, in the absence of knowledge of external events and actors, to make an assumption about this distribution, so that a distribution of power among actors within the system can be calculated relative to this assumption. That is what I will do here.

There is one assumption under which the external actors' interests serve only to preserve that distribution of power which would obtain in their absence, and I will outline that assumption here. Consider a system with n actors and m events in which one or more actors have less than complete interests in the set of events within the system. There is an additional event, indexed by $m + 1$, in which the remaining interests are placed, so $\Sigma_j^{m+1} x_{ji} = 1.0$ for all i. There is also another actor, indexed by $n + 1$, added to the system, with full control over that event.

The interest and control matrices for the system of n actors and m events are $\mathbf{X}$ ($m \times n$) and $\mathbf{C}$ ($n \times m$). The distribution of interests of actor $n + 1$ in events in the system that does not change their relative values or the relative power of actors is that distribution in which interests of actor $n + 1$ are identical to the values that would otherwise obtain. If these values are v_j, then $x_{j,n+1} = v_j$ for all j.

Solving for $\mathbf{r}$ involves first creating the $n \times n$ matrix $\mathbf{Z}$ (equal to $\mathbf{CX}$), then adding an $n + 1$ row:

$$z_{n+1,i} = \sum_{k=1}^{m+1} c_{n+1,k}x_{ki} = c_{n+1,m+1}x_{m+1,i} = x_{m+1,i}$$

An additional column is also added:

$$z_{i,n+1} = \sum_{j=1}^{m+1} c_{ij}x_{j,n+1} = \sum_{j=1}^{m+1} c_{ij}v_j = r_i \qquad (25.23)$$

That is, $z_{i,n+1}$, the control actor i has over actor $n + 1$, is simply the power of actor i. For $i = n + 1$,

$$z_{n+1,n+1} = v_{m+1} = r_{n+1} = 1 - \sum_{j=1}^{n} r_j$$

The addition of the row and column as indicated above gives an expanded matrix $\mathbf{Z}^*$, consisting of the matrix $\mathbf{Z}$ (equal to $\mathbf{CX}$) with an additional row, in which the entries $z_{n+1,i}$ are equal to $x_{m+1,i}$ for $i = 1, \ldots, n$, and an additional column, in which the entries are r_k for $k = 1, \ldots, n + 1$.

The additions, however, make the system no longer linear in r_j; a typical equation will look like this:

$$r_k = \sum_{j=1}^{n} z_{kj}r_j + r_k r_{n+1}, \qquad k = 1, \ldots, n + 1 \tag{25.24}$$

If this is divided by r_{n+1} and r_i^* is defined as r_i/r_{n+1}, then

$$\mathbf{r}^* = \mathbf{Z}\mathbf{r}^* + \mathbf{r} \tag{25.25}$$

or alternatively,

$$\mathbf{r} = \mathbf{Z}^*\mathbf{r} \tag{25.26}$$

The vector $\mathbf{r}$ can be found by a simple iterative method, given in the appendix to this chapter.

Control by External Actors

A question also arises about the application of the model to a situation in which one or more events are less than fully controlled within the system of actors under examination and is partially controlled by external actors. If there is to be equilibrium, the external events in which external actors are interested must be under the partial control of actors in the system. There is one assumption about the distribution of that control of external events which preserves the distribution of power that would otherwise obtain. This is the assumption that each actor's control over those events is equal to that actor's power. Under this assumption the last column in the matrix of control having elements $c_{i,m+1}$ is equal to r_i. In this case the system is closed by expanding the matrix $\mathbf{C}$ by one more row for actor $n + 1$, who has all the control over event j (that is, $c_{n+1,j}$) which is not held by actors in the system. That is,

$$c_{n+1,j} = 1 - \sum_{i=1}^{n} c_{ij}$$

The matrix $\mathbf{X}$ is expanded by an additional row and column containing all zeros except for $x_{m+1,n+1}$, which equals 1.

The expanded product matrix $\mathbf{W}^*$, consisting of expanded $\mathbf{C}$ left-multiplied by expanded $\mathbf{X}$, is the matrix $\mathbf{X}\mathbf{C}$ with an added row having entries $w_{m+1,j} = c_{n+1,j}$ and an added column having entries $w_{k,m+1} = v_k$. (The latter arises because the product for the last row is $w_{k,m+1} = \sum_{i=1}^{n} x_{ki}r_i$ and the right-hand side of this equation is equal to v_k by definition.) The equation for finding $\mathbf{v}$ is $\mathbf{v} = \mathbf{W}\mathbf{v}$, but, as was true for $\mathbf{Z}^*$ in the preceding section, $\mathbf{W}^*$ is not wholly exogenous but has v_i as elements. The typical equation for element v_j of $\mathbf{v}$ is

$$v_j = \sum_{k=1}^{m} w_{jk}v_k + v_j v_{m+1}, \qquad j = 1, \ldots, m + 1 \tag{25.27}$$

This equation, written in matrix notation, is

$$\mathbf{v} = \mathbf{W}^*\mathbf{v} \tag{25.28}$$

The set of equations defined by eq. 25.27 may be solved by the iterative methods described in the appendix to this chapter.

The model described in this chapter constitutes the basis for much of the subsequent work in this part. I will apply the model to empirical data in some illustrative data analyses (Chapter 26) and will extend it to cover kinds of action systems that do not meet the conditions of the idealized perfectly competitive market. This will entail allowing for events that do not have all the properties of divisible private goods, introducing social-structural constraints into the system, and other modifications. I will also examine dynamic aspects of the system of action, for the move from the initial distribution of control to the final distribution.

Appendix: An Iterative Method for Solving for **r** or **v** Given **X** and **C**

The solution of the system of equations $\mathbf{r} = \mathbf{CXr}$ or $\mathbf{v} = \mathbf{XCv}$ can be obtained through application of a simple iterative algorithm. When **CX** (equal to **Z**) satisfies the Markovian constraints that all $z_{kj} \geq 0$ and $\Sigma_{k=1}^{n} z_{kj} = 1$ for all j, then the system is ergodic. This means that, beginning with an arbitrary vector $\mathbf{r}_0$, successive multiplications by **Z** give asymptotically an equilibrium vector **r**, independent of the initial vector. That is,

$$\mathbf{r}_1 = \mathbf{Zr}_0$$

$$\mathbf{r}_2 = \mathbf{Zr}_1 = \mathbf{Z}^2\mathbf{r}_0$$

and

$$\mathbf{r} = \mathbf{Z}^{\infty}\mathbf{r}_0$$

In general,

$$\mathbf{r}_{j+1} = \mathbf{Zr}_j$$

This forms the basis for a simple iterative algorithm for obtaining **r**, given **Z**. The steps of the algorithm are as follows:

1. Choose an initial vector $\mathbf{r}_0$ with elements $r^{(0)}$ and define $\mathbf{r}_j = \mathbf{r}_0$. [A simple choice for $\mathbf{r}_0$ is provided by $r_k^{(0)} = (1/n) \Sigma_{j=1}^{n} z_{kj}$.]
2. Left-multiply $\mathbf{r}_j$ by **Z** to give $\mathbf{r}_{j+1}$.
3. Test whether $\max |r_i^{(j+1)} - r_i^{(j)}| < \varepsilon$, where ε is arbitrarily small and chosen for the desired degree of accuracy. If test succeeds, end iteration.
4. Replace $\mathbf{r}_j$ with $\mathbf{r}_{j+1}$ and return to step 1.

The iterative algorithm for obtaining **v** is identical to that for obtaining **r**, but with **v** in place of **r** and **W** (equal to **XC**) in place of **Z**.

Modification of the Iterative Method When Not All Interests Are Located within the System

When not all interests are located within the system of events, that is, when $\sum_{j=1}^{m} x_{ji} < 1$ for one or more actors i, and the assumption is made that the distribution of external actors' interests in events within the system is identical to the values for those events that obtain within the system, the system is described by eq. 25.24:

$$r_k = \sum_{i=1}^{n} z_{ki} r_i + r_k r_{n+1}, \qquad k = 1, \ldots, n + 1.$$

The modification of the solution algorithm is given by the following iterative equation

$$r_k^{(j+1)} = \sum_{i=1}^{n} z_{ki} r_i^{(j)} + r_k^{(j)} r_{n+1}^{(j)}$$

The steps of the iterative algorithm are as follows:

1. Choose an initial vector $\mathbf{r}_0$ with elements $r_i^{(0)}$ and define $\mathbf{r}_j = \mathbf{r}_0$. [Again, a simple choice for $\mathbf{r}_0$ is provided by $r_k^{(0)} = (1/n) \sum_{j=1}^{n} z_{kj}$ for $k = 1, \ldots, n$, and $r_{n+1}^{(0)} = 1 - \sum_{k=1}^{n} r_k^{(0)}$.]
2. Augment $\mathbf{Z}$ by row $n + 1$ with elements $z_{n+1,i} = 1 - \sum_{k=1}^{n} z_{ki}$, for $i = 1, \ldots, n$.
3. Augment $\mathbf{Z}$ by column $n + 1$ with elements $z_{k,n+1} = r_k^{(0)}$ for $k = 1, \ldots, n$ and $z_{n+1,m+1} = 1 - \sum_{k=1}^{n} r_k^{(0)}$
4. Left-multiply $\mathbf{r}_j$ by $\mathbf{Z}^*$ to give $\mathbf{r}_{j+1}$.
5. Test whether $\max |r_i^{(j+1)} - r_i^{(j)}| < \varepsilon$, where ε is arbitrarily small and chosen for the desired degree of accuracy. If test succeeds, end iteration.
6. Replace the last column of $\mathbf{Z}^*$ (having elements $z_{k,n+1}$) with $\mathbf{r}_{j+1}$ (having elements $r_k^{(j+1)}$).
7. Replace $\mathbf{r}_j$ with $\mathbf{r}_{j+1}$ and return to step 4.

This system with endogenous elements of $\mathbf{Z}^*$ is not ergodic; however, convergence to an equilibrium value independent of $\mathbf{r}$ seems to occur under a wide set of conditions. I will assume convergence for all cases considered here.

AN EXAMPLE OF AN ITERATIVE SOLUTION An example of the iterative procedure for solving for $\mathbf{r}$ when $\sum_{j=1}^{m} x_{ji} < 1$ for one actor is given below. The iterative procedure for $\mathbf{r}$ when $\sum_{j=1}^{m} x_{ji} = 1$ for all i can be seen from this example as well, for it involves a subset of the steps shown. That is, steps 1, 4, and 5 of the more extended procedure constitute all the steps of the less extended procedure.

$$\mathbf{Z} = \begin{bmatrix} .25 & .125 & .25 \\ .25 & .5 & .5 \\ .20 & .375 & .25 \end{bmatrix} \begin{matrix} \text{Row 1} \\ \text{Row 2} \\ \text{Row 3} \end{matrix}$$

$$\phantom{\mathbf{Z} = }\;\; .70 \quad\; 1.0 \quad\;\; 1.0 \qquad \text{Column sums}$$

Steps

1. $r_0 = (.2396, .3958, .2896, .075)$
2. Fourth row of augmented Z is $(.30, 0, 0)$
3. Fourth column of augmented Z is given by r_0 (step 1)
4. $r_1 = (.2068, .4276, .2937, .0719)$
5. Compare r_1 with r_0; test fails: max $|r_i^{(1)} - r_i^{(0)}| > .002$
3_1. Fourth column of augmented Z is given by r_1 (step 4)
4_1. $r_2 = (.1934, .4431, .2963, .0672)$
5_1. Compare r_2 with r_1; test fails: max $|r_i^{(2)} - r_i^{(1)}| > .002$
3_2. Fourth column of augmented Z is given by r_2 (step 4_1)
4_2. $r_3 = (.1908, .4478, .2988, .0625)$
5_2. Compare r_3 with r_2; test fails: max $|r_i^{(3)} - r_i^{(2)}| > .002$
3_3. Fourth column of augmented Z is given by r_3 (step 4_2)
4_3. $r_4 = (.1903, .4490, .2995, .0611)$
5_3. Compare r_4 with r_3; test succeeds: max $|r_i^{(4)} - r_i^{(3)}| < .002$

The equilibrium power distribution is given by r_4.

Modification of the Iterative Method When Not All Control Is Located within the System

When not all control is located within the system of actors, that is, when $\sum_{i=1}^n c_{ij} < 1$ for one or more events j, and the assumption is made that the distribution of control over external events held by actors in the system is identical to the distribution of their power within the system, the system is described by eq. 25.27:

$$v_j = \sum_{k=1}^m w_{jk}v_k + v_jv_{m+1}, \qquad j = 1, \ldots, m + 1$$

The algorithm for finding v is formally identical to the algorithm for finding r. The iterative equation is

$$v_j^{(i+1)} = \sum_{k=1}^n v_{jk}v_k^{(i)} + v_j^{(i)} v_{n+1}^{(i)}$$

The steps of the iterative algorithm are identical to those for finding r except that r is replaced by v, Z is replaced by W, X and C are interchanged, and m and n are interchanged.

« 26 »

Empirical Applications

The model presented in the preceding chapter serves not only as a formal framework within which theoretical issues examined in earlier chapters of the book can be examined but also as a framework for quantitative data analysis. Figure 26.1 is similar to Figure 1.2 in relating the micro and macro levels and shows where the concepts of the model are located. Actors and resources are at the micro level; actor i's interest in resource j (x_{ji}) and actor i's control over resource j (c_{ij}) are micro-level concepts. Interests can be said to have a system referent in the sense that the interest of actor i in resource j is relative to i's interest in all other resources in the system, and control can be said to have a system referent in the sense that the fraction of j over which i has control depends on the amount of j held by the other actors in the system. But as Chapter 25 showed, it is possible to specify the equations of the model when interests are given per unit of the resource, unconstrained by the total quantity of resources in the system, and control is given in terms of units of the resource held, unconstrained by the quantity of that resource in the system. Thus interests and control of actors are fundamentally micro-level concepts, properties of the relation between a single actor and a single resource.

In contrast, the value of resource j (v_j) is a system-level concept, as is the power of actor i (r_i). Value and power depend on the structure of interests and control, as well as on assumptions about the social processes through which exchanges take place (all exchanges occurring at equilibrium value, which is achieved by a recontracting process or through a central clearinghouse for offers, without any transaction costs). Value and power can be seen as resultants of actions of a particular constellation of actors, having particular interests and holdings, in a setting in which there is free and unconstrained exchange, with each maximizing utility subject to the constraints of his initial holdings. This, of course, describes a perfectly competitive economic market, in which exchanges involve goods that are fully divisible, alienable, and without externalities. Later chapters will introduce complications that create systems of action which differ from such simple markets. Since much of social exchange does conform reasonably well to perfect-market assumptions, it is possible to make empirical applications while retaining the strong assumptions of the simple system described in Chapter 25.

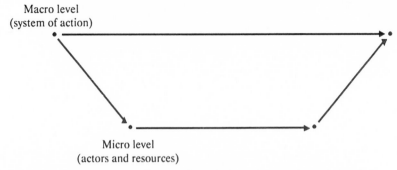

Macro level
(system of action)

Micro level
(actors and resources)

Figure 26.1   Causal diagram for relating micro and macro levels.

Estimation of Value with Perfect-Market Assumptions

In a perfect market there is a single price vector $v = (v_1, \ldots, v_m)$ for m resources. If c_{ij} is the amount of j held by i, then the total value of i's resources is given by this definitional equation (eq. 25.6):

$$r_i = \sum c_{ij} v_j$$

This equation holds for any perfect market, independent of the form of the utility functions of the actors in the system. Furthermore, since in a perfect market equal value is gained and given up in all transactions, the value of an actor's resources remains constant throughout exchange. Thus, if c_{ij0} is the amount of j held by i at time 0 and c_{ijt} is the amount held at a later time, t, after exchange, it is possible to write

$$r_{i0} = \sum_j c_{ij0} v_j = \sum_j c_{ijt} v_j = r_{it} \qquad (26.1)$$

In a system of action with n actors, there are n equations of the form of eq. 26.1, for $i = 1, \ldots, n$. If the number of actors, n, is at least as great as the number of resources, m, and if there are data on the holdings before exchange, c_{ij0}, and the holdings after exchange, c_{ijt}, it is possible to estimate the relative value of each of the resources in the system. If $n = m$, there are exactly as many actors as resources, and except for special cases in which all actors or all resources behave identically, there will be $n - 1$ independent equations and $n - 1$ (or $m - 1$) independent values, v_j. The values are, of course, relative, and as indicated in Chapter 25, the constraint is imposed by setting the sum of v_j equal to 1.0. That there are only $n - 1$ independent equations can be seen by supposing that the initial holdings and the holdings at time t are known for the first $n - 1$ actors. Then the gains and losses for the nth actor are determined for each resource, since no resources have been added to or lost from the system.

If the number of actors exactly equals the number of resources, the values may be found by successive elimination of variables from the equations. An example can be seen in the market for baseball and football cards described in Chapter 25.

EXAMPLE 1: TWO ACTORS AND TWO RESOURCES   If, for the trading-card example introduced in Chapter 25, it is observed that Tom began at (95, 4) and John began at (5, 96), and that after exchange Tom was at (77, 46) and John at (23, 54), an equation could be written for Tom in the form of eq. 26.1:

$$95v_1 + 4v_2 = 77v_1 + 46v_2$$

Since there is only a single exchange rate, v_1/v_2, this becomes

$$\frac{95v_1}{v_2} - \frac{77v_1}{v_2} = 46 - 4$$

Solving for v_1/v_2 gives 7/3, that is, 7 baseball cards for 3 football cards. Arbitrarily setting $v_1 + v_2 = 1.0$ gives $v_1 = .7$ and $v_2 = .3$. In Chapter 25 the point (77, 46) was found to be (after rounding to integral numbers of cards) the competitive equilibrium in a system in which the relative values of football and baseball cards were .704 and .296. What has been done here is to recover, from the initial distribution and the competitive equilibrium, the values of the cards. With the values of the cards, once they are obtained, it is possible to use eq. 26.1 to calculate the value of Tom's and John's initial holdings. When the sum of all values is taken to be 1.0, the total value of Tom's cards is .677 and that of John's is .323, a little less than half of Tom's.

Note that in calculating the values of resources, **v**, and power of actors, **r**, from the initial and final control, C_0 and C_t, no assumption about the form of the utility function is made; for this two-actor case, even an assumption of utility maximization is unnecessary (although, as will become evident, the latter assumption is necessary in systems with three or more actors). The fact that the distribution taken as the after-trading distribution happened to be the competitive equilibrium under the assumption of Cobb-Douglas utility functions, (.8, .2) for Tom and (.5, .5) for John, is irrelevant. Any distribution that involved some exchange could have been chosen.

For this example, as for any case with only two traders and two resources being traded, it is possible to find the exchange rate merely by observing what either of the traders had to give up for what he got. Tom gave up 18 football cards and got 42 baseball cards, giving an exchange rate of 18:42, or 3:7, in football cards for baseball cards. The ratio of values is the inverse of this, or $v_1 : v_2 = 7:3$. When the number of traders exceeds two, something more than such an observation becomes necessary.

Estimation of Value When There Are Two Resources and More Than Two Actors

When the number of actors is greater than the number of resources, it is possible that the empirical data will show that not all exchanges have occurred at the same exchange rates. Different subsets of $m - 1$ of the $n - 1$ independent equations will in that case give different exchange rates. A reasonable approach for the case where $n > m$ is to find that set of values which is best in the sense of minimizing some error function. That is, this equation can be written:

$$r_{i0} = r_{it} + \varepsilon_i \tag{26.2}$$

where ε_i is the difference between the value of i's resources before and after exchange. The problem then is to find the vector of values, $\mathbf{v}$, that in some sense minimizes the errors.

One standard approach is to minimize the sum of squared errors:

$$\min \sum_i \varepsilon_i^2 = \min \sum_i (r_{i0} - r_{it})^2 \tag{26.3}$$

The right-hand side of eq. 26.3 may be rewritten in terms of c_{ij} and v_j:

$$\min \sum_i (r_{i0} - r_{it})^2 = \min \sum_i \left[\sum_j (c_{ij0} - c_{ijt}) v_j \right]^2$$

For convenience d_{ij} may be defined as $c_{ij0} - c_{ijt}$, giving

$$\min \sum_i (r_{i0} - r_{it})^2 = \min \sum_i \left(\sum_j d_{ij} v_j \right)^2$$

The quantity $r_{i0} - r_{it}$ can be written in matrix form as $\mathbf{Dv}$, where $\mathbf{D} = \mathbf{C}_0 - \mathbf{C}_t$. Thus the quantity to be minimized is $\mathbf{v}'\mathbf{D}'\mathbf{Dv}$. The product of the two inner matrices, $\mathbf{D}'\mathbf{D}$, can be seen as a familiar cross-product matrix, in which a product of two $n \times m$ matrices (where $n > m$) is reduced to an $m \times m$ matrix. In a survey, for example, where n is the sample size, $\mathbf{D}'\mathbf{D}$ becomes a cross-product matrix for the sample with rows and columns representing resources being exchanged.

The quantity $\sum_i (\sum_j d_{ij} v_j)^2$, or $\mathbf{v}'\mathbf{D}'\mathbf{Dv}$ written in matrix form, can be expanded, and in the case of n actors ($n > 2$) and two resources it can be solved directly by simple algebra, since $v_2 = 1 - v_1$:

$$\min_{v_1} \sum_i (r_{i0} - r_{it})^2 = \min_{v_1} \sum_i (d_{i1}^2 v_1^2 + 2 d_i v_1 d_{i2} v_2 + d_{i2}^2 v_2^2)$$

The minimum is found by taking the first derivative of the expression with respect to v_1:

$$\min_{v_1} \sum_i (r_{i0} - r_{it})^2 = 0 = \sum_i [2 d_{i1}^2 v_1 + 2 d_{i1} d_{i2} (1 - v_1) - 2 d_{i1} d_{i2} v_1 - 2 d_{i2}^2 (1 - v_1)]$$

Solving for v_1 gives

$$v_1 = \frac{\displaystyle\sum_i d_{i2}^2 - \sum_i d_{i1} d_{i2}}{\displaystyle\sum_i d_{i1}^2 - 2 \sum_i d_{i1} d_{i2} + \sum_i d_{i2}^2} \tag{26.4}$$

Equation 26.4 can be used in an analysis of a market with two resources and any number of actors, to find the best-fitting exchange rate, v_1/v_2, in the market.

EXAMPLE 2: FOUR ACTORS AND TWO RESOURCES   The trading-card example can be modified so that there are four actors trading two types of cards. Suppose that two more boys enter the exchange system: Steve has 100 football cards and 40 baseball cards, and Dan has 60 baseball cards. The holdings before trading and after the four actors have made all the trades they want to make are given in Table 26.1. As the table shows, the exchange rates of football cards for baseball cards differ sharply among the four boys. Tom gave up 1.79 football cards for 1 baseball card, John got .81 for 1, Steve gave up 1 for 1, and Dan got 3 for 1. These differences can be seen as deviations from a perfect market, in which there is a single value for each resource. Such deviations from a perfect market may have a psychological source, that is, lack of rationality on the part of some actors (Tom, John, and Steve) in accepting a poorer exchange rate than others (Dan) got. The deviations may have a social source, in either of two ways: Dan may have been especially well placed in a communications network, facilitating his exchanges and effectively increasing his power in the system; or Tom and Steve may have given especially good terms to Dan because he began with fewer resources.

Despite the differences in exchange rate, which demonstrate that the perfect market assumption on the basis of which eq. 26.1 can be written is not satisfied by these data, eq. 26.2 can be used, assuming deviations from a perfect market. In that case eq. 26.4 can be used to calculate the value v_1 which minimizes the sum of squared deviations of r_{it} from r_{i0}. Carrying out this calculation using eq. 26.4 gives $v_1 = .488$. With this, eq. 25.6, which defines r_i, can be used to calculate the values of the resources of each boy before and after exchange. These are shown in Table 26.2. As these results show, Dan improved his relative position through exchange (all, of course, increased their levels of satisfaction, under the assumption of voluntary exchange) at the expense of Tom and John, whose exchanges were made at disadvantageous rates.

Both this example and the one in the preceding section are based on hypothet-

Table 26.1   Control of football and baseball cards for four traders before and after exchange.

	Before		After		Gained or lost	
	Football	Baseball	Football	Baseball	Football	Baseball
Tom	95	4	70	18	−25	14
John	5	96	44	48	39	−48
Steve	100	40	56	84	−44	44
Dan	0	60	30	50	30	−10

Table 26.2   Power (value of resources) of four actors before and after exchange.

Actor	Before	After
Tom	.24	.22
John	.26	.23
Steve	.35	.35
Dan	.15	.20

ical data and do not exhibit the way this model can be used in conjunction with real data. The next example indicates how real data may be used in analysis.

EXAMPLE 3: EXCHANGE BETWEEN TEACHER AND STUDENTS   In the social system of a school, one major process is an exchange between teacher and students. At the simplest level that exchange can be described as an exchange of effort on the part of students for grades from the teacher. For this exchange system one can conceive of two roles, that of teacher and that of student, with all exchanges occurring between these two roles. There are, of course, other exchanges, such as those that occur among students. A first level of analysis, however, may ignore those and consider only the exchanges between the two identified roles.

Thus it may be useful in describing the functioning of a system to identify the kinds of exchanges to be studied by specifying the roles of which the system, as conceived, is composed. Specifying the roles of student and teacher as relevant for analysis but not the roles of boy and girl, for example, indicates that the only exchanges to be studied are exchanges between students, as students, and teacher, as teacher—and that exchanges between boys and girls in the classroom, or for that matter any other exchanges, are to be ignored. The concept of role becomes useful not only to signal the kind of analysis to be carried out, but also to aid in the design of data collection. Specifying the roles that will play a part in the analysis dictates that data should be collected on exchanges among (or role relations of) those roles.

Before exchange occurs, the teacher can be conceived as having control of grades, and the students as having control of their time. The students can be seen as having an interest in grades and also an interest in their time, for which they have other uses. The teacher may be regarded as also having an interest in grades, not in the sense in which students do, but in the sense that there is some rule restricting the average of the grades given out, so as not to debase the value of a high grade. (I will make an assumption about that rule in the analysis below.)

Table 26.3 presents data for sophomore students in an American high school (school 2 in Table 6.1) in the spring of 1980, showing, among other things, the average grade they received in the preceding grading period and the average time they spent on homework. The exchange may be conceived of as occurring through students giving up free time to do homework. There is no information on

Table 26.3 Characteristics of twenty sophomores in an American high school in the spring of 1980.

Student	Hours per week on homework	Average grade	Test score	Days absent	Teacher's interest
1	5	6	46.3	0	2
2	1	2	38.2	20	3
3	8	4	45.6	10	2
4	5	4	42.0	4	3
5	13	8	72.9	0	1
6	8	6	52.9	4	1
7	1	3	36.6	0	2
8	1	5	39.8	10	1
9	3	4	35.0	25	2
10	8	5	43.0	0	2
11	0	5	66.0	4	3
12	8	6	57.1	0	2
13	5	5	52.8	0	2
14	1	4	37.3	10	2
15	5	4	44.8	4	3
16	8	7	49.3	2	1
17	8	6	50.5	4	3
18	1	7	59.4	4	2
19	1	5	49.0	10	2
20	13	7	49.0	0	2

Source: Data are from a 1980 study of tenth- and twelfth-grade students in 1,015 American high schools, carried out for the National Center for Education Statistics. The study, titled *High School and Beyond,* is described in Coleman, Hoffer, and Kilgore (1982).

the amount of leisure time students have, so students are assumed to have 25 hours of leisure time each week. It is also assumed that teachers cannot give out grades that average higher than a B, which is equivalent to a 6 in the grades column in Table 26.3.

The grade received by each student can then be regarded as the control the student has of grades after exchange, and the amount of time spent on homework, as a fraction of the student's total leisure time, can be regarded as the control of the students' time by the teacher after exchange. Thus, for these twenty sophomore students, time spent on homework and grades received give values of c_{ijt}, that is, the matrix $\mathbf{C}_t$. In this way, if the system is conceived as consisting of an exchange of time on homework for grades, information exists for the matrix $\mathbf{C}_0$, control before exchange, and the matrix $\mathbf{C}_t$. $\mathbf{C}_0$ and $\mathbf{C}_t$ are found by a few simple calculations.

Each student begins with 25 hours of leisure time, which is 1/20 of the total time in the system. The teacher begins with all the grades. Thus $\mathbf{C}_0$, with dimensions 21 × 2, has 1/20 in the first twenty rows of the first column and 0 in the last row, and 0 in the first twenty rows of the second column and 1 in the last row.

After exchange, each student has given up a certain fraction of the 25 hours of time. For the first student in Table 26.3, this is 5/25, or .20. Thus that student retains .8 of the fraction of the total time held at time 0. The first row of the first column of C_t is therefore .8 of 1/20, or .04. The twenty-first row is augmented by .01 from this exchange. After the discretionary time still held by each student is calculated and those quantities are summed, the total time given up to the teacher is found by subtracting that sum from 1.0. In this case the teacher controls .206 of the time after exchange.

The second column contains the fraction of the total available grades held by each actor after exchange. The total available grades are 20 × 6, so the entry in the first row is 6/(20 × 6), or .05. The entry in the twenty-first row is the difference between the total available grades and the total grades given out, divided by the total available grades. Calculations from Table 26.3 show this to be .142.

Equation 26.4 may be used with these data to estimate **v**, the relative value of students' time and grades in the social system of this classroom. The first step in the calculation is taking the cross product **D'D**. This gives a symmetric 2 × 2 matrix with entries

$$\sum_i d_{i1}^2 = .0458 \qquad \sum_i d_{i1}d_{i2} = -.1867 \qquad \sum_i d_{i2}^2 = .7759$$

Use of eq. 26.4 shows that the value of students' time in the system relative to the value of grades is .805 : .195. This ratio differs little from the ratio of the total fraction of the available grades that the students get to the total fraction of the students' leisure time that the teacher gets. (The source of the minor difference is the fact that eq. 26.4 minimizes the sum of the squared deviations, rather than the sum of the absolute values of deviations.)

In this example I assumed the total amount of leisure time and the overall grade, and as a consequence this analysis does not provide empirical results of interest (except when compared with other schools). If data had been collected on these two characteristics, the example would have provided meaningful results.

The vector of values is only a first result of the application of the theory to data. A second result is a measure of the degree to which the theory, as applied, fits the data. All transactions in a perfectly competitive exchange system take place with an equal exchange of value on the part of the two traders. This implies that eq. 26.1 holds. But that would mean that students who put in the same amount of time on homework would all receive the same grade. As Table 26.3 shows, this is not true. Thus the theory fits the data only with error. The sum of the squared error is $\sum_i \varepsilon_i^2 = .000555$. If grades had been distributed as shown in Table 26.3 but independently of homework, the error would have been .0019. The actual error in the system is 29% of the error that would have resulted from grades being given independently of homework.

The fact that some students got higher grades than others without doing more homework means that although students' power is equal at the outset, their power as calculated (using eq. 26.1) from the value of the resources they held at time t is not equal. As Table 6.3 shows (for an analysis involving grades, homework, and attendance), it is not the students with the highest grades (students 5, 16, 18, and 20) who have greatest power in the system. High power in the system results from receiving reasonably good grades with little time spent on homework (as did students 8, 11, 18, and 19). This corresponds to what is ordinarily observed in studies of youth in high school. It is not the "grinds" who are popular, even when they make the highest grades (see, for example, Coleman, 1961).

Estimation of Value When There Are More Than Two Resources

When the number of resources is greater than two, minimizing the sum of squared differences between resources at time 0 and resources at time t subject to the constraint that $\Sigma_j v_j = 1.0$ can be carried out by use of Lagrange multipliers. The Lagrangian function is

$$L = \sum_i (r_{i0} - r_{it})^2 + \lambda\left(1 - \sum_j v_j\right) \qquad (26.5)$$

The minimum may be found by setting the partial derivatives of L with respect to each of the v_j and to λ equal to zero and solving the resulting $m + 1$ equations, which have the following form:

$$\sum_{k=1}^{m} \sum_{i=1}^{n} d_{ij}d_{ik}v_k - \lambda = 0, \qquad j = 1, \ldots, m \qquad (26.6)$$

$$\sum_k v_k - 1 = 0$$

The Lagrange multiplier, λ, may be eliminated from the first m equations by subtracting the mth equation from each, to give this set of m equations:

$$\sum_{k=1}^{m} \sum_{i=1}^{n} (d_{ij}d_{ik} - d_{im}d_{ik})v_k = 0, \qquad j = 1, \ldots, m - 1 \qquad (26.7)$$

$$\sum_{k=1}^{m} v_k = 1$$

These equations may be solved for v_k.

In matrix notation, let the cross-product matrix be

$$\mathbf{F} = \mathbf{D'D} \qquad (m \times m)$$

$$= \|f_{jk}\|$$

where $\mathbf{D}$ is as defined earlier. Then define

$$\mathbf{G} = \|g_{jk}\| \qquad (m \times m)$$

where

$$g_{jk} = \begin{cases} f_{jk} - f_{mk}, & \text{for } j = 1, \ldots, m - 1, k = 1, \ldots, m \\ 1, & \text{for } j = m, k = 1, \ldots, m \end{cases}$$

Writing out g_{jk} in terms of control, c_{ij0} at time 0 and c_{ijt} at time t, gives

$$g_{jk} = \sum_i [(c_{ij0} - c_{ijt})(c_{ik0} - c_{ikt}) - (c_{im0} - c_{imt})(c_{ik0} - c_{ikt})]$$

$$j = 1, \ldots, m - 1, k = 1, \ldots, m$$

Then define

$$\mathbf{y} = \|y_k\|$$

where

$$y_k = \begin{cases} 0, & \text{for } k = 1, \ldots, m - 1 \\ 1, & \text{for } k = m \end{cases}$$

Then eq. 26.7 may be written as

$$\mathbf{G}\mathbf{v} = \mathbf{y} \qquad (26.8)$$

The solution to this equation is found by left-multiplying both sides by $\mathbf{G}^{-1}$, giving

$$\mathbf{v} = \mathbf{G}^{-1}\mathbf{y} \qquad (26.9)$$

Thus the vector of values, $\mathbf{v}$, may be found by first creating the cross-product matrix $\mathbf{F}$, constructing $\mathbf{G}$ from $\mathbf{F}$, and then finding the inverse of $\mathbf{G}$. Because $\mathbf{y}' = (0, \ldots, 0, 1)$, the vector of values, $\mathbf{v}$, is the mth column of $\mathbf{G}^{-1}$.

EXAMPLE 4: EXCHANGE BETWEEN TEACHER AND STUDENTS INVOLVING MORE THAN TWO RESOURCES   The analysis of the preceding example can be elaborated by assuming that teacher and students employ additional resources in their exchange system. Table 26.3 gives students' absences and teachers' interest (as perceived by students). Students can be seen to begin with control of their school time; they retain control of that time when they are absent but give it up to the teacher when they attend school. Thus a student who is absent a great deal retains control of most of his school time, whereas a student who attends school regularly gives up that time to the teacher. Similarly, the teacher may be viewed as beginning with full control of interest in students. Insofar as the teacher shows an interest in a student, the teacher gives up part of the potential interest to the student.

The maximum school time available to each student is taken as 30 days;

the highest potential interest that the teacher can have in any student is coded as 3 in Table 26.3. Thus the total school time is $20 \times 30 = 600$, and the total interest is $20 \times 3 = 60$.

Adding these two resources to the analysis (using eq. 26.9 to find **v**) changes greatly the value of resources in the system, as shown below:

Resource	Value
Students' leisure time	.347
Students' school time	.285
Grades	.303
Teacher's interest	.065

These values show that when students' school time and teacher's interest in students are included in the analysis, the value of grades increases greatly, the value of students' school time is very high, and the value of homework declines greatly. What this implies is that in this exchange system presence in school is as important to getting good grades as is time spent on homework. It implies that teachers withhold good grades from students who are habitually absent as much as or more than they withhold good grades from students who do not get their homework done. (This, of course, is an incomplete analysis, because it omits students' performances on tests, which ordinarily constitute the most important resource that students exchange for grades.)

The exchange rates differ, of course, from school to school. For another school with twenty sophomores (also reported on in *High School and Beyond*; school 1 in Table 6.1), the value of resources was as shown below:

Resource	Value
Students' leisure time	.422
Students' school time	.225
Grades	.319
Teacher's interest	.033

In this school grades were given less for presence in school and more for doing homework. In both schools teacher's interest was essentially irrelevant to the exchange.

In this example, the relative values of leisure time and school time, and the relative values of grades and teachers' interest, are very sensitive to minor variations in data, because of the similarities of profiles of resources of different students. This sensitivity would not be present in a differentiated exchange system, such as a system that included exchanges among students in the role of peers.

Arbitrary Zero Points for Resources

The model as described so far is based on the assumption that for each resource the zero point is well defined. That, of course, may not be so. In the example involving exchange between teacher and students, the zero point of grades, or of teacher's interest, or even of leisure time and school time, is not well defined. For this reason it is useful to allow for arbitrary zero points. Assume that the relation between the true quantity of resource j and the quantity as measured is

$$c'_{ij} = c_{ij} + c_{.j} \tag{26.10}$$

where $\quad c'_{ij} \equiv$ true quantity of j held by i

$\quad\quad c_{ij} \equiv$ measured quantity of j held by i

$\quad\quad c_{.j} \equiv$ true quantity minus measured quantity

Then the fundamental equation (eq. 26.2) stating that the value of an actor's resources before exchange equals the value of that actor's resources after exchange can be written in terms of true quantities as

$$\sum_{j=1}^{m} c'_{ij0} v_j = \sum_{j=1}^{m} c'_{ijt} v_j + \varepsilon_i \tag{26.11}$$

or, equivalently, in terms of measured quantities as

$$\sum_{j=1}^{m} c_{ij0} v_j + \sum_{j \in S_{i0}} c_{.j} v_j = \sum_{j=1}^{m} c_{ijt} v_j + \sum_{j \in S_{it}} c_{.j} v_j + \varepsilon_i \tag{26.12}$$

where S_{i0} is the set of resources i holds before exchange and S_{it} is the set of resources i holds after exchange. If all the actors i and k in the set of actors included in the analysis hold the same set of resources, $S_{i0} = S_{k0} = S_0$ and $S_{it} = S_{kt} = S_t$. Then eq. 26.12 can be written as

$$\sum_{j=1}^{m} c_{ij0} v_j + \sum_{j \in S_0} c_{.j} v_j - \sum_{j \in S_t} c_{.j} v_j = \sum_{j=1}^{m} c_{ijt} v_j + \varepsilon_i \tag{26.13}$$

The quantity $\sum_{j \in S_0} c_{.j} v_j - \sum_{j \in S_t} c_{.j} v_j$ is a constant for all actors included in the analysis and can be regarded as an additional resource, labeled $m + 1$, which is constant for all m actors included in the analysis. The quantity of that resource held by each actor is $1/n$, and the value is v_{m+1}, which is unknown.

Thus eq. 26.11 can be written in terms of observed quantities and a constant:

$$\sum_{j=1}^{m} c_{ij0} v_j + \left(\frac{1}{n}\right) v_{m+1} = \sum_{j=1}^{m} c_{ijt} v_j + \varepsilon_i$$

or

$$\sum_{j=1}^{m+1} d_{ij} v_j = \varepsilon_i \tag{26.14}$$

where, as before, $d_{ij} = c_{ij0} - c_{ijt}$, for $j = 1, \ldots, m$, and $d_{i,m+1} = 1/n$. The constraint that the sum of the values of all quantities in the system equal 1.0 remains a constraint over the m measured resources, excluding the constant.

Minimizing the sum of squared errors in eq. 26.14 can be done as before by setting up the Lagrangian function, including the constant. The Lagrangian function is as shown in eq. 26.5, where the summation over j includes only the m resources, excluding the constant. Taking the partial derivatives of the Lagrangian function with respect to the $m + 1$ values v_j and to λ and setting them equal to zero gives, instead of eq. 26.6:

$$\sum_{k=1}^{m+1} \sum_{i=1}^{n} d_{ij} d_{ik} v_k - \lambda = 0, \qquad j = 1, \ldots, m \qquad (26.15)$$

$$\sum_{k=1}^{m+1} \sum_{i=1}^{n} \frac{1}{n} d_{ik} v_k = 0$$

$$\sum_{k=1}^{m} v_k - 1 = 0$$

The Lagrange multiplier, λ, may be eliminated from the first $m - 1$ equations by subtracting the mth equation from each, giving

$$\sum_{k=1}^{m+1} \sum_{i=1}^{n} (d_{ij} d_{ik} - d_{im} d_{ik}) v_k = 0, \qquad j = 1, \ldots, m - 1 \qquad (26.16)$$

$$\sum_{k=1}^{m+1} \sum_{i=1}^{n} \frac{1}{n} d_{ik} v_k = 0$$

$$\sum_{k=1}^{m} v_k = 1$$

To solve this set of equations, the cross-product matrix **F** may be defined as in the case without a constant:

$$\mathbf{F} = \mathbf{D}'\mathbf{D} \qquad [(m + 1) \times (m + 1)]$$

The matrix **G** is constructed with elements g_{jk} defined as follows:

$$g_{jk} = f_{jk} - f_{mk}, \qquad \text{for } j = 1, \ldots, m - 1, k = 1, \ldots, m + 1$$

$$g_{mk} = f_{m+1,k}, \qquad \text{for } k = 1, \ldots, m + 1 \qquad (26.17)$$

$$g_{m+1,k} = 1, \qquad \text{for } k = 1, \ldots, m$$

$$g_{m+1,m+1} = 0$$

Then, if the vector **y** is defined as before, but with $y_k = 0$ for $k = 1, \ldots, m$ and $y_k = 1$ for $k = m + 1$, eq. 26.16 can be written as eq. 26.8 and solved for **v**, as before, to give eq. 26.9.

EXAMPLE 5: LABOR MARKET ANALYSIS Sociologists' quantitative empirical research on social stratification has characteristically taken the form of either studies of status attainment or analyses of tables on occupational mobility. The first of these two approaches treats the acquisition of occupational prestige very similarly to the way that changes in attitudes are studied: The individual's occupational prestige is taken as a dependent variable in a linear regression analysis, where the independent variables are characteristics of the individual or of some aspects of his background. The second approach has used either a Markov process, in which each individual from a given origin is regarded as having a probability of ending up in each of the possible occupations, or log linear analyses, which examine patterns of deviation from baseline assumptions about occupational mobility (such as no inheritance of occupation or complete inheritance).

In both of these types of analysis, what is neglected is that occupational choice is a resultant of a complex set of factors: the preference of the employee for the particular job relative to other jobs, the preferences of other employees for the job relative to other jobs, the preference of the employer who controls the job for the employee relative to others, the preferences among other employers for this and other workers, and finally the relative power of employees and employers in the market, which depends on number of workers and number of jobs. Occupational choice is a process in which jobs are matched with workers in a competitive market.

This structural aspect of occupational mobility has been recognized by a number of investigators, although no models of the process that are satisfactory for empirical research have yet been proposed.[1] White (1970) in effect turned the Markovian approach on its head; instead of considering each individual from a given origin as having a particular probability of ending up in each occupation, he considered each vacant job (characterized according to variables defining its previous occupant) as having a particular probability of being filled by an occupant with given characteristics. This approach takes as given the distribution of occupations and the choice process used by the employer, but ignores the effect of variation in the distribution of workers among whom jobs must be filled as well as preferences among workers. Boudon (1974) has taken some steps toward conceiving of occupational mobility as a result of market processes, but without developing a method of analysis for pursuing the conception.

If occupational choice is viewed as a two-sided market, the market may be considered an exchange system in which workers exchange their time in return for a job. Each worker has particular characteristics that are resources for getting a job, and each job has particular resources for attracting workers. The market, however, differs in structure from that described for the exchange between students and teacher. In the exchange of homework for grades, each student has a certain amount of discretionary time, and the teacher has a certain total of grades. Price, or value, serves as a means by which the quantities of resources exchanged are adjusted to bring about market clearing. In a labor market each actor exchanges all of what he has in return for all of what the other

1. Sattinger (1984) has addressed a problem with similar structure. He begins with the problem of optimal assignment of workers to machines and shows that with data on the productivity of worker i with machine j, it is possible to obtain not only optimal assignments, worker wages, and machine rents, but also the amount of each of a set of "properties," or resources, possessed by each machine.

Table 26.4   Values of worker and job resources for analysis of labor market.

Resource	Value
Education level of worker	.23
Experience of worker	.05
Worker with 0 years of education and experience (v_{m+1})	.43
Salary or wage for job	.66
Occupational prestige of job	.05

Source: Values were calculated using data from *General Social Survey* (Davis and Smith, 1986).

has (assuming that employers do not adjust wages or conditions to attract a particular worker, that is, that a job's characteristics are fixed).

Value in this system plays a different role. With the assumption that each exchange involves equal value moving in both directions, the value of a worker is a quantity indicating the value of a job that worker can get, and the value of a job is a quantity indicating the value of a worker that job can get. That is, the values of workers and the values of jobs are defined relative to one another.

The way in which this model can be applied in labor market analysis can be illustrated using data from *General Social Survey 1986* (Davis and Smith, 1986). From a representative sample of 923 members of the employed labor force in the United States, data were obtained on personal characteristics and job characteristics. The analysis uses two job characteristics (occupational prestige as measured by the Duncan index and logarithm of pay) and two characteristics of workers (education and experience). The model which allows for a constant is used.

Table 26.4 shows the results of the analysis in terms of values normalized to sum to 1.0 plus the constant term. The analysis shows that on the job side pay has a much greater value in attracting workers than does occupational prestige. It also shows that the principal value on the workers' side is contained in simply being an employee, even without considering the resources measured in the analysis. This reflects the fact that workers' income does not go down to zero, but only to some minimum greater than zero. The values for persons' resources above this minimum show that education is by far the most important, with experience having about a fifth of the value of education.

Sampling and the Importance of the Population and Resource Distributions

Most methods of data analysis are conceptually at a single level. If the units of analysis are individuals, both the variables and the estimated parameters characterize individuals. For example, suppose one assumed that test scores are a linear function of amount of time spent on homework and number of absences, as shown below:

$$y_i = a + b_1 x_{1i} + b_2 x_{2i} + e_i$$

where y_i ≡ test scores
   x_{1i} ≡ time spent on homework
   x_{2i} ≡ number of absences

Then, using the data of Table 26.3 in an ordinary least-squares regression analysis, one could estimate a as the constant term (predicted test scores when there was no time spent on homework and no absences), b_1 as the effect of spending time on homework on test scores, and b_2 as the effect of absences on test scores. All of these estimated parameters are conceptually at the level of the individual. The sample of students is necessary in order to have enough variation in test scores, time spent on homework, and absences to separate out statistically the effects of each of the two variables on the third. Conceptually, any sample of students would be satisfactory, as long as the underlying relationships were the same for each student and there was sufficient independent variation in time spent on homework and absences to estimate the parameters.

In linear systems analysis as introduced in this chapter, the sample plays a fundamentally different conceptual role. In the system involving the exchange between students and teacher of homework for grades, the estimated exchange rate was .805:.195. This means that the ratio of the fraction of the total available grades the teacher gave out to the fraction of their total leisure time students spent on homework was .805:.195 in that school. The teacher had to give out a lot of the total available grades in order to get a much smaller fraction of the total discretionary student time. The students gave up 103 hours out of their total discretionary time of 500 hours, or .206 of their time, and the teacher gave out 103 grade points out of a total (assumed) of 120 possible points, or .858 of the possible grades. The ratio .858:.206 is approximately the same as the ratio of values estimated in the analysis.

These estimates, although they are based on data about individuals, are conceptually estimates of a property of the system: the ratio of exchange at which transactions between actors take place. That rate can be specified in terms of units of the resources, rather than as fractions of their totals. For example, the total of grade points given out is 103, and the total number of hours spent on homework is 103, or 1 grade point for 1 hour per week of homework. (When more than two resources are involved in the system, however, this kind of comparison cannot be used to discover the exchange rates.)

Note, however, that if a regression analysis of grades on homework (or homework on grades) were carried out, that result would show, *at the individual level*, how many grade points were forthcoming for each hour of homework. This can be seen by assuming the same totals for grade points and hours on homework, 103 for each, but with zero correlation between grades and homework. A regression analysis of grades on homework would show a regression coefficient of zero, but the exchange rate shown by linear systems analysis would remain approximately the same as it would be if there were a perfect correlation. In linear systems analysis the absence of an individual-level correspondence between grades and homework would show up not in the exchange rates, which are a system property, but in the fact that those rates vary, that some students get a much better rate than others do, thus improving their resource position while others' positions worsen.

The effect of the population distribution on exchange rate can be best seen by referring to the labor market analysis of the preceding section. In that example the jobs could be characterized by a bivariate distribution according to occupational prestige and pay. Suppose that the overall pay was increased, through a 10% increase in the salary or wage for each job. Then if relative interests of workers in prestige and in money remained the same, the predicted exchange rates or values of resources, expressed as fractions of the totals, would remain the same; but the value of $1 in the market (in terms of the resources of workers it would buy) would go down by 10%. The only distributional change predicted would be that each worker would get 10% more money.

If the education of workers increased, then assuming that the interest of employers in experience (and other worker characteristics) relative to education remained the same (that is, employers had no interest in workers' having particular levels of education, but only an interest in education relative to experience), the predicted value of the total education in the system would remain the same, and thus the value to a worker of an extra year of education would be less than before. An individual-level regression analysis would lead to different predictions. If the regression coefficient shows an increment of $1,000 in income per year of education, then a worker who added a year of education to his total would, *independently of* the change in educational levels of others in the sample, be predicted to increase his income by $1,000.

As the illustrations offered above indicate, population distributions of resources and actors are very important to the estimates produced by linear systems analysis. Sampling of populations for data analysis need not have distorting effects if careful attention is given to obtain a representative sample. If data from two sides of a market are to be obtained independently, correct estimation of values in the market requires that weights be used where necessary to produce a weighted sample with a constant sampling probability.

Estimation of Interests

The analysis in this chapter has made no assumption about the form of actors' utility functions. It has been assumed that actors maximize utility subject to initial resource constraints; that is implicit in the one substantive assumption used in the analysis, the assumption that equal value is given up and gained in each transaction.

Assuming that the utility functions take the form used in Chapter 25 (the Cobb-Douglas utility function) makes it possible to estimate interests of each actor in each resource. To do so, it is also necessary to assume that

$$\mathbf{C}_t = \mathbf{C}^* \tag{26.18}$$

that is, that the distribution of resources after exchange is the equilibrium distribution. With these assumptions, the derivations carried out in Chapter 25 are relevant, and eq. 25.11 may be used to estimate interests of actors. Rewriting that equation to solve for x_{ji} gives

$$x_{ji} = \frac{c_{ij}^* v_j}{r_i} \tag{26.19}$$

Equation 26.19, with c_{ijt} from the data used as c_{ij}^* (in accordance with eq. 26.18) and with v_j and r_{it} as calculated from the data used as v_j and r_i, may be used to estimate interests, x_{ji}. In Chapter 6 interests of students and teacher in students' leisure time, school time, and grades were estimated using eq. 26.19. They are shown in Table 6.4.

Estimated interests make it possible to predict changes in values and in the equilibrium distribution of resources. Interests are properties of the actors and, under many circumstances, can be assumed to remain constant even though the distribution of resources changes. Whether that assumption is reasonable depends on the setting in question. Once such empirical questions are answered (and the answers can be expected to be similar for different resources), information about interests can be used to predict the equilibrium distribution as the composition of the system changes. This becomes especially important in the study of labor markets as the distribution of jobs or workers changes, or in the study of marriage markets as the age distribution of the eligible population changes. For example, the marriage squeeze that results from abrupt changes in the birth rate or other changes affecting the relative supplies of marriageable men and women can be studied through first estimating interests of men in women of particular ages and interests of women in men of particular ages. Given the interests estimated from age-specific marriages under one distribution, the squeeze that would arise under a different distribution can be predicted.

This chapter has introduced a general strategy for data analysis. Succeeding chapters of this part will introduce variations on the model for exchange of private, divisible goods that was presented in Chapter 25. Those variations can in turn generate variations on, or extensions of, the methods of data analysis introduced in this chapter. For example, empirical study of norms or collective decisions can be carried out using the results of Chapters 30 and 31 to extend the data analysis methods described in this chapter. I will not undertake presentation of the extensions; however, examples in succeeding chapters suggest directions that such empirical analysis might take. Nor have I discussed other approaches to empirical analysis using this model or earlier versions of it. These have focused primarily on the prediction of outcomes of collective decisions when interests and initial control are known. Examples of this work include Hernes (1971), El Hakim (1972), Marsden and Laumann (1977), Pappi and Kappelhoff (1984), and Kim (1986).

« 27 »

Extensions of the Theory

Chapter 25 described a linear system of action in an institutional and structural setting that made possible a perfectly competitive market. But social exchange often involves resources that do not have the full properties of private, divisible, and alienable goods, and it often takes place in an institutional and structural setting with properties that make it not a perfectly competitive market. These properties are in some cases market imperfections to which all the connotations of that term apply, but in other cases they are properties intrinsic to the situation, which affect the functioning of the system in ways that are intended and generally regarded as desirable. As discussed in Chapter 17, the fact that in most election systems votes cannot legitimately be exchanged for money is not an imperfection in the sense that the barrier is unintended. The fact that social obligations cannot be passed on to a third party as bills of exchange can does not in itself mean that the social system functions less well than if they could.

Thus the task of an analyst of social systems is neither to assume that all markets function like perfectly competitive markets nor to show means by which market imperfections may be overcome. It is, rather, to build conceptual systems that mirror social systems as they exist. In some cases this work may suggest institutions through which the social system could come to better realize the goals of all participants. But in many cases this will not be so.

This chapter examines some properties of social systems which lead social exchanges to differ from economic exchanges that occur in highly rationalized markets with a medium of exchange.

A Perfect Social System

In succeeding chapters of this part, it will be useful to refer to a model of a social system that corresponds to economists' perfectly competitive market. I will use the term "perfect social system," or in some cases simply "perfect system" to refer to such a model. The term refers to a social system in which actors are rational, as defined in Chapter 2, and in which there is no structure to impede any actor's use of resources at any point in the system. In economists' terms there are no transaction costs. Free-rider problems do not exist, for actors are able to use their resources to induce others with like interests to contribute to the common good. As in a perfectly competitive market, there are no advantages to strategic behavior, because there are no contingencies of actions. Each actor is confronted with a set of goods or events having values that are systemwide. The systemwide values ensure that each actor's power is systemwide, and not specific to other actors.

The perfect social system differs in one major respect from a perfect market. It contains indivisible events, for which a positive outcome favors the interests of one subset of actors in the system and a negative outcome favors the inter- ests of another subset. This means that the kinds of potential activities in a perfect social system include not only exchange of divisible goods but also exchange of partial rights of control over indivisible events. Yet because the value of each outcome of each event is known (as is the value of each combina- tion of outcomes of all divisible events taken together), control over indivisible events can occur and outcomes can be determined without exchange of re- sources. In such a system there is no conflict because all confrontations are virtual. The weaker side sees that it will lose and deploys its resources else- where, rather than wasting them in a lost cause. Norms exist, and sanctions are potentially present but are never used, because target actors know whether or not their power-weighted interests are greater than those of the sanctioners. If not, the target actors will obey the norm; otherwise, they will disregard the norm, and potential sanctioners will not sanction because they know it would be a waste of resources.

One concept that is particularly important in defining a perfect social system is social capital. In a perfect social system social capital is complete. Also, conver- tibility of all resources is complete. Thus each actor's potential power is usable at every point in the system. There are no transmission losses, no transaction costs.

An economic system in which power is measured by wealth comes closest to a perfect social system. Because of the existence of money as a fungible medium of exchange, an economic system deviates from a perfect social system primar- ily in social-structural barriers or transaction costs between pairs of actors, rather than in nonconvertibility between pairs of resources. A major reason why an economic system most closely approximates a perfect social system lies in its very conception: Within such a system there is no intentional nonconvertibility of resources as there is, for example, between money and votes, or between votes by one decision-making body and votes by another, or even between votes on two different issues in the same decision-making body. Outside the economic system, and between the economic system and the rest of the social system, there is nonconvertibility of power between different arenas of activity, purpo- sively established to prevent power in one arena from determining outcomes in other. The absence of full convertibility of power, enforced in some arenas by legal sanctions, allows what might be described as a pluralism of power. There is pluralism of power among institutional areas, among organizations, and even among departments of organizations.

One might ask whether another sort of arrangement could exist to preserve pluralism of power while maintaining full convertibility of power between institutional or organizational areas. The defects of the use of legal and organizational barriers to convertibility arise principally because actors with power in one arena and interests in another arena that is insulated from the first have an incentive to use their power to implement their interests. Legal sanctions are necessary to prevent that use, but actors often find ways to circumvent those sanctions. For example, the fact that corporate actors have strong interests in legislative outcomes but no rights of control over those outcomes leads to extraordinarily intense activity in attempting to use economic power to influence the legislative outcomes: lobbying, campaign support for candidates, and other actions. One could conceive of a system in which economic power was legally convertible into political power, and the political power was legally convertible into economic power. Under an appropriate constitutional allocation of political rights to natural persons, the political power held by every citizen could be converted into economic resources through exchange processes in which the political power was acquired for use by corporate actors; this would provide a minimum economic resource base for every citizen.

Psychic Investment

It will be useful to introduce an elaboration based on the distinction made in Chapter 19 between different parts of the self as rational actor: the acting self, which controls events, exchanges control over events, and exercises control; and the object self, which experiences consequences of events. If there is such a separation of acting self and object self, then the acting self may be motivated to act by the expected consequences to an expanded object self, which incorporates objects outside the physical self, and not only by the expected consequences to the physical self. Such psychic investments may with little difficulty be incorporated into the theory of action by splitting the actor into the two selves. They are labeled A for acting self and O for object self in Figure 27.1.

In this expanded system actors have control over events that have consequences for the objects of action, in which the actors have psychic investments. Thus the interest matrix is separated into two analytic components: consequences of events for objects, and psychic investments of actors in objects. This allows the possibility that an actor's psychic investments are distributed among other persons, and not confined to his own physical self.

Figure 27.1 Relations between an actor and an event when there is psychic investment.

Formally this extension is a simple one. The consequence matrix has events as rows and objects as columns and shows the fraction of each object's consequences that arise from each event. The matrix resembles an interest matrix in both its formal properties and its meaning, and it may be thought of in exactly the same way. Thus I will denote it by X, with elements x_{kj} representing the proportion of object j's consequences that come from event k. The psychic investment matrix I will denote by S, with elements s_{ji} representing the proportion of actor i's total psychic investment that is invested in object j. The constraints on s_{ji} are like those for C and X: $s_{ji} \geq 0$, and $\Sigma\, s_{ji} = 1.0$. That is, s_{ji} represents the partitioning the actor i's psychic investment among various objects j.

In this expanded theory there are three matrices: C, X, and S. The product XS plays the same role that X plays in the basic theory. That is, the sum of products $x_{kj}s_{ji}$, over all objects in which actor i has a psychic investment, constitutes the motivating force, the interest the acting self has in gaining control of event k. This extension of the system allows writing these equations for r, w, and C^* in place of eqs. 25.15, 25.16, and 25.11*:

$$r = CXSr \qquad (27.1)$$

$$v = XSCv \qquad (27.2)$$

$$C^* = D_r(XS)'D_v^{-1} \qquad (27.3)$$

This expansion of the basic theory allows introduction of a concept which I will call the importance of the object in the system, denoted by p_j. This is defined as the total investment of all actors in the object, weighted by the power or wealth of each actor:

$$p_j = \sum_i s_{ji}r_i \qquad (27.4)$$

$$p = Sr = SCXp$$

The quantity p_j represents the fraction of the system's total resources that are devoted to object j (which is ordinarily, although it need not be, one of the actors in the system). According to the expanded theory, object selves and acting selves are different; individuals as objects may have different importance than they have power as actors.

The basic theory, in which the object and acting self are the same, may be seen as a degenerate case of the expanded theory, in which no actor has a psychic investment in others. This is reflected in the formal model when S is an identity matrix.

Dependence of Events

A straightforward extension of the basic theory that is formally similar to psychic investment but represents structure in the external world rather than structure within the self is direct dependence of events (or resources) on other events or resources. In the basic theory there is dependence of events on other events through actors: An event controlled by actors who have an interest in another event is dependent on that other event through those actors. The dependence of events on other events through actors is given by the product matrix XC, which shows the dependence of column events on row events. Apart from this dependence through other actors, however, there is sometimes direct dependence of events upon other events. This section treats the structure through which that dependence can be represented.

The events in which actors are interested are often not those over which they have control, but rather ones that are dependent on those over which they have control. Thus there are many circumstances in which there is a structure of dependency among events which intervenes between actors' control and their interests. In some cases, as for collective decisions or indivisible events, discussed in Chapters 14, 15, and 31, actors have an interest in introducing new events in which some actors are interested by showing that they are dependent on events already within the system. The formal apparatus for introducing this dependence of events is straightforward. If the set of events over which actors in the system have control is $E_1, \ldots, E_m$ and the set of events in which they have an interest that depend on these events is $E_1, \ldots, E_m, E_{m+1}, \ldots, E_s$, then the columns in the control matrix, C, represent the m events over which they have control, and the rows in the interest matrix, X, represent the s events in which they have an interest. These latter events may, but need not, include the events over which they have control. A third matrix, which I will call a dependency matrix and will denote by B, is necessary to connect these two matrices. The elements of B, b_{kj}, represent the fraction of dependence of event j on event k. Just as the psychic investment matrix resulting from differentiating between actor as subject and actor as object did, the dependency matrix generates a new concept, which I will call the consequentiality of the event and denote by f_k. The value of control over event j, given by v_j, shows the value of controlling that event, either for its direct consequences (when b_{jj} is great and x_{ji} is great for powerful actors) or for its consequences through other events (when b_{jk} is great for one or more events k and x_{ki} is great for powerful actors). Similarly, f_k, the consequentiality of event k, shows the impact of the outcome of event k on the system, through its consequences for powerful actors. When events are independent, the consequentiality of an event is the same as the value of control over it; in the more general case this is not so.

When dependence of events on other events plays a role in the system, it is often true that externalities will be introduced. For example, the common project involving three actors described in Chapter 10 is an event dependent on the contributions of each but with consequences for all which are inseparable. When this is the case, methods to be described in Chapters 30 and 31 must be used for analysis of the system.

For dependence which does not introduce such indivisibility into the system, the methods of Chapter 25 may be extended much as they were for psychic investment. In such a case (as shown in the first example in Chapter 28) $\mathbf{r}$, $\mathbf{v}$, $\mathbf{f}$, and $\mathbf{C}^*$ may be found:

$$\mathbf{r} = \mathbf{Cv} = \mathbf{CBf} = \mathbf{CBXr} \qquad (27.5)$$

$$\mathbf{v} = \mathbf{Bp} = \mathbf{BXr} = \mathbf{BXCv} \qquad (27.6)$$

$$\mathbf{f} = \mathbf{Xr} = \mathbf{XCv} = \mathbf{XCBf} \qquad (27.7)$$

$$\mathbf{C}^* = \mathbf{D}_r(\mathbf{BX})'\mathbf{D}_v^{-1} \qquad (27.8)$$

When $\mathbf{B} = \mathbf{I}$, the system reduces to the basic system of control and interest.

In some cases there is more than a single stage of dependence, and a second dependency matrix is necessary. Such a matrix in itself introduces no new principles into the system; it may be absorbed directly into the interest matrix as $\mathbf{BX}$ or into the control matrix as $\mathbf{CB}$, after which the system is analyzed as before.

There can, however, be further complexity, since the dependence of events is not always fixed. For example, when there are events for which the outcomes depend on collective decisions, there may be dependence among them, but it will be determined by the order in which the decisions are made. The outcome of one event may be wholly dependent on the outcome of another, but only if the decision on that other is made first. Thus it may not be possible to describe the dependence of events until the agenda is known. Such hierarchies of dependence will not be treated here.

Throughout Parts I–IV of this book are presented examples of events that are directly dependent on other events. One setting in which this occurs is when a public good is the result of actions by several actors. For example, the outcome of the common project described in Chapter 10 is an event of interest to each of the three actors, and it depends directly on three events, the contributions of each of those actors. Each of these three events is also of interest to the actor making the contribution. The matrices of control, dependency, and interest for this system are shown in Table 27.1. E_1, E_2, and E_3 are A_1's, A_2's, and A_3's contributions, respectively; E_4 is the common project, equally dependent on the three contributions. These matrices show that interests of each actor are in his

Table 27.1　Control, dependency, and interest for a three-actor common project.

	Control (C)				Dependency (B)					Interest (X′)			
	E_1	E_2	E_3		E_1	E_2	E_3	E_4		E_1	E_2	E_3	E_4
A_1	1	0	0	E_1	1	0	0	1/3	A_1	9/21	0	0	12/21
A_2	0	1	0	E_2	0	1	0	1/3	A_2	0	9/21	0	12/21
A_3	0	0	1	E_3	0	0	1	1/3	A_3	0	0	9/21	12/21

own contribution and in the project. Control, however, is over only the contribution. It is the dependency matrix that links the contributions and the project.

Thus, if each actor's interest is to serve its function in the theory of action as the driver to determine the events over which the actor will attempt to gain control, it must be filtered through the dependency matrix to obtain a derived interest in the events that are under some actor's control, in this case, E_1, E_2, and E_3. This derived interest is given by **BX**, which can be treated in the same way as was **X** in the basic model. In this example the matrix **BX** giving the derived interests shows that each actor has a derived interest of 13/21 in controlling his own contribution and a derived interest of 4/21 in controlling the contribution of each of the other two actors.

Analysis like that carried out in Chapter 25 would show that each of the three actors would end up with .619 of control of his own contribution and .191 of control of the contribution of each of the others. This, however, is not meaningful and does not correspond to what would happen in reality. (It would seem to imply that each would give up .19 of his own contribution for the disposition of each of the others.) Chapters 30 and 31 address the proper way to analyze structures of this sort, in which events have externalities, and Chapter 30 provides a correct analysis for this example.

Partitioned Systems of Action

Another extension of the general theoretical framework involves partitioning the system into two sets of actors, connected by the events over which they have control and in which they have interest. The usefulness of this partitioning lies in what it can tell about relations between the two subsets of actors, as well as relations among actors within each subset.

A system consisting of n actors can be divided into two parts: actors $1, \ldots, n_a$ and actors $n_a + 1, \ldots, n$. For concreteness, consider a university department divided into faculty and graduate students, groups a and b. In the notation introduced above, let $\mathbf{CX} = \mathbf{Z}$. The partitioning of the system means that $\mathbf{Z}$ is partitioned into four submatrices:

$$\begin{array}{c|c} \mathbf{Z}_{aa} & \mathbf{Z}_{ab} \\ \hline \mathbf{Z}_{ba} & \mathbf{Z}_{bb} \end{array}$$

where $\mathbf{Z}_{aa}$ is faculty control over what interests faculty, $\mathbf{Z}_{ab}$ is faculty control over what interests students, $\mathbf{Z}_{ba}$ is students' control over what interests faculty, and $\mathbf{Z}_{bb}$ is student control over what interests students. The basic equation $\mathbf{r} = \mathbf{Zr}$ can be written

$$\mathbf{r}_a = \mathbf{Z}_{aa}\mathbf{r}_a + \mathbf{Z}_{ab}\mathbf{r}_b$$

$$\mathbf{r}_b = \mathbf{Z}_{ba}\mathbf{r}_a + \mathbf{Z}_{bb}\mathbf{r}_b$$

where $\mathbf{r}_a$ is the vector of faculty power and $\mathbf{r}_b$ is the vector of student power, and

1.0 equals the sum of power in the full system.[1] Focusing attention on faculty power gives

$$\mathbf{r}_a = \mathbf{Z}_{aa}\mathbf{r}_a + \mathbf{Z}_{ab}\mathbf{r}_b \qquad (27.9)$$

$$(\mathbf{I} - \mathbf{Z}_{aa})\mathbf{r}_a = \mathbf{Z}_{ab}\mathbf{r}_b$$

$$\mathbf{r}_a = (\mathbf{I} - \mathbf{Z}_{aa})^{-1}\mathbf{Z}_{ab}\mathbf{r}_b \qquad (27.10)$$

The vector $\mathbf{Z}_{ab}\mathbf{r}_b$ represents the power that each faculty member brings into the set of faculty through the interest of powerful students in what he controls. If an element of that vector is called π_{kb}, where $\pi_{kb} = \sum_{h=n_a+1}^{n} z_{kh}r_h$, and an element of $(\mathbf{I} - \mathbf{Z}_{aa})^{-1}$ is called g_{ik}^b, then each faculty member's power can be written as

$$r_i = \sum_{k=1}^{n_a} g_{ik}^b \pi_{kb}$$

The quantity π_{kb} is the power faculty member k brings in from students' (group b's) interest in what he controls, and g_{ik}^b is the units of power faculty member i ultimately has in the system per unit of power that k brings in from group b. If, for example, the power i has is greatly dependent on k's interest in what i controls, and if k loses his external power (that is, if π_{kb} decreases), then i will lose his internal power.

It is also possible to split z_{kh} (the interest of actor h of group b in what is controlled by actor k of group h) into its component parts, in order to examine the degree to which a given actor's power depends on control of a particular resource. An element from eq. 27.10 can be expanded:

$$r_i = \sum_k \sum_j \sum_h g_{ik}^b c_{kj} x_{jh} r_h$$

If the first two factors of the right-hand side are summed over actors k (in group a), and the second two are summed over actors h (in group b), the equation can be written as follows:

$$r_i = \sum_j \left(\sum_k g_{ik}^b c_{kj} \right) \left(\sum_h x_{jh} r_h \right)$$

The quantity inside the right parentheses is the weighted interest in resource j among actors in group b, that is, its *value* in group b, and the quantity inside the left parentheses is actor i's direct and indirect control, amplified through the interdependencies in group a, of that resource.

---

1. Formally $\mathbf{Z}_{ab}$ resembles the matrix of technological coefficients in input-output analysis, and g_{ik}^n resembles an element of the Leontief inverse matrix. Because Leontief's system is an open one and models the production process and this system is closed and models an exchange system, the similarity is only formal. It is interesting to note that in his early work Leontief (1951) developed a model for a closed economy, as well as the one for the open system that has proved useful for input-output analyses.

For the faculty-student example, if resource j is research assistantships, the quantity inside the right parentheses represents the value of research assistantships within the group of graduate students, and the quantity inside the left parentheses is the degree to which i's power depends on research assistantships (per unit of value of research assistantships among the students), either through his control (c_{ij}) of assistantships or through the control of assistantships by other faculty members (c_{kj} where $k \neq i$) who are beholden to him (g_{ik}^b). His power from research assistantships might increase for any of several reasons:

1. The value of research assistantships among the graduate students (the quantity in the right-hand parentheses) might increase. This could be due to either
   a. an increase of interest in research assistantships among students or
   b. a redistribution of power within the group of students, by which those with a high interest in assistantships gain power
2. Actor i's control of research assistantships (the quantity in the left-hand parentheses) might increase. This could be due to
   a. an increase in c_{ij}, his own control of assistantships or
   b. an increase in c_{kj} for those faculty who are beholden to him (high g_{ik}^b) or
   c. an increase in g_{ik}^b, the degree to which faculty member k is beholden to him, among those faculty who have control of assistantships (high c_{kj})

A special case of the partitioning described above is that in which group b contains only one actor, that is, where the total system is of size n, group a consists of actors $1, \ldots, n - 1$, and group b consists of actor n. In this case Z_{ab} becomes an $(n - 1) \times 1$ vector composed of the first $n - 1$ elements of the last column of Z. This vector may be called z_n.

The equation for the power of the first $n - 1$ actors is then, from eq. 27.9,

$$r_a = Z_{aa}r_a + z_n r_n \qquad (27.11)$$

The meaning of $z_{in}r_n$, the ith element of $z_n r_n$, is actor i's control of what interests actor n times the power of actor n, or, in other words, the amount of resources i gets directly through n's interest in what i controls. The above equation may be solved for r_a by transposing and multiplying by the inverse, as was done to obtain eq. 27.10. Then one element of r_a may be written as

$$r_i = \sum_k g_{ik}^n z_{kn} r_n \qquad (27.12)$$

According to this equation, r_i, the power of actor i, is composed of a number of terms of the form $g_{ik}^n z_{kn} r_n$.[2] First, consider the term for which $i = k$. This is the

2. Note that if such an analysis is carried out where the number in each group is greater than 1, it is necessary to determine the total vector of power in the system as a whole in order to obtain the vector of power, r, or a portion of it, such as r_1. It is not necessary, however, to do this in order to examine the substructuring of the system by studying the elements $(I - Z_{aa})^{-1}$.

power that i ultimately gets through the resources he controls that interest n. Since $z_{in}r_n$ is the power that i gets *directly* through the resources he controls that interest n, g_{ii}^n shows the amplification of these resources. That is, g_{ii}^n is the units of power i has in the system per unit of power he gets directly from n. Suppose, for example, that the system is a classroom, and actor n is the teacher. Then g_{ii}^n is the power that student i gets through the teacher's interest in what he controls.

There is an additional contribution to the power of actor i through the terms for which $i \neq k$. In eq. 27.12 the term $g_{ik}^n z_{kn} r_n$ is the power i ultimately gets through k's control of resources that interest n. Thus g_{ik}^n is the units of power i gets per unit of resources of interest to n controlled by k. If k is viewed as an actor who controls resources of interest to another actor, n, he gets certain direct power from that. But every actor, including himself, gets a certain increment of power indirectly through the interest of actor n in what he controls. In a classroom in which each student is in a relatively independent relation with the teacher, g_{ik}^n is small when $k \neq i$. In a more general system this is not the case.

The quantity $\Sigma_k g_{ik}^n z_{kn}$ may be viewed in either of two ways. The first is from actor i's point of view. Then it is the power that i gets, directly or indirectly, through his control of things in which actor n is interested. The second is from actor n's point of view. Then this quantity is the ultimate control of i, direct and indirect, over what interests n. Thus the quantity may well be thought of as i's control over n.

But if eq. 27.12 is divided through by r_n, then the quantity $\Sigma_k g_{ik}^n z_{kn}$ is equal to r_i/r_n, actor i's overall power in the system relative to actor n's overall power. Thus in a closed system, in which all other actors are reachable by each actor (a necessary condition in order to be able to calculate $\mathbf{r}$ from $\mathbf{C}$ and $\mathbf{X}$), the power of one actor over another is nothing more than the ratio of the overall power of the two. This again demonstrates the unidimensionality of power in such a system, that is, the capability of power's having its effect at any point in the system, no matter how distant. This is not, of course, a property of real social systems (except to some extent in small isolated villages or modern totalitarian states), but it is a property of a perfect social system as defined earlier.

Taking n different inverses successively excluding $j = 1, \ldots, n$ would give, for actors i and k, $n - 1$ values of g_{ii}^j and $n - 2$ values of g_{ik}^j, respectively. Since g_{ik}^j is the power i gets through k's control of resources of interest to actor j, the sum of g_{ik}^j over all other $n - 1$ actors j gives the power i gets through k's control of resources. If this result is divided by the sum of g_{ik}^j over j and k, what is obtained is the fraction of i's power that arises ultimately from k's control of resources.

Partitioning between Sets of Goods or Events

A second kind of partitioning of the system is also possible, a partitioning into two sets of resources. Later in this chapter I will introduce an example in which certain resources are within the economic system (money and entertainment) and others are within the political system (citizens' votes for a legislator and the legislator's appeal, which consists in part of campaign promises). In such a system there is some exchange between resources in the two subsystems. A partitioning of the system between the two sets of resources facilitates examination of the indirect effects of the transactions between the two subsystems.

The equations for partitioning a system between two sets of resources are entirely analogous to those already given for partitioning between sets of actors. The potential value of partitioning of systems, both between sets of actors and between sets of resources, seems great; however, since little has been done along these lines in actual data analysis, it is uncertain how great the potential is or in just what directions it lies.

Losses in Exchange between Actors and between Resources

Differentiated Power

Not only is power manifested in structurally different arenas, it comes in a number of forms. One of these forms is money, which is the most fungible form of power, being usable to obtain an enormous array of things. Since every person and every corporate actor has an interest in at least some of the things money will buy, money might well be said to be a completely fungible form of power. Precisely because interest in the goods or services that money can control is so widespread, however, the fungibility of money is artificially restricted by legal and normative barriers. For example, in many countries it is illegal to exchange sexual services for money. In legislative arenas it is illegal for a legislator to sell his vote for money. In bureaucratic arenas it is generally illegal for an administrator to accept money in return for a particular decision outcome.

Although money has almost universal fungibility, many other forms of power have extremely limited fungibility. In general, control of any resource in which other actors are interested constitutes power, and the strength of the interests is a measure of the value of the resource, and thus of the power of the actor (or actors) who control it. In a perfect social system, in fact, one can express power of an actor in just these terms, as is done in eqs. 25.6 and 25.12.

In a system other than a perfect system, those equations cannot measure an actor's power, which must be characterized in a different way. In this section I will derive the power of an actor in an imperfect system. Actor i's power over actor k can be considered as being the sum of a number of components: first, i's control over those resources that are of direct interest to k; second, i's control over resources that are of interest to other actors who control things of interest to actor k, that is, i's control at one remove over things that interest actor k; and so on to two removes and further. But the components of power through other actors must be discounted by a factor representing the loss that occurs in indirect exchanges. How this can be done in a way consistent with the general linear model can best be seen by examining power in a perfect system more closely.

When there are no losses between pairs of actors or between pairs of resources, the power of actors in the system is given by eq. 25.18 as a function of the matrix of control and interest:

$$r = (I - CX + E_n)^{-1}e_{n1} \qquad (27.13)$$

Defining an $n \times n$ matrix Z (equal to CX) allows eq. 27.13 to be written as

$$r = [I - (Z - E_n)]^{-1}e_{n1} \qquad (27.14)$$

But for a matrix A the inverse of $I - A$, that is, $(I - A)^{-1}$, equals an infinite sum:

$$(I - A)^{-1} = \sum_{i=0}^{\infty} A^i$$

Thus eq. 27.14 is equivalent to

$$r = e_{n1} + (Z - E_n)e_{n1} + (Z - E_n)^2 e_{n1} + \cdots \qquad (27.15)$$

An element from this vector is

$$r_i = \frac{1}{n} + \frac{1}{n}\sum_{k=1}^{n}\left(z_{ik} - \frac{1}{n}\right) + \frac{1}{n}\sum_{k=1}^{n}\sum_{j=1}^{n}\left(z_{ik} - \frac{1}{n}\right)\left(z_{kj} - \frac{1}{n}\right)$$

$$+ \frac{1}{n}\sum_{k}\sum_{j}\sum_{l}\left(z_{ik} - \frac{1}{n}\right)\left(z_{kj} - \frac{1}{n}\right)\left(z_{jl} - \frac{1}{n}\right) + \cdots$$

which reduces to

$$r_i = \frac{1}{n}\sum_{k}z_{ik} + \frac{1}{n}\sum_{k}\sum_{j}\left(z_{ik} - \frac{1}{n}\right)\left(z_{kj} - \frac{1}{n}\right) \qquad (27.16)$$

$$+ \frac{1}{n}\sum_{k}\sum_{j}\sum_{l}\left(z_{ik} - \frac{1}{n}\right)\left(z_{kj} - \frac{1}{n}\right)\left(z_{jl} - \frac{1}{n}\right) + \cdots$$

Equation 27.16 gives a sense of how r_i can be conceived as being constructed. Apart from the scaling factor $1/n$ which multiplies each term, the power of actor i is his control of resources that interest other actors plus a term for indirect exchanges at one remove, a term for indirect exchanges at two removes, a term for indirect exchanges at three removes, and so on. The term for indirect exchanges at one remove is the sum of the products $(z_{ik} - 1/n)(z_{kj} - 1/n)$. This sum can be reduced to $\Sigma \Sigma z_{ik}(z_{kj} - 1/n)$, since $\Sigma_k \Sigma_j z_{kj} = n$. This means that i's power is augmented when the others who are interested in what he controls are themselves strong, when $z_{kj} - 1/n > 0$, and decremented when they are weak.

The sum of the products $(z_{ik} - 1/n)(z_{kj} - 1/n)(z_{jl} - 1/n)$, which represents the transactions at two removes, can be reduced to a similar form:

$$\sum_{k}\left(z_{ik} - \frac{1}{n}\right)\sum_{j}\sum_{l}z_{kj}\left(z_{jl} - \frac{1}{n}\right)$$

The second sum of products over j and l in this expression is positive if those (indexed by k) who are interested in what i controls are in exchange with those (indexed by j) who are themselves strong, that is, if $z_{jl} - 1/n > 0$, and negative when they are weak. When i's strength with respect to k (represented by the first quantity, $z_{ik} - 1/n$), is greater than average, that is, when $z_{ik} - 1/n > 0$, then i's power is augmented by k's exchanges with strong partners; when it is less than average, then i's power is decremented by k's exchanges with strong partners.

Thus each of the successive terms in the expansion of $\mathbf{r}$ given by eq. 27.16 constitutes a correction to the direct power of i, which is given by $\mathbf{Z}$ (which is equal to $\mathbf{CX}$). Each additional term represents an additional link in the indirect exchange. The first term in eq. 27.16 represents i's power in direct exchanges, the second term is an increment or decrement to that due to exchanges at the first remove, and so on to the pth term for exchanges at the $p - 1$ remove. The final result is, with a large enough set of terms, the power of i.

This decomposition of $\mathbf{r}$ can be used to understand what is meant by the i, kth element in the matrix $\Sigma_{i=0}^{\infty} (\mathbf{Z} - \mathbf{E}_n)^i$, or, equivalently, $[\mathbf{I} - (\mathbf{Z} - \mathbf{E}_n)]^{-1}$. Denoting this element by g_{ik} allows writing its first few terms from eq. 27.15. For $k \neq i$ these are

$$g_{ik} = \left(z_{ik} - \frac{1}{n} \right) + \sum_{j=1}^{n} \left(z_{ij} - \frac{1}{n} \right)\left(z_{jk} - \frac{1}{n} \right) \qquad (27.17)$$

$$+ \sum_j \sum_l \left(z_{ij} - \frac{1}{n} \right)\left(z_{jl} - \frac{1}{n} \right)\left(z_{lk} - \frac{1}{n} \right) + \cdots$$

For $k = i$ they are

$$g_{ii} = 1 + \left(z_{ii} - \frac{1}{n} \right) + \sum_{j=1}^{n} \left(z_{ij} - \frac{1}{n} \right)\left(z_{ji} - \frac{1}{n} \right) \qquad (27.18)$$

$$+ \sum_j \sum_l \left(z_{ij} - \frac{1}{n} \right)\left(z_{jl} - \frac{1}{n} \right)\left(z_{li} - \frac{1}{n} \right) + \cdots$$

For eq. 27.17, where $k \neq i$, it is clear that the terms on the right-hand side represent the gain (above 1) or loss (below 1) in power to i per unit of power held by k, at each stage in the sequence of exchanges. When these terms are summed to give g_{ik} and then divided by n, the result represents the total gain or loss in power to i due to k's dependence on i or lack of it. When $k = i$, as for eq. 27.18, the terms on the right-hand side represent 1 plus the gain or minus the loss due to i's dependence or lack of it on what he controls. Thus g_{ik}/n represents, for $k \neq i$, the increment above $1/n$ or decrement below $1/n$ in i's power due to i's control of what k is interested in at all removes. Similarly, $(g_{ii} - 1)/n$ represents the increment or decrement relative to $1/n$ of i's power due to his control of the things in which he is interested. An arbitrary $\mathbf{Z}$ matrix and the matrix of g_{ik}/n and $(g_{ii} - 1)/n$ derived from it are given in Table 27.2.

Table 27.2　Control and differentiated power of actors in an imperfect system.

		Z (equal to CX) Interested actor						Increment or decrement to i's power from k (k)			
		A_1	A_2	A_3	A_4			A_1	A_2	A_3	A_4
	A_1	.5	.1	.1	.2		A_1	.097	−.067	−.064	−.026
Controlling	A_2	.3	.2	.3	.2	(i)	A_2	.016	−.009	.012	−.009
actor	A_3	.1	.6	.4	.5		A_3	−.068	.103	.058	.066
	A_4	.1	.1	.2	.1		A_4	−.044	−.027	−.007	−.031

Modification of Power Due to Transaction Costs for Pairs of Actors

In Chapter 32 a question is raised concerning just how barriers to exchange modify the power of actors. The answer, in brief, is that as long as the resources being exchanged are fungible, with value that allows for indirect exchanges, and as long as all actors remain reachable for all others, the introduction of barriers to exchange will not affect equilibrium power. This prediction opposes the experimental findings of those who have investigated the effects of various limited communication structures on the power of actors. I discuss those differences in Chapter 32, where the theoretical results are presented. Here, however, the focus is not on barriers to exchange but on costs of exchange, or losses incurred in exchange. The term "transaction costs" is used in economics to identify these losses. What is referred to here are losses not recovered by either of the parties to an exchange.

When there are transaction losses for exchanges between actors i and k, there will be reduced volume of exchanges between them despite the fact that they may control goods or events of interest to each other. When exchange occurs only with a certain efficiency, α_{ik}, and i has something in which k is interested, then the dependence of k on i through i's control of what interests k is $z_{ik}\alpha_{ik}$. The quantity α_{ik} is 1.0 if k is able to make exchanges with i without loss of value. The quantity α_{ik} is the fraction of value held by i and exchanged with k that is lost, or the cost of the transaction to k. (Throughout this exposition and the following example, I assume that all resources are fungible, so the only losses are between pairs of actors; none are specific to pairs of goods.)

Ordinarily it would be assumed that $\alpha_{ki} = \alpha_{ik}$: Since the exchange is two-sided, even though only k's interests are represented by z_{ik}, i must receive something of comparable value from k for what he gives up to k. The possibility that α_{ki} may not be equal to α_{ik} may be left open, as I will do here.

Taking the products $z_{ik}\alpha_{ik}$ gives elements $z^{\dagger}_{ik}$:

$$z^{\dagger}_{ik} = z_{ik}\alpha_{ik} \tag{27.19}$$

Because some α_{ik} are less than 1.0 and because $\Sigma_i\, z_{ik}$ is equal to 1.0 for all k, $\Sigma_i\, z^{\dagger}_{ik} < 1.0$ for some k. A new matrix $\mathbf{Z}^{\dagger}$ having an additional row and column can be defined:

$$\mathbf{Z}^\dagger = \|z_{ik}^\dagger\| \qquad [\text{an } (n + 1) \times n \text{ matrix}]$$

where

$$z_{ik}^\dagger = \begin{cases} z_{ik}\alpha_{ik}, & \text{for } i = 1, \ldots, n, \, k = 1, \ldots, n \\ 1 - \sum_{i=1}^{n} z_{ik}\alpha_{ik}, & \text{for } i = n + 1, \, k = 1, \ldots, n \\ r_i, & \text{for } i = 1, \ldots, n + 1, \, k = n + 1 \end{cases} \qquad (27.20)$$

Thus at each transaction stage there is a loss due to the deficiency in some $z_{ik}^\dagger$. This deficiency can be viewed as the power deficiency in the system, defined as $r_{n+1} = 1 - \sum_{i=1}^{n} r_i$. Then because

$$\mathbf{r} = \mathbf{Z}^\dagger \mathbf{r} \qquad (27.21)$$

the following equation may be written:

$$r_i = \sum_{k=1}^{n} z_{ik}^\dagger r_k + r_i r_{n+1}$$

If this is divided through by r_{n+1}, and r_i^* is defined as r_i / r_{n+1}, the result, in matrix notation, is

$$\mathbf{r}^* = \mathbf{Z}^\dagger \mathbf{r}^* + \mathbf{r} \qquad (27.22)$$

This is the same as eq. 25.25 for an open system, except that here $\mathbf{Z}^\dagger$ replaces $\mathbf{Z}$. Equation 27.22 may be solved by the iterative method described in Chapter 25.

It is possible to calculate a quantity comparable to g_{ik} for this deficient system. After the power vector has been calculated by the iterative method, it is possible to create the augmented $\mathbf{Z}$ matrix to which an additional row and column have been added. The additional row represents dependence of each actor on the outside for realization of his interests, because of losses in transactions between him and those actors who control what interests him. For actor k, this dependence equals $1 - \sum_i z_{ik}^\dagger$. The additional column is the outside's dependence on each actor, which, as indicated above, is set to equal r_i for row i. This augmented $\mathbf{Z}$ matrix makes it possible to calculate the degree to which each actor's power is augmented or decremented by his control of what interests each other actor.

EXAMPLE 1: LOSSES IN TRANSACTIONS Suppose that Tom, John, Steve, and Dan are engaged in trading sports cards. Each has 1,000 of a particular type: Tom has 1,000 football cards; John, 1,000 baseball cards; Steve, 1,000 basketball cards; and Dan, 1,000 soccer cards. For simplicity, assume that most of the interest of each boy is in the cards he owns; in fact, each boy has seven times as much interest in the cards he owns as in the cards owned by others. Each has equal interest in the cards owned by others. Thus the resources are the types of

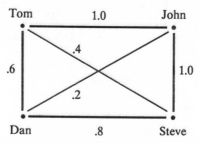

Figure 27.2 Transaction efficiencies among four traders.

cards, the control matrix is an identity matrix, and each column of the interest matrix has .7 on the main diagonal and .1 elsewhere. From symmetry, each boy has the same power, $r_i = .250$. Each of the boys, by symmetry, ends up with 700 of his own cards and 100 of the cards of each of the others.

Now suppose that the boys are not equally able to trade with each other, due to physical constraints. Shown in Figure 27.2 are the efficiencies for each of the pairs of boys in making trades. John appears best placed, except with respect to Dan. Dan is least well placed, having an efficiency of less than 1.0 for trades with each of the others.

These efficiencies multiply the corresponding z_{ik}, as indicated above, giving the elements $z^\dagger_{ik}$ of the matrix shown below.

$$\mathbf{Z}^\dagger = \begin{bmatrix} .7 & .1 & .04 & .06 \\ .1 & .7 & .1 & .02 \\ .04 & .1 & .7 & .08 \\ .06 & .02 & .08 & .7 \end{bmatrix}$$

Using the method described in Chapter 25 for calculating power when interests sum to less than 1.0 gives as the power vector $\mathbf{r} = (.226, .249, .241, .187)$. When $\mathbf{r}$ is augmented to give relative power, it becomes $(.250, .276, .267, .207)$, showing that the inefficiencies will reduce Dan's relative power. John's will be highest, Steve's next, and Tom's unchanged. The values from the vector $\mathbf{r}$ may be used to augment the matrix $\mathbf{Z}^\dagger$ as described above by adding a row with elements $1 - \Sigma_i z^\dagger_{ik}$ and a column with elements r_i. From this augmented matrix $\mathbf{Z}$ the inverse $[\mathbf{I} - (\mathbf{Z} - \mathbf{E}_n)]^{-1}$ may be calculated; its elements are g_{ik}. Then the values of g_{ik} can be used to show how much the power of each actor is incremented or decremented by each of the others. Shown below are values of $g_{ik}/5$ and $(g_{ii} - 1)/5$.

		Interested actor			
		Tom	John	Steve	Dan
	Tom	.271	−.039	−.123	−.089
Controlling	John	−.040	.266	−.050	−.147
actor	Steve	−.123	−.049	.261	−.060
	Dan	−.088	−.144	−.057	.297

This matrix shows that Dan, because of his isolated position, is more dependent on himself than are any of the others. John and Steve, who have greatest power, are less dependent on themselves than are Tom and Dan.

A more extreme situation is shown in Figure 27.3, where some of the pairs are altogether unable to carry out exchanges. Here Steve and John are in symmetric positions, as are Tom and Dan. The $\mathbf{Z}^\dagger$ matrix obtained from z_{ik} and α_{ik} is

	Tom	John	Steve	Dan
Tom	.7	.1	0	0
John	.1	.7	.1	0
Steve	0	.1	.7	.1
Dan	0	0	.1	.7

Using eq. 25.26 gives $\mathbf{r} = (.165, .266, .266, .165)$ and relative power as $(.191, .309, .309, .191)$. Thus the elimination of inefficient relations and strengthening of already efficient ones increases the power of John and Steve at the expense of Tom and Dan.

As before, using the augmented $\mathbf{Z}$ gives measures of the degree to which each actor increments or decrements the power of others, due to the combination of his structural position and his interests.

			Interested actor		
		Tom	John	Steve	Dan
	Tom	.343	.005	−.179	−.184
Controlling	John	.005	.278	−.067	−.179
actor	Steve	−.179	−.067	.278	.005
	Dan	−.184	−.179	.005	.343

This matrix shows that Tom's power is decremented by Steve and Dan, and Dan's is decremented by Tom and John. Dan and Steve decrement John's, and Tom and John decrement Steve's.

Note that this extension of the system to include transaction costs between actors does not affect the interest each actor has in different resources. Nor does it affect the equilibrium distribution of resources, except through the effect on relative power of actors and relative value of resources. The existence of indi-

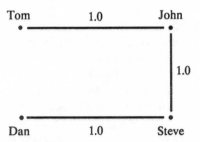

Figure 27.3 Transaction efficiencies among four traders when some are unable to exchange with others.

rect exchanges implies that if Dan cannot get football cards from Tom, he can get them from Steve, after Steve has gotten them from John, who had gotten them from Tom. Only relative value and relative power are directly affected by transaction costs, as long as paths of indirect exchange connect all pairs of actors. If that condition does not hold, the system is separable into isolated subsystems, which must be analyzed separately.

Transaction Costs between Pairs of Resources

Inefficiencies between pairs of actors often arise because of logistic or other barriers to communication. Costs of transactions involving pairs of resources, however, are ordinarily purposively created and maintained by laws, norms, or regulations. The formal treatment of such costs is similar to that for inefficiencies between pairs of actors.

First, it is useful to interpret value in a perfect system as arising through a sequence of indirect exchanges. If an $m \times m$ matrix $\mathbf{W}$ (equal to $\mathbf{XC}$) is defined, eq. 25.19 may be written as

$$\mathbf{v} = [\mathbf{I} - (\mathbf{W} - \mathbf{E}_m)]^{-1}\mathbf{e}_{m1} \qquad (27.23)$$

It is possible to write the right-hand side as an infinite sum:

$$\mathbf{v} = \mathbf{e}_{m1} + (\mathbf{W} - \mathbf{E}_m)\mathbf{e}_{m1} + (\mathbf{W} - \mathbf{E}_m)^2\mathbf{e}_{m1} + \cdots \qquad (27.24)$$

The first few terms for an element of $\mathbf{v}$, v_j, are

$$v_j = \frac{1}{m} + \frac{1}{m} \sum_{h=1}^{m} \left(w_{jh} - \frac{1}{m}\right) \qquad (27.25)$$

$$+ \frac{1}{m} \sum_{h=1}^{m} \sum_{k=1}^{m} \left(w_{jh} - \frac{1}{m}\right)\left(w_{hk} - \frac{1}{m}\right) + \cdots$$

Each exchange involves two goods, and the quantity w_{jh} represents the fraction of control over good h that is interested in good j. (Because action must be carried out by actors rather than by goods, the meaning of w_{jh} is more awkward to express in words than is that of z_{ik}.)

Like the expansion of r_i, the expansion of v_j, giving the value of j, begins with a mean value at the zeroth stage. At the first stage of transactions, this value is augmented if the values of w_{jh} (that is, the interest in j of actors who themselves have goods) are great. Then, analogous to the series for r_i, the value is augmented further if the goods that are held by those interested in h are themselves of interest to others who hold goods—and so on.

If the actor who controls h cannot use it to acquire j, because of legal or other restrictions, then a large value of w_{jh} will not lead to exchange of h for j. The quantity w_{jh}, which would otherwise be the engine for action, does not matter if there are effective barriers to exchanging h for j: In the series of eq. 27.25, through which j's value is modified, a quantity β_{jh} may be introduced as a multiplier to each w_{jh}, where β_{jh} is a nonnegative constant less than or equal to 1. This constant may be described as the convertibility of j to h and is ordinarily equal to either 0 or 1.

EXAMPLE 2: POLITICAL MONEY   In Chapter 6 I restated Ostrogorski's description of political transactions around the turn of the century, in which the party machine, legislators, interest groups, and voters all played a part. Here I will describe in highly simplified form an analogous set of transactions that appear to take place in a contemporary political system. The actors in the system consist of legislative candidates, voters, interest groups, and television networks. The last two are corporate actors. The legislative candidates are interested in getting elected and have two resources. One is their attention (as legislators), a resource in which the interest groups have an interest. The other is what might be described as their appeal, which consists of campaign promises, general appearance, and degree of trustworthiness (which gives the promises greater or lesser credibility and thus affects their value). Voters have interests in entertainment, money, and the promises of candidates (their appeal) and have two resources, their attention and their vote. Interest groups have a single resource, money, and an interest in the legislative attention of successful candidates and, to a lesser extent, an interest in the promises of candidates. Television networks have a single resource, entertainment, and a single interest, money.

The transactions that appear to characterize this system go something like this: Interest groups provide money to candidates (in the form of campaign support) in return for candidates' legislative attention and to a lesser extent their promises, with the value of the attention and promises affected by the candidate's probability of being elected. Candidates use this money in an exchange with television networks, buying with it the attention of voters. The voters have given up their attention to the television networks in return for entertainment (which the networks have purchased with money). Candidates use their appeal (that is, promises moderated by appearance and trustworthiness) in exchange for votes from the voters. But the votes are dependent (through a dependency matrix, as described earlier in this chapter) on the voters' attention as well as on the candidates' appeal. A diagram of the exchanges that take place in this highly simplified version of the campaign process is shown in Figure 27.4.

Note from the diagram that there are alternative exchanges that could, in principle, occur. Candidates want voters' attention, and voters could buy entertainment (or other things in which they are interested) with money. Thus, in principle, the intermediary of television, which acquires voters' attention with entertainment (which it has bought with money), could be replaced by a direct exchange between candidate and voter of money for attention, which would make possible the transaction involving appeal (that is, promises) and votes. This and other possible alternative transactions to those shown in Figure 27.4

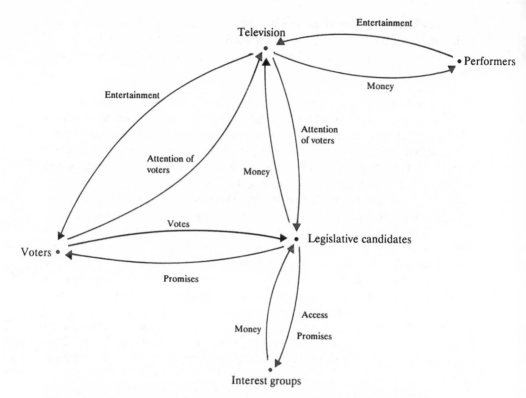

Figure 27.4   Transactions involving legislative candidates, interest groups, television networks, and voters.

illustrate the point that not all pairs of resources can be exchanged equally well. That is, in terms of the conceptualization introduced above, β_{jk} is not equal to 1 for all pairs of j and k and may be equal to 0 for some. For this system Table 27.3 shows how values of β_{jk} differ from 1 for particular pairs of resources. The transaction costs appear to be due to different sources for different pairs of resources.

The table implies a number of barriers to convertibility, most of which are due to legal or normative constraints. Some, however, are not, as is the case for the exchange of a vote for a candidate's promises. This is the basic political exchange between constituents and legislators, and it is neither legally nor morally proscribed. The low value for β_{13} shown in the table is due to the problem of the voter's inaccessibility to the candidate, a logistical constraint. The candidate must have the voter's attention in order for promises to bring a vote. It is for this reason that a column has been added on the right to the table, representing a combined resource, candidate's promises and voter's attention. Once the candidate has this combined resource, exchanging it for a vote is possible. And it is for

Table 27.3 Convertibility of pairs of resources (full convertibility indicated by $\beta_{jk} = 1$).

	Vote	Voter's attention	Candidate's promises	Candidate's attention	Money	Entertainment services	Candidate's promises and voter's attention
Vote		*	$\beta_{13} \ll 1$	$\beta_{14} = 1$	$\beta_{15} \ll 1$	$\beta_{16} \ll 1$	$\beta_{17} = 1$
Voter's attention			$\beta_{23} \ll 1$	$\beta_{24} = 1$	$\beta_{25} < 1$	$\beta_{26} = 1$	*
Candidate's promises				*	$\beta_{35} \ll 1$	$\beta_{36} \ll 1$	*
Candidate's attention					$\beta_{45} < 1$	$\beta_{46} = 1$	*
Money						$\beta_{56} = 1$	$\beta_{57} \ll 1$
Entertainment services							$\beta_{67} \ll 1$

*Since both resources in each of these pairs originate with the same actor, convertibility is irrelevant.

the same reason that in political systems in large social systems, the voter's attention, and thus the ability to deliver it (as television is best able to do), has come to be so valuable.

The necessity for introducing a combined resource, as I have done here, suggests that the conceptualization of resources for application of the theory may be an inferior one. What would appear to be a better conceptualization is to conceive of voters' attention as eliminating the barrier which keeps β_{13} close to zero, that is, as a resource which increases β_{13}. Similarly, the resource "candidate attention," or access to the candidate, which is what the interest groups purchase with money (campaign contributions), reduces the barriers to transactions involving legislative votes between the interest groups and the candidate (which are not shown in Table 27.3). Unfortunately, however, at this stage of development of the theory, there is no process for modifying the matrix of resource convertibility (or the matrix of social capital between pairs of actors). It is possible that resources of the character of voters' attention which make possible other transactions can be adequately treated merely through dependency as introduced in an earlier section. Further work is necessary in order to see how best to treat such resources.

Systems in Which Exchange Is for Use

In rationalized markets, where transactions involve goods that are divisible, private (without externalities), and alienable, various institutions have come into existence to overcome the need for the double coincidence of wants of which Jevons and other classical economists spoke. The most prominent of these, of course, is money as a medium of exchange. In the absence of money or some substitute, actors must receive in exchange things in which they have no interest but which they can use in further exchange with others who do.

In many social exchanges, however, the commodities being exchanged are intrinsically not capable of being further exchanged. For example, when one legislator promises another a vote on a particular bill in return for some future unspecified favor, the legislator who receives the promise cannot exchange it further, for promises are not negotiable. Thus on his side of the exchange at least, the exchange must be for use and cannot be for further exchange. In principle, there might be other legislators who, if the promise were in the form of a proxy, would want to cast the vote differently and would give up a greater favor for it. But this would not usually occur, for several reasons. First, the promise is ordinarily not in the form of a tangible proxy. Second, only political opponents would have an interest in gaining control of the promise. Even if the legislator who acquired it were willing in the end to give up the promise and were in a position to be able to do so, he would not ordinarily have acquired it with this end in mind.

This is only one example; there are many others. One general class is composed of personal services, attention one person gives to another, and other personal favors. Another general class consists of those resources having a highly restricted domain of use, such as a vote or delegated authority over a particular set of actions. The actor with such authority has power which can be exercised but can be given up in exchange only with great loss.

Several questions arise concerning systems which involve such commodities. First, if the system under consideration contains *only* such nonnegotiable commodities, how do its properties differ from those of a perfectly competitive market? Second, how much infusion of commodities that are negotiable is necessary to change the system into one in which the double coincidence of wants is no longer required? Third, when a system is an exchange system of this sort, what are the incentives to develop some device which breaks the necessity for the double coincidence of wants?

EXAMPLE 3: EXCHANGE OF ATTENTION   When exchange is for use and further exchange is not possible, the structure that is created differs from that in which there are barriers to exchange for pairs of actors or for pairs of resources. The example first introduced in Chapter 25 can be modified somewhat to illustrate this idea.

Suppose that the two persons engaged in exchange are, as before, Tom and John, but that the resources involved in the transactions are not football cards and baseball cards but Tom's attention and John's attention. Because the commodities being exchanged are the actors' attention, there is no barrier to exchange between Tom and John, and there are no barriers to exchange of Tom's attention for John's attention or vice versa. Neither actor can use the attention he had acquired from the other in an exchange with a third party, however. Suppose further that the exchange rate for attention is not constrained to 1:1 and, in fact, has no restrictions. That is, it is not necessary for Tom to give one unit of attention to John for every unit of attention John gives to Tom.

The initial control matrix is an identity matrix: Tom controls his attention, and John controls his. Suppose the interest matrix is (as shown in Table 25.1, case 1)

$$\mathbf{X}' = \begin{bmatrix} .8 & .2 \\ .5 & .5 \end{bmatrix}$$

Of Tom's interest, .2 is directed toward gaining John's attention, and .5 of John's interest is directed toward gaining Tom's attention. There are no other resources which either can use in the exchange, and no other actors; the system can be regarded as closed. Application of the model as carried out in Chapter 25 would show that the exchange rate at the competitive equilibrium is the inverse of the ratio of interests, .2:.5, and that Tom gets .5 of John's attention, and John gets .2 of Tom's. Tom's power is 5/7, and John's is 2/7.

Suppose that a third boy, Steve, enters the system and the interests change. John maintains his interest in Tom's attention at the same level, but Tom's interests shift: He now has no interest in John's attention, but .2 of his interest is directed to gaining Steve's attention. For Steve .6 of his interest is in gaining

Table 27.4   Three actors' interests in and equilibrium control of each other's attention.

			INTEREST (X') (Events) Attention of			EQUILIBRIUM CONTROL (C*) (Events) Attention of		
			Tom	John	Steve	Tom	John	Steve
(Actors)	Attention	Tom	.8	0	.2	.8	0	.6
	to	John	.5	.5	0	.2	.5	0
		Steve	0	.6	.4	0	.5	.4

John's attention. This system, composed of three actors and three resources, will be considered a closed one.

Table 27.4 shows the structure of interests and of control predicted at the competitive equilibrium, and Figure 27.5 shows the equilibrium diagrammatically (an arrow from *i* to *j* represents *i*'s control over *j* at equilibrium). Application of the model shows that at competitive equilibrium Tom would have .6 of Steve's attention, John would have .2 of Tom's, and Steve would have .5 of John's. Tom's power in the system (and also the value of his attention) is .58, John's is .23, and Steve's is .19.

There is no double coincidence of wants in this case; the equilibrium can be achieved only by means of a device which is limited to transactions involving alienable goods: One of the boys must accept in an exchange attention in which he is not interested solely in order to exchange it for attention in which he is interested. In such a situation this kind of indirect transaction could hardly occur, and there is no immediately apparent way that it could be achieved. There are, however, examples of attempts to realize some of the interests involved in such triangles. For example, Steve might give attention to Tom only on the condition that Tom would give attention to John in return for John's giving attention to Steve. Merely describing such maneuvering indicates how complex

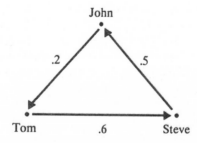

Figure 27.5   Relations among three actors.

such indirect exchanges can get. It is clear that in the absence of some medium of exchange, or some other obligations and expectations among the three persons in such a situation, nothing approximating the level of exchange predicted for the competitive equilibrium will occur; in fact, there may be no exchange at all.

Earlier I asked what the incentives are, when a system contains only nonnegotiable commodities like attention, to develop some device which allows exchange to take place. It is possible to assess what those incentives are by examining the difference between the overall satisfaction level from outcomes in the case of a perfectly competitive market and that from outcomes in the absence of exchange. This may be done by calculating the utilities of the outcomes in the two cases for each actor, using eq. 25.1. The utility is 0 for each actor in the absence of exchange, since inspection of eq. 25.1 shows that whenever $c_{ij} = 0$ for some event j for which $x_{ji} \neq 0$, then $u_i = 0$. At the competitive equilibrium the utilities are $u_1 = .76$, $u_2 = .32$, and $u_3 = .46$. Thus the utility gain if there were exchange would be .76 for Tom, .32 for John, and .46 for Steve. The difficulty, however, lies in giving some motivational meaning to these utility differences, since there is no baseline to which they can be compared. All that can be said is that everyone would be better off with exchange, so each has a motivation to facilitate exchange in some way.

One resolution of such a situation would be changes in interests; such adjustment of interests certainly operates in real social relationships. If a person cannot have attention from the person he wants, he may come to want attention from another person whose attention he can get. Another resolution of such a situation might be an attempt to develop something which makes such exchange possible. In Chapter 6 I discussed the devices which have arisen in economic systems: a particular good which can serve as a medium of exchange, or a particular actor who operates as a clearinghouse for credits and obligations. Another "solution" to the problem is one which is ruled out in specifying that these three actors and three resources constitute a closed system. This creates a situation in which no actor has social capital available to use to help realize his interests. Social capital of either of two kinds can facilitate transactions in a situation of this sort: social capital involving additional resources or events, or social capital involving additional actors.

Consider social capital from events: Suppose there are additional events under the control of Tom in which Steve has an interest (perhaps obligations Steve has to Tom), additional events under the control of John in which Tom has an interest, and additional events under the control of Steve in which John has an interest. Then, even if these events are also nonnegotiable, as attention is, they make possible the exchanges that are not possible in the example as stated. If these boys have been involved with one another in extensive activities, they will each have built up a supply of this form of social capital.

The second form of social capital involves other actors. If there is an actor who has obligations to Tom and to whom Steve has obligations, Tom can call in

Table 27.5 Modified interests of three actors in each other's attention and control of attention at competitive equilibrium.

			INTERESTS (X') (Events) Attention of			EQUILIBRIUM CONTROL (C*) (Events) Attention of		
			Tom	John	Steve	Tom	John	Steve
(Actors)	Attention	Tom	.78	.02	.20	.78	.047	.595
	to	John	.50	.48	.02	.213	.48	.025
		Steve	.02	.60	.38	.007	.473	.38

these obligations to gain Steve's attention. If there is another actor with obligations to John and to whom Tom has obligations, these can be used by John to gain Tom's attention; and similarly for Steve. If, for example, the boys are brothers, a parent will ordinarily serve in the capacity of the other actor for all three. Steve may call on the parent to "get John to pay some attention to me," and so on. In that case the parent constitutes social capital available to all three.

The value of either of these forms of social capital lies in its facilitation of social exchanges that increase satisfaction but would not otherwise take place. As indicated in Chapter 12, social capital exists in systems with a high degree of closure (in the example closure is achieved through a person with obligations to one actor in the system and to whom another in the system has obligations) and in systems in which the same persons have a number of relations with one another. Either of these forms of social capital can be brought into use when asymmetry of the sort exhibited in Table 27.4 and Figure 27.5 exists.

Clearly, without social capital, a medium of exchange, or an actor who can serve as a clearinghouse, there will be no exchange.[3] There is, however, a situation in which some exchange will occur, a situation closely related to that described by Table 27.4 and Figure 27.5, yet differing in that each actor has a very small interest in attention from the actor who wants his attention. Table 27.5 shows the interests as well as the predicted control of attention at equilibrium. For each actor .02 of his total interest is in gaining the attention of the actor who has the greatest interest in his attention. What difference does this make to the exchanges that take place?

Here again the competitive equilibrium disregards the lack of negotiability of the commodities. The predicted results are just as unreasonable as before and, in fact, differ only marginally from those shown in Table 27.4. Clearly there would not be an exchange in which Tom gets more than 50% of Steve's attention and

3. The medium of exchange and the actor who can serve as a clearinghouse may, on deeper analysis, turn out to be the two forms of social capital just described.

Table 27.6 Interests for three linked bilateral monopolies in exchange of attention.

		TOM-JOHN SYSTEM Attention of		TOM-STEVE SYSTEM Attention of		JOHN-STEVE SYSTEM Attention of	
		Tom	John		Tom	Steve		John	Steve
Interest of	Tom	.98	.02	Tom	.8	.2	John	.98	.02
	John	.5	.5	Steve	.02	.98	Steve	.60	.40

Steve gets less than 1% of Tom's. The interests suggest that Steve has power with respect to Tom, as long as the commodities are nonnegotiable; for example, as long as Tom cannot use John's interest in his attention as a means of getting some of Steve's attention (since Steve is interested in John's attention).

In fact, in the absence of negotiable commodities or social capital as described earlier, this is not a three-actor system at all. It is merely three linked bilateral monopolies of the sort described in Chapter 25, in which two boys are exchanging two commodities. The interest matrix (X') is given for each of the three systems in Table 27.6. The independence of these systems can be seen by comparing the structure of interests given in Table 27.5 with that for the Tom-John system in Table 27.6. Tom's interest of .20 in Steve's attention given in Table 27.5 is simply combined with Tom's interest in his own attention in Table 27.6; this is equivalent to specifying that Tom's interest in Steve's attention cannot be reached by John for use in implementing his own interest. To do so would necessitate using Steve's interest in John's attention; since that is not an alienable or negotiable commodity, however, John cannot use it. Thus interests for the Tom-John system are as given in Table 27.6.

What, then, will be the outcomes in these three systems? There are three bilateral monopolies, and contract curves can be calculated as in Chapter 25. The equilibrium in each case will lie somewhere on the contract curve. Where it will lie depends, as shown in Chapter 25, on whether some external norm dictates the rate of exchange. Table 27.7 shows the predicted outcomes according to competitive equilibrium and according to a 1:1 exchange rate.

These sets of predictions are strikingly different. With competitive equilibrium the differential interest gives the uninterested member of a pair power to pay little attention to the other and still receive his attention. With the 1:1 exchange rate, the external norm equalizes the power and thus the attention each pays to the other. Even in this case, however, attention paid is limited by the interest of the less interested actor.

These results are hardly satisfactory. The questions raised at the outset have not been answered. The character of the problem has been clarified, but there

Table 27.7 Predicted exchange of attention in three subsystems according to two principles.

	Competitive equilibrium (C*)					
	Tom's	John's	Tom's	Steve's	John's	Steve's
Attention	.02	.5	.20	.02	.02	.60
Power	.96	.04	.09	.91	.97	.03
	Exchange rate of 1 : 1					
	Tom's	John's	Tom's	Steve's	John's	Steve's
Attention	.125	.125	.067	.067	.149	.149
Power	.5	.5	.5	.5	.5	.5

remains uncertainty concerning just what happens in systems of the sort described by the example. No clear-cut answers as to what rational actors will do in such circumstances have been found by applying the theory. Further work is clearly warranted, because there are many resources in social systems that are usefully seen as being exchanged but not capable of being exchanged further. As the example suggests, the systems of exchange that develop for such resources may have quite different outcomes than are found in systems of exchange where there are no such constraints.

« 28 »

Trust in a Linear System
of Action

The condition under which an actor will place trust was specified in Chapter 5 as $pG + (1 - p)L > 0$, where p is the probability that the trust will be justified, L is the possible loss, and G is the possible gain. In this section I will examine the implications of this criterion for the functioning of a linear system of action as described in Chapter 25.

In the context of an exchange system, the actor who places trust must give up something, with certainty, in order to get back something he prefers, with some risk that he will not get it. Obviously what he stands to lose, what I have called L, is the utility of what he must with certainty give up. Not quite so obviously, what he stands to gain, what I have called G, is the difference in utility between what he will get if the trustee is trustworthy, and what he must give up to get that.

Ordinarily, for exchange to occur, what the actor gets must be worth to him at least what he must give up to get it. If his change in satisfaction through giving something up is denoted by s_1 (by definition a negative quantity) and the satisfaction he gets through receiving something in exchange is denoted by s_2, he will make the exchange if $s_2 > -s_1$. If, as in Chapter 25, the satisfaction to actor i is defined as $\ln u_i$, this means that for actor i to be willing to make an exchange of good 1 for good 2, the following inequality must be satisfied:

$$x_{2i} \ln \frac{c_{i2}}{c_{i20}} + x_{1i} \ln \frac{c_{i1}}{c_{i10}} > 0 \qquad (28.1)$$

where c_{i10} and c_{i20} are the quantities of goods 1 and 2 held initially and c_{i1} and c_{i2} are the quantities held after the transaction. In the case of two goods of equal interest to actor i, where $x_{2i} = x_{1i}$, this criterion reduces to $c_{i2}/c_{i20} > c_{i10}/c_{i1}$. Since c_{i2} can be written as $c_{i20} + \Delta c_{i2}$, where Δc_{i2} is the amount of good 2 gained in the exchange, and c_{i10} can be written as $c_{i1} + \Delta c_{i1}$, where Δc_{i1} is the amount of good 1 given up, the inequality becomes

$$1 + \frac{\Delta c_{i2}}{c_{i20}} > 1 + \frac{\Delta c_{i1}}{c_{i1}}$$

or

$$\Delta c_{i2} > \Delta c_{i1} \frac{c_{i20}}{c_{i1}}$$

747

That is, actor i must receive an amount of good 2 which is greater than the amount of good 1 he gives up multiplied by the ratio of the amount of good 2 he had *before* the exchange to the amount of good 1 he has *after* the exchange.

His before-and-after situation for an exchange for which $\Delta c_{i2} > \Delta c_{i1}(c_{i20}/c_{i1})$ can be seen by assuming he begins with .10 of good 2 and .11 of good 1 and gives up .01 of good 1, which makes the right-hand side of the inequality .01(.10/.10), or .01. This means he should get in return more than .01 of good 2, which would put him in the situation of having more than .11 of 2 and .10 of 1. Since, by assumption, the two goods are of equal interest to him, this would be better than the situation he was in before the exchange, having .10 of good 2 and .11 of good 1.

The dependence of the criterion for exchange on the amounts of the two goods initially held results from declining marginal utility, which makes a quantity of any good worth less to an actor if he already has a lot of it than if he has only a little.

When it is not certain that actor i will receive good 2, then the satisfaction he expects from good 2 becomes $px_{2i} \ln(c'_{i2}/c_{i20})$, and inequality 28.1 becomes

$$px_{2i} \ln \frac{c'_{i2}}{c_{i20}} + x_{1i} \ln \frac{c_{i1}}{c_{i10}} > 0 \tag{28.2}$$

The presence of p in this inequality means that c'_{i2} must be greater than c_{i2} in inequality 28.1 if this inequality is to hold whenever that one holds.[1]

What this formulation implies can be seen for the example in which credit was extended by the merchant banker Hambros to the Norwegian shipowner (first discussed in Chapter 5). Here the commodity given up, money, is the same as that to be gained.[2] The inequality that must be satisfied is $pG + (1 - p)L > 0$. In this case L is the loss in satisfaction (change in $\ln u_i$) due to the loss of £200,000. This is $x \ln(c_0 - 200,000) - x \ln c_0$, where x is Hambros's interest in money, and c_0 is its current assets. And G is the gain in satisfaction due to the present value of future gains to Hambros from extending the credit. This is $x \ln(c_0 + \Delta c) - x \ln c_0$. The criterion for extending credit is then

$$p[x \ln(c_0 + \Delta c) - x \ln c_0] + (1 - p) [x \ln(c_0 - 200,000) - x \ln c_0] > 0 \tag{28.3}$$

This reduces to

$$p \ln \frac{c_0 + \Delta c}{c_0 - 200,000} > \ln \frac{c_0}{c_0 - 200,000} \tag{28.4}$$

1. Setting the left-hand sides of inequalities 28.1 and 28.2 equal to each other and solving for c'_{i2} gives $c'_{i2} = c_{i2}^{1/p} c_{i20}^{(p-1)/p}$. If $c_{i20} = .10$, $c_{12} = .11$, and $p = .8$, then $c'_{i2} = .1127$.

2. If the good will of the Norwegian shipowner, which might lead to further profitable transactions, was the basis for the exchange, this can be expressed in terms of monetary gain to Hambros.

Suppose that the estimated probability of gain is .95, and assume that Hambros's current assets are £20,000,000. Then the value of Δc necessary for inequality 28.4 to become an equality is 10,580. Why? One might calculate what the necessary income would be if utilities were linear in money as follows:

$$.95\Delta c - .05(200,000) > 0$$

$$\Delta c = 10,526$$

Thus £10,526 is the amount Hambros would require as an insurance premium from the shipowner if Hambros expected no future gains from the relation. For example, if the habor authority had this expectation, they would have been in a position to let the ship sail for a fee of £10,526, since they would expect no future gain from extending the credit. This is the mathematical expectation of no gain, no loss, given that the probability was only .95 rather than 1.0. The difference between £10,526 and £10,580, or £54, is due to the fact that utility is not linear in money, and Hambros loses more in expected utility by a move from £20,000,000 to £19,800,000 with a probability of .05 than it gains by a move from £20,000,000 to £20,010,526 with a probability of .95. If Hambros's capital were unlimited, the utilities would be linear, and the critical amount would be £10,526. If Hambros's capital were only a tenth as large, that is, £2,000,000 instead of £20,000,000, the critical amount would be £11,121 instead of £10,580. Hambros would then require £595 beyond the mathematical expectation instead of £54, merely because the utility loss of £200,000 when their capital was only £2,000,000 would be greater than that loss when their capital was £20,000,000.

Of course, if Hambros had greater certainty that the money would be paid back, say .999 instead of .95, the insurance necessary to balance the mathematical expectation (with utility linear in money) would be less, only £201 rather than £20,526. The excess amount necessary because of the fact that a loss hurts more than a mathematically equivalent gain is worth would then be negligible if Hambros had £20,000,000 capital and £10 if it had only £2,000,000.

For other examples presented in Chapter 5, comparable quantities cannot be calculated because there is no quantitative measure of what the second farmer or the high-school girl was risking and no units in which to measure potential gain. In those examples, moreover, the exchange involved two different commodities, possibly of differing interest to the potential trustor, so if such an analysis could be done, it would be necessary to use inequality 28.2. In certain circumstances, such as in the Hambros example, the exchange involves a commodity being given up (ordinarily money) and the same commodity at some time in the future. The basic logic of the condition for placing trust is the same in both cases, but slightly different expressions are necessary.

As the Hambros example illustrates, there may well be transactions that will be carried out by a rational actor when trust is very high, but not when trust is lower. If, for example, the fees that can be charged for a transaction of the sort described in the Hambros example are small but the subjective probability that the trustee will repay the mor·:y advanced is sufficiently low to make a larger fee necessary, the transaction will not occur. In other situations the matter is even more straightforward. The terms of the transaction, assuming trustworthiness, are well established by precedent or custom, and if the level of trustworthiness as perceived by the potential trustor is sufficiently low, these terms will make the proposed transaction an expected loss for the trustor. For example, a girl learns roughly how much a relation with a boy will be strengthened by walking home with him, if all goes well. This puts her in a position to judge whether the likelihood of this benefit is more than offset by the possible jeopardy in which she places herself; she may, of course, judge incorrectly. The point is that the transaction, like many others, is not one for which the terms of trade are changed if the perceived level of trustworthiness changes. Instead, the terms are fixed; given these terms, trust is either placed or not placed.

Introducing Mistrust into a System

For the systems of action discussed in earlier chapters of this part, it has been assumed that transactions are not only costless but instantaneously consummated, so there is no possibility of nonpayment. For actual pairwise exchanges, it is obvious that one actor, expecting to receive a good from another actor, will have a subjective estimate of the probability that the other actor will actually live up to his part of the bargain.

A simple way to introduce lack of complete trust into a system of action is to separate the action into two parts: the promise and the delivery. The delivery is partially but not wholly contingent on the promise. In a system with two actors, A_1 and A_2, where A_1 makes his delivery immediately and A_2 later, there are three events: E_1 is A_1's delivery of good 1, E_2 is A_2's promise of delivery of good 2, and E_3 is A_2's delivery of good 2.

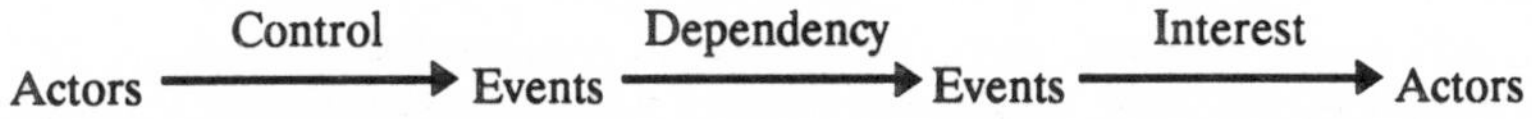

$$\text{Actors} \xrightarrow{\text{Control}} \text{Events} \xrightarrow{\text{Dependency}} \text{Events} \xrightarrow{\text{Interest}} \text{Actors}$$

Figure 28.1 Relations of actors and events when there is dependency of some events on others.

The model in this case makes use of the elaboration discussed in Chapter 27, in which there is a dependency of events in which actors are interested on events over which they have control, as shown in Figure 28.1. Here the dependency matrix **B** has elements b_{jk}, where b_{jk} is the probability that the outcome of event k will be determined by event j. This can be usefully illustrated by the example of the two-person exchange system.

EXAMPLE 1: CARD TRADING WITH SOME MISTRUST   Assume that the system is like that described in Chapter 25 except that Tom holds all the football cards at the beginning, and John holds all the baseball cards. Assume also that

John cannot deliver his cards immediately, but promises to deliver them in the future. Tom's trust in John's future delivery is less than complete: He believes that the probability of delivery is .7, and John operates as if the probability of delivery is only .7. The matrices of control, dependence, and interest are shown in Table 28.1, along with the product of the dependency and interest matrices, which shows the interests of Tom and John in the events they control. By definition of the events, Tom cannot gain control of the delivery. Consequently, his interest in this event must be set to zero. This reduces his total interests in the system below 1.0, which makes the system a modified one like the case described in Chapter 25 where quantities of goods vary. Equations 25.10′–25.21′ apply.

Application of the equations shows that the only change from the basic model in this case is a renormalization of Tom's interests so that they sum to 1.0. With eq. 25.18′ Tom's power is calculated as .77 and John's as .23; at the competitive equilibrium Tom has traded 15 football cards for promises of 59 baseball cards from John. These promises have an expected yield of 41 cards, so that while the explicit outcome from the trades consists of a promise of 59 baseball cards for 15 football cards, the expected outcome of what they are finally interested in (control of football and baseball cards) gives Tom 41 baseball cards for 15 football cards, while Tom keeps 85 football cards and John keeps 59 baseball cards.

A direct comparison of this outcome with the outcome for the example of Chapter 25, which does not involve lack of trust, is not possible, because this case was simplified by letting each boy begin with all the cards of one kind. But a comparison may be made with the competitive equilibrium for the comparable case in which there is complete trust, as shown in Table 28.2.

The outcomes shown have several important differences:

1. The actor whose delivery depends on not completely trusted promises (John) has reduced power in that case (.23 compared to .29).
2. There is less overall exchange in the case with incomplete trust (5 fewer football cards and an expected 9 fewer baseball cards).
3. The value of the promises is less than the value of the cards in the case without promises.
4. The value of the initial holdings of the actor who delivers immediately (Tom) is higher in the case with promises. (This follows directly from item 1).

All four of these differences hold in general for a two-person exchange system, as a little algebra would show. The competitive equilibrium for the case with promises and for the case without promises can be seen in Figure 28.2. The location of the former must always be between the initial point and the contract curve and must show an exchange rate more favorable to the party who delivers immediately.

EXAMPLE 2: A MORE COMPLEX CASE INVOLVING MISTRUST A sense of how a two-person exchange system functions in a slightly more complex situa-

Table 28.1 Control, dependency, and interest in trading-card exchange system with partial trust.

CONTROL (C)

	Football cards	Baseball cards	
		Promise	Delivery
	E_1	E_2	E_3
Tom	1	0	0
John	0	1	1

DEPENDENCY (B′)

	E_1	E_2	E_3
E_1	1	0	0
E_2	0	.7	.3

INTEREST (X′)

	E_1	E_2
Tom	.8	.2
John	.5	.5

(BX)′

	E_1	E_2	E_3
Tom	.8	.14	.06
John	.5	.35	.15

Table 28.2 Competitive equilibrium in exchange of football and baseball cards, with and without promises involving trust.

	WITH PARTIAL TRUST						WITH FULL TRUST		
	Exchange outcome			Expected final outcome			Exchange outcome		
	Football cards	Baseball cards promised	Power	Football cards	Baseball cards	Power	Football cards	Baseball cards	Power
Tom	85	59	.77	85	41	.77	80	50	.71
John	15	41	.23	15	59	.23	20	50	.29
Value per card or promise	.0077	.0020		.0077	.0023		.0071	.0029	

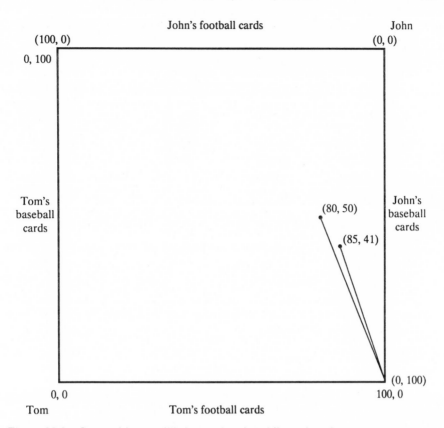

Figure 28.2 Competitive equilibrium points in a bilateral exchange system, without promises and with partially trusted promises.

tion can be gained by reconsidering the original trading-card example from Chapter 25 in which both actors hold some fraction of each of the goods at the beginning. In this case Tom controls two events: 95 football cards and 4 baseball cards (E_1 and E_2). John controls four: promises for the delivery of football and baseball cards (E_3 and E_4), and actual delivery of the two types of cards (E_5 and E_6). It is assumed, as before, that both Tom and John estimate the probability of delivery as .7. The initial control, dependency, and interest matrices are shown in Table 28.3. The modification of the basic model for cases where the quantities of goods vary must be used. Interests are determined by multiplying interest in each card (.008 and .002 for Tom, .005 and .005 for John) by the number of cards of each type held. As in the preceding example, interests of Tom in E_5 and E_6 of the **BX** matrix must be set to zero, since those are not involved in the exchange process.

With **C** and **BX** as the control and interest matrices, eqs. 25.10′–25.21′ apply. Using eq. 25.18′ to estimate **r**, with a dependency matrix included (that is, **X** is

Table 28.3 Control, dependency, and interest for exchange in bilateral monopoly with partial trust.

	Control (C)							Dependency (B′)								Interest (X′)			
	E_1	E_2	E_3	E_4	E_5	E_6		E_1	E_2	E_3	E_4	E_5	E_6			E_1	E_2	E_5	E_6
Tom	95	4	0	0	0	0	E_1	1	0	0	0	0	0		Tom	.76	.008	.040	.192
John	0	0	5	96	5	96	E_2	0	1	0	0	0	0		John	.475	.020	.025	.480
							E_5	0	0	.7	0	.3	0						
							E_6	0	0	0	.7	0	.3						

replaced by **BX**), gives $\mathbf{r} = (.739, .261)$. Then

$$\mathbf{v} = \mathbf{D}_c^{-1}\,\mathbf{BXD}_{bx}^{-1}\,\mathbf{r} = (.00766, .00290, .00536, .00203, .00040, .00039)$$

Calculating **C*** from eq. 25.11′ with **B** included gives

$$\mathbf{C^*} = \mathbf{D}_r(\mathbf{BX})'\mathbf{D}_v^{-1} = \begin{bmatrix} 78.8 & 2.2 & 4.2 & 52.7 & 0 & 0 \\ 16.2 & 1.8 & 1.8 & 43.3 & 5 & 96 \end{bmatrix}$$

The matrix **C*** gives the cards and promises traded. **C*B** gives the expected final distribution of cards after delivery:

$$\mathbf{C^*B} = \begin{bmatrix} 78.8 & 2.2 & 2.9 & 36.9 \\ 16.2 & 1.8 & 2.1 & 59.1 \end{bmatrix}$$

Combining the cards which originated with each actor with those acquired in exchange gives a final distribution of cards:

	Football	Baseball
Tom	81.7	39.1
John	18.3	60.9

Thus Tom ends up with 82 football cards and 39 baseball cards, and John with 18 football cards and 61 baseball cards. Comparison with the results for this same example without promises from Chapter 25 can be made by showing both equilibrium points on the same Edgeworth box, as in Figure 28.3.

What is not shown by Figure 28.3, but would be shown by calculating the indifference curves for Tom's and John's satisfaction levels in the cases with and without immediate delivery, is that the point (82, 39) is slightly above the indifference curve for Tom that passes through the competitive equilibrium for the case without promises. Thus Tom's expected final position for the case with promises is slightly better than that for the case without. That this can occur follows from John's weaker position in trading; he brings only promises to the market rather than immediately deliverable cards.

This example shows the increased complexity of calculating a competitive equilibrium when commodities that are being exchanged are in the hands of

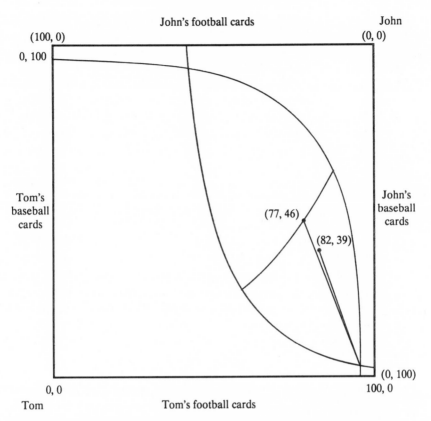

Figure 28.3   Competitive equilibrium points in a bilateral exchange system, without promises and with partially trusted promises: modified starting points.

actors for whom other actors have different levels of trust. And this is only one of the complications. Another lies in the assumption that *both* actors anticipate the possibility that a promise will not be kept. This means that not only is Tom less interested in the promises than he would have been in the cards themselves, but John is as well, and thus more willing to part with a promise than with a card.

Sometimes this is the actual state of affairs, but in other cases it is only the potential recipient who mistrusts. The person who has only promises to deliver fully intends to delivery on the promises and is as hesitant in making promises as in parting with the goods themselves. Such a case has a different outcome from that of the first example presented in this chapter. Suppose that John treats his promises as though they were cards, but Tom expects delivery only with probability .7. Then Tom's effective interest in baseball cards is reduced, as it was in the first example, but John's is not. The modification of the model may be carried out very simply by reducing Tom's interest in baseball cards from .2 to

.7 × .2, or .14, and then restandardizing interests to sum to 1.0. Tom's interests become .851 and .149, and John's remain at .5 and .5. The actors' power remains what it was in the first example, .77 for Tom and .23 for John (since they control the same goods), but the promises have a higher value (.0023 as compared to .0020) because they are discounted only by Tom, not by John. The same number of football cards, 15, passes from Tom to John, but in return for promises of only 50 baseball cards (rather than 59 as in the first example). If Tom's estimates of the probability of receiving the cards promised is correct, he will get only 35 (fewer than expected for the first example); if John is correct, Tom will get all 50 cards.

This example illustrates how differing levels of trust on the part of different actors can be introduced into an exchange system. The general specification of this is given in the next section.

Lack of Complete Trust in Larger Systems

The model for a system without complete trust must be limited to the case in which each commodity arrives at its ultimate destination after at most a single transaction. This restriction is necessary because without it the transaction path or the number of transactions for each good is not known. Since trust is a property of a specific transaction and affects the outcome of that transaction, a model which predicts system outcomes from initial conditions must assume a fixed transaction path.

This restriction is met by those action systems in which the commodity being transferred is the right to control one's actions (as long as the additional right to transfer the first right is not also transferred; see Chapters 3 and 7). It is also met by those systems that are monetized either by a single actor's promises which are completely trusted (that is, with $p = 1.0$) or by actor-specific promises, which serve as a medium of exchange in the transactions in which that actor is involved. In either of these sorts of systems, all commodities can reach their final destination in at most one transaction. I will examine several special cases: the case in which all transactions are mistrusted to the same degree by both partners to the transaction; the case in which particular trustees are mistrusted to the same degree by all trustors; and the case in which particular trustors mistrust all transactions in which they are engaged to the same degree.

A System in Which All Transactions Are Mistrusted to the Same Degree on Both Sides

When there is general mistrust in the system, this constitutes a mistrust of all transactions. Those goods and events which an actor controls without transactions are not mistrusted; those for which he must carry out a transaction in order to gain control are mistrusted. A real situation corresponding to this is one in which an individual finds himself in a strange country where all is different and new. Another is that of a psychologically pathological individual who has been traumatized in interactions with other persons and mistrusts all transactions.

In such cases how are an individual's actions affected by mistrust where the exchange rate is fixed? In actor i's exchange of a good which he controls (good k) for a good which he does not control (good j), he will give up k for j as long as $dU_i/dc_{ik} < 0$. In the absence of mistrust, from eq. 25.1,

$$\frac{dU_i}{dc_{ik}} = \frac{x_{ki}U_i}{c_{ik}} + \frac{x_{ji}}{c_{ij}} U_i \frac{dc_{ij}}{dc_{ik}}$$

Thus he will give up k for j as long as

$$\frac{x_{ki}U_i}{c_{ik}} + \frac{x_{ji}}{c_{ij}} U_i \frac{dc_{ij}}{dc_{ik}} < 0 \tag{28.5}$$

Multiplying by dc_{ik} (a negative quantity) reverses the inequality, giving

$$-\frac{dc_{ik}x_{ki}}{c_{ik}} < \frac{dc_{ij}x_{ji}}{c_{ij}} \tag{28.6}$$

Here the left-hand side is the magnitude of actor i's potential loss (L in Chapter 5), and the right-hand side is his potential return ($L + G$ in Chapter 5). He carries out the transaction if $p > L/(L + G)$. When $p = 1.0$, as in the case where there is no mistrust, he will carry out the transaction as long as $L < L + G$, or as long as the inequality of eq. 28.6 holds. At equilibrium that becomes an equality. But if $p < 1.0$,

$$-\frac{dc_{ik}x_{ki}}{c_{ik}} < p \frac{dc_{ij}x_{ji}}{c_{ij}} \tag{28.7}$$

The exchange rate with which he is confronted is

$$\frac{dc_{ik}}{dc_{ij}} = -\frac{v_j}{v_k}$$

which, when combined with eq. 28.7, gives

$$\frac{x_{ki}}{c_{ik}v_k} < \frac{px_{ji}}{c_{ij}v_j} \tag{28.8}$$

Thus he will carry out an exchange of k for j until the above inequality becomes an equality. In effect, this means that his interest in those goods and events that he does not control (j) is reduced from x_{ji} to px_{ji}.

The effect of this will differ, of course, depending on how much of what he is interested in is already under his control. The amount of j he will control at equilibrium, relative to the amount of k he already held, is reduced from

$$\frac{c_{ij}}{c_{ik}} = \frac{x_{ji}v_k}{x_{ki}v_j} \tag{28.9}$$

to

$$\frac{c_{ij}}{c_{ik}} = p \, \frac{x_{ji} v_k}{x_{ki} v_j} \tag{28.10}$$

He begins with c_{ik0} of k and exchanges it at the rate of v_j/v_k for j, so his equilibrium level of j is given by

$$c_{ij} v_j = (c_{ik0} - c_{ik}) v_k \tag{28.11}$$

Equations 28.9–28.11 can be used to compare the amount of the acquired good that he will hold at equilibrium in the presence of mistrust on his part with the amount that he will hold if he has complete trust. If c'_{ij} is the amount he holds in the presence of mistrust and c_{ij} is the amount he holds when trust is complete, then, when his interests in k and j sum to 1.0,

$$\frac{c'_{ij}}{c_{ij}} = \frac{p}{1 - x_{ji} + p x_{ji}} \tag{28.12}$$

Figure 28.4 shows this ratio as a function of his interest in the acquired good and his level of mistrust. The ratio increases as his interest in the good to be acquired increases and as his trust increases, but is more affected by the level of trust than by the level of interest.

The reduction in his level of satisfaction can be seen by comparing the satisfaction levels, $\ln U_i$ without mistrust and $\ln U'_i$ with mistrust, using eq. 25.3:

$$\ln U_i = \ln U'_i + \gamma \tag{28.13}$$

Equations 28.9–28.11 may be used to express the equilibrium levels of k and j in terms of c_{ik0}, the initial level of control of k. Using eq. 25.3 for satisfaction levels

$$\ln U_i = x_{ji} \ln c_{ij} + x_{ki} \ln c_{ik}$$

allows eq. 28.13 to be used to compare the satisfaction levels:

$$x_{ji} \ln \frac{c_{ik0} x_{ji} v_k}{v_j (x_{ji} + x_{ki})} + x_{ki} \ln \frac{c_{ik0} x_{ki}}{x_{ji} + x_{ki}} = x_{ki} \ln \frac{c_{ik0} x_{ki}}{p x_{ji} + x_{ki}}$$

$$+ x_{ji} \ln \frac{c_{ik0} p x_{ji} v_k}{(p x_{ji} + x_{ki}) v_j} + \gamma$$

Solving for γ gives

$$\gamma = (x_{ki} + x_{ji}) \left(\ln \frac{p x_{ji} + x_{ki}}{x_{ji} + x_{ki}} \right) - x_{ji} \ln p \tag{28.14}$$

Figure 28.5 shows relative utility as a function of x_{ji} and p. Relative utility is the multiplier by which his satisfaction is reduced when he mistrusts transactions by which he must acquire j.

These calculations and Figures 28.4 and 28.5 treat the situation of the single individual confronting a fixed environment, such as the cases mentioned before

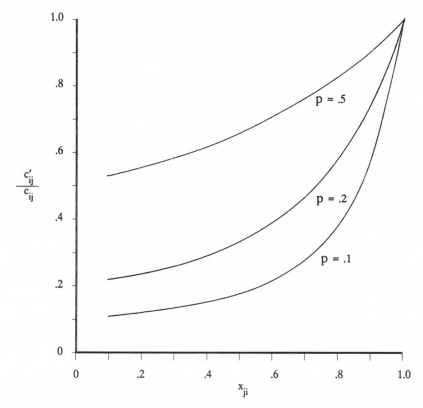

Figure 28.4 Ratio of control of an acquired good when there is mistrust to control of an acquired good when trust is complete, as a function of the level of trust and interest in the good.

of a person in a new and strange environment or a person with a pathological fear of interactions with others. Such persons will hold on to what they have and fail to acquire other things in which they are interested but which would require transactions, as shown in Figure 28.4. Their levels of satisfaction will be sharply reduced if their levels of trust are sufficiently low, as shown in Figure 28.5.

GENERAL EQUILIBRIUM For the case in which the whole system is infected with mistrust (each person trusts transactions only at a level $p < 1.0$), it is possible to compare the general equilibrium with that in the absence of mistrust. To do so requires the assumption that in the process of arriving at equilibrium exchange rates before transactions occur, actors adjust their interest levels according to inequality 28.8, so their interest in what they will acquire is reduced from x_{ji} to px_{ji}. Then interests must be renormalized in order to use the basic linear system, so the effective interests which determine actors' transactions will

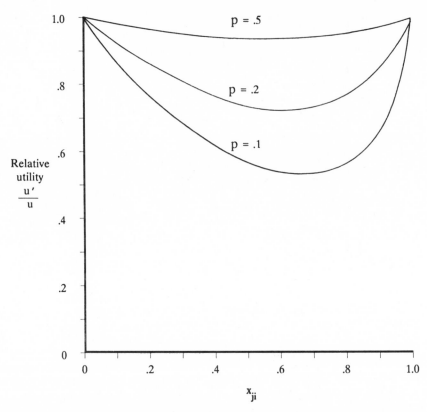

Figure 28.5   Ratio of the satisfaction level when there is mistrust to the satisfaction level when there is complete trust, as a function of the level of trust and interest in the good.

sum to 1.0. Effective interests are defined as follows:

$y_{ji} \equiv$ effective interests which govern actor i's transactions

$$y_{ji} = \frac{x_{ji}\, \delta_{ji}}{\sum_{j} x_{ji}\delta_{ji}}$$

where

$$\delta_{ji} = \begin{cases} 1, & \text{for those commodities which he will not acquire at} \\ & \text{the emergent prices} \\[2ex] p, & \text{for those commodities which he must acquire at the} \\ & \text{emergent prices through transactions} \end{cases}$$

With these new quantities y_{ij} in place of the true interests, the standard equations for equilibrium power may be found from eq. 25.18:

$$\mathbf{r} = (\mathbf{I} - \mathbf{CY} + \mathbf{E}_n)^{-1}\mathbf{e}_{n1}$$

$$\mathbf{v} = \mathbf{Yr}$$

$$\mathbf{C}^* = \mathbf{D}_r\mathbf{Y}'\mathbf{D}_v^{-1}$$

EXAMPLE 3: EFFECTS OF GENERALIZED MISTRUST OF TRANSACTIONS
Suppose that there are three persons in an action system—Tom, John, and Steve—and each begins with control over his own actions, a commodity which he is prepared to exchange with the others. But each does not trust the promises of the others in the exchange. Thus, if the interest matrix is $\mathbf{X}$, the effective interest matrix for the system of action, before normalizing to give column sums of 1.0, is

$$\mathbf{Y}' = \|x_{ji}\delta_{ji}\| = \begin{bmatrix} x_{11} & x_{21}p & x_{31}p \\ x_{12}p & x_{22} & x_{32}p \\ x_{13}p & x_{23}p & x_{33} \end{bmatrix} \begin{matrix} \text{Tom} \\ \text{John} \\ \text{Steve} \end{matrix}$$

Suppose the true interest matrix $(\mathbf{X}')$ consists of these values:

		Actions of		
		Tom	John	Steve
	Tom	.6	.2	.2
Interests of	John	.1	.8	.1
	Steve	.3	.3	.4

Thus John has the most interest in maintaining control of his own actions and Steve the least; and each one's interests in controlling the actions of the others are evenly spread. If the level of trust is complete, Tom, John, and Steve will each retain control of .6, .8, and .4 of their own actions, respectively, and their power in the system will be .27, .55, and .18, respectively. If the level of trust is only .6, calculations using eqs. 25.18' and 25.11' show that Tom, John, and Steve will each retain control of .714, .870, and .526 of their own actions, respectively, and their power is .263, .578, and .159, respectively. Thus reduced trust will lead to actors' retaining greater control of their own actions (and gaining less control of others' actions) and to an increased asymmetry of power in the system. The first of these effects follows directly from the increase in effective interest in what is already held compared to interest in what must be obtained from others. The second effect is less direct, for differential power arises from two sources: differential interests in what the actor himself controls (as in this case), and differential control of what others are interested in. Differential power arising from the first of these sources will increase with mistrust, because effective interest in what the actor himself controls is weighted by the power of the interested actor, and as the actor's own interest in what he controls becomes a larger fraction of the total interest in what he controls, the powerful become more powerful. Differential power arising from the second source will decrease as mistrust increases, because of the decrease in the interest of each in what others control.[3]

These results have important implications for social capital. If the social capital in a system of action in which each holds rights of control to others' actions is conceptualized as $\Sigma_{i \neq j} \Sigma_j c_{ij}^*$, where good j is rights of control over actor j's action and $i \neq j$, then the social capital declines as p declines. This can be seen by expanding c_{ij}^*:

$$c_{ij}^* = \frac{y_{ji} r_i}{v_j}$$

where y_{ji} is x_{ji} renormalized:

$$y_{ji} = \frac{p x_{ji}}{x_{ii} + p(1 - x_{ii})}$$

Neglecting the effects of p on r_i and v_j, and v_j, then y_{ji} is roughly p times x_{ji}, for $j \neq i$. Thus social capital in a system of this sort declines roughly in proportion to the level of trust.

EXAMPLE 4: TRUST AND MISTRUST BETWEEN TWO ACTORS   In a system of two actors, in which each offers for exchange with the other rights of control over his actions, the effect of lack of trust is particularly striking. Consider a girl Kay and a boy Jay who have very great interest in each other; each has an interest of .8 in the other and .2 in self. Figure 28.6 shows where the competitive equilibrium will be when their level of trust is .1 (point A), .4, .6, .8, and 1.0 (point B).

Observation of the actions of Kay and Jay when their level of trust is low, say at .2, would lead to the inference that their level of interest is much lower than it actually is. Because the level of trust is low, the actors' effective interests in each other and thus the control of each over the other's actions at equilibrium will be low.

If only one of the two has a low level of trust and the other is completely trusting, the situation is quite different. For example, suppose the two have equally strong interests in each other, but Kay is very trusting and Jay has little trust, say $p = .2$ for Jay and $p = 1.0$ for Kay. Jay's low level of trust has the effect, as indicated above, of sharply reducing his apparent interest in Kay, from .8 to .44 (point C in Figure 28.6). The end result with respect to their actions toward one another is that Jay remains largely in control of his actions, but gains control of a large portion of Kay's actions. The equilibrium point at (.2, .44) in Figure 28.6 represents Kay's control of only .2 of her actions and .44 of Jay's while Jay controls .56 of his actions and .8 of Kay's. Her power in the relation is

---

3. This analysis may be carried out more precisely by examining $\partial r_i / \partial x_{ji}$, where j refers to the goods actor i controls, and $\partial r_i / \partial p$.

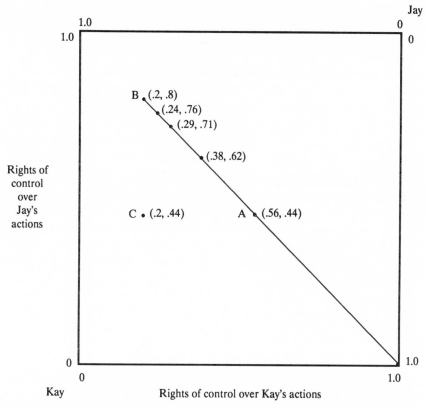

Figure 28.6   Equilibrium points in a bilateral exchange system with differing degrees of trust.

sharply reduced by the asymmetry in trust. Calculations would show a reduction of her power from .5 and .36, just as though there had been a wide asymmetry in interests.

If the actions of Kay and Jay at equilibrium were observed, without further information from them about their feelings toward one another and their levels of satisfaction in the relation, there would be no way to tell whether the locus of their actions was due to an asymmetry of trust or an asymmetry of interest.[4] As I will show shortly, however, if the *progress* of the relation from its beginning is observed, the two cases can be distinguished. The relation characterized by lack of trust takes a much longer time to reach its equilibrium state than does the relation in which interest is low but trust is complete. This is true, as Figure 28.6 suggests, even in the absence of any increase in trust itself.

4. I am excluding here other events which either actor might control that would be of interest to the other, which could show the power and thus the actions.

DYNAMICS IN A SYSTEM WITH MISTRUST   The effects of mistrust in a system examined so far have concerned the equilibrium state of the system. But the general level of trust also has an effect on the dynamics of the system.

The equation for change in the amount of value held by actor i in the form of good j can be expressed as a continuous-time Markov process with $n \times m$ states (see eq. 32.23). The equation for state ij (good j in the hands of actor i) can be written in terms of value as

$$\frac{da_{ij}}{dt} = \sum_k {}_iq_{jk}a_{ik}$$

where a_{ij} is the value of the amount of good j held by actor i and ${}_iq_{jk}$ is the instantaneous rate of movement of value from good k to good j. This equation expresses the movement of value from good k to good j. (The value held by actor i remains the same; in this process there is no flow of value between actors.[5]) For the case with two actors, indexed by 1 and 2, and four goods, indexed by 1, 2, 3, and 4, the matrix of transition rates, $\mathbf{Q}$, would have the following form in the absence of mistrust:

$$\mathbf{Q} = \begin{bmatrix} x_{11}-1 & x_{11} & x_{11} & x_{11} & 0 & 0 & 0 & 0 \\ x_{21} & x_{21}-1 & x_{21} & x_{21} & 0 & 0 & 0 & 0 \\ x_{31} & x_{31} & x_{31}-1 & x_{31} & 0 & 0 & 0 & 0 \\ x_{41} & x_{41} & x_{41} & x_{41}-1 & 0 & 0 & 0 & 0 \\ 0 & 0 & 0 & 0 & x_{12}-1 & x_{12} & x_{12} & x_{12} \\ 0 & 0 & 0 & 0 & x_{22} & x_{22}-1 & x_{22} & x_{22} \\ 0 & 0 & 0 & 0 & x_{32} & x_{32} & x_{32}-1 & x_{32} \\ 0 & 0 & 0 & 0 & x_{42} & x_{42} & x_{42} & x_{42}-1 \end{bmatrix}$$

$$(28.15)$$

The interests, x_{ji}, show, for actor i, the flow of value per unit time into good j given that actor i initially holds value in the form of another good, k. That flow is the same from all other goods k. If value is in state j, the flow of value is out of that state, and the transition rate is negative, that is, $x_{ji} - 1$. The flow of value is from the column state into the row state. As discussed in Chapter 32, in the form of the model in which quantities of goods vary, that is, when $\Sigma_k x_{ki} \neq 1.0$, the transition rate in the main diagonal $x_{ji} - \Sigma_k x_{ki}$, or $- \Sigma_{k \neq j} x_{ki}$. This form of expressing the main diagonal shows more directly that this transition rate is simply the negative of the sum of the flows into other states ik from state ij.

When there is mistrust (trust at $p < 1.0$), the goods with which actor i does not begin have a transition rate into state ij not equal to x_{ji}, but equal to px_{ji}. Thus, if actor 1 began with only goods 1 and 2, the first and second rows of $\mathbf{Q}$ would

---

5. The dual process, given in Chapter 32, describes the movement of value in the form of good j from one actor to another, with no flow of value between goods.

remain the same as shown, but the third row would become

$$px_{31} \quad px_{31} \quad -(x_{11} + x_{21} + px_{41}) \quad px_{31} \quad 0 \quad 0 \quad 0 \quad 0$$

and the fourth row would become

$$px_{41} \quad px_{41} \quad px_{41} \quad -(x_{11} - x_{21} - px_{31}) \quad 0 \quad 0 \quad 0 \quad 0$$

The reduced level of trust has the effect of reducing the transition rates for the movement of goods from one actor to another by a constant multiplier, p.

In the case of two actors and two goods, where actor 1's interests are x_{11} and x_{21} in the absence of mistrust, the rate of movement toward equilibrium is proportional to the sum of the transition rates, $x_{11} + x_{21}$. The following equation (see Chapter 32) shows the movement of value held by actor 1 between good 1 and good 2, where q_2 is the transition rate to good 2 and q_1 is the transition rate to good 1:

$$v_{11}(t) = v_{11}(0)e^{-(q_1+q_2)t} + \frac{q_1}{q_1 + q_2}(1 - e^{-(q_1+q_2)t}) \tag{28.16}$$

In this equation the quantity $q_1 + q_2$ determines both the rate of decline of the first term on the right-hand-side, which is the transitory component of $v_{11}(t)$, and the rate of increase in the second term on that side, which is the equilibrium component of $v_{11}(t)$. That quantity is simply the sum of the effective interests of actor 1, which in the case of complete trust is $x_{11} + x_{21}$. When trust is only at level p, the rate of movement is the sum of transition rates, $x_{11} + px_{21}$. Thus the rate of movement to equilibrium is reduced by an amount which depends on both p and x_{21}. The rate in the case where there is mistrust is a fraction, $(x_{11} + px_{21})/(x_{11} + x_{21})$, of the rate in the case where there is complete trust.

The change in rate of movement toward equilibrium cannot be so easily expressed for a larger system. What can be said, however, is that if $p < 1.0$ is the level of trust in a system, the rate of movement to equilibrium will be slower than if the level of trust were $p = 1.0$ and faster than p times the rate with complete trust. Thus the introduction of mistrust into the system not only changes the equilibrium, as indicated earlier, but also reduces the rate at which that equilibrium is reached.

Application of a model such as this is particularly appropriate to a system in which each has a single commodity of interest, control of his own actions (as in the earlier example involving Tom, John, and Steve and the one involving Kay and Jay). For a three-person system the matrix **Q** that is necessary is a 9×9 matrix of the form shown in Table 28.4. The matrix contains three submatrices of three rows and three columns; the first submatrix and the first row of the second are shown explicitly. Each submatrix describes a process by which value held by actor i flows from one commodity to another. Given the starting point, in which value held by i is all located in commodity i, it flows to j at rate px_{ji} and to k at px_{ki}. The matrix, however, describes the more general process, independent of the starting point, such that value would flow from j to i (at rate x_{ji}) or to k (at

Table 28.4 Matrix of transition rates (**Q**) for a three-person exchange system with mistrust.

		Origin state						
		11	12	13	21	22	23 $\cdots$	33
	11	$-px_{21} - px_{31}$	x_{11}	x_{11}	0	0	0 $\cdots$	0
	12	px_{21}	$-x_{11} - px_{31}$	px_{21}	0	0	0 $\cdots$	0
	13	px_{31}	px_{31}	$-x_{11} - px_{21}$	0	0	0 $\cdots$	0
Destination	21	0	0	0	$-x_{22} - px_{12}$	px_{12}	px_{12} $\cdots$	0
state	.	.	.		.	.	.	
	.	.	.		.	.	.	
	.	.	.		.	.	.	
	33	0						

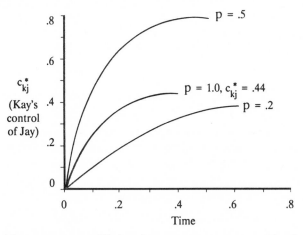

Figure 28.7 Movement to equilibrium in a two-actor system with a low level of trust.

rate px_{ki}). Obviously, because these are independent submatrices, the starting point, $\mathbf{v}(0)$, must have, in each subsection of the vector (that is, $i1$, $i2$, $i3$) the sum of value equal to that actor's equilibrium power (that is, $\Sigma_j v_{ij} = r_i$). This requires having calculated at the beginning the equilibrium vector **r**.

Figure 28.7 shows the movement of value for the two-actor system of Kay and Jay, for the case in which trust is complete and the case in which trust is at a level of only .2. Not only is the proportion of Jay's actions controlled by Kay at equilibrium reduced by almost half, but the rate of movement toward equilibrium is only about a third of that in the absence of mistrust.[6] In Figure 28.7 the curve with $p = 1.0$ and $c_{kj}^* = .44$ provides a comparison that allows seeing the

---

6. The rate of movement to equilibrium is the inverse of the total transition rate, so the ratio of the rates in these two cases is $1.0:.36$; that is, the rate is only .36 as great for the case with mistrust as for the case without mistrust.

lower rate directly. This curve is a line for a system with the same equilibrium point, (.56, .44), but that equilibrium is achieved through a lower level of interest rather than a lack of trust. This is, as I indicated earlier, a way of distinguishing systems in which there is a low level of interest in the other's actions from systems in which the level of interest is high but the level of trust is low. The latter system will reach the equilibrium more slowly than will the former, as shown by Figure 28.7.

A System in Which Particular Trustees Are Mistrusted to the Same Degree by All Trustors

The general framework used above can serve for examining the case in which one actor in a system is mistrusted by all others. For a system of three actors in which the first is mistrusted by the second and third, the effective interests before normalization are

	Interest in actions of		
	Tom	John	Steve
Tom	x_{11}	x_{21}	x_{31}
John	$x_{12}p$	x_{22}	x_{32}
Steve	$x_{13}p$	x_{23}	x_{33}

The effect is clearly to reduce the power of the actor who is mistrusted and to reduce his equilibrium control over those commodities in which he is interested. Comparing this system with the earlier example where Tom, John, and Steve all had reduced levels of trust toward one another shows this effect. Table 28.5

Table 28.5 Effect of general mistrust and of mistrust of one trustee on proportion of actions of each controlled by each at equilibrium in a three-actor system where each is interested in control of others' actions.

		INTERESTS (X') Actions of				FULL TRUST Actions of			
		Tom	John	Steve		Tom	John	Steve	Power
	Tom	.6	.2	.2		.6	.2	.2	.27
(Actors)	John	.1	.8	.1		.1	.8	.1	.55
	Steve	.3	.3	.4		.3	.3	.4	.18

		TRUST = .6 Actions of				TRUST OF TOM = .6 Actions of			
		Tom	John	Steve	Power	Tom	John	Steve	Power
	Tom	.72	.14	.14	.26	.6	.2	.2	.19
(Actors)	John	.07	.87	.07	.58	.06	.83	.10	.62
	Steve	.24	.24	.53	.16	.20	.34	.45	.19

shows the power of each actor and the equilibrium control of the actions of each by each of the others under three conditions: with no mistrust, with trust of each of the others by each at a level of .6, and with trust of Tom by the other two at a level of .6 while their trust in each other is complete. As the table shows, Tom's power is reduced when he is the only one mistrusted, compared to either of the other two scenarios, and he has less control of the others' actions, but their control of his remains at the same level as in the system with no mistrust.

A System in Which One or More Trustors Mistrust All Others to the Same Degree

The final case to be considered is a system in which one actor's level of trust in the others is below 1.0 and the others have complete trust. The effective interests before normalization in such a three-actor system are

	Interest in actions of		
	Tom	John	Steve
Tom	x_{11}	$x_{21}p$	$x_{31}p$
John	x_{12}	x_{22}	x_{32}
Steve	x_{12}	x_{23}	x_{33}

The effects of this form of mistrust in the system can be illustrated by modifying the preceding example so that Tom's interests reflect a reduced trust in either of the others. The result of this is to increase his effective interest in his own actions, to increase his power [giving the power vector (.34, .49, .16)], and to decrease John's and Steve's control of his actions from .2 each to .14 each (as in the case where each mistrusted the other). This result is as expected from the result for the preceding example.

« 29 »

Power, the Micro-to-Macro Transition, and Interpersonal Comparison of Utility

Interpersonal Comparison

The micro-to-macro transition imposes a requirement on social theory that has not yet been made explicit in this book. This requirement is that interests of different actors must be in some fashion aggregated. Such aggregation appears to violate the general maxim, long recognized by economists, that in a positive science the utility a good has for one person cannot be directly compared to the utility it has for another. That is, although it is simple to compare the utility an apple has for a given actor with the utility an orange has for that actor on the basis of the preference the actor exhibits for one over the other, it is not possible to compare the utility an apple has for one actor with the utility it has for another. The reason given is a very simple one: There is no behavior through which such a comparison can be made.

This generally held maxim is not true, however. Interpersonal comparison is not only possible; it occurs all the time. Yet the kind of interpersonal comparison that occurs in everyday life turns out not to be of value for the purpose to which many economists have wanted to put it.

The motivation for attempting to find a positive basis for interpersonal comparison of utility is ordinarily that of welfare economics, to provide a basis for saying that one distribution (of income, for example) is better than another in the sense that it provides greater overall welfare. This motivation has been and is a pervasive one. It is probably responsible, for example, for the extensive interest, throughout the social sciences but especially in economics, in Rawls's (1971) attempt to discover what kinds of inequalities are consistent with a just society.

The origins of welfare economics are found in the work of the utilitarians, beginning with Bentham, who assumed that utilities could simply be summed to find the maximum happiness. That general principle served as the basis for the welfare economics of Pigou and Bergson, who assumed that welfare was maximized when the marginal utility of money was the same for all, which occurred, by assumption, when all held the same amounts of money.

Although my aim is not that of welfare economics, the fact that interests of different actors are in some fashion aggregated, or combined, in the qualitative theory of Parts I–IV of this book and in the mathematical theory of Part V means that the issue of interpersonal comparison of utility must be explicitly addressed. It is useful to begin by examining discussions of economists on the subject.

Beginning in the 1930s there was extensive questioning of the easy assumption of interpersonal comparison of utility then made by welfare economists. Much confusion developed, and it has not yet been wholly dispelled. Perhaps the most important cause of this confusion was the perception of the role of the social scientist and the role of the subjects about whom the social scientist theorizes. Classically the role of the welfare economist was as policy advisor. Reflecting this position, Harrod (1938) said:

> Consider the repeal of the Corn Laws. This tended to reduce the value of a specific factor of production—land. It can no doubt be shown that the gain to the community as a whole exceeded the loss of the landlords—but only if individuals are treated in some sense as equal. Otherwise how can the loss to some—and that there was a loss can hardly be denied—be compared with the general gain? If the incomparability of utility to different individuals is strictly pressed, not only are the prescriptions of the welfare school ruled out, but all prescriptions whatever. The economist as adviser is completely stultified, and, unless his speculations be regarded as of paramount aesthetic value, he had better be suppressed completely. No; some sort of postulate of equality has to be assumed. (pp. 396–397)

Harrod recognized that if he was to advise on economic policy, he must explicitly make some assumption about the relative weight, or importance, of different persons' happiness. He was willing to apply equal weights, at least for policies involving restriction of competition. Robbins (1938), Harrod's principal antagonist in this argument, on the other hand, was not. He replied, reflecting on the evolution of his own views:

> But as time went on, things occurred which began to shake my belief in the existence between so complete a continuity between politics and economic analysis . . . I am not clear how these doubts first suggested themselves; but I will remember how they were brought to a head by my reading somewhere—I think in the work of Sir Henry Maine—the story of how an Indian official had attempted to explain to a high caste Brahmin the sanctions of the Benthamite system. "But that," said the Brahmin, "cannot possibly be right—I am ten times as capable of happiness as that untouchable over there." I had no sympathy with the Brahmin. But I could not escape the conviction that, if I chose to regard men as equally capable of satisfaction and he to regard them as differing according to a hierarchical schedule, the difference between us was not one which could be resolved by the same method of demonstration as were available in other fields of social judgment . . . "I see no means," Jevons had said, "whereby such comparisons can be accomplished." (p. 636)

Harrod and Robbins agreed that interpersonal comparison involves some judgment by the economist of the importance of different persons' utilities;

Harrod, in order to continue to give advice concerning government policies, was willing to make such judgments, but Robbins was not. Presumably most economic theorists felt similarly uncomfortable, despite the egalitarian origins of welfare economics, since they were quick to accept a point suggested by Kaldor (1939): In some cases two policies can be objectively compared without interpersonal comparison of utility, if a shift from the first to the second brings wide enough benefits to some groups that those who lose by the shift can be fully compensated by those who gain.[1] According to Kaldor's compensation principle, if compensation were in fact carried out (a matter left unclear in his proposal), everyone would be as well or better off under the second policy as under the first, and the move would be a Pareto-optimal move.

This approach, which formed the basis for further work by Hicks (1939), Scitovsky (1941), and Samuelson (1950), bypassed the question of whether the economist was to compare different persons' utilities but maintained the role of the economist as advisor on the welfare implications of economic policy. Samuelson showed that it was highly improbable that there were any moves that would pass sufficient tests to ensure that the second position was better than the first, and Kaldor's approach came to appear less profitable. Yet there was little or no resolution of the question of the economist's role and the question of interpersonal comparison of utility.

A slow shift in the interpretation of a social welfare function was taking place, however. The concept had always implicitly concerned the aggregate welfare, whether measured on an individual-by-individual basis without interpersonal comparison, as implied by the criterion of Pareto optimality, or measured through interpersonal comparisons of utility. But there was confusion concerning the answer to the question of who was to do the aggregating and how it was to be done. Arrow's book (1951), which purported to be about a social welfare function, discussed aggregating procedures that were tantamount to voting rules. Many economists initially refused to consider Arrow's approach as relevant to welfare economics. If it were to lead to some set of acceptable decision rules, the welfare economist would no longer play the role of economic policy advisor, since policy questions would be put in the hands of voters operating under an appropriate decision rule. The result was that some welfare economists disavowed the idea that a social welfare function should necessarily have any relation to individual choice. For example, Little (1952), in a critique of Arrow's work, said that "my interpretation of a Bergson [social welfare] function requires only that there should be an order. It does not require that it should be an order such that anyone would want to say of it that it represented the choice of society" (p. 424).

---

1. This compensation principle has attributes similar to those of a taxation scheme proposed much earlier by a Swedish economist, Knut Wicksell (1958 [1896]). Taxes to provide a public good would be levied in the same bill that created the good. Then, in order to ensure that the benefits outweighed the costs, the tax schedule would be adjusted until all benefited, as demonstrated by a unanimous vote in favor of the tax-and-benefit bill.

Unwilling to give up the economist's role as judge of what constitutes social welfare, Little also commented on Arrow's condition of nondictatorship:

> Let there be three men and two alternatives, x and y. Let the orders be xy for Tom and yx for both Dick and Harry. The [Arrow] conditions then preclude xy as the master-order. The two [economic] states may be such that in y Tom has one piece of manna, while Dick and Harry both have ninety-nine pieces; in x Tom has three pieces and Dick and Harry both have ninety-eight pieces. Might not then the master ranking xy be desirable? (p. 426)

The only answer to this is that obviously the master ranking xy would be desirable to Tom, and to Little, but not to Dick and Harry. This passage shows particularly well the peculiar assumption of welfare economists: that there is a god somewhere, standing outside society, in whose eyes something is better or worse for society, and it is the economist's role to be the expositor of that god's views to temporal rulers. Little at one point actually invokes someone he calls "superman" to carry out such judging.[2]

Although Arrow's book and the large volume of work spawned by it dealt with voting rules, most of the authors did not envision the loss of the role of policy advisor for the welfare economist. Yet Pareto optimality and Kaldor's compensation principle (where the policy includes the necessary compensation) imply that the criterion as to whether a new policy improves the social welfare should be an unanimous vote.

One of the disturbing aspects of the discussion of interpersonal comparison of utility by most authors is the failure to recognize the basis on which a concept in a theory may legitimately be endowed with certain properties, whether these are the ordinal, interval, or cardinal properties of real numbers. It is one of the achievements of economics that the appropriate criteria have been applied to choice under certainty, with the result that an ordinal conception of utility has come to replace the cardinal conception held by Marshall.

The appropriate criterion can be stated in several ways, but in essence, it is this: Does the behavior which the theory is designed to describe provide the basis for assignment of values and for testing of properties (such as ordinality and cardinality) that these values are assumed to obey? In economic behavior under certainty, with no assumptions about the preference function except that it obeys a declining marginal rate of substitution, the choice behavior of individuals does not allow testing a cardinal measure of utility, but only an ordinal measure.

There may, of course, be utility functions that *do* assume cardinal utility, thus implying behavior that allows that assumption to be tested. The Cobb-Douglas

---

2. Little is perhaps an extreme case, but the topic of interpersonal comparison of utility seems to bring out the worst in many who approach it. Even Sen (1979) appears eager to incorporate the policy advisor into economic theory through interpersonal comparison.

utility function, introduced in eq. 25.1 and used in this book, is an example. It implies something more specific than that each resource has the property of obeying a declining marginal rate of substitution: that the marginal rate of substitution of a resource is inversely proportional to the amount of the resource currently held. The constant of proportionality is the actor's *interest* in the resource, and when interests are normalized to sum to 1.0, they represent the fraction of the individual's total wealth that will be directed to acquiring and holding that resource. For example, if actor i begins with a resource in which he has no interest, and there are two resources, j and k, in which he does have an interest, x_{ji} and x_{ki}, respectively (where $x_{ji} + x_{ki} = 1.0$), he will, according to the Cobb-Douglas utility function, devote a fraction, x_{ji}, of his initial resource to acquiring j and a fraction, x_{ki}, to acquiring k.

This specific function allows one, on the basis of observing the fraction of actor i's resources devoted to each resource in which he has some interest, to assign a number representing x_{ji}, actor i's interest in resource j. Furthermore, by observing whether that fraction is affected by the total amount of resources held or by the amount of resources he must give up to acquire j (the price of j), one can test whether this particular cardinal utility function describes i's behavior. If one finds that the fraction is independent of the total amount of resources that i holds and independent of the price of resource j, then i's behavior is described by the Cobb-Douglas utility function. If not, it may nevertheless be described by another cardinal utility function.

The question of whether utilities have the property of cardinality is independent of the possibility of interpersonal comparison of utility, however. Because numbers can be added, it has often been assumed that cardinality and interpersonal comparison are synonymous. They are not. Neither implies the other. In the theory of this book, for example, eq. 25.1 gives a specific form for individuals' utility functions and can be tested empirically for particular individuals. Suppose that their behavior did meet its assumptions and numbers with full properties of cardinality could be assigned to them as their utilities, or satisfaction levels (see eq. 25.3). Equation 25.11 could be used for such tests, if r_i and v_j in that equation are taken to be exogenous. First, for an individual, i, one would assign values of x_{ji} for all j, based on observations of the amounts of j held (c_{ij}^*) for a particular level of resources, r_i, and set of prices, v_j. Then one would observe whether the quantities of c_{ij}^* varied as predicted when r_i and v_j were experimentally varied. Then, because the operation of addition has meaning for real numbers, it might be assumed that cardinality would imply that adding *different* individuals' numbers would be meaningful. But this is not so at all if the operations under the theory are limited to examining behavior of the *same* individual with different total resources and differing prices of goods.

It is only when a combination operation involving different individuals' actions is included in the theory that interpersonal comparison is implied. This does not occur in the development of the theory in Chapter 25 until eq. 25.12, where equilibrium price is given as a function of individuals' wealth and interests.[3] That equation shows that the interpersonal comparison *that occurs through the market* is one in which each actor's interests are weighted by his power (or wealth) in the system.

It is also true that interpersonal comparison of utility—that is, the conceptual capability of aggregating interests or utilities of different persons—does not imply cardinality of utility for a given person. Equation 25.12 could be used with a particular initial distribution of resources to assign interests (that is, fractions of wealth devoted to a good) on the basis of observed behavior. This would constitute interpersonal comparison; each actor's interests would still be weighted by his power (or wealth). This would not, however, imply that the individual's utility function has the property of cardinality. Under different initial distributions of resources, or with different distributions of tastes, the amount of each resource held at equilibrium by each actor might not obey any cardinal utility function, but only manifest the property of a declining marginal rate of substitution. Yet the aggregation, implying a particular set of weights for each actor's interests (although those interests could not be specified independently of the particular distribution of resources), would be possible and, in fact, would be implemented by the market processes themselves.

Despite the necessity for a combination operation if there is to be interpersonal comparison of utility, economists appear not to have explicitly applied the criterion of whether there is an operation in the theory itself involving some combination of different individuals' actions, and some have not even implicitly applied it. As a result, bizarre reasons have been given for accepting or refusing to accept interpersonal comparison. As is evident in the work cited earlier, Harrod accepted it in order to get on with the task of giving advice on policies. Robbins implicitly applied the criterion and rejected interpersonal comparison because disagreements could not "be resolved by the same method of demonstration as were available in other fields of social judgment." Jevons came closest to an explicit application of the correct criterion when he said, "I see no means whereby such comparison can be accomplished." In fact, the Brahmin in Maine's story was closer to the correct criterion than any of these economists when he said he was "ten times as capable of happiness as the untouchable over there." In the social system in which he lived, his interests counted perhaps ten times as much as did those of the untouchable's. The matter has by no means become clearer to economists in later work, as is evident from the earlier quotation from Little.

If one explicitly applies the criterion and asks whether there is any behavior

3. It may not be immediately apparent that eq. 25.12 does involve an assumption concerning interpersonal comparison. Equations 25.7–25.11 are specified for a single actor where prices are exogenously given. Only in eq. 25.12 is there summation over individuals (constituting interpersonal comparison) to make price endogenous. One can see, for example, that if price were set by external controls, eqs. 25.7–25.11 could hold for a given individual in the system. These equations do not imply interpersonal comparison; eq. 25.12 does.

among the actors as specified by the theory that allows calibration and testing of a utility that can be compared interpersonally, two answers are possible.

1. One can accept the conception of the welfare economist as policy advisor who judges whether a policy is better than another. In this case the individuals who are the subjects of the economist's advice carry out no actions that will allow interpersonal comparisons. They are merely passive recipients of policy outcomes. With this answer, interpersonal comparisons cannot legitimately be made, and the economist is forced to restrict his advice to those policy moves that are Pareto-optimal, withholding judgment on all those that would cause one or more persons to suffer.

2. One can reject the conception of the economist as policy advisor and state that the policy should derive from the behavior of the individuals in the society itself through whatever micro-to-macro processes translate individual interests into systemic outcomes. In markets these systemic outcomes are prices; in political systems they are collective decisions. In the latter case, decisions are often made and accepted only after extended struggle or conflict; thus it must be recognized that interactions other than those of exchange do occur, and that these interactions make manifest some sort of interpersonal comparison.

Furthermore, interpersonal comparison is not the passive concept that is implicit in economists' definitions of utility. Intrinsic to it is a notion of political power, that is, the power to realize one's goals. Thus the idea of interpersonal comparison of utility actually implies two comparisons. First, since the very concept of the utility of a good implies a willingness to sacrifice something to obtain the good, any interpersonal comparison must include a manifestation of the actor's willingness to sacrifice something, deriving from the utility he stands to gain or lose from the outcomes. (In the theory of this book, it is the individuals' interests that constitute the basis for such actions.) But the interpersonal comparison must also include a test of the relative efficacy of the actors' resources for realizing their goals. This dual comparison may take the form of conflict or the form of exchange; but whatever form it takes, it generates systemic outcomes through social processes.

Interpersonal Comparison through a Market

The interpersonal comparison of utility resulting from behavior in political systems is apparent; utility is weighted by the capacity to realize one's goals, that is, by power. What is less apparent is the fact that interpersonal comparison of utility is implied by any micro-to-macro transition. This is just as true in an economic market involving only voluntary exchanges as it is in a struggle over a collective decision whose outcome will benefit some and hurt others. The way interpersonal comparison arises in a perfect market can be seen by examining the structure of the basic model introduced in Chapter 25, that of a perfectly competitive market in which individuals have Cobb-Douglas utility functions.

In that model the individual's allocation of resources among different goods is determined by maximization of utility. For the case of exchange involving two goods, j and k, maximization of utility is given by those quantities c_{ij}^* which satisfy the following equation, obtained by taking the derivative of eq. 25.1 with respect to c_{ij}:

$$\frac{dU_i}{dc_{ij}} = \frac{x_{ji}}{c_{ij}^*} U_i + \frac{x_{ki}}{c_{ik}^*} U_i \frac{dc_{ik}}{dc_{ij}} = 0 \tag{29.1}$$

In a market with prices v_k and v_j for k and j, $dc_{ik}/dc_{ij} = v_j/v_k$, so eq. 29.1 reduces to

$$\frac{c_{ij}^*}{c_{ik}^*} = \frac{x_{ji}/v_j}{x_{ki}/v_k} \tag{29.2}$$

That is, actor i's relative holdings of j and k at equilibrium are proportional to the ratio of his interests in the two goods and inversely proportional to the ratio of their prices. Thus if relative prices in a system and the ratio of the quantities of two goods held are known, relative interests in these goods can be inferred. This results from the assumption that individuals' holdings of goods will be such as to maximize their utilities, and the specific form of the inference (the ratio of interests) results from assuming the Cobb-Douglas form for the utility function.

Thus eq. 29.2 expresses the behavior which allows intrapersonal comparison of utility, for the relative utilities of two goods for the same individual (or, for this model, the individual's relative interests in the goods).

On the basis of this behavior of individuals at market equilibrium, the general expression for the amount of each good controlled at equilibrium was derived in Chapter 25 and given in eq. 25.11:

$$c_{ij}^* = \frac{x_{ji} r_i}{v_j}$$

This equation can be used for two actors in the same system to carry out interpersonal comparison. Dividing eq. 25.11 for actor i by the same equation for actor h and rearranging terms gives an equation which is analogous to eq. 29.2:

$$\frac{x_{ji} r_i}{c_{ij}^*} = \frac{x_{jh} r_h}{c_{hj}^*} \tag{29.3}$$

Note that eq. 29.2 can be described as a balance of satisfaction for actor i between goods j and k and eq. 29.3 can be described as a balance of power between actors i and h. Rewriting the two equations shows directly the relation between intrapersonal comparison and interpersonal comparison:

$$\frac{x_{ji}}{x_{ki}} = \frac{c_{ij}^* v_j}{c_{ik}^* v_k} \tag{29.2'}$$

$$\frac{c_{ij}^*}{c_{hj}^*} = \frac{x_{ji} r_i}{x_{jh} r_h} \tag{29.3'}$$

Intrapersonal comparison of an individual's relative interest in two goods is given, in eq. 29.2', by the ratio of the amounts held, each multiplied by its price, or the ratio of the values held. Interpersonal comparison of two individuals' interests in a good is given, in eq. 29.3', by the ratio of the quantities held by each relative to their wealth; stated differently, the ratio of the quantities held by each is the ratio of their interests weighted by wealth.

This formulation shows formally the point made earlier: that interpersonal comparison of utility is not an ethical judgment carried out by a social scientist, but is inherent in the constitutional allocation of rights and resources and the actions carried out by the actors in the system.

The interpersonal comparison of utilities, or interests, necessary to make the micro-to-macro transition can be described quite simply as the relative impact of each actor's interests on the macro-level outcome. In a perfectly competitive market of the sort modeled in Chapter 25, this relative impact is given by a set of weights associated with individuals' interests, which are the r_i, the actors' wealth. For example, for eq. 25.12, the change in price of good j with respect to the interest of actor i in that good (which corresponds to the interpersonal comparison necessary to make this micro-to-macro transition, since the price of good j is a macro-level outcome) is

$$\frac{\partial v_j}{\partial x_{ji}} = \frac{\partial\left(\sum_{k=1}^{n} x_{jk}r_k\right)}{\partial x_{ji}} = r_i$$

The interpersonal comparison in this system derives from two starting points:

1. The distribution of interests within each individual (that is, the relative interests in different goods for an individual)
2. The distribution of rights and resources among individuals (that is, control of resources and events) as given in the constitution

The derivation of interpersonal comparison from these two starting points can be seen by eq. 25.18:

$$\mathbf{r} = (\mathbf{I} - \mathbf{CX} + \mathbf{E}_n)^{-1}\mathbf{e}_{n1}$$

The actor's control of events, one row of the matrix $\mathbf{C}$, constitutes a set of weights applied to the actor's interests in calculating the equilibrium distribution of wealth with this equation; once that distribution is known, the actor's wealth constitutes a single weight for all his interests.[4]

These derivations show that, for a perfectly competitive market with Cobb-Douglas utility functions, there is interpersonal comparison in the transition from micro level to macro level, which takes a very simple form: a weight

4. In game theory, Shapley (1967) has described two concepts of interpersonal comparison of utility which, under certain equilibrium conditions, coincide. Unlike the classical idea of interpersonal comparison of utility based on how strongly different persons feel about something, these concepts are very similar to the one in the theory of this book, for they are based on the actual positions that different players achieve in a game.

applied to the actor's interests, with the weight being the actor's wealth or power.

Cardinal Utility

Cardinal utilities associated with goods or resources (that is, utilities that are identifiable up to a linear transformation, $u_{ij} = a + bu_{ij}$, where a and b are constants and b is positive) are often seen to imply action under uncertainty, or risk. Rational action under certainty can lead to utilities that are specifiable only up to a monotonic transformation. There is no behavior that, modeled by the theory of rationality under certainty, can be used to distinguish between two utility functions that are monotonically related. This implies that utilities can make use of only that subset of the properties of numbers that involve ordinal comparison.

For action under risk, when probabilities of differing outcomes are known, von Neumann and Morgenstern (1947, p. 26) have provided the basis for cardinal utilities (von Neumann–Morgenstern utilities) through the use of expected utility in a risky environment. Various authors have described "lottery ticket" choice situations that would in principle allow specification of cardinal utilities. (See Mosteller and Nogee, 1951, for an early attempt at empirical measurement of von Neumann–Morgenstern utilities.)

Because the linear system of action presented in this part of this book requires more than ordinal utilities, there would appear to be a violation of the principle that actions under certainty can lead to specification of utilities that are identifiable only up to a monotonic transformation. The interests that play a central role in this theory are regarded as having all the properties of real numbers and are used with all operations permissible for real numbers. The explanation of this apparent violation lies in the fact that the linear system of action entails stronger assumptions than the theory of rationality under certainty does—just as the theory of rationality under risk based on the expected-utility hypothesis entails stronger assumptions than the theory of rationality under certainty does. It is these stronger assumptions that endow the concepts of the theory presented in this book (utilities and interests) with properties beyond the capability of being compared ordinally. The theory of rationality under risk entails the assumption that the individual's preference between two risky alternatives is based on the expected utility of each, where the expected utility of an alternative is the sum of the utilities of the possible outcomes, each weighted by its probability. It is these operations of multiplication and addition that require utilities that are specifiable up to a positive linear transformation.

The linear system of action entails the assumption that in choosing between alternatives under certainty, individual i will not merely exhibit consistency of (transitive) preferences, but will choose in such a way that there can be found quantities x_{ji} for goods j which when used in eq. 25.1 will predict i's choices between bundles of goods that differ in the quantities of each good held.

One empirical means by which this may be done is through a logistic regression based on outcomes of an individual's choices between bundles of goods. Suppose that an individual i is presented with n choices between pairs of bundles of m goods. For choice k there are in one bundle quantities $c_{ki1}, \ldots, c_{kim}$ and in the other bundle quantities $c'_{ki1}, \ldots, c'_{kim}$. If the individual chooses the first bundle, let $\delta_{ki} = 1$; if he chooses the second, let $\delta_{ki} = 0$. Then, assuming a two-state Markov process between choice of the first bundle and choice of the second bundle, with the transition rate toward each bundle equal to its utility, eq. 25.1 can be used in writing the logistic equation

$$\ln \frac{\delta_{ki}}{1 - \delta_{ki}} = \sum_j x_{ji}(\ln c_{kij} - \ln c'_{kij}) \qquad (29.4)$$

(See Coleman, 1981, Chapter 2, for derivation of this equation when the utility of the bundle is the transition rate toward choosing it.) Sufficiently numerous observations of diverse bundles make it possible to obtain estimates of the m values of x_{ji} by use of logistic regression. The test of the degree to which the model fits behavior is the frequency with which the estimated values x_{ji} lead to correct predictions of the individual's choices. A simple test is the proportion of correct predictions in the logistic regression.

Cardinal Utility and Interpersonal Comparison

Neither the cardinal utilities obtained from the von Neumann–Morgenstern expected-utility hypothesis nor the cardinal interests obtained from the Cobb-Douglas utility function concern social behavior. Thus they provide no information for interpersonal comparison of utility. It has sometimes been mistakenly believed, because the solution to a two-person zero-sum game in classic game theory requires transferable utility, that the von Neumann–Morgenstern cardinal utilities provide the basis for interpersonal comparison. This is not so. In a game the only basis for interpersonal comparison of utility is the resources the rules provide to each player, which implicitly give a weight to that player's interests; von Neumann–Morgenstern utilities show only the shape of each individual's utility curve for the good which constitutes the payoff in the game.

The theory of this book does imply interpersonal comparison, however, despite the fact that interests, as inferred from choices via eq. 25.1 and as estimated via eq. 29.4 or in another way, involve no social behavior. In the theory of this book, some actors' interests count more than others, just as in the caste system in India, a Brahmin's interests counted more than an untouchable's. The interpersonal comparison arises in moving from individual interests to a system of action, in which actors have interests in resources held by other actors. This kind of interest provides the basis for interpersonal comparison. This can be seen from eq. 25.15, rewritten below as a scalar equation:

$$r_i = \sum_j \sum_k c_{ij} x_{jk} r_k \qquad (29.5)$$

As this equation shows, the power of actor i is the sum of what he controls, weighted by the interests of others in what he controls, with the others' interests weighted by their power. Actor i obtains his power through the interests others have in what he controls. Power, thus defined, is the weight which, when applied to interests, constitutes the basis for interpersonal comparison. This is evident in Chapters 30 and 31, where power, defined as in eq. 29.5, plays an important role in determining whether a norm will exist or not and in determining the outcomes of collective decisions. The criterion for determining the outcome of an event j is always of the form of a comparison of $\Sigma\, x_{ji}r_i$ over the set of actors whose interests favor one outcome with the comparable sum over the set of actors whose interests favor the other outcome.

In the linear system of action, the distinction between interests as properties of individuals in relation to resources and power as a property of the individual *in a particular system of action* can be demonstrated by a two-stage process of estimation and testing. The first stage, shown by eq. 29.4, involves estimation and testing of the fit of individuals' interests and is purely individual, independent of any system of action. The second stage, shown by eq. 29.5, involves estimation of relative power once interests are known. It implies a particular system of action, characterized by a distribution of control of resources (**C**) and the possibility of free exchanges. The latter is implicit in eq. 29.4 because of the assumption that actor k's power-weighted interests in what actor i controls will contribute fully to actor i's power, however roundabout the path through which transactions occur. If there were transaction costs (and not the perfect social system assumed here), eq. 29.5 would not hold, and an actor's power in transactions with another actor would depend on the particular configuration of interest and control, which could not be summarized by a single measure of power.

Although eq. 29.5 can be used to estimate the power of actors from estimates of interests obtained independently of any system of action, together with the distribution of control of resources in the particular system, it cannot be used to test how well the conception fits empirical data. A test can be done using the observed distribution of resources, c_{ij}^{*}, *after* the social process has taken place. Just as testing of the individual property x_{ji} required observation of individual's actions, testing of r_i, a property of the individual in a particular system of action, requires observation of the functioning of that system. Application of eq. 25.6 with the observed distribution of resources after exchange will allow a second estimate of r_i. The two estimates, before exchange (assuming that exchange will take place in a perfect social system) and after exchange, can be compared to test the degree to which the assumptions of the theory are met.[5]

---

5. If the distribution of resources after exchange is regarded as the equilibrium distribution, **C***, a stronger test may be carried out. First, the power vector **r** is estimated, and interests are estimated by individual choices through a procedure like that used for eq. 29.4. Then eq. 25.11 will give a predicted distribution of control at equilibrium, $\mathbf{C}_{p}^{*}$, with which the observed **C*** may be compared. This provides a test of the consistency between interests as estimated on the basis of exchange behavior and interests as estimated on the basis of individual choice behavior.

Even though this two-stage process is useful for clarifying the point at which interpersonal comparison enters the theory, it is possible to collapse estimation into a single stage. The research strategy outlined in Chapter 26 does this. Observation of the distribution of resources before exchange (C_0) and after exchange (C_t) allows estimation of the vector of relative power, without any measurement of interests. If the distribution of resources after exchange is assumed to be the equilibrium distribution (C^*), then interests can be estimated as a second step, using eq. 25.11. (Such estimation was used for the interests given in Table 6.4.) This estimation procedure makes possible a test of the fit of the interpersonal comparison part of the measurement, because after the best-fitting vector of values is estimated, power may be estimated from both the initial distribution (C_0) and from the distribution after exchange (C_t), and the two estimates can be compared. Such a test is not possible for interests, however, unless they have been independently measured, for example, in an individual, nonsocial setting using eq. 29.4.

The above discussion of measurement is intended to demonstrate the way in which interpersonal comparison arises in this theory, not to provide a plan for empirical research based on the theory. Empirical research ordinarily collapses the measurement of X and r, as described in Chapter 26, through use of observations for both C_0 and C^*. This allows an estimate of the value vector, v, of the power vector, r, and of the interest matrix, X. The only test possible is a test of the power vector, since two power vectors can be estimated from v, one based on the observed C_0 and the other based on the observed C^*.

Power, through a Market and Otherwise

The most straightforward characterization of interpersonal comparison of utility is, as indicated in the formal theory of this book, relative power. It is very likely the comparative innocuousness of market power which leads otherwise astute theorists astray on this point. For example, Robbins, whose position in opposition to Harrod was the correct one, made this error when he extended his general argument to say about interpersonal comparison that it "is never needed in the theory of equilibrium and . . . is never implied by the assumptions of that theory" (1935, p. 139). To be fair, Robbins had in mind not the interpersonal comparison through which an equilibrium price is arrived at (that is, market power) but the normative conception for which welfare economists keep searching. In extending his argument against making interpersonal comparisons when the individual faces a fixed environment to cover the case in which the environment is itself determined by the aggregate of individual actions (that is, general equilibrium theory), Robbins made a crucial error. The general principle is that *every* micro-to-macro transition which results in systemic behavior involves some form of interpersonal comparison.

The more recent proofs of an equilibrium price, which are based on the concept of a core from game theory (in which coalitions and blocking of outcomes are central), introduce an imagery into general equilibrium theory which makes the role of power in interpersonal comparison more explicit. This can be seen by conceiving of a system like that described in Chapter 25 but with prices determined in a way other than that specified by the theory, that is, not as a sum of interests times wealth. The adjustment of prices to equal interests times wealth is an expression of the real demand that is exercised with respect to the goods. But suppose there is a managed economy in which prices of goods at time $t + 1$ are set to be proportional not to the wealth of those with an interest in them, as in eq. 25.12, but to the square of that wealth. The result would be that those items bought by wealthy persons would have a price higher than the market price (a result which could be brought about by imposing a high luxury tax) and those items bought by poor persons would have a price lower than the market price (which could be accomplished by a subsidy for goods bought primarily by the poor). In such a case market power which derives directly from wealth no longer determines prices. The interpersonal comparison in such a case includes not only market power, but also political power, in which the constitutionally allocated resources for persons with low incomes are relatively greater than their incomes.

Yet all of the above, with the exception of the last illustration, refers only to perfect markets and to market power. If the system of action is a perfectly competitive market and all the transactions are voluntary exchanges within that market, it is possible to characterize the power of each actor very simply, as is done in the model introduced in Chapter 25. It is the amount of wealth he brings to the market, either in the form of money (which is the measure of wealth) or in the form of goods and services desired by others who have wealth (which is measured by the extent of that demand). In such an individualistic, voluntary, and competitive system, power is well specified and consists of nothing more or less than wealth. In such a system money will buy anything, and thus the amount of power an actor can exert in the system (that is, the degree to which he can realize the outcomes he desires) is merely the amount of money (or other resources measured in terms of the money they can be exchanged for) he holds.

But in many systems of action there is far from a perfect market structure, and thus the power of a given actor depends on things other than the wealth he holds. A simple deviation from a perfect market occurs when a single producer has a monopoly over production of a given good. He can more fully realize his interests, that is, exchange his goods for greater amounts of money, than if he were in a perfect market. More generally, social systems involve numerous other kinds of activities, some involving exchange outside a market context and some involving collective decisions. Constitutions cover these, especially in addressing the rights various actors have to control collective decisions. Furthermore, it is in the context of actions of a collectivity as a whole (that is, governmental policies) that questions involving interpersonal comparison of utility have ordinarily arisen. For the differing forms and contexts of action systems discussed in Parts I–IV, the issue of interpersonal comparison of utilities must of course arise. The essential result is similar in all these contexts: Interpersonal comparison of utilities of different actors in a social system has meaning only in the context of a particular constitutional distribution of control over resources, and that meaning can be found, just as in the case of intrapersonal comparison, in the observed outcomes found in the system.

It is useful to gain an intuitive sense of how this occurs. When observing a disagreement over some issue between two participants, one's intuitive judgment of the strength of each participant's feeling derives from an assessment of how far one feels each might go to get his way. This can be seen most clearly for a strong disagreement between two persons that could lead to a fight. If one party seems uncontrollable, that is, he would stop at nothing to win, then in fact he will be more likely to win because he is willing to employ all his resources to that end. Another point also arises, however, concerning just what this party *could* do. If he has no power to help or hurt the other, then the other ordinarily need not worry, however uncontrollable the first may appear to be. That is, if the second party has much more power than the first, he can afford to pay no attention to the intensity of emotion. People behave quite differently toward a very small child who is uncontrollable and a large adult male who is uncontrollable.

Resolution of a disagreement between two individuals may occur through the perception by each of the other's intensity of interest and power to realize that interest. A husband may come home one night and perceive that it is very important to his wife that they go to the movies. Knowing that she has the power to cause him great discomfort, he will go unless going will discomfort him even more. This may be termed a virtual confrontation, since neither husband nor wife actually applies resources to win. A resolution might instead come about through a confrontation in which each actually applies resources; if such a conflict occurs, the outcome will be dependent on who applies the greater resources.

Thus two attributes of each individual are relevant in determining the resolution of a disagreement: first, what resources he has which give him the capacity to help or hurt the other; and second, how willing he is to use these resources in order to gain the outcome he prefers. This is precisely what is captured by the mathematical formulation in which interpersonal comparison depends on interests and on control of rights and resources.

Introduction of the notion of capacity to help or hurt the other, that is, of relative power, as the only source of interpersonal comparison of utility is so foreign to the usual ideas on this topic that some discussion is warranted. Consider again interpersonal comparison of utility between husband and wife. If a Bedouin husband rides while his wife carries a burden on foot, can the utility or disutility that each is experiencing be compared? If an American husband takes the bus to work while his wife uses the car, can the utility differences that each would experience from the two activities be compared? In both cases the answer is no. All that can be done is to observe the outcome and to infer from it not how important it is to one compared to how important it is to the other but something quite different: the power each has to realize his or her interest in the arena of decision making, and the amount of interest this event has for each relative to other things that are also of interest. In the case of the Bedouin husband and wife, it would be necessary to discover, first, the interests of each, relative to interests in other activities, by observing numerous choices of each among walking, riding, and other activities; and, second, the relative power of each by observing the outcomes of other events involving activities of varying levels of importance to each. Similar observations would be necessary in the case of the American husband and wife. Obviously, the main difference between these two examples is not in relative utilities but in relative power of the husband and wife. There is no standard for comparing their utilities other than the standard they (in their larger social context) establish for themselves, and this standard derives from relative power.

Thus the interests of some may count more than the interests of others in the social system as actually realized. Why is this so; why do not the interests of all count equally? The answer lies wholly in the constitution which dictates the distribution of control over resources and the distribution of interests in resources. One can then object, however, that this answer merely pushes the question up another level: Why does the constitution provide this degree of inequality (or equality)? This objection can only arise from the mistaken notion that there can be something outside society in terms of which its power distribution can ultimately be justified. Because a society is a self-governing system, the only answer leads into an infinite regress, moving at every point closer to fundamental sources of power, such as economic productivity, control of strategic resources, intelligence, physical strength, and historical development.

To have pushed the question up one level provides a valuable service in showing what the indirect consequences of a given constitution and particular government policies are. If the social system is in fact self-governing, it does not need social theory to inform a set of policy advisors or economic advisors. It needs social theory to inform those who have constitutional rights of control over social policy so that they can exercise those rights in an informed fashion. To conceive of a social system which depends on external advisors, or philosopher-kings, for its direction is to revert to an earlier and more primitive form of social organization, as envisioned by Plato or by Auguste Comte.

« 30 »

Externalities and Norms in a Linear System of Action

Chapter 10 introduced a different kind of event from those examined in earlier chapters: an event or good for which rights cannot be partitioned, so an actor's exercise of his rights has consequences only for himself. Such events sometimes generate norms to encourage or discourage action by the holder of rights, sometimes generate conflict, and sometimes result in collective decisions, where rights to control an event have been partitioned among interested actors. In this chapter I begin a formal examination of these kinds of events, using a version of the linear system of action.[1]

In a social system containing only divisible goods without externalities, actors are interdependent in only one way: in their exchange of goods. Since each good is fully divisible and individually consumable, there is no possibility of conflict, and the only source of disagreement is the terms of exchange. If terms are not agreed on, no conflict results; each actor simply keeps control of the goods he began with. Furthermore, if the market is highly developed, no room for bargaining remains, since the terms of exchange are the same for all traders.

This does not imply that such a system will be wholly satisfactory for all actors. Because each actor is able to satisfy his wants only up to the limit of the resources with which he begins, if different actors begin with different resources, their possibilities for consumption will differ.[2] As indicated in Chapter

---

1. This chapter might well be dedicated to Ronald Coase and Richard Posner. Coase (1960) argued that the legal allocation of rights does not matter for the social outcome; Posner (1986), an exponent of the same school of law and economics as Coase, argues that a major task of the law is to provide an allocation of rights that will lead to an efficient social outcome. This chapter addresses indirectly the apparent disagreement of these positions.

2. This in itself would generate conflict. I have assumed that no actor has any interest—positive or negative—in another's consumption. This is true under only one condition for private goods which have no objective external effects: when actors are not aware of one another's consumption. When they are, negative subjective interests may arise because of a sense of relative deprivation, even though no objective effects exist. Thus even in the absence of external effects of action in the usual sense, there exists the possibility of the psychological equivalent of external effects. These are wholly dependent on the degree of knowledge about the event (such as consumption) on the part of other actors, or the event's visibility. When that visibility is high, the system is one in which an event has consequences for more than one actor.

10, however, when there is no way of defining events such that an event has consequences for one actor only, a mode of social interaction arises that is fundamentally different from the exchange processes involving divisible, individually consumed goods. Since more than one actor can have interests in an event, more than one will attempt to acquire control of it. The way is paved for processes characteristic of social and political systems which go beyond exchange: collective decisions, coercion, and conflict.

Perhaps the simplest kind of situation of this sort is that characterized by individual actions that generate externalities. There are many externalities of actions by individual actors in both social and economic systems. In economic systems these often fall under the broad heading of pollution: air pollution from automobiles, water pollution from sewage, noise pollution from motorcycles and airplanes, and so on. In these cases an action has consequences beyond the direct and intended consequences for the actor himself, which constitute costs for other persons in the vicinity. In other cases an action will result in benefits to those others, and it becomes in their interest to encourage the action.

Furthermore, there is nothing intrinsic to the action itself which dictates that the right to carry it out must be held by the actor (I will call this actor the target actor, as in Chapter 10, and the action with externalities the focal action). The right to perform the action that causes pollution, for example, may lie in the hands of potential polluters in one legal regime, but then be taken by law from their hands, initiating a new legal regime. As Coase and others have pointed out (see Coase, 1960), in an economic system such rights are like any other rights and can therefore be bought and sold, as long as the focal action is not prohibited by law. If there is sufficient interest in the activity which generates the externalities and if the cost of preventing the externalities is sufficiently high, the focal action will continue to be carried out, despite the external costs it imposes on others.

As Coase also shows, the action may continue to be taken whether the right to impose the externalities is held by the target actors or withdrawn from them. In the first case the recipients of the social costs (sewage, air pollution, and so forth) must bear the cost; in the second case the target actors must pay a fee to compensate the recipients for the social costs, but find themselves better off paying the fee and continuing to carry out the action. For example, in certain situations there may exist effluent charges for discharging wastes into a stream. If the polluting actions are economically efficient, they will be carried out even if the target actors must pay a market price to compensate others for the disamenities created by the actions. If the disamenities are greater than the target actors can afford to compensate, the focal action is inefficient and will be discontinued.

Insofar as visibility of consumption increases in society, the externalities induced by it are increasing, and thus so is the potential for conflict. All this is apart from socialization, which leads persons' interests to be dependent on others' welfare, as discussed in Chapter 19.

I have described externalities imposed on others in the context of buying and selling rights, that is, in an economic context. Similarly, in a social context the question is whether or not the aggrieved parties will be able to prevent the focal action. If there is no norm, the right to act is held by the target actor. To prevent the focal action in that case, the aggrieved parties must appeal to the better nature of the target actor or offer some inducement to him to stop. If, however, there is a norm, the target actor must in effect use his resources to buy the right to carry out a focal action, if he has sufficient resources to do so. (This may take a simple form such as asking others in the vicinity if it is all right with them if one smokes. If they say it is, one incurs a slight debit toward them.) Ordinarily, prior to the existence of a norm, the actor who imposes externalities can be regarded as having a de facto right to carry out the focal action, so the aggrieved parties must use resources to buy the right to constrain the action.

In this chapter I introduce actions with indivisible consequences into the formal system of action presented in Chapter 25. I will treat the case where one actor imposes externalities on a set of others and will examine the conditions under which those others can prevent the action: in the economic context by buying or keeping rights to the action or by obtaining a legal reallocation of rights to the class of actions; in the social context by offering inducements not to carry out the action or by gaining a consensus that reallocates rights through creation of a norm against carrying out the action.

When Will Actions Having Externalities Be Taken? The Coase Theorem Revisited

Coase (1960) treated discursively the question of how the allocation of rights over an action which imposes costs on others (where rights are allocated either to the actor imposing the costs or to those hurt by it) allows the action to be carried out or prevents it. He drew the conclusion, surprising at the time, that if rights to the action could be bought and sold and if there were no costs of organization among those hurt by the action, the allocation of rights did not matter. The action would be carried out if it was economically efficient and would not be carried out if it was not. Since then, the Coase theorem has been taken as the correct way of viewing the allocation of rights in a social system (subject to the conditions stated above).

In this and the next section I will use the linear system of action to reexamine the problem of social costs and to show some necessary modifications to the Coase theorem. I will analyze a system containing an event (the focal action) with a positive outcome, in which the target actor is interested, and a negative outcome, in which the other actors are interested. There are two alternative conditions: First, the focal action is taken (positive outcome), or second, the action is not taken (negative outcome). In the first case the costs imposed on the aggrieved parties (their interests in the event) are deleted from the interest matrix. Their interests will no longer sum to 1.0 and must be treated as described in Chapter 25 for linear systems of action when quantities of goods vary, which amounts in this case to restandardizing other interests to equal 1.0. In the second case the interests of the target actor in the event are deleted, and his other interests are restandardized to equal 1.0.

The first analysis will show the amount of resources the target actor is willing and able to employ in order to keep or gain control of the rights so that he can carry out the action. The second will show the amount of resources the aggrieved parties are willing and able to employ in order to prevent the action, that is, to produce a negative outcome. If the value of the second set of resources is greater than that of the first, in a context in which rights are not legally allocated and there is no norm, the aggrieved parties will use their resources to induce the target actor not to carry out the action. If there is a norm, the target actor will not have sufficient resources to induce the others to let him carry out the action. If he attempts to do so anyway, they will apply sanctions, which will be effective.

If the value of the second set of resources exceeds that of the first and rights *are* legally allocated and marketable, the target actor will sell his rights to the focal action if he initially controls them or will fail to purchase them if he does not. The focal action will not be taken. If the value of the first set of resources is larger than that of the second, the target actor will take the action, since the aggrieved parties can neither offer sufficient inducements nor apply effective sanctions. In an economic context he will refuse to sell his rights, if he owns them, at the price the aggrieved parties are willing to pay, or will buy the rights at a price at which the aggrieved parties are willing to sell. The action will be taken. For the present I disregard the problem of organization, the second-order free-rider problem, faced by the aggrieved parties.

EXAMPLE 1: AN EVENT WITH EXTERNALITIES   The principles described above can be illustrated by again modifying the trading-card example first used in Chapter 25. Suppose that the set of traders is enlarged from two boys to three by adding Steve, who has basketball cards to trade. Tom begins with 1,000 football cards, John with 1,000 baseball cards, and Steve with 1,000 basketball cards. Suppose that there is also an additional event: During trading Tom is carrying on a telephone conversation with a girlfriend. This irritates both of the others, for it interferes with their exchanges. Tom has the right to talk on the phone; that is not the issue. But the others have an interest in his not doing so. Assume that the boys have no other relations outside this situation, nothing which one controls and the others have an interest in, nothing that could be used by John and Steve to persuade Tom to stop talking on the telephone. They can, however, offer Tom additional cards as an inducement to get off the phone. Will he accept their offer? This depends on how much they offer and on what will be sufficient to make him stop.

Table 30.1 shows the assumed distribution of interests in the absence of the telephone call and the initial distribution of control. Also shown are the interest matrices under two regimes: Under regime *a* Tom pursues his interests in talking

Table 30.1 Three actors' interest in and control of three types of cards and an additional event, a telephone call.

	CONTROL (C)				INTERESTS (X')				(X'_a)				(X_b)			
	E_1	E_2	E_3	E_4	E_1	E_2	E_3	E_4	E_1	E_2	E_3	E_4	E_1	E_2	E_3	E_4
Tom	1	0	0	1	.51	.255	.085	.15	.51	.255	.085	.15	.6	.3	.1	0
John	0	1	0	0	.27	.36	.27	.10	.3	.4	.3	0	.27	.36	.27	.10
Steve	0	0	1	0	.27	.18	.45	.10	.3	.2	.5	0	.27	.18	.45	.10
Value									.398	.282	.249	.070	.429	.290	.230	.052

to his girlfriend, but John's and Steve's interests are not pursued; they are eliminated from the matrix, and the other interests are restandardized. Under regime b Tom does not pursue his interests in talking to his girlfriend, but John and Steve pursue their interests by offering cards as an inducement to Tom to stop. The table also includes calculated values of each event under the two regimes. As these show, the value of the telephone conversation is greater under regime a than under regime b. John and Steve together would be willing to offer cards with a value of .052 (for example, 100 baseball cards with a value of .029 and 100 basketball cards with a value of .023), but the telephone conversation is worth more than that to Tom (.070, or 132 baseball cards plus 131 basketball cards), and he continues.

I do not raise here the question of how John and Steve would divide the cost of inducing Tom to get off the phone. The issue is moot, since they could not induce Tom to stop, even with an optimum allocation of costs. I will raise the question later, after Example 3, where it will be a real issue. The present example indicates how to apply the criterion for whether a focal action is taken.

The Formal Model

The formal model is as follows: Let X be the interest matrix, with one event, labeled m, of *positive* interest to one actor, actor 1, and of *negative* interest to others.[3] For each other event, j, x_{ji} is zero for all actors except one, or if not, the events are divisible resources, and could in principle be redefined as events in which only one actor has an interest (for example, i's consumption of j). More simply, we may say that there are no externalities in the system of events $j = 1$, $\ldots$, $m - 1$. Define two new interest matrices X_a (where the action is taken) and X_b (where the action is not taken): The first column (for actor 1) of X_a is identical to that of X. Elements of the matrix X_a are defined by

$$x_{aj1} = x_{j1}, \qquad \text{for } j = 1, \ldots, m$$

$$x_{aji} = \frac{x_{ji}}{\displaystyle\sum_{k=1}^{m-1} x_{ki}}, \qquad \text{for } j = 1, \ldots, m - 1 \text{ and } i = 2, \ldots, n$$

$$x_{ami} = 0, \qquad \text{for } i = 2, \ldots, n$$

X_b has all columns but the first identical to X and is defined by

---

3. In principle, the action may be of positive interest to persons other than the target actor: He may generate positive externalities for some, as well as negative externalities for others. In that case, disregarding the free-rider problems of organization for those experiencing the positive externalities, their interests in event m are treated like those of actor 1 (included in regime a and deleted in regime b).

$$x_{bji} = x_{ji}, \qquad \text{for } j = 1, \ldots, m \text{ and } i = 2, \ldots, n$$

$$x_{bj1} = \frac{x_{j1}}{\sum\limits_{k=1}^{m-1} x_{k1}}, \qquad \text{for } j = 1, \ldots, m - 1$$

$$x_{bm1} = 0$$

Let C be the control matrix, with initial control over event m held by actor 1 (the target actor) if actor 1 has control (legal or de facto) of the focal action, or distributed in some way over the other $n - 1$ actors if they have control of the focal action.

Then solve for v_a and r_a, using X_a and C; and for v_b and r_b, using X_b and C. The solutions to these systems show the value of events and the power of actors under the two different regimes:

> Under regime a actor 1's interest in a positive outcome of event m plays a part in the system, and any harmful consequences to other actors are not acted on by them.
>
> Under regime b only the interests of other actors in preventing a positive outcome of event m play a part in the system.

What, then, is the condition to be satisfied for the action to be carried out? Actor 1 must have resources that he is willing to commit to event m and that are greater than the resources that the other actors are willing to commit against it. In general, those resources are calculated as $x_{m1}r_{a1}$ for actor 1 and $\sum_{i=2}^{n} x_{mi}r_{bi}$ for the other actors.

Under regime a actor 1 can employ resources of value $x_{m1}r_{a1}$ to gain or maintain control of event m. He can use these resources to block sanctions or to induce others not to apply sanctions. In an economic context he can use these resources to gain control of the rights to carry out the action if others own the rights or to keep control of the rights if he owns them. If actor 1 has legal or de facto rights over the action, $x_{m1}r_{a1}$ gives the value of the resources others would have to provide in order to get him to relinquish those rights.

Under regime b the resources the other actors are able to devote to controlling rights over the action are $\sum_{i=2}^{n} x_{mi}r_{bi}$. If these are sufficiently great, they will pay up to this amount of resources to the target actor if he owns the rights or will refrain from selling the rights if they own them. "Sufficiently great" means greater than $x_{m1}r_{a1}$, the amount actor 1 is willing to employ to implement his interests under regime a, where their resources are deployed elsewhere. Thus they can use resources equal to $\sum x_{mi}r_{bi}$ to block the action (he having deployed his resources elsewhere in that circumstance), or he can use resources equal to $x_{m1}r_{a1}$ to carry out the action (they having deployed their resources elsewhere in that circumstance).

The criterion is this: The action will be carried out (disregarding free-rider problems of the aggrieved parties and, more generally, assuming a perfect social system as defined in Chapter 27) if and only if

$$x_{m1}r_{a1} > \sum_{i=2}^{n} x_{mi}r_{bi} \tag{30.1}$$

This criterion is equivalent to the criterion that v_{am}, the *value* of event m under regime a, in which the action is carried out, is greater than v_{bm}, the value of the event under regime b, in which the action is not carried out. For v_{am} is $x_{m1}r_{a1}$ and v_{bm} is $\Sigma_{i=2}^{n} x_{mi}r_{bi}$. Thus the criterion for action (regime a) can be restated as follows: Action m will be carried out if and only if

$$v_{am} > v_{bm} \tag{30.2}$$

where v_{am} is the value of the action when the event has a positive outcome (the action is carried out) and v_{bm} is its value when the event has a negative outcome (the action is not carried out).

The criterion as given in eq. 30.2 is Coase's (1960) central insight: In the absence of transaction costs, the action will be carried out if its value in the system (v_{am}) is greater than the costs (v_{bm}) it imposes. If the rights are held by the aggrieved parties and v_{am} is greater than v_{bm}, the action will be carried out, even though the target actor must give up something to acquire the rights to act. If the rights are held by the target actor and v_{bm} is greater than v_{am}, the action will not be carried out, even though the aggrieved parties must give up something to induce the target actor not to take the action.

This is the correct statement of the condition under which an action having externalities will be carried out. It is not the Coase theorem, which states that whether or not such an action will be carried out depends on its economic efficiency and is independent of the allocation of rights over the action. It is, however, what the Coase theorem should have stated. Later I will indicate the conditions under which the reallocation of rights can affect what is efficient and thus affect the carrying out of a focal action. First, however, some further implications of the above result should be examined.

Is it possible to go beyond the statement that the criterion given by inequality 30.2 ensures that the outcome with the greater total value in the system will take place? Can it also be stated that this outcome would in principle make it possible for each actor to be better off than he would be under the other outcomes? That is, if v_{am} is greater than v_{bm}, could the target actor redistribute the benefits he obtains from the focal action to the aggrieved parties to make them better off than they would be if the action were not taken? If the focal action were smoking, for example, could a smoker in principle compensate others in the vicinity sufficiently to make all better off than they would be if he did not smoke?

The criterion that the action will be taken if and only if v_{am} is greater than v_{bm} ensures that the action will be carried out if the target actor can devote more resources to its control than can those opposing it. This means that if he does not control the right to act, he will purchase that right from those who hold it. All parties will be better off than if, despite the fact that the criterion was met, he was unable due to legal or other restraints to purchase the right. The same holds true of the case in which v_{bm} is greater than v_{am} and the aggrieved parties do not hold the right: They will purchase it from the target actor, and all will be better off than if he carried out the action.

Reallocation of Rights: Does It Matter Who Holds the Rights?

An additional claim often made by economists, originating from the Coase theorem, is that the same state of economic efficiency will be achieved independently of who controls the rights to carry out the action that produces external diseconomies—assuming a perfect market, that is, no second-order free-rider problems or other transaction costs. The claim is that if an action is carried out when the rights are held by the target actor, it will also be carried out even if the rights are held by the aggrieved parties—because its being carried out under the first circumstance implies that it will be economically efficient for the target actor to purchase the rights. And if the action is not carried out when the rights are held by the aggrieved parties, it will also not be carried out even if the rights are held by the target actor—because if it is not efficient for him to purchase rights to carry out the action when he does not control them, it will be efficient for the aggrieved parties to purchase those rights from him when he does control them.

This argument implies, of course, a perfect market for the transactions, in which those who favor the same outcome have the ability to allocate costs of achieving it appropriately. Even if those conditions existed, however, this argument neglects the change in the distribution of resources that results from a shift of rights, either from target actor to aggrieved parties or the reverse. If the aggrieved parties hold the rights, then their interests have greater weight in the system, simply because they are backed up by a larger set of resources.

EXAMPLE 2: RIGHTS TO THE FOCAL ACTION NOT CONTROLLED BY THE TARGET ACTOR   An illustration is provided by reconsidering the example presented earlier, but with a single change: Rights to the offending action, talking on the telephone during the trading session, are differently allocated. There has been a prior agreement among the three boys that no one is to talk on the phone during the trading unless both others agree to allow it. In this case control over Tom's talking on the phone is held jointly by John and Steve.

Table 30.2 gives the revised control matrix, as well as recalculated values of events under the two regimes, based on this matrix and the interest matrices given in Table 30.1. As Table 30.2 shows, in this case it is not true that $v_{a4} > v_{b4}$; $v_{a4} = .057$ and $v_{b4} = .060$. The telephone conversation will not take place—not because interests have changed (they have not), but because the redistribution of rights away from the target actor, Tom, has sufficiently changed the distribution of resources that he no longer has enough resources to pay the others what it is worth to them to give up the right to prevent the call.

Table 30.2 Reallocation of control over telephone call and resulting values of events under two regimes.

	CONTROL (C)					VALUE OF			
	E_1	E_2	E_3	E_4		E_1	E_2	E_3	E_4
Tom	1	0	0	0	Regime *a*: Tom pursues interests	.380	.283	.280	.057
John	0	1	0	.5	Regime *b*: John and Steve pursue interests	.403	.285	.252	.060
Steve	0	0	1	.5					

Of course, in an economic system a redistribution of wealth in the system brought about by a reallocation of rights over one action is often not extensive enough to change the order relation of the values of the event calculated under the two different regimes. The shift from the telephone call's being efficient to its being inefficient does not directly follow from the shift of control from Tom to John and Steve. It is a second-order effect, resulting from the changed distribution of power. In the next example, in which all three have less interest in the telephone call, this point is illustrated.

EXAMPLE 3: REDUCED INTEREST IN THE FOCAL ACTION Suppose that the interest of each of the three boys in the telephone call is only half of what it was in the first two examples considered in this chapter, and that the other three events absorb the other half of that interest in proportion to their previous values. Thus the relative interests in all events remain the same, with the exception that Tom's interest in the phone call is only .075 rather than .15, and the interests of John and Steve against Tom's making the call are only .05 each rather than .1 each.

Table 30.3 shows the value to Tom of making the telephone call (v_{a4}, in regime *a*) and the value to John and Steve of its not being made (v_{b4}, in regime *b*). The values are given for the allocation in which Tom has the right to make the call and for the allocation in which John and Steve have the right to prevent him from doing so. As Table 30.3 shows, the value of the telephone call is greater to Tom than to John or Steve under both allocations. In this case the Coase theorem holds.

If John and Steve have the right to prevent the call, Tom will find it necessary to compensate them to induce them to withhold their veto, but it will be worth it

Table 30.3 Value of telephone call under two regimes and two rights allocations.

	VALUE OF CALL	
	Tom has right	John and Steve have right
To Tom (regime *a*)	.034	.030
To John and Steve (regime *b*)	.027	.029

to him to do so. How much will he have to give as compensation? Altogether he must pay the other two boys football cards worth .029. The value of each football card under regime *a* (the regime which obtains) is .0004. Thus, he must give up 73 football cards in order to make the call (but making it is worth 75 cards to him). How many cards does he have to give to John, and how many to Steve? Under regime *b*, which shows the value of the telephone call to John and Steve, John's interest is .05 and his power is .309; its value to him is the product, .015. Steve's interest is also .05 and his power is .275; so its value to him is .014. Tom must give John 38 football cards and Steve 35 to gain the right to make the call.

The Second-Order Free-Rider Problem in the Linear System: Sharing the Costs

There is, however, another problem that is not exhibited by the preceding examples. If Tom has the right to make the call, but it is worth more to John and Steve together for him not to make it than would be necessary to induce him not to make it, how are they to divide the costs of compensating him? This is the second-order free-rider problem discussed in Chapter 11: It is in Steve's interest for John to compensate Tom (if a norm existed, to pay the cost of sanctioning Tom), and it is in John's interest for Steve to do so.

EXAMPLE 4: THE PROBLEM OF SHARING COSTS   Another modification of the first example illustrates the free-rider problem that confronts John and Steve. Suppose that Tom's interest in the telephone call is .1, John's and Steve's interest is .1, and Tom has the right to make the call. The interest matrices under regime *a* and regime *b* are shown in Table 30.4, along with the value of the telephone call to Tom (regime *a*) and its value to John and Steve together (regime *b*).

Here the value of the telephone call if Tom pursues his interests is .046. The value of Tom's not making the call if John and Steve pursue their interests is .052. Thus they feel strongly enough that they can compensate Tom. The value to John is his power (.290) times his interest (.10), or .029. The value to Steve is his power (.230) times his interest (.10), or .023. Thus John and Steve would find

Table 30.4   Interests and power of three actors in exchange system under two regimes (*a* and *b*).

	X_a					X_b				
	E_1	E_2	E_3	E_4	Power	E_1	E_2	E_3	E_4	Power
Tom	.54	.27	.09	.10	.455	.6	.3	.1	0	.481
John	.3	.4	.3	0	.290	.27	.36	.27	.10	.290
Steve	.3	.2	.5	0	.256	.27	.18	.45	.10	.230
Value	.409	.290	.256	.046		.429	.290	.230	.052	

it worthwhile to give up cards worth .029 and .023, respectively. For John that would be .029/.00029, or 100 baseball cards. For Steve it would be .023/.00023, or 100 basketball cards. But they don't need to give up that much. Tom requires compensation valued at .046, which is 100 baseball cards and 74 basketball cards, or 100 basketball cards and 79 baseball cards, or some other combination.

What will happen? As indicated in Chapter 11, John and Steve have a problem of coordination, as well as a problem of how to share the burden of compensating Tom. If only John offers what it is worth to him, 100 baseball cards, Tom will not be deterred. If only Steve offers what it is worth to him, Tom will not be deterred. One solution is for John to carry out what was called in Chapter 11 a heroic sanction; but he will do this only if compensated by Steve. John can offer Tom 159 baseball cards (.046/.00029), but will do so only if he will be compensated by receiving at least 74 basketball cards (.00029 × 59/.00023) from Steve to make up for the extra 59 baseball cards he has to give Tom.

This is, of course, not the only solution; nor is it certain that John and Steve will find a way to induce Tom to give up the call. In the setting of the example, the boys are in direct communication with each other and could without difficulty work out some arrangement. But the necessity for closure of the social system, as discussed in Chapters 11 and 12, is directly relevant here: There are many comparable circumstances in which the counterparts of John and Steve are not in communication; thus, although the value to such actors of imposing a sanction to inhibit a negative externality (or encourage a positive one) is sufficient to allow them to impose an effective sanction, they are unable to do so.

This is the point at which social capital, in the form of communication which would allow coordination of sanctions or in the form of obligations and expectations, is important. Even in the examples presented above, where full communication was assumed, the existence of obligations and expectations among the three actors would have led to a much wider range of options. It was stipulated that the three actors had no relations outside of the exchange system. But if they had, there would have been no need to use cards to allow or prevent the telephone call. Obligations that each had toward the others and events that each controlled that were of interest to the others could have been used by Tom to make the call possible or by John and Steve to prevent it—and also by John to induce Steve to impose sanctions on Tom or by Steve for a similar purpose. These additional events, of interest to one or more of the actors and controlled by one or more of them, could be incorporated in the formal analysis, if knowledge of them were available—and clearly they would affect the outcome.

Externalities and Level of Affluence

It is useful to analyze the conditions in a society under which pollution and other undesirable side effects of personal or corporate actions will be tolerated. Such effects of action lead to discomfort and in some cases expenditure of time and energy in overcoming them. (For example, the soot from the burning of bituminous coal has created in some cities—for example, in the South Side of Chicago throughout the 1950s—extreme levels of dirt in houses, requiring extra cleaning.)

In an undeveloped economy, where persons' time is abundant (x_{ji} for time is low), and money is scarce (x_{ji} for money is high), the extra monetary expenditure to prevent pollution by corporate or personal action will often constitute a greater loss of utility than will the time expenditure or the discomfort it creates. But when money and goods are less valuable (x_{ji} for additional goods or money is lower) and time is more valuable (x_{ji} for time is higher), the utility cost of the extra monetary expenditure to prevent the side effects will be reduced, and the utility cost of experiencing those effects will increase.[4] This trend in the utilities of money, time, and comfort reaches a point at which the utility cost in time and comfort imposed by the externality is greater than that of the money lost by eliminating it, and then either the externalities are eliminated through monetary expenditure or the activity itself is stopped. Thus, in general, actions to eliminate pollution and other undesirable side effects of productive activity will be initiated by those persons who are most affluent and in those societies that are most affluent. It will be in the least affluent societies that pollution will be tolerated, and it will be in those societies where industries which create the greatest pollution continue to be economically efficient.

A similar statement can be made about social interactions. Members of a family or neighborhood with few economic resources will find it necessary to live in crowded quarters and to impose on one another. As they gain in economic resources, they can eliminate the actions which produce the negative externalities by reducing the necessity for asking for favors. They can purchase the services instead. The result will be a family or neighborhood with a less dense set of interactions, fewer obligations and expectations (for obligations and expectations are created when favors are requested and granted), and, overall, a reduced quantity of social capital. Thus the very changes which allow persons to reduce the externalities they experience at the hands of others lead them to reduce the social capital on which they and those around them can draw. (See Lindenberg, 1982, for discussion of some of these issues in sharing group theory.)

Regime a versus Regime b, and the Status Quo

One question was passed over in deriving the criterion for the conditions under which an action with externalities will be taken. The criterion was stated as $x_{m1}r_{a1}$ must exceed $\Sigma\ x_{mi}r_{bi}$. Actor 1's power, r_{a1}, is calculated under regime a

---

4. Interests in time and in money can be regarded here as being derived from interests in goods or events dependent on them, through a dependency matrix (see Chapter 27). If a person has already satisfied many of the wants that can be satisfied using money, then the person's interest in money, from that baseline, is low because of the declining marginal utility of the goods.

(when his interests in the actions are present), and the others' power, r_{bi}, is calculated under regime b (when their interests in the action are present). But why not use r_a in both cases or r_b in both cases? If, under regime a, the resources of the aggrieved parties become sufficiently smaller that even though $\Sigma\, x_{mi}r_{bi}$ is greater than $x_{m1}r_{a1}$ it is also true that $\Sigma\, x_{mi}r_{ai}$ is less than $x_{m1}r_{a1}$, then actor 1 would attempt to carry out the action and the others would apparently be unable to stop it, despite the fact that v_{bm} is greater than v_{am}. For the opposite case, where $x_{m1}r_{a1}$ is greater than $\Sigma\, x_{mi}r_{bi}$, but actor 1's resources under regime b are sufficiently smaller than those under regime a, it can be the case that $x_{mi}r_{bi}$ is less than $\Sigma\, x_{mi}r_{bi}$. The others would oppose the action, and actor 1 would appear not to be able to do anything about it. In Example 3, if the value of Tom's football cards has declined under regime b to the point that more than 75 were required to satisfy John and Steve, he could not compensate them.

Cases for which interests are calculated under one regime and power is calculated under the other raise questions that can be answered by considering just which regime represents the status quo. In deriving the criterion that v_{am} must be greater than v_{bm} for the action to be carried out, I assumed no status quo, that is, made no assumption about whether the action was being carried out or not (although a particular allocation of rights of control over the action was assumed).

If the action is currently being carried out (whether under an allocation of rights to the target actor or to the aggrieved parties), the system is in effect under regime a, and the power of actors under regime a is relevant in calculating whether the target actor will have enough resources to carry out the action or the aggrieved parties will have enough resources to prevent the action. If the action is not being carried out, the system is under regime b, and the power of actors under that regime is relevant. In Example 3, if Tom had already begun the telephone call and Steve and John demanded that he stop, he could compensate them with cards of the value required under regime a, even if more cards would have been required under regime b. If he were not already on the phone and offered to compensate them in order to make the call, the values under regime b would prevail.

In principle, this implies that oscillation could occur between the action's being carried out and its not being carried out. This would happen if $\Sigma\, x_{mi}r_{ai}$ exceeds $x_{m1}r_{a1}$ under regime a and $\Sigma\, x_{mi}r_{bi}$ is less than $x_{m1}r_{b1}$ under regime b. This pair of inequalities would arise only in the unlikely case where the target actor's resources were increased when he was not carrying out the focal action or the aggrieved parties' resources were increased when he was carrying out the target action, or both.

It is useful to consider a general change of the sort that occurs with increasing affluence. Suppose that a pollution-generating action is being carried out, for which v_{am} is greater than v_{bm}. Then there is an increase in interests harmed by the action, x_{mi}, relative to those benefited by it, x_{m1}, to the point where $\Sigma\, x_{mi}r_{bi}$ exceeds $x_{m1}r_{a1}$. That is, the interests of the actors harmed, weighted by their resources when the action is not carried out, come to exceed the interests of the actor benefited, weighted by his resources when the action is carried out. This point will ordinarily be reached before $\Sigma\, x_{mi}r_{ai}$ comes to exceed $x_{m1}r_{a1}$. This constitutes a case in which the status quo determines the outcome: The action will continue to be taken until $\Sigma\, x_{mi}r_{ai}$ exceeds $x_{m1}r_{a1}$. Until that point is reached, the aggrieved parties will not have sufficient resources to induce the target actor to stop the action (in an economic context, through purchase of the rights), though the value of the action's not being taken (regime b) is greater than the value of its being taken (regime a). After $\Sigma\, x_{mi}r_{ai}$ exceeds $x_{m1}r_{a1}$, and the aggrieved parties bring about a change to regime b, this change will ordinarily increase their resources slightly more (assuming that r_{bi} is greater than r_{ai} for the aggrieved parties).

What Is Meant by Efficiency?

This is a useful place to examine more closely the notion of efficiency. It is clear that there is an important sense in which the connotations of the term are appropriate: Given a particular distribution of resources and interests, certain actions are not efficient in the sense that the value they create is more than overbalanced by the costs they impose. It is important to see that in a perfect market those costs will be transmitted back to the actor who experiences the benefits so that the costs and benefits can be balanced against each other. In the formal model discussed above, this is represented by the balancing of the value of the event with a positive outcome against its value with a negative outcome. Thus it is possible to say whether a given action is efficient in that persons experience its benefits as greater than its costs.

But there is also a sense in which the connotations of efficiency obscure the role power plays in arriving at such a balance. The calculation of economic efficiency can be carried out only after a particular distribution of power or resources is taken as given. Another way of saying this is that all persons' benefits and costs are not counted equally. They are instead weighted by each person's power or resources, represented here by r_i. This is also evident in economists' calculations of costs and benefits. In a study done some time ago concerning the location of a third London airport, for example, persons' expenditures of time in getting to the airport were weighted by the market value of that time, that is, their incomes. Thus time expended by low-income workers counted for less than the same amount of time expended by high-income workers. If low-income workers lived on the southeast side of London and high-income workers on the northwest side, and if equal numbers of the two groups of workers used the airport, locating it on the northwest side would be, on these grounds, more economically efficient because lower-cost time would be expended in travel to the airport.

There is, then, a sense in which the use of the concept of economic efficiency to examine systems where the costs and benefits of an event are experienced by different persons hides an implicit struggle in which the strength of one's voice is determined by the extent of one's resources. It should be recognized that differential power of persons is intrinsically bound up with the concept of efficiency, and that any statement concerning the efficiency of an action is based on a particular distribution of resources. Such a statement should not be accepted without questioning the distribution of power on which the calculation is based. If that distribution is regarded as appropriate, then the calculation of efficiency based on it is appropriate. A different distribution of power may be brought about by the reallocation of rights, as in the second example above, and an action that was efficient under the old distribution may become inefficient under the new one. (These questions, along with their implications, have been discussed in more detail in Chapter 29.)

The Rationality of Norms

Conjoint Proscriptive Norms[5]

In the examples presented earlier in this chapter, two allocations of rights were discussed: In the first Tom had the right to make a telephone call during trading, and in order to prevent the call it was necessary for John and Steve to compensate Tom. In the second there was a prior understanding that Tom would not be on the phone during trading, and if it was sufficiently important to him to do so, he had to compensate John and Steve to gain the right.

A difference in allocation of rights is clear in a legal context. In contexts like that of the examples, there is no legal allocation of rights, but even so, understandings do exist that a person does or does not have the right to carry out an action that imposes negative externalities on others. It seems to capture the essence of what is meant by the existence of a norm to say that a norm against carrying out a certain action exists when the rights over that action are held by persons other than the actor. For the trading-card exchange system a norm exists when rights over Tom's phone call are held by John and Steve, as in Example 2.

What leads to this allocation of rights, rather than the "natural" allocation in which the actor holds the right to his action? A hint may be obtained from a statement of John Stuart Mill, quoted earlier in Chapter 13, about the condition under which society has the right to interfere with an individual's liberty: "As soon as any part of a person's conduct affects prejudicially the interests of others, society has jurisdiction over it" (1926 [1859], p. 142). Although Mill is vague about when this condition is met, he seems to have in mind some sort of balancing of the interests of the actor against the interests of society, or, more to the point, those in society who experience negative consequences of the action.

It is possible to go beyond the discussion of Chapter 10 and specify a kind of

5. Throughout this section it is assumed that the actions are carried out with equal frequency by each actor. That assumption may be easily dispensed with by letting the interests reflect the frequency of the actions.

norm for which a particularly strong condition holds. A pure conjoint proscriptive norm is a norm concerning a class of actions for which, *for every actor in the system*, the value of negative outcomes, calculated over the whole class, is greater than the value of positive outcomes. Thus, with a pure conjoint proscriptive norm, the move from a situation in which all carry out the action to a situation in which none do is a Pareto-optimal move.

The strong condition that holds for a pure conjoint proscriptive norm is this: If a pure conjoint proscriptive norm exists, this implies that the interests of those actors negatively affected by an action are greater than the interests of those actors carrying out the action. This proposition appears somewhat startling, because differential power does not enter. As will be evident below, the reason lies in the type of norm being considered.

To express this proposition formally in terms of the model requires some additional definitions:

a_j ≡ regime a for class J of actions; negative interests in actions of class J are set to zero, and other interests of actors having those interests are renormalized

b_j ≡ regime b for class J of actions; positive interests in actions of class J are set to zero, and other interests of actors having those interests (assumed here to be only the actor carrying out the actions) are renormalized

r_{ai} ≡ power of actor i in regime a
r_{bi} ≡ power of actor i in regime b

$$v_{a_j} = \sum_{k \in J} \sum_{i \in P_k} x_{ki} r_{ai}$$

$$v_{b_j} = \sum_{k \in J} \sum_{i \in N_k} x_{ki} r_{bi}$$

where P_k is the set of all actors who have a positive interest in actor k's action, k; N_k is the set of all actors who have a negative interest in actor k's action, k; and J is the class of actions covered by the norm. When, as assumed here, P_k has only one member, k, the definitions of v_{a_j} and v_{b_j} for a class of events J become

$$v_{a_j} = \sum_{k \in J} x_{kk} r_{ak} \quad \text{and} \quad v_{b_j} = \sum_{k \in J} \sum_{i \in N_k} x_{ki} r_{bi}$$

With these definitions, the criterion for a conjoint proscriptive norm (assuming second-order free-rider problems are overcome) is[6]

$$v_{b_j} > v_{a_j}$$

6. When there are positive interests in more than one action that would be covered by a norm (in this case a phone call by Tom, by John, and by Steve), then the actions are treated as separate events within the class J. A single regime a and a single regime b are created such that for each event in the class, there is a value. The quantities v_{a_j} and v_{b_j} are the sums of these values under each of the two regimes.

This inequality is not, however, the same as the proposition stated above. First, for a conjoint proscriptive norm, a comparison can be made for each actor i, whose interests appear both in v_b for actions of all other actors k and in v_a for his own action:

Interests against a norm	Interest favoring a norm
$x_{ii} r_{ai}$	$\displaystyle\sum_{k \neq i} x_{ki} r_{bi}$

If actor i's power is assumed to be essentially the same under the two regimes, then $r_{ai} \cong r_{bi}$, and it can be said that actor i favors a norm if and only if

$$r_i \left(\sum_{\substack{k=1 \\ k \neq i}}^{n} x_{ki} - x_{ii} \right) > 0 \qquad (30.3)$$

If this inequality holds for each actor in the system, this is equivalent to the condition for a pure conjoint proscriptive norm. But whether or not it is met for each, summing the left-hand side over all actors i gives a criterion for there being sufficient support for the adoption of a conjoint proscriptive norm (that is, a ceding to the collectivity of the right to carry out the action):

$$\sum_{i=1}^{n} r_i \left(\sum_{\substack{k=1 \\ k \neq i}}^{n} x_{ki} - x_{ii} \right) > 0 \qquad (30.4)$$

Note that inequality 30.4 does not imply that inequality 30.3 is met for each actor in the system. When inequality 30.3 *is* met for each member of the system, it is equivalent to the definition of a pure conjoint norm, for this is the case in which each actor in the system experiences the negative externalities from this class of actions as greater than the benefits. For this case summing over all actors i gives

$$\sum_{i=1}^{n} \left(\sum_{\substack{k=1 \\ k \neq i}}^{n} x_{ki} - x_{ii} \right) > 0 \qquad (30.5)$$

This inequality, stated earlier in words, is implied by a pure conjoint proscriptive norm. The interests opposed to the actions are on the left of the minus sign, and the interests of those same actors, favoring the actions, are on the right.

Since the summations on the left-hand side of inequality 30.5 are taken over all k and i except for the case where $k = i$, the subscripts of x_{ki} can be reversed to give an equivalent expression:

$$\sum_{i=1}^{n} \left(\sum_{\substack{k=1 \\ k \neq i}}^{n} x_{ik} - x_{ii} \right) > 0 \qquad (30.5')$$

Although this inequality holds for the system as a whole, the quantity in parentheses need not hold for each actor i, even though inequality 30.3, from which this inequality is derived, does hold for each actor i. Inequality 30.3 expresses the fact that actor i has a greater interest in others not carrying out the action than he does in carrying it out himself. A single term of inequality 30.5' would weigh the interests of an actor (i) in carrying out the action against the interests of other actors ($k = 1, \ldots, n, k \neq i$) against his carrying out the action. This comparison is meaningless, however, because it neglects the actors' relative power. The only meaningful comparison of this sort that can be made does include power. This inequality has meaning:

$$\sum_{\substack{k=1 \\ k \neq i}}^{n} x_{ik} r_k - x_{ii} r_i > 0 \qquad (30.6)$$

The meaning is that the interests of actor i in carrying out the action, weighted by his power, are less than the interests of others against his carrying out the action, weighted by their power.

Inequality 30.5 and the proposition stated earlier that is based on it appear to make such a comparison without taking power into account, but that comparison is different. The fact that inequality 30.3 holds for each actor in the system allows power to be eliminated in writing inequality 30.5. There are real systems in which inequality 30.3 does hold for each actor in the system, and therefore inequality 30.5 (and 30.5') also holds, but it is not true that inequality 30.6 holds for each actor. I will indicate later in the chapter the conditions under which inequality 30.5 holds and yet 30.6 does not hold for one or more actors in the system.

In the case of a pure conjoint proscriptive norm, where inequality 30.3 holds for each actor, the reallocation of rights away from the actors carrying out the focal action to the actors affected by the action is a Pareto-optimal move (assuming that the reallocation of rights to the collectivity does not reverse the inequality for some actor). Insofar as second-order free-rider problems and transaction costs are associated with inhibiting the action when rights are held by the target actor (for example, it is not easy, and possibly unpleasant, to induce a smoker to stop smoking in a place where he clearly has the right to do so), all are made better off by a transfer of the rights to those experiencing the negative externalities (for example, if all actors are smokers but find that their activities in a particular setting are more harmed by others' smoking than benefited by their own, then all will find themselves better off if no one smokes, although the best situation for each would be that in which only he smokes). This does not, however, mean that each will be constrained by the norm not to carry out the action, as a later section will show.

For a conjoint proscriptive norm that is not pure (that is, for which inequality 30.3 is reversed for one or more actors), the reallocation of rights to bring a norm into existence is not Pareto-optimal, except in one circumstance: if, for the actor(s) for whom inequality 30.3 is reversed, inequality 30.6 is also reversed. That is, when a conjoint proscriptive norm is not pure, it may still be Pareto-optimal if those whose interests are against the norm (reversal of inequality 30.3) also have sufficient power that they can continue to carry out the focal action in the presence of the norm (reversal of inequality 30.6).[7]

One might, however, ask a broad question: Why is it regarded as desirable that there be a transfer of the right over an action to those who experience its externalities? Since the criterion for the norm ($v_{b_j} > v_{a_j}$) and the stronger criterion for the pure conjoint proscriptive norm (inequality 30.3 for all actors) imply that the interests against the action are strong enough that those negatively affected by it can offer sufficient inducements to prevent it, why are they better off by not having to do so—by requiring the inducements instead to be offered by the one who wants to take the action? The same outcome would be predicted independently of the allocation of rights—unless, of course, that reallocation changed relative power sufficiently to reverse the inequality, which would not be expected for a conjoint norm.

The answer lies in the fact that a perfect social system has been assumed. Real social systems often lack the social capital necessary to overcome the second-order free-rider problem, and there are transaction costs that are absent if rights have been transferred. In a real system, where social capital is not complete, the outcome is not independent of the allocation of rights; a norm facilitates the socially efficient outcome.

EXAMPLE 5: MEETING THE CRITERION FOR A CONJOINT PROSCRIPTIVE NORM   The criteria for reallocation, as well as the interests of actors before and after reallocation, may be illustrated by again using the trading-card example. Example 1 showed that Tom had sufficient weighted interest in making the telephone call that John and Steve could not induce him to stop. But suppose there is a proposal that telephone calls are not to be made without agreement by all (thus requiring any one who makes a call to compensate the others). Whether the system meets the criterion for a norm may be decided by examining whether v_{b_j} is greater than v_{a_j} for class j, the class of telephone calls, which is the criterion for a conjoint proscriptive norm. To do this requires assessing the values of the three events representing telephone calls by the three boys under both regime a (calls are made) and regime b (calls are not made).

Table 30.5 shows the structures of interest and control which allow such an evaluation. Below those are the values for each event under regime a and under regime b. Shown also is the sum of values under the two regimes for telephone calls, the class of events which the norm would cover.

As Table 30.5 shows, the sum of the values of the calls if they are made

---

7. Strictly speaking, the inequality must be evaluated under the allocation of rights implied by the norm, although in the case of a conjoint proscriptive norm, this will ordinarily change the distribution of power only slightly.

Table 30.5 Control, interests, values, and power of three actors in exchange system under two regimes (*a* and *b*).

CONTROL (C)

	Cards			Calls by		
	Football	Baseball	Basketball	Tom	John	Steve
Tom	1	0	0	1	0	0
John	0	1	0	0	1	0
Steve	0	0	1	0	0	1

INTERESTS (X')

	Cards			Calls by		
	Football	Baseball	Basketball	Tom	John	Steve
Tom	.6	.3	.1	.15	.1	.1
John	.3	.4	.3	.1	.15	.1
Steve	.3	.2	.5	.1	.1	.15

VALUE OF CALLS

	Tom	John	Steve	Sum
Regime *a*	.056	.040	.035	.131
Regime *b*	.050	.058	.059	.167

POWER

	Regime *a*	Regime *b*
Tom	.429	.400
John	.304	.309
Steve	.268	.291

(regime a) is .131, and the sum of their values if they are not made is .167. The weighted interests against calls are greater than the weighted interests favoring calls. The criterion for a norm is met. This does not imply, however, that the value of each call is greater under regime b. As the table shows, the value of a telephone call by Tom is greater under regime a than under regime b. This suggests that Tom will continue to make calls if a norm is established, although this cannot be determined without a reexamination under the new rights allocation (which will be done in Example 8).

EXAMPLE 6: MEETING THE CRITERION FOR A PURE CONJOINT PROSCRIPTIVE NORM   A continuation of the preceding example will allow examining whether the condition is met for a pure conjoint proscriptive norm. The criterion is that the inequality of eq. 30.3 must hold for each actor: Each actor's interests against the class of actions in question must be greater than his interests favoring the class of actions, which are assumed to consist of only interests in his own action.

This may be determined without any calculations, simply by inspecting the interest matrix of Table 30.5. As that shows, the interests of each boy are .15 in favor of making a call himself and .1 + .1, or .2, against calls being made by others. Thus the inequality holds for each actor. The criterion for a pure conjoint proscriptive norm is met.

The importance of this test lies in the fact that in the case of a pure conjoint proscriptive norm the move to a norm is Pareto-optimal, so there is unanimous agreement that the norm is beneficial. All will agree that the norm is legitimate.

There appears to be an anomaly in the case of Tom. Tom does prefer a norm: The value to him of John's and Steve's not making a call is $.400(.1 + .1) = .08$, and the value to him of his making a call is $.429(.15) = .064$. Yet the value of his call under regime a (.056) is greater than its value under regime b (.050). This is not an anomaly; it arises because Tom's power is greater than that of John and Steve and, as a later section will indicate, corresponds to phenomena often found in social systems. In this case inequality 30.3 is met for each, but inequality 30.6 is reversed for Tom.

Disjoint Proscriptive Norms

For disjoint norms the targets and beneficiaries are different persons. Is there a comparable criterion for the emergence of such a norm? The target actors may or may not regard this kind of norm as legitimate, but its legitimacy is defined by the beneficiaries alone. Norms concerning what is proper behavior on the part of children are defined and determined by parents and other adults, and there is no requirement that children view these norms as legitimate. Thus the criterion for such a norm's emergence may at first appear to be much weaker, for example, that a particular type of action by a child has *any* externalities for adults.

Consider, however, what occurs if v_{a_j} is greater than v_{b_j}, that is, the value of the focal action in the system is greater than the loss of value it brings about. If that were true and there were a norm, with the rights held by those experiencing the externalities, then the rights would be bought back continuously by the target actors, and the action would be carried out anyway. If sanctions were imposed by the beneficiaries, they would be ineffective even though they imposed costs on the target actors; the actions would be carried out anyway, and the sanctions, without effect, would dwindle. The norm would become ineffective.

This consideration leads to the conclusion that the criterion for a disjoint proscriptive norm is like that for a conjoint proscriptive norm: If social-structural conditions are met, a norm will come into existence if and only if the sum of values v_{b_j} over all focal actions is greater than the sum of values v_{a_j} over the same actions. This can be expressed using the same notation as given in the earlier definitions: x_{kk} is target actor k's interest in carrying out the focal action, k, and x_{ki} is aggrieved actor i's interest in that action not being carried out.

$$v_{b_j} > v_{a_j}$$

or

$$\sum_{k \in J} \sum_{i \in N_k} x_{ki} r_{bi} > \sum_{k \in J} x_{kk} r_{ak} \tag{30.7}$$

where N_k is the set of actors who experience negative externalities from actor k's action, and J is the set of all actors whose actions that could be covered by a norm impose externalities on others (that is, all target actors).

For a disjoint proscriptive norm the interests on the right-hand side of inequality 30.7 are interests of a set of target actors, J, that is disjoint with the set of actors whose interests are on the left-hand side. The latter set includes all actors in the set N_k for at least one target actor k. In contrast, for a conjoint proscriptive norm, all actors who carry out the offending action (set J) are also in the set N_k for some k, that is, they are also among the aggrieved parties.[8]

When the beneficiaries or potential beneficiaries of a norm and the targets are not the same actors, differential power is important. The weights, r_i, applied to interests in bringing about interpersonal comparison by comparing v_{a_j} and v_{b_j} are different on the two sides. This means that, all other things being equal, a disjoint proscriptive norm will be more likely to come into existence if the potential targets are less powerful than the potential beneficiaries. In contrast, in the inequality of eq. 30.4, which holds for even an impure conjoint proscriptive norm, the same weights, r_i, are applied to both the interests benefited by the action and those harmed by it.

For inequality 30.7 note that if the sets N_k are themselves disjoint, this means that each of the potential target actors harms a different set of potential benefi-

8. Other logical possibilities exist, but they appear to add less that is theoretically different than is true for the disjoint and conjoint cases.

ciaries. For example, if the target actors are children and the focal action is carried out in the home, the potential beneficiaries of the norm are disjoint between households. In such a case a set of *different* norms will be established, one for each household. But there may be secondary externalities, such as when one child's action induces a similar action on the part of another. Then only if there is extensive social capital shared by the members of N_k and the members of $N_{k'}$ will the latter sanction actor k and the former sanction actor k'.

The way a disjoint proscriptive norm might become ineffective can be seen by examining how inequality 30.7 might be reversed over time. This can occur for any of four reasons:

1. The interest of beneficiaries against the focal action (x_{ki}) becomes weaker. For example, parents' activities become more separate from those of their teenaged children, so their interest against their children's underaged drinking weakens.
2. The interests of target actors favoring the action (x_{kk}) increase in strength. For example, as youth live more in a society of their peers, their interests in carrying out actions like those of peers increases.
3. The power of targets relative to that of beneficiaries increases $(r_{ak}/r_{bi}$ increases for the average target actor k and the average beneficiary i). For example, changes in the larger social structure reduce the power of parents over children.
4. The number of actors affected by a given target actor's action (the number of persons in set N_k for the average target actor) decreases. For example, in a nuclear family, compared to an extended household, N_k is reduced in size from greater than two to two. In a single-parent household, N_k is reduced in size to one.

How can inequality 30.7, which for a disjoint proscriptive norm pits the interests of one set against those of another, be a criterion for the rationality of a norm? Suppose that a norm is brought into existence when the criterion is not met, that is, when v_{a_j}, the total value to target actors of all actions that would be covered by the norm, is greater than v_{b_j}, the total value of those same actions to the aggrieved parties. This would mean that the target actors have sufficient interest in the actions (backed by sufficient power) to induce the aggrieved parties to let them do the actions or to do the actions anyway and withstand whatever sanctions are imposed. Thus the beneficiaries of the norm are powerless to prevent the focal action. A norm would be ineffective, and sanctions could not back it up.

Now suppose that a norm is not brought into existence when the criterion is met, that is, when v_{b_j} is greater than v_{a_j}. This means that those who experience the externalities must provide inducements to the target actor to discourage the focal action. This arrangement is clearly against the interests of the potential beneficiaries of a disjoint norm. They find it in their interest to assume the right to control the action, whether or not the target actors cede that right and thus accept the legitimacy of the norm—and the fact that v_{b_j} is greater than v_{a_j} means that the potential beneficiaries have the power, if necessary, to induce the target actors not to carry out the focal action or to provide sanctions that are effective.

This would suggest, following Coase, that even though the criterion that v_{b_j} must be greater than v_{a_j} is appropriate for the existence of a norm (that is, for rights to be held by the aggrieved parties), a norm is unnecessary. Nevertheless, it is to the interest of the aggrieved parties to establish a norm: The necessity to compensate the offending actor raises free-rider problems and transaction costs which could lead to the compensation not being paid, the actions being taken, and the set of actors being worse off (as indicated by the fact that the action is taken even though v_{b_j} is greater than v_{a_j}). If a norm is established when v_{b_j} is greater than v_{a_j} and rights are relinquished to the aggrieved actors, these potential "market failures" will not arise: Although effective sanctions are potentially present, they need not be used, as long as the target actor recognizes that his power is insufficient to counter the anticipated sanctions.

None of this, of course, addresses problems created by the lack of social capital. A target actor, when a norm does exist, may see that there is little social capital among those who experience the negative externalities of his action. Thus, he may see that he can violate the norm, and the beneficiaries will not be able to organize themselves sufficiently well to impose effective sanctions. Thus lack of social capital generates new problems. The criteria specified above assume the existence of a social structure which allows the full force of v_{b_j} to be mobilized, when necessary, to counter v_{a_j}, that is, the interests of the offending actor.

EXAMPLE 7: A DISJOINT PROSCRIPTIVE NORM   The system of card trading treated in earlier examples may be modified in yet a different way. Suppose Tom, John, and Steve are joined by a younger boy, Dan, with whom they share various activities but not the activity of trading cards. He creates a disturbance, disrupting the card trading. Tom, John, and Steve ask him to stop, but he fails to do so. Steve proposes that a rule be adopted that no one other than the traders may speak during trading without permission from the traders; Tom and John accept this proposal. Dan does not readily assent. He says that if they adopt such a rule, he may withdraw from their other shared activities. John, in turn, reminds him that they can reciprocate; any or all of the three older boys can withdraw from the activities they share with him.

The rule proposed by Steve, and agreed to by Tom and John, can be regarded as a disjoint proscriptive norm. It applies only to nontraders as targets; it is proposed by one of the traders as a norm to be held and enforced by the traders; and it is proscriptive, a rule against a certain action. Thus it fits the definition of a disjoint proscriptive norm. The question is whether the norm is enforceable and will be effective.

It is known that Tom, John, and Steve will favor such a norm, for each has no interest in carrying out the proscribed action. Thus inequality 30.3 holds for each because $x_{ii} = 0$ for each. It is also known Dan will oppose the norm, for he is the sole target, and therefore the only relevant quantity in inequality 30.3 is x_{ii} (since x_{ki} for all other actors k is zero), with the result that the inequality does not hold for him. For any disjoint proscriptive norm, then, the only question is whether the value of the proscribed action to the potential targets of the norm is greater than the value to the potential beneficiaries.

Table 30.6 shows a matrix of interests in which all have equal interest in shared activities, all the traders have equal negative interest in the disturbance, and Dan has strong positive interest in the disturbance. Also shown are calculated values for the events under regime a and regime b. Because there is only one potential target actor for the norm, the class of events to be proscribed consists of only one event, the disturbance (event 4). The results in Table 30.6 show that v_a is greater than v_b, so the norm cannot be established. Dan's threat to withdraw from the shared activities is stronger than the comparable threats of Tom, John, and Steve. This is not because he has greater power, for under either regime he is the weakest of the four. The reason lies in his greater interest in the disturbance, which is 5/7, or .714, as compared to the others' much weaker interest against it (for each .2/1.4, or .143). Thus the disturbance will continue, and no norm will be established. Nor will the three traders be able to buy Dan off by offering him trading cards: First, he has no interest in the cards; and second, stopping the disturbance is worth less to them, in the currency of this system, than continuing it is to him.

Why Do High-Status Persons Often Defy Norms?

In Chapter 11 the empirical generalization that high-status persons in a community may violate norms without being sanctioned was discussed. The criterion for emergence of a norm given above, that v_{b_j} must be greater than v_{a_j}, allows a simple explanation of this generalization. As long as there is heterogeneity, then for a particular offending actor and action i, the inequality shown below may coexist with inequality 30.7 for a disjoint proscriptive norm, or with inequality 30.4 for a conjoint proscriptive norm, or even with inequality 30.3 for a pure conjoint proscriptive norm.

$$\sum_{k \in N_i} x_{ik} r_{bk} - x_{ii} r_{ai} < 0 \qquad (30.8)$$

Note that inequality 30.8 includes all those terms involving interests in event i: the negative interests of aggrieved parties on the left-hand side of the minus sign, and the positive interests of target actor i on the right-hand side. (This inequality is simply a restatement, for the more general case, of inequality 30.6, reversed.) Inequality 30.3, in contrast, includes all those terms involving actor i's interests. Inequality 30.3 is relevant only for a conjoint norm (since one of the two terms will be missing for each actor in the case of a disjoint norm), but inequality 30.8 can be written for either a conjoint or a disjoint norm.

Table 30.6 Control, interests, values, and power in exchange system when a fourth actor with whom the traders have shared activities disrupts trading.

	CONTROL (C)					INTERESTS (X') (not normalized)				
	Football	Baseball	Basketball	Disturbance	Activities	Football	Baseball	Basketball	Disturbance	Activities
Tom	1	0	0	0	.25	6	3	.1	.2	.2
John	0	1	0	0	.25	3	4	.3	.2	.2
Steve	0	0	1	0	.25	3	2	.5	.2	.2
Dan	0	0	0	1	.25	0	0	0	.5	.2

VALUES					
	Football	Baseball	Basketball	Disturbance	Activities
Regime a	.294	.211	.192	.116	.186
Regime b	.241	.174	.162	.115	.308

POWER		
	Regime a	Regime b
Tom	.341	.318
John	.257	.251
Steve	.239	.239
Dan	.163	.192

Inequalities 30.7 and 30.8 express the fact that even though a norm is rational, or efficient, for the system as a whole, the weighted positive interests (regime a) in a particular actor's action (shown in inequality 30.8) are greater than the weighted negative interests (regime b) in that action. The simplest way for this to occur, in the face of the general inequality for a disjoint proscriptive norm (30.7), or for conjoint proscriptive norm (30.4) or for a pure conjoint proscriptive norm (30.3), is for actor i's power, r_{ai}, to be very large compared to the power of other actors, r_{bk}, where $k = 1, \ldots, n$ and $k \neq i$. Note that the power which weights the two kinds of interests in inequality 30.8 is the power of different actors; this is so whether the norm is disjoint or conjoint or even pure conjoint.

Thus a powerful member of a community may be free to violate a norm if he wishes, being able to shrug off any sanctions that other members find it in their interest to apply. He may, of course, not wish to violate the norm, so as to help ensure its maintenance; but the sanctions do not constrain him. If he is unconcerned about the existence of the norm, he would certainly find it in his interest to violate it. The existence of inequality 30.4 means, of course, that this freedom to violate is restricted in the case of a conjoint proscriptive norm to the few most powerful actors in the system (plus the few, if any, who have especially strong interests in carrying out the action that violates the norm).

This explanation of the empirical generalization stated at the beginning of this section allows certain predictions. For instance, the greater the variance in power in a community, the more likely it is that there will be high-status norm violators. In a relatively egalitarian community, no actors would be able to violate a norm without incurring effective sanctions (unless, of course, they remained undetected). Also, if more norm violation is found among the high-status members of one community than among those of another, this is an indication of greater variance in status in the first community than in the second.

EXAMPLE 8: VIOLATION OF A NORM BY A POWERFUL ACTOR   The trading-card example can be used to illustrate the effect of unequal power in leading to norm violation. Example 6 showed that all three boys favored a reallocation of rights over telephone calls such that rights to make calls would be held collectively. This was true even though, under the allocation in which rights over calls were held by the individual caller, Tom's call had a greater value for him (.056) than the value that would be lost by the others (.050) if he made it—so, under that rights allocation, they could not induce him not to make the call by offering him sports cards, and still benefit by doing so.

As shown in Table 30.7, after the allocation of rights to the collectivity, it remains true that continuing to make the call is sufficiently important to Tom (value = .054) that he can devote more resources to continuing it than the others can to stopping him (value = .049). Thus, if Tom has de facto control of the event (even though the others hold rights of control), he can violate the norm, and they cannot bring enough sanctions to bear to make him stop. Or if the transfer of rights of control to the collectivity included transfer of de facto

Table 30.7 Individual control over cards and collective control over telephone calls, interests, power of actors, and value of calls to those making them (regime *a*) and others (regime *b*).

CONTROL (C) (not normalized)

	Cards			Calls by		
	Football	Baseball	Basketball	Tom	John	Steve
Tom	1	0	0	1	1	1
John	0	1	0	1	1	1
Steve	0	0	1	1	1	1

INTERESTS (X')

	Cards			Calls by		
	Football	Baseball	Basketball	Tom	John	Steve
Tom	.6	.3	.1	.15	.1	.1
John	.3	.4	.3	.1	.15	.1
Steve	.3	.2	.5	.1	.1	.15

VALUE OF CALLS

	Tom	John	Steve	Sum
Regime *a*	.054	.040	.037	.131
Regime *b*	.049	.058	.060	.167

POWER

	Regime *a*	Regime *b*
Tom	.412	.407
John	.306	.307
Steve	.282	.285

control (through some device such as a locked telephone whose key is obtainable only after a unanimous vote), Tom will have to induce the others to allow him to make the call by giving them a sufficient number of cards to gain their assent. He can do so and still benefit because making the call is worth more to him than his not making it is to the two of them together.

Note that the difference between Tom's position in this example and that of John and Steve does not lie in their interests in favor of their own calls or opposed to the others' calls. It lies solely in Tom's greater power, which gives greater weight to his interests—both to his interests in making a call and to his interests in preventing the others from making calls.

Tom's immunity to sanctions in this case has precisely the same source as the immunity of powerful men in rural villages, as described for the Sarakatsan nomads of Greece by Campbell (1964). These men are immune to the sanctions of the other villagers, and their immunity lies in the greater resources they can bring to bear in furthering their interests, not in the intensity of their interests.

The Density of Social Relations, Norms, and Individualism

Note that the left-hand side of inequality 30.7 increases with N_k, the number of persons who experience externalities of action k. This provides an incentive for individualism, that is, an incentive to actor k to locate himself in settings where N_k is small. A smaller N_k does not imply, of course, a smaller group or community, but merely a smaller number of persons who are sufficiently close that their actions impose externalities on one another. That is, a smaller N_k implies a lower density of social relations.[9] When this density is lower, the left-hand side of the inequality will less often exceed the right, and actor k will more often find it not rational for there to be a norm (and others in that setting will also more often find it not rational for there to be a norm). This consideration, of course, is based only on negative externalities and proscriptive norms. As will be made evident shortly, a smaller N_k resulting in a reduced frequency of norms also operates for positive externalities and prescriptive norms. In those cases the move to more individualistic settings brings as a cost the loss of the positive externalities.

The Emergence of Norms and the Economic Analysis of Law

The development in recent years of the economic analysis of law provides an opportunity to examine the parallel between norms and laws for the linear system of action. The general argument of this school of legal theory is that the law allocates rights to their most economically efficient use. (See Posner, 1986, for development of this principle in various branches of law.) The analysis above, although it began from quite different premises, arrives at a similar conclusion

---

9. Durkheim (1947 [1893]) meant something like this by his term "moral density": "more individuals sufficiently in contact to be able to act and react upon one another" (p. 257).

with respect to norms. The general principle is that (given the existence of social capital) a norm arises which withdraws rights over an action from the hands of an actor when it is efficient for the rights to be in the hands of those who experience the externalities of the action. (Efficiency here means something broader than the usual economic efficiency, for it is based on all forms of social power, not merely on economic wealth.)

Furthermore, the emergence of a norm when the criterion is met is not mysterious or arbitrary. In the case of a conjoint norm, the criterion specifies precisely the condition under which persons find it to their longer-term interest to have rights removed from their hands when they are offending actors. In the case of a disjoint norm, the legitimacy of the norm may depend on the differential power of the beneficiaries and targets—and thus the conflict that is internal to each actor for conjoint norms becomes a potential conflict between beneficiaries and targets for disjoint norms. If the power relation changes, norms which were previously rational, or efficient, may no longer be so.

There is a similar difference in laws of two kinds: those corresponding to conjoint proscriptive norms (which might be called conjoint laws), and those corresponding to disjoint proscriptive norms (disjoint laws). For the former there is extensive overlap between those who are targets of the law's sanctions and those whose interests are affected negatively by the focal action (that is, those protected by the law). For the latter there is little such overlap. Any laws or rules that are specific to status or position are disjoint laws. Some examples are the rules and regulations of European universities that were challenged by the student revolts beginning in 1968. More striking examples are the different laws that were applied to the several Estates before the French Revolution or to slaves and free persons in the South prior to the Civil War in the United States. Even when a law does not apply specifically to particular statuses, a lack of overlap between targets of the law's sanctions and those negatively affected by the focal action creates what approximates a disjoint law. This occurs when certain kinds of crimes are committed at highly different rates according to the perpetrator's age, sex, racial or ethnic group, or social class.

The basis of popular legitimacy for disjoint laws is more problematic than that for conjoint laws. The power differential that may be responsible for their "efficiency" in the system must be maintained if disjoint laws are to be effective. If the power differential changes, a law that was efficient may become inefficient. This is not true for laws corresponding to conjoint norms, for the offenders and the aggrieved parties are the same persons.

The Meaning of Power and the Importance of Social Capital

An examination of the role of power (r_i) in the linear system of action will make apparent the importance of social capital to the maintenance of norms. As described in Chapter 25, r_i is actor i's control over whatever is of value in the system, that is, whatever interests others. The calculation of a single measure of power for the individual actor implies that he can use this power anywhere in the system—that there is a sufficiently rich set of social relations that no actor is insulated from any other, although he can of course counter the power of others with his own power, if it is sufficient. Thus packed into the concept of power, through its very definition and through the assumption that its effectiveness is undiminished by social distance, is the capability of applying sanctions to enforce one's interest. (See Chapters 27 and 32 for an examination of the way power can be diminished by social distance.)

If social capital is deficient in a system, this means that the assumption of generalized, or systemic, power is invalid. In this regard the contrast between a community such as that of the Sarakatsan nomads in Greece (referred to above and in Chapter 11) and a differentiated community in a modern Western society is apparent. In the former setting powerful fathers are able to establish and effectively enforce norms about their sons' behavior. In contrast, a set of fathers in a New York suburb may be very powerful in their jobs in Wall Street yet powerless to counteract the norms concerning behavior which develop among their sons or to establish their own norms for their sons' behavior.

The quantitative importance of social capital can be seen, after r_k is unpacked, in the term $x_{ik}r_{bk}$, which shows k's power to sanction i for an offending action (also labeled i). Neglecting the variation in r_k due to regime b gives

$$x_{ik}r_{bk} = x_{ik} \sum_j \sum_h c_{kj}x_{jh}r_h$$

The summation $\Sigma_j\, c_{kj}x_{jh}$ represents actor k's control of those events that are of interest to actor h. This is the leverage that actor k has in the system through actor h. But if indirect paths which k could use to exert pressure on i are not available (that is, if there is not sufficient closure of the system to provide social capital), then, as shown in Chapter 27, k has only one source of leverage: those events that are directly of interest to the offending actor, i. The sanctioning potential is reduced to

$$x_{ik} \sum_j c_{kj}x_{ji}r_i$$

Comparing this with actor i's power to act (which in the absence of social capital is reduced to his direct control of what interests others) and summing over all actors k who experience externalities from i's action gives a new criterion for the sanctioning potential in the absence of social capital:

$$\sum_{k \in N_i} x_{ik} \sum_{j=1}^{m} c_{kj}x_{ji} > x_{ii} \qquad (30.9)$$

The criterion for the emergence of a norm in the absence of social closure (except for the social capital that is necessary to overcome the free-rider problem of sanctioning) is that inequality 30.9 must hold over all actors i. In other words, an effective norm can exist when the interests of all actors experiencing externalities from the target actors' action, each weighted by what the actor directly controls that is of interest to the target actors, are greater than the target actors' interests in the action.

The tightening of the criterion for the emergence of a norm to inequality 30.9 (required to hold for all actors i) shows the importance of social capital in facilitating norms. The existence of extensive social capital as manifested in power remaining undiminished by social distance within the system is relevant to the problem of free riding on others' sanctioning (a problem to which I will return in a subsequent section). But the existence of social capital has further implications. If even the social capital necessary for overcoming the free-rider problem of sanctioning is absent, then the first summation of inequality 30.9 is not present. In such a case the notion of a norm becomes meaningless, and all that can be specified is the criterion that *some* single actor will sanction actor i:

$$\max_{k} \left(x_{ik} \sum_{j} c_{ki} x_{ji} - x_{ii} \right) > 0 \qquad (30.10)$$

That is, if there is an actor k^* whose interests against the action, weighted by his control of what interests i, are greater than i's own interests in the action, then k^* can carry out a heroic sanction to prevent the action. But unless there is someone for whom carrying out such a heroic sanction is rational, i will not be sanctioned. And unless inequality 30.10 holds for a large enough fraction of the target actors i in the system, it will not be rational to transfer rights of control to those experiencing the externalities, even though v_{b_j} is greater than v_{a_j}. Inspection of the inequality shows that it will hold only if the harm to at least one person, modified by the direct control of that person over what interests the target actor, is greater than the benefit to the target actor. The weak will be widely sanctioned, and the very strong will not be sanctioned at all. Inequality 30.10, in giving the condition for retaliation in the absence of social capital that could facilitate norms, expresses the law of the (individualistic) jungle.

Positive Externalities and Prescriptive Norms

The fundamental criterion for the establishment of either a conjoint or disjoint proscriptive norm by rational actors is given above as v_{b_j} must be greater than v_{a_j} for the action in question. Inequality 30.7 is given for disjoint norms, but it is in a form appropriate for either. In that inequality J is, as defined earlier, the set of offending actions, and equivalently, the set of actors who carry out the offending action, and N_k is the set of actors who experience the negative externalities from the action of k, a member of J. If J is disjoint with every set N_k, the norm is disjoint; if J coincides with every set N_k, the norm is conjoint.

Does this same criterion hold for norms that encourage actions that generate positive externalities? Answering this question requires distinguishing two cases. First, as in the common project discussed in Chapter 10, the actor whose action generates externalities may have an interest against carrying out the action. Second, the actor may have a positive interest in the action (for example, the action of cleaning snow off the sidewalk not only aids passers-by but provides a benefit to the homeowner, or the enjoyment of playing football may be sufficient that a boy will play in the absence of any rewards from others), but rewards from others increase that interest, leading to more activity (the homeowner may clean his sidewalk better and more often, or the boy may practice football longer and play harder) than would occur in the absence of such rewards.

For the first case the criterion would seem to be identical to that of inequality 30.7, but with N_k defined such that it is the set of actors who are benefited by the action. The interests of actor i, who creates the benefits for others, are opposed to the action, and the interests of actors k, who experience the benefits, favor it. Thus, as with negative externalities, the interests are opposed, and the norm is rational when the weighted interests on the left side, of those experiencing the benefits, exceed the weighted interests on the right side, of those carrying out the action. The only difference in this case is that the norm favors the action. If the criterion is met, it is rational for rights to the action to be in the hands of those experiencing the external benefits, and for the actor who carries out the action to be required to compensate the others or to suffer negative sanctions if he does not perform the action.

As with negative externalities, there may be an actor whose interests weighted by his power are sufficiently great that although the norm is rational for him (inequality 30.3 holds), it is also rational for him to fail to act to benefit others (inequality 30.8 also holds). Such a case arises when the negative consequences of the action for the actor are greater than the negative sanctions he would receive for not acting or the cost to him of the compensation he would have to pay for not acting. An instance of this occurred in earlier societies when a wealthy man bought his way out of military service by paying for another to serve in his place. This again illustrates the point made earlier concerning a proscriptive norm: Such a possibility is the exception rather than the rule, for otherwise the overall inequality $v_{b_j} > v_{a_j}$ would not be met, and the norm would not be rational in the first place. The fact that this practice was characteristic of societies with highly unequal distributions of wealth illustrates a second point made in an earlier section: The possibility that the most powerful can escape a norm because inequality 30.8 holds for each of them when inequality 30.7 does for the system as a whole is greater in a highly inegalitarian system than in a more egalitarian one.

Also, as in the case of a proscriptive norm, it may be to the longer-term interest of a person for whom inequality 30.8 holds while 30.7 holds for the system to carry out the action, despite the fact that he could safely fail to do so. For if his carrying out the action helps to reinforce the norm, then his interests as exhibited in inequality 30.7 (his interests in others acting so as to benefit him) are aided, despite the fact that he could get away with disregarding the norm. Again there appear to be examples: The fact that some who could have bought their way out of military service did not do so is one of many.

EXAMPLE 9: A PRESCRIPTIVE NORM IN A COMMON PROJECT   The three-person common project of Chapter 10 is an instance of a situation with positive externalities to which the criterion for a norm can be applied.

The scale for interests is arbitrary, so for convenience the interest in \$1 can be set at .1. Because each actor loses \$5 by contributing to the project, the interest x_{ii} for actor i is .5. Because each actor i gains \$4 from the contribution of each other actor, k, to the project, $x_{ki} = .4$, for all k and i. Thus the interest matrix ($\mathbf{X}'$, which is not normalized to make interests sum to 1.0) is

	E_1	E_2	E_3
A_1	.5	.4	.4
A_2	.4	.5	.4
A_3	.4	.4	.5

If a norm exists, giving half of the control of each actor's contribution to each of the other two actors, then the power of actor i when he acts and the others have directed their interests elsewhere (regime a) is $r_{ai} = .419$. Actor k's power, considering i's contribution and assuming that i has directed his interests elsewhere (regime b) is $r_{bk} = .296$. Then inequality 30.7 is

$$3[.4(.296) + .4(.296)] > 3[.5(.419)]$$

$$.71 > .63$$

Thus the criterion for a norm is met, and it is to the interest of each that all give up to the other two rights to decide whether to contribute.

That the only interests which entered this system (the only events linking these three actors) were interests in the project itself meant that the power of an actor under the two different regimes differed considerably (.419 versus .296), more than would ordinarily be the case. But such wide disparity in values of r_i is an artifact of the fact that the only resource which each actor had to use in relations with the others was control over contributions. There were no other events of the sort that ordinarily link individuals. Such events would, in this case, have meant that r_{bi} would have been approximately equal to r_{ai}, under whatever assumption about control.

If there were a norm giving the other two actors rights of control over each actor's contribution, what would this mean in reality? It would be meaningless if the project was a one-time occurrence with simultaneous contributions, unless each actually gave the contribution to the other two to dispose of. If, as is ordinarily true whenever the term "norm" is used, there was a continuing sequence of projects, then the existence of a norm would mean that there was an understanding that the other two would retaliate if any one of the three failed to contribute. Since, by assumption, the only events linking the three actors in the example are their contributions, the retaliation would necessarily take the form of a tit-for-tat withholding of contributions on the next project. In a more general case, however, the bundle of resources represented by r_i would allow actor i to pick some event which had little interest for him but a great deal for the actor to be sanctioned. (This brings up the public-good problem of sanctioning itself, the second-order free-rider problem. I will return to the common project from Chapter 10 when examining that problem in a later section of this chapter.)

When, as is not true of the example of the common project, the action not only provides benefits for others but the actor's own interests favor it, the matter is somewhat different. The actor and the recipients of the positive externalities have interests in the same direction. It would appear that a norm would always be rational in such a circumstance. That is, it would be rational for rights to control the action to be held by those experiencing its benefits. But why should rights not be held by the actor who produces those benefits? His interests lead in the same direction. There is no conflict of interest between that actor and those who experience the externalities. Thus there is no reason why individuals should transfer rights to act from themselves individually to themselves collectively. The criterion which would lead each to find it in his interest to do so is expressed by inequality 30.7; that, however, holds only for the situation in which the individual's interests as actor and as recipient of externalities are opposed, which is not the case here.

In this case, then, a norm is not expected to emerge. Instead there will be actions on the part of beneficiaries to increase actors' interest in carrying out the action: encouragement, expression of gratitude, and other rewards. These rewards, ordinarily not costly to the actor who gives them, can increase the level of action beyond that which would otherwise occur by in effect augmenting the target actor's interest in the action. This is seen empirically in the rewards provided by the fans of a sports team, as well as by the team members for one another's actions.

The argument might be made that a norm would be rational in this case whenever the total benefits to others exceeded the total benefits to the target actor. This would imply that the following inequality should be the criterion for the emergence of a norm in this case:

$$\sum_{i=1}^{n} \sum_{k=1}^{n} x_{ik} r_k > \sum_{i} x_{ii} r_i \qquad (30.11)$$

(Here regimes a and b are unnecessary because all interests are in the same direction.) The rationale behind this inequality is that rights over an event should be held by those actors with greatest (weighted) interest in the event.

I will not attempt to evaluate these two arguments concerning the rationality of a norm when the interests of the actor carrying out the focal action and of those experiencing externalities from it are in the same direction. Empirical evidence may provide additional insight.

Criterion for Overcoming the Second-Order Free-Rider Problem

In Chapter 10 and in an earlier section of this chapter, I discussed at some length the free-rider problem of sanctioning: that each of those who experience negative externalities from another's action also experience positive externalities from the sanctioning of that action by still another, although it is not in the sanctioner's own interest to sanction. I will continue the examination of this problem by reconsidering the common project of Chapter 10. The form of sanctioning discussed there assumed that rights are in the hands of the actor, not the recipients of the externalities: A_2 or A_3 (or both) had to compensate A_1 to induce him to act. If rights are instead in the hands of the recipients, the sanctions will be negative—in the example of the common project, retaliation by not contributing. That form of sanction does not exhibit the free-rider problem, because imposition of retaliation by not contributing imposes no costs on the sanctioner beyond those imposed on others. Thus, to examine the free-rider problem of sanctioning, I will modify the example from Chapter 10 slightly.

EXAMPLE 10: SHARING SANCTIONING COSTS IN A COMMON PROJECT
Assume that actors A_1, A_2, and A_3 have other resources which they can use for sanctioning; that is, each has control of other events that are of interest to the other two. The sanction for not contributing must impose a cost on A_1 which is the equivalent of at least \$5. If the cost to A_2 or A_3 of imposing such a sanction is assumed to be \$5 and it is further assumed that in the next project the sanction will bring a benefit of \$4 to A_2 and to A_3 (equivalent to the assumption in Chapter 10 that the sanction would change the project outcome for each of them from -1 to 3), then A_2's sanction (E_1) has an interest to him of .1 against sanctioning and an interest to A_3 of .4 favoring sanctioning. If A_2 has control of additional events (E_3) worth \$2 to him and \$8 to A_3 and A_3 is in a comparable situation, the interest matrix $\mathbf{X'}$ for A_2 and A_3 is as follows (as before, not normalized to sum to 1.0):

	E_1	E_2	E_3	E_4
A_2	.1	.4	.2	.8
A_3	.4	.1	.8	.2

If each retains control of his own sanctioning action, the control matrix ($\mathbf{C}$) is as shown below:

	E_1	E_2	E_3	E_4
A_2	1	0	1	0
A_3	0	1	0	1

With these matrices of interest and control, it is possible to calculate first $\mathbf{X}_a$ and $\mathbf{X}_b$ and then the power of A_2 (or A_3) under regimes a and b. These values are $r_{a2} = .476$ and $r_{b2} = .517$. The criterion for it to be rational for A_2 (or A_3) to transfer sanctioning rights to the other is

$$.4(.517) > .1(.476)$$

$$.21 > .05$$

Thus it is rational for A_2 and A_3 to reach a prior agreement that each has the right to commit the other to sanctioning A_1 if A_1 fails to contribute.

The Two Functions of Interests When Events Are Indivisible

Interests have two functions in the theory of rational action, deriving from the behavioral assumption that actors maximize utility. First, interests indicate the amount of utility to be realized from control of a particular event or good (see eq. 25.1); that is, the interest of actor i in good j is the partial elasticity of i's utility with respect to a change in the amount of j held. Therefore, under the assumption that actors maximize utility, interests provide guides to action. In the linear system of action x_{ji}, interest of actor i in good j, tells that actor to acquire more of good j at the expense of good k if x_{ji}/x_{ki} is greater than $c_{ij}v_j/c_{ik}v_k$, where v_j/v_k is the price ratio (the amount of k he must give up per unit of j gained) and c_{ij} and c_{ik} are the amounts of j and k already held.

The second function of interests in the theory is to provide a means of determining an actor's level of utility or satisfaction. Because actor i's utility is defined as $U_i = \prod_j c_{ij}\exp(x_{ji})$ (and his satisfaction is defined as the logarithm of that), his interests, together with the quantities of goods he holds (consumes), determine his level of utility.

When events are indivisible, however, these two functions of interests must be separated. The separation has somewhat different consequences depending on whether interests of two actors in an indivisible event are opposed or favor the same outcome. I will examine the two cases separately (although, as in the example where Tom's interests were opposed to those of John and Steve, but John's and Steve's were directed toward the same outcome, the cases sometimes occur together).

OPPOSED INTERESTS IN AN INDIVISIBLE EVENT   If two actors, i and k, both have an interest in the same indivisible event, but one favors a positive outcome and the other favors a negative one (for example, both Tom and John have an interest in Tom's telephone call, but Tom's interest is in continuing the call, and John's is in his ending it), one will end up with full control over the event, and the other will end up with no control over it. If both recognize this and both allocate their resources to maximize their utility, only one (determined by whether $x_{jk}r_{bk}$ is greater than $x_{ji}r_{ai}$ or vice versa) will allocate resources to controlling the event. It may not be the more powerful of the two; it will be the one for whom the interest weighted by power is greater.[10]

10. This will result in a level of realized utility for actor i given by $U_i = \prod_j c_{ij}\exp(x_{ji})$, where c_{ij} equals 1 if he gained control of the indivisible event j and 0 if he did not. This means that if he did not gain control of it, U_i equals 0 independent of whatever else he controls. This represents a conceptual inconvenience, which could be remedied in any of several ways. I will not pursue any of them because the absolute value of utility plays no role in affecting actors' actions according to the theory.

What this means, however, is that the original interests can no longer be the only guide to action. Because each actor is in a context in which he does not gain an increment of satisfaction, $x_{ji} \ln(c_{ij1}/c_{ij0})$, for each increment of resources, Δr_i, expended toward gaining control of event j, he must use a more complex guide to action. His interests will play a role, but so will his power and his assumption about what the other actor will do. In the normal case, where actor i assumes that the other actor, k, is rational, he will assume that k will act to gain control of the event if (and only if) $x_{jk}r_{bk}$ is greater than $x_{ji}r_{ai}$. If actor i holds rights of control over event j, he will give up these rights in exchange for resources from k; if he does not, he will not expend resources on j, despite the fact that a blind consultation of his interests would tell him to expend a quantity of resources equal to $x_{ji}r_i$ on the event.[11] Thus an actor's guide to action in this case makes use not only of his own interests, but also of his resources, the other actor's resources, and the other actor's interest in the indivisible event. If he has further information about the other, for example, that the other is especially timid or especially bold, he will, if he is rational, use that information as well in deciding whether to attempt to gain control of the event. Thus the criterion applied above may not, in a real system, be the sole basis for his decision about what to do. Because this theory is an abstraction from reality, that additional information is not included; I mention it only to help clarify the role of interests and of a more complex criterion as a guide to action. (The general problem that is an extension of this is discussed in the section titled "Population-Contingent Rationality" in Chapter 33.)

Where there is, in a system of events, an indivisible event to which an actor decides not to allocate resources (based on the criterion stated above), this implies that the resources are allocated among his other interests. Technically the allocation is found by simply renormalizing across the other interests, which are assumed to be interests in divisible goods without externalities, for which interest alone is a sufficient guide to action. (In Chapter 31 that assumption is relaxed when multiple indivisible events are considered simultaneously.)

LIKE INTERESTS IN AN INDIVISIBLE EVENT When interests of two actors in an indivisible event are in the same direction, it is again true that those interests alone are not a sufficient guide to action. For example, John and Steve have an interest in Tom's not continuing the telephone call, but each knows that if the other provides Tom with sufficient resources to get him to end the call, then he himself need not give up resources to do so. Thus each must take into account not only his own interests and resources, but also those of the other. In

---

11. Since the market for control of j does not have the virtues of continuity in such a circumstance because there are only two contending actors, there is the problem of indeterminacy of price that exists in a bilateral monopoly. The event is worth $x_{ji}r_i$ to actor i, which constitutes a minimum for the price, and $x_{jk}r_k$ to actor k, which constitutes a maximum. I have ignored this indeterminacy in calculating the value of j as the maximum under the regime for which v_j is larger, regime a or regime b.

addition, if either John or Steve sees that the other does not have sufficient interest weighted by resources to gain control of the event, and he also does not, he must ask himself whether, if they combined their resources, they could together bring sufficient resources to bear to induce Tom to end the call.

Where there are like interests in an indivisible event, then, the guide to action is even more complex. The actor whose interests in an indivisible event are like those of another will, if he is rational, consider at least three things in devising a guide to action:

1. His own resources and interests in the event
2. The resources and interests of the other actor with interests in the event like his own
3. The resources necessary to gain control of the event

If gaining control of the event involves allocation of more resources than will be allocated by another actor or actors whose interests favor the opposite outcome, then the actor must estimate those interests and resources and, if there is more than one actor with interests opposing his, the likelihood of those interests being combined.

One way of devising a guide to action is to compare the estimates of the values of the resources described in items 1, 2, and 3 above, which can be denoted v_1, v_2, and v_3. Then at least the following inequalities are relevant. Listed to the right of each are the action prescribed for the actor in that case and the expected outcome (a plus sign indicates the outcome he favors).

		Action	Outcome
1.	$v_3 > v_2 + v_1$	No action	−
2.	$v_2 > v_1, v_3$	No action (free ride on other's action)	+
3.	$v_1 > v_3, v_2$	Apply resources up to v_1 to gain control	+
4.	$v_2 + v_1 > v_3 > v_2, v_1$	Combine resources with the other up to v_1	+

As the various possibilities indicate, the appropriate guide to action is not at all straightforward in such a situation. Only with pattern 1 is there no ambiguity, assuming that interests and resources of the opposition have been estimated correctly. With pattern 2 the actor may decide to free ride, but the other actor may decide to do so also. With pattern 3 the actor decides not to free ride, and the other may also decide to employ resources rather than to free ride. With pattern 4 it is not clear what the contribution of each should be. Furthermore, like the difference between a single-play prisoner's dilemma and an iterated prisoner's dilemma, the appropriate action will depend on whether the event occurs only one time or will recur in the future.

In Chapter 33 the question is raised concerning what meaning rationality can have in such a circumstance, when an actor is in an environment where the outcome depends in a nonadditive way on the combination of his and others' actions. Here I want only to indicate that in these complex situations interest can no longer be the sole guide to action. Interest is one of the elements of such a guide, but the optimal action for actor i depends on what the other actor(s) will do; and as long as the outcomes for the other(s) are contingent on what actor i does, what is optimal for the other(s) depends on their anticipation of what actor i will do.

The Rationality of Voting and of a Norm to Vote

In Chapter 11 I discussed the way in which the paradox of voting is resolved by assuming that actors transfer to one another rights of control over the act of voting, that is, that they develop a norm which gives others the right to impose sanctions, such as expressing disapproval of a failure to vote. In this section I apply the derivations of this chapter to voting, to show the condition under which a norm to vote is rational.

Let there be n actors in a system in which event i is the action of actor i voting or not voting. There is an event $n + 1$, which is the election outcome. Assume that there are two candidates, and S_1 is the set of n_1 voters favoring outcome A and S_2 is the set of n_2 voters favoring outcome B. Assume also that actor i in set S_1 controls to the extent c_{ij} other events j of interest x_{jk} to other actors k in S_1. These are events outside the election with which he can sanction other actors k in S_1. Each actor i' in set S_2 also controls events j' of interest to other actors k' in S_2, with which he can sanction those actors. These latter assumptions imply that actors associate with, and can sanction, those actors who favor their candidate, but do not associate with, and cannot sanction, those actors who favor the opposing candidate. It is a minor simplification of the system, then, to see it as two independent subsystems consisting of the actors in S_1 and S_2, respectively. This is, of course, some distance from reality because in most democratic systems there is a considerable degree of intermixing among those who favor opposing election outcomes. Yet most persons' associations are strongly biased toward those favoring the outcome they favor. Beginning with distinct subsystems means that they can subsequently be allowed to penetrate one another partially, better reflecting the degree of positive bias in association which exists in real social systems.

Each actor i has an interest against voting, x_{ii}, which is for most a weak interest, imposed by the costs of time and effort the act of voting entails. Each also has an interest, $x_{n+1,i}$, in the election outcome in a direction favoring his candidate.

Consider first the set S_1 of actors favoring outcome A. Each actor in S_1 sees the election outcome (in which he has an interest, $x_{n+1,i}$) as equally dependent on each of the n_1 events which constitute voting or not voting on the part of the n_1 members of S_1. Thus the interest of actor i in actor k's voting is $x_{n+1,i}/n_1$, for all actors k in S_1. (It is also possible to specify an interest against the voting of actors in S_2, but since actor i's power extends only to the members of S_1, this interest is nonimplementable.) Thus each actor i in S_1 has a net interest against his own voting, which is $(x_{ii} - x_{n+1,i}/n_1)$ (and I assume that $x_{ii} > x_{n+1,i}/n_1$), and an interest in favor of each other actor's voting, which is $x_{n+1,i}/n_1$. This allows writing an expression for the value of actor i's vote under regime a, assuming he controls it (and does not vote, because his interest is opposed), and an expression for the value of his vote under regime b, assuming that it is controlled by others (which implies, because they favor his voting, that he votes).

$$v_{ai} = \left(x_{ii} - \frac{1}{n_1} x_{n+1,i}\right) r_{ai} \tag{30.12}$$

$$v_{bi} = \frac{1}{n_1} \sum_{\substack{k=1 \\ k \neq i}}^{n_1} x_{n+1,k} r_{bk} \tag{30.13}$$

Equation 30.12 gives the value of i's not voting, which is concentrated in i himself, and eq. 30.13 gives the value of his voting, which is spread among the other actors k in S_1.

The criterion for the emergence of a norm in favor of voting in S_1 is that v_b must be greater than v_a. This is given by summing v_{ai} and v_{bi} from eqs. 30.12 and 30.13 over all i in S_1:

$$\frac{1}{n_1} \sum_{i=1}^{n_1} \sum_{\substack{k=1 \\ k \neq i}}^{n_1} x_{n+1,k} r_{bk} > \sum_{i=1}^{n_1} \left(x_{ii} - \frac{1}{n_1} x_{n+1,i}\right) r_{ai} \tag{30.14}$$

This can be simplified if the minor differences in i's power under the two regimes are neglected, to give

$$\sum_{i=1}^{n_1} (x_{n+1,i} - x_{ii}) > 0 \tag{30.15}$$

The criterion for the individual is a very simple one. It will be beneficial for him that a norm to vote exists among the members of S_1 if his interest in the election outcome, not merely in his vote's effect on that outcome, is greater than his interest against voting. This is the ith term in the summation on the left-hand side of the above inequality.

If the sum of the interests in the election outcome of all the members of S_1 is greater than the sum of their interests against voting themselves, then a norm is rational. In many circumstances this criterion is certainly met: Nearly everyone has an interest in the election outcome that is greater than his disinclination to vote. Thus in such a case there is a norm among members of S_1 that others have a right to control whether one votes, which translates in practice into the right to express disapproval for not voting.

As with the earlier derivation, this result does not mean that it will be in the interest of all citizens to vote. The relevant terms must be extracted from inequality 30.14 to give a criterion analogous to inequality 30.8. That is, actor i can fail to vote without incurring effective sanctions if the following inequality holds:

$$\frac{1}{n_1} \sum_{k=1}^{n_i} x_{n+1,k} r_k < \left(x_{ii} - \frac{1}{n_1} x_{n+1,i} \right) r_i \tag{30.16}$$

Note that this inequality implies that the interest of other actors, k, in the election is weighted by their power, r_k. This assumes the existence of social capital, as discussed earlier, in order that the full force of r_k can be exercised. If there is not sufficient social capital to allow this, then the left-hand side of eq. 30.16 is reduced.

As indicated before in the discussion of the effect of actors' power in allowing them to escape sanctioning, it may be in actor i's interest to vote even if inequality 30.16 holds, if his voting has an effect on the maintenance of the norm. But those for whom inequality 30.16 holds and who are uninterested in the maintenance of the norm will be nonvoters.

Inequality 30.16 appears to predict, as suggested in an earlier section, that actors with greater power will be less likely to vote. Empirically there is, however, a small positive correlation between social status and voting in modern democracies where voting is not compulsory. That correlation is very likely due to the fact that both interest in the election and social capital are lower among lower-status persons. Thus $x_{n+1,k}/n_1$ and $x_{n+1,i}/n_1$, interest of friends and associates (k) and of self (i) in the election, are lower, and the lower social capital reduces the weight to be applied to $x_{n+1,k}/n_1$ to something less than r_k. The theory would predict that among lower-status persons whose social capital and interest in the election were equal to those of higher-status persons, the rate of voting would be higher than that among the higher-status persons.

The analysis for S_2 is the same as that for S_1. Thus two norms about voting, which appear to be a single norm, would be expected to arise: a norm within S_1 to vote, and a norm within S_2 to vote. (In practice, of course, there is not a single intercommunicating set of actors favoring a particular outcome but relatively distinct sets in each community or subsystem.)

The outcome of the election does not, under these assumptions, depend simply on numbers, that is, on n_1 and n_2. Because interest in the election may be higher in one of the sets, the norm may be stronger in that set. Or because social capital which can be used in sanctioning may be greater in one set than in the other, the turnout at the polls may be greater for that set even if the norms in the two sets are equally strong—simply because the social capital makes the threat of sanctions more effective in that set.

The assumptions stated above may be modified by allowing an interpenetration of the two sets of voters, S_1 and S_2. With the theory as specified here, some differential association is necessary if there is to be a norm to vote. But it should be evident from the above exposition that this differential association need not be full separation of the two sets of voters.

One prediction from this application of the theory is that a norm to vote should become weaker as the political bias of voters' association declines. Not only should the norm to vote decline in strength, but the fraction of citizens voting should decline as well. This weakened norm and lower rate of voting as the political bias of association declines should be greater for the smaller of the two sets of voters (see Coleman, 1964, Chapter 16, for elaboration), so social integration among those with opposing political allegiances should favor the larger party.

Another prediction from this application of the theory is that in those communities where a majority favors outcome A, those favoring outcome A should be more likely to vote (because the norm to vote will be stronger in S_1, the larger set). This phenomenon is well known in politics, where it has been termed breakage favoring the majority in a community (Berelson, Lazarsfeld, and McPhee, 1954).

Finally, for a system in which there is no differential association at all, this application of the theory predicts that there will be no norm to vote, as well as very low levels of voting.

31

Indivisible Events, Corporate Actors, and Collective Decisions

Chapter 30 treated a system in which there is one event with externalities. That chapter indicated how the optimal outcome might be arrived at when social capital is sufficient to overcome the free-rider problem of sanctioning the actor or actors controlling the event that produces externalities. This chapter examines systems in which a number of events have consequences for a number of actors, and there is competition for control of the events. For such a system several questions can usefully be examined:

1. What are the conditions under which it is rational (or efficient) for control of such events to be collectivized, so it is in the hands of a number of members of the system, rather than one?
2. When control of such events is collectivized, that is, rights of control are held collectively, what can be said about the optimal distribution of those rights of control?
3. When rights of control are held collectively, so outcomes of the events are determined by collective decisions, what is the consequence of varying the form of the rights of partial control held by individuals?
4. When rights of control over a class of indivisible events are held collectively, what is the optimal outcome for those events?
5. How can that optimal outcome be realized?

I will begin with a system which has a single event with consequences for many and in which all resources can be used to aid in gaining control of that event. Later in the chapter I will examine systems with more than one indivisible event of this sort. The overall purpose of the chapter is to introduce collective decisions and conflict into the linear system of action, through the introduction of indivisible events in which more than one actor has an interest and over which more than one may come to have partial control.

When Will Control of Events Be Collectivized?

Chapter 30 examined systems of action in which an indivisible event had consequences for more than one actor. In such circumstances the market processes through which actors realize their interests by gaining control of some amount of a divisible good in which they are interested cannot operate, because of the event's indivisibility. Actors can, however, apply their resources to gaining control of the indivisible event.

If an actor already controls the indivisible event, his action with respect to that event to bring about an outcome is governed by incentives that neglect the consequences to others. If he were affected by all the consequences, he might act to bring about a different outcome.[1] Thus action may not be efficient from the perspective of the system as a whole, because it is governed by only a portion of the consequences that it could be expected to bring.

Two separate activities are implied by the phrase "gaining control of an indivisible event." These activities correspond to what Buchanan and Tullock (1962) have called the constitutional stage and the postconstitutional stage. The first activity is bringing about what may be described as the constitutional allocation of rights of control over a class of events. This allocation specifies that the outcomes of a certain class of events are to be decided, for example, by collective decision among a particular set of actors using a particular decision rule (such as a majority vote in which all citizens 18 years of age or older have the right to cast a ballot). The second activity, the postconstitutional stage, consists of gaining control over a particular event within a class for which constitutional allocation has already occurred. This is a collective decision concerning a particular event, the existing constitutional allocation.

The Constitutional Stage

The examination in this section will be limited to a single class of events, as if the constitution dealt with only that single class. A subsequent section will examine the constitutional stage for multiple classes of events.

The constitutional stage can be seen as a component of the solution to the Hobbesian problem of social order. When the actions of each have extensive externalities for the others in a system, the creation of a social contract in which each gives over the rights to control his actions constitutes a solution to the Hobbesian problem. The question arises, however, of just what the conditions are under which the individual actors in a system of action will find it to their interest to give up those rights, forming a corporate actor which holds those rights and exercises them. (There is work in the theory of iterated games on the conditions under which cooperation will emerge among self-interested actors whose actions impose externalities on one another; see Raub and Voss, 1986, for

---

1. The question arises, of course, as to how the consequences to others should be weighted, the issue of interpersonal comparison of utility. As Chapters 29 and 30 show, this question is answered by the distribution of power in the system itself; that is, the weights are generated by the distribution of rights. If the system is fully interconnected, through what I have called social capital, then these external consequences will be taken into consideration appropriately by the actor who controls the indivisible event.

example.) Hobbes's vision of Leviathan, as well as totalitarian regimes in the real world, serves as a reminder that when rights have been collected under the control of a corporate actor, they are not necessarily exercised to the common benefit. Yet that possibility does not invalidate the question; it only complicates the answer.

In Chapter 30 a comparison of one regime, in which a particular action was carried out, with another regime, in which it was not, was used to determine whether the action would or would not be carried out and whether rights to the action should be held by the actor (no norm) or by the set of actors experiencing the externalities (a norm). This merged the two activities, the constitutional stage and the postconstitutional stage, that I want to distinguish here. The class of events under consideration at the constitutional stage is composed of indivisible events with consequences for a number of actors in the system. In the preconstitutional period (a Hobbesian war of each against all or a Rousseauean state of nature), all events are controlled individually, whether they have consequences for only one individual or for more than one.

Suppose that the class of events consists of drawing water from a common well serving a whole community. (See El Hakim, 1972, for application of an earlier version of the linear system of action to such a case in a village in Chad.) If the events are individually controlled, each person determines the amount of water he will draw. If the events are collectively held, the amount is determined collectively and supervised by an agent of the community or, alternatively, controlled by a norm governing how much water each person may take. This example is a good illustration of the close kinship between norms and formal collective decisions. In a case such as this, the choice between a norm and a formal collective decision with an agent of the community as the dispenser of water would probably depend on practical considerations such as the supply of water relative to total needs and the ease with which a person could draw water unnoticed by others, thus violating a norm without being apprehended. (In the case studied by El Hakim, the class of events was collectivized and was governed not by a norm, but by an agent of the community.)

In the period before the constitutional stage, the events are controlled individually, but each event has consequences for all. The question, then, is whether it is rational for the class of events to be collectivized, with control held by the collectivity and exercised via a norm with sanctions or a collective decision with an agent. The class of events under consideration at the constitutional stage may consist, as in this case of drawing water from a well in a village, of individual actions of all members of the system that impose externalities on others. Or it may consist of some single activity for which rights of control are held by one actor or a subset of actors, but which has consequences for many others. I will term it, as in Chapter 30, a class of events, each having a positive or negative outcome.

Definitions are consistent with those given in Chapter 30, except that changes in the definitions of regime a and regime b are necessitated by the existence of positive and negative externalities, or public goods and bads:

$J \equiv$ class of events under consideration, where each event has positive effects for one set of actors and negative effects for others

regime $a \equiv$ regime in which all events in class J have the outcomes favoring the interests of the actor with de facto control (Interests in each event in the class that oppose this outcome are ignored, and those actors' interests are renormalized over other events. In the case of events with negative externalities, or public bads, regime a will consist of positive outcomes on events in class J. In the case of events with positive externalities, or public goods, regime a will consist of negative outcomes on events in class J.)

regime $b \equiv$ regime in which all events in class J have the outcome opposed to the interests of the actor with de facto control (Interests in each event in the class that oppose this outcome are ignored, and those actors' interests are renormalized.)

$A_k \equiv$ set of actors with interests favoring the same outcome of event k in class J as does actor k, who has de facto control of event k

$B_k \equiv$ set of actors with interests opposing the outcome of event k in class J favored by actor k, who has de facto control of event k

$r_{ai} \equiv$ power of actor i under regime a

$r_{bi} \equiv$ power of actor i under regime b

$v_{ajk} \equiv$ value of the outcome of event k (in class J) that is favored by actor k

$v_{aj} \equiv$ the sum of v_{ajk} over all events k in class J

$v_{bjk} \equiv$ value of the outcome of event k (in class J) to which actor k is opposed

$v_{bj} \equiv$ the sum of v_{bjk} over all events k in class J

$v_{jk} \equiv$ value of the outcome of event k (in class J) actually realized

$v_j \equiv$ value of the outcomes realized for all events in class J

In addition, the rights allocation is introduced explicitly:

$\alpha \equiv$ allocation in which rights to control events in the class (class J) are held individually

$\beta \equiv$ allocation in which rights to control events in the class are held collectively by the incorporated collectivity

$\gamma \equiv$ allocation of rights that actually obtains (before the constitutional stage $\gamma = \alpha$; after the constitutional stage γ may equal α or β)

Both power and value depend on the rights allocation, which will be introduced as an argument of r_i and v_j when necessary for clarity. Comparison of v_{aj} and v_{bj} may be carried out with or without actual experience under the particular rights allocation for which they are calculated.

This notation can be used to express the net value, under rights allocation α, of outcomes of events in class J favoring the interests of the actor with de facto control of the action (indexed by k). The net value is positive if

$$\sum_{k \in J} [v_{ajk}(\alpha) - v_{bjk}(\alpha)] > 0 \qquad (31.1)$$

or

$$v_{aj}(\alpha) - v_{bj}(\alpha) > 0 \qquad (31.2)$$

where

$$v_{aj}(\alpha) = \sum_{k \in J} v_{ajk}(\alpha) = \sum_{k \in J} \sum_{i \in A_k} x_{ki} r_{ai}(\alpha)$$

$$v_{bj}(\alpha) = \sum_{k \in J} v_{bjk}(\alpha) = \sum_{k \in J} \sum_{i \in B_k} x_{ki} r_{bi}(\alpha)$$

Suppose that inequality 31.1 is reversed. Then under rights allocation α the outcomes opposing the interests of the actor in de facto control of the action are efficient. This means that the events in class J have sufficiently strong consequences for others, compared to their consequences for the actors controlling them, that those experiencing the externalities will be willing and able to compensate one another to bring control of the action out of the actor's hands and into the hands of those experiencing the externalities. This criterion is reminiscent of John Stuart Mill's statement that "as soon as any part of a person's conduct affects prejudicially the interests of others, society has jurisdiction over it" (1926 [1859], p. 86).

This suggests that greater efficiency may result if rights to the actions of each are held collectively. If rights are transferred to the collectivity, this eliminates the transaction costs involved when the members must provide to one another the resources necessary to induce each of them not to act counter to the interests of others (costs that are incurred under rights allocation α). In many circumstances the most significant of these costs are the costs of organization to overcome free riding, since it is often the case that small externalities are imposed on a large number of actors, with no single negative effect consequential enough to balance the actor's interest in his own action.

Elimination of the transaction costs through transfer of rights to the collectivity does not in itself imply that under that collective rights allocation (β) the value of the outcomes realized will always or more often be greater than the value of the opposing outcomes. Other considerations arise: Collective decisions are notorious for failing to transmit to a reasonable extent individual preferences to the level of the collectivity, as the literature cited in Chapter 15 indicated. There are also serious problems of agency for the implementation of collective decisions. Appropriate incentives for the agent are often difficult to devise, and providing those incentives will impose a cost on the collectivity. In addition, the collective rights allocation (β) may sufficiently shift resources among actors that even though the realized outcomes under that allocation satisfy the criterion of social efficiency under it, they would be further from social efficiency under the individual rights allocation (α) than were the preconstitution outcomes.

Because an evaluation may be carried out not only under rights allocation α but also under rights allocation β, it is possible to go beyond inequality 31.1. At the constitutional stage there are no realized outcomes under rights allocation β to be compared to the realized outcomes under the existing rights allocation, α. Nevertheless, comparison of the values of events in class J under regimes a and b may be carried out for rights allocation β, as it is in inequality 31.2 for rights allocation α:

$$v_{aj}(\beta) - v_{bj}(\beta) > 0 \qquad (31.3)$$

If this inequality holds, it implies that under rights allocation β outcomes favoring the interests of the actor in de facto control of the event are socially efficient.

There are four possible conclusions:

1. If v_{aj} is greater than v_{bj} under both rights allocations, then, independent of any effect of rights allocation on the distribution of power, outcomes favoring the interests of the actor with de facto control are socially efficient. This implies that in this situation the individual rights allocation (α) can be expected to give better outcomes (that is, outcomes favoring actors' interests) than the collective rights allocation (β) will.
2. If v_{bj} is greater than v_{aj} under both allocations, the above conclusion is reversed.
3. If $v_{aj}(\alpha)$ is greater than $v_{bj}(\alpha)$ but $v_{aj}(\beta)$ is less than $v_{bj}(\beta)$, the two different allocations of rights generate sufficiently different distributions of power that it can be expected that the outcomes under individual allocation of rights (α) will be closer than those under collective allocation (β) to social efficiency as evaluated under α, but will not be closer to social efficiency as evaluated under β.
4. If $v_{aj}(\beta)$ is greater than $v_{bj}(\beta)$ but $v_{aj}(\alpha)$ is less than $v_{bj}(\alpha)$, the two different allocations of rights generate different distributions of power such that conclusion 3 is reversed. Ordinarily this will not occur, however, for insofar as there is heterogeneity among actors in the value of the rights being reallocated, collectivization of rights of control over actions redistributes power, overall, away from those actors whose individually held rights were most valuable and toward those actors whose individually held rights were least valuable.

Thus, in practice, prior to actual experience under the two different allocations of rights, there are two possible conclusions (1 and 2) that are unequivocal (that is, independent of the status quo), one (conclusion 3) that depends on the status quo, and one (conclusion 4) that can be disregarded as irrelevant.

There is, however, an amendment that must be made if conclusion 2 is reached, that is, that the collective rights allocation is superior to the individual rights allocation. If the existing rights allocation is α, actors have experience with realized outcomes under this rights allocation. If these realized outcomes are those in regime b for most or all of the events in class J, this means that their value under the individual rights allocation, $v_j(\alpha)$, is at or close to the socially efficient value, $v_{bj}(\alpha)$. In such a case there is no reason to change to a collective rights allocation, β, because the free-rider problems and transaction costs which can inhibit the move to socially efficient outcomes are sufficiently small that those outcomes are already achieved under the individual allocation of rights.

A further statement may also be made about the condition that leads to conclusion 3, in which social efficiency depends on the rights allocation. Because social efficiency must be judged from the perspective of some allocation of rights, the only proper basis for its evaluation is the existing allocation of rights. If any other allocation is used for this evaluation, the distribution of power created by the existing allocation can prevent any reallocation which moves away from social efficiency as evaluated under the existing allocation.

This can be seen by comparing conclusions 2 and 3. If the existing rights allocation is α and comparison of equalities 31.2 and 31.3 leads to conclusion 2, then, even though some of those with greater power might lose power, the evaluation carried out under the existing allocation of rights shows that $v_{bj}(\alpha)$ is greater than $v_{aj}(\alpha)$. Thus the system can be expected to yield better outcomes overall under rights allocation β even when individuals' interests are weighted according to their existing power under α. Furthermore, the result of the evaluation shows that there is sufficient power in favor of the change to bring it about. This is the condition under which a Hobbesian state of nature would be replaced by a social contract. Under this condition actors with individual control over their actions would voluntarily give up those rights to themselves collectively as a corporate actor (although some compensation might be necessary, since each actor need not be better off under β.

On the other hand, if the existing rights allocation is α but v_{bj} is greater than v_{aj} only under rights allocation β (that is, conclusion 3 applies), then, according to the existing distribution of power, the existing rights allocation is better, and those who would gain by a reallocation do not have sufficient power to bring it about.

EXAMPLE 1: CONSTITUTIONAL REALLOCATION   Example 5 in Chapter 30 showed that in the system consisting of Tom, John, and Steve, under a preconstitution allocation of rights in which each boy had rights of control over his own phone calls, the value of a negative outcome for all calls was greater than that of a positive outcome. Table 30.5 shows the values of calls under regime a and regime b to be .131 and .167, respectively. This means that the first criterion for a change in rights allocation from α to β, given by inequality 31.2, is met. It is useful to examine the difference between v_{ajk} and v_{bjk} for each of the three actions separately, to determine whether the interests in each event are opposed to telephone calls.

The general equation is

$$v_{ajk}(\alpha) - v_{bjk}(\alpha) = x_{kk}r_{ak} - \sum_{i \neq k} x_{ki}r_{bi}$$

The values of the outcomes for each actor's calls and the total of these values are

Tom: $v_{aj1}(\alpha) - v_{bj1}(\alpha) = .056 - .067 = -.011$
John: $v_{aj2}(\alpha) - v_{bj2}(\alpha) = .040 - .051 = -.011$
Steve: $v_{aj3}(\alpha) - v_{bj3}(\alpha) = .035 - .048 = -.013$
Total: $v_{aj}(\alpha) - v_{bj}(\alpha) = .131 - .166 = -.035$

This shows that the interests in each of the three actors' phone calls are greater under regime b than under regime a. Thus the interests in each event pass the first criterion for a constitutional allocation that would give rights of control over this class of events to the collectivity; that is, the interests in each favor shifting from rights allocation α to rights allocation β for this class of events.

The second criterion is that of inequality 31.3, a comparison of the two regimes under the provisional postconstitutional rights allocation, β. This can be carried out using values provided in Table 30.7, which shows the value of each event under regimes a and b for a rights allocation in which all rights to all telephone calls are held by the three equally. Values for each of the three events and the total value are

Tom: $v_{aj1}(\beta) - v_{bj1}(\beta) = .054 - .068 = -.014$
John: $v_{aj2}(\beta) - v_{bj2}(\beta) = .040 - .051 = -.011$
Steve: $v_{aj3}(\beta) - v_{bj3}(\beta) = .037 - .048 = -.011$
Total: $v_{aj}(\beta) - v_{bj}(\beta) = .131 - .167 = -.036$

The collective rights allocation makes minor changes in the values of each event, but the overall evaluation of the outcomes is the same. The second criterion for a change in the rights allocation is also met. Thus at the constitutional stage the tests are passed for a change from rights allocation α to rights allocation β.

Regimes with Mixed Outcomes

The comparisons above included only regimes a and b. What about including regimes with mixed outcomes in determining what allocation of rights is most efficient? For the trading-card example with telephone calls, besides regime a (which can be denoted by 111 for all three outcomes positive) and regime b (which can be denoted by 000 for all three outcomes negative), there would be a regime denoted by 100 (Tom calls and the other two do not) and five others, for a total of eight regimes. If one of these regimes were to show the highest value (for simplicity, suppose that this were true under both rights allocations, α and β), this would seem to be justification for a rights allocation consistent with this regime. For example, in the case of the telephone calls, suppose that the regime denoted by 100 does show the highest value. Then why should there not be a rights allocation by which Tom has the right to make calls but for John and Steve the right is collectively held?

There are two answers to this question. The first is that in formal constitutions the rights allocation may differ between event classes, but not within such classes. This is what is meant by the statement "The law is no respecter of persons." If the law is to treat all equally, only rights allocations α and β, individually or collectively held rights over the actions of each person, are permissible.

A second answer is that in some circumstances, especially in informal settings, there is an allocation of rights by which some persons hold effective rights to their actions and others do not. For example, in some settings age brings certain rights or privileges. In premodern Europe, some estates, or classes of persons, held the legal right to carry out certain actions, and other estates did not. Those differences remain, sharply limited, in current legal conditions of children, criminals, military personnel, and others who do not have the full complement of civil rights enjoyed by the ordinary citizen.

One can conceive of a system of differential rights evolving over time in informal settings in such a way as to minimize transaction costs: If person A is powerful enough to nearly always be able to buy back the rights to control his own actions, and person B has so little power that he seldom can do so, there is some rationale for coming to an agreement that person A should have the right but person B should not. The principal argument in favor of such a rights allocation is that it recognizes what is already in existence. The principal argument against it is that it further exacerbates the already existing power differential.

Multiple Classes of Events

In the constitutional stage the question of individual or collective control ordinarily arises for a number of classes of events, not merely for one class. Thus the evaluation described above for class J must be carried out for all classes of events that are under consideration.

The technique of introducing regimes associated with particular combinations of outcomes may be used to discover which combination of outcomes yields the greatest value. The necessary definitions for doing so are as follows:

$t \equiv$ the number of classes of events $1, \ldots, J, \ldots, t$ under consideration for rights allocation

$k \equiv$ the index for the events in class J

$s \equiv$ an overall regime for the system consisting of regime a or b for each class J; represented by a string of ones (for regime a) and zeros (for regime b)

or the decimal representation of the binary number given by the string (For $t = 2$, the set containing class regimes b_1 and a_2 is represented by the binary number 10 or the decimal number 2.)

$s^+ \equiv$ the particular set s that is realized by constitutional choice

$s^* \equiv$ the particular set s that maximizes v_s under the existing rights allocation

$r_{si} \equiv$ the power of actor i under system regime s

$v_{sj}^i \equiv$ value of actor i's interests favoring the regime for event class J that is contained in system regime s

$v_s^i \equiv$ value of actor i's interests favoring the class regimes that are contained in s

$v_{sj} \equiv$ value of class J of events in system regime s

$v_s \equiv$ value of system regime s for all event classes

$\delta_{ski} = 1$,   if actor i's interests favor the outcome of event k in the regime (for class J) that is contained in system regime s

$\delta_{ski} = 0$,   otherwise

Then

$$v_{sj}^i = \sum_{k \in J} \delta_{ski} x_{ki} r_{si} \tag{31.4}$$

$$v_s^i = \sum_{j=1}^{t} v_{sj}^i$$

$$v_{sj} = \sum_{i=1}^{n} v_{sj}^i$$

$$v_s = \sum_{i=1}^{n} v_s^i = \sum_{j=1}^{t} v_{sj} \tag{31.5}$$

Throughout this section the rights allocation is left implicit. For a given class of events J, it is α or β; for the set s, it is γ, which consists of some combination of rights allocations over all classes of events.

Equation 31.5 assumes that there is no interdependence between interests in events in class J and interests in events in class J' (and no interdependence within a class): Each actor's interests in the combined class J and J' events equals the sum of his interest in events of class J and his interest in events of class J'. This does not imply, however, that the value of a given regime (that is, a given set of outcomes) for events in class J' is independent of the prevailing regime for events in class J. The power of actor i may differ with positive and negative outcomes of events in class J, so the value of positive outcomes of events in class J' may be quite different when combined with positive outcomes of events in class J than when combined with negative outcomes of events in class J. This means that v_s is not composed of the sum of the values of the outcomes considered separately. For the case where there are two classes of events, that may mean that $v_0 > v_3 > v_1 > v_2$. This would imply that system regime 3 (consisting of regime a for both class 1 and class 2) has a higher value than system regime 1 or 2 (consisting of regime a for one class combined with regime b for the other), despite the fact that system regime 0 (regime b for both classes) has the highest value of all.

The value of a particular system regime s shows which set of regimes for the classes of events under consideration will dominate in a perfect system with indivisible events, given a particular rights allocation. (Although I have left unspecified the rights allocation under which the system functions, some rights allocation is assumed.)

THE OPTIMAL SYSTEM RIGHTS ALLOCATION   When there is more than one class of events, the definitions given above may be used to state a criterion for an optimal system regime, as a generalization of inequality 31.2. The optimal system regime under rights allocation γ is given by $s^*(\gamma)$, that value of $s(\gamma)$ which maximizes $v_s(\gamma)$.

The system regime $s^*(\gamma)$ consists of a string of zeros and ones for event classes. A one for class J represents regime a for that class of events: the outcomes favored by the interests of those who hold rights to the events under α, the individual rights allocation for class J. A zero for class J represents regime b for that class: the outcomes opposing the interests of those holding rights under α.

Just as the system regime consists of a string of zeros and ones, the rights allocation may also be represented as a string of zeros and ones for event classes. A one for class J represents the individual rights allocation, and a zero represents the collective rights allocation. A system regime $s(\gamma)$ is thus consistent with a particular rights allocation if that allocation has the same string of zeros and ones as the system regime has. The socially efficient system regime $s^*(\gamma)$ under a given rights allocation γ is consistent with a rights allocation γ^* which has the same string of zeros and ones as does that system regime. Applying the criterion given by inequality 31.2 for a single class of events yields γ^* as a provisional constitutional allocation.

If $\gamma^* = \gamma$, then the constitution which replaces rights allocation γ with γ^* makes no change in the rights allocation. Also implied is that $s^*(\gamma^*) = s^*(\gamma)$. The reverse implication does not follow, however. The system regime that is optimal under the preconstitution rights allocation will be optimal under the postconstitution rights allocation if $s^*(\gamma^*) = s^*(\gamma)$, whether or not $\gamma^* = \gamma$. The rights allocation γ^* may be said to be internally consistent, since the socially efficient system regime $s^*(\gamma^*)$ is consistent with it. It also has the property of being consistent with the system regime that is socially efficient under the preconstitution rights allocation, since the preconstitution and postconstitution socially efficient outcomes are the same.

If the equality $s^*(\gamma^*) = s^*(\gamma)$ holds, then the conclusion that can be drawn about the provisional constitutional allocation is equivalent to conclusion 1 or 2 given earlier for the case of a single class of events. Then rights allocation γ^* places rights over each class of events in the hands of those whose interests, weighted according to their power under either rights allocation, γ or γ^*, give highest value for that class. One would expect this rights allocation to give outcomes of events that would be socially efficient under the original rights allocation. If so, then the rights allocation γ^* is stable and is an allocation that is optimal when evaluated under the original rights allocation, γ, given the existing state of information about what outcomes will actually be generated under a given rights allocation. It can be regarded as the optimal constitutional allocation.

It may be, however, that $s^*(\gamma^*)$ is not equal to $s^*(\gamma)$. This is a generalization of the indeterminate conclusions (3 and 4) for a single class of events. In this case further examination is possible. Just as $s^*(\gamma)$ may be used to create a provisional rights allocation, $s^*(\gamma^*)$ may be used to create a new provisional rights allocation, γ^{**}. In this allocation, all those rights allocations that are not α for event classes J in which regime a is contained in $s^*(\gamma^*)$ are changed to α, and all those that are not β for event classes in which regime b is contained in $s^*(\gamma^*)$ are changed to β.

If $s^*(\gamma^{**})$, the efficient set of regimes under γ^{**}, is equal to $s^*(\gamma^*)$, which was used to generate γ^{**}, then γ^{**} is internally consistent. It is a stable rights allocation, subject to experience under γ^{**}. It does not, however, meet the criterion that it is socially efficient under the original rights allocation, γ.

If $s^*(\gamma^{**})$ is not equal to $s^*(\gamma^*)$, but $s^*(\gamma^{**})$ is equal to $s^*(\gamma)$, then the rights allocation γ^{**} does not meet the criterion of internal consistency or the criterion of being socially efficient under the original rights allocation. The rights allocation γ^{***}, however, which is consistent with $s^*(\gamma^{**})$ and thus generated by it, is also consistent with $s^*(\gamma)$, so it constitutes a candidate for satisfying the criterion of social efficiency under γ [subject to the test for internal consistency: whether $s^*(\gamma^{***})$ is equal to $s^*(\gamma^{**})$]. This is the generalization of conclusion 4 for the single class of events.

The question of whether there will be convergence either to a rights allocation that is internally consistent or to some allocation γ' for which $s^*(\gamma')$ is socially efficient under the original rights allocation can only be settled by empirical investigation of the specific case. The possibility of indeterminacy in the case of a single class of events, as noted earlier in conclusions 3 and 4, indicates that neither type of convergence is assured.

There is a further question which applies not only to the case of indeterminacy, as described above, but even to the case in which there is internal consistency: Can there be instability in the outcome? The answer is no, given the assumptions that have been made of a perfect social system under a particular rights allocation. But there is a possible catch to this: An outcome of one or more of the events may constitute a change in the rights allocation. Can this lead to instability?

Under rights allocation β in a system of two events, there will be one ranking of the values of the outcomes. Suppose that it is $v_0 > v_3 > v_1 > v_2$. This ranking leads to outcomes in regime 0. But suppose that a positive outcome for event 2 would change the rights allocation to α. A positive outcome for event 2 is contained in regimes 2 and 3, but not in regimes 1 and 0. Suppose that the ranking of the values under rights allocation α is $v_3 > v_0 > v_2 > v_1$. Can those who favor a positive outcome of event 2 (whose power is strengthened under rights allocation α, quite apart from the impact of the positive outcome of event 2 on their interests) carry out exchanges that will lead regime 3 to be realized rather than regime 0? The answer depends on whether $v_3(\alpha)$ is greater or less than $v_0(\beta)$. If the value of regime 3 under rights allocation α exceeds that of regime 0 under rights allocation β, then those who would benefit under regime 3 could, when under that regime, still benefit after compensating those who prefer regime 0. For at least some of those who would benefit under regime 3, however, their benefits, after others have been compensated, depend on their being under the new rights allocation, α. Thus they may experience a temporary loss while still under rights allocation β, because of the necessity to compensate those who favor regime 0, in order to bring about a positive outcome of event 2. If the change in power due to moving to regime 3 is extraordinarily great, those who favor regime 3 might not have sufficient resources, under rights allocation β, to compensate those who would lose. In that case the system would remain in an inferior state and could not move to a state of higher value, regime 3.

CONSTITUTIONAL AMENDMENT Under a postconstitution allocation of rights (which I will call γ^*), the new basis for evaluating the allocation is the outcomes actually realized under it. Under the original rights allocation, γ, the outcomes realized have a value of $v_{sj}(\gamma)$ for class J of events and $v_s(\gamma)$ for all classes of events; under the postconstitution allocation, they have a value of $v_{sj}(\gamma^*)$ for event class J and $v_s(\gamma^*)$ for all classes of events. This value may of course be different from the value that would be predicted by the system regime s^* which leads to γ^*. If so, there is a new basis for comparison with the original rights allocation. Because there is a set of realized outcomes under both preconstitution and postconstitution rights allocations, it is no longer necessary to compare regimes consisting of combinations of possible outcomes. It is possible to compare the realized outcomes. To do so requires definition of a new quantity:

$v_s(\gamma, \gamma') \equiv$ the value of outcomes of constitutionally relevant events realized under rights allocation γ and evaluated using the power distribution under rights allocation γ'

Then, with γ as the preconstitution rights allocation and γ^* as the postconstitutional rights allocation, the following inequalities are relevant:

$$v_s(\gamma^*, \gamma) > v_s(\gamma, \gamma) \tag{31.6}$$

(The value of the postconstitution outcomes is greater than the value of the preconstitution ones when interests are weighted by preconstitution power.)

$$v_s(\gamma^*, \gamma^*) > v_s(\gamma, \gamma^*) \qquad (31.7)$$

(The value of the postconstitution outcomes is greater than the value of the preconstitution ones when interests are weighted by postconstitution power.)

$$v_s(\gamma^*, \gamma^*) > v_s(\gamma, \gamma) \qquad (31.8)$$

(The value of the postconstitution outcomes, when interests are weighted by postconstitution power, is greater than the value of the preconstitution outcomes, when interests are weighted by preconstitution power.)

If the first two inequalities (31.6 and 31.7) both hold, then the postconstitution outcomes are better than the preconstitution ones according to a criterion that bears a resemblance to that Pareto optimality (although it is of course much weaker). The postconstitution outcomes are better under both the preconstitution and postconstitution power distributions. Colloquially one might say that the postconstitution outcomes are preferred both by those with power before the constitution and by those with power after it.

If neither of those two inequalities holds, and if a constitutional change to γ^* has somehow occurred, then a constitutional amendment (to return to the preconstitution allocation of rights) will be proposed and will be adopted.

If inequality 31.6 holds but 31.7 is reversed, this implies that the existing rights allocation generates outcomes that are worse (given the power distribution under it) than outcomes under the other rights distribution. In principle, this would lead to oscillation between the two rights allocations, a succession of mutually reversing constitutional amendments.

If inequality 31.7 holds but 31.6 is reversed, this implies that from the perspective of the preconstitution rights allocation things are worse after the constitution, although they are better from the perspective of the postconstitution rights allocation. This would not lead to change.

If this were the case, could those who had greater power before the constitution bring about a constitutional amendment, to return the system to its earlier state? Indeed, could a constitutional change to rights allocation γ^* have occurred in the first place? It is here that the third inequality (31.8) becomes relevant. If the actual realized value of the postconstitution outcomes is greater than that of the preconstitution outcomes for the same classes of events, then the new constitution, once in place, is stable, even though it gives less satisfactory outcomes as viewed from the preconstitution position. However, the resources to bring about the new constitution do not exist within the system for those who would benefit by doing so. They can make the change only by borrowing against the future, since their preconstitution power is too little to bring about such a change, as shown by inequality 31.6. The resources borrowed must come from outside the system, because optimal borrowing is already assumed within the system among those who prefer the preconstitution state.

Similarly, if inequality 31.7 holds and 31.6 is reversed, and a constitutional change to rights allocation γ^* does take place, inequality 31.8 is relevant to the question of whether those who prefer the preconstitution state can move the system back to that state. If inequality 31.8 is reversed, there is potential gain to moving back. But this gain can be realized only by borrowing against the future and from the outside.

Finally, another question that must be asked before predicting that a constitutional amendment will occur under specified conditions concerns how rights are allocated over the class of events that bring about the constitutional change. The prediction that a constitutional change will occur from γ^* to γ when inequalities 31.6 and 31.7 are reversed, or when 31.6 and 31.8 are reversed, is based on the assumption that all interests, no matter where they are located in the system, will be transmitted with appropriate weights (the existing power of the actors) to those actors who hold rights of control over the class of events leading to the constitutional change. Yet in any actual system other than those that are very small and densely structured, that assumption is likely not to be correct. For example, the group who met in Philadelphia to frame the U.S. Constitution in 1787 did not include many powerful persons in the new nation who felt that the document created there would be ineffective and that the Articles of Confederation would stand as the constitution of the loosely federated system.

When power, wherever it is located in the system, is not fully transmitted, constitutional change cannot be predicted using the three inequalities discussed here. The outcome will instead depend on the decision rule, as well as on barriers to exchange, as will be discussed in a later section.

A final comment is useful: Although constitutional change is under discussion here, the logic of the analysis applies equally to revolutionary change by force. The rights allocation is equivalent to a power distribution, and comparison of the values of outcomes under rights allocations before and after a constitutional change can just as well be interpreted as comparison of the values of outcomes under distributions of power before and after a revolution. In particular, if the rights allocation is γ but both inequalities 31.7 and 31.8 hold and 31.6 is reversed, then those who prefer revolutionary change do not (since inequality 31.6 is reversed) have the power to bring it about. Only if they can borrow against the future and get aid from outside can they bring the reallocation γ^* into being. By inequality 31.8, however, once the revolution has occurred, and the constitutional allocation is γ^*, it is stable. This shows why aid from outside powers is important to the success of revolutions—even those revolutions that lead to highly stable systems.

EXAMPLE 2: A CHANGE IN INTERESTS LEADING TO REPRIVATIZATION
In the trading-card exchange system, suppose that the boys are a year older. Their interest in girls has increased, relative to their interest in sports cards. This change in interests can be expressed by leaving unchanged in Table 30.7 the interests in cards and the interests against phone calls (which are derivative from

their interests in cards, although I have not shown that via a dependency matrix) and increasing the interests in phone calls to .3 for each. The boys had established a constitution (see Example 1 of this chapter and Table 30.7) by which the rights to make telephone calls are collectively held and each must compensate the others in order to make a call. Because the boys' interest in girls has increased substantially, nearly all the calls that any one of them wants to make, as well as those he receives from girls, are of sufficient importance that he is willing to compensate the others for the delay in trading. But the boys begin to find this compensation cumbersome. Each wonders whether their constitution should be amended to reprivatize telephone calls. This would eliminate the need for continual compensation.

The fact that phone calls now generate compensation (regime a) rather than being deferred until the trading session is over (regime b), as they were a year ago, is sufficient to suggest to the boys that a constitutional amendment to reprivatize calls would be beneficial. Because this is a perfect social system, they have achieved the socially efficient outcomes even under collective control, but the need to compensate one another has introduced inconvenience. In a less perfect social system, where there was impermeability between actors and inconvertibility of resources, the socially efficient outcomes would not be achieved. The boys would feel that what they were getting (an uninterrupted trading session) was not worth what they were missing (telephone conversations with girls), and it would be this feeling of discontent (a feeling that they could better realize their interests) that would lead to the proposal for a constitutional change.

The matrices of interest and control are shown in Table 31.1. In the table are also shown the values of the events under regime a and regime b, with the existing constitutional allocation of rights (that is, collective control, or β). The events of class J (telephone calls) have a value of .230 under regime a and .167 under regime b. By this comparison there should be a reprivatization. Under private control (α) the values of events of class J under regimes a and b are almost the same as they were under the existing constitution. Thus by both tests there should be a constitutional change to rights allocation α, that is, individual rights of control over telephone calls.

The Postconstitutional Stage

Under a given constitutional allocation of rights, the question arises of just what set of outcomes will be realized for the actions within a given class. For the trading-card example with telephone calls, there are three events within the class of telephone calls, and thus eight possible combinations of outcomes, from 111 to 000. There are two ways of evaluating just what combination will have the highest value.

If there is a collective rights allocation (as in Table 30.7) and one of the boys wants to buy back the right to make a telephone call, the appropriate criterion is

Table 31.1 Control, interests, and power in trading-card system, with value of phone calls under two regimes and two rights allocations.

| | CONTROL (C) | | | | | | INTERESTS (X′) | | | | | |
| | Cards | | | Calls by | | | Cards | | | Calls by | | |
	Foot-ball	Base-ball	Basket-ball	Tom	John	Steve	Foot-ball	Base-ball	Basket-ball	Tom	John	Steve
Tom	1	0	0	1	1	1	.6	.3	.1	.3	.1	.1
John	0	1	0	1	1	1	.3	.4	.3	.1	.3	.1
Steve	0	0	1	1	1	1	.3	.2	.5	.1	.1	.3

POWER

	Regime *a*	Regime *b*
Tom	.407	.407
John	.307	.307
Steve	.285	.285

VALUE OF CALLS UNDER RIGHTS ALLOCATION β (above)

	To Tom	To John	To Steve	Sum
Regime *a*	.092	.071	.067	.230
Regime *b*	.049	.058	.060	.167

VALUE OF CALLS UNDER RIGHTS ALLOCATION α (see control matrix in Table 30.5)

	To Tom	To John	To Steve	Sum
Regime *a*	.099	.070	.062	.231
Regime *b*	.050	.058	.059	.167

whether, under this allocation of rights, the value of the event to him is greater than its value to the others. These values are given in Table 30.7, and it is apparent that the value of Tom's call to him is greater than the value of preventing it to the other two, but the reverse is true for John and Steve. Thus, as discussed in Chapter 30, Tom would make his call, compensating the others for doing so, and John and Steve would not make theirs. If rights are held individually for the same case (as in Table 30.5), similar considerations would show that Tom would make his call and that John and Steve would be compensated by the others for not making theirs.

This analysis is based on considering the values of each of these events, taken separately, and is appropriate for the situation in which only one event arises during the period under consideration. If more than one event comes up (for example, all three boys want to make telephone calls), a different kind of analysis, with possibly different outcomes, is necessary. Each actor will find it necessary not merely to use resources (in this case cards) to gain or keep control of a single event, but to use resources for all three events under contest. Thus, for example, under the individual rights allocation, the mixed outcomes 100 would require Tom and Steve to compensate John for not making his call, Tom and John to compensate Steve for not making his, and Tom to resist the offers of John and Steve to compensate him not to make his call. In this case Tom's resources would necessarily be extended over the three events. Would he get his desired outcome on all three (the regime with outcomes 100)? Examining the value of this regime of mixed outcomes shows that the value is .154 under the individual rights allocation, and .158 under the collective rights allocation. In both cases this value is lower than the value for regime *b*, in which none make calls. Thus, if all three events arise, the expected set of outcomes is 000, or no telephone calls, a result that occurs with either allocation of rights.

These initial considerations are merely an extension of the comparisons of values made in the institution-free setting implicit in the examination of norms in Chapter 30. In the postconstitutional stage rights are held collectively for some classes of events; this fact necessitates some form of collective or corporate action.

The postconstitutional stage is the actual exercise of corporately held control through authoritative actions, whether taken by an executive acting as an agent for the collectivity or as a result of collective decisions. There are two questions to be examined. The first concerns activity which is actually part of the constitutional stage but follows the constitutional allocation of rights: How should the corporately held rights be reallocated to best realize the constitutional intent? This reallocation includes establishing decision rules and institutions for each class of events for which rights are held corporately. The second question truly concerns the postconstitutional stage: Just how will decisions be made, given the decision rules and institutions?

Obviously the answer to the first of these questions should be informed by knowledge of the answer to the second. This suggests that the two may fruitfully be examined together, as I will do in this section. To do so, however, requires first addressing briefly what is meant by a term used above, constitutional intent.

Constitutional Intent and Barriers to Exchange

One question that should be asked about constitutional intent is a descriptive one: What was the constitutional intent of the set of framers of a particular constitution? A second question is normative: What would be the appropriate constitutional intent to best meet some criterion? One such criterion is social efficiency under the preconstitution allocation of rights. Another is social efficiency under the postconstitution allocation of rights. (This second criterion is somewhat incestuous, because it and the allocation are determined together.)

I eschew questions about optimal constitutional intent, but make use of two observations concerning existing constitutions in political democracies. The first is that constitutions always impose barriers to exchange which separate political rights and resources (in the form of legislative or executive or citizens' rights to participate in collective decisions) from other resources, particularly those in the private sector of the economy. The second observation is that these barriers are never absolute and always allow some exchange between control of collective decisions and control of other resources, particularly economic resources. Both of these observations raise questions concerning why these phenomena are universal. If constitutional intent is to insulate political power, such as control of legislation, from other resources in the society, why are the barriers everywhere so incomplete? If constitutional intent is to allow the use of other resources in political arenas, why are there barriers at all?

Although I will take constitutional intent as given, I will examine the effects of nonconvertibility, that is, the effects of barriers between rights to control a particular class of events and other resources in society. Under the constitutional rights allocation γ^*, the rights to control all event classes for which the collective rights allocation β is contained in γ^* have come to be collectively held and must be exercised. They may be exercised by an agent of the corporate body or by some set of actors who individually have rights of partial control (for example, as when a vote is taken).

Rights of Control over Corporate Actions

The problem of how to allocate collectively held rights so that outcomes are consistent with constitutional intent is a complex task, and I will address only one aspect of it: the question of how rights of control over corporate action are best partitioned if the total set of rights is 1.0 ($\Sigma c_{ij} = 1.0$). What actors should have control over the class of events, and how should that control be partitioned among them? I will assume that the postconstitution actors are the same as the preconstitution ones and will neglect the fact that new positions may be created for agents of these actors, which amounts to overlooking the creation of new interests that occurs whenever new positions are created (see Chapter 13, and Michels, 1949).

Some new notation is useful for the postconstitutional stage, including a new definition of regimes *a* and *b* for events in class *J*:

regime $a \equiv$ a positive outcome for events in class *J*

regime $b \equiv$ a negative outcome for events in class *J*

$P_k \equiv$ the set of actors whose interests favor a positive outcome for event *k* in class *J*

$N_k \equiv$ the set of actors whose interests favor a negative outcome for event *k* in class *J*

$v_{ajk} \equiv$ the value of a positive outcome on event *k* in class *J*

$v_{bjk} \equiv$ the value of a negative outcome on event *k* in class *J*

The first point to note is that if the system has the properties of a perfect social system, so r_i, the power of actor *i*, is the same when applied at any point in the system, then the only effect of the allocation of rights of control over events of class *J* is the effect on the distribution of power in the system. This effect is relatively minor if event class J covers only a small portion of the things in which actors are interested. If, under the rights allocation γ^*, $v_{aj}(\gamma^*)$ is greater than $v_{bj}(\gamma^*)$, there will be a positive outcome (regime a), whether or not those favoring this outcome have direct control of the class of events. If constitutional intent is to prevent collective decisions on outcomes of events of the class from being shaped by a single dimension of power, it is the allocation of rights, *together with* barriers to convertibility between resources or barriers to exchange between actors, which prevents a single dimension of power (which would be denominated as money) from determining the outcomes of the collective decisions. (One might ask whether it is useful to prevent a single dimension of power from determining the outcomes, but here I simply note that barriers to exchange are necessary if that is the intent.)

One way of discovering how barriers to perfect exchange have their effect is by examining the criterion for a positive outcome of event k in class J, that is, whether v_{ajk} is greater than v_{bjk}. Expanding v_{ajk} in successive stages gives

$$v_{ajk} = \sum_{i \in P_k} x_{ki} r_i$$

$$= \sum_{i \in P_k} x_{ki} \sum_h c_{ih} v_h \qquad (31.9)$$

$$= \sum_{i \in P_k} x_{ki} \sum_h c_{ih} \sum_g x_{hg} r_g \qquad (31.10)$$

Equations 31.9 and 31.10 are equations for a perfect social system. But if barriers, b_{kh}, representing high transaction costs between events k (in class J) and h (as described in Chapter 27) are inserted in the system between events of class J and other events h, then eq. 31.9 becomes

$$v_{ajk} = \sum_{i \in P_k} x_{ki} \sum_h c_{ih} b_{kh} v_h \qquad (31.9')$$

If these barriers are absolute ($b_{kh} = 0$ for all h not in class J), then the outcome would be determined simply by the strength of interests on each side, weighted by the fraction of constitutionally allocated control to each actor, that is, c_{ik}. No other resources would affect the outcome.

The function of interests, to allocate resources r_i among desired goods and events, cannot be carried out here, however, since no exchanges are possible. Thus if x_{ki} is greater than some threshold value, representing the cost to i (in interests forgone) of exercising his fraction of control, c_{ik}, over event k, x_{ki} can be replaced by 1.0. Assuming for the present that all interests in k exceed this threshold, the criterion for the value of k under regime a exceeding that under regime b can be expressed as follows:

$$\sum_{i \in P_k} c_{ik} > \sum_{i \in N_k} c_{ik} \qquad (31.11)$$

This is simply a counting of votes on either side, and the only role of interests is to determine whether actor i's interests favor a positive outcome (he is in P_k) or oppose it (he is in N_k). If the decision rule is a majority rule, the outcome is positive if the highly constrained value expressed in the above inequality is greater on the positive side than on the negative side. If the rule is a qualified majority rule, the constrained value on the positive side must exceed that on the negative side; for example, if the rule calls for a two-thirds majority, the constrained value on the positive side must be twice that on the negative side. This makes it easy to see why a highly asymmetric decision rule is seldom used in systems with highly constraining barriers to convertibility: With a unanimity rule no positive action would be taken as long as there was any interest against the action. As will be evident in later sections, a unanimity rule has no asymmetric effect at all in a perfect social system.

Can it be that as a criterion for the outcome of event k in class J inequality 31.11 is an accurate expression of constitutional intent? It is hardly imaginable that this could be so, since the inequality ignores not only strength of interests but also interests of all actors other than those who have a constitutionally allocated right of partial control (c_{ik}). Thus if the voting body is a legislature, only the legislator's own interests will affect the outcome. If the voting body is the citizenry holding voting rights, interests of children will not affect the outcome. And the barriers to convertibility will prevent the strength of interests from having any effect whatsoever on the outcome. Yet existing formal institutions for collective decisions appear to be reasonably well represented by inequality 31.11. The deficiencies of such a criterion, for which strength of interests plays no role, suggest potential improvements in the institutional forms through which constitutional intent is realized.

With respect to eq. 31.9′ it is possible to imagine barriers that are not absolute or that differ for different pairs of resources. For example, consider a system where $b_{kh} = 0$ for all events h outside class J, and there are no barriers for events k' within class J for which $b_{kk'} = 1.0$. This is a system in which vote trading is freely allowed for decisions on events of class J. One might expect that this would achieve outcomes closer to the constitutional intent: Through exchange actors would concentrate their votes on those events within class J in which their interests were strongest. As has been repeatedly demonstrated in the literature on social choice and as will be discussed later in this chapter, the indivisibility of the events in question largely destroys this potential benefit, by creating instability in the outcomes in the form of cycles that do not converge to a stable state.

When the barriers are lowered for other resources, that is, divisible goods without extensive externalities, then eq. 31.9′ moves in the direction of a perfect system, toward eq. 31.9. For example, within the political arena there are resources which do not have the extremely destabilizing properties of collective decisions: party support for reelection, financial and otherwise, committee memberships and chairmanships, and many others. Nevertheless, the barriers between political resources and resources in the private economy are substantial. I have examined the presumptive intent of establishing these barriers elsewhere (Coleman, 1986a, Chapter 10).

It is useful to examine another kind of barrier, barriers to free exchange between actors. The following modification of eq. 31.10 shows how such barriers operate:

$$v_{ajk} = \sum_{i \in P_k} x_{ki} \sum_h c_{ih} b_{kh} \sum_g x_{hg} a_{ig} r_g \qquad (31.10')$$

Equation 31.10' shows the value of a positive outcome of event k in class J when there is not only lack of convertibility between event k and resource h, but also barriers to exchange between actors i, who have direct control over event k or over other events with which it has convertibility, and other actors g. These barriers between actors, a_{ig}, appear to be infrequently imposed by constitutional intent (much more frequently are due to lacunae in social structure). Nevertheless, there are circumstances in which there are explicit barriers. When a decision-making body is closeted, or shut off from the outside, as is probably most frequently found with juries, this is usually intended to prevent any kind of exchange with actors outside that body. The principal source of low values of a_{ig}, however, lies in the lack of social capital linking actors i and g. This can result in attenuations and distortions, which can operate to differing degrees for those favoring positive and negative outcomes, and thus distort the outcome. The question that arises, then, if the constitutionally intended barriers to convertibility, b_{kh}, are temporarily neglected and only the unintended barriers, a_{ig}, are considered, is how to ensure that the amount of control actor i exercises over event k is proportional to $x_{ki} r_{ai}$ if he favors a positive outcome and to $x_{ki} r_{bi}$ if he favors a negative outcome. Since r_{ai} is ordinarily approximately equal to r_{bi}, the criterion becomes that control should be proportional to $x_{ki} r_i$.

One way of ensuring that control exercised by actor i over an event is proportional to $x_{ki} r_i$ is not to depend on exchanges through the social structure, but to establish rights of control over k proportion to $x_{ki} r_i$. One can state the following proposition: Social efficiency will be realized for the events of class J if the corporate body's rights of control over events in class J are allocated to actors i such that

$$c'_{ij} = \frac{x_{ji} r_i}{\sum_{k=1}^{n} x_{jk} r_k} \qquad (31.12)$$

Allocating control according to eq. 31.12 implies, crudely, putting control of the class of events in the hands of those most interested in the events. (This does not imply, of course, that when interests in one direction are concentrated among a few actors who have strong interests and those in the other direction are dispersed among many actors who have weak interests, social efficiency will occur when control is placed in the hands of those with strong interests. Nor does it even imply that when control in an imperfect social system is placed precisely according to eq. 31.12, social efficiency will result. The asymmetry of concentrated and dispersed interests is a classic and interesting problem on which the theory of this book can shed some new light. I will address it in the next section.)

Note that where interests are not opposed, eq. 31.12 is simply the equation for c_{ij}^*, equilibrium control of an event j by i (see eq. 25.11), since $v_j = \Sigma x_{jk} r_k$. In the present case, however, where interests are opposed, $v_j = \max(v_{aj}, v_{bj})$; that is, v_j includes only the interests on the more powerful side. For a particular event k in class J,

$$c'_j = \sum_{i \in P_k} c'_{ij} = \frac{\displaystyle\sum_{i \in P_k} x_{ji} r_i}{\displaystyle\sum_{i \in P_k} x_{ji} r_i + \sum_{i \in N_k} x_{ji} r_i} \qquad (31.12')$$

Under the condition that each actor's interest in event k in class J is proportional to (although it need not be in the same direction as) his interest in the class J to which k belongs, then $x_{ki} = x_{ji}$, and eq. 31.12' becomes

$$c'_j = \sum_{i \in P_k} c'_{ij} = \frac{v_{ajk}}{v_{ajk} + v_{bjk}} \qquad (31.12'')$$

If c'_{ij} is thought of as the fraction held by i of the total votes on decisions on events in class J, the left-hand side of eq. 31.12'' shows the fraction of votes cast in favor of a positive outcome for event k. That is, the fraction of votes in favor of a positive outcome for event k equals the value of a positive outcome divided by the sum of the value of a positive outcome and the value of a negative outcome. If a majority decision rule is used for a collective decision, this implies that there will be a positive outcome if the value of that outcome is greater than the value of a negative outcome, and a negative outcome otherwise.

This result appears to provide a justification for the use of a majority decision rule by a collectivity. Appearances are misleading, however. A majority rule ordinarily specifies that each voter counts equally, but here the majority is a majority of votes weighted by both interest in the class of events and power in the system. This result also raises a question about decision rules other than a majority rule, where more (or, less frequently, less) than a majority is required for a positive outcome. Under what conditions are such nonmajority decision rules socially efficient? I will return to this question later in this chapter.

Is there any evidence in social institutions that control over collective decisions is allocated in the way the theory indicates it should be? The answer is that there are many cases in which control is allocated roughly as the theory indicates, but also some cases in which control is allocated quite differently.

Perhaps the strongest evidence in support of the theory can be found in the practice of federalism in democratic systems. The reason such societies have such a large number of subgovernments, with differing and sometimes overlapping jurisdictions, appears to lie in the direction specified by the theory. For example, in the New York City metropolitan area, approximately 1,400 govern-ments (that is, public corporate bodies with rights of control over certain events) can be found (Wood, 1961). The theory that best explains why these exist, rather than one large governing body for the entire area, is fiscal federalism (see Breton and Scott, 1978). That theory is based on roughly the principle developed here: that social efficiency results when the decisions of a corporate body are made by the set of actors having interests in events that are under control of that corpo-rate body. This implies that there will be not only different bodies with control over events in different geographic areas, but different bodies with control over different classes of events: schools controlled by one set of bodies, sanitation by a different (possibly overlapping) set, port authority by another, water systems by another, and so on. The theory of this book goes beyond fiscal federalism, however, in its predictions (or, viewed normatively, in its prescription for social efficiency). It specifies that control will be weighted according to the product of the magnitude of an actor's interest in the class of events (x_{ji}) and his power in the system (r_i).

There are, however, many cases where rights of control are allocated in ways that are wholly out of accord with predictions based on this theory. In the examination of barriers to convertibility and to exchange between actors earlier in this section, some types of allocations were shown to be out of accord with the theory. The theory predicts that such a structure of control will engender serious problems of several sorts: Because interested parties have no rights of control over decisions, they will attempt to use their power to affect the outcomes of the decisions via informal or illegal channels (for example, bribery of inspectors). Because control over a decision is held in part by actors other than those inter-ested in it, some decision outcomes that are realized will be dominated, that is, will be inferior to another outcome for all interested parties. When that is the case, the interested parties will be expected to collude to evade the outcome, to substitute for it an outcome which dominates it. Finally, the interested parties without control of the decisions will attempt to exercise control over other outcomes that could negate the ones over which they lack control.

The Asymmetry between Concentrated and Dispersed Interests

A classic problem in political theory is that which arises when there is opposition of two sets of interests that are distributed very differently: very strong interests held by a few actors versus very weak interests held by many. In modern society the specialization of economic production makes this a common situation; there are often a few producers of a good or service and a large number of consumers. This occurs in manufacturing production, where, for example, automobile manufacturers are producers and car owners are consumers, as well as in other disparate areas: In medicine, hospitals and health professionals are the produc-ers and the general population comprises the consumers; in defense, defense contractors are the producers, and the general population comprises not pre-cisely the consumers but the intended beneficiaries; in education, teachers and school administrators are the producers, and children and parents are the consumers.[2] Thus, in the following exposition, I will sometimes refer to the concentrated interests as producers' interests and the dispersed interests as consumers' interests.

Many of the decisions that take place in such an asymmetric structure are not collective decisions, but individual ones made in the context of a market: Each actor has rights over his own action. Some of the matters to be treated in this section hold for outcomes of those decisions as well as for outcomes of collective decisions. I will consider explicitly, however, only collective decisions involving concentrated and dispersed interests, which are embodied in real systems in legislative decisions and decisions of regulatory agencies covering a particular industry, for example.

The theory presented in this chapter implies that social efficiency will be achieved when the rights of control over decisions involving concentrated and dispersed interests are held in part by producers and in part by consumers. Because these are two sides of the same market, the theory would specify that the total weight of interests on each of the sides should be the same. This follows from the fact that the value exchanged in the economic transactions in that market is equal to $\Sigma_{i \in P_j} x_{ji} r_i$, where P_j is the set of all consumers in the market, r_i is consumer i's wealth, and $x_{ji} r_i$ is the value of i's purchases in the market. That value is also the value of the goods, j, provided by the producers. Thus if the resources employed in the transactions are to be taken as the weights to be applied to interests, the two sides should have equal weights of interests. If there were a board with rights of control over the decisions, it should include exactly one consumer's representative for each producer's representative. If instead votes were allocated among all participants in the market, each producer and each consumer should have a number of votes proportional to the amount of money received or spent in the market, and the total number of votes held by producers should equal the number held by consumers.

If there were such a board or such an allocation of votes, two activities might be expected to occur. The first would be the use of votes to express one's interests, and the second would be attempts by actors on each side to use their control over other events to gain control of some of the votes held by actors on the other side of the market. As an example of the first activity, if there were a board of the sort described, and there were only the two sets of interests and a number of issues (events) within the event class constituting the board's jurisdiction, there would be trading of votes between the two sides, each giving up rights of control over issues that were of lesser interest to it in return for rights of control over those of greater interest. If regime a (positive outcome) is arbitrarily defined as expressing consumers' interests in events in class J, and regime b (negative outcome) is defined as expressing producers' interests in the same events, then the consumers will tend to gain control of those events h for which

---

2. There are, of course, chains of production in which intermediate consumers (or in some cases final consumers) are more concentrated than producers. Agriculture is an example; food-processing firms are more concentrated than farmers.

v_{ajh} is greater than v_{bjh}, and producers will tend to gain control of those events k for which v_{ajk} is less than v_{bjk}.

I say "tend to gain control," because the structure is a bilateral monopoly, like that examined in Chapter 25. As the examples in that chapter illustrate, the outcome will depend on various factors. The competitive equilibrium can be found as follows: Suppose that there are m_j issues (events). Since for every issue the two interest blocs on the board begin with equal numbers of votes, power in the system is equal. Thus the trading of votes will be such that if the m_j events are put in order of decreasing difference $\Sigma_{i \in P_j} x_{ji} r_i - \Sigma_{i \in N_j} x_{ji} r_i$, that will be the order of decreasing difference $v_{ajk} - v_{bjk}$. If votes are exchanged between the two blocs at their value to the bloc for which they are of less value, equilibrium will occur with event k^* being the last event controlled by consumers, where k^* is that value of h which minimizes θ_h, and θ_h is defined as follows:

$$\theta_h = \left| \sum_{k=1}^{h} v_{bjk} - \sum_{k=h+1}^{m_j} v_{ajk} \right| \tag{31.13}$$

The total value in the left-hand summation is the value given up by producers in the vote trading, and the total value in the right-hand summation is the value given up by consumers. The above treatment fits the structure of collective bargaining in the United States since the National Labor Relations Act of 1936 reallocated rights over the class of events covered by the employment contract; equal rights were given to the firm and, corporately in the form of the legally recognized bargaining agent, to the workers. The theory would predict that the outcome would be such that the value given up by workers equals the value given up by employers, over all issues covered in the negotiations, and that the issues given up by each side would be those on which the value difference was greatest, as in the above treatment.[3]

The foregoing analysis is subject to two limitations:

1. It concerns only the use of votes to express one's interests. It does not consider use of other resources which are part of each actor's total power, r_i.

2. It does not treat concentrated and dispersed interests differently but assumes that all interests that are alike are able to be combined. Thus, in effect, it treats the system as a two-actor system.

The first of these limitations has been discussed in the earlier section on constitutional intent and barriers to exchange. The second is discussed below.

DISPERSAL AND CONCENTRATION OF INTERESTS   Final control of an event over which rights of control have been transferred to a corporate actor

---

3. This assumes that there is a well-defined set of issues at the start of negotiations. How that set of issues, the agenda, is established, is a matter I will not treat here, despite its importance (see, for example, Plott and Levine, 1978).

may be distorted in two ways by the concentration of interests favoring one outcome among a few actors and the dispersal of interests favoring the other outcome among many actors. One of these arises when the reallocation of collectively held rights takes the form of votes giving equal rights of control (that is, equal votes) to all actors who meet certain qualifications. This will tend to shift rights of control away from strong concentrated interests toward weak dispersed interests. Thus, if collective decisions are made on events within a class, and no resources other than the votes are used to gain control of an event, positive and negative votes will be in approximate proportion to the numbers of actors with positive and negative interests in the event, respectively—not in approximate proportion to the amount of interest on each side. This will bias the outcome against the concentrated interests (known in U.S. politics as special interests) and in favor of the dispersed interests (known as the general interest).

Bias in the opposite direction has its source in the losses involved in combining small amounts of resources from each of many actors that reflect their levels of interest in a class of events. A major component of this source of bias is the free-rider problem that exists when many actors have similar interests. Even if there were no free-rider problem, there would be organizational costs associated with concentrating the resources. In addition, the fact that an actor has limited attention means that weak interests may never exert sufficiently strong demands to gain the actor's attention.

For all these reasons (the free-rider problem is perhaps the most important), dispersed interests are less likely to mobilize resources reflecting those interests, which in the theory are given merely by summing over actors their interests multiplied by their power: $\Sigma\, x_{ji} r_i$. The summation ignores the losses involved in combining resources from different actors. Thus the model does not reflect the bias against dispersed interests. The bias favoring dispersed interests, however, is directly reflected in the theory by the allocation of rights of control over the collective decision to members of the collectivity.

It is useful to attempt to locate where the theory fails to mirror reality by ignoring the losses involved in combining resources. Consider the simplest case: One actor favors one outcome of an indivisible event, and two other actors favor the opposite outcome. For Tom's phone call of the first example in Chapter 30, Tom favored making the call and John and Steve were opposed to his making the call. The value of the event under regime a is $x_{41} r_{a1}$, which in that case was .070. The value under regime b is formed from the sum $x_{42} r_{b2} + x_{43} r_{b3}$, which was .052. As was pointed out, this sum is made up of .029 from John and .023 from Steve. What social assumptions are implicit in this summation but often not realized in reality? This question was dealt with in Chapter 30 in the discussion of the second-order free-rider problem, although the context of collective decisions is somewhat different from that of norm enforcement. The social assumptions are simply that there are no barriers between pairs of resources or between pairs of actors of the sort expressed in eqs. 31.9' and 31.10'. Thus nonconvertibility of resources and social-structural barriers (often due to the absence of social capital) which depress b_{kh} and a_{ig} toward zero bring about this power asymmetry between concentrated and dispersed interests.

Social Choice by Various Decision Rules

The preceding analysis in this chapter and that in Chapter 30 provide tools for examining some institutions of social choice. By social choice I mean decisions that are made by some body in which rights to control the outcomes are partitioned among more than one actor. This is the rights allocation β over a class or classes of events, by which rights to control the outcomes of the events are vested in the collectivity as a corporate actor. The decisions are then made by a body to which the rights have been delegated and among whose members they have been partitioned in some way. The most common means of partitioning the rights other than the right to establish the agenda is through endowing each member of the body with votes. Then the outcomes of the events are decided by casting of votes followed by application of a decision rule to the aggregate vote count.

In this section I will denote the rights allocation by γ, that is, whatever allocation exists in the postconstitutional stage. This will in general mean that rights over some classes of indivisible events are collectively held (rights allocation β) and rights over other classes of indivisible events are individually held (rights allocation α). For the classes of events under rights allocation β, outcomes are decided by an agent of the corporate actor, a decision-making body. I will analyze several widely used decision rules: consensus, simple majority, qualified majority (where some fraction greater than half is specified), unanimity, and weighted voting (as in shareholder voting).

It is important to recognize that in a perfect social system the decision rule used for social choice does not matter, except as the allocation of rights over the particular event class affects the distribution of power in the system as a whole. For a single class of events among many, this effect is small (although it may be large if replicated over many event classes, so the system may be described as democratic or oligarchic or dictatorial). But if only a single class of events among many is considered, so power is unaffected by the rights allocation of the decision rule for that class of events, the outcomes of those events are nearly unaffected by the decision rule in a perfect social system. Control of the decision may be in the hands of one actor, or a few, or many; the outcomes will be the same. If control is in the hands of many, the outcome will be unaffected by the number required for a positive outcome. No asymmetry between positive outcomes (taking action) and negative outcomes (not taking action) will be introduced by an asymmetric decision rule, even an extreme one such as each member of the collectivity having the right to commit it to one action in the event class or each having a veto. All this is another way of saying that in a perfect social system the socially efficient outcome does not depend on the decision rule and that it will be reached.

Obviously in real systems the outcome does depend on the decision rule used, a fact which justifies the attention paid to the decision rule. Nevertheless, because the outcome also depends on the amount and kind of imperfections in the social system, attention should be directed not only toward arriving at a tolerably satisfactory decision rule (none of which are very satisfactory in imperfect social systems, and all of which are satisfactory in perfect systems), but also toward eliminating the system's imperfections. Thus the examination of decision rules in this section will focus on the joint effect of the decision rule and imperfections in the system on outcomes.

Consensus

In Chapter 14 I discussed some properties of a rule which specifies (formally or informally) that decisions are to be made by consensus. One fact about such rules is that they are ordinarily used only in small decision-making bodies. They are especially often found in bodies with dense relations among members, such as communes or small work groups. Groups of this sort probably come as close as any to being the kind of densely related collectivity that is assumed in a perfect social system. Thus the analyses above, which are based on such a system, should be especially applicable to the settings in which consensus rules are found. I will consider those settings to be collectivities in which there are no barriers for pairs of actors or for pairs of resources, conditions that define a perfect social system.

In an informal setting without established institutions, there should evolve procedures which facilitate social efficiency, that is, procedures such that the value of the alternative chosen is greater than that of the alternative rejected. In the notation of this chapter, this means that when a decision is made on a class of events J, $v_j(\gamma) = \max[v_{bj}(\gamma), v_{aj}(\gamma)]$, and when decisions are made on all events considered together, the regime that is actually realized, s^+, is such as to maximize $v_s(\gamma)$ over all regimes for all classes of events.[4]

Does a consensus decision rule have properties which make it particularly likely to result in the socially efficient outcome? I believe so. A consensus decision rule may be defined by two properties:

1. There is no explicit voting procedure.
2. No outcome is chosen until there is general agreement, or consensus, after a discussion. This is ordinarily not the same as unanimity, for ordinarily no explicit polling is done, and agreement is assumed when no one objects to the proposed outcome.

---

4. Although I do not consider explicitly modifications of, or amendments to, proposals during the deliberations of decision-making bodies, a set of events considered together can be regarded as corresponding to a single complex decision of this sort, with each proposed modification as one of the events in the total set of events. Regarded in this way, a regime consists of a particular combination of outcomes of proposed modifications (accepted or rejected) and thus as one of the 2^m possible regimes which may be the result of the deliberations (where m is the number of proposed modifications).

A consensus decision rule may be seen as one in which implicit weights are associated with actors, taking into account both their differential power and their differential interests. The differential power is implicitly understood by members of the collectivity, and the strength of interests is elicited in the discussion. (When the decision has more than one component, so there are more than two regimes, consisting of different combinations of outcomes for the different components, the discussion also allows comparison of the various regimes.) The result is that, as discussion proceeds, each of the members of the collectivity learns the total power that each other member is willing and able to bring to bear in favor of each regime: The power actor i has to support regime s is $\Sigma_j \delta_{sji} x_{ji} r_{si}$, that is, his interest in all the outcomes he favors that are included in that regime, weighted by his power in that regime. After the discussion, when all the regimes have been examined and all the interests elicited, each member has an estimate of $v_s(\gamma)$ for each regime s. Consensus is achieved when each member has the same perception of power and interests; that is, the estimates of $v_s(\gamma)$ by different members are approximately the same. When this is so, all will select the same s, which is the socially efficient regime, s^*. Each will realize that the power-weighted interests that could be brought to bear in favor of this set of outcomes is sufficient to defeat all other sets, so there is no basis for disagreement—despite the fact that the interests of some, perhaps even a majority, favor a different regime, s'.

Other commonly used decision rules differ in several respects from consensus. Each actor is given one or more votes, which he can cast in favor of a particular regime. The regime chosen will depend, based on the decision rule in effect, on the aggregate number of votes cast for each regime. The votes that are allocated can be viewed as fractions of control over the decision, if they are divided by the total number of votes necessary to control the outcome.

Decision rules differ not only in the transformation by which the votes cast are made into a collective decision, but also in other procedural aspects. One difference among rules is the extent of discussion permitted before votes are cast. Another is the degree of separation between various issues which are to be decided by the collectivity. If there is no discussion prior to the vote, neither an actor's intensity of interest nor his power will serve as a weight. If there is extended discussion, as with a consensus rule, and if the system is a perfect social system, power and intensity of interest will serve as weights. In the extreme case each actor will discover the regime with highest value, s^*, and will vote for that outcome whatever his personal preferences, recognizing that it is backed by enough power to defeat any other. Short of this extreme, when the system is less than perfect (and particularly when there are barriers to exchange between the events being decided on and other resources in the system), any decision rule other than consensus will introduce weights which distort the outcome, giving a realized regime, s^+, which may have a lower value than the socially efficient regime.

Thus a decision rule other than consensus can be thought of as introducing a *priori* weights which determine each actor's fraction of control over the outcome, independent of that actor's interest in the event and power in the system. These weights are most often 1 and 0; a vote has a weight of 1 for all those with the right to vote and 0 for all others. These weights, however, do not correspond to each actor's power in the collectivity, r_i, or his interest in the event, x_{ji}. Thus a collective decision arrived at using weights other than r_i may give an outcome other than the maximally efficient one. That is, the outcome chosen, s^+, may not be s^*, the outcome which maximizes $v_s(\gamma)$. What does this mean for the collectivity? Loosely, it can be said that the outcome will not have the full weight of the collectivity behind it. Its implementation will be weaker than would that of outcome s^*. In addition, because there are resources not reflected in the weights, there is the possibility that some actors attempt to overturn outcome s^+, through use of resources not reflected in the weights by which it was arrived at. If s^+ is overturned in favor of s', then s' may also be overturned, because still other resources may be used to bring about another outcome. Cycling among different outcomes may occur, as different actors bring additional resources into the contest, to supplement the weights the decision rule has given them.[5]

In the small, close-knit, undifferentiated collectivities in which consensus rules are most often used, these additional resources (the difference between each actor's power and the amount of control the actor was able to exercise over the decision) are immediately and directly available to overturn the outcome. If the weights used are actors' power, r_i, the outcome is given by $s^+ = s^* = s$ which maximizes $v_s(\gamma)$. If the weights used are $w_i \neq r_i$, and if no resources outside the set of events under consideration are used in negotiations, so w_i constitutes actor i's effective power to determine the outcome, the outcome is given by

$$s^+ = s \text{ which maximizes } \sum_{j}^{m} \sum_{i}^{n} \delta_{sji} x_{ji} w_i \qquad (31.14)$$

The value (power) that is available to overturn outcome s^+ in favor of s^* is $v_{s^*}(\gamma) - v_{s^+}(\gamma)$. The actors who prefer outcome s^* to s^+ are those whose support for regime s^* is greater than their support for regime s^+, where support for a regime is the sum of the actor's interests in outcomes contained in that regime. Formally, the actors who favor regime s^* over regime s^+ are all those actors for whom this inequality holds:

$$\sum_{j} \delta_{s^*ji} x_{ji} > \sum_{j} \delta_{s^+ji} x_{ji} \qquad (31.15)$$

The resources that any such actor will be willing to devote to overturning the outcome are given by the difference between the two sides of inequality 31.15,

5. A special case of cycling occurs when the other resources are votes on other issues by the same decision-making body and the decision rule is a majority rule. There is an extensive literature on cycling, which cannot exist with a consensus decision rule. Much of this literature may be found in the journal *Public Choice*.

multiplied by r_i. (This neglects differences in r_{si} under the two regimes, s^* and s^+. As long as neither of the two regimes will lead to a reallocation of rights, and most interests of actors are in resources other than the m events covered by this social choice, $r_{si} \approx r_i$ for all s.) By definition, this difference will be positive for those actors who prefer regime s^* to regime s^+, and negative for those actors who prefer regime s^+ to regime s^*. And because $v_{s^*}(\gamma)$ is greater than $v_{s^+}(\gamma)$, the sum of that value over all actors who prefer s^* is greater than its sum over all actors who prefer s^+. The difference between the two sums is simply $v_{s^*}(\gamma) - v_{s^+}(\gamma)$.

If the *number* of actors favoring s^+ is greater than the number of actors favoring s^* despite the fact that $v_{s^*}(\gamma)$ is greater than $v_{s^+}(\gamma)$, then either the interests of those favoring s^+ in those outcomes contained in s^+ but not in s^* are weaker than the analogous interests of those favoring s^*, or their power in the system is less, or some combination of the two. Whatever the source of the potential weakness of those favoring s^+, if the outcome were to be decided by their numerical superiority, it would be vulnerable to those favoring s^* [as well as to those favoring any other regime s for which $v_s(\gamma) > v_{s^+}(\gamma)$].

For this fundamental reason any weighting other than that using r_i in a closely knit undifferentiated collectivity will give outcomes that are not more stable or more implementable than outcomes for which r_i are used, and under some conditions will give outcomes that are unstable and less implementable. A consensus decision rule in such a collectivity uses weights r_i, for these are the weights automatically applied by members of such collectivities to each others' preferences.

As is evident from the above, a majority rule is socially inferior to a consensus rule, but what about a unanimity rule? With a unanimity rule each actor i has a vote, and unanimity is required for a positive outcome. The first question that arises is whether there is any operational difference between a unanimity rule and a consensus rule.

With a consensus rule no action is taken until a consensus is reached. The consensus implies that s^* has been found.[6] Until then, there is virtual confrontation between pairs of regimes, s and s', until one regime, s^*, is found which has a higher value than any of the others brought up for consideration. Then, because $v_{s^*} = \max_s[v_s(\gamma)]$, those who prefer another outcome do not object to s^* because they know that greater weight could be brought to bear in its favor than for any other outcome which had been considered. This appears no different from an explicit unanimity rule, because no decision results until all agree on the regime to be chosen. According to one rationale, however, there is a difference. With a consensus rule no additional rights are allocated for making decisions on the set of events under consideration. With a unanimity rule, however, explicit rights

6. It is interesting to note that in communes where a consensus decision rule is used, something like this conception is apparent in the language the members use to describe the process of arriving at a decision. They speak of "searching for the right decision" and "finding the right decision," not of persuading or influencing one another.

are allocated; each actor is given a weight of 1 for the events under consideration by the decision-making body.

The explicit allocation of rights given by the unanimity rule over the events in question makes more egalitarian, at least in principle, the power distribution among members of the decision-making body. It gives each member $1/n$ of the control over a set of events in which members are interested, where that interest is reflected in $v_{s*}(\gamma)$. Thus the power of each actor is modified, to become

$$r_i' = \frac{r_i + v_{s'}(\gamma)/n}{1 + v_{s'}(\gamma)}$$

If this modification has much effect on the distribution of power, use of the unanimity rule may give outcomes that are different from those achieved with the consensus rule. When the unanimity rule is used, there is a new definition of $s*$ because the rights allocation has changed from γ to γ'. The new $s*$ may not include the same outcomes as did $s*$ under γ. It will, however, be the regime achieved with the unanimity rule.

In practice, the terms "unanimity" and "consensus" are often used interchangeably for decision making within small, close-knit, undifferentiated groups. With such usage the difference described above would of course not appear. In a collectivity of that sort, however, if there were an explicit announcement, accepted by consensus of the group, that henceforth all decisions of a particular type would be voted on and no action would be taken until the vote was unanimous, then outcomes would shift in an egalitarian direction. The way this would occur, according to the model, is that some persons who had little power in the group otherwise would assert their newly acquired veto rights, and thus outcomes would have to move in a direction they favored, with the amount of movement depending on the amount of rights acquired, which depends in turn on the importance of the events under consideration relative to other events and goods internal to the system.

The potential instability of outcome s^+, which is arrived at through a decision process in which interests are not weighted by r_i (or in which there is a vote in which not even the magnitude of interests plays a role), decreases as the system moves further away from a perfect system, that is, as the coefficients a_{ik} for pairs of actors i and k and b_{jh} for pairs of events or goods j and h move away from 1, representing barriers (as discussed in an earlier section). The possibility of overturning s^+ in favor of $s*$ depends on actors being able to bring to bear power from within the system but from outside the body to which decision-making rights with respect to the events in question have been constitutionally allocated. If there are barriers between other actors in the system and actors who constitute that body, then the resources in the system that are not represented in the decision-making body cannot exert influence on the outcomes determined within it. Nevertheless, even when social capital is low or convertibility between resources is low, the existence of the more efficient outcome $s*$ implies the existence in the system of resources available to actors with interests in overturning outcome s^+, resources that are greater than resources held by actors interested in defending it. This may not only have an effect in weakening the implementation of the outcome, but may also lead to a longer-term effect toward overturning the outcome.

Asymmetric Decision Rules

Among discontinuous decision rules, a majority rule is symmetric; each vote represents the same fraction of control whether it is cast in a positive or negative direction. If there are n voters, where n is odd, then $(n + 1)/2$ votes are necessary to win, and each vote represents $2/(n + 1)$ of the control necessary to win. If a discontinuous decision rule is asymmetric, then kn votes are required for a positive outcome, where k is some fraction between 0 and 1, and $(1 - k)n + 1$ votes are required for a negative outcome. Each vote cast in a positive direction represents $1/kn$ of the control necessary to achieve that outcome, and each vote cast in a negative direction represents $1/[(1 - k)n + 1]$ of the control necessary to defeat it. If, for example, $k = 3/4$, each positive vote represents $4/3n$ of the control necessary, and each negative vote represents $4/(n + 4)$ of the control necessary. If the decision rule in force is unanimity, each positive vote represents $1/n$ of the control necessary, and each negative vote represents all of the control necessary, that is, has veto power.

When an asymmetric rule is used in a perfect system, the greater number of votes necessary for passage than for defeat does not affect the outcome. This can be seen by considering the extreme case of a unanimity rule. Suppose that $n - 1$ actors favor a positive outcome and 1 actor favors a negative outcome. In a perfect system any subset of actors has the full power of all members of the subset; there are no losses due to boundaries between actors. Thus the subset of $n - 1$ actors favoring a positive outcome can act as a single actor. For event m, if the sum of all their weighted interests is greater than the weighted interests of the single opponent, there will be a positive outcome. Because of the much greater power of a negative vote, they may have to compensate him for not using his prospective veto, but the inequality of interests implies that they will be able to do so. If the single actor's weighted interests are greater, the outcome will be negative, of course. But this would be so even with another decision rule.

This result raises three questions, however. First, why is a qualified majority rather than a simple majority sometimes required, if it will lead to the same outcomes? Second, why is it true that collective decisions less often lead to positive outcomes when k is greater than 1/2? Third, why is it that extremely asymmetric decision rules, such as the unanimity rule, are less widely used in large groups than in small ones?[7]

7. In Poland in the sixteenth through eighteenth centuries, every noble was a member of the parliament, and each had a veto right over the election of the king and certain actions of the king. This unanimity rule, which had been initiated when the number of nobles in Poland was small, came to be extensively used, with a sometimes paralyzing effect on the country.

The answers to these questions appear to be related to the degree of imperfection of the system. For example, there may be imperfections in the system which prevent solution of the free-rider problem. Then suppose that the weighted interests on the negative side were greater than those on the positive side but were equally distributed among the opponents of the outcome, and that the weighted interests on the positive side were better organized (either because they were initially concentrated in one actor or because there was greater social capital among the actors). If anything less than unanimity were required, it is possible that the negative side would lose in a vote, not because their weighted interests were weaker, but because their organization, or social capital, was less. Thus requiring a majority greater than half can be seen as insurance that any positive action which is taken is an action for which the weighted interests favoring it are in fact greater than those on the opposite side. The proximity of k to 1 measures the degree to which the insurance is absolute.

The answer to the second question asked above follows from this. The qualified majority rule with k greater than $1/2$ constitutes an attempt to unbalance the errors due to poor social organization. If social organization is weak, leading to difficulties in amassing the full resources possessed by actors on the two sides, this produces errors that, in conjunction with the different distributions of interests on the two sides, will lead to negative actions being taken more often than positive ones. Thus, insofar as there is weak social organization, there will more often be negative outcomes. (This suggests that the asymmetry of outcomes under an asymmetric decision rule may be used as a measure of the weakness of the social organization.)

The answer to the third question above appears to follow from the paralyzing consequences of using extremely asymmetric rules when social capital is low. According to the theory presented here, an asymmetric rule leads to asymmetry of outcomes (inaction rather than action) only when social capital is low. When social capital is complete, use of an asymmetric rule has no effect on the outcomes. If, then, social capital declines as the decision-making body increases in size, an asymmetric decision rule, which has no paralyzing effect when the body is small, does lead to inaction when the body is large.

Majority Rule

Majority rule is the most widely used decision rule for collective decisions. The outcome of a social choice when a majority rule is used can be considered under three conditions:

1. When there is no discussion or negotiation, so actor i merely examines the direction of his interests and casts a vote in that direction
2. When there is a perfect system, so all power, in no matter what form, is used in arriving at the social choice
3. When there is negotiation, but votes are the only resources used in the negotiation

The set of elementary events (each with outcome 0 or 1) is indexed by 1, . . . , m, and each actor has a single vote on each event. Each set of possible outcomes is a sequence of zeros and ones representing outcomes of the elementary events. The set chosen, s^+, is a particular string of zeros and ones. I assume no interdependence among the outcomes, so the elementary events are independent.

CONDITION 1   Under condition 1 the outcome of event j is determined simply by counting the number of actors in P_j and N_j. The set of outcomes s^+ is the set containing ones for all events j for which the number of actors in P_j exceeds the number in N_j, and zeros for all other events.

CONDITION 2   Under condition 2, with a perfect system, the set of outcomes s^+ is s^*. Both interests and power are taken into account here, giving that set of outcomes s^* for which the following quantity is maximized:

$$v_s = \sum_{j=1}^{m} \sum_{i=1}^{n} \delta_{sji} x_{ji} r_i \tag{31.16}$$

where $\delta_{sji} = 1$ if actor i favors the outcome in s on event j, and $\delta_{sji} = 0$ otherwise.

The necessity for the set of outcomes chosen to be s^* in this case can be seen by considering a set s' which contains all outcomes in s^* except that for event j, which is reversed. The value of s' is the same as the value of s^*, except for event j. Suppose that the outcome of event j is negative in s' and positive in s^*. The contribution of event j to the value of s' is $v_{bj} = \Sigma_{i \in N_j} x_{ji} r_i$, and its contribution to the value of s^* is $v_{aj} = \Sigma_{i \in P_j} x_{ji} r_i$. Because $v_{s^*} > v_{s'}$, it must be true that $v_{aj} > v_{bj}$. Thus, in a perfect system, those actors who favor a positive outcome could buy sufficient votes from those opposing it (having excess resources equal to $v_{aj} - v_{bj}$ to do so) in order to control the outcome.

It is important to recognize that this purchase of votes is done with divisible resources without externalities, which prevents the problems of instability that arise when votes are purchased with votes on other events over which there is collective control. Those problems arise under condition 3, considered below.[8] Also, in this discussion of the consequence of the majority rule under condition 2, I asume that the fraction of total value in the system that is contained in the set of events being decided collectively is sufficiently small compared to the power over other resources to which rights are held individually that $r_{si} \approx r_i$, independent of the set of outcomes s.

CONDITION 3   Under condition 3 a perfect system is assumed *within* the set of m events over which there is collective control based on a majority rule. Also assumed, under this condition, are effective barriers to exchange *between* the set

---

8. Note that in the procedure for demand revelation in social choice with continuous variation in outcomes (such as a tax bill with a continuum of alternatives representing the tax rate) proposed by Groves and Ledyard (1977) and Tideman and Tullock (1976), it is the use of a private divisible resource (money) that makes the procedure possible.

of *m* events and events and goods outside this set. Because of these barriers, the set of *m* events can be considered to be a separate system, one in which the rights allocation is β (collective control).

Nearly all of the extensive literature on social choice has focused on the special case where the only resources present in the system are those events for which rights of control are held collectively, and the outcome is decided via a rule involving the casting of votes. Furthermore, much of the literature is concerned with only the majority rule, and examination is further restricted to a single event for which a collective decision is to be made (although in many cases the event has more than two possible outcomes). As the analysis carried out here will show, it is these artificial abstractions from real systems that create the voting paradoxes and decision rule inadequacies with which so much social choice literature is concerned.

I will distinguish between normative power and positive power under condition 3. By normative power, I mean power that derives directly from the allocation among actors of partial rights of control over social choices. In a wholly egalitarian system of direct democracy with *n* actors, for example, each actor has $1/n$ of the rights of control for each of the events in the system. More generally, if there are n_j votes on event *j* and actor *i* has been allocated n_{ji} votes, then actor *i* has n_{ji}/n_j of the rights of control over event *j*. In such a system normative power depends not only on the constitutionally allocated rights of control but on the distribution of interests across events. If actor *i* has rights of partial control over event *j*, in the form of a vote, and actor *k* has rights of partial control over event *h*, then their relative power will depend on the relative amounts of interests that various actors have in event *j* and event *h*. Calculation, using eq. 25.18, will give the normative power of each actor if rights of control over events and interests in events are specified. Furthermore s^*, the optimal outcome, where $v_{s^*}(\beta) = \max_s[v_s(\beta)]$ (based on normative power, which is in turn based on constitutionally allocated rights of partial control), can also be found. In principle, this optimal outcome is valuable as a criterion against which to measure the actual outcome; however, since there is not a behavioral process that leads to s^*, as there is in systems discussed earlier, s^* cannot be discovered by observation. An independent measure of interests is required in order to find s^*.

Positive power, on the other hand, is based on outcomes achieved. In the system under consideration here, it is not true (as it is in the systems examined earlier) that power calculated from control and interests constitutes a resource that the actor can unconditionally use to realize his interests. The value of a partial right of control (in the form of a vote, for example) is conditional on the actions of others, which are in turn conditional not only on the distributions of interests and rights of control, but also on anticipation of what other actors will do. Thus, for this kind of system it is not possible to specify the value of an outcome as a sum of products of actors' interests and power, conceived as being independent of the outcomes.

Why this is so may be seen by proceeding as follows: *A priori*, each actor's power is the same, since each has one vote on each event. Then the value of event j should be the maximum of v_{aj} and v_{bj}, where

$$v_{aj} = \sum_{i \in P_j} \frac{x_{ji}}{n} \text{ and } v_{bj} = \sum_{i \in N_j} \frac{x_{ji}}{n}$$

Then, if there is a positive outcome, all power is in the hands of those favoring that outcome, so the set of actors P_j have positive power v_{aj}.

There are, however, two problems with this. First, although it might be specified that the set of actors has a certain amount of power, dependent on the interests of those who favored that outcome, it is not correct to say that an actor in that set has $1/n_a$ of this power (where n_a is number of actors in P_j). His power is the interest of others in what he controls, and unless he has decisive power over the outcome, he controls nothing. Thus power resides intrinsically in the decisive set, P_j, of which he is a part, and cannot be partitioned. The second problem lies in the fact that the value v_{aj}, on the basis of which the power of the set of actors in P_j is calculated, is itself derived from a different assumption about power, which is that each actor has $1/n$ of the total power. This problem can be illustrated by considering a case where there are only two events, with four possible outcomes: 11, 10, 01, and 00. Then there are eight distinct interest groups, as indicated in Table 31.2. Suppose that $n_{21} + n_{22} + n_{31} + n_{32}$ exceeds $(n + 1)/2$. This implies, if actors directly vote their interests, a positive outcome for event 2. Suppose also that $n_{11} + n_{12} + n_{31} + n_{32}$ exceeds $(n + 1)/2$. This implies a positive outcome for event 1. Now suppose n_{12} is less than n_{11} and n_{21} is less than n_{22}. Then there is no coalition that could propose outcomes other than positive ones for both events and gain a majority.

In this case, how can the power of actors, either individually or as a body, be conceived of and calculated? The outcomes realize the interests of actors in groups 3, 4, 7, and 8 on event 1 and the interests of those in 5, 6, 7, and 8 on event 2. The outcomes realize the stronger interests of those in groups 3 and 6 and both interests of those in groups 7 and 8. They realize no interests of those in

Table 31.2   Interests of subgroups in collective decisions on two events.

Group	Size	Strength of interest	Outcomes favored E_2	E_1
1	n_{01}	$x_2 < x_1$	0	0
2	n_{02}	$x_2 > x_1$	0	0
3	n_{11}	$x_2 < x_1$	0	1
4	n_{12}	$x_2 > x_1$	0	1
5	n_{21}	$x_2 < x_1$	1	0
6	n_{22}	$x_2 > x_1$	1	0
7	n_{31}	$x_2 < x_1$	1	1
8	n_{32}	$x_2 > x_1$	1	1

groups 1 and 2. All that can be said beyond that is that those in groups 1 and 2 have no power and those in 3, 6, 7, and 8 have all the power. No individual or subset of actors has power that will allow him or them to realize greater interests than those realized by positive outcomes for both events. Those in groups 3 and 4 would prefer a negative outcome for event 1 and a positive outcome for event 2, but they cannot bring this about by forming a coalition with those in groups 1 and 2 because $n_{11} + n_{12} + n_{01} + n_{02}$ is less than $(n + 1)/2$; similarly for those in groups 5 and 6.

Suppose the value of each of the two events is calculated in the normal way for indivisible events, as the sum of the interests that are realized by the outcome chosen, with each actor favoring that outcome given equal weight, say $1/n$ for simplicity. Is it true, in this case, that the value of each of the two events is the same as the value given for an event in earlier sections (the greater of two values, calculated over those favoring and opposing the event, where each actor is given a power of $1/n$)? The answer is, not necessarily. The interests of the actors in group 4 against a positive outcome for event 2, where they lose, may be much greater than their interests favoring a positive outcome for event 1, and the interests of actors in group 3 in the two events may be nearly the same, with x_1 only slightly greater than x_2. This could mean that v_{b1} is greater than v_{a1} despite the fact that the positive outcome on event 1 is stable. Because neither $n_{11} + n_{12} + n_{01} + n_{02}$ nor $n_{12} + n_{21} + n_{01} + n_{02}$ is greater than $(n + 1)/2$, the actors in group 4 cannot implement the great interest differential they have. Their prefer-ence for two negative outcomes over two positive ones is thwarted by the numerical superiority of group 3, despite the small difference in x_1 and x_2 which makes those in group 3 only weakly prefer two positive outcomes to two nega-tive ones. A similar result holds for actors in group 5 and the value v_{b2} compared to v_{a2}.

Thus even when, as in the case, there is a stable outcome (a Condorcet winner—see Chapter 15, and Young, 1987) among the set of possible outcomes, this does not ensure that the event with the highest value (if everyone is given equal weight) will be achieved. Whether or not it is achieved depends on the sizes of the numerical majorities and the balance of interests among those whose less important event loses compared to the balance of interests among those whose more important event loses.

A question arises, however: Of what use is it to calculate value and then power of actors in this case? The functional meaning of power is useless here, for that meaning lies in the resources which give strength to an actor's interests. Value and then power are defined here only after the fact and in terms of nothing beyond those interests. Thus the tentative conclusion must be that these two concepts are not useful in this case.

The foregoing has treated a situation for which the outcome is stable, resulting in a Condorcet winner from among the set of possible outcomes. Suppose, however, that n_{12} is not less than n_{11}, but greater, and n_{21} is not less than n_{22}, but greater. This would not change the majorities favoring positive outcomes for both events. The substantive meaning of this change is that among those who are in the majority on one event and in the minority on the other, the number who lose on their more important event exceeds the number who lose on their less important event. Actors in these two groups have an incentive to exchange with each other their vote on their less important event for their vote on their more important event. Thus those in groups 4 and 5 might either exchange votes physically, if proxy voting is allowed, or promise to vote in a direction opposed to their interest on their less important event, that is, to vote for negative outcomes for both events.

In this situation it may be the case that $n_{12} + n_{21} + n_{01} + n_{02} > n_{11} + n_{12} + n_{31} + n_{32}$. If this inequality holds, a negative outcome for both events can get a majority over a positive outcome for both. The actors in groups 4 and 5 gain more from the negative outcomes than they lose. This, however, can lead to further instability (assuming that no actual trades of votes have occurred) since those in groups 7 and 8, losing on both events if both have a negative outcome, have an incentive to gain on one by offering to join either with those in groups 3 and 4 or with those in groups 5 and 6 to form a majority in favor of a negative outcome for the first event and a positive outcome for the second, or vice versa. This is only the third step in a cycle of unstable outcomes.[9] As in the case of stable outcomes, the outcome actually achieved may not have the greatest value (where value is calculated by giving a weight of $1/n$ to each actor's interest).[10] In this case, in fact, all four possible outcomes are in the cycle, and any one might be the outcome realized.

Thus it is evident that a system in which the only events are those under collective control and the rights to control the outcomes take the form of votes cannot be analyzed through minor modifications of the linear system of action. Furthermore, the difficulties do not lie in the theory but in the very procedures through which social choices are made. These procedures have various undesirable properties, one of which is the instability discussed above. More important, even under conditions where the outcome is stable, there is no process that moves toward an optimal outcome (that is, the set of outcomes s^*), as there is for

9. The instability of outcomes produced by vote exchanges has been treated by a number of authors. In 1966 I proposed implicit vote exchanges as a way of overcoming the cycles implied by the Arrow impossibility theorem. Park (1967), in a comment on that paper, showed that the exchange led to an unstable outcome. (As Weesie, 1987, has shown, however, this instability vanishes if a probabilistic decision rule of the sort described in Coleman, 1986a, p. 115, is employed.) Subsequent authors (Schwartz, 1981) showed that the conditions under which vote exchanges could change the outcome were exactly the conditions under which there was no Condorcet winner, and under which Arrow's paradox was exhibited. Tullock (1981) has asked why, in view of the theoretical instability, there is a relatively high amount of stability in legislative outcomes. Various authors (Coleman, 1982a; Shepsle and Weingast, 1981) have proposed answers to this question. The literature on these topics is extensive and may be found in journals such as *Public Choice, Journal of Economic Theory*, and *Social Choice and Welfare*.

10. The rationale for using such a weight is normative: The rights of control over the collective decision are distributed so that each actor has one vote. Although the value calculated in this way has no positive meaning (unlike earlier cases where the theory would predict that the outcome with greatest value would be chosen), it does have normative meaning as the value under the constitutional allocation of rights.

private goods, for events with externalities embedded in a system of private goods, and for sets of social choices embedded in a system with private goods (see condition 2 above).

It is clear that the difficulty lies in the fact that in any system that is wholly insulated from divisible goods which actors could use as resources to aid in realizing their interests, the only resources that remain are the rights of partial control over events under collective control. These rights, however, do not have inherent value deriving from the interests of the actors in what they control: Their value is discontinuous and is conditional on others' actions, which in turn depend on both their interests and their anticipation of what others will do. Such a system has all the mutual contingencies of action that are relatively easily eliminated in a system that includes divisible goods without externalities. In the latter type of system, there are mutual contingencies, which can lead to a situation in which the core is large (as in an exchange system with a bilateral monopoly where, as shown in Figure 25.3, the core is the whole contract curve). The core will contract rapidly, however, with the addition of more actors to the system, as long as the system contains only divisible goods without externalities.

A system containing only indivisible events under collective rights of control has more than mutual contingencies of action. There are instabilities that can be expressed by the statement that the core is empty. That is, for every outcome there is a set of actors having sufficient resources to overturn it and each having an interest in doing so. This instability arises because the very value of one's resources in realizing one's interest is contingent, in discontinuous fashion, on the actions of others.

The analysis of this section appears to indicate that social choices are not only analytically intractable (as work in social choice has demonstrated) but incapable of assuring reasonable outcomes. Matters are not, however, as hopeless as that. I see two possible avenues of escape. One is to eliminate the barriers between indivisible events determined by social choice and divisible goods under individual control, for the latter constitute resources that can aid in realizing interests and in overcoming the instability described above. The second avenue of escape is to recognize that, in a system with many indivisible events over which there is collective control, there are ways of allocating rights of control other than giving a single vote on each event to each actor in the system. Both of these avenues of escape make use of the fact that the absence of a core in insulated systems where social choices are decided by votes hinges on the kinds of resources actors have.

Conflict

The analysis in Chapter 30 assumed that interests on one side of an event with externalities will be pursued, and the interests on the other side will be withdrawn by the actors who hold them, in return for compensation if they initially hold the rights to control the outcome. Some withdrawal in the presence of an opposition that can mobilize more powerful resources is a rational action, but expenditure of resources that are either less than those of the opponent or are greater than is warranted by one's interest constitutes a diversion of resources from other events that would bring greater gain and is not rational. That is, for event j with externalities, if v_{bj} is less than v_{aj}, it is not rational to expend resources equal in value to v_{bj} on the event, because opponents will expend more resources and win. Nor is it rational to expend enough resources to exceed v_{aj}, because the extra resources spent in that way, even if they are sufficient to gain control of the event, will bring less satisfaction than if they are employed to gain control of other resources, in each case to the degree dictated by interests.

It may well be, however, that v_{aj} and v_{bj} are close enough that both sides will estimate that they will be able to gain control of event j. If, as in the trading-card examples with telephone calls, control is gained through a market process in which the losing side can recover its offered resources, the system will operate as described earlier, and the recovered resources will be deployed in alternative ways. But if there is a struggle for control of the event, as is often the case in noneconomic transactions in society, the resources employed, or some large part of them, are lost and constitute a waste.

In effect, three levels of social functioning can be specified for a system where the value of a positive outcome of a given event exceeds that of a negative outcome (that is, $v_{aj} > v_{bj}$). The first level is where the positive outcome occurs without employment of any resources by those who oppose that outcome, who will be compensated if they initially held rights of control over the event, but in any case will use the resources they would have directed toward this event (a quantity equal to v_{bj}) in other ways.

The second level is where the negative outcome occurs and the actors favoring a positive outcome employ elsewhere the resources (of value v_{aj}) they would have used to bring about that outcome. In this case the magnitude of the loss is a function of $v_{aj} - v_{bj}$, for it is this extra amount of resources that is being redirected to events that produce lesser utility.

The third level of social functioning occurs when both sides employ their resources to gain control of the event, in a struggle for control in which the resources of the losing side are used up. In this case the loss is not merely $v_{aj} - v_{bj}$, due to deployment of resources on events that bring lesser utility, as in the second level of functioning; it is a total loss of the resources of lesser value. The resources lost in this case cannot be calculated under regime a or regime b, because both of those regimes assume redeployment of resources by the losing side, to give a set of values which sum to 1.0 over all events. This implies that all resources in the system are employed at their most valuable use. What actually applies is a single regime in which both resources of those favoring a positive outcome and resources of those favoring a negative outcome are employed, despite the fact that one side will lose. The value of the interests favoring a positive outcome is

$$v_{+j} = \sum_{i \in P_j} x_{ji} r_i \approx v_{aj}$$

The value of the interests favoring a negative outcome is

$$v_{-j} = \sum_{i \in N_j} x_{ji} r_i \approx v_{bj}$$

A positive outcome wins if $v_{+j} > v_{-j}$, and a negative outcome wins if $v_{-j} > v_{+j}$. The winner will ordinarily, but not necessarily, be the same as the winner when there is nondestructive use of resources to gain control of the event, as in regime *a* or regime *b*. The lack of complete correspondence arises because, under this different resource deployment, other events will have different values, and thus those who control them will have different resources. In particular, when resources of both sides are deployed to gain control of event *j*, that event is of greater value than when resources of only one side are so deployed.[11]

Processes That Expand Conflicts

When there is a single event over which a struggle for control occurs, a number of processes that expand the conflict have been identified. One of these is the proliferation of issues (Coleman, 1957), which refers to the introduction of new issues into a conflict, leading to a situation in which the original event has been supplemented by a number of others. The new issues are characteristically introduced by actors whose interests are already engaged by the conflict, on one side or the other.

An example introduced in Chapter 15, concerning a conflict over the curriculum in Pasadena schools, can be elaborated to illustrate how the introduction of new issues affects conflict. The school superintendent, who had rights of control over the curriculum (within specified limits), had introduced a progressive education curriculum into the Pasadena schools. A small group of women in the community with strong anticommunist orientations saw this new curriculum as subversive. They came to have strong interests in changing this curriculum. In the framework of the theory, the event over which interests are in conflict is changing or not changing the curriculum. The first action taken by the women was to attempt to induce the superintendent to change the curriculum. They were unsuccessful.

Their second action was to introduce a new event on which the first was (in

---

11. The fact that the outcomes may be different when the resources of both are employed to gain control of event *j* as opposed to when the weaker retires could be the basis for saying that conflict is rational for the side that would lose in the absence of conflict (that is, through comparison of regimes *a* and *b*) *if* the value of its resources employed when there is conflict is greater than the value employed by its opponent. This circumstance could arise when a large fraction of the interests of the weaker (when comparing regimes *a* and *b*) are in resources controlled by the stronger. This means that the latter's power is increased when the weaker's resources are redirected away from the event under contention. The increase may be enough to tip the scales in his favor when comparing regimes *a* and *b*, even though he does not win when both sides devote resources to this event.

view of the first failure) seen to be wholly dependent: continuation or change of the superintendent. The board of education had rights of control over this event. The group of women attempted to gain control of it by inducing the board to terminate the superintendent's contract. They were also unsuccessful in this. The methods they used are illustrated at the next stage, after introduction of another new event.

The next stage was the election of board members, an event on which the termination of the superintendent's contract was highly dependent. Rights of control over this event were held by individual citizens of Pasadena, in the form of votes for board members. Here the group of women introduced a new issue (that is, a new event) unrelated in content to any of the others: reading achievement of children in early grades of school. They called a meeting of parents who were concerned about this issue, that is, interested in improvement in their children's reading achievement. At the meeting the principal activity was to establish for the attending parents, first, a link between low reading achievement and the progressive curriculum, then, a link between the curriculum and the superintendent, next, a link between the continuation of the superintendent's contract and the school board, and, finally, a link between the school board's actions and the election of its members. All the links but the first were straightforward, because those dependencies were already well known. It was the first link which, if established, would connect the group's interest through the other links to the school board election. The group was more successful at this stage, principally through introducing new issues (events) such as children's reading achievement, which connected the interests of a large number of voters to the school board election. Board members who opposed the superintendent were elected, the superintendent's contract was terminated, and the curriculum was changed.

This example indicates that processes in conflict ordinarily expand the number of events and the number of actors involved in the conflict over control of the original event. Thus if an analysis does not take into account the possibility that new, previously unrelated events may be brought into a conflict through the capacity of interested actors to establish new dependencies in the minds of other actors, the analysis will be incomplete. These new dependencies (such as the dependency of low reading achievement on the progressive curriculum) are established by interested parties in order to draw in new actors or new interests which can aid their goals. The theory cannot predict when the capacity for establishing new dependencies will exist or what dependencies will be established (although it can indicate what dependencies would be most in the interest of interested parties to establish). It can show the effect of their establishment on the outcome of the conflict.

There are additional processes through which conflicts are expanded beyond the initial actors and events, but I will not examine them here. This sketch of the application of the theory to conflict over events with externalities merely indicates the direction of a much broader investigation of conflicts and indicates how conflicts might be treated within the present framework of ideas. The examination has addressed two points.

The first point is that when there are indivisible events with externalities, either of two kinds of social processes might occur: market valuation of the two outcomes of the event, with only one side devoting resources to gaining or keeping control of the event; or conflict, in which both sides devote resources to the event, and those of the losing side are wasted. In the latter case the level of social efficiency of the system will be lower than it would be if the same side had won but there was redeployment of the potentially opposing resources by the losing side.

The second point is that research on conflict shows that certain processes expand the conflict so it encompasses additional events and actors. One of those processes involves changes in the cognitive structure of some actors through the establishment, by actors interested in the conflict event, of a perceived dependency of other events on the outcome of the conflict event. That dependency, if successfully incorporated into the cognitive structure of actors in the system, gives some actors additional derived interests in the conflict event.

32

Dynamics of the Linear
System of Action

There are two kinds of dynamics in a system of social exchange which may be separated analytically. One is the adjustment of values of different resources such that, for each resource, the value of the quantity of the resource that is available equals the value of other resources actors are willing to give up to get it. The value of the quantity available is the supply; the value of other resources actors are willing to give up is the demand. An equilibrium of values, or prices, exists when the values have been adjusted so that demand equals supply for all goods. In terms of the model introduced in Chapter 25, this process consists of making changes in v_j to get an equilibrium vector of values, v. This is equivalent to what economists call price adjustment, or Walrasian adjustment (after Leon Walras).

The second kind of dynamics is a rearrangement of goods among actors through a process of exchange. This process is one in which c_{ij} changes over time, as actor i gives up some goods to gain others. The exchange involving resources j and k occurs at the current ratio of values of j and k. This is not the same as quantity adjustment in an economic system (sometimes called Marshallian adjustment, after Alfred Marshall), for that implies change in the overall level of each of the resources, as a result of variations in production. There is no production in this model. The redistribution that occurs through exchange is ordinarily viewed in economics as occurring immediately or automatically when the equilibrium prices are established for the quantities of goods in the system. I will assume here that the redistribution must occur through processes operating over time, once the equilibrium prices have been established.

The dynamic processes in this model are assumed to be sequential: The adjustment of values is assumed to take place first, and then all exchanges occur at the equilibrium values. If not all exchanges occur at the equilibrium values, much of the simplicity of the model vanishes. The value of an actor's resources would change over time if he gains or gives up something when its value is above or below the equilibrium value. The final equilibrium state of the system would not be independent of the starting point.

The second process, exchange of resources among actors, will be treated first, assuming v to be constant at its equilibrium value for all resources j. This, together with the competitive market assumption that in all exchanges equal value is given up and gained, implies that the value of the resources held by actor *i* does not change during the exchange process. Thus, throughout the process of exchange of resources, both **v** and **r** are assumed to be fixed. The dynamics of prices (the Walrasian adjustment) will be examined in a later section.

Exchange of resources between actors can be seen from two perspectives. One is the change in the mix of resources held by a given actor. The second is the change in the set of actors holding a given resource. For the case where there are two actors and two resources, the same equations describe these two perspectives; for the case where there are more actors or resources, this is no longer true. I will treat first the two-actor, two-resource case, then change in the mix of resources held by a single actor, then exchange of a single resource among actors, and finally the two processes taken together. In all this it will be assumed that a price equilibrium has already been established before exchange occurs. (For a more formal treatment of dynamics for this system, see Braun, 1990.)

Exchange with Two Actors and Two Resources

As a first step in studying the dynamics of the exchange process, I will treat the basic system of action as described in Chapter 25, for the case where the transactions involve private, divisible, and alienable goods. The first general point is that there are many paths through which an equilibrium can be realized. In a two-person system of bilateral exchange involving two goods, the point which is reached on the contract curve is compatible with some paths but not others. As shown in Figure 32.1, if Tom and John reach point *D* on the contract curve, they could not have done so by any paths below the curve *TT'* or by any above the curve *JJ'*—for a move to *D* from a point outside these limits would not be beneficial to one or the other of the traders. It would not be a Pareto-optimal move and thus would not be taken voluntarily.

A comment must be made here concerning strategic behavior. In general, persons may engage in strategic behavior by taking a short-term loss to achieve a longer-term gain. The opportunity to do so is particularly likely to arise in a contingent social environment (as in a game when a player fakes to one side to induce a response from his opponent and then makes his move toward the other side). The environment is ordinarily most highly contingent when it consists of only one other person. Thus it is the case that especially in two-person settings, such as that for which an Edgeworth box is constructed, strategic behavior may arise. Because of the use of strategies, treatment of the action in two-person exchange systems as always ascending upward in utility, never taking a longer-range view of a global optimum that can be attained by ignoring a local optimum, may be particularly unrealistic. It is done here to aid intuitive understanding of the dynamics in larger systems, in which actors have less opportunity for gain through strategic behavior, and in which the assumption of reactive rationality is likely to be more valid.

There are many paths that are compatible with an equilibrium point at *D* in

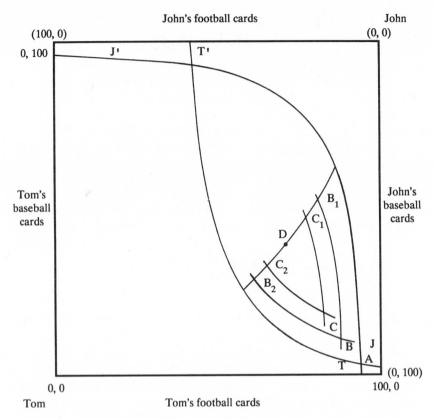

Figure 32.1   Exchange envelopes from three starting points in a system of bilateral exchange.

Figure 32.1. Starting at point A, any movement which keeps within the envelope of the indifference curves which pass through the current point traces a feasible path (a path that benefits both) but reduces the set of feasible equilibria. Because the indifference curves are convex, a straight line from any initial point to point D on the contract curve, where point D lies between the indifference curves that pass through the initial point, will remain within the envelope. If the initial point is B, this envelope is given by B_1BB_2, and the equilibrium can be at any point on the contract curve in the segment B_1B_2. Starting at point C narrows the envelope to C_1CC_2, and the segment representing the feasible equilibria is reduced to C_1C_2.

Since there are many paths to an equilibrium point on the contract curve, there is no basis for specifying one of the feasible paths rather than another, without further information about the rules governing actions or the institutions within which they take place. In the absence of such a basis, I will focus on the competitive equilibrium rather than another point on the contract curve.

Changes in the mix of resources held by an actor can be studied by beginning with the two-actor case and then moving to the general case. I assume that the ending point on the contract curve will be the competitive equilibrium, as derived in Chapter 25. This is where Tom's control of good 1 is c_{11}^* and his control of good 2 is c_{12}^*, and John's control is represented by the complements of these two quantities. What occurs in reaching that point as Tom gives up good 1 and gains good 2 at market exchange rates?

For good 2, which Tom acquires, the equilibrium quantity is $c_{12}^* = x_{21}r_1/v_2$, and I will assume that he acquires good 2 at a rate proportional to the difference between the current quantity he holds and the equilibrium quantity. (This assumption is a natural one and has the additional virtue of leading to linear differential equations, which are mathematically tractable.) Expressed in value terms, this assumption is

$$\frac{dc_{12}(t)v_2}{dt} = \gamma_1[x_{21}r_1 - c_{12}(t)v_2] \tag{32.1}$$

where γ_1 is an arbitrary positive constant and $c_{ij}(t)$ is written as an explicit function of time. Because Tom's holdings of good 1 change at the same time, a second equation can be written:

$$\frac{dc_{11}(t)v_1}{dt} = \gamma_1'[x_{11}r_1 - c_{11}(t)v_1] \tag{32.2}$$

Since the exchange occurs at equal value, there must be a value balance:

$$\frac{dc_{11}(t)v_1}{dt} = -\frac{dc_{12}(t)v_2}{dt} \tag{32.3}$$

Since by eq. 32.3 the left-hand sides of eqs. 32.1 and 32.2 are equal in absolute value and opposite in sign, the right-hand sides must be equal in absolute value and opposite in sign. Expanding r_1 [equal to $c_{11}(t)v_1 + c_{12}(t)v_2$] and comparing the quantities in brackets shows that they are equal and opposite in sign if $\gamma_1' = \gamma_1$. Thus eqs. 32.1 and 32.2, with $\gamma_1' = \gamma_1$, give the rate of change of value in Tom's hands from football cards to baseball cards as he engages in exchange with John.

But this change of value in Tom's hands also has implications for the change of value in John's hands: Every unit of value of good 1 that Tom gives up is acquired by John; that is,

$$\frac{dc_{21}(t)v_1}{dt} = -\frac{dc_{11}(t)v_1}{dt} \tag{32.4}$$

The equation which describes John's acquisition of good 1 is analogous to eq. 32.1 for Tom:

$$\frac{dc_{21}(t)v_1}{dt} = \gamma_2[x_{12}r_2 - c_{21}(t)v_1] \tag{32.5}$$

Again, since the left-hand side of eq. 32.5 equals the negative of the left-hand side of eq. 32.2, the right-hand side of eq. 32.5 must be equal to the negative of the right-hand side of eq. 32.2. What does this imply about the relative values of γ_1' and γ_2? Substituting $v_1 - x_{11}r_1$ for $x_{12}r_2$ allows expressing the quantity in brackets in eq. 32.5 as $[-x_{11}r_1 + v_1 - c_{21}(t)v_1]$. Since $v_1 - c_{21}(t)v_1 = c_{11}(t)v_1$, this gives $[-x_{11}r_1 + c_{11}(t)v_1]$, which is the negative of the quantity in brackets in eq. 32.2. This implies that $\gamma_1' = \gamma_2$. Thus all equations for changes in value of Tom's and John's holdings of goods 1 and 2 can be written with a common rate constant.

Figure 25.6 showed the competitive equilibrium for the exchange of football cards for baseball cards; the rate of movement from the starting point to the equilibrium point can be determined using eqs. 32.1 and 32.2. First, however, these equations can be put in somewhat more useful form. If $c_{ij}(t)v_j$, for the value of good j held by actor i, is replaced with

$$a_{ij}(t) = c_{ij}(t)v_j$$

and if r_i is expanded in terms of the quantities $c_{ij}v_j$ (that is, a_{ij}) of which it is composed, and the fact that $x_{11} + x_{21} = 1$ is used, then eqs. 32.2 and 32.1 may be rewritten as follows:

$$\frac{da_{11}(t)}{dt} = \gamma[-x_{21}a_{11}(t) + x_{11}a_{12}(t)] \tag{32.6}$$

$$\frac{da_{12}(t)}{dt} = \gamma[x_{21}a_{11}(t) - x_{11}a_{12}(t)] \tag{32.7}$$

Equation 32.7 is redundant, since the right-hand side is the negative of the right-hand side of eq. 32.6. Equation 32.6 has a unique solution, $a_{11}(t)$, as a function of the starting point, $a_{11}(0)$:

$$a_{11}(t) = a_{11}(0)e^{-\gamma(x_{11}+x_{21})t} + \frac{x_{11}r_1}{x_{11} + x_{21}}(1 - e^{-\gamma(x_{11}+x_{21})t})$$

$$= a_{11}(0)e^{-\gamma(x_{11}+x_{21})t} + \frac{x_{11}r_1}{x_{11} + x_{21}}(1 - e^{-\gamma(x_{11}+x_{21})t}) \tag{32.8}$$

Using eq. 32.8 with information from Chapter 25 which gives r_1 as .681 and $a_{11}(0)$ as .669 (with $x_{11} = .8$ and $x_{21} = .2$), and assuming $\gamma = 1$, allows calculating values of $a_{11}(t)$. In Figure 32.2 are plotted values of $a_{11}(t)$ and $a_{12}(t)$ [equal to $r_1 - a_{11}(t)$] from the starting point to equilibrium. The quantities $c_{11}(t)$ and $c_{12}(t)$ could have been obtained by dividing $a_{11}(t)$ by v_1 and $a_{12}(t)$ by v_2.

Change in Resources Held by One Actor

The usefulness of the rationalized process described by eq. 32.6 lies in its simplicity, and in its generalizability to a greater number of actors and a greater number of resources. Some properties of the process will become evident by

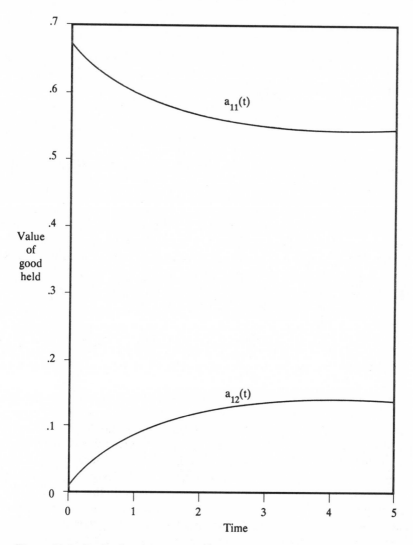

Figure 32.2 Paths for changes in value in a two-good system over time.

expanding the system from two goods to three. In such a case the interests of actor 1 in goods 1, 2, and 3 are x_{11}, x_{21}, and x_{31}. These equations may be written:

$$\frac{da_{11}(t)}{dt} = \gamma[-(1 - x_{11})a_{11}(t) + x_{11}a_{12}(t) + x_{11}a_{13}(t)] \qquad (32.9)$$

$$\frac{da_{12}(t)}{dt} = \gamma[x_{21}a_{11}(t) - (1 - x_{21})a_{12}(t) + x_{21}a_{13}(t)]$$

$$\frac{da_{13}(t)}{dt} = \gamma[x_{31}a_{11}(t) + x_{31}a_{12}(t) - (1 - x_{31})a_{13}(t)]$$

Because the sum of $a_{ij}(t)$ over j equals r_i, eqs. 32.9 can be written more simply as

$$\frac{da_{11}(t)}{dt} = \gamma[x_{11}r_1 - a_{11}(t)] \tag{32.10}$$

$$\frac{da_{12}(t)}{dt} = \gamma[x_{21}r_1 - a_{12}(t)]$$

$$\frac{da_{13}(t)}{dt} = \gamma(x_{31}r_1 - a_{13}(t))$$

These equations may be solved independently to give equations analogous to eq. 32.8:

$$a_{ij}(t) = a_{ij}(0)e^{-\gamma t} + x_{ji}r_i(1 - e^{-\gamma t}) \tag{32.11}$$

As is evident from the derivation, eq. 32.11 is not restricted to three goods but holds for any number of goods. Since the rate constant, γ, must be the same for all actors, the equation holds not only for all goods j, but also for all actors i.

If $\mathbf{D}_v$ is defined as the $m \times m$ diagonal matrix with v_j as the jth diagonal element, and $\mathbf{D}_r$ as the $n \times n$ diagonal matrix with r_i as the ith diagonal element, then the following set of (independent) equations of the form of eq. 32.11 can be written:

$$\mathbf{C}(t)\mathbf{D}_v = e^{-\gamma t} \cdot \mathbf{C}(0)\mathbf{D}_v + (1 - e^{-\gamma t}) \cdot \mathbf{D}_r\mathbf{X}' \tag{32.12}$$

where $\cdot$ denotes multiplication of each element of the matrix by the scalar quantity [either $e^{-\gamma t}$ or $(1 - e^{-\gamma t})$].

The set of equations represented by eq. 32.11 or 32.12 is highly specialized because of the assumption that an actor's acquisition of good j draws from each of the goods he holds in proportion to the value of it he holds. (This assumption is evident in eq. 32.9 in the fact that da_{11}/dt is augmented by the same multiplier, γx_{11}, applied to a_{12} and to a_{13}.) It is useful, however, to see what a system of equations for change in a_{ij} (or, equivalently, in c_{ij}) would look like if this assumption were not made, if the process were more general, in that the acquisition of value in the form of good j came differentially from the other values held. The usefulness of doing this lies in the fact that there may be barriers between pairs of resources or, in contrast, propensities for exchange between pairs of resources. These barriers or propensities between resources j and k manifest themselves in an actor's giving up a lesser or greater proportion of value held in resource k than of other resources in acquiring resource j.

As an aid in extending the model in this way, it is useful to note that the process described by eq. 32.9 has the same form as a continuous-time Markov process with restrictions on the transition rates. A diagram for such a process is given in Figure 32.3, which shows three states, or forms, in which actor 1 can hold value: in the form of good 1, good 2, or good 3.[1] In a general Markov

---

1. Although the stochastic interpretation of the model is not important here, it can be described this way: a_{ij}/r_i is the probability that a given unit of value held by actor i is in the form of good j.

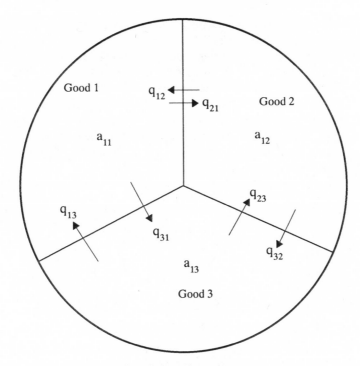

Figure 32.3   Movement of value held by one actor among three goods.

process, as pictured in Figure 32.3, there are six independent transition rates [$m(m - 1)$, where m is the number of goods, or forms in which value can be held]. Inspection of the figure and eq. 32.9 shows that the equation describes a continuous-time Markov process with two transition rates, q_{jk} and q_{jh} from states k and h, respectively, to state j, for individual 1, where restrictions of the form $q_{jk} = q_{jh} = \gamma x_{j1}$ apply.[2] That is, in this simple exchange system, the transition rate into a state is independent of the state of origin. For the three-state process for actor 1, then,

$q_{13} = q_{12} = \gamma x_{11}$ (from good 2 or 3 to good 1); $q_{11} = -\gamma(x_{21} + x_{31})$

$q_{21} = q_{23} = \gamma x_{21}$ (from good 1 or 3 to good 2); $q_{22} = -\gamma(x_{11} + x_{31})$

$q_{31} = q_{32} = \gamma x_{31}$ (from good 1 or 2 to good 3); $q_{33} = -\gamma(x_{11} + x_{21})$

The substantive meaning of the assumption is that an actor is as likely to acquire good j in exchange for good k as in exchange for good h if he holds equal value in the form of k and h: The rate of acquisition depends not on the form in which he holds value but only on his interest in good j. This gives some insight

---

2. Here the destination state is the *first* subscript; the origin state is the *second*. This is the reverse of the common usage for Markov processes and is used in order to conform to the notation for the linear system of action.

into one of the assumptions underlying models of perfect markets: There are no special relationships among goods. When a good j is acquired, the likelihood that a good k will be given up in acquiring it depends only on the amount of k that is held. Recognizing this, and recognizing also that it is not true that this assumption always holds empirically in social exchange processes (for example, doing a favor for another is more likely to be repaid by a return favor than by a material payment), allows generalizing the process by letting the transition rate differ according to not only the state of destination but also the state of origin.

For the general case an $m \times m$ transition matrix $\mathbf{Q}_i$ can be defined for a given actor i with elements representing rates of the movement of value held by that actor from state j to k, that is, from good j to good k. The elements of $\mathbf{Q}_i$ are[3]

$$_iq_{kj} \equiv \text{transition rate from good } j \text{ to good } k, \text{ where } k \neq j$$

$$_iq_{jj} \equiv - \sum_{\substack{k=1 \\ k \neq j}}^{m} {_iq_{kj}}$$

The equation governing the process is

$$\dot{\mathbf{a}}_i(t) = \mathbf{Q}_i\mathbf{a}_i(t) \tag{32.13}$$

where $\mathbf{a}_i(t)$ is the vector of values held by actor i in states $1, 2, \ldots, m$, and $\dot{\mathbf{a}}_i(t)$ is the vector of first derivatives of the elements for $\mathbf{a}_i(t)$ with respect to time. The solution for the general equation is

$$\mathbf{a}_i(t) = e^{\mathbf{Q}_i t}\mathbf{a}_i(0) \tag{32.14}$$

which gives the vector of values at time t as a function of the vector at time 0. The notation $e^{\mathbf{Q}t}$ is the convergent infinite matrix series which generalizes the infinite series that defines the scalar e^x:

$$e^{\mathbf{Q}_i t} = \mathbf{I} + \mathbf{Q}_i t + \frac{\mathbf{Q}_i^2 t^2}{2!} + \frac{\mathbf{Q}_i^3 t^3}{3!} + \cdots \tag{32.15}$$

At equilibrium eq. 32.13 gives

$$\dot{\mathbf{a}}(t) = 0 = \mathbf{Q}_i\,\mathbf{a}(t)$$

For the special form of $\mathbf{Q}_i$ under consideration, with $_iq_{jk} = \gamma x_{ji}$, independent of k ($k \neq j$), this equation takes an especially simple form in which each of the m equations are independent:

$$a_{ij} = x_{ji} \sum_{k=1}^{m} a_{ik}$$

---

3. The restrictions given earlier imply that all rows of $\mathbf{Q}_i$ are alike except for the elements on the main diagonal.

Expressing a_{ij} as $c_{ij}v_j$ gives

$$c_{ij}v_j = x_{ji} \sum_{k=1}^{m} c_{ik}v_k = x_{ji}r_i$$

From eq. 25.11 this is the equation for the equilibrium value of c_{ij}.

For the case of a general $\mathbf{Q}_i$ the equations are no longer independent but constitute a system of interdependent equations. In this case $a_{ij}(t)$ does not depend only on $a_{ij}(0)$, x_{ji}, and t, as is true for the system given by eqs. 32.9 and 32.11. It depends on the whole vector $\mathbf{a}_i(0)$, since the rate at which value in form k is exchanged for value in form j is in general different from the rate at which value in form h is exchanged for value in form j. These rates are no longer determined solely by x_{ji}, actor i's interest in j, and may differ. It will be necessary to introduce more general rates when systems in which there are barriers between pairs of resources are examined in a later section.

Empirical Use of Dynamic Data

Dynamic analyses of the linear system of action can proceed from eq. 32.11 or, for the unrestricted process, from eq. 32.14. The way these equations are used depends on what data are available. To use eq. 32.11 to estimate the restricted model, either of two types of data are necessary:

1. Interests of actors and control of events by actors at one point in time
2. Control of events by actors at two points in time

If data of type 1 are available and the restrictions shown in eq. 32.9 are accepted, the data may be used in conjunction with eq. 32.11 to calculate $a_{ij}(t)$ [and then $c_{ij}(t)$] for a given value of t by assuming a particular rate constant, γ. First, however, $\mathbf{v}$ and $\mathbf{r}$ must be found by using eqs. 25.18 and 25.19 with the empirically known interest and control matrices to calculate the values, v_j ($j = 1, \ldots, m$), and power, r_i ($i = 1, \ldots, n$), for the system.

Note that there is nothing in the specification of interests or control which has the dimension of time. This means that although these quantities may be used to describe the process through which control over goods is redistributed from those individuals who originally control them toward those who will finally control them, they tell nothing about the rate at which this redistribution takes place.

Calculating $a_{ij}(t)$, and thus the rate of redistribution from an initial control matrix $\mathbf{C}(0)$ to a later one $\mathbf{C}(t)$, requires either having some independent information on the rate of movement or assuming a rate constant, γ. Doing the latter, of course, means that the empirical analysis cannot be used to make any valid statements about the overall rate of redistribution. It is possible, of course, to make valid statements about *relative* rates of redistribution by examining the relative rates of movement toward equilibrium from different initial interest and control structures.

If data of type 2, that is, control of events by actors at two points in time, are available, additional steps are necessary. If control is measured at time 0 and at equilibrium, the identity $C(0)v = C^*v$ may be used to find the best-fitting v by eq. 25.21, and r may be found from v and C^*. Then $X = D_r C^* D_v^{-1}$, where D_v and D_r are diagonal matrices with v_j and r_i as their diagonal elements, respectively.

If control is measured at time 0 and at time t, however, to give the two control matrices $C(0)$ and $C(t)$, this method can be used to find v and r, but not X. Because the system is not at equilibrium, $C(t)$ cannot be used to find X once v and r are known. It is, however, possible to obtain an estimate of X, if there are observations of $C(0)$, $C(t)$, and $C(\tau)$, that is, data on control at three points in time: before exchange and at two points during the process of exchange.

Applying eq. 32.11 at times t and τ gives two equations in x_{ji} and γ. It is possible to eliminate γ, giving

$$\frac{a_{ij}(\tau) - x_{ji}r_i}{a_{ij}(0) - x_{ji}r_i} = \left(\frac{a_{ij}(t) - x_{ji}r_i}{a_{ij}(0) - x_{ji}r_i} \right)^{\tau/t} \tag{32.16}$$

Given values of $C(0)$, $C(t)$, and $C(\tau)$, it is possible to obtain best-fitting values of v and r. Then $a_{ij}(t)$ [equal to $c_{ij}(t)v_j$], $a_{ij}(\tau)$, r_i, τ, and t may be used to estimate x_{ji} through numerical analysis. If $\tau = 2t$, eq. 32.16 can be solved for x_{ji} explicitly:

$$x_{ji} = \frac{a_{ij}(0)a_{ij}(\tau) - a_{ij}(t)^2}{r_i[a_{ij}(0) + a_{ij}(\tau) - 2a_{ij}(t)]} \tag{32.17}$$

Since there are $2mn$ degrees of freedom and only $mn + 1$ parameters to estimate (X and γ), an optimization procedure can be used to fit the model to the data.

The More General Case

If much richer data are available, eq. 32.14 may be used to estimate the transition rates $_iq_{jk}$ for the movement of value held by actor i from state k (good k) to state j (good j). Because the absence of special relationships among goods is not assumed in the more general case, the data necessary include both data on the distribution of control held by each actor at two points in time and data which give some evidence about the actual transactions. For example, for each unit of value held in the form of good k at time 0, if the number of units of value held in the form of each other good at time t were known, then eq. 32.14 could be used, following methods described in Coleman (1981), to estimate Q_i for each actor i.

More simply, if data on transactions exist, they can be used directly to find Q_i. This can be done as follows: Data for $C(0)$ and $C(t)$ are used to calculate v and r, by methods described in Chapter 25 (eq. 25.21). The transition rate $_iq_{jk}$ is the instantaneous rate of transfer of value for actor i from state k to state j. Under Markovian assumptions (which are implied by the form of eq. 32.14), this rate is constant and equal to the inverse of the expected time that value will remain in state k before moving to state j. Under the same assumptions this expected waiting time is the same for all destination states. Thus $_iq_{jk}$ for $j \neq k$ may be estimated as

$$_iq_{jk} = \frac{\sum\limits_{s} c_{ik}(j,s)}{\sum\limits_{h}\sum\limits_{s} t_s c_{ik}(h,s)} \qquad (32.18)$$

where $c_{ik}(j,s)$ is the quantity of k that actor i exchanges in exchange s for value in state j, and t_s is the length of time that actor i held value in state k before exchanging it in exchange s, for all exchanges s for which actor i held value in state k.

If, at the final observation time, t, there remains some quantity of k, this is included in the denominator of eq. 32.18, multiplied by the length of time it has been held since observation began.

Movement of a Resource among Actors

The preceding section dealt with the dynamics of exchange of value for one actor from one good to another. The equations derived say nothing about the exchange between actors which is implied by the shift for one actor from holding value in the form of one good to holding it in the form of another, or about the shifts implied for other actors from value held as one good to value held as another. In this section I will describe the movement of a resource among actors and in the next section will turn to the full-scale process which mirrors both change in the form of value held by the individual actor and exchange among actors.

For a system of exchange involving three actors who exchange good 1 among themselves, the following equations of the form of eq. 32.2, but with v_1 in the last term on the right-hand side expanded, can be written:

$$\frac{dc_{11}(t)v_1}{dt} = \gamma\left[x_{11}r_1 - c_{11}(t)\sum_{i=1}^{3} x_{1i}r_i\right] \qquad (32.19)$$

$$\frac{dc_{21}(t)v_1}{dt} = \gamma\left[x_{12}r_2 - c_{21}(t)\sum_{i=1}^{3} x_{1i}r_i\right]$$

$$\frac{dc_{31}(t)v_1}{dt} = \gamma\left[x_{13}r_2 - c_{31}(t)\sum_{i=1}^{3} x_{1i}r_i\right]$$

I will assume that the rate constant γ is the same in all these equations; this can be shown to be implied by the constancy of v and r over time.

The general equation for exchange of good j among actors can be rewritten by extracting from the summation the term corresponding to $x_{11}r_1$, $x_{12}r_2$, or $x_{13}r_3$ in eq. 32.19 and multiplying and dividing the right-hand side by v_j, to give,

$$\frac{da_{kj}(t)}{dt} = \gamma\left([v_j - a_{kj}(t)]\frac{x_{jk}r_k}{v_j} - a_{kj}(t)\sum_{i \neq k}\frac{x_{ji}r_i}{v_j}\right) \qquad (32.20)$$

Equation 32.20 can be seen as a Markov process, with constraints on the transition rates, for the flow of value in the form of good j between actor k and other actors. The term $x_{jk}r_k/v_j$ is the interest of actor k in good j multiplied by his power relative to the value of j. When multiplied by γ, this constitutes, according to the model, the transition rate at which actor k acquires j:

$$_jq_{ki} = \frac{\gamma x_{jk}r_k}{v_j}, \qquad \text{for } i \neq k \qquad (32.21)$$

Note that, just as the transition rate for change of value held by one actor is independent of the resource from which the value comes, the transition rate of resource j to actor k is independent of which actor i it comes from. As a result, this transition rate, common to all actors from whom resource j comes, multiplies the total value of resource j not held by actor k, which is $v_j - a_{kj}(t)$. Thus, because of the constraint, the general expression for the rate of flow of resource j to actor k, on the left in the following equation, simplifies to the expression on the right, where i does not appear:

$$\sum_{i \neq k} {_jq_{ki}a_{ij}(t)} = \frac{\gamma x_{jk}r_k}{v_j}[v_j - a_{kj}(t)]$$

The term

$$a_{kj}(t)\sum_{i \neq k}\frac{\gamma x_{ji}r_i}{v_j}$$

from eq. 32.20 represents the value of j held by actor k, that is, $a_{kj}(t)$, multiplied by the transition rate from actor k to all other actors i, which is the product of the rate constant and the demand from other actors for j. The constraints on the transition rates are reflected by the fact that the demand by actor i for the value in form j held by actor k depends only on i's interest in j and his wealth or power. It does not depend on any special relationship between actors k and i.

Note that, analogous to the case of change in resources held by an actor, the constraints imply that eq. 32.20 for resource j is independent of equations for movement of other resources among actors. The equation may be written more simply, since $\Sigma_i x_{ji}r_i = v_j$:

$$\frac{da_{kj}(t)}{dt} = \gamma[x_{jk}r_k - a_{kj}(t)] \qquad (32.22)$$

which is of the same form as eq. 32.10. The solution is given by eq. 32.11.

When the constraints on the transition rates do not hold, the process may be described by a more general equation:

$$\frac{da_{kj}(t)}{dt} = \sum_{i \neq k} {}_jq_{ki}a_{ij}(t) - \sum_{i \neq k} {}_jq_{ik}a_{kj}(t) \tag{32.23}$$

In eq. 32.23 ${}_jq_{ik}$ is the transition rate at which value in the form of j moves from actor k to actor i, and $a_{kj}(t)$ is the amount of value in form j held by k. The restrictions inherent in eq. 32.19 can be expressed as ${}_jq_{ki} = {}_jq_{kh} = x_{jk}r_k/v_j$ for all actors i and h.

A diagram for the general process is shown in Figure 32.4, where the transitions are movements of good j (expressed in value terms) from one actor to another. Nothing is specified about the reverse movement of other goods which accompanies every such movement.

For the general process of movement of good j between actors, an $n \times n$ transition matrix $\mathbf{Q}_j$ can be defined, with elements

${}_jq_{ki} \equiv$ the transition rate at which value in the form of j moves from actor i to actor k, for $i \neq k$

$$_jq_{ii} \equiv -\sum_{\substack{k=1 \\ k \neq i}}^n {}_jq_{ki}$$

The equation for the process is

$$\dot{\mathbf{a}}_j = \mathbf{Q}_j\mathbf{a}_j(t) \tag{32.24}$$

The solution is

$$\mathbf{a}_j(t) = e^{\mathbf{Q}_jt}\,\mathbf{a}_j(0) \tag{32.25}$$

where $e^{\mathbf{Q}_jt}$ is defined as shown in eq. 32.15.

As described for the movement of value among goods for a single actor, empirical data can be used to estimate $\mathbf{Q}_j$. If, for each unit of good j held by any actor at time t, the actor who held it at time 0 can be identified, the data have the form of a two-wave panel, and $\mathbf{Q}_j$ may be estimated by methods described in Coleman (1981). If each transaction can be traced, the methods described in the preceding section for estimation of $\mathbf{Q}_i$ may be used, making use of the fact that the expected time value will remain in a state is the inverse of the sum of transition rates out of the state.

Logical Constraints on Transition Rates in Pairwise Exchange Systems

A barter process of the sort described in the preceding sections implies certain relationships among the rates of flow of resources. The assumption that there is

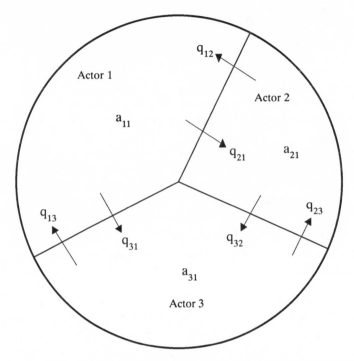

Figure 32.4   Movement of one good (good *j*) among three actors.

constant value in the form of good *j* and that an exchange involves equal flow of value in both directions implies that the amount of value held by actor *i* remains constant, for all actors.

The general process may be seen for three actors and three goods by characterizing the state in which value resides according to actor and good. In Figure 32.5 arrows show which states are connected by exchange; the states are labeled with numbers corresponding to *ij*, or actor *i* holding good *j*. Horizontal arrows represent movements of value among goods for the same actor, and vertical arrows represent movements of value among actors for the same good. The equations for the horizontal arrows for actor 1 are given by eq. 32.9, and those for the vertical arrows for good 1 are given by eq. 32.19.

For this system of exchange a particular exchange cannot be described independently of others, because of the necessity of maintaining constant value in each column and row. This can be seen by assuming that there is movement of value into state 12 (good 2 in the hands of actor 1) due to a transfer of good 2 from other actors (vertical arrows toward 12 in the center column of Figure 32.5). In order to maintain the horizontal value balances (constant power of each actor), this implies vertical movement from state 11 to states 21 and 31 or from state 13 to states 23 and 33, or both. That is, it must be that $\Delta a_{11} + \Delta a_{12} + \Delta a_{13} = 0$. Suppose Δa_{12} is wholly due to transfer from actor 2 (that is, $\Delta a_{22} =$

Goods

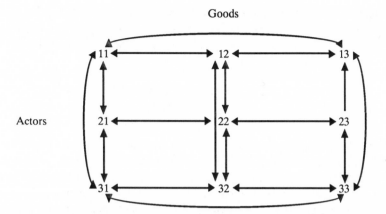

Figure 32.5 Movement of goods among actors and of actors among goods in a three-actor, three-good system.

$-\Delta a_{12}$) and compensated by a transfer from state 11 to state 21 ($\Delta a_{11} = -\Delta a_{21}$). This implies an equal movement of value from state 11 to state 12, and from state 22 to 21.

The existence of these logical constraints on the transition matrices for a system of pairwise exchange shows the importance of a clearinghouse of credit or a medium of exchange in facilitating actors' realization of interests in such a system. If there were a central clearinghouse with which exchanges could be made, none of the balancing described above would be necessary. The initial movement of value into state 12 through transfers of good 2 from actors 2 and 3 to actor 1 would be balanced by a debit to the central clearinghouse for actor 1 and a credit for actors 2 and 3. At the end of transactions no debits and credits will remain because the process of reaching an equilibrium of value before exchange ensures that there will be market clearing when all actors pursue their interests and when debits are incurred at equilibrium values.

The kind of pairwise credit system that arises for pairs of actors who have an ongoing relationship does not serve this purpose, as Chapter 6 indicated. What is necessary is a central clearinghouse, which can go beyond pairs of actors to balance a first actor's obligations to a second, and the second's obligations to a third, and the third's to the first. This is what, in effect, a monetary system with a single medium of exchange does. In social transactions which do not involve money, there is no comparable medium or clearinghouse. It is true, however, that in certain arenas, such as a legislature, a central figure (such as the Speaker of the House) does serve as an imperfect form of clearinghouse.

A Description of the Path of Values: Walrasian Adjustment

The dynamics of the process through which an equilibrium set of values is reached can also be described. Consider a procedure in which there are no exchanges until there is a set of values (or prices) at which market clearing occurs for all goods, and a central agent posts current prices at each time period and registers the demand at those prices. Then, if the central agent posts arbitrary prices $v_j(t)$ for goods j at time t, the tentative wealth of actor i can be written as

$$r_i(t) = \sum_j c_{ij} v_j(t)$$

If actor i allocates a fixed portion, x_{ji}, of his wealth to good j and this is true for all actors, the demand for j at time $t + 1$ is given by $\Sigma_j x_{ji} r_i(t)$. If there is not market clearing, the quantity of j demanded will be greater or less than the total quantity available (set arbitrarily at 1). If the total quantity demanded is written as $1 + \varepsilon_j$, where ε_j is the excess demand for j (possibly negative), then the value of the demand for j can be written as

$$v_j(t)\,(1 + \varepsilon_j) = \sum_i x_{ji} r_i(t) \tag{32.26}$$

Equation 32.26 may be rewritten to express the excess demand for j in terms of the difference between value of the demand for j and the value of the supply of j, which is $v_j(t)$:

$$\varepsilon_j v_j(t) = \sum_i x_{ji} r_i(t) - v_j(t) \tag{32.27}$$

The central agent establishes new values of v_j at time $t + 1$, depending on the demand at time t in relation to the supply. A reasonable way to do that is by adjusting v_j by ρ, a fraction of the excess or deficient demand. If that fraction is equal to 1, then $v_j(t + 1)$ is simply $v_j(t)\,(1 + \varepsilon_j)$, and eq. 32.27 shows the change in value from time t to $t + 1$. Assuming that the process moves toward an equilibrium, eq. 32.27 describes the path of that movement.[4] As the exchange process continues, if actors continue to devote the same fraction of their resources to good j, the quantity ε_j declines, approaching zero. The transactions take place at equilibrium (say at time τ), when the following equality holds:

$$v_j(\tau) = \sum_i x_{ji} r_i(\tau) \tag{32.28}$$

The process is slightly more general if the central agent does not set ρ equal to 1, but sets it at some fraction of the excess or deficient demand. In that case the

4. This assumption is valid because the process is Markovian, that is, because $\mathbf{XC}$ has the properties of a transition matrix in a Markov chain and eq. 32.23 can be written as $\Delta v(t) = \mathbf{XC}v(t) - v(t)$, or $v(t + 1) = \mathbf{XC}v(t)$. A fully communicating Markov chain always converges to an equilibrium, independent of the starting point.

equation for change in value can be written as

$$\Delta v_j(t) = \rho \left[\sum_i x_{ji} r_i(t) - v_j(t) \right]$$ (32.29)

Equation 32.29 describes the path of change in value as it approaches the equilibrium at which exchange takes place. If the exchange process were continuous in time, there would be a continuous change in value, described by

$$\frac{dv_j(t)}{dt} = \rho \left[\sum_i x_{ji} r_i(t) - v_j(t) \right]$$ (32.30)

where ρ is a constant of dimension t^{-1} expressing the rate at which equilibration occurs.

It is also possible to derive eq. 32.30 from eq. 25.11 for utility maximization. If an arbitrary price vector at time 0 is assumed and it is further assumed that actors express a demand which maximizes their utility, the demand expressed by actor i, summed over all actors, is

$$\delta_j(0) = \sum_i \frac{x_{ji}}{v_j(0)} \sum_k c_{ik} v_k(0)$$

where $\delta_j(0)$ is total demand for good j at time 0. The total supply of good j is, by assumption (see eq. 25.4), equal to 1. Expressed in terms of current value of j, the difference between demand and supply is

$$\delta_j(0) v_j(0) - v_j(0)$$

If the value adjustment is continuous, at a rate proportional to the difference between demand and supply, this gives the right-hand side of eq. 32.30.

Substituting for $r_i(t)$ in eq. 32.30 and writing the result in matrix notation gives

$$\dot{v}(t) = \rho[\mathbf{XC}v(t) - v(t)]$$ (32.31)

Defining $\mathbf{Q}$ as the matrix $\rho(\mathbf{XC} - \mathbf{I})$ allows eq. 32.31 to be written as

$$\dot{v}(t) = \mathbf{Q}v(t)$$ (32.32)

The solution of eq. 32.32 is

$$v(t) = e^{\mathbf{Q}(t)} v(0)$$ (32.33)

Comparing eq. 32.33 with eq. 32.14 shows that the process for reaching an equilibrium set of values by means of bids and price adjustments before the exchanges take place is described by the same type of equation as that for the exchange process among actors at the equilibrium prices.

The equilibrium values are realized when $\dot{v}(t) = 0$. Thus from eq. 32.32, at equilibrium,

$$\mathbf{Q}v = 0$$ (32.34)

Then, if **1** is an $n \times n$ matrix of ones and $\mathbf{1}_1$ is an $n \times 1$ vector of ones, since $\mathbf{1v} = \mathbf{1}_1$, this equation can be written:

$$\mathbf{Qv} + \mathbf{1v} = \mathbf{1}_1$$

Its solution is

$$\mathbf{v} = (\mathbf{Q} + \mathbf{1})^{-1}\mathbf{1}_1 \qquad (32.35)$$

Since $\mathbf{Q}$ has been defined as $\rho(\mathbf{XC} - \mathbf{I})$, this solution for $\mathbf{v}$ is the same as that given in eqs. 25.16–25.19.

Obviously an analogous equation can be written for change in the nominal wealth of each actor at current values. This entails beginning with an equation similar to eq. 32.27 but showing the change in r_i rather than the change in v_j. The rate equation analogous to eq. 32.31 is

$$\dot{\mathbf{r}}(t) = \rho(\mathbf{CX} - \mathbf{I})\mathbf{r}(t) \qquad (32.36)$$

Dynamics of Systems with Social-Structural Barriers

Earlier sections have described general models in which the rate of acquisition by actor i of value in the form of good j may not be independent of the form in which actor i currently holds value (that is, $_iq_{jk} \neq {}_iq_{jh}$ for other goods k and h) or may not be independent of the other actors from whom actor i gets good j (that is, $_jq_{ik} \neq {}_jq_{ih}$ for other actors k and h). There may be real social structures, however, such that certain pairs of goods are more or less capable of being exchanged or certain pairs of actors are more or less likely to engage in transactions. The presence of these relations, or barriers, has certain implications. The rate at which an actor acquires a good depends either on something (other than value) about what he must give up for it or on something about whom he must trade with to get it. These pairwise relations constitute a structure superimposed on the exchange process. They are common in social systems, as well as in most kinds of economic exchange systems (see Baker, 1983). They imply something other than a fully competitive market. It is these relations or barriers to which the term "social structure" or "social networks" is often applied.

The dynamics of such a system may be examined by treating both barriers between pairs of actors and barriers between pairs of resources. These barriers (or partial barriers) can be regarded as introducing a deterrent to the effective demand ($z_{ik}r_k = \sum_j c_{ij}x_{jk}r_k$) of actor k for goods held by actor i or a reduction in the effective value of good h in transactions involving good j ($w_{jh}v_h = \sum_i x_{ji}c_{ih}v_h$). First the effects on the price (and power) distributions in the equilibration before exchange will be examined, and then the effects on the exchange itself.

Effects of Barriers between Actors on Distribution of Power

Barriers between actors may be represented by introducing quantities α_{ik}, where $0 \leq \alpha_{ik} \leq 1$. These quantities represent the reduction in the intensity of interest for all transactions in which k acquires something controlled by i. Using these quantities as multipliers for z_{ik} gives

$$z_{ik}^* = z_{ik}\alpha_{ik}$$

From eq. 32.36 the equation for the rate of change of r_i in a perfect system, prior to the exchange process, is

$$\frac{dr_i(t)}{dt} = \rho\left[\sum_{j=1}^m c_{ij} \sum_{k=1}^n x_{jk}r_k(t) - r_i(t)\right], \qquad \text{for } i = 1, \ldots, n \quad (32.37)$$

$$= \rho\left[\sum_k z_{ik}r_k(t) - r_i(t)\right]$$

The quation for the general process is

$$\frac{dr_i(t)}{dt} = q_{ik}r_k(t), \qquad \text{for } i = 1, \ldots, n, k \neq i \qquad (32.38)$$

where

$$q_{ii} = -\sum_{k \neq i} q_{ki}$$

This constraint on q_{ii} is necessary for conservation, that is, in order that r_i will sum to 1.0 over all states of the system (that is, over all actors). In this special case

$$q_{ik} = \rho z_{ik}, \qquad \text{for } k \neq i$$

and

$$q_{ii} = \rho(z_{ii} - 1)$$

Because $\sum_{k=1}^n z_{ki} = 1$, $\rho(z_{ii} - 1) = -\rho \sum_{k \neq i} z_{ki}$, satisfying the constraint on q_{ii}.

When barriers are introduced, with $\alpha_{ik} < 1$ for some i or k, then for some i, $\sum_{k=1}^n z_{ki}^* < 1$. For conservation this implies that q_{ii} is greater than $\rho(z_{ii}^* - 1)$ for some i. In general,

$$q_{ii} = \rho\left(z_{ii}^* - \sum_{k=1}^n z_{ki}^*\right)$$

What does this mean substantively? Consider z_{ki}, which is k's control over what i is interested in. In a perfectly competitive system this is i's propensity to trade with k. But if α_{ki} is less than 1, this is a partial or complete barrier to i's getting something from k. This implies that demand for, or effective interest in, the resources held by k is reduced. Effective interest is reduced to the extent that $\sum_{k \neq i} z_{ki}^*$ is less than 1. Does this mean that k's power is reduced? Answering that question requires seeing whether introduction of symmetric parameters α_{ik} into

$_jq_{ik}$ affects the equilibrium. At equilibrium, when $dr_k/dt = 0$ for all k, the rate of flow of value between each pair of states

$$z_{ik}r_k = z_{ki}r_i + \Delta r_{ki}$$

where Δr_{ki} is zero if there are no compensating flows involving three or more states (see p. 889 for discussion). Introducing barriers gives

$$z_{ik}\alpha_{ik}r_k = z_{ki}\alpha_{ri}r_i + \alpha_{ki}\Delta r_{ki}$$

As long as $\alpha_{ik} = \alpha_{ki}$, the second equation reduces to the first. Thus introducing parameters α_{ik} of any size into the system does not affect the equilibrium state as long as $\alpha_{ik} = \alpha_{ki}$ for all i and k.

The absence of effect on the equilibrium power distribution does not imply, however, that there is no effect on the path from the initial power distribution to the equilibrium power distribution. What that path would be can be seen by first defining

$$\mathbf{Q} = \|q_{ik}\| \qquad \text{(an } n \times n \text{ matrix)}$$

where

$$q_{ik} = z_{ik}\alpha_{ik}, \quad \text{for } i = 1, \ldots, n, \quad k = 1, \ldots, n, \quad k \neq i$$

$$q_{ii} = -\sum_{h \neq i} z_{hi}\alpha_{hi}$$

Then this equation, analogous to eq. 32.33, can be written:

$$\mathbf{r}(t) = \mathbf{e}^{\mathbf{Q}t}\mathbf{r}(0)$$

The effect of the barriers to exchange is to make the movement to equilibrium slower. The barriers reduce the transition rates, so the initial distribution of resources will persist over a longer period of time. Because the equilibration of value and power is seen as occurring rapidly, prior to the exchange itself, the rate at which it occurs is irrelevant for the analysis of exchange. The equilibrium states are unaffected by barriers to exchange.[5]

Because of the formal correspondence between value and power, the results described above also hold for the effects of barriers between pairs of goods. There is an effect in delaying the movement of values to equilibrium, but no effect on the equilibrium state itself.

Effects of Barriers between Actors on Exchange

The equation for the rate of change of the amount of value in the form of good j in the hands of actor k is given as eq. 32.23 for the general case where $_jq_{ki}$ are unconstrained by the competitive market assumption that the demand for good j

---

5. If the barriers were asymmetric (that is, if $\alpha_{ik} \neq \alpha_{ki}$), they would have an effect on the equilibrium distribution.

by actor k is independent of the actor who currently holds that good. (When that assumption is made, the transition rate is given by eq. 32.21.) If the assumption is not made and barriers represented by $\alpha_{ik} < 1$ are introduced, then eq. 32.21 becomes

$$_j q_{ki} = \alpha_{ik} \frac{\gamma x_{jk} r_k}{v_j} \qquad (32.39)$$

What is the effect of barriers between actors on the equilibrium distribution of resources among actors and on the rate of exchange of resources?

As with power and value, each comparison of flow rates (here the flow of resource j in and out of the hands of actor k) shows that there is no effect of these barriers on the equilibrium distribution of resources, as long as $\alpha_{ik} = \alpha_{ki}$ for all i and k. In the absence of barriers, for good j in the hands of actor k, at equilibrium the flow of value from actor i to actor k equals the flow from k to i:

$$_j q_{ki} a_{ij} - {_j q_{ik}} a_{kj} = 0$$

At equilibrium, $a_{ij} = c_{ij}^* v_j = x_{ji} r_i$, and substituting for $_j q_{..}$ and $a_{..}$ gives

$$\frac{x_{jk} r_k}{v_j} x_{ji} r_i - \frac{x_{ji} r_i}{v_i} x_{jk} r_k = 0$$

The relative flows are unaffected if the two rates are multiplied by α_{ik} and α_{ki}, respectively, as long as these coefficients are equal.

As with power and value, barriers between actors have an effect on the exchange of resources prior to equilibrium. Here, however, because the process is assumed to operate more slowly, this effect may be a lasting one. Many social subsystems never reach equilibrium before being changed by the introduction of new events. Thus nonequilibrium distributions may be important; and social-structural barriers can have important effects on these states.

How Do Power of Actors and Values of Events Change?

In the system of action as I have described it, there are no changes in the equilibrium values of events and the equilibrium power of actors. The preceding sections showed how, given the distributions of control of events and interests in events, the nominal value and power will change from an arbitrary starting point to an equilibrium, before any exchanges take place. All this is conceived to take place before exchange in a process by which actors feel each other out and set values at which exchange will take place. But nothing has been said about how there can be a change from one equilibrium to another.

The substance of the matter is straightforward. There are several sources of such change:

1. New events or goods can enter the system under control of one of the actors.

2. New actors, who have a particular distribution of control of events, can enter the system. The simplest such case is that in which the entering actor has partial control of events or resources already in the system and previously under the control of the actors already there or in which a leaving actor relinquishes control of events to the actors who remain in the system.
3. New actors can enter the system bringing new goods or events in which actors already in the system have some interest, or actors already in the system can leave, taking with them the events or goods over which they have control.

As an example of change of the first type, consider the exchange system of the trading-card example of Chapter 25, in which there were 100 cards of each type. Tom had an interest of .008 in each football card and an interest of .002 in each baseball card, and John had an interest of .005 in each type of card. Then 100 more baseball cards came into the system, 96 under John's control and 4 under Tom's. This brought about both a change in the relative values of football and baseball cards and a change in the relative power of Tom and John. Tom's power in the original system was .681, and it was reduced to .499 in the new system. The value of each football card in the original system was .0070, and it was reduced to .0050; the value of each baseball card was reduced from .0030 to .0025. The example can be worked out to show the path from the old equilibrium vectors of values and power to the new. This change occurs, according to the model, before any exchanges but after the new cards enter the system.

Equation 32.31 describes the rate of change of values during the period preceding exchanges for particular distributions of interest and control. If the starting point, $v(0)$, is not an arbitrary vector of values, as assumed earlier in describing the movement to equilibrium, but the equilibrium vector for the original system, then the solution to eq. 32.31, using the new X and C matrices, describes the path of values from the old equilibrium to the new. In the trading-card example being considered, the original value of football cards was .704, and that of baseball cards was .296. In the new system these values were .498 and .502, respectively. The equation giving the vector of values at time t as a function of the vector of values at time 0 is

$$v(t) = e^{Qt}v(0)$$

where Q for the new system is $XC - I$. Using the normalized power and value matrices gives

$$Q = \begin{bmatrix} .667 & .333 \\ .333 & .667 \end{bmatrix}\begin{bmatrix} .95 & .04 \\ .05 & .96 \end{bmatrix} - \begin{bmatrix} 1 & 0 \\ 0 & 1 \end{bmatrix} = \begin{bmatrix} -.35 & .3467 \\ .35 & -.3467 \end{bmatrix}$$

Using eq. 32.15 to find e^{Qt} for different values of t allows calculating the predicted path of the change in values of football and baseball cards as they approach the new equilibrium. The paths are shown in Figure 32.6: a smooth exponential decline or increase to the new equilibrium value.

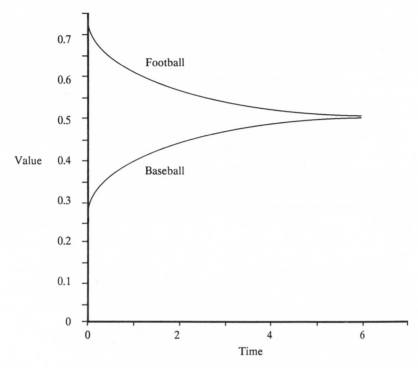

Figure 32.6   Change in total values of two types of trading cards after numbers of cards in the exchange system change from 100 of each type to 100 baseball and 200 football.

More generally, when wholly new events or goods come into a system under a particular distribution of control, the new distribution of control and interests will in general lead to a new equilibrium, and the path toward the new equilibrium may be described as above.

The third type of change listed earlier can be illustrated by again referring to the trading-card exchange system. If Tom, John, and Steve are within the system, each holding a set of trading cards and if Steve leaves after cards have been traded, the relative power of Tom and John will change, as will the relative values of the cards they hold. A new exchange process will take place. A more realistic example of a social system is a school. If a new girl enters a high school, with a particular set of resources and a particular set of interests, the relative power of those currently in the system will change. The magnitude of that will change depending on the interests of those in the school in what she brings into the system and on the degree to which her interests in others in the system coincide with their current values in the system. Chapter 27 shows how partitioning of systems of action can illuminate the sources of such changes.

In addition to the three kinds of changes listed earlier, where actors or resources or both migrate in or out of the system, there are changes by which new events enter the system, which are of interest to some actors and have some dependency relations with events already in the system. In such a circumstance there may be a struggle for control of the new indivisible event, with existing power in the system determining the outcome. This case is treated in the examination of conflict in Chapter 31.

33

Unstable and Transient
Systems of Action

The social system that is described by the formal theory presented so far has a particular property that is produced by the constraints of exchange. Control over goods and events is limited, and the systemic functioning is dependent on a balance of power among those who are interested in gaining control. That functioning consists of actors using resources under their control to gain control of other resources of greater interest to them, in competition with others also interested in gaining control of the same resources. The equilibrium that is achieved is one in which each actor's resources are pitted against, or balanced against, the resources of other actors in the system.

That balance is represented by the ratio of control that two actors, i and k, have at equilibrium over resource j, where the resource is divisible and has no externalities (from eq. 25.11):

$$\frac{c_{ij}^*}{c_{kj}^*} = \frac{x_{ji}r_i}{x_{jk}r_k}$$

The ratio of equilibrium control of the resource is the product of i's power and interest relative to the product of k's power and interest. Subject to the constraints imposed by properties of the resources, by the social structure, and by the institutional rules under which exchange takes place, the system functions to allocate control so as to give an efficient equilibrium, one which has the same effective meaning for the system as maximization of utility does for the individual. That is, goods and events come into the hands of the actors who are most interested in them, relative to the actors' initial control of resources.

The systemic constraints which induce this balance are actors' limited control over events and goods, which operate for the system in just the way that a budget constraint operates for an individual. It is in this sense that economics has been described as the science of the allocation of scarce goods; and it is in this sense that Arrow and Hahn are to be understood: "A social system moved by independent actions in pursuit of different values is consistent with a final coherent state of balance" (1971, p. 1).

But suppose there is a system in which individuals still engage in their internal balancing, but this does not lead to a system balance. How could that be? The nature of the internal balancing carried out by the individual is ordinarily stated as the individual's balancing of utility gained from using scarce resources to acquire one good with utility gained from using those same resources to acquire another good. More generally, it can be stated as the individual's allocation of resources in such a way as to maximize utility. The difference between the more general statement and the narrower one lies in the assumption that the allocation of scarce resources requires the acquisition of goods which are in demand by others.

It is this assumption which translates the individual's allocation of scarce resources into a systemic allocation of scarce resources, and the individual's balance into a systemic balance. But the assumption is not always met. It is not met when the individual's decision about how to allocate resources so as to maximize utility does not require using resources to acquire goods or control over events that are in demand by others. The individual may still be confronted with a budget constraint, that is, a decision about how to allocate scarce resources, but the resources may not be in demand by others. In such a circumstance the attempts on the part of individuals to establish internal equilibria may not lead to equilibration at the system level but to something quite different.

One kind of decision that the individual may confront is whether to allocate control over his actions to himself or to another. If the expected benefits of allocating control to another are greater than the expected benefits of allocating control to himself, then he is rational to allocate control to the other. That is, in the terms of Chapter 5, if he trusts the judgment of the other more than he does his own and the other's judgment is freely available to him, he will transfer control to the other. For example, if a person hears that a firm in which he holds stock is about to fail and he trusts the source from which he learned this more than he trusts other sources of information, he will sell his stock immediately. If others who hold stock hear the same information, they too can transfer control over their action to the source of the information, and immediately sell their stock.

There are no systemic constraints in such a case. The system can "run wild" because there is no competition for scarce resources within it. The usual equilibrating constraints are missing. Thus, in such a case, there is an individual-level balancing that does not lead to system-level balancing. The result at the system level is, in a wide variety of circumstances, the phenomena loosely grouped under the heading of collective behavior. In this chapter I will examine some of these phenomena using a mathematical treatment in which the individual criterion of rationality remains but there is no system-level constraint as introduced in eq. 25.12 in the form of relative prices of goods. The individual's decision about allocating control over his own actions is not subject to that systemic constraint; he has only to apply the criterion of which allocation will bring the greatest expected return.

Single-Contingency and Double-Contingency Collective Behavior

The various phenomena known as collective behavior appear to have two properties in common. One property, stated above, is that the resource that actors can be regarded as allocating rationally is control over their own actions, which in these settings is a resource not in demand by others and therefore not subject to exchange in a competitive context.[1] The other property is that an actor's allocation of this resource, although not subject to market constraints, may be dependent on others' actions.

The dependence of this allocation on others' actions may be due to any of several sources. For example, others' actions may constitute additional information for an actor in an uncertain environment. In the period during which a run on a bank develops, withdrawals by others may increase an actor's beliefs in the bank's insolvency. Others' actions may instead directly change for an actor the expected outcomes of his action. Looting on the part of members of a crowd is initially held in check by the threat of punishment from authorities. The looting done by other crowd members, once it begins, reduces this danger for the actor, both by providing a shield hiding his actions from authorities and by making punishment of any of the participants less likely.

The systemic instability that characterizes collective behavior arises from this interdependence of different actors' actions. There are, however, two levels of interdependence. One occurs when the collective behavior involves a single action on the part of each actor, and the other arises when there is a sequence of actions on the part of each actor. I will call these single-contingency and double-contingency collective behavior, respectively. Single-contingency collective behavior is exemplified by a bank panic, in which each depositor either takes the single action of withdrawing his funds or does not. Double-contingency collective behavior is exemplified by a physical escape panic or a hostile crowd.

There is a structural difference between single-contingency and double-contingency collective behavior. In the case of single contingency, an actor's action is contingent on that of others, but it affects his outcome directly and not through its effect on the actions of others (that is, for example, he either gets his money or does not when he goes to withdraw it from the bank). Thus to act rationally in such circumstances requires only that he estimate the expected outcome of his actions in an uncertain environment. He may use others' actions as an aid in doing so.

In double-contingency collective behavior, however, the actor's action affects

---

1. In other settings this resource is in demand by others: There is competition for control over actors' actions, and an actor will give up this control to the highest bidder. In most forms of collective behavior, however, the actor allocates control over his actions based not on what others offer him, but on the benefits he sees as accruing to him from the allocation; the two things are the same from his point of view, but not from the system perspective.

his outcome not only directly but also indirectly, through the actions of others. The outcome for him is thus contingent on the actions of others, which are in turn contingent on his actions. Each of the others is in similar circumstances, attempting to choose the best actions, given that one's action has its effect in part through its effect on the actions of others. This creates a feedback process among a set of rational actors, which greatly complicates the very concept of what constitutes rational or optimal action.

The greater indeterminacy about just what action is rational in structures of action characterized by double contingency can be seen as follows: In single-contingency behavior there is a feedback loop from the actor's current action through its consequences to the actor's future actions. He uses information about others' previous actions to better predict those consequences. But in the case of double-contingency behavior, the feedback loop contains the strategic actions of others. The actor acts; his action affects others, who act in such a way as to influence his future actions in a way that will be beneficial to them. Recognizing this, he in turn acts in such a way that their actions will be beneficial to him.

To anticipate how to achieve one's goal, and thus to act rationally, in a single-contingency situation involves predicting outcomes in the presence of risk or uncertainty. To act rationally in a double-contingency situation involves predicting what actions others will take, that is, what strategies they will pursue. The simplifying assumption of von Neumann and Morgenstern (1947), which made possible solutions to two-person zero-sum games, was that each player would assume that the other would respond optimally to actions of an opponent. This in turn would cause each player to respond optimally to what would be the optimal response to an optimal response (which can usefully be described as a sequence of best replies).

But such an assumption is not always appropriate. It is not appropriate when one actor has information about the other's actions that is inconsistent with the assumption. Thus, in a double-contingency situation, if one is in a population of others about whose past actions one has some information, such an assumption is not valid. Also, the assumption is probably not appropriate for knife-edge situations, in which small deviations from actions consistent with the assumption produce large variations in consequences.

Because of such considerations, it is necessary to develop and apply models and theories that are less mathematically elegant and parsimonious but accord more with reality. The rationality that must emerge in such situations is action that differs depending on one's assumptions about the strategies of others, or population-contingent rationality. The recognition of this has led to the introduction of various concepts in evolutionary biology: evolutionarily stable strategies, invadability of populations, and other related concepts (see Maynard Smith, 1974; Axelrod, 1984).

Thus the difference between single-contingency and double-contingency collective behavior is a fundamental one; it leads to a difference in what constitutes rational action. As will be evident in subsequent sections of this chapter, the double-contingency case requires the more extensive analysis.

A note on game theory is relevant here. Although game theory generated a great amount of interest from its birth, it has until recently been of little value to social scientists. The reason why recent applications have been of value probably lies in the shift of theorists' attention from single-play to sequential games. For example, the single-play prisoner's dilemma is of little use other than as a demonstration of the additional gain that can sometimes be realized from joint action (or the loss that is sometimes incurred from individual maximization). The prisoner's dilemma becomes of considerable interest, however, when it is made into a sequential game, an iterated prisoner's dilemma. Similar statements are true for other two-person games, such as coordination games or the game called "chicken." Bargaining theory makes use of the theory of games, but again sequential games rather than single-play games. Furthermore, even the heuristics surrounding single-play games employ sequential thinking. In von Neumann and Morgenstern's 1947 book, the notion of a minorant game in which the player must play first, and a majorant game in which he plays second, are used as heuristic devices to justify the minimax solution for a single-play game.

In a single-contingency panic, an actor's decision whether to transfer control over his actions to others or to act unilaterally is rather straightforward. The only question in the case of a bank panic is whether to trust the information that the bank is insolvent. Other persons' actions can aid in making this decision, by confirming or disconfirming the initial report; and other persons' actions can affect the actor's estimate of how quickly he must withdraw if he is to recover his money. Since other persons' actions are not contingent on his own in any way that can affect the outcome for him, he need not take into account the possible effects of his action on theirs.

Thus a property of any single-contingency panic, in which the individual carries out a single action which leads to an outcome for him, is that others' actions may be contingent on his (for example, they may use it to confirm the information they have), but his action will have brought about the outcome of interest to him before the actions contingent on his have taken place. Single-contingency panics are therefore simpler to analyze than double-contingency panics.

Transfer of Control in Single-Contingency Panics

Because individuals' attempts at internal equilibration do not necessarily lead to system equilibrium, what is relevant here is not the equilibrium state of the system, but its dynamics. For binary actions (for example, withdraw money from a bank or not) the appropriate stochastic model is a continuous-time, discrete-state Markov process (see Coleman, 1964; Cox and Miller, 1965; Tuma and Hannan, 1984). The appropriate deterministic model at the level of the system is a differential equation.

The single-contingency panic is useful for demonstrating the transition from the micro level (the individual actor), at which the process is specified, to the macro level (the system of actors), at which the systemic behavior is observed. The two situations which may occur are that in which a single source of information leads to action, with each individual acting independently, and that in which the actor also uses others' actions as a way of confirming the initial information. I will treat the former, which is simpler, first.

A Single-Contingency Panic with Information from a Single Source

For the model of a process by which a single individual moves between two states, 0 and 1, the necessary definitions are

$p_1(t) \equiv$ probability of being in state 1 at time t

$q_{10}(t) \equiv$ transition rate (of dimension t^{-1}) at time t for movement from state 0 to state 1; $q_{ij_t}(t) = \lim_{\Delta t \to 0} [p_{ij}(\Delta t)/\Delta t]$, where $p_{ij}(\Delta t)$ is the probability of being in state i at time $t + \Delta t$ given occupancy of state j at time t

$q_{01}(t) \equiv$ transition rate at time t for movement from state 1 to state 0

In this notation the subscripts on transition rates are in reverse order from the way they usually appear in notation for stochastic processes. This is consistent with the notation used in Chapter 32, which is in turn consistent with the equilibrium models of earlier chapters. Except where necessary for clarity, I will write $p_i(t)$ as p_i.

The equation defining a two-state Markov process for the individual is

$$\frac{dp_1(t)}{dt} = -q_{01}(t)p_1(t) + q_{10}(t)[1 - p_1(t)] \tag{33.1}$$

A diagram representing such a process is shown in Figure 33.1.

If the process is governed by transition rates that are constant over time, $q_{ij}(t) = q_{ij}$. (For the two-state case I will drop the subscript referring to the state of origin, so q_{10} becomes q_1, and q_{01} becomes q_0.) When the rates are constant

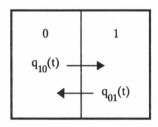

Figure 33.1   Transition rates between two states for an individual.

over time, eq. 33.1 may be solved for the probability of being in state 1 at time t:

$$p_1(t) = p_1(0)e^{-(q_0+q_1)t} + \frac{q_1}{q_0 + q_1}(1 - e^{-(q_0+q_1)t}) \qquad (33.2)$$

The right-hand side of this equation has a transient term (to the left of the plus sign) and a nontransient term (to the right). As $t \to \infty$,

$$p_1 = \frac{q_1}{q_0 + q_1} \qquad (33.3)$$

If the process consists of movement in only one direction, eq. 33.2 reduces to

$$p_1(t) = 1 - e^{-q_1 t}[1 - p_1(0)] \qquad \text{if } q_0 = 0 \qquad (33.4)$$

or

$$p_1(t) = p_1(0) \, e^{-q_0 t} \qquad \text{if } q_1 = 0 \qquad (33.5)$$

This process is stated at the level of the individual. Suppose that there are a number of individuals who have deposits in the same bank and identical responses to a signal that the bank is insolvent, which they all receive at the same time. Suppose further that this response is withdrawal of deposits. Then there is a system of action consisting of independent individuals all governed by the same process, as described by eq. 33.1. If state 0 is the state in which money is left in the bank and state 1 is the state in which the money has been withdrawn, then all are in state 0 at time 0 (when the signal is given that the bank is insolvent). With $q_{01} = 0$ and q_{10} represented as q_1, eq. 33.1 becomes

$$\frac{dp_1}{dt} = q_1(1 - p_1)$$

and the probability that any actor has withdrawn his money at time t is

$$p_1(t) = 1 - e^{-q_1 t} \qquad (33.6)$$

For a set of n individuals, the stochastic process may be described as the probability of moving in and out of system state i, which is the state in which i persons have withdrawn their funds. The probability of the system's being in state i is defined as s_i, which is a function of time (with t suppressed in the notation). Because the individual-level processes are independent, the transition rate between states is simply the sum of the transition rates for those individual actors who are still in state 0. Those rates are

$$\frac{ds_0}{dt} = -nq_1s_0 \qquad (33.7)$$

$$\frac{ds_i}{dt} = (n - i + 1)q_1s_{i-1} - (n - i)q_1s_i$$

$$\frac{ds_n}{dt} = q_1s_{n-1}$$

Figure 33.2 is a diagram representing this macro or system level, where n individuals are all governed by the process represented in Figure 33.1.

Solving the above set of equations gives:

$$s_i(t) = \binom{n}{i}(1 - e^{-q_1 t})^i e^{-q_1 t(n-i)} \tag{33.8}$$

which is the binomial distribution with probability of success on a single trial equal to $1 - e^{-q_1 t}$.

That the transition rates between states for the system-level process may be written as simply the sum of the transition rates for the individual-level process follows from the fact that the transition rates are instantaneous rates, and are therefore unbounded from above and have only a lower bound at 0. The expected value of i, the system-level state, is given by the sum of the probabilities of the individual states. From eq. 33.6,

$$E(i) = np_1(t) = n(1 - e^{-q_1 t}) \tag{33.9}$$

To write an equation for the deterministic process at the system level of change in the number who have withdrawn requires defining m and ϕ:

$$m \equiv \text{number who have withdrawn (t is implicit)}$$

$$\phi \equiv \text{rate of withdrawals (of dimension t^{-1})}$$

If ϕ is constant over time, the rate equation is

$$\frac{dm}{dt} = \phi(n - m)$$

Dividing through by n gives an equation for change in the proportion who have withdrawn, where that proportion is denoted by p_1^*:

$$\frac{dp_1^*}{dt} = \phi(1 - p_1^*)$$

Solving for p_1^* gives

$$p_1^*(t) = 1 - e^{-\phi t} \tag{33.10}$$

Comparing eq. 33.10 with eq. 33.9 shows that $m = E(i)$ if $\phi = q_1$. That is, the

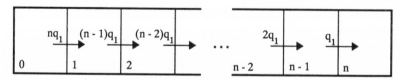

Figure 33.2   Transition rates among $n + 1$ states for a system.

number who have withdrawn at time t in the deterministic equation is the same as the expected value of the number who will have withdrawn at time t in the stochastic equation. This follows from the fact that each individual is responding independently to the signal. In such a circumstance the process as described at the system level is of the same form as the process as described at the individual level. The micro-to-macro transition consists of nothing more than aggregation of the individual-level processes.

This is an instance in which (to resuscitate the individualism-holism debate) the holistic, or system-level, "law" is identical to the individual-level "law." It is not always true that a process of the same form can be specified at individual and systemic levels. When the individual's action depends on others' actions, a deterministic analog of the individual-level process does not give results that correspond to the expected value for the individual-level stochastic process. This will be made apparent in the next section.

The assumptions made here that individual responses are identical and that transition rates are constant over time are obviously assumptions that simplify reality. The same processes can be specified without these two assumptions, but the mathematics becomes more difficult. (Models which introduce these complexities may be found in Bartholomew, 1973.) It is important to examine one assumption made here, however, for its relaxation involves introducing the first level of interdependence between actions of different actors. In the next section I will relax the assumption that actors attend only to the initial signal and do not use one another's actions to confirm it.

A Single-Contingency Panic with Information Confirmed by Others' Actions

The preceding section dealt with a situation in which each actor responded individually to a single signal of danger. Even in a single-stage panic, however, actors may make use of information from others' actions. The simplest case where they do so is described by a process which is an extension of that described in the preceding section. In this case the transition rate $q_1(t)$ is not generated solely by the initial signal, but is increased by observation of the actions of others in moving from state 0 to state 1 (in a bank panic the action of others in withdrawing funds). The following simplifying assumptions may be made:

Each actor responds in the same way.
Each actor's action constitutes the same degree of confirmation of the initial information, thus augmenting transition rates to the same degree.
Each actor treats each other actor's action as information independent of the information provided by others' actions.
Transition rates change only in response to additional information.

These assumptions allow specifying each actor's transition rate to state 1 when i actors have already moved to state 1:

$$q_1 = \alpha + i\beta$$

where

$\alpha \equiv$ transition rate to state 1 due to initial signal

$\beta \equiv$ transition rate to state 1 due to another actor's being in that state

Then the process for an individual may be stated as

$$\frac{dp_1}{dt} = (\alpha + i\beta)(1 - p_1) \tag{33.11}$$

Solving for p_1 gives

$$p_1 = 1 - e^{-(\alpha + i\beta)t} \tag{33.12}$$

Here the first complications due to the interdependence of actions become evident. Equation 33.12 can be written only if i has remained constant over the interval from time 0 to time t. But in the present context this is explicitly not the case. In such a circumstance the move from the individual to the systemic level cannot be accomplished by a simple aggregation of the outcomes of the individual-level processes to give a system-level outcome, as is done in writing eq. 33.12. What is necessary instead is first to aggregate the instantaneous-level processes which have the form of a differential equation like eq. 33.11 to obtain a system-level process, and only then to obtain the system-level solution, or outcome. This will not, in general, give a system-level "law" that is a structural analog to the "law" obtained at the individual level. In this kind of circumstance a deterministic process specified at the system level does not in general correctly correspond to the expected value for the system-level stochastic process.

The individual-level instantaneous equation (33.11), with the four assumptions given above, leads to equations for the system-level process:

$$\frac{ds_0}{dt} = -n\alpha s_0 \tag{33.13}$$

$$\frac{ds_i}{dt} = (n - i + 1)[\alpha + (i - 1)\beta]s_{i-1} - (n - i)(\alpha + i\beta)s_i,$$
$$\text{where } i = 1, \ldots, n - 1$$

$$\frac{ds_n}{dt} = [\alpha + (n - 1)\beta]s_{n-1}$$

A diagram of the process is shown in Figure 33.3. This system of equations leads to a complicated distribution function, which will not be reproduced here. (It may be found in Bailey, 1963.)

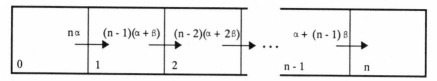

Figure 33.3 Transition rates among $n + 1$ states for a system with transfer of control.

The asymptotic expected value of i, the number who will have withdrawn by time t, is given, for large n and for i not near 0 or n, by the following equation (from Bartholomew, 1973, p. 304):

$$E(i) \approx n \left(\frac{e^\lambda - \alpha/\beta + 1}{e^\lambda + n} \right) \qquad (33.14)$$

where

$$\lambda = (\beta n + \alpha)t - \gamma + \theta(\alpha/\beta - 1)$$

$$\gamma = .5772 \ldots \qquad \text{(Euler's constant)}$$

$$\theta(x) = \sum_{i=1}^{\infty} \left(\frac{1}{i} - \frac{1}{i + x} \right)$$

For the two processes given by eqs. 33.7 and 33.13, the expected number who will have withdrawn by a given time is shown in Figure 33.4; the values plotted were obtained using eqs. 33.9 and 33.14. The transition rate to withdrawal due to the initial signal is the same for each process; in addition, the transition rate for the second process is augmented by an amount equal to 1/10 of the rate due to the initial signal for each depositor who withdraws. The group size assumed for the figure is 100. Thus, for the second process, the transition rate for the first to withdraw is the same as the rate for all actors in the first process; the transition rate for the last to withdraw is 10.9 times that for the first. As comparing eq. 33.14 with eq. 33.9 indicates, the interaction among actors produces a very different process.

Figure 33.4 shows that there are two differences. First, the process goes to completion at a much greater speed when each actor uses others' actions to confirm the initial information. Second, the process takes a different form over time. Without the interaction among actors, the number withdrawing per unit time declines continuously as the number at risk shrinks (even though each actor has the same constant rate); with the interaction the number withdrawing per unit time accelerates for the first half of the period, until the number at risk declines enough to overcome the increasing transition rate for each.

Another consequence of the interdependence of actions can be seen by writing an equation for the system-level deterministic process, as was done for the case

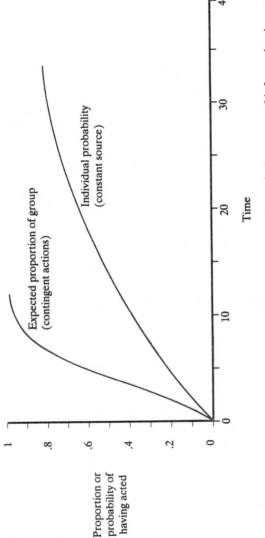

Figure 33.4 Probability that an individual will respond to a single source of information in a single-contingency panic and proportion of group (of size 100) expected to respond.

of noninterdependence in eq. 33.10. I define m and ϕ as before and add a new definition:

$\psi \equiv$ increment to transition rate to withdrawal per additional actor who has withdrawn

Then

$$\frac{dm}{dt} = (\phi + m\psi)(n - m) \tag{33.15}$$

Dividing through by n gives an equation for the change in the proportion who have withdrawn, where that proportion is denoted as before by p_1^*:

$$\frac{dp_1^*}{dt} = (\phi + \psi np_1^*)(1 - p_1^*) \tag{33.16}$$

The solution of eq. 33.15 for m, the number who have withdrawn, is

$$m = n\left(\frac{e^{(\psi n + \phi)t} - 1}{e^{(\psi n + \phi)t} + \psi n/\phi}\right) \tag{33.17}$$

Note that in this case (in contrast to the earlier case) comparison of the individual-level stochastic process given by eq. 33.11 and the system-level deterministic process given by eq. 33.16 shows a difference. For eq. 33.11 to be comparable to eq. 33.16, the quantity i in eq. 33.11, which is the number who have acted, would instead have to be $E(i)$, the expected number who will have acted. But then eq. 33.11 would represent a process in which the individual's change in probability of withdrawing would be dependent on the expected number who have withdrawn rather than the actual number, which is meaningless in this context.

The consequence of this difference is that the system-level "law" (eq. 33.17) based on a system-level analogue (eq. 33.15) of the individual-level process is not the same as the system-level "law" derived from the individual-level process (eq. 33.14). The deterministic equation written at the system level will in general understate the rate of change.

The difference between the stochastic process and the deterministic one at the system level can be seen in Figure 33.5. The magnitude of the difference (with $n = 100$ for this illustration) is not large; it would be larger for a smaller n. What is important is that the interdependence of actions generates a system-level process (eq. 33.14) that is different from the system-level process (eq. 33.17) that is not derived from the individual-level process.

Double-Contingency Panics

In a single-contingency panic, rationality plays only a small role in the analysis, for the actor's task is merely to estimate which of two possible states is true (for

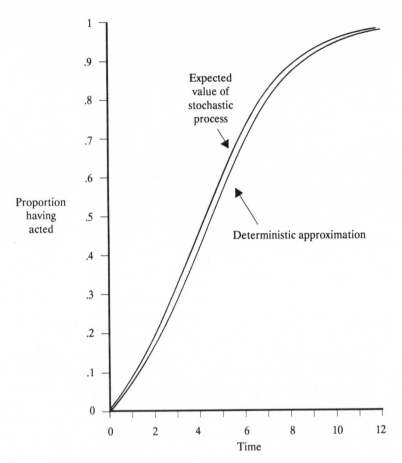

Figure 33.5 Proportion of a group (of size 100) expected to respond in a single-contingency panic, compared to a deterministic approximation.

example, the bank is or is not solvent). In double-contingency collective behavior, the orientation of the actor changes drastically, and to capture that the analysis must change as well. Thus matters are more complicated, and it is helpful to examine first the simplest case: two actors in a sequence of actions that correspond to an escape panic.

Two-Person Escape Panic

A case that can be seen as the prototype of actions that are doubly contingent is an iterated prisoner's dilemma. I suggested in Chapter 9 that this structure corresponds to that of a physical escape panic; here I will use a physical escape panic as an example. Suppose there are two actors, Jay and Kay, and run and

Table 33.1   Reward structure for two persons in escape panic.

Kay

		Walk	Run
Jay	Walk	Ww_j, Ww_k	Wr_j, Rw_k
	Run	Rw_j, Wr_k	Rr_j, Rr_k

walk are the two possible actions. I will assume there are rewards at each stage, as shown in Table 33.1 (the capital letter represents the action of the actor denoted by the subscript, and the lowercase letter represents the action of the other actor; for example, Rw_j represents the value of Jay's reward if he runs and Kay walks). The rewards for each are ordered $Rw > Ww > Rr > Wr$. If the only two possible strategies for Kay and Jay are to walk or to run, then the fact that for each $Rw > Ww$ and $Rr > Wr$ means that each should run. But if these are not the only possible actions, it may not be the case that running dominates. For example, if Jay knows that Kay may make her action at time 2 contingent on his action at time 1, it may be to his advantage to walk at time 1. And he knows that it may be to her advantage to walk first and see what he does, that is, to make her action contingent on his.

More generally, this setting can be viewed as Kay and Jay having n plays in an iterated prisoner's dilemma (corresponding to the n instants between the starting point of the escape panic and the final exit). Each recognizes that, considering each stage separately, the dominant strategy at each stage is to run (which I will label S_1). But because of the possible gains from making his action contingent on Kay's preceding action, Jay devises the following strategy (S_2) as an alternative to running: walk until Kay runs and then, on the next play and from then on, run. He assumes that Kay will use a strategy of walking for the first n_1 plays (unless he runs, whereupon she will run on the next play), until, at play $n_1 + 1$, she sees it to her advantage to run from that point on. (The strategy of running from the first play onward, on Kay's part, is simply the case in which $n_1 = 0$.) Jay can ask then himself two questions: Given that Kay uses the strategy of walking for the first n_1 plays, is there a critical value such that if n_1 is greater than this value, it is better for me to use S_2 than to use S_1, and, if so, what is the critical value? At which play is it optimal for Kay to begin to run if she believes I am using either strategy S_1 or S_2?

To answer the first question, Jay can start by considering extremes: Clearly if

$n_1 = 0$, that is, if Kay decides it is better for her to run at the beginning, Jay is better off using S_1, that is, running, from the beginning—for to do otherwise imposes a cost equal to $Rr_j - Wr_j$ on the first play. This is the cost of not starting to run until the play after Kay does. At the other extreme, if Jay believes that Kay will set $n_1 = n$, that is, will never run unless Jay does, until the last play, it is better for Jay to use strategy S_2. Thus it is rational for Jay to use one strategy at one extreme of Kay's possible actions and to use the opposite strategy at the other extreme. This indicates that there is some value of n_1 beyond which it becomes rational for Jay to use S_2 rather than S_1. This value may be found by determining at what point, as n_1 increases, the reward from S_2 becomes greater than that from S_1. The rewards from S_1 and S_2 are

$$\text{From } S_1: \quad \begin{array}{ll} Rw_j + (n - 1)Rr_j & \text{if } n_1 > 0 \\ nRr_j & \text{if } n_1 = 0 \end{array}$$

$$\text{From } S_2: \quad n_1 Ww_j + Wr_j + (n - n_1 - 1)Rr_j$$

When does the reward from S_2 exceed that from S_1 under each of the conditions, $n_1 > 0$ and $n_1 = 0$? If $n_1 = 0$,

$$\text{Reward from } S_2 - \text{reward from } S_1 = Wr_j - Rr_j < 0$$

If $n_1 > 0$,

$$\begin{aligned} \text{Reward from } S_2 - \text{reward from } S_1 = {} & n_1 Ww_j + Wr_j \\ & + (n - n_1 - 1)Rr_j - Rw_j - (n - 1)Rr_j \end{aligned}$$

If $n_1 = 0$, the rewards from S_1 are greater than those from S_2; but if $n_1 > 0$, there is some n_1^* such that Jay is better off using S_2 if Kay's value of n_1 is greater than n_1^*:

$$n_1^* = \frac{Rw_j - Wr_j}{Ww_j - Rr_j} \tag{33.18}$$

Inspection of eq. 33.18 shows that because of the ordering of the payoffs, the numerator must always be greater than the denominator; thus n_1^* is always greater than 1. For example, suppose that the rewards to Jay and Kay are as shown in Table 33.2. With these rewards $n_1^* = (2 + 1)/(1 + 0) = 3$. This means that if Jay believes that Kay will not start running until after play 3, he is better off using S_2, that is, walking until Kay begins to run. Otherwise, he is better off running.

Now, what is the optimal value of n_1 for Kay if she believes Jay is using strategy S_2? Kay's strategy, walking until an optimal play, n_1^*, and then running, I will call S_3. The reward from S_3 is

$$\text{Reward from } S_3 = n_1(Ww_k - Rr_k) + Rw_k + (n - 1)Rr_k$$

Inspection shows (since $Rw_k > Ww_k > Rr_k$) that the reward from S_3 is maximized when $n_1 = n - 1$. When n_1 is set at $n - 1$, the reward to Kay is $(n - 1)Ww_k + Rw_k$. Thus it appears that Kay should set n_1 at $n - 1$, and only start running at the last play.

Table 33.2 Possible values for rewards to Kay and Jay in the escape panic situation.

		Kay	
		Walk	Run
Jay	Walk	1, 1	-1, 2
	Run	2, -1	0, 0

But Kay knows that Jay will be using S_2 only if n_1 is greater than 3. At each round of play Jay reassesses whether to use S_1 or S_2. Thus Kay knows that as the number of plays approaches n, Jay will no longer find it advantageous to use S_2. If the current play is i, Kay knows that unless $n - i > n_1^*$, it is to Jay's benefit to run, since he assumes she will run on the last play. Thus the optimal play on which Kay should run is that denoted by the largest integral value of i such that

$$n > i + n_1^* \qquad (33.19)$$

I will call the value of i which satisfies this criterion i^*.

Thus from this analysis the optimal strategies for Jay and Kay seem to be as follows: Jay uses S_2 until play i^* and then, on that play, uses S_1; Kay uses S_3 with n_1 set to i^*, which she determines using the value of n_1^* she knows Jay uses. Thus with the rewards as given in Table 33.2, $n_1^* = 3$ and both Kay and Jay would walk until the fourth play from the end, on which both would start to run. Jay's running would not be pushed back to play $i^* - n_1^*$ (and then back and back, to the beginning) because if he anticipates the play on which Kay will run and runs on that play, he will not experience the worst outcome for him, Wr_j. Is it rational for Kay to attempt to preempt Jay by running on the next earlier play? Or for Jay to do so? The conventional wisdom argues that it is (see Luce and Raiffa, 1957). I will come back to this point later and will show that it could hardly be rational for either Jay or Kay to plan to do so.

The situation can be described heuristically in this way (and if it could not be described in a substantively meaningful fashion, it could hardly be correct to say that the individuals would think along such lines): Jay divides the difference between the payoff from running when Kay is walking and the payoff from walking when Kay is running by the difference between the payoff if both walk and the payoff if both run (see eq. 33.18). If the number of plays remaining is not greater than this result, he starts running. Kay knows he will do this and starts running on the same play. If Jay and Kay have exactly the same reward structure, this could be the end of the matter: Each will walk until the ratio of payoff differences shown on the right-hand side of eq. 33.18 is as great as the number of plays left; and then they would both begin to run.

If the reward structures for the two are different, however, further analysis is necessary. Note that, as the case has been described, the individuals are in an asymmetric position. Jay assumes that Kay will carry out an initiatory strategy and he will carry out a reactive one. He makes his actions contingent on hers, and it is only because of that contingency that her strategy is contingent on his at a second order. This leads to the same action by both, beginning to run at i^*; perhaps they would take different actions if their roles were reversed.

There is no reason for an asymmetric analysis. It would be likely that both would be prepared to employ an initiatory strategy and a reactive one. That is, suppose that both Jay and Kay have available to them strategies S_1, S_2, and S_3 and that each is prepared to use any of these three strategies on any play.

First, if Kay were to use S_2, she would also have a critical value of n_1, based on the assumption that Jay will use S_3. Because her reward may be different from his (she may have more or less to lose than he does by walking), her critical value, n_1^*, may be different from his. Different values of n_1^* would produce different values of i^*, which can be denoted by i_j^* and i_k^*.

To see this difference, suppose that Kay has a lot more to lose than Jay does by not being the first to run—perhaps because she begins in a disadvantaged location. Then the reward structure is like that of Table 33.2 but with one exception, as shown in Table 33.3. In such a case, although n_1^* remains at 3 for Jay, for Kay it becomes $(2 + 9)/(1 - 0) = 11$. Thus if Kay were reacting to the possibility of Jay's running by using S_2, she would begin to run on the twelfth play from the end (if $n \leq 12$, she would run from the beginning). Jay, using S_3, would also begin to run on the twelfth play from the end—not because it was

Table 33.3   Alternative values for rewards to Kay and Jay in the escape panic situation.

		Kay	
		Walk	Run
Jay	Walk	1, 1	-1, 2
	Run	2, -9	0, 0

important to him not to have Kay run first, but because he knows she will begin to run on that play.

Now suppose that each uses a mix of S_2 and S_3 (S_1 is merely a special case of S_3). What I mean by a mix is this: Jay knows that if he uses strategy S_2 and Kay uses S_3, both will run on i_j^*. If he uses S_2 and Kay uses S_2, she will run on i_k^* and he on $i_k^* + 1$. If he uses S_3 and she uses S_2, both will run on i_k^*. If both use S_3, he will run on i_k^* and she on $i_k^* + 1$. With the reward structure given in Table 33.3 and 100 plays the results would be as shown in Table 33.4; rewards if Jay runs on first play (S_1) and if Kay runs on first play (S_1) are also given.

There are two kinds of mismatches here: one in which he runs first, and the other in which she runs first. In this case i_k^* is 89 and i_j^* is 97. Jay's gains by running on i_k^* when Kay would have run on i_j^* (row 4 of Table 33.4 compared to row 1) are $Rw_j - Ww_j - (i_j^* - i_k^* - 1)(Ww_j - Rr_j)$. That is, he gains on the first play when he runs, and then incurs a loss on the remaining plays separating i_k^* and i_j^*. With the rewards given in Table 33.3, this is $1 - 7$, or -6. Jay's losses by not running on i_k^* when Kay does run (row 2 of Table 33.4 compared to row 3) are $Wr_j - Rr_j$, or -1. Kay can make a similar evaluation: For the mismatch for which Jay's gains (possibly negative) are $Rw_j - Ww_j - (i_j^* - i_k^* - 1)(Ww_j - Rr_j)$, her gains are $79 - 96$, or -17. For the opposite mismatch (row 2 compared to row 3), her gains (possibly positive) are $Rr_k - Wr_k - (i_j^* - i_k^* - 1)(Ww_k - Rr_k)$, or 2, and Jay's losses are $Wr_j - Rr_j$, or -1. In this example Jay loses 6 if he runs too soon and 1 if he runs too late. Kay also loses 6 by running too soon, but loses 17 by running too late.

What is rational for each to do? I cannot say (a position I will justify in the next section), for it is not clear that either S_2 or S_3 or some mix is rational. What I would do if I were in Jay's place in the example is to use S_2, which involves planning to run on the third play from the end. If I were in Kay's place, I would also use S_2, which involves planning to run on the twelfth play from the end. Then, if I were Jay, I would get a total reward (from 100 plays) of 87, and if I were Kay, I would get 90.

It is possible to evaluate at a still deeper level: If Kay recognizes that running

Table 33.4 Rewards to two players (Jay and Kay) in an iterated prisoner's dilemma with 100 plays, depending on the strategy used.

Strategy used		Play to run on		Total reward	
Jay	Kay	Jay	Kay	Jay	Kay
S_2	S_3	97	97	96	96
S_2	S_2	90	89	87	90
S_3	S_2	89	89	88	88
S_3	S_3	89	90	90	79
S_1	S_2	1	2	2	-1
S_2	S_1	2	1	-1	2

too late causes little harm to Jay, compared to the harm of running too early, and Jay recognizes the opposite about Kay, then Kay might plan to run later than on the twelfth play from the end, and Jay might plan to run earlier than on the third play from the end. But carrying the evaluation to this level forces a recognition that what Kay and Jay are engaged in is the use by each of information about the other to determine what is an optimal strategy.

This recognition also reveals that restricting the information available about Jay and Kay to that contained in a payoff matrix has been tantamount to making a false assumption that this is the only information about each other they will use in discovering what actions the other is likely to take. It is evident that they will not make the standard game-theoretic assumption that the other player is exactly like oneself except that he confronts a different payoff structure. Rather, each will also use additional information about the other, such as the depth of analysis the other is likely to engage in. If Kay saw that Jay was less likely to devote attention to this matter, she could exploit this fact and gain by so doing. For example, having carried out the above assessment, she might also realize that Jay will stop at the assessment that on any round his maximum loss from walking is only three times his maximum gain, and thus she might wait until the play 97 or 98 to run.[2]

Escape Panic with More than Two Persons

In Chapter 9 it was pointed out that a physical escape panic does not have the properties of a prisoner's dilemma, because the sequential nature of the former allows each to make his actions conditional on what others do. A result of the fact is that, under a certain condition, it is rational not to run to an exit (it would be rational to run if the physical escape panic did have the structure of a prisoner's dilemma) but to make one's action contingent on what others do, that is, to transfer control over one's action to others. The condition is that each of the others has transferred a certain amount of control over his action to oneself.

The process, which occurs over a period of time, must be modeled as a dynamic one. The result given above, however, can be shown by modeling the decision of an actor in the system at any point from the time at which an alarm is first sounded. Four assumptions are necessary:

The actor has two alternative actions from which to choose: to run or to walk toward an exit.

He sees others as having the same two alternatives.

---

2. It is likely that the depth of assessment also depends on the potential gain or loss from playing the game. In personal relationships women appear to carry out deeper analytical assessments of strategies than do men and appear to be able to exploit this deeper assessment—perhaps because of the fact that ordinarily the successful play of this "game" has a greater potential gain or loss for women (because their social position has, throughout much of history, depended more on it) than for men.

Any reaction of the actor will be to the actions of others considered as a single body, although he will use individuals' actions as indicators of what that body will do.

He sees the probabilities of escape as being ranked in the following order: $p_{21} > p_{11} > p_{22} > p_{12}$, where p_{ij} is the probability of escape given that he takes action i and others take action j (1 = walk, 2 = run).

If "run" and "walk" are seen as equivalent to "defect" and "cooperate" in a two-person prisoner's dilemma and if escape is a better outcome for the actor than not escaping, then the expected payoffs are equivalent to those of a prisoner's dilemma. In a prisoner's dilemma defection (running) dominates cooperation: If others walk, his expected payoff is higher if he runs; if others run, his expected payoff is higher if he runs.

The following definitions are necessary:

$U_a \equiv$ his utility if he escapes
$U_b \equiv$ his utility if he does not escape
$\Delta U = U_a - U_b \quad (\Delta U > 0)$
$U_w \equiv$ the expected utility of walking
$U_r \equiv$ the expected utility of running
$f_i \equiv$ his estimate of the probability that others will walk given that he carries out action i

His expected payoff if he walks (takes action 1) is

$$U_w = [p_{11}f_1 + p_{12}(1 - f_1)]\Delta U + U_b \tag{33.20}$$

If he runs, it is

$$U_r = [p_{21}f_2 + p_{22}(1 - f_2)]\Delta U + U_b \tag{33.21}$$

If $f_1 = f_2 = f$, that is, if he sees others' walking as not conditional on his own action, then

$$U_r - U_w = [(p_{21} - p_{11})f + (p_{22} - p_{12})(1 - f)]\Delta U \tag{33.22}$$

Since $p_{21} - p_{11} > 0$, $f > 0$, $p_{22} - p_{12} > 0$, and $\Delta U > 0$, eq. 33.22 implies that $U_r - U_w > 0$. This is a first result. If the structure of action is only singly contingent (his action is contingent on the previous actions of others, but there is no subsequent action of others that may affect him and that is contingent on his action), he is always better off if he runs.

Suppose, however, that he estimates that $f_1 > f_2$. The others' probability of walking conditional on his walking is greater than the others' probability of walking conditional on his running. Specifically, assume that $f_2 = f_1 - \gamma f_1$, where $\gamma \leq 1$. The definition of γ is the fraction by which the others' probability of walking is reduced if he runs. When γ is near 1, others' action is highly conditional on his own; his running will sharply decrease their chance of walking. Then, from eq. 33.22,

$$U_r - U_w = \{[(1 - \gamma)p_{21} - p_{11}]f_1 + p_{22} - p_{12} - [(1 - \gamma)p_{22} - p_{12}]f_1\}\Delta U \tag{33.23}$$

If the actor's expected return from walking is to be greater than his expected return from running, $U_r - U_w$ must be less than zero. Forming an inequality by setting the right-hand side of eq. 33.23 to be less than zero and solving for γ gives

$$\gamma > \frac{p_{21} - p_{11}}{p_{21} - p_{22}} + \frac{1 - f_1}{f_1}\left(\frac{p_{22} - p_{12}}{p_{21} - p_{22}}\right) \tag{33.24}$$

Thus, if his expected utility of walking is to be greater than that of running, his estimate of the fraction by which the others' probability of walking is reduced by his running must be greater than the right-hand side of this inequality.

The interpretation of the expression on the right-hand side of inequality 33.24 is as follows: The first term is the increase in his probability of escape by running, given that others are walking, *relative to* the increase in his probability of escape when others walk rather than run, given that he is running. The second term is the product of two ratios: the ratio of the probability that the others will run if he walks to the probability that the others will walk if he walks; *and* the increase in his probability of escape when he runs rather than walks, given that others are running, relative to the increase in his probability of escape when others walk rather than run, given that he is running.

Inequality 33.24 yields the critical value, γ^*, of the conditionality parameter, γ. If the actor estimates that his running will reduce others' probability of walking by more than this critical value, then he is better off if he walks. The first term of the right-hand side can be described simply as what he gains by running when others walk, relative to what he gains by their walking when he runs. If he does not gain much by running when the others are walking, or if he gains a lot from their walking when he's running, then this reduces the critical value of others' conditionality, increasing the range of settings in which he is better off if he walks. The first ratio of the second term, $(1 - f_1)/f_1$, is simply the odds that, if he is walking, others will run, relative to the odds they will walk. When that ratio is high, he has little to gain by not running. The second ratio in that term is what he gains by running when others are, relative to what he gains from their walking when he's running.

Inequality 33.24 shows how conditional others' actions must be on his own action for him to find it beneficial to walk rather than to run. But he might use another strategy: to walk as long as others walk, but to run if he sees them running. What would make this a better strategy than that of running unilaterally? It is always a better strategy than that of walking unilaterally, since he is more likely to escape if he runs once others are running ($p_{22} > p_{12}$), a condition assumed at the outset. I will assume that his chance of escape is not reduced if he is not the first to run, that he can react quickly enough that, using this strategy, his probability of escape when others run and he joins them is p_{22}.

His expected utility from this conditional strategy is

$$U_c = [p_{11}f_1 + p_{22}(1 - f_1)] \Delta U + U_b \tag{33.25}$$

If U_c is to be greater than U_r, that is, if $0 < U_c - U_r$, then

$$0 < \{[p_{11} - (1 - \gamma)p_{21}]f_1 + [(1 - \gamma)p_{22} - p_{22}]f_1\}\Delta U \tag{33.26}$$

Solving for γ gives

$$\gamma > \frac{p_{21} - p_{11}}{p_{21} - p_{22}} \tag{33.27}$$

The second critical value of γ is γ^{**}, the value which is equal to the right-hand side of inequality 33.27. If γ is greater than γ^{**}, it is rational for the actor to make his action conditional on that of others. If γ is less than γ^{**}, it is rational for him to run, independent of what he sees others doing.

Thus there are three regions into which γ can fall, shown in Figure 33.6. If γ is below γ^{**}, it is rational for the actor to run, whatever others do. If γ is above γ^{**} but below γ^*, it is rational for him to walk, conditional on others' walking—in effect, to transfer control over his action to them. If γ is above γ^*, it is rational to plan to walk unconditionally if he is unable to make his action conditional on theirs.

Inequality 33.27 shows how conditional he must see others' action being on his own action if it is to be rational to make his action conditional on theirs. The right-hand side of inequality 33.27 is the gain he expects from running when others walk, relative to the gain he expects from their walking when he runs. If he gains nothing by running when others are walking ($p_{21} = p_{11}$), then he should always transfer control if the others' action has the slightest conditionality on his own. If he gains nothing from their walking when he runs ($p_{21} = p_{22}$), then it is never rational for him to make his action conditional on theirs.

Comparing inequality 33.27 with inequality 33.24 shows that the right-hand side of 33.27 contains only the first of the two terms on the right-hand side of 33.24. Since the second term on the right-hand side of 33.24 is always positive, there is a range of values of the conditionality of others' action on his own (γ), in

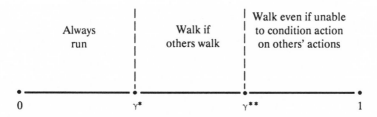

Figure 33.6 Behavior regions for double-contingency escape panics.

which it is rational to walk unless others run but not rational to walk unilaterally if one must choose between running unilaterally and walking unilaterally.[3]

A Deeper Level of Reflexivity

If the individual in an escape panic sees the others as being like himself, can he estimate how conditional their actions will be on his, given that he has established a criterion by which his actions should be conditional on theirs? Answering this requires first making more explicit what is meant by the collective term "others." It has been assumed in the exposition to this point that the individual is responding to the others as a single actor, not as individual actors. He may use one actor's running as a signal that the crowd, considered as an entity, will begin to run, or he may merely regard that action as increasing the probability that others will begin to run. In general, the process of a crowd beginning to run can be conceived as a continuous-time stochastic process in which the states are the number of persons running, and the system is initially in state 0. Figure 33.7 is a diagram of such a process, showing the transition rates between states i and $i + 1$ as q_i. I assume that there are n persons in the crowd other than the individual, who is estimating what the crowd, consisting of the n other people, will do.

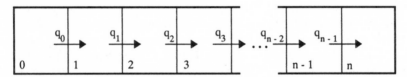

Figure 33.7 Running in a crowd of size n as a continuous-time, stochastic process.

The volatility of the crowd is given by the values of q_i. If each of the n other persons has a propensity to run, α, independent of what anyone else does, then $q_0 = n\alpha$. If τ is the length of time it takes for one person to get out as the crowd files out, the probability of being in state 0 (no one running) at time t, s_0, can be found as follows:

$$\frac{ds_0}{dt} = -q_0 s_0 = -n_t \alpha s_0$$

Since $n_t = n - t/\tau$, for $t \leqslant n\tau$,

$$\frac{ds_0}{dt} = -\left(n - \frac{t}{\tau}\right)\alpha s_0 \tag{33.28}$$

3. Walking unilaterally is not, in fact, a rational action under any circumstance, if he can observe the others' actions and sees that they are running. The rationality of walking unilaterally depends on f_1 being greater than zero. If he sees others running, f_1 immediately becomes zero.

Integrating eq. 33.28 from time 0 (when $s_0 = 1$) to time t gives

$$s_0(t) = e^{-\alpha t(n - t/2\tau)} \tag{33.29}$$

Equation 33.29 gives the probability, as estimated by an individual in the crowd, that no one will be running at time t. If the fraction of the crowd ahead of the individual is g, the individual can expect that at time $t_g = gn\tau$, which is when he will reach the door if no one runs, the probability that no one will be running will be $s_0(t_g)$:

$$s_0(t_g) = e^{-\alpha n^2 \tau g(2 - g)/2} \tag{33.30}$$

This quantity decreases as g (the proportion of the crowd ahead of him) increases, and as n (the absolute size of the crowd) increases. Thus s_0 may be much smaller if the individual is toward the rear of the crowd than if he is toward the front. If he assumes that he will get out only if he is the only one to run and that others' running is not contingent on his own, then, by eq. 33.30, he will be more likely to start running if he is near the rear than if he is near the front.

If there is a high degree of contingency of others' action on the action of the first person to run, then $q_1 = (n - 1)(\alpha + \beta)$, where β is very large. If each additional person running increases the transition rate for each nonrunner by β, then $q_1 = (n - 1)(\alpha + i\beta)$. Of course, q_1 may change nonlinearly, with succeeding runners having either successively greater impact on the remaining nonrunners or successively less.

The individual may ask himself: If I start running, what is the probability that the system will remain in state 1? This may be found by assuming that at time 0 the system is in state 1, with this transition rate:

$$q_1 = (n_t - 1)(\alpha + \beta) = \left(n - 1 - \frac{t}{\tau}\right)(\alpha + \beta)$$

Then integrating $ds_1/dt = q_1 s_1$ between times 0 and t, with $s_1 = 1$ at time 0 gives

$$s_1 = e^{-(\alpha + \beta)t(n - 1 - t/2\tau)} \tag{33.31}$$

If s_0 is regarded as equal to f_1, the probability that others will walk if he walks, and s_1 is regarded as equal to f_2, the probability that others will walk if he runs, then $s_1/s_0 = f_2/f_1 = 1 - \gamma$. Then, from eqs. 33.29 and 33.31,

$$\frac{s_1}{s_0} = e^{-\beta n^2 \tau(2 - g - 2/n)/2 - \alpha n \tau g} \tag{33.32}$$

(If $\beta n \gg \alpha$, the term $\alpha n \tau g$ in the exponent can be neglected.)

The question posed at the beginning of this section can now be stated more specifically: Can the individual estimate β (or, equivalently, γ, given n, τ, and g) if he assumes that others know the critical values of conditionality below which he will run unilaterally (γ^{**}) or will run if they begin to run (γ^*)? That question remains unanswered.

What Effect Do Fire Drills Have?

Several variables used in this analysis are subject to manipulation that can increase or decrease the likelihood of an escape panic. In practice, fire drills are often used to reduce the likelihood of panic. What do fire drills do to reduce the chance of a panic? Fire drills are intended, at minimum, to induce each individual not to run unilaterally and, at maximum, to induce each individual to walk unilaterally. Thus in terms of this analysis fire drills are an attempt, at minimum, to reduce the right-hand side of inequality 33.27, so the critical value γ^{**} will be lower, and thus each individual will be less likely to run unilaterally. At maximum, they attempt to reduce the right-hand side of inequality 33.24, so the critical value γ^{*} will be lower, and each will be more likely to walk, even if he is not able to make his action contingent on that of others.

One variable whose value may be increased by fire drills is p_{11}, the perceived probability of escape if one walks and others walk as well. An increase in the value of p_{11} will reduce both γ^{*} and γ^{**}. Timing how long evacuation takes in fire drills should have an effect, according to this analysis, not merely in reducing the time it takes to clear the building, but in demonstrating to each that the length of time necessary for orderly evacuation is small. Thus announcement of the evacuation time to all involved should be an intrinsic part of a fire drill, as a way of increasing p_{11}.

None of the other escape probabilities that appear in inequalities 33.24 and 33.27 seem to be directly affected by fire drills. But f_1, the probability that others will walk, given that he walks, appears in inequality 33.24. If f_1 is increased, the first critical value, γ^{*}, declines toward the second critical value, γ^{**}, increasing the region in which the individual will walk even if he cannot make his action contingent (see Figure 33.6). If f_1 is 1.0, the contingency region between γ^{*} and γ^{**} vanishes, and he will walk unilaterally unless his estimate of γ is less than $(p_{21} - p_{11})/(p_{21} - p_{22})$. Fire drills appear to have a strong effect on f_1, for they demonstrate to each individual that the others will walk out in an orderly fashion. They create the expectation on the part of each that others will walk; that is, they raise f_1 for each of the individuals.

There may be some unintended effects of fire drills, as well as effects not reflected in the model. Perhaps the most important unintended effect is on γ, the individual's estimate of the fraction by which the others' probability of walking will be reduced by his running, or his estimate of the contingency of their actions on his own. It is this contingency which creates the possibility that something besides unilateral running is rational for him. Yet a fire drill may have the unintended effect of making each believe not only that f_1 is high but also that γ is very low, that none of the others will run even if he does. This could lead each to be more likely to run in a real panic, thus defeating the purpose of the fire drills.

A possible effect of fire drills that is not reflected in the model is the emergence of a norm against running. If such a norm does come into existence, accompanied by sanctions, it would impose an extra cost on running when others are walking. The expected utility of that action would then not be $p_{21}\Delta U + U_b$. It would instead be (assuming that p_{21}, the estimated probability of escape, is unchanged) $p_{21}\Delta U + U_b + U_s$ where U_s is the cost due to imposition of the sanction.

Time-Contingent Rationality

The conventional wisdom as to what is the optimal strategy for an iterated prisoner's dilemma with two persons and a finite number of plays stems from an argument stated by Luce and Raiffa (1957): For the last play the optimal action is to run (defect). But if the optimal action for the last play is to run, each player knows the other will run on that play. This makes running the optimal action for the next-to-last play, for both players. This unravels back to the beginning, with the result that the optimal strategy is to run from the beginning.

The defect in that argument can be seen by reconsidering the two-person panic situation discussed earlier. At the starting point Kay does not know what kind of boy Jay is. She can evaluate the rewards to her from strategy S_1 compared to those from S_2 or S_3 (which are alike in this case) if Jay uses S_1, a strategy of running from the beginning. By using S_2 or S_3 she will get the reward Wr_k on the first play, instead of Rr_k from S_1. If Jay uses what I will call a Luce-Raiffa strategy, she will be worse off by the difference between Rr_k and Wr_k (with the numbers from Table 33.2 this is 1). If Jay uses any strategy which does not dictate that he run on the first play, but defers running until play n^*, this means that if Kay uses S_2 or S_3, she gets reward Ww_k on the first $n^* - 1$ plays and Wr_k on play n^* (assuming the worse case, where Jay runs first). If she uses S_1, she gets Rw_k on the first play and Rr_k on the next $n^* - 1$ plays. Thus the gain (possibly negative) from using S_2 or S_3 rather than S_1 is $Wr_k - Rw_k + (n^* - 1)$ $(Ww_k - Rr_k)$. With the numbers from Table 33.2 Kay's gain from using S_2 or S_3 rather than S_1, if Jay does not run until n^*, is $-1 - 2 + n^* (1 - 0)$, or $n^* - 3$. If the number of plays and Jay's strategy are such that $n^* > 3$, then Kay is better off not to use a Luce-Raiffa strategy. As is shown by comparison of the last two rows of Table 33.4 with the first four rows, a Luce-Raiffa strategy could bring extensive loss. Thus, although it would be rational for Kay to use a Luce-Raiffa strategy if she was certain that Jay was also using that strategy, she would incur a loss by doing so if Jay was not using that strategy. And the argument that it is rational for Jay to use a Luce-Raiffa strategy is a faulty one, because if he does so and Kay is using S_2 or S_3 or another strategy that does not dictate running on the first play, he will do less well, as long as the number of plays is not very small relative to the payoff extremes.

From the perspective of the starting point rather than the perspective of the last play, it certainly does not appear rational to use a Luce-Raiffa strategy.

PRECOMMITMENT   In an iterated prisoner's dilemma why does a strategy of pure defection arise from taking the perspective of the player at the last play in the iteration, and the strategy of nondefection arise from taking the perspective of the player at the first play? I suggest the reason lies in the following: An action for time t ($t > 0$) which is rational at time 0 may not be rational when the actor is at time t; an action for time t which is not rational at time 0 may be rational at time t. If I am at time 0, I have available the rational strategy at time 0 or that at time t. Since I have more options at time 0, the rational strategy at time 0 is at least as good as the rational strategy at time t. If the two strategies differ, I must choose the one that is rational at time 0, a strategy which dictates my play at time t. This strategy is obviously as good as or better than the rational strategy I would choose at time t, because at time t I am in an inferior position: I no longer have the possibility of choosing between the rational strategy at time 0 and the rational strategy at time t. Thus, recognizing this at time 0, I must choose the strategy that is rational at time 0. This is a precommitment strategy. This type of precommitment is different from the usual precommitment in anticipation of weakness of will at time t (see Elster, 1979).

The Sanctioning Problem in a Common Project

In Chapter 11 the problem of developing a credible threat for sanctioning actors who fail to contribute to a common project was discussed, but was not treated systematically. What is missing in that treatment is specificity about how and when sanctioning for not contributing can take place. The problem is intrinsically one of doubly contingent actions, because the contributor's own action affects him not only directly but indirectly, through the actions of others whose actions (sanctioning, future contributions) are contingent on his own. Similarly, the sanctioners' actions affect themselves not only directly but also through the sanctionee's actions, which are contingent on theirs. The focus in Chapter 11 was on the emergence of norms, which involves a transfer of rights from the actor who has de facto control of the action to those affected by the action. Further insight into the conditions governing the effectiveness of norms can be gained by examining the sanctioning process more carefully.

In the common project of Table 10.2, each of three actors, A_1, A_2, and A_3, contributes \$9 (or fails to do so), and each of the three receives \$4 back for each \$9 contributed. If A_1 fails to contribute, it is in the interest of A_2 and A_3 that A_1 be punished for that in some fashion, but only if that punishment is likely to have a deterrent effect on A_1's future defections. This ordering of noncontribution and sanction implies that there must be anticipation of a future project on the sanctioner's part. Effectiveness of the sanction implies that the sanctioned noncontributor must have anticipation of a project after the next and belief in the motivation of the sanctioners to sanction in that project. Motivation to apply the sanction implies an awareness of this anticipation on the part of the sanctioners. (The threat of sanction can, of course, precede the contribution stage, but if there is no future project, the threat will not be credible to the potential noncontributor, who knows that the potential sanctioners have no incentive to sanction in the absence of a future action which their sanction could influence.)

The recognition of all this is what led Luce and Raiffa (1957) to the argument stated earlier in this chapter: For any finite sequence of iterated prisoner's dilemma games, mutual defection for all games is the only rational strategy. But this need not be the case, as demonstrated in the discussion of the two-person panic situation. There is another source of nondefection strategies. Anticipation of a future project can exist without there being an infinite sequence of projects: There may be a next project, occurring with probability less than 1.0. In the simple case each next project has the same probability, p, of occurring, conditional on the existence of the preceding project. Then no matter how small one wishes the probability of a future project to be, one can find a number of projects such that the probability of another project is less than this probability. If k is the probability of an nth project occurring, the number of projects, n, necessary to decrease the probability to this level is merely the smallest n such that $k < 1 - p^n$. Even for high p and low k, n is fairly small. For $p = .8$ and $k = .01$, for example, n is only 21.

Some idea of how sanctions might operate in such a setting can be gained by examining the potential cost the credible threat of a sanction could impose on the potential noncontributor, compared to the incentive for the potential noncontributor not to contribute. If the loss expected due to the sanctioner's credible threat is larger than the potential noncontributor's expected gain from withholding contribution, then sanctioning constitutes an equilibrium, and the threat of the sanction can be expected to be effective. If the threat does not exceed the expected gain, then noncontribution without sanctioning is an equilibrium and can be expected to proliferate.

As a concrete example, consider a sequence of three-actor common projects, in which each project is followed by a next project with probability p. A single iteration of the project consists of two stages: a contribution stage and a sanctioning stage. Noncontribution in the next project could be used as the sanction. This would make the sequence of three-actor common projects a three-player iterated prisoner's dilemma. There is, however, a difficulty with this, one that greatly complicates choice of strategy in any iterated prisoner's dilemma: The same action, noncontribution, can be interpreted in any of three ways. It can be seen as a sanction which punishes a player who failed to contribute in the preceding game, as an exploitative attempt to free ride on the others' contributions, or as defense against repeated noncontribution on another's part. If the sanction must take this form, estimation of its cost becomes very difficult, both for the actor who is deciding whether to sanction and for the theorist. Interpretation of the noncontribution by the person it is meant to sanction is also difficult.

Thus I will introduce a second stage, a sanctioning stage, into the three-actor common project. The sanction imposes a cost on the actor being sanctioned and is made at a cost to the sanctioner. The rule is that actors who have contributed on a given project have the right to sanction (at a cost) actors who have not. The contribution stage of the project produces resources, $4 for every $3 contributed; the sanctioning stage consumes resources if sanctioning is carried out. To impose a sanction on a noncontributor that loses him $3 costs the sanctioner $2.

Table 33.5 Reward structure for a three-person common project with a
sanctioning stage: (a) when A_1 does not contribute or (b) when A_1 and
A_2 do not contribute.

	A_3			A_3		
	Sanction	No sanction		Sanction both	Sanction A_1	No sanction
A_2 Sanction	(2), -3 -3	(2), -5, -1		(2), (2), -9	(2), (8), -5	(8), (8), -1
No sanction	(2), -1, -5	(8), -1, -1				
	(a)			(b)		

Thus, since each contributor must put in $9, a noncontributor is $5 better off by
not contributing; the minimum sanction which would make him worse off is $6.

The reward structure for the project is given in Table 33.5 both when there is
one noncontributor and when there are two. The table shows the net results after
both stages, with payoffs for noncontributors in parentheses. First, consider the
case of two noncontributors. The cost to A_3 of making a credible sanction of A_1
and A_2 (a sanction that imposes on each of them a cost of $6) is $8. The benefit, if
each contributes next time, is $8 ($4 from each). Thus, if A_2 and A_3 respond to
the sanction by contributing, the benefit to A_3 is $8p$, since the probability that
there will be a next project is p and the cost is 8. As long as p is less than 1.0, the
expected benefit cannot equal the cost, even if A_3 were certain that the sanction
would make A_1 and A_2 contribute in the next project. In any case it would not be
rational for them to do so unless they believed they would be sanctioned in that
project, which implies some probability of a project beyond that, as indicated
earlier.

It is not rational, then, for an actor to sanction two noncontributors in the
three-actor common project, given the cost of doing so and the potential benefit,
unless the benefit extends beyond the next project.[4] Similar considerations hold
for an actor's sanction of only one of two noncontributors.

4. One might conjecture that the single sanction would lead A_1 and A_2 to contribute in all
succeeding projects, because of the continuing threat of sanction. If so, then A_3's expected
benefit would be $8p/(1 - p)$, which is the sum of expected benefits from the whole sequence of
projects. If that was A_1's and A_2's strategy, the expected return to A_3 from a sanction would be
positive as long as $p > .5$. Would that be a rational strategy for A_1 and A_2? It depends on their
assessment of A_3's strategy.

For the case of one noncontributor, where, for example, A_1 is a noncontributor and A_2 and A_3 are potential sanctioners, is it rational for A_2 and A_3 to jointly sanction A_1, at a cost to each of \$2? First, note that Table 33.5(a) shows only the cost of a sanction; the benefits depend on the strategy used by the noncontributor and are not included. The table shows that nonsanctioning on the part of each is not only an individual optimum; it is a social optimum for A_2 and A_3. If A_2 and A_3 both sanction, the cost to each is \$2, and the benefit to each is $4p$ if A_1 contributes on the next project. Thus if they expect A_1 to contribute as a result of the sanction, the expected return from both sanctioning is $4p - 2$. This is positive as long as p is greater than .5.

But will A_1's strategy be to contribute on project $i + 1$ if sanctioned on project i, given the probability p that there will be a next project? If the sanction on project i is a signal to A_1 that a noncontribution on project $i + 1$ will be sanctioned, then the expected return to A_1 of a contribution is the expected benefit from not receiving the sanction minus the net cost of contributing, or $6p - 5$. Thus if p is greater than 5/6, or .83, it is rational for A_1 to contribute to project $i + 1$ if A_2 and A_3 sanction in project i, making it rational for them to sanction, if they can jointly do so.

If p is greater than .83, the question becomes how A_2 or A_3 can ensure that the other sanctions—the only condition which would make it rational for each to sanction. In Chapter 11 this problem was termed the second-order free-rider problem. It can be solved if the project is expanded to a third stage: sanctioning the nonsanctioner. If the costs to sanctioner and sanctionee are the same as given earlier for the sanctioning of noncontribution, then A_3 will lose \$2 by sanctioning A_2, and A_2 will lose \$3 by being sanctioned. The expected benefit to A_3, if A_2 responds by sanctioning A_1 on project $i + 1$, is $4p^2$ (because A_1's response does not occur until two projects hence). This gives A_3 a positive expected return only if $p > .71$. Thus the situation depends on the value of p. If $p > .83$, it is rational for A_1 to respond to a sanction, and that makes sanctioning rational; thus A_2 and A_3 can police each other to ensure joint sanctions. If $.71 < p < .83$, it is not rational for A_1 to respond to a sanction by contributing, and thus not rational for A_2 and A_3 to sanction. If A_2 and A_3 believe that A_1 will respond to a sanction by contributing, even though that is not the rational action, it is rational for them to sanction jointly, and they can police each other to ensure a joint sanction. If $.5 < p < .71$, it is rational to sanction only if A_2 and A_3 believe that A_1 will respond by contributing and if each has some external means to ensure that the other will join in a sanction, such as a continuing relationship outside the project (as illustrated in Figure 11.1). If $p < .5$, it is not rational to sanction.

By symmetry, the above arguments also hold when A_2 or A_3 is the noncontributor. Thus, if each actor acts according to the above considerations, there will be contributions if $p > .83$, and no contributions if $p < .83$.[5]

_____

5. A caveat to this statement derives from footnote 4. If each sees the expected benefit of a sanction as being the contributions in all succeeding projects, then a sanction is rational, and

A norm which transfers the rights over contributions and sanctions from the potential contributors and potential sanctioners to those potentially benefited by the contributions and the sanctions would be valuable in this situation. If the logistics make it feasible for the exchange of rights to contribute to be accompanied by an exchange of control over the action of contributing, then contributions will come from all. If that is not feasible, but it is feasible for the exchange of rights to sanction to be accompanied by an exchange of the capacity to sanction, then A_2 can exercise A_3's sanction and A_3 can exercise A_2's. If that is not feasible, the transfer of rights allows A_3 and A_2 to use other resources (if each has some social capital toward the other, as implied in Chapter 11) to exercise control over the other's action. This is ordinarily how there can come to be a second or third stage to such a project, with sanctions for not contributing and sanctions for not sanctioning. Only when each actor has social capital allowing him to discipline others without too great a cost to himself can a norm which gives each the rights to exercise such discipline be effective. Inherent in that social capital is the existence of a future (which, as shown above, need not be a certain future) in which that discipline can be exercised.

The foregoing analysis has made certain assumptions, as the actors themselves in such a system must, about the strategies of the actors being sanctioned. To attempt to go beyond this and specify what strategies might be rational for those actors entails getting into bargaining theory, which provides no determinate answer. The most productive direction of work is that which examines the evolution of populations of strategies, to be discussed briefly below.

Population-Contingent Rationality

The double-contingency panic, exemplified by the physical escape panic, illustrates a general point: In settings where there are doubly contingent actions and in which outcomes are non–zero-sum, rationality cannot be defined independently of the population with which the individual actor is interacting.

A useful illustration of this is provided by Axelrod's tournaments of iterated prisoner's dilemma games, discussed in Chapter 9. The players were computer programs submitted by a set of individuals made up mostly of social scientists, computer scientists, and game theorists. (The number of plays was not known to the players in advance but was to be determined by a random-number generator, and to have an expected value of 200. The absence of a predetermined number of plays seems not to have had a great impact on the strategies, however, as indicated by qualitative comments made by Axelrod and by those who designed the programs.) In this population and setting, the game strategy which ended up with the highest overall score was not a strategy of pure defection but a tit-for-tat

---

contributions will continue, as long as $p > .5$. If members of pairs have the means to police each other's sanction, then contributions will continue if $4p/(1 - p) > 2$, or $p > .33$. Such a group would have greater survival value than those discussed in the text.

strategy with cooperation as the action on the first play—a strategy very much like the S_2 and S_3 strategies described earlier, but without their end-game element. Furthermore, in general, the strategies which did not defect early and were not the first to defect (called nice strategies by Axelrod) ended up with higher scores than the strategies which were quick to defect.

In another population composed largely of players using a Luce-Raiffa strategy, these nice strategies would show less superiority, and in some populations would be inferior to a Luce-Raiffa strategy. Thus knowledge about the population is necessary in order to say what a rational strategy will be in such settings.

Evolution of Strategies

Based on work by population biologists, especially Maynard Smith (1974), one can ask about the survival value of strategies in populations, the ability of new strategies to invade existing populations, and the evolutionary stability of strategies. The evolutionary stability of a strategy is dependent on the environment within which interactions take place (the reward structure and the degree of closure in interaction patterns). For a large range of reward structures within the prisoner's dilemma constraints, a Luce-Raiffa strategy has low survival value and a tit-for-tat strategy has high survival value (see Axelrod, 1984; Swistak, 1987, Chapter 4).

In a double-contingency setting, where the very definition of what constitutes rationality is population-contingent, the notion of rationality is of questionable value as either a prescription for a course of action or a description of the course of action that individuals take. As a prescription for action, it requires extensive data on others' actions, as well as extensive calculations. As a description of action, it seems lacking, given that the actors are limited both in data and in calculating ability. In such a circumstance the idea that strategies can evolve through a process of selective survival is a highly appealing one. Evolutionary processes may not lead to an optimal strategy in a given population, but they will result in strategies that do well in that population. Because the strategies of all in the population are changing through the same evolutionary processes, the adaptive process constitutes a reasonable way to track the social environment. The necessity to track a changing environment of course makes the calculation of a rational strategy more complex.

For these reasons the development of theories of evolution of strategies appears particularly promising for double-contingency situations in social systems.

« 34 »

The Internal Structure
of Actors

The analysis of this book has treated actors as purposive, that is, as unanalyzed entities characterized by a utility function that each actor seeks to maximize. The only properties of the actor that are taken into account are interests, the parameters of the utility function (see eq. 25.1 and Chapter 29). Interests are conceptualized as the springs of action guiding the actor.

For a number of reasons, this approach is not completely satisfactory: It provides no basis for modeling socialization, internalization, or, more generally, internal change of the springs of action. It provides no insight into certain deviations from rationality identified by cognitive psychologists and referred to in Chapter 19 (weakness of will, precommitment, preference reversals with changes in proximity, failure to meet the criterion of independence from irrelevant alternatives, and others). It gives no basis for understanding actions (such as addiction) that must be modeled by use of bizarre or unusual utility functions.

In addition, this approach does not facilitate the connection between levels in conceiving of corporate actors. From one perspective a corporate actor is a system of action containing actors, resources, and events and leading to outcomes. But considered as an actor with a utility function, this same system is, like a natural person as actor, an unanalyzed entity. Although the actions of a corporate actor would seem to correspond to outcomes of indivisible events in a system of action, these two perspectives have not been made consistent. In other words, there has not been made explicit any means of mapping between event outcomes in a system of action and utility functions (or even indifference curves) for that system of action considered as a corporate actor.

There are, however, some aids available for developing a model of the internal structure of actors. The fact that the theory of this book includes as actors both natural persons and corporate actors means that the modeling of natural persons' internal structure may be aided by modeling the internal structure of the corporate actor, which is equivalent to the system of action explicated in Chapters 25 through 33. To do so, however, requires making the conceptual transition between event outcomes in a system of action and utility functions of a corporate actor.

In this chapter, therefore, I will first address the conceptual transition between event outcomes in a system of action and utility functions for that same system considered as a corporate actor. This will provide a basis for modeling multilevel systems, in which systems at one level are actors at the next higher level. I will use this in modeling the internal structure of the natural person as actor, conceptualizing the actor as a system of action having the same form as the systems of action developed in Chapters 25 through 33.

Event Outcomes as Actions of a Corporate Actor

Chapters 30 and 31 introduced a device which makes possible the modeling of outcomes when indivisible events have two outcomes and some actors' interests favor one and other actors' interests favor the other. This device consists of finding the value of the event to those actors whose interests favor a positive outcome (suppressing the interests opposing this outcome) and the value of the event to those actors whose interests favor a negative outcome, and then choosing the outcome with the higher value in the system. In a more complex situation conceived as consisting of the joint outcomes of m events, there are 2^m joint outcomes, each having a value that follows from the interests that favor its particular combination of event outcomes. All this is described in Chapter 31.

If the outcome of an event is regarded as an action, and the system of actors and resources within which the outcome is generated is regarded as an actor, this gives the elements necessary to conceptualize a corporate actor. If, however, the corporate actor is to be conceived as a unitary actor, it is necessary to see it as part of a larger system defined by actors and resources internal to that larger system and to regard it as having a certain set of interests and resources.

I set aside for the present the problem of how to go from the resources held by actors in the smaller system (the corporate actor), which according to Chapters 30 and 31 should be regarded as closed, to the resources of the larger system of which it is a part. The first question I will pose concerns interests. How can the corporate actor be conceived as having interests when all that can be calculated from the internal functioning of that system are values, power of (internal) actors, the equilibrium distribution of resources among the (internal) actors, and the outcomes of indivisible events? One possibility arises by recognizing that, according to the principle of revealed preference, interests are known only by inference from actions. Consider a situation in which a corporate actor is confronted with an event having two outcomes that are mutually exclusive and exhaustive. As a concrete example, take the case of the Ford Motor Company in the 1920s and 1930s, first discussed in Chapter 19. Assume that the event is the hiring of a new employee, and the alternatives are to add an engineer to the manufacturing engineering staff (outcome A) or to add a designer to the product design staff (outcome B). The cost to the company is the same in either case. Following Selznick's (1957) simplified account of Ford in the 1920s, I will treat the company as consisting of only two actors: the manufacturing engineering department as actor 1 and the product design department as actor 2. I will assume that actor 1's power in the company is r_1 and actor 2's power is r_2.

According to Selznick's account, r_1 is much greater than r_2. Actor 1 has an interest, x, in the welfare of the manufacturing engineering staff and favors outcome A. Actor 2 has an equal interest in the welfare of the product design staff and favors outcome B. At what level of relative existing investment in manufacturing engineering and product design will the company be indifferent between outcomes A and B?

As a first approach to the problem, the procedures used in Chapters 30 and 31 to determine the outcome of an event can be applied. This leads to calculation of the values of regime a (outcome A) and regime b (outcome B). The value of regime a is the value of the interests that favor it, or $r_1 x$. The value of regime b is the value of the interests that favor it, or $r_2 x$. Since the interests are equal and the power differs, the outcome, by this calculation, will always be A because of the greater power of those favoring that outcome. According to this analysis, Ford would hire no employees in product design and make no investment in product design, unless the interest of that department increased sufficiently to offset the difference in power.

This kind of analysis is appropriate when the event in question is unrelated to the existing resources in the system. As stated above, however, the problem concerns the level of existing resources, some devoted to project design and some devoted to manufacturing engineering, at which the company would be indifferent between the two outcomes. This specifies that the event in question is not unrelated to the existing resources in the system. There already exist resources of two types within the company, and the event involves an incremental addition to one of the two sets of resources.

Such a situation requires deeper consideration of the criterion for determining the outcome of an event: that outcome is chosen which has the higher value for the system, where value is defined as interests weighted by power. This implies that when there are two actors in the system with interests in opposing outcomes, each will devote to securing the outcome he favors (as implied by the Cobb-Douglas utility function) a fraction of his total resources (that is, of his total power, r_i) equivalent to his interests in that outcome. For an independent event in which actor i has interest x, this is $r_i x$, as indicated earlier. When the event outcome involves an increment to some resource already existing in the system, however, it is necessary to use the Cobb-Douglas utility function given in eq. 25.1 to find the change in actor i's utility when the quantity of resource j changes. Taking the derivative of U_i with respect to c_{ij} gives

$$\frac{dU_i}{dc_{ij}} = \frac{x_{ji}}{c_{ij}} U_i \qquad (34.1)$$

In terms of the derivative of the logarithm of utility, or satisfaction, from eq. 25.1,

$$\frac{dU_i}{U_i \, dc_{ij}} = \frac{d(\ln U_i)}{dc_{ij}} = \frac{x_{ji}}{c_{ij}} \qquad (34.2)$$

From this equation (or, equivalently, from eq. 25.22), it is reasonable to postulate that the increment of actor i's resources he will be willing to devote to acquiring an increment dc_{ij} of resource j will be proportional to the increment of satisfaction this increment of resource j will bring, which is $x_{ji} \, dc_{ij}/c_{ij}$. This is consistent with maximization of utility, as given by eq. 25.8.

This result implies that when there are two actors with differing resources, r_1 and r_2, favoring opposing outcomes of an event that will increment either resource j (outcome A) or resource k (outcome B), the amount of resources each is willing to devote to the event is $r_1(x_{j1} \, dc_{1j}/c_{1j})$ and $r_2(x_{k2} \, dc_{2k}/c_{2k})$, respectively. Outcome A will occur when the first of these quantities is greater, and outcome B will occur when the second is greater. Thus there is system equilibrium (that is, the corporate actor is indifferent between outcomes A and B) when this equation holds:

$$\frac{r_1 x_{j1} \, dc_{1j}}{c_{1j}} = \frac{r_2 x_{k2} \, dc_{2k}}{c_{2k}} \tag{34.3}$$

Note that eq. 34.3 may be derived in another way. In a perfect social system containing actors i and h and resources j and k, the competitive equilibrium is achieved when (by eq. 25.11)

$$c_{ij}^* = \frac{x_{ji} r_i}{v_j} \quad \text{and} \quad c_{hk}^* = \frac{x_{kh} r_h}{v_k}$$

Combining these two equations and rearranging gives the following equation. The corporate actor is indifferent between outcome A (resource j) and outcome B (resource k) when

$$\frac{x_{ji} r_i v_k}{c_{ij}^*} = \frac{x_{kh} r_h v_j}{c_{hk}^*} \tag{34.4}$$

Since the exchange rate, v_k/v_j, is equal to the amount of j that i must give up (dc_{ij}) relative to the amount of k that h must give up in exchange (dc_{hk}), eq. 34.4 becomes identical to eq. 34.3 if $i = 1$ and $h = 2$, and dc_{ij}/dc_{hk} is substituted for v_k/v_j.

Equation 34.4 represents the balance of power between actor i, interested in resource j, and actor h, interested in resource k. It is analogous to eq. 29.3, which shows interpersonal comparison, except that in Chapter 29, the balance of power involved a struggle over the same resource. Because eq. 29.3 involves only resource j, the prices fall out; eq. 34.4 involves resources j and k, so the price ratio must remain.

The transition from a system in equilibrium to a corporate actor requires one more modification. In a system of exchange of private goods among independent actors, actors realize their interests (maximize their utility) by acquiring or gaining control of the resources in which they are interested. When actors are part of a system of action, that is, a corporate actor, and there is an event in which these actors are interested, an action taken in one direction or another by the corporate actor, the actors realize their interests through the outcome of the event, not through personal acquisition of a resource. This is true for the kinds of events treated in Chapter 31, which are indivisible events unrelated to other resources in the system. It is also true for the kind of event treated here, which is acquisition by a corporate actor of an additional increment of an existing resource.

Thus, when actors i and h are opposed to one another in a struggle over a corporate action or a collective decision involving the corporate actor's acquisition of an increment of resource j or resource k, private control of j and k by actors i and h, respectively, is replaced by the corporate actor's control of resources j and k. The quantities c_{ij} and c_{hk} in eqs. 34.3 and 34.4 are replaced by $c_{.j}$ and $c_{.k}$, where $c_{.j}$ is the quantity of resource j controlled by the corporate actor.

For the Ford example the quantity $c_{.j}$ represents the existing corporate resources in manufacturing engineering, and $c_{.k}$ represents the existing corporate resources in product design. The increments $dc_{.j}$ and $dc_{.k}$ represent the addition of an engineer or a designer, outcomes A and B of the event. For the example it is assumed that the cost of the outcomes is the same, that is, that the market confronted by the company values engineers and designers equally, so the exchange rate imposed on the company from outside is $dc_{.j}/dc_{.k} = 1.0$. (If the market priced one engineer the same as two designers, the externally imposed exchange rate would be $dc_{.j}/dc_{.k} = 1/2$.)

With the exchange rate $dc_{.j}/dc_{.k} = 1.0$, eq. 34.4 implies that the company, considered as an actor, will be indifferent between the two outcomes when

$$\frac{c_{.j}}{c_{.k}} = \frac{x_{ji}r_i}{x_{kh}r_h}$$

that is, when the ratio of existing resources of the sort favored by the manufacturing engineering department (actor i) to those of the sort favored by the product design department (actor h) equals the ratio of interests in these two resources weighted by the power of the two actors. If the interests are the same, indifference occurs at the point at which the ratio of the resources of the two types equals the ratio of the power of the two actors. This corresponds to what one might intuit; but what is important is that it is not postulated ad hoc. It is implied by the system of action within the corporate actor, assuming Cobb-Douglas utility functions and that the system is a perfect system in the sense discussed in Chapter 27. (I will discuss the latter assumption shortly.)

How can the interests (considered as the driving forces, or the subjective interests, in the terms used in Chapter 19) of the corporate actor be characterized? Equation 34.4 can be generalized by considering not merely i and h, two actors internal to the corporate actor, but J, the set of actors internal to the corporate actor who favor acquiring resource j, and K, the set of actors internal to the corporate actor who favor acquiring resource k. Making this modification to eq. 34.4 and substituting $c_{.j}$ and $c_{.k}$ for c_{ij}^* and c_{hk}^*, respectively, gives the following as the criterion for indifference between acquiring an increment of j and acquiring an increment of k:

$$\frac{\sum_{i \in J} x_{ji} r_i}{c_{\cdot j} v_j} = \frac{\sum_{i \in K} x_{ki} r_i}{c_{\cdot k} v_k} \tag{34.5}$$

Equation 34.5 gives the equilibrium holdings of j and k for the corporate actor, given the price ratio, v_j/v_k, it faces in its environment. Comparison of this equation with eq. 25.9 for a unitary actor shows that they are the same if the corporate actor's interest $x_{j\cdot}$ is defined as the power-weighted interests of those actors in set J, and the corporate actor's interest $x_{k\cdot}$ is defined as the power-weighted interests of those actors in set K. Equation 34.5 for indifference between acquiring an increment of j (at price v_j) and an increment of k (at price v_k) then becomes similar in form to eq. 25.9, which gives the amounts of two resources j and k held at equilibrium by a unitary actor:

$$\frac{x_{j\cdot}}{c_{\cdot j}^* v_j} = \frac{x_{k\cdot}}{c_{\cdot k}^* v_k} \tag{34.6}$$

The asterisk on $c_{\cdot j}$ and $c_{\cdot k}$ indicates that these are the equilibrium holdings of j and k by the corporate actor.

The result, then, is straightforward. If there is a perfect social system at the lower level (within the corporate actor), the interest of the higher-level actor (the corporate actor) in a given resource is the power-weighted sum of interests of lower-level actors in that resource. If there are m lower-level actors in the system that comprises the corporate actor, the corporate actor's (subjective) interests are given by

$$x_{j\cdot} = \sum_{i=1}^{m} x_{ji} r_i \tag{34.7}$$

These interests lead the corporate actor to act, in exactly the way interests of a unitary actor lead him to act, as the derivation indicates. That is, the indifference curves (the equilibrium holdings) for the corporate actor bear the same relation to its interest in resources, as defined by eq. 34.7, and its control of resources as the indifference curves for a unitary actor do to its interests in and control of resources. This means that if a corporate actor is composed of unitary actors with Cobb-Douglas utility functions and is a perfect social system internally, the corporate actor itself can be regarded as having a Cobb-Douglas utility function.

Corporate Outcomes and Public-Good Problems

In a system of actors and private divisible resources, each actor pursues his interests by acquiring those resources in which he has an interest. If such a system is regarded as a corporate actor taking an action (modeled as an event in the system), each lower-level actor pursues his interests by trying to induce the corporate actor to acquire the resources in which he has an interest. As a result, the outcome is a public good (or, more properly, a corporate good), and thus leads to free-rider problems. This is true for events unrelated to existing resources (examined in Chapter 31), and it is equally true for events that consist of acquiring or giving up increments of existing resources (treated above). In the derivation of the preceding section, the shift from individual acquisition to corporate acquisition can be seen in the replacement of c_{ij} and c_{hk} in eq. 34.4 by $c_{\cdot j}$ and $c_{\cdot k}$ in eq. 34.5. As long as only one actor favors each outcome, the public-good problem is obscured; in the general case described by eq. 34.5, however, the power-weighted interests of all actors favoring a particular corporate outcome (that is, acquisition by the corporate actor of a particular resource, j or k) were simply aggregated.

This aggregation, which depends on the assumption of a perfect social system, is problematic in the functioning of a corporate actor that is not dictatorially governed. In fact, dictatorial governance does not solve the problem if there is power on the part of any other actor within the corporate actor who is interested in a corporate outcome. For although the dictator may determine the direction of action taken by the corporate actor, this does not ensure that the interests of others favoring that outcome will lead them to implement it. This problem is characteristic of dictatorial governance of social systems. It is the source of the low levels of effort by workers in socialist states (relative to market economies) and the low levels of effort by workers in large firms (relative to small firms). In general, this public-good problem is solved just as others are, by an incentive structure that brings some satisfaction of the individual actor's interest when the corporate actor achieves the outcome of interest to it as a corporate actor.

The free-rider problems involved in attaining the corporate good have been discussed in earlier chapters (especially Chapters 14, 15, and 31) and I will not discuss them further here. It is sufficient to note that the direct transition between levels, with actions (and thus interests) at the higher level derived from interests at the lower level via eq. 34.5, occurs only in a perfect social system. The decision rules used in democratic political systems can be seen as attempts to approximate a perfect system, but, as has been clear since Condorcet's analysis, they do so only incompletely. Their defects are apparent from eqs. 34.6 and 34.7. If $x_{j\cdot}$ is seen as the interest of the collectivity in outcome j, an appropriate decision rule would generate numbers proportional to $x_{j\cdot}$ for each outcome j, from which an outcome could be determined using eq. 34.6, if $c_{\cdot j}^*$ and v_j are known. The decision rule does not even need to generate numbers to be compared (as current formalized decision rules do, through vote counts); all that is necessary is that the procedure generate that outcome j for which, for all outcomes $k \neq j$,

$$\frac{x_{j\cdot}}{c_{\cdot j} v_j} > \frac{x_{k\cdot}}{c_{\cdot k} v_k}$$

As discussed in Chapter 14 and elsewhere, informal decision making in small groups probably comes closest to such a procedure and does so without generating any numbers.

Current decision rules in nation-states deviate from the logic of eqs. 34.5–34.7 in at least two ways. First, interests are ordinarily not weighted according to power in the system, but are given either zero weight (ineligible to vote) or equal weight (eligible). As a result, actors whose interests have zero weight (such as corporations and trade unions) exercise their power outside the formal political system, and many of those whose interests are counted (eligible voters) fail even to register their preference. Second, most such decision rules aggregate preferences rather than interests, failing to take into account strength of interest (or, as it is usually expressed, intensity of preference).

The Value of Resources and the Interests of a Corporate Actor

The value of resource j in a system of action is the sum of actors' interests in the resource, each interest weighted by the actor's power, as given by eq. 25.12. But eq. 34.7 shows that if the system of action is considered to be a corporate actor, the interest of that actor in resource j, that is, $x_{j.}$, is given by the same equation. Thus the interests of a corporate actor in resources are equal to the values of those resources in the system of action comprised by that corporate actor. This allows conceiving of a system of corporate actors, each of which comprises a system of internal actors and resources, where the internal actors have interests that generate values for the corporate actor. These values are then the interests of the corporate actor.

To conceive of this correctly, however, it is necessary to recognize that the quantity of resource j in a given system (a given corporate actor) can no longer be arbitrarily set to 1.0. In the larger system consisting of corporate actors, each of those actors has a certain quantity of resource j, and these quantities vary as the corporate actors engage in exchange. Thus it is necessary to use the version of the model of a system of action in which quantities of resources vary, as described in Chapter 25. In that version the interests of the internal actors are specified as interests per unit of the resource, and control over a resource is specified in units of the resource.

The functioning of such systems of systems can be described as follows. These definitions apply to corporate actor i:

$\mathbf{X}_i = \|x_{ijk}\|$ (an $m_i \times n_i$ matrix of the interests of internal actors, k, in each of m_i resources j)

$\mathbf{C}_i = \|c_{ikj}\|$ (an $n_i \times m_i$ matrix of the control of internal actors, k, over each of the m_i resources j)

$\mathbf{v}_i = \|v_{ij}\|$ (an $m_i \times 1$ column vector of the values of a unit of resource j in the system comprised by corporate actor i or, alternatively, interests of corporate actor i in a unit of resource j)

Then, for the lower-level system within actor i, beginning with X_i and C_i, v_i can be calculated using eq. 25.19':

$$v_i = (D_{ci} - X_i D_{xi}^{-1} C_i + E_{mi} D_{ci})^{-1} e_{m1i} \qquad (34.8)$$

Then the vectors v_i, regarded here as interest vectors for each of the corporate actors, are used to find the values of each of the resources in the higher-level system. Definitions for the higher-level system are as follows:

$m \equiv$ number of resources in the system of corporate actors; $m \geqslant \max_i m_i$

$n \equiv$ number of corporate actors in the system of corporate actors

$V = \|v_{ji}\|$ (an $m \times n$ matrix of values (interests) in which elements in column i are elements from v_i for the m_i resources internal to actor i, and for the other $m - m_i$ elements, $v_{ji} = 0$)

$B = \|b_{ij}\|$ (an $n \times m$ matrix in which the i, jth element is the number of units of resource j held by actor i, that is, $b_{ij} = \Sigma_{k=1}^{n_i} c_{ikj}$

$D_v \equiv$ an $n \times n$ diagonal matrix with diagonal elements $\Sigma_{j=1}^{m} v_{ji}$

$D_b \equiv$ an $n \times n$ diagonal matrix with diagonal elements $\Sigma_{j=1}^{m} b_{ij}$

$y = \|y_j\|$ (an $m \times 1$ vector whose elements are the values of a unit of resource j in the higher-level system)

$p = \|p_i\|$ (an $n \times 1$ vector whose elements are the relative power of corporate actor i in the higher-level system)

The elements of v, b, D_v and D_b known from analysis of the lower-level systems are used to find the value of a unit of each resource in the higher-level system by a second application of eq. 25.19':

$$y = (D_b - V D_v^{-1} B + E_m D_b)^{-1} e_{m1} \qquad (34.9)$$

With the values in this system, it is possible to find the relative power of each actor, using eq. 25.6:

$$p = By \qquad (34.10)$$

This completes the analysis of the functioning of two-level systems. At the lower level are actors k with interests x_{ijk} and control c_{ikj} over resources j, confined within subsystem i, which constitutes corporate actor i. These lower-level configurations of interest and control generate values within each corporate actor, which constitute interests of that corporate actor. Together with the resources held within corporate actors, these generate values and power in the higher-level system of action.

The model of two-level systems described above has certain characteristics that may prevent it from reflecting accurately the functioning of some real two-level systems of action. First, it works from the lower level up to the higher one, taking the lower-level distributions of control of resources and interests as given. This implies a correspondence between resources internal to the corporate actor

(m_i resources for corporate actor i) and resources in the higher-level system. Because the interests of the corporate actors that comprise the higher-level system are based on the resources held at the lower level, the model provides no way for other resources to enter at the higher level and be part of the higher-level system of action. A second characteristic of the model that also results from taking the lower-level system as the starting point, or foundation, for the two-level system concerns the derivation of the corporate actor's interests. This aspect merits more detailed attention.

Subjective and Objective Interests of a Corporate Actor

According to the preceding analysis, the action of the corporate actor from which interests are to be inferred is the outcome of exchanges within—or the interplay of forces within—that corporate actor. The corporate actor's action might be described as expressive rather than rational, for it appears not to be based on feedback from the higher-level system, but to depend only on the interests and control of resources of the internal actors. The action of the corporate actor does take into account the values or prices in the higher-level system, as well as the budget constraint, but its interests (generated as values in the lower-level system) are taken as fixed and as independent of the functioning of the higher-level system.

To regard the corporate actor's action as expressive rather than rational because it seems to be based on internally generated interests is to impose a more stringent criterion for rational action than is ordinarily implied by the concept of rationality. The usual concept, applied throughout this book, regards an actor's interests or utilities as given and does not require them to be in harmony with the environment in some fundamental way, so as to provide the best outcomes for the actor in the long run. The problem this conception creates for the actor may be a serious one; it is examined in the literature on subjective versus objective interests referred to in Chapter 19. Yet, according to the principle of revealed preference, an actor is regarded as rational when that actor's actions are consistent with transitive preferences, when the actor prefers more of a resource to less of it and is willing to give up less of other resources for a unit of that resource when he already holds more of it.[1] In short, the actor's interests or utilities as expressed through action are taken as given, as long as they exhibit consistency.

It is nevertheless true that some corporate actors are designed so that the expressive action resulting from internal functioning is not only consistent with a set of transitive preferences but also optimal (or rational) in the environment in

---

1. These last two conditions represent positive marginal utility and declining marginal utility, respectively. Although these are not ordinarily regarded as necessary conditions for rationality, they hold for the particular utility function used in this book. Other conditions are sometimes imposed as criteria for rationality, such as exponential discounting of future benefits or consistency with expected utility axioms (see von Neumann and Morgenstern, 1947, pp. 15–29).

which the corporate actor commonly finds itself. The discussion so far has provided no insight into how this stronger criterion of rationality might be met. The two-level system may, however, provide a means of going beyond the weak criterion of rationality to examine more fully the disparity between subjective and objective interests.

The Ford Motor Company example used earlier can provide a concrete illustration. The subjective interests reflected in the actions of Ford in the 1930s expressed principally the power of the manufacturing engineering department, but these actions led the company toward demise until reorganization increased the power of product design and marketing. This reorganization once again made Ford competitive. Examining what happened through the perspective of the two-level system discussed above yields the following analysis.

The system of markets within which the corporation acted placed values on four resources relevant to this analysis: automotive engineers, automotive designers, automotive engineering, and automotive design. Actors in the system other than Ford provided a supply of engineers and designers at a value established in the system, and Ford had some interest in each, as inputs to its production process. These interests led to the company's actions in the way described earlier. Other actors in the larger system had an interest in automotive engineering and in automotive design as aspects of the finished product, creating a value for each of these two resources, which constituted outputs from Ford's production process. Ford's problem was that its internal organization, which determined its hiring actions and other actions, led to a low output of attractive design (which was valued highly in the system external to Ford) and a high output of engineering refinements (valued less in the system external to Ford).

The disparity between Ford's outputs and the external system's values could have arisen from various sources, but was in fact a result of the lower power of those actors within the corporation who were producing the output more highly valued in the environment. Thus the company lost viability as the resources it acquired from the external system were unable to produce resources valued highly enough outside (attractive design) that it could sell them in the market for sufficient revenue to cover the costs of production, that is, the costs of those resources it acquired, its factor inputs such as manufacturing engineers.

After the reorganization, in which the distribution of power within Ford was changed, the company acted differently, exhibiting preferences for different input resources. It combined them differently in its production process and produced output resources that did reinstate its viability in the market. The reorganization gave power within the corporation to various actors (such as designers, marketers, and engineers) on a basis that corresponded more closely to their contributions to creation of those resources that had high market value. The internal values of resources constituted in effect the subjective interests of Ford as expressed in its actions. After the reorganization the subjective interests were closer to what might be termed the objective interests of the corporation, in that if pursued, they would provide the highest chance of viability.

Nearly all the elements necessary to mirror this process are present in the two-level system described earlier. One component, however, is missing: In the example a transformation, or conversion, process takes place inside the corporate actor. It consumes certain resources as inputs and produces other resources as outputs. Manufacturing engineers and automotive designers were the input resources, and product design and engineering refinements were the outputs. The introduction of such a production process into the system of action that constitutes a corporate actor in effect creates a fundamentally different system. The linear system of action modeled in this book is a closed system of exchange. Nothing is created, and nothing consumed. To introduce a production process into such a system is to transform it into an open system, which ingests one set of resources from the environment and returns a different set to the environment.

Incorporating a production process into the linear system of action requires introducing a production function into the model. Introduction of a production process will facilitate the linking of objective interests and subjective interests. It can be posited that the ultimate objective interest of any actor is to maximize viability, that is, likelihood of survival. For corporations operating in an economic market, this is approximated by profit maximization. (For other kinds of corporate actors and for natural persons, there is no comparably simple approximation, but one can nevertheless posit viability maximization.) Then the overall process linking subjective and objective interests can be conceived as follows:

1. *Exchange*: The actor pursues subjective interests by exchanging resources already held and acquiring other resources from actors in the external system.
2. *Production*: The acquired resources are consumed in a production process that both sustains viability and produces other resources.
3. *Exchange*: As in step 1, the actor uses the resources produced in step 2 in exchange for others, and the process continues.

In this overall process involving exchange and production, two properties are important in maintaining the actor's viability. One is the set of subjective interests (the matrix X in the linear system of action), which are the springs of action. The other is the production process which transforms a set of resources into a different set of resources that can be used in exchange. If viability is to be sustained, the production process must be capable of producing resources that will, when guided by the appropriate set of subjective interests, both sustain viability and allow acquisition of other resources that, as inputs to the production process, will be sufficient to maintain production.

If the corporate actor is viewed as a system of action composed of internal actors, then for it to be viable requires, first, that the relative power of internal actors brings about an interest of the corporate actor (via eq. 34.7) which will lead to acquisition of the appropriate resources and, second, that the production process is capable of taking those resources as inputs and generating outputs that will be in demand in the larger system (valued in the market more highly than the inputs).

The Ford example as I have described it (although not of course in reality) represents an especially simple case. It is assumed there are only two actors; each actor has an interest in Ford's acquiring only a single resource; each of the two resources acquired produces only one output, which has a value in the market. This simple system can be described by the model by extending the earlier analysis. For two resources, j and k, the relative quantities acquired by the corporate actor in the external market are, from eq. 34.6,

$$\frac{c^*_{.j}}{c^*_{.k}} = \frac{x_j.v_k}{x_k.v_j} \tag{34.11}$$

where $x_j.$ and $x_k.$ are interests of the corporate actor, and v_j and v_k are the values of j and k in the market. If, within the corporate actor, actor 1 has interests x_{j1} in resource j and none in resource k, and actor 2 has interests x_{k2} in resource k and none in resource j, then $x_j. = x_{j1} r_1$ and $x_k. = x_{k2} r_2$. Assuming for simplicity that $x_{j1} = x_{k2}$ makes eq. 34.11

$$\frac{c^*_{.j}}{c^*_{.k}} = \frac{r_1 v_k}{r_2 v_j} \tag{34.12}$$

Equation 34.12 says, in effect, that the relative amounts of j and k acquired by the corporate actor are equal to the relative power of the two actors interested in them, adjusted by their price ratio.

Now suppose that resources j and k are used in a production process to produce resources i and h. The production process is assumed to operate via Cobb-Douglas production functions:

$$c_{.h} = c^{y_{.jh}}_{.j} c^{y_{.kh}}_{.k} \tag{34.13}$$

$$c_{.i} = c^{y_{.ji}}_{.j} c^{y_{.ki}}_{.k} \tag{34.14}$$

For the simple example being considered here, $y_{.jh} = 1$, $y_{.ji} = 0$, $y_{.kh} = 0$, and $y_{.ki} = 1$. With these values for the parameters, the quantity of h produced equals the quantity of j used to produce it, and the quantity of i produced equals the quantity of k used to produce it. Production is maximized if all of j is used for h and all of k is used for i.

The corporate actor can exchange h and i in the external market, where their values are v_h and v_i, respectively, to obtain resources whose value is given by

$$v(h, i) = c_{.h} v_h + c_{.i} v_i \tag{34.15}$$

The corporate actor seeks to maximize this value subject to the resource constraints with which it begins. The problem in the example is that $v_h \gg v_i$, but Ford's acquisition and production processes generated quantities of h and i such that $c_{.h} \ll c_{.i}$.

Three kinds of variables that can be changed within the corporate actor to maximize $v(h,i)$ represent successively greater changes in the actor's internal structure:

1. Allocation of j and k to the production of i and h can be varied, given the market values v_h and v_i, the total quantity of j, $c^*_{.j}$, the total quantity of k, $c^*_{.k}$, and the production coefficients $y_{.ji}$, $y_{.jh}$, $y_{.ki}$, $y_{.kh}$. In the example this change is precluded, since the coefficients are either 0 and 1. Maximization occurs when $c^*_{.j}$ is allocated to the production of h and $c^*_{.k}$ is allocated to the production of i, with none of j allocated to i and none of k allocated to h.
2. The relative interests of the corporate actor in resources j and k can be changed, given the production coefficients and the market values, v_j, v_k, v_h, and v_i. Since the corporate actor's interests in j and k are determined by the relative power of actors 1 and 2 (assuming the interests of actors 1 and 2 to be concentrated in j and k, respectively), a change implies that, if the interests of actors 1 and 2 do not change, their relative power, r_1/r_2, must change.
3. The production coefficients can be changed to bring about more efficient production of those resources that are highly valued in the market.

Because of the production coefficients specified in the example, each unit of resource j produces one unit of resource k, and each unit of resource k produces one unit of resource i. Thus the value of $v(h,i)$ is given by

$$v(h,i) = c_{.j} v_h + c_{.k} v_i \tag{34.16}$$

Since the trade-off between j and k is given by market valuations of j and k, $v(h,i)$ can be expressed wholly in terms of $c_{.j}$ and values of the four resources:

$$v(h,i) = c_{.j} v_h + c_{.j} \frac{v_j v_i}{v_k} \tag{34.17}$$

Equation 34.17 shows that for every unit of j that the corporate actor acquires, it realizes a value of v_h, and for every unit of k, it realizes a value of $v_j v_i/v_k$. Thus the corporate actor should acquire only j if $v_h > v_j v_i/v_k$ (or, equivalently, if $v_h/v_j > v_i/v_k$) and should acquire only k if that inequality holds in reverse. The ratios v_h/v_j and v_i/v_k are the ratios of selling price of product to purchase price of factor of production. Thus the condition reduces to saying that the corporate actor should acquire only that resource dictated by the direction of the inequality.

For the Ford example this implies that only designers should be hired, since $v_j = v_k$ by assumption, and $v_h > v_i$. This is a corner solution, an extreme produced by the fact that the production coefficients for both products were 0 or 1 for both factors of production. In general, the production coefficients would not be 0 or 1, and some quantity of both input resources should be acquired in order to produce the output mix with maximum value.

The case of Ford is a simple one not only because 0 and 1 are taken as the values of the production coefficients. Altogether there are five simplifications:

1. Each of the actors within the corporate actor has only a single interest in one resource.
2. Interests of the two actors favoring the two resources are taken as equal.
3. There is only one actor with an interest in each resource, so there are no problems associated with organization of the interests favoring a particular resource.
4. Each resource has a nonzero production coefficient only for one output resource.
5. There are only two input resources and only two output resources.

There are problems in bringing about the maximization of viability: organizing so that power will be distributed appropriately, ensuring that actors will have interests which, given their power, are consistent with maximization of viability, and efficiently organizing the production process. The general problem also includes the problem of devising an appropriate incentive structure, which is sometimes regarded as the central problem of productive organizations.

This extension of the two-level system to incorporate a production process illustrates the connection between subjective interests as pursued by a corporate actor and objective interests as interests that would lead to actions that maximized the actor's viability. It is, of course, ordinarily true that the actions that will maximize viability are not known; if they were known, no organizations would fail, and all would be at maximum levels of performance.

What I have given here is only a statement of the problem. It is, however, useful in suggesting how one might conceive of the internal structure of the self of natural persons, to which I now turn.

The Internal Structure of Persons as Actors

The model described above has been presented as a model for corporate action, beginning with actors at one level, generating corporate actors which take action at a second level. The model can be applied with systems of action among persons as the higher level and a system of action within the person as the lower level. What does this suggest for the internal characterization of persons?

The usefulness of this conceptualization may lie in several areas. It opens the possibility of overcoming a central weakness of theory based on rational action. A first step toward realizing this possibility is to ask how to conceive of a person's action when the person is regarded as a system consisting of internal actors. According to the conception developed earlier in the chapter for corporate actors, an action with two possible outcomes can be conceived as the result of a comparison between the value of an event under regime a (when only the interests of actors favoring a positive outcome are considered) and the value of the event under regime b (when only the interests of actors favoring a negative outcome are considered). This leads to the question of how to conceive of these internal actors who have interests in a positive or a negative outcome.

A start toward answering this may be made by reconsideration of the trading-card example in Chapter 30 in which Tom, John, and Steve each have an interest in making a telephone call and an interest against each of the others making a call. If the existing allocation of rights is (as in Example 5 of Chapter 30) one in which each holds the rights over his own action, then, in the absence of exchange, each will simply make a phone call. If there is exchange, both John and Steve will give up their phone calls in return for sports cards from the others, but Tom will make his call, since the value of his interest in the call is greater than the value of John's and Steve's combined interests against the call.

Up to this point each actor is considered as a unitary actor, with no internal structure. But suppose that, as in Example 8 of Chapter 30, rights of control over the calls are held collectively, with a norm against making calls. As Table 30.7 shows, it is still true under this rights allocation that John and Steve do not make a call, and Tom does (since with the power distribution that exists under this rights allocation, the value of interests in favor of Tom's making the call remain greater than the value of interests against his making the call). John and Steve will obey the norm, and Tom will not obey it; he will either violate it without regard for its maintenance or will compensate John and Steve to regain the right to make the call. (If he sees it as being in his long-run interest to have this allocation of rights maintained, that is, to have the norm maintained, he will pay compensation rather than simply violating the norm, for if he violates it, John and Steve may dissolve the norm and claim the right to make their calls, which would force him to compensate them not to do so.) But just what is meant by collective control in this circumstance? Each remains in de facto control of making the call. What is meant is that each recognizes the right of the others to sanction him if he makes the call and to be compensated if he wants to make a call. Each assesses the interests and power of the others, and then either refrains from making the call or (as in the case of Tom) goes ahead and makes it.

Saying that each makes this assessment is equivalent to saying that each has cognized the system of action. Each has brought it inside himself cognitively. In doing so, each internalizes the distribution of rights of control, as he perceives that distribution. For an actor to internalize a distribution of rights of control is in effect to create a constitution within himself. In that constitution some of the events are his own actions, and the rights of control over those actions are held in part by others.

It is not necessary that each sees the rights of control as being distributed in the same way; each may have an internal constitution that differs from that of the others. Each will act or attempt to act, however, on the basis of the constitution he has internalized. John, for example, having internalized the distribution of rights, carries out in some fashion the calculations carried out in Chapter 30 to determine whether he will make a phone call or not. But in doing so, he does not act as if he holds the right of control over his call but acts according to the constitution he has internalized, in which (if he accepts the reallocation of rights as specified in the example) that right is held by the three boys collectively.

The process illustrated by this example can be seen as the first step toward creating an internal system of action that is partially independent of the external system of action. In the example there was an agreement that rights to phone calls would be held collectively, with the result that the system of action that each internalized simply reflected the external system. As discussed in Chapter 4 (on authority relations), Chapter 9 (on collective behavior), and elsewhere in this book, however, an actor may transfer rights of control over his actions unilaterally, as long as he holds both the right to control the action and the right to transfer that right. Such transfers imply that there is an internal system of action, with a constitution created by the set of transfers.

For example, Chapter 9 discusses the milling of a hostile crowd as a process during which members of the crowd individually transfer rights of control over their actions from the authorities to the collectivity that is the crowd, after feeling out the crowd to determine the extent of common sentiments. This transfer will occur at different times for different members of the crowd (ordinarily the first to transfer will be those who have least to lose if apprehended by the authorities; the transfer can be seen as the result of the actor's comparing, in the internal system, the value of the rights being held by the crowd and by the authorities). Before an actor makes the transfer, he will have one internal constitution; after he makes it, that constitution will be a different one. Whether or not to take an aggressive action is decided by comparing the value of taking the action (regime a) and the value of not taking the action (regime b). Before the transfer the actor's internal constitution will yield a higher value under regime b; after the transfer outcome under regime a may have a higher value, leading the actor to take the aggressive action.

If individuals can create constitutions for their own internal systems of action, this can provide a basis for modeling the general process of internalization that occurs in socialization. It is useful to distinguish two kinds of internalization that are ordinarily confounded in discussions. One is internalization of another person's perceived directives, as when a child internalizes a mother's wishes as perceived by the child. The second is internalization of norms that specify that a certain action is right or wrong.

The first of these kinds of internalization, which follows directly from the conceptual structure described earlier, can be described as a transfer of rights of control, in one's internal constitution, to a particular other person for a broad class of actions. Of course, this does not say anything about the conditions under which an actor will transfer rights of control to another; the general principle of rational action is that an actor will do so when transferring has a higher expected utility than retaining control oneself. Once rights of control have been transferred to another, the actor may appear not to be acting rationally but acting under control of another; however, rationality must then be sought at a higher level, in construction of the internal constitution.

The second kind of internalization (internalization of a belief that a certain action is right or wrong) can be seen as a transferring of rights of control over that action to a generalized other, whose interests favor or oppose the action. The creation of a generalized other in the internal constitution appears to be a long-term process resulting from the actor's having been in a relatively consistent social environment over some period of time. Schmeikal (1976) has described a somewhat different process from the one discussed here, through which such internal changes may occur.

The conception of the internal structure of persons as actors developed in this section is one in which each actor has an internal system of action that corresponds in part to the external system. The actor's actions arise not from interests, taken as fundamental, but from this internal system. An action comes about as the result of the relative value of the event of which the act consists when interests favoring different outcomes are taken into account. The internal system of action is based on a constitution constructed by the actor, in which various actors have rights, resources, and interests, as perceived by the actor. Rights of control over the actor's actions are either held by the actor or held by others to whom they have been transferred. The actor will thus appear sometimes to be acting in his own interests, sometimes to be acting in the interests of particular others, and sometimes to be guided by a norm concerning what is right or wrong. Rationality consists not in acting according to his interests, but in constructing the internal constitution so that the actions generated by the internal system of action will bring him maximum viability.

This model of an internal structure of actors that is consistent with the linear system of action developed in earlier chapters does not eliminate purpose, but pushes it back to a deeper level, the construction of an internal constitution. This is the starting point for a theory of the self.

References

Abrams, C. 1951. The time bomb that exploded in Cicero. *Commentary* 12:407–414.

Adcock, F. E. 1964. *Roman political ideas and practice.* Ann Arbor: Ann Arbor Paperbacks.

Ainslie, G. 1984. Behavioral economics II: motivated involuntary behavior. *Social Science Information* 23:247–274.

———. 1986. Beyond microeconomics: conflict among interests in a multiple self as a determinant of value. In *The multiple self,* ed. J. Elster, pp. 133–176. Cambridge: Cambridge University Press.

Ainslie, G., and R. J. Herrnstein. 1981. Preference reversal and delayed reinforcement. *Animal Learning and Behavior* 9:476–482.

Ainsworth, M. D., R. G. Andry, R. G. Harlow, S. Lebovici, M. Mead, D. G. Prugh, and B. Wooten. 1965. *Deprivation of maternal care.* New York: Schocken Books.

Allport, G. W. 1937. The functional autonomy of motives. *American Journal of Psychology* 50:141–156.

Alwin, D. 1988. From obedience to autonomy. *Public Opinion Quarterly* 52:33–52.

American Law Institute. 1958. *Restatement of the law second agency 2nd.* St. Paul: American Law Institute.

Ariès, P. 1962. *Centuries of childhood.* New York: Knopf.

Arrow, K. J. 1951. *Social choice and individual values.* Cowles Commission Monograph 12. New York: John Wiley.

Arrow, K. J., and F. H. Hahn. 1971. *General competitive analysis.* San Francisco: Holden Day.

Asch, S. 1956. *Studies of independence and conformity.* Washington, D.C.: American Psychological Association.

Ashton, T. S. 1945. The bill of exchange and private banks in Lancashire, 1790–1830. *Economic History Review* 15, nos. 1, 2:25–35.

Avorn, J. 1970. *Up against the ivy wall.* New York: Atheneum.

Axelrod, R. 1984. *The evolution of cooperation.* New York: Basic Books.

Bailey, F. G., ed. 1971. *Gifts and poisons: the politics of reputation.* New York: Schocken Books.

Bailey, N. T. J. 1963. The simple stochastic epidemic: a complete solution in terms of known functions. *Biometrika* 50:235–240.

Baker, W. 1983. Floor trading and crowd dynamics. In *The social dynamics of financial markets,* ed. P. Adler and P. Adler, pp. 107–128. Greenwich, Conn.: JAI Press.

Balbus, I. 1971. The concept of interest in pluralist and Marxian analysis. *Politics and Society* 1 (February):151–177.

Bandura, A. 1982. The self and mechanisms of agency. In *Psychological perspectives in the self* 1:3–40, ed. J. Suls. Hillsdale, N.J.: Lawrence Erlbaum Associates.

———. 1986. *Social foundations of thought and action: a social cognitive theory.* Englewood Cliffs, N.J.: Prentice-Hall.

Banfield, E. 1967. *The moral basis of a backward society.* New York: Free Press.

Banfield, E. C., and J. Q. Wilson. 1963. *City politics.* Cambridge, Mass.: Harvard University Press.

Baram, M. S. 1968. Trade secrets: what price loyalty? *Harvard Business Review* 46:66–74.

———. 1982. *Alternatives to regulation.* Lexington, Mass.: Lexington Books.

Barnard, C. 1938. *The functions of the executive.* Cambridge, Mass.: Harvard University Press.

Bartholomew, D. 1973. *Stochastic models of social processes.* 2nd ed. London: Wiley.

Baumrin, B. 1988. Hobbes's egalitarianism: the laws of natural equality. In *Thomas Hobbes: proceedings of the second Franco-American conference of the International Hobbes Association.* Nantes: University Press of Nantes.

Becker, G. 1964. *Human capital.* New York: National Bureau of Economic Research, Columbia University Press.

———. 1973. The theory of marriage, part 1. *Journal of Political Economy* 81, no. 4:813–846.

———. 1974. The theory of marriage, part 2. *Journal of Political Economy* 82, no. 2:511–526.

———. 1976. *The economic approach to human behavior.* Chicago: University of Chicago Press.

———. 1981. *A treatise on the family.* Cambridge, Mass.: Harvard University Press.

Becker, G. S., and K. M. Murphy. 1988. A theory of rational addiction. *Journal of Political Economy* 96, no. 4: 675–700.

Becker, G. S., and N. Tomes. 1979. An equilibrium theory of the distribution of income and intergenerational mobility. *Journal of Political Economy* 87:1153–1189.

———. 1986. Human capital and the rise and fall of families. In *Approaches to social theory,* ed. S. Lindenberg, J. S. Coleman, and S. Nowak, pp. 129–143. New York: Russell Sage Foundation.

Ben-Porath, Y. 1980. The F-connection: families, friends, and firms, and the organization of exchange. *Population and Development Review* 6:1–29.

Bentham, J. 1983 (1841). *The collected works of Jeremy Bentham: constitutional code, vol. 1.* Oxford: Clarendon Press.

Bentley, A. E. 1953 (1908). *Process of government.* Chicago: University of Chicago Press.

Berelson, B., P. Lazarsfeld, and W. McPhee. 1954. *Voting.* Chicago: University of Chicago Press.

Berle, A. A., and G. C. Means. 1933. *The modern corporation and private property.* New York: Macmillan.

Berndt, R. M. 1965. The kamano, usurufa, jate and fore of the eastern highlands. In *Gods, ghosts and men in Melanesia,* ed. P. Lawrence and M. J. Meggitt, pp. 78–104. London: Oxford University Press.

Berne, E. 1964. *Games people play.* New York: Grove Press.

Bernholz, P. 1987. A general constitutional possibility theorem. In *Economic imperialism,* ed. G. Radnitzky and P. Bernholz, pp. 383–400. New York: Paragon House.

Bettelheim, B. 1953. Individual and mass behavior in extreme situations. *Journal of Abnormal and Social Psychology* 38:417–452.

———. 1982. *Freud and man's soul.* New York: Knopf.

Biernacki, R. 1988. A comparative study of culture in nineteenth century German and British textile mills. Ph.D. dissertation, University of California, Berkeley.

Black, D. J. 1958. *The theory of committees and elections.* Cambridge: Cambridge University Press.

———. 1970. Lewis Carroll and the Cambridge mathematical school of P.R.: Arthur Cohen and Edith Denman. *Public Choice* 8:1–28.

———. 1976. *The behavior of law.* New York: Academic Press.

Black, R. D., A. W. Coats, and C. D. W. Goodwin, eds. 1973. *The marginal revolution in economics.* Durham: Duke University Press.

Blau, P. 1963. *The dynamics of bureaucracy.* 2nd ed. Chicago: University of Chicago Press.

———. 1964. *Exchange and power in social life.* New York: Wiley.

Blau, P., and R. Schoenherr. 1971. *The structure of organizations.* New York: Basic Books.

Booth, C. 1891. *Life and labour of the people in London.* 4 vols. London: Macmillan.

Bott, E. 1971. *Family and social network.* 2nd ed. New York: Free Press.

Boudon, R. 1974. *Education, opportunity, and social inequality.* New York: Wiley.

Bourdieu, P. 1980. Le capital social. Notes provisaires. *Actes de la Recherche en Sciences Sociales* 3:2–3.

Bowlby, J. 1965. *Child care and the growth of love.* Baltimore: Penguin Books.

———. 1966. *Maternal care and mental health.* New York: Schocken Books.

———. 1969. *Attachment and loss.* London: Hogarth Press.

Bowles, S., and H. Levin. 1968. The determinants of scholastic achievement—an appraisal of some recent evidence. *Journal of Human Resources* 3:3–24.

Bradley, R. T. 1987. *Charisma and social structure.* New York: Paragon House.

Brams, S. J., and P. C. Fishburn. 1978. Approval voting. *American Political Science Review* 72, no. 3:831–847.

———. 1983. *Approval voting.* Boston: Birkhauser.

Braun, N. 1990. Dynamics and comparative statics of Coleman's exchange model. *Journal of Mathematical Sociology* 15.

Brennan, G., and J. M. Buchanan. 1985. *The reason of rules.* Cambridge: Cambridge University Press.

Breton, A. 1974. *The economic theory of representative government.* Chicago: Aldine.

Breton, A., and A. Scott. 1978. *The economic constitution of federal states.* Toronto: University of Toronto Press.

Brinton, C. 1965. *The anatomy of revolution.* 2nd ed. New York: Vintage Books.

Brown, R. 1965. *Social psychology.* New York: Free Press.

Buchanan, J. 1975. *The limits of liberty.* Chicago: University of Chicago Press.

Buchanan, J., and G. Tullock. 1962. *The calculus of consent.* Ann Arbor: University of Michigan Press.

Bulmer, M. 1984. *The Chicago school of sociology: institutionalization, diversity, and the rise of sociological research.* Chicago: University of Chicago Press.

Burns, A. F., and W. C. Mitchell. 1946. *Measuring business cycles.* New York: National Bureau of Economic Research.

Cain, G., and H. Watts. 1970. Problems in making policy inferences from the Coleman report. *American Sociological Review* 35:228–242.

Campbell, J. 1964. *Honor, family, and patronage.* Oxford: Clarendon Press.

Carter, J. C. 1907. *Law, its origin, growth, and function.* New York and London: G. P. Putnam's.

Chandler, A. D. 1962. *Strategy and structure: chapters in the history of the industrial enterprise.* Cambridge, Mass.: Harvard University Press.

Chandler, R. 1955. *The little sister.* Harmondsworth: Penguin Books.

Charnes, A., and A. C. Stedry. 1966. The attainment of organizational goals. In *Operational research and the social sciences,* ed. J. R. Lawrence. London: Tavistock Publications.

Clark, R. 1979. *The Japanese company.* New Haven: Yale University Press.

Clements, K. W. 1987. Alternative approaches to consumption theory. Chapter 1 of *Applied Demand Analysis,* ed. H. Theil and K. W. Clements. Cambridge, Mass.: Ballinger.

Coase, R. H. 1960. The problem of social cost. *Journal of Law and Economics* 3:1–44.

Coleman, James Samuel. 1956. Social cleavage and religious conflict. *Journal of Social Issues* 12, no. 3:44–56.

———. 1957. *Community conflict.* New York: Free Press.

———. 1961. *The adolescent society.* New York: Free Press.

———. 1964. *Introduction to mathematical sociology.* New York: Free Press.

———. 1966. The possibility of a social welfare function. *American Economic Review* 56, no. 5:1105–1122.

———. 1968a. Equality of educational opportunity: reply to Bowles and Levin. *Journal of Human Resources* 3, no. 2:237–246.

———. 1968b. The marginal utility of a vote commitment. *Public Choice* 5 (Fall):39–58.

———. 1969. The symmetry principle in college choice. *College Board Review* 73:5–10.

———. 1970a. Reply to Cain and Watts. *American Sociological Review* 35, no. 2:242–249.

———. 1970b. Social inventions. *Social Forces* 49, no. 2:163–173.

———. 1971. Internal processes governing party positions in elections. *Public Choice* 11:35–60.

———. 1972a. The evaluation of equality of educational opportunity. In *On equality of educational opportunity,* ed. F. Mosteller and D. P. Moynihan, pp. 146–167. New York: Random House.

———. 1972b. Policy research in the social sciences. Morristown, N.J.: General Learning Press.

———. 1973. The university and society's new demands upon it. In *Content and context: essays on college education,* ed. C. Kaysen, pp. 359–399. New York: McGraw-Hill.

———. 1974a. Inequality, sociology, and moral philosophy. *American Journal of Sociology* 80:739–764.

———. 1974b. *Power and the structure of society.* New York: Norton.

———. 1978a. A theory of revolt within an authority structure. *Papers of the Peace Science Society* 28:15–25.

———. 1978b. Sociological analysis and social policy. In *A history of sociological analysis,* ed. T. Bottomore and R. Nisbet, pp. 677–700. New York: Basic Books.

———. 1980. The structure of society and the nature of social research. *Knowledge: Creation, Diffusion, Utilization* 1:333–350.

———. 1981. *Longitudinal data analysis.* New York: Basic Books.

———. 1982a. Recontracting, trustworthiness, and the stability of vote exchanges. *Public Choice* 40:89–94.

———. 1982b. *The asymmetric society.* Syracuse: Syracuse University Press.

———. 1983. Predicting the consequences of policy changes: the case of public and private schools. In *Evaluating the welfare state: social and political perspectives,* pp. 273–293. New York: Academic Press.

———. 1985. Schools and the community they serve. *Phi Delta Kappan* 66 (April):527–532.

———. 1986a. *Individual interests and collective action.* Cambridge: Cambridge University Press.

———. 1986b. Social structure and the emergence of norms among rational actors. In *Paradoxical effects of social behavior: essays in honor of Anatol Rapoport,* ed. A. Diekmann and P. Mitter, pp. 55–83. Vienna: Physica-Verlag.

———. 1988a. Free riders and zealots: the role of social networks. *Sociological Theory* 6:52–57.

———. 1988b. Social capital in the creation of human capital. *American Journal of Sociology* 94:S95–S120.

———. 1988c. The family's move from center to periphery, and its implications for schooling. In *Center Ideas and Institutions,* ed. L. Greenfield and M. Martin. Chicago: University of Chicago Press.

Coleman, J. S., and T. B. Hoffer. 1987. *Public and private high schools: the impact of communities.* New York: Basic Books.

Coleman, J. S., V. Bartot, N. Lewin-Epstein, and L. Olson. 1979. *Policy issues and research design.* Report to National Center for Education Statistics. Chicago: NORC, University of Chicago.

Coleman, J. S., E. Q. Campbell, C. J. Hobson, J. McPartland, A. M. Mood, F. D. Weinfeld, and R. L. York. 1966. *Equality of educational opportunity*. Washington, D.C.: U.S. Government Printing Office.

Coleman, J. S., T. B. Hoffer, and S. Kilgore. 1982. *High school achievement*. New York: Basic Books.

Coleman, J. S., E. Katz, and H. Menzel. 1966. *Medical innovation*. Indianapolis: Bobbs-Merrill.

Coleman, James Smoot. 1958. *Nigeria: background to nationalism*. Berkeley: University of California Press.

Commons, J. R. 1951. *The economics of collective action*. New York: Macmillan.

Conard, A. F., and S. Siegel. 1972. *Enterprise organization*. Mineola, N.Y.: Foundation Press.

Cook, K. S. 1982. Network structure from an exchange perspective. In *Social structure and network analysis,* ed. P. V. Marsden and N. Lin, pp. 177–199. Beverly Hills, Calif.: Sage Publications.

Cook, K. S., R. M. Emerson, M. R. G. Gillmore, and T. Yamagishi. 1983. The distributive power in exchange networks: theory and experimental results. *American Journal of Sociology* 89:275–305.

Cooley, C. H. 1902. *Human nature and the social order*. New York: Scribner's.

Cox, D. R., and H. D. Miller. 1965. *The theory of stochastic processes*. London: Chapman and Hall.

Cox Commission. 1968. *The crisis at Columbia*. New York: Random House.

Cressey, P. G. 1932. *The taxi-dance hall*. Chicago: University of Chicago Press.

Crozier, M. 1964. *The bureaucratic phenomenon*. Chicago: University of Chicago Press.

Dahl, R. 1961. *Who governs?* New Haven: Yale University Press.

Dahrendorf, R. 1968. *Essays in the theory of society*. Stanford: Stanford University Press.

Davies, J. C. 1962. Toward a theory of revolution. *American Sociological Review* 27, no. 1:5–19.

Davis, J. A., and T. W. Smith. 1986. *General social survey, 1986* (machine-readable data file). Chicago: National Opinion Research Center.

Debreu, G. 1960. Review of R. D. Luce, *Individual choice behavior: a theoretical analysis. American Economic Review* 50:186–188.

Debreu, G., and H. Scarf. 1963. A limit theorem on the core of an economy. *International Economic Review* 4:235–246.

Denman, D. R. 1958. *Origins of ownership*. London: Allen and Unwin.

Deutsch, M. 1962. Cooperation and trust: some theoretical notes. In *Nebraska symposium on motivation,* ed. M. R. Jones, pp. 275–319. Lincoln: University of Nebraska Press.

Dorfman, R., P. Samuelson, and R. Solow. 1958. *Linear programming and economic analysis*. New York: McGraw-Hill.

Downs, A. 1957. *An economic theory of democracy*. New York: Harper.

Drake, S., and H. Cayton. 1946. *Black metropolis*. New York: Harcourt Brace.

Dreyfuss, C. 1952. Prestige grading as a mechanism of control. In *Reader in bureaucracy,* ed. R. K. Merton, A. P. Gray, B. Hockey, and H. C. Selvin, pp. 258–265. New York: Free Press.

Durkheim, E. 1947 (1893). *Division of labor,* trans. G. Simpson. New York: Free Press.

———. 1951 (1897). *Suicide.* Glencoe, Ill.: Free Press.

Eccles, R. G., and H. C. White. 1986. Firm and market interfaces of profit center control. In *Approaches to social theory,* ed. S. Lindenberg, J. S. Coleman, and S. Nowak, pp. 203–220. New York: Russell Sage Foundation.

Edgeworth, F. Y. 1881. *Mathematical psychics.* London: Kegan Paul.

Einzig, P. 1966. *Primitive money.* 2nd ed. London: Pergamon Press.

Eisenstadt, S. N. 1978. *Revolution and the transformation of societies.* New York: Free Press.

Eisenstadt, S. N., and M. Curelaru. 1976. *The form of sociology: paradigms and crises.* New York: Wiley.

El Hakim, S. 1972. Collective decisions in a south Saharan village. Ph.D. dissertation, Johns Hopkins University.

Elias, N. 1982. *The history of manners.* New York: Pantheon.

Elkana, Y. 1974. *The discovery of the conservation of energy.* London: Hutchinson Educational.

Elster, J. 1979. *Ulysses and the Sirens.* Cambridge: Cambridge University Press.

———. 1983. *Sour grapes.* Cambridge: Cambridge University Press.

———. 1985. *Making sense of Marx.* Cambridge: Cambridge University Press.

Esch, J. 1950. A study of judgments of social situations. Unpublished term paper, University of Kansas.

Fama, E. F. 1980. Agency problems and the theory of the firm. *Journal of Political Economy* 88:288–307.

Fanon, F. 1967. *The wretched of the earth.* London: Penguin Books.

Faris, R. E., and H. W. Dunham. 1939. *Mental disorders in urban areas.* Chicago: University of Chicago Press.

Ferejohn, J. A., and M. P. Fiorina. 1974. The paradox of not voting: a decision theoretic analysis. *American Political Science Review* 68:525–536.

Festinger, L., S. Schachter, and K. Back. 1963. *Social pressures in informal groups.* Stanford: Stanford University Press.

Fiester, K. 1980. How labor unions view and use codes of ethics. In *The ethical basis of economic freedom,* ed. I. Hill. New York: Praeger.

Finley, M. I. 1983. *Ancient slavery and modern ideology.* New York: Penguin Books.

Fishburn, P. C. 1977. Condorcet social choice functions. *SIAM Journal of Applied Mathematics* 33:469–489.

Flap, H. D., and N. D. De Graaf. 1986. Social capital and attained occupational status. *The Netherlands' Journal of Sociology* 22:145–161.

Form, W. H., and D. C. Miller. 1960. *Industry, labor, and community.* New York: Harper.

Frank, R. H. 1985. *Choosing the right pond.* New York: Oxford University Press.

———. 1988. *Passions within reason.* New York: Norton.

Frankenberg, R. 1951. *Village on the border: a social study of religion, politics, and football in a North Wales community.* London: Cohen and West.

Friedman, J. W. 1977. *Oligopoly and the theory of games.* Amsterdam: North Holland.

Friedman, M. 1956. *Studies in the quantity theory of money*. Chicago: Chicago University Press.

Friedman, M., and L. J. Savage. 1952. The expected utility hypothesis and the measurement of utility. *Journal of Political Economy* 60:463–474.

Friedrichs, R. 1972. *A sociology of sociology*. New York: Free Press.

Fromm, E. 1941. *Escape from freedom*. New York: Farrar and Rinehart.

Galaskiewicz, J. 1985. *Social organization of an urban grants economy: a study of business philanthropy and nonprofit organizations*. Orlando, Fla.: Academic Press.

Gale, D., and L. Shapley. 1962. College admissions and the stability of marriage. *American Mathematical Monthly* 69:9–15.

Garfinkel, I., ed. 1982. *Income-tested transfer programs: the case for and against*. New York: Academic Press.

Garnsey, P. 1973. Legal privileges in the Roman Empire. In *The social organization of law*, ed. D. Black and M. Mileski, pp. 146–166. New York: Seminar Press.

Gauthier, D. P. 1986. *Morals by agreement*. Oxford: Clarendon Press.

Geertz, C. 1962. The rotating credit association: a "middle rung" in development. *Economic Development and Cultural Change* 10:240–263.

Gibbard, A. 1973. Manifestation of voting schemes: a general result. *Econometrica* 41, no. 4:581–601.

Gierke, O. von. 1868–1913. *Das deutsche genossenschaftsrecht*. Berlin: Weidmann.

———. 1934 (1913). *Natural law and the theory of society 1500–1800*, trans. E. Barker. Cambridge: Cambridge University Press.

———. 1968 (1900). *Political theories of the Middle Ages*, trans. F. W. Maitland. Cambridge: Cambridge University Press.

Glasstone, S. 1946. *Textbook of physical chemistry*. 2nd ed. New York: Van Nostrand.

Gluckman, M. 1955. *Custom and conflict in Africa*. New York: Free Press.

———. 1963. Gossip and scandal. *Current Anthropology* 4:307–316.

Goel, M. L. 1975. *Political participation in a developing nation*. New York: Asia Publishing House.

Goldberg, A. J. 1971. Debate on outside directors. *New York Times*, October 29, 1971, p. 1.

Goldstone, J. A., ed. 1986. *Revolutions: theoretical, comparative, and historical studies*. Orlando, Fla.: Harcourt Brace Jovanovich.

———. 1989. Deterrence in rebellion and revolutions. In *Perspectives on deterrence*, ed. R. Axelrod, R. Jervis, R. Radner, and P. Stern. Oxford: Oxford University Press.

Goode, W. J. 1960. Norm commitment and conformity to role-status obligations. *American Journal of Sociology* 66:246–258.

———. 1978. *The celebration of heroes*. Berkeley: University of California Press.

Granovetter, M. 1978. Threshold models of collective behavior. *American Journal of Sociology* 83:1420–1443.

———. 1985. Economic action, social structure, and embeddedness. *American Journal of Sociology* 91:481–510.

Grant, G. 1973. Shaping social policy: the politics of the Coleman report. *Teachers College Record* 75:17–54.

Groves, T. 1973. Incentives in teams. *Econometrica* 41:617–633.

Groves, T., and J. Ledyard. 1977. Optimal allocation of public goods: a solution to the "free rider problem." *Econometrica* 45:783–809.

Gurr, T. R. 1970. *Why men rebel.* Princeton: Princeton University Press.

——. 1986. Persisting patterns of repression and rebellion: foundations for a general theory of political coercion. In *Persistent patterns and emergent structures in a waning century,* ed. M. Karns. New York: Praeger.

Guttentag, M., and P. F. Secord. 1983. *Too many women? The sex ratio question.* Beverly Hills, Calif.: Sage Publications.

Habermas, J. 1971. *Toward a rational society.* London: Heinemann.

Hacker, A., ed. 1964. *The corporation take-over.* New York: Harper and Row.

Hanushek, E. A. 1986. The economics of schooling: production and efficiency in public schools. *Journal of Economic Literature* 24:1141–1177.

Hanushek, E. A., and J. F. Kain. 1972. On the value of equality of educational opportunity as a guide to public policy. In *On equality of educational opportunity,* ed. F. Mosteller and D. P. Moynihan, pp. 116–145. New York: Random House.

Hardin, G. 1968. The tragedy of the commons. *Science* 162:1243–1248.

Hare, R. M. 1981. *Moral thinking.* Oxford: Clarendon Press.

Harrod, R. F. 1938. Scope and method of economics. *Economic Journal* 48:383–412.

Haworth, L. 1960. The experimenting society: Dewey and Jordan. *Ethics* 71:27–40.

Hayek, F. A. von. 1973. *Law, legislation and liberty,* vol. 1. London: Routledge and Kegan Paul.

——. 1976. *Law, legislation and liberty,* vol. 2. London: Routledge and Kegan Paul.

Hechter, M. 1983. *Microfoundations of macrosociology.* Philadelphia: Temple University Press.

Heider, F. 1958. *The psychology of interpersonal relations.* New York: Wiley.

Hernes, G. 1971. Interest, influence, and cooperation: a study of the Norwegian parliament. Ph.D. dissertation, Johns Hopkins University.

Herrnstein, R. J. 1981. Self-control as response strength. In *Quantification of steady-state operant behavior,* ed. E. Szabadi and C. Lowe. Amsterdam: Elsevier/North Holland.

——. 1982. Melioration as behavioral dynamism. In *Quantitative analyses of behavior,* vol. II: *Matching and maximizing accounts,* ed. M. L. Commons, R. J. Herrnstein, and H. Rachlin. Cambridge, Mass.: Ballinger.

Herzog, D. 1985. *Without foundations: justification in political theory.* Ithaca: Cornell University Press.

Hicks, J. R. 1939. The foundation of welfare economics. *Economic Journal* 49:696–712.

——. 1957 (1932). *The theory of wages.* Gloucester, Mass.: Peter Smith.

Hilgard, E. O. 1956. *Theories of learning.* 2nd ed. New York: Appleton-Century-Crofts.

Hirschman, A. O. 1970. *Exit, voice, and loyalty: responses to decline in firms, organizations, and states.* Cambridge, Mass.: Harvard University Press.

——. 1977. *The passions and the interests: political arguments for capitalism before its triumph.* Princeton: Princeton University Press.

———. 1986. The concept of interest: from euphemism to tautology. In *Rival views of market society and other recent essays*, pp. 35–55. New York: Viking Penguin.

Hirshleifer, J. 1978. Exchange theory: the missing chapter. *Western Economic Journal* 16:129–146.

———. 1987. On the emotions as guarantors of threats and premises. In *The latest on the best: essays in evolution and optimality*, ed. John Dupré. Cambridge, Mass.: MIT Press.

Hobbes, T. 1960 (1651). *Leviathan*. Oxford: Blackwell.

Hoffer, T. B. 1986. *Educational outcomes in public and private high schools*. Ph.D. dissertation, University of Chicago.

Hogue, A. 1985 (1966). *Origins of the common law*. Indianapolis, Ind.: Liberty Press.

Hohfeld, W. 1923. *Fundamental legal conceptions as applied in judicial reasoning*. New Haven: Yale University Press.

Hollingshead, A. B. 1949. *Elmtown's youth*. New York: Wiley.

Holmes, S. 1989. The secret history of self interest. In *Against self interest*, ed. J. Mansbridge. Chicago: University of Chicago Press.

Homans, G. 1950. *The human group*. New York: Harcourt Brace.

———. 1958. Social behavior as exchange. *American Journal of Sociology* 65:597–606.

Honoré, A. M. 1961. Ownership. In *Oxford essays in jurisprudence*, ed. A. G. Guest. Oxford: Clarendon Press.

Hume, D. 1985 (1778). *The history of England*. Indianapolis, Ind.: Liberty Press.

Hurlburd, D. 1950. *This happened in Pasadena*. New York: Macmillan.

Ivamy, E. R. H. 1971. *Casebook on agency*. London: Butterworth's.

Janis, I. 1972. *Victims of groupthink*. Boston: Houghton Mifflin.

Jensen, M. C., and W. H. Meckling. 1976. Theory of the firm: managerial behavior, agency costs and ownership structure. *Journal of Financial Economics* 3, no. 4:305–360.

Jevons, W. S. 1875. *Money and the mechanism of exchange*. London: D. Appleton.

Kahneman, D., and A. Tversky. 1979. Prospect theory: an analysis of decision under risk. *Econometrica* 47:263–291.

Kahneman, D., P. Slovic, and A. Tversky. 1982. *Judgment under uncertainty; heuristics and biases*. Cambridge: Cambridge University Press.

Kaldor, N. 1939. Welfare propositions of economics and interpersonal comparisons of utility. *Economic Journal* 49:549–552.

Kanter, R. M. 1973. *Communes: creating and managing the collective life*. New York: Harper and Row.

Kantorowicz, E. H. 1957. *The king's two bodies*. Princeton: Princeton University Press.

Kappelhoff, P., and F. U. Pappi. 1982. *Restricted exchange in Altneustadt*. Kiel: Institut für Soziologie der Universität Kiel.

Kardiner, A. 1945. *The psychological frontiers of society*. New York: Columbia University Press.

Katz, E., and S. Eisenstadt. 1960. Some sociological observations on the response of

Israeli organizations to new immigrants. *Administrative Science Quarterly* 5:113–133.

Katz, E., and P. F. Lazarsfeld. 1955. *Personal influence*. New York: Free Press.

Kaufmann, C. B. 1969. *Man incorporate*. New York: Doubleday/Anchor Books.

Kim, Y. H. 1986. Resource mobilization and deployment in the national policy domains. Ph.D. dissertation, University of Chicago.

Klein, L. R., and H. Rubin. 1948. A constant-utility index of the cost of living. *Review of Economic Studies* 15:84–87.

Kohn, M. L. 1977. *Class and conformity*. 2nd ed. Chicago: University of Chicago Press.

Kramer, G. H. 1972. On a class of equilibrium conditions for majority rule. *Econometrica* 41:285–297.

Kreps, D., P. Milgrom, J. Roberts, and R. Wilson. 1982. Rational cooperation in the finitely repeated prisoner's dilemma. *Journal of Economic Theory* 27:245–252.

Kroeber, A. L. 1973 (1957). *Style and civilizations*. Westport, Conn.: Greenwood Press.

Lancaster, K. 1966. A new approach to consumer theory. *Journal of Political Economy* 74:132–157.

Laqueur, W. 1976. *Guerrilla: a historical and critical study*. Boston: Little, Brown.

Laumann, E. O., and F. U. Pappi. 1976. *Networks of collective action: a perspective on community influence systems*. New York: Academic Press.

Laver, M. 1976. *The theory and practice of party competition: Ulster 1973–75*. Beverly Hills, Calif.: Sage Publications.

Lawrence, P. 1967. *Road belong cargo*. Melbourne: Melbourne University Press.

Lazarsfeld, P., M. Jahoda, and H. Ziesel. 1933. *Die arbeitslosen von Marienthal*. Leipzig: S. Hirzel.

Lazear, E. P., and S. Rosen. 1981. Rank order tournaments as optimum labor contracts. *Journal of Political Economy* 89:841–864.

Le Bon, G. 1960 (1895). *The crowd*. New York: Viking.

Lecky, P. 1945. *Self-consistency: a theory of personality*. New York: Island Press.

Lederer, E. 1940. *State of the masses*. New York: Norton.

Leites, N., and C. Wolf, Jr. 1970. *Rebellion and authority*. Chicago: Markham.

Lenin, V. I. 1973 (1902). *What is to be done?* Peking: Foreign Language Press.

Lenski, G. E. 1954. Status crystallization: a non-vertical dimension of social status. *American Sociological Review* 19:405–413.

Leontief, W. W. 1951. *The structure of the American economy, 1919–1939*. New York: Oxford University Press.

Lévi-Strauss, C. 1964. *Structural anthropology*, vol. 1. New York: Basic Books.

Lewis, J. D. 1935. The Genossenschaft theory of Otto von Gierke. University of Wisconsin Studies in the Social Sciences and History, no. 25. Madison: University of Wisconsin Press.

Lifton, R. J. 1961. *Thought reform and the psychology of totalism*. New York: Norton.

Lin, N. 1982. Social resources and instrumental action. In *Social structure and network analysis*, ed. P. Marsden and N. Lin, pp. 131–145. Beverly Hills, Calif.: Sage Publications.

―――. 1988. Social resources and social mobility: a structural theory of status attainment. In *Social mobility and social structure,* ed. R. L. Breiger. Cambridge: Cambridge University Press.

Lin, N., W. M. Ensel, and J. C. Vaughn. 1981. Social resources and strength of ties: structural factors in occupational status attainment. *American Sociological Review* 46:393–405.

Lindenberg, S. 1982. Sharing groups: theory and suggested applications. *Journal of Mathematical Sociology* 9:33–62.

―――. 1986. The paradox of privatization in consumption. In *Paradoxical effects of social behavior: essays in honor of Anatol Rapoport,* ed. A. Diekmann and P. Mitter, pp. 297–310. Vienna: Physica Verlag.

Lipset, M., M. A. Trow, and J. S. Coleman. 1956. *Union democracy.* New York: Free Press.

Little, I. M. D. 1952. Social choice and individual values. *Journal of Political Economy* 60:422–432.

Locke, J. 1965 (1690). *Two treatises of government.* New York: New American Library.

Loewenstein, G. F. 1985. Expectations and intertemporal choice. Ph.D. dissertation, Yale University.

Lomasky, L. E. 1987. *Persons, rights, and the moral community.* New York: Oxford University Press.

Loury, G. 1977. A dynamic theory of racial income differences. Chapter 8 of *Women, minorities, and employment discrimination,* ed. P. A. Wallace and A. Le Mund. Lexington, Mass.: Lexington Books.

―――. 1981. Intergenerational transfers and the distribution of earnings. *Econometrica* 49:843–867.

―――. 1987. Why should we care about group inequality? *Social Philosophy and Policy* 5:249–271.

Luce, R. D., and H. Raiffa. 1957. *Games and decisions.* New York: John Wiley and Sons.

Lynd, R. 1939. *Knowledge for what?* Princeton: Princeton University Press.

Lynd, R., and H. Lynd. 1929. *Middletown.* New York: Harcourt.

Machina, M. J. 1983. Generalized expected utility analysis and the nature of observed violations of the independence axiom. In *Foundations of utility and risk theory with applications,* ed. B. P. Stigum and F. Wenstop, pp. 263–293. Dordrecht: D. Reidel.

Mackay, C. 1932 (1852). *Extraordinary popular delusions and the madness of crowds.* New York: Farrar, Straus, and Cudahy.

Macpherson, C. B. 1964. *The political theory of possessive individualism.* Oxford: Oxford University Press.

MacRae, D., Jr. 1976. *The social function of social science.* New Haven: Yale University Press.

―――. 1985. *Policy indicators.* Chapel Hill: University of North Carolina Press.

Maitland, F. W. 1904. *Trust and corporation.* Cambridge: Cambridge University Press.

————. 1908. *The constitutional history of England*. Cambridge: Cambridge University Press.

————. 1936. Moral personality and legal personality. In *Maitland: selected essays*, ed. H. D. Haseltine, G. Lapsley, and P. H. Winfield. Cambridge: Cambridge University Press.

Malinowski, B. 1922. *Argonauts of Western Pacific*. London: Routledge.

Malinvaud, E. 1972. *Lectures on microeconomic theory*, trans. A. Silvey. Amsterdam: North-Holland.

Mandeville, B. de. 1772 (1714). *The fable of the bees: or, private vices, public benefits*. Edinburgh: J. Wood.

March, J. G., and H. A. Simon. 1958. *Organizations*. New York: Wiley.

Margolis, H. 1982. *Selfishness, altruism, and rationality: a theory of social choice*. Cambridge: Cambridge University Press.

Markoff, J., and G. Shapiro. 1985. Consensus and conflict at the onset of revolution. *American Journal of Sociology* 91:28–53.

Marsden, P. V. 1981. Introducing influence processes into a system of collective decisions. *American Journal of Sociology* 86:1203–1235.

————. 1983. Restricted access in networks and models of power. *American Journal of Sociology* 88:686–717.

Marsden, P. V., and E. O. Laumann. 1977. Collective action in a community elite: exchange, influence resources and issue resolution. In *Power, paradigms and community research*, ed. R. J. Liebert and A. W. Imershein. London and Beverly Hills, Calif.: Sage Publications.

Marx, K. 1963 (1847). *The poverty of philosophy*. New York: International Publishers.

————. 1973 (1858). *Grundrisse*, trans. M. Nicolaus. London: Allan Lane.

Mauss, M. 1954. *The gift*. New York: Free Press.

Mayer, P. J. 1944. *Max Weber and German politics*. London: Faber and Faber.

Mayhew, H. 1861. *London labour and the London poor*. London: Griffin.

Maynard Smith, J. 1974. *Models in ecology*. Cambridge: Cambridge University Press.

Mead, G. H. 1934. *Mind, self and society*. Chicago: University of Chicago Press.

Mecham, F. R. 1952 (1933). *Outlines of the law of agency*. 4th ed. Chicago: Callaghan.

Merry, S. E. 1981. *Urban danger: life in a neighborhood of strangers*. Philadelphia: Temple University Press.

————. 1984. Rethinking gossip and scandal. In volume 1 of *Toward a general theory of social control*, ed. D. Black, pp. 271–302. New York: Academic Press.

Merton, R. K. 1940. Bureaucratic structure and personality. *Social Forces* 18:560–568.

————. 1968. *Social theory and social structure*. 3rd ed. New York: Free Press.

————. n.d. Study of World War II housing projects. Unpublished manuscript. Columbia University, Department of Sociology.

Merton, R. K., and A. S. Rossi. 1950. Contributions to the theory of reference group behavior. In *Continuities in social research*, ed. R. K. Merton and P. F. Lazarsfeld, pp. 40–105. New York: Free Press.

Michels, R. 1949 (1915). *Political parties*. New York: Free Press.

Mill, J. S. 1926 (1859). *On liberty*. New York: Macmillan.

Miller, D. C. 1970. *International community power structures*. Bloomington: Indiana University Press.

Miller, D. C., and W. H. Form. 1980. *Industrial sociology*. 3rd ed. New York: Harper and Row.

Miller, D. R., and G. E. Swanson. 1958. *The changing American parent*. New York: Wiley.

Mills, C. W. 1959. *The sociological imagination*. New York: Oxford University Press.

Mintz, A. 1951. Non-adaptive group behavior. *Journal of Abnormal Social Psychology* 36:506–524.

Mogi, S. 1935. *Otto von Gierke*. London: King and Son.

Montesquieu, C. L. de S. 1977 (1748). *The spirit of laws*. Berkeley: University of California Press.

Mosteller, F., and P. Nogee. 1951. An experimental measurement of utility. *Journal of Political Economy* 59:371–404.

Mueller, D. C. 1979. *Public choice*. Cambridge: Cambridge University Press.

Muller, E. N. 1985. Income inequality, regime repressiveness, and political violence. *American Sociological Review* 50:47–61.

Murray, C. 1984. *Losing ground*. New York: Basic Books.

———. 1988. *In pursuit: of happiness and good government*. New York: Simon and Schuster.

Nagel, E. 1970. A formalization of functionalism. In *Systems thinking*, ed. F. E. Emery, pp. 297–329. Harmondsworth: Penguin.

Nanson, E. J. 1883. Methods of election. *Transactions and Proceedings of the Royal Society of Victoria* 19:197–240.

National Research Council (Committee on Youth Employment Programs of the Commission on Behavioral and Social Sciences and Education). 1985. *Youth employment and training programs: the YEDPA years*. Washington, D.C.: National Academy Press.

Newell, A., and H. A. Simon. 1972. *Human problem solving*. Englewood Cliffs, N.J.: Prentice-Hall.

Niou, E. M. S. 1987. A note on Nanson's rule. *Public Choice* 54:191–193.

Noll, R. 1983. The feasibility of marketable emissions permits in the United States. In *Public sector economics*, ed. J. Finsinger, pp. 189–225. London: Macmillan.

Norwood, R. 1985. *Women who love too much*. Los Angeles: J. P. Tarcher.

Nozick, R. 1974. *Anarchy, state and utopia*. New York: Basic Books.

Nurmi, H. 1987. *Comparing voting systems*. Dordrecht: D. Reidel.

Oberschall, A. 1973. *Social conflict and social movements*. Englewood Cliffs, N.J.: Prentice-Hall.

———. 1978. Theories of social conflict. In *Annual Review of Sociology* 4:291–315.

O'Flaherty, W. D., and J. D. M. Derrett, eds. 1978. *The concept of duty in South Asia*. New Delhi: Vikas Publishing.

Okun, A. M. 1975. *Equality and efficiency: the big tradeoff*. Washington, D.C.: Brookings Institution.

Olson, M., Jr. 1965. *The logic of collective action.* Cambridge, Mass.: Harvard University Press.

Ostrogorski, M. 1964 (1902). *Democracy and the organization of political parties,* vol. 2: *The United States.* Chicago: Quadrangle Books.

Ostroy, J. M., and R. M. Starr. 1974. Money and the decentralization of exchange. *Econometrica* 42:1093–1113.

Pace, C. R. 1964. *The influence of academic and student subcultures in college and university environments.* Los Angeles: University of California at Los Angeles Press.

Pappi, F. U., and P. Kappelhoff. 1984. Abhängigkeit, tausch, und kollective entscheidung in einer gemeindeelite. *Zeitschrift für Soziologie* 13:87–117.

Park, G. K. 1974. *The idea of social structure.* New York: Anchor Books.

Park, R. E. 1967. The possibility of a social welfare function: comment. *American Economic Review* 57:1300–1304.

Patterson, O. 1977. The study of slavery. *Annual Review of Sociology* 3:407–449.

Payne, J. 1976. Task complexity and contingent processing in decision making: an information search and protocol analysis. *Organizational Behavior and Human Performance* 16:366–387.

Pitt-Rivers, J. A. 1971. *The people of the Sierra.* 2nd ed. Chicago: University of Chicago Press.

Plott, C. R., and M. E. Levine. 1978. A model of agenda influence on committee decisions. *American Economic Review* 68:146–160.

Plott, C. R., and V. L. Smith. 1978. An experimental examination of two exchange institutions. *Review of Economic Studies* 45:133–153.

Pollock, F., and F. W. Maitland. 1968 (1898). *History of English law.* 2 vols. Cambridge: Cambridge University Press.

Popper, K. R. 1963. *The open society and its enemies.* 4th ed. Princeton: Princeton University Press.

Posner, R. A. 1986. *The economic analysis of law.* 3rd ed. Boston: Little, Brown.

———. 1987. The constitution as an economic document. *George Washington Law Review* 56 (November):4–38.

Pryor, E. J., Jr. 1972. Rhode Island family structure, 1875–1960. In *Household and family in past time,* ed. P. Laslett, pp. 571–589. Cambridge: Cambridge University Press.

Public Opinion. 1979. October/November,p. 30.

Rapoport, A., and A. Chammah. 1965. *Prisoner's dilemma.* Ann Arbor: University of Michigan Press.

Raub, W., and T. Voss. 1986. Conditions for cooperation in problematic social situations. In *Paradoxical effects of social behavior: essays in honor of Anatol Rapoport,* ed. A. Diekmann and P. Mitter. Vienna: Physica Verlag.

Rawls, J. 1958. Justice as fairness. *Philosophical Review* 67:164–194.

———. 1971. *A theory of justice.* Cambridge, Mass.: Harvard University Press.

Reich, C. 1964. The new property. *Yale Law Journal* 73:733–787.

Reitz, J. 1973a. The gap between knowledge and decision in the utilization of research. Bureau of Applied Social Research, Columbia University. Mimeographed.

———. 1973b. Social interaction between policy makers and social scientists. Bureau of Applied Social Research, Columbia University. Mimeographed.

Riesman, D., N. Glazer, and R. Denney. 1953. *The lonely crowd.* Garden City, N.Y.: Doubleday.

Riker, W. H., and S. J. Brams. 1973. The paradox of vote trading. *American Political Science Review* 67:1235–1247.

Riker, W. H., and P. C. Ordeshook. 1973. *An introduction to positive political theory.* Englewood Cliffs, N.J.: Prentice-Hall.

Rivlin, A., and P. M. Timpane. 1975. *Planned variation in education.* Washington, D.C.: Brookings Institution.

Robbins, L. 1935. *An essay in the nature and significance of economic science.* 2nd ed. London: Macmillan.

———. 1938. Inter-personal comparisons of utility. *Economic Journal* 48:635–641.

Robinson, J. 1956. The industry and the market. *Economic Journal* 66:360–361.

Roethlisberger, F., and W. Dickson. 1939. *Management and the worker.* Cambridge, Mass.: Harvard University Press.

Rosen, S. 1986. Prizes and incentives in elimination tournaments. *American Economic Review* 76:701–715.

———. 1988. Promotions, elections, and other contests. *Journal of Institutional and Theoretical Economics* 144:73–90.

Rossi, P. H., and K. C. Lyall. 1976. *Reforming public welfare: a critique of the negative income tax experiment.* New York: Russell Sage Foundation.

Roth, A. E. 1984a. Misrepresentation and stability in the marriage problem. *Journal of Economic Theory* 34:383–387.

———. 1984b. The evolution of the labor market for medical interns and residents: a case study in game theory. *Journal of Political Economy* 92:991–1016.

———. 1985a. The college admissions problem is not equivalent to the marriage problem. *Journal of Economic Theory* 36:277–288.

———. 1985b. Common and conflicting interests in two-sided matching markets. *European Economic Review* 27:75–96.

Rotter, J. B. 1966. Generalized expectancies for internal vs. external control of reinforcement. *Psychological Monographs: General and Applied* 80:1–28.

———. 1971. External control and internal control. *Psychology Today* 5:37–59.

Rousseau, J. J. 1950 (1756). *The social contract.* New York: E. P. Dutton.

Runciman, W. G. 1966. *Relative deprivation and social justice.* Berkeley: University of California Press.

Sabine, G. H. 1937. *A history of political theory.* New York: H. Holt.

Samuelson, P. A. 1950. Evaluation of real national income. *Oxford Economic Papers* 2:1–29.

———. 1954. The pure theory of public expenditures. *Review of Economics and Statistics* 36:387–389.

Satterthwaite, M. 1975. Strategy-proofness and Arrow's conditions: existence and correspondence theorems for voting procedures and social welfare functions. *Journal of Economic Theory* 10, no. 2 (April):187–217.

Sattinger, M. 1984. Factor pricing in the assignment problem. *Scandinavian Journal of Economics* 86, no. 1:17–34.

Schmeikal, B. 1976. The internalization of collective values and bounds of interest matrices. *Quality and Quantity* 10:225–240.

Schoen, R. 1983. Measuring the tightness of a marriage squeeze. *Demography* 20, no. 1 (February):61–78.

Scholem, G. 1973. *Sabbatai Sevi, the mystical messiah.* Princeton: Princeton University Press.

Schon, D. 1970. The future of American industry. *The Listener* 2 July 84: 8–12.

Schultz, T. 1961. Investment in human capital. *American Economic Review* 51 (March):1–17.

Schultze, C. T. 1977. *The public use of private interest.* Washington, D.C.: Brookings Institution.

Schumpeter, J. 1954. *History of economic analysis.* London: Allen and Unwin.

Schwartz, T. 1975. Vote trading and pareto efficiency. *Public Choice* 24:101–109.

———. 1981. The universal-instability theorem. *Public Choice* 37, no. 3:487–501.

Scitovsky, T. 1941. A note on welfare propositions in economics. *Review of Economic Studies* 9:77–88.

Seeman, M. 1963. Alienation and social learning in a reformatory. *American Sociological Review* 69:270–284.

———. 1971. The urban alienations: some dubious theses from Marx to Marcuse. *Journal of Personality and Social Psychology* 19:135–143.

Selznick, P. 1957. *Leadership in administration.* Evanston, Ill.: Row, Peterson.

Sen, A. 1970. The impossibility of a Paretian liberal. *Journal of Political Economy* 78:152–157.

———. 1979. Interpersonal comparisons of welfare. In *Economics and human welfare: essays in honor of Tibor Scitovsky,* ed. M. Boskin, pp. 183–201. New York: Academic Press.

Shaplen, R. 1950. Scarsdale's battle of the books. *Commentary* 10:530–540.

Shapley, L. 1967. *Utility comparison and the theory of games.* Paper no. 582. Santa Monica, Calif.: Rand Corporation.

Shepsle, K. A., and B. R. Weingast. 1981. Structure-induced equilibrium and legislative choice. *Public Choice* 37, no. 3:503–520.

———. 1984. Uncovered sets and sophisticated voting outcomes with implications for agenda institutions. *American Journal of Political Science* 28:49–74.

Sherif, M. 1936. *The psychology of social norms.* New York: Harper.

Sigelman, L., and M. Simpson. 1977. A cross-national test of the linkage between economic inequality and political violence. *Journal of Conflict Resolution* 21:105–128.

Sills, D. 1957. *The volunteers, means and ends in a national organization.* New York: Free Press.

Simmel, G. 1908. *Soziologie.* Leipzig: Dunker und Humblot.

———. 1950. *The sociology of Georg Simmel,* ed. K. Wolff. New York and Glencoe, Ill.: Free Press.

Simon, H. A. 1947. *Administrative behavior.* New York: Macmillan.

———. 1955. A behavioral model of rational choice. *Quarterly Journal of Economics* 59:99–118.

———. 1957. The compensation of executives. *Sociometry* 20:32–35.

Simon, H. A., D. W. Smithburg, and V. A. Thompson. 1951. *Public administration.* New York: Knopf.

Simpson, D. 1975. *General equilibrium analysis.* Oxford: Basil Blackwell.

Skocpol, T. 1979. *States and social revolutions.* Cambridge: Cambridge University Press.

Skocpol, T., and A. S. Orloff. 1986. Explaining the origins of welfare states: a comparison of Britain and the United States, 1880s–1920s. In *Approaches to social theory,* ed. S. Lindenberg, J. S. Coleman, and S. Nowak. New York: Russell Sage Foundation.

Smelser, N. J. 1959. *Social change in the industrial revolution.* Chicago: University of Chicago Press.

———. 1963. *Theory of collective behavior.* London: Routledge and Kegan Paul.

Smith, A. 1937 (1776). *The wealth of nations.* New York: Random House, Modern Library.

———. 1976 (1753). *The theory of moral sentiments.* Indianapolis, Ind.: Liberty Classics.

Smith, V. L. 1982. Economic systems as an experimental science. *American Economic Review* 72:923–955.

Snow, C. P. 1951. *The masters.* Garden City, N.Y.: Doubleday/Anchor Books.

Sorokin, P. 1928. *Contemporary sociological theories.* New York: Harper.

Starr, J. 1978. *Dispute and settlement in rural Turkey.* Leiden: E. J. Brill.

Steiner, H. 1977. The natural right to means of production. *Philosophical Quarterly* 27:41–49.

Stene, E. K., and G. K. Floro. 1953. *Abandonment of the manager plan.* Lawrence: University of Kansas.

Stephenson, R. B., Jr. 1980. *Corporations and information.* Baltimore: Johns Hopkins University Press.

Stevens, S. S., ed. 1951. *Handbook of experimental psychology.* New York: Wiley.

———. 1957. On the psychophysical law. *The Psychological Review* 64:153–181.

Stigler, G., and G. Becker. 1977. De gustibus non est disputandum. *American Economic Review* 67:76–90.

Stinchcombe, A. 1968. *Constructing social theories.* New York: Harcourt Brace and World.

Stone, C. 1975. *Where the law ends: the social control of corporate behavior.* New York: Harper.

Stone, L. 1970. The English revolution. In *Preconditions of revolutions in early modern Europe,* ed. R. Forster and J. P. Greene. Baltimore: Johns Hopkins University Press.

Stouffer, S. A., E. A. Suchman, L. C. DeVinney, S. A. Star, R. M. Williams, Jr., A. A. Lumsdaine, M. H. Lumsdaine, M. B. Smith, I. L. Janis, and L. S. Cottrell, Jr. 1949. *The American soldier,* vols. I and II. Princeton: Princeton University Press.

Stuart, J. 1950. *The thread that runs true.* New York: Scribner's.

Swann, W. B., Jr., and S. J. Read. 1981. Self-verification processes: how we sustain our self-conceptions. *Journal of Experimental Social Psychology* 17:351–372.

Swistak, P. 1987. *Theory of models and the social sciences*. Ph.D. dissertation, University of Chicago.

Talmon, J. L. 1952. *The origins of totalitarian democracy*. London: Secker and Warburg.

Tawney, R. H. 1947. *Religion and the rise of capitalism*. New York: Penguin Books.

Thaler, R. H. 1980. Towards a positive theory of consumer behavior. *Journal of Economic Behavior and Organization* 1:39–60.

Thaler, R. H., and H. M. Shefrin. 1981. An economic theory of self-control. *Journal of Political Economy* 89:392–406.

Thrasher, F. M. 1936. *The gang*. 2nd ed. Chicago: University of Chicago Press.

Tideman, N., and G. Tullock. 1976. A new and superior process for making social choices. *Journal of Political Economy* 84:1145–59.

Tilly, C. 1978. *From mobilization to revolution*. Reading, Mass.: Addison-Wesley.

Tilly, C., L. Tilly, and R. Tilly. 1975. *The rebellious century: 1830–1930*. Cambridge, Mass.: Harvard University Press.

Tocqueville, A. de. 1955 (1860). *The old regime and the French revolution*, trans. S. Gilbert. Garden City, N.Y.: Doubleday.

Tullock, G. 1974. *The social dilemma: the economics of war and revolution*. Blacksburg, Va.: University Publications.

———. 1981. Why so much stability? *Public Choice* 37, no. 2:189–204.

Tuma, N., and M. Hannan. 1984. *Social dynamics*. New York: Academic Press.

Turnbull, C. 1972. *The mountain people*. New York: Simon and Schuster.

Turner, R. H., and L. M. Killian. 1957. *Collective behavior*. Englewood Cliffs, N.J.: Prentice-Hall.

Tversky, A. 1972. Choice by elimination. *Journal of Mathematical Psychology* 9:341–367.

Tversky, A., and D. Kahneman. 1981. The framing of decisions and the rationality of choice. *Science* 211:453–458.

Ullmann, W. 1966. *The individual and society in the Middle Ages*. Baltimore: Johns Hopkins University Press.

Ullmann-Margalit, E. 1977. *The emergence of norms*. Oxford: Clarendon Press.

U.S. Bureau of the Census. 1931. *Census of population, 1930*. Washington, D.C.: U.S. Government Printing Office.

———. 1940, 1947, 1949, 1951, 1980, 1984. *Statistical abstracts of the United States: 1940, 1947, 1949, 1951, 1980, 1984*. Washington, D.C.: U.S. Government Printing Office.

———. 1975. *Historical statistics of the United States, colonial times to 1970*. Washington, D.C.: U.S. Government Printing Office.

U.S. Bureau of Labor Statistics. 1972. *Handbook of labor statistics*. Washington, D.C.: U.S. Government Printing Office.

Vanberg, V. 1986. De moribus est disputandum. George Mason University, Fairfax, Va. Mimeographed.

von Neumann, J., and O. Morgenstern. 1947. *The theory of games and economic behavior*. 2nd ed. Princeton: Princeton University Press.

Walaszek, Z. 1977. Use of simulation games in development of formal theory. In *Problems of formalization in the social sciences*, pp. 51–76. Warsaw: Ossolineum.

Waller, W. 1938. *The family, a dynamic interpretation*. New York: Cordon.

Walras, L. 1954. *Elements of pure economics*. London: Allen and Unwin.

Walzer, M. 1977. *Just and unjust wars*. New York: Basic Books.

Watson, T. 1978. *Will you die for me?* Old Tappan, N.J.: Fleming H. Revell.

Weber, Marianne. 1926. *Max Weber: ein lebensbild*. Tübingen: Paul Siebeck.

Weber, Max. 1947 (1922). *The theory and social and economic organization*, trans. A. M. Henderson and T. Parsons. New York: Oxford University Press.

————. 1958 (1904). *The Protestant ethic and the spirit of capitalism*. New York: Scribner's.

————. 1968. *Economy and society*. New York: Bedminster Press.

Wechsberg, J. 1966. *The merchant bankers*. Boston: Little, Brown.

Weede, E. 1981. Income inequality, average income, and domestic violence. *Journal of Conflict Resolution* 25:639–653.

————. 1986. Income inequality and political violence reconsidered. Comment on Muller. *American Sociological Review* 51:438–441.

————. 1987. Some new evidence on correlates of political violence: income inequality, regime repressiveness, and economic development. *European Sociological Review* 3:97–108.

Weesie, J. 1987. On Coleman's theory of collective action. University of Utrecht, The Netherlands. Mimeographed.

Weiszacker, C. C. von. 1971. Notes on endogenous change of tastes. *Journal of Economic Theory* 3:345–372.

White, H. 1970. *Chains of opportunity*. Cambridge, Mass.: Harvard University Press.

Whiting, B. B., and J. W. M. Whiting. 1975. *Children of six cultures*. Cambridge, Mass.: Harvard University Press.

Whyte, W. H. 1956. *The organization man*. New York: Simon and Schuster.

Wicksell, K. 1958 (1896). A new principle of just taxation. In *Classics in the theory of public finance*, ed. R. A. Musgrave and A. T. Peacock, pp. 72–118. New York: St. Martin's Press.

Williamson, O. E. 1975. *Markets and hierarchies, analysis and antitrust implications*. New York: Free Press.

————. 1981. The economics of organization: the transaction cost approach. *American Journal of Sociology* 87:548–577.

Willmott, P., and M. Young. 1967. *Family and class in a London suburb*. London: New English Library.

Wirth, L. 1928. *The ghetto*. Chicago: University of Chicago Press.

Wood, R. C. 1961. *1400 governments: the political economy of the New York metropolitan region*. Cambridge, Mass.: Harvard University Press.

Wu, S. C. 1974. *Distribution of economic resources in the United States*. Chicago: National Opinion Research Center.

Yoors, J. 1967. *The gypsies*. New York: Simon and Schuster.

Young, H. P. 1987. Condorcet. In *The new Palgrave*, pp. 566–567. New York: Stockton Press.

Young, H. P., and A. Levenglich. 1978. A consistent extension of Condorcet's election principle. *SIAM Journal of Applied Mathematics* 35:285–300.

Zablocki, B. 1971. *The joyful community*. Baltimore: Penguin Books.

———. 1980. *Alienation and charisma*. New York: Free Press.

Zagorin, P. 1982. *Rebels and riders 1500–1660*, vol. 1. Cambridge: Cambridge University Press.

Zand, D. E. 1972. Trust and managerial problem solving. *Administrative Science Quarterly* 17:29–39.

Zorbaugh, H. W. 1929. *The gold coast and the slum*. Chicago: University of Chicago Press.

Name Index

Subject Index

Acting self: or actuator, 504; interests for, 509; maximizes utility, 510; separation of interests from object self, 510. *See also* Self

Action choices: transfer of control over resources, 32–33. *See also* Control; Preferences; Resources or events; Social choice; Social system of action

Action-potential, 375

Action research. *See* Research

Action-rights bank, 267–268, 371

Actions or events: types of, 32–33; purposive, 34, 36; with externalities, 37, 249–250, 786; allocation and control of indivisible, 47–48; inability to transfer, 66; free-rider problem for indivisible, 375

Action system or structure, 36; for each individual actor, 50; with individual-level and system-level concepts, 133; power of actor in, 381; in formal organization, 426; in perfect competition, 426; relations among persons in external, 520; two-person exchange as, 673; multilevel, 933–941

Actor: as element in social system of action, 28–29; interdependence among, 29–34; control over resources or events by, 33–34; distinction between simple and complex relations among, 43; private world of, 50; relevance of, 68; role in a system, 132; in complex authority structure, 165; interest in a norm, 256; as actuator and as receptor, 504; object self and acting self of, 504; development of identification by, 519–520; responsibility to others of, 557; as clearinghouse, 744. *See also* Object self; Self

Actors, external: in open system, 695–697; distribution of control by, 697

Addictive behavior. *See* Behavior

Advisors: as intermediaries in trust, 180–185; as intermediaries in large trust systems, 189, 192, 194

Affine agency: definition and examples of, 158–160; as benefit to principal's interest, 161. *See also* Identification

Agency concept. *See* Concept of agency

Agency relations: cases establishing principles governing, 149–151; employment relation as example of, 154

Agenda control, 395–396

Agent: delegation to, 81–82; actions and interests of, 148–152; constraints on, 152, 155; usage rights of, 156; affine, 157–161; in complex authority structure, 166; socializing, 295, 296; interface in corporation among, 444–445; internalizing corporation interests by, 445–446; self as object of action, 507–508

Alienability: of goods, resources, or events, 33–34, 66; of capital, 562–563, 564

Allocation, 681. *See also* Contract curve; Equilibrium, competitive; Exchange system or structure

Altruism, 32, 518

Applied research. *See* Research

Approval voting, 415

Arrow's set of axioms, 374–375, 378, 383, 398, 408–409. *See also* Independence from irrelevant alternatives (Arrow)

Associations: example of rational transfer of authority, 73, 78; voluntary organizations with social capital, 312–313; for mutual protection, 328–330. *See also* Credit

Asymmetry: in vested authority relation, 145; in employment relation, 167n; in trust relations, 178–180; converted to sym-

with guarantor as intermediary in trust, 186–187; of social capital, 302; forms of power with limited, 729; of money as power, 729

Gains: probability of, 103; from being trusted, 114; with transfer of rights of control, 291; in participation in revolt, 500
General will, 338
Generational conflict, 603–604
German Social Democratic Party, 360–361
Golden Rule, 333, 384, 385
Goods: economic, 44; generating externalities, 47; divisible without externalities, 59; indivisible, 371, 720; value of, 689, 692. *See also* Private goods; Public good
Gossip, 283–286
Government: services of, 61; policy of, 784
Great Society, 622
Gresham's law, 106
Group interest theory of politics, 135
Guarantors, 180–188

Half-transactions, 120–131
Hare system, 411n, 415
Heroic sanctions. *See* Sanctions
Heroism, 494
Heterogeneity: in power, 214–215; of reward structure, 225–226; prediction of crowd behavior given, 229; and concept of social optimum, 260–262
High schools, 349–352
High-status persons, 810–814
Homogeneity: of behavior, 201; effect of crowd, 214–215; of reward structure, 225–226; and concept of social optimum, 260–262; of individual orientation, 496
Human capital, 305; underinvestment in, 297; social capital in development of, 300–301; versus social capital, 304, 316

Identification, 157–161; of authority of a position, 168–169; with socializing agent in socialization, 295; with corporate actor, 515; process and definition of, 517–520
Ideology: and social capital, 320–321; effect on revolutionary activity of, 487–489; utopian, 494–495
Imagery of a balance, 333
Immunity to sanctions, 810–814
Importance of the object in the system, concept of, 722
Imports in open system, 695–696

Imposed optimality, 353–354
Inalienability: of rights of control, 33, 66; of social capital, 315
Incentives, 43, 45, 54; pay, 154, 431n; in trust relations, 178; in escape panic structure, 212; in free riding and zeal, 275; selective, 493–494; changes for mutual dependency of, 585; for individualism, 814
Income distribution, 587–590
Incremental sanctions. *See* Sanctions
Independence, 171
Independence from irrelevant alternatives (Arrow), 398–400, 932; in individual decisions, 399–400
Independent contractor: as form of agency in common law, 148–149
Indifference curves: for preferences, 670, 672, 675; calculation with two goods of, 676–677
Individual: behavior, 1–2, 479; control by, 337; vesting of rights in, 442; as holder of rights, 531; positions in and exchanges with corporate actors, 597–598
Individualism of benefit, 337–339
Indivisibility: of resources, events, or goods, 47–48, 60, 64; of actions or events, 59–60, 371, 720, 822–825, 932
Inflation, 120
Information: and rationality of action, 30; and role in allocation of rights, 54–57; objective and subjective nature of, 55n; effect on probability of gain of, 103, 104; decision by trustee to provide, 114; role in trust relations of, 189–194; in individual decision making, 238; source as form of social capital, 310, 317; provided by approval voting, 415
Initial control matrix, 741
Innovations: conditions to foster or impede, 112; ownership rights to, 439–441
Input-output analysis, 726n
Insider trading, 566–567n
Instability, 318
Institutional design: problem in micro-to-macro transition, 375–376
Institutions: social, 114; economic, 302
Intangibles, 36
Intensity of preferences. *See* Preferences
Interdependence, 29–31, 207
Interest: of person awarding status, 130; in a resource, 133–134; effect of conflict between long- and short-term, 601–602
Interest matrix, 721–722, 787, 788